WELLINGTON

RORY MUIR, a renowned expert on the Duke, has researched Wellington and subjects close to his life for thirty years. He is a visiting research fellow, University of Adelaide. His previous books include a highly praised study of Wellington's great triumph at Salamanca (published by Yale) and the edited letters of Alexander Gordon, Wellington's confidential aide-de-camp. He lives in Australia.

Wellington

WATERLOO
AND THE FORTUNES OF PEACE
1814–1852

RORY MUIR

YALE UNIVERSITY PRESS
NEW HAVEN AND LONDON

Front cover: Sir Thomas Lawrence, *Arthur Wellesley, 1st Duke of Wellington* (*c.* 1821). Private Collection / Photo © Christie's Images / Bridgeman Images.

Back cover: Felix Philippoteaux, *Cuirassiers Charging the Highlanders at the Battle of Waterloo on 18th June 1815* (1874). Apsley House, The Wellington Museum, London / Bridgeman Images.

Published with assistance from the Annie Burr Lewis Fund.

First published in paperback in 2018

For information about this and other Yale University Press publications, please contact:
U.S. Office: sales.press@yale.edu   yalebooks.com
Europe Office: sales@yaleup.co.uk   yalebooks.co.uk

Set in Minion Pro by IDSUK (DataConnection) Ltd
Printed in Great Britain by Hobbs the Printers Ltd, Totton, Hampshire

Library of Congress Cataloging-in-Publication Data

Muir, Rory, 1962-
    Wellington / Rory Muir.
      pages cm
    Includes bibliographical references and index.
    ISBN 978-0-300-18665-9 (v. 1: alk. paper) — ISBN 978-0-300-18786-1 (v. 2: alk.
    paper)
    1. Wellington, Arthur Wellesley, Duke of, 1769-1852. 2. Great Britain. Army—History.
3. Great Britain—History, Military—1789-1820. 4. Generals—Great Britain—
Biography. 5. Prime ministers—Great Britain—Biography. 6. Great Britain—Politics
and government—19th century. I. Title.
DA68.12.W4M85 2013
941.07092—dc23
[B]
                                                                            2013018606

A catalogue record for this book is available from the British Library.

ISBN 978-0-300-23282-0 (pbk)

10 9 8 7 6 5 4 3 2 1

CONTENTS

LIST OF ILLUSTRATIONS
AND MAPS

Maps

PREFACE

IN THE FIRST forty-five years of his life Arthur Wellesley rose from being the disregarded younger son of an obscure Irish nobleman to the most famous and successful British soldier for at least a century. There had been little sign of promise even when he was in his mid-twenties, when he had appeared to be nothing more than a poor and unremarkable young officer, a hanger-on at Dublin Castle and an insignificant member of the Irish Parliament. But from his arrival in India he showed great confidence and an unusual breadth of vision; and when the arrival of his brother as Governor-General gave him great opportunities he took full advantage of them, displaying remarkable ability in a variety of military, diplomatic and civil roles. He returned to England in 1805 with sufficient fortune to make him independent, and some fame, although achievements in India were heavily discounted in England. The defence of his brother's reputation brought him into close contact with many of the leading politicians of the day, and he became an active member of the House of Commons while not renouncing his military career. In 1807 he was appointed Chief Secretary for Ireland, an important position which was often a stepping stone into the Cabinet. He combined this post with active service, first in Denmark and then in Portugal in 1808.

Wellington led the first British troops ashore in the Peninsular War and his victories at Roliça and Vimeiro persuaded the French to negotiate their withdrawal from Portugal. The British public reacted badly to the resulting Convention of Cintra, and Wellington was savagely attacked only a few weeks after he had been celebrated as a hero. He vindicated his conduct to an official inquiry and returned to Portugal in the spring of 1809, remaining in command of the British and allied army for the next five years, and leading it to an unbroken succession of victories including Oporto, Talavera, Busaco, Fuentes de Onõro, Salamanca, Vitoria, the Pyrenees, the passage of the Bidassoa, Nivelle, the Nive, Orthez and Toulouse. His foresight and planning were demonstrated by the rebuilding of the Portuguese army in 1809–10 and the construction of the Lines of Torres Vedras which enabled him to defeat the French invasion of Portugal in 1810–11. Throughout all his campaigns he worked constantly to improve the quality of his army, insisting that junior officers attend to the welfare of their men, and taking great pains to enforce discipline in order to protect the civilian population from abuses by his troops. But his attention extended well beyond his army: he put pressure on successive British governments to supply him with more men, money and resources; he engaged closely with the Portuguese and Spanish governments on a broad range of subjects far beyond direct military co-operation; and he closely observed events in central and eastern Europe which had a direct impact on the strength of the French forces he was facing. He proved a capable diplomat and a highly effective administrator as well as a consummate general, establishing this mastery on the battlefield, in conducting a campaign, and more broadly in his understanding of grand strategy. By the close of the war in 1814 his reputation was second only to that of Napoleon.

After the war Wellington turned to diplomacy, serving at Paris and at the Congress of Vienna, but resumed arms following Napoleon's escape from Elba. There followed the crowning victory of Waterloo which raised him from eminence to pre-eminence: no British monarch, soldier or statesman had achieved such power, influence and fame in Europe since Henry V after Agincourt. Wellington used his position to support Castlereagh's efforts to consolidate the peace by imposing moderate terms on France and encouraging co-operation among the great powers.

After commanding the allied Army of Occupation in France for three years, Wellington returned to England at the end of 1818 and joined Lord Liverpool's Cabinet. He went on to play a major part in British and international politics for the next thirty years, as a senior and influential Cabinet minister, as prime minister for three years, one of the two leaders of the Opposition between 1830 and 1841, as leader of the government in the Lords in Peel's government from 1841 to 1846, and as a senior statesman in the last years of his life. Nonetheless his career in these years has often been neglected. In 1931 Philip Guedalla noted that, 'when Waterloo is passed', biographies of the Duke 'nearly always falter, and the story dies away in a desultory stream of anecdote.'[1] And it was only in the 1980s, after Wellington's correspondence was deposited at the University of Southampton, that academic historians began to reassess his political career. Since then, work by many scholars including Neville Thompson, Norman Gash, Peter Jupp, James Sack, Christopher Woolgar, Richard Gaunt, Russ Foster and, above all, Richard Davis, has transformed our understanding of the Duke from a politically naïve, public-spirited servant of the Crown, to a shrewd and capable party leader who had strong and considered views on a wide range of policies, but who always remained essentially pragmatic. At the same time he gained the reputation of a politician who was prepared to defy the wishes of his own supporters for the greater national good. He was a far more complex and interesting figure than the stiff, ingenuous hero of Victorian memory. One purpose of this book is to build on this scholarly work and to explore in some detail Wellington's role as a politician. This does not require arguing that all his views and actions were right or successful; but they were seldom if ever absurdly wrong-headed or simply inexplicable. By approaching events from Wellington's point of view we get fresh insights into a narrative that has too often been written from the other side of the hill. It is not the only way that the story can be told, but by neglecting it for so long we have distorted and misunderstood British history between Waterloo and the Crimea.

However, Wellington was much more than a politician, and a second strand of the work charts the evolution of his reputation from the extraordinary praise that was heaped upon him from all directions on his return from the Peninsula, to the sharp reaction that followed hot on the heels of the first euphoria after news of Waterloo broke, and so on to the national mourning after his death. Wellington's reputation affected the way his actions were perceived at the time and subsequently, just as he sometimes shaped his actions to live up to his reputation, on one occasion telling a friend: 'I am the Duke of Wellington, and *bon gré mal gré* [like it or not], must do as the Duke of Wellington doth.'[2] His reputation also has much wider implications, for it proved a powerful ingredient in British culture throughout the nineteenth century influencing everything from the definition of gentlemanly conduct to the role of army officers in British politics and society, and the standards of probity expected from figures in public life. Wellington was a very British hero, and his character helped shape not just what the Victorians, and later generations, meant by a 'hero', but also what they felt it meant to be British.

The third main strand of this volume is to see how the hard-working, high-spirited, indiscreet man who commanded the army in the Peninsula in his early forties, adapted to the very different milieu of London society. How did he respond to the many intelligent cultivated women who played such a prominent role in British political and social life, after five years in the Peninsula (and even more in India) where he had been almost totally deprived of educated female society? How did he treat his wife and sons, his extended family and friends, when the demands of the war no longer made the perfect excuse for neglect? And how did he cope with periods of enforced leisure when he was out of office and so deprived of the official business that at other times filled his days?

Choosing the exact point at which to divide Wellington's life between two volumes was not as simple as it might seem. Waterloo is the high point of a sequence of events that begins with Napoleon's departure from Elba and ends with the withdrawal of the allied Army of Occupation of France at the end of 1818. Ending the first volume as night fell on 18 June 1815 would have had a fine dramatic effect, but it would also interrupt the story halfway through, and impede rather than help the reader to understand the significance of events. This leaves a choice of two natural breaks in the narrative: Wellington's return from the Peninsula in 1814, and his return from France in 1818. And while the second would mean that all his battles were included in the first volume, a great many of the themes of the second volume have already come into play by 1818. A secondary but still significant consideration was that, at over 300,000 words, the first volume was already long enough when it concluded in 1814, and I hoped (mistakenly as it proved) that volume two would prove to be shorter.

In writing this volume I felt that almost every chapter could have been the subject of a substantial monograph, and I never finished a chapter without wishing that I had sufficient time to consult a few more sources. The first draft of the text was more than two-thirds complete when *Wellington. The Path to Victory, 1769–1814* was published, and I began writing it as long ago as 2007. As with the first volume, a great deal of additional material, including detailed arguments explaining my interpretation of events and supplementary evidence including many first-hand accounts, is available in the online commentary at www.lifeofwellington.co.uk.

I have now been working on the two volumes of this biography for fifteen years and I cannot hope to thank all the individuals and institutions who have assisted me over this time. Throughout these years I have been a visiting research fellow at the University of Adelaide and I am very grateful to the university, and to the Barr Smith Library (and in particular to Margaret Hosking), for giving me such a suitable base of operations and for making the immense resources of the library readily available. Looking back I am surprised just how much has changed while I have been writing about Wellington. In the early years I would visit the library frequently to borrow books, photocopy articles and look at *The Times* or one or two other newspapers on barely legible microfilm; now, via the internet, I access the library's resources predominantly from home – as well as a vast array of scholarly articles, books (both old and obscure and current) and early nineteenth-century newspapers. Future scholars will take this all for granted, but to anyone who has lived through this change the abundance and accessibility of source material only a few clicks away is still astonishing.

A very detailed calendar of the Wellington Papers for 1819–32, prepared by the expert staff of the Hartley Library of the University of Southampton, is freely available online; but it is still useful to see the manuscripts, while the later years can, at present, only be studied in person. My visits to Southampton over the years have always been marked by the kindness, efficiency and good humour of the staff of the Archives and Special Collections of the Hartley

Library. Professor Christopher Woolgar is both a friend and wise counsellor whose published articles on Wellington are full of fresh insights and new perspectives, and whose private comments have been immensely useful. Karen Robson's work on early nineteenth-century patronage is relevant to both volumes of this biography, while her article on Wellington's appearance in nine-teenth-century ballads opened a completely new line of enquiry which subsequently sprouted in several directions. For this, and for all her assistance both when I was in Southampton and in response to my subsequent enquiries, I am most appreciative. I would also like to thank all the other staff of the Archives and Special Collections, including Pearl Romans, Sarah Maspero, Laura Joy, Mary Cockerill, Sabrina Harder and Emily Rawlings, both for their help on my visits and for their work organising successive Wellington Congresses.

I am very grateful to the many other archivists and librarians who have answered my queries and assisted me in person over the years, and in particular to the staff of the Special Libraries and Archives at the University of Aberdeen, the British Library, the National Archives, the National Army Museum, the National Library of Scotland, the Staffordshire Record Office, the University of Reading and the Centre for Buckinghamshire Studies. I would like to thank the Trustees of the Wellington estate for permission to reproduce images from their collection; and also Jane Branfield, the archivist at Stratfield Saye, for all her help with the illustrations and answering other queries.

I have benefited enormously from the generosity of other historians who have fielded questions and freely shared the fruits of their own research, both when meeting in person and by correspondence. Conrad Kent followed up a fascinating talk at Southampton with a series of e-mails providing details of popular ephemeral publications (ranging from prints to fans and stationery) that celebrated Wellington's victories and contributed to the growth of his reputation at home during the course of the war against Napoleon. Erwin Muilwijk expanded on some of his discoveries relating to the role of the Dutch-Belgian army in the Waterloo campaign, and shed a good deal of light on the early part of the battle of Quatre Bras and allied movements especially on 15 June 1815. Russ Foster has provided me with much information about Wellington's later life, including such recondite matters as Lord Charles Wellesley's activities as a member of the Commons. Greg Roberts and Tim Couzens have filled in my knowledge of other branches of the family, including Wellington's nephew, the 'wicked' William. Alexander Mikaberidze provided me with a copy of a hard-to-find article that I needed in a hurry, and located the source for Napoleon's remarks on Castlereagh's diplomacy which are discussed in the Commentary to Chapter 5. Years ago S.G.P. Ward added greatly to my understanding of George Murray's political career. Angus Hawkins answered my queries about Lord Stanley and the politics of the 1850s, and helped discover the true origins of the phrase 'The Who? Who? ministry' (not Wellington at all, but a Liberal journalist writing a generation later). Richard Gaunt, Peter Jupp, Huw Davies, John Severn, Andrew Lambert, Christopher Bryant, D.G. Graves, John Cookson, Nicholas Dunne-Lynch, Marcus Beresford, Kevin Linch and Charles Fremantle have all given valuable help, advice and encouragement at different times. One of the pleasures of working in this field is the enthusiasm and friendship of other historians and the sense of camaraderie this creates.

I am very grateful for the support the project has received over the years from the staff at Yale University Press in London, and in particular Robert Baldock, Heather McCallum, Rachael Lonsdale and Oli Dillon. Jonathan Asbury has been an exemplary editor, making the task of revising the original script of this volume much less laborious and painful than I expected, and resolving my doubts over a late draft of the Conclusion. Martin Brown has prepared the maps with his customary skill and deftness. At an earlier stage of the process I was enormously helped by Dr Penelope Eate of the University of Adelaide, whose efficiency and friendship were invaluable. And my agent, Bill Hamilton of A.M. Heath, has helped ensure that everything progressed smoothly towards publication.

My working life has been enlivened and my enthusiasm sustained by correspondence with friends including Mark Thompson, Zack White, Giles Hunt, John Malcolm, Bob Burnham and Arthur Murchison. Ron McGuigan has continued to give me the benefit of his encyclopaedic knowledge of the lives and careers of British army officers of the period, and read the whole manuscript, alerting me to a variety of slips and mistakes. Howie Muir has sent me his unpublished essay on the use of four-deep line at Waterloo, among much other material, and lifted my morale when it faltered. And Charles Esdaile, whom I met when I first began working on the Wellington Papers in 1986, and who has been a true and valued friend ever since, has shared the pleasures and pains of research and writing on this fascinating period.

I owe the discovery of my vocation as a historian to my mother, Marcie Muir, who died in 2007 when I was writing the early chapters of this volume. She understood better than anyone the way that scholarly projects can grow far beyond their initial scope, and the importance of enjoying the journey while still ensuring that you reach the destination. My sister Kathie Muir and her partner Anthony Psarros have given me love, support and encouragement through all the many changes and challenges that have occurred in my life over the years that I have been working on this book. And finally I am grateful to my beloved wife Robin Muir, who has not only endured but encouraged and sustained my preoccupation with Wellington ever since we first met, and who, particularly over the last twelve months, has done so much to ensure that the book has finally been completed. Thanks to her, life after Wellington is an exciting prospect.

Prologue

A T TEN O'CLOCK on the morning of 6 July 1814, just two months after Napoleon's abdication and the end of the long war, the Duke of Wellington arrived at the studio of Thomas Lawrence to sit for his portrait. 'He came on horseback attended by an old Groom, and in the plainest manner; wearing a Blue Coat & a round hat. – Nobody was apprised of his coming, and the few people who were passing had no knowledge of His being the Duke of Wellington.'[1] The portrait was commissioned by Sir Charles Stewart and shows Wellington in plain civilian dress; and Lawrence was soon at work on another, for the Prince Regent, showing Wellington in the uniform of a field marshal and holding aloft the Sword of State with St Paul's in the background – a reference to the Service of Thanksgiving for the victory which was held there that same July. But it was a third, much smaller half-length portrait of Wellington, which in the twentieth century became the best-known image of the Duke, and which has helped to shape our impressions of Regency society. In this portrait Wellington wears his scarlet coat with lavish amounts of braid and decorations, but there is no doubt that the man dominates the costume, the picture and the viewer. Arms folded, body at a slight angle but face almost full, the Duke stares forth. Lawrence has made him look more severe, but nobler than in previous portraits – not softening the features but refining them a little, the chin less heavy, the nose a little less dominant, the gaze direct and the small mouth without a hint of a smile. Yet the overall effect is not off-putting – Lawrence's colours are too warm and conception too beguiling, so that the viewer delights in the picture and is led to admire Wellington without resentment.[2]

Lawrence's portraits represent one contemporary view of Wellington: as the embodiment of nobility, grandeur and the triumph of Britain in the war against Napoleonic aggression. But there was another perspective held by many radicals and other critics of the government which was expressed by George Cruikshank with a satirical brilliance not far short of Gillray in a number of elaborate caricatures published in 1815 and 1816. In November 1815 Cruikshank produced a print significantly titled *The Afterpiece to the Tragedy of Waterloo* in which Wellington and other allied leaders tie a feminine embodiment of France to the ground in order to torture and rape her, while literally forcing miniature versions of the Bourbons down her throat. In the background their soldiers carry off loot while a broken shield inscribed 'Napoleon le Grand' is in the foreground.[3] And the following August Cruikshank produced *The Royal Shambles or the Progress of Legitimacy & Re-establishment of Religion & Social Order–!!!–!!!–!!!* – the largest and most complicated caricature of his career. While it was directed primarily against the Bourbon restoration, which Cruikshank depicts as a triumph of religious bigotry and political oppression, Wellington is also attacked as the ally of the ultra-conservatives in France, and the instrument, with his army, of despotism. He is dressed in an elaborate uniform and pulls along a cannon on which is mounted the corpulent figure of Louis XVIII, while trampling a prostrate man under the spiked sole of his boot.[4]

The conflict between these two views of Wellington, the hero and the instrument of tyranny and oppression, lasted for a generation or more after his return from the Peninsula in 1814. The radical view was probably always a minority opinion in the country as a whole, but on a number of occasions when the political atmosphere became heated it dominated the press, the prints and the popular mood in London. Until the closing years of his life Wellington remained a controversial, divisive and vital figure in Britain, only slowly retiring from centre stage in the 1840s. His death, in 1852, produced an extraordinary outpouring of national mourning that united the country and elevated his memory into a Victorian pantheon where there was little room for politics, controversy or error. But the real Wellington was never a dull paragon of worthiness, driven only by a sense of selfless duty; and the deference paid to his memory obscured the nature of both the man and the role he played in shaping the course of British history in the years between 1814 and 1852.

PART I

WAR AND PEACE IN EUROPE (1814–18)

CHAPTER ONE

CELEBRATIONS AND DIPLOMACY
(April 1814–March 1815)

THE LONG WAR was finally over. The battle of Toulouse had been fought on 10 April 1814, and two days later Wellington had learnt of Napoleon's abdication. It took another week before Soult submitted to the new French government, but there was no further fighting, except for a pointless and costly sortie by the garrison of Bayonne on 14 April. On 21 April, before Wellington had even begun to think about his future, Sir Charles Stewart arrived from Paris carrying a letter from Castlereagh offering him the Paris embassy, 'if you have no other object immediately in view, repose after such exertions being in itself a very natural one'. Castlereagh argued that Wellington's authority and prestige would give Britain added influence in France and in the affairs of the Continent as a whole. There would be no need to take up the position for some time but it would be helpful if he could come up to Paris for talks fairly soon.[1]

Wellington was genuinely surprised by the offer, replying that he was 'very much obliged and flattered by your thinking of me for a situation for which I should never have thought myself qualified'. This was unduly modest; he had been at the centre of diplomatic negotiations with Spain and Portugal for the last five years, and before that in India, while it was common at the time for important diplomatic positions to be filled by soldiers. Despite his protest he had no hesitation in accepting, explaining to Henry that 'I must serve the public in some manner or other'.[2]

He left Toulouse at the end of April and arrived in Paris on 4 May. Castlereagh, seeing him for the first time in five years, commented: 'He looks perfectly well, and does not show the effects of his campaigns as much as I expected in his countenance.' He was immediately the centre of attention. Byron's friend, John Cam Hobhouse, a radical with no sympathy for Wellington's politics, was in Paris at the time and admits: 'I felt, for my own part, an insatiable desire to see him, and ran many chances of being kicked and trampled down to get near our great man. Two Englishmen near me showed as much eagerness as myself to approach him, and one of them as he passed by me said, "Oh, for God's sake, let me see him! – I know you will excuse me, sir, for this; but I must see him!"' Nor was the excitement limited to British visitors; when Wellington went to the opera with Castlereagh and his party, he 'was in plain clothes, without any decoration to attract notice, and sat in the back of the box; but he was almost immediately recognised by someone in the pit, and a voice cried out, "*Vellington*." The cry was taken up by others, and at last the whole pit rose, and turning to the box, called out "*Vive Vellington!*" nor would they be satisfied till he stood up and bowed to them, when he was cheered and applauded'.[3]

Wellington spent barely a week in Paris, discussing the peace settlement and the affairs of Spain and Portugal with Castlereagh, and making arrangements with the French authorities for the British cavalry to march from Toulouse to the Channel Ports – the infantry would ship home from Bordeaux. He also met the Emperor Alexander of Russia and Metternich who, possibly prejudiced by Castlereagh, enthused to his wife that Wellington was 'Austrian in his soul'.[4]

And it was in Paris too that he learnt that the British government had marked his most recent victories and the coming of peace with another, final, step in the peerage of the United Kingdom; on 3 May 1814 he had been made Duke of Wellington. He at once wrote thanking the Prime Minister in suitable terms and stressing his pleasure that his principal lieutenants Hope, Graham, Cotton, Hill and Beresford had been raised to the peerage at the same time. While military honours always meant more to Wellington than civil distinctions, he was not indifferent to this latest reward for service, and mixing in Paris with the princes, rulers and statesmen of Europe, he would have been conscious of the importance of rank in an aristocratic age and society. The famously nonchalant announcement of the news to Henry in a postscript – 'I believe I forgot to tell you I was made a Duke' – came almost a fortnight later when, on signing a letter on other questions, Wellington realised that it had hitherto been overlooked. Still, not many men *would* overlook such an honour, certainly not Lord Wellesley for whom the comparison with his own despised Irish marquessate must have been both inescapable and unbearable.[5]

The subject that dominated Wellington's discussions with Castlereagh in Paris was the state of Spain, where unfolding events would have a significant effect on Wellington's reputation at home, and sow the seeds for much subsequent radical criticism. When Ferdinand had been released by the French on 24 March 1814 he had proceeded to Valencia amidst acclamations of joy. He did not fail to notice that the *liberales* and their constitution of 1812 were unpopular in the country. At Valencia on 16 April General Elio had publicly declared his determination, and that of the army, to uphold the King in the unrestricted exercise of his powers. And at the same time, Ferdinand received a 'Manifesto of the Persians' signed by ninety-six 'servile' members of the Cortes condemning the constitution.[6] This was enough to overcome Ferdinand's habitual caution. On 4 May he issued a proclamation abolishing the constitution including freedom of the press, and declaring acts of the Cortes void; and a week later on the night of 10 May, Elio's troops occupied Madrid and arrested many leading *liberales*.

Henry Wellesley was careful to avoid any involvement in Ferdinand's coup. He had no love for the *liberales*, but believed that they had strong support in parts of the country and in some sections of the army, and feared that direct action might precipitate a revolution. Ferdinand ignored his warning and did not inform him of his intentions. Wellington had no prior knowledge of the coup at all, and once it had happened, his main concern, shared by Castlereagh, was the danger of civil war. There were rumours that the Third and Fourth Spanish armies, which were in France under Wellington's command, favoured the *liberales* and were preparing to act in their support. With Castlereagh's approval, Wellington proposed to attempt to nip this problem in the bud, and then go on to Madrid 'in order to try whether I cannot prevail upon all parties to be more moderate, and to adopt a constitution more likely to be practicable and to contribute to the peace and happiness of the nation.'[7]

Travelling south, Wellington was reassured to find no signs of impending civil war: the Spanish generals had been anxious not to commit themselves prematurely rather than actively opposing the King. He went on and reached Madrid on 24 May. His first impression was: 'Nothing can be more popular than the King and his measures, as far as they have gone to overthrow the Constitution. The imprisonment of the *Liberales* is thought by some, I believe with justice, unnecessary, and it is certainly highly impolitic; but it is liked by the people at large.' However, the King had failed to follow up his 'great act of vigor' by establishing any new system of government.[8] Wellington urged the King to honour his promise to prepare and issue a new constitution, and warned him that the arrests would provoke widespread criticism, especially in England. He even presented the King with a lengthy memorandum – characteristically forthright and lucid – arguing that Britain not France was the ally vital for Spain's future, and warning that British help, including loans and the arrears of the subsidy, would depend on a relaxation of his measures against his domestic opponents.[9]

Privately Wellington told Castlereagh that while the King and his ministers had been 'very civil' to him, he thought that they looked to France and did not depend much on a close alliance with Britain.[10] This proved a little too pessimistic. Within a few months Henry Wellesley had negotiated an important treaty with Spain, but the two countries were on diverging paths with little legacy of goodwill on either side from the struggle against Napoleon. While Spain attempted to return to eighteenth-century absolutist government, in Britain an increasingly vocal, liberal and confident public emerged, which not only condemned Ferdinand's political oppression at home, but was morally outraged that Spain had not abandoned the slave trade. When Wellington was the guest of honour at a Guildhall dinner in London in July, only three months after the war had ended, the Lord Mayor warned him that any attempt to toast the King of Spain would either be positively refused or 'at least received with so much disgust as to render it very disagreeable to me and to every well wisher to the Spanish government'.[11]

Wellington's mission to Madrid is significant for the insight it provided into his political outlook: his dislike of the unbridled absolution espoused by many of Ferdinand's supporters was as strong as his irritation with the ideologically driven folly of the *liberales* when they had been in power in 1813. The lack of moderation and tolerance appalled him, especially as he believed it was bound to lead to a reaction. Many values that were taken for granted in a British context were in question in Spain, so that Wellington was reduced to instructing the Minister of War on the importance of the rule of law and the separation of the judicial and executive branches of government, so that consequently captain generals should not interfere in the proceedings of the law courts. Above all Wellington upheld the importance of the army standing aloof from politics and accepting its subordination to the government of the day, which in turn refrained from using the army, or its patronage, to pursue the interest of a political faction or party. The rejection of these values contributed greatly to Spain's misfortunes over the next century and a half.[12]

However, Wellington received little credit for these views at home and he was often accused of having tolerated, if not actively supported, Ferdinand's coup, while the faults of the Spanish *liberales* were ignored by a public which knew little of their actual conduct but found their rhetoric appealing. There was a particularly unpleasant element to an article in *The Times* in November which, in the course of defending Henry Wellesley, condemned Wellington for accepting honours from Ferdinand at a time when the leaders of the Cortes who originally proposed the honours 'had been carried from their homes to dungeons'. The chronology on which the charge depended was hopelessly inaccurate, but that hardly mattered for any refutation would simply give the accusations added life. Wellington could point out that he had offended the editor of *The Times* by refusing to accept a friend of Mr Walter's as a chaplain. But that was not the whole story: Mr Walter's nomination had come via Benjamin Sydenham, and Lord Wellesley had a long-standing and close connection with *The Times*. 'I cannot drive from my mind that this paragraph comes from Apsley House [Lord Wellesley's residence],' Wellington told Pole. 'There is in it such a knowledge of facts connected with Henry's transactions in Spain, & with the cause of his stay at Madrid after he had obtained leave of absence, which can be got only from his family . . . God forgive me if I am wrong; and indeed the idea of such a thing is painful enough to carry with it its own punishment.' Lord Wellesley's bile could be contained no longer, and he had revenged himself for Wellington's success. It would take some years for the brothers to be reconciled.[13]

After a fortnight in Madrid Wellington turned his face towards England, pausing for a few days at Bordeaux to farewell the proud army that he had led for the past five years, and which was already being broken up and sent in all directions. He left Bordeaux on 15 June and landed at Dover early on the morning of 23 June. It was less than six years since his last homecoming in the autumn of 1808. Then he had been at the centre of the storm over the Convention of Cintra, lampooned in the prints, and execrated by the press, the lightning rod for the nation's disappointment. Now the mood of the country was completely different, drunk with excitement and pleasure at the rapid end of a war that had lasted for so long and which, only two years before, had seemed interminable. At that moment even the Whigs and radicals were delighted with the peace, and for a brief period Wellington was celebrated as a national hero on all sides, without any dissenting voice making itself heard.

After a clamorous early-morning reception at Dover, Wellington reached London that afternoon, and found Kitty and the boys (Arthur, Lord Douro was now seven; Charles, six) at 4 Hamilton Place, just off Park Lane and around the corner from Apsley House. A crowd gathered by the street, cheering in the hope that Wellington would come to the window, but he had already slipped out the back and gone to visit his mother in Upper Brook Street.[14] The Prince Regent and the allied sovereigns and dignitaries, who were nearing the end of their visit to England, had gone down to Portsmouth for a naval review, and on the following day, 24 June, Wellington followed them. Here he was greeted by rapturous crowds who took the horses from his carriage and drew it to the Regent's abode. 'When he went in,' a newspaper reported, 'the voices of a glad-dened public resounded from the streets and ramparts; and, after the lapse of a few minutes, his Grace, the Duke of Wellington appeared publicly on the balcony and bowed repeatedly. He looked well, and showed strongly his feelings at what he heard and saw. He wore his British uniform, with several orders.'[15] After weeks of cheering foreign leaders, the public was eager to celebrate Britain's own hero.

On Tuesday 28 June, Wellington took his seat in the House of Lords with the Lord Chancellor, Lord Eldon, commenting that never before had a man risen through every step in the peerage, with each step commemorating a separate and worthy triumph. It was an occasion of dignity and state. A large crowd including many members of the Commons had assembled to watch, while the peers' benches were unusually crowded. Both the Duchess of Wellington and the Countess of Mornington (Wellington's mother) were present, and saw Wellington enter the House soon after three o'clock preceded by the Duke of Norfolk, Earl Marshal of England, Sir Isaac Heard, Garter King-at-Arms and Sir Thomas Tyrrwhit, Usher of the Black Rod, and with the Dukes of Richmond and Somerset accompanying him as his supporters. His patents of creation were then severally read – which took 'a considerable time' – before the usual oaths were administered, he signed his name and took his seat. The Lord Chancellor then addressed him to convey the Thanks of the House which had been voted the previous evening and Wellington replied with a suitable, and therefore not strictly accurate, speech in which he paid tribute to the unwavering support he had received from the government, the ample resources entrusted to him, and the 'cordial assistance' he had received from 'the gallant officers who shared my campaigns'. After a few minutes in which he was congratulated by many of the peers he retired to unrobe and returned dressed in his field marshal's uniform with all his decorations, and the House proceeded to consider a petition from the Roman Catholics of England, and the Treaty of Peace with France.[16]

In May the Prince Regent had informed Parliament of Wellington's elevation to a dukedom and asked it for a grant to enable him to support the honour. The ministers, working from precedents, proposed £300,000 in addition to the £100,000 already granted. This ran into opposition of an unexpected kind. Samuel Whitbread, the most radical of the leading Whigs, who had often been scathing in his criticism of Wellington and the Peninsular commitment, now declared that 'there was no man so wicked, so stupid, or so envious, as to venture to detract from the glory of the Duke of Wellington'. And George Ponsonby, the leader of the Whigs in the Commons, went further and proposed that the new grant be raised to £400,000. A somewhat bemused Chancellor of the Exchequer agreed and the vote was passed without dissent.[17]

On 1 July Wellington personally thanked the Commons, being received with immense enthusiasm and continued acclamation. That night there was a grand masked ball held in his honour at Burlington House attended by all the *haut ton* and some of the more fashionable and daring of the *demi-monde* safe behind dominoes (masks). Byron was there, looking 'very well' in the becoming, if incongruous, costume of a monk, while Hobhouse wore his Albanian costume. Supper was held in a temporary room which sat 1,700 persons with ease, and looking back over a long life Hobhouse declared that it was 'the most magnificent thing of the kind ever seen'. Wellington was reported to be 'in great good humour . . . and not squeezed to death'.[18]

A week later came a national service of thanksgiving at St Paul's Cathedral. This was a state occasion on the grandest scale, with a cavalcade of the members of the Commons, the Lords, foreign ambassadors and other dignitaries, mostly in full dress, proceeding through the streets. Soon after eleven o'clock a salute of twenty-one guns announced the departure of the Prince Regent from Carlton House. Wellington accompanied the Prince in his carriage, but not even the presence of the hero of the hour could prevent the crowds from hissing the Regent, for his continuing unpopularity had sharpened in recent months because of an escalation of the long-standing feud with his wife, and the head-strong behaviour of his daughter.[19]

The Regent arrived at the cathedral at about noon, and Wellington walked on his right hand carrying the Sword of State. The service lasted several hours and the artist Joseph Farington recorded that the sermon lasted for thirty-five minutes, but not anything that it contained. He was more interested in observing the dignitaries who were present, and his long list includes Lord Wellesley, Wilberforce, Whitbread, Canning and Picton as well as most of the Cabinet. He also had time to observe that 'the Gold or Gilt service of Plate on the Communion Table was very splendid, and the whole scene [was] magnifi-cent'.[20] When the service was over and the Almighty had been thanked for his discernment in favouring the British cause, the cathedral slowly emptied and the Regent and many of those present returned to Carlton House.

Two days later Wellington's old enemies in the Corporation of the City of London gave him a splendid dinner at the Guildhall and presented him 'with a sword of exquisite workmanship'. Many dignitaries were present and the galleries were crowded with ladies so it is perhaps not surprising that Charles Abbot found it 'very noisy'. Amid the multitude of guests Wellington spotted a face he had not seen in fifteen years: the Captain Eastwick who had carried him from Madras to Fort William so expeditiously in May 1798. Wellington drank a glass of wine with him, and reminded him of a favourite saying to slow sailors: 'What is the delay, you lubber? Are you cutting sticks with a wooden hatchet?'[21]

The celebrations continued all through July and into August with many smaller events filling the intervals between the grand occasions. For example, a dinner was given for Wellington on 11 July by 'the gentlemen of India' with Warren Hastings, then seventy-two and in frail health, in the chair. Naturally Wellington was praised as 'our own Indian-taught general', and it is clear that he retained a warm sense of friendship for many of his old comrades in India, not least for John Malcolm who was in London at the time, and was deputy chairman of the dinner.[22] The culmination of the festivities came on 21 July when the Prince Regent gave a superb fête in the gardens of Carlton House in Wellington's honour. Mrs Calvert, who was present, noted with pleasure: 'The Duke of Wellington was there – just the same good-humoured, unaffected creature he ever was. He met me very kindly, enquiring after Felix [her son, an officer who had been ADC to Sir Thomas Graham].'[23]

The pace slackened after the fête and Wellington was able to get out of London. Yet even here he was the centre of attention and on display, with crowds following him, cheering and calling out blessings. At Salisbury the enthusiasm was overwhelming, and the crowd pressed close so that Wellington's arms were 'almost pulled off in the eagerness of the people to shake hands with him!' Yet Wellington was not annoyed by the incident; indeed he treated it 'with the most perfect good humour'. And this seems to have been typical of his attitude towards all the celebrations and pomp of these weeks; there is no evidence that he viewed them with disdain or cynicism, while his one recorded comment suggests that he felt a good deal of relish in the pleasure of the moment, without taking it too seriously. As he was escorting Lady Shelley from their box at the Opera one night the crowd parted before them with the greatest respect, and Wellington remarked 'in the gayest tone: "It's a fine thing to be a great man, is it not?"'[24]

Lady Shelley was one of the new friends Wellington made in these weeks who would have an important place in his life over the next few years. She was twenty-seven, married, and with a family. Her husband Sir John Shelley was three years younger than Wellington and had served in the army in his youth and in Parliament in 1806, but was best known for his connections with Carlton House and the Turf. Lady Bessborough thought that he seemed a good-natured fool rather than a rogue, although not everyone agreed. Gossip accused them both of blatantly pursuing Wellington in London and later, in Paris, in 1815. If so, they were certainly not alone, and Wellington enjoyed Lady Shelley's company more than most, for she was lively and vivacious, and her flattery was sufficiently subtle to appeal.[25]

If only Kitty, the Duchess of Wellington, had possessed the nerve and zest for society of Lady Shelley! But at forty-two Kitty had long since lost her youthful vivacity without gaining any compensating self-assurance. Five years of independently managing her own household and affairs had done nothing to strengthen her confidence or resilience; she still shrank from high society and was liable to be thrown into a panic by trivialities. Her health and spirits were not robust. It is possible that she was battling clinical depression; certainly she spent far too much time dwelling on her own failings. She was happiest in the country, staying in or near Tunbridge Wells, and devoting herself to her two boys and to Gerald, Henry Wellesley's son.[26]

The long separation had seen no diminution of Kitty's affection for Wellington; he may even have been easier to love *in absentia*. But nor did it diminish the fatal ineptitude and over-eagerness with which she expressed her feeling. For example in the autumn of 1813 she learnt that Wellington was suffering from rheumatism and lumbago while campaigning in the Pyrenees, and asked John Malcolm to get her some Cazaputta oil for her to send him. There was nothing wrong with this, but her comments in a subsequent letter on the subject are all too revealing: 'Thank you, my dear Sir, for your efforts to get me the Cazaputta oil. I hope you may succeed, for though Lord W. is considerably better and will probably receive my offering with scorn, yet it may be of use to him, as those who have once severely suffered from rheumatism are liable to a return.' But if she expected Wellington to receive the oil with scorn, why put everyone to considerable trouble and expense by sending it? And above all, why thus confide in his old friend?[27]

Her reaction to his wound at Orthez was relatively restrained: 'His contusion was, thank God, nothing of consequence, though more than enough to electrify me. I have always seen him in my mind protected by a transparent, impenetrable, adamantine Shield, and settled that he could not be *even touched*; so precious a life, so invaluable – surely the almighty hand of God will protect him.' And in her quiet way she exulted in his victories and in the honours they brought. In August 1813 she was disappointed that victory in the battle of the Pyrenees had not been followed by some 'distinguished mark of approbation', even though it was less than a year since Wellington had been made a marquess, and a few weeks since he had been promoted to field marshal. It is hard to imagine that Kitty had any real desire to be a duchess, for nothing about such eminence suited her, but the thought had stirred and as the months that followed brought tidings of fresh victories, it did not disappear. In March 1814 she confided to Malcolm that she was impatient: 'This Dukedom is such a time a-coming.'[28]

After the war was over Wellington wrote to Kitty from Madrid announcing that he had accepted Castlereagh's offer of the Paris embassy and asking if she would like to accompany him or stay at home. By the standards of the day he was being more than commonly fair in giving her a perfectly free choice, but that very fairness must have wounded her; how she would have welcomed a warm expression of his desire that she should come, or even a confident anticipation that she would! However, she was not well suited to the role of an ambassador's wife who, especially in Paris in 1814, needed to be a hostess on a grand scale and to cut a figure in society, and both he and she knew it. Nonetheless she accepted without hesitation, and she was right to do so. Staying at home would have marked a public separation and would have been tantamount to an open admission that the marriage was all but over. Kitty was not ready for that, and whatever Wellington's feelings may have been, he would not force the issue.[29]

With the end of the season, and fashionable society heading out of London for the country, it was time for Wellington to leave for Paris to take up his new position. He travelled through Belgium which, under the peace settlement, had been united with the Netherlands. Britain viewed the new country as an essential bulwark against renewed French expansion, and had championed its interests in the peace negotiations. She had returned to it the fabulously wealthy Dutch East Indies, and while she retained the poor but strategically important Cape of Good Hope, she paid £2 million in compensation, on condition that this money be spent building fortresses in southern Belgium. The threat of invasion from the Low Countries had haunted British strategic policy for centuries, and experience of Napoleon's naval building programme at Antwerp only sharpened the concern. The small British army taken to Holland by Sir Thomas Graham at the beginning of 1813 had not been withdrawn, although its command was about to be given to the young Hereditary Prince of Orange (son of the ruling Prince of Orange), Wellington's former ADC. The extent of British interest in the Netherlands aroused some jealousy in both Russia and Prussia, but the greatest resentment was naturally felt in France where the loss of Belgium was felt keenly as a blow to national pride and a breach of the doctrine of 'natural frontiers'. The situation was not helped by the fact that many Belgians, especially in the southern, French-speaking part of the country, regarded themselves as French and disliked their incorporation in the United Netherlands.

Wellington's visit was intended to be an affirmation of British support for the Netherlands in the wake of the breakdown of the proposed marriage between Princess Charlotte and the Hereditary Prince of Orange; and it gave him the opportunity to tour the Belgian frontier and advise both governments on the construction of the 'barrier fortresses'. He did not have time to inspect the whole frontier but noted that the west, and in particular the centre between Mons and Namur, were the most vulnerable points. Considering possible lines an invading French army might take, he identified a number of positions in which it might be checked, including 'the entrance of the *forêt de Soignes* by the high road which leads to Brussels' – a position which he himself would successfully defend less than twelve months later.[30] This possibility was in no one's mind in 1814, but even without it Wellington was convinced that his visit had been worthwhile. 'Whatever may be the military consequences of our tour,' he told Bathurst, 'we have made noise enough in the country, and the people are convinced of our intention to defend it.'[31]

Wellington reached Paris on 22 August and on the very next day, even before he had formally presented his credentials, he raised the issue of the slave trade with Talleyrand. In the peace settlement the French, under pressure from Castlereagh, had agreed to abolish the trade within five years, but this had not satisfied Wilberforce and other campaigners, and their protests gained wide support from the press and public. The British government was shaken by the strength of this reaction, and instructed Wellington to endeavour to persuade the French to accept immediate abolition.[32] Both Louis XVIII and Talleyrand were personally sympathetic, but could do little in the face of a powerful West Indian lobby that was supported by public opinion which was almost universally cynical and hostile on the question. British pressure, especially the very public pressure exerted by the newspapers in London, only hardened this resistance, and Wellington asked Wilberforce to quieten their attacks while he endeavoured to change perceptions in France. Convinced of his sincerity and impressed by his commitment to the issue, Wilberforce agreed, and over the next few months Wellington spent much time studying papers and pamphlets on the subject, selecting those most suitable for translating into French and organising their widespread distribution. Wilberforce, Clarkson and Zachary Macaulay were all involved in the resulting campaign, but progress was slow and results meagre – which was not surprising, for it had taken more than twenty years to change opinion in England, and Wellington had barely twenty weeks in France. The British government did all it could to support him, offering £2 million, or even £3 million in compensation, if this would secure immediate abolition or, if money was unacceptable, the valuable colony of Trinidad instead. In the end Wellington secured a ban on the trade north of Cape Formosa, and reiteration of the intention to abolish it at the end of five years, but nothing more. In this respect, if in no other, Napoleon's return from Elba proved fortunate, for he summarily abolished the trade on 29 March 1815.[33]

While the question of the slave trade dominated official business in Wellington's first months in Paris there were many lesser, often mundane, topics which received his careful attention. He was also responsible for acquiring a new British embassy: the splendid Borghese Palace, purchased from Napoleon's sister Pauline. This became a centre of social life, especially for the huge influx of British visitors who were flocking to Paris after the long war. The French shopkeepers naturally benefitted from this flood of tourists, and the initial impact was pleasantly startling – the current English fashion for ladies to wear small bonnets caused a great stir – but it did not take many months before the visitors had become very unpopular, especially among those who regretted Napoleon's fall. There were too many English, with too much money and far too much self-confidence. This resentment was much increased by the marked favour shown to the British by Louis XVIII. Stories circulated that he wore the Garter more often than the French decoration, and that English visitors, however badly dressed, were granted access to court and admitted to the Chapel Royal, while his own subjects were excluded. Lord Hardwicke noted with simple complacency that although the gallery at the Louvre was shut to the public 'yet the English who are desirous of seeing it, have no difficulty in procuring admission'. No wonder that a police report of 2 November stated: 'Hatred for the

English is growing daily. They are regarded as the destroyers of French industry . . . it is said that the King and the princes do not like the French.'[34]

This hostility to the English was part of a much broader wave of discontent that gripped Paris in the autumn of 1814. The bitterest feelings belonged to thousands of unemployed officers, many of them former prisoners of war released from Britain and Russia, who returned home but who could find no niche in civilian society. They were often still young, healthy and ambitious, but their dreams of wealth and glory had fallen with the Empire, and they could see no way to make a living, let alone to recover their hopes. They congregated in the cafés of Paris, eking out tiny pensions and indulging in loose talk against the Bourbons and of – often imaginary – conspiracies. Such men did not represent the majority of the population in Paris, let alone the provinces. They may not even have represented the majority of the army, but their desperation and volatility made them a more dangerous and unstable element than mere numbers would suggest.

Beyond this core of discontent there was a much wider and more pervasive uneasiness. The restoration had yet to put down roots and had dangerously few active partisans. The great majority of the population, and of the political class, gave it tepid acquiescence but no real loyalty. Many royalists were disappointed to see so many of Napoleon's officials still in place, which limited their own hopes of office and promotion. For their part the marshals and other dignitaries of the Empire smarted at social snubs delivered with venom by well-bred ladies and gentlemen with ancient pedigrees, and faced the loss of a large part of their income, for Napoleon had deliberately given them estates outside the ancient limits of France – estates which were now forfeit. Liberals feared that the King and his ministers would seek to emulate Ferdinand VII and govern without parliament, while ministers acted without cohesion or sense of common purpose. None of this was particularly surprising; it was only a matter of months since Napoleon had abdicated and the Bourbons had come to power, more by default and outside pressure than by the choice of the French public. No one, including Louis XVIII and Talleyrand, had a master plan for what to do next, and on the whole the regime was commendably cautious, realising that it was easier to make enemies than friends. Time would help to consolidate its hold on power, but its first year would not be easy.

Wellington's mere presence in Paris was regarded by some Frenchmen as a gross insult – a constant reminder of their defeat and the triumph of their most hated and implacable enemy. Improbable stories circulated, and were eagerly repeated by visiting British Whigs and radicals, of his insufferable behaviour and of his privileged access to the King. He was said to have come to a formal dinner at Marshal Berthier's fresh from hunting and with his 'great coat and boots bespattered with mud'. Hobhouse heard that 'his nod is unsupportable', while James Mackintosh recorded that 'the negligence of the Duke of Wellington's manner and the familiarity of his nods are quoted in every company as proofs of his insolence . . . he has neither courtesy nor display enough to be popular at Paris'.[35] Lack of manners and good breeding was not an accusation made against Wellington at any other point in his life, but if people are determined to feel themselves insulted they will always find a pretext. Whether Castlereagh had made a mistake in sending Wellington to Paris is more debatable. It had been intended as a signal of British support for the restoration, and to help maintain British prestige and influence in Paris, and it had succeeded in these objects. Such prominence was bound to be provocative to those who were not reconciled to the regime. But the Bourbons suffered far more from the appearance of weakness than of strength, and while Wellington's presence may have alienated some waverers and embittered some enemies, it also gave much-needed assurance and confidence to the friends of the new government.

Wellington went out of his way to lessen the personal animus against him by the lavish hospitality he extended to former enemies, some of whose loyalty to Louis XVIII remained rather doubtful. Lady Dalrymple Hamilton dined with Wellington on 3 November and met Marshals Soult, Victor, Macdonald and St Cyr, the first two with their wives. Lady Bessborough commented, with a touch of weariness, that dining at the Duke's on 6 November she met 'more Marshals and Ministers', although she was grateful for an introduction to Masséna who proved entertaining company when she visited in Marseilles later in the year. But it was left to a much younger English visitor to hint at the underlying tensions: '[Soult] and several other marshals who were there cannot but owe Lord Wellington many a grudge, and their countenances are not of the most placid cast.' He had a much greater success in an equally unpromising quarter, winning lavish praise from Madame de Staël, the great liberal intellectual. She had been flattered when he dined with her when he stopped briefly in Paris in June, and this favourable impression was strengthened by further meetings in the autumn. At the end of September she wrote that 'he is very much the fashion here and his manner is simple and noble', while a few weeks later she was even more decided: 'Lord Wellington treats me with great distinction and I am proud of it.' Like most British men he found her political talk a little too earnest and overpowering, but otherwise she was not only 'excessively brilliant' but even 'the most agreeable woman he had ever known.'[36]

Kitty joined Wellington in October and took an active part in the social round. She described the embassy as 'splendid and comfortless', and wrote an amusing account of her presentation at court which poked fun at her own, very real, discomfort, but felt that in a fortnight she had made more progress than she had in three years in England. Others were more critical, and Elizabeth Yorke praised her with all the condescension of youth:

The Duchess of Wellington has arrived to take her station here. Her appearance, unfortunately, does not correspond to one's notion of an ambassadress or the wife of a hero, but she succeeds uncommonly well in her part, and takes all proper pains to make herself and her parties agreeable. Last night we had a pleasant ball there, given on the model of all I have seen here – fiddles and lemonade, but no regular supper, which is better than our London custom, where the expense prevents people enlivening their assemblies with dancing, because of the requisite food and wine it entails upon them.[37]

It was not a life Kitty enjoyed, and Wellington's behaviour made it much worse as Lady Bessborough – herself no stranger to extra-marital affairs – sadly noted:

The D. of W. is so civil to me, and I admire him so much as a hero, that it inclines me to be partial to him, but I am afraid he is behaving very ill to that poor little woman; he is found great fault with for it, *not* on account of making her miserable or of the immorality of the fact, but the want of *procédé* and publicity of his attentions to Grassini.[38]

Wellington's attentions to Grassini, the famous contralto, were far from discreet, especially as she had been a former mistress of Napoleon. One later observer has commented that there was something in the Hôtel Borghese that encouraged romantic indiscretions – Pauline Bonaparte's love life had been flamboyant – and it is rather strange that Wellington, who had been so disciplined and careful in the Peninsula, should have been so incautious in Paris.[39] Still, his behaviour was no different, or just a degree more open, than that of Metternich and the Emperor Alexander at Vienna in these same months. The first whiff of Victorian prudery was in the air, but it was still an age of licence.

Wellington's months in Paris coincided with the first and most important part of the Congress of Vienna, and he kept Castlereagh informed of the views of the French government, which was eager to co-operate with Britain and gain re-admission to the inner councils of the great powers. This was achieved when Castlereagh signed a formal alliance on 3 January 1815 uniting Britain, France and Austria in opposition to Prussia's claims to Saxony; and after a heated confrontation, in which war was freely threatened, the Prussians were forced to give way, although Castlereagh then ensured that they received generous compensation in the Rhineland. Britain's underlying objective was to create powerful barriers to any future French expansion: to the north with the United Netherlands, and to the east with Prussia's new possessions on the Rhine. Wellington advised Castlereagh on some of the strategic issues at stake, such as the importance of the fortress of Luxembourg, and he worked hard to smooth the path for close co-operation between the British and French representatives in Vienna, but even so his role was limited to that of a supporting player, well off centre stage.[40]

While the main focus of the negotiations at Vienna was on central and eastern Europe, the French government was eager to see Murat, Napoleon's brother-in-law, removed from the throne of Naples, and the Neapolitan Bourbons restored. Its hostility to Murat was due less to legitimist ideology or Bourbon family solidarity than the fear that Naples, would become a haven for Bonapartist exiles from France and a centre of disaffection and instability affecting both Italy and France. Spain would give enthusiastic support for the proposal, which also had considerable appeal for Britain, for Sicily had been a British ally throughout the war. On the other hand some Whigs and radicals were attracted to Murat, and managed to regard him as both an Italian patriot and a liberal, despite ample evidence that he was a ringletted *beau sabreur* from Gascony and nothing more. Wellington agreed with Talleyrand that 'Murat's continuance at Naples increases the chance of disturbance in France, which would again disturb all Europe'. But the British government was unwilling to countenance any action and the question was left open for the moment.[41]

At the beginning of November the British government received several reports from France of plots to kill or kidnap Wellington, possibly as part of a wider plan to murder the royal family. The Cabinet decided that Wellington should leave Paris as quickly as possible, with Liverpool, the prime minister, giving him the choice of going to Vienna to advise Castlereagh in the negotiations over the frontier of the Netherlands, or taking command of the British forces in North America with full powers to bring the war to a close either by negotiation or active operations. However Wellington proved reluctant to agree, arguing that his departure would be seen as a defeat for the royalists and for British influence. Liverpool was not persuaded, and while not giving Wellington a direct order, he made it clear that the government was determined to have its way. Wellington at once withdrew any opposition, writing that he would 'make immediate arrangements for quitting Paris', although he could not resist adding: 'No man is a judge in his own case; but I confess that I don't see the necessity for being in a hurry to remove me from hence.' And yet he remained in Paris. Newspaper reports of his impending departure caused a sensation, and he wrote home that leaving would have the worst effects, and that he felt that it would impugn his character by making it look as if he was running away. This was decisive, and Liverpool immediately backed down. By procrastination, persistence and in the end invoking the prerogatives of honour, Wellington had got his own way in the face of the explicit and repeated wishes of the government and without completely sacrificing the appearance of subordination. However, the incident shows that there were clear limits to Wellington's oft-repeated willingness to serve in whatever capacity was required.[42]

Over the next few weeks the ferment in Paris gradually calmed, partly due to the strong measures enforced by Marshal Soult, the newly appointed minister for war. This improvement eased the way for Wellington's departure from Paris in the New Year. There was no need to invent a pretext, for Castlereagh had to go home to lead the government in the Commons when Parliament resumed in February, and Wellington was the obvious replacement.

Wellington's arrival in Vienna at the beginning of February caused considerable excitement. After four months the brilliant round of balls, dinners, receptions and outings had grown rather stale; the vast majority of the distinguished visitors to Vienna had little or no say in the main negotiations, and were growing bored and impatient, while the handful of central players were exhausted. Even Metternich, the chief conductor of the whole Congress, was reported to be 'no longer gay, his colour is grayish, that readiness of speech is gone, his habits have changed'.[43] Wellington was a novelty, a completely new figure of genuine distinction who was nonetheless almost unknown to most observers; and his arrival and the impending departure of Castlereagh gave hope that the Congress was finally drawing towards its conclusion.

The day after Wellington arrived in Vienna the Emperor of Russia called on him and began by saying: 'Things are going on very badly in France, are they not?' 'By no means,' replied the Duke. 'The King is much loved and respected, and behaves with admirable circumspection.' 'You could have told me nothing,' rejoined the Emperor, 'which could have given me so much pleasure. And the army?' 'For foreign wars, against any Power in the world,' said Wellington, 'the army is as good as it ever was; but in questions of internal policy it would probably be worthless.' This at least is how a delighted Talleyrand reported the exchange to Louis XVIII a few days later, and he had his information, in whole or in part, from Russian sources. He added that Alexander was more impressed by the information than he allowed himself to show, and that Russia had soon made further concessions on the details of the settlement of Saxony. Clearly Alexander had hoped to be able to discount French strength because of the discontent in Paris, but had been forced to revise his opinion in the face of Wellington's assurance. Wellington had passed his first test with flying colours.[44]

Castlereagh left Vienna in the middle of February having thoroughly briefed Wellington on all the subjects where negotiations remained unresolved. Little progress had been made since the Duke's arrival largely because Wessenberg, Metternich's deputy and indispensable assistant, had been ill. Once negotiations did revive, in the second half of February, they covered a whole range of subjects. Perhaps the most difficult was the final settlement of Germany, where Metternich was having trouble finding sufficient compensation for Bavaria to balance the return from Salzburg to Austria; and where many details of frontiers in Saxony and the Rhineland remained unresolved. Wellington played a useful secondary part in these negotiations, urging the virtues of moderation and sweet-reasonableness with the philosophy that comes from detachment; Britain had nothing at stake except the desire to achieve a settlement that would leave everyone reasonably satisfied.[45] She was a little more involved in the question of Norway, whose population was stoutly resisting its forcible transfer from Denmark to Sweden. Public opinion and the Opposition in Britain sympathised with the Norwegians, while even Castlereagh, and the government, disliked the deal which had been Bernadotte's price for support against Napoleon in 1812. Wellington's part consisted simply of warning the Swedes that they in turn must honour their pledge to give up Swedish Pomerania (which would be passed on to Prussia in exchange for territorial concessions to Denmark), and in soothing the Emperor of Russia's hostility to the Danes.[46]

Another unresolved question moved much closer to settlement in late February and early March when reports of French determination to act against Murat, and that Murat in turn was increasing his army, led to a dramatic reversal in Austrian policy: not only would Austria stop protecting Murat, she would remove him from the throne of Naples herself. What is more, she acted rapidly: on 4 March Wellington could report that the 'army is in full march; and Metternich appears astonished at his own decision and firmness'.[47] Naturally a request for funding accompanied the news – it sometimes seemed that a corporal's guard could not be changed anywhere in Europe without some statesman appealing for British guineas – although in this case the Austrians asked only for the payment of the subsidy already due to them. It was probable that their request would be viewed favourably, for Castlereagh thought that Austrian action, even if in conjunction with the French, would greatly reduce the risks of acting against Murat.[48]

In the second week of March Wellington and Talleyrand accompanied Metternich to Pressburg to obtain the King of Saxony's consent to the treaties that deprived him of one-third of his kingdom. It was an unpleasant task made worse by the vehement and repeated objections of the King, who showed no gratitude whatever to the three powers which had risked war to ensure that he was left with any kingdom at all.[49] That task done, and with other questions progressing steadily if slowly towards a solution, Wellington might have felt that he was helping the Congress move towards its conclusion, and even speculated on what he would do when it was over. But already, on 7 March, news had reached Vienna which upset all previous calculations, and promised at least a great deal of trouble and uncertainty: Napoleon had escaped from Elba.

CHAPTER TWO

THE RETURN OF NAPOLEON
(March–June 1815)

A T ABOUT THE same time Wellington arrived in Vienna, Napoleon made his decision to escape from Elba. He had quickly tired of his pocket-sized realm and had listened eagerly to reports of discontent in Paris, unrest in Italy, and the quarrels of the allies in Vienna. He missed his wife and child who had failed to join him; while the French government had not honoured its obligation to pay him a substantial pension, and was instead pressing for his removal to a more remote place of exile. He had recovered from the first shock of defeat and, at least superficially, from the exhaustion and strain of the campaigns of 1812–14. At forty-five he was unwilling to abandon all his hopes and ambitions, and instead resolved to attempt to regain all that he had lost. The odds against success were considerable, but not as steep as those against a penniless lieutenant of artillery becoming emperor of the French and arbiter of Europe. The faith in his star that had always sustained his boldness had not deserted him even now.

Napoleon left Elba on the evening of 26 February accompanied by some 1,100 men, most of them veteran troops whom he had been allowed to keep in his service. The flotilla of seven small ships escaped detection and headed for France, landing near Fréjus on 1 March; by midnight Napoleon was master of Cannes. He could have raised his banner in the south and waited for his supporters to rally to it, but instead he took the initiative and marched rapidly north over mountain roads towards Grenoble. Memories of the hostile crowds he had encountered the previous year in his journey through southern France to Elba were too fresh for him to delude himself with hopes of popular support in the region and, in any case, he knew that his best chance was to catch the government by surprise and build up an appearance of irresistible momentum that would impress waverers and discourage opponents. On 7 March at the pass of Laffrey outside Grenoble a battalion of 5ᵉ *Ligne* and some engineers blocked his path. In a scene that would be immortalised in a superb – and wildly unrealistic – piece of artistic propaganda by Carl Steuben, Napoleon advanced and invited the soldiers to shoot their emperor, and, after a momentum of hesitation their discipline dissolved and they flocked to join him. Other troops soon followed suit and Napoleon entered Grenoble without a shot having been fired.

The first reports of Napoleon's escape reached Vienna that same morning, 7 March, in a despatch to Metternich from Lord Burghersh who was now British envoy to Tuscany. No one as yet knew where Napoleon had gone, although some form of combined action with Murat in Italy seemed a likely possibility. Metternich promptly informed the allied sovereigns and ministers who issued orders to mobilise their forces, while the Emperor Francis personally ordered Bellegarde to destroy Napoleon if he landed in Italy. No public statement was issued, but rumours soon began to circulate and Wellington thought it necessary to warn the King of Saxony against pinning his hopes on a chimera and losing the chance of salvaging the best part of his realm.[1]

Metternich, Talleyrand and Wellington returned to Vienna from Prague late on 11 March and learnt that Napoleon had landed in France. Talks during the following day resulted in the Emperors of Austria and Russia and the King of Prussia writing to Louis XVIII offering him the assistance of their forces, if needed, to deal with the threat. The plenipotentiaries of the eight powers who had signed the Treaty of Paris (Britain, France, Austria, Russia, Prussia, Spain, Portugal and Sweden) resolved to publish a declaration of their determination to maintain the settlement. This was issued on 13 March and not only pledged a united effort to maintain the general peace, but proclaimed confidence 'that all France, rallying round its legitimate Sovereign, will immediately annihilate this attempt of a criminal and impotent delirium'. It also declared that Napoleon had voided the terms of the treaty that granted him sovereignty of Elba, and that this 'destroys the only legal title on which his existence depended: by appearing again in France with projects of confusion and disorder, he has deprived himself of the protection of the law, and has manifested to the universe, that there can be neither peace nor truce with him. The Powers consequently declare, that Napoleon Buonaparte has placed himself without the pale of civil and social relations, and that as an enemy and disturber of the tranquility of the world, he has rendered himself liable to public vengeance.' This language was a compromise; the initial French proposal, 'which virtually called Napoleon a wild beast and invited any peasant lad or maniac to shoot him down at sight', was softened by the opposition of Metternich, who had not forgotten that Napoleon was still the son-in-law of the Emperor Francis, and Wellington, who denounced the idea of encouraging assassination or murder as a private sport.[2]

Preliminary plans for military action were drawn up in case Napoleon was able to have some success against the forces of Louis XVIII, and their scale shows that the Powers took the potential threat of Napoleon very seriously indeed. The Austrians would form an army of 150,000 men in Italy which would need to keep the country quiet, and an eye on Murat, as well as to guard the border with France. Bavaria, Württemburg and Baden would provide the initial nucleus of an army of the Upper Rhine, which would be brought up to some 200,000 men when Austrian reserves had time to arrive. A third army would be based in the Netherlands and on the Lower Rhine and would include Kleist's Prussian corps and the British, Dutch and Hanoverian troops already in Belgium. Wellington was designated as commander of this force. A Russian army of 200,000 men would form a central reserve based in Wurtzburg, a prospect which did more to alarm than reassure Metternich, who felt that it might leave the Russians with an overwhelming predominance as the last man standing. The remainder of the Prussian army was to form a similar reserve on the Lower Rhine. The Emperor Alexander floated the idea that he should be given the supreme command, but finding that this was 'not relished' by anyone, let it drop and was reconciled to 'the old System of managing the great concern in a council consisting of Himself, the King of Prussia and Schwarzenberg'. Wellington also reported that the Emperor 'expressed a wish that I should be with him, but not a very strong one; and as I should have neither Character, nor occupation in such a Situation, I should prefer to carry a musquet'.[3]

Despite his knowledge of the discontent in France, Wellington was remarkably optimistic, telling Castlereagh on 12 March: 'It is my opinion that Buonaparte has acted upon false or no information, and that the King will destroy him without difficulty, and in a short time.' Although he added the caveat: 'If he does not, the affair will be a serious one.' Wellington was pleased with the reaction of the allies in Vienna and assured Castlereagh: 'I don't entertain the smallest doubt that, if unfortunately it should be possible for Buonaparte to hold at all against the King of France, he must fall under the cordially united efforts of the Sovereigns of Europe.'[4]

By the time that this despatch reached London it was clear that there would be work for 'the Sovereigns of Europe' and their armies. Every attempt to block Napoleon's march north failed, and the royalists all too obviously lacked the necessary determination and coolness to rally support. Soult was dismissed as minister of war on suspicion of treachery; Ney was caught in a conflict of loyalties and deserted to Napoleon rather than risk precipitating a civil war or finding that his men would not follow him. With all hope gone, the court prepared to embark on its travels again; in the early hours of 20 March Louis XVIII fled from Paris, crossing the frontier into Belgium a few days later. The *Moniteur* reported events with superb insouciance: 'The King and princes left in the night. H. M. the Emperor arrived this evening at 8 o'clock in his palace of the Tuileries at the head of the same troops which had been sent to block his route this morning.'[5]

In England the news was greeted with dismay across the political spectrum. Queen Charlotte condoled with her son for the 'disastrous catastrophe', and condemned the 'Emperor of Russia & King of Prussia' who 'had it in their power to prevent this tyrant to do any more mischief, by crushing him when . . . it was in their power'.[6] And Samuel Romilly, the humanitarian reformer and radical, wrote in his diary that 'After twelve days of most painful and increasing anxiety' it was clear that Napoleon's venture would succeed:

> So sudden, complete, and bloodless a revolution more resembles fiction than history. Napoleon seems, as it were at his pleasure, and just at his own season, quietly to have resumed his empire. But what a dreadful prospect is thus suddenly opened to mankind! What dismay must not these tidings strike into the hearts of hundreds of thousands of human beings in every station of life, from the throne to the cottage! What a deluge of blood must be shed! How various and how terrible the calamities which are now impending over states and over individuals.[7]

Only J.W. Ward, writing from Rome, admitted to mixed feelings:

> As an Englishman one must wish him to fail. His restoration would occasion a renewal of the war, and the income tax renewed with it would be piled upon the last budget to break the backs of the unfortunate people of England. This is reason enough for wishing him at the Deuce, if there were not twenty more. And yet the actions of the greatest captain that ever lived have been so glorious and astonishing . . . and the enterprise in which he is now engaged is so unexpected, so rapid, so brave and so chivalrous, that I cannot help harbouring some feelings with respect to him which are neither very reasonable nor very patriotic.[8]

There was less unanimity over the course Britain should take. The ministers and most of their supporters, Lord Grenville and his connections, and many Whigs believed that Napoleon's return made war inevitable, and that any delay beyond that needed to mobilise the allied armies would simply allow him to consolidate his position in France. But Wilberforce had doubts, being torn between his inclination to negotiate with Napoleon and the recognition that this would almost inevitably lead to the break-up of the alliance which had won the war in 1814. As late as 10 May he wrote in his diary: 'If Buonaparte could be unhorsed, it would, humanly speaking, be a blessing to the European world; indeed to all nations. And government ought to know both his force and their own. Yet I greatly dread their being deceived, remembering how Pitt was.' Lord Grey went further, writing privately that he could see no justification for a war directed against Napoleon as an individual, and that Britain had neither an obligation under a treaty, nor a right to take arms to seek to determine who governed France.[9] Grey was not eager to debate the question, for it would reveal divisions within the Opposition, but Whitbread seldom allowed such tactical considerations to influence him when he felt strongly on an issue. On 7 April, in a debate on the Regent's address, he launched a scathing attack on the government's policy and the likelihood of war, praising Napoleon for his abolition of the slave trade, and denouncing Wellington for signing the allied declaration. Even allowing for the broad licence of parliamentary oratory it was an extraordinary personal attack:

He could not help expressing his regret, that one of the greatest names of which England could boast had been sullied, by setting his seal to such a deed on the Declaration of the Allies. All the brilliancy of his achievements, and all the splendor of his character, would not be sufficient to drag him out of the abyss of shame into which he had plunged himself, by setting his name to this Declaration.

. . .

He maintained that lords Cathcart, Clancarty and Stewart, and the duke of Wellington, deserved impeachment for putting their names to such an instrument.

. . .

If words meant anything, that Declaration went to designate an individual for assassination. Much might be said (and he trusted would be said by some of his hon. and learned friends) of its inconsistency with the law of nations, as well as of its hostility to every principle of social order. It led directly to a war of extermination.[10]

Castlereagh might assure Wellington that 'Whitbread did not make much last night of his attack upon your declaration',[11] but Wellington could read the speech for himself in the newspapers and in subsequent attacks, for Whitbread did not abandon the issue despite having the support of only a small minority of Parliament. Wellington was understandably irritated and hurt by the criticism, telling Pole that:

The mode of attacking a servant of the public absent on the public service, day after day in speeches in Parliament, which has been lately adopted by Mr Whitbread, appears to me most extraordinary and unprecedented.

If I have done anything wrong or unbecoming my own character, or that of the station I filled, I ought to be prosecuted, or at least censured for it, in consequence of a specific motion on the subject; but it is not fair to give to the act of any individual a construction it will not fairly bear, a construction which no man breathing believes it was intended to bear; and to charge him home with being an assassin day after day in speeches, and never in form.[12]

The Duke went on to dispute the published translation of '*vindicte publique*' as 'public vengeance' rather than 'public justice', but added that even if this was accepted: 'When did the dagger of the assassin execute the vengeance of the public?'

Wellington's discomfort was much increased by Lord Wellesley's stance. Not that the Marquess supported Whitbread's attacks – that would have been too blatant – but he opposed a renewal of the war, arguing that the country was too exhausted to make a fresh effort, and that the Bourbons were so discredited that even in the event of complete success they could only be kept on the throne by a prolonged British military commitment for which there was neither the funds nor the requisite popular support. These arguments, which might have been unremarkable coming from Huskisson or Lord Auckland, were so out of tenor with Lord Wellesley's whole career that they raise doubts as to his motives, and arouse the suspicion that jealousy of Wellington was more influential in shaping his view than a new-found concern for the national finances.[13]

Notwithstanding this opposition the government had large majorities in all the debates, and the ministers were confident the country as a whole supported them. They were careful to limit their war aims to the overthrow of Napoleon, rejecting pleas from Talleyrand to uphold the principle of legitimacy. This restraint sat well with moderate opinion in Britain and with the attitudes of the allies, for the ease with which Louis XVIII had been overthrown revived all Alexander's contempt for the Bourbons, while Metternich, as usual, sought to preserve the maximum room to manoeuvre. However, neither Alexander nor Metternich had a definite alternative to offer, and while the British government had no doubt that its preferred outcome was the restoration of the Bourbons, it would not make this a *sine qua non* of peace. Wellington agreed and was confident that 'the great majority of the population in France are decidedly adverse to Buonaparte, and that many Generals and other officers, the whole of the National Guard, and even some regiments of the line, have remained faithful to the King.'[14] Still, there was no denying that the Bourbons had been damaged by their eleven months in power, and Wellington believed that the government should seriously consider a compromise figure such as the Duc d'Orléans if Napoleon was overthrown by the Jacobins or the army – a possibility raised by many rumours that April.[15]

Meanwhile preparations for war continued. Wellington remained at Vienna until 29 March absorbed in negotiations on a variety of subjects, of which the most difficult was whether troops from the small states of northern Germany should be attached to his army in the Netherlands or the Prussian army on the

Lower Rhine. This should have been a relatively simple question solved by compromise and goodwill, but the Prussians were feeling extremely sore and discontented in the spring of 1815 and were ready to make difficulties. Their main grievance, of course, was Saxony; all the other powers had got what they most wanted from the Vienna settlement; only Prussia had been deprived of the fruits of victory. Exacerbating this feeling was the sense, particularly strong in the army, that they had never received full recognition for their role in the defeat of Napoleon in 1813–14. Senior soldiers spoke with contempt of their diplomats and statesmen, although they must have known in their hearts that the real weakness was in the King, not his ministers. Eventually a compromise was reached after Wellington left Vienna, by which the Nassau contingent went to Wellington, the Hessians to Kleist, and the Saxons were divided, with those men coming from the parts of the country ceded to Prussia going to the Prussians, and the rest to Wellington. This last proved hopelessly impractical as Saxon regiments had to be split in half. Their already precarious morale collapsed as the reality of partition hit home and the men mutinied in early May, giving the Prussians a not entirely unwelcome opportunity to impose their authority and punish the trouble-makers.[16]

Naturally the Prussians blamed British interference for stirring up trouble and for giving small states ideas above their station. Other issues contributed to this sense: for example Wellington insisted that the commissaries of his army buy supplies at the market rate, while the other allies all expected to get their needs at low fixed prices. The discrepancy did not affect the Austrians and Russians, who were far away, but it naturally disadvantaged Prussian commissaries looking for provisions in the Netherlands, while the German contingents of Wellington's army were forced to pay high prices for the supplies they consumed, while their families at home had no choice but to sell cheap to the Prussians. Again a compromise was devised which resolved this difficulty (Wellington's Germans were allowed to pay low prices and the difference was made up by the government of the Netherlands), but it was just another example of how insufferable the British were: too rich, too full of themselves, and all too ready to put everyone else into the wrong![17]

Still, it is important not to get this irritation out of perspective. There was no serious conflict between the national interests of Prussia and Britain, and the friction caused by these disputes cannot compare to Prussian hatred of France, or even her long-standing rivalry with Austria. Among the great powers Prussia felt closer to Britain than to any except Russia, and Russia had betrayed her over Saxony. For their part the British looked to Prussia as a valuable bulwark against French expansion on the Rhine or in the Low Countries. They may have been patronising, but no more so than they were towards the rest of the world, and at least their condescension was backed by cash.

Wellington's search for troops for his army extended well beyond the small states of Germany. At one point there was even a suggestion that he be given 15–20,000 Austrians, although given Austria's other commitments it is no surprise that this came to nothing. Before he left Vienna he warned Castlereagh that the army in the Netherlands was 'very short' in numbers, 'and the troops in that quarter are not of the best description'. To remedy this he proposed bringing 12,000–14,000 Portuguese troops to Belgium by sea. The British government feared that this might prove both slow and expensive, while the idea was greeted with marked lack of enthusiasm by the Regency Council in Lisbon despite Beresford's support, and although some preparations were made the troops never sailed.[18]

Wellington reached Brussels on the evening of 4 April, although he did not formally take command of the allied forces from the Prince of Orange until 11 April. The twenty-two-year-old Prince, and his even younger brother Frederick, were both given senior commands in the army for obvious political reasons – although the latter's authority was probably more nominal than real. Nonetheless Wellington's relations with the princes' father, the new King of the United Netherlands, were strained. The central problem was that the King had not made Wellington Commander-in-Chief of his army, and objected to Wellington's desire to mix Dutch-Belgian units with those of the other allied contingents, rather than keep them together. Adding to the tension was British distrust of a number of the King's senior officers and advisors – men who had spent many years loyally serving Napoleon – and the belief that the Dutch-Belgium army as a whole (and especially the Belgian units) were far from reliable. Sir John Colborne (military secretary to the Prince of Orange) had warned on 21 March: '*I would not trust the Belgian Troops an inch.* Some of the men of the 2 Regiments at Mons began the cry of *Vive Napoleon* on the first arrival of the news.' As a result the British firmly insisted on maintaining their own garrisons in Ostend and Antwerp – an essential precaution but one which was bound to arouse resentment. Nonetheless most of these issues were gradually resolved; Wellington was made a field marshal in the Netherlands service in May, and despite the points of friction the alliance worked quite well on the whole.[19]

Throughout the spring of 1815 the allies were torn between two conflicting ideas. On the one hand they believed that Napoleon had little support in France outside the army, and that the sooner he could be attacked the less chance he would have of consolidating his position. On the other, they were acutely aware of the simmering discontent in many parts of Europe, from Belgium to Poland, Saxony to Italy, and among the 'Jacobins' and 'liberals' of many nations. They feared that if Napoleon achieved even a temporary success this discontent might burst into flame and engulf all Europe in another prolonged war. This view favoured waiting until the allies had a crushing preponderance of force before beginning any advance. So fine was the balance between these ideas that both Castlereagh and Wellington repeatedly veered from one to another as each fresh piece of news strengthened their hopes or their fears. This indecision was never entirely resolved, but the commencement of the allied offensive was constantly postponed, although by early June Wellington was able to hope that by the middle of the month the Russian and Austrian armies would be ready to begin the campaign.[20]

At the same time Wellington frequently complained that the British government was not acting with sufficient energy especially in building up his army. It was easy for Wellington to say that he would be 'satisfied' with '40,000 good British infantry, besides those you insist upon having in garrisons', 12,000 British cavalry, 'and 150 pieces of British artillery fully horsed'; such demands simply could not be met, or at least not for some months. Too many of the best troops from the Peninsular army had been sent to America and were still on the other side of the Atlantic; while many others had already been discharged with the coming of peace. The troops from America were being brought home as quickly as possible – Bathurst announced the arrival of the ill-fated New Orleans expedition on 16 May and sent troops fit for immediate service straight on to Ostend – but others would not arrive until September when the campaign would probably already have been decided. And if 40,000 British infantry was an optimistic demand, 12,000 cavalry and 150 guns was quite unrealistic – more than the highest strength of either arm in the Peninsula. Still, it appears that the pressure Wellington applied encouraged both the Horse Guards and the Ordnance to redouble their efforts to support him, and while the final totals fell short of Wellington's demands they considerably exceeded what Torrens believed would be possible in April.[21]

However, questions remained over the quality of some of these contingents. British doubts over the loyalty of the Belgian troops have already been mentioned, while the Duke of Cambridge, who was governor of Hanover, warned Wellington that:

> although this corps has been raised about a year, the men have been together hardly above six weeks, having been upon the peace establishment, according to which the greater part of the men are upon furlough for eleven months of the year: they are, therefore, not in that state of drill I could wish them; the officers for the most part have never served; and indeed many vacancies have been kept open . . . I must do both the officers and men the justice to say that there is the greatest good will in them, and I have every reason to hope that they will do their duty.[22]

Even the British troops did not merit unqualified praise, in Colborne's view: 'The British Regiments are in good order,' he told Bunbury on 21 March, 'but composed of Young Soldiers who have never been on service except in Holland, in 1814. Could not the Guards be gradually changed? The Officers are almost all Boys, the Men Recruits, and have never heard a shot fired, except 3 or 400 who are too infirm for hard service. The Cavalry and Infantry of the [King's German] Legion are excellent.'[23]

Given this it is not surprising that Wellington himself complained in early May that 'I have got an infamous army, very weak and ill equipped and a very inexperienced Staff'. Like many of Wellington's most memorable phrases this expressed only part of the truth and the army improved significantly before the campaign began in the middle of June. Still there is no doubt that the army of 1815 was much inferior to the Peninsular army of 1812–14, and it is easy to see why Wellington was so keen to have his old troops – British and Portuguese – back again. It was less a question of courage than of cohesion, discipline and confidence, and with so many less experienced troops Wellington was much less inclined to manoeuvre or attack, even if the strategic situation had called for it.[24]

Staff appointments proved another sore point, mostly because there was already a numerous and not very efficient staff in place, and the Horse Guards, in the first anxiety that Napoleon might attack immediately, made a number of additional appointments without consulting Wellington. This created a considerable obstacle, for in such matters possession was at least nine parts of the law, and Wellington shrank from wholesale dismissals simply to make space for officers he preferred. The Horse Guards exacerbated the problem by continuing to appoint officers from home – an exercise of authority which the Duke of York would have been wiser to forgo. Wellington was mortified at having to tell many officers who had served him well on the staff in the Peninsula that he had no vacancy for them in Belgium, especially as it was universally assumed that all such decisions rested with him personally, so that he had the opprobrium of refusal without the benefit of patronage. This led to a sharp complaint to Bathurst in early May:

To tell you the truth, I am not very well pleased either with the manner in which the Horse Guards have conducted themselves towards me. It will be admitted that the army is not a very good one; and, being composed as it is, I might have expected that the Generals and Staff formed by me in that last War would have been allowed to come to me again: but instead of that, I am overloaded with people I have never seen before; and it appears to be purposely intended to keep those out of my way whom I wished to have. However, I'll do the best I can with the instruments which have been sent to assist me.[25]

Despite this outburst Wellington did manage to secure the appointment of officers he knew and trusted to most of the key posts on his staff before the campaign began. The senior places in his immediate household were filled with familiar faces: Fitzroy Somerset as military secretary, Colin Campbell as headquarters commandant, and Alexander Gordon, Charles Fox Canning and John Fremantle heading the list of aides-de-camp. The vital post of Quartermaster-General would be filled by Sir George Murray as soon as he returned from Canada, and in the meantime Wellington secured the removal of Sir Hudson Lowe and his replacement by William Howe De Lancey. The junior ranks of the staff included many experienced and capable officers, but whatever their ability as individuals the machinery could not be expected to run smoothly from the outset, while the campaign was so brief and bloody that the staff was completely disrupted by casualties before it could become fully effective. This was not a problem limited to Wellington's army; the French and Prussians also suffered from poor staff work because officers had no time to find their feet.[26]

The selection of subordinate generals to serve under Wellington was also full of difficulties and awkwardness. Henry Paget, now Lord Uxbridge, and Stapleton Cotton, Lord Combermere were both eager to command the cavalry. The Prince Regent had always favoured Paget, and Wellington made no objection despite his loyalty to Combermere and Paget's role in the break-up of Henry Wellesley's marriage.[27] Rowland Hill, Henry Clinton and Charles Colville had already been sent out to Belgium, and would be given senior commands, while Sir Thomas Picton and Charles Alten joined before the campaign began. The major-generals included such well-known names from the Peninsula as James Kempt, John Byng, Denis Pack and Lord Edward Somerset, while at a slightly lower level Colborne commanded his beloved 52nd and Frederick Ponsonby the 12th Light Dragoons. Few British generals have opened a campaign with so much proven experience at their command, and Wellington's one real grievance in this respect was his most senior artillery officer, Sir George Wood. It has been suggested that Wellington had blocked Wood's appointment to the Peninsula, and he had instead served under Graham in the Low Countries in 1814 which meant that he was already in place in Belgium in 1815. It is not clear if Wellington endeavoured to have him removed, but after the battle he complained to Bathurst that 'the Com[mandin]g Officer of the Artillery knows no more of his business than a child, and I am obliged to do it for him; and, after all, I cannot get him to do what I order him'.[28]

By the middle of June Wellington's army amounted to about 110,000 men. Some troops were detached in garrisons or held in reserve, but the great majority served in the main field army. This was organised into three corps, commanded by the Prince of Orange, Rowland Hill and the 'Reserve' under

Wellington himself. Each corps contained two 'British' divisions, and a roughly equal number of foreign troops: two Dutch-Belgian divisions in the first corps, one and a half in the second, and the Brunswick and Nassau contingents in the Reserve. Most 'British' divisions however were themselves made up of two British or King's German Legion brigades and a Hanoverian brigade so that the British and King's German Legion infantry, on which Wellington most depended, were spread evenly throughout the army. There were seven British, one Hanoverian and three Dutch-Belgian brigades of cavalry, but only the latter were organised into a division. And there were 203 guns and a section of rockets – a figure which does not include the Dutch-Belgian Reserve artillery nor the British siege train. Altogether Wellington had under his command 129 battalions of infantry (approximately 87,000 men), 106 squadrons of cavalry (16,000 men) and 8,600 artillerymen.

British	36,176	all ranks	(33.1 per cent)
King's German Legion	8,322	all ranks	(7.6 per cent)
Hanoverian	24,554	all ranks	(22.5 per cent)
Dutch-Belgian and Nassau	33,205	all ranks	(30.4 per cent)
Brunswick	6,894	all ranks	(6.3 per cent)
	109,151	all ranks[29]	

Whether standing on the defensive or in an invasion of France, Wellington's army would act in co-operation with the Prussians under Blücher. The Prussians were still upset by the results of the Congress of Vienna, with Blücher declaring that Napoleon's return was 'the greatest piece of good luck that could have happened to Prussia! Now the war will begin again! The army will fight and make good all the faults committed in Vienna!' A few weeks later Wellington reported that the Prussians had learnt of details of the alliance between Britain, Austria and France signed at the beginning of the year to resist, by war if necessary, Berlin's claim to Saxony. Although this discovery 'has rendered them excessively indignant against us', it did nothing to lessen Prussian hatred of Napoleon or affect their willingness to co-operate against him.[30]

Staff talks began well before either Wellington or Blücher reached Belgium, and while the Prussians were just as concerned with covering Mainz and the middle Rhine as with Brussels, they were conciliatory. In essence the Prussians believed that the best plan was to agree to concentrate the two armies at Tirlemont east of Brussels if Napoleon launched an offensive, while the British, worried about the political implications of uncovering so much of Belgium, favoured a more forward concentration near Genappe, Fleurus or Gembloux.[31] This was dangerously close to the frontier, meaning that the armies would have little time to concentrate before facing the French in battle, although the

Prussian plan would leave the two lines of communication (which lay in opposite directions: the British north to Antwerp and east to Ostend, the Prussians
east through Liège) more vulnerable. On the whole the Prussian plan was
probably better; if Napoleon attacked the campaign would be quickly decided
by a battle or series of battles, and the temporary loss of Brussels would matter
little if it was followed by Napoleon's defeat. But Gneisenau yielded to
Wellington before Blücher arrived, although it was never likely that the old
Marshal would object to a forward move. Gneisenau's letter of 7 April to Sir
Hudson Lowe announcing the decision shows a conscious determination not
to put the narrow interests of the Prussian army ahead of the allies as a whole:

> On the 11th our troops will be in those points whence they may succour
> yours and cover the capital, in case the enemy should be in too great numbers.
> This movement is dangerous to us Prussians in case of a reverse. Our army
> would then be forced to pass the Meuse on a single bridge, to repass it at Huy
> to be on the same bank with the enemy, and to pass the river for the third time
> at Liège. You feel, General, how great must be our confidence in the talents
> and character of the duke of Wellington.[32]

The Prussian army subsequently took up position between Charleroi and
Liège, with its outposts on the French frontier and its first line along the Sambre
from Charleroi to Namur. This was further forward than Wellington's army
which was in quarters as far north as Brussels and stretching well to the west.
Wellington and Blücher met at Tirlemont on 3 May and Blücher visited
Wellington in Brussels at the end of the month. Future operations were bound
to have been discussed at these meetings but there is no record of any detailed
contingency planning beyond a determination to stand or fall together.[33] In
part this was because both generals were gaining confidence in their ability to
withstand an attack and were looking forward to an allied invasion of France.
On 8 May Wellington told Charles Stewart: 'I say nothing about our defensive
operations, because I am inclined to believe that Blücher and I are so well
united, and so strong, that the enemy cannot do us much mischief.' And on
2 June Henry Hardinge, Wellington's liaison officer with the Prussians, wrote
that 'this head quarters [is] very impatient to begin operations . . . Marshal
Blücher, in talking of the reported state of things in France, said to me pretty
publicly that he was quite ready to begin if the Duke would'.[34]

Amid all the military preparations Brussels enjoyed a thriving social life in
which the large expatriate British community and officers from the army
played a prominent part. Fanny Burney saw Wellington at a recital by Catalani,
and 'was charmed with every turn of his countenance, with his noble and

singular physiognomy and his eagle eye. He was gay even to sportiveness all the evening, conversing with the officers around him. He never was seated, not even a moment, though I saw seats vacated to offer him frequently. He seemed enthusiastically charmed with Catalani, ardently applauding whatsoever she sung, except the Rule, Britannia; and there with sagacious reserve he listened in utter silence.' Spencer Madan, the tutor to the Richmond children, described him in April:

> The Duke of W. was in the highest spirits, full of fun and drollery, and made himself the life & soul of the company . . . In the drawing room before dinner he was playing with the children, who seem to look up to him as to one on whom they might depend for amusement & when dinner was announced they quitted him with great regret saying 'Be sure you remember to send for us the moment dinner is over' which he promised he wd. do, and was good as his word.[35]

Thomas Creevey was less impressed after a dinner in April at which Wellington maintained that the Jacobins were about to overthrow Napoleon and establish a republic. 'I thought several times he must be drunk; but drunk or sober, he had not the least appearance of being a clever man. I have seen a good deal of him formerly, and always thought the same of his talents in conversation.' However, Lady Capel (Lord Uxbridge's sister) was reassured by Wellington's high spirits and the fact that he encouraged his niece, Emily Somerset, Fitzroy's wife, to remain in Brussels even though she was pregnant (her daughter Charlotte was born on 16 May). Wellington gave two balls in close succession in early June, and Lady Capel noted that he 'has not improved the *Morality* of our Society, as he has given several things & makes a point of asking all the Ladies of Loose Character – Every one was surprised at seeing Lady John Campbell at his House & one of his Staff told me that it had been represented to him her not being received for that her Character was more than Suspicious. "Is it, by ___" said he, "then I will go & ask her Myself". On which he immediately took his Hat & went out for the purpose.' A fortnight later she added: 'I should suppose the Commencement of Hostilities (If they ever do begin) cannot be far distant – But Nobody can guess Lord Wellington's intentions, & I dare say Nobody will know he is going till he is actually gone. In the meantime he amuses himself with Humbuging [*sic*] the Ladies, particularly the Duchess of Richmond.'[36] It would not be long before he had been 'humbugged' himself.

CHAPTER THREE

QUATRE BRAS
(15–17 June 1815)

W HEN NAPOLEON ARRIVED in Paris on 20 March 1815 he encountered no
open resistance. Attempts to raise the royalist standard at Bordeaux
flickered fitfully then went out, although there would be more serious trouble
in the Vendée in the months to come. However, genuine active support for the
Emperor was also very limited; the army and veterans were, with some notable
exceptions, enthusiastic. More surprisingly those on the left of politics, whom
he had little favoured when in power before, were inclined to prefer him to the
Bourbons. Although they continued to be known as Jacobins, these politicians
had greatly moderated their views, and had much more in common with the
liberales of Spain, British radicals, and similar groups across Europe, than with
Robespierre and the Jacobins of 1793. Napoleon sought to conciliate them with
fair words, promises of constitutional rule and gestures such as the abolition of
the slave trade, but it was essentially a marriage of convenience and neither side
could place much reliance on the other.

Napoleon professed to want peace and France was certainly war-weary, but
the allies made it plain that they would not quietly accept his return, while he
could only satisfy his supporters in the army by reversing all the peacetime
reductions imposed by the Bourbons, and this could only be paid for by
unpopular and unsustainable increases in taxation or by war. Napoleon's whole
regime had always rested on making war profitable, if not for France, at least
for the French army and his new ruling elite. France in 1815 was simply not
wealthy enough to satisfy the appetites and expectations of his supporters, and
if war had been avoided then, it would have followed within a year or two.[1]

On his return to power Napoleon wasted no time in mobilising the army
and equipping it to take the field, so that the spring of 1815 saw a race between
France and the allies to collect their military forces and get them into position.
In theory Napoleon might have waged a defensive campaign as he had done in
1814. This would have brought some strategic advantages, but it would almost

certainly have been a mistake in military terms to allow the allies to delay the fighting until they were ready, and it would have been politically disastrous to attempt to fight the war on French soil. Napoleon's best, almost his only, hope for survival lay in a quick successful offensive that would bring some immediate booty to the army, affirm his prestige, cause dissension and doubts among the allies, and possibly open the way for peace negotiations. The most suitable field for such an operation lay to the north in Belgium.

By early June Napoleon was ready to strike with a field army of some 120,000 men including a high proportion of cavalry and artillery. The components of the army were excellent, although the logistical and other support services were less efficient. The spirit of the lower ranks was good, but there was considerable distrust towards and among the senior officers, with tension between those who had adhered to Napoleon's cause early, and those who only joined him when he was again the effective ruler of France. Both Soult, whom Napoleon employed as his chief of staff, and Ney, who was given command of the left wing at the last minute, had much to live down before the army as a whole would be convinced that they deserved their places.[2] To hold Paris and guard his rear Napoleon chose Marshal Davout, whose iron hand and complete loyalty could be relied upon to keep intrigue in check, at least until news from the front showed which way the wind blew. A likely source of that intrigue was Fouché, whom Napoleon restored to his old position at the head of the police as a sop to the Jacobins, and whose combination of subtlety and disloyalty was a stark antithesis to Davout.

Napoleon left Paris early on 12 June and travelled rapidly north to join the army, which had been concentrated on the frontier near Beaumont. The campaign began at first light on 15 June with the French driving in Prussian outposts on the frontier, crossing the Sambre and taking Charleroi, then pushing on further north. The fighting was quite heavy in places, for the men of Zieten's corps resisted stoutly and sustained some 1,200 casualties. Blücher's reaction to the news was to order his whole army to concentrate around Sombreffe in order to give battle at Ligny on the following day; however, the order sent to Bülow failed to convey the necessary sense of urgency and Bülow did not order his men to march until the following morning, which made it impossible for them to reach Sombreffe on 16 June. It was just the first of many errors that would affect all three armies during the campaign.[3]

The few days of the Waterloo campaign have been studied so intensively that the original documents have been probed and tested beyond breaking point, with the result that trivial anomalies and inconsistencies, together with gaps in the evidence, have assumed an unwarranted significance, and even led to talk of conspiracies, fabrication and cover-ups. In fact there is nothing unusual in such contradictions in first-hand testimony, and if the few days leading up to

Salamanca, Vitoria or the battle of the Pyrenees (or Jena-Auerstädt, Lützen or Dresden and Kulm) were examined in this detail, similar discrepancies would be revealed. The problem is greatly compounded by the acrimony aroused by many of the controversies surrounding the campaign. Some Prussian officers felt, with reason, that their army never received sufficient credit for its role in the campaign, and this sense of grievance was heightened by their dissatisfaction with the leniency of the peace terms granted to France after Napoleon's defeat. Anglo-German rivalry in the two decades before the outbreak of the First World War infected the spirit with which the subject was discussed in both countries at a time when many of the most important operational studies of the campaign were written. And the revival of the controversy in the late 1990s was marked by personality clashes and heated exchanges which tended to obscure some excellent scholarly work on both sides.

The intense scrutiny of the campaign has another effect: it highlights the errors made by all three commanders and their subordinates – errors that can appear almost wilfully foolish with the benefit of hindsight. Yet both Napoleon and Wellington were generals of the finest quality at the height of their powers, and even Blücher was far from the buffoon of some popular histories. They made mistakes, not because they were incompetent, but because waging war is not easy. They acted under intense pressure, generally with little sleep and amid a cloud of partial and misleading information. A common analogy compares war to chess, but for this to have some relation to reality each piece would be capable of moving at the same time; each move would need to be dictated several moves in advance; one in three pieces would not move as directed or not move at all; and the player would only get the occasional glimpse of the board! Historians necessarily clarify and simplify the story they tell, and it takes a conscious effort to remember just how much more confused and unclear was the picture facing the generals at the time.

In the weeks before the opening of the campaign the allies had received numerous warnings that an attack was imminent. However, such reports had been common ever since Napoleon's return and were obscured by many false reports, some spread deliberately, so that by June the allied commanders were inclined to dismiss them.[4]

However, as the evidence of an impending attack accumulated the Prussian attitude began to shift. On 13 June Colonel Pfuel was sent to consult Wellington in Brussels, and on the following morning Gneisenau issued preliminary orders for the army to prepare to concentrate. At half past eleven on the night of 14 June, before the first shots of the campaign had been fired, these orders were confirmed, while Zieten's corps, which held the outposts, was already on full alert.[5] Wellington was slower to react to the signs of an impending attack,

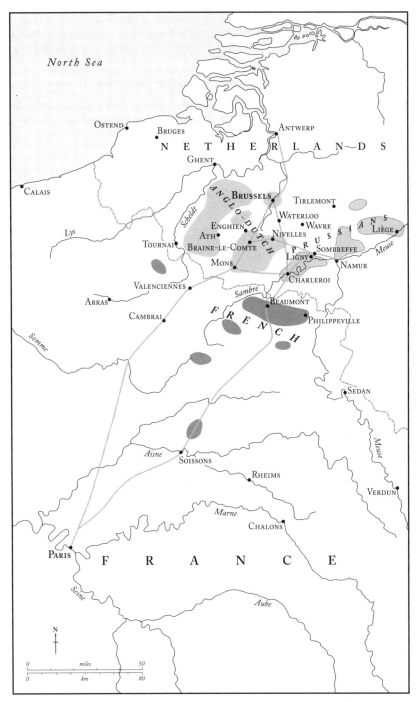

1   The Waterloo campaign: the situation before operations began with troops still dispersed in cantonments.

partly because there was less activity opposite his outposts, and possibly also because he relied too heavily on intelligence from Paris. As a result his army was still widely scattered in its cantonments to the south and west of Brussels when the campaign began.

Napoleon's line of advance was by no means predictable. He might have followed the main highway from Paris to Brussels which passed through Valenciennes, Mons and Braine-le-Comte to the west of Charleroi and Waterloo. A successful advance on this route would cut Wellington's army in half, for all this country was held by his forces. Or he could have advanced much further to the east, through Namur, in order to strike at the heart of the Prussian army and threaten its line of retreat. Instead he chose to strike at a point where the two armies overlapped, in the hope of driving them apart; the Prussian line began at Binche, two or three miles west of Charleroi, while the most easterly of Wellington's men were further north on the road which ran from Charleroi through the crossroads at Quatre Bras to Genappe, Waterloo and Brussels some 34 miles away. (This road, from Charleroi to Brussels via Waterloo, has a retro-spective significance in all accounts of the campaign which was far from obvious at the time, when other routes, including that through Braine-le-Comte, appeared just as important.)

There has been much controversy over when Wellington learnt of Napoleon's attack at Charleroi, with claims that a messenger from Zieten arrived quite early in the morning of 15 June, but that his news was either disregarded or even deliberately ignored in the hope that this would lead to the Prussians bearing the brunt of the fighting. However, the evidence for this message is scanty, and it is simply unbelievable that Wellington would have failed to react if he knew that the campaign had begun; self-preservation (if nothing else) would have ensured that he lost no time in getting his army ready for action.[6] This is exactly what he did in orders issued at around six o'clock that evening, ordering each division and the cavalry to concentrate and be ready to move at short notice. The original text of these orders is missing and they need to be treated with some care, but their gist is clear enough.[7] Very few troops were actually ordered to move, other than to their assembly point, although some of the troops furthest to the west were ordered to a more central position.

These orders included one serious mistake: instructions for the 2nd and 3rd Dutch-Belgian Divisions to concentrate at Nivelles, which if obeyed would have led to the withdrawal of Prince Bernhard of Saxe-Weimar's brigade from Quatre Bras, opening the road from Charleroi to Brussels, and the loss of a good defensive position south of Nivelles which Chassé's division had occupied that morning. Fortunately for Wellington these orders were not obeyed, and on the following morning Wellington approved this act of independence by his Dutch-Belgian subordinates. It was one of the few occasions in Wellington's long military career in which the independent initiative of subordinates in flagrantly disobeying his orders worked to his advantage.[8]

A few hours later, probably around ten o'clock at night, a second set of orders, known as the 'After Orders', were issued. It is not certain whether they were prompted by fresh intelligence, and if so what, or simply by reflection. The most plausible suggestion is that it was a combination of a letter from Gneisenau confirming the seriousness of the French attack and announcing Blücher's intention to concentrate his army and give battle near Sombreffe, with further reports that all remained quiet near Mons, but this is largely supposition. These After Orders dictated a general shift of the army east towards Nivelles. So the Third Division (Alten) would move from Braine-le-Comte to Nivelles, while the First Division (Cooke) would move from Enghien to Braine-le-Comte. The Second and Fourth Divisions in Hill's Corps would move on Enghien, as would the cavalry, while the Reserve in Brussels, including the Fifth and Sixth Divisions, would march south on the Charleroi road as far as Mont St Jean, where the road to Nivelles diverged from the road south through Quatre Bras to Charleroi.[9]

Having issued these orders Wellington went to the Duchess of Richmond's ball. It was Byron who made the ball famous and emblematic of one facet of the romantic age in the third canto of *Childe Harold's Pilgrimage*, published only eighteen months later and immensely successful right across Europe. Thirty years after the publication of *Childe Harold* the fame of the ball was refreshed for a new generation of readers in Thackeray's *Vanity Fair*. Prose replaced verse, romantic enthusiasm had given way to a sardonic, if not wholly cynical view of the world (a tone which owed a good deal to Byron's *Don Juan*), but the work was just as popular and remained so for the rest of the century. No educated English man, let alone an educated English woman, in 1900 would not have heard of the battle of Waterloo or linked it indissolubly in their mind with the Duchess of Richmond's ball and the sound of revelry by night, although by then few people knew anything of the Duke of Richmond.

The reality could hardly match these heightened depictions, and the first-hand accounts of the ball which we possess suggest rather less grandeur and more confusion and dismay than Byron or Thackeray admit. William Verner of the 7th Hussars arrived fashionably late and only had time to quickly survey the room before 'Lord Uxbridge came to the door . . . [and] said, "You gentlemen who have engaged partners, had better finish your dance and get to your quarters as soon as you can."' And Katharine Arden, daughter of Lord Alvanley, told her aunt a few weeks later:

When on our arrival at the ball, we were told that the troops had orders to march at 3 in the morning, and that every officer must join his regiment by that time, as the French were advancing, you cannot possibly picture to your-self the dismay and consternation that appeared in every face. Those who had brothers and sons to be engaged, openly gave way to their grief, as the last parting of many took place at this most terrible ball . . . We staid at this ball as short a time as we could, but long enough to see express after express arrive to the Duke of Wellington, to hear of Aides de Camp arriving breathless with news, and to see, what was much more extraordinary than all, the Duke's equanimity a *little* discomposed.[10]

Wellington's dismay and the premature break-up of the ball were caused by the arrival at about half past midnight or one o'clock of Captain Henry Webster, ADC to the Prince of Orange. He brought with him a despatch from General Constant-Rebecque at Braine-le-Comte dated 10.30pm. It contained news that the French had advanced as far as Quatre Bras, and that Constant had sent orders to Perponcher to try to hold the crossroads by concentrating his whole division there.[11] This was startling. The previous reports had suggested that Zieten would hold a line from Gosselies to Gilly, blocking the Charleroi road almost ten miles south of Quatre Bras. If the French had really pushed so far north they had made an extraordinary advance on the first day of the campaign and gained an important strategic advantage, for the crossroad which ran through Quatre Bras was the road from Nivelles to Sombreffe and provided the best line of communication between the two allied armies. Little wonder that Wellington was reported to have been most reluctant to believe the news at first, or that he took the Duke of Richmond aside and said: 'Napoleon has *humbugged* me (by G__d), he has gained twenty-four hours' march on me.'[12]

In fact Constant's message was exaggerated. The French were not in Quatre Bras nor, in any great strength, anywhere much to the north of Gosselies. Late on the afternoon of 15 June, probably between five and seven o'clock, the leading cavalry of Ney's wing of the French army had pushed forward to Frasnes, and the 2/2nd Regiment Nassau Usingen had lost its outlying picquet and been forced to withdraw as far as the Gemioncourt farm a mile south of Quatre Bras. By the time the leading battalion of French infantry reached Frasnes night was falling and the weary soldiers were very sensibly allowed to rest. Prince Bernhard of Saxe-Weimar's brigade was in possession of the cross-roads, although the Prince felt anxious and exposed, writing to Perponcher (his immediate superior) at nine o'clock that the terrain prevented him from seeing the strength of the enemy's force. He reported that morale was good among his troops, but undermined this assurance with claims that two of his battalions were critically short of ammunition and could not easily be re-supplied because their muskets and rifles were of French and mixed calibres respectively.[13] Perponcher responded by reinforcing Prince Bernhard during the night with the bulk of his other brigade (Bijlandt's) and instructing him to maintain his position as long as possible, but that if he was forced to give way he should retreat north to Mont St Jean rather than west to Nivelles.

The Prince of Orange reached Quatre Bras about six o'clock on the morning of 16 June. Despite many hours in the saddle and little rest he was cheerful and optimistic. He did not order all his men to come to Quatre Bras as quickly as possible; instead he kept the bulk of his forces (two of his three brigades of cavalry, Alten's British and Chassé's Dutch-Belgian divisions) at or around Nivelles. There was no guarantee that the small French force near Frasnes signalled that the principal French thrust would come on the Charleroi-Quatre Bras road; it might just as easily come along the road through Nivelles, where it would completely disrupt the concentration of the allied army.[14]

Wellington snatched a few hours' sleep after the Ball, and left Brussels early on the morning of 16 June. He overtook the Reserve marching on the road south, its leading units breakfasting near Waterloo from whence it could march south to Quatre Bras or south-west to Nivelles as circumstances demanded. He reached Quatre Bras about ten o'clock in the morning and must have been pleased to find that all was still quiet, although the Prince and some of his senior officers were becoming disturbed by the lack of French activity, fearing that it might conceal a move on Nivelles. The Duke approved the deployment of Perponcher's division at Quatre Bras; the orders to Chassé and Alten to cover Nivelles; and those summoning Cooke and the First Division from Braine-le-Comte to Nivelles.[15]

He then rode forward and reconnoitred the French position near Frasnes, but because of the high ground to the south and the extensive wood beyond it, he could see little, although there did not seem to be much evidence of French activity or large forces. From this spot at half past ten he wrote a note to Blücher in which he gave a misleading account of the location of his troops, suggesting that they were more concentrated and closer to the front than they actually were. (Various implausible explanations have been offered for the inaccuracy of this letter, which is certainly strange – perhaps the least unlikely is that he was saving face, minimising the consequences of his slow start to the campaign. Such inaccuracies were not uncommon – the Prussians made similarly optimistic statements – and it is very hard to argue that the letter from Frasnes had any significant consequences.)[16] He then ordered the Reserve forward to Quatre Bras, but not the troops at Nivelles.[17]

As the French at Frasnes remained quiet, Wellington decided to ride over to Ligny to discuss his next move with Blücher, and probably also to see for himself the strength of the French forces facing the Prussians. The two generals met near the windmill of Brye at about one o'clock and conversed in French for

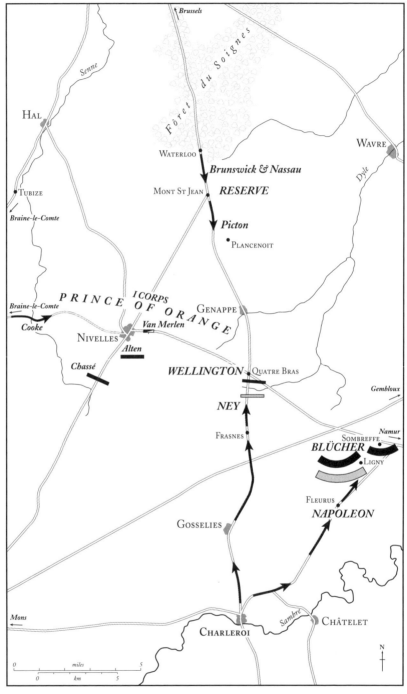

2   The Waterloo campaign: the early afternoon of 16 June 1815.

some time. Inevitably the accounts of their discussions are surrounded by controversy, but it seems probable that Wellington told Blücher that he did not expect to be attacked at Quatre Bras, and that they discussed the best way that he could assist the Prussians: Wellington initially proposing an advance on Gosselies to operate against Napoleon's flank, but accepting, or seeming to accept, Gneisenau's objection that there would not be time for this to take effect and that a direct reinforcement would be preferable. Accounts differ whether any time was mentioned or a figure put on the number of men, and while Müffling makes explicit Wellington's proviso 'I will come so long as I am not attacked myself', others are silent on the point – although everyone must have understood that as an implicit condition. Whether Wellington criticised the Prussian deployment either directly to them, or privately to Hardinge, the British liaison officer, is much more doubtful. Years later both the Duke and Hardinge told stories to this effect, even adding that Wellington had predicted that the Prussians would be 'damnably mauled'; but this smacks of hindsight and there is no trace of it in other accounts of the meeting. Possibly Wellington had some reservations about the position at Ligny that he expressed privately to Hardinge, or in such diplomatic language to the Prussians that it made little impression, but there is no reason to believe that he rode away from the meeting at Brye expecting his allies to be defeated or with any intention other than coming to their assistance in the course of the afternoon.[18]

At Brye Wellington had seen that Blücher was faced with a substantial French force, but none of the allies yet knew where the larger portion of Napoleon's army was, or what his intentions were. They could not rule out the possibility that he was about to strike a heavy blow along the Binche-Nivelles or Mons-Braine-le-Comte roads, or even against the Prussian right by attacking Namur; although we know that almost all the French army was concentrated close to the Frasnes-Fleurus-Charleroi triangle. On the other side, Napoleon also had to operate in a fog of uncertainty and partial knowledge, guessing at the allied plans from scraps of information, much of it misleading. On the morning of 16 June he did not expect to fight a major battle that day. He thought that the Prussians would continue to retreat, and ordered Grouchy and Gérard, commanding the troops of his right wing, to drive them back from Sombreffe to Gembloux and beyond. This should ensure that they retired east on the lines of communication towards Liège, rather than north towards Wavre and Brussels. Napoleon believed that Ney with the left wing of the army was also unlikely to face any serious resistance, and should bring his troops forward to occupy Quatre Bras in strength, and push one division forward as far as Genappe. If all went well Napoleon intended to join him with the Guard that evening and make a forced march so as to arrive in Brussels very early on 17 June. This would completely disrupt the concentration of Wellington's army, split the allies apart and probably send them both into headlong retreat. It would also make great demands on the marching ability of the French soldiers, but all three generals asked for the barely possible from their men at times in the campaign.

Napoleon's plans were flexible however, and he rapidly adjusted them when he found that the Prussians intended to stand and fight at Ligny. The opportunity of beating their army at the outset of the campaign was welcome and the Emperor's only disappointment was that Gérard's corps was unable to get into position to attack until the afternoon. At two o'clock, as he was preparing to open his assault on the Prussians, Napoleon wrote to Ney instructing him to 'attack whatever force of the enemy is directly opposed to you, and after having driven it aside . . . turn in our direction, so as to bring about the envelopment of [the enemy]'. Even now Napoleon was not quite sure that the Prussians would make a determined stand, for he added that if they were quickly overthrown he would manoeuvre to assist Ney's operations.[19]

Ney had already received several previous orders from Napoleon, although apparently none before the morning was well advanced. Some historians, particularly those who sympathise with Napoleon, have strongly criticised Ney's 'inactivity' on the morning of 16 June, pointing out that he could have occupied Quatre Bras with little difficulty if he had advanced early in the day. But it was not for Ney to set the pace and direction of the campaign without orders, and his critics would have condemned him even more strongly if he had brought on a disadvantageous fight against Napoleon's wishes by his 'impetuosity'. Besides, his troops were tired after a long march on 15 June, and faced another long march that night, so there was good reason to let them take their time. At eleven o'clock Ney reported to Soult from Frasnes: 'All information to hand tends to show that there are 3,000 hostile infantry at Quatre Bras and very few cavalry. I think that the Emperor's arrangements for the advance on Brussels will be carried out without great difficulty.'[20] At that point Ney had few troops at Frasnes and only a single division of infantry (Bachelu's) north of Gosselies with which to support his cavalry. He gave orders for the remainder of his wing of the army to march, and about noon Foy's division left Gosselies, followed by Kellermann's cuirassiers and Jerome's division of infantry. It is worth adding that throughout the day, and indeed the whole campaign, Ney was hampered by the lack of a proper staff answerable to him – a consequence of his late appointment to the command.

It was probably a little before two o'clock that Ney began his attack, although we cannot be sure, for the timing and sequence of events in the battle are exceptionally hard to determine with many apparently reliable first-hand sources contradicting each other, and very few detailed accounts giving a bird's-eye view of the whole action. Many incidents are described well, sometimes by more than one source; the difficulty lies in constructing an accurate framework in which to set them. Sir John Fortescue, who wrote one of the most

careful accounts of the battle, remarked that 'few engagements are more difficult to follow and to understand than the battle of Quatre Bras.'[21] Historians
will continue to differ over what happened when, and how the battle unfolded,
and it must be understood that any reconstruction of the events of the day is
unusually tentative and provisional.

Wellington seems to have returned from Ligny soon after the French attack
began, and he must have been surprised at the strength of the French force now
visible and its advance. He sent orders to Charles Alten to bring two of the three
brigades of the Third British Division to reinforce the troops at Quatre Bras, while
leaving the remaining infantry brigade to support Chassé's force covering
Nivelles.[22] He probably also sent word to Cooke with the First Division and to the
cavalry to hasten their march, although even now it was not clear that Ney's attack
would be pressed home or that a full-scale battle would ensue. Fortunately other
reinforcements were already beginning to arrive: the Reserve from Brussels, with
Picton's Fifth Division in the lead, followed by the Brunswick Corps and the
Nassau contingent, which came marching south from Waterloo, while van
Merlen's brigade of Dutch-Belgian light cavalry trotted along the road from
Nivelles. Wellington ordered Picton's men to turn left at Quatre Bras and form a
line along the Namur road. The 1/95th in the lead was sent a little further east and
south in the hope that it could occupy the farm at Pireaumont south of the Materne
pond. At the other end of the line the 92nd Gordon Highlanders secured their
flank on the buildings of Quatre Bras. Best's Hanoverian brigade formed in reserve
north of the road. The Brunswick Corps arrived a little later and formed to the
west of the Charleroi road, between it and the Bois de Bossu. Two companies of
Brunswick riflemen were sent into the wood to assist the Dutch-Belgian defence,
and a light battalion was sent to the other flank of the army to support the 95th.[23]

The initial French attack was around the farm of Gemioncourt, and
the Belgian and Dutch troops fought bravely before being forced to give way.
The Prince of Orange led an unsuccessful counter-attack, while a charge by the
Hussars of van Merlen's brigade intended to cover their retreat was unsuccessful. Wellington and his staff were caught up in the flight of the hussars and
Fitzroy Somerset recalled that 'the Duke leaped a bank and ditch, and on a
worse horse he might not have escaped.'[24]

The fighting that followed was fierce. George Simmons, veteran of a score
of Peninsular battles, wrote home: 'A more bloody or obstinately contested
thing had seldom or never been seen. This convinced me that the French would
fight for Buonaparte.'[25] Another British officer in Picton's division described
what happened in a letter written on 25 June:

> A little before four the action commenced, on the side of the French. We lay
> down in the cornfield till they came within forty yards of us, when a shout

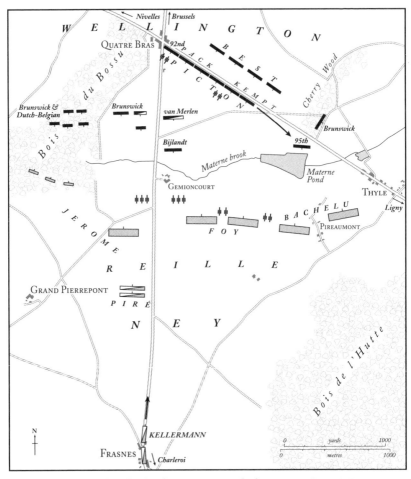

3   The early stages of the battle of Quatre Bras, mid-afternoon, 16 June 1815.

from our right caused us to rise. We fired a volley and charged them down to the ditch, in getting over which they lost numbers. When we got down the bugle sounded for us to return and form in line upon the colours, which we did, and were pursued by them again; we charged them a second time, and actually the ground was covered with dead and wounded bodies.[26]

Even after the initial attack was repulsed the British line remained under heavy fire from French skirmishers who took cover behind the hedges, and overwhelmed the British light companies.

To the west of the road the three battalions of the Brunswick corps were much exposed to the French artillery. The Duke of Brunswick set his young soldiers an example of steadiness, quietly smoking his pipe and giving orders for more than an hour while appearing to ignore the enemy. Part of a British battery was sent to his assistance but was soon silenced by the French guns and withdrew. The French infantry then pushed forward, and the Duke of Brunswick, doubting that his infantry were in a state to repel the enemy, led his lancers against the leading column but they were driven back in confusion by the French fire. Seeing this the Brunswick infantry began to fall back, with orders or without them. Piré's light cavalry, which accompanied the advancing French infantry, found the perfect moment to charge and Brunswick's troops turned and fled. The Duke, desperately trying to rally his men, fell mortally wounded, less than nine years after his father had fallen in similar fashion at Auerstädt. Most of the 846 Brunswick casualties probably occurred at this time.

Piré's horsemen then swept onwards towards the crossroads, catching the Verden Landwehr battalion of Best's brigade in line and inflicting heavy casualties, but the Lüneberg and Osterode battalions drove the French off without difficulty.[27] Part of the cavalry then charged the flank and rear of Pack's brigade, but were repulsed by the 42nd and 44th Regiments, even though they were caught at a disadvantage. The rest of the cavalry then bore down on the crossroads where Wellington was watching the action beside the 92nd Highlanders. He was standing behind the centre of the regiment and said, '92nd, don't fire until I tell you', and waited until the oncoming French were within twenty or thirty yards before giving the order. The resulting volley brought down an 'immense' number of men and horses, and the surviving French 'faced about and galloped off'.[28] One French officer actually tried to escape by riding along the rear of the regiment, which was still in line. Wellington called out 'Damn it, 92nd, will you allow that fellow to escape?' whereupon several men turned and fired at once, killing the Frenchman's horse and wounding him in each foot. Curiously, an officer of the 92nd who was himself subsequently wounded was billeted with the Frenchman in Brussels, where they both recovered and became good friends.[29]

The battle had reached a stalemate. The French attacks had placed great pressure on the allied line, but had generally been repulsed, and even where the allied troops had broken, the French had been unable to exploit their advantage. There was a great deal of skirmishing and artillery fire along the whole line from Bossu Wood in the west to the Thyle in the east, and both sides were being worn down as their casualties mounted. Both looked to the arrival of reinforcements to strengthen their position.

Ney felt under acute pressure. He knew that Napoleon's confidence in him was fragile and now, on only the second day of the campaign, he risked disrupting the Emperor's plans by failing to achieve a task which he himself had described only a few hours before as a matter of course. The pressure was intensified when he received a letter from Soult ordering him to fall on the Prussian flank and rear immediately so that the French would gain a decisive victory, and declaring dramatically 'the fate of France is in your hands'.[30] At the same time he discovered that d'Erlon's corps, almost half his force, had turned aside and was already marching against the Prussians rather than assisting Ney in securing Quatre Bras. With the Olympian detachment of hindsight it is easy to criticise Ney for not recognising that this solved his problem; d'Erlon could give Napoleon the support he needed while Ney contained Wellington at Quatre Bras. A cool operator might even have added the finesse of sending d'Erlon some orders, backdated an hour or so, instructing him to do what he had already done, apparently on his own initiative, and so secure a good share of the credit. But Ney was not that sort of man, and his whole will and determination had become focussed on seizing Quatre Bras, forgetting that this was merely the means to an end, not the end in itself. He lost his temper and sent peremptory orders to d'Erlon to return at once. It was a terrible mistake, for by the time d'Erlon received the order he was on the edge of the battlefield of Ligny and his unheralded appearance was causing alarm in both armies. Napoleon suspended a critical attack while he discovered whether the newcomers were friends or foes, but before he could bring d'Erlon into his plans the First Corps had withdrawn back into the haze in obedience to Ney's summons. Yet, although d'Erlon obeyed Ney at once, night was falling by the time his weary men reached Quatre Bras, having spent the whole afternoon marching between two battlefields entirely ineffectively, when their presence at either would have been decisive.

Meanwhile Ney needed to secure victory and could not expect d'Erlon's men for some time at least. Reille's corps had already been committed to the fight and while not exhausted needed some fresh impetus if they were to break through. Ney had few reserves in hand, but Napoleon had entrusted him with Kellermann's two divisions of heavy cavalry – a magnificent force – and he had already seen how effective Piré's light cavalry had been. Summoning Kellermann he ordered him to attack and overthrow the allied army, and echoed the Emperor's injunction: 'The fate of France is in your hands.' When Kellermann protested that he had only one of his four brigades at the front and could hardly be expected to win the battle with a mere 800 cuirassiers, Ney would not listen – although he promised to support the attack with every man. Kellerman had no choice but to obey and may not have been altogether without hope; after all Murat had saved the day at Eylau in far worse conditions albeit with a much larger force, and he himself had delivered the decisive blow at Marengo fifteen years before with a much more ragged body of cavalry than the superb cuirassiers he now commanded.[31]

Time was running short for the French, for allied reinforcements were already beginning to arrive and more were on their way. Charles Alten's Third British Division arrived at Quatre Bras probably a little before five o'clock; Cooke with the First British Division was not very far behind and Wellington still hoped that the allied cavalry would appear before the long summer evening was over.

Alten's British brigade consisted of four rather inexperienced battalions (2/30th, 33rd, 2/69th, 2/73rd) under Sir Colin Halkett, who had commanded the light battalions of the King's German Legion with much distinction in the Peninsula. Halkett's men were sent to take the place of the Brunswickers, between the Bossu Wood and the Charleroi road south of Quatre Bras. Piré's cavalry had disappeared before he arrived, and he endeavoured to provide cover for the Brunswick troops to rally and to relieve the pressure on the 42nd and 44th who were running short of ammunition and feeling the effects of the fire of the French artillery and skirmishers.

Years later Halkett described how he had ridden ahead of his brigade to reconnoitre and had observed a large body of French cavalry moving forward in small groups, as if to water their horses. He took this to be a ruse to conceal preparations for an attack and alerted his men to prepare to receive cavalry.[32] Scarcely had he done so before the French artillery opened a tremendous fire on the allied line, and soon afterwards Kellermann's cuirassiers, supported by Piré's four regiments and possibly some other French cavalry, moved forward to the attack. The first blow fell with tremendous force on Halkett's brigade. The 69th, which had been detached a little to the left to take the pressure off Pack's brigade, was broken when not in square, and its King's Colour was captured. The 30th and the 73rd formed square in time and the French cavalry made no impression upon them. The 33rd was less fortunate, for the ground on which it formed square was particularly exposed to the French artillery; the men broke and fled into the nearby Bois du Bossu.

Kellermann's charge penetrated as far as the crossroads of Quatre Bras itself but the horsemen could not hold the ground they had overrun, or break the stalwart squares they had left in their rear. The Gordon Highlanders, and beyond them Best's Hanoverians, held the Namur road and were undaunted. Kellermann's horse was shot under him and it was with difficulty that he escaped hanging on to the stirrups of two of his troopers. Almost the whole British line, from Kempt's brigade on the left, to Halkett's on the fringes of the Bois de Bossu, was in square at this time, and the French cavalry made repeated charges, although never with the same impetus or success as their initial onslaught.

For all its heroism Kellermann's charge had failed to turn the tide of the battle. As afternoon gave way to evening the fighting continued and the French light infantry made progress towards gaining control of the Bois de Bossu. Then, probably between six and seven o'clock, the First British Division under George Cooke arrived on the Nivelles road after a long march from Enghien. Maitland's brigade (2nd and 3rd battalions, 1st Foot Guards) was at the head of the column and was ordered to clear the wood, which it did, apparently without too much difficulty, although inevitably becoming disordered in the process. An attempt to advance beyond the wood was checked by heavy French fire, and the Guards withdrew back into the wood. There was evidently some hard fighting at this point for both battalions lost heavily (285 casualties in the second battalion; 262 in the third), and an officer admits that 'our loss was very severe, and we found great difficulty in forming our line again'.[33]

At the same time the rest of the allied line pushed forward and recovered most of the ground they had lost in the course of the day – including Gemioncourt – before nightfall. It is not clear whether the French put up much resistance, or whether they were happy to break off the battle and withdraw a little, accepting that neither side could gain a decisive advantage in the last hour of the day.

Wellington described Quatre Bras as a 'desperate battle', and Sir Augustus Frazer wrote home that 'I have never seen a hotter fire than at some times of yesterday, nor seen more of what is called a melée of troops'. The fighting had been intense, with troops on both sides displaying great courage and determination. Frazer declared: 'The enemy's lancers and cuirassiers are the finest fellows I ever saw; – they made several bold charges, and repeatedly advanced in the very teeth of our infantry. They have severely paid for their spirit – most of them are now lying before me.'[34] Ney probably never had 25,000 men in the field, while by late in the day more than 35,000 allied troops had been present at one time or another, although Wellington probably never had 30,000 men ready to fight at once.[35] The allies lost almost 5,000 casualties – as many as at all but the bloodiest of Wellington's Peninsular victories. Of these casualties almost exactly half were British, one-quarter Dutch-Belgians, and the rest Brunswickers and Hanoverians. There are no such reliable figures for the French, but that evening Ney told Napoleon that he had lost 'about 2,000 killed and 4,000 wounded'. This was clearly nothing more than a rough estimate (both the proportion and the absolute number of dead are excessive) and it may even be too high, for most accounts put the French losses at between 4,000 and 4,500 casualties.[36]

Wellington's role in the battle is curiously obscure. He did not give a detailed account of the fighting in his Waterloo despatch and there are relatively few references to him in first-hand accounts of the action. Presumably he decided where each body of reinforcements would be sent as it arrived and kept a close watch on the battle as was his custom, but we have only a few glimpses of him during the course of the afternoon and evening. Equally the whole course of the battle is too shrouded in uncertainty to permit any serious tactical criticism of the conduct of either general.

The most striking difference between Quatre Bras and Wellington's battles in the Peninsula was the effectiveness of the French cavalry. In part this was because the French cavalry in 1815 was simply much better; Kellermann's cuirassiers were an elite force of heavy cavalry – strong men on strong horses in fine condition – quite different from the dragoons and chasseurs in the

Peninsula, whose mounts and morale had been worn down by years of hard service and poor fodder. But it was also because the battlefield of Quatre Bras was relatively open; neither army was fully settled into a position and each threw fresh units into the fray as soon as they arrived, and this created better opportunities for cavalry to act than a battle where each army had time to deploy fully before the fighting began. The battle as a whole was much more fiercely contested than most actions in the second half of the Peninsular War, and it is clear that the French army was better than any Wellington had faced at least since 1809 and Talavera, while the allied army lacked the coherence and confidence that the Peninsular army showed from at least 1811.

Strategically the allies undoubtedly benefitted from Quatre Bras, but only because of the French failure to use d'Erlon in either battle. Wellington had absorbed the attention of roughly two-fifths of the French army, thereby giving the Prussians far more assistance than they had ever expected. The equation would have been very different if Ney had used one corps to keep Wellington at bay and sent the other to assist Napoleon in inflicting a crushing defeat on the Prussians, or had used both at Quatre Bras so that Wellington had been on the back foot, struggling to concentrate his army at a position that was really too far forward. By the evening of 16 June Wellington had largely, although not completely, recovered from his slow start to the campaign; the allied cavalry had begun to arrive at Quatre Bras and other troops were getting closer, but he did not know how the Prussians had fared at Ligny.

That night Wellington and his staff rode back to Genappe and managed a few hours' sleep before returning to Quatre Bras early on the morning of 17 June. He had still received no word from the Prussians since a message had arrived late on the previous day that they were under pressure but hoped to maintain their ground.[37] If they had done so the prospects for the allies were excellent, for Bülow would join Blücher and the rest of Wellington's army would arrive, enabling them to go onto the offensive and decide the campaign that day.[38] Early on the 17th Wellington sent Alexander Gordon, escorted by a troop of the 10th Hussars, towards Ligny to re-establish contact with the Prussians. Gordon encountered French outposts where the Prussians had been the day before and, avoiding them, headed north where he found the Prussian rear-guard near Tilly. Here he learnt that the Prussians had been defeated and forced to retreat, although they had not been broken. In fact Blücher's army had lost more than 10,000 casualties, and a further 8,000 troops, mostly men new to Prussian uniforms, had fled east in disorder.[39] But the core of the army remained with the colours and in relatively good spirits. Crucially it was retreating north, towards Wavre, not east along its lines of communication to Liège. The initial decision to head north had been taken by Gneisenau when Blücher was incapacitated (his dying horse had rolled on him); it kept open the possibility of further co-operation between the allied armies without fully committing the Prussians – for, of course, Gneisenau did not know what Wellington would do. Amid the stress and confusion of organising the retreat of the defeated army in the fading light Gneisenau had not forgotten to send news of his intentions to Wellington, but his ADC had been wounded at Pireaumont and so failed to deliver the message. A second Prussian message, despatched on 17 June, reached Wellington an hour or two after Gordon made his report.[40]

Wellington had no doubt that he must withdraw in conformity with the Prussian movement. Whether he would be able to make a fresh stand at Mont St Jean just south of Waterloo, or whether he would be forced to uncover Brussels and withdraw further north towards Antwerp, would depend partly on the force the French showed in the course of the day, but principally on whether the Prussians would be willing and able to come to his assistance. At nine o'clock he issued orders for the army's retreat, taking care that the troops still around Nivelles should get away in good time. It was fortunate that there was a separate road from Nivelles to Mont St Jean so that the whole army was not forced to crowd onto the Quatre Bras to Brussels road.

Some troops, part of the Fourth British Division and Prince Frederick's Dutch-Belgian corps, were still west of the Nivelles near Braine-le-Comte and Enghien respectively. Wellington left them there, either deliberately or inadvertently, and that evening sent them orders from Waterloo to withdraw to a good defensive position at Tubize south of Hal, on the main Mons to Brussels road. Here they would guard against any French attempt to turn his flank or strike directly at Brussels, and they were instructed to hold their position 'as long as possible'.[41] He could have ordered them to join the army at Mont St Jean on the morning of 18 June but did not do so. It was far from certain that a battle would be fought on 18 June, and if not their presence would greatly increase the difficulty of the retreat as the whole army crowded onto the road north through the Forest of Soignes. And he still feared a French attempt to turn his right flank and relied on the detachment to at least delay and impede, if not completely block, such a move.[42]

There was some skirmishing between the outposts of the two armies during the night of 16 June and at first light on the following morning, before it became obvious that neither side was interested in renewing the battle of the day before. Ney was waiting for orders from Napoleon which were slow to arrive, and his men badly needed food and rest. This allowed Wellington to gradually thin his forces, as the infantry and artillery took the road north until only the cavalry and horse artillery remained. The day was oppressively hot, building to a thunderstorm, and one witness says that Wellington spent most of the morning laughing over the English newspapers and even napping, although he would mount, ride forward and examine the French lines through his telescope every now and again to make sure that nothing was stirring.[43]

Napoleon made his plans late that morning. His reconnoitring parties had failed to discover that the main body of the Prussian army was marching north, and he presumed that they were heading east towards Namur. He decided to detach Grouchy with a whole wing of the army – more than two corps of infantry and three divisions of cavalry, some 32,000 men[44] – to press them back. This was a large detachment, but he must have known that Bülow's strong corps had not been at Ligny and that plenty of fight remained even in the three corps that he had defeated. If Grouchy was too weak he might be defeated, offsetting whatever advantages Napoleon gained with the rest of the army. Meanwhile he would join Ney with the Guard and part of Lobau's corps and the cavalry and push on to Brussels, forcing Wellington back to the north or west. It must have seemed unlikely that the British would stand and fight either at Quatre Bras or further north, but any chance to defeat them would be most welcome. On the whole the campaign appeared to be going well, although it was unfortunate that the opportunity of inflicting a really crushing defeat on the Prussians had been missed.

It was early on the afternoon of 17 June that the French at Quatre Bras finally began to stir and the outlying allied picquets were forced to withdraw. By then the infantry was well away and had nothing to fear from the enemy in its march to Mont St Jean. The rear-guard of cavalry and horse artillery was pressed and hustled at times however, and there was a sharp skirmish at Genappe where Uxbridge's own regiment, the 7th Hussars, was embarrassed and the Life Guards had to intervene to cover their retreat. It may be, as some critics have alleged, that Uxbridge was over-eager to contest the ground and delayed his movements so that when they came they were made with some hurry and confusion, but a lengthy withdrawal in the face of a pressing enemy strong in cavalry was never easy, and Uxbridge accomplished it with fewer than a hundred casualties, and without his own cavalry being daunted or intimidated by the enemy.[45]

The thunderstorm broke early in the retreat so that the manoeuvres, artillery fire and clash of swords and lances were overwhelmed by vivid flashes of lightning, tremendous claps of thunder and torrential rain. All the troops suffered, finding it impossible to keep dry and difficult to light or maintain a fire, but Wellington's infantry had made most of their march on dry ground and some received supplies from their commissariat, while the French troops had to slog their way through mud and largely depended on the food they could find for themselves. Part of the army – the infantry of Reille and Lobau and Kellermann's cuirassiers – got no further than Genappe, while the rest camped near the road with Jacquinot's cavalry and d'Erlon's corps near the village of Placenoit two or three miles south of Mont St Jean.[46] Although Napoleon knew that Wellington's army remained in front of him, he had no reason to suppose that the allies would stand and fight on the following day rather than continue their retreat.

CHAPTER FOUR

WATERLOO
(18 June 1815)

U NLIKE MOST OF his men, Wellington spent the night of 17 June in relative
comfort at Waterloo. He rose early, between two and three o'clock, on
18 June and wrote letters to the Duc de Berri, Sir Charles Stuart, the governor of
Antwerp, and to Lady Frances Webster who was in Brussels. Although he advised
Lady Frances to make preparations to flee to Antwerp in case he was obliged to
uncover Brussels, he was full of confidence, assuring Stuart that the Prussians
would be 'ready again in the morning for anything'. The only danger that he
acknowledged was that the French might turn his right, or western, flank; this
was lessened by the dreadful state of the roads, and he had guarded against it by
leaving Prince Frederick's corps at Hal and Tubize.[1] A few weeks later in Paris, he
explained: 'I think that if I had been Bonaparte I should have respected the
English infantry more after what I must have heard of them in Spain; and that I
should not have taken the bull by the horns. I should have turned a flank, the
right flank. I should have kept the English army occupied by a demonstration to
attack or by slight attacks, while in fact I was moving the main army by Hal on
Brussels.'[2] Wellington has often been criticised both for making this detachment
and for not recalling it on the morning of 18 June when it was 'obvious' that
Napoleon was intent on nothing more than a frontal assault. However this criticism reeks of hindsight, for even when battle was joined at Waterloo Wellington
could not be sure that Napoleon had not detached 20,000 men to turn his flank;
and far from this being inherently unlikely such a manoeuvre was an integral
part of Napoleon's favoured tactics from Montenotte and Castiglione in 1796 to
at least Bautzen in 1813.[3] In any case the bulk of the force at Hal was made up of
Dutch-Belgian troops who would have been of limited value in the cauldron at
Waterloo although, as Quatre Bras has shown, they were quite capable of delaying
the advance of a French column. They were stiffened by a single brigade of
British infantry and one of Hanoverians, so that the real cost of guarding against
the danger of a turning movement was not unduly high.

Wellington's confidence was underpinned by the assurances he had received of Prussian support, in particular a letter from Blücher to Müffling written at midnight promising that Bülow's corps would march at daybreak and be followed immediately by II Corps. That was more than half the Prussian army and Blücher indicated that more might well follow.[4] Familiarity obscures the boldness of Blücher's commitment, for his march to Wellington's aid on 18 June was one of the most daring and courageous strokes by any general in the entire Napoleonic Wars. His army had been defeated in a hard-fought battle only two days before and had yet to recover fully. A powerful French column was pursuing him, and his lines of communication were already in jeopardy. Ignoring all arguments of caution or even self-preservation he deliberately placed his army between two French forces with no good line of retreat in the event of defeat. There could be no turning back; if Wellington's army was over-whelmed or forced to retreat Blücher would be lost, but if Wellington could maintain his position it would be the French who would be placed in an impossible position. Blücher had the courage to stake everything on a fair chance of victory and was rewarded for his spirit; but it was a less obvious or easy choice than it now seems.

About six o'clock Wellington mounted his horse and rode forward with his staff to where his army was shaking itself into life after a miserably wet and hungry night. Calculations of the strength of the allied army on the morning of 18 June vary from a traditional figure of around 67,000 men down to 63,000 given by Fortescue and up to the 74,000 proposed by Scott Bowden.[5] As this suggests, the problem is less simple than it appears and any statement involves making some debatable assumptions, while – as in any army – there were men who were present for the morning roll call who absented themselves on one pretext or another before the first shots were fired. Napoleon's army was, by all accounts, a little stronger: 74,000 men according to Houssaye, 74,500 according to Bowden.[6] The allies had between 150 and 185 guns; the French around 250.[7] Certainly the French had a marked superiority in both artillery and cavalry, in numbers and in quality. If Napoleon's army had a weakness it was that it was rather short of ordinary line infantry: four divisions in D'Erlon's corps amounting to just over 16,000 men; three divisions in Reille's corps (much stronger on average, but they had been heavily engaged at Quatre Bras); and two divisions under Lobau, some 7,000 men at most. In addition there was the Imperial Guard which amounted to almost one-quarter of the army with Napoleon on 18 June including its own cavalry and artillery.

Wellington's men occupied a front running little more than three miles from Braine l'Alleud in the west, past Hougoumont and La Haye Sainte, to Papelotte, La Haie and Smohain in the east. It was open, unremarkable country the natural features of which were gentle, even tame. The 'ridge' which marked the allied position was little more than a gradual swelling of the ground – a noticeable rise to a pedestrian or horseman but no impediment to any movement. Its tactical significance was considerable, for it provided a skyline and some dead, or at least sheltered, ground beyond, but it does not begin to compare with the terrain at Talavera, Busaco or Sorauren. A cross road running along the line of the allied front had some importance to the east of the *chaussée* to Brussels where it was lined with stout hedges, and for a little way to the immediate west, where it ran through a cutting. Far more important were the outlying posts which were soon converted into strongholds: the château of Hougoumont with its enclosures, a wood, a walled garden and an orchard; and the farm of La Haye Sainte in the centre. Because each could be sealed (albeit imperfectly in the case of La Haye Sainte) they were easier to defend than a village and proved of the utmost value to the defence. The flanks of the position were also well protected: by the village of Braine l'Alleud and the high ground which overlooked it on the right, and by the intricate country around Papelotte, La Haie and Smohain on the left. Nonetheless it was not a remarkable or a particularly strong position. Wellington had taken note of it before and asked his engineers to prepare a detailed survey, but later denied reports that he had always intended to fight there if he could. 'The fact is,' he told John Malcolm in Paris just a few weeks later, 'I should have fought them on the 17th at Quatre Bras, if the Prussians had stood their ground. My retiring to Waterloo was an act of necessity, not choice.'[8]

On the morning of 17 June Wellington gave orders that Lieutenant Faris commanding a company of sappers should put Braine l'Alleud in a state of defence by constructing earthworks to cover its entrances or other field works. However, for reasons that are unclear Faris neglected the order and although he was placed under arrest by Colonel Smyth his men retired to Brussels of their own accord.[9] Nothing was done to fortify Braine l'Alleud and when Wellington ordered that some cover be thrown up behind La Haye Sainte on the following morning neither the sappers nor their tools could be found.[10] Some measures were taken to strengthen Hougoumont and the 2nd Light Battalion of the King's German Legion, which was garrisoning La Haye Sainte, did its best to prepare the post but without tools it could not make good the destruction of the great barn door which had been torn down and used as firewood the previous night.[11] A crude abatis was also constructed blocking the *chaussée* level with the farm and a few gaps in the hedges were cut for the allied artillery, but otherwise the battlefield remained in its natural 'unimproved' state.

It was a very small battlefield given the size of the armies. Wellington had well over 20,000 men per mile of front compared to 8,000 at Salamanca. This affected both how the battle was fought and how it was remembered. Essentially it was a crude slogging match, 'hard pounding' in Wellington's famous phrase,

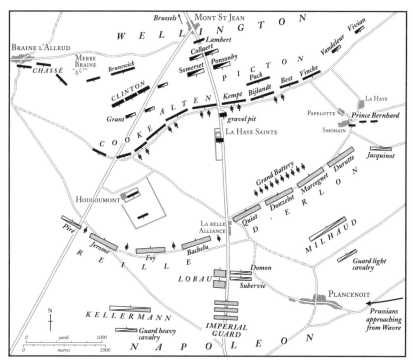

4   The battle of Waterloo: deployment of the armies before the battle began.

in which the French attempted to batter the allies into submission and the allies tried to endure until their enemies were exhausted, with only the occasional quick counter-punch to ease the pressure. This limited Wellington's role; he could make no grand plans or direct sweeping strokes, but he could move among his men, encouraging and inspiring them, making small adjustments to the position of units and feeding his reserves as slowly as possible into the fray, for in such a battle of attrition victory was likely to go to whoever had fresh reserves towards the end of the day.

At Waterloo, unlike at Salamanca, the same ground was repeatedly fought over, and for the defending troops one French attack merged into another without the obvious pattern created by an advance across a battlefield against successive enemies. This, and the sheer intensity of the battle, the noise and the smoke, explains why so many first-hand accounts of the fighting, especially those written soon afterwards, are so confused. Later eye-witness accounts are often much clearer, but only because the original recollection has been shaped and polished into a coherent, entertaining narrative by frequent repetition, and by the influence of histories and other accounts of the battle that the veteran has read or heard. This is a problem with all battles, of course, but it is much worse with Waterloo simply because it eclipsed all previous triumphs in fame and accounts of the events of the day were so pervasive.[12]

Wellington was well aware of the problem. His own account of the battle in his official despatch was much vaguer and more generalised than usual and included the supremely unhelpful line that the French made 'repeated attacks of cavalry and infantry, occasionally mixed, but sometimes separate'.[13] Later, in other contexts, he would not be so reticent, although his version of events is sometimes contradicted by other equally credible sources. He discouraged attempts to write the history of the battle, largely because 'every man you see in a military uniform is not a hero; and that, although in the account of a general action, such as that of Waterloo, many instances of individual heroism must be passed over unrelated, it is better for the general interests to leave those parts of the story untold, than to tell the whole truth'. But he also pointed to the practical difficulty of the task:

> The history of a battle is not unlike the history of a ball. Some individuals may recollect all the little events of which the great result is the battle won or lost; but no individual can recollect the order in which, or the exact moment at which, they occurred, which makes all the difference as to their value or importance.[14]

This objection needs to be taken seriously, and while the broad outline of the narratives of the battle that was gradually put together over the months, years, and even decades which followed, is probably fairly close to the truth, it is important to realise that our knowledge of the events of the day is much more provisional and uncertain that it sometimes seems from popular accounts. Purported precision, especially on questions related to the time at which events occurred, should arouse a suspicion that we have crossed the line from history, based on intractable sources, to imaginative reconstruction where the author selects the evidence to suit their fancy.

The allied army was distributed unevenly along its three miles of front. The flanks were held by Dutch-Belgian infantry: Chassé's division on the right around Braine l'Alleud and Prince Bernard of Saxe Weimar's brigade at Papelotte, La Haie and Smohain. Vivian's hussars supported Prince Bernhard and sent out patrols to watch for the arrival of the Prussians. Within the main line the army was very heavily weighted to the right behind Hougoumont where the First Division in the front line was supported by Clinton's Second Division, the Brunswick Corps and several brigades of British light cavalry. This clearly reflected Wellington's expectation that Napoleon would manoeuvre against this flank but it meant that the centre – and in particular the centre-left – was thinly manned. The three-quarters of a mile of open front east of the *chaussée* was held by Picton's battered division and Bijlandt's Dutch-Belgian brigade. The only reserve of infantry in this part of the field were Vincke's Hanoverian brigade (which was sent to the eastern end of the line to support Prince Bernhard) and Lambert's British brigade, which only reached Mont St Jean late in the morning. Otherwise there was only the army's heavy cavalry: Somerset's Household brigade to the west of the *chaussée* and Ponsonby's Union brigade to the east, with Collaert's two Dutch-Belgian brigades further back. This was a powerful force and one which might have been preserved until later in the battle if there had been a second line of infantry behind Picton.

Although Wellington is said to have instructed his subordinates simply to form up in the usual way, many of the troops were neither deployed in line nor stationed behind the skyline. Indeed it was not until well after the battle had begun that Wellington ordered the infantry between La Haye Sainte and Hougoumont to take shelter behind the 'ridge' – a movement which some accounts suggest was mistaken by Ney for the beginning of a retreat.[15] As for their formation we have unequivocal evidence for the Third Division at least in the form of the official report of its commander, Charles Alten, written on the day after the battle. His division was in the centre, west of the *chaussée* with Picton on his left and the First Division on his right. 'In compliance with your Grace's orders, and those of His Royal Highness the Prince of Orange, to form the division for the attack in two lines of contiguous columns, I placed them in columns of two battalions together at quarter distance, the right regiment on its left company, the left on its right company, so as to deploy right and left into line, or to form squares as necessary: the columns composing the 1st and 2nd lines chequered.'[16] Throughout the battle the allied infantry changed from column, to line, to square and back to column as circumstances required; what mattered was the spirit and courage of the men, and the discipline that enabled them to make these changes while retaining good order despite their steadily mounting casualties. Wellington made one tactical innovation for the battle: even in line most of his infantry formed four-deep. This reduced their fire power but greatly speeded up the transition from line to square, and, by reducing the unit's frontage, brought officers and NCOs close together, tightening the bonds of discipline.[17]

One aspect of the position has attracted considerable discussion: the presence of the Forest of Soignes close behind the allied line has suggested to some commentators that in the event of defeat the army would not have been able to execute an orderly withdrawal. Various counter-arguments have been made including the suggestion that Wellington would have withdrawn the bulk of his army, not north through Waterloo and the Forest but west-north-west past Braine l'Alleud to Hal. This might have worked if a retreat had become necessary early in the day before the armies were seriously engaged, although even then it would have been an extremely delicate and difficult operation, but once the battle had become serious there was little hope of salvaging much from defeat, forest or no forest. The French cavalry was too powerful, and experience suggests that while the British troops who formed the core of Wellington's army were indomitable on the battlefield, they lacked the resilience of the French, or the Prussians, in the case of defeat. For Wellington, as for Blücher and Napoleon, there would be no second chance; victory or defeat, the campaign would be decided that day.

As the morning passed Wellington inspected the position, giving detailed directions for strengthening Hougoumont, reconnoitring down the Nivelles road, and then riding along the whole line as far as La Haie before returning to the First Division. About ten o'clock Captain Taylor of the 10th Hussars brought word to Wellington that the Prussians were approaching. Taylor had been commanding an outlying picquet of Vivian's brigade when he had been met by a Prussian officer with a patrol who informed him that the leading elements of Bülow's corps had arrived at St Lambert three-quarters of a league away. According to Taylor, Wellington was 'vastly pleased' with the news. Fresh supplies of ammunition and rations for at least part of the army arrived, and the soldiers looked to their weapons, endeavoured to make themselves comfortable, and thought of home and their families.[18]

One young officer reflected on the ways of the world and found them strange:

> It is an awful situation to be in, to stand a sharp edged instrument at one's side, waiting for the signal to drag it out of its peaceful innocent house to snap the thread of existence of those we never saw, never spoke to, never offended.
> On the opposite ascent stand hundreds of young men like myself whose feelings are probably more acute, whose principles are more upright, whose acquaintance would delight and conversation improve me, yet with all my soul I wished them dead as the earth they tramped on and anticipated their total annihilation.[19]

Most men were probably more pragmatic, hoping to survive unscathed while performing their duty with credit, or at least not disgracing themselves. For young officers in particular, facing their baptism of fire, it was an uncomfortable morning as they wondered how they would react when put to the test.

A couple of miles to the south of La Haye Sainte Napoleon had breakfasted outside the little inn of Le Caillou. He was feeling confident and dismissed reports that the allies had begun to retreat with easy assurance: 'You have seen wrong and it is too late now. Wellington would expose himself to certain loss.

He has thrown the dice and they are in our favour.' When Soult urged that part of Grouchy's force be recalled the Emperor snubbed him: 'Because you have been beaten by Wellington, you consider him a great general. And now I tell you that Wellington is a bad general, that the English are bad troops, and that this affair is nothing more serious than eating one's breakfast.' This was, of course, partly bravado, for a general, particularly one like Napoleon, could not admit to doubts or hesitation; yet it really does seem that he underrated both Wellington and the allied army. Reille tried to warn him: 'Well posted, as Wellington knows how to post it, and attacked from the front, I consider the English Infantry to be impregnable, owing to its calm tenacity, and its superior aim in firing. Before attacking it with the bayonet, one may expect half the assailants to be brought to the ground. But the English Army is less agile, less supple, less expert in manoeuvring than ours. If we cannot beat it by a direct attack, we may do so by manoeuvring.'[20]

Napoleon might have attempted to turn one of Wellington's flanks – an attack to the west by Braine l'Alleud was unlikely to succeed, but the eastern flank was rather more promising despite the good defensive cover provided by Papelotte, La Haie and Smohain[21] – but instead chose a frontal assault designed to shatter the allied army. He had ordered his men to be ready to begin by nine o'clock but this proved overly optimistic; with few supplies and after the misery of the previous night the army was still widely scattered, with only Reille's corps approximately in position at nine o'clock. Even two hours later many units were far to the rear and Napoleon was forced to accept that his army would not be fully concentrated until towards one o'clock.[22] There would still be plenty of time to win a great victory before the long June day was over, and the delay would at least let the ground dry out, facilitating the movement of cavalry and artillery. But the passing hours brought a new problem: the Prussians, whom Napoleon had confidently dismissed from his calculations at breakfast as good for nothing for at least another two days. First, in the middle of the morning, came a letter from Grouchy with the news that the Prussians had retreated north to Wavre, not east, and so were not all that far away. Then, about one o'clock, the appearance of unidentified troops in the distance to the east, in the direction of Wavre. And finally, not long after, a captured Prussian subaltern who cheerfully admitted that he belonged to Bülow's corps. There was no disguising that this was bad news, although Napoleon made the best of it: 'This morning we had ninety odds in our favour. We still have sixty against forty, and if Grouchy repairs the terrible fault he has made in amusing himself at Gembloux, and marches rapidly, our victory will be all the more decisive, for Bülow's corps will be completely destroyed.'[23]

By then the battle had begun with a preliminary attack on Hougoumont. Different accounts, all written by officers who were present, give different times for the opening of hostilities, ranging from ten o'clock to twelve noon exactly, while Marshal Ney, writing just eight days later, made it one o'clock. Two officers who made special note of the exact moment were Rowland Hill, who put it at ten minutes before noon, and Edmund Wheatley who made it 'just eleven o'clock', and others could be quoted, each confident in the accuracy of both his watch and his memory. Yet this was a simple thing to remember: a clear, sharp, well-defined event coming early in the day, before the senses were overwhelmed and exhausted. If our witnesses cannot agree on this we must not be surprised if there is confusion and contradiction in their accounts of what followed.[24]

Napoleon appears to have intended the attack on Hougoumont to be nothing more than a diversion, but as often happens, especially when a tangible prize is at stake, the operation developed a momentum of its own and eventually absorbed more than half of Reille's corps as the commanders on the spot, particularly Prince Jerome, called for fresh troops after each setback, or in the hope of pressing home a temporary advantage. Much of the fighting was at very close range and there were many acts of conspicuous courage and valour on both sides. The struggle lasted all day, although probably in a series of violent spasms rather than continuously. Wellington watched it closely and Pozzo di Borgo (the exiled French diplomat in the service of Russia) was struck by his cool reaction when the Nassau troops defending the wood gave way. Sir Augustus Frazer then brought up Bull's troop of howitzers and proposed firing over the heads of the defenders into the French. Wellington said: "'Colonel Frazer, you are going to do a delicate thing; can you depend upon the force of your howitzers? Part of the wood is held by our troops, part by the enemy." . . . I answered that I could perfectly depend upon the troop; and, after speaking to Major Bull and all his officers, and seeing that they, too, perfectly understood their orders, the troop commenced its fire, and in ten minutes the enemy was driven from the wood.'[25]

Fresh attacks were made, and it is said that the wood to the south of the château changed hands three times. But it was the house and its enclosures that was the kernel of the defence and shortly before three o'clock – according to Colonel Frazer – the buildings caught fire. Chance has preserved the written order which Wellington sent to the garrison soon afterwards. Written in pencil on a slip of asses' skin which could be wiped clean and used again, it shows his attention to detail and willingness to bypass the usual chain of command. There was neither address nor signature:

> I see that the fire has communicated from the Hay stack to the roof of the Chateau. You must however still keep your Men in those parts to which the fire does not reach. Take care that no Men are lost by the falling in of the Roof

or floors – After they are both fallen in occupy the Ruined walls inside the Garden; particularly if it should be possible for the Enemy to pass through the Embers in the inside of the House.[26]

In his official despatch Wellington paid a warm tribute to the defence: 'I am happy to add that it was maintained throughout the day with the utmost gallantry by these brave troops, notwithstanding the repeated efforts of large bodies of the enemy to obtain possession of it.'[27]

But however fierce the fighting and brave the defence, Hougoumont was essentially a sideshow; Napoleon's main thrust was always going to be made on the allied centre, where D'Erlon's corps would lead the attack with some of Milhaud's cuirassiers in close support. The French artillery was brought up and began to pound the centre and left of the allied line. British troops had not encountered such a weight of fire in the Peninsula and it made a marked impression, with Thomas Dyneley commenting that the 'rascals certainly did this beautifully' and two of his fellow artillery officers describing it as 'a tremendous cannonade' and 'tremendously heavy'.[28] The number of actual casualties produced by such a bombardment, at longish range and against troops either lying down or under some cover, was probably rather small, but each casualty made a great impression on the tense, anxious troops, who had no way of replying and generally no activity to distract them. The strain proved too much for some men. William Tomkinson of the 16th Light Dragoons records the instance of Private Price in his troop who 'got off his horse and ran away to the rear before we were engaged, being deranged. He was an old soldier, yet not the wisest, and had been shoemaker to the troop for many years. The men after the day was over did not resent his leaving them, knowing the kind of man and his weakness'.[29] Evidently Tomkinson himself saw no need to take official action against Price; the tolerance of his fellow soldiers apparently secured his immunity. Sergeant William Lawrence of the 40th shows that this tolerance was unusual:

During this movement a shell from the enemy cut our deputy-sergeant-major in two, and having passed on to take the head off one of my company of grenadiers named William Hooper, exploded in the rear not more than one yard from me, hurling me at least two yards into the air, but fortunately doing me little injury beyond the shaking . . . I remember remarking to a sergeant who was standing close by me when I fell, "This is sharp work to begin with, I hope it will end better": and even this much had unfortunately so frightened one of the young recruits of my company, named Bartram, who had never before been in action, and now did not like the curious evolutions of this shell so close to him, that he called out to me and said he must fall out of rank as he was taken very ill. I could easily see the cause of his illness, so I pushed him into rank again, saying, "Why, Bartram, it's the smell of this little powder that has caused your illness; there's nothing else the matter with you;" but that physic would not content him at all, and he fell down and would not proceed another inch. I was fearfully put out at this, but was obliged to leave him, or if he had had his due he ought to have been shot.[30]

The sequel is instructive. Bartram returned to the regiment some months later with a contingent of men who had recovered from their wounds. Lawrence immediately reported him and he was arrested, court martialled and sentenced to three hundred lashes 'and received every lash!' When Bartram returned from hospital after three weeks Lawrence, on the orders of his captain, inspected his kit and knapsack and, as he expected, found them empty. Bartram was sentenced to another three hundred lashes and again received them all, with Lawrence commenting that 'it may be pretty well taken for granted that the drummers did not fail in their duty towards such a man as this, for there is no one they feel more strongly against than a coward'. Even this did not close the affair 'for all his comrades shunned his society and would scarcely speak to him at all', and his pay was docked for the missing equipment so that he was reduced to the depths of misery and penury. Not surprisingly the unfortunate man went absent without leave and when he returned was found to have sold his kit for a few days' food and drink in Paris. A third flogging was followed by a fourth when the regiment returned to Scotland and he was then discharged in disgrace from the regiment.[31] It is an ugly but illuminating story. The disgrace and punishment of Bartram showed all the other young soldiers in the regiment the price they might pay if they let their fears overwhelm them. At the same time it allowed them to define themselves in contrast to him; he was a coward, they were good soldiers. It is noticeable how little sympathy there was for Bartram, either from Lawrence or from his fellow soldiers in the ranks. This was the harsh, unedifying side of the group cohesion that underpinned discipline in action and which is rather obscured by the pleasant phrase *esprit de corps.*

Soldiers who displayed such blatant cowardice as Price and Bartram were rare, but as the battle went on many more would fall out of the ranks and drift to the rear on one pretext or another – helping a wounded comrade to a dressing station was a favourite – and few returned before the end of the day. The French bombardment began the process of wearing away each man's reserves of courage, fraying strand by strand the ties of loyalty, discipline and self-esteem that kept him in the ranks. As with the actual casualties it inflicted, the effect was small at first but accumulated over the hours, sapping the strength of the allied army. This was part of what was meant by a battle of attrition.[32]

The bombardment continued all day, waxing and waning in intensity and shifting its main focus from the left-centre of the allied line to the right-centre. This first phase may have lasted only half an hour,[33] although it probably seemed longer to the allies, before D'Erlon's corps moved forward to the attack. All four divisions were employed in the attack. Quiot's Division advanced close to the *chaussée*. Its leading brigade attacked La Haye Sainte, driving the garrison out of the orchard and gardens but not from the enclosed farmhouse, stables and barn. The second brigade under Baron Bourgeois drove the riflemen of the 95th from the gravel pit on the other side of the road from the farm. On Bourgeois's right, to the east, came the divisions of Donzelot and Marcognet, and beyond them Durutte's division attacked the allied outposts in Papelotte and La Haie. Quiot's left flank was protected by Travers' brigade of cuirassiers advancing to the west of La Haye Sainte. The attack was, initially at least, in echelon with Quiot's division leading. Unaccountably the main columns of Bourgeois, Donzelot and Marcognet were all formed by a closely packed succession of battalions each deployed in line, one behind another, only a few paces apart. This formation had nothing to recommend it; the troops could not easily form square, extend their frontage or even advance very rapidly, and the whole division was reduced to the firepower of a single battalion while presenting a monstrous target for the allied artillery. Even worse, it meant that the entire corps was committed to a single assault without any supports or reserves. It would have been much more effective to have had fewer men in the first wave of the attack but with a second and third wave of fresh, well-formed troops ready to exploit any disorder in the allied lines. The mystery of who ordered this formation and why has never been solved, but it has been fairly pointed out that it took time for the divisions to form these columns and that both Ney and Napoleon had the opportunity to intervene if they had wished.

A Swiss officer in the *45e Ligne* in Marcognet's division describes the advance:

At length our time has come, a frantic shout of *Vive l'Empereur* is our answer to the order to advance. The four columns step off with arms supported, and with ranks well closed up we descend the slope into the hollow ground which divided us from the English whose batteries thunder upon us. The intervening space is but small, an ordinary pedestrian would have crossed it easily in five or six minutes, but the soft saturated ground and the tall rye we had to pass through much retarded our advance, and gave the English batteries ample time to do their work of death upon us. Yet there was no flinching, and when we at length reach the position, the drums beat the change, the pace is quickened, and with a thousand cries of *Vive l'Empereur* we rush on the batteries.[34]

William Gomm, serving on the staff of Picton's division, picks up the tale:

> Three solid masses of infantry ... advance with rapidity across the gentle
> ravine that separates the two positions, his left column directing its attack
> upon the great road, the other two between the great road and height which
> formed our left. The horse artillery are forced to withdraw their guns after
> having done dreadful execution against the enemy's column advancing along
> the road and to our immediate left of it. The 95th, light troops, and skir-
> mishers are forced to withdraw before the French column, which reaches the
> top of our position in compact order, the head of it crossing the lane along
> which our line had been originally formed. At this moment the 32nd and
> 79th Regiments, posted on our right, which had retired some paces, and
> which had hitherto kept up a destructive fire upon the enemy's column
> without seeming to shake it, advanced to the charge with shouts. The column
> hesitates, turns and breaks, hurrying in disorder down the hill.[35]

What seems to have happened is that Donzelot's column halted at the
summit of the ridge in a vain attempt to deploy and was overtaken by Marcognet,
who pushed through the hedges without pausing. Bijlandt's brigade of Dutch-
Belgian troops, mostly militia who had already suffered heavily at Quatre Bras,
crumbled and gave way, but Pack brought his brigade forward and filled the
gap. The French infantry was then attacked by Picton's men (at least some of
whom were formed in four-deep line) who fired one or more volleys and then
charged, Kempt's brigade against Donzelot, Pack's against Marcognet.[36] Picton
was killed, shot through the head moments after he gave the order to charge.
The French columns hesitated, quivered and began to give way, but the decisive
blow was struck when William Ponsonby's brigade of heavy dragoons charged
into them: the Scots Greys cutting into Marcognet's column; the Inniskillings
into Donzelot; and the Royals into Bourgeois. The French broke and fled, two
Eagles were taken (those of the *45ᵉ* in Marcognet's division by Sergeant Ewart
of the Scots Greys and that of the *108ᵉ* in Bourgeois's brigade by Captain Clark
of the Royals), and more than 2,000 prisoners were taken.[37]

The Swiss officer of the *45ᵉ* gives a vivid sense of what happened:

> As I was pushing one of our men into his proper place in the ranks he suddenly
> sank under a sword cut, turning briskly round I saw the English Dragoons
> riding into our column, in every direction cutting our men down right and
> left ... In vain did our poor fellows try and defend themselves with their
> bayonets, they had not a chance against these dragoons mounted as they were
> on powerful horses. The few shots this hapless and bewildered crowd could
> fire proved as dangerous to our own men as to the Cavalry. We were totally

defenseless before those terrible dragoons, who in their fury cut down every one they could reach, even to our poor drummer boys. It was then we lost our eagle, and then death stared me in the face, for my best and dearest friends were falling fast around me, and though still mechanically brandishing my sword I every instant expected to share their fate.[38]

At the same time the Household Brigade under Lord Edward Somerset charged the French cuirassiers who were covering D'Erlon's western flank, and caught them at a disadvantage as they endeavoured to cross the sunken road near the crest of the rise above La Haye Sainte. Many of the French gave way at once, and those who could escape did so, but others were caught in a corner between a solid fence and the road and were cut down – although not without difficulty, for their cuirasses provided them with useful protection in the melée.

The disordered British cavalry galloped forward, without control or direction, driving the French infantry and cavalry before them and over-running some of the French artillery. Their impetuosity led to disaster as French cavalry reserves – including some lancers – were sent against them and found them easy prey. Scattered parties of over-excited men on blown horses could not hope to resist fresh troops capably deployed, and very often they could not even manage to escape. William Ponsonby and many of the officers and men of both brigades were killed or wounded far in advance of the allied position. The exact losses will never be known, for all the regiments went on to suffer casualties later in the day, but it seems likely that when they finally collected again near their starting point there were fewer than half the men in the ranks who had been there only an hour or two before. Not all the others were casualties – some had simply been unhorsed, or felt that they had done their bit for the day and took advantage of the confusion to make their way to the rear, either to shelter in the Forest of Soignes or to go on as far as Brussels. Many of these stragglers would return to the colours before the casualty returns were prepared. Nonetheless the official figures are grim enough: of the 2,407 officers and men of the two brigades present on the morning of 18 June, 359 were killed, 558 wounded and 288 missing by the end of the day, a total of 1,205 or almost exactly half.[39]

These losses have led to some criticism of the charge, but it was no surprise that British cavalry should escape control once released into action; the same thing had happened before in the Peninsula, even in Le Marchant's great charge at Salamanca. Theoretically it might have been possible to hold one squadron of each regiment, or one regiment of each brigade, back in support, but in practice there was such a choice of temptingly disordered enemy formations to charge that it was inevitable that the whole force would sweep forward to exploit the opportunity to the utmost. The failure, in so far as there was one, lay in not bringing forward fresh bodies of cavalry quickly enough to shelter the withdrawal of the two brigades once the charge was exhausted. Some steps were taken, but they proved inadequate and belated. Otherwise the 'blame' rests with the initial deployment of the army which meant that there was no other substantial body of troops in place to support Picton in the face of D'Erlon's corps. Yet the whole question is ill-conceived. The charge of the Union and Household brigades was a magnificent exploit, perfectly timed and executed with great courage and élan. Two and a half divisions of French infantry were broken, losing heavily in men and even more in morale, cohesion and confidence. Nor can the sight of their comrades fleeing from the allied position in terror while being hacked at by the British horsemen have done much to inspire the soldiers in the rest of the French army, knowing as they did that they too would have to climb that slope, unaware of what trouble might be brewing just out of sight.[40]

A pause seems to have followed the British charge as both sides regrouped and their commanders considered what came next. Wellington looked anxiously to the east for some sign of the Prussians, for it was now several hours since news of Bülow's approach had been announced. However, there is a great difference between the leading squadron of cavalry or battalion of infantry reaching a point, and a whole army, or even a corps, being ready to advance from it, and the roads and terrain between Wavre and the battlefield, especially in the later stages around Lasne, were difficult and congested, and made even worse by the rain and the passage of troops. The Prussians came as quickly as was humanly possible and by four o'clock had reached the Paris wood, behind Napoleon's flank, but there was no point launching a feeble, piecemeal attack with the first troops in hand when a little delay would enable them to strike with much greater force. Even so Napoleon had already been forced to detach two divisions of light cavalry (under Domon and Subervie) to observe their movements, with Lobau's infantry in support. This was no small help to Wellington, for in the wake of D'Erlon's mishap Lobau's infantry could have been very useful in renewing the assault upon Mont St Jean.[41]

As soon as some of the least affected of D'Erlon's battalions had rallied, Ney renewed the attack on La Haye Sainte with Quiot's brigade, supported to the east by an advance against the gravel pit and up the slope – although this time the French infantry went forward without enthusiasm and mostly in open order. Accounts of this fighting are particularly vague, but it seems that throughout the rest of the afternoon there was almost continuous skirmishing around this part of the allied line.[42]

Meanwhile the French had brought more artillery into action and the bombardment now extended along the whole allied line from opposite Hougoumont to Papelotte in the east. In response the front line of allied troops between Hougoumont and La Haye Sainte withdrew one hundred yards or so behind the skyline. It is said that this movement, combined with glimpses of large numbers of wounded, prisoners, ammunition carts and the like making their way to the rear, convinced Ney that Wellington had begun to retreat, and that he sought to convert this retreat into a rout with a massive attack by the French cavalry on the allied centre.[43] In fact he had little real choice: D'Erlon's corps was, if not completely spent, then incapable of striking a heavy blow; half of Reille's corps had been sucked into the fight for Hougoumont, and he could not hope to defeat the main body of the allied army with the division and a half which remained; Lobau had been sent to ward off the Prussians; and Napoleon would certainly not release the Guard this early in the day. For better or worse it was up to the cavalry to make the next attack. Theoretically it might have been best for it to strike east of La Haye Sainte where the defence had already been tested, but that part of the battlefield was littered by the detritus of D'Erlon's attack and the British cavalry which would impede cavalry advancing to the charge, while the hedges lining the Ohain road at the summit would further rob the attack of the momentum that was vital to its success. The ground to the west of the farm was more promising – open and uncluttered – even if the allied troops in that sector were relatively fresh and numerous.

Almost 3,000 cuirassiers and 2,000 elite light cavalry advanced to assail the centre of the allied line. Wellington had some warning of the impending attack and strengthened his centre with troops from his right flank and reserve. Four battalions of Brunswick infantry were added to the main line while Mitchell's and Adam's brigades took up the ground overlooking Hougoumont, the Guards shifting a little to the left, closer to the centre. Lieutenant James Hamilton, of the 2nd Line Battalion of the King's German Legion in the second line, described the initial onslaught in a letter written just over a month later:

> Our Brigade was formed in open Column of Companies on the right and a little in rear of the first Division – we continued in this Position suffering much from the Cannonade until two, when we observed the Regiments of the first Line form Squares to repel Cavalry – this movement was scarcely executed when the French Cavalry made a dashing charge. They were received with a severe and galling Fire, that did much execution. They did not however retire immediately, but finding that they could make no impression on the 52nd [Regiment] which received their charge They galloped down the Line of Squares, perhaps in the Idea of finding some Corps in Confusion but they were at every point repulsed with the greatest Steadiness.
>
> . . .
>
> [O]ur Cavalry observing the opportunity cut in amongst them and completed the Havock previously made by the Infantry. Those that escaped

were immediately supported by numerous Forces, and our Cavalry were obliged to retire in their turn. At this charge the French had passed within our Artillery, and many of the men were cut down at the Guns, others escaped by creeping under and the moment the French had repassed jumped up and fired with the greatest coolness and gallantry.[44]

Hamilton also gives us a glimpse of Wellington at this moment:

It was also at this charge the Duke of Wellington and his Staff were exposed to considerable hazard of being taken Prisoners. He had been riding on the Summit of the Hill (where some Batteries of Artillery were placed) the whole morning. The best spot where a general View could be had of the Battle – but certainly by far the most dangerous Post in the Field – The French Cavalry came on so rapid[ly] that the Duke had scarcely time to get within the protection of the Squares[.] His personal danger, great exertions, and Gallantry were conspicuous to the whole Army throughout the Day.[45]

The charge had failed to break a single allied square, but neither Ney nor his men would give up. Driven from the allied position they rallied and returned time and time again, without the impetus or menace of the initial attack but with astonishing courage and determination. Napoleon thought the initial attack was premature, but seeing it fail ordered Kellermann to support it with his corps, and ultimately even the heavy cavalry of the Guard joined in.[46] This was much more of a mistake than the initial attack; these additional troops had little chance of success advancing over the churned-up, muddy, casualty-strewn field against infantry whose confidence had been bolstered by weathering the initial storm, while if even a few regiments of heavy cavalry had been preserved intact they might have been used with much greater effect later in the day. Nonetheless we must not fall into the trap of supposing that the infantry in the squares in the allied centre felt easy or secure. The menace and ferocity of the cavalry was palpable and between their charges came the bombardment by the French artillery, and in the tightly packed squares every man was aware of the mounting toll of casualties. Surgeon James records that the men he treated said that 'the terrific cannonading was worse than anything they had ever experienced'.[47]

The battlefield had become an unimaginably horrible place. Edmund Wheatley wrote that:

An ammunition cart blew up near us, smashing men and horses. I took a calm survey of the field around and felt shocked at the sight of broken armour, lifeless bodies, murdered horses, shattered wheels, caps, helmets, swords, muskets, pistols, still and silent. Here and there a frightened horse would rush across the plain trampling on the dying and the dead. Three or four poor wounded animals standing on three legs, the other dangling before [them]. We killed several of these unfortunate beasts and it would have been an equal Charity to have performed the same operation on the wriggling, feverish, mortally lacerated soldiers as they rolled on the ground.[48]

It all proved too much for some men to bear. The Duke of Cumberland Hussars, a regiment of volunteers from Hanover, most of whom had seen little or no previous service, and who were sufficiently wealthy to own their own horses, began moving to the rear about five o'clock. Uxbridge sent his ADC to halt them but without success, nor would they even obey a subsequent order to form up on the road out of range of the French artillery; having once allowed themselves to give way they were determined to escape completely.[49] A much more surprising example of misconduct occurred in the 95th Rifles. According to their commander Andrew Barnard, writing only three days after the battle:

I regret to say that a *great* number of our men went to the rear without cause after the appearance of the Cuirassiers, there were no less than 100 absentees after the fight and this vexes me very much as it is the first time such a thing has ever happened in the regiment. Kincaid says very few if any quitted the corps after the charge of the cavalry. Many of those that went to the rear were men that I little expected to have heard of in that situation.[50]

The historian of the 95th attributes this flight to combat fatigue – the idea that veteran soldiers in the regiment had seen too much fighting and found that their courage had been exhausted.[51] This is plausible, but there is another possibility. The veterans of the 95th thought they knew what a battle was like from their experience in the Peninsula; and they were so shocked and appalled by the much greater intensity of the fire at Waterloo that some of them took to their heels. An officer of the Royal Dragoons, Alex Kennedy Clark, made the comparison explicit: 'I never was in such a fire! Anything I saw in Spain was child's play compared with Waterloo'; while even Marshal Ney, the 'bravest of the brave' and most renowned fire-eater of the age, declared that it was 'the most dreadful carnage I have ever witnessed'.[52]

Six months after the battle, in December 1815, Wellington described an even more serious instance of troops absconding, in a letter to the Master-General of the Ordnance:

To tell you the truth, I was not very well pleased with the artillery in the battle of Waterloo. The army was formed in squares immediately on the slope of the rising ground, on the summit of which the artillery was placed, with orders not to engage with artillery, but to fire only when bodies of troops came under their fire. It was very difficult to get them to obey this order. The French cavalry charged, and were formed on the same ground with our artillery, in general within a few yards of our guns ... We could not expect the artillery-men to remain at their guns in such a case. But I had a right to expect that the officers and men of the artillery would do as I did, and as all the Staff did, that is to take shelter in the squares of the infantry till the French cavalry should be driven off the ground, either by our cavalry or infantry. But they did no such thing; they ran off the field entirely, taking with them limbers, ammunition, and everything; and when, in a few minutes, we had driven off the French cavalry, and had regained our ground and our guns, and could have made good use of our artillery, we had no artillerymen to fire them; and, in point of fact, I should have had no artillery during the whole of the latter part of the action, if I had not kept a reserve in the commencement.[53]

This letter did not become public until 1872 when it provoked a storm of denials from the surviving veterans of the artillery in the battle, but the most recent historian of the British artillery admits that there is good evidence that at least three allied batteries did withdraw from the front line at this time, and that it is not clear who, if anyone, gave them permission to do so. Many individual gunners, like many infantrymen and cavalrymen, also found their way to the rear on one pretext or another. Wellington's comments were probably too sweeping and too harsh – as his private pronouncements often were – but equally the well-known tales of heroism at Waterloo, such as Mercer's immensely readable *Journal*, need to be balanced with the untold stories of soldiers who may have fought bravely for a time, but who left the field before the battle was over.[54]

There is less room for doubt about other instances of individual misconduct. When Rowland Hill's brother Clement was making his way towards Brussels, having been wounded, he encountered an acquaintance headed in the same direction although apparently unscathed: '"Eh, my good fellow," cried the Colonel, "I thought you were wounded: were you not?" "No, no!" said he, "but *I had some very narrow escapes!*"'[55] While another officer, Lord Portarlington, is reported to have quitted the regiment he commanded (the 23rd Light Dragoons) soon after the battle had begun, saying that it was a bad business, and that he did not know what he was doing there, service or no service, and that he was unwell and so on. Writing of this case to the Duke of York, Wellington said: 'I should think it would be best not to bring him to trial, but to desire him privately to retire from the service. I confess that I feel very strong objections to discuss before a General Court Martial the conduct of any individual in such a battle as that of Waterloo. It generally brings before the public circumstances which might as well not be published; and the effect is equally produced by obliging him who has behaved ill to withdraw from the service.'[56] This seems to have reflected existing practice in the army, for we have evidence from several regiments of officers who were suspected of misconduct being privately required to explain themselves and, if unable to do so satisfactorily, being forced to resign. Private Bartram of the 40th would have wished that similar consideration and discretion had extended to the ordinary soldiers of the army.[57]

There are many first-hand accounts of the extraordinary state of confusion in the rear of the allied army during the battle as throngs of fugitives, some wounded, some not, crowded onto the road to Brussels or sought shelter among the trees of the forest. These fugitives came from all contingents of the army and included officers as well as men, although there was a tendency in some later British reminiscences to describe them all as Belgians and to quietly ignore the red coats among the blue. Two days after the battle Wellington issued a General Order admitting that 'soldiers, and even officers, have quitted their ranks without leave, and have gone to Bruxelles, and even some to Antwerp, where, and in the country through which they have passed, they have spread a false alarm, in a manner highly unmilitary, and derogatory to the character of soldiers'. He called for a report on those officers and men still absent without leave, and no doubt in time some were punished, although most had returned to the colours soon after the battle.[58]

Such scenes were not unique to Waterloo, although the small size of the battlefield and the intensity of the fighting made them much more obvious. In the end what really mattered was that the panic did not spread to the troops in the front line, and that enough officers and men remained with their units for the army to be able to maintain its position. This was not a foregone conclusion, for as each hour passed the allied army was being steadily eroded. But so too was the French, for it was not only allied troops whose courage was exhausted and who left the ranks in despair long before the battle had been decided. The great cavalry charges put immense pressure on the allied centre, but at a high cost. After some time Ney did attempt to support them with infantry, pushing forward Bachelu's division and Janin's brigade of Foy's division, the only fresh infantry he had left. Their attack was repulsed with little difficulty even though the allied infantry then had to form swiftly back into square to face another cavalry charge. The day was still far from over but some idea of the scale of the 'wearing away' can be gathered from James Hamilton's statement that in his battalion, which had mustered more than 300 bayonets in the morning, there were by the close no more than six officers and thirty-four private soldiers left with the colours. 'Many joined us the next day who had assisted to convey away the severely wounded.'[59]

When the cavalry charges were at their height, the French gained an important success capturing La Haye Sainte, whose garrison had fought with great heroism and tenacity until their ammunition was completely exhausted.[60] Possession of the farm emboldened the French skirmishers to push forward against the allied line, and a battery of artillery came forward to support them. James Kempt, who had taken command of the 5th Division on Picton's death, reported: 'A desperate struggle and fire now took place. I directed all the broken ground that afforded the least cover to be completely lined with troops; but in addition to this I found it absolutely necessary to increase our fire by moving up the greatest part of the 27th regiment . . . it was unavoidably much exposed. The regiment behaved nobly, and suffered exceedingly. The 95th and 32nd were also near this point, and suffered also great loss. The struggle at the point continued for some hours.'[61]

The fate of the 1/27th attracted particular attention. It was a strong battalion, with more than 750 all ranks at the beginning of the day, and only took its place at the front after the fighting had begun. But its position was exposed and it suffered some 478 casualties in the space of a few hours, mostly without being able to retaliate. This was an extreme example, but the problem was general. One officer of the 5th Division believed that it had been reduced from 6,000 officers and men to 1,800, 'and the men were so completely worn out that it required the greatest exertion on the part of the officers to keep up their spirits'. While another wrote in his memoirs: 'Our division, which had stood upwards of five thousand men at the commencement of the battle, had gradually dwindled down into a solitary line of skirmishers.'[62]

Wellington was in the thick of this fighting. He had taken his station by an elm tree a little to the west of the *chaussée* overlooking La Haye Sainte, although he was often on the move, encouraging wavering soldiers and watching for fresh developments. One of Wellington's ADCs who survived the battle unscathed wrote home the next day: 'The Duke did wonders and earned well his victory, we were near losing the day four times, and I assure you that nothing but his countenance kept the matter going; you will see that great havoc has been made among our Staff. . . . how the Duke escaped we are at a loss to know, for he was in the thick of it from morning till night.' Lord Bathurst's son, Lord Apsley, who was present at the battle as an amateur, agreed: 'The Victory was entirely won by the Duke's own personal courage and conduct. He stood in the squares as the French Cavalry charged them, and led them on, when the cavalry retreated.' Thomas Wildman, one of Uxbridge's ADCs, told his mother: 'Three separate times, I believe, all hopes were given over by everyone, except the Duke of Wellington, who only said, "we will beat them yet before night."' And Augustus Frazer wrote on 20 June: 'His Grace exposed his person, not unnecessarily but nobly: without his personal exertions, his continual presence wherever and whenever more than usual exertions were required, the day had been lost.' This exposure alarmed Wellington's staff. Two or three times Alexander Gordon led the Duke's horse out of severe fire when he was using his glass, coolly ignoring his commander's expostulation: 'Damn it, I must see!'[63]

As the long day drew towards its close both armies teetered on the edge of exhaustion. Wellington wrote to Beresford a fortnight later: 'Never did I see such a pounding match. Both were what the boxers call "gluttons".'[64] The last allied reserves had gone, thrown into the furnace hours before to sustain the wilting line. Now, needing to reinforce his crumbling centre, Wellington called in troops from both flanks: Chassé's division from the right and the light cavalry brigades of Vivian and Vandeleur from the left. They were not the troops Wellington would have chosen for such a situation, but they helped fill the gaps and give heart to the battered infantry who were ready to waver. Not that the whole of the centre was on the brink of collapse; some units, such as Adam's brigade in Clinton's division, had not been much exposed and had, as yet, suffered only a few casualties. Others, such as the Guards, had suffered more but remained in good order and spirits. But many others, particularly those closest to La Haye Sainte, were beginning to lose heart.

The French were in just as bad a plight; all the line infantry and all the heavy cavalry had been thrown into the fray, driven back with heavy losses, rallied and advanced again, only to suffer even more. The gunners manning the batteries had suffered relatively few casualties but their stamina was flagging after hours of hard labour. There remained only the Guard, and not all of that. The Prussians had launched their assault against the French flank and rear, probably between four and five o'clock. The French light cavalry was driven back but Lobau counter-attacked with some success. Bülow brought up fresh reserves and, driving the French infantry before him, stormed the village of Plancenoit behind Napoleon's flank. The Prussians could not be permitted to retain it, and Napoleon sent the Young Guard to Lobau's aid. The fighting in the village was fierce but the Prussians were forced to give way. However they rallied on their reserves and returned to the attack, and in its turn the Young Guard had to give ground; house by house the ruined village changed hands again. Napoleon had no choice but to draw on his reserves and despatched two battalions of the Old Guard (1/2nd Grenadiers, 1/2nd Chasseurs), who charged through the village brooking no resistance and checked the Prussian menace for a time.[65]

This left Napoleon with a dozen battalions of the Grenadiers and Chasseurs of the Guard. It is often said that if he had used this final reserve for a decisive attack on the allied centre in the hour after La Haye Sainte had fallen the allies would have been unable to resist, and the French would have gained the victory.[66] Possibly. Such scenarios are very tempting and, because they are purely hypothetical, there is no way of testing them or of knowing what problems might have arisen if they had been attempted. But such an attack would not have come without warning and it would be unsafe to assume that Wellington would not have taken steps to guard against it. Whether those steps would have been sufficient, however, is unknowable.

The details of the final French attack which led to 'the Crisis and Close' of the battle are shrouded in controversy, myth and uncertainty. It was late in the day, and visibility was limited by clouds of smoke from gunpowder and the burning buildings and haystacks of Hougoumont and La Haye Sainte; men were tired, their senses already battered to numbness. Most of the first-hand accounts written soon after the event lack clarity when describing the events of the late afternoon and evening unless some particularly vivid incident or image stands out. But as time went on regimental pride asserted itself and retired officers took to claiming that *their* regiment had struck the decisive blow and defeated Napoleon's famed Imperial Guard. Twenty, thirty, even forty years after the event middle-aged and elderly men embarked on furious controversies as they repudiated the claims of their rivals and became ever bolder in their own assertions. Someone who, on 18 June 1815, was a teenage subaltern, almost dropping with fatigue and nervous strain, intent on keeping his courage up, his men in line and not missing his captain's next order or forgetting the words of command, would, thirty years later, confidently state that he had carefully observed the enemy he was facing, and be certain that it had been infantry of the Guard, not the line; that they were formed in column not square; and that they numbered 10,000, not 2,000 or 600.[67] The officers of the 52nd believed that they had received insufficient credit, that their flank attack was decisive, and that Wellington had done them a grave injustice by not publicly acknowledging their pre-eminent role in winning the battle in his official despatch. Their bitterness was heightened by the credit given to the Guards both by Lord Bathurst, in Parliament, less than a week after the battle, and by the Horse Guards, which bestowed the title of 'Grenadier' upon the 1st Foot Guards to commemorate their triumph. Sir John Colborne, commander of the 52nd and, by some accounts, the originator of the flanking movement that routed the Imperial Guard, wisely abstained from official protest or public controversy, but went out of his way to excuse the negligence of Wellington's despatch while indicating that the whole subject was inexpressibly painful.[68] Some of his juniors were less discreet, provoking pamphlet wars which reflected little credit on any of the participants. Officers who had served in other parts of the field, and who noted that the 52nd had suffered proportionately fewer casualties than most regiments in the battle, felt slighted by the elevation of one incident in the long day to transcendent significance. Even Harry Smith, proud veteran of the Light Division and good friend of Colborne, could not refrain from commenting: 'The Battle of Waterloo has been too often described, and nonsense enough written about the Crisis, for me to add to it. Every moment was a crisis, and the controversialists had better have left the discussion on the battlefield.' Smith had been Lambert's brigade-major at the battle and the memory of the fate of the 1/27th may have lessened his sympathy for the wounded pride of the 52nd. And then there were the thousands of Peninsular veterans who had not been at Waterloo and who saw all their great triumphs and years of hard campaigning eclipsed by a single bloody afternoon, and who reflected sourly that not all glory was equally appreciated.[69]

The 52nd was the most plausible, but not the only, rival of the Guards for the honour of defeating Napoleon's final attack. Sir Richard Hussey Vivian maintained that his brigade of hussars had struck the decisive blow, and there were almost as many well-connected officers in the fashionable hussar regiments willing to support his version as in the Guards or the 52nd. Colin Halkett's brigade of infantry, which had suffered much at Quatre Bras and even more at Waterloo, thought that it had played a part as well, while some Brunswickers and even Chassé's Dutch-Belgian division had the temerity to attempt to gatecrash what was clearly a British-only party. The respected French historian Henry Houssaye tied himself in knots trying to reconcile all these different claims. Although almost all sources agreed that the Guard had attacked in either one or two columns Houssaye was forced to postulate that it made no fewer than four separate attacks, each with just one or two battalions, in order to allow each of the claimants its turn at 'beating the Guard'.[70]

This all seems highly implausible but we are most unlikely ever to unravel the tangle of claim and counter-claim to discover what really happened. Sir Augustus Frazer, writing at eleven o'clock that night, says only that 'the contest was severe beyond what I have seen, or could have fancied. I cannot describe the scene of carnage. The struggle lasted even by moonlight.' Fitzroy Somerset, writing later, tells us: 'The Duke went to Adam and made him form his brigade [including the 52nd] in line four deep. With this brigade the Duke crowned the crest of the hill before the French infantry came up to it. Adam moved on the right of the Guards and advanced beyond the line of our infantry, at that time all exposed and suffering much from musketry as well as from the enemy's artillery.' And Captain Robert Batty of the Guards, writing a few days after the battle, states that:

> It was now about seven o'clock. The French infantry had in vain been brought up against our line, and, as a last resource, Buonaparté resolved upon attacking our part of the position with his veteran Imperial Guard, promising them the plunder of Brussels. Their artillery covered them, and they advanced in solid column to where we lay. The Duke, who was riding behind us, watched their

approach, and at length, when within a hundred yards of us, exclaimed, 'Up, Guards, and at them again!' . . . The Enemy did not expect to meet us so soon; we suffered them to approach still nearer, and then delivered a fire into them, which made them halt; a second, like the first, carried hundreds of deaths into their mass; and, without suffering them to deploy, we gave them three British cheers, and a British charge of the bayonet. This was too much for their nerves, and they fled in disorder.[71]

Almost every detail of this account can be disputed (including Wellington's words, which he later denied), and we cannot really be sure of anything beyond the simple fact that Napoleon's final attack was defeated and broken.

When the Guard fell back, the underlying confidence and spirit of resistance which had sustained the French army so well through the day finally failed. Wellington ordered a general advance along the allied line and the French, who had fought so bravely, now turned and fled. Wellington pressed on until he met Blücher, supposedly near the inn called La Belle Alliance, although that seems too good to be true, and handed over the pursuit to the Prussians who, weary as they were, conducted it with great energy and ruthlessness.[72] In his despatch, written only hours later, Wellington paid tribute to his allies for their role in deciding the fortunes of the day:

I should not do justice to my own feelings, or to Marshal Blücher and the Prussian army, if I did not attribute the successful result of this arduous day to the cordial and timely assistance I received from them. The operation of General Bülow upon the enemy's flank was a most decisive one; and, even if I had not found myself in a situation to make the attack which produced the final result, it would have forced the enemy to retire if his attacks should have failed, and would have prevented him from taking advantage of them if they should unfortunately have succeeded.[73]

Not that he gave the Prussians all the credit, as his private letter to William Wellesley-Pole, written on 19 June, makes clear:

You'll see the account of our Desperate Battle and victory over Boney!! It was the most desperate business I ever was in; I never took so much trouble about any Battle; & never was so near being beat.

Our loss is immense particularly in that best of all Instruments British Infantry. I never saw the Infantry behave so well.[74]

Others praised Wellington. Sir Augustus Frazer: 'The Duke's forte is in the pursuit of a beaten enemy. Where, indeed, and what is not his forte? Cold and indifferent, nay, apparently careless in the beginning of battles, when the moment of difficulty comes intelligence flashes from the eyes of this wonderful man; and he rises superior to all that can be imagined.' Another gunner, Lieutenant-Colonel May, agreed: 'In the battles of the 16th and 18th instant the Duke of Wellington has even exceeded himself, and adorned his brows with that one laurel more that was wanting to complete his fame and glory in the entire defeat of Bonaparte. The battle of the 18th was one of the most gigantic struggles it is almost possible for the Mind to form an idea of.' Horace Churchill, one of Hill's ADCs, told his father: 'I believe in the whole army Lord Wellington was the individual who *fought* the hardest.' And Thomas Wildman, who served on Uxbridge's staff, declared: 'I firmly believe that under any other man but the Duke of Wellington even British valour would have been unavailing.' Uxbridge himself, according to one source, 'said that [Wellington's] coolness and decision in action surpassed everything he cd. have conceived', while Lord Apsley told his father that Uxbridge 'is in ecstasies about the Duke, says there never was such a man', and adds that 'indeed the whole army give him the whole credit'.[75]

There are no comprehensive, reliable figures for French casualties at Waterloo, but some insight into the scale of their losses can be gained from the fairly accurate records of officer casualties. This would suggest that Napoleon's army suffered between 25,000 casualties and 30,000 casualties on 18 June, not including some 7,500 unwounded prisoners, so that 40–50 per cent of its strength was *hors de combat* by the end of the day.[76] By comparison Marmont's army appears to have suffered approximately 25 per cent casualties in its complete defeat at Salamanca. Whatever the cause of the French defeat at Waterloo, lack of courage and determination by the officers and men in the ranks played no part.

The figures for the allies are more accurate but still not without difficulties. Wellington's army suffered between 14,000 and 17,000 casualties, or around 20–25 per cent of its strength. The British contingent had just under 7,000 casualties with 1,500 more in the King's German Legion. The Prussians are reported to have lost almost 7,000 casualties, indicating the intensity of the fighting around Plancenoit. Altogether the allies suffered between 21,000 and 24,000 casualties, so that something like 50,000 men, and perhaps as many as 10,000 horses, were killed or wounded in a small tract of Belgian countryside in an area not much more than three miles by three miles, on a single summer's day in 1815.[77]

Grim stories of amputations and other operations conducted without anaesthetics or antiseptics by exhausted doctors with blunted instruments in makeshift dressing stations suggest that the prognosis for the wounded was dire. However, one official return concerning the fate of 7,687 British and KGL soldiers wounded during the campaign is relatively reassuring. By the time this return was prepared in April 1816 5,068 men, or almost two in three, had rejoined their regiments. Of the remainder only 856 (or 11 per cent) had died, while 854 remained in hospital. A few others had been transferred to Veteran or Garrison battalions, and 506 had been discharged from the army. Of course it is possible that British and KGL wounded received better treatment than those of other allied contingents, and certainly they would have been given priority over the French. Even so it seems safe to assume that only a relatively small minority of the wounded died as a consequence of their wounds.[78]

Wellington was deeply moved by the carnage especially, but not only, among those close to him. In the senior ranks of the army Picton and William Ponsonby had been killed, and Uxbridge, the Prince of Orange, Cooke, Kempt, Pack, Adam and Colin Halkett had been wounded. Both the senior staff officers in the army, the Quartermaster-General (William De Lancey) and the Adjutant-General (Edward Barnes) were wounded, as was the latter's deputy (Sir John Elley), while De Lancey's wound proved mortal. Fifteen of the fifty 'assistants' in two staff departments were casualties.[79] But most grievous of all were the losses among his personal staff: Fitzroy Somerset had his arm amputated; Charles Canning was killed; and Alexander Gordon was wounded, carried from the field and had his leg amputated, but died in the night. Dr Hume took Wellington the news: 'He had, as usual, taken off all his clothes, but had not washed himself; and as I entered the room, he sat up in his bed, his face covered with the dust and sweat of the previous day, and extended his hand to me, which I took and held in mine, whilst I told him of Gordon's death and related such of the casualties as had come to my knowledge. He was much affected. I felt his tears dropping fast upon my hands, and looking towards him, saw them chasing one another in furrows over his dusty cheeks. He brushed them suddenly away with his left hand, and said to me in a voice tremulous with emotion, "Well, thank God! I don't know what it is to lose a battle, but certainly nothing can be more painful than to gain one with the loss of so many of one's friends."'[80]

On the following day, with all the other demands upon him, he made time to write to the families of Fitzroy Somerset and Alexander Gordon, telling the former that 'the losses I have sustained have quite broken me down; and I have no feeling for the advantages we have acquired', and the latter: 'I cannot express to you the regret and sorrow with which I look around me, and contemplate the loss which I have sustained, particularly in your brother. The glory resulting from such actions, so dearly bought, is no consolation to me, and I cannot suggest it as any to you and his friends.'[81]

CHAPTER FIVE

PEACEMAKING IN PARIS
(June–December 1815)

THE PRUSSIANS TOOK up the pursuit after Waterloo, driving the demoralised wreck of Napoleon's army south, giving it no opportunity to rally or recover from its defeat. Wellington's army slept on the field of battle, and on the morning of 19 June advanced, but only as far as Nivelles. The Duke himself spent the night of 18 June in his quarters at Waterloo before riding into Brussels the following morning, where he completed his despatch and assured the Richmonds and other British visitors that the danger was past. This brief escape from the horrors of the battlefield may have been therapeutic, for it seems that Wellington was shaken by the ferocity of the fighting and the scale of the losses. However, the campaign had to go on; it was obvious that the best way to end the war was a rapid advance on Paris, before the French had time to recover from their defeat. On 21 June the army crossed the frontier 'with three cheers, on passing the line of demarcation. The Duke of Wellington rode thro' the Army, and was repeatedly cheered.'[1] Charles Colville, whose division had been at Hal on 18 June, records a conversation with Wellington on 22 June as his troops were marching into Le Cateau. The Duke 'spoke with much enthusiasm of the battle of the 18th, which he says, and all other accounts agree, was one of the most determined ever fought. In respect to individuals lost upon the occasion, we spoke only of Sir Thos. Picton and Col. Ellis, but he said that when he considered the valuable lives that had been closed, . . . [if] the sacrifice was not attended with all the results expected, it would break his heart.'[2]

As always Wellington was determined to do all he could to protect the civilian population from plundering and issued a General Order informing the army that they entered France not as conquerors but as allies of the King of France, and that it must therefore be regarded as friendly territory; nothing was to be taken without full payment, and the army would be supplied by the commissariat 'in the usual manner, and no requisition is to be made direct on the country or its magistrates by any officer or soldier'. To help enforce this order he re-established Staff Corps Cavalry, a precursor to the military police, which had been abolished in the post-war reductions even though it performed valuable service in the closing campaigns in the Peninsula. These measures proved remarkably effective with the British troops, largely because officers and men alike knew that they were meant seriously and would be strictly enforced. The behaviour of other contingents, where officers were much more inclined to turn a blind eye while their men oppressed the local population, was less good, with the Dutch-Belgians being described by a British surgeon as 'little better than a rabble while on the march'.[3] The Prussians were much worse and their officers, even at the highest level, set the men a bad example rather than attempting to restrain them. In Prussian eyes France had failed to benefit from the clemency she had received in 1814 and needed to be taught a lesson so that she would feel the cost of war and be deterred from again disturbing the peace of Europe. The French naturally preferred the British approach, making Wellington and the British relatively popular in France for a time, while the Prussians were hated – a contrast which could not help but heighten the resentment in the Prussian army, where it was felt their role in the allied victory had not received due recognition.

Nonetheless Wellington was far from satisfied with his army in these first days in France. On 23 June he complained sharply about the inefficiency of the junior branches of the commissariat, and two days later sent Bathurst an extraordinary broadside in which he declared: 'I have not got only the worst troops, but the worst equipped army, with the worst staff, that was ever brought together in the shape of an Army.' And concluded: 'I never was so disgusted with any concern as I am with this; and I only hope that I am going the right way to bring it to an early conclusion in some way or other.' To their infinite credit the ministers swallowed the complaint, as they had swallowed so many previous complaints, without any apparent effect upon their admiration and goodwill towards Wellington.[4]

After Waterloo Napoleon had abandoned his army and raced to Paris, where he arrived soon after the news of the defeat. Although some of his supporters urged him to declare martial law, he abdicated in favour of his son on 22 June. Political opinion in Paris was divided: there was some support for a Bonapartist regency among government officials and in the army; others looked to a liberal monarchy under the Duc d'Orléans; while there were still many who regarded the return of Louis XVIII as providing the best chance for peace and stability. The allies were not committed to a restoration of the Bourbons, and the British government had gone out of its way to emphasise that it was not fighting to impose a particular regime in Paris, but rather to depose a usurper who had broken the treaty exiling him to Elba and who posed a threat to all Europe.

However, it is clear that Wellington, Castlereagh and the whole British government believed that the restoration of the Bourbons offered the best solution to
the problem, although they faced constraints in playing an active part in
attempting to bring it about. Wellington urged Louis XVIII to follow the allied
advance into France as quickly as possible.[5]

In Paris, Napoleon's abdication had been followed by the creation of a
provisional government in which Fouché soon gained the upper hand. This
government approached Wellington and Blücher on 24 June seeking an armi-
stice in the name of Napoleon II. The allied generals had no hesitation in
rejecting the overture, as it did not offer 'that description of security which the
Allies had in view'.[6] The fate of Napoleon now became an issue; the French
authorities suggested that he be allowed to go into exile in the United States,
but Wellington denied that he had any authority to issue a free passage. The
Prussians were said to be eager to catch and shoot him, and there were some in
England and even in the British army who sympathised with this view.
Wellington was not among them, informing Charles Stuart that:

> Blücher wishes to kill him [Napoleon]; but I have told him that I shall remon-
> strate, and shall insist upon his being disposed of by common accord. I have
> likewise said that, as a private friend, I advised him to have nothing to do with
> so foul a transaction; that he and I had acted too distinguished parts in these
> transactions to become executioners; and that I was determined that if the
> Sovereigns wished to put him to death they should appoint an executioner,
> which should not be me.[7]

Fortunately Napoleon fled from Paris to Rochefort before the allies approached.
At Rochefort he found that there was no escape, and surrendered to Captain
Maitland of HMS *Bellerophon* on 16 July. The British government, acting on
the suggestion of John Barrow of the Admiralty, proposed that he be exiled to
St Helena, and the allied sovereigns accepted this solution without demur.
Wellington was not consulted – not that he would have had any objection, for
his own idea was that Napoleon be imprisoned in Fort St George (Madras), a
much less suitable choice on both strategic and humanitarian grounds.[8]

By the beginning of July the allied armies were approaching the gates of
Paris and the mood in the city was feverish with rumours and uncertainty.
Marshal Davout had more than 80,000 men in place to defend the capital, but
while he might hope to repulse the initial attack there was no prospect of
lasting success against the second and third wave of allied forces now pouring
over the frontiers. Besides, for what or whom would the French be fighting?
The infant Napoleon II safe in his grandfather's custody in Vienna? To keep
Fouché at the head of a provisional government? Was it worth exposing Paris

to the horrors of being stormed and sacked for a cause such as that? Davout hoped to gain concessions in return for accepting a Bourbon restoration but he consistently pitched his demands too high, for example initially stipulating that no allied troops approach within thirty leagues of Paris. In any case both royalists and the allies preferred to negotiate with others, for Davout spoke for the army, and it was the disloyalty of the army which was seen as being primarily responsible for the success of Napoleon's return in March. In the negotiations which followed Davout was marginalised, but his known willingness to accept the inevitability of the return of the Bourbons was an encouraging sign for their partisans.[9]

Meanwhile Fouché had been playing faction against faction with consummate skill. His personal preference was probably for an Orleans monarchy which would have plenty of places for his liberal allies; but his overriding need was to be seen as the indispensable midwife of the new regime, whatever form it took. He released Vitrolles the royalist agent from prison and used him to make contact with the legitimate party, persuading them to abstain from any open move which would force men to take sides opening divisions and so hindering a seamless transition. And he approached the allies to discover their attitude. Wellington responded:

> that I had no authority to talk upon the subject, even from my own government, much less from the Allies; and that all I could do was to give them my private opinion . . . I conceived the best security for Europe was the restoration of the King, and that the establishment of any other government than the King's in France must inevitably lead to new and endless wars; that Buonaparte and the army having overturned the King's government, the natural and simple measure, after Buonaparte was prisoner or out of the way, and the army defeated, was to recall the King to his authority, and that it was a much more dignified proceeding to recall him without conditions, and to trust to the energy of their constitution for any reforms they wished to make either in the government or the constitution, than now to make conditions with their Sovereign; and that, above all, it was important that they should recall the King without loss of time, as it would not then appear that the measure had been forced upon them by the Allies.[10]

Pressed upon the point Wellington explicitly declared that the allies would not accept Napoleon II, but refused to comment further on whether some other Bourbon prince (that is, the Duc d'Orléans) might be acceptable, although in a second interview he stated – again as a private opinion – that 'if any person excepting the King were called to the throne of France . . . [he] must be considered an usurper whatever his rank and quality'.[11]

The message could hardly have been plainer, yet it is not quite true to say – as Fouché subsequently did – that the allies had insisted upon the restoration of Louis XVIII. Wellington had certainly expressed a strong preference for the legitimate monarchy, but in the name of the allies he had only ruled out Napoleon and Napoleon II. If the French had united behind an alternative – Orleans being the only credible possibility – it was probable that the allies would have accepted it, even if only grudgingly. The very fact that Wellington would express only personal views on this possibility was a clear indication that the allies would not be united or determined in their opposition to it. But while support for Orleans was quite widespread, it was almost entirely tepid: the second choice of many but the first choice of few. Even Louis XVIII had more resolute partisans, and so Fouché discarded the Orleans cause as he had already discarded that of Napoleon II and Napoleon.

The Convention of Paris, signed on 3 July, covered the evacuation of the capital and the withdrawal of the French army behind the Loire. Two of its clauses were later to expose Wellington to accusations of bad faith: one offered an amnesty to all those who had turned their coats and joined Napoleon earlier in the year; the other guaranteed all public property except military stores. Fouché deliberately misrepresented the first to the Chambers by claiming that the immunity it offered would bind the restored monarchy as well as the allied armies; and this caused concern in London, where the British government was convinced that Louis could not re-establish his authority without spilling the blood of at least a few traitors. Wellington responded that the Convention could only bind the parties to it – in other words the allied armies – and that he had no power or authority to promise anything on behalf of the restored monarchy; a point which was clearly understood by all those who took part in the negotiations. At one level it would have been better if this had been made explicit in the Convention, but the ambiguity was useful to Fouché at a moment when the balance of forces in Paris was very delicate. It is most unlikely that his lie actually deceived anyone; the King had already published a proclamation which, while generally very conciliatory, had explicitly reserved the right to punish the instigators and authors of the plot to overthrow him, but talk of an amnesty backed by the allies helped the Chambers swallow the pill of the restoration.[12]

The second clause – the protection of public property – has attracted rather less attention. The difficulty was that this would appear to cover all the artworks looted from across Europe and which were filling the galleries and squares of Paris – works which the allies subsequently reclaimed. Apparently there was talk of specifically protecting these artworks by a distinct guarantee, but Blücher refused to agree and Wellington would not accept a clause excepting only Prussian art. According to Wellington the subject was left open for the allied sovereigns to decide, but although this may have been understood by all involved in the negotiations, it was not explicitly mentioned in the Convention, leaving an opening which the restored French government did not scruple to exploit when it discovered how strongly the population of Paris resented the loss of these treasures.[13]

There was some surprise and even criticism in Britain that Wellington was prepared to work closely, and to dine, with Fouché who, as one of the regicides of 1793 and Napoleon's minister of police, had an evil reputation. Wellington responded to this with some impatience, telling his friend John Malcolm: 'They do not know what they want in England; but if they think an administration of honest and honorable men can be found in France, they are fools – there are no materials; and where all are rascals, you must take those who are most useful. If I had not settled with Fouché when I did . . . the Duke of Orleans would have been proclaimed king next day, and that would have been a new trouble.' In fact Wellington had been secretly corresponding with Fouché even before Waterloo, as part of a wider British policy of pressing Louis XVIII to broaden his base of support by showing a willingness to work with at least some of the French *liberales*. This was the same advice Wellington had given King Ferdinand in Madrid the previous year, and as in Spain it did not convince the French ultra-royalists. After the unexpected success of the French royalists in elections in August they succeeded in forcing Fouché from office. Yet at the same time Wellington and Castlereagh were endeavouring to persuade the French and Spanish governments to be more liberal, they were attacked by British radicals, and in caricatures such as Cruikshank's *Royal Shambles*, as being responsible for the triumph of ultra-royalism on the Continent.[14]

The allies made their entrance to the city quietly, without ceremony on 7 July, and on the following day the King returned and was received with considerable enthusiasm by crowds of his supporters. The Prefect of the Seine, the Comte de Sabrol, showed a fine ear for rhetorical effect if not for mundane accuracy when he greeted the King – 'A hundred days have passed since the fatal moment when Your Majesty left his capital' – and the phrase struck although the true figure was one hundred and eleven.[15]

The mood in Paris in those first days of the Second Restoration was uncertain and rather ugly. Charles Stuart wrote on 7 July: 'I do not like the look of things here; there is a sulky ill humour in the place which does not promise tranquillity, and I do not think the King's party have the upper hand.' A week later he felt rather less anxious, but as late as the second week of August a British officer recorded that 'odds are offered that the Duc d'Orléans is King of France before this time twelve months'. The misbehaviour of the Prussians and some other allied troops was deeply resented, but their ubiquitous presence and the constant arrival of more allied troops gradually brought home to the French that they had indeed been conquered, and that any attempt at resistance would simply give their enemies the excuse some of them wanted to adopt much harsher measures. A Prussian officer, General Müffling, was governor of Paris; allied troops stood sentry outside public buildings, and the British were camped in the Bois de Boulogne and on the Champs Elysées. The none-too-subtle message was driven home by a succession of military reviews in and near the capital which convinced even the most ardent Bonapartist to delay any hope of revenge until a more promising season. Tensions were eased by the news that Davout and the army had submitted to the King on 14 July, and of Napoleon's surrender, although consoling rumours circulated that the Emperor was really in hiding and that one of his brothers had impersonated him to deceive the allies. At the same time, in parts of southern France royalist mobs took their revenge on local opponents in riots and disorder in which hundreds died: the so-called 'White Terror'. Liberals and Bonapartists across the whole country were intimidated; there would be no ostentatious parading of their dissent as in 1814.[16]

The excellent behaviour of its troops, the inclination of some of their officers to spend freely, and recognition that Wellington was much more sympathetic to France than, for example, Blücher, created a superficial popularity for the British. Still, the relationship between such old enemies could not become easy and harmonious overnight, especially as each was inclined to assume that their innate superiority was obvious. One British officer wrote: 'We English are more sombre in our looks and manners, honest and just in our dealings, strict in discipline, conscious of our superiority: all of which the French acknowledge, but they do not like us notwithstanding.' And: 'Our time passes away merrily enough, but the vicinity to Paris will not improve our morals. Too many lures thrown out: the French people study amusement and pleasure, I will add, refined vice. The Palais Royal is a sink of iniquity, gambling and licentiousness.' A civilian British visitor saw another side of things: 'There were never people more mortified more subdued and apparently more broken in spirit. They submit with sad civility to the extortions of the Prussians and Russians and avenge themselves at the expense of the English whom they charge three prices for everything because they are the only people who pay at all.'[17]

As in 1814 a flood of British visitors crossed the Channel to enjoy the sophisticated pleasures of the French capital; only in 1815 there was an added delight, a chance to savour an almost unimaginable moment of national glory with British troops quartered in the capital of her ancient enemy, and a British general the undisputed hero of the hour. For even when the Emperors of Russia and Austria, the King of Prussia and assorted lesser royalty, with all their attendant statesmen, generals, mistresses and religious guides had taken up residence, there was no doubt that Wellington was the greatest lion of the hour, the one whom everyone was most curious to meet. He took this celebrity in his stride. John Malcolm was delighted by a greeting which 'showed me at once that his astonishing elevation had not produced the slightest change. The tone – the manner – everything was the same.' Walter Scott told his wife that Wellington 'is the most plain & downright person you ever knew', while Lowry Cole's new wife wrote in her journal that the Duke 'spoke with much openness and simplicity of himself'.[18]

The British Parliament had thanked Wellington and the army for the victory of Waterloo, and voted for a national monument to the officers and men who had fallen (which was never built). A silver medal was issued to every member of the British army who had fought in the battle, and it counted as two full years' service. The Regent proposed that Wellington be granted an additional £200,000 towards the purchase of an estate and this was approved without any dissent. Foreign governments also bestowed fresh honours, so that Wellington became a knight of another half-dozen orders of chivalry, and was made Prince of Waterloo by the King of the Netherlands, with the revenue from an estate to support the dignity.[19]

Wellington's life during the summer and autumn of 1815 in Paris was spent in 'a perfect whirlwind & tempest of gaiety', with balls, dinners, receptions, the opera and theatre jostling one another to fill his evenings, while the days were spent in a mixture of work – the peace negotiations and administration of the army – military reviews and other diversions.[20] Among the British visitors to Paris were Sir John and Lady Shelley. Wellington greeted them warmly, calling on them as soon as they arrived, inviting them to use his box at the theatre and opera, and, most extraordinarily, having Lady Shelley by his side as he took part in many of the grand military reviews that took place. Obviously he enjoyed the presence of this smart, fashionable, good-looking young woman, who made no secret of her admiration for him but who had enough sense to conceal the intensity of her feelings. Her diary leaves no doubt that she was more than half in love with him, or that their relations remained friendly, but chaste. The closest moments of intimacy she records came when she cut off a lock of his hair as a keepsake, and she makes it plain that she would not have been so bold if her husband had not been present.[21] She saw Wellington at his most relaxed, genial and sociable, writing after one evening: 'The delight that I felt in sitting next to the hero of Waterloo, listening to his cheerful conversation, is not easily expressed in words. He seemed to be the youngest, and the gayest of the party.' After the theatre he took her to see Madame Crauford where, although 'at first everything was stiff, the Duke soon enlivened the company. We laughed and he had a great deal of fun, which continued as we drove homewards.' Enquiries soon confirmed her suspicion that Madame Crauford's circle was not quite the top drawer of French society, and she had to acknowledge that her hero had a flaw: 'As much as I admire the Duke of Wellington, I own that he shows no taste by going so often to her house.' But hot on the heels of the criticism came the exculpation: 'after all, he is a true soldier, and likes lively society where he can be at his ease.' And it is notable that Lady Shelley herself continued to visit Madame Crauford even when not with Wellington.[22] Many of the established leaders of Paris society had left the city or were staying quiet during the allied occupation, and while the parties given by Lady Castlereagh may have been very respectable, they were also notoriously dull.

Lady Shelley's attendance at military reviews raised a few eyebrows. The Emperor Alexander 'looked rather surprised' at her appearance at the grand review of 150,000 Russian troops on 10 September, but soon recovered his poise 'and spoke to me most graciously, during intervals, for the rest of the day'. Harriet Countess Granville, daughter of the famous Duchess of Devonshire, went further in reporting the gossip of Paris to her sister soon after she arrived in late July: 'Sir John and Lady Shelley ran after the great Duke in a very disgusting manner.' And later she added: 'But as they were together, "sans peur et sans reproche."' And: 'Lady Shelley pursues her pursuit with the most unremitting diligence, and makes herself really ridiculous . . . There is no harm in her, I am sure, beyond inordinate vanity . . . Sir John is quite charmed with it.' As the Shelleys were relatively obscure figures in English society, it is not surprising that their sudden elevation to prominence should arouse some irritation and pique.[23]

Wellington's relations with another woman, Lady Frances Webster, also aroused some comment which found its way into the press. According to the *St James Chronicle* the outraged husband Captain James Wedderburn-Webster had demanded £50,000 and the case was headed to the divorce court. However, the only legal proceedings which actually took place were when the husband and wife united to sue the paper for libel. The editor offered no defence and £2,000 was awarded against him. It seems likely that this result was just; Lady Frances was seven months pregnant at the time of the alleged affair, and had earlier had a flirtation with Byron which was never consummated. Inevitably the affair refreshed the Duke's dislike of the press. 'We talked also about the newspapers.' Lady Shelley recorded a little later:

> The Duke expressed himself with great warmth, against the licentiousness of the Press; especially as regards its attacks upon the private affairs of individuals. Although he is aware of the difficulty of checking libellous insinuations, he seemed to be very sore indeed. I knew what was in the Duke's mind; he keenly felt the scandalous reports that had been circulated about himself and Lady Frances Wedderburn Webster – reports which every day convinces me are absolutely untrue.[24]

If Wellington had an affair with anyone in Paris in 1815 the most likely candidates are Grassini, who was again much in evidence in accounts of parties at this time, and Lady Charlotte Greville. Harriet Arbuthnot later described Lady Charlotte as 'full of grace & talent and the charm of every society she went into'; and commented that she was widely supposed 'to have conquered the Conqueror of France'. Charles Percy writing from Paris in September 1815 was much less sympathetic: '*Horrid Charlotte Greville* makes the most filthy & *disgusterous* love to the Duke of Wellington, sitting on his knee, patting his head & *wrinkling* her face into lascivious smiles.' The surviving evidence is scanty, but strongly suggests that Wellington did have an affair with Lady Charlotte at some time between 1815 and 1820. If the affair began in Paris it may have continued intermittently for several years before evolving into a warm friendship; one of Wellington's ADCs commented in 1818 that 'the Duke is always in such good spirits when she is with him', and in 1820 Princess Lieven noted that the Duke kept Lady Charlotte's portrait in his study. A few years later Wellington appointed her son Algernon Greville (brother of the famous diarist) to his staff at the Ordnance, and then as his confidential private secretary.[25]

Among other activities in Paris in these months Wellington had his portrait painted by Gérard. The pose is very still, impassive, though not stiff, and the face rather heavy and inanimate. The result is dignified and respectable but not at all inspiring – almost anti-heroic in its calmness. The contrast with the highly romantic portraits of Napoleon is marked and probably intentional (on the part of the artist, if not the sitter), but the result is unconvincing; this is not the Wellington we know from his despatches, although it does resemble a French (and occasionally English) misconception of him as a master of patient Fabian warfare lacking both sensibility and nerves.[26]

Behind the public scenes of gaiety and military reviews were tough, often acrimonious negotiations among the allies over the terms of peace they would impose upon France. Wellington was in the midst of this, working in close and harmonious co-operation with Castlereagh, who had joined him on 6 July and who remained until late November. It was Castlereagh who determined the direction of British policy, but it is clear that Wellington concurred wholeheartedly in it, and had no hesitation in committing himself fully to the cause. The central issue of contention was the overall approach towards France; Prussia, with the support of most of the small states of Germany and to some extent of the Netherlands, urged a punitive peace with large territorial transfers. The provinces stripped from France would be ceded to the small states, who in turn would yield ground further north and east to Prussia. Sheer greed and dynastic ambition were powerful motives behind these plans, but not the only consideration. The Prussian army, which had a great influence on her policy, was eager for revenge and wished to punish and humiliate France as an object in itself. And there was an argument that France would never accept defeat on any terms, and that the only safe course was to weaken her so much that she would be incapable of posing any threat to her neighbours. Castlereagh vehemently opposed this, pointing out that the Netherlands and the small German states would never be strong enough to defend themselves and would depend on Prussian and British guarantees for their security. He knew that there was no willingness in London to undertake such a permanent commitment and made this plain to Baron Gagern, who had been pushing the claims of the Netherlands rather further than his King wished. He told Liverpool in August, 'it is not our business to collect trophies, but to try if we can bring back the world to peaceful habits,' and this would be the underlying theme of the foreign policy he and Wellington would continue to pursue for many years.[27]

The Prussian generals were outraged at British opposition to their demands, and were especially bitter about Wellington's role; they were inclined to view all civilian statesmen, including their own, with contempt, but expected better from a fellow soldier. Gneisenau had already denounced Wellington's 'theatrical magnanimity' towards Napoleon, and all the resentment aroused by the dispute over the partition of Saxony came bubbling back to the surface.[28] They vented their feelings through the press in attacks which Wellington bore with his customary lack of stoicism. 'The *Rhenish Mercury*', he told Malcolm in October,

is a paper set up and patronized by the Prussian military Jacobins, having in view to be established in Germany, and eventually all over Europe, the dominion of Prussian military jacobinism; a tyranny rather more degrading than that from which we have lately escaped. They began to attack me the day after the battle of Waterloo, not because, as they now assert, I was jealous of the Prussian military successes, as I had been unsuccessful and they had not, but because they were jealous of mine, and they saw in me, as I hope they will find in me, the great obstacle to the attainment of their object.[29]

If this seems an over-reaction it is worth remembering that even the Prussian Chancellor Prince Hardenberg professed himself alarmed at the army's pretentions, and told a British diplomat that he felt himself 'in the midst of Praetorian bands'.[30]

Fortunately the Emperor Alexander strongly favoured magnanimous terms towards France, and went out of his way to conciliate Castlereagh and to repair the damage he had done in his visit to London. He remained popular in Paris and the press readily gave him the credit for every concession, but this was a small price to pay for his indispensible co-operation in restraining Prussian demands. Metternich played a much less obvious part; he seems to have been exhausted by the demands of the Congress at Vienna and all that had preceded it, while it would only have provoked the Prussians further if he had led the fight against them. When necessary Castlereagh could depend on his support and that was what mattered.

The support of the British government, however, could not be taken for granted. The Prince Regent, the press and the public at large had no inclination towards moderation in their hour of triumph, and Liverpool, Bathurst and the other ministers were strongly inclined to agree. Liverpool felt that there was little prospect of firmly re-establishing Louis XVIII upon the throne – 'For what is a King unsupported by opinion, by an army, or by a strong national party?' – and this led him to think of large territorial reductions; all the conquests of Louis XIV were mentioned.[31] Castlereagh was unmoved by these arguments and slowly, patiently, persuaded Liverpool and the Cabinet to yield point after point until they had accepted most of his arguments.

Wellington's support was crucial in this battle; if the victor of Waterloo threw his weight behind a moderate peace it would be very hard for anyone in Britain to mount an attack on the government over it, while his opinion carried great weight with the members of the Cabinet who might not have yielded to Castlereagh's lone judgement. In a long letter of 11 August, nominally written to Castlereagh but clearly intended for the Cabinet and perhaps a wider public, Wellington set out cogent arguments of both principle and expediency in favour of a moderate peace. He claimed that while the French people had submitted to Napoleon 'it would be ridiculous to suppose that the Allies would have been in possession of Paris in a fortnight after one battle fought if the French people in general had not been favourably disposed to the cause which the Allies were supposed to favour'. That was debatable, but Wellington then moved onto stronger ground:

> we ought to continue to keep our great object, the genuine peace and tran-
> quility of the world, in our view, and shape our arrangement so as to provide
> for it. Revolutionary France is more likely to distress the world than France,
> however strong in her frontier, under a regular government; and that is the
> situation in which we ought to endeavour to place her.[32]

Privately Wellington showed more exasperation, telling Beresford: 'I am sorry to add that our own government also are taking up a little too much the tone of their rascally newspapers. They are shifting their objects; and, having got their cake, they want both to eat it and keep it.'[33]

However, even Wellington's prestige might not have been enough by itself to allay the concerns of the British – and other – governments. A solution was found in the proposal to ensure France's return to peaceful ways by maintaining an army of occupation of 150,000 men on her territory and at her expense for some years; after some discussion the term was set at five years, with the possibility of withdrawal after three. The four main allies would each contribute 30,000 men to this army, with a further 30,000 from the smaller states of Germany and Denmark, which would have the additional advantages for them of softening the inevitable economic dislocation caused by rapid post-war demobilisation and permitting them to keep a larger standing army than they could otherwise afford. By common consent the command of this army would be entrusted to the Duke of Wellington – a task which he readily undertook.[34]

Some reduction of French territory was still felt to be necessary and this was placed on a regular basis by making it a return to the frontiers of 1790 rather than 1792. This led to the loss of Savoy, a small strip of land near Geneva, the suzerainty of Monaco, some territory on the Belgian frontier and, most significantly, the Saar Valley and Landau. Whether these cessions were worth the potential irritation and sense of grievance they created may be doubted, but most negotiations result in some compromises that make little sense when viewed in the cool light of day, and it does not seem that much real harm was done in this instance. France was also required to pay an indemnity. The Prussians wanted to set this at 1,200 million francs; Castlereagh proposed 600 million and in the end the total was agreed at 700 million (£28 million), a result which fairly reflects the balance of the negotiations overall. Wellington successfully resisted pressure from Liverpool for an explicit link between payment of the indemnity and the withdrawal of the Army of Occupation although it was generally understood that the army would not be withdrawn until the indemnity was paid.[35]

The British government also pressed the French to take action against some of those who had betrayed the King and joined Napoleon in the spring. Liverpool explained his reasoning earlier in August:

> one never can feel that the King is secure upon his throne till he has dared to spill traitors' blood. It is not that many examples would be necessary; but the *daring* to make a few will alone manifest any strength in the government. It is a curious circumstance that, after the sanguinary scenes which we recollect at the beginning of the French Revolution, all parties appear now to have an insuperable repugnance to executions. This arises not from mercy but from fear.[36]

It is not clear that Wellington agreed with this argument, or whether British pressure was decisive, but Fouché reluctantly drew up a list of fifty-seven individuals who were excluded from the royal amnesty and against whom action would be taken. He then proceeded to warn all those on the list and to facilitate their escape into exile, so that it was only through bad luck and over-confidence that three were arrested. The first was Colonel La Bédoyère, who had led his regiment over to join Napoleon on 7 March at Grenoble, and who was tried before a court martial and executed on 19 August. The second was Marshal Ney, one of the most illustrious and beloved of all the marshals and a man famous throughout Europe as a fine fighting soldier and no politician. Ney had been caught in a conflict of loyalties in the spring, and his desertion symbolised the collapse of royal authority, so his inclusion on Fouché's list was inevitable; but he had not taken part in any of the conspiracies against the King and his execution at the hands of a French firing squad on 7 December did the new regime no credit. The third was a civilian, Count Lavalette, whose role in the Emperor's return was much less obvious. Although sentenced to death he escaped on 21 December with the aid of several Englishmen including Sir Robert Wilson. Unfortunately Wilson, whose talents as a self-publicist and a braggart far exceeded any real ability he possessed, wrote a long account of the affair, naming all those who had taken part, and entrusted it to the ordinary French post. Naturally it was intercepted by the police who, with a signed confession in their hands, felt compelled to act. Lavalette was safely out of the country, but Wilson and his fellow conspirators were arrested, tried and sentenced to a few months in prison. The radical press in Britain treated Wilson as a hero and a martyr to the cause of liberty and helped ensure his election for Southwark in 1818. Fortunately the affair, while intensely irritating at the time, did no real harm to Anglo-French relations.[37]

Wellington's popularity in Paris suffered less from these executions than from his role in the removal of looted art from the museums and squares of the city and its return to its country of origin. This blow to French pride was felt keenly even though it was only the stolen works which were taken; if the allies had followed Napoleon's precedent the galleries would have been stripped of all their treasures which would have been taken to London, Berlin, Vienna and St Petersburg, rather than to Florence, Rome, Venice, Amsterdam and Brussels. Britain received nothing, but she helped pay the cost of removal and her engineers carefully took down the famous horses of St Mark and packed them to return to Venice, while a watching crowd groaned in dismay. In fact neither Castlereagh nor Wellington were in favour of the measure, believing that it would cause more discontent that it was worth, but this was a tussle they lost, and as a result the Duke was hissed in the theatre while one British visitor declared that 'the glory of the battle of Waterloo is effaced by the storming of the Louvre.'[38]

Wellington was not indifferent to public opinion and no more relished unjust criticism or blame than most men, but he did not let it shape his conduct.

If he had, he might well have rested on his laurels after the fighting was over, content to leave the messy business of negotiation to others, especially as he was offered only a subordinate role; but he liked and trusted Castlereagh, agreed with the policy he was pursuing, and could not resist the chance to be working for the common cause. It is easy, particularly in hindsight, to take this for granted but an entry in John Malcolm's diary makes the point that it was not inevitable:

> [Wellington] is now displaying his character in what I deem the finest point of view. He was at the summit of fame; and as they chose, instead of employing him to settle affairs, to send Lord Castlereagh, he might well have stepped aside, and said, 'I would rather confine myself to my military duties;' for it must be as evident to himself as to others that by lending his name to the negotiations he may, as far as he values popularity in England, do himself a world of injury, and can derive no additional reputation; for the utmost that can be said is that he assisted Lord Castlereagh. When the negotiations are attacked, the Ministers will defend themselves with his name as with a shield. Of all this there can be no doubt he is aware, and he knows that many of his real friends groan over the part he is acting. But he thinks of nothing but serving his country. He is confident that his opinions may do good, and cannot do harm; and he is ready to encounter all the abuse that can be poured upon him rather than show that prudence which fights more about personal character than public interests.[39]

CHAPTER SIX

THE OCCUPATION OF FRANCE
(1816–18)

For three years following the signing of the Second Peace of Paris in November 1815 Wellington commanded the allied Army of Occupation in France. It was a responsible position with many potential sources of acrimony among the allies themselves and with the French authorities. It gave Wellington a considerable voice in the domestic politics of France and, because Paris was one of the focal points of European diplomacy, he also played an important part in international disputes involving the Netherlands, Spain and Portugal. He had a unique position on the European stage in these years, being regarded not simply, or even principally, as a *British* statesman, but as a figure apart whose integrity was unimpeachable, and who could be relied upon to settle disputes without regard to any special interests. At the same time, as both the victor of Waterloo and the chief representative of the allied occupation of France, he attracted the resentment and even the hatred of those Frenchmen who remained unreconciled to their defeat, leading to several plots and one attempt on his life. These years would form the high point or culmination of the career of most men, but in Wellington's life they appear as a relatively quiet interlude between the tension and bloodshed of his military campaigns and the different strains he was to face as a major figure in British politics when he returned to England.

The Army of Occupation was originally conceived as a guarantee for the security for the Netherlands while the fortresses guarding her southern frontier in Belgium (the 'barrier fortresses') were rebuilt; and, more broadly, to ensure that France abided by the terms of the peace. But even before the Treaty was signed this idea had been extended to include the hope that the presence of the army would help to stabilise France, and give Louis XVIII implicit protection while he demobilised the Napoleonic army and constructed a new one which might direct its loyalty to him. Being temporary the occupation contained an obvious incentive for good behaviour, and a few years of quiet might bring the French back into habits of peace and tranquillity. The allies were not blind to the likelihood of friction with the local population, of wounded *amour propre*, and of the risk that the occupation would undermine the standing of Louis XVIII, making him appear as no more than a foreign puppet, but after the Hundred Days they needed a substantial guarantee of France's future behaviour and a temporary occupation was less likely to sow the seeds of future conflicts than the extensive territorial cessions that were initially considered.[1]

As the unanimous choice to command the army, Wellington played a large part in drawing up the terms of the occupation. It would be confined to a broad swathe of territory running from the Channel to the Swiss border and, with the exception of certain fortresses which would retain their native garrisons, no French troops would be permitted within this zone. On the other hand French civil authorities would remain in place and the local magistrates would deal with complaints against civilians, just as the allied military authorities would try and punish soldiers accused of committing crimes. The cost of the occupation was to be borne by France, but the extent of this obligation was clearly defined both to avoid disputes and to prevent exploitation. The total cost was some 50 million francs per annum, or about £2 million, which, while a heavy burden, was certainly not exorbitant for an army of 150,000 men. The Austrian contingent was quartered in Alsace, the most southerly part of the occupied zone; north of it were the contingents from Bavaria and Wurttemburg; then the Prussians with their headquarters at Sedan; to their west were the Russians, and finally the British stretching to the coast. The Danish, Hanoverian and Saxon contingents were close to the British, and Wellington had his headquarters at Cambrai, for he commanded the British contingent as well as the army as a whole. In practice it seems that the allied contingents very largely managed their own affairs and that Wellington was only occasionally called upon to intervene in their disputes with the local authorities. Even with the British contingent he used a relatively light rein, delegating much more to his subordinates than had been his custom when the army was on campaign – although he was still quick to express his displeasure if the orders he issued were not obeyed or if problems with the local population were carelessly handled.[2]

The Peace was signed on 20 November 1815 and within a few days the allied troops began to move, many marching home, others taking up their new quarters in the occupied territory. The last troops did not leave the environs of Paris until the end of January. The new Royal Guard was not yet capable of dealing with a serious disturbance in the capital, and the French government asked Wellington to wait a few weeks while some controversial legislation passed through the Chambers. Wellington stayed in Paris until April, convinced that his presence gave some comfort to the moderates and *libéraux* who had been shocked by the triumph of the ultra-royalists in the elections, and also helped to strengthen the position of the Duc de Richelieu, the moderate royalist prime minister. The British government was rather unhappy at Wellington's decision, fearing for his safety and worried that his presence might be provocative, but he brushed their concerns aside, writing to William Wellesley-Pole: 'I wish the British Cabinet would lay aside the notion that I am anxious to be assassinated by a French Mob; I hope they will allow me to do my own duty in the way I think best myself.'[3]

Another source of tension between Wellington and Liverpool was more personal, and is less well documented. We know that late in 1815 Wellington again approached Liverpool seeking clerical promotion for his brother Gerald, and that this was refused in terms which Wellington found deeply offensive. Months later Wellington told John Malcolm that he could not ask Liverpool for any favour, or even correspond with him except on purely official business, because 'he wrote what I may call a very *impertinent* letter in answer to an application which I made through Arbuthnot, for promotion in the Church for my brother Gerald. He may have refused, but I think I deserve, & at all events I must have, civil terms. I have therefore had no further communication with him.' Unfortunately neither the original application nor Liverpool's letter appear to have survived, but on 23 December 1815 Liverpool told Bathurst: 'Arbuthnot has had another letter from the Duke of Wellington on the subject ['his brother being a bishop' – note by Lord Bathurst] I mentioned to you on Monday, which makes me most unwilling to remain at the head of the Government. The Prince's conduct has been quite abominable.' Liverpool did not, of course, resign, but the two men were not reconciled until the following August. Although their different attitudes to the patronage of the Church made disagreement on the question unsurprising, it is remarkable that it was handled so badly that it caused such ill feeling; but it is evident that there was never much real warmth or personal compatibility between Liverpool and Wellington, despite their extensive contact ever since 1807.[4]

Cambrai was conveniently located between London, Paris and Brussels, and Wellington made many journeys to each of the three cities. He generally spent the first months of the year in Paris, moving to Cambrai in the spring (April or early May) and using it as a base for short visits to England, tours of the fortresses in Belgium, and brief trips to Paris during the middle of the year when the roads were best for travelling. But even at other seasons he was often on the move and a break of just a few days in his correspondence may conceal a quick trip across the Channel or to Paris. He was in Paris in February 1816 when Charles Stuart got married, and again in June for the wedding of the Duc de Berri, the King's nephew, to Princess Caroline of Naples. He celebrated the anniversary of Waterloo on the following day with a dinner for fifty guests, and a week later gave a grand ball, which was not disrupted despite an attempt to set the ballroom on fire.[5]

Wellington spent most of July at Cheltenham taking the waters and living quietly with his family. Kitty soon reported that he was 'considerably better both in looks and spirits', and noted with delight that the boys (now aged eight and nine) 'are as fond of and as familiar with their noble and beloved Father as if they had never been separated from him. They accompany him on his walks, *chat* with him, play with him. In short they are the chosen companions of each other'.[6] This may have been an idealised picture, although Wellington was always good with children. The few days he had spent in London en route to Cheltenham had passed in a whirl of dinners and social engagements, although his attempt to use his prestige to secure the re-admission of Lady Caroline Lamb into polite society had ended in failure which only narrowly avoided public humiliation.[7]

It was on this same visit to England in the summer of 1816 that Wellington met Marianne Patterson and her sisters Bess and Louisa Caton. They were American (although their father, Robert Caton, was English), and came with a warm recommendation from Wellington's niece Mary Bagot, the wife of the British envoy in Washington, who had been impressed by their poise and sophistication. Mary's mother Katherine Wellesley-Pole invited them to dinner with Wellington, and the whole party then went on to Almacks. Arriving late in the season, when society was bored and jaded, the young women attracted a great deal of attention, most of it very favourable, despite a common English prejudice which assumed that all Americans were boorish and ill mannered. Wellington was strongly attracted to Marianne, the oldest and most beautiful of the sisters, and relished the self-confident assurance with which she discussed public affairs as much as the admiration which shone in her 'brilliant yet melting black eyes', and the genuine sweetness of her character. It was for her that he commissioned the half-length portrait by Lawrence that has become the most famous image of him, and at the same time one of her which he kept. It is probable, although not certain, that they became lovers; and it is quite clear that he was more than half in love with her, and that the feeling was reciprocated. The ties were strengthened when her sister Louisa married Felton Hervey, one of Wellington's aides-de-camp, in April 1817, with the Duke giving the bride away. Nonetheless, Marianne sailed home to America with her husband Robert in the spring of 1818, and it seemed unlikely that they would ever meet again, although Wellington continued to write long letters to her, and sent her books and other presents, all travelling safely through the diplomatic bag.[8]

Wellington sat to Lawrence several times in the spring of 1817, and also visited David Wilkie, a young Scottish artist who was already making a name for himself with his paintings of village life. Wellington was sufficiently impressed with his work to commission a large painting of old soldiers at their ease, telling stories or playing skittles outside a public house. After a little discussion Wilkie suggested the rather too appropriate idea of introducing the *Gazette* with the news of Waterloo as the focal point of the scene, and Wellington agreed. The result was an exuberant work which took Wilkie sixteen months' work over four years. *The Waterloo Gazette; or, the Chelsea Pensioners reading the Gazette of the Battle of Waterloo* proved the highlight of the Royal Academy exhibition of 1822; crowds queued for hours to see it and special barriers had to be installed to protect it from the throng. Wellington bought it for twelve hundred guineas – an astonishingly high price at the time – paying the artist in person and with cash. The conception and execution of the work may not have been very subtle, but it has proved enduringly popular, and it is interesting that Wellington chose to commemorate his greatest triumph thus obliquely, and with the vision of ordinary soldiers relaxing and enjoying the fruits of victory.[9]

These visits to England also enabled Wellington to see his family. His mother, Lady Mornington, had been ill in the spring of 1817 and had 'become at last *old* in proportion to her advanced age' (she was seventy-five). Evidently age had not mellowed her, for she complained to a visitor that the 'tumult of joy and congratulations' on Wellington's many victories 'had shaken her nerves and contributed to her late illnesses'. She regretted that she did not see more of her son, and then proceeded to recount a string of embarrassing, even disparaging, stories about his youth. Sweet she was not, and never had been.[10]

Waterloo had been a crowning mortification for Lord Wellesley; the days of basking in reflected glory were long over, and there was the added humiliation of having publicly opposed the renewal of the war with Napoleon and predicted that it would end in disaster. His political career seemed over, while his private life provided no consolation. His estranged wife Hyacinthe died on 5 November 1816, but this offered no solution to the financial problems that now threatened to overwhelm him. His sensible son Richard, who bore the brunt of attempting to untangle the mess, reported that the Marquess was 'totally ruined' and that the remaining Irish estates were all to be sold, and that his pension from the East India Company was placed in the hands of trustees for his creditors. Lord Wellesley sank his pride and appealed to Wellington for £10,000, but the Duke insisted that he first cut back his establishment to a sustainable level. This evidently helped bring the Marquess to reason, and in 1817 Wellington purchased Apsley House from his brother for £42,000. Given that Lord Wellesley had paid only £16,000 for it a decade earlier it seems likely that the price included a substantial fraternal premium. Nonetheless the symbolism could not have been starker; Wellington had taken Wellesley's place in the sun. Henceforth the Duke would have the best address in London on

Hyde Park Corner, while the older brother could slink off to lodgings in Ramsgate, or wherever else took his fancy and suited his straitened means.[11]

Meanwhile Gerald's wife Emily is said to have had an affair with the Marquess of Anglesey and then to have discarded him for Lord Wallscourt, who was still in his teens and half her age. The affair with Anglesey was particularly squalid for, of course, he was not only married to her sister but had precipitated the break-up of the sister's marriage to Henry Wellesley. Gerald did not seek a divorce – it was suggested that his own behaviour had not been irreproachable – but we can see why Liverpool did not think him suitable for the Episcopal bench. Yet not all was gloom; Henry Wellesley, home on leave from Spain, married Georgiana Cecil, daughter of the Marquess of Salisbury. The families were already close; Lady Salisbury was a great friend of Lady Mornington, and Wellington often visited Hatfield and enjoyed hunting there. Fortunately this marriage proved happy.[12]

As well as Apsley House, Wellington needed a country estate. Parliament had voted the money for its purchase, and Wellington had indicated to his trustees that he would prefer to buy an estate and build a palace than buy and extend an existing great house. Several properties were considered. Wellington wanted to be fairly close to London, but when Miserden in Gloucestershire was proposed he realised that it would not be an advantage to be just a morning's ride from a fashionable spa like Cheltenham. Then it was discovered that Lord Rivers might be willing to sell his estate of Stratfield Saye in Hampshire, not far from Reading and some forty miles west of London. The location was perfect and Benjamin Dean Wyatt, the architect, who had been Wellington's private secretary in Ireland, was enthusiastic: 'I feel no hesitation in saying, that the estate possesses great beauty & dignity; is capable of being made a princely Place.' The estate was in good condition with fine plantations, a magnificent park, beautiful prospects and happy tenants.[13] Wellington made a flying visit at the beginning of November 1817 and gave his approval; the trustees proceeded with the purchase, paying £263,000 for the existing house and 5,000 acres, although Wellington did not gain possession until the spring of 1819.[14] Wyatt set about plans for a great palace, surpassing even Marlborough's Blenheim, that would give permanent expression to the nation's gratitude for Waterloo.[15]

But for the moment Wellington's headquarters were at Cambrai, and he spent more time there, and at the nearby château Mont St Martin, than anywhere else during these years. The British contingent of the Army of Occupation was widely dispersed in scores of small detachments, most amounting to fewer than one hundred men, some with little more than a dozen. This eased the burden on the countryside, but made it much harder for officers to supervise the men, and the smallest detachments were vulnerable in the event of serious trouble with the local population. Inevitably some locals resented the presence of foreign troops and there were brawls and quarrels, particularly on Sundays and feast days, but the accounts of soldiers who served in France in the Occupation give an overwhelmingly positive impression. According to John Douglas: 'The French people were greatly attached to the British and I assure you I never spent so pleasant a time during my soldiering. I have seen the old and young shed tears in abundance at our leaving them and numbers of men, being discharged, went back and got married, and are there to this day.' And many years later John Morgan recalled the kindness of the people in the little village near Arros where he was quartered; he would help them in the fields, or dig their gardens, or cut wood, and in return they would give him their nice white bread, while the hard dark ration bread went to feed the pigs! Tales of such happy co-operation do not of course figure in Wellington's correspondence, where courts martial and disputes with the locals are a constant if not overwhelming refrain. In fact the trouble was kept well within bounds, but this is a testament to Wellington's precautions and assiduity rather than a sign that they were unnecessary.[16]

One persistent French grievance that was hard to avoid was the damage to crops caused by soldiers engaged in training exercises. Wellington collected the entire British contingent, together with the Danes, Hanoverians and Saxons, for large-scale manoeuvres over several days each autumn on the uncultivated plains near Denain between Cambrai and Valenciennes. The experienced soldiers seem to have generally disliked these mock battles, but they were probably useful, especially for the staff and some regimental officers. More routine training went on throughout the year, with Wellington issuing occasional orders to practise this or that manoeuvre.[17]

Wellington made few significant innovations in the army in these years, partly at least because his power to do so was quite limited; all the army's permanent rules and regulations were the responsibility of the Horse Guards, which showed no great eagerness to look to him for advice. One area in which Wellington was responsible was the extensive brevet promotions of officers after Waterloo, and again in 1817. Inevitably those who missed out complained loudly, while those who were promoted took it as no more than their due. When Sir Thomas Graham (now Lord Lynedoch) wrote on behalf of two disappointed protégés Wellington could only reply that he knew that both were worthy men who had been unfortunate, but that he had spent more than a month working over the lists, consulting senior officers, trying to get the fairest result, but that even so 'I confess that I am not satisfied with my own work, and that I know I have omitted some more deserving than those whose names are in the list; but I cannot now help it'. Senior subordinates could be very pressing in advancing the claims of their ADCs and personal favourites, and Wellington was acutely aware that if all these claims were granted worthy officers serving with their regiments in the line would miss out.[18]

Nonetheless life at Cambrai was not all work, and Wellington was able to relax with less pressure than he had felt for years. 'I never saw anyone so well or in such spirits as our Duke', George Bowles of the Guards wrote home in June 1816, 'no schoolboy was ever more eager for fun of every description than he is'.[19] There were private theatricals and exuberant horseplay with ladies sitting on rugs being dragged along the corridors of the Château Mont St Martin amid squeals of laughter – a game which they called 'riding in the coach'. Wellington's own account of this, in a letter to Georgiana de Ros (the Duke of Richmond's daughter) catches him at his most unguarded:

Dearest Georgy,

. . . We are going on here as usual – 'Riding in the coach', dancing the Mazurka, &c, &c. The house is as full as it can hold. Yesterday was a very bad day, and I went to Cambray; and I understand that they hunted Lord C___ through all the corridors, even that in the roof. At night we had an improvement on the coach. Two goats were brought in and harnessed, but instead of being horses and assisting to draw, they chose to lie down and be drawn. The night before, the ladies drew me in the *petty* tour [i.e. the shorter route], and afterwards Lord Hill the *grand* tour, but the 'fat, fair and forty', and M___ were so knocked up that some of us were obliged to go into the harness, although we had already run many stages.[20]

A less unexpected, but still revealing, view of Wellington at this time comes from the journal of Catherine Mure, the sister of Charles Colville's young wife:

At first I was rather disappointed at his appearance. He is no dandy in dress and looks older than I had expected. His hair is grey and his teeth not good. His looks improve much when you know him better. He has the most animated, intelligent and expressive countenance I ever saw. He is like the pictures one sees of him, but not so tall as they lead one to suppose. He is stout made, with broad shoulders: his figure is best on horseback, his bust being fine. He is fair, eyes a fine grayish blue: this does not sound fine, but they are so animated and keen. They look quite through you and are the beauty of his face. He handed Jane to dinner.

The Duke was in great spirits. He is very lively, talked and laughed a great deal and told us all the gossip of Cambray, which he seems to enjoy as much as the young men on his staff. It seems odd to see so great a man with so many important concerns to transact, amusing himself with such trifles, but they say he has the most extraordinary powers during his hours of recreation to banish from his mind all serious matters and that during the most awfully important periods of the war he could at any time, when he had a spare hour, amuse himself like a schoolboy. He seems much liked by those about him and on such a pleasant footing with them. What a pity, with such talents and powers of pleasing, he should not be equally estimable in private life.[21]

It was probably gossip about Wellington's affairs and his treatment of Kitty which provoked Catherine Mure's comment about his private life; and it is clear that his neglect of her and attentions to other women – whether they were full-blown affairs or not – caused her considerable pain and some humiliation. Equally she continued to irritate him whenever they were together, and while they were often under the same roof in Paris, Cambrai, London and Cheltenham, they were also often apart. In December 1815 John Fremantle, one of his ADCs, commented on his ill humour and added: 'I do not think it can be the duchess for poor soul she never sees him except across the table at dinner.' A few weeks later Fremantle noted the great improvement in Wellington's temper after the Duchess had returned to England. And in 1817 Kitty's jealousy of the newly married Louisa Hervey was plain to all; but she also had her friends among the ADCs and evidently played an active part in the gossip and party games of the château when she was there.[22]

Other accounts show Wellington acting as a pleasant host to a variety of guests, British and foreign, teasing the Duchess of Richmond, and talking politics to Creevey with a frank directness that rather startled Lady Frances Cole, who was used to the more guarded diplomatic conversation at her father, Lord Malmesbury's, table. His relations with his principal subordinates seem also to have been much more cordial and relaxed than when subject to the strain of active operations. Early in 1816 Rowland Hill's father became involved in financial difficulties and Wellington immediately offered to lend whatever sum was needed to settle the problem, writing a difficult letter with unusual tact and warmth. Hill did not need to take up the offer but was evidently touched by Wellington's concern.[23]

When the Occupation ended and the army was going home Sir Denis Pack wrote a farewell letter in which, having recalled his long service under Wellington in the Peninsula, he described:

the confidence and delight with which I have always met your Grace, and reflect that in this long and eventful period I have never seen you discomposed or heard a harsh expression from you to any one under your command, I am beyond all bounds impressed with feelings of admiration for your Grace's character and with deep regret for the separation that has just taken place. I beg that your Grace will accept my best acknowledgments for the kind attentions, that I have ever experienced from you, and the best wishes from my heart that you may enjoy many years of honour and happiness.[24]

Even when every discount has been made for the nostalgia of the moment, and the relative position of the author and the recipient, it is clear that there was much real feeling underlying this letter. Wellington's last command had been a happy one.

From the outset it was obvious that the success of the allied occupation would be decided more by events in Paris than by those in Cambrai, and in particular by the ability of the King to form an effective and stable government, which would ensure that the Bourbons were not overthrown as soon as the last allied troops left the country. Castlereagh and Wellington initially viewed the appointment of the Duc de Richelieu as prime minister in September 1815 with misgivings. They would have preferred to retain Talleyrand and Fouché in office in order to reassure the *libérals* and Bonapartists, hoping that this would give the new regime the broad base of support that it would need to survive. Richelieu by contrast was almost unknown in France and represented an obvious shift to the right, while his close connection with the Emperor Alexander suggested that he might be little more than a Russian puppet. However, these fears quickly evaporated; Richelieu might have lacked finesse in political intrigue, but his integrity, moderation and sincerity impressed all observers and particularly appealed to Castlereagh and Wellington. And they were pleased by his determination to pursue a middle course despite the opposition of the ultra-royalists who dominated the Chamber after the election of 1815. Throughout the Occupation Wellington consistently opposed the ultra-royalists, seeing them as a divisive force which was overly partisan and none too scrupulous in its means. As late as the beginning of 1818 he bluntly told a royalist sympathiser: 'I entertain no doubt how this contest will end. The descendants of Louis XV will not reign in France; and I must say, and always will say, that it is the fault of Monsieur [the Duc d'Artois] and his adherents.'[25] This, while not bad as prophecy, was a typically exaggerated expression of Wellington's view. He did not see an immediate threat to Louis XVIII in 1818, but realised the vision of the ultras hovering in the wings led by the King's brother and heir to the throne, ensured that many *libérals* gave only provisional support to the regime and kept alive the possibility of an alternative, more liberal, settlement under the Duc d'Orléans.[26]

Many Whigs and radicals in Britain, and not a few officers in the British contingent of the Army of Occupation, would have welcomed such a revolution, and in late 1815 and early 1816 their activities gave Wellington some trouble. Much of this was essentially harmless: loud talk by officers who had no appreciation that publicly advocating the overthrow of the existing government might be frowned upon by French officials unaccustomed to the notion that a British gentleman should be free to speak his mind without thought or discretion, sober or otherwise, in whatever country he happened to be.[27] Still, the publicity surrounding the role of Sir Robert Wilson and Captain Hely Hutchinson in the escape of Count Lavalette showed that not all officers would limit themselves to mere talk, while several great Whig Lords in England were active in encouraging and patronising liberal opponents of the established government not just of France but also of Spain and Naples. Their free use of the ambassador's diplomatic bag to avoid police censorship of their correspondence raised doubts among some royalists whether the British government itself was inclined to favour the Orleans option. Wellington's presence in Paris and forthright support for the King and Richelieu's government soon scotched this idea, although the doubts lingered, with rather more justification, over Sir Charles Stuart's attitude. However, as Stuart knew only too well and naturally resented, his significance as ambassador was greatly diminished by Wellington's presence.[28]

Wellington's personal relations with Louis XVIII were particularly good. The King was grateful not just for Waterloo but for the summons to join the army in the advance on Paris, which, despite the contrary advice of Talleyrand and others, had greatly simplified the Second Restoration. The displeasure felt by the King over the removal of the foreign art treasures left no permanent scars, and he showered Wellington with attention and marks of royal favour. Wellington was accorded the rare honour of being invited to dine with the King, and in late 1815 Louis expressed the wish to give him the house and estate of Grosbois. Reporting this to London, Wellington professed to see no reason why the King of France should not give him an estate, any more than any other monarch, but fortunately others were more alert to the obvious indelicacy of the gift and it was never made. The King found a more appropriate way of thanking Wellington when he made him a Chevalier du Saint Esprit, a high order of chivalry which included other foreigners. The award was not purely honorary, for the plaque of the order given to Wellington was set in diamonds which were said to be worth 600,000 francs (approximately £24,000). This was not the only valuable present Wellington accepted from the King. In 1818 he was given a magnificent Egyptian service of china, one hundred and two pieces in all, which has been described as 'one of the most original and entrancing services ever made at the Sèvres factory'. After the occupation was over the Duke received one of six collections of medals set in gold, silver, platinum and bronze; and in 1823 a service of forty-eight blue and gold Sèvres dessert plates. These were princely gifts – it is said that Wellington received almost as much from Louis XVIII as Madame de Pompadour had received from Louis XV – which reflected magnificence on both the giver and the recipient. The age when such gestures could be made without suggestions of impropriety or overtones of corruption was already drawing to a close, but in this as in many other respects both Wellington and Louis XVIII embodied the assured values of the eighteenth century rather than the anxious self-consciousness of Victorian propriety.[29]

The King did not resent, or else forgave, Wellington's respectful but rather blunt warning that the behaviour of the ultra-royalists in the Chambers and at court was damaging the monarchy in early 1816. And Wellington and the allies generally approved the bold decision taken by the King and Richelieu together, to dissolve the Parliament and hold fresh elections. These produced a much more balanced chamber, dominated by moderate royalists, in which Richelieu's ministry had a comfortable majority; but which also permitted the ultras to indulge in irresponsible opposition fuelled by a sense that the renewed opportunities of 1815 were being squandered. The King had traded the fervour of the ultras for the tepid support of more reasonable men; and the durability of the gain was open to doubt.[30]

Poor harvests in 1816 and 1817 led to simmering discontent, and Richelieu pressed for a reduction of the size of the Army of Occupation to help the government's finances. While broadly sympathetic, Wellington resented being pressed and managed to delay a concession until the spring of 1817, when the size of the occupying force was reduced to 120,000 men. Richelieu's government rather added to the problems it faced with a new electoral law passed in February 1817 which reduced the power of the ultras by limiting the influence of conservative rural voters. It also required that elections for one-fifth of the Chamber of Deputies be held each year. This naturally made it much more difficult for any ministry to maintain a stable majority, and heightened the political atmosphere when it most needed to be cooled. The result was a steady influx of *libérals* into the Chamber who had no real loyalty to Richelieu's ministry, while at the same time the hostility of the ultras was intensified by their sense of betrayal. Richelieu continued to hold the centre ground, but under increasing pressure from both flanks.[31]

Wellington's influence extended beyond France; he had an important role at several levels in the internal affairs of the Netherlands. He was responsible for supervising the rebuilding of the barrier fortresses in the Netherlands, and although he delegated much of this work to Colonel J.T. Jones R.E. (and the actual planning and construction was undertaken by Dutch-Belgian engineers), Wellington was ultimately accountable for the £6.5 million which had been set aside for the project. (Of this, £2 million came from Britain, £2 million from the Netherlands under the 1814 Peace Treaty, and £2.5 million from the

Netherlands' share in the war indemnity paid by France.) He conducted annual tours of inspection, and was satisfied that good progress was being made and that most of the works would be completed by 1820.[32]

The technical excellence of the barrier fortresses could not, however, do anything to correct the fundamental weakness of the new Kingdom of the Netherlands. The union was very unpopular in Belgium and not embraced with any great enthusiasm in Holland. A whole generation of Belgians had been brought up as Frenchmen, had served with pride in Napoleon's armies, and now felt that they had been relegated to second-class status in a second-class power. Their discontent was inflamed by the presence of many Frenchmen who had either been exiled or who had refused to remain in the France of Louis XVIII. The King of the Netherlands was well aware of the problem and endeavoured to conciliate his Belgian subjects without alienating or offending his Dutch ones, holding court in Brussels for part of each year, although the great majority of his most trusted advisors continued to be Dutch. His son, the Prince of Orange, was inclined to go further. Wellington succeeded in dissuading him from establishing a rival court in Brussels, but the Prince continued to cultivate contacts among Belgian liberals and even among the French exiles. Yet as Wellington forcefully pointed out, there was no hope of winning real support in such quarters: 'Your Royal Highness's family and its interests in the world are the most obnoxious to the revolutionary party in every kingdom in Europe; and that whatever this party in France or their adherents in the Netherlands may say to your Royal Highness, their first object after success in France – an object the attainment of which is absolutely necessary to their existence – is the destruction of the dynasty of your Royal Highness's family in the Netherlands.'[33]

The presence of the French exiles in Belgium, and a relaxed censorship regime, permitted a vigorous – frequently outrageous – liberal francophone press. This attracted the notice both of the French government, which was the principal target of the libellous attacks that filled these papers, and of the allied powers. The allies, acting through the regular meetings of their ambassadors to Paris, asked Wellington to represent their concerns to the King of the Netherlands, and he showed no reluctance to act as the spokesman for the Concert of Europe on the subject. In doing so he may have gone a little further than Castlereagh might have wished, for the Foreign Secretary had strong although not consistent scruples about the Great Powers interfering in the internal affairs of smaller states.[34] And he risked offending the growing liberal consensus in Britain in favour of the 'freedom of the press'; but in Wellington's view this was more than outweighed by the mischief created by irresponsible and unaccountable newspapers, especially where, as in the Netherlands, the political system did not rest upon secure foundations. From the summer of 1816 onwards Wellington pressed the King of the Netherlands to strengthen his press laws but the King proved reluctant to act, possibly due to the difficulty of getting such legislation through Parliament or from the fear of driving an influential slice of society into outright opposition. Wellington's hand was strengthened when he himself was libelled, and even more so when the resulting prosecution failed in the courts, but the King gave ground only slowly, using time-honoured tactics of procrastination and half-measures to defuse the pressure.[35]

Early in 1818 the underlying hostility to Wellington in France flared briefly into action. Just after midnight on the night of 10–11 February, as he returned in his carriage to his residence on the Champs Elysées a well-dressed man fired a pistol at him at close range but missed, then escaped into the night. No one was hurt; the shot did not even hit the carriage and for a moment Wellington did not even realise what had happened, thinking that one of the sentries at his gate had accidently discharged his musket when picking it up. Two of Wellington's servants who were coming home at the same time let the man pass in the street because there was no immediate outcry. Reflecting on the attempt later Wellington concluded that it had been carefully planned; the moment when the carriage halted before entering the gates was well chosen, and with a slightly cooler head and steadier hand the assassin could have succeeded.[36]

Over the next few days evidence emerged that the attempt was part of a wider conspiracy, with reports of Wellington's death or some other dramatic event having circulated in different parts of the country well before the news from Paris could arrive. Wellington was not satisfied with the initial reaction of the French government – he particularly resented the suggestion that the attempt had not been serious – but as the police investigations began to make progress, the ministers became more decided in their condemnation. The plot had its origins among the French exiles in Belgium and had been in preparation for some time – a previous plan to strike when Wellington was in Brussels had been thwarted because Wellington had chosen to stroll in a different part of the park in the company of Lady Charlotte Greville. In the middle of March a half-pay officer named Cantillon was arrested. He was tried in Paris in May 1819 but unanimously acquitted by the jury; there was no real doubt of his guilt, but the prosecution never had enough evidence which it could produce in court to prove the case. Cantillon's name would soon have been completely forgotten if Napoleon had not left him 10,000 francs (£400) in his will on the strange grounds that 'Cantillon had as much right to kill that oligarch, as the latter had to send me to die on that rock of St Helena'. Few even among Napoleon's greatest admirers could stomach the poor logic or the poor taste of the gesture; nor was their embarrassment lessened by the fact that the legacy was not paid.[37]

The British government reacted with alarm to the attempt on Wellington's life tinged with a little perverse satisfaction that the ministers' long-held forebodings had been justified. They were worried by his continued presence in Paris, and when they learnt that he was not satisfied by the immediate response of the French authorities they sent him formal, unequivocal instructions to leave the capital and proceed at once to Cambrai. Wellington reacted as he always did when he received instructions with which he disagreed: he refused to obey, prevaricating and arguing that he should instead be permitted to handle things in his own way. 'It is very hard to place me in the situation of being obliged to disobey, or even to delay to obey, the positive order of the Prince Regent; but I must do the latter at all events, as I conceive the public interests require it.' He claimed that the French were now taking the case much more seriously; that he would be no safer in Cambrai than in Paris; and that his withdrawal would undermine the French government and encourage all the disaffected opponents of the regime. As usual his intransigence was rewarded and Bathurst rescinded the order, while making it plain that the Cabinet had only given way with extreme reluctance and entirely against its better judgement: 'The danger of your protracted residence at Paris consists in this: that your presence there is constantly inflaming the malignant passions of a large mass of needy, desperate, and unprincipled villains, who cannot be kept under any control except by the unceasing exertions of an active, vigilant, and faithful police.' However, the British ministers' concerns were rather exaggerated; as in 1814–15, distance magnified the perceived threat, and there can be little doubt that Wellington's withdrawal would have been a mistake, while his cool unruffled presence in Paris helped preserve the impression of normality.[38]

The affair shed light on the precautions Wellington routinely took for his own safety when in France. The previous year he had told Beresford that in Paris: 'I never go into any blackguard mob or place in which a fellow might insult me with impunity. In other respects, I ride or walk alone, and unattended, and go to the theatres and everywhere as other people do.' Immediately after the attack he sought to reassure the government: 'I have always been much more careful than people imagine. I know that no person in these degenerate days will risk his own life to take mine, or even that of a more obnoxious person; and therefore I conceive I run no risk by day, or in those public places which are under the immediate guardianship of the police. I never go to any suspicious place and have no particular place of resort at which an assassin might lie in wait for me.' Perhaps realising that this was not entirely convincing he added that he had decided that in future he would use a plain carriage at night, whose doors had been altered so that they could not be opened from the outside, with some arms (presumably pistols) inside, and an armed guard in the box; and that he would be escorted by gendarmes when going to official functions or anywhere else where his presence was predictable. His underlying attitude was spelt out towards the end of the year when a plot to kidnap or murder the Emperor Alexander on a visit to the Netherlands was thwarted, and Wellington successfully argued against employing large numbers of troops to guard the tsar: 'I am certain that it is desirable in such cases as this not to demonstrate unnecessary apprehension, by taking unnecessary precautions; and that it is better with such miscreants as those with whom we have the misfortune to deal to incur some risk rather than to appear to be afraid of them.' Fortunately he knew that Alexander agreed and would be displeased by obtrusive security precautions.[39]

The attack on Wellington was only the most obvious symptom of the troubled state of France in the winter of 1817–18. Wellington was dismayed by the weakness of Richelieu's government and the impossibility of persuading the ultra-royalists to give it even tacit support. He did not credit reports of a possible uprising, but warned Bathurst:

> I confess that I have a very bad opinion of the stability of things here. The government have certainly not got on since the year 1815, and in my opinion they have gone backwards in the last six months . . . the Ministers are running as hard as they can in pursuit of a low, vulgar popularity, which they think the best support of the King's authority and their own . . . But it must not be supposed that in this race they can run as fast as the liberal Jacobins, or as any of those factions whose object is to overturn the existing order of things. Every step they take tends to weaken the Royal authority, and I think it is much to be apprehended that as soon as the Allies will withdraw from France the whole fabric will crumble to pieces.[40]

This was Wellington at his most pessimistic, but the ministers in London were inclined to view things even more darkly. Bathurst wrote that 'a sudden insurrection at Paris, or in the interior of France', was 'by no means impossible'. That was in the aftermath of the attempt on Wellington's life, but even some months before, at the beginning of December 1817, Bathurst had expressed the fear that the French government might be so weak that it might give way to a popular clamour for war when the occupation ended.[41] A century of rivalry and a generation of almost continuous war could not be quickly forgotten on either side of the Channel. In October 1815 Liverpool had remarked, as an obvious truth: 'We ought never to lose sight for a moment of the consideration, that with whatever humanity and indulgence the French may have been treated by us, they hate us far more than any other nation; and that they would most willingly embark in any project for the destruction of the force which has saved them, if they only thought that it was likely to prove successful.'[42]

Nonetheless during the closing months of 1817 and the first months of 1818 a consensus emerged in favour of bringing the Occupation to a close at the end of the third year (November 1818) rather than continue it for the full five years. Wellington favoured an early withdrawal, largely from a fear that the mood of the country was changing from a sullen but essentially passive discontent to a more active opposition. He feared that the Occupation was at risk of no longer contributing to the stability of France, and instead becoming a grievance which might even lead to a low-level guerrilla war. These concerns were overstated, possibly even consciously, in order to convince those in London, like Bathurst, who were inclined to oppose an early withdrawal, but even so they undermine the comfortable assumption that the Occupation was ended early because it had been a success, and that France was so stable that it was no longer needed.[43]

The British government and the allies agreed that the occupation should end in 1818 provided that France pay the indemnity of 700 million francs stipulated in the peace treaty, and the compensation to private individuals and institutions for the exactions and damage committed by Napoleon's armies. It was almost universally assumed that if the occupying troops left before these claims were settled the French government would have little hesitation in dishonouring them, but it took some optimism to believe that the complicated negotiations for their settlement could be completed, and the enormous sums of money required raised, in less than twelve months. France could not possibly pay the indemnity and compensation outright, whether in one year or in three, but she might be able to borrow the money, and the success of three substantial loans in 1817, raised through the British and Dutch banks of Barings and Hope, was encouraging. Barings had undertaken the 1817 loans with the approval of the British government and Wellington's co-operation; they had originally hoped for an allied guarantee, but that was never even a remote possibility. Alexander Baring was a well-respected Whig MP as well as a banker, and he was soon on confidential terms with Wellington, discussing political as well as financial questions with considerable candour. Wellington worked comfortably with him, but was far too shrewd to take all Baring's statements at face value and firmly resisted an attempt to alter the terms of the first loan in the bank's favour.[44]

At the beginning of 1818 Wellington reported that Baring was confident in financial prospects in France, and in his ability to raise the money 'notwithstanding the political gloom'. However over the next couple of months the banker's enthusiasm waned, and he began to talk of the need to extend the period of raising money into 1819 or even 1820. Part of this was probably just a negotiating ploy, but Baring must also have been affected – and knew that the markets would be affected – by the signs of discontent in France, and in particular by the attempt to assassinate Wellington. The French government also made the task more difficult; the success of the 1817 loans had triggered a speculative boom and the government was criticised for allowing foreign banks to make large profits at the expense of France. It responded by trying to secure better terms for the 1818 loan, and by including French banks and municipalities in the loan. Wellington reported to Liverpool at the end of February: 'I saw Mr Baring again yesterday. He is not very well pleased with the French government, who, it appears, having made all the use of him they could, now think themselves independent of him, and, as usual, are treating him ill.' Nonetheless an agreement was reached by the end of May, although Wellington insisted upon some changes and explanations on other points; these seem to have related to clauses included by the French government for political effect rather than anything which concerned the financial terms of the loan. Events proved that Barings had paid too much – demand for the loan was sluggish and in September it traded at a discount, triggering a further sharp fall as the speculative boom collapsed.[45]

The negotiations over compensation for allied subjects should have been quite separate from those for the loan, but as they took place at the same time and involved many of the same people it is not surprising that they became intertwined. Wellington was annoyed by the French government's prevarication – its refusal to accept its responsibility and explain the justice of the demands to the public. On the other hand he accepted that many of the individual claims being made were unjustified and that their gross total was so inflated that it would have to be substantially reduced if any settlement was ever to be achieved. He proposed that the allies arbitrarily set a figure for the total compensation (he suggested 500 million francs, or rather less than half the gross total of the claims) and then divide it among themselves. Castlereagh objected that this would simply set the allies quarrelling among themselves if no sound principle could be found to divide the total (it could not be a simple proportion of the gross claims, as some of the allies had already subjected their claims to considerable scrutiny while others had not). After much fruitless discussion the Emperor of Russia proposed that Wellington take charge of the issue, and it is a mark of the respect with which he was regarded that this proved acceptable to all parties.[46] Wellington demanded that the claims of each nation be reduced to a bare minimum; and those which he still thought were inflated he sent to arbitration. This ultimately reduced the claims to just over 240 million francs, or less than one-sixth of the gross.[47] The French had secured an extraordinarily good bargain, but rather than show any gratitude they at once began to haggle over the interest. Wellington told Castlereagh: 'I think that both the King and his Ministers have behaved shabbily in this concern. The Ministers of the Allies have certainly come down as low as they can, or ought, and they all reckoned upon and have a right to the back interest; but the King and his Ministers take advantage of the general eagerness to obtain a settlement to refuse any reasonable accommodation upon the question.' Still, French grumbling was not wholly unjustified, for the total cost of their defeat in 1815, including the indemnity reparations and feeding and paying the Army of Occupation, came to a daunting 1,863 million francs or some £75 million, without including anything for all the French lives lost, men maimed, and property damaged. Napoleon's last adventure had been a glorious failure that caught the whole world's imagination, but when the show was over others had to pick up the bill.[48]

The allied sovereigns decided to hold a meeting in the autumn where they would formally take the decision to end the occupation, lay the basis for their future policy towards France, and have the opportunity to discuss other problems. They soon agreed that this should not be another congress on the Vienna model, to which all the Princes of Europe would flock, but a much smaller, briefer, more businesslike meeting. Partly with this in mind, and for its central location and historical connotations, they chose to meet at Aix-la-Chapelle, which offered only limited accommodation. There had been some realignment of the European powers since 1815: Prussia was now much closer to Austria, and Castlereagh was not without fear that the Russians might champion the claims of France, and particularly Spain. For their part, the French were very eager to see the final dissolution of the wartime alliances as well as the immediate end of the occupation. Wellington acted as a principal in discussions over the Army of Occupation, and on the settlement of financial questions, while on other questions he loyally supported Castlereagh. In general the talks went smoothly, but Castlereagh faced an embarrassing dilemma when Alexander brought forward a plan for a universal guarantee of the existing governments in Europe from any threat, whether internal or external. It was not hard to see that in practice this would tend to permit the interference of large powers in the internal affairs of their neighbours with no real reciprocity, and that it would lead to endless further disputes. But even if it had been less intrinsically objectionable Castlereagh had clear instructions from Liverpool to avoid any additional continental commitments. The mood in Britain had swung sharply against European diplomacy since 1815 and towards a more independent self-serving line of policy. Castlereagh's achievements at Vienna and Paris had never been properly appreciated at home, and he had always lacked the oratory and flair for public relations needed to convince the public, which much preferred Byron's witty sarcasm and the shallow bombastic rhetoric of the press. In the face of Castlereagh's opposition Alexander reluctantly put aside his plan, but general positions adopted at this time would persist. Throughout the closing years of the war it had seemed quite possible that Alexander might emerge as the champion of European liberalism, while Britain had been the most committed supporter of the restoration of the Bourbons. But by 1818 the conservatism inspired by the Emperor's religious enthusiasm had largely overcome the legacy of his liberal education and he was ready to throw his full weight against the threat of disaffection and subversion. Castlereagh welcomed the change, writing to Bathurst:

> I must render justice to the Emperor, and to his *Faiseurs*, in all this business, that they have been most handsomely anxious to court an irreparable breach with the Jacobins of all countries, and to uphold everything you have done. This . . . will bring all the democratic fire of Europe upon the Emperor, and we must stand by him accordingly.[49]

Not everyone in Britain, or even in Liverpool's Cabinet, agreed, but for the moment Castlereagh's view of foreign policy prevailed, and Britain and Russia were able to co-operate quite harmoniously in preserving the peace of the Continent.

The withdrawal of the army went smoothly; British troops began to sail home in October and by the end of November only a few stragglers were left: some sick, commissaries and other officials settling the final loose ends. Wellington farewelled the army in a General Order dated 10 November in which he praised the soldiers for 'their uniform good conduct' and expressed regret at parting from them after almost ten years of service together.[50] This order marks the end of Wellington's last active command, but the transition from soldier to statesman was a gradual one. Even in India he had been closely involved in the civil government of Mysore and diplomatic negotiations with the Marathas; in the Peninsula a large part of his time was generally occupied by relations with the allies and the authorities in London; while ever since the spring of 1814, except for the few weeks of the Waterloo campaign, he had been preoccupied by the problems of peace, not waging war.

As Wellington made the now familiar journey from Paris to London in December 1818 he may have reflected on the past; ten years before he had been in Chelsea defending his reputation before the Board of Inquiry into the Convention of Cintra; ten years before that he had been in Madras making preparations for the campaign against Tipu Sultan and mourning his friend Colonel Aston, killed so pointlessly in a duel; looking even further back, to 1788, he was an insignificant subaltern on the staff at Dublin Castle. It had been an extraordinary rise to fame, wealth and glory far beyond his most extravagant hopes. He undoubtedly owed part of his success to good fortune – being born in the right decade, having sufficient rank and experience (if only just) to allow him to hold the commands he was given – and to his brother, whose blatant favouritism gave him opportunities that might more fairly have gone to others. But he had taken every opportunity with both hands, meriting the confidence that was reposed in him and achieving success after success, often in the face of formidable difficulties. Waterloo raised him beyond equal: not just the greatest British soldier of his generation but the most famous and powerful Briton for at least a century. He had reached the very summit of the mountain, and now it was time to go home and face a fresh challenge of making a new life on a smaller domestic stage. In a few months he would turn fifty and he felt full of life and energy, gaiety and self-confidence. He enjoyed the good things that his success brought – the grand houses, the money, the orders of chivalry, the Sèvres china, and the flattery and attention of beautiful, intelligent women – but he enjoyed the work itself even more. He was not going home to grow cabbages, or waste his talents as Richard had done; he would remain at the centre of affairs, influencing if not determining government policies, and expressing his opinion in his unique, trenchant style.

PART II

IN CABINET (1819–27)

CHAPTER SEVEN

POLITICS AND THE DUKE

I N THE AUTUMN of 1818 while the foreign troops still occupied France, and the allied sovereigns were gathered together at Aix-la-Chapelle, Lord Liverpool turned his thoughts to Wellington's future and invited him to join the Cabinet. His initial idea was that Wellington would serve as a 'minister without portfolio', but Lord Mulgrave offered to vacate the Ordnance in favour of the Duke. This was a particularly appropriate office, for the Master-General of the Ordnance was invariably a senior soldier, and the precedent of Lord Chatham in 1809 showed that it need be no bar to Wellington taking an active field command in the unlikely event of a new war requiring his immediate services. Rumour reported that Wellington had said that it was the only office that he would accept, while Mulgrave's own declining health made a reduction of his duties highly desirable.[1]

Wellington evidently felt that the offer was a little precipitate – he might even have anticipated a brief holiday between giving up the command of the army and taking on a new task – but he seems to have had no hesitation in accepting the proposal. He did stipulate that if the government was at any time forced from office, he should be free 'to take any line I may at the time think proper'. He felt 'sincerely attached' to the party in office but had no taste for opposition:

> The experience which I have acquired during my long service abroad has convinced me that a factious opposition to the government is highly injurious to the interests of the country; and thinking as I do now I could not become a party to such an opposition, and I wish that this may be clearly understood by those persons with whom I am now about to engage as a colleague in government.[2]

Although later generations have found this stipulation remarkable, Liverpool did not. He readily conceded that 'there are many special circumstances in your situation which render it of the utmost importance, in the event to which your refer, that you should be at full liberty to adopt that line of conduct which you may at that time judge most proper and advisable, with a view to the country and to yourself'. In other words Wellington was a national, not merely a party, figure whose prestige should not be lowered by being used in pursuit of purely party ends. But Liverpool went further, declaring that he would not expect *anyone* who joined the ministry necessarily to follow the party into opposition if it lost office. In many ways the Pittites remained essentially a party of government. Their experience of opposition was brief and unhappy, and they did not accept the ideological value that the Whigs placed on party spirit as an essential check to the power of the Crown. Rather than being a demand for special, favoured treatment, Wellington's stipulation showed that he shared one of the central tenets of the ministers he was joining.[3]

Wellington never spelt out his political principles or understanding of the British constitution in any great detail, but scattered references in his correspondence in the years before he joined the Cabinet suggest that his views were largely those of a conventional Pittite. On a central point he believed 'that the King has a right, and must be supported in the exercise of the right, to choose his own servants'.[4] In other words the King would nominate his ministers, who would use the influence of the Crown to help form a government with a majority in both Houses of Parliament. But many of the MPs who helped make up that majority were sufficiently independent to vote against the government on individual questions and, in extreme cases, to express a complete lack of confidence in it and call upon the Crown to select new ministers. No government in the early nineteenth century could take the Commons for granted; its measures would be judged on their merits, and if it lost the confidence of the country that would soon be reflected in the votes in the House. The concept of party threatened this balance. If a sufficient number of MPs banded together and agreed to always vote the same way, they would be able to force the King to select their nominees as his ministers, and keep them in office irrespective of their performance.

This doctrine was challenged by the Whigs who argued, in the words of Dunning's motion of 1780, that 'the influence of the Crown has increased, is increasing, and ought to be diminished'.[5] Only party discipline could act as an effective restraint on an ambitious monarch (as the Whigs believed George III to be in the first half of his reign), or a domineering executive (which seemed a little more plausible in the early nineteenth century). At the same time the Whigs pressed to reduce the power of the executive to influence the composition of Parliament. These proposals often had broad support; Pitt himself introduced many such 'reforms', while subsequent ministers either chose not to oppose, or failed to block, others. Over the course of a generation or two the number and reputation of the office-holders who provided the core of any government's most dependable support had been greatly reduced. A century earlier, Sir Robert Walpole would parade his train of dependents, blatantly advertising his hold over the Commons; but later generations had grown squeamish, and ministers liked to think that they could win arguments on their merits, and were half ashamed if their majority on an important question shrank to the point where everyone knew that they had depended on the office-holders to secure their success.[6] An important strut supporting the system was knocked away by Curwen's Act of 1809, which prohibited the sale of seats in Parliament. Worthy as this sounds, it effectively applied only to the government, which was forced in future to take precautions against knowing anything of the money transactions which MPs on all sides continued to conduct with the borough-mongers who controlled one or more seats in the House, and which they were prepared to make available to a gentleman in return for a consideration.[7]

The most recent step in this campaign against the power of the Crown was a move to abolish sinecures, which governments had always used to reward their supporters, and to replace them with pensions. The ministers had repulsed attempts in 1812 and 1813, but felt compelled to yield to the mood in the House in 1817. Wellington regretted this concession, telling Castlereagh:

> . . . what you say on the subject is unanswerable. I cannot, however, but think that the loss of this patronage is a misfortune to the Crown, for which no system of pension, however expensive, can be a remedy. People in England are ready enough to attend to reason, more particularly when it is obvious that no expense can be saved by a favourite measure; and I would earnestly recommend you to get some *hard-headed* friend to reason the whole question, to show how sinecures have been employed, and in what manner the pensions would operate, and the expense of both systems. People would probably be inclined to pause before they should determine to destroy what is certainly good and cheap in order to establish what will be a bad substitute and more expensive, and without convicting yourselves you may be able to retain for the Crown the valuable patronage.[8]

Of course it was easy for Wellington, far from the parliamentary fray, to feel that the ministers had not made their case with sufficient vigour and that a more positive line would have swayed the Commons. In this instance he was almost certainly wrong – the feeling in the country was running too strongly against sinecures – but it is interesting to see his belief in the importance of making the argument. Back in the dark days of 1810 he had told Villiers: 'I wish that the ministers could strengthen their government; and that somebody would take pains to inform the public and guide their opinion, and not allow every newswriter to run away with the public mind, upon points essential to the interests of the country.' And even before this, in 1806 when he had been defending his brother's reputation, he had looked to the press and pamphlets as a way of influencing the climate of opinion as a preliminary to taking up the question in Parliament.[9]

Ten years after joining Liverpool's government Wellington told the Lords that his fundamental political principles were to maintain 'the prerogatives of the Crown and the rights and privileges of the Church and its union with the State'.[10] As this suggests, the religious settlement made after the Restoration in 1660 was central to the British constitution in the eighteenth and early nineteenth centuries. The supremacy of the Anglican Church was entrenched in both the state and the country. Political and many other offices were, in theory, reserved for Anglicans, although a series of annual indemnity bills extended a broad degree of toleration to other Protestants. The result was curiously patchy; a number of prominent non-conformists, including Unitarians, sat in the House of Commons, but they were excluded from local government in most but not all county towns and provincial cities, causing increasing resentment. Catholics were excluded from Parliament and all senior offices, but many held commissions in the army without the question of their religion ever being raised. The private practice of religion was permitted to all, and this was the era in which both Quakers and Jews gained a much more assured place in British society.

This embedded hostility to the Catholic Church dated back to Tudor times, but had been sharpened in the seventeenth century and particularly the reign of James II, which had cemented the perceived link between Catholicism and political tyranny. Throughout the eighteenth century the proud boast of British liberty was to be a 'true-born Protestant Englishman'. The connection was strengthened by the contrast with France, where an absolutist monarchy and the Church were both believed to demand complete subservience from their subjects. Two hundred years of Protestant preaching and propaganda had created a storehouse of popular 'knowledge' and beliefs: the horrors of the Inquisition; fat friars and lecherous monks preying upon the people; beautiful girls locked away in nunneries against their will; religious processions and services that bordered on idolatry. All these ideas were still widely current in the early nineteenth century, as can be seen in the comments of many of the junior officers and men who served under Wellington in Portugal and Spain, and who often reacted with a mixture of horror and startled fascination to their first sight of monks and friars, or of the host being paraded through the streets.[11] The upper classes were generally more sophisticated, and their opposition to Catholicism both weaker and more intellectual. A minority still felt an intense distaste for some of the religious doctrines of the Catholic Church (such as transubstantiation and purgatory), but this was becoming less common, and the Gordon Riots in 1780 had created political taboo over any attempt to mobilise popular hostility to Catholicism. When Spencer Perceval emphasised his strong religious principles in 1807 – a pertinent point given that the Talents had just been dismissed for proposing Catholic Emancipation – he was vehemently attacked for risking the peace of the country by rousing the inflammatory cry of 'No Popery!'[12]

Wellington's own opposition to Catholic Emancipation was grounded mainly on his knowledge of Ireland, but also on a more general belief that 'the Roman Catholic religion in its natural state is not very favourable to Civil Government in any part of Europe'.[13] Two intertwined ideas lay behind this: that the loyalty of the Catholic clergy and hierarchy was primarily to the Church, not to the King or nation; and that the subservience of Catholics to their priests extended beyond religion to political questions. Both threatened to create a party within the state and one that might, in the last resort, owe its loyalty outside the country. The experience of Irish elections, especially during Wellington's tenure as Chief Secretary, confirmed that priests had the potential to mobilise and direct their congregations in parliamentary contests, even if it was only occasionally used.[14] These difficulties might be lessened by some form of concordat with the Pope, as many Catholic rulers had obtained, which would give the national government some influence over the Church, but it would not be easy to make such an agreement without impinging on the establishment of the Anglican Church, or expecting the Pope to yield his claim to head the one true universal Church. The issue of Catholic Emancipation was not quite as simple and obvious as it appears in hindsight in a secular age. As Wellington told the Lords in 1828:

> we, who look with some jealousy [i.e. suspicion] at the Catholic subjects of the King in Ireland, have some reason for feeling that jealousy; and ought not to be accused of bigotry, or of acting upon surmises, when the fact really is, that it has been found that, till some connexion is formed between the Government and that Church in any country in which the Roman Catholic religion exists, the Government cannot be carried on.[15]

If Wellington's main political principles can be summed up in the old cry of 'Church and King', there were other, more distinctive aspects of his outlook, habits of mind rather than principles as such, which affected his approach to politics. His primary concern was almost always pragmatic – the good government of the country – and his instincts lay with the executive rather than the legislature. He had a strong distrust of theory and arguments from first principles, regarding intellectuals in politics, particularly the 'philosophical radicals' who came to the fore in these decades, as impractical and dangerous. His preference was always to take an existing structure and, by a combination of his own energy and purpose, and necessary changes, make it function efficiently, rather than demolish the whole and begin anew. This reflected his experience as an officer commanding an army in the field who simply did not have the power to make sweeping changes to the way it was organised and run; even in 1815 he could not, had he wished, abolish flogging, change the way junior officers were promoted, or restructure the commissariat. But this approach suited him, and when, in later years, he did have much more extensive powers, he was generally reluctant to initiate sweeping reforms, and was inclined to be sceptical of proposals for improvement. Not that he was ever the rigid opponent of all change as he is sometimes depicted; indeed he was a keen supporter of new technologies that promised practical benefits, whether steam navigation, Brunel's tunnel under the Thames, or domestic gadgets.

Wellington believed in the value of good sense and moderation, and that they were most likely to flourish in longstanding institutions with well-established traditions, while he had no faith in either enthusiasm or democracy. In the autumn of 1809, when the Spanish government was preparing to summon a Cortes, he told his brother:

I acknowledge that I have a great dislike to a new popular assembly. Even our own ancient one would be quite unmanageable, and, in these days, would ruin us, if the present generation had not before its eyes the example of the French revolution; and if there were not certain rules and orders for its guidance and government, the knowledge and use of which render safe, and successfully direct its proceedings.[16]

A year later and experience had only sharpened his distrust:

The natural course of all popular assemblies, of the Spanish Cortes among others, is to adopt democratic principles, and to vest all the powers of the State in their own body; and this assembly must take care that they do not run in this tempting course, as the wishes of the nation are decidedly for a monarchy: by a monarchy alone can it be governed; and their inclination to any other form of government, and their assumption of the power and patronage of the State into their own hands, would immediately deprive them of the confidence of the people; and they would be a worse government, and more impotent, because more numerous, than the Central Junta.[17]

While in 1811 he told Lord William Bentinck: 'The enthusiasm of the people is very fine, and looks well in print; but I have never known it produce anything but confusion.'[18]

This distrust of popular enthusiasm may have contributed to Wellington's marked dislike of grandiloquence and jingoism. In 1810 he sharply criticised the draft of a proclamation to the Portuguese people urging that it should be 'in plain language, without bombast, and ought, above all, to be short'.[19] His own style was consciously plain and simple, with a strong emphasis on factual details and avoiding literary artifice. This helped shape his public image in a way which suited him, and served as a sharp contrast to Napoleon's *Bulletins* which were far less accurate, but much more romantic and inspiring. Given that this was an age that accorded far greater fame and success to the works of Walter Scott and Lord Byron than to Jane Austen's novels, Wellington might have benefitted if his style had been more highly coloured. In time William Napier would do the job for him, describing the campaigns in the Peninsula, and especially some battle scenes, in rich emotive prose which was intensely admired for two or three generations, and which ensured that Wellington's victories were not forgotten. Meanwhile Wellington continued to write and speak in Parliament in his own way, while his sharp dry wit and staccato dismissal of inanities built up an increasingly appreciative audience and were even parodied in *The Times*.[20]

Wellington had little interest or expertise in economic problems in 1818, as opposed to the financial and even budgetary issues he had handled at different points in his career. He was tolerably familiar with high finance, having negotiated with Barings and Rothschilds over their loans to France, and struggled to find ways to overcome the chronic deficiency of the revenue of Portugal; but unlike Liverpool or Huskisson he had not studied the works of Adam Smith as a young man, and had no great insight into the underlying forces shaping the economy. His diagnosis of the post-war economic problems was far from penetrating:

> As for our distress, I believe it consists principally in the reduction of our war establishments, in the rage for travelling for all our gentry, which have deprived some of our people of employment, and lastly and principally in the idleness, dissipation, and improvidence of all the middling and lower classes in England, produced by a long course of prosperity and of flattery of their vices by the higher orders and the government.[21]

Wellington's Cabinet colleagues might have been more cautious in expressing their views, but only a few leading politicians of his generation, in government or opposition, had any real interest in or understanding of economics. Castlereagh was capable of making himself unintelligible upon any subject, but this did not, in itself, make him an economist; and while Canning had been alerted to the importance of the subject through his friendship with Huskisson and his electoral connection with the great port of Liverpool, his real interests lay elsewhere, in politics, intrigue, literature and diplomacy. The younger generation, reared on statistics and the spirit of rational enquiry, found the subject far more palatable; Peel was their brightest light, but they were only just beginning to edge towards the centre of the stage.

Wellington's greatest interest and expertise, outside the army, lay in foreign policy. He had dominated British policy towards Portugal and Spain throughout the war, and had an unrivalled knowledge of all the issues that might affect relations, from the slave trade to tensions between the two countries over Olivenza, as well as all the leading personalities in the two countries. Ever since 1814 he had worked closely and harmoniously with Castlereagh, supporting his policy of close engagement with the great continental powers in order to preserve the hard-won peace. Wellington was a major figure at any gathering of allied sovereigns, fully equal in prestige, if not formal status, with the Emperor of Russia or Austria, and he had an intimate knowledge of French domestic politics. Like Castlereagh he believed that Britain should use her influence to help resolve international problems by negotiation, and far from pursuing narrowly British interests (which had already been largely secured by the time Napoleon first abdicated in 1814), both men believed in promoting compromise and accommodation. Wellington had a far better appreciation of Castlereagh's foreign policy than any other member of Cabinet, and shared his outlook, while Liverpool (and in particular Canning, although his influence on foreign policy in these years was negligible) was much more inclined to play to public opinion in Britain and to pursue a much narrower, more self-interested line, in part because it had popular appeal.[22]

Wellington also believed that it was the duty of the government to protect the country against revolution – something which no one of his generation could take for granted. In his view the French Revolution had been an unmitigated disaster, for France and for Europe: 'In France, what was called enthusiasm was power and tyranny, acting through the medium of popular societies, which have ended by overturning Europe, and establishing the most powerful and dreadful tyranny that ever existed.'[23] As this suggests, Wellington saw little or nothing to admire in Napoleon's regime, although he had enough common sense and good taste to avoid public criticism of his fallen foe, and was usually content simply to praise his military ability, for example remarking that Napoleon's 'presence on the field made the difference of forty thousand men'. In private he was occasionally more forthcoming, telling Croker in 1826:

> I never was a believer in him, and I always thought that in the long-run we should overturn him. He never seemed himself at his ease, and even in the boldest things he did there was always a mixture of apprehension and

meanness. I used to call him *Jonathan Wild the Great*, and at each new *coup* he made I used to cry out 'Well done Jonathan,' to the great scandal of some of my hearers. But, the truth was, he had no more care about what was right or wrong, just or unjust, honourable or dishonourable, than *Jonathan*, though his great abilities, and the great stakes he played for, threw the knavery into the shade.[24]

When Segur's account of Napoleon's invasion of Russia was published in 1825 Wellington wrote a long commentary on the campaign in which he was highly critical of Napoleon's strategy and whole approach to the war. This was purely for his own satisfaction, for he had no intention of publishing it. He despised Napoleon's tricks for winning popularity, such as appearing to recognise a soldier in the ranks and recollect his service record, when he had just been briefed on it by an aide. He commented on Napoleon's lying and bullying, going so far as to say: 'Buonaparte's whole life, civil, political and military, was a fraud. There was not one transaction, great or small, in which lying and fraud were not introduced.' He praised French soldiers as 'upon the whole the best, the most orderly and obedient, and the most easily commanded and best regulated body of troops that ever existed'. And he accused Napoleon of treating them badly by neglecting their needs and waging war in order to raise money. This was the gist of his references to Jonathan Wild, for Wild was a London criminal on a grand scale in the early eighteenth century who, through a mixture of deception, extortion and intimidation, was not only for a time immensely successful, but also respectable before he went too far and was betrayed by his confederates. The parallels were not exact, of course, but Wellington seems to have seen Napoleon as preying on the whole of Europe in the same way, and lavishly rewarding his family and close associates with the proceeds of plunder and extortion. It was a partial, hostile view held by a man who had little sympathy for the (often betrayed) ideals espoused by the French Revolution and (to some extent) embodied in Napoleon's regime, but it also reflected the reality of the wars waged in Napoleon's name in the Peninsula; unlike most of Napoleon's British admirers, Wellington had seen the burnt villages and slaughtered civilians left behind by Masséna's retreating army in 1811.[25]

The French example also gave him a strong distaste for political extremism of any kind, and Wellington did not believe that party differences should be allowed to interrupt private friendships or social intercourse. He himself was on excellent terms with many Whigs, including some who had vehemently attacked him in the past. Thomas Creevey recalled that when he met the Duke in Brussels in 1815 he was unsure of his reception, having been a vocal supporter of Paull's attacks on Lord Wellesley's government of India, 'which produced such angry words between Sir Arthur and myself that I was quite prepared for there being no further intercourse between us. . . . however, he not only did not seem to resent or recollect these former bickerings, but . . . he behaved with the most marked civility and cordiality to myself and to all who were connected with me'.[26] Creevey became a good friend and something of an admirer, while never ceasing to disagree, often strongly, over politics. In a similar way Wellington was on excellent terms with Lady Bessborough, her daughter Lady Caroline Lamb, and her niece, Harriet, Lady Granville; with Lady Jersey; and with many other significant figures in Whig society. Creevey was surprised at the lack of partisanship with which Wellington discussed politics, recording a conversation in 1818 when they discussed the oratorical skills of leading members of the Opposition in the Commons. 'He said much in favour of Lord Grey's and Lord Lansdowne's speaking. Of the former he said that, as *leader* of the House of Commons he thought his manner and speaking *quite perfect*; and of Lord Lansdowne he said that, had he remained in the House of Commons he *must* have been minister of the country before this time'.[27]

Wellington had gone to considerable trouble in the Peninsula to keep party spirit out of the army. He worked hard to overcome the party prejudice of Whig officers whom he valued, such as Richard Bourke (whom he sent as liaison officer to Cuesta's army in 1809), Robert Craufurd (to whom he gave the plum command of the Light Division), and Sir Thomas Graham, whom he welcomed as his second-in-command. These men were all converted from initial hostility or scepticism to warm admiration. Even Wellington's personal staff came from a broad range of political backgrounds; they included the son of one Pittite Cabinet minister (Lord Burghersh, son of Lord Westmorland), and the cousin of another (Charles Fox Canning, cousin of George Canning), but also John Fremantle whose family were closely aligned to the Grenvillites, and Lord William Russell, scion of one of the greatest of Whig families, and himself an MP whose politics were more radical than Whig.[28]

The example of France also made Wellington very hostile to the idea of the army as a separate corporate body with political interests and influence of its own, rather than firmly integrated into the state and subservient to civil government. This was never a problem in Britain, partly because Wellington, and the Duke of York, had taken pains to keep politics out of senior military appointments; but also because senior British officers regarded themselves first and foremost as gentlemen, and when they entered Parliament were far more influenced by their personal opinions, their families and their patrons, than their profession. However, the role of the army was a problem in some other countries, and Wellington was clear that after the chaos of a revolution or in the midst of a restoration the first necessity was 'to form a government of such strength as that army and people can be forced by it to perform their duty'.[29] When he joined the Cabinet in 1818 Wellington did so as an individual, not as a representative of the army, nor as the advocate of the officers and men who had served under him in the Peninsula and at Waterloo. This disappointed some veterans and even led to some resentment, but it properly reflected the spirit of the constitution and was undoubtedly beneficial to the country as a whole.

Wellington's close connections to the Pittites had always added a partisan edge to the controversies surrounding his career. Whigs and radicals had relished the opportunity to attack a member of the government, and of a politically prominent family, in the outcry over Cintra; while they had vehemently criticised his return to Lisbon in 1809 and the government's commitment to the defence of Portugal in 1810. Masséna's retreat in the spring of 1811 confounded their predictions of disaster and led to a public *volte face*, but in private the Opposition continued to take a gloomy view of the war. The peace celebrations in 1814 brought a brief season of harmony with even Whitbread, the most radical of the leading Whigs, lauding his achievements. But this was soon ended by Napoleon's return from Elba, and the allied declaration outlawing him, which provoked Whitbread's extraordinary personal attack on Wellington.[30] Some Whigs and many radicals opposed a renewal of the war, arguing that it was purely a matter of internal French politics, while a few openly sympathised with Napoleon, seeing him as a champion of liberty.

News of Waterloo and the collapse of Napoleon's new regime confounded the dire predictions commonly made by the Whigs of a new and prolonged conflict; and the country, while mourning the long list of casualties, breathed a sigh of relief. Only five days after the battle, ministers moved thanks to Wellington and the army in Parliament. Lord Lansdowne, a prominent Whig peer, supported the motion, describing the victory as 'one of those events which formed the most valuable part of the national property and history', while in the Commons the vote was passed unanimously and with 'loud and long cheering'.[31] Specific motions thanking the officers, NCOs and private soldiers of the army and Britain's allies were also passed, with leading radicals such as Sir Francis Burdett and Whitbread speaking in their favour – the latter now going out of his way to heap praise on Wellington's courage and skill. The non-conformist MP for Norwich, William Smith, not only supported the grant of an additional £200,000 for Wellington, but said that he would support an even larger grant to ensure that a palace equal to Blenheim in magnificence was constructed, and this was supported by William Wilberforce.[32]

Nonetheless, critical voices did not stay silent for long, and 1816 saw a sharp reaction against both government spending and the reputation of the army and Wellington. 'Waste', 'corruption' and 'extravagance' proved a rewarding line of attack for the Opposition, winning widespread support both in the Commons and the country, which was suffering from an inevitable post-war economic slump. A wave of petitions and county meetings (some organised by MPs otherwise friendly to the government) urged the abolition of the wartime Property (or income) Tax, and despite the pleas of the ministers, the Commons voted it down in March 1816. This, combined with other reductions in taxation conceded under pressure at the same time, cut the disposable income of the government (once interest on the national debt had been paid) by almost a third. The ministers had no choice but to make deep cuts in their expenditure, most of which was on the army and navy. Inevitably this austerity had the effect of worsening the economic depression, although given that national debt amounted to approximately double the annual output of the entire economy, and that the government's share of the economy had risen from between 8 and 10 per cent in 1793 to as much as 20 per cent in the last years of the war, a contraction was probably necessary. However, the success of the campaign in 1816 encouraged the government's critics to press for further economies in subsequent years, and this debate dominated politics for several years.

The pressure to economise encouraged a narrowing of public attitudes and growing opposition to any close involvement in the affairs of the Continent. This mixed a sense of disenchantment – times were tough, victory in the war brought no tangible gain – with arrogance born of victory; Britain was secure enough to be able to ignore the Continent with impunity. Castlereagh's notorious inability to articulate his policy opened the door to this, for he could not catch the public imagination or explain that his aim was to create a much more harmonious and peaceful Europe, where the Great Powers would work together rather than act as rivals, resolving problems through consultation and lessening tensions through periodic meetings of leading statesmen.[33] This was obscured in his convoluted speeches and lost completely due to the unpopularity of the government and the invective poured upon Castlereagh (by Byron and Shelley among others), as the ministry's leading spokesman in the Commons. At the same time the public's attitude to the continental powers had changed; they were no longer seen as allies, or even as friends, but as despotic regimes which oppressed their people. This concept of 'despotism' was very useful; the term carried enormous pejorative overtones, but was sufficiently vague to be applicable to any and every country in Europe, and even at times to Britain itself. Only the United States could not be tarred with the same brush, and most British radicals found other grounds for dismissing the Americans with patronising praise or pure scorn.

There had been signs of this change of outlook as early as July 1814 with the hostility to Ferdinand VII which Wellington encountered at the Guildhall; while the caricaturists subsequently associated the Spanish King with symbols of Catholicism and gibbets, and the press gave sympathetic coverage to *liberale* exiles. Ferdinand offended opinion in Britain on two counts: not only had he dissolved the Cortes, abolished the Constitution of 1812, and imprisoned some *liberale* opponents; he had also refused to follow Britain in abolishing the slave trade. The campaign against slavery was a formidable force in the early nineteenth century, with the passionate commitment of well-connected leaders in Westminster and a vast network of activists, as well as the active goodwill of a large part of educated opinion. It was not satisfied when Britain renounced her part in the trade in 1807, and in 1814 eight hundred petitions signed by 750,000 people demanded that the British government insist that all the European powers agree to the ban without delay.[34] In the process the campaign played a major role in broadening the British political public, and creating a sense of moral superiority compared to the rest of Europe that was to grow stronger as the years passed.

But it was France that attracted the most attention from liberal and radical critics of the government's policies. Napoleon's defeat had been followed by the Second Restoration of Louis XVIII, a result which, while certainly not unpopular with the bulk of the British people, was regarded with dismay by many radicals. This was the view expressed by George Cruikshank in a series of caricatures including one showing France being tied to the ground and raped by the allies while having the Bourbons forced down her throat, and another where Louis reaches the top of the greasy pole by standing on Wellington's sword-point. Cruikshank's later prints attacking the Bourbons, including the extraordinary *The Royal Shambles* (August 1816), mixed motifs of popular radicalism with old-fashioned anti-Catholicism, depicting France as a bloody, priest-ridden despotism, whose government was only kept in place by British troops paid for by poor, long-suffering John Bull. Wellington figures prominently in these prints as the ally and instrument of oppression, the conquering hero Cruikshank had celebrated at Vitoria long forgotten.[35]

Remarkably, Cruikshank's work was scarcely more violent or extreme than the private views of many leading members of the Opposition, who displayed a vehement hostility towards Wellington which is hard to explain. Lord Holland took up the cause of Marshal Ney, arguing that his execution was a violation of the Convention of Paris and that 'nothing but Wellington's name could carry down so foul a transaction, so the whole odium of the breach of faith will fall on him and him only'. According to Wellington, who saw the original letter, Holland went on to accuse him of allowing that 'accomplished soldier to be judicially murdered, because I could not beat him in the field', although this does not appear in the version of the letter Holland printed in his memoirs. Wellington was always remarkably tolerant of political attacks upon him, but this was too much even for him to swallow, and he refused to speak to Holland for several years, although after he returned to England civilities were restored.[36]

Lord and Lady Holland were both leading liberal Whigs and great admirers of Napoleon; so their view of Wellington might have been expected to be jaundiced, especially in the months after Waterloo. But Lord Grey was scarcely more restrained, writing privately in 1816 that the growth of radical disturbances:

> seems to me to be tending, and is pushed by Burdett and his adherents, to a contest between the crown and the mob; in which those who ought to be the leaders of the people, and would be so if they could, will be driven from a sense of their own security to the support of the Crown; the success of which, with the assistance of the Duke of Wellington, and the worst army in spirit and principle that I believe ever existed in the world, will be probably the utter extinction of all Liberty.[37]

The Opposition was scarcely more restrained in public. Lord Grenville, of all people, opposed the presence of British troops in the Army of Occupation of France on the curious grounds that it would expose them to 'debauchery & vice', and that, because the expense was met by France, it undermined Parliament's constitutional control over the army. The young Lord John Russell went further, arguing in Parliament in February 1816 that:

> It might happen that evil counsellors should persuade a King of France to trample on his subjects, and British soldiers might be engaged as the instruments of detested tyranny. Already in Spain the prediction had been nearly verified. Sir William Blackstone had held, that the army only existed for the protection of the people; and after having been employed successfully in France in quelling the rising energies of a great people, our soldiers on their return would be well qualified to act the same disgusting scenes in England.[38]

The idea that the British army posed a danger to the constitution and traditional freedoms was taken up by many speakers in Parliament in 1816. Lord Lansdowne called for an enquiry into the size of the army, arguing that statesmen of all parties in the previous century had agreed that a large standing army was a threat to civil liberties. Lord Milton complained of the use of troops to police the streets on court days, protesting that this was a new and alarming innovation and that a trooper in the Horse Guards had, that very morning, behaved in an insolent manner to him. This trivial incident was used as the peg for a lengthy debate, with George Tierney accusing the ministers of attempting to accustom the populace to the sight of the soldiery being used on ordinary occasions. It was then raised in the Lords with Grenville, Grey and Holland – the most senior members of the Opposition – all treating it as a matter of great significance. Lord Holland declared that 'it was of the last importance that the people of the metropolis should not be familiarised to the sight of troops acting on such occasions without the control of the civil power, lest they should begin to look upon the military, not as their servants, which they really were, but as their masters'. In another debate the radical Lord Folkestone went even further, stating his apprehension that 'a military government was growing up in this country, and that there existed in certain quarters a wish and design to substitute a military despotism for the free constitution of this country'.[39]

In such a climate it is hardly surprising that the proposal to establish a London club for officers of the army and navy was viewed with grave suspicion, even though its chief proponent was Sir Thomas Graham, who was not only one of Wellington's most distinguished subordinates, but a lifelong Whig. Graham put forward the idea in May 1815 and received support from the Dukes of York and Wellington as well as a considerable number of senior officers. But even in November 1815, before the Opposition had begun their attacks on the army in Parliament, the Prime Minister was sensitive to the way such a club might be portrayed, and refused to lease it Crown Land, describing it as 'a most ill-advised measure, and so far from its being serviceable to the army, it will inevitably create a prejudice against that branch of our military establishment, and we shall feel the effects of it even in Parliament'. He was right. On 4 March 1816 Thomas Foley, a Whig MP and a colonel in the militia, presented a petition from the inhabitants of Leominster in Herefordshire expressing their alarm at the news of the formation of the club, and humbly hoping that the House of Commons 'will watch over, with a true constitutional jealousy, the proceedings of such a formidable military body, which appear to the petitioners to be too well calculated to render the military power of the country a body too distinct from the people, and consequently inconsistent with the true principles of a free government'. Opposition speakers supporting the petition dominated the lengthy debate which followed, and hammered away at the same theme: that the army, as the instrument of the ministers and the Crown, threatened to undermine the free constitution of the country and replace it with a military despotism.[40]

It is hard to know what effect these attacks had on the general public. On the one hand we are told that when Wellington visited England in 1816 he was 'follow'd and Huzza'd' and was as popular as he had been in 1814; but on the other, the petitions which flooded into Parliament denouncing the Property Tax also frequently condemned the retention of a large standing army as, to quote one example, 'hostile to the spirit of the *British* Constitution, and highly injurious to the best interests of society'.[41] What is striking is the weakness of the government's defence against these charges; none of the ministers rose to the occasion and rejected the allegations with scorn or indignation. They did little to defend the honour and reputation of Wellington or the army, or even make the obvious point that many of those who claimed to fear the establishment of a military despotism in Britain were open admirers of Napoleon, the very model of a military despot. Faced with incessant calls to slash spending on the army there was little effort to beat the patriotic drum and remind the House that the regiments which would be reduced, and the soldiers who would be discharged, were the very same who had triumphed at Waterloo less than a year before. The British army had never been as good as it was in 1814–15; substantial reductions were undoubtedly necessary to place it on a peace establishment and the government's finances in order, but Palmerston, the responsible minister, did nothing to make MPs and the country feel that these reductions were a painful necessity, not something intrinsically desirable. Whether from weakness or cool judgement that the spirit of the times was running too strongly in the other direction, the ministers abandoned their best ground without a fight and left the initiative almost entirely to their ideological opponents.

Throughout the post-war years the radical press disparaged Wellington and derided his achievements. For example, on the second anniversary of Waterloo, 18 June 1817, when most of London was preoccupied with the festivities associated with the opening of the new 'Waterloo' bridge over the Thames, Wooler's *Black Dwarf* published a song, 'The Waterloo Man', which savagely attacked the miseries of war: 'Humanity sickens to hear of the glory / Achieved on the day the dread slaughter began.' And it went on to suggest that the battle was a victory, not for freedom and justice, but for oppression. The *Examiner* reacted with embarrassment to news of the attempt on Wellington's life in 1818, relegating it to second place in the foreign news behind the death of the King of Sweden, suggesting that it may have been prompted by a private quarrel, and finally reminding its readers that an attempt had been made upon Napoleon's life by an 'infernal machine' (a bomb) in 1800. And in 1819 Cobbett told his readers: 'Napoleon was not put down by our armies ... but by perfidy, purchased with banknotes ... Wellington had no more to do, as to the putting down of Napoleon, than I had. It ought not to be called "Waterloo Bridge"; but "Paper-money Bridge".'[42]

When reports began to circulate that Wellington was to join the Cabinet in late 1818 the *Examiner* declared that 'the Duke of Wellington is a mere soldier, who manages things well enough when they are in a barrack-state, but no further'. The *Black Dwarf* went further:

This Duke is a very fortunate fellow! The King of France has rewarded his services to that country by a blue cord, and a diamond worth *twenty thousand pounds sterling!* To be sure his Grace has helped a little in the glorious endeavour to thin France of its population as much as possible; and it is but fair that he should have his share of the spoil produced by the friendly executions of Ney, Labedoyère, etc; but one could hardly think it would have amounted to Twenty Thousand Pounds! Besides a rope![43]

And the following year saw the publication of the first cantos of Byron's *Don Juan*, which opened with a sly dig at Wellington:

I want a hero: an uncommon want,
When every year and month sends forth a new one,
Till, after cloying the gazettes with cant,
The age discovers that he is not the true one.[44]

Radicals, and radical poets, represented only one strand of opinion in Britain, and many other people of all classes continued to take pride in the victory over Napoleon and to admire Wellington. But although he continued to be surrounded by cheering crowds on his visits to England after 1815, there seems little doubt that the criticism of him and the army made a considerable impression, and that his reputation was once more a matter for party feeling, after the almost universal acclaim which he had received in the summer of 1814.

The Opposition had faced a problem in 1814–15. It had always been half-hearted and defeatist in its attitude to the war, while many on the radical fringe were open in their sympathy for Napoleon. This put it at odds with the great bulk of the public, who were delighted with the victory and predisposed to give the credit for it to the ministers who had kept their nerve through so many difficulties.[45] One way in which the Opposition could regain political momentum was to recast the debate and depict the army and Wellington not as military heroes who had triumphed over the country's enemies, but as a financial burden on the struggling taxpayer, and as a threat to civil liberties and an instrument of oppression and despotism. This line of attack proved extraordinarily effective, partly because it tapped into a long-standing British tradition of anti-militarism which dated back to the seventeenth century. The financial position of the country was genuinely difficult, and the government accepted the need for large spending cuts which inhibited ministers from taking a more assertive line in defence of the army. And the press, caricaturists and at least a slice of the public were strongly inclined to favour liberal and even radical views. There is no reason to believe that the Opposition took this line cynically; on the contrary, the private correspondence of senior Whigs suggests that they really believed that the Regent, his ministers, Wellington and the army were a danger to the constitution, just as, a few years earlier, they had really believed that Napoleon was a man of peace and liberal views whose outlook on the world reflected the values of the Glorious Revolution of 1688!

In the summer of 1818, almost six years after the 1812 election, Britain went to the polls. Although there was little enthusiasm for the Whigs, the government did quite badly, especially in the prestigious county seats and those with a large, relatively open franchise. The old power of the ministry of the day to influence an election heavily in its favour (which was one of the bedrocks of the constitution, for the King's ability to choose his servants ultimately rested upon it) had been severely eroded, if not worn completely away. The government could still expect to have a majority on questions of confidence and most important issues of policy, but party allegiances were far from clear cut and the strength of each party would remain uncertain until it was tested on the floor of the Commons. Wellington's prestige might give the government some assistance, but its fate would depend on its measures, the performance of the leading ministers (especially those in the Commons), and whether it succeeded in conveying a sense of competence and purpose both to Parliament and to the wider public.

CHAPTER EIGHT

THE RADICAL CHALLENGE
(1819)

WELLINGTON ARRIVED IN London from the Continent on 21 December 1818. It was a cold, dismal Christmas with a hard frost and unrelenting fog so dense that the artist Joseph Farington required candles at noon. Road accidents were frequent, and ten people were said to have been fatally injured after being run down by carriages in just a few days. Nonetheless Wellington was out and about, spending his first afternoon in long discussions with Castlereagh at the Foreign Office, Bathurst at the Colonial Office, and the Duke of York at the Horse Guards. On the following day he attended Cabinet at the Lord Chancellor's house, and then rode to Carlton House to pay his respects to the Regent. He formally took office as Master-General of the Ordnance on 26 December and was soon hard at work mastering the intricacies of his new department.[1]

Wellington's first seven months in office passed quietly. He made no attempt to dazzle the House of Lords with his oratory. His years in the Commons a decade before had established him as a workmanlike speaker at best, and he had not been taking lessons. His only speech of real significance was on 17 May when he spoke near the end of a long debate on the Catholic Question, declaring his opposition to any concession. He argued that none of the proposed securities offered to protect the Protestant Establishment was remotely adequate, and went on: 'I believe that no doubt can be entertained, considering their present feelings, that if the Roman Catholics were admitted to the enjoyments of political power, their first exertion would be to restore their religion to its original supremacy, and to recover the possessions and property of which they were stripped by the Reformation.' Faced with such uncompromising rhetoric, it is unlikely that anyone paid much attention to the opening of the speech, in which Wellington declared that for him, 'the whole of this question turns upon the expediency of removing the disabilities of which the Irish Roman Catholic complain, and upon what concessions can safely be made to them'. Yet this was important, for it made plain from the outset that Wellington's opposition to

Catholic Emancipation was essentially pragmatic; the risks and disadvantages of granting concessions outweighed the advantages. Neither issues of abstract justice nor the theological merits (or de-merits) of either Church weighed heavily with him; and, while sceptical, he would continue to look with interest at any proposal that offered the promise of solving the question without endangering the Protestant Establishment.[2]

Although Wellington opposed Catholic Emancipation, he disapproved of the Orange Order and the vehement, anti-Catholic sectarianism it promoted, arguing that he could not support any society from which 'a large proportion of his Majesty's subjects must be excluded, many of them as loyal men as exist, and as much attached to the Constitution'. He added that his 'life had been passed in transactions with persons of that and of all other religious persuasions', and that he had never found that 'the religious persuasion of individuals or of nations affected their feelings of loyalty to their Sovereign, or of attachment to the laws and constitution of their country'.[3]

Wellington took a much more prominent role in London society than in Parliament. On 28 May he took the chair at the annual dinner of the Pitt Club in London. Pitt Clubs tended to be annexed by the more conservative wing of the party, preferring to emphasise the 'Pilot who weathered the Storm', rather than the reformer of the 1780s, or the politician who throughout his life regarded himself as a Whig. Pitt's promises of Catholic Emancipation as part of the union with Ireland, and his resignation in 1801, were quietly forgotten, and toasts were drunk to 'Protestant Ascendancy'.[4] This was an overtly political occasion, but Wellington was also besieged by invitations to chair or take part in many other public dinners, often in aid of good causes, and he had already accepted honorary positions on many hospitals and other charities which hoped his prestige would give them an added éclat. As always the competition among such bodies was fierce, and Wellington had the added advantage of novelty where many of the 'lions' were not only rather shabby but all too familiar. W.T. Fitzgerald, who was helping to organise the dinner of the Royal Literary Fund in 1819, expressed this hierarchy in his reaction to the news that the Duke of Kent had withdrawn due to the advanced state of the Duchess's pregnancy: 'I really fear that we shall make but a bad figure without a Royal Chairman . . . the lying in Hospital found means to put in their chair the greatest of all Great Guns! The Duke of Wellington – most heartily do I wish we could do the same.'[5]

Wellington also took an active part in the whirl of society and evidently enjoyed it. Lady Shelley found him at Mrs Edward Bouverie's one evening in March. He was 'in high spirits . . . [and] talked to me almost the whole evening, a distinction not only great in itself, but also valuable, because it promotes the *agréments* of London life. It is a relief from dullness, and it excites attention from others. Alas! poor human nature! that such despicable vanities should be able, even for one moment, to increase the sum of human happiness! but so it is'. A week later she saw him again and had another long conversation. 'It is agreed that we are to meet the Duke every day about five o'clock in the Green Park; at which hour he always takes a gallop between the duties of his office and his attendance at the House of Lords.'[6]

Maria Edgeworth, visiting from Ireland, was rather less impressed, and even failed to recognise her old acquaintance: 'He looks so old and wrinkled I never should have known him from likeness to bust or picture.' (Given that he was not quite fifty when this was written, it may be a little exaggerated, although equally there is little doubt that most portraits of the period rather flattered their subjects.) 'His manner', Edgeworth continued, was 'very agreeable perfectly simple and dignified. He said only a few words but listened to some literary conversation that was going on as if he felt amused laughing once heartily. It was lucky for me that I did not know who he was for the very fear of falling on dangerous subjects about husbands and wives in various novels we discussed would have inevitably brought me into some scrape had I known who he was. On the contrary I talked on quite at my ease.'[7]

For all its pleasures London life did not entirely agree with Wellington. The late nights, stuffy rooms and – despite his daily gallop in the Park – lack of physical exercise made him sleep badly and feel unwell. Travel and a return to his old habits might effect a cure, and as soon as he could be free of London, he set off for the Continent, early in August 1819. The principal purpose of the trip was to inspect progress on the barrier fortresses in the Low Countries. He reached Brussels on 8 August after a 'tolerably good' passage to Ostend of fourteen hours. Nonetheless he admitted to Mrs Arbuthnot: 'I was not what is called sick, but very miserable instead & not able to move from a Mattress on which I lay from the moment I embarked till I quitted the ship.' Once ashore he set a lively pace, inspecting the works at Ostend, Nieuport and Antwerp in two days and having talks with the King and the Prince of Orange before moving on.[8]

While Wellington was on the Continent, the simmering discontent and reform agitation which had been building since the start of the year in the manufacturing parts of Britain came to a head, presenting the government with a serious problem that would dominate politics for the next two years. Wellington played an active part in devising the government's response, drawing on his experiences of actual and potential civil unrest in India, Ireland and France. At the same time his reputation, and that of the army, was the subject of fierce debate in the ideological struggle which was waged with great intensity as the government's authority was challenged more directly.

This outbreak of popular radicalism had long antecedents, stretching right back to the outcry over Cintra in 1808 and the Mary Anne Clark affair in 1809.

It was often associated with mass demonstrations which could easily turn into riots. In 1810 Piccadilly was occupied by crowds for three days, preventing the arrest of Sir Francis Burdett for contempt of Parliament; while between 1810 and 1812 much of the midlands and the north of England was affected by the Luddite disturbances. In May 1812 the news that the Prime Minister, Spencer Perceval, had been assassinated in the lobby of the House of Commons was greeted in some parts of the country with popular rejoicing; while in 1815 the introduction of the Corn Laws led to extensive rioting in London. Radical agitation increased in 1816, fed by the hard times that followed the end of the war and the adjustment to peace. This culminated in a series of mass meetings at Spa Fields in London. At the second of these meetings a breakaway group of extreme radicals headed into the City behind a tricolour and began looting the shops of gunsmiths, seizing arms and killing a bystander for no obvious reason. Order was eventually restored, but the revolutionary intent was obvious and was supported both by the evidence collected by the Home Office and by the rhetoric of the radicals themselves.[9]

The government had limited means of responding to such trouble. The police force in London was tiny and fragmented, amounting to only 250 officers, divided between five different organisations for a city of 1.3 million inhabitants. Yet increasing the force even to this level had been denounced by Romilly, Brougham and other champions of civil liberty. The only alternative was calling out the army, but this was a crude measure which often led to a poorly calibrated response. The role of the troops was sharply defined and circumscribed. They could only act at the behest of a magistrate who must first read the proclamation prescribed in the Riot Act to the crowd, taking care to do so exactly, and then give protesters a full hour to disperse. (In practice it was usual for the proclamation to be read repeatedly and several hours to be given – bluff being infinitely preferable to the use of force.) Only when this warning went unheeded might the magistrate order the soldiers to clear the streets and, when they did so, their usual course was to fire in the air or use the butts of their muskets and the flat side of their sabre rather than more lethal force. Sometimes greater violence was used and demonstrators were killed or wounded, and this was frequently followed by legal proceedings against the soldiers. Officers and even common soldiers knew that the law would not necessarily protect them, which was one reason why they hated the duty. There were others: even if they were not required to act against the crowd they were likely to be taunted, abused and pelted with mud, filth and stones possibly for hours without being allowed to make any response. They would normally be very heavily outnumbered and had no special equipment with which to protect themselves, while their muskets and swords were not that much more effective than brickbats and paving stones in a scrimmage. And the service was wholly negative; neither glory nor plunder was to be gained however well they did their duty when faced with a mob of their own countrymen, and if things got out of hand the inhabitants of the town were likely to bear them a grudge and blacken their name. Like most soldiers Wellington disliked the use of soldiers to deal with civil disturbances, and at the time of the Burdett Riots pointed to another disadvantage when he commented: 'Let [the ministers] take care that they don't set fire to the extinguisher, or that the soldiers don't join the mob.'[10]

The Spa Fields riot in 1816 convinced the government it had to act. Parliament's prejudice and demands for economy meant that there was no possibility of establishing a strong, effective police force, so ministers introduced repressive legislation including the suspension of Habeas Corpus following the precedents employed by Pitt in the 1790s. Committees of both Houses, whose members included a number of moderate Whigs and Grenvillites, supported the proposals, convinced by the evidence of danger of revolutionary activity. On paper the new legislation was draconian and posed a serious threat to cherished liberties, but in practice this was softened by the great difficulties of launching successful prosecutions. A few unfortunate souls were punished with excessive severity, but many more were never even charged because magistrates felt unsure of the law or feared local unpopularity. The celebrated trial and acquittal of William Hone, the radical bookseller and publisher, in 1817, showed that whatever the facts of the case, and however flagrant the guilt of the accused, British juries would not convict in political cases when they sympathised with the defendant or felt that the judge was biased. Nonetheless the legislation, and a reaction against the extremism of some of the radicals associated with the Spa Fields meetings, led to a reduction in radical activity in 1817 and 1818.

Ministers were far less insulated or protected from these disturbances than they are in a modern bureaucratic democracy; Westmorland was pelted with mud from head to toe during the Burdett Riots and, three days before Waterloo, Castlereagh was chased through the streets by a radical mob and only escaped because he kept his head and was well mounted. During the Corn Law riots Lord Eldon, the Lord Chancellor, had to flee his house with his family, escaping through the back wall into the grounds of the British Museum, while rioters vandalised his drawing room. Eldon then returned with a handful of soldiers, who cleared the house with bluff rather than force. The Lord Chancellor personally seized two men by the collar and told them they would be hanged, whereupon one responded that the people were far more likely to hang him! Both men were sent before a JP but the soldiers coolly declined to give evidence and the prisoners had to be released. The Prince Regent was frequently hissed and booed when he opened Parliament, and in the years to come Wellington would be both cheered and abused by a populace that was never afraid to give voice to its opinion.[11]

Fresh trouble erupted in March 1819 at a by-election for Westminster caused by the suicide of Samuel Romilly. The Whig, George Lamb, defeated the radical John Cam Hobhouse (Byron's friend), with the even more radical 'Orator' Hunt running a distant third. A mob set fire to the house containing Lamb's committee-room, forcing him to escape through an upper window and across the rooftops, before being escorted home to Melbourne House by a detachment of Life Guards. Brooks's club, the Whig bastion, was defended by a curious mixture of constables, strong sedan-chairmen and 'gentlemen of the ring'. This deterred an attack and the crowd contented themselves with throwing stones, breaking all the windows of Castlereagh's house, and forcing his neighbours to flee through their garden and over its walls.[12]

But the most sustained radical activity in 1819 was in the north of England – in Lancashire, Yorkshire and a few surrounding districts. In January 'Orator' Hunt had addressed a meeting of some 8,000 people at Manchester and encouraged them, not to petition the Prince Regent for reform, but to issue a remonstrance to him for denying them their rights, which were now asserted to include annual Parliaments and universal suffrage. Subsequent meetings were held in many towns across northern England where the worsening trade slump created many grievances. On 7 June delegates from twenty-eight towns met at Oldham and agreed to have a national meeting in London. The challenge to Parliament's legitimacy was deliberate and driven home by holding mock elections for towns which were unrepresented in the Commons. Three weeks later at a meeting at Stockport Sir Charles Wolseley declared that he had been present at the storming of the Bastille and 'was not idle on that glorious day', while the Rev. Joseph Harrison told the crowd that the people were being checked by the barrier of corruption and 'must blow it up or blow it down'. At Blackburn a Waterloo veteran spoke from the platform and 'begged pardon for having fought in so bad a cause'. The agitation spread to London where, on 21 July, a mass meeting at Smithfield resolved that Parliament was not properly constituted and that its Acts would cease to be binding on 1 January 1820.[13]

The Manchester magistrates were seriously alarmed and repeatedly warned the Home Office that matters were moving towards a crisis. A huge meeting was planned for Manchester for 9 August, but it was banned by the magistrates – so that the organisers postponed it for a week. Warned of impending trouble the Home Secretary, Lord Sidmouth, ensured that troops were at hand to maintain order, but advised the magistrates against any attempt to disperse the crowd. All through the morning of 16 August people poured in to St Peter's Fields just outside Manchester; they were generally peaceful and orderly, for the organisers had gone to great pains to minimise the usual rowdiness of a late

Georgian gathering. Contingents from many nearby towns marched in, led by banners and accompanied by musical instruments, while seats on the main platform were already occupied by representatives of the press – both local and London papers. By the time Hunt arrived at one o'clock the crowd was calculated to be 60,000 strong, although there is no way that this estimate can be verified. The magistrates then decided that the meeting 'bore the appearance of an insurrection', and ordered that Hunt be arrested. Joseph Nadin, the Deputy Constable of Manchester, not unnaturally requested military assistance to execute the warrant, and forty men from the Manchester and Salford Yeomanry Cavalry were given the task. Exactly what happened next is much disputed, but it seems that Hunt was arrested and that the Yeomanry either got into trouble while trying to withdraw, or attempted to disperse the crowd. The people panicked and there was a stampede; a detachment of the 15th Hussars was sent in to help extricate the Yeomanry; and sabres were drawn and used. In the end eleven people were killed and some four hundred injured, many of the latter being hurt as the crowd panicked.[14]

News of these unfortunate events reached Sidmouth on the following day and after consulting the few other ministers who were at hand, he recommended that the Prince Regent formally congratulate the authorities, both civil and military, for the 'firmness', 'zeal' and 'alacrity' with which they had 'preserved the peace of the town upon that most critical occasion'. It is probable that this encomium was written on the basis of partial and misleading information, and there is little doubt that it did as much as the events in Manchester themselves to arouse indignation and offend wavering opinion. Yet even in private the ministers showed no inclination to retreat from their stand. Canning, who was not present when the decision was taken, thoroughly approved, while Wellington cheerfully tolerated Lady Shelley's 'twitting' him with the rumour that attributed the decision to him personally. In fact he had yet to return from the Continent when the decision was taken, but agreed with its necessity. None of this means that the ministers actually believed that the magistrates had handled the situation well – there was a good deal of quiet muttering over their tactics, but also a strong sense that this was not a moment for recriminations or any sign of weakness. As Wellington remarked: 'Unless the magistrates had been supported in this instance, other magistrates on future occasions would not act at all; and then what a state the country would be in!'[15]

News of the events in Manchester and the Regent's message spread across the country, unleashing a wave of indignation and support for the radicals which was greatly encouraged by the press. There were riots in Macclesfield on 17 August in which the houses of yeomen and special constables were attacked, and disturbances in Stockport. The atmosphere in Manchester itself was highly charged, with troops patrolling the streets and much talk of preparations for an insurrection. On 25 August a meeting at the Crown and Anchor Tavern in London raised a subscription of almost £4,000 'for prosecuting the authors of the outrages at Manchester, and relieving the sufferers'. The radicals themselves were delighted that for once they could appear as the innocent victims, not the instigators of violence and disorder, and were determined to milk the occasion for all it was worth. Day after day newspapers recycled the tale of the 'massacre', as it was soon called, with the crowd becoming larger and more peaceful, and the soldiers becoming more brutal and bloodthirsty, with every retelling. The caricaturists took up the cause with glee, with half a dozen prints driving home the same message. George Cruikshank's *Massacre at St Peter's or "Britons Strike Home!!!"* has become one of the best-known prints of the era, constantly reproduced, and accepted by many casual viewers as an accurate representation of events, rather than a far from subtle piece of party propaganda. On 21 August the *Manchester Observer* coined the term 'Peter Loo' as a name for the event, and despite the evident absurdity of equating the mishandling of a crowd which resulted in fewer than a dozen deaths with a battle which saw 50,000 casualties, the name, reduced to a single word, has stuck.[16]

On 9 September the Common Council of the City of London resolved that the Manchester meeting was lawful and blamed the violence exclusively on the magistrates and yeomanry, addressing the Regent to express their 'strongest indignation . . . [at the] unprovoked and intemperate proceedings'. Four days later Hunt, free on bail, entered the city in triumphant procession with a large red flag inscribed 'Liberty or Death'. At the end of the month the election of a new Lord Mayor gave the populace the chance to express their feelings, not by voting but by stopping the carriages of the well-to-do and abusing those inside. And on 2 October the *Democratic Recorder and Reformists Guide* wrote: 'If ever it was the duty of Britons to resort to the use of arms to recover their freedom and hurl vengeance upon the heads of their tyrants it is now.'[17]

More alarming for Wellington and the other ministers were reports from northern England, especially those by Major-General Sir John Byng, which warned of further serious trouble. Byng was a capable and experienced officer who has been praised by a historian sympathetic to the radicals for his 'shrewdness and impartiality', and for 'his firmness combined with sympathy for the springs of the discontent'.[18] He was principally responsible to the Home Secretary, but he also wrote to Wellington, for the Ordnance was answerable for the security of arms depots and fortified places, and for the artillery under Byng's command. Moreover Byng had served under Wellington as a young man in the 33rd in the 1790s, and again in the Peninsula, and clearly valued his judgement. In September he was anxious about Hull, where there was a substantial magazine of arms and ammunition. Radical agitators had been active there in 1817 and had recently returned, giving soldiers seditious tracts and pamphlets and apparently reconnoitring to see if they might capture the weapons by a *coup de main*. As the weeks passed he saw no sign of the danger lessening. In late October he reported: 'By the accounts received today, the Radicals are much divided about their meetings for Monday next, but the majority are decidedly in favour of Thistlewood, who has superseded Hunt in their idolatry, a convincing proof how anxious they are for immediate revolution.' A week later he was able to confirm that the 'disaffected leaders in Lancashire are quarrelling among themselves', and added: 'I cannot but think it desirable they should come to extremities. I cannot hope the country will return to a state of peace without it. I am satisfied with my force, but I wish that I had more efficient magistrates in Lancashire. They are in general very inefficient.'[19]

Wellington responded by taking action on specific points such as ordering the repair of the defences of many castles and other strongholds, reinforcing Byng with additional artillery and some spring carts from Leith which might transport a modest force more rapidly than they could march, and by at least one long letter of general advice. Writing on 21 October he expressed the fear that 'a general and simultaneous rising' aimed at the 'plunder of the rich towns and houses which will fall in their way' might be imminent. It was most important that Byng not succumb to the temptation to disperse his force in small detachments in an effort to guard every town and place of importance. That would simply invite defeat in detail which would embolden the troublemakers and undermine the prestige and confidence of the soldiers.

> As long as no misfortune happens to them, the mischief will be confined to plunder and a little *murder* and will not be irretrievable. But it is impossible to foresee how far it will go if the mob should in any instance get the better of the troops. I put out of the question them corrupting the troops, unless they are remarkably changed since I knew them about a twelvemonth ago, and unless the mob should have some success against them.[20]

Nonetheless he advised against quartering the troops on the population; better to use large barns, warehouses or even bivouac them in huts, so long as they had ample material for fires or else they would find their way to the nearest public house, which might result in trouble. He also recommended that cavalry only be used when infantry be available to support them, and that detachments not be smaller than two or three hundred men, except when garrisoning a stronghold. This was not only excellent advice in itself, it would also be useful in helping Byng to withstand the many pressing applications for assistance he was bound to receive from local mill owners and others for small bodies of troops to guard their properties, for it was something to be able to cite Wellington's opinion in support of his own when refusing their importunities.[21]

A few weeks later, in mid-November, Wellington told Robert Plumer Ward, the capable Clerk of the Ordnance, that 'the Radicals no longer concealed their true object', which was 'that the gentry had possessed their estates long enough and it was now their turn. This object they might carry had they arms, which we know . . . they have not, and must take care to prevent their getting them.' He went on: 'public opinion was everything; and if a piece of cannon, or 1500 stand of arms were once taken by the mob, no matter with how little exertion, it would go far to produce a revolution at once'. Yet when Plumer Ward suggested that a partial rising, firmly suppressed, might clear the air, Wellington strongly disagreed, pointing not only to the direct suffering of innocent as well as guilty, but the fact that it would inevitably cause much economic damage which would increase distress and so fuel further discontent. Besides, radicals throughout the country would exploit trouble for their own political purposes, just as they had done with the events in Manchester.[22]

While the government took precautions against a general insurrection the Whigs hesitated for some time, uncertain whether to try to take the lead in the protests, or to stay quiet in the hope that this would help calm the situation. Eventually Earl Fitzwilliam threw his immense local prestige behind the call for a Yorkshire meeting, and the rest of the party swung obediently into line behind one of the greatest of Whig magnates. The government responded by dismissing Fitzwilliam as Lord Lieutenant and by recalling Parliament. Government lawyers set to work drafting legislation to limit seditious meetings, ban secret military training, limit the right to bear arms, and try to check the flood of cheap seditious newspapers and literature, while not pressing too hard on traditional support for the freedom of the press. The result was the 'Six Acts' that made the law rather more effective, while never amounting to the straitjacket of repression that radical writers and politicians loved to denounce.[23]

Before Parliament met, Liverpool and Arbuthnot, the Treasury Secretary, went to some pains to test the feeling of a range of independent or unaligned MPs, and were much encouraged by the results. The Grenvilles were firmly in support of the government's proposals, with even Tom Grenville, Fox's friend and the most liberal member of the family, having no doubt that the Manchester meeting posed a serious threat to the stability of the country. This was part of a wider reaction against the radicals, whose extravagant language and menaces had cost them much of the sympathy they had received in August. Brougham told Grey: 'The Radicals have made themselves so odious, that a number even of our way of thinking would be well enough pleased to see them and their vile Press put down at all hazards.' Even the caricaturists wavered, attacking the whole cause of reform as threatening to plunge the country into revolution. This change of heart was only transitory – the Six Acts galvanised George

Cruikshank into some of his most influential and radical work – but it represented an important check in the tide of opinion.[24]

The new session opened quietly on 23 November. In the weeks that followed the Whigs argued in favour of moderation and conciliation; called for an inquiry into the events at Manchester; and re-affirmed their commitment to civil liberties and British freedom: all of which was excellent for their self-esteem and would help their reputation in years to come, but which did nothing to convince the waverers in Parliament who had come up to London convinced that strong measures were needed to save the country from anarchy. Overall the ministers were surprised with the progress their legislation made, and the few concessions they were required to make (one of the bills was given a 'sunset clause' limiting it to five years). Wellington spoke once on 10 December on a point of detail, and took an unusually keen interest in the debates in both Houses, commenting that Canning's speech was 'remarkably good in every point but length': two hours would have been quite sufficient. He also praised Lord Eldon's speech on the Address, and Lord Grenville's speech a few days later which 'put the Manchester case much higher than it was put by the Government'; but he showed less enthusiasm for Lord Wellesley's speech on the same occasion, evidently finding it too high-flown and lacking in practical arguments.[25]

On the day of the opening of Parliament Lady Shelley mentioned in her diary a cheap, simple little booklet of twenty-four pages that had recently been published. 'The Political House That Jack Built is the best, and yet the most dangerous satire ever written; its sale has been prodigious. It went through twenty editions in a month. Its author is supposed to be [William] Hone.'[26] No doubt she exaggerated, but not without cause. Modelled on a familiar children's nursery rhyme, which had often been used in the past by satirists, Hone's work was nonetheless revolutionary in almost every sense. The simple text, where each verse repeated and added to what had gone before, was easy to read and understand, while the thirteen woodcuts by George Cruikshank illustrated and added to the argument, often exploiting the traditional immunity of an artist to make more explicit the message of the text. 'This is the House that Jack built'; 'This is the wealth that lay in the House that Jack built' (a treasure chest containing, not gold and silver, but Magna Carta, Habeas Corpus and the Bill of Rights); 'These are the Vermin that Plunder the Wealth that lay in the House that Jack Built' (a Court Chamberlain, two soldiers, a clerical magistrate, a tax collector and a barrister – some possibly intended as recognisable portraits of individuals). And so on, with the printing press hailed as the 'poison' for the vermin, but under threat from 'the public informer' and 'the Reasons of Lawless Power' (the army). The most famous verse, and sharpest drawing, attacks the Prince Regent:

This is THE MAN – all shaven and shorn,
   All covered with Orders – and all forlorn;
THE DANDY OF THE SIXTY,
   who bows with a grace,
And has *taste* in wigs, collars,
   cuirasses and lace;
Who to tricksters, and fools,
   leaves the State and its treasure,
And, when Britain's in tears,
   Sails about at his pleasure . . .

The next page shows 'The People all tatter'd and torn, who curse the day wherein they were born . . . Who, peaceably Meeting to ask for Reform, were sabred by Yeomanry and Cavalry'. Another page attacked the ministers, singling out Sidmouth, Castlereagh and Canning. And Wellington? He appears in the most prominent place of all, a drawing on the title page where he drops his sword into a balance on the side which already holds the legal instruments of repression, but which is nonetheless outweighed by a single feather: the writer's quill.[27]

   The radical press had continued its personal attacks on Wellington in 1819. In February the *Black Dwarf* criticised his appointment to the government on the grounds of extravagance: 'The Waterloo Duke has become head clerk of the Ordnance Department, and signs his name twice or four times a year for his salary.'[28] And, four months later, it struck another chord:

It is said our burthens should be borne patiently. Be it so, when *all* consent to *bear them alike*. Why should the peasant suffer, and the prince be exempt from suffering? Why should the artist want bread, and the public pensioner wallow in luxury? Why must the magnificence of the court, be purchased by the misery of the cottage? Why should the Duke of Wellington amass a princely fortune, while his fellow soldiers are begging their daily subsistence, and would be thankful for the refuse of his table?[29]

   In the wake of 'Peterloo' the old attacks on Wellington and the army as the instrument of oppression and despotism were revived with redoubled force. In *The Political House that Jack Built* 'Reform' is the panacea 'that the WATERLOO-MAN's to crush with his sword', if the Whigs and the people don't stop him. Elsewhere Wellington is depicted as a butcher about to slaughter a bull (John Bull) that is weighed to the ground by a pyramid of placemen, courtiers, soldiers and parsons, with the crown surmounting the whole. And in another print he is 'Waterloo-Man' with a placard on his chest inscribed 'Coruption [*sic*] Prize Money £60,000 Allowances £200,000 & c & c'. He holds a dagger which transfixes a bleeding heart and on his back a label reads 'Inquisition'. The associated text claims that he saved the Spanish nation only to send them to perdition under Ferdinand. All the emotive newspaper accounts of 'Peterloo' and subsequent prints such as *Britons Strike Home!!!* depicted the army as the enemy of the people. Later prints frequently show military symbols as the bulwark of the Crown, with a print of late 1820 showing Wellington directly advocating the violent suppression of all dissent.[30] A simpler and more potent design came in *The Man in the Moon*, a sequel by Hone and Cruikshank to *The Political House That Jack Built*, where one illustration shows the soldiery brutally thrusting their swords and bayonets down the gaping mouths of terrified civilians. The heading 'Steel Lozenges' plays upon a popular patent medicine, while the design points to the threat to free speech and the press as well as to the use of the army against demonstrations. (However, the very power and force of this and other radical literature of the period makes any threat to freedom of expression appear somewhat hypothetical.)[31]

Conservatives did not stay silent in the face of this flood of subversive literature, and the caricaturists were often equally ready to abuse both sides. They were helped by the venomous divisions among the radicals themselves, and by the innate conservatism of a society that, for example, found the idea of working-class women radicals inherently ridiculous.[32] And much as clerical magistrates were hated, the irreligion or outright atheism of some extreme radicals was also the cause of alarm and even horror.[33] The strong sympathy shown by many of the radicals for Napoleon and France, especially in 1815, provided good grounds for questioning their patriotism and loyalty. These themes were picked up in many of the replies-in-kind to Hone's work, such as *The Real or Constitutional House That Jack Built* where 'Order is heaven's first law'. Here the dedication is to 'The lovers of Peace and the True Friends of Old England'; the 'Treasure' of the house includes not just the Bible, but an early steamship and a fruitful harvest; Napoleon is one of the thieves who would plunder the treasure; and Wellington is the most prominent of a group of patriots, 'the Heroes of Britain – the Gems of her Crown', who defended the country.[34]

Attempts were also made to establish newspapers that would challenge the radicals and proclaim the benefits of the existing order of society, although such efforts were frequently still-born or transitory. Early in 1819 Wellington gave some financial assistance to one such proposal for an 'independent weekly' whose views would reflect those of Lord Wellesley; and in the following year he encouraged an abortive attempt to establish a 'patriotic' paper in Southampton. In 1820 he subscribed £25 for the Constitutional Association for Opposing the Progress of Disloyal and Seditious Principles, which was intended to encourage the enforcement of the libel laws; and unlike some of his colleagues, he saw no need to conceal his identity behind misleading initials.[35]

Despite this highly charged partisan atmosphere, not all the popular depictions of Wellington at this time were overtly political. Richard Dighton produced a print of the Duke as 'Master-General of the Ordinance [*sic*]' which was a straightforward, if somewhat heavy, full-length portrait. And in the spring of 1819 a brief fashion for velocipedes led to a number of mostly good-humoured prints that poked fun at great men without any edge of hostility. 'The Master of the Ordnance Exercising his Hobby' shows a handsome Wellington astride a large cannon which is aimed at three fashionable ladies who affect to take alarm. One lady remarks: 'Bless us! what a Spanker! I hope he won't fire it at me – I could never support such a thing!' Her friend consoles her: 'It can't do any harm, for he has fir[e]d it so often in various Countries, that it is nearly wore it [*sic*: worn out].' This ribaldry was disrespectful and hardly flattering, but no worse than any public figure had to expect in Regency England.[36]

In late September and early October 1819 Wellington paid a visit to the West Country to inspect a small estate he owned in Somerset and to meet the Prince Regent at Plymouth. It was six weeks after 'Peterloo', which *The Times* had covered in great and indignant detail. Nonetheless it gave lavish and indulgent coverage to Wellington's expedition, reproducing articles from local papers without jibbing at their fulsome tone. When the Duke arrived in Bath, 'the intelligence was no sooner become public than crowds assembled to obtain a sight of this illustrious warrior'. Introduced to an old comrade in arms, 'he shook him most heartily by the hand, and made several enquiries about all his family'. He visited the Masonic Hall 'and remained there upwards of a quarter of an hour: he expressed himself more highly pleased with its splendid appearance than with that of any foreign lodge he had visited'. Three long reports in the space of a week described his activities in the inane detail and fawning manner that the press was to use for royalty and other celebrities for the next two centuries. But it is just this comfortable complacency, at the very moment that Sir John Byng was devising his plan against an imminent insurrection, that is significant. The rural counties of southern England were relatively prosperous and untroubled in 1819, while even in London support for the radicals was tinged with ambivalence.[37]

By the end of 1819 the ministers could feel a little reassured. The wave of radical agitation was not over, but the crisis precipitated by the events at Manchester had passed without further serious violence, and while there was still much talk of revolution, moderate opinion had rallied behind the existing constitution. Early in the New Year Wellington told a colleague: 'Radicalism was for a time completely got under, that the public were pleased with Ministers for it, and were in tolerable humour.'[38] However, this was overly optimistic, for the radicals remained full of vitality and were still popular in many parts of the country, while the ideological struggle continued with redoubled intensity. 1820 would be a tumultuous year.

CHAPTER NINE

THE QUEEN'S AFFAIR
(1820–21)

O N 29 JANUARY 1820 George III, the half-forgotten, half-revered, 'mad' old King at Windsor, died in the sixtieth year of his reign, and the Prince Regent at last came to the throne as King George IV. His accession at once precipitated a dispute over the official position of his estranged wife Caroline of Brunswick that almost led to the fall of the government. George had wanted a divorce even before the death of their daughter, Princess Charlotte, in 1817, although it is not clear whether he had serious thoughts of remarriage, or simply wished to sever himself utterly from the wife whom he loathed and abhorred. The ministers were most reluctant to have anything to do with the question. It was true that there were many reports in circulation of the indiscretion and indelicacy of Caroline's behaviour since she left England in 1814, but it might still be difficult to prove infidelity in court, while George's series of mistresses and personal unpopularity ensured that the public would almost certainly sympathise with the wife, not the husband. In 1819 Brougham, acting for Caroline, proposed a negotiated settlement on moderate terms: a formal separation, but not divorce; renouncing her right to be crowned, and taking some other title such as Duchess of Cornwall; and undertaking never to return to England in exchange for a guaranteed income for life of £50,000. Unfortunately the Regent was not satisfied, and interpreted (correctly) the very moderation of these proposals as an admission of weakness.[1]

George IV's succession to the throne meant that the problem could no longer be deferred; either Britain had a new queen, with all the rights and privileges which that entailed, or it did not, and some explanation was necessary. The most pressing question was whether the Queen's name should be included in the liturgy read in Anglican services across the country. Precedent suggested that churchgoers should pray for 'our gracious Queen Caroline', but the new King was adamant that she should not be mentioned in this or any other way, in the service. The Archbishop of Canterbury and the Speaker of the Commons (who was the Archbishop's son) both disagreed. Canning thought that it was unfair and prejudicial to omit the Queen from the prayers before any case against her had been made, and his views needed to be treated carefully. He had been a good friend to Caroline years before – indeed there were widespread suspicions that he had been more than a friend – and might well break with his colleagues if they took up the King's cause against her. Nonetheless after much debate the whole Cabinet, including Canning, decided to give way to the King over the liturgy, for a much more serious battle was looming.[2]

The King demanded that the ministers agree to bring forward a divorce, and they refused. The terms Brougham had proposed in 1819 seemed quite reasonable to them, and they would not risk the precarious tranquillity of the country or the reputation of the monarchy simply to satisfy the King's personal feelings. For several days the King talked of dismissing the government or of retiring to Hanover, but eventually he gave way, although with a strong sense of grievance and considerable resentment towards Liverpool in particular.[3]

George III was buried at a solemn torchlit ceremony at Windsor on 16 February. The following morning brought news of another, more troubling, royal death: the Duc de Berri, second son of the Comte d'Artois and third in the line of succession to the French throne, had been assassinated as he left the opera in Paris. It was a reminder of the underlying instability of France four-and-a-half years after the Second Restoration, which Wellington attributed to the continuing discontent of some 25,000 army officers who had lost the privileged and affluent positions they had held under the Empire.[4]

Any illusion that Britain was immune to such dangers was shattered on 23 February with the revelation of a plot to murder the whole Cabinet. The Cato Street Conspiracy, as it has become known, was the work of Arthur Thistlewood and other extreme radicals who had been plotting revolution since before the Spa Fields Riots of 1816. Although they had long-standing contacts with 'Orator' Hunt, and received some funding from Jeremy Bentham, these extremists were on the fringes of the radical movement, and in the wake of 'Peterloo' Hunt had sharply distanced himself from them. Nonetheless they retained some influence and connections in Lancashire, Yorkshire and around Glasgow, and would not have lacked support if their initial blow had succeeded. Thistlewood's plan was ambitious. With forty heavily armed confederates, he would storm Lord Harrowby's house and murder all the Cabinet who were dining there. At the same time a second group of radicals would meet in Shoreditch and seize the Artillery Ground and its cannon, while a third group led by John Palin, a chair-maker, would meet south of the river, set fire to large oil warehouses at Horsley Down, then cross the Thames and set fire to Furnivals and Staples Inns. Having murdered the Cabinet the main group would proceed to set fire to the King Street barracks, meet Palin's party in Cavendish Square, and storm the Bishop of London's house. They would carry with them the severed heads of Castlereagh and Sidmouth and would display these trophies to the crowds at every opportunity in the confident hope that this would gain them support. They planned to capture the Light Horse Barracks in Gray's Inn Lane and distribute the weapons it contained to their new followers, before all three parties converged on the Mansion House to establish a provisional government and seize the Bank of England. Thistlewood expected that this would trigger a general rising, and there is some evidence that his contacts in the north of England and Scotland had been alerted that an important blow was about to be struck so that they could be ready to take advantage of the confusion.[5]

However, the execution of the plan was much less formidable than its outline. Only about eighteen men assembled in the loft in Cato Street on 23 February, rather than the forty Thistlewood had hoped would comprise the principal party; and two men who had been involved in the plot recoiled as the day approached, and alerted the authorities. The news did not come as a surprise, for the Home Office had been aware of the plot from the outset since one of the ringleaders, George Edwards, was a government informer. But no jury in 1820 was likely to convict on the evidence of an informer alone, so the Home Office let the plot develop until the last possible moment, eliminating the doubt that the conspiracy was nothing more than idle talk. On the evening of 23 February the police, backed by troops, stormed the loft. Thistlewood killed the first constable who climbed the narrow ladder and then managed to escape with half his fellow conspirators. He tried to find the other parties, but soon realised that they had been forestalled or had failed to act, and was arrested on the following day thanks to intelligence from Edwards. When Croker saw some of the prisoners at the Home Office the next day 'they looked so intensely miserable that I pitied them'. But this was unusual; the almost universal reaction was of intense revulsion and condemnation, and Croker records that the 'mob exclaimed that Thistlewood ought to be hanged'. Wellington agreed, telling Marianne Patterson that it was 'probably the most desperate & bloody [plot] that ever yet entered the Minds of Men'. 'It is really quite shocking to read the Reports of the discussions of these Miscreants. They talk of Murder & Blood as they would of their common occupations; & two of them actually prepared Sacks to carry off our Heads after we should be murdered; & then they discussed their preferences & I think it turned out that the greater number wished to murder Lord Castlereagh & myself . . . You can form no idea of the Horror which these disclosures have occasioned in this Town. There is not the smallest doubt that if we had not had accurate Information & if those to whom it was communicated had not kept the Secret admirably the scheme must have succeeded.'[6]

Radical sympathisers soon recovered from the shock caused by the discovery of the conspiracy and portrayed the plotters as deluded victims of Home Office intrigue. Nonetheless the affair helped to discredit the extreme radicals, who had been losing momentum ever since the autumn of 1819, but did nothing to increase the popularity of the government or lessen support for the more moderate 'constitutional' radicals such as 'Orator' Hunt and Alderman Matthew Wood, one of the MPs for the City of London, who gained prominence in 1820.[7]

Meanwhile events in Spain showed that other governments were more vulnerable to internal subversion, and produced an important declaration of British foreign policy on the delicate question of whether one country had the right to intervene in the internal affairs of another in the event of a revolution or other domestic upheaval. On 1 January 1820, troops who had assembled at Cadiz in order to be sent to South America to combat colonial pretensions to independence, rebelled and proclaimed a restoration of the Constitution of 1812. The uprising was a slow-moving affair with no evidence of popular interest outside the army. Wellington was at first inclined to dismiss the revolt, taking comfort in the lack of support for the *liberales* or the Constitution, and believing that the Spanish people would not let a 'Praetorian Guard' dictate to them how they were to be governed; although he foresaw dangerous implications, including the temptation to attack Portugal, arising from any forced renunciation of Spain's colonial empire. However the revolt did not fizzle out with the soldiers deserting their officers as Wellington expected, and the Spanish government proved incapable of any effective action against it. The impasse was resolved when other military units around the country eventually joined the rebels, forcing the King to give way and accept the Constitution on 7 March.[8]

France and Russia viewed these events with consternation, seeing in the success of the military Jacobins of Cadiz uncomfortable parallels to Napoleon's return from Elba in 1815. Before Ferdinand's final capitulation they proposed a meeting of the allied ambassadors in Paris to consider how they should respond if the King appealed to his allies for assistance. Not that either France or Russia were entirely happy with Ferdinand's absolute rule; they favoured a moderate constitution similar to the French *Charte*. Prussia was quite happy to agree, but Metternich, the most conservative of all the leading statesmen, held back, largely in deference to Britain's special interests in Spain. And the British had no hesitation in opposing any foreign intervention in Spain. From the outset Wellington was quite clear that it would be counter-productive – the one thing that might actually mobilise the population in favour of the *liberales* – and he spelt this out in letters to the French government. In a lengthy memorandum he prepared for Castlereagh in the middle of April, he considered the practical difficulties of intervention, highlighting the many almost insurmountable problems that had bedevilled Napoleon's attempt to conquer the country. He also argued that as the King had by then accepted the Constitution and not appealed for any assistance, there was little or no justification for foreign interference.[9]

Castlereagh and the Cabinet accepted all this and went further in the state paper that was the result of their discussions. Among other objections they argued that outside intervention could only be justified when internal troubles posed a direct and imminent danger to other states, and that Spain was clearly too weak and decrepit to pose a threat to anyone (an argument which was only plausible if Portugal was deliberately ignored). And they acknowledged that public opinion would necessarily play a large part in determining British policy – Ferdinand being so unpopular in Britain that her support for any policy designed to restore him to absolute rule was inconceivable. At the same time the ministers were clearly jealous of the interest France and Russia were showing in Spain, reflecting a desire to regard it as falling into a British sphere of influence.[10]

However foreign policy, like many other important questions, was relegated to the sidelines when the Queen unexpectedly returned to England on 6 June. She was received with great enthusiasm in London, not for her own virtues, which were hard to find, but as a symbol of opposition to her unpopular husband. The press had refrained from reporting the many stories of her misconduct which freely circulated in the higher reaches of London society, so that most ordinary people honestly believed that she was the innocent victim of a cruel and hypocritical husband.

The King was initially pleased by the Queen's return since it revived the possibility of a divorce, and he had little appreciation for the depth of his own unpopularity. But the ministers were dismayed, foreseeing that nothing but trouble could arise from the affair. Nonetheless Liverpool and Castlereagh moved at once to establish secret committees of each House to examine the Queen's conduct. This was carried in the Lords, but the Commons instead urged that further negotiations for a settlement be attempted. Canning warned his colleagues that his former friendship with the Queen might compel him to take a separate line, and in debate spoke warmly of his 'unaltered regard and affection' for her. He then offered to resign; but Liverpool refused to let him go. The King was furious, and his latent dislike of the Prime Minister flared. On 12 June he sent for Lord Sidmouth and pressed him very strongly to accept the premiership, but Sidmouth stoutly declined. The King then asked who else might fill the role and suggested Wellington, 'but Lord S. begged to be excused from offering any opinion on that subject, and pressed on H.M. the expediency of continuing to confide in Ld. L[iver]pool'. The rift was patched over, and Canning remained in Cabinet after apologising to the King, although on the understanding that he would take no responsibility for its proceedings against the Queen.[11]

Wellington and Castlereagh negotiated with Brougham for a compromise settlement in talks that lasted from 14 to 19 June, but the Queen, emboldened by her popularity and encouraged by her radical advisors, increased her demands and rejected their proposals. Meanwhile an alarming incident occurred when soldiers of the first battalion 3rd Foot Guards refused to obey orders on 15 June. Although first reports talked of a 'mutiny', the soldiers regarded it more as a strike in protest at their move into barracks recently fitted up in the King's Mews near Charing Cross, and at the extra duty they were having to perform supporting the civil authorities in the streets. The Duke of York immediately ordered the battalion to Portsmouth. One wing marched at four o'clock on the following morning, while the other was confined to barracks. A crowd gathered outside the Mews on the Friday evening and threatened to break down the gates and let the soldiers out, before it was dispersed by the Life Guards. The remaining wing marched on the following morning without further trouble, although, according to Henry Hobhouse at the Home Office, 'the battalion on its march have betrayed instances of indiscipline, and have used expressions in derogation of the King and approbation of the Queen'.[12]

Inquiries suggested that discipline in the regiment had been poor for some time and a good deal of blame was directed at the Duke of Gloucester, who had been its colonel since 1806, for his 'ill-advised humanitarian ideas' and attempts to dispense with corporal punishment. It was especially alarming that there had been no warning of the trouble; the officers were unaware that anything was wrong, and those NCOs who did know said nothing. Wellington went to see the second wing begin their march on the Saturday morning, and reported that the men were obedient and in perfect order, but did not show as much pleasure at the sight of him as they had always done in the past.[13]

Publicly the Horse Guards and the government played down the incident, attributing it to a few isolated malcontents, but in private the Commander-in-Chief admitted to great uneasiness about the Coldstream Guards as well. Wellington took the problem very seriously and warned Liverpool that the danger of further trouble could not be discounted. And he urged that the government immediately reduce its dependence on the Guards either by forming a larger and more efficient force of police, or by having available some body of troops other than the regular army. Wellington's idea for the creation of a new police force was not taken up at this time, probably because it would take too long to be effective.[14]

Throughout the summer London was awash with rumours of disaffection among the troops, attempts by the Queen's supporters to suborn them, and dangerous foreign precedents. Liverpool himself sent Wellington a report that 'in the low public houses the example of the Spanish army is strongly and zealously preached up'. W.H. Fremantle told Buckingham: 'The press is paid for her abundantly, and there are some ale-houses open where the soldiers may go and drink and eat for nothing, provided they will drink "Prosperity and health to the Queen". The K___ grows daily more unpopular, and is the only individual in the Kingdom insensible to it.' Henry Hobhouse agreed: 'Great pains have also been taken both by her friends and by the Radicals (who are anxious to avail themselves of her popularity for the advancement of the revolution, which they contemplate) to seduce the soldiery to their views.'[15]

Doubts about the reliability of the army were increased by a breakdown in the discipline of the 90th Foot when a large number of soldiers conspired together to release a comrade from custody, where he had been placed for insubordination. Although the incident was not overtly political the regiment had been stationed in Manchester for some months and the authorities worried that the men had been corrupted by radical ideas. Some thought was given to dissolving the regiment, but the Horse Guards preferred to send it to the Mediterranean instead.[16]

The concern was increased by the news, in the middle of July, that the army in Naples had imitated that of Spain, overthrown the government, and forced the King to accept a new constitution. Tom Grenville told his nephew: 'I hope you observe the *Morning Chronicle*'s congratulations on the Naples revolution without loss of life, "in consequence of its being achieved by the *soldiery*, since *wherever* they raise *their voice*, it is *imperative*." And this is the Whig and Opposition printer!!!' Still worse, a handbill distributed by the radical printer William Benbow took the same message to a much wider audience.[17]

Anxiety focussed on the meeting of Parliament in the middle of August, when formal proceedings against the Queen would be commenced in the House of Lords, and when whatever trouble was brewing was most likely to reach boiling point. According to Wellington several foreign diplomats had mentioned their apprehensions to him, believing that the army was unreliable and that consequently the government lacked the means to restore order in the event of serious rioting in London. The Lord Chancellor was reported to have said that 'there was no Peer who should go down to the House of Lords the first day who could be certain of returning', while the attempts of the Home Office to establish a local defence force based on streets and parishes in the capital had come to nothing. On the other hand, by the end of July Wellington was able to write to Liverpool: 'I have great pleasure in telling you that I have the best accounts to give of all ranks of the Army. I am quite certain that Everything at Woolwich is right, as well as in the Horse Guards, Blues & all the Light Cavalry in the neighbourhood of London. The Guards likewise do their duty remarkably well & I believe there is nothing among them excepting the loose talk of some in Public Houses; and I entertain no doubt that all will do their duty under any circumstances when called upon.' And this reassuring assessment was confirmed by several reviews of troops held near London in late July and early August, attended by the King.[18]

Concern about the loyalty of the troops subsided as rapidly as it had arisen. News of yet another military coup leading to a liberal constitution, this time in Portugal in September, caused no more than a brief shiver of sympathy, although Wellington was very annoyed that Beresford had left the country for Rio despite his strongly worded advice: 'If ever Man lost a Country, he has lost that by this foolish voyage.' The Duke detested the idea that an army that he had led for so long and with such success should overthrow the established government of its country:

I cannot bear the pusillanimity & supineness of General [John] Wilson, General Blunt & the other English Officers who, if they had exerted themselves, might & would have taken the Soldiers from the Portuguese Officers, & would have saved all. But there are some Men who have no spirit excepting in a field of Battle! All the Audacity & boldness is on the side of the Revolutionists. On the other, no one will risk even his own Paltry life to save a Country from the Horrors to which these miserable Countries are devoted. At Lisbon, instead of calling out the Troops & putting somebody at their Head on whose fidelity & Courage the Government could rely, they were preparing to submit to the Insurrection! Then in Spain I see that the Army in the Isla de Leon refuses to break up; the Government & Cortes submit; and there is nobody bold enough even to raise up his voice against such a degrading Tyranny! I declare it makes me sick![19]

Nothing could be more offensive to Wellington's political principles than the army acting as an independent entity in politics, pursuing its own views and interests, something which he saw as the very essence of Napoleon's regime.

Following the failure of the negotiations with the Queen, the government had little real choice but to proceed against her in Parliament. Discussions between the Cabinet and law officers concluded that the most appropriate procedure was by a Bill of Pains and Penalties which, if passed, would punish her for the damage her misconduct had done the nation, and only incidentally include a divorce for the King. The bill would be introduced into the Lords where evidence was able to be taken on oath, and where both sides were represented by legal counsel, so that the Queen was virtually put on trial. The preliminary Secret Committee unanimously reported in early July that there was a prima facie case – the Opposition members had withdrawn from it – but the main proceedings were delayed until 17 August to permit both sides to prepare their evidence.[20]

Public opinion remained overwhelmingly in favour of the Queen with frequent large meetings, processions and addresses from all over the country in her support. Cobbett acted as her chief publicist and most of the other radicals were active in her cause. Sales of radical papers such as the *Black Dwarf* rose sharply, and violent handbills and placards conveyed the absurd message that the Queen's life was at stake. Tensions rose as 17 August approached and rumours abounded that there would be trouble on the streets, if not an attempted revolution. Large crowds gathered around the approaches to Parliament, and Creevey observed that when Wellington arrived there was 'an uproar, with hissing and shouting', and that the Duke was 'evidently annoyed'. Fortunately the crowd dispersed peacefully in the evening.[21]

The immediate crisis was passed although London remained in a ferment throughout the 'trial'. Wellington continued to be a particular object of abuse from the crowd. Back in June, when the Queen first arrived in London, the windows of his coach had been broken when he was in it, and the hissing and shouting which Creevey observed on 17 August were constantly repeated in the days and weeks ahead. On 24 August his sister-in-law wrote that 'I am sorry for our national credit to say that the Duke of W. is daily abused, hissed, and treated with the most opprobrious language on his way to and from the House of Lords'. While on 29 August Lady Granville recorded a rather more serious incident: 'The mob direct all their violence against the Duke of Wellington. They tried yesterday to pull him off his horse. The police interfered and some of the mob were knocked down, some hurt in the struggle'. Even as late as 7 November Creevey casually noted: 'I had a very good-humoured nod from Wellington this morning, while the people in the Park were hooting him'.[22]

Wellington made light of this unpopularity. After one incident he told Lady Shelley: 'The mob are too contemptible to be thought about for a moment! About thirty of them ran away from me in the Park this morning, because I pulled up my horse when they were hooting!' And on another occasion he told Mrs Arbuthnot: 'The people had shouted to him as he went down to the House in the morning, "No hero! We want no hero!!" He seemed much amused by it.'[23] But Wellington was never quite as indifferent to popular opinion as he pretended, and the constant flow of abuse, where before there had been praise, was depressing, and probably encouraged his natural predisposition to take a gloomy view of the state of the country.

Others were shocked at his reception. Robert Plumer Ward recorded his 'grief at the scoundrel spirit of the times that such a man should meet with the treatment he did', and 'almost regretted that the Duke had ever taken office, his only crime'. Plumer Ward was a friend and a colleague, but even those who had never met Wellington were dismayed. Sara Hutchinson, Wordsworth's sister-in-law, wrote: 'Only think of the D. of W. being *insulted* so late their idol – but it is ever so & why wonder? Alas how soon are benefits forgot!' And the artist Benjamin Robert Haydon wrote in his diary on 19 August:

> Went to the House of Lords to see the Queen come & saw an English mob disgrace itself by hooting at *Wellington*! . . . As he & Anglesea [sic] rode by, I thought, 'There go two beings who will be remembered as long as this Earth remains undestroyed by another Flood'. Wellington took [it] with great good humour, & seemed, as he turned from side to side, mocking their noise. Directly after a scoundrel had been hollowing, he turned round to me & said, 'Who *is it*? *Who* is it?' With as much contempt as I could muster, I said, '*Wellington*'. '*What a shame!*' said he – though he had that moment before been hooting with the rest.

While Wellington maintained his composure and ignored the jeers Anglesey was inclined to make 'them speeches about his duty' which had little or no effect. But it was Anglesey, not Wellington, who had the wit to respond to the demand that he cheer the Queen with the famous line: 'God save the Queen – and may all your wives be like her!'[24]

The case against the Queen was led by Sir Robert Gifford, the Attorney General, with Brougham and Denman cross-examining the witnesses and endeavouring to damage their credibility. This part of the 'trial' was completed at the end of the first week of September and, after a little more legal jousting, proceedings were adjourned until early October when the defence presented its evidence. All the twists and turns of the case were followed avidly by the public, and the newspapers were filled by testimony of the witnesses, often given in full. Writing to her sister on 22 August Lady Granville conveys something of the entertainment which the affair provided: 'The interpreter is the man that delights them all. His name is Spinetto; he is an Italian teacher at one of the Universities, as quick as lightning, all gesticulation, and so eager he often answers instead of the witness. Between them they act all the evidence, and at times they say this is so irresistibly comic that the noble lords forget all decorum and are in a roar of laughter.'[25]

Very few Lords, on either side, sincerely believed in the Queen's innocence, but many found ways of justifying opposition to the bill: it was inexpedient; the case had not been proved beyond all possible doubt; the King's own misbehaviour was too notorious simply to ignore; or, particularly among the bishops, disapproval of divorce on principle. Among the general public on the other hand, a genuine and passionately held belief in the Queen was widespread and remained completely unshaken by the evidence, which was taken as simple proof of the depths of the conspiracy against her. Brougham destroyed the credibility of Majocchi, a key witness against the Queen, by asking a long succession of questions designed to elicit the response '*non me ricordo*' ('I don't remember'), a phrase derided in chapbooks and songs and which lasted in general currency for several generations, regardless of the fact that most of the questions were completely irrelevant. People on all sides had long before made up their mind about the Queen; very few were going to let the evidence influence them.[26]

By October the strain was beginning to tell on the ministers. There were fresh reports that the King was considering dismissing them in the hope that the Whigs would bring the trial to a rapid conclusion and secure a divorce in return for office. Wellington took this seriously, for he thought that the Opposition might agree to such a proposal, and had heard that the King 'said that he had ruined himself by his adherence to us, that *we dragged him through the mire*, & that he shd. be the most popular sovereign that ever sat on the throne if he dismissed us & took other Councillors'. Other ministers dismissed this as nothing more than self-indulgent grumbling, although Castlereagh commented that 'such conduct & feelings entirely destroyed any pleasure there might be in serving him'. But he blamed Lady Conyngham, the King's mistress, for encouraging his folly.[27]

The ministers were uncertain and divided whether to persist with the bill as it stood or drop the divorce clause, for it was plain that there were many peers for whom this was an obstacle. According to Plumer Ward: 'The D. as vehement as ever that the case is proved, and the Bill ought to go on: this is his straightforward way. *Il ne sçait pas ménager*. Never had any man more of the simplicity of honesty'. And, a few weeks later when the government managers were anxiously considering what to do if the bill passed the Lords and headed to the Commons, Arbuthnot noted: 'The Duke feels that it wd. be disgraceful to get rid of it by any trick. So it wd., but I wish some honourable mode cd. present itself . . .' Yet no one was more impatient and weary of the whole affair than Wellington. On 16 October Plumer Ward saw him 'just come from the H. of Lds., and tired and disgusted, if not resentful, at all the factions and insolent spirit that showed itself there'.[28]

More generally Wellington was dismayed by the state of the country and the weakness of the government. The apathy of the middle and upper classes in the face of constant popular protest and agitation disheartened him, and in words which echoed his comments on events in Portugal, he lamented to Plumer

Ward that there was 'audacity and insolence on their side, and tameness on ours. We go to the House seemingly on purpose to be insulted; the opposition know it, and act accordingly.'

> But, continued he, with some vehemence, the mischief is we are no Government, but afraid of using our own power, or this spirit might be put down in the House and out of the House; – in the House, by retorting upon our enemies what they deserve; and asserting ourselves, out of the House, by executing the laws. Last Parliament we passed laws and got power enough, and now we are afraid to use it. I believe, added he, with warmth, everyone of these meetings for addresses are contrary to the Act, and yet we are tame. Libel upon libel comes out, which the law might lay hold of, yet nobody is touched.[29]

At the same time Wellington's confidence in Liverpool's leadership had been shaken by a mistake over tactics in the Lords, which left Wellington and Eldon voting against the other ministers on a relatively minor matter. And he complained to Mrs Arbuthnot: 'Ld. Liverpool was so fretful & so ill tempered it was impossible to say anything to him; that he, for his part, never did; that Lord Liverpool never consulted with or spoke to any of them; never wd. listen to any argument or remonstrance & took the most important steps without consulting with them.'[30]

Wellington was not alone in complaining about a deterioration of Liverpool's temper. The strain of many years in high office, culminating in the extraordinary stresses of 1819 and 1820, undermined Liverpool's habitual self-control and even temper. He suffered a good deal of discomfort from a painful condition in his left leg (probably a form of thrombo-phlebitis), and his wife Louisa was seriously ill throughout the summer and autumn of 1820. In September he told Canning: 'In the whole course of my life I do not recollect to have undergone such continued fatigue as during the three weeks of the proceedings in the House of Lords.' October was as bad or even worse, and in November there was a 'terrible scene' in Cabinet. Liverpool 'was in a phrenzy, & his rage got so high that for a time it stopped all deliberation. He abused the Chancellor. He complained of the ill usage he had received from several in the room, without particularizing them; & ended by crying.' Eldon considered resigning, but Liverpool patched things up with an apology. Hobhouse commented that 'these gusts of passion, so utterly inconsistent with the calm and even cold manner, wch. Ld. L. exhibits to the public, have lately broken out several times in the meetings of Cabinet.'[31]

But even at the height of the affair Liverpool's public performances remained impressive. Charles Arbuthnot told his wife on 4 November: 'Lord Liverpool began the debate in continuation of his speech, & a magnificent one it was. I was nervous about him yesterday, for he was hoarse & seemed embarrassed. Today he was admirable, & made her guilt as glaring as we know it is.' Charles Greville remarked on the strength of party feeling and the violence of speakers on both sides, but hastened to exempt Liverpool who was 'a model of fairness, impartiality, and candour'. And, looking back over the months of wrangling, Francis Burton declared: 'It is easy to see now that, if the whole were to be done over again, many things might be done better, but among these I should not include Lord Liverpool's speeches, or his conduct in the House, which seem to have been quite unexceptionable, and becoming a judge as well as a statesman. They have accordingly raised him in the opinion of most men, and have extorted compliments from the chief of his opponents.'[32]

This was one reason why Liverpool was indispensable to the government. He might not be a dominating figure giving charismatic leadership to the whole country, but he could speak, and speak well, across the whole range of government business, week after week. By contrast Wellington seems to have made only one brief contribution to the Parliamentary debates in 1820, when a question relating to regulations affecting the wearing of uniforms by Austrian officers was raised in evidence in the Queen's 'trial', and even then his contribution was secondary to Liverpool's.[33] But incumbency was even more important. Liverpool's ministry was in fact, although not in name, a very broad coalition held together by the glue of office and a shared history encapsulated by the memory of Pitt. While few ministers or members felt any great personal allegiance to the Prime Minister, all recognised him as the fulcrum of the government, and a leader who scrupulously maintained a balance between its different component parts. It would not be easy – it might not be possible – for the ministry to continue under any other leader, and if it were dissolved it would be very difficult to rebuild it. For all his frustration with Liverpool and with the weakness of the government, Wellington recognised that there was no alternative; and when Plumer Ward mentioned the possibility of a new administration formed on the broadest possible basis, possibly under his leadership, he replied:

Even that will not do, for there will be no leader and no submission. It is a mistake to suppose *I* can be the man. Since the days of Mr Pitt there has been no individual who could command such confidence as to rally people round him with implicit devotion, so as to sacrifice their own opinion to a leader's; and when every man is to follow his own counsel, or think it ought to be followed, we know what that is. No; there is no one man in the state, of whatever party, who can command the spirits of others.[34]

On 6 November a second reading of the bill was carried by 123 votes to 95 and the ministers, after some discussion, determined to press forward with a third reading. This was passed on 10 November, but by such a small majority that Liverpool at once announced that the government would not proceed further. According to Plumer Ward, Wellington was delighted and felt that they had escaped from an impossible position with ' "safety and without dishonour. The votes put the question of guilt or innocence out of doubt; the withdrawing is grounded upon mere expediency, and has nothing to do with the verdict; had we given up before the third reading, it would have been different".' That night, and over the next few days, the Queen's supporters celebrated their victory. According to Anne Cobbett, within half an hour of the news being reported 'guns were firing in all directions, bells ringing, and illuminations in every street and suburb'. All the ships on the river were decked with lights on their masts and rigging; processions marched behind bands triumphantly playing 'God save the Queen' and with busts of the Queen crowned in laurel at their head. Stones and bricks were thrown through the windows of the pro-Government *Courier* and *Morning Post*, and there were a few clashes between the police – supported by the Life Guards – and the crowds, but in general the revelries were remarkably good-humoured. Wellington refused to illuminate Apsley House and spent the whole evening at home undisturbed 'and so quiet, he said, that he began to think he was a popular Minister'.[35]

Nonetheless the government's standing was seriously weakened by the failure of the bill, and there was much talk that the ministers would, or should, resign. Liverpool wanted to prorogue Parliament until the end of January to give the country time to quieten down, and Members of Parliament some perspective. Oddly, the King violently disagreed, precipitating the fourth major crisis in his relations with his government in this, the first year of his reign. Superficially the dispute was over tactics: the King argued that it was vain to hope that the country would be quiet until a settlement for the Queen had been agreed. But underneath was exasperation and resentment that the long, degrading affair had achieved nothing – a feeling which the ministers recipro-cated, for they could not help but blame the King for the whole ghastly mess.

On 16 November the King wrote to Liverpool dismissing the government, but could not bring himself to send the letter. Instead he made an approach to the Opposition in an effort to discover just how many bitter pills he would be forced to swallow if he gave them his confidence. Typically Grey was out of town, but Lord Donoughmore suggested that a new government would wish to repeal the Six Acts, reduce government spending, increase the Queen's allowance beyond £50,000 per annum, restore her name to the liturgy, and make substantial concessions to the Catholics.[36] Not surprisingly, the King's

enthusiasm for a change of ministers soon cooled. He must also have been influenced by an extraordinary Memorandum presented to him by Wellington in
which the Duke urged him 'for the sake of your own honour' not to dismiss the
ministers until the Queen's affair was finally settled. Wellington stressed the
importance of proroguing Parliament – which meant that the Bill of Pains and
Penalties would lapse – and avoiding a discussion of the King's use of his British
and Hanoverian servants to gather evidence against the Queen. With the best
will in the world a Whig government would be unable to resist pressure from the
Queen's supporters to pursue these matters, while the outgoing ministers would
be forced to defend their reputation by explaining that their role in these activities was very limited. Inevitably the King would be embroiled in another more
dangerous controversy, which would damage his reputation and the standing of
the monarchy. While this was no doubt meant as an honest warning, it would
not be difficult to construe the letter as blackmail – 'dismiss us, and you'll be
sorry' – and it is not surprising that the King was reported to be 'furious' and
declared it to be a letter which should not have been written to an equal, let alone
to a sovereign. But if unpalatable, it was also true; and the reference to the King's
honour, coming from Wellington, touched a sensitive spot, for the King was not
totally unaware of the difference between tinsel and sterling.[37]

The King, as so often, gave way, and there was no change of government
and Parliament was prorogued over Christmas; but even this was not the end
of the crisis.[38] Canning had avoided the 'trial' by travelling on the Continent.
Now he returned and announced that he must resign. Those who disliked and
distrusted him – and there was no shortage of them – immediately detected a
typically unprincipled bid for personal advantage and power. He saw that the
ministerial ship was sinking and hoped that by scuttling it he would be well
placed to collect the flotsam and jetsam. But it was Liverpool who was most
dismayed. Only a fortnight before he had written forlornly to Arbuthnot 'I feel
I have few, very few, publick friends in the world', and now the oldest, the ablest,
the most brilliant of them, whose career he had revived in 1816 and whom he
had protected from the King earlier in the year, was going to desert him. Tired
and disillusioned, he complained that 'this proceeding of Canning's was of a
piece with all his former public conduct. He has no moral principle in public
affairs; he looks only to this private advantage and never considers himself
bound in honour to act fairly with his party.'[39]

Liverpool made a half-hearted overture to Peel to replace Canning, but was
rebuffed. This was hardly a surprise; no one was likely to join the government
until it had shown that it could survive the resumption of Parliament and finish
the Queen's affair. The general view was still that the government could hardly
stand without substantial reinforcements, and no one could see from whence
they could come. Loose talk by the King did not help, and rumour and

speculation abounded. Nonetheless the ministers scattered across the country to spend a few weeks relaxing and visiting friends. Arbuthnot, Bathurst and Liverpool gathered at Stratfield Saye just before Christmas and 'they passed one evening playing charades, at which Lord Liverpool was very expert; and another time the Duke's boys played blind man's buff and caught Lord Liverpool, who, however, refused to join in that sport, thinking, I suppose, that such amusements wd. not sound well just now'.[40] Amid scenes such as these the tensions and half-suppressed animosities of the year could dissolve, or at least fade into the background and be replaced by a renewed sense of camaraderie and common purpose.

Whether they knew it or not the ministers had reason to rejoice that Christmas, for at long last the tide of opinion in the country was turning. The very success of the Queen deprived her of her greatest asset, and as early as 15 November a deadly little rhyme was in wide circulation:

> Most Gracious Queen, we thee implore
> To go away and sin no more;
> But, if that effort be too great,
> To go away, at any rate.[41]

Many of the Queen's supporters, especially among the upper classes and in Parliament, would have secretly agreed with the sentiment; and others, reflecting over the positions they had endorsed over the last few months, must have felt qualms. Mrs Arbuthnot had tartly identified one such concern back in August: 'All one can say is, if the Whig lords do not consider the disgusting details they have heard *proof*, the Whig ladies may in future consider themselves very secure against divorces, for it wd. be impossible to conceive a case in which more proof could be established.' Nor were many radicals – even leaders of the most advanced stripe – entirely comfortable with the way that women had rallied to support the Queen. Henry Hunt and William Cobbett were men of their time, and even Richard Carlile, the ultra-radical atheist, believed firmly that what 'every honest and virtuous woman considers to be her duty . . . [is] to obey the voice of her husband'.[42] And above all there was the loss of a clear objective. For months the Queen's supporters had concentrated their hopes and energies on her defence. With the dropping of the Bill of Pains and Penalties they were left rudderless. Campaigning for a lavish allowance, a palace, a title, inclusion in the liturgy, or even the punishment of her accusers, simply did not have the same appeal as defending the heroine of romance from unjust persecution. The movement in favour of the Queen did not suddenly collapse – it continued to attract substantial support into the new year – but it dwindled, losing the energy and vitality that had distinguished it in 1820.

Conversely, there was a revival of public support for the King and of hostility to the Queen. The caricaturists were quick to sniff the wind and anticipate the change. During the trial they had depicted the Queen as virtue personified; now they began a sustained and intense campaign of denigration which, untroubled by accuracy or decency, was elaborately amusing and cruel. Loyalists across the country organised addresses in favour of the King which at least equalled and probably surpassed those still appearing in supporting the Queen.[43] And almost as soon as the trial was over a new weekly paper appeared called *John Bull*, which attacked the Queen and her supporters with the same low personal abuse and invective that the radical press had been publishing for years. *John Bull* was the idea and largely the work of Theodore Hook, although his identity and that of the other contributors was carefully concealed. The ministers appear to have had no hand in the paper and regarded it with distaste, but the King understandably relished this unexpected ally. Its success was great and immediate – its circulation rose to 10,000 – and its crude attacks on the character and morals of Whig ladies who dared visit the Queen sent a shudder of revulsion through London society. The radical MP H.G. Bennet sued it for libel and moved that it breached Parliamentary privilege and that the Attorney General should be instructed to prosecute; however, to their credit, Brougham and Burdett showed greater commitment to the principles of free speech, and the printer and nominal editor (a man of straw) were merely imprisoned in Newgate until the end of the Session two months later.[44]

Parliament resumed on 23 January 1821 and the King's Speech encouraged waverers and disarmed critics by its moderation and conciliatory tone. The expected trial of strength came almost at once on a motion condemning the removal of the Queen's name from the liturgy. This was decisively defeated 310 to 209, and the government was secure. Subsequent votes only confirmed the fact with the majority rising to almost 150. Early in February the King was emboldened to visit the theatre and was greeted with great enthusiasm. 'Hats and handkerchiefs in the air, and shouts almost the whole time. Twice a voice called out "Queen", and once, "Where's your wife, Georgie?" But the hissing, "Shame, shame", "Turn him out", instantly stopped this.' A few weeks later Lady Granville wrote: 'The Queen is entirely forgotten. They have got up a thing at Drury Lane all full of justice, innocence, spies, and servants bribed to ruin their masters, but not a single hint is taken or applied.'[45] The Queen's most ardent supporters were disillusioned when she accepted the government's offer of £50,000 per annum, on the same terms she had been offered the previous April. Partisans on all sides could hardly help wondering what all the drama and anxiety of the proceeding nine months had been about, or what their efforts had achieved. As for the Queen, surely she must have regretted that she ever left Italy and her lover to return to England.

Her remaining supporters attempted to organise protests on the day of the King's coronation (19 July) but their efforts fell flat, and the occasion was the King's greatest triumph, with huge and enthusiastic crowds filling the streets of London and hardly a murmur of discontent.[46] The Queen's death on 7 August provoked a revival of sympathy based on remorse and guilt that she had been so quickly abandoned. The radicals mobilised huge crowds, which diverted her funeral cortège through the streets of London amid scenes of considerable violence and disorder. But this proved the last hurrah of the popular radicalism which had been such an important feature of British politics since 1808. The next few years would be much quieter and more peaceful as politics left the streets. No single explanation for the change is entirely convincing. The Six Acts and repression – the arrest and imprisonment of many leading radicals – was probably an important factor, although it had not prevented the huge outburst of activity in 1820. An improving economy undoubtedly helped, but prosperity generally came a little after, not before, the waning of the radicals. Perhaps, though, it was the very success of the radicals in gaining support in 1819 and 1820 that in the end exhausted the movement. Time and time again ordinary men and women had answered the call, attended meetings and marched in procession or demonstrations. They had eschewed violence and had striven to be peaceful, orderly and respectable. They had wept over the poor martyrs of 'Peterloo', and feared that a gracious Queen might be beheaded on Tower Hill if they did not protest against such infamy. And in the end it was hard to see what their efforts had achieved. Their lives were no better because the Queen had her pension, or her coffin had passed through the city. Parliament had not been reformed, nor the Six Acts repealed, but perhaps neither seemed to matter quite as much in the summer of 1821 as they had a year before. It was time to move on.

CHAPTER TEN

THE KING AND HIS MINISTERS
(1821–22)

WHILE THE QUEEN'S affair preoccupied the British public, the revolutions in Spain and Naples were provoking a reaction from the other great powers that threatened to undermine the foreign policy that Castlereagh and Wellington had pursued ever since 1813. British influence in Europe was weakened by her domestic political problems; throughout the second half of 1820 and into 1821 a change of ministry, and with it a change of foreign policy, appeared likely, and a revolution not impossible. Metternich, unable to rely upon Britain, his preferred ally, was forced to move closer to Russia. At the same time, the weakness of the government forced Castlereagh to take more account of British public opinion in shaping his policy than he might have wished. It was not a moment to add more fuel to the bonfire of radical and Whig excitement that was threatening to engulf the government.

The revolutions in Spain and Naples sharply divided British opinion. Wellington, Castlereagh and the other ministers viewed both revolts with alarm and dismay. Some Whigs, led by Lord and Lady Holland, viewed events through the prism of 1688 and believed that the new 'liberal' regimes should be embraced with enthusiasm. The extreme radical, John Gast, misled by an ill-informed press, regarded the Neapolitan Carbonari as 'like austere Scotch Presbyterians, foes of gambling and advocates of continence and a primitive Christianity that rejected the Roman Church'. But there was also a wide swathe of public opinion that had come to view with distrust any close involvement with the Continent, seeing it as extravagant, self-indulgent and probably unnecessary. This was the public which had turned increasingly against Castlereagh's diplomacy in the years since 1815, which viewed most foreign regimes with distaste, disliked the congresses and meetings with allied sovereigns, but which was equally ready to turn against foreign liberals. These attitudes were shaped partly by the sense of security and superiority following British success in the war, particularly Waterloo; partly by press criticism of the

Holy Alliance which often suggested that all Europe was groaning under one form of despotism or another, and that only Britain was truly free; and partly by the memory of the huge subsidies provided to the continental powers in the closing years of the war, recollected in the light of endless post-war financial stringency and economic distress. It was an outlook which naturally favoured non-intervention, strict neutrality and a narrow conception of national interests, and by 1820 it had become too powerful to be ignored.[1]

Official British policy towards Naples was the same as towards Spain, urging restraint, warning against any ill-treatment of the royal family, and opposing outside interference. Privately, however, Wellington, Castlereagh and other ministers signalled that they would welcome prompt action by Austria to crush the revolution and restore a government which had a much better reputation than that of Spain. These signals were not particularly subtle or ambiguous; when the news of the revolt was still fresh Wellington told the Austrian *chargé d'affaires* 'that in his opinion there was not a moment to lose in suppressing the Neapolitan Revolution, and that we [that is Austria] could now do with 80,000 men what we could not effect later with 200,000'. Six months later Princess Lieven reported to Metternich that Wellington 'is not satisfied with what is happening. He says: "Things ought to be hurried up. What is to be done should be done at once: as it is, it will turn out ill." '[2]

But Metternich could not, or would not, act without the agreement of the other powers, if only to avoid creating a precedent for unilateral action which might prove highly inconvenient in future in the hands of Russia or France. The result was the meeting or Congress at Troppau in the autumn of 1820, where the rulers of Austria, Prussia and Russia discussed the state of the world, and Britain and France chose to send only low-level observers and disassociated themselves from the proceedings. Metternich secured Russian approval for action against Naples, but only by yielding some ground to Alexander's desire to make it a precedent for settling other problems by collective agreement – a fairly clear reference to Spain.

The British government reacted very strongly to the decisions reached at Troppau, with Castlereagh issuing a diplomatic circular on 19 January 1821 condemning in sweeping terms the doctrine of collective interference in the internal affairs of other countries, except when they posed an immediate threat to their neighbours. While partly written with an eye to public opinion the rift between Britain and her allies on the question was real and ran deep. Wellington had expressed it with characteristic bluntness in discussion with Mrs Arbuthnot: 'The Duke told me he thought it very unfortunate that we had not had a more efficient representative at Troppau than Lord Stewart . . . They have had all sorts of wild schemes of establishing a general police all over Europe & sending the troops of one country to keep order in another; & any Englishman of good sense & conduct wd. have been able to shew them the folly of such schemes.'[3]

If ministers as conservative and pro-European as Castlereagh and Wellington reacted this strongly to the meeting at Troppau, it is not surprising that the Whigs, radicals and press responded with a storm of indignation. When Parliament met early in 1821 the Opposition took up the issue with more gusto than discretion. Lord Holland attacked 'the Troppau Tyrants' and demanded that Austria repay a huge loan she had received more than twenty years before in the early years of the war against France. And in a speech in February he went beyond the generous bounds traditionally granted to debates in Parliament, by accusing Alexander of complicity in the death of his father – 'unless men were utterly degraded and brutalized, would they consent to take their notions of public morality from such a quarter' – and was forced to withdraw the remark and apologise in *The Times*.[4]

Even within the government there were shades of opinion, if not open disagreement. Wellington and Castlereagh had always been the most pro-European of ministers, favouring close co-operation with the continental powers in order to preserve the peace settlement. Liverpool was more sceptical, more concerned with purely British interests, with commercial considerations, and with how Parliament and the public would regard such foreign entanglements. He gave Castlereagh loyal and constant support, and very seldom even hinted at overriding his judgement, but there was no doubt on which side of the scale he threw the weight of his influence. And Canning, who was out of office for part of the time, and had little personal contact with foreign statesmen, was on Liverpool's other flank, always preferring an assertive British policy with little concern for the fluctuations of influence and power in central Europe.[5]

The Congress of Troppau was closely followed by a further meeting at Laibach attended by King Ferdinand of Naples, who formally requested Austrian intervention. Wellington made a self-indulgent mistake when he responded to a request from the Austrian ambassador for his comments on the plan of the campaign, and was fortunate that this did not find its way into the newspapers.[6] News of a revolt in Piedmont arrived just as the campaign was beginning, and raised liberal hopes in Britain to fever pitch. According to the *Examiner* of 18 March 'the liberation of Italy is almost certain, and the liberation of all Europe will be its inevitable consequence', while Sir Robert Wilson boasted of his plans to travel to Naples in order to give its government the benefit of his military genius.[7] However, the Austrians met almost no resistance. Far from enabling the revolution to establish itself, the long delay had brought out divisions among its leaders, proved their incompetence at governing, and thoroughly disillusioned their supporters. The Austrians may not have been popular, especially when they insisted that Naples pay all the costs of the campaign, but for the moment they seemed the less bad alternative. And with the collapse of the revolution at Naples, order was quickly restored in Piedmont. The news was deeply disillusioning for British radicals, and contributed significantly to the shattering of their hopes in the spring of 1821.

The Queen and foreign policy were the principal subjects of debate in Parliament in 1821, and the government's majority proved secure against direct attack. Yet the House was restless and discontented, and delighted in harassing the ministers on lesser questions. Part of the problem was undoubtedly the weakness of the front bench, for with Canning and Peel both out of office, Castlereagh was too often the only minister who could carry the burden of debate.[8] The ministers responded to the discontent by promising further economies and by swallowing the occasional humiliation, such as when the country gentlemen combined with the Opposition to repeal the tax on farm horses, and came perilously close to abolishing the increased malt duty imposed in 1819. A more surprising symptom of disaffection was the sign of some tentative but growing interest among the country gentlemen in some of the schemes for Parliamentary Reform being discussed by the Opposition. The government was actually defeated by a majority of sixty on the question of whether the two seats stripped from the borough of Grampound for blatant corruption should be transferred to the county of Yorkshire (as the ministers proposed), or to Leeds (as the Opposition wanted). The defeat was rectified in the House of Lords, but to a careful observer like Liverpool it suggested that the retreat of radicalism might end up loosening the government's hold on some of its more marginal supporters.[9]

Wellington made only one intervention in debate in the session, defending himself against Opposition complaints that as Lord Lieutenant he had attempted to thwart the wishes of the freeholders of Hampshire to hold a county meeting in favour of the Queen. In the course of his remarks he incautiously said that 'it was not necessary to go through the farce of a county meeting'; and the Opposition immediately exploited the slip, despite a hasty apology from the Duke. The story was picked up by the press and revived for months whenever a paper wished to disparage Wellington, and it was even the subject of a rough but effective caricature. Creevey commented: 'Was there ever such a goose to get into such a mess? He was pummelled black and blue by Carnarvon, Lansdowne and Holland, and had not only to apologize himself, but to get Liverpool to do the same for him.' Lady Granville, with more sympathy, told her sister: 'The poor dear Duke of Wellington has put his foot in it, and the joke is "that the curtain will never be drawn over that farce".'[10]

The government's difficulties in Parliament were dwarfed by its troubled relations with the King, which continued to cast a shadow over the ministry's

future through most of 1821. Much of this ill humour can be attributed to sour-
ness left over from the Queen's affair, but behaviour on both sides added to the
problem. The ministers were resentful and suspicious of Lady Conyngham's
influence, complaining that the King showed her all his papers, however secret,
and that his infatuation showed no signs of waning. They strongly suspected
her of having close links with the Opposition, and at least an inclination to
intrigue to bring about a change of government. Her prolonged public quarrel
with Lady Castlereagh further added to the resentment felt on both sides, while
adding another strain on the already over-burdened Foreign Secretary.[11]

Wellington felt none of the moral aversion which Liverpool and perhaps
even Castlereagh felt for Lady Conyngham, but he did not find her attractive:
'In my life I never saw so vulgar a Woman as she is. I am not fastidious; but she
gave me the feeling which I think I should have if I were to experience a revulsion of Blood!' Nonetheless he was able to listen to her grievances and
complaints with more patience than the other ministers, and in reply gave her
some plain-spoken direct advice, which risked causing offence but which was
probably beneficial.[12]

The King's indiscretion and fondness for empty talk added greatly to the
distrust with which he was viewed by the ministers. According to Wellington
the King 'liked to talk grandly, to make people imagine that his Prime Minister
was a sort of *maitre d'hotel* which he might dismiss at any moment that
happened to suit him, & that it was the mere love of talking nonsense that made
him so absurd'. And it was not to be expected that a man such as Lord Liverpool
who had devoted his whole life to public service should not feel resentment at
such remarks, or refrain from contrasting, in his own mind, his assiduity and
discipline with the self-indulgent bombast of his royal master. Pittite devotion
to the Crown never depended solely on the personal qualities of the monarch,
but in the course of 1821–22 both Liverpool and Castlereagh were driven to
talk of resignation by their disgust at the behaviour of the King towards them.[13]

In Wellington's opinion all these problems were exacerbated by the King's
reluctance to see his ministers in person and discuss business directly with the
Prime Minister and his colleagues. Months passed without Wellington or other
senior Cabinet ministers seeing the King, while business was transacted by
correspondence and through intermediaries such as Sir Benjamin Bloomfield,
the King's private secretary. In such circumstances there was little hope of
re-establishing mutual confidence and harmonious relations.[14]

But not all the blame rested with the King and Lady Conyngham. Liverpool's
behaviour at this time was remarkably pugnacious and assertive, almost
seeking out disputes in which he could humiliate the King and assert his own
authority. A few months later Mrs Arbuthnot, whose sympathies lay squarely
with the Cabinet, not the court, noted that: 'One cannot much wonder at the

King. Lord Liverpool abhors him & takes every opportunity to thwart & vex him, & often fails most seriously in the attention & respect that is due to him. The King hates Lord L[iverpool], & there is constant & incessant bickering between them.' While Croker thought that 'no reformers, if they knew the whole secret, would wish to reduce the monarch lower in real and effective state and power than his Ministers place him'.[15]

The best explanation for Liverpool's behaviour is that he was exhausted and sick at heart; that he had lost his taste for the game and the patience needed to deal with the King, as well as all the other problems of government. He had been prime minister for more than eight years and almost continuously in high office for a decade before that, and the last two years (1819 and 1820) had been exceptionally taxing. His wife was now plainly dying, and even his most loyal allies began to take his talk of resignation seriously and consider who might succeed him. (Wellington thought that the best solution would be Castlereagh as prime minister, Canning as foreign secretary and Liverpool remaining in Cabinet as president of the Council and leader of the Lords, although he acknowledged that Castlereagh's unpopularity would be a problem, and it was unlikely that Liverpool would be willing to retain such a prominent position. However, any combination involved great difficulties.)[16]

Nothing came of this, but as the Session drew towards its close Liverpool looked to strengthen the government. Canning had returned from Paris and as the Queen's business had been concluded might rejoin the Cabinet, while Sidmouth was anxious to retire, and it was thought that Harrowby and Bragge Bathurst might join him.[17] At the end of May Liverpool commissioned Wellington to approach William Wellesley-Pole about retiring in exchange for a peerage. Pole did not take the suggestion well; indeed, he 'was quite frantic at the proposal for his quitting the Cabinet. He abused the Duke furiously, said that he ought not to have allowed such a proposal to be made him, that he never in his life had done any thing for him; in short, was quite beside himself, positively refused to listen to the proposal & burst out of the room after declaring that the Duke owed his advancement in life to him!'[18] Stoicism in the face of disappointment was never a leading characteristic of the Wellesleys, but Wellington had always got on well with William, and was taken aback and then seriously offended by his brother's tantrum. And yet, curiously, it worked; Pole remained in Cabinet for another two years and even received his peerage (becoming Lord Maryborough) in the coronation honours.

Pole's removal was, at most, a sideshow. Liverpool's main aim was to bring back Canning despite the King's well-flagged objections. Canning was unwilling to return to the Board of Control, which was a second-tier post. He felt that time was passing, and younger men, such as Peel, were rising rapidly; if he did not return to the front rank now he never would. Yet he clearly could not go to the Home Office, where he would be brought into constant contact with the King. Liverpool's solution was to shift Melville from the Admiralty. Canning agreed and so, with considerable reluctance, did Melville. The King did not, pointing out that he was going to lose the minister he most liked and trusted (Sidmouth) and replace him with a man he abhorred (Canning). Just as negotiations reached this impasse, Liverpool was summoned to his wife's deathbed and was unable to attend to business for some days as pent-up emotions found release in grief and outbursts of rage. None of his colleagues shared his eagerness to bring Canning back into the government. They agreed that it was desirable, and would strengthen the ministry in the Commons, but they were not willing to dissolve the government over it, especially when the King made clear that his veto was not necessarily permanent. Liverpool took this lack of support badly when he was able to attend to business again, and seemed positively whiggish in the subordination he required from his sovereign.

Wellington's view was summarised in a memorandum by Arbuthnot:

> We should do our utmost to persuade the King to admit Canning, but I cannot be a party to breaking up the Government for the sake of Canning. My conviction is that the country will be ruined, & all the foreign interests of the country destroyed if the Whigs come into power, therefore my first & main object is to keep the Whigs *out*.[19]

For a politician who frequently proclaimed his indifference to retaining office, the discovery that the Opposition would ruin the country, and that it was therefore a patriotic duty to keep them out, was a great comfort; but this does not make it insincere, or even untrue.

Further negotiations, including a rather heated interview between Wellington and the King, failed to shift the impasse and at the end of June Liverpool returned to work.[20] The crisis had not been resolved but simply put to one side. Sidmouth agreed to remain at the Home Office, and ministers hoped that a few months of tranquillity would enable a fresh solution to be found.

News of Napoleon's death reached London at the beginning of July 1821, but failed to create more than a ripple of interest. Indeed, the most common remark in contemporary diaries and letters was surprise at the indifference which greeted it. Wellington told Mrs Arbuthnot, 'Now, I think I may say I am the most successful Genl. alive', but he was much more interested in the affairs of the day. The only strong emotion produced by the news was the grief and dismay felt by the small number of Napoleon's admirers who remained steadfast in faith; they were most common among the extreme radicals, but were overshadowed by the extravagant partisanship of Holland House, and particularly Lady Holland, whose devotion to the exiled Emperor had become a rather threadbare joke. Few other Whigs shared this commitment, or even looked upon it with much patience, while the radicals were divided on the question; only a few months earlier Joseph Hume had called for a drastic reduction (90 per cent was the figure he had in mind) in the money spent in keeping Napoleon at St Helena.[21]

George IV's coronation followed on 19 July and went off remarkably well despite the undignified behaviour of the new King, who 'was continually nodding & winking at Ly Conyngham & sighing & making eyes at her'. Wellington, as Lord High Constable of England, played a prominent role and commented, with an unexpected degree of self-consciousness: 'The Spectacle was truly magnificent and everyone was satisfied. The ridicule which would have been occasioned by the individual costumes was shared by all, no one was seen in relation to his real self; and people were so delighted with the general effect that everyone was consoled for the slight feeling of ridiculousness caused by his individual costume.'[22]

The coronation marked the end of the London season of 1821 and gave the signal for society to disperse to country houses or further afield. Among Wellington's circle of female friends and admirers Mrs Arbuthnot now held pride of place, while Lady Shelley was less prominent and Princess Lieven more so. A hint of Princess Lieven's attraction can be found in a letter Wellington wrote soon after she left for the Continent in early June: 'Lady Granville will have told you how much we miss you. Really I have no more pleasure in Society for I have no one in whom to confide what strikes me as ridiculous in our best of all possible worlds.' The rest of the letter is filled with a mixture of social and political gossip of high order – entertaining and indiscreet, even if it had not been written from a Cabinet minister to the wife of a foreign ambassador.[23] Another friendship formed at this time was inherently indiscreet; Lady Jersey was a leading figure in London society, and had taken up the Queen's cause with zest in 1820. She was the daughter of Lord Westmorland, and Wellington had many ties with the Fanes, and in 1821 he admitted to 'a sort of tenderness' for her. Taxed by Mrs Arbuthnot who told him that it was ridiculous, and that the world would say he was in love, he just laughed. But as with his fondness for Lady Caroline Lamb, it is probable that his affection for Lady Jersey was at least in part sympathy for someone whose tongue ran away with her and got her into trouble.[24]

Wellington enjoyed the company of intelligent, well-informed women who shared his interest in politics and public affairs. They may have flattered him with their attention, but he also listened to them, and took their opinions seriously. This was not particularly unusual; few men in British high society at that time discounted the intelligence of women (at least the actual women they knew) simply because of their gender, although some men were more comfortable in predominantly male company. Others, such as Canning and Peel, whose marriages were unusually happy, did not seek other female confidants, while Wellington's many women friends helped fill the void created by his poor relations with Kitty.

Wellington spent August on the Continent, making his annual inspection of the barrier fortresses in the Netherlands, and visiting Paris, where he thought that things were in a relatively good state. At the same time George IV visited Dublin, where he was received with immense popular enthusiasm. The triumph did nothing to soften his attitude to his ministers, and Liverpool in particular, and there was much talk of the possibility of his changing the government. The ministers left in London fretted under the strain, but Liverpool's taste for office revived and his colleagues united behind him.

The King paused only briefly in London before setting off to visit Hanover, this time without Lady Conyngham. At the last minute he had the idea of commanding Wellington to accompany him as far as Brussels and guide him over the field of Waterloo. The King's mood began to improve as soon as he left England. Wellington reported that he reached Brussels on the evening of 27 September 'in very good humour and spirits'. Evidently he was flattered by his reception, although officially he was travelling incognito. An informal dinner that night went on until almost midnight and, again according to Wellington, the King 'was very blackguard and entertaining!' Apparently he ate '& drank himself so sick he kept his bed for two days'. The lingering effects of this over-indulgence may explain why the tour of the battlefield fell flat. 'His Majesty took it very coolly', Wellington said later; 'he never asked me a single question, nor said one word, till I showed him where Lord Anglesey's leg was buried, and then he burst into tears.'[25]

This chore accomplished, Wellington was free to go home while the King, accompanied by Castlereagh (now Lord Londonderry following his father's death), went on to Hanover. Metternich joined the party in Hanover and had extended informal talks with Londonderry about Greece. The two ministers were concerned by the implications of a revolt against Turkish rule, which had begun in April, and which would be a major issue in European diplomacy for the rest of the decade, complicating relations among the great powers, shaping public attitudes, and closely involving Wellington. Both sides in the revolt behaved with extreme brutality, massacring large numbers of civilians in what a later era would call 'ethnic cleansing'. Turkish reprisals extended to the Greek population in Constantinople where the Patriarch, his bishops and congregation were slaughtered while celebrating Easter mass; and to the prosperous, peaceful island of Chios, where the men and the elderly of both sexes were killed, and the women and children were abducted and sold in the slave markets.

Reports of these events reaching western Europe were marked by a combination of ignorance and extreme bias; the descendants of Pericles and Socrates could do no wrong, especially in the eyes of Whigs and radicals, while the Turks were depicted as uncivilised barbarians. Nonetheless, the response to the news varied; strongest in Germany and France, while being quite slow in Britain where distrust of Russia acted as a countervailing force. Prince Esterházy, the Austrian ambassador to London, wrote: 'The public here of course look on the question as one of Liberalism, but they are not prepared to see the liberty of Greece bought at the price of Russian supremacy in the Mediterranean.'[26]

Russia was the great complicating factor; her long-standing hostility to Turkey, her territorial ambition, and her sympathy for other Orthodox Christians left no doubt of her predilection to intervene in the revolt, by diplomacy and perhaps by force of arms. But restraining Russia in the Balkans was the most fundamental plank of Austrian foreign policy, comparable to British determination to keep France out of the Low Countries. Metternich abhorred the revolt as he abhorred any challenge to established authority, and because it created dangerous instability in the most dangerous quarter possible.

Londonderry was happy to support the Austrians on the question; indeed he took a much more assertive line in warning Russia against interference in Turkey. The roots of this policy can be traced back to Pitt and the Ochakov Crisis of 1791, but it also reflected Londonderry's own readiness to view central and eastern Europe from an Austrian perspective, and his long record of disagreements and tussles with Alexander. In fact the Tsar had behaved with great restraint over Greece, resolutely resisting pressure at home, and from some of his diplomats abroad, to exploit the opportunity to revive his grandmother's ambitions. The argument put forward by Londonderry and Metternich that the Greek Revolt was another example of revolutionary liberalism, like Spain and Naples, was hardly credible; but there was more force in the point that Austria had not acted against Naples without consulting her allies, and Russia should be equally respectful of the alliance. But Russian policy was still fluid, the diplomatic position at Constantinople explosive, and every piece of news from Greece, good or bad, added to the pressure on Alexander to intervene.

At Hanover Londonderry and Metternich were able to discuss the problem in detail and work out their tactics. They agreed to avoid joint action, which would only antagonise the Russians, but each to apply pressure in their own way in something not far removed from the 'good cop, bad cop' technique. Their talks put an end to the rift created by Troppau and Laibach, much to Metternich's relief, although this could not hide the fact that Britain was much less firmly attached to the alliance than she had been before 1820.[27]

The meetings between Metternich and George IV were also significant. Neither man was famous for his modesty and a great deal of mutual flattery soon convinced the King that Metternich was a statesman of rare discernment and judgement. He confided in him all his accumulated grievances with Liverpool and his other ministers, and tossed around the idea of Londonderry as prime minister. This was tempting bait for Metternich, who was well aware that Liverpool had much less sympathy for Austria than Londonderry, but he was too wily and cautious to overplay his hand; rather than help the King set one minister against another, he praised ministers and sovereign alike, convincing George that all Europe looked to him for leadership, and was enchanted by the policies pursued by his government. The King was delighted, and back in England was heard to say: 'I regard Prince Metternich as the first statesman in Europe, and after him Lord Londonderry; these two Ministers understand one another so perfectly, and their agreement is so important in the present state of Europe, that this circumstance alone ought to outweigh all other considerations.'[28]

From this moment the King's attitude to his ministers changed; old resentments were allowed to slip away and he looked to make a fresh start. Liverpool, having recovered from the first shock of his wife's death, also became more conciliatory, and agreed that Lord Conyngham should become Lord Steward of the Household, an appointment which satisfied Lady Conyngham. She also allowed earlier grievances to evaporate, and used her influence to support, not oppose, the ministers, even telling Wellington that she had more than once saved them from summary dismissal. According to his wife, Charles Arbuthnot reported that 'the King says the day of his reconciliation with Lord Liverpool is the happiest of his life!'[29]

The other great problem – what to do with Canning – had also been solved, when he agreed to succeed Lord Hastings as Governor-General of India. This allowed Liverpool to proceed with strengthening the ministry in other directions. Sidmouth handed over the Home Office to Peel (who had always been the successor he preferred), but remained in Cabinet without portfolio as an elder statesman. The Buckingham-Grenville connection was finally being brought back to the Pittite fold, with Charles Wynn taking the Board of Control and a seat in Cabinet; the Marquess of Buckingham was elevated to a dukedom; and a few minor offices were given to the spear-carriers. At the same time, although independently, Lord Wellesley was appointed Lord Lieutenant of Ireland, with Henry Goulburn as his Chief Secretary. Wellesley's inefficiency was well known – Wellington commented that 'great energy cannot now be expected of him, that he never was diligent, and that his indolence has increased with his years' – but it was hoped that Goulburn would compensate for that, while Lord Wellesley would make a splendid and popular vice-regal figurehead.[30]

The improvement of relations with the King and the strengthening of the ministry meant that the government began 1822 with more confidence and brighter horizons than at any time since the summer of 1819. Nonetheless the mood in the Commons when it met in February was surly, for the state of agriculture and the economy had deteriorated, and there was strong pressure for the government to economise. A reduction in official salaries caused discontent and in some cases real hardship to lowly paid clerks in government service, while all the ministers and great officers of state surrendered 10 per cent of their income. This raised the delicate issue of the Civil List, and Liverpool and Londonderry went to see the King in March to discuss it with him. Wellington had gone down a little in advance and prepared the ground so that the King was not taken by surprise, and this precaution produced a handsome dividend when the King, without pressure or ill humour, told the three ministers: 'I cannot as a Gentleman make my servants pay ten per Cent, and not make a similar sacrifice myself.' Writing to Mrs Arbuthnot, Wellington added: 'He really did it with more feeling than I have ever known him shew.' She commented in her journal: 'The Duke of Wellington was present at this audience &, as he has the greatest possible contempt for the King, it is well that he should for once see him in a more favourable point of view.' However, another entry little more than a month later records that 'the Duke came away from Brighton', after a visit in which the King abused Bloomfield extravagantly, 'more disgusted than ever with him.'[31]

The discontent which made the parliamentary session a severe trial for Londonderry was not apparent away from Westminster. Cheap food was not a cause for complaint for the urban population, while even in the countryside (outside Ireland) it seems that the weight of the depression fell most heavily on landlords and farmers, not the rural poor. (This was in marked contrast with the depression at the end of the decade which triggered the Captain Swing riots.) Wellington was once again a popular figure in London as well as outside it. Princess Lieven told Metternich that when he attended the theatre in May 'he was now cheered to the echo. At first, he did not want to take any notice; when he was compelled to go forward to satisfy the audience, he gave two little nods, as if to say "How do you do", and then left them to clap their hands without giving them another look.' By contrast, the King spent a good quarter of an hour bowing to the audience and luxuriating in a popularity which was as recent as it was mysterious.[32]

The erection of a statue in Hyde Park, opposite Apsley House, to commemorate Wellington's victories aroused a good deal of comment and amusement. Paid for by subscription of the Ladies of England, it consisted of a copy of a large and completely naked Achilles in Rome. Given that the subscription was organised by Lady Spencer, 'the most prudish of all the English great ladies', and that the names of the subscribers were to be inscribed on the base, it is not surprising that Princess Lieven thought it 'a quaint idea', or that the caricaturists exploited the potential for broad humour with relish. At the last moment prudence and propriety prevailed and a fig leaf was added to the statue, but this could not avert criticism, especially as the press and public were already in the habit of ridiculing the King's architectural and artistic 'follies' on grounds of both taste and economy.[33]

The relative good humour of these caricatures reflects a softening in attitudes to the army as the intense radical agitation of the post-war years faded away. This was the year in which Wilkie's *Chelsea Pensioners* drew large and enthusiastic crowds to the Royal Academy exhibition; and over the next few years memoirs of the Peninsular War, which had previously been greeted with neglect if not hostility, began to receive favourable reviews and considerable commercial success.[34] The anniversary of Waterloo was commemorated in 1822 not just by the troops mounting guard in public wearing laurel in their caps, but by a grand dinner given by Wellington at Apsley House to some sixty officers who had served in the battle, and the Duke of York and Lord Bathurst. The officers wore their uniforms, and the magnificent service of Portuguese plate was used. These dinners became an annual tradition which gained prestige as the years went on.[35]

Parliament finally rose for the year on 6 August. Wellington prepared for his visit to the Low Countries, and the King, who had contemplated another jaunt to the Continent, decided to go to Scotland instead. Cabinet met to consider the instructions which Londonderry had drafted for his own guidance in the meeting of allied sovereigns and ministers which was to be held in Vienna in September. Originally this meeting was a mere preliminary to a meeting to be held in Florence (later changed to Verona) to discuss the state of Italy; however, Londonderry had indicated that he would not attend the Italian discussions, believing that the Italian states should be allowed to find their own solutions to their internal problems without foreign interference. But Metternich was eager to have Londonderry's support in restraining Russia over Greece – hence the two separate meetings in rapid succession. The character of the Vienna meeting was transformed and its importance much increased by dramatic events in Spain in July, where a botched attempt by royalists to regain power was thwarted, and the extreme radicals came to power. Britain's whole policy of non-interference, based on the argument that the Spanish revolution would soon burn itself out if only it was left alone, suddenly appeared to be little more than wishful thinking; and it did not require much prescience to realise that Russia, and probably France, would use the Vienna meeting to press for concerted allied action to restore stable government to Spain.[36]

The added pressure of events in Spain came at a time when Londonderry was already greatly overworked and showing symptoms of severe strain. As early as the beginning of June he had felt disgusted with public life, driven to distraction by the continuing quarrel between his wife and Lady Conyngham, and beset by fears that his colleagues were plotting against him. Oddly enough his suspicions were not directed at Liverpool and Canning, but towards Peel, whom he saw as a rival in the House of Commons, and Wellington, who he thought was cultivating the King. A few days later, on 10 June, Princess Lieven noted sadly: 'Londonderry looks ghastly. He has aged five years in the last week; one can see that he is a broken man.' But he rallied and at a dinner on 15 June it was said that he was 'in very high spirits', and that he had satisfied himself that his suspicions were unfounded. On 31 July Princess Lieven also found him 'in good spirits' and delighted with the prospect of his trip to the Continent.[37]

However, in early August his condition deteriorated and his behaviour became odd, although he continued to discuss business with all his accustomed authority and sense. Just before Wellington left for Belgium on 9 August he saw Londonderry and was shocked at his condition. 'It appears to me', the Duke wrote to Charles Arbuthnot before he left town, 'that his Mind and Body have been overpowered by the work of the Session; and that he is at the moment in a state of mental Delusion'. Wellington told him plainly that he was unwell, upon which the Foreign Secretary broke down in tears, confessing that it was so, and promising to go home and send for his doctor. The Duke offered to stay with him, and when this was refused, wrote himself to Dr Bankhead who at once visited Londonderry, bled him, and sent Wellington a reassuring note.[38] Nonetheless Wellington was severely shaken, as he admitted to Mrs Arbuthnot in a letter written from Calais the following day: 'I cannot describe to you the Impression it has made upon me. To see a Man with such a sober mind, who one would think could not be influenced by any Illusion, in a state bordering upon Insanity is not calculated to raise one's opinion of the strength of the Human mind. Poor Human Nature! How little we are after all.'[39]

Londonderry went down to Cray Farm, his place in the country, with his wife and doctor in the hope that quiet and rest would soon restore him. They were sufficiently concerned at his state to lock away his pistols and razors, but early on the morning of 12 August he cut his carotid artery with a small penknife they had overlooked, and died in the doctor's arms. His death left a void in the government, and the King in Scotland, and Liverpool in London, each sought assurances that the other would take no decisive step until they were able to discuss it in person after the King's return. Nonetheless it was obvious that there were two possibilities. The simplest and most natural was that Wellington would take the Foreign Office and Peel the leadership of the Commons, leaving Canning to proceed to India as planned. The other was that Canning would step into Castlereagh's shoes, taking both the Foreign Office and the leadership of the Commons.

The King, of course, wanted Wellington at the Foreign Office, partly for his own sake, and partly to block Canning. And there was much to be said in favour of this move: Wellington was Londonderry's obvious heir; he had worked closely with him ever since 1814, and shared his outlook and approach to foreign policy. He had vast experience of international diplomacy – dealing with allied governments had been one of his principal occupations from 1809 to 1818 – excellent personal contacts with foreign statesmen, and unequalled international prestige. Canning, by contrast, had spent thirty months as Foreign Secretary when Britain was at war with so much of the world that she had diplomatic relations with a bare handful of states, and had since been sent on a diplomatic mission to Lisbon which proved (through no fault of his) a complete failure. Moreover there was no doubt that Britain's allies would welcome Wellington's appointment, while they would view Canning with considerable reservation and distrust.[40]

But there were also arguments against Wellington's appointment. He was ineffective in Parliament, and while this mattered less because he was in the Lords, it still made a sharp contrast to Canning's excellence in the Commons. Liverpool also had a sense, which he had expressed as early as March 1821, that Wellington should be kept removed from the worst of the rough and tumble of politics lest it damage his reputation as a national figure:

> the Duke of Wellington was by his talents, his comprehensive mind & his clear & sound judgment the most important member of the Cabinet, & the most fit for the highest situation, yet that he belonged too much to the country generally to be put into any situation which might render him an object for party violence to attack; & that, tho' he was most fit for the highest military situations, yet that he shd be kept for them & that it wd not be fair by the country to make him solely a politician.[41]

It is not clear how this attitude can be reconciled with Wellington's inclusion in the Cabinet, or with the intense radical and press attacks on him, but Londonderry had agreed with Liverpool, and Wellington himself seems to have been influenced by the argument. Indeed the most compelling reason for not giving Wellington the Foreign Office in 1822 was that he made it clear that he did not want it. On 21 August, when discussions were still in their earliest stage, Princess Lieven asked Wellington directly: 'Are you going to be Minister for Foreign Affairs?' To which he replied:

> No, I don't want to be; that would mean deviating from my position and my career. I should be compelled to adopt the opinions of my party and my individual opinion would no longer be free. My ideas are more independent

as I am now; I would rather stick to them. If the King's service demands that I should assume this post, I will take it, but only if the worst comes to the worst; and I do not think we shall come to such a pass as that. I have no ambition; so little that I am ready to take any position, even though it is subordinate, if I see that I can be useful . . .

He went on to say that he had lost the habit of speaking in Parliament, which was necessary in a foreign secretary, and concluded:

In any case, they need not worry about finding Londonderry's successor. No man here is responsible for the policy of his country. That policy is already marked out, and the Cabinet cannot turn aside from it. I have already said this to Liverpool today; and I say it again on every possible occasion. Let England abandon that policy, and you plunge Europe, and consequently yourselves, into chaos. This truth must be grasped, for it is self-evident. Listen – I have such confidence in the system that I believe that, if Lord Grey were to become Minister today, he would maintain it just as we do.[42]

This moment marks Wellington's great refusal – the failure to accept that his active career as a soldier was over, and to embrace his position as a leading politician and Cabinet minister. If he had demanded the Foreign Office he would probably have got it, although there was a risk that Liverpool would resign and bring down the government rather than yield. But the reluctance to take the crucial step was genuine, and to justify this indulgence to himself, he argued that whoever was foreign secretary would inevitably see the world much as he and Londonderry saw it, and would pursue similar policies. He was deluding himself.[43]

Wellington's refusal was only one side of the story; the other was Liverpool's determination to bring in Canning. In part this can be explained by a lifelong friendship, admiration for Canning's ability, and perhaps also a response to Canning's emotional warmth and intensity of feeling. But political calculation also played a part. Liverpool feared that if Canning were excluded, even if he was happy in India, many of the less committed supporters of the government, especially those who supported Catholic Emancipation, would drift away. Already the Duke of Buckingham was murmuring that his connection would need to reconsider their participation in the government if Peel became leader of the Commons, and there were many younger, more liberal MPs who would see the elevation of Peel and Wellington as giving the administration a much more conservative character. Liverpool also had doubts about Peel's ability to dominate the Commons, and while Peel might serve under Canning without disgrace, there could be no thought of subordinating Canning.

Wellington himself accepted these arguments and used them to try to reconcile Londonderry's family to Canning's elevation, although without success.[44]

There was also a third layer to Liverpool's thinking: he wanted a change in foreign policy. Wellington would continue Londonderry's approach, if anything striving to co-operate more closely with the continental powers, and showing even less sympathy for liberal revolutions. Canning would favour a more assertive policy, one which would pay greater attention to the sensitivities of the House of Commons than to Britain's allies. Liverpool probably did not want or expect an immediate, dramatic change of direction, but under Canning the tendency of British politics would be away from, not towards, Europe. A few months later the Prime Minister wrote of Wellington: 'The truth is, he is rather *more continental* than we either are or ought to be *permanently*. I say *permanently*, because from circumstances we were brought into a course which was quite right at the time, but to which (with our different prejudices and form of Govt) we never could expect to adhere indefinitely'.[45]

There remained the opposition of the King supported by Lords Eldon and Sidmouth to be overcome. Wellington's disinclination to take the Foreign Office himself cut the ground from under them, but it was important that the King's consent not be too rudely extorted, or all the old resentments would flare back into life and the poisonous atmosphere of 1821 would return. At this crucial point Wellington fell gravely ill. According to Mrs Arbuthnot, he had found that his hearing was deteriorating in his left ear and submitted to treatment by an aurist named Stevenson who 'poured lunar caustic into his ear, put him to excruciating torture, threw him into a violent fever, & so great was the inflammation on the membrane leading to the brain that the physicians were frightened to death lest he should have a brain fever'. Liverpool admitted to feeling 'the greatest anxiety respecting the Duke' as 'the opinions of the medical men are not comfortable', while Princess Lieven told Metternich that the Duke 'has been in the gravest danger'. That may have been slightly exaggerated, but Wellington himself told Mrs Arbuthnot: 'I never was so unwell ... All my efforts to bully & bluster failed for the first time; and strange to say! I was near fainting in the effort to dress myself, & was obliged to give it up'.[46] His recovery was rapid but he did not give himself enough time to recuperate, and for the rest of the year and into 1823 his health was the subject of discussion and concern to his friends and colleagues. Liverpool, who was a year younger than Wellington but considerably less robust, remarked in November: 'We must make the Duke of W[ellington] take care of himself ... He has had a strong warning which comes upon every man a little sooner or later when he approaches or is past fifty. [Wellington was fifty-three], and he will feel himself compel'd to alter his mode of life. It is most unlucky that he should not find in domestick comforts a proportion at least of that repose he now so much wants'.[47]

Yet it was when the illness was at its worst that Wellington's influence on the King was greatest. Too ill to go and see His Majesty as the other senior Cabinet ministers did, Wellington admitted Knighton into his sickroom in his dual capacity as doctor and King's friend, and discussed the delicate question of how far the King's personal honour might be affected by Canning's return to the Cabinet. The Duke's advice, committed to paper on the following day, was that the personal honour of the Sovereign 'consists in acts of mercy and grace, and I am convinced that your Majesty's honour is most safe in extending your grace and favour to Mr Canning upon this occasion if the arrangement in contemplation is beneficial to your Majesty's service'.[48] No explanations need be embarked upon; it was quite sufficient for the King to say 'I forgive' and the matter would be closed.[49]

The King was delighted with this argument, which not only allowed him to reverse his veto on Canning without loss of face, but made it appear an act of grace not weakness. Yet he could not quite live up to the role, and when he wrote to Liverpool on 8 September he included a letter to be read to Canning which included the deliberately provocative phrase: 'The King is aware that the brightest ornament of his crown is the power of extending grace and favour to a subject who may have incurred his displeasure.' Canning naturally bridled at this, declaring it as being just the same as receiving a ticket for Almack's inscribed 'Admit the rogue', but it was now really too late for either side to withdraw without appearing ridiculous, and so the affair was smoothed over, and Liverpool was free to sit back and admire his handiwork: Canning was back in Cabinet, and nothing would ever be the same again.[50]

CHAPTER ELEVEN

VERONA AND SPAIN
(1822–23)

WITHIN DAYS OF Londonderry's death, and long before his successor was appointed, Liverpool indicated that Wellington would represent Britain in the important talks that the allied powers were about to hold in Vienna. The principal subjects for discussion at these talks would inevitably be the affairs of Spain and Greece, and Wellington was the obvious choice: well known to all the allied sovereigns and their ministers, familiar with Londonderry's thinking and the issues which were to be discussed, and able to speak on the affairs of Spain with unequalled authority. Wellington took with him the instructions Londonderry had drawn up for his own guidance, but his departure was delayed by his illness and the negotiations over Canning's appointment, so that he did not reach Paris until 20 September 1822.[1]

British interest in the talks was dominated by the problem of Spain, where the 'constitutional' regime established after the military revolution of 1820 had not been a success. It had the active support of only a narrow band of Spanish society, and widespread initial indifference had turned to hostility when promises to reduce taxes and abolish conscription were either never honoured or quickly reversed. The *liberales* who should have been the mainstay of the government were deeply divided, as much along generational as ideological lines, with fierce competition for the perks of office soon overwhelming any sense of common purpose. The authority of the central government was very weak, and while many progressive measures of social and economic reform were discussed, most did not become law, and even those that did were seldom implemented. Frustrated local officials sometimes acted arbitrarily and with violence, attacking both the Church and landowners, adding to the sense of anarchy and chaos. Royalist partisans took to the hills, together with many men whose motives were primarily economic and who behaved more as brigands than as guerrillas (although the distinction between the two had always been blurred). However, the army remained loyal to the new regime and had some success against the insurgents. Mina, the famous guerilla leader who had been noted for his humanity in the war against the French, now displayed extreme brutality in a campaign against royalists in Catalonia. Governments came and went in Madrid, and only made the situation in the countryside worse. Many of the older, more moderate *liberale* politicians came to admit that the famous Constitution of 1812 was virtually unworkable and should be revised, but any hint of the move in this direction simply gave an opening to their more radical opponents, who were supported by political clubs in the capital and sections of the army. Meanwhile the King remained implacably opposed to the new regime and aroused the distrust of even the most moderate and practical of the *liberales*. In July 1822 the Royal Guards made an incompetent attempt to seize power in Madrid, only to be defeated by the Urban Militia. Inevitably Spanish politics swung sharply to the left as the radicals celebrated their triumph and demanded that the King's power be further curtailed. The parallels with events in France thirty years earlier seemed obvious.[2]

The European powers watched the unfolding of events in Spain with dismay. In deference to Britain they had left Spain alone in the hope that the revolution would produce a stable and peaceful government, but instead it had simply gone from bad to worse. The contagion had already spread to Portugal and to Naples; ominous conspiracies had been detected in the French army; and discontented officers and radicals all across Europe took heart from the example of Spain as they plotted to overthrow their own governments. The events of July in Madrid were the last straw, and it was obvious that the other powers were growing impatient with the British policy of non-interference.[3]

At the same time the British public had grown increasingly hostile to the 'Holy Alliance', making any compromise very difficult. The underlying problem was Britain's inability to influence events in Madrid; she had pressed strongly for changes to the constitution which would make it both more efficient and less radical, and she had urged Ferdinand to work with the moderate *liberales* for the good of the country, and in both cases had received nothing but empty promises. This left Britain playing the dog in the manger: unable to help Spain herself, and unwilling to let any other power do so.

Wellington had remarkably frank talks in Paris with Villèle, the dominant figure in the French government. Villèle openly admitted that his Cabinet was divided between those who advocated an invasion of Spain to liberate the King and crush the revolution, and those – including himself – who preferred to do nothing for the moment. He saw this as a choice of evils; those who called for an invasion hoped that French troops would be well received by the populace, would not have to advance beyond Madrid, and could be able to withdraw from Spain as soon as their job was done, leaving Ferdinand restored to his full powers. Obviously all these assumptions were distinctly optimistic, and the

Peninsular War showed just how badly things could go wrong. If the Spanish people resisted as they had done between 1808 and 1814 the campaign would be a humiliating failure and the loyalty of the French army to the Bourbons, which was already open to question, would be placed under even greater strain. On the other hand, a policy of inaction would be condemned as a shameful failure if, as seemed all too likely, Ferdinand was deposed or the royal family came to harm.

Villèle was confident that he could resist the pressure to intervene for some time, but he had already agreed to assemble an army of 100,000 men in southern France to encourage the Spanish politicians to make concessions before it was too late. Wellington responded that French actions, including the assembly of troops and the aid which had been covertly supplied to royalist insurgents, had only increased tensions in Spain, strengthening the hand of the radicals in Madrid and making war more likely.[4]

Villèle cautioned that the meeting of the allies had aroused expectations, and that it could hardly end without making some declaration or taking some action over Spain without appearing impotent and encouraging radicals across Europe. Wellington can scarcely have welcomed this, for there was almost no common ground between Britain and the allies on the issue, but nonetheless he was thoroughly pleased by his meeting with Villèle. It was no small comfort to find that the French minister was working to avoid French intervention in Spain, and was keen to maintain good relations with Britain if at all possible. And Wellington, whose opinion of French politicians was not generally very high, was impressed by Villèle, reporting to London that 'he displayed more ability, candour, and fairness than I have ever observed in any French minister'.[5]

After only a few days in Paris Wellington left for Vienna, which he reached on 29 September. His health suffered on the last stage of this journey with a recurrence of the pain in his head and he had to be bled on his arrival. It was only three weeks since his life was thought to be in danger.[6] Nonetheless, once at Vienna he plunged straight into further negotiations and problems. He found that Charles Stewart, the new Lord Londonderry, was incensed at Canning's appointment, and had already resigned as British ambassador to Vienna without even waiting to speak to Wellington. Stewart remained bitter for years, a loose cannon, impulsive, wrong-headed, slightly ridiculous, but quite capable of damaging his friends if not his enemies.[7]

Wellington spent less than a week in Vienna, for the allied ministers and sovereigns were impatient to move to Verona where the main congress was to be held. But in these preliminary talks Metternich was comforting; he abhorred the Spanish revolution, wished that it might be overthrown, but felt that foreign intervention would risk doing more harm than good. Alexander was, predictably, much more difficult: 'He said that he considered that country [Spain] as the headquarters of revolution and Jacobinism; that the King and Royal Family were in the utmost danger; and that so long as the revolution in that country should be allowed to continue, every country in Europe, and France in particular, was unsafe.'[8] Alexander's vehemence was partly explained by the knowledge that Spanish diplomats had played an active role in fomenting the revolutions in Portugal and Naples, and even more by claims that 'the late Spanish minister in Russia laid out large sums of money to corrupt my officers and troops; I was obliged to send him away'.[9] Wellington repeated the familiar British arguments against interference in the internal affairs of other countries, and cited Lord William Bentinck's constitutional experiments in Sicily in the final years of the war against Napoleon as evidence for the failure of solutions imposed from the outside. Unconvinced by this the Emperor moved on to specifics, commenting that he did not think that the French army could be trusted to undertake an operation against liberal Spain, and made it clear that he hoped to see a pan-European, but predominantly Russian, army employed. He was obviously eager to use his army somewhere, and Wellington warned that if he was thwarted in Spain it might be more difficult to restrain him in Greece, for reports of the Turkish massacres had aroused strong feelings in Russia. Nonetheless Wellington was confident that the French would refuse to allow any Russian troops near Spain, and had the satisfaction of seeing that Alexander had not anticipated this problem and had no answer for it. Wellington was reasonably pleased with these initial meetings. It was clear that it would be chiefly up to Britain to restrain the Russian Emperor's eagerness for action, just as it had been at Aix-la-Chapelle, but he hoped that with quiet support from Austria and Prussia this could be achieved. Much would depend on the stance taken by France, but Villèle's desire to retain his freedom of action suggested that the French would be unlikely to press for a united allied policy on Spain.[10]

Wellington arrived at Verona on 15 October and at once began further informal talks. His position was not helped by the arrival of news from Spain, where an extraordinary session of the Cortes had listened with enthusiasm to inflammatory speeches from several leading ministers denouncing the allied meeting and hinting that Spain might actually declare war on France. At the same time the allies learnt that Britain had sent Sir William À Court as her new envoy to Madrid – a step which they felt conveyed a measure of support for the Spanish government. It looked to them that Britain wished to be free to pursue an independent policy of her own in Spain, while expecting them to hold back in deference to her wishes. This was being rather oversensitive, for it was only through a mission such as À Court's that Britain could use her influence and friendly persuasion to convince the Spaniards to make concessions; but the timing was unfortunate, appearing to pre-empt any decisions made at Verona, and in allied eyes À Court was tainted by his (actually rather limited) sympathy for Neapolitan liberals in his previous posting.[11]

Despite these developments the negotiations over Spain might still have taken the course Wellington desired if the French had followed the policy outlined by Villèle in Paris. However, the French delegation was led, not by Villèle but by his rival, Montmorency, the Foreign Minister, who viewed war with Spain as both probable and desirable. Montmorency was happy to sacrifice some freedom of action in return for the support of the Eastern Powers, which might be used to counter the inevitable British opposition to any French interference in Spain. Far from wishing to avoid discussion of Spain he placed it squarely before the allies on 20 October, by formally enquiring how they would respond if France was attacked by Spain.[12]

The responses were fairly predictable. Alexander leapt on the idea with enthusiasm, and talked of forming a Russian army of 150,000 men in Piedmont at short notice to help France. Privately Alexander acknowledged that his army might also be used to restore order in France itself if the war triggered a military revolt or Jacobin revolution, but had little appreciation that the mere presence of such an army on the frontier would destabilise the country and undermine the legitimacy of the Bourbons.[13] The British position was just as extreme in the opposite direction. Wellington said that he would not comment on how his government would react in hypothetical circumstances, while suggesting that France bore most of the blame for the troubled state of her relations with Spain. This stand attracted a good deal of criticism. The allies, and particularly Metternich, condemned Wellington for obstinate intransigence that made useful negotiations impossible. Conversely the British public, led by the Opposition, would soon accuse him of 'contemptible tricks' and playing 'a low, truckling and cowardly part', because he did not summon his carriage and abandon the Congress the moment Spain became the subject of discussion. In fact Wellington's response was dictated by his instructions, which had been made more explicit by Canning, who wrote in late September: 'I am to instruct your Grace at once frankly and peremptorily to declare, that to any such interference, come what may, his Majesty will not be a party.' Not that this represented more than a marginal hardening of British policy on Spain, which had barely shifted since Castlereagh's state paper of 1820.[14]

Austria and Prussia valiantly tried to find some common ground on which to frame a compromise, but the British and Russian positions were simply irreconcilable. If he had been able to consider the question in isolation Metternich would probably have sided with Britain and carried Prussia with him. But Greece and the Balkans were far more important to Austria than Spain, and he would not squander his influence restraining Russia in the west when he might need it to restrain her closer to home. So he did the minimum possible to help France and satisfy Russia, in the hope that if Britain was alienated she would soon get over it and resume her part as a vital ally, just as she had done after Troppau and Laibach. It was not a comfortable choice, but it was understandable.[15]

The result was that Britain was largely excluded from the talks on Spain which took place at Verona in the first three weeks of November. Everyone knew where she stood, and her disapproval of the final outcome was virtually taken for granted. This does not mean that her stance did not have influence, but that it provided a constant steady pressure in one direction. Metternich used it to extract concessions from Alexander that gradually removed the most effective, and hence obnoxious, elements from his policy. In the end the army of 150,000 men in Piedmont had disappeared, and been replaced by a co-ordinated diplomatic protest by the ambassadors of the four powers (France, Russia, Austria and Prussia) in Madrid, which would probably result in their recall. This did not amount to war, but it was a strong signal of allied solidarity with France, virtually amounting to a promise of allied approval if she chose to intervene in Spain.

Wellington was presented with this result almost as a *fait accompli*. He did all that he could to argue against it, warning that war might lead to disaster, and that the proposed diplomatic action would only make Spain more hostile, and reveal to the world that the alliance was irreconcilably divided on the question. Metternich could sympathise with these arguments, privately deplored the need to take any action on Spain, but still felt compelled to do so. Ironically, the knowledge that the French government was not committed to war made it very much easier for Austria and Prussia to support her, for it allowed them to hope that they would never be called upon to honour their promises.[16]

Wellington found the negotiations at Verona a strain. Before the end of October he told Canning that none of the previous meetings he had attended equalled the 'difficulty and embarrassment' of the discussions over Spain, and he found his exclusion from many of the subsequent talks galling, even though it was obvious that he would have been perpetually the odd man out. The fragility of his health added to his troubles. Princess Lieven told her brother on 23 October: 'His health is much broken, and I am really afraid lest the Congress should give the finishing stroke.' That was unduly pessimistic, but other observers were almost equally anxious.[17] Fortunately he was not alone. Fitzroy Somerset accompanied him and could be trusted to handle much official business which Wellington did not want to entrust to the subordinate British diplomats at the Congress. And Wellington's favourite niece Priscilla and her husband Lord Burghersh arrived from Florence and stayed with him until the end of the Congress, providing some much-needed domestic comfort and amusement.[18] When his health and spirits were good enough there was no shortage of society, and Wellington could pay court to Princess Lieven one night, and dine with seven sovereigns the next. Nonetheless, almost from the outset he looked forward to the end of the Congress and the chance to go home. He had achieved some success on subsidiary questions such as measures to enforce the ban on the slave trade, and the final outcome on Spain was not quite as bad as it might have been, but the fact remained that the allies had broken with Britain over Spain, and that war was now more likely than ever. That was not Wellington's fault – he could not stop Montmorency raising the issue or convince Metternich that Spain mattered more to Austria than the Balkans – but there was little satisfaction to be felt in the result.

Wellington left Verona on 30 November and spent eleven days in Paris trying to strengthen Villèle's position and discourage the war party. Villèle was still in the ascendant; he had been formally appointed president of the Council of Ministers since Wellington's previous visit, and the King and the Duc d'Angoulême agreed with his opposition to war. But the royalist press and public opinion were extremely bellicose, denouncing Villèle as craven, attacking British influence, and portraying events in Spain in the most lurid and inflammatory light. Villèle had almost no support from within his own party, and the limited support he received from French liberals was counter-productive, further damaging his credibility in royalist circles. In his talks with Wellington, Villèle made it plain that he was fighting a rearguard action and that the only hope of peacefully defusing the crisis was if the Spanish government made substantial concessions which he could use to placate French opinion and justify a step back from the brink. Wellington also did his best to change the climate of opinion in the elite circles of ultra-royalists who had a direct influence on the government's foreign policy. This naturally annoyed the Russians, who were working in the same way in the opposite direction. According to Princess Lieven, Pozzo di Borgo 'is very much incensed with the Duke of Wellington, who everyone says behaved like an intriguer while he was here'; while, with a fine lack of self-consciousness, she angrily denounced him for 'paying marked attentions to Madame du Cayla', the King's favourite.[19]

Wellington landed at Dover on the morning of 22 December 1822 and reached London on the following day. He continued to suffer from the effects of his illness and exertions. In January it was said that he 'looks older and thinner', while a month later Canning told Bagot: 'The Duke is not ill, but very deaf.'[20] At the end of January he was slightly injured in a traffic accident – knocked to the ground and badly shaken by a gig or cabriolet. A few weeks later Creevey was shocked at his appearance: 'I never saw a man's looks so altered. He is a perfect shadow, and as old looking as the ark.'[21] For once this even affected his work, and on 20 March he apologised for not forwarding some papers to Canning because he had been too unwell to attend to them. The nature of the illness is unclear, but as he described them as 'inflammatory attacks' and complained 'a good deal of his head' it was probably related to the mistreatment of his ear the previous year.[22] By the beginning of April he was feeling sufficiently recovered to resent Mrs Arbuthnot's anxiety and the attention of his doctor:

All Doctors are more or less *Quacks!* and there is nothing more comical than that Dr Hume should have made you believe that I am an *Idiot!* rather than the truth, that he as well as others of the Medical Profession is a little bit of a *Charlatan!* I know very well that my Head has been out of order ever since that other *Charlatan* doctored my Ear; and I know what is good for me as well [as] Dr Hume or any Doctor of the Profession . . . Then I know . . . that to lay in bed does and always has done me more harm than anything else. I am never unwell but at night; and I get well from the moment I rise in the morning, & better till I go to bed again. The whole Medical profession cannot tell me the reason any more than they can tell me now whether I am deaf or not, or whether I shall ever hear again, or what I am to do to hear. I am put to torture with blisters, only because they will do me no harm; and then I am to be told that Doctors are not *Charlatans.* You know as well as I do that they are! and that what they talk is neither more or less than *nonsense & stuff* . . .[23]

It was not Wellington's way to suffer in silence, but the shocking thing is that his scepticism is probably justified, for it is hard to believe that bleeding or blisters would have done anything to improve his condition. His natural toughness and abstemiousness did far more than medical science to help him recover from the illness, and his health was considerably better for the rest of 1823, although he could not take it for granted as he had previously done, and suffered several other brief spells when he was unwell. Yet he was still in his prime, turning fifty-four that spring.

Neither Wellington's health nor his temper were improved by the cool reception he had received from Liverpool and Canning on his return from the Continent, or by his growing concern at Canning's conduct of foreign affairs. As early as 12 January Mrs Arbuthnot recorded that 'the Duke says that Mr Canning is upsetting all our Foreign policy, and doing things in so hasty & unreflecting a manner as will get him into innumerable scrapes; he settles things without half understanding his subject & unsettles them in an equally hasty manner'. And in February she noted that 'the Duke of Wellington, who was the most eager to have him, is now the most uneasy at all that is going on & says he had no conception what a man he was'. Wellington was particularly unhappy that Canning was doing nothing to heal the rift which had opened between Britain and the continental powers. Before the end of January the Duke was sending conciliatory messages to the Courts of Russia and Austria through their ambassadors in London and even showing them confidential papers, intending to reassure them that the British government had not suddenly been converted to Jacobinism. This was not done with the intention of undermining Canning's policy, but it plainly exposed the divisions within the British government and so damaged the Foreign Secretary's authority.[24]

Meanwhile France and Spain continued to drift towards war. British pressure, including an ostensibly private mission by Fitzroy Somerset, failed to persuade either party in Spain to make concessions. King Ferdinand eagerly anticipated a French invasion which would restore him to absolute power, while the *liberales*, trapped by their own rhetoric and the passion of their supporters, affected to despise the threat of foreign intervention and made much of claims that the French army would rebel and overthrow the government rather than be used to put down the sacred cause of liberty.[25]

The balance of forces in France was also swinging towards war. On 28 January Louis XVIII's speech at the opening of the Chambers pointed to the likelihood of war in order to 'save the throne of Spain for a [descendant] of Henry IV . . . let Ferdinand VII be free to give his people institutions which they cannot hold but for him'.[26] This produced a furious outcry in Britain where the legitimist doctrine that political institutions could only come from the Crown, and talk of a Bourbon family compact, were seen as equally provocative. Canning and Liverpool led the British reaction against the French. Liverpool told Marcellus, the French chargé d'affaires in London, that the Cabinet had been forced to revise George IV's speech to Parliament and remove the word 'neutrality'; the navy was increased from 21,000 to 25,000 men; and the embargo on the export of arms to Spain and South America was lifted. Canning denounced Louis's speech and French intervention in Spain in a despatch of 3 February, which re-affirmed the principle of non-intervention and maintained the complete independence of Spain regardless of dynastic ties. A few days later, in a public speech at Harwich, he said that while Britain sought peace she was fully prepared for war.[27]

It is not entirely clear whether Canning and Liverpool really believed that such crude public threats would force the French to back down, or whether they were more concerned with opinion at home, especially in Parliament. Canning's language in the Commons certainly stole the Opposition's thunder and deprived it of a popular cause, but it simply strengthened the war party in Paris. By February the chance of avoiding French intervention in Spain had shrunk to almost nothing, but the pressure applied by Britain made it even harder for Villèle to craft a compromise that would not be seen as a humiliating backdown. Chateaubriand, who had replaced Montmorency as foreign minister, responded to the Harwich speech and other British blustering by consulting the allied ministers in Paris, who made clear their full support for France. Alexander went further, sending out a diplomatic circular stating that he would regard a British declaration of war on France as 'a general attack against all the allies and that he would accept without hesitation the consequences of this principle'. With great satisfaction Chateaubriand wrote to Marcellus: 'Let my honourable friend Canning fume as much as he pleases. He is foiled. He had dreamed of war and is powerless to make it. That is the secret of his ill humour.'[28]

In fact neither Canning nor Liverpool had any intention of going to war in defence of the discredited Spanish government. Wellington had warned them strongly that they would face most or all of Europe, and that Britain's vital interests in the Netherlands and Portugal would be placed in jeopardy. He plainly loathed their cavalier talk of war: 'It is the greatest mistake to suppose that if we enter into this or any war we can do it by halves, or confine our operation to one branch of our military power and resource.'[29] He argued instead that Britain should adopt a much more cautious, conciliatory policy which would make the best of a situation that was clearly beyond her control:

It must be our policy not to offend [the allied] Sovereigns. We must wish and endeavour to remain at peace with them, and, remaining at peace, we must desire and endeavour to be on good terms with them. In proportion as we are on good terms with them, we may hope that we shall influence their conduct in the expected contest between France and Spain; and that at all events the best mode of alleviating the evil which must be the consequence of a successful result of the invasion of Spain by France will be to prevail upon the Powers of the Continent hereafter to join with us to prevent France from profiting by that result by obtaining objects of French or family ambition.[30]

Wellington's advice was not taken, setting Britain up for an ignominious diplomatic defeat when her bluff was called. Yet it would be unfair to dismiss Canning's policy as nothing more than a populist appeal to the gallery. He had a long-standing distrust of the system of allied co-operation in Europe that Castlereagh had helped forge, and which Wellington still sought to maintain. He derided it as an *Areopagus* that aspired to rule the world, and preferred instead a system of open competition between the powers where Britain could use her natural advantages to pursue her own interests. In November 1822, he expressed this in a private letter to his old friend, the diplomat Charles Bagot, who was at St Petersburg: 'You know my politics well enough to know what I mean – when I say that for "Europe" I shall be desirous now and then to read "England".'[31] Canning was acutely sensitive to public opinion, and felt that the

British government had paid a high price at home for its close co-operation with the continental powers, and received little in return. Like most foreign ministers he craved freedom of action and resented the constraints imposed by the need to work with the allies. And he felt that in general British interests would best be served by keeping a greater distance from European affairs, and hoped that by doing so he could make British intervention rare but decisive. Unfortunately this theory was particularly ill suited to the situation he faced in early 1823, where Britain needed to exert more influence than she possessed in Paris and Madrid, and where her erstwhile allies were ranged against her.

As the French prepared for war, opinion on both sides of the Channel became more heated. French liberals, including General Foy, predicted that any attack on Spain would provoke a national uprising which would combine the excesses of the Peninsular War with the political radicalism of the height of the French Revolution. Attempts were made to subvert the French troops, but without success, and the spirit of the army improved markedly with the prospect of action.[32] In Britain the atmosphere was intensely pro-Spanish; hostile, but almost contemptuous of France; and reserving its greatest venom for the Eastern Powers, especially Russia, who were blamed for driving the French into war. The subject dominated the news in the early months of 1823; more than half of the political caricatures of the year were given to it, and they were almost all sympathetic to the Spanish cause. Spain was identified without hesitation or qualification with the cause of liberty; France and the continental powers with that of tyranny and oppression, often with an element of uninhibited anti-Catholicism thrown in for good measure. Several prints showed strong Bonapartist sympathies, and looked to the failure of French armies in Spain bringing about a revolution in France which would lead to the elevation of Napoleon's twelve-year-old son to the imperial throne.[33] The finest prints were four by George Cruikshank, all produced between 17 and 26 February, in which he ridiculed Louis for attempting to emulate Napoleon, blamed allied pressure on France for causing the trouble, attacked Ferdinand's treachery while lauding the Spanish constitution, and predicted the complete defeat of any French attack. It is striking that none evoked memories of Wellington's Spanish campaigns or called for British military aid to Spain. As radicals Cruikshank and his peers had spent years calling for lower taxes and less spending on the army while sniping at 'the Waterloo Man' and the whole idea of military glory. It was too much to reverse direction in an instant, and besides Wellington's lack of sympathy for the Spanish cause was an open secret.[34]

The rhetoric of the Opposition in Parliament was at least as intemperate as that of the press and the caricatures. Many Opposition members were strongly tempted to call for Britain to go to war in defence of Spain, while others were torn by conflicting impulses. Canning had already occupied the Opposition's natural ground, leaving it little choice but to tamely support his policies or risk divisions in its own ranks and getting ahead of public opinion. After a little hesitation, the cooler heads among the Whigs prevailed, and rather than committing themselves to advocating a war which would have been at odds with so many of their other policies, they preferred to criticise the detail of the government's conduct. They soon turned to the Congress of Verona and demanded to know why Wellington had failed to avert French action then. This led to an attempt to censure the government at the end of April which resulted in three nights of debate in which Canning swept the floor with his opponents, and reduced the Opposition to the expedient of voting with the government to conceal their lack of support. The censure was defeated by 372 votes to 20.[35] A similar motion had already been defeated in the Lords, where Wellington had spoken in his own defence. The result was a comfortable but less one-sided victory (142 to 48) with the minority including a royal duke (Sussex) and Lord Lynedoch – Wellington's old Peninsular comrade Sir Thomas Graham. Despite these majorities, the debates and the discussions surrounding them damaged Wellington's reputation at the time and subsequently. They left an impression that he had been ineffective if not incompetent at Verona, and that his opposition to foreign intervention in Spain had been lukewarm. Lord Acton, the great nineteenth-century liberal historian, lent his weight to the idea with the accusation that Wellington had deliberately sabotaged Canning's policy at Verona. Later research showed that this was nonsense, but until recently British diplomatic history of these years has been overwhelmingly presented from Canning's perspective, and little account is taken of those who argued that another approach might have produced a better outcome.[36]

The French army commanded by the Duc d'Angoulême crossed the Bidassoa into Spain on 6 April 1823. The Spanish people who, only a decade before, had resisted the French so passionately, greeted their return with cheers and enthusiasm. The French were careful not to spoil their reception, maintaining strict discipline especially in their behaviour towards civilians, and paying promptly for all their supplies. On 24 May Angoulême entered Madrid amid a shower of flowers, with cheering crowds crying out 'Death to all Liberals'. The Spanish government had fled, dragging Ferdinand with them, first to Seville where the King was 'temporarily' deposed and a regency declared, and then on to Cadiz. The French followed and on 1 October Cadiz capitulated and Ferdinand was restored to power. He promptly rejected French advice to pardon all but the worst of his enemies and give his people a moderate constitution, instead setting an example of proscriptions and executions which was taken up with enthusiasm by his supporters in the provinces. Angoulême went home in disgust and refused all honours for his remarkable triumph, while a French army of occupation remained in Spain, peacefully and without trouble until 1828. France was unable to ensure that Spain was well governed in these years, but she provided an interlude of calm and stability which appears relatively attractive compared to the preceding and following periods.[37]

As soon as the invasion began Canning had announced that Britain would remain neutral on three conditions: that any French occupation of Spain be temporary, not permanent; that the French did not attempt to assist Ferdinand to regain control over his colonies in the Americas; and that the independence of Portugal was respected. The French simply ignored this statement, and its hollowness was made evident by the lack of resistance to their advance in Spain. Britain could hardly fight to defend a Spanish constitution that plainly aroused no feelings of loyalty within Spain itself, while the idea that French troops should quit Spain as soon as Ferdinand was released was obviously absurd, and would have condemned the poor distracted country to more years of anarchy and civil strife.[38]

The French success in Spain was humiliation for British foreign policy. Spain would now inevitably fall back into the French sphere of influence, and probably forge an even closer alliance than the 'Family Compact' of the eighteenth century. At the same time the French government emerged much stronger. The loyalty of the army had been tested and proved sound; and while the campaign had been almost bloodless, there was deeper satisfaction in expunging memories of Napoleon's disastrous war in Spain and replacing them with an operation that could not have succeeded better. Angoulême's campaign helped establish the Bourbons in France on a much more secure footing. From the point of view of the British government, that was all to the good; although its corollary, that France would be much more self-confident, assertive and unresponsive to British influence, was naturally less welcome in London.

The lack of support for the 'constitutional' government in Spain, following similar events in Naples, ought to have dealt a fatal blow to the pretension of radicals to speak on behalf of 'the people'. However any effect, at least in Britain, was transitory. Enthusiastic partisans of the Spanish cause like Lord Holland were surprised and disappointed at the turn events had taken, but soon took comfort in the excuses offered by liberal refugees, who naturally fashioned a tale which accorded remarkably well with their host's prejudices. If there was a lingering effect on British political attitudes it was an increase in insularity and contempt for foreigners who had failed to live up to the hopes and expectations they had aroused. This was well expressed by a paragraph in the *Morning Herald* in October:

> The game appears to be completely up in Spain, and every revolutionary symptom appears to be at an end. In viewing the conduct of those who took a part in opposing the invasion of the French, when we consider the treachery of some, the cowardice of others, and the imbecility of almost all, we are

inclined to entertain the same feeling for them as for the Neapolitans. Among the Spanish Constitutionalists there are undoubtedly many individuals who displayed a great deal of intrepidity; but as a people, the Spaniards appear to be sunk low in the scale of natural degradation . . .[39]

The demise of the 'constitutional' government in Spain triggered a similar change in Portugal, but without any direct foreign involvement. Lord Holland and his friends may have been dismayed, but Canning, who had more personal knowledge of Portugal than of any other foreign country, was not. He told Bagot on 14 July that the overthrown 'revolutionists were the scum of the earth and the Portuguese earth – fierce, rascally, thieving, ignorant ragamuffins; hating England, and laboring with all their might and cunning to force or entrap us into war. They are gone, gone out like a candle, a tallow-candle, and in their stead reigns Palmella, the very best of Portuguese.'[40] Palmella and the King of Portugal promptly appealed to Britain for aid, specifically a naval squadron in the Tagus and a force of 6,000 troops to ensure stability while the army and militia were re-modelled, for the threat of a renewed revolution came less from the people than from the soldiery. Wellington warmly supported the request and was amazed when Liverpool and Canning proved willing to send the ships but not the troops, claiming that none were available. Wellington knew that the British army had been so reduced as to be almost incapable of any exertion, but believed that if the will existed this difficulty could be overcome; temporary expedients could cover a shortfall while some fresh troops were raised. He was in Cheltenham at the time, taking the waters, and two forceful letters went up to London in three days putting his case:

If we have not the troops and cannot get them, we cannot give them. But if we have the troops I cannot see how we can refuse them, allied as we are to the King of Portugal, unless we make up our minds to give up our position in Europe, and to leave France to act the part which had hitherto been ours.[41]

The advantages to be derived from the measure are, the saving of Portugal from the influence of France; and likewise from the tyranny of a despotism established under French influence on the one hand, or from that of the mob on the other; the assertion of the influence of this country, and the demonstration of its power in a cause of which no reasonable man can doubt the justice, which in its consequences may, and indeed must, tend to give this country all the weight it would desire to have in the settlement of the affairs in the Peninsula, and of those between Portugal and the Brazils.

I confess that it opens a scene of operations for us in our neutral character, and affords an opportunity which I am astonished that you don't seize.[42]

Faced with Wellington's vehemence the Foreign Secretary called a Cabinet meeting to consider the question, but when the Duke arrived in London he found that neither Canning nor Liverpool would discuss Portugal with him in advance of the meeting, and that the whole thing was settled whether he liked it or not. Seething with resentment he stormed back to Cheltenham, and the breach inside the government yawned wider than ever.[43]

Even before the abortive trip to London Mrs Arbuthnot reported, 'I have never seen the Duke so annoyed about anything in my life', and it is clear that he felt that Canning was principally to blame, even though it was Liverpool who had made the case against sending troops to Portugal. The Prime Minister was worried that the initial commitment of 6,000 men would not be enough and that Britain might soon find itself taking sides in a civil war.[44] He may also have feared that Britain's role in Portugal would not appear all that different from that of France in Spain and Austria in Naples, and that the Opposition would exploit this in Parliament to associate the ministry again with the unpopular force of reaction. Pressure from London prevented Palmella appealing to France for aid, and for a few months it seemed that Portuguese affairs would slip back into their customary obscurity, although any careful observer could see that further trouble was almost inevitable.

It is hardly surprising that relations between Wellington and Canning should have become a source of constant tension and difficulty within the government by the summer of 1823. Both were highly intelligent men, accustomed to the admiration and attention of their friends and used to getting their own way. Each believed that he had a superior understanding of foreign affairs and Britain's place in the world, and these outlooks differed quite sharply. Yet they had made a real effort to work constructively together. Wellington was generous with his advice – too generous, for he could not avoid sounding patronising and Canning was far too acute not to notice, and far too proud not to resent, it. In his first months in office the Foreign Secretary bit his tongue and treated the Duke with courtesy and even some appearance of deference – frequently giving at least some ground to conciliate Wellington, and, where conflict could not be avoided, hiding behind Liverpool wherever he could. He also appointed Henry Wellesley to take Londonderry's place in the Vienna embassy – a step entirely justified on merit and experience, but which was nonetheless also a gesture of goodwill to the Duke. None of this was nearly enough to bridge the gap between the two men; Wellington, like most of the political world, distrusted Canning and believed that he was pursuing his own advantage rather than that of the government. Canning's history and conduct provided ample ammunition for his critics, who laughed at the blatancy of some of his manoeuvres, whether it was appointing Lord Francis Conyngham, son of the King's mistress and a regular presence at Brighton and Windsor, as his under-secretary; or his cultivation of the press and public opinion, so that some Conservative back-benchers might have been tempted to mutter that he was 'friend of every party but his own'. Certainly there were many on the government benches who felt distinctly uncomfortable with the language and attitudes used by the new leader of the House, and who felt the large majorities enjoyed by the ministry in 1823 had been bought by a large sacrifice of principles and policy.[45]

Inevitably Wellington 'again & again repented having advised [Canning's] having the Foreign Seals & said, if it was to come over again, he wd. cut his hand off rather than recommend such a measure'.[46] But Wellington's anger was almost equally directed at Liverpool, who had pressed so hard for Canning's inclusion and who now failed to restrain him. In July he burst out in public 'My Lord Liverpool is neither more nor less than a common prostitute', and while he was embarrassed when he realised that ladies were present, he did not disavow the sentiment. A month later, after the row over Portugal, Charles Arbuthnot privately warned Liverpool 'that it was *he* and not *Canning* who had given the offence. Arbuthnot confided to Bathurst: 'I think I have done good. [Liverpool] is evidently very anxious to be well with the Duke, and I took care to let him feel that it depended upon himself to be so.'[47]

Wellington's concern and resentment were shared by the other senior ministers in the government. Eldon had, of course, always been opposed to Canning's return to the ministry, and the enmity between the two men was unabated. Bathurst was 'excessively uneasy' at Canning's conduct of affairs as early as the beginning of February, and looked to Wellington to help keep him under control. And Peel, the other Secretary of State, 'has great suspicions of Canning; and it annoys him not a little that Lord Liverpool should be under such subjugation to him'.[48] Outside the ministry, the heir-presumptive to the throne, the Duke of York, whose influence was increasing in 1823, was decid-edly hostile to the Foreign Secretary. A few of the younger, less influential ministers, especially those in the Commons such as Fredrick Robinson, may have begun to look to Canning in 1823, but he remained essentially an isolated figure in Cabinet with none of his own loyal band of followers to second his views. Not that this mattered much so long as he retained Liverpool's confi-dence. Most important government decisions were taken not in full meetings of the fourteen-man Cabinet, but in smaller groups whose composition varied according to the subject. Charles Wynn, who was acutely conscious of his exclusion from the inner councils of the government, said that 'the only real and efficient Cabinet upon *all* matters, consists of Lords Liverpool and Bathurst, Duke of Wellington and Canning, and that the others are only more or less consulted upon different businesses by these four'.[49] This was simplifying matters a little too much; Wellington had little interest in economic or financial questions at this time, and it is unlikely that Bathurst or Canning had much either, except where they related to foreign or colonial trade. Here Liverpool would consult Robinson, Huskisson and also Herries, who was appointed financial secretary to the Treasury in 1823. Wellington had a greater interest in Irish affairs, but Peel was obviously the most influential minister when they were discussed, although the Prime Minister here and everywhere would have the last word if he chose to use it. Liverpool did not dominate his government in the obvious way that Pitt had done, if only because he was in the Lords and never did much to project himself as the personification of the government, but his was no government of equals, and there was no question of disagreements being resolved by votes in Cabinet.[50]

The King's personal dislike of Canning remained as strong as ever and was now reinforced by disquiet over his policies. The King's sympathies were all with France, not Spain, and he continued to look on Metternich as 'the first statesman of Europe'.[51] He was indiscreet enough to reveal this to foreign ambassadors, and treated Princess Lieven as a confidential member of his inner circle.[52] Still, in general his relations with his ministers were much better than in previous years. Canning saw no advantage in making difficulties with the King, and overlooked much that would have provoked another foreign secretary to protest, while the King's objections to Liverpool were largely in abeyance in the first half of the year.

Liverpool's own position was much stronger than in 1821. Canning had divided the Cabinet and made the government much less cohesive and happy, but paradoxically this had ensured the Prime Minister's indispensability. He was the vital link between the two wings of the government and was the only man capable of forcing them to work together. Neither wing was able to make a viable government on its own, but together they formed the strongest and most successful ministry to govern Britain since the 1790s. Whether by accident or design – Liverpool is too opaque a figure for us to know which – he had succeeded in guarding his flank against any intrigue.

Twelve months after Canning took office, the government's position had been transformed. Internationally Britain was isolated and had lost her influence over Spain. The continental powers still hoped to re-establish the alliance and to co-operate in solving outstanding difficulties such as the Eastern Question, but they would have been blind not to recognise Canning's hostility or to assume that he would be brought to heel by his colleagues. But what the government lost abroad it gained at home. The country was more prosperous and peaceful than at any time since the end of the war. Its majority in the Commons was secure, and Canning's foreign policy gained at least as much applause from the Opposition as from the government benches. Beneath the surface a new, broad consensus was emerging in public opinion. The old confrontational radicalism was, for the moment at least, in eclipse; but equally the government appeared to have moved closer to its opponents, adopting more liberal stances on foreign policy, economic and trade issues, and also in Ireland, where Lord Wellesley was quarrelling vigorously with the government's traditional Protestant supporters. In fact these were quite separate unrelated developments, but they gave the government a fresher, refurbished look which was much enhanced by Canning's bold oratory both in the Commons and, most unusually, in the country more generally. This was the genesis of the idea of a new age of 'liberal toryism', which helped strengthen the government's standing, but only at the cost of appearing to slight many of its most senior ministers, including Wellington.

CHAPTER TWELVE

LATIN AMERICA AND THE
CATHOLIC QUESTION
(1823–25)

A T THE BEGINNING OF 1824 Wellington was alienated from the Prime Minister and the Foreign Secretary, and to a lesser extent from the rest of the Cabinet. He was still smarting from his treatment in the discussions over Portugal the previous August, and resented the reluctance of colleagues who agreed with him to stand up to Canning and Liverpool in Cabinet meetings. As a result he felt let down and isolated, unhappy with the policies the government was pursuing, and even more unhappy with the processes by which they were decided. In August 1824, he told Princess Lieven that he had been on bad terms with the Prime Minister for a year, and admitted that they scarcely spoke to one another except at Cabinet meetings. At the same time he wrote to Mrs Arbuthnot: 'I don't mind Lord L[iverpool]'s conduct to me. I think mine to him was just as bad, and probably worse. I certainly do feel the utmost contempt for him, and I am afraid that when I have that feeling I am too apt to show it; and I am not surprised that he should not be very fond of me, although he must know that I have always done what is right by him.'[1] A few weeks later Mrs Arbuthnot noted that:

[Wellington] always grows warm when Ld L[iverpool] is subject of conversation as he thinks he has been shamefully & unfairly used by him. He said to me . . . that Ld Liverpool had *changed his politics*, that he had treated all the Cabinet & his colleagues shamefully, for that he had abandoned all the principles upon which his government was formed, that he had completely adopted Mr Canning's policy, that he was endeavouring to break with all the Powers of Europe in order to league himself with the revolutionary rascals and blackguards of Europe and America . . . He said that Lord Liverpool had completely alienated every member of the Government except Mr Canning, that they all felt as if they were treading on a mine, that every question was studied between Ld Liverpool & Mr Canning & only such parts mentioned as suited them. In short, things were no longer managed in that fair, honest, open way which he had been accustomed to, & that he was completely disgusted with the state of affairs.[2]

Wellington's differences with Canning were more fundamental, but lacked the edge of bitterness aroused by Liverpool's apostasy. In April 1825 he wrote:

> The truth is this respecting Mr Canning. I stand exactly in the *Antipodes* in relation to him. I differ from his way of thinking, acting and conducting himself upon every subject. I dislike to seek popularity and to court the vulgar, so much as almost to dislike Popularity itself, particularly when I know and feel it is not merited; and I cannot endorse the practice of insulting Sovereigns and others who have not the Power of avenging their own Cause, only because there happens to be a Cry against them. As soon as I discovered what sort of Man Mr Canning was, and what his mode of thinking and acting, I ought to have quitted the Government . . .[3]

These differences meant that every disagreement over policy – and there were many – was exacerbated by the distrust and dislike each man now felt for the other. In early 1824 Cabinet discussions over the King's Speech grew heated even though Wellington entirely agreed with Canning's central point, that Britain should refuse to take part in a proposed European Congress called to discuss the future of Spain's American colonies. But where Canning wished the Speech to include a long partisan account of the government's actions in response to the French invasion of Spain, which would play well with the British public but which would rub salt into the still open diplomatic wounds, Wellington saw no need to be so provocative and offensive to countries which he still regarded as allies.[4] After prolonged discussions – in the course of which Liverpool flatly contradicted Wellington, and Canning showed great irritation – the Duke gained most of the concessions he wanted and was quite satisfied. But he told Mrs Arbuthnot that, 'in discussing every question, Ld L[iverpool] & Mr C[anning] had always some *arrière pensée* besides what met the eye':

> I assure you, when I am with these two gentlemen, I feel like a man who, going into a crowd, thinks it prudent to button up his pockets. I button myself up & take the utmost care what I say, because I know that they are always upon the watch to twist one's expressions into some sense at variance with the true one. If an unguarded word is uttered, they note it down & quote it against one the next week or the next month.[5]

For his part Liverpool complained of Wellington's 'violence' and 'thought he carried too far his desire to keep up a strict alliance with the Continental Powers'. However, both Bathurst and Peel told Charles Arbuthnot: 'Nothing could be more perfect than the Duke was in the discussions. Mr Peel said that he was very strong in his language, but did not lose his temper & argued his point with the utmost calmness & clearness. Mr Peel said that Ld Liverpool's meanness & subjection to Canning was beyond expression contemptible & disgusting, that for his part he had entirely left off speaking to him . . . even on matters of his own business.'[6] But Wellington felt that other ministers were slow to join him in opposing Liverpool and Canning, even though they agreed with him. Towards the end of March Arbuthnot told Bathurst:

the only way to keep the Duke right will be to support him in the Cabinet when he delivers an opinion in accordance with your own. I know that he thinks he is deserted; and that some of his colleagues, who agree with him, are afraid of saying so . . . This idea also has been strengthened by his having been told *after* the Cabinet by some of his colleagues that his opinion had been the right one, but that as the leaders in the two Houses had taken a different view they had thought it better to acquiesce. I know that both Lord Sidmouth and Lord Harrowby have agreed with him after the Cabinet was over, though they were silent during the deliberation. He himself is so plain spoken, so frank, and so open that he does not understand this sort of management . . . It would be very painful to *you*, I am sure, and very injurious to all were he to retire. Do pray therefore speak out when he delivers opinions consonant with your own . . .[7]

Paradoxically Wellington's position was greatly embarrassed by the outspoken support of the King, who was reported to have said that he relied upon the Duke to restrain Canning and thwart his wild schemes. Wellington believed, probably correctly, that this actually deterred other ministers from supporting him in Cabinet in case they were accused of joining an intrigue and favouring the court over prime minister and Parliament. Nor did he care for the implication that he represented the interests of the crown or the view of the King when he spoke in Cabinet – thinking, not unreasonably, that his views carried more weight if they were unencumbered by royal baggage.[8]

Liverpool, Canning and Wellington were all the same age, part of a remarkable cohort of men born in 1769–70 which also included Napoleon, Castlereagh, Huskisson, Lawrence, Wordsworth and Beethoven. The Prime Minister's health had been giving him trouble and concern for several years, in particular a painful vascular problem in his legs. At the end of March 1824 he was ill and

1 In 1817 Wellington commissioned this portrait by Sir Thomas Lawrence as a gift for Marianne Patterson. It was little known for many years, but in the twentieth century it became the most familiar image of Wellington in his prime.

2 Wellington in civilian dress, painted by Lawrence in 1814 for Sir Charles Stewart, Castlereagh's brother, who had served as Adjutant-General under Wellington in the Peninsula and later went on to hold a number of diplomatic positions. This was the first of Lawrence's portraits of Wellington, begun in July 1814 in the midst of the peace celebrations.

3 Wellington holding the sword of state with St Paul's in the background, by Lawrence, commissioned by the Prince Regent in 1814 to commemorate the victory over Napoleon and the Service of Thanksgiving held in the cathedral. Unfortunately the sword's highly decorated scabbard resembles a bell pull, so that it rather appears that the Duke is summoning the servants to show out an unwelcome visitor.

4 William Heath's *Centre of the British Army at La Haye Sainte during the Battle of Waterloo*, a coloured aquatint published in 1816. A contemporary, although not eyewitness, depiction shows British cavalry counter-attacking the French, while the British infantry are in square in the foreground. The print conveys something of the intensity and confusion of the fighting at Waterloo, although the scene is a little more crowded than would have been the case.

5 Denis Dighton's *The Battle of Waterloo*, showing Wellington (telescope in hand) ordering the general advance following the defeat of the final French attack by Napoleon's Imperial Guard. Dighton was a specialist painter of military uniforms and scenes who visited Waterloo a matter of days after the fighting, producing this picture within a year of the battle.

6 *The Field of Waterloo as it appeared on the Morning after the Memorable Battle of 18th June 1815,*
a coloured aquatint by Dubourg after John Heaviside Clark. Approximately 50,000 men and 10,000
horses were killed or wounded within a few square miles on a single summer's afternoon. The
armies moved on, but it was many days until the last of the wounded were transported to Brussels
and the corpses, stripped of their clothes, rings and other possessions, and even their teeth, were
crudely buried in mass graves.

7 The Waterloo despatch, Wellington's draft of his official report on the battle, begun on the night of the battle and completed the following morning in Brussels. Wellington wrote drafts of his most important despatches on a folded sheet of paper, leaving a wide margin for corrections, so this opened sheet shows the first and fourth pages of the draft with a number of corrections.

8 The radical reaction after Waterloo, 1: George Cruikshank's *Afterpiece to the Tragedy of Waterloo*, published on 9 November 1816. This print shows a female embodiment of France tied to the ground while the victorious Allies literally force the Bourbons down her throat. Wellington (front right) hammers an iron staple round her wrist into the ground and says '"We enter France as Friends" – well, I've crippled her Arms if that will do her any good.' Other figures represent the allied sovereigns, Blücher (pulling a miniature of Napoleon from France's neck), and Castlereagh holding aloft symbols of the Revolution and the French crown. Allied troops plunder the country while in the distance John Bull watches with delight.

9 The radical reaction after Waterloo, 2: *The Royal Shambles or the Progress of Legitimacy* (1816) is the largest and most elaborate caricature of Cruikshank's career, equating the restoration of the Bourbons with oppression and tyranny (including a strongly anti-Catholic element), and depicting Wellington (centre-left, in a blue coat) grinding innocent victims under foot. Wellington pulls forward a cannon on which Louis XVIII is insecurely perched; they are preceded by monks and priests who beat down the people, while two raised platforms show opponents of the Restoration having their hands and heads cut off. John Bull (centre) marches over a woman and child but is distressed and angry at the scene.

10 A French view of Wellington: a stiff portrait by Baron François Gérard (see p. 92).

11 The Duchess of Wellington hated being painted and few images of her survive. This is a pencil sketch by John Hayter drawn in 1825.

12 *The Eton Boys* by Richard Barrett Davis, painted around 1820. Wellington's sons Arthur, Lord Douro and Lord Charles Wellesley, and his nephew Gerald Wellesley, in their Eton uniforms, with Stratfield Saye in the background.

13 *The Waterloo Gazette, or the Chelsea Pensioners reading the Gazette of Waterloo* by David Wilkie, commissioned by Wellington in 1817. The group of old soldiers includes veterans of many previous wars and from all over the United Kingdom.

14 George Cruikshank's *Britons Strike Home!!!* (1819), a contemporary print dramatising the 'Peterloo Massacre'.

15 George Hayter's depiction of the trial of Queen Caroline, in the House of Lords. The King's attempt to divorce his detested wife dominated British politics in 1820 and provided a focus for radical agitation.

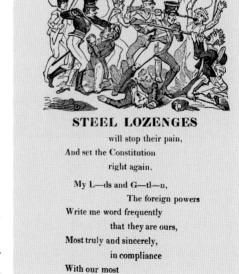

16 The title page of William Hone's pamphlet *The Political House That Jack Built*. This was influential radical propaganda, showing Wellington throwing his sword onto the scales against the demands of the people.

17 A page from *The Man in the Moon*, a second radical pamphlet by Hone with illustrations by Cruikshank, showing the army being used to suppress dissent. The phrase 'Steel Lozenges' was a pun on a popular patent medicine of the day.

18 Marianne Patterson by Sir Thomas Lawrence, commissioned by Wellington at the same time as the portrait of himself (Plate 1) intended as a present for her. Marianne was described by a contemporary as 'Tall, lithe and extremely graceful, her figure was perfect and her face one of the handsomest I have ever seen ... [She had] large and wondrous eyes of deep hazel, with hair that corresponded, every feature regular, and a mouth, the sweetness of whose expression was unequalled, with teeth faultless in form and colour ... [her] beauty was a thing not to be forgotten.' She was also remarkably calm and sweet-natured.

19 A portrait of Lord Liverpool by Sir Thomas Lawrence. The longest-serving British prime minister since Pitt the Younger and the most underrated politician of the nineteenth century, Liverpool's relations with his colleagues and the King were not always easy or harmonious, but he was indispensable to the survival of his government.

20 Harriet Arbuthnot by Lawrence. Mrs Arbuthnot was one of Wellington's most trusted friends. She admired him immensely but did not hesitate to disagree with him or tell him unpleasant truths.

the Cabinet met at his house. During the Easter recess he took the waters at Bath and his condition improved, only for it to worsen when he returned to London. His pulse sank to fifty and his doctors were unable to raise it. Sir Henry Halford, the leading physician of the day, was called in and took a gloomy view, warning the King that Liverpool would be unable to hold office much longer. Early in June Knighton was reported to have told the King that Liverpool 'cannot *live* long, even if he quits office . . . the blood vessels are all becoming *grisly*, that he is in constant pain if he hangs down his legs, that the circulation about the heart is very defective, and that his head is now affected in a manner that caused the death of his father & Grandfather'.[9]

The Prime Minister's illness naturally gave rise to speculation about possible replacements, speculation which he fuelled by talk of possible retirement and the need to put his private finances in order. The obvious candidates were Wellington and Canning, and there was no doubt whom the King would prefer, even if Canning had not chosen this moment to ruffle royal feathers by attending the Lord Mayor's banquet hosted by Robert Waithman, an erstwhile champion of Queen Caroline. Wellington was extremely reluctant to discuss the possibility even with the Duke of York, to whom he was said to have replied curtly that 'until his colleague retired, he refused to lay himself open to the suspicion of coveting his cast-off office; that, when the time came, he would know what to do, and that would be to await the King's commands'.[10] But there was one person who could not be put off in this way, and in June the King sent for Wellington and informed him of Knighton's dire prognosis:

> The King told the Duke that he was the person he looked to, & in whom he reposed all his confidence. The Duke replied that he was at the disposal of the King, that he shd. feel it his duty to serve him in any way His Majesty pleased; that as a soldier he had all the confidence which he thought he had a right to feel in himself; but that, in civil office, he felt that he was deficient in many important respects; that, however, he wd. do his best & that he wd. never be party to any scheme for recommending *any* minister to him; that, if the Cabinet proposed it, he wd. protest against it & maintain the King's right to a free & unbiassed choice. He urged the King not to make up his mind till the event occurred & especially not to utter upon the subject to anyone, for that if his opinions were known before they were acted upon, he wd. [be] thwarted & impeded at every step.[11]

If anything this went a little beyond conventional Pittite doctrine in respect for the Royal Prerogative, for in both 1809 and 1812 the Cabinet had indicated to the monarch the most appropriate choice to lead a new government, while in 1801 Pitt himself had encouraged, if not suggested, the selection of Addington

as his successor. Underlying this attitude was a genuine reluctance to undertake the task and a hope that the need would not arise. But when Princess
Lieven suggested that his lack of experience speaking in Parliament might
make him incapable of replacing Liverpool, he sharply rejected the idea, confidently asserting: 'Even if I can't, the Duke of Portland had no more idea of
speaking than I have; and yet he was at the head of the administration.'[12]
Portland was hardly the model of an ideal prime minister, or comparable to
Wellington in character and talent, but the significant point of the remark is
the contrast with Wellington's stance less than two years before when he had
advanced his lack of parliamentary oratory as a reason why he was not the right
choice to replace Londonderry as foreign secretary. Changing circumstances
called for a changed response, and Wellington adapted his arguments
accordingly.

The alternative to Wellington was Canning, assuming that the King's aversion to the Opposition was greater than his dislike and distrust of the Foreign
Secretary. Yet Canning would receive only limited support from the ranks of
Liverpool's government; it was most unlikely that senior ministers including
Wellington, Bathurst, Peel and Eldon would agree to serve under him. This
would leave him no choice but to seek support from the Opposition, and there
was much speculation that he had already come to an understanding with
some moderate Whigs, including Lord Lansdowne and Sir James Mackintosh,
that they would join a coalition government. If Princess Lieven is to be believed,
even Lord Grey was willing to join such an administration if offered the Foreign
Office; although given Grey's entrenched hostility to Canning this is so
surprising as to raise the suspicion that someone was simply making mischief.[13]
Whether such a coalition ministry would succeed or prove stable was open to
debate, with most verdicts reflecting the observer's own prejudices: those who
admired Canning imagined him triumphing over adversity; while those who
disliked him questioned even the strength of his existing influence over the
Commons. The only suggestion for a successor to Liverpool other than
Wellington or Canning came from Princess Lieven a little later in the year,
when Canning paid a visit to Ireland. This led her to speculate that he might
put forward Lord Wellesley as a compromise prime minister, arguing that it
would be hard for Wellington to object to the choice of his brother, while
Knighton might welcome the elevation of his former patron. The idea is
intriguing but unconvincing, as Princess Lieven herself recognised: 'All this
means nothing. The doctor will readily sacrifice his benefactor, and the Duke
does not love his brother. The Ministers hate him; in fact it won't do.'[14] Lord
Wellesley's time had passed; his tenure in Ireland had simply confirmed his
utter inefficiency and lack of judgement; while Canning was most unlikely to
accept second place in any new administration.

The succession stakes were complicated by doubts over the health of both candidates. Wellington was ill again in December 1823, and W.H. Fremantle reported: 'Nothing could look more wretchedly or broken. I really thought him twenty years older than when last I had seen him.' In January he had a return of the giddiness which had periodically affected him ever since the mistreatment of his ear. Although that passed, Mrs Arbuthnot wrote in her journal: 'We are very uneasy about him; he is dreadfully thin & does not sleep. Unfortunately his spirit is so high he is always disposed to fight against illness & not to take proper care of himself. His life is so precious, & he is so inexpressibly dear to me, that I cannot look in his pale face & wasted form without the deepest sorrow.'[15] This outburst of feeling, which is almost unique in her journal, underlines just how alarming Wellington's condition seemed to those who knew him best. A month later he was better, but in April went to Cheltenham 'for his health', and was complaining that he could not sleep. According to Croker, 'he looks very ill, and really before the recess looked extremely ill, withering and drying up; but he is better'. In May he had a serious stomach and bowel complaint, and Fremantle reported that it was feared that it might be cholera.[16] This was probably the nadir of his health at this time; he had subsequent attacks later in June and July, but by September he was clearly getting better. Mrs Arbuthnot was delighted – 'All the symptoms of the affection in his head are becoming mitigated' – while a month later she could report that he was 'in high spirits &, I hope, every day regaining his former health & strength'.[17] Fortunately the recovery proved sustained, and while his health continued to cause some concern, the series of illnesses from which he had suffered since the summer of 1822 were now largely behind him.

Canning's health was not nearly as troubled as Liverpool's or Wellington's, but he was so affected by gout over the winter that the Prime Minister told Arbuthnot that he did not think he could last many more sessions of the House of Commons. And in August he was ill with a bilious fever, prompting Princess Lieven to comment: 'It was not enough to kill him; what an opportunity missed.'[18] Nonetheless he clearly seemed the most robust of the three ministers; the one least likely to die first. The Prime Minister's health improved in the middle of the year, even before the end of the parliamentary session eased the burden which was weighing him down. Once the recovery was sustained and London emptied of its gossips, the speculation over the succession faded away, but not without having exacerbated the existing tensions in the Cabinet.

The parliamentary session of 1824 was remarkably quiet, with the Opposition lacking purpose and the country gentlemen somnolent. On 20 February Mrs Arbuthnot noted: 'They [The House of Commons] last night voted the Navy &

Army estimates, & Mr A. was home before eleven o'clock, the Army estimates alone having, two years ago, taken *six weeks* to vote.'[19] The country was peaceful and prosperous – the economy entering a boom which eased all other sources of tension – while the public had become fascinated by the mirage of quick profits to be made by speculation, especially in new ventures listed on the stock exchange. Inevitably trouble was brewing, but for the moment everyone, even the farmers, seemed to be doing well. In March Wellington wrote to Princess Lieven (who was visiting in Italy): 'There has never been anything to equal the wealth and prosperity of the country. There is no talk of "agricultural distress" and "starving people"! No one knows what to do with his money, and if we must complain we shall soon be grumbling because the general prosperity is too great; and that it does not give enough occasion to certain people to spend part of their capital. In the meantime popularity, that Divinity to whom some of us pay court with so much assiduity, seems to be attached to the Government. There is no longer any Opposition in Parliament.'[20]

This domestic harmony left foreign policy as the principal subject of contention, and even here the real arguments occurred within the government, not between it and the Opposition. The unresolved instability of Portugal ensured that it would soon be brought back to the attention of the British Cabinet. Even before the end of 1823 Palmella put forward a request that Britain guarantee the Portuguese government's position while it introduced a programme of domestic reforms. This was unrealistic; not even Wellington was willing to support such an open-ended commitment, pointing out that it would destroy the Portuguese confidence in themselves, and open the way for the British Parliament to demand a say in the reforms which were adopted.[21] In any case, that battle had been fought and lost in August, and there was nothing in Palmella's proposal to make Canning and Liverpool reconsider their stand. Denied help by his ancient allies, the King of Portugal had little choice but to proceed as best he could and hope for the best. In February he summoned the ancient Cortes of the Kingdom in the hope that this would go some way towards satisfying the liberal and radical parties without outraging the champions of absolutism. Unfortunately it simply alienated everyone and triggered weeks of turbulence, culminating at the end of April with a palace coup led by the King's second son Dom Miguel, hero of the ultras. The King was kept in seclusion, while many of Miguel's opponents were beaten or murdered. Beresford and the diplomats representing all the leading powers of Europe forced their way into the palace, found and liberated the King, who then took refuge with Palmella and Subserra (his pro-French rival) on board the British warships in Lisbon harbour. From this sanctuary the King summoned Miguel to appear before him, and much to everyone's surprise, the errant Prince came, submitted to his father's authority and was banished from the realm.[22]

During the crisis the French ambassador Hyde de Neuville gained great credit by resolutely supporting the King rather than Dom Miguel, whose absolutist views might have been expected to appeal to this protégé of Comte d'Artois. Neuville even went so far as to summon French troops from Spain to assist the restoration of the King. It was true that the French commander at Badajoz did not act on this summons, but no one knew that for some time, and Neuville's action emboldened the King's adherents and discouraged Miguel and the ultras. Palmella and Sir Edward Thornton, the British ambassador, were as pleased as anyone at the defeat of the coup, but were naturally dismayed that the credit should go to the French. In the hope of re-establishing the predominance of British influence they made a renewed appeal to London for British troops.

Cabinet considered the request in a series of meetings at the beginning of July. As might be expected, Canning remained opposed while Wellington favoured the proposal. Again there was some doubt whether any troops were available, even though the army had been increased by 5,000 men late in 1823 following trouble in the Caribbean. Still, fears that another outright rejection would drive the Portuguese King into the arms of France persuaded the Cabinet to do something. A solution was found in the idea of employing Hanoverian troops, which even Canning was willing to endorse. However, the plan was attacked in the press as a betrayal of the principle of non-intervention, an interpretation which gains some credence from Princess Lieven's reaction: 'England is sending 6000 Hanoverian troops to Portugal. Bravo, she is on our side! What has become of the Ministers' speeches against the principle of intervention and occupation? . . . England is once more linked up with the European system.'[23] Alarmed by the reaction to the plan, Canning extracted from the French ambassador in London an official disavowal of Neuville's actions, and assurances that France would not intervene in Portugal. This enabled him to re-open the question in Cabinet, and after further heated meetings he succeeded in overturning the decision to send troops to Lisbon. Wellington was furious:

What a noble, what a generous figure we are cutting! An unlucky King, who thinks rightly that he is surrounded by dangers, asks protection and help of his oldest ally. We reply, Yes; you shall have it, if France will give it instead of us; but, if France agrees not to help you, we shall leave you in the lurch too, and you can get out of your difficulties as best you may. Well, I have told the Cabinet what I thought. Nobody had a word to say in reply, but nobody would support me.[24]

Canning's admirers regard this as a great triumph, arguing that he succeeded in checking French influence in Lisbon without violating his much-proclaimed commitment to the principle of non-interference.[25] But the actual result was that Portugal was left distracted and unstable, with nothing to show for her loyalty to the British alliance. Nor did Canning's commitment to non-interference stretch very far; over the next few months he applied great diplomatic pressure on France to recall de Neuville from Lisbon, and on the King of Portugal to dismiss Subserra. Eventually the King gave way, but with a nicely judged gesture of resentment dismissed Palmella at the same time, appointing Subserra ambassador to London and Palmella ambassador to Paris! (Having made his point he relented and sent Palmella to London and Subserra to Madrid, while a new anglophile ministry took office in Lisbon.)[26]

Wellington felt this defeat keenly and even talked of withdrawing from Cabinet. He grumbled that Canning produced or withheld papers from the Cabinet depending on whether they would strengthen or weaken the argument he was making on the day, and feared that the breakup of the Quintuple Alliance would be followed by war which would plunge all Europe into chaos. He was convinced that Portugal would soon be plunged into another crisis and that Britain would ultimately be forced to send troops, or see it in the hands of France. He said that 'his whole life had been spent in fighting against the Liberals; that all his honours had been gained in fighting for Spain & Portugal; that the Treaties he had made had promised a long & prosperous peace, & now the work of his life is undone from Mr Canning's mere *love of undoing*, from his dislike to a settlement not made by himself, & to gratify his own spleen. For *principle* he has none, he has no fixed project, no plan of action; it is a mere vague desire of change.'[27]

The other issue which seriously divided the Cabinet in 1824 was whether Britain should recognise the independence of Spain's American colonies. During the Peninsular War independence movements had sprung up in many parts of Latin America, with very mixed results. One of the principal grievances of the Spanish Americans was that they were not allowed to trade directly with Britain or other countries, even when most of Spain had been overrun by the French. The British government struggled to balance its obligations to Spain as an ally, with the need to find new export markets to fund the war at a time when Napoleon's Continental System had closed most of Europe to British goods. Unfortunately the Spanish *liberales* were heavily influenced by commercial interests in Cadiz who were implacably opposed to any change which would undermine their, now largely notional, monopoly on trade with the American colonies; while royalists and 'serviles' could not swallow the humiliation they saw as resulting from the loss of empire, so that neither party in Spain was willing to make meaningful concessions. After the defeat of Napoleon the Spanish government was able to send some reinforcements to its forces in America, but never enough to re-establish her authority. Fighting continued with mixed results and sudden reversals of fortune, and it sometimes appeared that the real issue was not loyalty to Spain or independence, but rather a civil war over who would wield power in the vice-royalties which were now emerging as autonomous countries. Many British and European adventurers crossed the Atlantic and joined the struggle, some inspired by liberal or radical ideas, others fired by Napoleonic dreams and ambitions, and still others looking for a fortune, or at least a living. The British government, professing neutrality, attempted to ban the export of arms and the enlistment of men for either side, but numerous well-known examples, none more famous than the radical admiral Lord Cochrane, made a mockery of these restrictions.

Liberal opinion in Britain, and across Europe, was inspired by the limitless potential of Spanish America once the shackles of despotism, ignorance and Catholicism were struck off, and the people were reinvigorated by the pure clear air of freedom and unrestricted commerce. Canning sympathised with this view, writing to Wellington at Verona in November 1822:

> Every day convinces me more and more, that in the present state of the world, in the present state of the Peninsula, and in the present state of this country, the American questions are out of all proportion more important to us than the European, and that if we do not seize and turn them to our advantage in time, we shall rue the loss of an opportunity never, never to be recovered.[28]

Wellington was much more sceptical; he accepted that Britain must ultimately recognise the Latin American governments once they had clearly established their independence, which he regarded as inevitable, but he held it to be a point of honour that Britain should not be in too much of a hurry to do so.[29] He thought it only fair that Spain be given every opportunity and encouragement to take the lead in the hope that she might salvage some pride and perhaps some commercial concessions, or protection for those colonies, such as Cuba, which had remained loyal, in return for officially recognising the loss of her other colonies. He had little sympathy for the cause of the colonists, and disliked the revolutionary origins of the new states. His discussions with Miranda in 1807–08 had not convinced him that the Spanish American patriots understood the art of government or would be able to create a stable political system; and the prominence of so many adventurers with links to the radicals and Bonapartists naturally aroused his suspicions. He also argued that the exports of the new states, especially Colombia, would directly compete with those of Britain's struggling West Indian colonies.[30]

The push for recognising the independence of the Spanish American colonies was led by Liverpool and Canning, who talked of its importance for British trade and the danger that delay would allow the United States, which had

already recognised them, to establish a permanent predominance in the
western hemisphere or, alternatively, encourage French and Russian intrigues.
The difficulty with these arguments is the assumed link between diplomatic
recognition and trade. In fact British trade with Spanish America had been
flourishing for years and was already booming in 1824.[31] In October 1823
Canning had appointed consuls to many towns and cities in Latin America,
and Wellington made no objection. Indeed he was quite happy to support any
similar measures which gave practical support to British trade, even if they
amounted to *de facto* recognition.[32] What divided the Cabinet was the final
step of formally extending recognition to the new states, something which
would make little practical difference, but which would delight the liberal press
in England and annoy the continental powers.

Feelings on both sides were exacerbated by the fact that the discussions in
July 1824 closely followed the arguments over Portugal, which left the ministers out of patience with each other. Liverpool took a much more prominent
position on the American question than on Portugal, where Canning had
made the running. Both the Prime Minister and the Duke hinted at resignation
if they did not get their way, and Wellington began to suspect that Liverpool
was anxious to make a quarrel for some, unspecified, ulterior reason.
Nonetheless, on this occasion the Duke did not stand alone, receiving powerful
support from Bathurst, Eldon, Westmorland, Sidmouth and Peel, while all the
ministers were aware of the King's entrenched opposition to the proposal. In
the face of this determined resistance Liverpool and Canning were forced to
give ground and accept a compromise. Breaking Spanish America into its five
separate parts, the ministers had no difficulty agreeing that Peru was out of the
question because the struggle there continued; that their information about
Chile was insufficient; and that Mexico was 'unsatisfactory'. They were divided
over Colombia, but Canning and Liverpool agreed to wait for the results of
Bolívar's expedition into Peru before pressing for a decision. This left only
Buenos Aires where Spanish loyalists had long since ceased to have a presence,
which appeared to have a relatively stable and well-established government
and with which extensive commerce was already conducted. Rather than
immediate, unconditional recognition Canning proposed that full powers be
sent to Mr Parish, the Consul-General in Buenos Aires, to conclude a commercial treaty which would convey recognition when it was ratified. Even this was
going a little too far for Wellington, Eldon and Sidmouth, but the rest of the
Cabinet agreed to the proposal and they then accepted defeat. Canning then
added to his reputation for duplicity by endeavouring to conceal the disagreement from the King and imply that the decision was unanimous. The King
discovered the trick, but none of the three conservative ministers chose to
reopen the dispute by insisting on a formal correction.[33]

The struggle was renewed early in December when Liverpool proposed that the King's Speech announce the government's intention of recognising Mexico and Colombia. Wellington responded that he could see no change since July which would justify such a step, and further that if the ministers had been better informed of the situation in Buenos Aires then, they would not have approved even of the commercial treaty. He also cited the King's entrenched opposition, and concluded with an offer to resign. But Liverpool would not give way, insisting that 'if we allow these new states to consolidate their system and their policy with the United States of America, it will in a very few years prove fatal to our greatness, if not endanger our safety'. As for the King's 'strong prejudices', the Prime Minister felt that it was time that he 'should be set right upon this point, as well as made to feel that the opinions which he sometimes avows on the subject of legitimacy would carry him to the full length of the principle of the Emperor of Russia and Prince Metternich'.[34]

Although most of the ministers remained unconvinced by his arguments, the Cabinet yielded to the Prime Minister's determination. Wellington contemplated resignation but decided that he could still do more good in the government than out of office. Swallowing the pill was made a little easier by the fact that what was proposed was again not immediate recognition but commercial treaties on the Buenos Aires model, and by his success in restraining Canning on a separate matter: a protest over the continuance of French garrisons in Spanish fortresses, which the Foreign Secretary wished to use as an opportunity to beat the patriotic drum.[35] What is more, he accepted defeat with good grace. Peel, Bathurst and even Frederick Robinson told Arbuthnot that the Duke had shown 'extraordinary good temper & moderation and fairness', in marked contrast to Canning's 'extreme ill-temper'. And Wellington told Mrs Arbuthnot that he 'did not care a pin' about Canning's impertinence. 'He knew Mr Canning's object was to drive him out of the Cabinet that he might have the coast clear to do as he pleased; but that, feeling that by remaining he certainly moderated every measure, & considering that if he quitted the Cabinet the King would certainly break it up, he was determined to remain as long as it was possible for him to do so with any regard to his own honour.'[36]

This time, Liverpool went to see the King in person to explain the Cabinet's recommendation. The King's first question was whether the ministers were all agreed, and Liverpool announced that there was a wide divergence of views and that Wellington remained decidedly opposed to recognition. The King responded that he wished to consult Wellington, who accordingly went to Windsor on the following day. The Duke's advice was that the King could scarcely refuse to approve the proposal to negotiate commercial treaties without dismissing the government, and that he could see no prospect of forming an alternative administration without resorting to the Opposition. The King should therefore yield, but 'watch Mr C[anning] narrowly and keep him as straight as possible'.[37] This resulted in a stiff letter from the King to Liverpool which made plain that His Majesty believed that the policy pursued by his ministers 'upon this subject has been erroneous', but declined to oppose the current proposals provided that they were justified to the public as being designed for 'the benefit of his subjects and for the promotion of the navigation of the country', and not 'as measures of war or retaliation against other powers'. He also required that Spain and the allied powers be promptly informed of the proposed step 'and in such language and manner as may make the communication as little obnoxious to their feelings as possible'.[38] Canning was delighted, telling Granville:

> The fight has been hard, but it is won. The deed is done. The nail is driven. Spanish America is free; and if we do not mismanage our affairs sadly, she is English, and
>> *Novus saeclorum nascitur ordo* [A new age begins]
> You will see how nobly Liverpool fought with me on this occasion . . . it matters not whether I go out of town or out of office; for it was the one thing needful in the present state of the world. And I most assuredly would have gone out of office, if I had been thwarted in it.[39]

But if Canning absurdly overrated the future benefits of the connection with Latin America, Wellington erred in the other direction. The following April found him noting with ill-concealed relish a report of a speech from the President of Colombia to Congress which was 'remarkable for the insolent tone which it adopts towards England'. Wellington told friends that 'the Cabinet will soon find that all these states are our natural enemies & that he was right in foretelling that they wd not treat us with common civility after they had got from us an acknowledgement of their independence'.[40] But Wellington's fears proved as unfounded as Canning's hopes. Throughout the nineteenth century Latin America was an important destination for British investment and a lucrative trading partner, as it had already been for a decade or more in 1824. Canning's grandiloquence filled the newspapers, gladdened the hearts of British liberals, and added fresh fuel to the already overheated speculative bubble that was overtaking the economy, but he was no more capable of calling a new world into existence than he was able to redress the balance in the old world.

The discussions over Latin America were made more heated by the troubled state of Ireland, where Protestant fears had been aroused by the poor judgement and erratic behaviour of Lord Wellesley, and by the immense success of the Catholic Association led by Daniel O'Connell. The link between the two issues was highlighted by O'Connell himself at the most inopportune moment, when he praised Bolívar in a speech on 16 December and declared that 'Ireland, if persecuted to madness, will not want a like leader'. This revived the King's opposition to the recognition of Colombia and led to further talks with the ministers before he was finally pacified. Wellington played a careful mediating role but admitted to Peel that he sympathised with the King: 'At the moment at which we are going to prosecute Mr O'Connell for exciting the people of Ireland to rebel, we have authorised our agent in Colombia to decide whether he will or will not recognise Bolívar in the name of the King … We are all right in Ireland; but the mischief is that we are wrong elsewhere.'[41]

O'Connell was charged over his remarks but the case was thrown out by a Grand Jury, and the government resolved to bring in fresh legislation to suppress the Catholic Association in the parliamentary session of 1825. The debate on the bill in the Commons lasted for four days, but the result was never in doubt, with it being passed by a majority of well over a hundred votes. Lacking support in the House on the particular measure, the Opposition broadened the debate to encompass the wider question of Catholic Emancipation. This was comfortably familiar ground, but as Mrs Arbuthnot pointed out with some asperity it was also irrelevant to the real problems afflicting the Irish population:

> The ignorant & almost starving population of Ireland have been made to believe that obtaining Catholic emancipation wd. cause riches & comfort to flow in upon them while, in fact, to the lower orders of the Irish it wd. not make the slightest difference. The misfortune of Ireland is the system of absenteeism, by which 100s of 1000s [of pounds] are yearly drained from the country & no return made. It is quite disgusting to hear men like Ld Fitzwilliam & Mr Agar Ellis giving £10 to the Catholic Rent & holding forth upon the oppressions & miseries of Ireland, while they yearly draw thousands from Ireland & think they do great things by devoting a few pounds of their enormous wealth to charities which, [in] fact, do no good. Let them reside on their princely estates, employ the population, eat upon the land that produce which is now exported to pay their rent, encourage the manufacturers & gain the affections of their dependents; they wd. soon find the distresses of Ireland become ameliorated, & such *reform* wd. have ten times the effect of the Catholic emancipation.[42]

Her view may have been influenced by Wellington, for the previous May she had written that:

> The Duke of Wellington came here yesterday even[in]g & got upon the subject of Ireland; a subject he said he considered of such importance that he

said he really could hardly sleep for thinking of it. He says Ireland will be the destruction of England if something is not done to make the capital of the country some what more on a par with the population. The Irish peasantry, by the system of paying their labour by giving them an acre of potato garden at £9 per acre, never see a farthing of money &, if a wet season happens and the potatoes fail, they starve & England has to keep them. They pay no revenue, have no taxes, & the year of scarcity had between two & three millions from England. This evil of general pauperism is every day increasing, & the Duke seems convinced, if the system is not changed, all Ireland will be a nest of paupers dependent upon England for food. His ideas are to enforce residence in the proprietors of land in Ireland, & to subject those who do not reside to an enormously heavy tax, 50 per cent – to pass a law obliging Irish labourers to be paid for their work in money. He wd also enforce the residence of the clergy & restrict them to one living each. I have no doubt, if the Duke was Minister, these measures wd be partly if not wholly adopted, but they are far too strong & vigorous & wd bring too heavy a strain upon the Govt from the Irish absentees for Ld L[iverpool] to face.[43]

There is no evidence that Wellington discussed these ideas with Liverpool or Peel, let alone that he took any detailed proposals to Cabinet, for, as Mrs Arbuthnot recognised, the political obstacles facing them were immense. However they show that even in 1824 Wellington, far from being the staunch defender of the status quo in Ireland, was open to much more radical change than anything being proposed by the Whigs.

For more than thirty years the debate over Ireland had been framed in terms of the civil disabilities imposed on the Catholic population – laws which prevented Catholics from becoming KCs, or MPs, or (in theory, though not in practice) officers in the army, but which never touched the lives of the great majority of Irishmen. Self-interest played a part in the commitment of the Whigs to emancipation; it was a way of appearing as the friends of Ireland and claiming the moral high ground without endangering their Irish estates, or even requiring the trouble and inconvenience of visiting them. But there was much more to it than this. The greatest appeal of the Catholic Question for the Whigs had nothing to do with Ireland; it was rather that it provoked such intense resistance on the part, first of George III and then of his son, making it the perfect policy on which to unite the party around its central tenet: that the King should be forced to submit to the will of Parliament and his ministers. The Irish leaders themselves accepted the centrality of Emancipation to their problems, but they were aristocrats like Lord Fingall, lawyers like Daniel O'Connell, or members of the Catholic Church hierarchy, and were inevitably almost as remote from the common people as the ministers in London. When

politicians came to discuss or even think about Ireland, they almost irresistibly
fell into their accustomed stances and attitudes, repeating arguments which
they had first made years before, reinforced by the approval of their friends and
reassured by the familiarity of the counter-arguments put forward by their
opponents.

At the end of February Sir Francis Burdett called for a committee of the
whole House to examine the Catholic Question, and this was soon followed by
the introduction of a bill granting Emancipation, which passed its second
reading in the Commons on 21 April by 268 to 241 votes. There was nothing
very remarkable about this. Similar proposals had been passed by the Commons
in almost every Parliament since 1807, only to see them defeated in the Lords,
and the proponents of emancipation had gone out of their way to be conciliatory. Daniel O'Connell had come to London and was at pains to appear a model
of moderation and gentility. To win over waverers and lessen the hostility of
opponents he agreed that two 'wings' be annexed to the principal measure: one
was for the state to pay, and so secure influence over, the Catholic clergy; the
other was to disenfranchise the forty-shilling freeholders who made up the
great majority of the Irish Catholic electorate, and who were beginning to exercise considerable influence on their members. These were the same voters for
whose enfranchisement the young Arthur Wesley had spoken and voted in the
Irish Parliament in 1793.[44]

The majority in the Commons on the question was not particularly large,
but the opponents of Emancipation were very conscious that the tide of opinion
was running against them, and that while the Lords might block the measure
again on this occasion, they could not continue to do so indefinitely. As early
as February 1825 Wellington had decided that the time had come when the
government should take the lead in settling the issue once and for all,[45] and
over the next two months he worked on a paper setting forth his views at some
length. Characteristically he wasted no time on abstract principles or fundamental rights, but concentrated on the practical problems facing the government. He began by noting that the activities of the Catholic Association had
not led to any significant backlash of opinion in England; that the public
appeared apathetic on the question; and that 'new and young' members of
Parliament were more inclined to support emancipation than the older generation. The Lords would continue to oppose the measure so long as a government led by Liverpool and Eldon called upon them to do so, but this was a
diminishing asset which in time would disappear. He argued that circumstances would never be more propitious to make a permanent settlement on
favourable terms: the country was at peace and prosperous; the Catholic
Association had been put down; and concessions now would appear as a boon.
If the opportunity was lost there was a great risk that Ireland would become

troublesome as soon as the country faced other difficulties, and the government would be forced to cobble together a settlement in a position of relative weakness. This was an important early exposition of the doctrine of 'timely concession' which went on to play an influential part in Conservative thinking in Britain for the next hundred years and beyond, until it became something approaching an ingrained reflex.[46]

Wellington went on to make the case that it would be far better for the existing government to draft the terms of a new settlement, rather than leave it to the Opposition, which was so associated with advocacy of Catholic claims. The Protestants in Ireland, the public in England, the King and the Church would all be more likely to accept proposals as necessary and as containing suitable safeguards if they were brought forward by such firm friends of the Protestant cause as Peel and Liverpool. He recognised that this would be a bitter pill for such ministers to swallow, laying them open to recrimination, charges of apostasy and excessive love of office, but countered this with the claim that if the measure was introduced by the government it would 'be no party triumph' for the Opposition, would not cause weakness on other questions, and that 'it is surely more manly and consistent with our duty to our Sovereign and the public so to conduct ourselves as to be able to render most service in the particular crisis of the time, than to be looking about'. This was a little too calm and pragmatic to be entirely realistic, taking insufficient account of the passions aroused by politics, and the fact that most politicians felt that a large part of their honour rested upon their consistency to their principles and loyalty to their friends. It was much easier for the Duke of Wellington to disregard such hostile imputations than for any mere mortal, whose career had been centred on the Houses of Parliament, and who had no other claim to the public's regard.[47]

Having made his case for the government to embrace the question, Wellington proceeded to discuss the state of Ireland. He readily acknowledged the entrenched fear and antipathy between Catholics and Protestants, and the immense influence of the Catholic Church to make or prevent trouble. The Catholics in Ireland were alienated from the British state and were heavily influenced by a foreign power (the papacy) which in the past had often been hostile to Britain. The Protestant Ascendancy was maintained not by the consent of the governed, but by force. He proceeded to discuss the penal laws and civil disabilities imposed on the Catholics, going to some pains to show that most of them either pre-dated or post-dated the reign of King William; in other words that they were not an integral part of the Glorious Revolution of 1688, and that their alteration or even removal was not contrary to its principles. He noted that between the 1770s and 1790s the restrictions imposed on the Catholics had been greatly eased, and concluded that neither harshness nor concessions had done any good; the Catholic party remained as formidable and as hostile as it had been in King William's day.[48]

Wellington did not believe a satisfactory settlement could be reached by the British Parliament acting unilaterally or in consultation with the Irish Catholics, for the Church in Ireland was ultimately answerable to Rome. He believed that the government should first defeat the Opposition's proposals in the Lords and then, in the last week of the Session, repeal the laws which prohibited intercourse with the papacy; it should then use the parliamentary recess to negotiate a concordat with the Pope such as that already established by most European states. This would enable the most contentious issues to be met and faced squarely, with Emancipation providing the incentive for the papacy and the Irish Catholics to make concessions. He was particularly concerned to protect the position of the Anglican Church of Ireland, and argued that this could best be done if the Catholic Church was established as a missionary not a national church, with bishops *in partibus* and vicars apostolical rather than diocesan bishops. Since the French Revolution the power of the Catholic Church in most European societies had greatly diminished and the population gave its first loyalty to the state, not the Church. The role of the Church in Ireland was anomalous and Wellington was clear that 'our view must be . . . to bring the Roman Catholic religion in that country under the control of the Crown'. It is evident that he anticipated more opposition from the Irish Catholics than from the papacy, but believed that if all the main structural problems were anticipated and resolved in negotiations with Rome, time would favour the new regime.[49]

Mrs Arbuthnot, who heard many of these ideas as they were being formed, entreated Wellington to speak in the Lords debate on the question and set on record his grounds for opposing the current bill. Presciently she remarked: 'As it is possible that he may be called upon to pass a Bill of Relief for the Catholics upon his own view of the case, I am very anxious he shd state his opinion publicly that it may be impossible hereafter to say that he changed his opinions in preference to quitting office.'[50] Unfortunately circumstances made it impossible for him to follow this advice without bringing down the government, which was already, very quietly, tottering behind the scenes. Such a speech would surely have been seen as an attempt to distance himself from Liverpool and the more committed Protestants, undercutting their support and setting himself out as an alternative prime minister.

Neither Liverpool nor Peel were willing to consider abandoning one of the leading principles of their political careers in the spring of 1825; they dismissed Wellington's proposals and came very close to resignation. Peel felt the Commons vote very keenly. Ireland was his responsibility as home secretary; he had made his name as a Protestant champion; and he was alone among the

Cabinet ministers in the Commons in opposing Emancipation. Feeling isolated and forlorn, his inclination was to quit even before the proposal went to the Lords. But Liverpool declared that he could not remain if Peel resigned, for it would leave no minister in the Commons to express his view of the case. This made Peel pause, but both ministers remained determined to resign if the measure passed the Lords, and continued to talk of leaving office even if it was rejected. The secret was tightly held by a small circle which included Wellington, Bathurst and the Arbuthnots, but not Canning or any other supporter of the bill. Repeated meetings failed to make any impression, and Wellington wryly told Mrs Arbuthnot that 'no man had ever worked so hard *to be* Minister as he had *not to be*', and she added that 'he wishes very much to keep everything as it is, but I doubt his keeping Mr Peel'.[51] The King's attitude oscillated unpredictably; at one point he was ready to welcome Liverpool's departure and looked to a government that would include both Wellington and Canning (the Duke as prime minister), which would tackle the Catholic Question; at another showing signs that Canning was in favour; and then suddenly raising the issue of the Coronation Oath on which his father had founded his opposition to Emancipation.[52]

The Duke of York had no such hesitation, and on 25 April he made an emphatic speech against any further concessions when presenting a petition to the Lords. This created a sensation, for he was the heir-presumptive to the throne, and the Whigs claimed that he had breached constitutional proprieties. Even so staunch a Protestant as Mrs Arbuthnot felt that he 'would have been wiser perhaps to have held his tongue', although she could not resist adding that lectures on discretion came oddly from an Opposition which did not hesitate to agitate such a dangerous subject with the most inflammatory rhetoric. But the Duke's speech probably had a considerable effect; if not upon the actual votes in either House of Parliament, then in rallying the spirits of those who opposed Emancipation and giving them fresh heart.[53]

The debate in the Lords took place on the night of 17–18 May 1825, lasting until after five o'clock in the morning. Strangely, neither Lord Holland nor Lord Grey spoke, possibly in the hope of avoiding the sense of a party contest. Liverpool by contrast made 'the most vehement anti-Catholic speech' of his career, unusually forceful not only in its content but its delivery. The bill was defeated by 178 votes to 130, and the majority of 48 was almost double that which Liverpool had anticipated. It was a great triumph for the Protestant cause, winning the opponents of Emancipation a little more time, but Liverpool admitted to the King that in some respects the majority was hollow and would not necessarily last.[54]

The Prime Minister hesitated, but did not immediately give up his intention to retire. Canning then complicated the issue by calling a Cabinet to consider the Catholic claims, arguing that it could not be left an open question any longer. Wellington tried to persuade him to let it rest, but failed; and Liverpool and Peel held their hand, calculating that it would damage the Catholic cause if it could be blamed for the breakup of the administration. Possibly Canning made the same calculation or received a hint about what had been going on, for when the Cabinet met he did not press the issue, instead contenting himself with the empty assertion that he had established his right to raise the subject. This backdown was just the salve for wounded pride that Liverpool and Peel needed and, together with the size of the Lords majority, it reconciled them to remaining in office at least until the question was raised again. And so the government survived, and the real problems of Ireland slowly got worse as its population increased.[55]

The months following the crisis over Catholic Emancipation were quiet, with most interest in the political world centred on whether Liverpool would call an election in the autumn or wait until the following year. It was most unusual for Parliaments to last their full seven years, and with the country prosperous the argument for an October poll appeared compelling. However, there was also a widespread perception that Protestant feeling in the country had been aroused by the recent debate, and that the supporters of Emancipation would suffer from an early election. This led Canning to press Liverpool to wait until 1826, offering in return to stifle any further discussion of the issue in the meantime. Conversely Wellington wanted an early poll to strengthen the Protestant party in Parliament, not in order to block change, but to control it. In the end Liverpool left the election until the following year, perhaps fearing that the smouldering animosity among his colleagues would ignite in an election where the contest would be as much among the government's supporters as with the Opposition; and perhaps also from a desire simply to play for time and so postpone as long as possible the problems which threatened to bring down the ministry.[56]

CHAPTER THIRTEEN

THE LAST YEAR OF LIVERPOOL'S GOVERNMENT

(December 1825–February 1827)

T HE BRITISH ECONOMY, which was already dangerously overheated in 1824, accelerated madly towards the precipice in 1825, fuelled by a speculative binge in foreign loans, and shares in new companies – many of them connected to Latin America. Before the boom there were only 156 public companies with a total capital of just under £48 million, with most being in insurance and infrastructure: roads, canals, docks and the like. During 1824 and 1825 a further 624 companies were formed with a projected total capital of £372 million, covering almost every imaginable aspect of the domestic economy from dairies to steam-powered laundries, as well as foreign ventures, with mining companies being especially popular. The inevitable crash came before most of these companies could be brought to market, while even in those that actually were floated, investors generally only paid the first instalment (often 10 per cent) of the nominal value of their shares. Nonetheless some £17.6 million was actually raised – and largely lost. Princess Lieven told Metternich in January 1825: 'You cannot imagine how mad everyone here has gone over the companies in South America. Everybody is buying shares. Everybody, from the lady to the footman, is risking pin-money or wages in these enter-prises. Huge fortunes have been made in a week. Shares in the gold-mines of Rial de Monte, bought at £70, were sold, a week later, for £1,350.'[1] Two months later Liverpool warned Parliament against 'this rash spirit of speculation', while Huskisson predicted that the huge increase in foreign loans being raised in the City would 'turn out the most tremendous Bubble ever known'. Despite these sage words, the policies of the government had played a significant part in creating the frenzy. A loosening of monetary policy by the Bank of England and the Treasury in 1822–24 stoked the boiler, while a reduction of the interest paid on government debt had sharpened the appetite of investors for new opportunities. The uncritical publicity given to the new states of Spanish America, often generated by those hoping to raise loans for them on very dubious security, was given tacit endorsement by the government's recognition of their independence, although Canning was always careful to make clear that the government would not intervene to protect the interests of British bond-holders. The policies of deregulation and free trade being pursued by Liverpool and Huskisson, and the ebullient optimism of Frederick Robinson, the popular Chancellor of the Exchequer, had far more influence on the public mood than occasional warnings against the dangers of speculation. The crowning act of official folly, at least at a symbolic level, came in June when the Bubble Act, passed more than a century before in the wake of the South Sea Bubble, was repealed.[2]

An entry in Mrs Arbuthnot's journal for March 1825 records not only Wellington's view of the boom but also some of the excitement of the moment. Having described the rage for Mexican, Peruvian and Brazilian mining companies on the back of the spectacular gains by Real del Monte shares, she continues:

Many of these Companies will no doubt end in smoke & many foolish persons will be ruined; but the Duke of Wellington & I have long disputes upon the subject.

He thinks the greatest national calamities will be the consequence of this speculating mania, and all the companies are bubbles invented for stock jobbing purposes & that there will be a *general crash*, which [would] be almost as fatal as the failure of Law's schemes [the Mississippi Company in France in 1720]. I differ with him altogether. I think that all these new companies are so many modes of investing money which will relieve the public funds & facili-tate the paying off the debt; the 3 per cents would long since have been above par but for this new mode of employing money, & great distress wd have been felt when scarcely any interest could be got for money. The Duke is not averse to those which are formed for improvements in our own Island, tho' some of those are carried to a ridiculous extent. There is a railway going to be made between Liverpool & Manchester which promises to answer immensely. We have 10 shares in it for which we gave £3 a piece & which are now worth £58 each, and they are expected soon to be worth above £100. I am very fond of these speculations & shd *gamble* greatly in them if I could, but Mr Arbuthnot does not like them & will not allow me to have any of the American ones as their value depends upon political events & he thinks in his official situation it wd be improper.[3]

Despite his general scepticism Wellington became quite closely involved in one of the largest and most respectable enterprises launched during the boom: the American and Colonial Steam Navigation Company. The company proposed to establish a fortnightly transatlantic service of steamships running between Valentia in south-west Ireland and Halifax, Nova Scotia, with feeder services connecting it to Quebec and New York at one end and Glasgow, Liverpool, Bristol and London at the other. A separate route, to Jamaica via Madeira, was also contemplated. The company had a projected capital of no less than £600,000 (six thousand £100 shares, on which the first payment was £10). The plan was bold, far-sighted and imaginative – all alarming words in a financial context – and depended on the very latest technology. Steam-powered ships were now well established on short routes – the Channel, the North Sea, and between Liverpool and Dublin – but the first crossing of the Atlantic by the *Savannah*, which was partially, not wholly, steam-powered, had been made as recently as 1818. The American and Colonial Steam Navigation Company would need to begin from scratch, building its own ships and facilities. The eighteen directors were more notable for their social and professional eminence than their experience of business: two admirals, two naval captains and four MPs including Wellington's old friend Sir Pulteney Malcolm, the banker Walter Boyd, and the economist and statistician G.R. Porter. Wellington was approached in July 1824 by Maurice Fitzgerald, the hereditary Knight of Kerry, an old family connection from the days of his youth in Ireland, but more recently a Whig MP. Fitzgerald stressed the economic benefits of the plan for southern Ireland and the strategic advantages of being able to send substantial numbers of troops to Canada much more rapidly and reliably than by sail. Wellington was convinced, and lobbied Huskisson in support of the company's petition for an exclusive royal charter (which was nonetheless not granted), and consulted Lord Eldon on the relative advantages of a charter, as opposed to a bill, to incorporate the company.[4] He also agreed to act as one of the two 'patrons' of the company (the other was the Duke of York), while the appointment of the Whig Lord Lansdowne as its 'President' advertised both its political neutrality and the strength of its connections. Whether any of these dignitaries received or subscribed to shares in the company is unclear, although it is sufficiently obvious that hope of financial gain was not the motive for Wellington's participation.

The market peaked in the summer of 1825 but subsided only gently in the autumn, following a pattern set a few months before by the Latin American loans. The bubble finally burst in the middle of December when two important private banks in London failed, precipitating a panic. Within days even the best security with the most stable and reputable firms was looked at askance, and there was a run on the banks as depositors sought to withdraw their money in cash. Banks failed, often the failure of one triggering a wave of others as country banks relied on those in London to hold part of their funds and handle many of their transactions. So great and so sudden was the demand for specie (gold and silver coin) that the reserves of the Bank of England itself were almost exhausted, and the directors approached the government, asking it to authorise a temporary suspension of cash payments. If this was granted it would be a terrible further blow to confidence; but if it was not, the Bank itself might fail. Huskisson and other economic ideologues were willing to countenance the failure of the Bank – indeed at one level they welcomed it, for it would open the market to more competition – but to Wellington, who was receiving advice from Herries and, either directly or indirectly, from Rothschild and Barings, this seemed madness. At a heated Cabinet meeting which lasted until the early hours of the morning:

> He told Lord Liverpool while there was life there was hope; that there was a chance of the Bank standing &, while that chance remained, he wd not despair; that the Government were bound to support them to the very utmost of their power & that, if they were forced to suspend their payments, it must be done in the manner most beneficial to the Bank, for that their interests were those of the country & their difficulties caused by no imprudence on their part but by the fault of the Govt in encouraging foreign speculations & allowing the country banks to inundate every district with one & two pound notes.[5]

In the end the Cabinet refused to take upon itself the odium of suspending cash payments, but Wellington's strong stand had changed the character of the debate within the government, and reassured the Bank's directors, and other leading City figures, that Huskisson did not represent the view of the government. This helped ease the panic, but nonetheless the Bank came perilously close to running out of cash before the crisis was solved by the arrival of large sums of specie brought over from the Continent by Rothschild. Many stories, some certainly apocryphal, others probably true, were later told about just how narrow the escape had been, and it is clear that it was as close-run a thing as any of Wellington's battles.[6]

But although they had ridden out the immediate crisis, ministers faced the inevitable aftermath of a severe depression as the sharp contraction of credit and failure of banks brought down over-extended businesses all over the country. 1826 was a year of hardship, of short hours and of unemployment, of bankruptcy and anxiety, of some rioting but little renewed radicalism. In February Mrs Arbuthnot noted: 'The distress which pressed so severely on the country in the month of December seems returning again with almost renewed violence. The manufacturers are almost entirely at a stand, credit is totally destroyed, the funds are today at 76, having this time last year been at 97, & every person in the City is in despair.' The number of bankruptcies recorded in the *London Gazette* rose from an average of between two and three hundred a quarter in 1825, to over eight hundred in each of the first two quarters of 1826, and was still well over five hundred in the last quarter of the year. The most famous individual casualty was Sir Walter Scott, ruined by his financial involvement with the printers Ballantyne, but there were thousands of equally poignant if more obscure cases in an age before limited liability was common, and when bankruptcy frequently meant impoverishment and shame for the whole family.[7]

The American and Colonial Steam Navigation Company had no hope of sailing through the storm. In March 1826 a 'tumultuous' meeting of shareholders was told that of the 6,000 shares offered, only 2,680 had been issued, raising rather less than £27,000. There was much criticism of the conduct of the company secretary and some directors before the meeting was adjourned, 'amidst the greatest scene of uproar'. Further meetings were held which revealed that expenditure to date amounted to £6 14s 5d per share, and those shareholders who wished to salvage what remained of their investment (presumably £3 5s 7d per share) were permitted to do so. Attempts to revive the company in 1827 and 1828 failed.[8]

It is unlikely that the failure of the company attached any opprobrium to Wellington's name; it was much too common a story to blame any individual. But nor did the crash do much to discredit the economic policies of Huskisson and Liverpool, or Canning's foreign policy. Liberal enthusiasts for Latin America who subscribed to the loans floated by the new republics had ample cause to repent their folly; by the end of 1828 only Brazil was not in default, while loans issued by liberal regimes in Greece, Portugal and Spain had also failed, but Austria, Russia, Prussia, Denmark and Naples continued to honour their obligations. But Wellington's prediction, made in February 1825, that when the 'false glitter' of prosperity 'vanish[ed] in smoke' Canning's popularity would vanish with it (as those who had failed to take their profits before it was too late blamed him for their losses), proved overoptimistic.[9] No doubt there was some disillusionment – it was the mood of the moment – but the commitment of the press and a large slice of the public to a broadly liberal view of events, which included admiration of Canning, seems to have been hardly dented by the financial misery of 1825–26.

In the midst of the financial crisis in December came the news of the death of the Emperor Alexander of Russia at the age of only forty-eight. He had no children and it was believed that his brother Constantine had renounced his rights to the throne, so that the new emperor would probably be a younger brother Nicholas, of whom little was known except that he was reported to be 'very anxious for military glory'.[10]

The uncertainty over the Russian succession and the direction of her future policy would have been troubling at any time, but it came at a particularly delicate moment. The Greek Revolt was faltering. Unable to suppress it themselves, the Turks had invited assistance from their nominal vassal Mehemet Ali, the Pasha of Egypt, whose forces were relatively well trained by European (largely French) officers, and much better equipped and organised than those of the Greeks. An Egyptian army commanded by Mehemet's son Ibrahim had reconquered a considerable part of Greece, and although Greek ships held their own at sea, they appeared at least as interested in privateering as in fighting the enemy. But Ibrahim's success led to increased pressure in Russia and from Western liberals for intervention in favour of the Greeks, encouraged by lurid stories of Turkish atrocities and reports that Ibrahim planned to enslave and deport the entire population of southern Greece and replace them with Muslim colonists from Egypt.[11]

British policy was divided between traditional fears of Russian expansion and liberal support for the Greek revolt. Canning personally does not seem to have been much interested in Greece, at least compared to Spain and Latin America. He was strongly inclined to remain aloof rather than become embroiled in a problem which would require close co-operation with the other powers. Greece was an issue which would almost inevitably set Austria and Russia at odds, and so break up the Holy Alliance. For Castlereagh or Wellington that would have been grounds for Britain to take a leading part, absorbing Russian hostility while helping Austria restrain her, and preventing tensions among the powers reaching such a level that co-operation became impossible. But Canning, who never in his life had seen a battlefield or travelled in the wake of an army, viewed discord among the continental powers with equanimity, even enthusiasm.[12]

Wellington believed, well before 1826, that neither the Greeks nor the Turks would be able to obtain a complete victory, and his view was unshaken by the successes obtained by the Egyptian army. He was confident that in the end the Sultan would be forced to concede a form of autonomy which fell only marginally short of full independence for a relatively small, weak Greek state. It was not a prospect which he viewed with enthusiasm; the new country was likely to be unstable, pro-Russian and possibly influenced by the liberal outlook of its Western supporters, but these problems could be managed. Wellington's greatest concern was that Russia would use the Greek Revolt as an excuse to attack Turkey, and gain a dominant position in the Balkans, perhaps even seizing Constantinople.[13]

Canning shared some of these fears and came to accept that Britain needed to play a more active role if she wished to influence the outcome. But while Wellington and Bathurst believed that Britain should act in conjunction with

Austria and France, and present Russia with a united stand, Canning's aversion to 'Congress diplomacy' was unshakeable, especially if it involved co-operation with Metternich. He preferred to pursue an independent policy, opening talks with the Russian ambassador in London, who received his approaches warmly, for the Russians knew that if they could neutralise Britain, Metternich would not dare stand in their way.[14]

In the wake of Alexander's death, Canning proposed that Wellington go to St Petersburg to convey the King's condolences and to discuss future Russian policy with the new Emperor. The mission was given urgency by rumours that Russia planned to attack Turkey in the spring of 1826. Even so, some of Wellington's friends were dismayed when he agreed to undertake the mission. Croker went to see Mrs Arbuthnot 'in a state of frenzy . . . He said we had one great treasure & we squander it in the most absurd way; that politically the Duke was invaluable, the only person with mind & character to oppose any popular cry'. And the King seemed most uncomfortable when he authorised Canning to broach the idea to Wellington in the first place, and accompanied it with a private letter insisting that Wellington had an entirely free choice to accept or refuse the task.[15] The Duke himself seems to have had no hesitation in accepting, even though his expectations for what he could achieve were limited. He explained to Bathurst:

> Excepting in the way of conciliation, which is certainly very desirable at the commencement of a new reign, I don't expect to do much good in my mission. But I don't see how I, who have always been preaching the doctrine of going wherever we are desired to go . . . could decline to accept the offer of this mission; more particularly as I believe it will be satisfactory to the young Emperor; and, if it produce no other effect, it will afford the best information and means of judging from facts of his future intentions.[16]

He set out with a small suite and reached Berlin on 17 February where he had useful talks with the King and Count Bernstorff the Prussian minister, who believed that war between Russia and Turkey was highly likely. Wellington travelled onwards overland; he was pleased with his carriage (a little *calèche*) which he had brought with him from England, and he assured Mrs Arbuthnot: 'I was never cold in the Carriage, or in fact at all in Russia; & in Prussia only upon arriving in the Inns.' As an experienced campaigner, he did not trust the inns and took his own camp bed with him, with 'the mattress made of silk, in order to prevent vermin from penetrating into it; and of a light colour, that they might be seen upon it'. He reached St Petersburg on 2 March and was evidently surprised to find it 'the most beautiful town in the World, and nothing can be more picturesque than its appearance. It is like the Dream of an Eastern Town.

The Palace & Public buildings are beautiful, and the Neva about the breadth of some of the Reaches of the Severn which we saw from the Heights in the Forest of Dean'.[17]

He was received with 'the utmost kindness and cordiality' by the Emperor Nicholas, his family and the government; and not surprisingly, for it was most unusual for such a distinguished visitor to make the arduous journey to St Petersburg in winter. Wellington attended the Emperor's funeral and many of the preceding ceremonies as an honoured guest, and found that: 'A Greek Funeral is certainly calculated to rouse one's feelings to a degree far exceeding any other Ceremony of the Kind. But in this case it might really have been believed that the Deceased had been carried off only the preceding Week, instead of nearly four Months ago.'[18]

The business of the visit took place in a series of meetings with the Emperor and his ministers beginning the day after Wellington's arrival. He was impressed with the young Emperor who was, he thought, as clever as, but considerably calmer and more sensible than, Alexander.[19] They had several long informal conversations in which Nicholas was remarkably frank. Wellington was very relieved to find that the Emperor disclaimed any interest in the Greek cause, describing the Greeks as rebellious subjects of the Turks. Nor did there appear to be much general support for the Greeks in St Petersburg, although Wellington found the Russian ministers non-committal on the subject, evidently wishing to keep the Greek card up their sleeve in case it became useful later. Nicholas was more assertive on other Russian disputes with Turkey, and while he professed a desire to avoid war, made it clear that he did not think that this would be possible. Most of these grievances were quite limited, and in private conversation Nicholas declared that in the event of a victorious war he would not add even a single village to his dominions, or endeavour to establish greater Russian influence in Constantinople or the Balkans. This was certainly going further than he intended – the result of inexperience and the desire to impress the man he looked up to as the foremost soldier of the day. When Wellington tried to get the declaration on paper, Nesselrode, the Russian foreign minister, prevaricated and added conditions and clauses which significantly weakened its meaning. But even an informal verbal undertaking, when given by the Emperor in person to an interlocutor of Wellington's standing, carried great weight. The issue was not whether Russia might hang on to a small tract of territory near the frontier, but the assurance that she would not attempt to drive the Turks out of Europe and so risk precipitating a wider war. There was still the danger, as Wellington pointed out to the Emperor, that even a limited war might precipitate the collapse of Turkish rule and that Russia would be dragged into the chaos which would follow. Coming from a soldier of Wellington's experience this could not be ignored and helped to strengthen

Nicholas's own intrinsic caution. Wellington was in no position to do more; the only chance of forcing the Russians to remain at peace with the Turks was if all the European powers had been united, and Canning had prevented that. Not that Nicholas would necessarily have listened even then, for Russian patience with such opposition had worn thin, and the new Emperor could not be seen to be weak. In the end Wellington was quite pleased with the result: 'I hope we shall have no war; and I am certain that if we should have war it will be upon purely Russian and Turkish grounds, and that no power in Europe will have any reason to interfere, or to be apprehensive of its consequences.'[20]

Detailed negotiations concentrated on Wellington's attempts to soften the terms of the ultimatum the Russians were planning to present to the Turkish government, and developing proposals for joint Anglo-Russian mediation between the Greeks and Turks. On the first the Russians made a few small concessions which may have made it a little easier for the Sublime Porte to yield. The disputes were not resolved but war was averted for the moment, although it finally broke out in 1828. The British government had already made strong representations at Constantinople and directly to Ibrahim Pasha to disown the alleged scheme of enslavement and deportation, and orders had been issued to the Royal Navy to intervene and prevent it if there was any sign of an attempt being made to implement it.[21] The mediation would propose a solution on terms which were understood to be acceptable to the Greeks: they would accept nominal Turkish suzerainty and pay a token annual tribute in return for effective self-government and independence. The catch was that this mediation had to be accepted by both parties, and that the Turks would certainly not do so while they retained any hope of suppressing the revolt by force. Wellington's hope was that the Protocol would act as an effective brake on Russian ambitions even if she went to war with the Turks. To this end the third article stipulated that the terms of the proposed settlement for Greece would remain fixed even in the event of war, while Article V bound both Britain and Russia not to seek 'any increase of Territory nor any exclusive influence, nor advantage in Commerce . . . which shall not be obtainable by all other Nations'.[22] However, the effectiveness of these clauses was weakened by the failure to define the extent of Greek territory and by granting both Britain and Russia the right to continue to pursue the issue separately as well as acting together. Wellington has been much criticised for these flaws, but he was negotiating with a very weak hand and it is unlikely that any amount of diplomatic finesse would have gained significantly better terms. After several years of virtual isolation Britain had returned to the centre stage of European diplomacy, but at Canning's insistence she continued to play a solo part in a role that could not succeed without a supporting cast.[23]

Wellington left St Petersburg on 6 April 1826 and arrived home on the evening of 27 April. Mrs Arbuthnot expressed her delight in a letter to Lady Shelley on 1 May:

He is actually arrived, *sain et seuf*! I could hardly believe it possible he really was come, though I held his hand and looked in his face, which I assure you is quite ruddy and fat. I never saw him look better, and he is in excellent spirits . . . I suppose he will be torn to pieces by all the ladies in their joy to have him back. He did not go out last night, but said he would go to Mrs Hope's tonight. She will be *très glorieuse* at being the first. He says he has not had a day's illness, and did not seem the least tired with his long journey.[24]

On the whole Wellington was satisfied with the success of his mission. He told Mrs Arbuthnot that when he stopped at Berlin on the return journey and explained the result of his talks, the King of Prussia had said: 'You have done everything we could desire. We are no longer on the brink of a precipice.' Canning was, not surprisingly, less effusive in his praise, but gave unqualified official approval to the Duke's conduct. The public was much less impressed, largely because it had completely misunderstood the purpose of Wellington's journey. Even a usually well-informed gossip like Greville believed that the Duke had gone to St Petersburg to arrange with the Russians the most convenient way for both countries to recognise the independence of Greece. When neither this nor any other obvious result followed it was all too easy to conclude that the mission had failed.[25]

On his return to Britain, Wellington found the economy still in the doldrums and the political world abuzz with rumours that Canning was engaged in an intrigue with the Opposition, and particularly the moderate Whigs clustered round Lord Lansdowne. It was not quite clear what the purpose of this intrigue might be, but it did not seem inconceivable to some that Canning might be plotting a coalition, and even have ideas of promoting Lansdowne as Liverpool's successor if the Prime Minister finally acted on his oft-repeated talk of retirement.[26]

This was less improbable than the transformation of the King's attitude to Canning, which was now plain for all to see. Ever since he had taken office Canning had wooed the King with one hand while slapping him in the face with the other. The policies he championed abroad and at home were anathema to the King, and the Foreign Secretary did not hesitate to trample on the King's feelings in order to maintain his popularity; but where he could do so cheaply, he sought to ingratiate himself at Court, and in the end he triumphed. His methods were not subtle. When he took the seals of the Foreign Office in 1822 he at once appointed Lord Francis Conyngham as his under-secretary. The King's mistress laughed at the blatancy of the gesture, but told Princess Lieven: 'I should have been a fool not to take advantage of it.' The post had an income of £2,000 and Mr Canning was immediately granted the honour of an invitation to dine with the King and Lady Conyngham at Brighton.[27] The King continued to hate Canning but Lady Conyngham was softened, and Canning could be sure that through Lord Francis something of his view of events would be conveyed to the Court.

By May 1825 Wellington was conscious that the King's regard for him was waning, and he ascertained that His Majesty had opened a direct line of communication with Canning through Knighton. This was not really surprising. The King had given Wellington and the other Conservative ministers his unequivocal support in their struggle against the Foreign Secretary, and nonetheless they had been defeated in almost every major test of strength. When the King proposed breaking up the government and forming a more conservative administration, he had been told that such a ministry could not stand in the Commons and that neither Wellington, nor any other minister would undertake it. At the same time Canning pleased the King and Lady Conyngham by appointing Lord Ponsonby, an old lover of hers, to be British minister at Buenos Aires, and ensuring that her incriminating letters disappeared (allegedly purchased with the Foreign Office secret service funds). The King was relieved, Lady Conyngham immensely grateful, and they both felt that life went on more smoothly when they were on good terms with the Foreign Secretary, and even that diplomatic relations with South American republics had some advantage after all![28]

There was a curious subplot in the story, one which probably hurt Wellington's feelings much more than the King's tergiversations. Princess Lieven, the arch-conservative champion of continental absolutism who had poured such scorn and derision on Canning for years, suddenly changed her tune and became his enthusiastic champion. The volte-face occurred in March and April 1826, while Wellington was in Russia, and was the result of some assiduous courtship on Canning's part. The fact that Britain and Russia were drawing closer together facilitated the entente, but it seems clear that personal attraction counted for more than policy concerns. Princess Lieven was bored. It was years since she had seen Metternich, her lover; her husband and Wellington were both away; she was tired of the follies of the court and the amusements of society; and Canning offered novelty and the access to information and power which she always craved. There is no reason to assume that they became lovers, but her behaviour was so indiscreet as to excuse any amount of gossip. Wellington was naturally piqued by her defection, and it is unlikely that he was really deceived by her excuse that she was motivated purely by political concerns.[29]

While all this was going on behind the scenes, or at least in the semi-privacy of London drawing rooms and the Court, the country was going to the polls. The strange thing about the general election of 1826 was that it was so uneventful. Despite the economic woes afflicting the whole country there was comparatively little disorder or high feeling. Radicalism was comatose and there was little sign of strong Protestant feeling in England. The Whigs appeared apathetic and the most celebrated contest was between three members of the government for the two seats returned by Cambridge University, where Palmerston was returned as the second member despite arousing opposition by his support for Catholic Emancipation. In Ireland the Catholic clergy exerted their influence on an unprecedented scale, opposing candidates unsympathetic to Emancipation and forcing others to pledge themselves further to the cause.[30] Nonetheless these gains were more than offset by losses in Britain, and Wellington is reported to have said that he believed there would now be a majority of fourteen votes in the Commons to oppose Emancipation. Other estimates broadly agreed, although the political landscape would undergo a remarkable transformation before these calculations could be put to the test.[31]

The election did nothing to resolve the simmering discontent within the government and among its supporters. Mrs Arbuthnot expressed the feeling of many when she wrote in May: 'Our party, as a party, is entirely broke up, and it remains to be seen how long the Whigs will give us *support* without *places*. Messrs Canning & Huskisson have certainly most completely destroyed the confidence which the country had in Lord Liverpool's administration. I am so disgusted at the state of affairs that I quite wish we were out of office.' And again in September: 'The state of the Cabinet & of the whole party, the sort of fusion Mr Canning has effected with the Opposition, & the ill-humour, & almost open hostility, of the old supporters of the Tory Party make the whole concern so very disagreeable that I wd give anything to be out of it & to see the Govt broke up. I hope & believe it will happen soon.'[32] Such feelings were too slow-moving and usually too incoherent to create a crisis that would bring down the government, but when a crisis arose from other causes, they would have a profound influence on the way the government's supporters behaved. Already in 1826 a great many 'Tories' were exasperated and disillusioned by their leaders, and were beginning to question their loyalty. The seeds of future trouble had been sown and had taken root.

Meanwhile the ordinary business of government continued and in August Lord Wellesley raised an old source of discontent by asking Wellington to discover if Liverpool's attitude to their brother Gerald had softened with five years of exemplary conduct, as several Irish bishoprics might soon be vacant. Wellington took up the cause with more energy than prudence – apparently goaded on by other members of the family, possibly including Gerald himself – only to run into Liverpool's adamant opposition. The Prime Minister did not believe that a man who had separated from his wife but not divorced her was suitable to be a bishop, for the world would always assume that he had acted not from Christian forbearance, but because he feared that details of his own misconduct would emerge in court. This seemed a poor argument to Wellington, who was well aware of episcopal misconduct far more serious than marital infidelity, and who favoured the raising of standards but without Liverpool's zeal or priggishness. Bathurst shared Wellington's outlook and sympathised with Gerald Wellesley, but noted that Liverpool had the support of the Primate of Ireland and of both Peel and Goulburn. As on previous occasions the dispute aroused much acrimony and ill-feeling between Liverpool and Wellington, with neither man displaying much tact, while Lord Wellesley, having stirred the issue up, promptly abandoned it.[33] But this story, at least, had a happy ending. In February 1827 a batch of clerical promotions and appointments finally enabled Liverpool to provide a handsome consolation prize for Gerald Wellesley. There was still no mitre but the combination of the living of Bishop Wearmouth and an exchange of his prebend of St Paul's for that of Durham would provide dignity, convenience and an income of some £3,000 a year. It was one of Liverpool's last acts as prime minister, and it mollified Wellington and satisfied the Wellesley clan; the issue of Gerald's promotion was never revived.[34]

Another old source of contention, Britain's relations with Portugal, reappeared in the autumn of 1826, although in a new form which led the leading British protagonists to reconsider the roles they wished to play. King João died on 10 March and his eldest son Pedro preferred to remain as Emperor of Brazil rather than attempt to reunite the two possessions. But before he renounced his rights to the Portuguese throne he imposed a liberal constitution on the country, and nominated as his successor in Lisbon his seven-year-old daughter Maria. The powers of regent were to be exercised in the first instance by Pedro's sister Isabella, but under the terms of the King's will and Pedro's constitution, Dom Miguel had a claim to become regent when he turned twenty-five in 1827, provided that he first swore to uphold the constitution. Isabella was already in Lisbon and the regency was soon dominated by liberal veterans of the revolution of 1820, while their absolutist opponents looked to the formidable widowed Queen Carlotta, and longed for the return of Miguel from his exile in Vienna.

The new regime had little support in the country, while attempts to purge the army of Miguel's supporters led to widespread desertion, with many soldiers finding a refuge in Spain. The Spanish government strongly opposed the liberal government in Portugal, while tensions in Lisbon were raised further by the news that Miguel had taken the oath of loyalty to the constitution and evidently intended to assert his rights to the regency as soon as he turned twenty-five. Beresford, who had returned to Lisbon, wrote home that support for the constitution was growing but remained weak. 'I can have no hesitation in saying that were Dom Miguel to come now he might act exactly as he pleased, yet he would have fewer supporters against the constitution than ten days since; and I am almost doubtful if in a year hence he would be able to overset it, and certainly not but by the assistance of the army.'[35]

In late November 1826 a small force of Portuguese deserters, armed and equipped in Spain, crossed back into Portugal and attempted to raise an insurrection against the government. The first effort, near Castello Branco, was a failure, but a second larger attempt in the north of the country had greater success, and soon the whole of Tras os Montes was in arms, and most of the government forces in the area had deserted. There was no doubt that the rebels had received a good deal of help from Spain, but it was not clear whether this meant that the insurrection could be defined as an attack on Portugal, and so justify British assistance.[36]

In London, Canning had no hesitation, sensing that the public would welcome a dramatic gesture in favour of a liberal regime, and that the defence of poor little Portugal against the autocratic governments of the Continent, and specifically against Spain, home of the Inquisition and the reviled Ferdinand VII, would make good fodder for the newspaper writers. 'This moment is ours,' he told Liverpool; 'if we use it, we shall settle the dispute; but if we miss it I foresee a series of growing difficulties, and the very war which we wish to avoid, in the distance.' Wellington was more doubtful, and evidently wished for more information from Beresford before making the commitment. He thought that diplomatic pressure would force the Spanish government to back down, and worried over the cost of mounting an expedition when the government's revenue was depleted by the depression. Unspoken but unmistakable was his distaste at being tied to the defence of such a weak, unpopular and essentially artificial regime as the liberal government in Lisbon, which was likely to be overthrown as soon as Miguel became regent. But despite all these doubts, in the end he felt that Britain's obligation was clear and that she had no real choice but to come to the aid of her ancient ally.[37]

Once the decision had been made Wellington busied himself with the practical preparations of mounting an expedition at short notice, working closely with the Horse Guards, who were responsible for finding the troops, and Lord Bathurst who would issue the instructions to their commander. The expedition amounted to little more than 5,000 men under Sir William Clinton, whom Wellington had found painfully conscientious and under-confident in the Peninsula thirteen years before. His instructions would not be easy to interpret for he was to take the field against the insurrection, providing that it was being conducted by the Portuguese deserters from Spain, but not to intervene otherwise unless an insurrection in Lisbon threatened the personal safety of the royal family. The impossibility of identifying the personal history of every Portuguese rebel was self-evident, as was the inevitability that the blame would fall upon Clinton if anything went wrong, but such are the perils of attempting to marry the limited, conditional use of force to an ambiguous foreign policy.[38]

The decision was announced to Parliament on 11 December and discussed the following night. Canning made a point of asking Wellington to speak in the Lords debate and to repeat the arguments in favour of the expedition which he had used in Cabinet. It would, he said, 'do infinite good, not in this country only, but on the continent'. With Wellington publicly advocating the expedition, it would be much harder for Metternich or other champions of absolutism to argue that it was an ideological crusade inspired by Canning. Wellington readily agreed and made his first speech of any consequence for three and a half years – not that it was either long or momentous, amounting to a bare column in *Hansard* and doing little more than expressing his agreement that Portugal had been attacked and that as a consequence the provisions of the alliance had been triggered, but that he earnestly hoped that war with Spain would be avoided. Even Mrs Arbuthnot's enthusiasm was restrained, although she added a significant rider: 'The Duke spoke very well, & I am certain quite well enough to be Prime Minister.'[39]

That same night in the Commons Canning made one of the most famous and electrifying speeches of his career on the same question, culminating with the words: 'Let us fly to the aid of Portugal, by whomsoever attacked, because it is our duty to do so; and let us cease our interference where that duty ends. We go to Portugal, not to rule, not to dictate, not to prescribe constitutions, but to defend and preserve the independence of an ally. We go to plant the standard of England on the well-known heights of Lisbon. Where that standard is planted, foreign dominion shall not come.'[40] Palmerston's enthusiastic reaction was typical of many, and shows how easily the principle of non-interference, which Canning professed, was submerged in relish for action to support a liberal 'constitutional' regime:

I confess I heard that speech with peculiar delight; it is most gratifying to hear avowed by the ministers of the country as the guide of their conduct those principles one feels & knows to be true ... The principles of constitutional freedom are not only the elements of strength to the country which carries them into practice, but the best guarantee of peace to neighbouring nations & it is much for our interest therefore to favour their extension on the Continent.[41]

This was to become in time the standard, conventional view: the complacent idea that the British way of doing things was the only right, proper and enlightened way, and that those misguided foreigners who clung to their foolish traditions scarcely even deserved pity, for they were being wilfully wrong-headed.

At the time however the applause for Canning's speech was not universal, and Greville noted that it was 'much more cheered by the Opposition than by his own friends'.[42] Mrs Arbuthnot went much further, calling Canning's speech 'abominable':

> He said [she wrote in her journal] . . . that if England made war it wd be a war of opinion & that all the discontented of Europe wd range themselves under the banner of England, & that it behoved Europe to beware how she forced England to wield this tremendous engine. This is a Minister who professes to be anxious for peace & to want the King of France to declare in his speech to the Chambers that he will act in conjunction with us! I think it behoves *England herself* to beware how she enters upon a war upon exactly the same principles as those professed by the French in 1792. They proffered fraternity & alliance to all the discontented of other countries, & dearly have they & all Europe paid for the offer & the acceptance. It behoves her, too, to be beware how she upholds a Minister who dares, publicly, in his place, to avow such sentiments & to hold out such dark threats to Europe. Mr Canning was most loudly & vehemently cheered by the Opposition, those on his own side were deadly silent.[43]

Exaggerated and unfair as this was, it reflects the bitterness of those government supporters who could not follow Canning's embrace of liberalism. The personal triumph of his speech only widened the fissures splitting the government even further.

Clinton's force sailed by 21 December and the mere report that British troops were on their way transformed the political landscape in Portugal.[44] The insurrection collapsed and when the British troops arrived they had nothing to do, although their presence sustained the regency and guaranteed an interlude of calm. Unfortunately the Portuguese liberals were quite incapable of using this opportunity to achieve national reconciliation, preferring to triumph over their enemies and so perpetuate the cycle of civil strife. The British intervention of 1826–27 was a flamboyant gesture which made a great splash in England and on the Continent, but in the end did nothing to resolve the troubles besetting Portugal.

On 5 January 1827 the Duke of York died, aged sixty-three. He had been seriously ill since the previous spring and had suffered greatly from retention of fluid and gangrene in his legs. His death was an event of considerable political significance for it had long been assumed that he would outlive the King, and in his reign give unyielding support to conservative defenders of the Anglican Establishment. Mrs Arbuthnot deeply regretted his loss on both personal and political grounds. Wellington's reaction is harder to assess; he praised the Duke lavishly – they had mixed much together in society and their views of politics were not very dissimilar – but they were not close, there being an undercurrent of resentment and rivalry running in both directions, although the royal Duke naturally envied Wellington's eminence more than Wellington minded being kept at arm's length by the Horse Guards. The new heir-presumptive was William, Duke of Clarence, who had spent his youth in the navy. He was not generally regarded as among the abler or more intelligent sons of George III, and Princess Lieven told Metternich with some sarcasm: 'The Duke of Clarence will be a fine King! The King said to me at table the other day: "Look at that idiot! They will remember me, if he is ever in my place." '[45]

The Duke of York's funeral took place on the night of 20 January at Windsor. It was badly managed and far from imposing. The long delays in the extreme cold of the Chapel Royal were blamed for the illnesses that affected a number of those who attended. The Bishop of Lincoln died and Wellington took a chill which led to a return of sickness and the pain in his head which forced him to spend several days in bed and left him, a fortnight later, 'better but not yet well'.[46] Canning suffered even more and was reported to be dangerously ill; he was unable to attend Parliament when it resumed on 8 February, leaving Peel in charge of government business in the Commons.

York's death created a vacancy at the Horse Guards, with Wellington the obvious successor as Commander-in-Chief. Four months previously the King had told Wellington that he intended to appoint him to the position, and Wellington indicated that he would accept, although he advised His Majesty to make no commitment until the time came.[47] Yet in January 1827 the King toyed for a time with the idea of acting as his own Commander-in-Chief, despite his notorious reluctance to attend to any official business. He was probably motivated mainly by his sense of self-importance and perhaps a reluctance to make the appointment outside the royal family, although Wellington later attributed it to Lady Conyngham and more sordid views. 'But we must not think of this subject, and particularly not talk about it. My lady was concerned! I believe she had patronage in view; possibly the sale of it!' Liverpool nipped this scheme in the bud, and the King gave way, although he displayed some lingering resentment by not writing to Wellington about the appointment. Wellington retained his position as Master-General of the Ordnance and his seat in the Cabinet.[48]

Wellington was much gratified by the strong support he had received from Liverpool, Bathurst and Peel in the affair. Canning was understood to be unhappy with the appointment, or at least at Liverpool's failure to consult him over it, and Mrs Arbuthnot thought he might use it as a pretext to press for Wellington's removal from Cabinet. And there were genuine constitutional objections to the Commander-in-Chief being an active politician and a member of Cabinet. However, there appears to have been a general consensus in 1827 that Wellington's case transcended normal rules. Even Lord Grey thought it was simple: 'It appears to me to have been impossible, with decency, to appoint anyone but the Duke of Wellington to succeed the poor Duke of York.'[49]

By the middle of February the political world of Westminster was just beginning to settle back into its accustomed pattern after the Duke of York's death. Parliament had resumed on 8 February, although without Canning. Within a week anticipation turned to the Catholic Question and Liverpool began to talk again of retiring. The following night, 16 February, he moved the motion in the Lords to increase the income of the Duke of Clarence, and his friends 'remarked upon the unusual inefficiency of his manner'.[50] The next morning, while opening his post after breakfast, he suffered a massive stroke. He was only fifty-six, but he had been prime minister for almost fifteen years and he was irreplaceable.

CHAPTER FOURTEEN

MASTER-GENERAL OF THE ORDNANCE
(1818–27)

FOR MORE THAN eight years (December 1818 to April 1827) Wellington sat in Cabinet as Master-General of the Ordnance, and while his main concern was with the national and international issues of these years, he also devoted a great deal of time and attention to his department. As Master-General he proved an effective and economical administrator, turning a moribund organisation notorious for its sloth into a model of efficiency; and recognition of this success considerably enhanced his reputation in political circles in London.

The Ordnance was an ancient institution, considerably older than the standing army, which was responsible for supplying the army and navy with weapons, ammunition and equipment, and for the Royal Artillery, Engineers and related troops. Answering to the Master-General was a board of five officers: the Lieutenant-General, the Surveyor-General, the clerk of the Ordnance, the principal storekeeper and the clerk of deliveries. The Lieutenant-General was a senior, if not always a distinguished, soldier, and acted as the Master-General's deputy in his absence or when he was busy with other matters, besides having immediate responsibility for the Artillery, Engineers and other Ordnance troops. The responsibilities of the four civil officers on the board were less clearly defined in 1818, but broadly speaking the Surveyor-General supervised the letting of contracts and answered for the quality of supplies received or produced, whether of weapons, gunpowder or other equipment. The clerk of the Ordnance looked to expenditure and the payment of accounts and, by logical extension, justified the Ordnance Estimates in the Commons and was the principal spokesman for the department in Parliament. The principal storekeeper received reports from a large network of outstations and depots scattered across Britain and the Empire which held Ordnance supplies; while the clerk of the deliveries, the junior member of the board, handled issues from the stores to the troops who needed them and all the paperwork that this entailed. As this suggests, the board was supported in its work by a considerable bureaucracy; in 1820 there were 504 civil officers and clerks in its principal offices in Pall Mall and at the Tower of London.[1]

The department had expanded rapidly in the 1790s, the early years of the war against France, and had continued to grow more slowly in later years, becoming in the process more cumbersome and inefficient. Neither Lord Chatham (Master-General 1801–06 and 1807–10) nor Lord Mulgrave (1810–18) had the energy or inclination to introduce extensive changes. In 1813 Henry Torrens told Wellington:

> Nothing connected with the executive government of the country requires reform more than this Ordnance Department. It is, as now constituted, the greatest clog about the State. It is a mélange of jealousy, intrigue, and stupid prejudice ... There are two powers in the Ordnance Department always acting in opposition and in contradiction to each other: the one is that of the Master-General himself and his secretary, the other is the Board and their secretary. They are jealous of each other; and although the former is generally as efficient as the latter is the contrary, yet the Board, upon the subject of supply in particular, possess an independence at variance with prompt control the chief *ought to exercise.* The constitution of the whole thing is radically bad.[2]

In fact the board was, legally, entirely subordinate to the Master-General so that the problem was not with the formal constitution of the Ordnance, but with the bad practices which had grown up under the weak leadership of Chatham and Mulgrave. It was never likely that Wellington would prove so passive, and his arrival was anticipated with some apprehension as he himself recognised, telling Lady Charlotte Greville on the day before he took up his duties:

> I hear that the Department in London, as well as the Officers at Woolwich, are very much alarmed at my appointment. I understand that some wag stuck up a bulletin in a sort of coffee-house they have there, the morning after they heard of it, stating, 'The Field-Officers and Captains, after passing a very restless and uncomfortable night, are as well as could be expected this morning!'[3]

Wellington recognised that if he was to succeed in introducing any effective improvements in the department he would need at least one man of his own on the board. He had no wish to remove Sir Hildebrand Oakes, the Lieutenant-General, who had a good service record and whom he would have welcomed as his second-in-command in Portugal in 1810. Nor would it make any sense to lose Robert Plumer Ward, the clerk of the Ordnance, who was a capable and experienced junior minister in the government. He would have liked to remove Mark Singleton, the principal storekeeper, who had been appointed to the position twenty-three years before when his father-in-law, Lord Cornwallis, was Master-General, but Liverpool intervened; and instead it was Vice-Admiral Robert Moorsom, a family connection of Lord Mulgrave's, who was forced to make room for Ulysses Burgh, Wellington's old ADC. Even this modest change was not implemented until 1820, and it gave Wellington an early taste of the established interests that would oppose any change to the department.[4]

There are signs that Wellington encountered even greater resistance from the senior permanent officials of the department. Unfortunately the full story of the Ordnance has yet to be written, and without it the evidence is too patchy for us to see the whole picture clearly. We know that the secretary of the board, the most senior civil servant, was Robert H. Crew; that he held that position from 1794 until 1823; and that Wellington's correspondence with him appears professional rather than confidential. We have a little more information on the military side, where the most senior figures were Lieutenant-General Gother Mann, the Inspector-General of Fortifications, and Lieutenant-General John Macleod, the Deputy Adjutant-General of the Artillery. Both men were considerably older than Wellington (Mann turned seventy-two in 1819, Macleod sixty-seven and Wellington fifty). Mann had last seen action in 1793 and had risen slowly through the Engineers to reach the position of Inspector-General in 1811, which he would retain until his death in 1830. Macleod had displayed more obvious ability in his career, winning the support of both Cornwallis and Moira for his energy, courage and spirits in the American War, and serving on the artillery staff since the 1780s and as deputy adjutant (the most senior purely artillery position) since 1795. He had played a large part in the creation of both the Horse Artillery and the Artillery Drivers, and deserves a good deal of credit for the high standards British artillery achieved in the last years of the war. But equally he cannot escape all responsibility for its deficiencies, and it seems likely that he had simply been in office for too long and found it too painful and difficult to dismantle his own creations. In the midst of one dispute Wellington was driven to declare: 'It is very little use my seeing him, for he neither understands me nor I him.'[5]

Wellington lost no time getting down to work. Even before he formally assumed his office on 26 December 1818 he had been sent the Ordnance Estimates by Robert Plumer Ward, which would be presented to Parliament in the New Year, and over the following weeks Wellington prepared plans for the reduction of the artillery, engineers and other Ordnance troops consequent on the return of the Army of Occupation. Ward was greatly impressed by his diligence and was fond of describing an incident in the early days of the new regime when he encountered his chief just as Wellington was mounting his horse at the end of the day. Ward mentioned that there were some outstanding questions which could be discussed later, but the Duke at once dismounted and dismissed his horse, remarking 'No time like the present', and led the way back to the office, where they remained till past eight o'clock and the business was done.[6] Nor did this early enthusiasm soon flag; towards the end of the year Ward wrote in his diary that the Duke's 'promptitude, decision, intelligence, and manner were charming', and again a little later, 'he was full of business, having five Cabinet boxes before him, yet stopped to talk of a long report I had made him upon shells (only the day before), all of which he had read, though so busy a day'. Although the two men had little in common – Ward would go on to a second career as a novelist producing works which combined silver-fork snobbery with long passages of religious and philosophical discussion – they had a close, friendly working relationship. At the end of 1819 Ward's wife was ill and, returning to work after a month's leave, Ward found that he was still not up to business. He went to see Wellington and 'told him I was overset, and begged off. I shall not soon forget the kindness of his look and manner, when getting up from his chair he squeezed my hand with friendliness and postponed the subject'.[7]

Ward retired from the Ordnance in April 1823. Wellington selected as his replacement Henry Hardinge, who had attracted his notice as an enterprising staff officer in the Peninsula and who had served as liaison officer with the Prussians in 1815, being wounded with the loss of his left hand at Ligny. He had entered Parliament as member for the city of Durham in 1820, and in the following year had married Emily James, Castlereagh's widowed sister. Given the intense scrutiny of the Ordnance Estimates in Parliament at the time it was a bold choice, but Wellington's judgement was vindicated for Hardinge handled hostile questioning with great aplomb, being calm, courteous and extremely well briefed. Canning, who, as leader of the House, had been ready to intervene to protect him if he floundered, assured Wellington that Hardinge had needed no assistance and that his performance had won general approval. And in 1828 the Finance Committee – which was dominated by radicals who had no sympathy for military spending or military men – concluded that the duties of clerk of the Ordnance 'have been most efficiently performed by the able and intelligent officer who lately held that situation'. Hardinge himself told Mrs Arbuthnot in 1824 that 'under the Duke's auspices, their office was become (from a state of utter confusion) the most efficient, but the most economical, of all the departments'. However, he added a significant caveat: 'tho' under the Duke's eye & management the arrangement answered perfectly, yet whenever it came to be superintended by a less extraordinary mind . . . it wd be found that too much business devolved on each person'.[8]

The administrative burden on Wellington was eased by his official secretary: initially Felton Hervey and, following his death in September 1819, then Fitzroy

Somerset. For artillery questions Wellington seems to have relied heavily, although at first unofficially, on advice from Alexander Dickson. In February 1821 the Duke offered Dickson the post of brigade major in Ireland, candidly adding that he hoped Dickson would decline, but that he had nothing else to offer for the moment. Fortunately Dickson was able to be patient and in the following year was appointed inspector of artillery and succeeded Macleod as Deputy Adjutant-General in 1827, a post which he held until his death in 1840. In May 1825 Wellington had the opportunity to nominate two Ordnance officers to the honour of serving as ADCs to the King, and he selected Dickson from the artillery and John T. Jones from the Engineers. Dickson's elevation in the Peninsula had aroused some resentment and jealousy in the artillery both there and in London, despite his undoubted efficiency and considerable tact; and it seems at least plausible that his influence on Wellington in the 1820s had a similar result.[9]

In the middle of 1821 Wellington implemented a major restructuring of the civil side of the Ordnance. Possibly the most important change was that the board members were given much clearer and more direct responsibility for their individual departments, while the supervisory responsibility of the board as a whole was reduced. This proved most successful; as the Finance Committee reported in 1828, 'where there is collective responsibility, each individual is disposed to consider himself as in a great degree relieved from personal responsibility; but that where there is individual responsibility, no such feeling can exist; responsibility is then brought home to each individual, and is a constant motive to render him faithful in the discharge of his public duty'. The staff at each Ordnance depot was regulated and in most cases reduced, while their method of doing business was set upon a new footing, which combined simplicity and accountability through the recording of all transactions in a daily journal. A monthly return of all stores and their state ('serviceable, repairable and unserviceable') was to be sent to London, and printed forms were to be prepared and distributed containing a 'complete vocabulary of stores' to help ensure the standardisation of records. New clerks were to be employed on a three-year probation period, and their subsequent promotion was dependent on the recommendation of the chief clerk of the section or department, not on seniority alone. At the same time the pay of most of the clerks was reduced, with the saving paid into their pension fund.[10]

Underlying all these changes was the need for economy, as Wellington explained to the board:

The publick [will] has been so clearly expressed as well in Parliament as out of doors respecting the expense attending the transaction of the publick business in every department of the state, and particularly in the Ordnance, and the transaction of it is really so expensive that it is absolutely necessary to consider of the mode of curtailing this expense at present and of keeping it down in future.[11]

Some of the specific proposals, such as those relating to the number and pay of the clerks, probably did not originate with Wellington. The Finance Committee had made an adverse report on the Ordnance in 1817, and since then a number of administrative reforms had been set in train under pressure from the Treasury.[12] But Wellington took a close interest in the reforms and restructuring – the drafts of memoranda working out the proposals are in his own hand, not that of a secretary – and the Ordnance adopted the changes ahead of other government departments. Having been notorious for its inefficiency before Wellington took charge, the Ordnance became the exemplar of the benefits of reform by the late 1820s. For example, in 1829 a report into the keeping of official accounts stated that:

> The general efficiency of the system by which the business of the Ordnance Department has been of late years conducted, with reference to the important objects of the security of the Public Money, the regularity of the Payments, and the speedy delivery and examination of the Accounts, is most satisfactorily shown by its practical effect, as stated on a Return from the Ordnance Office, dated 20th March 1828 . . . 'The Department has no arrear Accounts; no debt; its payments are made in ready money within 16 days of the Bills being allowed, and for the last four years the loss to the Public, by defalcations, has not exceeded £100.'[13]

The Finance Committee agreed, praising the 'efficient and economical dispatch of business' at the Ordnance, and recognising the 'great exertions' made by Wellington and the board in effecting improvements over the previous eight years.[14]

In Wellington's early years at the Ordnance the annual passage of its Estimates had been the subject of constant criticism and debate in Parliament led by the indefatigable, if slightly ridiculous, Joseph Hume. No item of expenditure was too small for Hume to question, and he constantly argued that Ordnance expenditure – and that of other government departments – should be reduced back to the levels of 1792. He made no allowance for Britain's increased colonial commitments, the inclusion of the Irish Ordnance (which until 1801 was on a separate establishment), or, indeed, whether the Royal Artillery and Engineers (and the army and navy in general) were more efficient in the early 1820s than they had been at the outbreak of war with Revolutionary France thirty years before. Hume had more support in the press than in Parliament, although many members who did not much like or respect him, nonetheless felt that he played a useful role in holding the government to account. Nonetheless he frequently overplayed his hand, as when he told the House in 1823 that he 'attached no importance to what the Duke of Wellington might say on such a subject . . . He would not give a fig for such authority.'[15]

The position of Lieutenant-General of the Ordnance was often attacked in Parliament as an unnecessary sinecure. When Sir Hildebrand Oakes died suddenly in September 1822 Wellington, who was ill at the time and about to set off for the Congress of Verona, offered the vacancy first to Lord Hopetoun (formerly Sir John Hope) and then Lord Hill. Wellington explained: 'The office is worth about £1500 per annum; but the business is constant, and, I am afraid, will render necessary your residence in London during a great period of the year, probably the whole of it.' Both Hopetoun and Hill declined, but Beresford, Wellington's third choice, accepted. The appointment led to a sharp debate in Parliament, but an excellent speech from Canning ensured that Hume's criticism was defeated by a large majority. Unfortunately Beresford left for a prolonged visit to Lisbon a few months later, and Wellington was slow to accept his subsequent resignation; while his successor, George Murray resigned after only a year in office, and William Clinton combined the office with the command of the 1827 expedition to Portugal. Although Wellington always argued that the post was efficient and important, it is not surprising that in 1828 the Finance Committee recommended that it be abolished, and that this was done by Grey's government in 1831.[16]

Unless members of Parliament were themselves officers in the armed forces or had close ties to them, they would have had little real sense of the impact of the reductions imposed since 1814. In 1815 the Royal Artillery had amounted to 23,085 officers and men. By 1823 this had been cut by more than 70 per cent to 6,365 all ranks, a rather higher level of reduction than that imposed on the army as a whole.[17] Care was taken to preserve a substantial number of skeleton units rather than keeping only a small number at full strength, the theory being that it was quicker and more effective to expand an existing unit rather than to create new ones from scratch. So only seven troops of horse artillery disappeared entirely, while the remaining seven were each reduced from six to two guns. A similar system was adopted with the foot artillery, although the historian of the regiment says that insufficient attention was paid to keeping the best and most experienced men and units. He also claims that money was wasted on new recruits when many old soldiers were still being discharged. However, it is at least arguable that the artillery would benefit from some inflow of new blood even in a period of severe contraction, rather than be limited entirely to officers and men who had already seen much action and who were likely to become jaded and disillusioned with the inactivity of peace-time soldiering.[18]

Wellington was well aware of the danger of stagnation, and did the little that was in his power to alleviate it by ensuring that the reductions were carried out in such a way as to keep open the road of promotion and advancement for officers who remained in the service, although inevitably their progress would be very much slower than in wartime. He gradually reduced the number of cadets at the Woolwich academy by imposing a rule that only one new cadet could be admitted for every two who were appointed to the artillery or engineers, and extended this into the officer corps so that only every second vacancy would be filled.[19] There was no escaping the fact that such reductions were painful and that many a man who had been an active, brave and hopeful young officer in 1812 or 1813, would be thoroughly soured and disillusioned a decade later if he was forced to exist – and perhaps support a family – on the meagre pay of a subaltern or captain. Wellington viewed such officers not merely with compassion but also some apprehension, as he explained to Sir Herbert Taylor in April 1821 when refusing an application for a place at Woolwich for one young man:

> It appears that Mr Chetwood Eustace has nothing to depend upon excepting the pay which he may eventually get from his commission. I confess that I have long thought that we have too many officers in the Artillery and Engineers of this description. These are, in fact, of the description of those officers who have revolutionized other armies; that is, having no connexion with the property and rank of the country, they are the more easily disposed to destroy its institutions, of which the primary object is to maintain the rights and protect the property of the whole community. I have therefore invariably endeavoured to put in my list of candidates for admission into the Academy at Woolwich, from which all the officers are taken, only those connected in some degree with the property of the country, in order to diminish, as far as may be in my power, the chance in these corps of the evils which have occasioned so much mischief elsewhere.[20]

It must be remembered that this was written in the wake of the Queen Caroline affair when serious doubts had been raised about the reliability of the troops in London, and when Spain, Naples and Portugal had all been convulsed by military revolts proclaiming liberal objectives. Nor could Wellington be unaware of the appeal to disgruntled officers of any nation of the example of a penniless artillery officer who had risen from neglect and obscurity to become Emperor of the French and master of Europe.

If the fear of the effects of discontent made Wellington guarded on his choice of candidates for the academy at Woolwich, it also encouraged him to be scrupulous in ensuring that the rewards of service went to officers according to merit, not their connections. In March 1821 he wrote to Melville refusing an application on behalf of a Captain Sabine: 'I never recommended, nor ever will recommend, any officer for promotion by brevet excepting for repeated distinguished service before the enemy in the field. I don't wish to depreciate Captain Sabine's service, but if I was to give way upon this occasion, we should have men promoted for their services in the barrack-yard at Brighton.'[21] He loathed the habit of officers who had distinguished themselves under his command soliciting promotion through supposedly influential third parties, telling the unfortunate John Malcolm who had written on behalf of a friend:

> What I object to is, that officers who have served, and who know that I have noticed them, should go and expose themselves for sale, and come to me upon electioneering and other jobs, and claim troops of Horse Artillery, etc. This practice really degrades them and me, and I take every opportunity of letting them know that I don't approve of it.
>
> When I was in India, and with the army, nobody ever thought of applying for anything, knowing that I would do justice to all as fast as I could. But these confounded corps of Artillery and Engineers are so accustomed to look to private patronage and applications, that I am teased out of my life by them; and there is not a woman, or a member of parliament, or even an acquaintance who does not come with an application in favour of some one or other of them.[22]

When, in 1824, a much sought-after vacancy arose in command of a troop of horse artillery (which was not only a prestigious elite, but also exempt from colonial service) Hew Ross, who had distinguished himself in the Peninsula, wrote to Fitzroy Somerset asking how he could advance his claim to the position. Somerset replied that he should do nothing; the Duke knew that he would like to return to the Horse Artillery and would dislike any importunity. Such advice was not easy to follow, but Ross held his nerve and in due course was appointed to the position.[23]

Wellington lived at a time when attitudes to patronage were changing from the unabashed use of nepotism and influence in the eighteenth century to the growing austerity and professionalism of the mid and later nineteenth century, and his example encouraged the trend. Nonetheless he was still quite prepared to oblige his friends in areas such as the appointment (or trial) of junior clerks or of barrack masters where there was no established method of recruitment.[24] He was even willing to write to Lord Melville on behalf of a nephew, William Wellesley, who had passed his exams and served his time as a midshipman, and was now anxious for promotion and foreign service. That he was conscious of some inconsistency here may be deduced from his admission that he had been harried into writing by pressure from his family, and it is to Melville's credit that he replied promptly with an assurance that the young Wellesley would be immediately promoted, and without even the faintest allusion to Captain Sabine.[25]

In private life Wellington delighted in new inventions and conveniences, but he was much more sceptical of their value when it came to armaments. In 1824 he warned Sir William Congreve that he would 'most positively object' to the trial of new weapons on board naval vessels before they had been approved by the committee of artillery and naval officers appointed to consider them. He went on:

> If a life passed in the service and much practical experience had not taught me the value of most of these new inventions, the circumstances which have come to my knowledge since I have been Master-General, and some with which I became acquainted in my recent visit to Portsmouth, have proved how very cautious both Boards ought to be before they adopt them. You must pardon me, therefore if I don't enter into the consideration of them with the same sanguine expectations of their success as their ingenious parent does, and if I consider them, as I ought, rather with a view to discover objections to them than to cover their defects.[26]

Remarks such as these feed the image of Wellington as an arch-conservative, but that ignores the inevitable bias of hindsight, which picks out the early stages of inventions which later became successful while the much greater number which failed are quietly forgotten. To all appearances the most promising new weapons being developed in the 1820s were not rifled muskets and Paixham's shell-firing guns, but an improved version of Congreve's rockets and the steam-powered gun developed by the American inventor Jacob Perkins which attracted much attention in London in 1825. Neither proved successful in the long run, and it was fortunate for the Ordnance that the Master-General did not divert scarce resources from the existing artillery to pursue weapons which appeared to some to have the potential to revolutionise warfare.[27]

A far more valuable innovation that Wellington fully supported, despite its cost, was the Ordnance Survey of Ireland. The initiative for the project appears to have come from the Irish government, but it was undertaken and paid for by the Ordnance. In 1820 Wellington had appointed the thirty-six-year-old Captain T.F. Colby R.E. to the head of the Ordnance Survey on the recommendation of 'D. Hatton and indeed every scientific man in London'.[28] Colby had worked closely for many years with his predecessor, William Mudge, but had no sooner taken charge at the Survey than he set about raising standards and increasing the sales of the maps. A crucial decision was made at the outset in undertaking the survey of Ireland; whereas Britain had been mapped on a scale of two inches to the mile, in Ireland it would be six inches to the mile. This naturally meant slower work and more expense, and for this reason it was condemned by the Finance Committee in 1828, but the greater detail enabled the maps to be used to adjust the inequitable system of land tax and to settle property disputes. It took years for the first maps to be published and the survey was not completed until 1847, but it was not the least important legacy of Wellington's tenure at the Ordnance.[29]

One of the first tasks Wellington faced when he arrived at the Ordnance was to prepare a comprehensive plan for the defence of Canada, based on numerous papers and reports already in the office, and the result was presented to Lord Bathurst on 1 March 1819. Wellington identified the keys to Canada as Quebec, Montreal and Kingston, and recommended a number of fortifications to guard against an American attack. He accepted the view of naval officers that Britain was unlikely to retain control of the Great Lakes – America had so many more resources on the spot that she would almost certainly be able to outbuild the British – and recognised that this imperilled communications with Upper Canada. And he placed as much emphasis on lines of communication (from Britain to Nova Scotia, from Nova Scotia to Quebec and thence further into the interior) than on troops, or even fortifications. With the St Lawrence and the Lakes too exposed to the enemy to be relied upon for the passage of troops and supplies, Wellington proposed the development of an interior line of communication making extensive use of rivers and canals and even, for short passages, of railways, although these had yet to be combined with steam locomotion. Provided that the local population remained loyal, Wellington believed that Canada could be defended by a force of only 13,000 regulars plus militia, which he would divide into two bodies of approximately 5,000 regulars and 3,000 militia each, with the remaining regulars being employed in garrisons.

> As far as I can judge of the operations of any future war in these countries, from what took place in the last war, I should say that an American corps of strength and efficiency to contend with a corps consisting of 5,000 regular troops and 3,000 militia and Indians, which is what I suppose these corps would consist of, would not readily be formed, and that if such a force could be collected and put in operation, its own size would distress it and oblige it to retire from the country without effecting anything.

The whole memorandum, and this paragraph in particular, have clear echoes of Wellington's plans for the defence of Portugal in 1810, and although there was no imitation of the Lines of Torres Vedras, there was the same exploitation of the logistical difficulties an invading army would inevitably face. Wellington ended the Memorandum with the unequivocal statement that he regarded any 'notion of attacking the United States on their frontier' as impractical.[30]

The government adopted Wellington's plans and work on many of the proposals soon began, but proved vastly more expensive than the estimates made on the spot had suggested. Not everyone in Britain thought that Canada was worth such sums, while even some officers who had considered the question before 1819 when stationed in North America had considered it an encumbrance rather than an asset. However, the British government was committed to its defence not only for its own sake, but because if Canada was abandoned American ambitions would probably turn elsewhere, most obviously the Caribbean.[31] Ministers had few doubts of the underlying hostility of the United States; relations between the countries varied from year to year, improving with Castlereagh's careful diplomacy, then deteriorating as Canning preferred rivalry to co-operation, until they were strained almost to the limit in the mid-1820s. The public on each side of the Atlantic viewed the other with great antipathy, so that it was easy for politicians or journalists in either country to gain cheap popularity by provoking the other. Wellington fully shared the prevailing view, writing to a colleague in 1826:

> We are much mistaken if we believe that any settlement of any existing question of difference with the United States, or that any sacrifice on our parts, will ever soften their jealousy of, or their hostility towards, us or will prevent them from breaking with us at the moment at which it shall be most convenient to them and most disadvantageous to us.[32]

This belief in American hostility, combined with the conviction that Britain had extended her finances to the limit, strengthened Wellington's desire to avoid any conflict in Europe while at the same time not reducing the armed forces too far. At the end of 1824 he told Sir Herbert Taylor:

> Our wars have always been long and ruinous in expense, because we were unable to prepare for the operations which must have brought them to a close, for years after they were commenced. But this system will no longer answer. We cannot venture upon any great augmentation of our debt, if we did we should find the payment of the interest impossible, together with the expense of our peace establishments. We must, therefore, first take great care to keep ourselves out of disputes if possible, and, above all, too keep our neighbours quiet; and next to put our resources for war on such a footing as

that we may apply them hereafter at a much earlier period of the contest than we have ever done hitherto.[33]

The Ordnance department had a significant presence in most of Britain's colonies, and there were frequent clashes of authority between colonial governors and Ordnance officers which often resulted in both parties sending home voluminous vindications of their conduct. Wellington's response to these disputes was not always tactful, and there was a considerable amount of friction between the Ordnance and the Colonial department, which grew noticeably sharper in tone when Robert Wilmot replaced Henry Goulburn as under-secretary at the end of 1821. Wellington and Bathurst (the colonial secretary) continued to get on well personally, although there were occasions when Wellington's impatience or asperity inflicted a wound which took some time to heal. Not that Bathurst was always blameless, but he was usually considerate of Wellington's feelings and did his best to defuse disputes, which typically centred on colonial governors taking over land which had been set aside for the Ordnance, or interfering in the work undertaken by the engineers.[34]

One element in the disputes between the Ordnance and the Colonial Department was that Ordnance officers, generally Royal Engineers, were often employed to advise upon, design and even construct works for which the Ordnance had no official knowledge, leading to a hopelessly confused chain of command.[35] Much of this work was done for the Barracks Department and this was one reason why in 1821 Wellington proposed that it and the Stores Department of the Commissariat be transferred from the Treasury to the Ordnance. There was a large duplication of effort between the Ordnance and Commissariat stores and it seemed reasonable that the barracks might be inspected by Engineer officers already stationed in the district rather than by a separate network of inspectors. But the primary motive behind Wellington's suggestion was that both departments were notoriously badly run, and long overdue for reform. After some discussion the Treasury agreed to the plan without apparent reluctance, although it appears that the Duke of York would have liked the Horse Guards not the Ordnance to be the recipient, and Gother Mann, the Inspector-General of Fortifications, expressed strong reservations.[36] Nonetheless the plan had been accepted by the government before the end of 1821 and the transfer took place in 1822, although some colonial properties took much longer. Initially the internal structure of the Barracks department was kept unchanged, with little more than a symbolic financial saving arising from the abolition of the posts of comptroller and deputy comptroller, but in the summer and autumn of 1823 Wellington issued a series of regulations designed to improve efficiency, eliminate corruption and save money. Enquiries into the Irish barrack department (hitherto a separate establishment) revealed some of the problems of the old system, as Wellington explained to Goulburn:

> I have been lately wading through the reports on the different barracks in Ireland, in which the most flagrant of the abuses are occasioned by the neglect and insufficiency of the persons recommended by the gentlemen of the county to be barrack-masters, and by the abuse of those persons of the trust and confidence reposed in them, with a view to forward their own interests or that of their patrons, in hiring land or houses, or the purchase of articles of consumption for the barracks, etc.
>
> The simplest mode of getting the better of these abuses would be to refuse to appoint as barrack-master of any barrack a gentleman belonging to the county in which it is situated, or recommended by a gentleman of that county. But I hope I am too powerful for these petty abuses without the assistance of such a rule.[37]

Wellington's solution to these problems was to increase the pay of the barrack masters and insist that they performed their duties effectively, enforcing this by a reorganised system of inspection and detailed regulations for how they were to be run and records kept of all expenses.[38]

Abuses were by no means limited to Ireland and after enquiring into one case of alleged corruption in Kent, John Burgoyne reported that while he had yet to master the full intricacies of the financial system, 'I could see enough to feel convinced that the system was a bad one. The accounts are all mixed together, in a manner which renders it impossible to separate the expense of any one job from that of the whole mass of work, and which consequently prevents investigation into any specific abuse that may be suspected or pointed out.' As a result Burgoyne was convinced that the Ordnance's system of auditing, which he had previously felt to be tiresome and laborious, was a necessary and effective safeguard. As with all of Wellington's other reforms at the Ordnance the new regulations for the barracks emphasised a clear, simple system of keeping records, especially of public money, with built-in checks. This could not, in itself, prevent peculation, but it made it much easier to detect and acted as a substantial deterrent.[39]

There were also problems with the quality of buildings and other works constructed by the Engineers, as Wellington admitted in a confidential memorandum to General Mann in 1823:

> I beg General Mann to observe the number of works, buildings, etc, now useless or going to decay, on account of their having been constructed with bad or improper materials, or badly, or upon insufficient foundations, or in a

manner not calculated to insure the purposes for which the buildings were intended.

I wish him to look at the expense annually demanded and incurred for each repairs.

Is this system to go on? Is there no remedy? Are the public to be without a remedy?

An individual can dismiss his architect or his builder if he finds fault with him. Can the public dismiss the whole corps of Engineers?[40]

Some problems may have been caused by wartime haste or post-war economies and might be solved with more care and supervision, but Wellington diagnosed a deeper problem: the lack of personal responsibility felt by officers who received no individual recognition for their work. His solution was elegantly simple and economical: whenever any public building was constructed under the direction of an officer of the Engineers 'a brass plate may be affixed in some conspicuous part of it, stating its dimensions, the amount of the estimated expense, the amount of the cost, the date of the commencement, and that of the conclusion of the work, and the name of the officer who has executed or superintended it'.[41] Naturally this aroused considerable opposition from the engineers – the potential for embarrassment was all too obvious – and if it was ever carried into force it was soon watered down, but at the very least the proposal indicated that the Master-General was determined to raise professional standards within the department, and that individual officers would receive credit for their successes and be held accountable for their failures.[42]

Yet the emphasis on accountability had its disadvantages, especially in a time of financial stringency. In the years after Wellington left the Ordnance the procedures for gaining approval for spending money on public works, especially in distant colonies, became painfully slow and bureaucratic, with detailed estimates having to be submitted to the Ordnance where they might languish for extended periods before being referred on to the Treasury, which might further delay them. This contributed to the gradual decline in the reputation of the Ordnance from its apogee under Wellington's leadership, so that during the 1830s and 40s the department again became the object of criticism for sloth and inefficiency.[43]

Ordnance troops saw no significant active service during Wellington's years as Master-General (there was fighting in India and Burma, but the Indian artillery had its own separate establishment). However, the need to mount an expedition to Portugal at short notice at the end of 1826 revealed many problems caused by years of under-funding. It was a small force and the artillery consisted of only three batteries each of four guns amounting to about 270 men and 200 horses. Even so it was necessary to take the horses from two troops of horse artillery to equip the batteries, and the expedition had no sooner landed at Lisbon than a stream of complaints began to flow home: the horse shoes were too large, the nails of poor quality, the harness execrably bad, and the gunner-drivers overweight and unfamiliar with the handling of horses. The commander of the artillery, Lieutenant-Colonel Webber Smith, then decided that six-horse teams were inadequate for his 9-pounders, and took the horses from the reserve ammunition train to give his beloved guns more mobility, while forcing the ammunition to rely on whatever horses or mules it could find locally. Wellington was not impressed and recalled Webber Smith, sending out Sir John May with a draft of sixty men and forty horses to make up the deficiencies and to try to infuse a more positive spirit into the force. In the eyes of some of his colleagues Webber Smith joined the long line of artillery officers martyred by Wellington, and the affair even made its way into the press in a crude attempt to suggest that the Duke had attempted to sabotage the expedition to Portugal because he disapproved of its liberal aims. That was too absurd to be given credence, but it is more legitimate to ask whether the faults and poor morale revealed by the expedition suggest failings on the part of Wellington's administration of the Ordnance, or whether they were the inevitable result of excessive economy combined with years of peacetime inactivity. It is a question which must be left open until the internal workings of the artillery in the 1820s are examined in far more detail than can be attempted here.[44]

Wellington's years at the Ordnance show him in the unexpected role of an administrative reformer in the mould – although not of the stature – of Sir Robert Peel. Clearly these ideas were in the air at the time and the reform of the Ordnance was undertaken, at least in part, in response to considerable external pressure; but it is striking that, under Wellington's leadership, the department was roused from its accustomed lethargy and became a model of efficiency and economy. There is no room to doubt Wellington's personal role in this success; his papers bear ample testimony to the fact that many of the most significant changes were first drawn up in his own hand, and in any case everything we know of his nature points to the same conclusion – he was not a man to hand over a department to subordinates. Not all the changes at the Ordnance were successful, but the same can be said of almost any scheme of extensive reform, let alone one implanted in the midst of a very sharp reduction in funding. And if one criticism is to be made of Wellington's performance as Master-General, it is not in the detail of the changes he made inside the department, but rather in his reluctance to engage with the public in an attempt to lessen the rage for economy and to persuade Parliament and the nation that more money should be found for the armed forces, and the Ordnance in particular. The tide was running too strongly for such an effort to be very productive, but it is striking that in eight years Wellington did not make even one speech in the Lords, let alone reach out to a broader public, on the subject of national defence. Wellington was not alone in this reticence; Liverpool, Castlereagh and some of the other ministers spoke frequently in Parliament, but their speeches had little resonance beyond Westminster, and their other efforts to influence opinion were fitful and lacked conviction, while none of them strongly challenged the assumptions which underlay the pressure for economy. Of all the ministers, only Canning knew how to catch the public imagination with a memorable phrase or to persuade it that it was embarked on a high and noble purpose, and that it would be churlish to question the cost. But Canning usually preferred to point in a direction to which public opinion was already inclined, and would not squander his hard-won popularity where there was little prospect of success or personal advantage.

CHAPTER FIFTEEN

FAMILY AND FRIENDS
(1819–27)

W HEN WELLINGTON RETURNED to England at the end of 1818 the problems which had always existed in his marriage became harder to ignore. The fundamental incompatibility of the Duke and the Duchess was entrenched, and while there was no open breach, they were often apart. When they moved into Stratfield Saye the Duke's bedroom was on the ground floor, just off the library, in the bottom left-hand corner of the house; the Duchess's was upstairs in the top right-hand corner.[1] Maria Edgeworth, Kitty's old and loyal friend, found some of her other friends rather too eager to discuss the state of the marriage, and concluded sadly that 'the Duchess has been more hurt by her friends than her enemies and more by herself than by both put together'. This lends some weight to Wellington's accusation that 'you & your family have complained of my conduct towards you without Reason'; although there is no doubt that he was primarily to blame for their difficulties becoming common knowledge through his obvious neglect of her, and public attentions to other women.[2]

An unhappy marriage usually brings out the worst in both parties, and neither Wellington nor Kitty was a saint, so that their relations were often dismal and unedifying. He complained that she used the servants to spy upon him: 'It really makes my life a Burthen to me. If it goes on I must live somewhere else. It is the meanest dirtiest trick of which anybody can be guilty.' And: 'I don't care what your object was. If you are to continue to ask and obtain information of what I do from any servant or dependent of mine or anybody else excepting myself I'll not live in the same house with you.' To which Kitty replied with righteous indignation: 'I am as incapable of any mean or dirty action as you are yourself . . . I do not deserve that you should harbour [such suspicions, and I hope] that I may not again be subjected to offensive accusations for which there is positively no grounds whatever. I hope this subject so painful to you and so injurious to me now be dismissed forever.'[3] Unfortunately Kitty could not leave it at that, and two months later convinced herself that she was dying, and wrote a farewell letter to her husband, all too obviously designed to sear him to the soul and make him repent his cruel injustice:

> I hope that I forgive you. I would and I am sure I could have made you happy had you suffered me to try, but thrust from you I was not allowed, for God's sake for your own dear sake for Christ sake do not use another woman as you have treated me never write to a human being such letters as those from you which I now enclose they have destroyed me.
>
> God in heaven bless you my husband and bless and guard and guide you and my Children.[4]

But, as many a child has found, the 'You'll be sorry when I'm dead' argument looks rather foolish the following day, and it is unlikely that Wellington's soul was singed, let alone seared, once assured that his wife was still breathing and appeared in no great danger.

We can only hope that these letters marked the nadir of their relations, and that they did not waste more time and energy tormenting each other, although there is no hint of any real rapprochement. The Duchess, declared Mrs Artbuthnot in 1825,

> certainly is the silliest woman I have ever met with, & I must own that I think she now does not appear to have the slightest desire to please him. She does not comply with any of his fancies in the arrangement of his house, & in truth it is so bad a *ménage* it is quite disagreeable to be in the house. It is hopeless, too; if she had good sense, all wd. now be right, for what he now wants is a comfortable home, but she is totally unfit for her situation. She is like the housekeeper & dresses herself exactly like a shepherdess, with an old hat made by herself stuck at the back of her head, and a dirty basket under her arm. The Duke says he is sure she is mad.[5]

Mrs Arbuthnot may not have been impartial, but she was a clear-eyed observer whose fondness for Wellington did not make her uncritical, and her account of life at Stratfield Saye a few months later rings true:

> The parties at his house are certainly spoilt by the Duchess, for she is the most abominably silly, stupid woman that ever was born; but I told the Duke I thought he was to blame, too, for that all wd. go on much better if he wd. be *civil* to her but he is not. He never speaks to her & carefully avoids ever going near her. He protested that he always was very civil to her & never said a harsh word to her in his life. I dare say he thinks this is true, but he is not aware that his manner is abrupt to the greatest degree to every body, particularly to her;

and, as she is frightened to death at him (a thing he detests) she always seems *consternée* when he comes near her. Then she will talk & complain of him to every body, which enrages him to the greatest degree. He says he shd not care if she abused him to his face, but he cannot bear that his affairs shd be talked over with any body she can get near. Poor woman! I am sorry for her; she cannot help being a fool, & never was a person so mismatched. I am sorry for him too; it drives him from his home & he is getting tired of running about the world.[6]

Lady Shelley confirms many of these details and adds: 'It seemed to be the one object of her life to pose as a cruelly neglected wife.' It is all too easy to go along with this, to list Wellington's undoubted flaws as a husband, and to pity Kitty as a powerless victim. But she was far from powerless, and had the opportunity within broad limits to do what she wanted with her life. If she had wished to learn Hebrew and travel to the Holy Land Wellington would have been surprised, but he would not have forbidden it; indeed he would soon have been advising her on the details of her itinerary! As it was, she devoted herself to her children, both her two sons and several orphans and wards that were placed under her care, on whom she doted, and whom she encouraged to bully her. She was also more generous than she could afford to old servants and other poor people who came to her attention, and evidently enjoyed the quieter country life at Stratfield Saye more than the demands of high society in London. But this does not mean that Kitty was indifferent to her position; she remained immensely proud of Wellington, resented criticism of him, and enjoyed the honours and titles he brought her. In 1824 she told her niece: 'I have an old regard for Broadstairs. I have heard there of many a victory. It was there that I first was called Viscountess Wellington. It was on a Sunday, for the *Gazette* came out on Saturday night. I recollect holding the plate at Church on that day in my new character for a charity sermon.'[7]

The unhappiness of the marriage naturally affected Wellington's relations with his sons, although probably not as much as his prolonged absence in the Peninsula in their childhood and continuing preoccupation with public affairs subsequently. Still, in 1816 Kitty described the boys (aged eight and nine) walking, chatting and playing with their father when the family was at Cheltenham with as much affection and confidence as if they had never been separated.[8] Both boys were sent to Eton, which Kitty described with enthusiasm as 'the only school in the world'. Wellington was much more sceptical, telling Lady Shelley 'that I have known so many instances of boys going through Eton without learning anything, that I should not like to send one there without a private tutor who should force him to learn something'. He recommended that she send her son to Charterhouse, 'which I believe is the best school of them all'.[9]

The Duke had strong and enlightened views on the education of young men destined for the army, that clearly reflect his regret at his own haphazard education. As early as 1809 he told the Duke of Richmond:

> I am decidedly of opinion that the best thing to do with boys who are to be officers, particularly with those who are likely from their station in the country to command armies in the course of their lives, is to give them a finished education; and I would recommend you not to hurry your boys from school till their education will be more nearly complete. To see service with a regiment is important, but not when they are very young, so much so as to complete their education.[10]

And in 1817 he told J.W. Gordon that he intended his own boys to have 'the education usually given to English gentlemen, notwithstanding that they will both serve the King'. He also made clear to his sons that they needed to study and apply themselves if they were to succeed at anything; birth and inheritance would give them opportunities and a position in the world, but nothing more, and 'Ignorance' would be a 'perpetual drawback upon you'.[11]

Accordingly both boys went from school to Christ Church, Oxford. Wellington was not quite as unrealistic and demanding a father as might have been expected. He provided both his sons with handsome but not extravagant allowances, and gave them a stiff warning against gambling and getting into debt, but his tone was more practical than moralising, and he did not extend his homily to the other vices which young men might find tempting. When, in 1825, Lord Charles got into serious trouble at Christ Church, suspended for a year for a drunken frolic, the Duke made it plain that he thought the sentence excessive and that the lax discipline of the college had contributed largely to the offence; and he withdrew both his sons and sent them to Trinity College, Cambridge instead. He succumbed to the temptation to compile wildly unrealistic reading lists, and outlined a programme of study that might have given James Mill pause, but even professional pedagogues can fall into that trap. He was certainly not particularly close to his sons, but that was common enough at that time in that class of society, and has been known even in other times and classes.[12]

Lady Granville heard that Douro, then aged eighteen, was 'a stick', but William Napier, who met him at Stratfield Saye praised his 'great kindness and good nature'. Napier went on to tell his wife: 'I like the sons of the Duke much. Lord Charles I delight in; he is such a fine, laughing, playful, spirited boy, without the least pride or impertinence about him. Lord Douro is more grave, very amiable and gentlemanlike, very resembling the Duke without his *devil*.' Mrs Arbuthnot agreed, describing Douro as 'remarkably gentlemanlike &

pleasing, very sensible in his conversation, and . . . wonderfully like the Duke, not only in face but in every action; his way of sitting, standing, speaking, every movement is the Duke again'.[13]

Douro accompanied his father on his visit to France in 1824, but Wellington complained that he showed little interest or curiosity about the country they travelled through and slept most of the time in the carriage. He was at university, but neglected his studies and was idle. The Duke implausibly claimed that he would not mind this 'if he saw him eager and energetic about other things, but that he is listless & indifferent about every thing & does nothing but "loll on a sofa & chatter"'. Mrs Arbuthnot, the recipient of these grumbles, sensibly responded that the Duke was being too severe. Douro 'is but 18, just let loose from school, falling in love with every woman he gets near &, I think, is just the age when young men generally do nothing; he is no longer *forced* to study & he is not yet man enough to do it of his own accord'. And 'I have understood that the Duke himself was not a clever boy and, besides that, he must not expect that a young man born in the highest rank & heir to a princely fortune will exert himself & turn all his talents to account in the same way that he, a younger brother without fortune did'.[14]

Two years later Wellington felt that his sons neglected him, but reflected that 'the only thing to do is to keep a steady, quiet and patient course with them, to say or do nothing harsh or unkind by them & omit nothing that is kind, & there leave them to their own devices . . .'[15] If this sounds rather too good to be true, it is also clear that Wellington was prepared to give his sons more latitude than many fathers of his generation. Douro appears to have felt oppressed, not by his father's neglect or conduct towards him, but by a sense of inferiority and an excessive consciousness of the greatness of Wellington's achievements – attitudes which he had learnt from his mother. As so often, the shrewdest observation comes from Mrs Arbuthnot:

> The Duke is not upon the terms I wish to see him with his eldest son, who is really a very nice person, & I am very fond of him because he is so very like the Duke. I am afraid that that very conformity of character may tend to keep them separate. He is also excessively shy and very much afraid of his father. The Duke imagines that the D[uche]ss has set his son against him, which only makes him more irritated against her & mortifies him to the greatest degree. He is unjust, for the D[uche]ss wd do anything she possibly cd to put him & his children well together if she knew how, but she is such a fool that she does not.[16]

Charles, the younger son, had a happier temperament and was less burdened by his inheritance: 'He is a wild, rattling, high spirited boy, full of tricks & not in the least afraid of his father, who is amused by his nonsense.'[17]

Throughout the 1820s Wellington's principal source of domestic comfort and emotional support came not from his wife and children but from his close friendship with Charles and Harriet Arbuthnot. He could relax and talk politics and social gossip with them with complete confidence. It is clear from Harriet Arbuthnot's journal that her relations with the Duke were enriched and enlivened by an undercurrent of sexual attraction, but that it remained an undercurrent. He called on them frequently when they were in London, went riding with them every Sunday, and saw much of them in the country. He also wrote frequently whenever they were apart: 1,488 letters to Mrs Arbuthnot and 144 to her husband have survived, covering a fifteen-year period. They generally began 'My dear Mrs Arbuthnot' and ended 'God bless you and believe me ever yours sincerely'; they are not the letters of a lover, but a close friend who delighted in sharing news and experiences relating to a world which engrossed them both. The letters are highly entertaining, written to amuse and pass on the latest news whether from London, Brighton, Vienna or St Petersburg with a well-justified expectation that she would understand the significance of every eddy in society or shift in the political wind.[18]

After having Wellington as a guest for a fortnight in September 1823 Mrs Arbuthnot wrote in her journal: 'The Duke was, as usual, charming. He is the pleasantest person possible in a house, he is so simple & so easily amused & pleased. We rode & walked & drove in his curricle every day, & I shall miss my agreeable companion very much.' Her only complaint was that: 'Since he has been here I have not been able to write in my Journal, for I have but one sitting-room here in which he always is &, as I do not let anyone know I keep a Journal, I had no means of writing it without his seeing me. Besides which, if I am out of the room where he is for five minutes, he asks where I have been & does not like my being absent.' Yet often it was Wellington who had letters to write, and sometimes Mrs Arbuthnot acted as secretary, making a fair copy sometimes of extremely sensitive material. Three years later, faced with a house overflowing with guests, she noted that 'the Duke (who is always the person who makes the fewest difficulties) brings his own little travelling bed & is to sleep in my new room which is not yet furnished'.[19]

Mrs Arbuthnot's journal shows the great freedom with which Wellington discussed all aspects of politics with her, and gives ample evidence of her willingness to express her own opinions, even when they were contrary to those of the Duke and of her husband. Wellington took her views seriously and knew that they approached politics, in much the same way, so that their differences were commonly over tactics, or the necessity to adopt some measure that went against his natural inclination. In 1828, when he was prime minister, she recorded: 'We had what he calls a grand breeze [i.e. an argument] & I thought the people on the Mall wd have thought he was mad, he talked so loud; but we ended as we always do. We made up our quarrel & were very good friends, & I must do the Duke justice to say that, tho' he gets into a passion for a moment, he never likes one a bit the less for telling him unpleasant truths.'[20]

Wellington's friendship was with both the Arbuthnots, and a modern historian who has made a close study of the relationship compares it to 'an equilateral, not an isosceles triangle'. Charles Arbuthnot was a tactful, discreet man, with immense experience of the workings of government and knowledge of the political world, who could give Wellington valuable advice ranging from the best way to put any particular policy into practice (citing administrative and legal precedents), to the character and inclinations of obscure members of the House of Commons. He was also very good company and may well have been Wellington's closest male friend in these years, but the record of their friendship lacks the vividness and intimacy of his wife's journal, which inevitably means that we see the friendship most clearly through her eyes. There is no doubt of the warmth of Mrs Arbuthnot's attachment to the Duke. In 1830 she wrote in her journal:

> I sometimes think it is most unfortunate but it is quite true that, excepting my husband & his children, I have no feeling of warm interest for any human being but the Duke. There is something about him that fascinates me to a degree that is silly, but which I cannot resist. He is so amiable, so kind hearted with a great appearance of roughness, & so frank, that I always feel I wd die for him . . . & it makes me miserable that he should have anything to vex him . . .[21]

A few years later Henry Greville, Lady Charlotte's youngest son, wrote that the friendship 'has been [the Duke's] greatest resource . . . I believe him to be equally attached to husband and wife and there was no matter personal or political in which he was concerned or interested that he did not freely discuss with them in the most unreserved manner'.[22]

The Arbuthnots were Wellington's closest friends in these years, but he was on excellent terms with many other figures in high society. His friendships with women are most obvious because so many of them left vivid records of their lives in letters and diaries. These give a good impression of his relations with Lady Shelley, Princess Lieven, Lady Cowper (later Palmerston), and Lady Granville, to mention just those best documented. Other women, and many of Wellington's male friends, survive as not much more than frequently recurring names, with little sense of their personality. His friendships cut across party lines – he mixed a good deal in Whig as well as Tory society – while he was perfectly happy to defy convention and lend his support to someone (particularly a lady) whose behaviour had attracted censure.

An old flame reappeared in Wellington's life in 1824 when the recently widowed Marianne Patterson returned to England to visit her sisters Louisa and Bess. Wellington greeted her warmly and visited her frequently in South Audley Street, but she only stayed in London briefly before heading on to France, where she and her sisters remained for the rest of the year. In the summer of 1825 Marianne and Bess visited Ireland where Lord Wellesley was Lord Lieutenant. He entertained them royally and was enchanted by Marianne, while she found him charming, attentive and charismatic. After a courtship lasting a few weeks he proposed and she, after some slight hesitation, accepted. Wellington was astonished, mortified and dismayed by the news. Mrs Arbuthnot was probably correct in writing that 'his love for her has long been at an end', but that did not mean that he could see her marry his brother with equanimity. When Mrs Arbuthnot, who was not surprisingly a little jealous, told him that 'it was pretty well for the widow of an American shopkeeper to marry a Marquis, the Ld Lieutenant of Ireland and a Knight of the Garter', he replied that 'the honours were all empty ones and that the real facts were that Ld Wellesley was a man totally ruined; when he quitted Ireland, which he must soon do, he wd not have a house to take her to, or money to keep a carriage; that he had not a shilling in the world &, moreover, was of a most jealous disposition, a violent temper & that he had entirely worn out his constitution by the profligate habits of his life'. The jealousy and sibling rivalry were blatant, heightened by the fact that the news came as a surprise, and probably also with a sense of disappointment: 'He had given her credit for more real good sense than to make such a preposterous match.'[23]

There were other possible grounds for objecting to the match which evidently carried less weight in Wellington's eyes. Unlike Mrs Arbuthnot he did not regard Mrs Patterson as socially inferior to his brother, despite her nationality and her father's failed business ventures. Nor did he mention the difference of ages: Lord Wellesley was sixty-five; Mrs Patterson, thirty-seven. And there was the fact that she was a Roman Catholic – a matter of considerable political significance in the wife of the Lord Lieutenant of Ireland, and one which might have had serious repercussions if she had not handled it with great tact and discretion.

Wellington wrote, with more real friendship than prudence, to Marianne, outlining his objections to the marriage, while he told his brother: 'I have long known Mrs Patterson intimately, and have felt the greatest regard and affection for her ... in disposition temper sense acquirements and manners she is equal if not superior to any Woman of any country with whom I have ever been in Society.'[24] She did not take Wellington's advice to break off the engagement, but kept his objections to herself and always strived to improve relations between the brothers. The marriage took place on 29 October 1825, and Wellington's forebodings were soon justified. By the summer of 1827 Marianne used the socially acceptable excuse of her health to spend substantial periods of time away from Lord Wellesley, and while a public separation was avoided, they soon led independent lives. Fortunately she had ensured that her fortune was protected from her husband (and his dependents) before they married, and she never received any money from him. Wellington remained a good and loyal friend, but the fervour of 1816–17 had faded forever.[25]

Wellington's relations with his other brothers appear to have been friendly, although not particularly close, in these years. He made no attempt to dissuade Liverpool when the Prime Minister finally manoeuvred William (now Lord Maryborough) out of the Cabinet and into the court appointment of Master of the Buckhounds. William was dismayed at first, and even used the dreaded, inevitable phrase himself, complaining that they were 'sending him to the dogs'; but he seems to have adapted to his new life quite happily. He took little further part in politics, seldom attending the Lords and not seeking fresh office when Wellington became prime minister, but he became a significant figure at court for the rest of George IV's reign and sometimes acted as a link between Wellington and the King.[26]

Henry remained ambassador to Spain until 1821, and in 1823 Canning appointed him ambassador to Austria – a more senior and a more pleasant position, although Canning's dislike of any significant dealings with Metternich reduced its importance so long as he remained at the Foreign Office. Wellington and Henry corresponded, although not particularly frequently, throughout these years; exchanging a mixture of public and family news. Although closer to home Gerald appears even less frequently in the records of Wellington's life at this time, except when his promotion in the Church was being discussed.[27]

Wellington saw more of his nieces and nephews than of his brothers and was an excellent, attentive and helpful uncle. He was always particularly fond of William's three daughters and wrote pleasant, light-hearted letters to Mary and Priscilla when they were abroad accompanying their husbands on diplomatic postings. Anne's daughter Georgiana had married Wellington's ADC Lord Worcester in 1814, but the marriage broke down, and he ran up huge debts and the bailiffs moved in, so that 'if the Duke of Wellington had not given her rooms in his house she wd not have had a hole to put her head into'. In May 1821 she fell ill and died in great pain a week later at Apsley House. She was only twenty-eight, 'one of the handsomest women in England', and had been 'flattered, followed & admired by all the world'. Wellington accompanied Worcester to the funeral at Badminton and was, not surprisingly, reported to be 'very much out of spirits'.[28]

Many of the younger generation of Wellesleys followed in their parents' footsteps with marriages that broke down in a variety of scandals, but none attracted as much notoriety or opprobrium as William's son, subsequently known in the family as 'Wicked William'. In 1812 William married Catherine Tylney Long, a great heiress said to be worth more than £1.5 million. He added her surnames to his own to produce the much-ridiculed mouthful of 'Pole Tylney Long Wellesley', and proceeded to run through as much of her fortune as he could while making her extremely unhappy. By the 1820s William was deep in debt and living abroad, separated from his wife and children. Wellington tried to act as mediator, and after Catherine's death accepted her wish that he act as guardian of the children. This led to a protracted series of court cases as William endeavoured to obtain custody; while in 1827 William wrote a scurrilous pamphlet in 1827 in which he accused Wellington and almost every other member of his extended family, and just about everyone else involved in the case, of an extraordinary range of moral failings and sexual misdemeanours. However, the accusations were too numerous, and the malice too obvious, for them to be taken seriously even by Wellington's greatest enemies.[29]

John Malcolm, Wellington's old friend from India, was in England from 1822 to 1827, and the Duke endeavoured to assist him in his attempts to secure the governorship of Bombay or Madras, although Malcolm did not always take his advice, and had his heart set on becoming Governor-General of India, a prize which would remain beyond his reach. Malcolm was the prime mover in the establishment of the Oriental Club in London in 1824, and Wellington accepted the position of the inaugural president of the club, and remained a member until his death. The Duke was also a member of many other clubs including the Athenaeum, the Army and Navy, the Carlton, the Oxford and Cambridge, and the United Service Club, although there is little evidence that he spent much time at any of them.[30]

Wellington provided a home for Don Miguel Alava, the Spanish liaison officer who had been attached to his headquarters in the Peninsula, and who had been forced to leave Spain because of his liberal views. Wellington introduced him into society, let him live at Apsley House, and helped him financially until he was able to receive his own income from Spain regularly. Alava became a well-known figure in London society, and was welcomed at first but eventually came to be regarded as little more than a gossip, and something of a bore, who exaggerated his intimacy with Wellington.[31]

The Duke also took a kindly interest in Frederick Ponsonby, Lady Bessborough's son, who had served with distinction in the Peninsula and was fortunate to survive multiple wounds at Waterloo. The family weakness for gambling left Ponsonby seriously in debt, and in 1822 Wellington arranged for him to go to the Ionian Islands as Inspecting Officer, in the hope that a few years there would enable him to break the habit and recover his fortune. At the same time he wrote a difficult letter of advice:

> I cannot conclude this letter without urgently entreating you to recollect what it is that has obliged you to separate yourself from your family and friends, and to quit the most advantageous and agreeable position that can fall to the lot of any man in England. I am afraid that you can go to no part of the world, whether near or distant, in which you will not find means and opportunities of getting into similar scrapes; and you may rely upon it that their only result will be to occasion fresh and increased regret to yourself, and sorrow to your family and friends, and to none more than to him who subscribes himself yours most sincerely and affectionately, Wellington.[32]

Ponsonby replied: 'I have quite given it up . . . and if there is any faith in man, I promise that your advice shall not be forgotten.' He returned home on leave in 1824 and married Lady Emily Bathurst in the following year; and Wellington lent them £1,000 as neither had much money. After Ponsonby's sudden death in 1837 Wellington took an interest in the career of his son Henry Frederick who, after serving in the army, became private secretary to Queen Victoria.[33]

Lady Shelley records her gratitude for a smaller but still significant kindness. She was ill and unhappy in the spring of 1825 and Wellington called every day 'sometimes for one minute only – on his way to the Horse Guards [and] with his cheery: "How are ye today?" kept up my spirits, and was a better cordial than any which my physician could devise'. At other times Mrs Arbuthnot and the Duke would come together and stay much longer discussing all the news of the day and he would leave pamphlets, letters and other papers to amuse the invalid.[34]

Despite being extremely busy Wellington was always ready to help resolve private quarrels, and was frequently consulted over delicate matters, including marital disputes. His advice, as Lady Burghersh records, 'was always in favour of conciliation and indulgence, and many family feuds have been stifled and family misfortunes mitigated by his beneficent interference'. When Lord Wellesley's daughter Anne left her dull husband Sir William Abdy for the even duller Lord Charles Bentinck in 1815, Wellington comforted her sister Hyacinthe: 'I am not astonished at your feeling for your sister; but you must not allow these feelings to keep you out of the World or make you believe that people will on that account think the worse of you; nor on the other hand should you regret any good-natured act you may have done by her, or be induced to abandon her in her misfortunes.' His attempt to act as mediator in a bitter dispute between Lord and Lady Westmeath in 1819 ended badly, but it is notable that he was willing to spend four or five days carrying messages and proposals from the wife in the drawing room to the husband in the dining room and back again. Despite his pleasure in gossip, his discretion and integrity in such matters were absolutely reliable. Although she had already quarrelled with him and aligned herself with Canning, it was to Wellington that Princess Lieven turned when she was desperate to retrieve her compromising love letters to Metternich. Her confidence was justified and he handled the affair with tact and *savoir faire*, just as in later years he helped resolve the quarrel between the young Queen Victoria and her mother, the Duchess of Kent, and ensured the departure of Sir John Conroy, the Duchess's favourite. In all these cases Wellington's enormous prestige helped; quarrelling spouses, or parents and children, would be ashamed if he saw them behaving in a petty or mean-spirited manner, while his wide experience as a man of the world meant that he was unlikely to be shocked or censorious at their revelations.[35]

Wellington's social life in the 1820s followed the familiar pattern of British high society, with the season being tied to the sitting of Parliament, which usually began in January and rose in July, with a short recess at Easter. He would spend these months in London, living at Apsley House, working at his office at the Ordnance, attending Cabinet meetings, going for a ride in the park, calling on his friends, and then either attending debates in the Lords (which sat less often than the Commons) or at a dinner, a ball, or theatre. On 18 June he would host the annual banquet for a selection of officers who had served at Waterloo, an occasion that was rapidly gaining éclat and becoming an important fixture in the calendar. He would also spend several days or a week in June staying with the King and attending the races at Ascot, a party which he described in 1824 as 'very stupid'.[36]

As the season drew towards its close and the days lengthened and weather improved, pleasure parties were organised in which the Duke frequently took part. For example, in early August 1822, Wellington held a 'breakfast' or garden party for the Duke of York at Woolwich at which the Ordnance demonstrated the use of rockets and a new method of attacking fortifications. Mrs Arbuthnot missed this part of the festivities, but came in the afternoon and 'saw all the models & all the armour etc taken at Paris ... We had a most magnificent dinner and afterwards there was a great deal of dancing. We got back to London about 12 o'clock at night. It was the prettiest fete I ever saw.' And on 12 July 1825 Wellington arranged a pleasure jaunt on the Ordnance barge to Greenwich with a party which included Mrs Arbuthnot, Lady G. Fane, General Alava and a number of other ladies and gentlemen. On the way they stopped to inspect the tunnel which Marc Isambard Brunel was constructing between Rotherhithe and Wapping. Wellington had encouraged and supported the project, but it ran into difficulties and was not completed until 1843. They also viewed the East India Docks before dining at Greenwich and walking in the Park. The weather was perfect and the river bustling with merchantmen and pleasure craft. On the return trip Lady Georgiana Fane and Alava amused the company by singing Spanish songs.[37]

In August, once Parliament had risen, Wellington would visit the Continent to examine progress on the barrier fortresses in the Netherlands, and possibly go on to Paris. He would usually be home in time to stay with the Arbuthnots at Woodford (their modest house in Northamptonshire) to celebrate Harriet's birthday on 10 August. (In 1822, when he was detained in London, he gave her an emerald and pearl bracelet made from the stones in the hilt of a sword which had been presented to him by a Maratha chief after the defeat of Dhoondiah Waugh, on that day in 1800.)[38] A succession of visits to other country houses would follow, sometimes with Kitty, more often without. He would also host one or more parties at Stratfield Saye, and would often see in the New Year at Apethorpe (Lord Westmorland's seat) where, at least in 1822, he and Mrs Arbuthnot attended the servant's ball and even joined in the dancing.[39]

On his return to England Wellington took up shooting, which had become increasingly fashionable and provided important opportunities for informal conversation and strengthening friendships. Even Robert Peel, classics scholar, intellectual and art collector, was passionately fond of it and would not hesitate to boast of his daily total of slaughtered birds, for shooting was highly competitive and Wellington had no wish to be left on the sidelines as a non-starter, nor to be regarded as a dunce. An early outing, while staying with Sir John and Lady Shelley at Maresfield in October 1819, was not a great success, with Lady Shelley recording that on the first afternoon the casualties included a wounded retriever, a gamekeeper with peppered gaiters, and an old woman innocently doing her washing at the window of her cottage. Fortunately the light birdshot they were using did no serious harm, and a generous tip was sufficient to convince the woman that to be shot by the victor of Waterloo was an honour to treasure. (The keeper was probably accustomed to such accidents, but one hopes that the dog got a large bone.)[40] Sir John was a keen sportsman and seeing the problem, appointed himself Wellington's tutor, the Duke meekly accepting his instruction. With this assistance the next day's shooting was more successful and with practice Wellington steadily improved, adding reports of his triumphs and failures to his letters to Lady Shelley for the rest of the season: 'We had one day's very good shooting at [Blickling] and I killed fifty-one head, of which half were pheasants and partridges, and I think that Shelley would have been very well satisfied with his scholar.' And: 'I have been shooting pretty well lately, I killed twenty-seven head at Woburn; and the Duke of York, with his five guns, only killed thirty five!'[41]

Hunting features less prominently in his letters in these years, but he told Mrs Arbuthnot after a good run at Belvoir in 1822: 'I enjoyed it so much that I have serious thoughts of breaking out in a New Place, & of buying some Horses and of establishing a Stud next year in Leicestershire, & even of sending some Horses down there this year.'[42] Nothing seems to have come of this plan, although Wellington continued to hunt when the opportunity arose. He also played real tennis, in a court at Stratfield Saye which had previously been the riding school. His most frequent partner was Mr Wagner, his sons' tutor, who recalled: 'One occasion I remember to have made a chance, back-handed, violent return of the ball, which was so rapid and twisting that he could not get out of its way. It struck him on the side. I jumped over the net, and expressed my regret; secretly wishing that I, and not he, had received the blow. He rubbed the place, and referred to a custom in India, of rubbing for a variety of ills. He then resumed the game, and would not leave off till he had played out the set.'[43]

Not all Wellington's recreations were as energetic as this and he could be just as happy indoors as out. In 1821 Lady Granville described him taking part in charades with Lady Worcester, Princess Lieven and others and as 'happier than when he won his battles'. In 1820 she had told her sister: 'I quite love the Duke of Wellington. He is neither an agreeable man nor in my eyes a *héros de roman*, but he is the most unpretending, perfectly natural and amiable person I ever met with. We had an old admiral from Ipswich to dinner yesterday, whom he had known very early in his military career, and you never saw anything like his kind and cordial manner to him.' And in 1822 when he was again staying at Wherstead she noted: 'The Duke and the Lievens stay till Sunday. The Duke is as merry as a grig. We were occupied all yesterday evening with conjuring tricks and patiences of every kind.' And: 'Madame de Lieven was for a whole week invariably gay and agreeable, and with the *bonhomie* and adorable qualities of the Duke, and the *agréments* of F. Lamb, Lord Clanwilliam, and Francis, the enjoyment of the last ten days . . . has been very great.' Samuel Rogers agreed, noting: 'The Duke of Wellington has, naturally, a great gaiety of mind; he laughs at almost everything, as if it only served to divert him. Not less remarkable is the simplicity of his manner. It is, perhaps, rather the absence of everything like affectation. In his account of himself he discovers [i.e. reveals], in no instance, the least vanity or conceit, and he listens always readily to others. His laugh is easily excited, and it is very loud and long, like the whoop of the whooping-cough often repeated.'[44] Even when the society was less compatible and agreeable than at Maresfield or Wherstead Wellington was ready to enjoy whatever amusement was to be had. A few years earlier he had written to his niece, Mary Bagot, when she was in Washington: 'As for your being bored I don't mind [i.e. believe] that . . . I believe that you are like me in that respect, viz., that you can find amusement with blackguards if you cannot find gentlemen to keep company with . . .'[45]

But if Wellington was an excellent guest, he was not quite so successful as a host. Stratfield Saye was not a particularly good house – the intention had always been to demolish it and replace it with a palace to rival Blenheim – although Wellington was delighted with the improvements he made in it, especially the central heating. Philipp von Neumann, the Austrian diplomat, was scathing: 'The house is not very comfortable, the park ugly, the living mediocre, the whole indicating the lack of sympathy existing between the Duke and his Duchess'; while in 1826, after the heating was installed, Peel told his wife: 'The house is a wretched one, wretchedly furnished, but warm and not uncomfortable.' Still, Peel was pleased with the shooting; on the first day of his visit he killed 12 rabbits, 16 hares and 39 pheasants, while on the following day the tally was 28 pheasants, 21 hares and 10 rabbits.[46]

Years later Lady Shelley recalled that the Duchess 'invariably called all the party "the Duke's company," and sat apart from her guests, dressed, even in winter, in white muslin, without any ornaments, when every one else was in full dress!' She made little effort at conversation, talking mostly to the boys' tutor or to a country neighbour, and appeared uneasy when taken into dinner by the most high-ranking male guest, usually a royal duke or foreign ambassador. 'She seldom spoke, but looked through her eyeglass lovingly upon the Duke, who sat opposite to her. When the ladies went to the drawing-room, she retired to her own room.'[47]

In September 1824 Wellington gave Mrs Arbuthnot an account of a particularly difficult evening:

My Company are still here, and appear disposed to stay. It is however very difficult to amuse them, and I am sometimes quite at a loss. One would think that Mme de Lieven would have no *amour proper* about playing the Harpsichord, but it was her own proposition last night to sit down to it; and I was in a situation in which it was quite certain that I should not fall asleep, as you will recollect that I did once before, as I filled the ignoble Office of turning over the leaves for her. But after she had played for some little time, others began to talk, & she got up immediately saying that she played very seldom, but that if she was not attended to she would not play at all. As the Duchess does not like cards on a Sunday, I was then obliged to amuse them as I could till they went to bed. Really, the call upon me for amusement is so constant that I am tired of having people in the House.[48]

And so he used the difficulty of keeping his friends entertained as the basis of a letter to amuse another friend.

Wellington thoroughly enjoyed society and felt particularly comfortable where the worlds of politics, high society and diplomacy overlapped. He relished the company of intelligent, fashionable women and, unlike some men, he listened to them and took their opinions seriously. He was a good friend, willing to make time in an extremely busy life to give advice and practical assistance when it was needed, and to write frequent entertaining letters, which were also often remarkably indiscreet. The unhappy state of his marriage certainly encouraged him to rely quite heavily on his friends for amusement and comfort, and as he grew older he was increasingly conscious of this loss, despite his surrogate home with the Arbuthnots. He did not hanker to withdraw from society, except in rare moments of *ennui*, but he regretted the absence of a wife who would share and enhance his political and other interests and whom he could love, respect and admire. Nonetheless his private life in these years was relatively happy, although somewhat marred by his increasing deafness.[49]

CHAPTER SIXTEEN

THE INS AND OUTS OF 1827

L IVERPOOL'S STROKE ON 17 February 1827 brought to an end a premiership of almost fifteen years; only Walpole and Pitt of his predecessors, and none of his successors, have held the office for longer. The remaining ministers played for time. It was immediately obvious that Liverpool would not be able to resume his duties, but it was felt that he might be able to recover sufficiently to be able to resign, or conversely a second stroke might kill him. Peel went down to Brighton to inform the King, who took the news well at first but became more and more agitated as he contemplated its implications, so that he had to be dissuaded from sending an urgent summons to Wellington in the small hours of the following morning.[1]

The choice of Liverpool's successor was not simple. Canning's claim, as leader of the government in the Commons and a dominant figure in Cabinet, was obvious; and as early as 20 February *The Times* was loudly trumpeting his merits. Indeed the paper went further, not just talking of him as the natural heir, but going on to speculate on a junction with Lansdowne and the moderate Whigs, while questioning Wellington's capacity to act even as leader of the Lords, and praising Frederick Robinson's 'high character and unimpeachable integrity'. Two days later it cast any pretence of objectivity aside: 'There is in one part of the Ministerial body, a strong disinclination to give to a certain Right Honourable Gentleman, in form, the official dignity which his talents must confer upon him in effect – namely, that of Prime Minister.' And: 'The Right Hon. Gentleman, whatever his powers may be, labours under one disad-vantage in these bickerings, which is, that he feels, he is sensitive; the brutes who thwart him are callous, and impenetrable to acute sensation.' Given that *The Times* was well known to have close ties to the Foreign Office, some readers may have felt that Canning was making his pitch a little too obviously, espe-cially as there had, in fact, been no discussions as yet in Cabinet over the succession. Certainly the obvious bias of the press would not have endeared

Canning to his more conservative colleagues, although we now know that in this case *The Times* was probably taking its lead from Brougham, not the Foreign Secretary.[2]

Despite the enthusiasm of *The Times* there were significant difficulties to the choice of Canning as the new prime minister. His support for Catholic Emancipation would unsettle the balance in the government on the question and lead to Peel's resignation from the Home Office.[3] It also constituted the King's greatest personal objection to Canning. All the old resentments over the Princess and other grievances had been forgotten, while his dislike of Canning's foreign policy had faded, but the King's opposition to Catholic Emancipation remained strong, buttressed by memories of the determination of his father and the Duke of York on the question. Against this the King's closest associates, Sir William Knighton and Lady Conyngham, had been won over by Canning, while the King himself could confidently anticipate that Canning would be more inclined to indulge him on questions of patronage and his building projects than Liverpool or Wellington.

It was not clear that Canning would be able to hold the government together. He was associated with policies both foreign and domestic that won much applause from the Opposition, but which were met with glum dislike from the traditional supporters of the ministry. Catholic Emancipation; support for liberal governments abroad of doubtful legitimacy; a reduction in tariffs; financial deregulation; and the undermining of the Corn Laws, was not a programme which held much appeal for Conservative country gentlemen. More seriously, the other senior ministers simply did not trust him. Years of working closely together had made them doubt his temperament, his judgement and his character; and it was this, at least as much as their dislike of the liberal policies he pursued, that provoked their opposition. These doubts were strengthened in early March when, during a debate on Catholic Emancipation, Canning damaged his own cause by losing his temper and launching an extraordinary attack on the Master of the Rolls, John Singleton Copley.[4] In some cases hostility to Canning seems to have been heightened by social snobbery, but it is significant that the famous jibe attributed to Lord Grey that 'the son of an actress [is] incapacitated *de facto* for the premiership of England', and Londonderry's description of him as a 'charlatan parvenu', both came from men who had long nursed a deep personal animosity. The fact was that Canning had always been a divisive figure, arousing great admiration and loyalty in some, dislike and distrust in others; and this had little or nothing to do with his family background.[5]

Wellington was the obvious alternative to Canning. None of the other ministers remotely equalled his range of experience or grasp of policy across a broad range of the government's activities. Mrs Arbuthnot was naturally enthusiastic about the idea, and it is interesting to see the grounds she chose on which to make out the case:

> The Duke is as great a statesman as he is a soldier, and I am certain he wd be the best Minister we ever [had]; for, while he wd be really efficient & wd really govern the country (which has not been the case of late years), he wd be honest as the day and wd be *excessively economical* which is, I think, what we want more than anything; he wd introduce order into the chaos of the Treasury & all our public departments, make them really efficient & do, at the head of the Govt, the same good that he has already done in the office over which he has presided for some years & which is now the cheapest & best regulated of any.[6]

But against this there was Wellington's lack of confidence speaking in the Lords; and grave doubts whether Canning would serve under him, or whether the government could survive in the Commons with Canning neutral or in opposition. Another more recent objection to Wellington was his appointment as Commander-in-Chief. Even many of his closest supporters thought that this put him out of the running. Sir Henry Hardinge, who was 'warmly attached personally & politically to the Duke', felt that it created an insuperable obstacle, and Charles Arbuthnot agreed, although he had told Knighton in 1826 that the two roles were not incompatible. The Duke of Rutland and the Marquess of Buckingham, both of whom were eager to find an alternative to Canning, reluctantly accepted that it was impossible, and Peel appeared to take it for granted.[7] Mrs Arbuthnot acknowledged the difficulty, but refused to regard it as insurmountable:

> It need not be so if they did not make the bugbear for themselves. There is nothing unconstitutional in it; and, tho' as a general principle it would be most objectionable to heap so much power on one person, yet in a case of such extreme difficulty it appears to me to be the greatest possible weakness to fear facing the storm of unpopularity which, no doubt, such an appointment in the first instance wd cause. We have but the alternative of him or Mr Canning or some *man of straw* chosen from the mere purpose of keeping the party together. There can be no doubt of the Duke's capability; he is just the man which the circumstances of the moment require.[8]

Wellington's own attitude was ambivalent. He never disputed or contradicted statements that he was out of contention, but watching him closely Mrs Arbuthnot was convinced that they irritated him. She believed that 'the Duke is haunted with the dread of being supposed to enter into anything like an intrigue; he says he has never in his life asked for anything or put himself forward in any way for political aggrandizement & that, please God!, he never will, & that he would rather serve under Mr Canning than be supposed to quit from anything like personal pique'. As early as 22 February she recorded that 'he himself thinks his being Minister impossible on account of his situation as Cr in Chief', but she immediately undercut the remark with the rider, '& at all events he will not stir a finger to become so'.[9] This seems to be the key to Wellington's attitude to the succession battle; he would not put himself forward or actively canvass for support, but he knew that he might nonetheless be called upon to play a role in forming a government, and that if asked it was not in his nature to refuse. This does not mean that he hankered for the responsibility, for the evidence suggests that he was torn between fears for the future if the government was formed by Canning and the Whigs, and a desire to concentrate on his role as Commander-in-Chief. Mrs Arbuthnot is again our best source:

> I am very uneasy about it, for I see the Duke will break his heart if he is forced to resign the command of the army &, tho' I think he will like being Minister if he cd. be both, he wd. rather 100 times over go out of the Govt altogether than give up that great military position which he feels is his natural place, where he is beloved & respected & for which he feels himself so indisputably fit. I am afraid he wd be made to give up the Command in Chief if he was made First Lord of the Treasury.[10]

Certainly he did nothing to court the King's favour at this crucial time, and on 20 February seemed almost to go out of his way to pick a quarrel over the appointment of a new colonel to the 4th Dragoon Guards. Such colonelcies were lucrative honours rather than active commands, and the King indicated that he wished the place go to Lord George Beresford, but Wellington, as Commander-in-Chief, objected. In part this was a matter of principle – a tussle to preserve the Commander-in-Chief's right to control such appointments free of royal interference in the face of the court's attempt to regain patronage it had lost years before. But there were other political implications: Beresford was a member of a family that gave the government consistent support in Parliament; while the alternative was Lieutenant-General Sir George Anson, who was a Whig MP. The Duke of York had established and entrenched the principle that officers were to receive promotion, and the honours and rewards of their profession, regardless of their political affiliations; and if, in one of the first appointments made by Wellington at the Horse Guards, Beresford was preferred to Anson, the Opposition would certainly cry foul, especially as Anson had served in the Peninsula and Lord George had never seen action.

Challenged with this argument the King backed down and Anson was appointed, but it is unlikely that His Majesty relished the incident or that it endeared Wellington to him. It is also worth pointing out that the whole idea of promotion on merit irrespective of political ties was antipathetical to the eighteenth-century constitution, and that its gradual spread through government over the previous half-century had contributed substantially to the erosion of the Crown's ability to command a majority in the Commons, and hence to the King's right to select a minister of his choice. Why should military officers or other placemen continue to give loyal support to the ministry of the day if this support was to count for nothing when it came to their own advancement? Not that this was how Wellington saw it; both in practice and in theory he was scrupulous in treating colleagues and subordinates fairly, if anything, making a particular effort to welcome those whose political views differed most sharply from his own.[11]

The interregnum following Liverpool's stroke lasted seven weeks. Parliament continued to sit, and on 5–7 March there was a debate on the Catholic Question. This was the first test of feeling in the new Parliament, and to almost universal surprise the motion was narrowly defeated. The result shocked and outraged liberal opinion and produced a violent reaction in the press, while both *The Times* and the *Morning Chronicle* published stories accusing Wellington of looking to the reconquest of Ireland as the only solution to its problems. Wellington was understandably furious and took legal advice about suing both papers. Although he was prepared to swear that he had never made the remark, the lawyers advised against an action because he was not explicitly named, and the papers might pretend that they were really referring to somebody else. Such was the oppression of the press under the Six Acts of 1819![12]

The papers, and Canning's friends, also blamed Wellington for an ill-judged effort by a group of 'high' or 'ultra' Tories, including the Duke of Newcastle and Lord Colchester, to persuade the King that there was a strong party of 'King's friends' ready to support him in maintaining the Protestant constitution. In fact, Wellington had discouraged their activity, believing that it infringed the King's prerogative and was likely to be counter-productive.[13]

During the interregnum there was naturally intense speculation over whom the King would name as Liverpool's successor, and the names of numerous possible compromise figures – some of them very dark horses indeed – were discussed. As early as 21 February Wellington and Peel had agreed that 'they must be quite quiet, leave the King alone to do just what he pleased, & decline to give any opinions or state their own intentions until he had named the person he meant to make Minister; that it wd. not do for them to take the responsibility of advising the King for or against any person, for that he was not to be trusted & that, moreover, it was not their business'. By and large they stuck to this line and rebuffed several attempts by the King to pass the responsibility for choosing the minister on to the Cabinet.[14] Canning was less restrained. Princess Lieven claimed to have conveyed a message from Canning to the King that 'his resolution was taken. He had decided to become head of the Cabinet or to leave the party'. And Canning told the King directly on 28 March that he would resign unless he was given the premiership, or at least the 'substantive power of First Minister'. By then, if not from the outset, he was convinced that the game was his, and that he only had to hold firm to gain the prize that he had coveted for so long. Still he did not completely close the door on other arrangements and on 3 April floated the possibility that if the King asked him to form a government he might send Robinson to the Lords and give him the office of prime minister. Wellington did not encourage this scheme, for it was obvious that whatever the form, the real power in such a government would have rested in Canning's hands.[15]

On 5 April the King came to London from Windsor and over the next few days more intensive discussions were held among the ministers. When these failed to produce a solution which would satisfy everyone, the King formally commissioned Canning to form a government on the afternoon of 10 April. Canning then wrote to, or arranged to see, all of his Cabinet colleagues, asking them to remain in office. His letter to Wellington was noticeably stiff and uninformative: it gave no information about the proposed ministry, nor suggested a meeting to discuss it; or expressed any active wish that Wellington would remain. The Duke's reply was carefully guarded – it is clear that he expected some ambush or trick but did not know what form it would take, and felt the need to make sure of his ground: 'I anxiously desire to be able to serve his Majesty as I have done hitherto in his Cabinet, with the same colleagues. But before I can give an answer to your obliging proposition, I should wish to know who the person is whom you intend to propose to his Majesty as the head of the government'.[16] Canning took umbrage at this and replied that it was 'so generally understood' that the person asked to form a government would head it, that he had seen no need to spell this out. The tone of the letter was clearly and deliberately insulting, and this was magnified by the fact that Canning had submitted it to the King and obtained his approval before sending it. Wellington responded with studied courtesy, going out of his way to credit Canning with the best of intentions, but declining to serve in his government. And on the following day he wrote to the King resigning the command of the army.[17]

The most puzzling aspect of the affair is why Canning's behaviour was so gratuitously offensive. Even if he was working on the assumption that Wellington would resign, and if he secretly was eager to see Wellington go, it would surely have been better to have made a show of conciliating him in order to appeal to government supporters hesitating over which leader to follow. However, the point which attracted most discussion at the time and subsequently was Wellington's decision to resign the command of the army as well as the Ordnance. It is often said that this was unnecessary and risked politicising a purely professional office. Wellington explained his decision by referring to the King's approval of Canning's second letter, which implicated His Majesty in the insult, and pointed out that the Commander-in-Chief had to work closely with the prime minister on many issues ranging from the expansion or reduction of the army to its deployment overseas, most immediately to Portugal. 'How was it possible,' he asked the Lords, 'for me to consider that I was likely to possess the Right Honourable gentleman's confidence on any of these points, after receiving from him, in his Majesty's name, such a rebuke as was contained in his letter to me of the 11th?'[18] Moreover, the Commander-in-Chief was also in constant contact with the King, discussing promotions, appointments, uniforms and many other aspects of the army, and it would be difficult to limit such discussions to purely professional matters or to avoid the accusation that he was using such meetings to intrigue against Canning. It is not hard to imagine that if he had remained at the Horse Guards he would have been accused of clinging to office for purely selfish reasons, and been confronted with demands that he either support the government or withdraw entirely from active politics. And certainly there would have been something more than a little awkward in having the Commander-in-Chief in open opposition to the government of the day.[19]

News of Wellington's resignation was greeted with dismay in the army and especially at the Horse Guards. Canning did not attempt to fill the vacancy and the King got his wish of having a personal command, with the actual work divided between Sir Herbert Taylor and Palmerston, who remained as Secretary-at-War but who gained a seat in the Cabinet. The Ordnance went to Anglesey who then had to be persuaded to sit in Cabinet. Possessing all the presumption for which the Pagets were famous, he had little experience or talent for politics, but his acquisition was nonetheless useful to Canning, for he had recently voted against Catholic Emancipation (having previously supported it) and was one of the very few 'protestants' willing to serve in the new government.[20]

Almost all the senior ministers in the government resigned at the same time as Wellington: Peel, Bathurst, Melville, Eldon, Westmorland and Bexley. Only Canning, his old friend Huskisson, Robinson, Wynn (who had quarrelled with his patron Lord Buckingham) and Harrowby remained. Comparing the two lists left no doubt where the balance lay, and the withdrawal of Bexley's resignation under strong pressure from the King only emphasised the reluctance of Canning's equals to serve under him. At the same time several dozen junior ministers and other office-holders also quit, some out of loyalty to their chiefs, others over the Catholic Question. Many others remained for the moment, reluctant to take an irrevocable step but with strong reservations.[21]

Canning did not find it easy to form a government. The only significant recruit of any standing he could find was the Master of the Rolls, John Singleton Copley, whom he had abused and ridiculed a few weeks before, and whom he now made Lord Chancellor with the title of Lord Lyndhurst. Copley was ambitious; he had already been marked out as Eldon's most likely successor, but incumbency, especially in that office, carried great weight, and he knew that if he declined Canning's offer he might be overtaken by a rival, so he swallowed his pride, accepted the Great Seal and, by his presence, indicated that the King remained determined not to make concessions to the Catholics. Other appointments were embarrassingly insubstantial. The choice of the Duke of Portland as Lord Privy Seal was unobjectionable, but his only qualification for office, other than his title, was that he was Canning's brother-in-law. After offering the Home Office to a number of staunch 'protestants' and being rebuffed by them all, Canning was finally forced to entrust it to his prep-school friend William Sturges Bourne, who had never previously been thought equal to even a junior ministry. The new Foreign Secretary was J.W. Ward, now Viscount Dudley and Ward – a brilliant, unstable dilettante, painfully aware of being out of his depth, and who was widely reported to have accepted the position only after receiving assurances that Canning would continue to supervise the office and 'write & think for him'.[22]

But the *pièce de résistance* was the appointment of the Duke of Clarence, the heir to the throne, as Lord High Admiral. Clarence had served in the navy in his youth forty years before, and had hankered to meddle with it ever since. The idea of being made Lord High Admiral had been raised by him in 1823, when Croker had squashed it with the magnificent retort that there was a precedent: 'James II had done the same.'[23] Having dined out on the story for years, Croker now revived it in earnest. His patron, Lord Hertford, had accepted a special diplomatic mission from Canning, and Croker had long supported Catholic Emancipation, so it is not surprising that he had no qualms retaining his office at the Admiralty. Canning leapt on the idea, which was applauded by his admirers as a stroke of genius, pleasing the King and ensuring the favour of his successor. But the ministers who had just resigned saw in it ample vindication of their decision. To them it was an act of naked opportunism which sacrificed the future efficiency of the navy for a partisan political advantage. Clarence was, as all England except himself well knew, incompetent to perform the duties of the office, and unlikely to submit for long to the guidance of his subordinates. The problem was not just his lack of intelligence but also his inexperience of official business; he was sixty-two years old and had never held office before. Entrusting him to such an important position, one whose powers were ill defined and open to wide interpretation, was almost bound to lead to disaster.

Ever since 1822 the Whigs, especially Brougham and Lansdowne, had been encouraging divisions within the government by supporting Canning's more liberal measures in Parliament, and it was generally expected that at least part of the Whig party would join him in office at the end of the parliamentary session. Indirect negotiations had begun within days of Liverpool's stroke, and fuelled the suspicion of Canning among his more conservative colleagues; but Canning would make few promises and in the end the Whigs offered their support in return for whatever crumbs Canning chose to give them. Curiously, some leading radicals were among the strongest advocates of the rapprochement: Sir Francis Burdett, Sir Robert Wilson and Brougham himself were more associated with the wilder fringes of the party than the moderate centre of British politics. On the other hand Joseph Hume and John Cam Hobhouse held aloof, while Cobbett attacked the proposed coalition with his accustomed vehemence. Over the next few months a trickle of Whigs took office individually rather than as a party, leaving them very under-represented in the ministry compared to their strength in the Commons, and the party impatient for a greater share in the spoils of office.[24]

Canning's greatest advantage was the support of the press, which largely took the form of abuse of the ministers who resigned. The *Examiner* criticised 'the old hacks of office' for attempting to dictate to the King, and proceeded to compare Wellington and his colleagues to fleas or bugs, and urged the King to 'crush them under his nail for their audacious enterprise' – a curious stance for a paper more commonly associated with cries for popular liberty than a defence of the royal prerogative. The *Morning Chronicle* was more decorous in its language, but equally dismissive of the men who had governed the country since the dark days of 1807: 'Who, for instance, cares for such men as Lord Westmorland or Lord Bathurst? . . . The Duke of Wellington is only respectable as a General. As a Statesman, he is far from eminent; and his talents as a debater can confer little benefit on his associates.' The *Times* agreed: 'We can solemnly affirm that the retreat from political office of Lords Eldon, Bathurst, Westmorland, the Duke of Wellington, and Lord Melville, is a blessed relief from a whole bundle of nuisances, as in our own time, and through natural means, we had scarcely ever hoped to see accomplished.'[25]

The message was reinforced by a flood of caricatures which responded to the heightened public interest in politics. Almost all these prints favoured Canning, or at least derided his opponents. Two depicted the retiring ministers as a multi-headed dragon being slain by Canning, either as St George or in the company of King George and St George. Another depicted Canning as Cicero, dressed as a Roman senator, enjoying a ceremonial triumph for his victory in defence of the British constitution, with Wellington in chains, leading the procession of his captives. Others showed Wellington variously as a high-wayman, a peacock, a bandsman, a dismissed carpenter and a dunghill; in almost every case the stance was hostile, with several having him lament the perks of office. One of the best of the prints criticises Wellington's resignation as Commander-in-Chief by depicting him as *Achilles in the Sulks after his Retreat; or, The Great Captain on the Stool of Repentance*. Wellington, made ridiculous by his enormous boots and outsize hat, is sitting in a petulant sulk, staring at the letter from the King accepting his resignation. A broken baton inscribed 'Comr in Chief' is on the floor, a picture of Waterloo is on the wall, and through the open window on which Wellington has turned his back is the statue dedicated to him of Achilles in Hyde Park.[26]

Peel was concerned that this torrent of abuse might decide public opinion before the resumption of Parliament gave the former ministers the opportunity of justifying their resignations, and he urged Wellington to publish a simple statement of his case to clarify the record. Wellington refused, preferring to claim the high moral ground: 'I have never had any concern with newspapers. I hate the whole tribe of news-writers, and I prefer to suffer from their false-hoods to dirtying my fingers with communications with them. I may be wrong, but I have always acted upon this principle, and I have generally found that it succeeded at last.'[27] This was neither strictly accurate (he had dealt with the press when defending Lord Wellesley's conduct in India and as Chief Secretary for Ireland, although never in pursuit of personal advantage), nor realistic, and when Wellington took office as prime minister in the following year he accepted the distasteful necessity of cultivating the press.

Wellington told Mrs Arbuthnot on 20 April that he intended to stay out of London during the parliamentary recess and avoid any involvement in 'all the foolish Mischief of Lord Londonderry & others':

My opinion is that the Policy which I wish to pursue is that which suits our Party best. Our Party consists of the Bishops & Clergy, the Great Aristocracy, the landed Interest, the Magistracy of the Country, the great Merchants and Bankers, in short the *parti conservateur* of the Country. It can never suit that Party to enter into a Factious opposition to the Government. The Government has fallen into the hands of an unworthy Individual, the tendency of whose Politicks & views & personal Interests would lead him to unite with the Whigs. Our object should be to gain time; not to hurry that Union, but to give the King time to reflect upon the Measures into which he is about to involve himself, and upon the consequences to his own personal Interests and ease of the steps which he is about to take.[28]

This suggests that there was more strategy behind his rejection of Peel's suggestion than appeared on the surface, and that he had already charted a course of moderate opposition that would allow him to defend his reputation without making it too difficult for the King to turn back to his old ministers when the time came.

Parliament resumed after Easter on Tuesday 1 May, and the transformation of the government was make starkly apparent, for immediately behind the Prime Minister sat the radical stalwart Sir Francis Burdett and the Whig George Tierney, while Brougham also took his seat on the ministerial side. Once the formalities had been completed Peel rose and made a long speech explaining and justifying his conduct and that of the other ministers who had resigned. Mrs Arbuthnot, listening in the loft, declared that 'nothing could be more triumphant or more perfect'. She was especially delighted by 'a beautiful & most eloquent compliment' to Wellington. By a happy coincidence the tribute came on Wellington's birthday and according to Mrs Arbuthnot he was 'much pleased', having been more hurt and provoked by the newspaper attacks than he would admit.[29] Peel concluded his speech with a peroration which became famous:

I may be a Tory – I may be an illiberal – but the fact is undeniable, that when I first entered on the duties of the Home Department, there were laws in existence which imposed upon the subjects of this realm unusual and extraordinary restrictions: the fact is undeniable, that those laws have been effaced. Tory as I am, I have the further satisfaction of knowing that there is not a single law connected with my name, which has not had for its object some mitigation of the severity of the criminal law; some prevention of abuse in the exercise of it; or some security for its impartial administration ... Where change and restoration were deemed necessary, they have been applied, thus recommending those ancient institutions to the long enduring attachment and veneration of the country.[30]

The speech was a triumph, raising Peel's standing in Parliament and the country and ensuring that the contest for public opinion ceased to be one-sided. Canning could not conceal his chagrin, although the Duke of Rutland complained that 'Peel wound up his speech by too much trumpeting forth of his own public services'.[31] A more serious criticism is that he conceded too much to his opponents, in effect claiming to be just as good a reformer and as liberal as they were, rather than contesting their assumption that change equated to improvement. The speech he made suited the mood of the time and the place, but it also established a pattern of Tories apologising for being conservative which has proved remarkably enduring.

The other ministers who had retired made their explanations on the following night in the Lords, where interest focussed almost entirely on Wellington's speech, in part because an important speech by him was a novelty, and because if he failed his reputation as a serious figure in domestic politics would be seriously damaged. The House was packed, with men crowded on the steps of the throne and twenty or thirty ladies at its side. Behind the new ministers sat Lansdowne, Holland and other Whigs; but Grey, Lauderdale and their friends remained in their old places on the Opposition benches where they were joined, rather uncomfortably, by the High Tories Newcastle, Kenyon, Mansfield and Winchilsea, as well as by Londonderry. Wellington and the other ex-Ministers sat on the cross bench signalling at least a theoretical neutrality. Wellington's speech was plain, simple and straightforward, with few rhetorical flourishes or attempts at passion or fine oratory. But on this occasion at least the style worked well as he went through the sequence of events, reading aloud each letter in full and drawing attention to the significant points or omissions in each. He addressed many of the criticisms which had been made of him, firmly denying any conspiracy or attempt to dictate to the King his choice of minister. Colchester described the speech as 'clear, forcible, and conclusive', while Mrs Arbuthnot declared that 'partiality entirely put aside, . . . I never heard a better speech or one more ably delivered'. Even the Duke of Newcastle who, for all his conservatism, had viewed Wellington with some suspicion and dislike, praised it unreservedly: 'I never heard a better Speech, it was well arranged, compleat in all its parts, Strong, fluent, well expressed & most entirely Satisfactory – He was loudly cheered by the house & I rejoiced to witness it.'[32]

Nonetheless, Wellington's speech contained one serious error of judgement which would cause embarrassment later on. In denying the accusation that he had resigned out of pique because the King would not make him prime minister, Wellington said: 'My Lords, his Majesty never offered to me to make me his minister. His Majesty knew as well as I did, that I was, and must be, totally out of the question; and so I considered myself, and so stated myself repeatedly.' Having risen to the summit of his chosen profession, 'I could not be desirous of leaving it in order to seek to be appointed to be the head of the government, a situation for which I am sensible that I am not qualified'. He expounded upon this theme for some time, fortunately producing no disqualification more serious than his lack of practice at addressing the Lords, before stating, much too memorably: 'My Lords, I should have been worse than mad if I had thought of such a thing.'[33] This was foolish and unnecessary, breaking the golden rule of politics, 'never say never', and it reflected his own deep ambivalence; after eight years in Cabinet he still clung to the idea that he was not really a politician.

Party spirit ran high over the next few weeks, and Canning struggled with his temper as the Commons grew increasingly restless with his half-formed government. But there was no direct test of strength; Wellington, Peel and the other Tory leaders would not countenance anything approaching a motion of confidence which would force members to take sides and which would be represented as an attempt to regain office by force. Their view was that Canning's ministry was unsustainable and that it would either collapse of its own accord or rely so heavily on the Whigs for support that it became essentially a Whig administration with the infusion of a few Canningites. But this did not mean that they felt obliged to give free passage to all the government's proposals, and in June a row erupted over modifications to the Corn Laws. This had been discussed in Cabinet the previous November, with Wellington and some of the other ministers accepting the new scheme rather reluctantly and with some reservations. Since then a select committee of the Lords which Wellington attended had heard much evidence about abuses in the warehousing of imported 'bonded' grain, and the ease with which the market prices on which the legislation depended for its operation could be manipulated by importers. Towards the end of May Wellington wrote to Huskisson outlining the problem and proposing some amendments to the legislation. Huskisson replied rejecting Wellington's ideas but putting forward a scheme of his own. Wellington gladly adopted this and with Huskisson's letter in his pocket moved an amendment based closely on it in the Lords on 1 June, carrying it against the government by 78 to 74. This unleashed a tide of recrimination from which it appears that Huskisson had never intended his idea to be more than a temporary expedient or transitional measure, and that he had not informed his colleagues in the Lords that he had suggested any alteration in the law, or even kept a copy of the letter himself. For his part Wellington seems to have regarded the change as a technical modification that would improve the operation of the law without significantly affecting its principle. In other circumstances a compromise might have been devised, and Wellington offered to withdraw the amendment if the government would undertake to deal with the problem of price manipulation. But after almost a fortnight of confusion and growing acrimony, both sides dug in their heels and a second vote was held in a very full House which again carried Wellington's amendment by 133 to 122 votes (including proxies). The government then announced that it would abandon the measure and a temporary scheme was passed without difficulty.[34]

The ministers were infuriated by their defeat and the press embraced the cause with unrestrained zeal. On 19 June the *Morning Chronicle* wrote: 'Let the Duke of Wellington enjoy the rewards of his services to his country; but do not let him think that any services can screen him and his colleagues from the consequences of conduct, which will fill every well-constituted mind with inexpressible loathing and disgust.' On the following day it took up Canning's suggestion that Wellington was nothing more than a tool in the hands of others, declaring that 'after the evidence of incapacity amounting almost to imbecility which he has himself given, the supposition that he was played upon carries with it much probability'. Three caricatures widened the argument and opened a line of attack which would become a staple in years to come. In one a tall, handsome Wellington, in full uniform, holds a loaf of bread impaled on his sword aloft out of the reach of a starving crowd below; while in a second Canning presents a huge bag of bonded wheat to John Bull and his hungry family while Wellington cuts a hole in it from behind with a sword inscribed Revenge; the print is titled *The Rats at the Corn!!!*[35]

But if Wellington's amendment exposed him to attack in London, its success was greeted with delight in many parts of the country. In Hampshire there was talk of a subscription for a piece of plate to commemorate the victory, and addresses of congratulation were begun in many counties, although Wellington did his best to discourage them so as not to offend the King. Peel initially had doubts about Wellington's stand, but returned from the country in the middle of July in high spirits and convinced that 'the Duke's conduct upon the Corn Bill has been productive of great good, and that it has made him most popular with all the landed interest'. This encouraged Peel to think that the Tories 'must have a systematic opposition next session, and keep no terms with the Government'; while Billy Holmes, the long-serving government Whip under Liverpool, had prepared a formidable list of likely supporters.[36] Wellington may not have agreed with this – he had always been reluctant to mount a consistent opposition to the government of the day – but he made no secret of his hostility to Canning.

These months in 1827 were important in the gradual emergence of a Tory party distinct from the established support for Liverpool's administration as the government of the country. The process was far from complete at the end of the year, and many setbacks and divisions lay ahead, but some of the old inhibitions and objections to the idea of 'party', which the Pittites had inherited from the eighteenth century, faded from view in 1827 and were not seen again. This was as much evident in the provinces as in London, and the network of 'Pitt Clubs' across the country became an important vehicle for building a sense of cohesion and common purpose. It is impossible to make any estimate of the level of support enjoyed by any of the parties in the country at this time, but it is clear that the metropolitan press, even more than usual, gave an incomplete sense of the national mood.

Canning's health suffered from the strain of his position, and on 20 July he went to stay at the Duke of Devonshire's Palladian villa at Chiswick to rest and recuperate. Instead of regaining his strength he rapidly became much worse and died on the morning of 8 August. He had been prime minister for just under four months: the shortest tenure of any British premier before or since. Canning died leaving the eggs broken but the omelette unmade. If he had died a year earlier Liverpool's government would have survived a relatively simple transition to an administration dominated by Wellington and Peel. If Canning had lived another year or two the experiment of a liberal coalition government would have had a fair trial and either succeeded in reshaping British politics or failed amid disappointment and acrimony. But dying when he did, Canning left too many questions unanswered and too many wounds still open and bleeding.

The King did not, as some naïve observers expected, at once send for Wellington. There had been too much acrimony over the past few months to put back the clock and pretend that nothing had happened, while the King himself had not forgiven Wellington and the other ex-ministers for 'abandoning' him. Instead he turned to the amiable but lightweight Frederick Robinson, Viscount Goderich, the leader of the government in the Lords. The King also insisted that Goderich appoint John Charles Herries, a Conservative financial expert and staunch opponent of Catholic Emancipation, as his Chancellor of the Exchequer. This infuriated the Whigs, who pressed for the appointment of Lord Holland as Foreign Secretary as compensation. The King refused, and after much indecision the Whigs backed down, while Huskisson took Goderich's position of Secretary for War and the Colonies and also became leader of the Commons. Given the weakness of the government when Canning was alive, this clearly would not do; it was not just *Hamlet* without the Prince: most of the rest of the cast were second-string understudies.[37]

Goderich wasted no time in asking Wellington to resume command of the army. There had been several previous approaches in Canning's lifetime, but they had been primarily designed to score political points in the press and to encourage the King's sense of grievance, and were dismissed or evaded without difficulty.[38] However, Wellington had always made clear that his objection was personal to Canning, who had insulted him, and with Canning gone he felt that he had no choice but to accept. 'I am aware of the delicacy of the position in which I shall be placed,' he told Lord Westmorland, '[b]ut I think I can overcome that difficulty more easily than I could the abandonment of my professional position, or any inconsistency upon the reasons of my resignation.' The issue sharply divided his friends and allies. Peel and Bathurst both felt that he was right, although they accepted with regret that it would force Wellington to limit his opposition to the government. Melville, Hardinge, Londonderry, Rutland and the Duke of Cumberland all either expressed the hope that he would refuse, or regretted his decision once it was known.[39] But the strongest reaction came from Mrs Arbuthnot:

Mr Arbuthnot and I were very much annoyed, not at his accepting it for, with his feelings about the army, he could not well refuse it, and indeed it was not desirable; but it appeared to us that he did not sufficiently guard himself against being considered friendly to the new Govt. He came here from

Cirencester to dine and sleep; and, coming so soon after we had received the
news, I could not conceal how little I was satisfied. He was very much annoyed
and said I (with the exception of Ld Falmouth, who he always considers a fool
& who is a stupid fellow) was the only person he had seen of that opinion; that
Mr Bankes, Lord Ellenborough, the Bathurst family, all were delighted at what
he had done. I told him I believed the fact was that I was the only one who
spoke *truth* to him, for that I cd. not credit that Lord Bathurst had any such
opinion, as he had been, when we were at S. Saye, quite of a contrary opinion.
He was very angry, said he could not & wd. not do otherwise; that he was *no
politician* but a soldier, that the army looked to him as their protector; and that
he had a right to act as he pleased without anybody's interfering. I told him it
was all very well and that he had a right to accept the command of the army if
he chose, but that it was ridiculous nonsense for him to stand up and tell me
he was *no politician*; that I had known him intimately as a member of the
Cabinet for nine years, that he had taken a most active part in both our home
and foreign politics, that a large body in the State looked to him as their
protector against the political economists, and that he must be quite aware that
they did not do so on account of his military talents; that, with his view of the
subject, he might not perhaps be able to refuse, but that I thought it wd. have
been more fair & honourable to have stated his disapprobation of the present
Govt. He said he had stated it, and in the very manner recommended formerly
by Mr Peel himself. I remarked that that was recommended under different
circumstances, & that just remarking in parenthesis to Ld Goderich that he
did not think political differences of opinion ought to prevent his taking office,
was not saying he was opposed to the Govt; that, by accepting the command,
he had struck a most fatal blow at that party with whom he always had hitherto acted; and, tho' I admitted & always had felt that he could not refuse, yet
I positively thought that he ought clearly & explicitly to have told Lord
Goderich that he could not & wd not support his Govt, that, if he had done
that, his own friends wd not have been injured and that he wd have avoided
giving strength to a Govt whose principles I have heard him repeatedly say he
thought most dangerous. We had a desperate *scene* for he was excessively
angry, *swore* (which he never does) & said he wd do as he liked, while I cd not
conceal from him that I thought he had shewn more eagerness to resume the
Command than was consistent with his character as a politician.[40]

Reading this one is struck by Mrs Arbuthnot's courage in holding her ground,
by her fairness as a reporter, and by the shrewdness of her argument. They
parted company next morning, when Wellington went to Windsor to take up
his appointment formally. He wrote to her reiterating his position rather defen-
sively, and again the following day to Mr Arbuthnot expressing the hope that

the subject could be dropped and would not spoil their friendship. For her part Mrs Arbuthnot wrote a long letter in which she said that 'I cannot set up my judgment in opposition to [yours]', a statement which was then contradicted over several pages. Neither apologised more than superficially; neither backed down; but the friendship which had given them both so much pleasure emerged unscathed. Wellington, at least when it came to politics, was always remarkably tolerant of criticism and harboured few resentments. How many other politicians of that or any other time would swallow such criticism from a woman twenty-four years their junior?[41]

The reaction in the press to Wellington's return to the Horse Guards was curiously muted; *The Times* even expressed conditional approval because the army had suffered from the absence of an effective Commander-in-Chief, although as it coupled this with a demand that the Duke withdraw from politics, its motives look a little suspect. Two caricatures were issued on the occasion, but even they lack any sharp political edge. Both were the work of William Heath ('Paul Pry'), who had recently returned to London from the provinces and was beginning a short career which would breathe new life into the old form and emulate the success of Gillray and Cruikshank. The first of these prints, *The Two Happiest men Alive*, showed Wellington lending his arm to the King and saying 'Proud to be your _____ty's Staff', while the subtitle 'A Friend in need is a Friend indeed' shows how far the hostile mood towards Wellington had softened. The second is probably the most famous of all the caricatures of Wellington, so that overfamiliarity dulls its impact. *A Wellington Boot or the Head of the Army* shows Wellington's head, complete with elaborate cocked hat, emerging from the top of an eponymous boot. The face is in profile but the one visible eye looks sidelong at the viewer with a sardonic expression. The effect is unsettling and almost surreal, but again not hostile.[42]

Wellington's contact with the government as Commander-in-Chief was limited almost exclusively to official business and it did not result in any real rapprochement. On 1 September he told Eldon: 'In my opinion they, equally with the late administration [i.e. Canning's], are *falsehood personified*.' Goderich's personal weakness and propensity to tears invited ridicule. Mrs Arbuthnot recorded a story which she must have heard second or third hand, that the King was so exasperated with one tearful scene that he 'got into a violent passion, called Ld Goderich a blubbering fool, [and] said he wd make *Ld Bexley*! his Prime Minister'. And at the same time Londonderry wrote, with more than a touch of the schoolyard bully, 'as to Goody, he is so shabby; he is only a driveling, blubbering puppet in their hands'. While even Huskisson, one of Goderich's closest colleagues, said that there had never been a prime minister 'so weak, undecided, and utterly helpless'.[43]

Wellington spent the last week of September and the first days of October on a tour of northern England organised and arranged by Lord Londonderry, who had large estates in County Durham. The visit was marked by a succession of civic occasions, public dinners and other celebrations, all of which ostensibly commemorated victories in the war against Napoleon, but which provided ample opportunity to praise the Duke, and Lord Bathurst, who accompanied him on the tour, and the memory of Castlereagh. Huge crowds turned out to watch the fun as his open carriage was unhorsed and pulled through the streets, under triumphal arches and past banners and flags, escorted by outriders and greeted by cannon firing salutes and bands playing 'See the Conquering Hero Comes'. The crowd cheered, addresses were presented, speeches made and dinners eaten. Wellington inspected the Northumberland Yeomanry and was shown over the colliery at North Pittingdon, taking particular interest in the pumping engine and winding gear. At Wynyard, Londonderry's seat, the Duke laid the foundation stone of a memorial arch commemorating his visit and recording for posterity his friendship with Londonderry and appreciation for his service in the Peninsula. This was certainly one purpose of the visit: to enhance Londonderry's standing in the region by showing off his influential friends and displaying his wealth and power. But beyond this, the intention was probably to respond to the abuse and denigration of Wellington and the Tories in the press, by reminding the country not just of Wellington's part in the victory over Napoleon, but also the part played by the ministers of the day. While never overtly political, there was an implicit contrast between Wellington and the hapless Goderich. The latent politics of the tour was recognised by the London press, which could barely conceal its irritation and took to printing stories denying that the huge crowds were really cheering or enthusiastic at all. Wellington endured rather than enjoyed much of the fuss but, when it was over, reported that 'upon the whole I am very well pleased with my tour which I believe will have done good'.[44]

Until late in the autumn attention in Britain was almost entirely absorbed by the drama of domestic politics, but in November news from Greece came as a sharp reminder that the rest of the world could not be ignored forever. During the spring and summer Canning had given way to pressure from Russia and France for intervention in the Greek Revolt. Wellington expressed grave misgivings over this policy in March, pointing out that while the St Petersburg protocol had offered friendly mediation between Greeks and Turks if both parties consented, the new proposals pointed towards armed intervention against an old ally and in favour of insurgents. Naturally his objections were disregarded and Canning proceeded with the negotiations which resulted in the Treaty of London (6 July 1827). While Canning's admirers delighted at this fresh proof of his brilliant statesmanship, his opponents were dismayed. Bathurst complained that 'we are, by requiring the expulsion of the Turks from Greece, practicing towards our Allies in time of peace the same measure, which we declared to be too bad for the Turks to commit against their antagonists in time of war'. And he forecast that it would be much easier to invite the Russian fleet into the Mediterranean than to ensure that it would leave again.[45]

The British Mediterranean fleet, under Vice-Admiral Sir Edward Codrington, duly arrived off the coast of Greece in July and was joined by the French squadron a few weeks later and the Russian squadron in October – a combined force vastly more powerful than the Egyptian-Turkish fleet, which was anchored in Navarino Bay. Using the excuse that an attempt to blockade the bay at that season of the year was impractical, Codrington sailed in on 20 October with guns loaded and the men at their quarters. Inevitably the Turks began firing, and a one-sided battle followed in which their fleet was destroyed with at least 4,000 casualties, compared to 650 suffered by the allies.[46]

First reports of the action reached London on 10 November, and Clarence, without considering the implications, at once persuaded the King to give Codrington a GCB before the ministers had any chance to consider their response.[47] Wellington was dismayed by news of the battle:

> It is quite clear that our admiral was bamboozled into it by Heyden the Russian; that having got into the port and taken a position, as it is called, that is to say anchored within pistol shot of the Egyptian fleet, and the *Dartmouth* being too near the fireship sent a boat to force the latter to remove; that fireship resisted and fired and thus the battle, which was and must have been the inevitable consequence of *the position*, began. They then endeavour to lay the blame upon Ibrahim's cruelties, of which they could not have been informed by Captain Hamilton till after the battle; and they endeavour by a threat without date to force the Musselmen to admit that they were the aggressors!
>
> Then as a military feat it is mere humbug! The Allies had eleven sail of the line against three, and on the whole more large ships than the Turks.[48]

It was not only the Tories like Wellington who felt no inclination to rejoice. Creevey wrote to his step-daughter: 'Well! so the magnanimous Allies have really destroyed the Turkish fleet, and a more rascally act was never committed by the great nations, nor upon more false and hypocritical pretenses.' While Lord Bathurst wrote that: 'I was at Howick when news came of the Navarino victory; which threw Lord Grey into a state of great irritation. Notwithstanding his hatred to the Turks, he thought the whole proceeding unwarrantable, as the Turks were fully justified in resisting our advance, which, by Sir Edward's own account, was for the express purpose of so stationing the Allied fleet as to be able to destroy the Turkish fleet if they did not submit to our terms...'[49]

Navarino placed an impossible strain on a government that was already on the brink of collapse. Rumours abounded that the Whigs were pressing for full-scale war on Turkey in alliance with Russia; and that Goderich had threatened to resign if it came to war, while Huskisson replied that he would go if it did not. The Whigs revived the question of giving Lord Holland – whose loathing of Turkey exceeded even his hatred of Russia – the Foreign Office, and the King and Knighton had begun to lose faith that the administration could be kept afloat.[50] Parliament would meet in January; the Prime Minister was laughed at and despised by everybody, and there was barely a figure in the government who could command respect. Goderich virtually resigned in the middle of December but was too weak even to succeed in that, and the farce dragged on into January when a furious row between Herries and Huskisson over the choice of a new chairman of the Finance Committee proved the final, long overdue, straw. Although there was some talk of making Dudley, Harrowby or even Lord Wellesley prime minister, the King's patience with cunning plans and ingenious expedients was finally exhausted. On 8 January he accepted Goderich's resignation and on the following day he sent for Wellington and asked him to form a government.

PART III

PRIME MINISTER (1828–30)

CHAPTER SEVENTEEN

CABINET-MAKING
(January–June 1828)

O N THE MORNING of 9 January 1828 the King saw Wellington and commissioned him to form a new government. Wellington accepted, but warned the King that his professional position as Commander-in-Chief might prevent his serving as prime minister; he would need to consult his prospective colleagues. He then asked if His Majesty had any specific requirements. The King replied that he thought that the new ministry must include both supporters and opponents of Catholic Emancipation, and indicated that the Duke should look to members of the Canning and Goderich administrations as well as those who had resigned the previous spring. He also mentioned his wish that the Duke of Devonshire and Lord Carlisle remain in office – men who had not served under Lord Liverpool and had been appointed as part of Canning's overture to the Whigs. The King's motives were partly personal, but he was also indicating his preference for a broadly based administration which would not depend on the support of the High Tories. The King went on to praise Lansdowne and Dudley, but made it clear that these wishes were not commands; with one exception the Duke would have a free hand to form a ministry as he thought best. The exception was a ban on Lord Grey, and it is curious that where so many other bitter and more personal grievances could be forgiven – even Brougham – Grey remained beyond the pale.[1] One other stipulation was implicit rather than explicit: the summons from the King had been conveyed by Lyndhurst, the Lord Chancellor, and it was understood that he would retain his office in the new ministry, something which suited Wellington as well as the King.

On the Catholic Question the King laid down that it should not be made Cabinet policy; ministers might champion or oppose Emancipation as individuals, but the government as a whole should not propose it, and that the Lord Chancellor, the Lord Lieutenant of Ireland and the Lord Chancellor of Ireland all be 'protestants' (that is, opponents of Emancipation). Wellington appears to have accepted these conditions without discussion, although he was privately convinced that significant movement on the Question could not be postponed much longer; but the King would take time to be reconciled to change and it would clearly be unwise to add to the difficulties of the moment by venturing onto such dangerous territory. On the whole Wellington was well pleased, telling Mrs Arbuthnot that 'the case cannot stand better', and that the King had given him 'Carte blanche in respect to everything and everybody' – an interpretation which evidently reflects the spirit more than the letter of the interview.[2]

Wellington left the King at Windsor and returned to London where he at once wrote to Peel whose co-operation was essential, for he would inevitably be the mainstay of the new government in the Commons. Peel was in the country but got to town that evening and saw Wellington who was, he told his wife, 'most reasonable and friendly and satisfactory in every way'. Between them the two men soon agreed on the basis of the new government. Peel told the Duke that he was happy to serve under him, and that it was 'for the advantage of the public service, as tending to reconcile animosities and jealousies, that a new Government should have the advantage of your name at the head of it' and that 'my view is to reunite the old Party, which was in existence when Lord Liverpool's calamity befell him. I cannot undertake the business in the House of Commons without more assistance than the mere Tory Party, as it is called, would afford me'.[3] An attempt to include at least the Canningite ministers from Goderich's government was obviously necessary. While their credibility had been damaged and they were too weak to stand alone, they retained significant support both in the Commons and the country, and to refuse an overture to them would suggest that the new government would be hostile to the liberal policies, particularly on trade and foreign policy, that they had championed. On the other hand it was neither necessary nor wise to go so far as to make an approach to Lansdowne; such a move would alienate the Tories on whom the government would depend (and who would have enough difficulty swallowing the retention of Huskisson and his friends); while it was highly likely that Lansdowne would refuse, and that he would use his refusal to help reunite the Whig party which had been shattered by his coalescence with Canning. Besides Lansdowne's few months in office had left his reputation in tatters; an offer would only revive it and even without him there were not enough offices to go around.[4]

Some other decisions were easily made. Of the stalwarts of Liverpool's government, Wellington included Bathurst in consultations from the outset, and summoned Melville from Scotland, so that already there was a solid core of the new Cabinet: Wellington, Peel, Lyndhurst, Bathurst and Melville. Henry Goulburn was soon added to this list as Chancellor of the Exchequer in place of Herries. Although he had no record of financial expertise, Goulburn's probity, hard work and efficiency made him an excellent choice, relieving Wellington of much of the routine work of the Treasury. If Huskisson and the other leading Canningites agreed to remain in office they would fill four more places (Huskisson, Dudley, Palmerston and Charles Grant), for Goderich was too damaged to remain in office. And if Huskisson remained in, it would be necessary to retain Herries, although not at the Exchequer, to satisfy the Tories and the King. With eleven seats at the Cabinet table filled almost by default it was not easy to find room for much new blood. This and the need to broaden the base of the government led to the decision to exclude Eldon, Westmorland and Bexley. Eldon had accepted that he would not return to the Woolsack; he was seventy-seven and Lyndhurst was unlikely to be displaced. But he was disappointed not to be offered a less demanding office in the Cabinet, and hurt not to be consulted over the formation of the ministry. His exclusion was felt as a snub by the High Tories and, together with the inclusion of the Canningites, meant that they viewed the new ministry with considerable reservations from the outset. Yet, as Wellington later explained to the King, Eldon had never been the ideal colleague, being slow to defend the government's policies when they came under attack or to identify himself with the common line agreed to by the Cabinet.[5] Westmorland was politically less significant, but the Canningites loathed him and Wellington reluctantly agreed to leave him out of office. No one seems to have felt a pang at, or even really to have noticed, Bexley's retirement except the King, and even his regret was fleeting.[6]

These exclusions enabled Wellington to offer places to three new ministers: Aberdeen, Ellenborough and Rosslyn. The forty-three-year-old Earl of Aberdeen was best known as a classical scholar and aesthete who had served as British ambassador to Austria in 1813–14, when he had fallen under Metternich's spell. He had impeccable political connections (in his teens Pitt and Dundas had been his guardians), but had previously been reluctant to devote himself seriously to politics. There was also a personal connection with Wellington, for his brother Alexander Gordon had been one of Wellington's most trusted ADCs in the Peninsula and had been killed at Waterloo. Ellenborough and Rosslyn were both closely associated with Grey. At thirty-seven Ellenborough was the youngest member of the new Cabinet, full of self-assurance and ambition; he was handsome, charming and prosperous thanks to a sinecure worth some £8,000 a year, the fruit of his father's judicial career. In 1813 he had married Castlereagh's sister Octavia (when he was twenty-three and she twenty-one), and had been drawn into his orbit. Lady Octavia had died in 1819 and following Castlereagh's death he had transferred his loyalty to Grey, for his views were liberal and he detested Canning. In 1824 he married the beautiful Jane Digby but the marriage was to be engulfed in scandal in 1829. Ellenborough was not popular; his ambition and conceit were a little too obvious even for the world of politics where neither characteristic was uncommon, but he had consciously made himself an effective speaker, and had undoubted ability.[7] Rosslyn was a complete contrast; almost twice Ellenborough's age (he turned sixty-six in February), he was a distinguished soldier who had been unable to take the field under Wellington because he out-ranked him. A Foxite Whig since 1781, he had as a young man been one of the managers of the trial of Warren Hastings, and had remained a good friend of Grey's ever since, but was also on excellent terms with Wellington. The offers to Ellenborough and Rosslyn were partly designed to conciliate Grey, and to keep alive the tentative sympathy which had been established between the Duke and some of the aristocratic Whigs by their common opposition to Canning. Ellenborough accepted office with Grey's blessing, but Rosslyn declined and Wellington then offered the Ordnance to Beresford, but without a seat in the Cabinet.[8]

Neither Ellenborough nor Aberdeen were entirely satisfied with the offices given to them (Lord Privy Seal and Chancellor of the Duchy of Lancaster respectively), but all the positions with more real business attached to them were reserved either for the Canningites who already occupied them, or for senior figures from Liverpool's government. At least they were *in* Cabinet. Charles Arbuthnot was intensely disappointed to be offered nothing more than his old office as Commissioner of Woods and Forests (which he had grown to dislike), outside the Cabinet. His annoyance was exacerbated by Mrs Arbuthnot's disapproval of the overture to the Canningites, and for a moment it looked as though the friendship which was the cornerstone of Wellington's private life was in peril. He reacted strongly and without false pride, telling Mrs Arbuthnot 'I would have cut my Tongue out of my Mouth' before offering Arbuthnot a position that would lower his standing in the world, and that whether he had accepted or not, 'I see clearly that my peace & Happiness in this World are at an end'. Faced with his appeal the quarrel was resolved; Charles Arbuthnot accepted the offer comforted with the knowledge that Wellington knew he was not satisfied with it and would endeavour to find him something better when an opportunity arose. The incident added greatly to the strain Wellington felt in the political negotiations, and when it was settled he wrote to Arbuthnot: 'God knows that I have disgust enough in all these affairs, to desire to avoid the augmentation of that which must be the consequence of the break up of the only private & confidential Relation I have in Life.'[9]

As this suggests, the task of forming the government proved full of frustration and annoyance. Peel complained that 'every blockhead is for the complete predominance of his own opinions, and generally with a vehemence proportional to their impracticality'. Wellington was forced to ask the King to prorogue Parliament for an extra week to give time for the arrangements to be completed.

The negotiations with the Canningites were particularly tiresome for Huskisson and his friends set a high price on their support, refusing to recognise the fact that they had lost much of their political capital with the collapse of Goderich's government. Far from being grateful for the chance to retain their offices – and they included some of the most important places in any government – they demanded further promises and assurances. Some of these were easily given – Wellington had no intention of retaining Herries at the Exchequer or abolishing the Finance Committee, while it was understood from the outset that the Catholic Question must be left open – but it was insulting and politically dangerous to expect the Prime Minister to pledge himself to divide Irish patronage according to the recipients' opinions on the Emancipation. As it was, Wellington did not reverse the recent appointment of Anglesey as Lord Lieutenant and retained William Lamb as Chief Secretary, so that the Irish executive was headed by two Catholic sympathisers, but the tone of the discussions did not bode well.[10]

This was the major hurdle, but there were differences of emphasis and priority closer to home, as Wellington explained on 13 January to Mrs Arbuthnot:

> On the one hand I have the King, who cares for nothing excepting to keep the Duke of Devonshire. On the other there is Mr Peel, who cares for nothing excepting to surround himself on the Treasury Bench in the House of Commons by the best Speakers he can get; and if he is thwarted, or *your* principle is suggested, says, 'Very well! I will support you in everything, but I will not take Office'. And then Lord Bathurst cares for nothing excepting to bring back His Old Colleagues, even to Lord Eldon, who would come back; and I am the Instrument to be used in everything disagreeable to be done by any party or Individual whatever.[11]

But in the end, when the government was finally settled on the night of 20 January, it was pretty much as Wellington and Peel had envisaged from the outset. In an ideal world Wellington might have made less effort to include the Canningites and more to bring in Lord Grey and his friends, but the liberal mood of the Commons and the press, Peel's need for front-bench support, and the King's prejudices all made this difficult, and Wellington was above all a pragmatist.

One crucial question remained unresolved: could Wellington remain Commander-in-Chief while serving as prime minister? There was no legal obstacle to his doing so, and a partial precedent: in the early 1790s Lord Amherst had sat in Cabinet, but the suspicion of the army, which had been cultivated by the radicals ever since Waterloo, and the discussions of the previous year, created a serious political hurdle. At first Wellington's friends thought that he might stare down the criticism; Hardinge told Mrs Arbuthnot on 15 January that he found opinion generally favourable, and 'I had rather see a hero high-spirited than politic'. But ten days later he admitted that even those most convinced that there was nothing unconstitutional in the combination hoped that Wellington would yield to public opinion.[12] The press and the cartoonists were already running hard on the theme, depicting Wellington as *The Prime Lobster* ('lobsters' being a common slang term for soldiers), and accusing him of concentrating all the patronage of the state, military as well as civilian, in his hands, and wielding the sword of despotism as he rode poor ragged John Bull into the mouth of hell. Wellington raised the subject at the first formal meeting of Cabinet on 24 January. 'His feelings were strongly excited, and he evidently would have been desirous of retaining the army', but he placed his decision in the hands of his colleagues, who would meet on the following day in his absence. To his great disappointment they decided, unanimously, that he must resign the command.[13] This was a great sacrifice on Wellington's part, for he still liked to think of himself primarily as a soldier rather than as a politician; but the part he had played in politics ever since his return from the Continent at the end of 1818, and his position in the country, made it almost impossible for him to choose the army over the state. As for combining the two roles, there was nothing inherently outrageous about this – it is integral to the constitution of many modern liberal democracies, including France and the United States – but it ran counter to the tradition of anti-militarism which had marked British political culture since the seventeenth century, and which had gained a renewed vigour in the years since 1815. Nonetheless Wellington's decision, and the comment and debate which surrounded it, mark an important moment in the gradual professionalisation of the army and the withdrawal of its officers from active participation in politics.

Once the pill had been swallowed it became necessary to find a replacement for Wellington at the Horse Guards. Sir Herbert Taylor examined the precedents and suggested that a general be appointed to do the business of the Horse Guards as the senior officer on the staff, rather than that he be formally made Commander-in-Chief. This would both provide a financial saving to the public and keep open the door for Wellington to return to the Horse Guards in the future. Wellington approved the proposal in part at least because it facilitated the appointment of Rowland Hill to the position despite his lack of seniority. As Hill was a distinguished soldier and a careful and prudent man, famous for his concern for the welfare of his men, and had played little part in politics, he was an excellent choice. Nonetheless critics derided him as a man of straw, Wellington's puppet, and claimed that 'every body knows Lord Hill's incapacity for the situation & his entire subserviency to the D. of W. Lord H. is a quiet, inoffensive, obedient, heavy man who will take orders & give none.[14] The army knew better, although Hill's ability to improve the life of the soldiers and the careers of the officers was tightly constrained by the severe economies imposed by Parliament, especially in the 1830s.

Wellington's renunciation of the Horse Guards lessened but did not end criticism from those who felt that, as a soldier, he was virtually ineligible for such a high office. Opponents quoted his speech of the previous May in which he proclaimed that he would be 'worse than mad' if he aspired to become prime minister. Other reactions were more diverse and even eccentric; Lord Ashley (later, as Lord Shaftesbury, to be famous for his reforms of working conditions in factories and mines) was delighted by Wellington's appointment – 'I love and respect him from the bottom of my soul' – but was deeply troubled by the fact that he was a member, if an inactive one, of Crockford's, the fashionable gambling club.[15] Less unexpected was Hardinge's delight:

> What a glorious triumph of our glorious hero! What a year! If he had remained *in* with Canning, he wd. have been degraded by the connexion – & now what an honourable wreath of civil honours encircle[s] his brow almost covering the laurels of his military glories. I shall turn optimist . . . but then the Duke's good fortune is in this as in every other instance founded upon great sagacity, intuitive judgement, & the most incorruptible integrity.[16]

And Creevey reported that his friend Sefton, who had inclined towards Canning's coalition government the previous year, was now 'quite convinced that Wellington will turn out the greatest *Economical* Reformer the Country can produce, and he thinks that after he had proved himself to have such dispositions, Grey will come into office, but *I* say *not* without Ireland being set at rest, and even then at Grey's time of life, it is idle to speculate on such matters'.[17]

Overall there was considerable goodwill towards the new government from most parts of the political spectrum. Canning's death and the ignominious failure of Goderich's administration had created an appetite for a strong, effective government while leaving the Opposition divided and incoherent. At the beginning of April Wellington wrote to the Prince of Orange: 'Up to the present moment, the government have been very successful. There is in fact but little, if any, opposition to it . . . There is no party remaining. The ladies and the youth of the country in particular are with us, and I could also count upon my fingers those who are hostile to the government.'[18] This gilded the lily a little for foreign consumption, but the most serious weakness in the government's position lay beneath the surface, for although the government benefitted from broad goodwill, it had a relatively narrow base of committed supporters. The High Tories were at best lukewarm, and while most were happy to support the ministry on individual questions, they felt no allegiance to it; which left only an ill-defined party of moderate Tories who could be relied upon in adversity. Many ministries, including Liverpool's, had been equally weak at first and had gone on to gain strength with time and success, but the fractured state of politics in the late 1820s, and the strong undercurrent of liberalism affecting the press and many MPs, meant that Wellington and his colleagues would need both skill and good fortune if they were to succeed.

The first task facing the new ministers once they had taken office was to decide the main policies of the government as they would be set out in the King's Speech at the opening of Parliament. These talks began over dinner at Apsley House on 22 January, where Huskisson and Dudley agreed that the expedition to Portugal should be withdrawn now that the threat from Spain had evaporated, but pressed that this should not be announced in a way which implied any criticism of the original decision to send it. At the next meeting, on 24 January, Huskisson expressed his conviction that there must be another bill on the corn question and said that he was so pledged to the principle of the measure he had brought forward the previous year that he would have to resign if it was not adopted. For a senior minister to talk of resignation within two days of the formation of the government was decidedly ominous, especially when the issue was one on which he had previously clashed with the new Prime Minister, but a row was avoided, and Ellenborough emerged from the meeting with a little more confidence than before: 'If we can get through the Corn Laws we shall do very well.'[19] Subsequent meetings considered how the government should respond to Navarino; after some discussion it was decided not to disavow Codrington or to announce his immediate recall, largely because this would separate Britain from her allies and might encourage the Turks to demand compensation just when they seemed content to let the matter rest. Nonetheless the government distanced itself from the battle, describing it not as a 'victory', but as 'wholly unexpected' and an 'untoward event'. The King questioned this language, and Peel thought (rightly) that it would provoke much discussion, but as it was acceptable to the Canningite ministers, it was left unaltered.[20]

Parliament met on 29 January and, according to Ellenborough, 'the impression produced by the Speech was that we came off with flying colours, but that Dudley would have a difficult task'. Most of the discussion which followed concentrated on Navarino, but a direct question from Lord King prompted a short speech from Wellington in which he announced the government's commitment to the introduction of a Corn Bill, before moving on to Turkey and Greece, where he went a little farther than his colleagues expected in defending Codrington. Ellenborough's verdict on the debate was decidedly positive: 'Everybody seemed in good humour . . . The evening passed off as if the Administration had been established [for] years.'[21]

The session which followed was relatively easy for the government. The Opposition lacked direction and leadership. Lord Grey did not support the ministers but was not unsympathetic to them, a stance which Wellington encouraged by some adroit use of patronage (making Grey's brother-in-law an Irish bishop and Lord Rosslyn Lord Lieutenant of Fife) and by personal courtesy.[22] Brougham and Lansdowne had been seriously damaged by the events of the previous twelve months – the former being widely regarded as devious and untrustworthy, while the latter's energy and competence had been thrown into doubt. The Finance Committee in the Commons absorbed the energy of many habitual critics of the government, while many questions which might have provoked debate in the House were diverted to the Committee. This was potentially dangerous, for the Committee might have led the attack upon the government, but it concentrated its attention on an enquiry into the Ordnance and, possibly to its surprise, found the department to be a model of efficiency. The reputation of both Wellington and Hardinge was much enhanced by this scrutiny, and by their manner and command of detail when giving evidence to the Committee. The Committee did recommend abolishing the position of Lieutenant-General of the Ordnance but when Wellington over-ruled Peel's doubts and insisted on rejecting this recommendation, the vote was a triumph for the ministers. At a time when any hint of extravagance in government was extremely unpopular, the reputation of the government as a whole benefitted from this proof of Wellington's efficiency in administering his department.[23]

Nonetheless the government's performance in the Commons was disappointing. Mrs Arbuthnot commented at the end of February: 'In spite of all Mr Peel's fuss about speakers, we are lamentably deficient. Mr Herries never utters, and last night there was a laugh of derision when he was named as a Minister, Ld Palmerston scarcely ever speaks, Mr Grant never, [and] Mr Goulburn never.' And, a few weeks later: 'Mr Peel has lost ground in a manner that is quite surprising since he has been Leader. The Tory Party find him ill tempered & cowardly, and the liberals, who see his weakness, say they will worry him to death & drive him into greater liberalities than even their own party w[oul]d venture upon.'[24] This was probably unfair – Mrs Arbuthnot had both personal and political grounds for disliking Peel at this time, and showed little understanding or sympathy for the difficulties he faced in the Commons – but even allowing for that it is clear that he had not done as well as might have been expected.

Wellington by contrast had adjusted to his new role with aplomb. Again Mrs Arbuthnot's verdict needs to be taken with a pinch of salt to allow for her warm friendshi,p but it is broadly supported by other sources. '[T]he Duke encreases daily in popularity. All parties are agreed in admiration of his talents, his good sense, his industry & his temper. He is felt by everybody to be the only person capable of being Minister in these difficult times.' The liberal E.J. Littleton, no friendly critic at this time, wrote in May that there was 'an almost universal belief of his fitness for his post; which has greatly surprised people'. And Creevey reported in February: 'Huskisson fell 50 per cent in last night's jaw, and the Beau gained a corresponding degree of elevation. In short the latter will do capitally; his frank, blunt and yet *sensible* manner will beat the shuffling, lying Huskisson and Brougham school out of the field . . . My sincere opinion is – and I beg to record it thus early – that the Beau *will* do something for the Catholics in Ireland.' And five weeks later he added: 'The Beau is rising most rapidly in the market as a practical man of business. All the deputations come away charmed with him. But woe be to them that are too late! He is punctual to a second himself, and waits for no man.'[25]

The impression that the government was not entirely in control of the Commons was increased by the repeal of the Test and Corporation Acts – a measure proposed by a leading member of the Opposition and carried rather against the government's wishes than with its support. The Test and Corporation Acts were part of the Restoration settlement (passed in 1673 and 1661 respectively), and were designed to exclude Dissenters as well as Catholics from public offices. However, since the early eighteenth century regular indemnity acts made them largely irrelevant except as a symbol of Anglican supremacy.

In 1827 the young Lord John Russell revived the issue, partly from a sincere commitment to religious liberty, but also as a way of embarrassing Canning and impeding his junction with Lansdowne. Reactions to the question were unpredictable; a significant minority of supporters of Catholic Emancipation opposed immediate repeal, fearing that once their own grievances were met the Dissenters would oppose any concessions to the Catholics. Conversely some opponents of Emancipation were willing to support repeal, either because they were specifically anti-Catholic or from tactical motives.[26] Even within the Dissenting community there were initially many doubts at the wisdom of stirring an issue which had little practical effect and which might ignite an Anglican backlash. Nonetheless Russell's motion attracted a good deal of support: 1,200 petitions were sent to Parliament in its favour in a striking demonstration of the wealth and confidence of Dissenting communities, both evidently much increased over the previous generation or two. Once the issue had been raised, even those Dissenters who wished to let it lie felt it had to be carried or they would lose ground. Canning came out in strong opposition to repeal and succeeded in deferring the issue until 1828. By then he was dead and Wellington was prime minister. On 7 January the United Committee, which represented most but not all Dissenters, announced that it would not make common cause with the Catholics, and leading Dissenting MPs stressed the point in Parliament. This bore early fruit when the Protestant Society announced that it would support repeal.

Although a major debate on the question was clearly inevitable the government was ill prepared, only deciding at the last minute to oppose repeal and then not communicating this clearly to its backbenchers in the Commons.[27] Russell spoke well in the debate, arguing that toleration would protect the Church of England better than exclusions, and that the existing tests encouraged hypocrisy and profanation of the sacrament, while the response of the ministers was lame, conceding the questions of principle and virtually inviting defeat. Russell's motion was carried by 237 to 193 votes, amidst loud cheering. The government could still have blocked repeal in the Lords, although the strength of the majority and lack of any public feeling in defence of the Acts would have made this difficult. Within the Cabinet only Wellington and Bathurst favoured further resistance, and they gave way because of the number of other difficult issues facing the government at the time.[28]

By the time the question was debated in the Lords in late April the High Tories, and other defenders of the Anglican Establishment, had recovered from their initial surprise and gained support in part of the press. *John Bull* warned that it would establish a precedent 'of which those dreaded Papists will instantly afterwards avail themselves to renew their clamour', and declared that 'a more complete subversion of the principles upon which our Constitution has been supposed to be founded, we cannot imagine'. The *Standard* went further: 'Where is the constitutional boundary to be fixed? at this side of Judaism? or Mahommedism? or Deism? or Unitarianism? or Atheism? or Devil-worship?'[29] In the Lords debates the ministers had to hold the centre ground supporting repeal, but adding amendments which afforded greater protection for the Church in the face of fierce opposition from the High Tories, led with great skill by Lord Eldon, and with the tepid support of liberals and Whigs who wished to go even further. The bishops who had previously refused to defend the Acts now began to waver, goaded by Eldon's taunts, but the government carried the critical vote comfortably (70 to 43, or 117 to 55 if proxies are included). In the course of the Third Reading Debate on 28 April Lord Holland alarmed the Lords by proposing that the measure be broadened to include Jews, while Eldon endeavoured to add the words 'I am Protestant' to the declaration. Wellington opposed this arguing that there were already enough barriers to the Catholics and that he would not support any more, and again the government secured a comfortable majority (154 to 52).[30]

At one level the immediate effects of the bill were minimal; many town corporations remained effectively closed, while Dissenters continued to play a prominent part in others. But there were significant political consequences.

The issue greatly widened the rift between the government and the high or 'ultra' Tories, although some very significant figures including the Duke of Cumberland and Lord Londonderry retained their faith in Wellington, if not in Peel. The High Tories learnt the lesson of the debate and set about mobilising opinion in advance of any discussion of the Catholic Question. A Protestant Dinner was held on 4 June and a Protestant Club formed a month later. More generally the debates added to the sense of the government's weakness; it had accepted an important measure that it did not want because it did not think that it could resist it. As Newcastle wrote after the first debate in February: 'The Ministry suffers itself to be led instead of leading.'[31]

In the long run the repeal of the Test and Corporation Acts appears as the first step in the constitutional revolution of 1828–35 which transformed the Anglican settlement, which dated back to the Restoration of 1660. The connections were primarily psychological; advocates of Catholic Emancipation were emboldened and its opponents discouraged to find that even Peel and Wellington were more flexible and vulnerable to pressure than had been assumed. The weakness of the arguments put forward in defence of the old order on this question helped to undermine support for it more broadly, while the lack of popular feeling on the question challenged conventional assumptions about the likely response to an appeal to 'Church and King' sentiment. When put to an unfamiliar test, the Anglican Establishment and its supporters had shown themselves to be weaker and less self-confident than anyone had supposed. Led by the High Tories they might yet rally, but they had lost important ground.

Although the repeal of the Test and Corporation Acts appears in retrospect the most important event in the first months of Wellington's government, at the time the ministers were equally or more concerned with other issues, especially tensions within the Cabinet which threatened to tear it apart. To a large extent these disputes saw the four Canningite ministers acting as a group and pressing for a continuation of the previous government's policies, against the wishes of more conservative ministers including Wellington, while Peel and other moderates varied according to the question.[32] The problems were made worse by Huskisson's remarkable lack of tact and clumsiness in personal relations, and by his public claim that he had only joined the government after receiving guarantees that it would continue Canning's policies. This inevitably led to a rebuttal by Wellington which added to tension inside the Cabinet. Palmerston was also alienated and felt out of place, telling Mrs Arbuthnot that he felt closer to the Whigs than the Tories, while in May he gave a speech in the Commons extolling Canning's principles and declaring that the government deserved support only to the extent that it abided by them.[33]

By contrast Dudley was soon at his ease in the new Cabinet. He had no difficulty working closely with Wellington and was grateful for the Duke's close involvement in foreign policy. He told a close friend:

My experience of [Wellington] is too short for a just judgement, but hitherto I have found it very pleasant to do business with him. He is as quick as lightning, clear, decisive, and at the same time simple and good humoured. I see no symptom of his not meaning to behave quite fairly to all his colleagues. He has no zeal for liberty, that is true, but on the other hand he is quite free from the prejudice of the old Tories, both as to the Church and the State. I am very much mistaken, too, if he does not turn out to be as economical a minister as Lamb can wish[.][34]

Nonetheless, when an issue was disputed in Cabinet Dudley generally supported his fellow Canningites, even when he privately admitted that he thought they were in the wrong. It was this perpetuation of a semi-detached party inside the Cabinet that most frustrated and annoyed Wellington and made him regret their inclusion in the government. In late March Mrs Arbuthnot noted that he 'has had a complete sickener of them', and thought their behaviour was 'excessively unfair'. And in May Ellenborough understood that Wellington was 'broken-hearted' about the Cabinet. 'Palmerston is always *pecking*. Grant is obstinate and useless. However, he is seldom there, and takes little part. Dudley would never give the least trouble if it were not for Huskisson, who sets him on. Huskisson is not to be trusted.'[35]

There were serious divisions in Cabinet over the Eastern Question. Palmerston and Huskisson were insistent on continuing Canning's policy embodied in the Treaty of London; while Wellington and the other ministers were alarmed by the dangers that a Russian attack on Turkey would pose for the peace of the Balkans and Europe as a whole, and by the injustice, as they saw it, of Canning's policy towards Turkey. This led to prolonged and painful discussions in Cabinet which exacerbated the irritation between ministers. For example, Palmerston described a Cabinet dinner on 2 April where there was '*As usual much discussion and entire difference of opinion*; the Duke, Ellenborough, and Aberdeen being for cutting down the Greeks as much as possible; Huskisson, Dudley and myself for executing the treaty in the fair spirit of those who made it . . . so we parted at half-past one, Huskisson very angry, and the Duke ill-pleased.' A month later Palmerston added: 'The Duke has the strongest dislike to Russia – more, I think, from personal feeling than from political. Ellenborough is even more adverse than the Duke: Aberdeen is Austrian, and Bathurst anti-Russian and Austrian; all these would give anything to get out of the Greek treaty, which they hate, and they set about it dexterously.

The Duke I believe to be in correspondence with Metternich, and tries to play his game of delay and procrastination – a system so unlike his natural temper about anything which he wishes really to accomplish.'[36] It is striking that Palmerston, who had sat in Cabinet for barely twelve months and had no great knowledge of the Continent or experience of diplomacy, felt no hesitation in dismissing the views of Wellington, Bathurst and Aberdeen, two of whom had been at the heart of British foreign policy for more than a decade, while Aberdeen had personal knowledge of the most intense negotiations among the great powers in 1813–14.

There was less real disagreement over Portugal, where all the ministers accepted that the British force which had been sent to Lisbon at the end of 1826 should be withdrawn now that there was no longer any hint of a foreign threat to justify its presence. Yet this was not a comfortable decision for the Canningite ministers, who still had their late chief's delusive phrases about planting the standard of liberty on the ramparts of Lisbon ringing in their ears. A further complication was that the British ambassador to Lisbon was Frederick Lamb, brother of the Canningite Chief Secretary for Ireland, and that he had completely identified himself with the Constitutionalist Party in Portugal and argued strongly that the British troops should remain to protect these liberals from Miguel and the absolutists. Not even Palmerston was willing to go this far, as he explained on 25 April:

> Miguel seems to be going to the devil as fast as he can . . . It is provoking, but we cannot help it. Our troops did not go to interfere in the affairs of Portugal, or to dictate a Government to the nation. We went to defend them from Spanish aggression in compliance with the obligation of a treaty, and that duty being performed, it would have been a departure from all the principles we have ever maintained to have kept our troops there in order to impose upon the people any form of government, or, indeed, to meddle at all in their domestic concerns. If they like an absolute king and an usurper it is their own affair, and if they don't, they ought to say so, and to resist.[37]

However, the worst dispute inside the Cabinet was over corn. The clash between Wellington and Huskisson the previous year meant that this was always going to be dangerous ground, but the government had to bring forward a measure that both men could endorse without loss of face. Again there was a succession of Cabinet meetings as proposals were put forward, discussed and then abandoned amid a good deal of exasperation and ill humour. It is notable that Wellington made no attempt to use his authority as prime minister to impose a solution on his colleagues, but argued his case and made concessions as one minister among many. Eventually a compromise was devised which both Wellington and Huskisson could accept, only for it to be thrown into doubt by the objections of Charles Grant, the president of the Board of Trade, and the minister who would have to introduce the bill into Parliament. Although Grant was the least significant of the Canningites it was clear that if he resigned Huskisson, Palmerston and Dudley would all follow him out of office.[38] Grant's friends put him under great pressure to yield, but he remained obstinate and the crisis dragged on with him seldom attending Cabinet and creating such confusion that other ministers were uncertain whether or not he had already resigned. Eventually he backed down and accepted the compromise bill, but by then some of the other ministers were so irritated by the affair that they felt more regret than relief at its resolution. According to Mrs Arbuthnot Wellington was 'disappointed & vexed' at the news for he had nearly settled in his own mind how he would restructure the government. This may be coloured by her own feelings, but Ellenborough was unequivocal: 'I much regret this termination . . . if the Canning leaven had gone out we should have gone on so comfortably together, and have been so much stronger.' It is unlikely that Peel would have gone this far, but he was disappointed at the lack of support he received from his colleagues in the Commons, and while he worked hard to frame a compromise that would keep them in office, he was quite willing to carry on without them.[39]

Ironically, the proposal which emerged from these tortuous negotiations was well received. The High Tory Duke of Newcastle wrote that 'it presented a manly, wise & patriotic view of the necessity of upholding the landed interest – it will restore confidence to the sinking farmer & will tend more to alleviate the distress of the country than anything that had been done for years.'[40] And Palmerston told his brother:

> Our new Corn Bill will pass without any serious difficulty, although there will be many alterations suggested from both sides. It is not what I should have liked, being still further removed from the principle of Free Trade than the measure of last year. But a compromise was unavoidable. Last year's Bill would not have passed the House of Lords. The agricultural gentlemen, and especially those in the Upper House, are not yet sufficiently advanced in the 'march of intellect' to understand how little their own real interests are promoted by the restrictions and prohibitions for which they are struggling . . . But these wiseacres look only to the price in the 'Gazette', and think every man who has half an idea more than they have, a wild theorist. This party, however, is going down fast, and the reign of Toryism is drawing to a close.[41]

Evidently Palmerston was as confident of his understanding of agricultural economics as he was of his insights into diplomacy, and with as much reason.

Nonetheless Toryism was not yet dead, and the triumph of the principles of free trade would coincide with an agricultural depression which lasted several generations and did much to further impoverish one of the poorest groups in Britain: the agricultural labourers.

Huskisson and the other Canningites would have been wise to adopt a more conciliatory line after inflicting such a succession of troubles on their colleagues, but they were curiously oblivious to anything but their sense of self-importance, and remained preoccupied with vindicating their record of personal consistency whatever the cost to the government as a whole. The question that finally led to their resignation was less significant than many previous issues of dispute, but in four months they had exhausted the patience and goodwill of their colleagues. Two boroughs, Penryn in Cornwall and East Retford in Nottinghamshire, had been proved to be corrupt. The established cure in such cases was to broaden the franchise from the borough to include all of the hundred in which it was located – the larger electorate being less easily corrupted. But in this case liberal reformers wanted to remove entirely the right of these boroughs to send members to Parliament and transfer it to Manchester and Birmingham – large new cities which had no representation except through their county members. Tories objected that this was unfair to the uncorrupt voters in Penryn and East Retford, and that if this was established as a precedent it could not be contained. (Many more allegations of corruption were likely to be made if large, wealthy but unrepresented towns might hope thereby to gain seats in Parliament.) They also questioned the assumption that cities such as Manchester would benefit from the franchise. 'In practice nothing can exceed the folly of giving members to these populous towns. It causes riots & loss of lives & property at every election & is not needed, for the great merchants get returned for the rotten boroughs & can attend to the interests of their town much better than if they were obliged to pander to the passions of an interested mob.'[42] This view gained some credibility from the recent refusal of two members by Leeds, which were instead added to Yorkshire's county seats. Nonetheless, opinion in the Commons was running strongly in favour of giving seats to at least one of the new cities, while the Lords were widely expected to resist any such move.

At a Cabinet dinner on 19 March, in the midst of the crisis over corn, and while the repeal of the Test and Corporation Acts was being discussed by a committee of the Commons, Peel proposed a compromise: East Retford should be thrown into the surrounding hundred, while Penryn's seats should go to Manchester. This should have been generally acceptable, for Canning had always firmly opposed parliamentary reform, and Huskisson agreed with Peel on the need to avoid establishing a rule that the seats would always go to large towns without the franchise.[43] But the Lords stalled over Penyrn and made it clear that they might reject the transfer of its seats to Manchester. This led to further Cabinet discussions and a good deal of confusion, with Palmerston believing that it had been agreed that ministers could vote whichever way they liked in the Commons. On 19 May he voted against the government over East Retford, and Huskisson impulsively joined him in crossing the floor.

Palmerston went home with a clear conscience, but Huskisson was anxious and this increased to alarm when he discussed the vote with Joseph Planta, the government Whip, who took a very serious view of the likely damage to the government's standing of yet another open rift in the Cabinet. Impressed with this, Huskisson wrote to Wellington as soon as he got home, tendering his resignation. It is clear that Huskisson intended this purely as a matter of form – a token apology to make amends for 'the injury to the King's service which may ensue from the appearance of disunion in his Majesty's councils, however unfounded in reality, or unimportant in itself, the question which had given rise to that appearance'.[44] But for Wellington, it was the last straw. He knew that the reputation of the government had already been seriously damaged by the divisions in its ranks, and that the task of keeping a majority in the Commons was made much more difficult by the sight of ministers frequently crossing the floor or speaking on opposite sides of a question. If he told Huskisson not to worry about his vote he would, in effect, condone his behaviour and make a mockery of the principle of Cabinet solidarity. Besides, it would certainly be said in the press that he had asked, even begged, Huskisson to remain. For months Wellington had treated the Canningites with extraordinary indulgence, behaving almost as if he was sharing the premiership with Canning's ghost, allowing them plenty of time to adjust to the new regime. They had responded with arrogance and selfishness, making little attempt to make common cause with the rest of the government, and he decided that the time had come to assert his authority and give them a choice between submission and resignation. He waited until the early afternoon of 20 May, making enquiries as to the events of the previous night and giving Huskisson a chance to have second thoughts and either ask to see him or withdraw the resignation. When he heard nothing further he laid the resignation before the King and informed Huskisson that he had done so.[45]

This was a deliberate escalation of the affair, but it did not mean that Wellington was determined to force Huskisson and, by extension, the other Canningites out of office. That may have been his preferred outcome, but he made it clear that the door was open for Huskisson to remain simply by begging permission to withdraw his resignation. Huskisson and his friends were astonished and bemused by this turn of events. At first they assumed that it was all a misunderstanding and they had only to persuade Wellington that Huskisson had not really meant to resign for him to beg them to remain, and the whole affair would blow over. They had waved the stick of collective resignation so often that they had ceased to believe that their bluff might ever be called, let alone on a matter as trivial as the East Retford question. (That, of course, was Wellington's point: it was one thing to divide the Cabinet and weaken the government over an issue as important as Greece or Catholic Emancipation; but it would be impossible to govern if ministers insisted on going their individual way on every second- or third-order question.) Palmerston and the other Canningites spent days trying to discover a compromise that Wellington would accept which would save Huskisson's face, and were genuinely puzzled to find Wellington gnomic and unco-operative, for Wellington would not tell them plainly that nothing less than some loss of face would do, because these exchanges were bound to become public. Three days later Ellenborough wrote in his diary: 'The Duke's spirit is up, and he is quite determined . . . He said he knew the men he had to deal with. The Canningites all entertained an erroneous and exaggerated view of their own consequence, which existed in the minds of none but themselves. They were always endeavouring to lord it. In this case, if he had solicited Huskisson to remain, Huskisson would have been Minister instead of himself.'[46]

After waiting nearly a week Wellington saw the King and Huskisson's resignation was made final on 25 May. As expected, the other Canningites followed, although Dudley at least was not happy: 'I do not pretend not to be sorry to quit so splendid, and in many respects so agreeable, a station. Indeed there are some circumstances peculiar to myself which make resignation a greater sacrifice. I have an unbounded admiration and reverence for the Duke, a great confidence in his genius for business as well as for war.' Why then resign? Because all his friends were leaving; loyalty to Canning's memory and a sense that he had only taken office in the first place as one of Canning's party; and the fear that if he stayed he would be accused of pursuing self-interest.[47] A number of junior ministers and other officials (including William Lamb, Chief Secretary for Ireland) also resigned, and were more missed than their superiors.

On the whole, public opinion supported Wellington, not the departing ministers. Two caricatures by William Heath both present Huskisson repenting his folly; in the first he is a mutineer drummed out of Wellington's regiment, while in the second he is a truant schoolboy begging for readmission, which Wellington as schoolmaster sternly denies.[48] When Wellington attended a Lord Mayor's dinner on 21 May he was 'received extremely well. He looked ill, and as if he had been annoyed; but he was quite in good spirits with his reception, *elated*.' On 24 May Ellenborough believed that 'the country looks to the Duke alone, and cares little who are the other ministers', but, he added, 'should Huskisson remain in, it will not be easy to make it clear to country that the

Duke is really Minister'. And in June, after the correspondence had been published, Creevey wrote to his step-daughter: 'Well, have you read Huskisson's charming compositions of letters that he read of his own accord and as his own defence. Never was there anything so low and comtemptible throughout, either in intellectual confusion or mental dirt. In short, thank God! he is gone to the devil and can never shew again. The Beau, both in talent and plain dealing, in his letters and conduct, is as clean and clear as ever he can be.'[49]

Long before the final rupture with the Canningites there had been a good deal of speculation about how Wellington might reshuffle his ministry if they left office. In the event he sprang a complete surprise when he nominated Sir George Murray, his old Quartermaster-General in the Peninsula, to succeed Huskisson as Secretary of State for War and the Colonies. Reactions to the choice were generally favourable; Ellenborough, who might have resented his advancement to such a prominent position, was warm in his praise: 'A better man could not have been found. He is able; a good man of business; a good speaker (as far as he is known), and he brings a high established character into the service of the country. He is, besides, a Catholic [that is a supporter of Catholic Emancipation]. My expectation is that next session he will be the most efficient man in the House of Commons.' And Mrs Arbuthnot agreed: 'Sir George Murray will make an excellent Colonial Secy. He is very clever, an excellent man of business, a very good speaker &, from having been in Canada, knows that Colony (which is now so important) well &, in short, is in every respect well qualified. He is also quite unpledged, a new man who has never been mixed up in any party squabbles & who can do his duty without looking to one side or the other.'[50] Inevitably the Opposition complained at the appointment of a soldier to high office, but the most hostile reaction came, oddly enough, from the opposite end of the political spectrum. The Duke of Newcastle was incensed by the choice of Murray:

> Coming from the D. of Wellington it will have a very bad appearance in the country that he should be putting into the chief situations of the Country Soldiers of fortune & who are only Known to the public as having Served well in the field – it will excite alarm in the Country & the cry Will be, [']we are to have a military despotism['] – The D. of W. could not have taken a more impolitic step, it will Justly make him unpopular & give a vantage ground to his opponents, which will not be lost by them.[51]

Wellington gave the Foreign Office to Aberdeen who had more experience and was less violently anti-Russian than Ellenborough, although his strong sympathies for Austria were well known. The Duke probably judged that, while both men were conceited, Aberdeen was the more cautious and less likely to object to the Prime Minister's active involvement in the work of the office. It proved a good selection and the two men worked well together. Ellenborough was disappointed and gave full vent to his feelings in his diary – a safe outlet for his jealousy – but the highly critical picture he paints of Aberdeen needs to be taken with a substantial pinch of salt. He also expressed his disappointment, presumably more moderately, to Wellington, who soothed him, and assured him that he would be given a more active office as soon as an opportunity arose.[52]

Other appointments included Vesey Fitzgerald, Peel's friend, as president of the Board of Trade, and Lord Francis Leveson Gower (later Earl of Ellesmere) as the new Chief Secretary for Ireland. Sir Henry Hardinge went to the War Office, but without a seat in the Cabinet. This reduced the Cabinet to eleven members, the smallest it had been since 1807, making a more cohesive and efficient body. There was room for recruits if the government gained reinforcements, but after the experiment of living with the Canningites the ministers were reluctant to invite a fresh source of discord into their ranks, for they had learnt that there was as much weakness as strength in numbers.

The reshuffle enabled Wellington to gratify his closest friends; Charles Arbuthnot was moved from Woods and Forests to the Duchy of Lancaster. His wife reacted with unequivocal delight: 'Our change is very agreeable to us & will put Mr A. quite into good humour, which he was not before. He hated the office of Woods & Forests to a degree that amounted to antipathy & in which there was no reason, for it is not in fact at all a disagreeable office.' But her husband, while pleased at the change, was well aware of the significance of this second failure to enter the Cabinet: 'Had I exerted myself in Parlt. I shd. not have been so left behind by others; but tho' it is my own fault, it does not the less mortify me.'[53]

The government which Wellington led in June 1828 had a slightly narrower base but was much more united and efficient than that which he had formed in January. This does not mean that the inclusion of the Canningites was a mistake; rather, it was an experiment which had to be tried to satisfy opinion in Parliament, in the country and inside the ministry itself, even though its success was always doubtful. It failed because Huskisson and his allies had an unrealistic sense of their own importance, and because there was a legacy of too much irritation and bad blood, not just from the events of 1827, but from the later years of Liverpool's government. Their resignations did not seriously damage the government, for there was a general recognition that they had over-played their hand and that Wellington and the other ministers had treated them with remarkable forbearance. But the weakness which the government had from the outset remained: it was dangerously dependent on the goodwill of MPs who did not see themselves as owing it any great loyalty. There was still no clear alternative, but the only group who identified themselves with the ministry were the moderate Tories, and even they included many who felt an equal attraction either to the High Tories or to Canningite liberals. This had little to do with Wellington; politics were still in a state of flux after the relaxation of party allegiances in recent years, and it was impossible to reconstruct a government that would embrace opinion from the High Toryism of the Duke of Newcastle to the liberalism of Huskisson and Palmerston. Time might produce a more settled and substantial base of support for the ministry, or its enemies might coalesce against it, but in the meantime an old problem burst anew onto the political scene when the Catholic Daniel O'Connell defeated Vesey Fitzgerald and won the by-election for County Clare.

CHAPTER EIGHTEEN

CATHOLIC EMANCIPATION
(1828–29)

T HE ATTITUDE OF Wellington's government to the Catholic Question had been the subject of speculation from the moment it took office. The High Tories were alarmed by the exclusion of Eldon from the Cabinet and the repeal of the Test and Corporation Acts, and while advocates of Emancipation did not expect much from Wellington or Peel, they were determined to press the government. A debate in May 1828 convinced Wellington and Peel that despite the election of 1826 there was now an entrenched majority in favour of concession in the Commons. In the Lords Wellington argued firmly against Emancipation, but it was noticed that he based his arguments entirely on the practical difficulties of satisfying Catholic claims while safeguarding the position of the Established Church, rather than on questions of principle.

Behind the scenes Wellington had already sought the advice of Henry Phillpotts, the Dean of Chester and an established controversialist, who acted with admirable discretion, consulting a range of opinion without giving any hint that he was doing so on behalf of the Prime Minister. This does not mean that Wellington took office having made up his mind to introduce Catholic Emancipation at the first opportunity, and it is more probable that he felt that whether he took the initiative or not, he would soon be forced to confront the question and that he needed to be prepared.[1] The Commons debate convinced Peel that the government needed to reconsider its whole policy towards Ireland when Parliament rose, but he warned Wellington that he might feel compelled to resign whatever policy was adopted: it was inappropriate for the leader of the House to be personally responsible, as home secretary, for a policy which the Commons had repeatedly disavowed, while he was too committed to the Protestant cause to preside over its defeat. This was not unexpected; Peel had taken the same stance in 1825, and his conscience was always going to be one of the chief difficulties Wellington would face if he was to concede Emancipation.[2]

None of this was apparent to the public, especially in Ireland, where the Catholic Association regarded Wellington and Peel as the leading opponents of Emancipation and decided to oppose the election of any government supporters. Vesey Fitzgerald's appointment as president of the Board of Trade – which required that he resign and stand again for his seat of County Clare – created an early opportunity to test this resolution. Nonetheless it was only at the last moment, eight days before the polls opened, and after it had been unable to find a suitable Protestant candidate, that the Association decided that its leader, Daniel O'Connell, would stand. If elected he would be unable to swear the necessary oaths to take his seat, but there was no legal impediment to his contesting the election.

Although Fitzgerald was a relatively popular landowner with a long record of supporting Catholic Emancipation, the by-election proved an unqualified triumph for O'Connell. After five days of polling Fitzgerald withdrew from the contest, trailing by over one thousand votes (936 to 2,057). The great mass of electors – poor forty-shilling freeholders enfranchised by their landlords in a complicated game to gain influence both locally and with the government in Dublin – had defied their masters and voted for O'Connell. Voting was not secret and individuals were accompanied to the poll by large crowds of supporters, friends and family. In normal times it was this lack of secrecy which enabled landlords to intimidate their tenants into voting as required; but at Clare in 1828 it would have been more daunting for a poor man to defy the wishes of his neighbours and friends and to break ranks by voting for Fitzgerald. A large part of this success was due to the Catholic Church, both the hierarchy which gave its unequivocal blessing to O'Connell's cause, and the local priests who exhorted their parishioners to vote as directed. It is said that only one priest in the county campaigned for Fitzgerald, and that he was ostracised as a result.[3]

But the most remarkable thing about the election was that it did not descend into violence or serious tumult. The police and troops which the Irish government had stationed nearby were not needed, and the thousands of voters and their supporters who flocked to Ennis (the County town) were housed and fed and kept in good order. While welcome at one level this discipline was disconcerting, even frightening, to anyone familiar with Irish politics. Months later Peel told Sir Walter Scott:

I wish you had been present at the Clare election, for no pen but yours could have done justice to that fearful exhibition of sobered and desperate enthusiasm. 'Be true' was the watchword which, uttered by a priest or an agitator, calmed in an instant 'the stormy wave of the multitude', and seduced the freeholder from his allegiance to his Protestant landlord.

We were watching the movements of tens of thousands of disciplined fanatics, abstaining from every excess and every indulgence, and concentrating every passion and feeling on one single object; with hundreds of police and soldiers, half of whom were Roman Catholics – that half, faithful and prepared, I have no doubt, to do their duty. But is it consistent with common prudence and common sense to repeat such scenes, and to incur such risks of contagion?[4]

The Clare election convinced Wellington that the government had no choice but to consider the Catholic Question during the recess and present proposals to Parliament in the New Year. On 1 August he wrote to the King enclosing a detailed memorandum in which he argued that Ireland was completely in the hands of the Catholic Association rather than the government, and yet no laws appeared to have been broken which would enable the government to reassert its control by prosecuting O'Connell. With the support of the priests the Catholic Association had a far more effective and widespread organisation than the rebels in 1798, and it rested entirely in their hands 'whether the people shall rise in rebellion or shall remain quiet'. The government could not risk any action which would lead to a fresh election in Ireland, so that it was unable even to appoint a county member to a position in the government or give him a peerage, while the obvious power and success of the Catholic Association was terribly destructive of the natural authority of the government throughout the country. Wellington did not offer any simple solution to the problem. It might not have arisen if the Catholic Association had been put down as soon as it was reconstituted in 1825, and if the forty-shilling freeholders had been disenfranchised, but that moment had passed, and it was now too late for such measures to break the influence of O'Connell and his associates over the mass of the Catholic population.

Wellington was convinced that the Commons would refuse to pass any coercive legislation except as part of a plan to grant Emancipation. Even if Ireland broke into rebellion it was likely that MPs would insist on granting equal rights to Catholics as part of a settlement. And there was no possibility of dissolving Parliament and calling a general election in the hope of gaining a more Protestant Commons, for at the very least a general election in Ireland would be accompanied by extensive civil unrest and the loss of almost all the county seats, while there would be a dreadful risk of provoking outright civil war in Ireland if the government in England appealed too stridently to Protestant opinion. The Lords had blocked Emancipation for more than a decade but public opinion as expressed through the Commons continued to support concession, and the state of Ireland meant that question could not be postponed any longer. Here, as over the abolition of the Property Tax in 1816, the subsequent post-war economies, and the repeal of the Test and Corporation

Acts, the government had to accept the will of the political nation and shape its policy accordingly, rather than demand that the Parliament yield to the views of the executive.

Wellington did not believe that granting Emancipation would solve Ireland's problems, but Parliament and the public would not support the government in dealing with any crisis in Ireland if this had not first been conceded.

It may be very doubtful whether the concession of Roman Catholic Emancipation, with any guards or securities, or in any form, would pacify the country, or would save us from the civil contest hanging over us.

But whatever the King and his ministers may think of the chances of pacification which Roman Catholic Emancipation would afford, it is the duty of all to look our difficulties in the face and to lay the ground for getting the better of them. We must endeavour to conciliate Parliament and the public to our measures, in order that if we should be involved in this contest we may enter into it with the support of the large majority of the Parliament and of the people of England.[5]

After this apocalyptic diagnosis, Wellington's prescription verged on being an anti-climax. Far from calling for immediate action he simply asked the King's permission to discuss the whole state of Ireland with Peel and Lyndhurst, and then to speak to the King again before taking anything to Cabinet. Comforted by this reassurance that events were not speeding out of control the King cordially agreed to the proposal that Lyndhurst and Peel be consulted, while reserving the right to refuse to countenance any further discussion of the subject even within the Cabinet.[6] Such elaborate deference to royal authority and formal procedures was highly unusual, and has been attributed to Wellington's 'antique notions of constitutional behaviour' and the rights of the Crown. Certainly the defence and preservation of those rights was one of his, and the Pittite party's, guiding principles; but this did not prevent Wellington's and other Cabinets freely discussing other subjects when they arose without prior royal permission. The Catholic Question was unlike any other; George III had twice dismissed governments for pressing it upon him, and on both occasions his objections were much increased because ministers had not kept him fully informed of their plans. Wellington would not repeat this mistake, and evidently believed that his best chance of overcoming the King's deep-seated opposition to Catholic Emancipation was to accustom him to the idea gradually and lead him gently forward step by easy step, rather than confronting him with a bald demand that he yield his opinion to that of his ministers. In the event this conciliatory approach delayed but did not prevent several bruising confrontations with the King over the question, and probably did little to lessen the King's ultimate resentment, but it was still useful that Wellington had kept the King reasonably happy until early 1829, rather than have him encouraging the rise of Brunswick Clubs and other popular opposition to concession.[7]

In fact Wellington did not limit himself to consulting Peel and Lyndhurst: Bathurst and both Mr and Mrs Arbuthnot knew of his plans and proposals in detail, and it is possible, even likely, that there were a few other confidants. But Wellington had no wish to take the question to Cabinet at this stage. He had first to persuade Peel not just that the concession should be granted, but to remain in office and to steer the measure through the Commons; and he was convinced that the success of the measure depended on secrecy.[8]

Wellington's ideas for the terms of a settlement of the question had evolved since 1825, partly in response to Phillpott's advice. He had dropped the idea of a concordat with the Pope, and instead hoped that the government could gain the loyalty of the Catholic clergy and influence over the Church in Ireland by requiring that all priests be licensed and paid by the Crown. The position of the Anglican Church would be protected by a ban on the Catholic Church employing any existing ecclesiastical titles. All offices in the government would be open to Catholics except a few senior positions that dispensed extensive patronage in the Anglican Church (including prime minister, Lord Chancellor and Lord Lieutenant of Ireland), and he rejected the idea of a limit on the number of Catholics who could be elected to Parliament, arguing that it would simply perpetuate a sense of grievance and so prove counter-productive. On the other hand he was tempted by the idea of suspending rather than abolishing the restrictions on Catholics, and renewing them annually at least for a probationary period. He thought that the forty-shilling franchise should be greatly tightened, but not entirely abolished, and was unashamed in declaring that 'the restoration of the influence of property in the election in Ireland is the result to which we ought to look in this arrangement'. But he was deliberately and consciously tentative in framing all these ideas, telling Mrs Arbuthnot that they 'were his first crude notions, which reflection & discussion wd probably change & improve'.[9]

No one Wellington consulted at this stage objected to the principle of granting Emancipation, for O'Connell's election made some resolution imperative, and the likely consequences of an attempt to maintain the status quo were all too obvious; but everyone had their own ideas. For example, Bathurst, who was widely if mistakenly regarded as a narrow-minded Tory of 'the old school', favoured a concordat with the Pope; while Lyndhurst wanted to limit the number of seats open to Catholics for a trial period of seven years.[10] Peel favoured a more generous settlement than Wellington proposed with fewer restrictions, although he too was tempted by the idea of a limit on the number of Catholic MPs, comparing it to the number sitting for Irish or Scottish seats.

He also objected to Wellington's plan to license and pay the Catholic clergy, arguing that this would prompt demands for payment from Dissenting ministers in Britain, while he believed that the licence would rapidly become purely nominal, giving the government no real influence over the priests yet giving them official recognition. More seriously, he showed no sign of wavering in his determination to resign, while promising his wholehearted support for the measure when out of office. Wellington could not accept this, for if Peel resigned there was an obvious danger that he would, however reluctantly, become the focus of Protestant opposition to the measure.[11]

Wellington spent the second half of August in Cheltenham, recovering from the exertions of an exceptionally demanding twelve months, and then hosted a party at Stratfield Saye from 1 to 8 September which included Peel, Lyndhurst and the Arbuthnots. There was much discussion of the Catholic Question but no real progress. At the same time Wellington's relations with the King were put under great strain by a prolonged and unpleasant dispute between the Duke of Clarence, the Lord High Admiral, and his board at the Admiralty. In essence Clarence wanted to exert more real power over the navy and demonstrate his independence from his professional advisers, but lacking experience in the ways of bureaucratic warfare, he put himself thoroughly and repeatedly in the wrong. Wellington had little choice but to force him to back down and the Royal Duke tendered his resignation. The King had few illusions as to his brother's competence, and he fully supported Wellington, but he did not relish his brother's fall or the blow to the royal dignity which it involved. Nor was the affair quickly resolved; Clarence took his time vacating his office and there was much talk of a possible compromise, and even of his retaining his office with enhanced powers, while his opponents were consoled with senior operational commands. Some of Wellington's closest friends were inclined to favour such a settlement, which would certainly have pleased the King, but Wellington would not sacrifice the efficiency of the navy simply to conciliate the King and his heir. The most he was prepared to offer was to retain Clarence with even less power as a figurehead, and when this proved unacceptable he sent a somewhat reluctant Melville back to the Admiralty and gave Ellenborough the Board of Control for India. The dispute first erupted in July, lasted all through August, and was not finally resolved until the middle of September, while the feelings it aroused took a little longer to dissipate.[12]

Another reason for delay was, paradoxically, the state of Ireland, where tensions had risen sharply in the wake of O'Connell's triumph at Clare. On the one hand the Catholic Association sought to maintain the momentum it had gained through a series of blatant provocations which ranged from deliberately circulating reports that troops in the Dublin garrison were being subverted, to

O'Connell's boast at a large public meeting in August that 'with a hundred thousand of my brave Tipperary boys, I would soon drive them [the Protestants] into the sea before me'.[13] All this inflamed the fears of the Protestants, who had already been alarmed by the rise of the Catholic Association, the obvious inclination of Lord Anglesey to favour the Catholics, and reports from their friends in London that even Wellington and Peel could not be trusted. The consequence was an outburst of strident Orangeism every bit as provocative and threatening to the general peace as O'Connell's speeches. The rapid growth of Brunswick Clubs, dedicated to the defence of the constitution and the House of Brunswick, with their none-too-subtle reminder that George IV and his family owed the throne to their Protestant faith, added to the growing air of crisis.

Lord Anglesey, the Lord Lieutenant, wrote directly to Wellington in September saying that things were 'rapidly getting worse' with a 'revolutionary spirit' abroad, and a growing risk that O'Connell, the leaders of the Catholic Association and the priests would soon lose control over their followers. He asked that three or four battalions of infantry and a regiment of cavalry be made ready for immediate despatch to Ireland if trouble erupted, and made plain that in his opinion the whole problem could be simply and easily settled by granting Emancipation and conciliating the Catholic leaders.[14] Neither Peel nor Wellington had any confidence in Anglesey's discretion or loyalty, while they were alarmed by his willingness to outrage the Protestants in his attempts to conciliate the Catholics. They had already stationed troops close to ports from which they could be despatched to Ireland, but were frustrated that the Irish government had ignored repeated instructions to prosecute some of the leading agitators of the Catholic Association. Fortunately Anglesey's alarm proved unfounded and as the months passed the agitation slowly subsided, so that by the end of the year the Chief Secretary could report to London that with 'the exception of Tipperary and Roscommon, I think I may say the country is tolerably quiet'.[15] This was excellent news, for Wellington had always been convinced that concession could only be safely granted if a degree of calm and tranquillity had been established so that it would not be seen to have been extorted under threat of violence.

But as Ireland grew gradually a little quieter, there was growing resistance to any concession in Britain. A group of high or ultra Tory peers established a Protestant Club in London in June, which soon changed its name to the Brunswick Constitutional Club. Many Tories had serious doubts about the propriety of such political associations, while others were reluctant to doubt the steadfastness of Wellington and Peel, so the movement was slow to gain momentum. The first provincial club was not established until the middle of September after a heated meeting at Maidstone, but others then followed more rapidly and much of the Tory press gave the movement vocal backing.

On 24 October a huge open-air meeting was held at Penenden Heath near Maidstone with estimates of attendance ranging from 25,000 to 60,000 people, including organised parties supporting both sides of the question. Speakers included Cobbett, 'Orator' Hunt and O'Connell's lieutenant R.S. Sheil, but it was an anti-Catholic ultra Tory, Lord Winchilsea, who expressed the mood of the meeting and whose arguments secured a large majority when the question was put to the vote. However, the anti-Catholics proved unable to follow up this success with other equally impressive meetings, and it was clear that while they had considerable support in the country they amounted to a formidable, but by no means irresistible, movement.[16]

Wellington viewed the Brunswick Clubs and other anti-Catholic activities with considerable disdain, telling Westmorland:

> The truth is this – the Irish gentlemen have lost all influence in Ireland. If we were to dissolve the Parliament the [Catholic] Association would return sixty out of the hundred members for Ireland. The remainder would be divided between us and the Whigs. These sixty, in addition to the Radicals already in the House of Commons, would be too much for any government.
>
> . . . [W]hat use will be a cry in favour of the Protestant religion? Can we avail ourselves of it to dissolve the Parliament? If we cannot, we can do no good with it. The difficulties of the times have been accumulating for nearly forty years; and I must find a way out of them!!! It is not by means of Brunswick Clubs.[17]

The King, on the other hand, took some comfort in the rise of the Brunswick Clubs and the Protestant loyalist views they expressed. He was ill in the second half of September and much irritated by Anglesey's refusal to act against the Catholic agitation in Ireland. On 10 October he subjected Wellington to an extended monologue in which he urged Anglesey's recall, and suggested the introduction of Eldon into the Cabinet and resistance to all Catholic demands. The government should welcome the resurgence of Protestant feeling in Britain, dissolve Parliament, and fight a 'Church and King' election. Wellington was given no opportunity to respond at the time, so wrote to the King a few days later justifying his position and pointing to the dangers of fighting an election on nakedly sectarian grounds. Even if the election was successful Wellington did not believe that any government could be formed on this basis. And he pointed out that the Catholic leaders had other weapons at their disposal apart from electoral influence and the threat of rebellion; they might use their great popularity to instigate a campaign of non-payment of rents and tithes. 'The clergy and the landlords might have recourse to the law. But how is the law to be enforced? How can they distrain for rent or tithes millions of tenants.' Altogether he saw no alternative to 'a consideration of the whole state of Ireland' – the now well-established code by which he meant Catholic Emancipation with certain safeguards. And he concluded with an apology which made his determination to carry the question quite clear: 'This is the real state of things which it is my painful duty to bring under your Majesty's view. I am aware of the pain which I give your Majesty by stating these facts; but I should not deserve your confidence if I did not state them, and I entreat your Majesty to consider them coolly and dispassionately.'[18]

Wellington gave the King a few weeks to digest this and for his health to improve before pressing him again on the subject. In the middle of November he wrote to the King, enclosing a copy of the proposals he had put forward in August, including licensing and paying priests. He did not ask the King to make any judgement or decision on the plan, simply that he consider it and permit Wellington to discuss it with the leading bishops in the Church of England. This was not enough to alarm the King – the bishops were unlikely to sympathise with any concessions to the Catholics – and he readily granted permission, provided that Wellington made it clear that the plan had not been approved by the King; and he reiterated that he reserved his decision for the moment.[19]

Wellington lost no time in seeing the Archbishop of Canterbury and the Bishop of London, and repeated to them the arguments he had used to the King. According to the Duke's account, written immediately afterwards, both clerics conceded that the plan offered sufficient safeguards for the Church if it could be implemented in full, but the Archbishop thought that it would be displeasing to the country in general, while the extent of power given to the Crown over the Catholic Church 'would revive the old Cry of Popery and Arbitrary Power; to which I answered that the danger now was from Popery and Democracy'. Wellington asked them to consider his proposals more fully and to let him know their conclusions, 'but above all to keep the Secret'.[20] This immediate reaction was quite encouraging, for the Church was the natural centre of opposition to any relaxation of the penal laws, and its influence in Parliament and the country was still very powerful. It was most unlikely that the Anglican Church as a whole would ever support Wellington's plan, but if its opposition was muted, half-hearted or divided, the chances of success, and of minimising lasting damage to the Tory Party, would be much improved. The results of overtures to other leading churchmen were also relatively favourable; Charles Sumner, Bishop of Winchester, expressed positive support for the plan, believing that it offered the best means of promoting the reformation, although he quibbled at some details. His brother, the Bishop of Chester (and a future Archbishop of Canterbury), was more cautious, objecting to the idea of paying and licensing Catholic clergy as it would imply a degree of official recognition of the Roman Church and its hierarchy which he felt was dangerous. Still, he did not object to the underlying principle of the plan, merely to the means by which it accomplished its goal. And Charles Lloyd, the Bishop of Oxford, also felt that the plan adequately protected the position of the Church. This was doubly important, for Oxford was the home of strong Anglican feeling and the likely centre of clerical and lay opposition, and Lloyd was Peel's oldest and most influential friend; if he had been vehemently hostile to the plan it would be much less likely that Peel could be persuaded to stay in office.[21] Wellington also consulted the Bishops of Durham and Lincoln with similar results, but the hopes which this aroused were disappointed; reflection, the chance to test the mood of their parish clergy, and the activity of the Brunswick Clubs and other High Tories, produced a reaction, and by early January it was clear that the majority of the Church and the bench of bishops would oppose the proposals, although it seemed unlikely that the leaders would be intemperate.[22]

At the same time Wellington was embarrassed and annoyed by the publication of a letter he had written to Dr Curtis, the Catholic Archbishop of Armagh. Although Wellington's language was cautious – he said that he would like to see a settlement of the question, but could see no prospect of one, partly because it had become such a subject of controversy – the mere fact that he had written to the leader of the Catholic Church in Ireland on such a subject aroused a great deal of speculation and discussion. Anglesey then added to the trouble by writing an open letter to Curtis thanking him for publishing Wellington's letter as it was only from it that he had learnt of the Prime Minister's true sentiments for the first time![23] This would certainly have been the last straw, except that Anglesey's fate had been sealed weeks before, when he had responded to a rebuke in language which no prime minister could tolerate. Wellington had decided then that he must be recalled, but waited until the Cabinet had gathered again in late December to endorse his decision.[24]

By the end of the year Wellington was feeling the strain, and complained to Mrs Arbuthnot:

The Bishops will not support me in the R. C. Affair. Peel is now all for it, and as eager as he was before indifferent and indeed opposed to the Concession. The King, who was all for the dismissal of Lord Anglesey, is now afraid of removing him. I am going to Windsor at this moment, as he says he cannot write to me. I am really sick of my life . . . I was five hours with the Bishops yesterday. I shall be eight this day on my excursion to Windsor, and have all the business to do besides. It is really too much for any man.[25]

Nonetheless office had its consolations as well as its demands, and Wellington had recently received one of the most delightful gifts that was in the power of the Crown to bestow. Poor forgotten Lord Liverpool died on 4 December, thereby vacating the office of Lord Warden of the Cinque Ports, and Wellington, who was normally so reluctant to ask for anything for himself, lost no time in indicating to the King that he would be glad to receive the appointment. He justified the claim, as much to himself as to his royal master, by pointing out that it was an office of considerable influence and power but no salary; it was held for life, and the three previous holders had each been the minister of the crown when it was vacated. But the great attraction of the office was not its antiquity or the pomp, ceremony and patronage of the association of the five coastal towns, but possession of Walmer Castle – a small, comfortable residence, right on the beach between Deal and Dover, where Pitt and Dundas had often drunk the night away during the invasion scare of 1804–05, and Liverpool had escaped the relentless demands of office. Walmer was to be a third home for Wellington, in many ways more purely enjoyable than either Apsley House or Stratfield Saye, while in December 1828 its gift was an important public gesture of royal favour, especially as the King's letter on the subject was 'perfect'.[26]

Parliament was due to meet in early February so that when the Cabinet began to collect in London in the New Year they had only about a month to settle their plans for the coming session. Most of the ministers still knew nothing of Wellington's proposals, although they must all have been well aware that in one way or another the Catholic Question would dominate the coming session of Parliament. Wellington had three problems to solve before he would be ready to introduce legislation into either House. First he had to persuade Peel to remain in the government and to take responsibility for guiding the measures through the Commons. Second, he had to obtain the King's consent. And third, he had to settle the details of the measure in consultation with Peel and the rest of the Cabinet. Ideally he would also have time to win over many wavering Tories to an idea they had grown up opposing, but this could hardly be done without sacrificing the secrecy which he still regarded as vital to the success of the measure. In the end the secret was very well kept, but the result was that friends and allies as well as the Opposition and the ultra-Tories were disconcerted, and sometimes even indignant at not being consulted.[27]

The first problem was solved on 12 January when Peel announced that if Wellington really thought that it was imperative that he remain in office he would do so, even though he would still prefer to resign and support the measures from outside the government. We do not know exactly what brought him to this decision, but in his letters he cited the increased difficulties facing Wellington from the opposition of the bishops and the recall of Anglesey, and it may be that it was only now that he realised that his resignation was a luxury which the government could not afford. Still, it is hardly surprising that Peel had hesitated so long; he was rightly proud of his reputation for disinterested integrity, and he would have known that he would be accused of apostasy and selling his principles to stay in power – and that these accusations would come less from old enemies than from old friends. He had long been the champion of the Protestant party in Parliament, and all the political capital he had built up in this role would not merely be lost but would count against him when he brought into the Commons the measure which it was dedicated to oppose. He was one of the two MPs for Oxford University and he felt obliged to resign and re-contest this seat when he publicly announced his volte-face. The result was a hard-fought by-election which absorbed much time and energy and destroyed many old friendships, and in the end he was defeated and returned to Parliament as member for the pocket borough of Westbury.[28]

Peel's letter announcing his decision was accompanied by a long, forceful memorandum intended for the King, which spelt out his reasons for coming to the conclusion that 'matters cannot remain as they are', and that there was no real alternative to concession. Many of the arguments were the same or similar to those used by Wellington, although there was probably an even greater emphasis on the House of Commons. Peel argued, just as Wellington had done, that it would be impossible to form a government on the basis of outright opposition to the Catholic claims, and that if an attempt were made and it failed the result would be wholesale concession without any safeguards or securities.[29]

Wellington announced Peel's decision to the King and gave him the memorandum to read. At the same time he intimated that the time had now come for the King to permit the Cabinet to consider the state of Ireland. This was a critical moment, for there was no real doubt what advice the Cabinet would give. The King hesitated, and then required a separate interview with each of the ministers who had hitherto opposed Emancipation. Wellington, Peel, Lyndhurst, Bathurst, Goulburn and Herries saw the King at Windsor on 15 January and slept there that night together with the other ministers – Ellenborough noted that the rooms 'were cruelly cold' and it is unlikely that the King's reception was much warmer. Faced with a united front of his responsible advisers the King gave way and gave his consent for the subject to be considered, but again reserved his right to reject their advice when it was given, 'even if it should concur unanimously in the course to be pursued'.[30]

The Cabinet began its deliberations on 17 January. Only Goulburn expressed any serious qualms about the idea of concession, and he reserved his decision on whether he could support the measure or not until he saw the details of the final plan. There was general agreement on some points: that a bill to suppress the Catholic Association was a desirable and necessary preliminary; that almost all offices should be opened to Catholics, as well as the right to sit in Parliament; and that Anglican ecclesiastical titles should be protected. But many elements in Wellington's plan provoked disagreement, and he frequently yielded in the face of objections from his colleagues. For example, his idea of retaining but tightening the forty-shilling freeholder franchise was dropped in favour of its simple abolition. And the central provision of Wellington's plan, the licensing and paying of priests, which he had always felt provided the principal security both for the Anglican Church and for the peace of Ireland, aroused strong opposition from Peel, who was supported by most but not all of the other ministers. Their argument was that this provision would be unpopular with both sides; many Anglican churchmen felt that it gave too much recognition to the Catholic Church, while some Catholics might object to the level of influence and control it gave the government. Yet without it, and without a concordat with the Pope, the government's proposals contained fewer securities for the Anglican Church than the scheme put forward by the advocates of Emancipation in 1825. The government, gained little if any influence over the Catholic Church, and there was no incentive for the priests in Ireland to withdraw from politics, so that the argument that it was better for Emancipation to be introduced by a Tory government, which would protect the interests of the Established Church, appeared decidedly hollow. Still, after much discussion Wellington 'very reluctantly' gave way. It is significant that Wellington conceded such an important point, and it is just one of many examples which disprove the accusation that he treated his colleagues like subordinates and demanded obedience rather than collaboration.[31]

The proposals were completed and presented to the King on 29 January, followed by a draft of the King's Speech on 1 February. At a Council meeting on the following day the King made a few verbal difficulties, and a mischievous but hardly serious suggestion that the direct reference to the Catholic Question be omitted from the Speech from the Throne, but in the end approved the measures without a scene and even expressed himself as quite satisfied with it.[32]

Despite this surprisingly ready compliance, the King made it clear to all the world that he was not happy with his ministers. He gave an interview to Lord Anglesey as soon as he reached London, and pretended to have opposed his recall. And he invited a large party of Whigs and Canningites to the Castle where, gossip reported, they 'passed the whole time plotting against the Govt & settling how their *expected Cabinet* shd be formed! Ld Melbourne [William Lamb] was to be Prime Minister.' Not that the King was present at these discussions, but even so it produced a great deal of excitement and some real damage to the government.[33] On the other hand Wellington was very pleased that the King sent Knighton to Berlin to discourage the Duke of Cumberland from coming over to Britain as he planned, for Cumberland would inevitably prove a focus for ultra-Tory resistance to the government's plans. And the King made no objection to the selection of the Duke of Northumberland as Anglesey's replacement in Ireland. This was generally regarded as a good choice, for although Northumberland was 'a stupid, prosing man', he was 'as rich as Croesus', and his wife was 'excessively good humoured & has very popular manners'. Northumberland's views on the Catholic Question were moderate and flexible, and he fully understood, as Anglesey had not, that his function was to act as a magnificent figurehead and to patronise the shopkeepers of Dublin, not to pursue a different policy from the government in London.[34] Wellington also tried to fill the office of Lord Privy Seal, which he had kept open in case it was needed as part of a reconstruction of the government if he had failed to persuade Peel to stay. He wanted a High Tory nobleman and approached the Duke of Beaufort and Lord Westmorland, but both declined – the latter with many a pang of regret but finding it too difficult to accept office and immediately support a measure he had always opposed.[35]

The secret of the government's intentions only trickled out in the last few days before Parliament met on 5 February, and was confirmed at a dinner for government supporters in the Commons the night before. The reaction varied widely; most Whigs and liberals were pleased, if a little ambivalent at seeing their long-cherished project brought forward by Wellington and Peel. However, the extent of the anger and sense of betrayal among some Tories would be hard to overstate. The Duke of Newcastle wrote in his diary on 4 February: 'I learn to my horror, indignation & disgust that my suspicions have been all along well founded & that the *Duke of Wellington* is actually going to bring in a bill to remove almost all disabilities from the Papists – many apostasies have taken place & it is said that Mr Peel retires – The whole affair appears to be of the blackest & most disgusting nature & will lead to consequences fatal to the happiness of many.' And when he learnt that Peel would not resign, he added: 'This cotton Spinner is a degraded wretch, one could not spit upon him, he is so fallow, supplicating & grovelling.'[36] By contrast, Lady Holland told her son:

It is a delightful concession, & so surprising that one feels in a dream. Peel is the only *honest* one. The great Duke is what one always thought, devoid of principle, gratitude, generosity; but he is the only man who could now carry the measure, & as such will be supported in it by all who are really attached to the welfare of the Country. The King has been circumvented, as he ought to be when great benefits are necessary for the country.[37]

And Creevey, writing a month later, declared: 'Well, the Whig croaking must end now. The Beau is immortalized by his views and measures as detailed by Peel last night.'[38]

Wellington was disappointed by the immediate reaction to the King's Speech. He told Croker that the mood in the Lords was 'sullen and sour', and that if the Opposition had moved an amendment the government might have been defeated, so alienated were the Tory peers.[39] In order to rally support he wrote to the Duke of Rutland and to Lord Lonsdale, both High Tories, but much more moderate than extremists like Newcastle, and after explaining at some length the reasons behind the government's decision, went on to warn them: 'If this government is not supported by those highly respected individuals and parties in this country who are the main pillars of the monarchy, it is time that I should take my leave. I cannot submit to be the puppet of the rump of the Whigs and of [the friends of] Mr Canning.'[40]

It is clear that Wellington underestimated the strength of the opposition he would face from the ultra Tories. The necessity of the measure, and the lack of any practical alternative, appeared so obvious to Wellington, Peel and the other ministers, that they struggled to understand how so many Tories could remain obdurate. But most of the ultras had little experience of high office and the compromises it required. They were men of strong principle who understood clearly that granting Catholic Emancipation would destabilise the constitution and open the way for further changes. They had grown up believing that there was strong popular support for the Protestant constitution, and they felt that it would be a shameful betrayal to yield to the implicit threat of insurrection in Ireland rather than to defy O'Connell and, if necessary, fight for what they believed. Their views were not always wise or realistic, but they were no more ridiculous than the liberal argument that Emancipation would solve Ireland's problems, and were probably more representative of British opinion as a whole.[41]

Fortunately for the government the initial trial of strength was in the Commons, where strong backing from Whigs and liberals more than compensated, at least in the short term, for the lost votes of the ultra Tories. There was no opposition to the first measure, the bill to dissolve the Catholic Association, which passed both Houses without a division. Disenfranchisement of the forty-shilling freeholders produced scarcely more resistance. O'Connell and other Catholic leaders made a feeble pretence of opposition, but in reality were easily reconciled to the sacrifice of the peasantry who had given them such whole-hearted support. Huskisson, Palmerston and the High Tory Henry Bankes voted against it in the Commons, but Peel carried the measure with a thumping majority: 223 votes to 17. But behind the impressive majority lay the seething discontent of many of its nominal supporters, including a number of junior ministers, and the doubts of the King.[42]

Knighton's mission had failed, and the Duke of Cumberland arrived in London on 14 February and went straight on to Windsor to see his brother.

Mrs Arbuthnot anticipated the consequences: 'It is a great misfortune for it will do great mischief, keep the King in hot water & worry him to death, besides giving heart and resolution to the Protestants in their opposition.' Wellington saw Cumberland and urged him to 'keep himself quiet' and 'not allow himself to be made the head of a party' in opposition to the King's ministers, and Cumberland agreed to follow this advice.[43] Perhaps for the moment he meant it, for he had a real respect, even admiration, for Wellington personally, but this was dwarfed by the passion of his commitment to the Protestant constitution, and any restraint was short-lived. On 19 February he spoke in the Lords saying that the question was simply 'whether this country was to be a Protestant country with a Protestant government, or a Roman Catholic country with a Roman Catholic government'. This produced an angry debate, but the real threat posed by Cumberland was more insidious. He told leading ultra Tories that the King did not really support the measures and would be glad to be helped to escape them, and he used all his influence at Windsor to make this true.[44]

The result was a serious row at the end of February which stretched into early March, with the King vacillating between Cumberland and Wellington. After one interview Wellington is said to have written to Knighton 'that if the Duke of Cumberland thought he could make a Government, he had better give that advice to the King at once, and so end matters'.[45] But as Wellington well knew, Cumberland and the ultra Tories could *not* make a credible government even with the unequivocal support of the King. They might make a fair showing in the Lords, but they had no one of the first or even the second rank to lead them in the Commons. It had been hard enough in 1784 with the young Pitt to defy Opposition majorities in the Commons, and George III had vastly more courage and obstinacy than his son. However, the High Tories were emboldened by the belief that they had the country if not Parliament with them, and were elated by the news of Peel's defeat at Oxford, which arrived late on 27 February.[46]

A second interview with the King lasted five hours, and Wellington told Mrs Arbuthnot that he 'never had so painful or so distressing a scene in his life to go thro[ugh]'. 'The King, as usual, began with a long history of his own life, of his political sentiments, of what his father had said of him, of his honesty, his uprightness, his good temper, his fairness, &c., &c., and, having talked in this strain for an hour & a half till he was out of breath, he said, "Now what have you got to say to me?"' Wellington then went through the government's measures in detail, and the King made many difficulties and talked of his conscience, the Coronation Oath and of the opinion of his father. In the end he gave way, shedding tears, praising Wellington as the only minister in whom he could feel confidence, and giving him permission to write to the Household requiring them to support the government. At Wellington's suggestion the King even promised to ask Cumberland to return to the Continent, and when the Duke offered to kiss the royal hand on parting as usual 'the King put his arm around him & kissed him'.[47]

But the victory was only temporary, and a few days later Wellington was back at Windsor finding the King obstinate and violent in his language, and even talking of abdicating and retiring to Hanover. The King admitted that he had looked around for an alternative prime minister, but could not find one, and even asked Wellington 'if he thought he could trust old Eldon! The Duke shook his head and laughed, and said he would not advise His Majesty to do so.'[48] In London Wellington saw the Cabinet, which was united in its determination to persist, and refused to agree to recommend that Royal Assent be given to the bill suppressing the Catholic Association without firm assurances that the King would give his support to the relief measures as well. Wellington, Peel and Lyndhurst went back to Windsor on 3 March where they spent five hours with the King, during which he talked almost the whole time while drinking copious quantities of brandy and water. He spoke 'of his conscience & his determination not to yield, said he had not understood what the measures were & objected particularly to granting seats in Parliament'. At one point he talked of postponing the bill until he had consulted the Archbishop of Canterbury and the Bishop of London, but then changed his mind; while at another he confused the Coronation Oath with the Oath of Supremacy. Wellington pointed out that the nature and extent of the concessions had been discussed and agreed to in January, that the government was committed to the measure, and that if it did not have the King's support the ministers would have no choice but to resign and to tell Parliament why they had done so. 'The King said then he must try to find other Ministers &, if he failed, he supposed he must come back to them. With this they parted.'[49] The three ministers returned to London and announced to their colleagues that they were out of office, but within hours the King's determination had collapsed and he finally gave an unequivocal pledge of his support for the measure, which enabled Peel to introduce it into the Commons that evening.[50]

The Cabinet had succeeded in imposing its will on the King, but the contest had left considerable ill-feeling on both sides. In the midst of it Mrs Arbuthnot asked Wellington if he thought that the King 'really had a conscientious feeling about it'. Wellington replied 'no, but [the King] had been worked upon & excited by the Duke of Cumberland till he fancied he had'. Mrs Arbuthnot was even more forthright in her journal, declaring that 'every body knows he has no more conscience than the chair he sits in'.[51] That was clearly too cynical – the King's distress was genuine if facile – but his vacillations had posed a considerable strain upon the loyalty of his ministers. Ellenborough wrote: 'It is impossible not to feel the most perfect contempt for the King's conduct. We should be justified in declaring we will have no further intercourse with one who has not treated us like a gentleman.'[52] The pressure on Wellington in particular was enormous. On 2 March he was described as looking 'much exhausted', and as soon as the crisis was over he succumbed to a heavy cold and was forced to stay home, while on 9 March Ellenborough wrote that he 'did not seem at all well . . . He looked very pale, and was languid and silent.'[53]

The struggle now shifted to Parliament. The High Tories lacked the numbers to block the government's proposals in the Commons, but in the first important vote they still mustered a surprisingly large minority of 160 (to 348 in favour, which included almost all the Opposition).[54] The forces were more evenly balanced in the press and in the country as a whole. The *Quarterly Review,* the most serious and successful intellectual journal of the day, and long associated with a range of moderate and liberal–Tory views, failed to offer the support which the government would have expected. The *Standard* and the *Morning Journal,* two Tory dailies which had supported Wellington in 1828, now opposed him with intemperate vehemence, calling for his impeachment and the fall of the government even if it was followed by the Whigs. Both papers, but especially the *Standard,* were believed to have ties to the Duke of Cumberland. Five other Tory newspapers or journals including *Blackwood's* and *Fraser's Magazine* came out against the government at this time, and were to persist in their hostility long after Emancipation had passed into law. One Dublin paper, the *Star of Brunswick,* described Wellington as a 'military desperadoe [*sic*]', compared him to Cromwell, and finally took to referring to him as 'the Dictator' – abuse which he was more accustomed to receive from the radical press. The *Standard* went even further, suggesting that he intended to 'perpetuate his power by dangerous designs connected with the succession to the crown', while other papers cast aspersions on Wellington's relations with Mrs Arbuthnot, described the Duchess of Wellington as disfigured by smallpox, and impugned Wellington's generalship at Waterloo.[55]

Not all the Tory papers broke with the government over Catholic Emancipation; *John Bull,* its scandalous fiery heyday now a faded memory, the *Morning Post* and the *Courier* followed the Treasury line, although it is unlikely that anyone took their views very seriously. Wellington received far more effective, if unreliable, support from the liberal press and in particular from *The Times,* whose stature had risen steadily throughout the 1820s, although never managing to catch up with its own idea of its importance. To wavering MPs and to the public as a whole, the press would have appeared predominantly favourable to Emancipation and sympathetic to the government, but it is likely that Wellington perceived it differently and was much more aware of the equivocation of allies and the real hostility of his former admirers, who were now his most savage critics.[56]

The prolonged and intense political debate produced a rich crop of caricatures; more than 120 were devoted to the Catholic Question in the first four
months of 1829, completely swamping every other issue. Here the balance lay
with the opponents of the measure, partly because there was such a well-
stocked tradition of no-popery motifs for artists to draw on, and partly because
satire always inclines to the negative. The Pope and the Devil make frequent
appearances, usually in harmony and sometimes interchangeably, while
O'Connell and the Irish peasantry are depicted as either menacing or ridiculous. Several prints used the other great news story of the day – the trial of
Burke and Hare, for committing a series of murders in order to sell their
victims' bodies to Dr Knox's anatomical school – to telling effect. For example,
William Heath's *Burking poor Old Mrs Constitution Aged 141* shows Wellington
and Peel in the act of smothering the Constitution of 1688, while a Catholic
priest waits eagerly at the door ready to purchase the corpse. Another print by
Heath, *Doing Homage*, shows Wellington on bended knee, rosary in hand,
humbly kissing the Pope's toe while Peel waits anxiously to follow suit. More
interesting and fairer, but less well designed and executed, is a slightly later
print, *A Long Pull A Strong Pull and a Pull Altogether*, which depicts the King
being pulled in one direction by Wellington and Peel who use a green ribbon
labelled 'Expediency', while Eldon and Cumberland tug equally hard in the
other direction using an orange ribbon labelled 'Coronation Oath'. The King
himself appears red-faced and in great discomfort, without any preference of
his own, while his crown falls from his head towards Wellington.[57]

The anti-Catholic movement fostered by the Brunswick Clubs had
continued through the winter, expressing itself through county meetings,
pamphlets and above all petitions. By the end of February 720 anti-Catholic
petitions had been presented to Parliament, compared to only 220 in favour.
One petition from Glasgow had over 36,000 signatures; one from Bristol,
38,000; from Kent 81,000; and from Ireland 168,000, all opposing concession.
Anglican and Methodist clergy often played a prominent part in organising
and supporting local activities, but most other Dissenting ministers, grateful
for the repeal of the Test and Corporation Acts, either supported Emancipation
or kept out of the strife. The feeling in the country was strong but not overwhelming. Crowds hooted and jeered at Wellington as he went to or from the
Lords, and they cheered Newcastle and other leading Protestants, but these
demonstrations were not on the same scale as those during the Queen Caroline
disturbances. The High Tories hoped to organise a huge popular march from
London to Windsor to present anti-Catholic petitions directly to the King, and
the government took a variety of steps to discourage attendance and warn
against the scheme. Wellington even told Mrs Arbuthnot that if the Duke of
Cumberland did anything to disturb the peace or frighten the King he would

send him to the Tower! Her comment that 'they won't find it an easy matter to get 20,000 men to walk as far as Windsor unless they opened the alehouses for them when they get there' was justified when the march fell flat.[58]

None of this slowed the steady progress of the bill through the Commons, but the debates were marked by great passion and personal feeling, while Wellington, Peel and other ministers were excoriated by members of both Houses who had previously admired and praised them. Relations between Wellington and Cumberland were now marked by open hostility, with the latter criticising the Prime Minister on grounds far removed from the Catholic Question, for example accusing him of monopolising the patronage of the army and treating Lord Hill as a cipher – remarks which Hill naturally resented.[59] One of the most prominent and forceful speakers among the ultras was the thirty-seven-year-old Earl of Winchilsea, who had first made a name for himself at the public meeting at Penenden Heath the previous October, where his self-confidence and stentorian voice made him an impressive figure. On 10 March he attacked Wellington in the Lords, accusing him of acting in a more arbitrary and dictatorial manner than any former minister in the country's history even in the most despotic times, and declared his support for Lord Grey and parliamentary reform as the votes on the Catholic Question had proved the Commons to be corrupt and unrepresentative of the country.[60] And on 16 March a letter from Winchilsea was published in the *Standard* in which he described Wellington's support for King's College, London, as a trick to mislead Tories designed to conceal for a time his intention of breaking down the constitution of 1688 so that he might 'the more effectually, under the cloak of some outward show of zeal for the Protestant religion, carry on his insidious designs, for the infringement of our liberties, and the introduction of Popery into every department of the State'.[61]

This was too much even for Wellington, and he wrote to Winchilsea asking if he had indeed written the letter and given permission for its publication. When Winchilsea confirmed both points Wellington demanded a formal apology: 'No man has a right, whether in public or in private, by speech, in writing, or in print, to insult another by attributing to him motives for his conduct, public or private, which disgrace or criminate him.'[62] Winchilsea declined to apologise, privately explaining to a friend that he knew that he had been wrong to publish the letter, but that the insult had been so gross that nothing less than a comprehensive and humiliating apology would suffice, and that he feared that such a climb-down would cost him his character if it was seen to be made under pressure.[63] Faced with this obduracy Wellington had little choice but to challenge Winchilsea to a duel and place the management of the meeting in the hands of his second – a role which he asked Sir Henry Hardinge to fill. Hardinge and Winchilsea's second, Lord Falmouth, did what they could to prevent the duel, but Falmouth was a poor creature quite unable to prevail upon Winchilsea to apologise, or to refuse to act for him as a consequence. Wellington took the affair very coolly but must have been extremely annoyed to find himself placed in this position. Throughout his long career in the army he had always avoided any involvement in duels. No doubt the death of his friend Colonel Aston in India in 1798 helped to shape his attitude, but it also reflected the changing opinion in society. George III's opposition, the rise of evangelicalism, and changing mores had led to the gradual decline of duelling, but they continued to be fought from time to time in the worlds of politics and high society, as well as in the army. Pitt had fought a duel in 1798, when he was prime minister; the Duke of York one in 1789 when he was second-in-line to the throne; Canning and Castlereagh had their celebrated encounter in 1809; and in 1822 the Dukes of Bedford and Buckingham fought over some remarks the former made at a county meeting. None of these duels had fatal results, nor did any of the participants suffer serious consequences in the eyes of society – the meeting had vindicated their honour and cast the offence into oblivion. Even Peel had only been prevented from fighting O'Connell in 1815 because the affair received premature coverage in the press and the police intervened, much against the wishes of both men.

Wellington's duel was fought early on the morning of 21 March 1829, and we have a detailed account written later that day by Dr John Hume who was asked to attend by Hardinge. Hume met Hardinge at the latter's house in Whitehall Place before seven o'clock in the morning and travelled on in the carriage while Hardinge rode, so that it was not until he arrived at Battersea Fields half a mile south of the river that he discovered who the principal was, and he confesses that this left him 'overwhelmed with amazement and so greatly agitated that I could scarcely answer' Wellington's laughing greeting. Winchilsea and Falmouth arrived a little later, their coachman having taken them by Putney rather than Battersea Bridge. There was some conversation between the seconds in which Hardinge made it clear that he thought that the duel ought to have been avoided and Falmouth, all too aware that he would be blamed if Wellington was killed or wounded, 'seemed agitated and very much affected'. Hume loaded the pistols for Hardinge (who had lost a hand in 1815), and nearly had to do the same for Falmouth, who was shaking so much that he could scarcely get the ball into the mouth of the pistol or ram it home. As Falmouth continued to express his regret at what was happening Hume could not resist saying: 'But surely, Sir, it might have been prevented? Could you not have prevented it? Is not Lord Winchilsea entirely to blame? As for the Duke, I know so well his discretion and temper in all great matters that I am certain that he could never either say or do anything to offend or to hurt any man's feelings whatever.' Hardinge then placed the two principals twelve paces apart, and, taking his ground midway between them, read a paper protesting against the duel. Winchilsea murmured something about '*rather strong language*' and Falmouth, with tears in his eyes, implored everyone to believe that he had done everything he could to prevent it, and that he had never approved of the publication of the letter, to which Hardinge replied: 'Indeed, my Lord Falmouth, I do not envy you your feelings.' Through all this Wellington remained silent and aloof, with what Hume described as 'a smile of good nature upon his countenance'. Each second then gave his principal a loaded pistol, and stepped back a few paces. Hardinge said, 'Then gentlemen, I shall ask you if you are ready, and give the word *fire* without any further signal or preparation', which, a few seconds after, he did, announcing, 'Gentlemen, are you ready? *Fire!*' Wellington raised his pistol immediately, hesitated for a moment when he saw that Winchilsea's arm was still by his side, then fired and missed. Winchilsea then slowly raised his arm to point straight up and fired into the sky.[64]

Falmouth then came forward and said: 'Lord Winchilsea, having received the Duke's fire, is placed under different circumstances from those in which he stood before, and therefore now feels himself at liberty to give the Duke of Wellington the reparation he requires.' And when Hardinge said that Wellington would not be satisfied with less than an unconditional acknowledgement by Winchilsea of his error, Falmouth assured him, 'I mean an apology in the most extensive or in every sense of the word', and pulled from his pocket a paper to this effect. However, upon reading it over the word 'apology' did not appear and Wellington, intervening, said quietly to Hardinge: 'This won't do; it is no apology.' Hardinge then took it to Falmouth, who appeared puzzled how to insert the word without rewriting the whole letter until Hume pointed out where it could fit, albeit awkwardly.[65] Wellington then touched the brim of his hat with two fingers and said, 'Good morning, my Lord Winchilsea; good morning, my Lord Falmouth', but did not shake their hands, before mounting his horse and riding off, closely followed by Hardinge. Hume was left to collect the pistols and to listen to Falmouth's prattling on about his unbounded admiration for Wellington and more of his regrets. The good doctor was left with a favourable opinion of Winchilsea – 'His manner throughout was exceedingly becoming; no haste, no forwardness, no presuming. His demeanor was gentle, calm and unobtrusive' – while for Falmouth he evidently felt pity tinged with contempt.[66]

It was fortunate for all present that neither party was killed or wounded. Indeed Falmouth only agreed to attend when he received an assurance in writing from Winchilsea the evening before the duel that he would not fire on the Duke, and would apologise amply after standing the Duke's fire.[67] As for Wellington, according to Ellenborough: 'The Duke said he considered all the morning whether he should fire at him or no. He thought if he killed him he should be tried, and confined until he was tried, which he did not like, so he determined to fire at his legs. He did hit his coat.' The ruthless pragmatism and unwavering egoism of this do not seem altogether implausible in the circumstances, but there is no way of knowing how accurate a reflection this was of Wellington's thoughts at the time – he may simply have been looking for an excuse for missing![68]

None of Wellington's family or close friends, except Hardinge, knew of the duel in advance, but even with the assurance that he was unharmed it was not comfortable news. The Duchess wrote to her friend Mrs Fremantle:

> From the day on which I received it, which was on Saturday, I have been incapable of writing or even thinking on any subject but *one*. You know, my dear Mrs Fremantle, the extent and depth of my love to my dear and noble husband and can imagine with what horror I heard that his most precious life had been endangered. I cannot now think of it without shuddering, but thank the God who protects him all is now well . . .[69]

According to Greville many of Wellington's female friends in society, particularly Lady Jersey, 'have been very ridiculous, affecting nervousness and fine feelings, though they never heard of the business till some hours after it was over. Mrs Arbuthnot was not so foolish, but made very light of it all, which was in better sense and better taste'. But Mrs Arbuthnot told Lady Shelley: 'I am very glad I had no suspicion, for I should have died of fright; but I am sure the Duke was right, and that such an impudent letter *could not* be overlooked . . . The Duke seems quite well, and in good spirits, and seemed to think it an excellent joke, but I was ready to cry.'[70]

Hardinge published the correspondence which preceded the duel, and Winchilsea's apology, in the *Courier,* and it was reproduced by the other papers on Sunday and Monday; readers were quick to apportion praise and blame. There was almost universal agreement that Winchilsea's letter had been grossly insulting and should never have been published, but more argument over whether Wellington was right to challenge him or should have treated it with contempt. Greville inclined to the latter view: 'I think the Duke ought not to have challenged him; it was very juvenile, and he stands in far too high a position . . . [but] it is impossible not to admire the high spirit which disdained to shelter itself behind the immunities of his great character and station, and the simplicity, and almost humility, which made him at once descend to the level of Lord Winchilsea.' The King was much less ambivalent, thoroughly approving Wellington's conduct and even saying that if he had seen Winchilsea's letter he would have drawn it to Wellington's attention.[71] *The Times* was emphatic: 'By the *manner* of conducting his whole correspondence, [Wellington] established the highest claims to general respect and admiration, for the inimitable dignity, temper, and even kindliness of his expostulations with the man who had wantonly insulted him.' Even the two caricatures which soon appeared on the subject were relatively restrained – although Heath could not resist depicting Wellington as a lobster (that is, a soldier) in a monk's habit with a rosary hanging from his belt.[72] Only the ultra Tories took a different line, with Newcastle regretting that Winchilsea had apologised and admitting in his diary: 'One is almost tempted to wish that a life So dangerous had been taken away – but one must not indulge in such unchristian feelings . . . The D of Ws time may not yet be come but it may & that shortly & terribly for assuredly he is a villain & a Sinner.' But this was untypical, and the best summary of public reactions comes from Ellenborough: 'The first feeling of everyone is that the Duke should not have gone out; but when they read the letters they think he was right, as somehow or other he always is.'[73] As this suggests, the duel had considerable political benefits, and cost the ultra Tories sympathy, support and momentum. Nonetheless they continued to fight the bill every step of its way through Parliament.

The bill passed the Commons before the end of March and was sent straight to the Lords. By now the only hope of the High Tories lay in delay: if they could drag out proceedings until the Easter recess, they might whip up more feeling in the country and work upon the King's doubts; but Wellington saw the danger and pushed the bill through its successive stages in the Lords with a brusqueness which made even some of his supporters blink. The Second Reading debate began on 2 April and lasted three days, with opposition being led by some of the bishops and Lords Mansfield and Falmouth. Wellington spoke at the beginning of the debate, introducing the bill. The liberal John Cam Hobhouse wrote in his diary:

I had never heard the Duke speak before, and was much struck with the man and with the occasion – both the one and the other being such as history has seldom, if ever, furnished. The Duke spoke slowly but without hesitation or embarrassment of any kind. He did not refer to notes at all, and only once read from a paper containing an extract from the Journals of the Scottish Parliament. His speech was clear and satisfactory in every part, except perhaps when he referred to the Revolution settlement, when he did not appear quite at home.

The most striking part of his speech was when he alluded to his own experience of the horrors of civil war, and said that he would willingly lay down his life to avoid one month of it. The effect of this in the mouth of the great soldier was visible in all who heard him. The words were not the boasting of an orator, but the expression of real feeling from one who had seen thousands die around him, and was, as Lord Grey afterwards said, 'red with the blood of a hundred battles'.[74]

Wellington had become, not a great orator like Peel, but a thoroughly competent and effective speaker.

The government forced the Lords to sit on Saturday 6 April in order to close the Second Reading debate and bring it to a vote. The result was a majority of 105 (217 to 112), far exceeding the most optimistic ministerial calculations. Wellington was delighted and dined with the Arbuthnots afterwards in high spirits, but although prepared for the blow, Newcastle was mortified: 'What base, unworthy wretches must these *noble* lords be who thus throw away their Constitution & for what [?] literally for no reason whatever but to please that ambitious traitor & assuming Scoundrel the Duke of Wellington – I am hurt, cut to the heart, ashamed, disgusted at my truckling, time-serving, unprincipled Countrymen . . .'[75] The King was scarcely more pleased at this vote of confidence in his administration and told Lord Aberdeen that the House of Commons had long since disgraced itself, the Lords had now followed suit, and that he felt like Louis XVI on the eve of the French Revolution. Cumberland was even more violent, accusing Wellington of tyranny and insolence, and swearing that though the bill must pass he would then try to bring down the government. Meanwhile the bill sailed through the committee stage in the Lords without difficulty and passed its Third Reading on 10 April by a majority of 104 (213 to 109). Three days later the King signed it into law, telling the Chancellor that he had 'never *before* affixed his name, with pain or regret, to any act of the Legislature'.[76]

For more than a generation Catholic Emancipation had been advocated as the solution to all Ireland's problems. In the event it did not even bring a season of tranquillity, while O'Connell and the other Catholic leaders lost little time in unveiling a programme of new demands that were equally irrelevant to the real needs of the Irish people, including repeal of the Act of Union with Britain, and dis-establishing the Anglican Church of Ireland and plundering its assets. Meanwhile the Irish poor continued to grow poorer and more dependent on their crops of potatoes, as the growth of the Irish economy failed to keep pace with the increasing population.

Wellington and Peel never believed that Emancipation would make Ireland peaceful and prosperous; that is why they resisted it for so long. They yielded the concession because they had become convinced that there was no longer sufficient support in the governing class in Britain, as reflected in the House of Commons, to resist the Catholic demands, and because the situation in Ireland required a decisive step towards either coercion or conciliation. Catholic

Emancipation was not a small concession; it touched the fundamentals of the British constitution, and went a considerable distance along the road that led towards the separation of Church and State. Wellington and his colleagues had no wish to embark upon a constitutional revolution but, like many other ministers before and since, they made long-term concessions in order to deal with an immediate crisis, and given the state of Ireland following O'Connell's election in 1828 it is hard to see that they had a real choice. But it is not surprising that the High Tories found their apostasy hard to forgive. It was unfortunate for Wellington that he was prime minister just when Ireland finally became un-ignorable. If Canning had lived another two years he might have passed Catholic Emancipation and held office at the head of a liberal-Whig government, while Wellington and Peel would have led a united Tory Party in opposition, and the politics of the 1830s and 1840s would have been very different. But no prime minister can choose the crises they will face, and Wellington had successfully navigated the state through perilous rapids at considerable political cost to his reputation and the stability of his government.

CHAPTER NINETEEN

THE FOREIGN POLICY OF WELLINGTON'S GOVERNMENT
(1828–July 1830)

ALTHOUGH DOMESTIC ISSUES dominated British politics between 1828 and 1830, foreign affairs played an important part in shaping attitudes towards the government, especially after the passage of Catholic Emancipation. It was a field dominated by Wellington; no British prime minister before or since has taken office with such credentials.[1] He had been a major figure in Europe for fifteen years, dealing personally and as an equal with the leading monarchs and statesmen of the time, and brought with him the immense prestige of his military victories and a reputation for unimpeachable integrity. His foreign secretaries were dwarfed by comparison. Dudley admired Wellington greatly and was happy to subordinate himself to the Duke, despite his Canningite pedigree and liberal views. Aberdeen was a more substantial and independent figure, but still new to high office, and his outlook and approach were quite close to Wellington's. They generally differed, when they differed at all, on details and methods, not objectives, and there was never any question who would have the last word. This does not mean that Wellington's approach was autocratic; he listened to advice and suggestions, not just from Aberdeen but from other colleagues, and he was careful to gain the support of Cabinet for important decisions, sometimes giving way on significant points to do so.[2]

The central objective of Wellington's foreign policy was to keep Britain at peace, and in particular to extract her from the dangerous positions Canning had taken on Portugal and Greece at the least cost, while reviving co-operation with the other great powers of Europe. It was not a policy which had much appeal for journalists or the reading public; there was no soaring rhetoric, no ideological crusade, no collection of conquests or other tangible trophies, not even a chance to beat the patriotic drum by making enemies of Britain's neighbours, but much slow, patient work defusing bombs and containing fires that had to be doused before they set the whole neighbourhood ablaze. The work was important but unglamorous, tiresome in its detail, and seldom very satisfying even for those who undertook it.

When the ministers took office in January 1828 both Portugal and Greece required their urgent attention, and both problems would continue in parallel for the life of the government, although Portuguese affairs reached their crisis sooner (in the summer of 1828) and had a longer denouement. Miguel, the prospective regent of Portugal, had arrived in England on 20 December 1827, disembarking at Greenwich and being received with honours and attention. He went out of his way to please his hosts and in private talks renewed his promises of abiding by the constitution, and even asked that the mooted withdrawal of the British expeditionary force be delayed a little. Wellington entertained him at Stratfield Saye and the government used its influence with Rothchilds to ensure that he was able to raise a modest loan (£50,000) for his immediate expenses.[3] Frederick Lamb, the newly appointed British ambassador to Portugal, who was to accompany Miguel on his return to Lisbon, was condescending but not alarmed by his first impression of the Prince: 'If we can keep him among gentlemen when he gets to Lisbon, it will do very well. This is what I doubt and fear. He shows no cleverness, and a great facility of disposition. I am sorry for it. I wish he were more determined . . .' Nor did Lamb initially warm to Palmella, who had joined Miguel at Vienna: 'I much distrust Palmella. He seems to me to have nothing in view but his private ends which, God knows why, he unites in his own mind with the maintenance of the Constitution at all events.'[4]

Miguel and his party sailed from England on 9 February 1828 and landed at Lisbon thirteen days later. On 26 February he again swore allegiance to the constitution and was installed as regent, although already some eager supporters were acclaiming him as king. Whatever his real intentions in England, once in Lisbon he soon fell under the influence of his mother and the absolutist faction. Palmella and other liberal ministers were dismissed, the army was purged of leading liberal officers, and the absolutist exiles in Spain were not only welcomed home but restored to their old positions of power and influence. Some of this was only to be expected as the wheel turned, but many of Miguel's actions, and those of his supporters, destabilised his regime and lent it a precarious air. Royalist mobs roamed the streets at night attacking those suspected of sympathising with the previous government, while there was constant discussion of the constitution and whether Miguel had not a better claim to the throne than his niece.

The Portuguese absolutists had no love for Britain, which they felt had favoured their liberal opponents, and which was, by Portuguese standards, an inherently liberal society. Miguel and his ministers treated Lamb with scant courtesy and made obvious their disregard for his advice and his protests at their actions. After less than a month in Lisbon, Lamb urged his government either to take 'this country in hand and [set] it to rights' or openly to wash their hands of Miguel by recalling their ambassador. Lamb's conclusion may have led some at home to wonder if he had mistaken his vocation: 'Such a set of cowards as both parties have shown themselves I had never beheld before. My belief is they are all to be managed by a horsewhip, and by nothing else.'[5]

Wellington was almost equally forthright in his assessment of the situation:

> As far as I can judge of the state of affairs at Lisbon, both parties are fright-ened out of their senses. On the one hand Don [*sic*] Miguel has listened to the tales of all the old women, who have told him that the house of every nobleman contains a Freemason's lodge, or is the place of meeting of a secret society, whose object is to concert plans to assassinate him, and to overturn his government; and, on the other, the constitutional party believe that Don Miguel must intend to overthrow the charter, and to usurp his brother's kingdom; that the changes of government, and that of the officers commanding in the provinces, and of certain regiments in Lisbon, are the evidence of such an intention; and that the next step will be to arrest, imprison, and murder them.[6]

He was highly critical of Miguel's actions, especially his provocative dissolution of the legislative chambers, his dismissal of moderate men of proven ability, and the failure to maintain order on the streets, but he did not believe that Britain had any right to complain if Miguel preferred one party rather than another to form his government. A few weeks later he spelt this out even more explicitly in another letter to Lamb:

> It is my opinion not only that we have no right to interfere . . . but that the less we interfere in the internal affairs of Portugal the better for both parties. We are bound to defend Portugal against a foreign enemy, and we have a right to give our advice in respect to the measures of foreign policy, and possibly in respect to those measures of internal policy which may in their consequences affect the tranquillity of the country, and its political and military strength. The penalty of omitting to follow our advice must be that such omission puts it out of our power to fulfil the obligations of treaties. We have no right, nor, indeed, have we the means of using force; and my opinion is that we ought to confine our exertions strictly to the objects of keeping the country quiet, and in a state to enable us to assist efficaciously in its defence, if we should unfor-tunately be called upon to defend it. All the existing mischief has originated in our departure from the strict line above laid down; and the sooner we resume it the better.[7]

This reluctance to interfere too much in the internal affairs of Portugal led the Cabinet to decide to withdraw the British expeditionary force, a decision which was supported by Palmerston and the other Canningite ministers.[8] However, Frederick Lamb was unhappy that this diminished his already marginal influence. During March and April he had come to sympathise warmly with the Portuguese liberals, and assisted many to flee to England. He quarrelled with Wellington and on his return to England did much to influence British Whigs and liberals in condemning the government's policy.

The announcement of the British withdrawal was greeted with delight by the absolutists in Portugal, especially by the more extreme party which looked to Queen Carlotta Joaquina (mother of Pedro and Miguel) rather than to Miguel for guidance. On her birthday, 25 April, her supporters in the Portuguese senate passed an address imploring Miguel to take the title of king in his own right. This was treason, but rather than accept the offer or reject the proposal with indignation, Miguel prevaricated and urged his friends to have patience. Lamb, believing that affairs had reached their crisis, suspended the embarkation of the troops for a few days, and gained the support of all the diplomatic community in Lisbon in protesting against any usurpation of the crown which properly belonged to Maria. This was sufficient for the moment, although no one was left with much doubt that it was only a matter of time before Miguel took the throne.

The radicals in Oporto chose not to wait and on 18 May rose in revolt against Miguel's government, which was still the legitimate regency of the country. The rebels advanced as far as Coimbra, but found that they had little support from the population at large, and dared not press on to Lisbon. Miguel's government reacted slowly, for it distrusted the regular army, which was still strongly liberal in spirit. But on 25 June Miguel recaptured Coimbra – the same day that the new Cortes he had summoned offered him the crown. Again he hesitated but on 30 June he accepted the petition and declared himself the legitimate king, arguing that Pedro had forfeited his rights and those of his family when he chose Brazil over Portugal in 1822. Lamb and all the other diplomats in Lisbon, even the Spanish ambassador, announced that they refused to recognise the new regime and left the country, but this was overshadowed by the fall of Oporto a few days later. Palmella and the other leading liberals fled back to England almost as soon as they arrived, while some of their supporters went home and the rest marched north into Galicia, and from there made their way to England as well. The triumph of the absolutists appeared complete.[9]

In England the increasingly liberal press stridently supported the constitutionalist cause. For example, *The Times* described Miguel's seizure of the throne as 'the grossest perversion of public law . . . a usurpation which probably had never been matched in the history of civilized nations, for the baseness, ingratitude, and perfidy by which it is distinguished'. And, when the revolt appeared to be prospering, the *Morning Chronicle* hoped that when it succeeded the 'Intriguing Queen and her Son will, it is presumed, be at least expelled, if they escape the severer punishment which they deserve'. This commitment wavered briefly in the immediate wake of the fall of Oporto; *The Times* was impressed that no atrocities had been committed by the victorious absolutists, and felt that Miguel might be given *de facto* recognition as the ruler of Portugal if he would grant an amnesty to his enemies and restore their confiscated property.[10] This conciliatory stance did not last long. On his return from Oporto Palmella worked assiduously to influence the press and found it very receptive. Over the following months many articles appeared, often in the form of letters from Lisbon or Oporto. One example gives their flavour: 'As the public prints teem with the atrocities which have been hourly perpetrated ever since the usurpation, I shall merely say on this subject, that so far from being exaggerated, none of the accounts yet promulgated contain anything like an adequate picture of the cruelties to which all and every age and sex continue to be exposed from the infuriated bigots in power'. Commenting on this, *The Times*'s leader writer condemned the British government's conduct towards Portugal since the beginning of the year, while other writers did not hesitate to suggest that the withdrawal of the British expedition had facilitated Miguel's accession to power and persecution of his enemies, and to call for active intervention in favour of Pedro, his daughter and the liberals.[11]

The government did not share this sympathy for the Portuguese liberals, and Wellington was irritated at Palmella's 'newspapering'.[12] He did not believe that Britain had any right to intervene but looked for a negotiated settlement which would recognise both the reality of Miguel's success and Maria's claim to the throne. (There was an incongruity here: Miguel, the absolutist, effectively although not in theory, founded his claim to the throne on the popular will and the declaration of the Cortes; while Maria's liberal supporters had to emphasise the laws of dynastic succession and the recognition of foreign powers when arguing her case. Not surprisingly, British Whigs such as Lord Holland, who enthusiastically embraced Maria's cause, studiously ignored the parallel with the Glorious Revolution of 1688.) In August the British government sent Lord Strangford on a special mission to Brazil to stress to Pedro that Britain would not countenance any attempt to revive his claim to the throne or to reconquer Portugal in the name of his daughter. If Brazil did attack Portugal or her Atlantic dependencies it was possible that Miguel might appeal to Britain for aid, and if Britain failed to respond he might have more success with Spain or France. As Wellington stated with remarkable directness in a memorandum at this time: 'Our object must be, first, that Portugal should be independent of all; secondly, that she should be on good terms with her neighbour; because as long as she is so, she can be no burthen on us.'[13] This could best be achieved through national reconciliation establishing domestic peace and tranquillity, which in the view of the British government required the completion of the marriage between Miguel and Maria, with all acts to be in their joint names, and a general amnesty for all but the most prominent liberal exiles and the restoration of their property. But neither side was willing to accept such a reasonable compromise; the liberal exiles continued to plot ways of destabilising their country and reviving the civil war, while Miguel would not pardon his enemies, or marry his niece, as the price of international recognition.[14]

The Portuguese exiles proved a serious problem for Wellington and the British government. Individual refugees of any nation or description could claim asylum in Britain,[15] but following the defeat of the Oporto insurrection large numbers of rank and file soldiers found their way to Britain, where they were disarmed but remained in regular units under their officers. By late October Wellington was informed that there were at least 4,000 men collected near Plymouth and that they were being paid by Palmella from funds provided by Brazilian diplomats in London.[16] To Wellington's intense frustration the government was advised that it lacked the legal power either to disperse or expel these foreign troops.[17] Palmella responded to remonstrances with bland assurances, while continuing to recruit foreign soldiers from Germany and other parts of the Continent, and hiring transport ships. Finally this small private army sailed for the Azores where it was only prevented from landing on Terceira by a British warship, after a theatrical scene in which one man was killed. As intended, the incident caused a flurry of excitement in the press and liberal circles in London, and led to much further criticism of the government.

Public interest in Britain had already been much increased by the unexpected arrival of the nine-year-old Queen Maria at Falmouth on 24 September 1828. Her father, Pedro, had sent her to Europe to be educated in Vienna, at the court of her maternal grandfather the Emperor Francis, but her escort had diverted to London in the hope of giving the appearance of British support for the liberal cause in Portugal. Wellington was furious, telling Aberdeen: 'The arrival of this young Queen in England is the work of an intrigue, and is intended to give and will give us a good deal of trouble.'[18] But again there was little the government could do other than receive her with all due honours. The King held a party for her at Windsor and was reported to have been 'enchanted', while *The Mirror of Literature, Amusement and Instruction* assured its readers that she 'has not the slightest tinge of a tropical complexion; her hair is extremely light, her face pale, her eyes light blue and very sparkling'.[19] Even with such publicity the public at large probably cared little for Portugal, but it was a significant issue among the political class, and helped align the press more firmly with the Opposition and against the ministers.

Throughout the rest of 1829 and 1830 Britain continued to press Miguel to grant an amnesty to his opponents as the implicit cost of recognition. The idea of the marriage to Maria seems to have faded, possibly because the liberals had lost interest in compromise and because it had been excoriated in the British press. Palmella and his allies shifted their base to France and from thence to the Azores, where the local liberals had gained the upper hand and proclaimed a regency for Queen Maria. Nonetheless Miguel remained in firm control of mainland Portugal and by July 1830 he had been recognised by the governments of Spain, Russia and the United States, and by the papacy; while some other governments held back in deference to British wishes. In October 1830 Miguel appeared ready to grant the amnesty and Wellington had already decided to send Beresford to Lisbon as British ambassador, but before this could happen the British government fell, and the new ministry, with Grey at its head and Palmerston at the Foreign Office, adopted a much more hostile attitude.

The other issue which dominated British diplomacy during Wellington's government was the 'Eastern Question', and in particular the future of the Ottoman Empire. The victory of the British, French and Russian fleet at Navarino achieved little. The Turks did not press their justified anger into war, and although Count Lieven talked of the allies extending their operations and dictating peace 'under the walls of the Seraglio', this was a negotiating ploy not a serious proposal, and was easily brushed aside by Wellington.[20] In fact the Russian government had less interest in supporting the Greek Revolt than in establishing its own influence in Constantinople, and it recognised that the sympathy for the Greeks felt in Britain and France, and consequent hostility to Turkey, gave it a favourable opportunity.

In February 1828 Russia made peace with Persia, freeing troops and commanders for operations in the Balkans and Caucasus. War was declared two months later with the Russians pointing to the Turkish failure to implement fully the terms of the one-sided Treaty of Akkerman which they had imposed on the Turks in September 1826. It is possible that Nicholas thought that as in 1826 the Turks would give way to threats or come to terms after only token resistance, for neither his army nor public opinion had been properly prepared for a serious war.[21] Nesselrode, the Russian minister, and Nicholas were well aware of the alarm which their war would cause throughout Europe, and felt that they needed a quick victory and an early peace if they were to avoid the risk of Britain, France and Austria combining against them and forcing them to disgorge their conquests.

Wellington feared that however limited Russia's aims, any advance through the Balkans would trigger an irreversible collapse of Ottoman power. He explained this in a letter to the French foreign minister, the Comte de la Ferronays, at the end of February:

The invasion of the Turkish dominions in Europe and the occupation of Constantinople must not be viewed in the same light as other invasions and occupations which we have witnessed in our days.

In all these invasions and occupations the invaders were the enemies of the invaded, and every inhabitant of the invaded country considered each day's delay of the departure of the invaders as an injury to himself. The restoration of the power of the invaded government, and of order and regularity in the country, was not difficult after the departure of the invading troops . . .

But in the case of the invasion of the Turkish dominions, we may be assured that no declaration, no power of remonstrance, of influence, nor of action on the part of the Allies will prevent a general insurrection of all the different people subjected to the Turkish government in Europe . . .[22]

He had therefore done all he could to deter the Russians, but without success. When war came he looked to close co-operation with France, strict adherence to the provisions of the Treaty of London, and a pointed emphasis on admittedly vague Russian assurances that their aims were modest, as providing the best hope of preventing the war spreading. A few years earlier he might have endeavoured to work with Metternich, but the Austrian minister had exhausted his credit in St Petersburg and was regarded with aversion by British liberals, and some distrust even by Wellington and fellow Tories. Any obvious attempt at collaboration was likely to reduce support for the policy in Britain and France and give it less, not more, weight in St Petersburg. In this dance Metternich would be little more than a wallflower, even though Austria had more at stake than Britain, France or even Russia.[23]

The Russians occupied most of the Principalities (Moldavia and Wallachia, modern Romania) with ease, but then encountered serious resistance on and south of the Danube. An attempt to storm the important fortress of Braila on the great river failed on 15 June, and in the summer heat the Russian troops began to suffer from sickness and shortage of supplies. Dysentery ravaged the army, and the Emperor, who had taken the field with his men, found the reality of war much less glamorous and satisfying than the parade-ground exercises of which he was so fond. For more than four months, throughout the summer and early autumn, the Russian advance was checked by the Turkish defence of Braila, Shumla and Varna, while enthusiasm for the war in St Petersburg faded. Eventually, on 11 October, Varna fell, but by then it was too late to do much more that season, and any excitement the population of the Balkans may have felt at the prospect of throwing off Turkish rule had cooled. The Russians had done better in the Caucasus, where Kars had fallen on 5 July. On their side the Turks had suffered enormously and were facing immense difficulties collecting and supplying their forces; they saw little or no prospect of victory, but they

were not yet ready to give way, and they made no attempt to open peace negotiations, probably fearing that this would be seen by the Russians as a sign of
weakness.

Russia's war was very unpopular in Britain. Mrs Arbuthnot wrote in her
journal at the end of August: 'I think the aggression upon Turkey so shamefully
unjust & so contrary to the interests of England that I am desirous beyond
measure of hearing that the Russians are defeated. They are said to suffer very
much from the climate.' And the Duke of Rutland went further, telling Lady
Shelley: 'If they were to get a good thrashing, I believe the whole of this
Kingdom would be illuminated. There is a great feeling against the Russians.'
The caricatures support this, with almost all the prints being hostile to Russia,
while attitudes to the Ottomans vary more widely. Inevitably the theme of a
bear about to devour a turkey features repeatedly, with the best example being
The Nest in Danger by Heath, while *The Turkey at Bay* shows the bird with the
Sultan's head, scimitar in claws, boldly defying the Russian bear while the other
powers of Europe hover, waiting for their share of the carcass if the turkey is
slaughtered. Russia's unexpected discomfiture in the field is reflected in a
magnificently grotesque print in which the Turk's head fills one half of the plate
while the much smaller Emperor Nicholas, his trousers in tatters, flees, leaving
his coattails between his opponent's teeth. Only a few liberals, radical Whigs
and enthusiastic phil-hellenes were inclined to favour Russia in 1828.[24]

This public mood made life difficult for Princess Lieven and her husband
and encouraged them to draw closer to the liberals, the one section of British
society where they might receive a sympathetic hearing. Ever since her break
with Wellington in 1826 Princess Lieven had derided him in public and in
private while lauding Canning, her new best friend. She exulted when Canning
became prime minister, convinced that she had switched horses at just the right
moment and was perfectly placed not only to learn all the secrets of British
policy but to help shape it. Canning's death was a serious blow to her hopes,
and possibly a real grief as well, while Wellington's appointment as prime
minister was bitter, even humiliating. She made an effort to regain her place in
his esteem, but while he treated her with courtesy he would not discuss politics
or diplomacy with her, and where he could he avoided her company. Thwarted,
she set about cultivating some of the younger generation and was soon in
regular correspondence with Palmerston, although Lord Grey was the most
important, although not the best informed, of her contacts. She was openly
hostile to the government, especially after the resignation of the Canningites,
and in 1829 she encouraged the Duke of Cumberland and the other ultras in
their campaign. Wellington did not attribute this to personal malice or a belief
that the government was inherently hostile to Russia, but rather to its opposition to Russian expansion in the Balkans. 'The person to whom she looks is

Lord Grey! Why? Because Lord Grey entertains some old opposition opinions of Mr Fox's that the Turks ought to be driven out of Europe.'[25] Wellington informed Lord Heytesbury, the British ambassador to the Russian court, of the problem, but told him not to make any complaint, as this would be badly received in British society and transform the prevailing exasperation at the Lievens into sympathy. 'Besides that, to tell you the truth, I am perhaps vain enough to think that I am too strong for Prince and Princess Lieven, and that I prefer to suffer a little inconvenience to taking a step which might require from me some explanation.'[26]

Russia's attack on the Ottoman Empire caused considerable disquiet in France as well as Britain, although many Frenchmen were more concerned that France might miss out on her share of the plunder than with preserving the peace of Europe. A dozen years of peace had left France restless and ready for adventure. All parties subscribed to a more or less assertive nationalism, and there was a strong desire, especially but not only among the liberals, to conquer the left bank of the Rhine and even Belgium, and so regain France's 'natural' frontiers. There was also keen interest in the eastern Mediterranean, and Mehemet Ali's Egyptian army and navy were trained by many French (and some British) officers. Liberal sympathy for Greece was stronger than in Britain, and the itch for action stronger still. This led the French government in the middle of 1828 to propose sending a military force to southern Greece to compel the Egyptians to withdraw from the Peloponnese and so settle the long conflict. This would be a hard blow to the Turks, but even Metternich, their strongest champion, approved the proposal in the hope that it would then enable Britain and France to give effective diplomatic support to the Porte against Russia. Wellington evidently disliked the scheme, but after receiving emphatic assurances from Polignac that the troops would be quickly withdrawn he agreed to it, although the British government was not willing to see the French advance north of the Gulf of Corinth. According to Ellenborough: 'Our consent to the French going to the Morea has been received as a personal favour by the King of France. He thinks it of great importance to his Government, the feeling was so strong in the country and in the Chambers in favour of it.' That was reasonable, but he was probably too cynical when he added: 'Whatever may happen the French army will go to the Morea, not to save Greece, but to save the French Government.'[27]

By early September the French had 11,000 men in the Peloponnese and soon brought this up to 20,000 men. The Egyptian forces made no attempt to resist them, and good relations were maintained while the details of how to organise the repatriation of Ibrahim's men were agreed. Ibrahim went so far as to attend a French military review incognito, and then had a little too much to drink afterwards when, according to gossip, he 'became very entertaining. He asked whether some of the French regiments had not come from Spain, and on being told that the greatest part of the army had been in that country, he said the French were a curious people, to send the same army to establish slavery in Spain and liberty in the Morea.'[28] Less satisfactory was the failure of the French to restrain the Greeks, who took advantage of the paralysis of their opponents to push into territory previously untouched by the revolt, so that once again Western intervention was, in effect if not by design, extremely one-sided and partisan.

At the same time the British, French and Russian ministers formerly at Constantinople met on the island of Poros to discuss the terms of a settlement of the Greek revolt that should be put to the Turkish government. Wellington and Aberdeen made a mistake accepting this arrangement, for the British minister was Stratford Canning, cousin of the late Prime Minister, who openly favoured the Greeks, and was far more interested in giving advantages to their new state than in conciliating or preserving the Ottoman Empire.[29] As the French and Russian ministers were naturally even less sympathetic to the Turks the resulting agreement was decidedly unfair, requiring the Turks to surrender many parts of the country where they were in unchallenged control. On the other hand the proposal did not grant Greece full independence; it was to be autonomous, headed by a hereditary prince from a yet-to-be-determined European dynasty, but it was to pay an annual tribute to the Porte. Wellington strongly objected to the injustice of this scheme, which he thought was bound to prolong the struggle for the Turks would not accept it and could only be made to do so by force, which might lead to outright war between France and the Ottoman Empire, with Britain obliged to support France.[30] This led to further negotiations in London and a compromise agreement in the form of a protocol signed on 22 March 1829 which reduced Turkish losses but still included Attica, Euboea, and other parts of the country still in their hands. Months of talks had failed to produce an agreement which the Turks would accept and so open the door for the British minister to return to Constantinople.

As 1828 drew towards its close Wellington was despondent: 'It is quite clear to me, however, that the Turkish power in Europe will be annihilated in the next campaign if something cannot be done for their relief. They have no chance of retaking Varna.' If Metternich could induce the Turks to make concessions on Greece, Britain and France might bring pressure to bear on Russia to bring the war to a quick end on generous terms, but this was a forlorn hope. 'The truth is that the French have two or three objects in view, and they seek to attain each in its turn as it appears to suit the opinion of the *salons* at Paris. But the uppermost one in the mind of Monsieur de la Ferronays is to keep upon good terms with the Emperor Nicholas, and to seek the attainment of other objects only as they will be compatible with this one.'[31]

The Russian Emperor did not take the field with his army in 1829. On his return to St Petersburg in late 1828 he had set in train rigorous enquiries into the causes of the poor performance of the forces, and these had led to extensive changes in the senior command of the army and some reform in its logistical services. The new campaign opened in early May with Russian armies crossing the Danube under the energetic but unpopular General Diebitsch. They gained an important victory at Kulcheva on 11 June and Silistria fell soon after. Diebitsch then took his army south across the Balkan mountains and on 19 August Adrianople fell without resistance and the road to Constantinople seemed open. On 7 September leading Russian units reached the Aegean, while to the east their forces were marching on Trebizond on the southern shore of the Black Sea.[32]

The Turkish defeats and the Russian advance on Constantinople caused great alarm in London, Paris and Vienna. The Lievens openly exulted in the prospect of its fall, and told everyone that they should rely on the moderation and restraint of the Emperor, who would devise peace terms that would satisfy all reasonable concerns. Wellington told Aberdeen:

I confess that it makes me sick when I hear of the Emperor's desire for peace. If he desires peace, why does he not make it? Can the Turks resist him for a moment? He knows that they cannot. Why not state in conciliatory language his desire for peace, and reasonable terms to which the Porte can accede? This would give him peace tomorrow. He is looking to conquest; and by-the-bye, the plunder of Constantinople, if nothing else, would satisfy more than one starving claimant upon his bounty, besides what it would give to the public treasury.[33]

Aberdeen recognised that it was now too late for Britain to do anything to halt the Russian advance, and that it had probably never been possible given the position in which she had been placed – he did not add, though he might have, 'by the Treaty of London'. Expecting Constantinople to fall, he believed that 'a new epoch is about to arrive', and that the whole framework of British policy would need to be reconsidered, but he did not elaborate. Wellington was more forthcoming, writing on 11 September that if Constantinople fell the 'world must then be reconstructed' and that a satisfactory result would only be achieved through close co-operation between Britain and France. As for the shape of such a settlement, it was too soon to be certain, but he was inclined to think a strong new power should be made from the ruins of the Ottoman Empire, that it should control Constantinople, the Bosphorus, the Dardanelles and the mouths of the Danube, and that it should be independent of Russia. 'We must reconstruct a Greek empire, and give it Prince Frederick of Orange, or Prince Charles of Prussia; and no Power of Europe ought to take anything for himself excepting the Emperor of Russia a sum for his expenses.'[34]

However, the Russians did not take Constantinople, or even press their advance right to its walls. Senior figures in the Russian government were well aware of the dangers that would be unleashed if the Ottoman Empire collapsed, and with commendable self-restraint Nicholas listened to their advice and went without a triumph of immense symbolic importance. The growing unpopularity of the war inside Russia, and the fact that the military position was not quite as secure as it looked, may have made this choice easier, but they certainly did not compel it and they might even have been used as arguments in favour of pressing onward. Nicholas halted from a sense of enlightened self-interest; he could demand and gain everything he really wanted from a peace dictated at Adrianople, but if he took Constantinople the other powers of Europe would unite against him, forcing him to choose between a humiliating withdrawal and the risk of a general European war, while the fall of the Ottoman capital would surely unleash chaos throughout the Balkans and perhaps beyond.

The terms which the Russians imposed were by no means moderate, although they can appear so in comparison with the complete destruction which was the implicit alternative. Notwithstanding the Emperor Nicholas's personal assurance to Wellington in 1826 that he would not take one village of Turkish territory, Russia demanded strategically significant slices of territory south of the Caucasus and around the mouths of the Danube. More humiliating and dangerous to the authority of the Sublime Porte, Russian vessels were to be granted unhindered passage through the Bosphorus and Dardanelles, under the very walls of Constantinople, and Russian merchants were given a special privileged position throughout the Ottoman Empire. The government of the Principalities was recast on lines dictated by the Russians, and Turkish authority over them became little more than a fiction. Serbia, which also enjoyed a special status only a little below independence, was enlarged, and finally, a massive indemnity was imposed which would keep the Turkish government in hock to the Russians for years and cripple any attempt to rebuild and modernise their army.[35]

Both Wellington and Metternich regarded the treaty as a disaster, reducing the Ottoman Empire to little more than a puppet state in thrall to Russia, and Wellington even went so far as to say that it would have been better if Constantinople had fallen.[36] That was clearly an exaggeration and in the event the ramshackle, rickety Turkish Empire showed an unexpected capacity for survival and regeneration – a capacity helped by a reduction in the indemnity which Nicholas granted in an effort to soften the hostility which had greeted the terms of the peace in the rest of Europe.

This still left Greece unsettled. The Russians had forced the Turks to accept the London protocol of 22 March 1829, but there was growing support – even in Vienna – for a slightly larger and fully independent country which might be more stable and less dependent on foreign (that is, Russian) support. There was also a sovereign to be chosen; at one point all parties agreed on Leopold of Saxe-Coburg, the widower of Princess Charlotte, but after enquiring into the state of the country he wisely declined the offer. The Greek revolt did not bring happiness to its people. The country was even poorer, more lawless and beset by banditry and violence than under Turkish rule. Capodistria attempted to impose a modern central government but failed, and was murdered in October 1831, which unleashed a civil war. Eventually in February 1832 Britain, France and Russia agreed on the seventeen-year-old Prince Otto of Bavaria as the King of Greece (although his Catholicism at once alienated him from almost all his new subjects), and the presence of a few thousand Bavarian troops permitted the last contingent of the French force to go home. In July 1832 the Sultan recognised the new country, although Greece continued to take every opportunity to attempt to gain more territory from its neighbour until the disaster of 1919–22.

The British government's handling of the Eastern Question won few plaudits at the time; even Wellington made many comments which suggested that he was unhappy with the way events were unfolding, and although he justified the government's conduct in Parliament his tone was defensive, not triumphant.[37] Lord Ellenborough went further, writing in his diary that 'our foreign policy has certainly been most unsuccessful. We have succeeded in nothing . . .' (although that was written in August 1829 when the Russians appeared to be about to take Constantinople, and is further coloured by Ellenborough's jealousy of Aberdeen). Liberals were vehement in their criticism, treating Canning's Treaty of London with unwarranted reverence, and bestowing on the Greek cause much retrospective enthusiasm. For example, Palmerston wrote to his friend Laurence Sulivan in October 1829:

So at last peace is made between Russia & Turkey and upon Russia's own terms; I hope & trust that Greece will now be placed upon a proper footing and our Govt will find that they have failed at both their objects, having succeeded neither in preventing the establishment of Greece, nor in protecting the Sultan from the arms of Russia. We shall therefore have lost our influence both with the free, & the despot. This is the fate of those who are unable to pursue a straight course, because their inclination leading one way, & necessity driving the other they are forced into the diagonal.[38]

This outlook influenced many later accounts of British foreign policy, especially those written in the early decades of the twentieth century which took for granted a liberal perspective and priorities. There is a useful correction to this view in Paul Schroeder's magisterial history of international politics in Europe, which is all the more convincing, as he is in general no great admirer of British policy. Schroeder argues that while Russia clearly won the contest, nothing she gained was worth the costs and risks of the war and the antagonism it aroused in the rest of Europe. Metternich was an acute observer of events but unable to influence them, while the French did little more than bolster their prestige and self-esteem. Schroeder argues that the greatest share of the credit for Europe avoiding disaster in 1828–30 rests with Wellington and Aberdeen:

> Nothing is easier than to criticize them for lacking the energy and decisiveness of Canning and Palmerston . . . Yet to read their correspondence is to recognize that they understood what needed doing, namely, making the best of the bad situation they had inherited, sticking with France, holding back Russia, not falling in with Metternich's schemes, fulfilling Britain's treaty obligations so that others had no excuse to break theirs, and thereby saving both peace and the system. They understood and practiced the art of damage control, the use of pacts of restraint, and the wisdom of accepting the inevitable and muddling through.[39]

The Eastern Question and the troubles in Portugal dominated British foreign policy during Wellington's government, but Wellington and Aberdeen also faced a number of less significant problems. The wonderful new countries of Latin America, which Canning had been so eager to recognise, proved unstable and quarrelsome. There was civil war in Chile (where the liberals refused to accept the election of a conservative vice-president), and war between Peru and Colombia (where Bolívar declared himself dictator after the constitutional assembly refused to accept his proposals). The United Provinces of the River Plate (Argentina) were so far from united that Britain sometimes could not tell who constituted the legitimate government. This was in the wake of a war between Brazil and Argentina which destabilised both countries, as well as seriously disrupting British trade and encouraging the rise of piracy in their waters. And talk of renewed war between Spain and Mexico raised the spectre of an attack on Cuba, either by Mexico or the United States, which would threaten the stability of Britain's colonies in the West Indies.[40]

Wellington and Aberdeen successfully avoided becoming entangled in these disputes, while preserving British interests. They firmly discouraged any attack on Cuba from Mexico or Colombia, and conversely Wellington 'repeatedly urged the Spanish government . . . not to think of making war upon Mexico, or any of its ancient dominions on the continent of South America'. Nonetheless a small Spanish expedition landed in Mexico in July 1829, but achieved nothing and was soon forced to surrender. Fortunately this failure did not lead to a retaliatory attack on Cuba and the island remained in Spanish hands – a result which Wellington described as 'a material object to us'. British pressure and restraint was also useful in deterring French, American or even Russian intervention in the region.[41]

Relations with the United States generally improved in these years, although an attempt to resolve the long-running dispute over the precise border between Maine and British North America proved unsuccessful. Here, as in Europe, Wellington was eager to smooth feathers ruffled by Canning's pugnacity and want of tact, and felt that Britain had more to lose than to gain by international tension and disputes. Even when a dispute could not be avoided, as with a threat to exclude British shipping from the Rhine and impose prohibitive tariffs on some of her leading exports to the Netherlands and north Germany, Wellington's instinct was to argue Britain's case forcefully but quietly, behind the scenes, rather than through the newspapers. The results vindicated his preference, but did nothing to impress the public.[42]

A far more serious problem, both for the stability of Europe and the public perception of Wellington's government, arose from developments inside France. Despite a very restricted franchise and blatant official manipulation, the *libérales* had made great gains in the elections of 1827. Villèle's government resigned, but a moderate ministry under Martignac only gave the *libérales* greater confidence. Wellington was alarmed, telling Aberdeen: 'The meaning of liberality in France is war; with England, if war cannot be obtained without war with England; but war and bullying and boasting are essential. It is lamentable to see a country in such a state.' Even Palmerston, a far more sympathetic observer, concluded on a visit Paris in the winter of 1828–29 that:

> The tendency of a more liberal government would be less friendly to England. There are many motives which point to war; a strong desire to regain the country on the north east between France & the Rhine; a great hankering after Savoy & Piedmont & the Milanese; a wonderful itching for promotion in the army, who all declare that three years more of peace will superannuate every rank & put them *hors de combat* as a military nation.[43]

In August 1829 Charles X accepted the resignation of the Martignac ministry and formed a new government in which the Prince de Polignac, the French ambassador in London, was the dominant figure. French opinion interpreted this, correctly, as a sharp shift to the right; but also believed, incorrectly, that Wellington was in some way behind the appointment, and this view spread back to Britain. Wellington had worked well with Polignac, and thought that he was a man of more ability and with a better understanding of British policy than his predecessors, but he did not believe that he would be able to manage the *libérales* in the Chambers.[44]

The appointment of Polignac heightened political tensions in France, and produced a feverish atmosphere of rumour and speculation. The *libérales* proved very effective at managing the press and mobilising opinion, mounting a campaign claiming that Polignac would inaugurate a counter-revolution similar to the reaction in Spain. Many British liberals were caught up in the excitement, identifying strongly with their French counterparts, blaming Wellington for Polignac's appointment, and giving a ready ear to wild talk of international conspiracies against liberty. Palmerston wrote home that soon after Polignac took office he approached the other great powers to see if they would support the abolition of the constitution. 'England & Austria of course were delighted with the idea', but the Emperor Nicholas refused to consent as the constitution had been established under the auspices of his brother Alexander! And this was reported not as a joke or an example of the folly of the moment, but in all earnest.[45]

The French Parliament met at the beginning of March 1830 and a motion of no confidence was soon passed in the ministry, with 221 *libérales* voting for it. Charles X refused to dismiss Polignac and instead dissolved Parliament, proclaiming his support for the constitution and calling for fresh elections in late June and early July. The already excited atmosphere became even more heightened, with the press filled by provocative stories and rumours. In an attempt to gain popularity, and perhaps also to reduce the risk of the army leading a liberal revolution, the French government despatched an expedition to attack Algiers. Foreign governments were reassured that 'our aim is humanitarian. We are seeking, in addition to satisfaction for our own grievances, the abolition of the enslavement of Christians, the destruction of piracy, and the end of humiliating tributes that the European states are having to pay . . .' An army of 37,000 men in 350 transports, escorted by more than a hundred warships, was collected with remarkable speed and efficiency. The troops began landing a few miles west of Algiers on 14 June, and on 5 July the French flag was flying above the forts of the city, and by the end of the month it was clear that the French were there to stay.[46]

Wellington strongly disapproved of the expedition. He had warned against it as early as January 1830, and told Aberdeen in April: 'Prince de Polignac seems to have made a strange mistake in thinking that we can allow France to seek safety from domestic troubles in foreign conquests, even on the coast of Africa. Neither Bonaparte nor the Directory behaved worse than the French government have in this case.' He repeated this view as late as 1848, telling George William Chad: 'The taking of Algiers was a most unprincipled act, Napoleon never did anything so bad. He made Wars of aggression and ambition, but He never did anything so bad as Algiers. It was all done for the sake of producing effect at home.' At a time when it was facing a political crisis at home, the government of Charles X had thoroughly alienated one of its closest allies.[47]

Wellington's foreign policy was essentially defensive. He endeavoured to preserve rather than expand British territory and influence, and to accommodate the interests of the other powers rather than compete with them. His aim, above all, was to keep Britain at peace and preserve the post-war settlement. This had the disadvantage of making his policy often appear passive, reacting to events rather than shaping them. It was also sometimes unsuccessful, for British influence was limited. Wellington could put pressure on Miguel to grant an amnesty to his opponents, but could not compel him to do so; he could warn Russia of the risks of an aggressive war in the Balkans, but not prevent it; and he could not even stop the French launching their attack on Algiers. Against these failures are set the success of managing problems created by others, containing the damage and risks of wider conflict, and maintaining the importance of abiding by treaties. They were dull, prosaic virtues but they helped gain the trust and confidence of the other powers, reducing the level of international tension and aiding co-operation when it was most needed. By late 1830 London had replaced Vienna and Paris as the centre of diplomatic negotiations.[48]

But whatever its virtues, Wellington's foreign policy did nothing to strengthen the government at home, instead encouraging liberal criticism both in Parliament and in the press. It was too easy to argue that the ministry favoured the tyrannical Dom Miguel rather than the innocent child-queen Maria II; that it supported the despotic Turks rather than the enlightened Greeks who had given the world the idea of freedom; and that it was behind the appointment of Polignac in France, who was intent on abolishing the Charte and restoring absolutist rule. Canning had taught the public to view foreign affairs through a crude ideological lens – virtuous liberals and villainous reactionaries – and Wellington, like Castlereagh before him, lacked the flair, and perhaps the desire, to interest them in a more complex and realistic story.

CHAPTER TWENTY

DOMESTIC DIFFICULTIES
(May 1829–July 1830)

THE CATHOLIC QUESTION absorbed the attention of Parliament in the session of 1829 almost to the exclusion of anything else. After it was passed Lord Holland attempted to mount an attack on the government's foreign policy, but received little support; Whigs and liberals were still well disposed towards an administration that had finally passed their favourite measure, while no one had much energy left so late in the session. This preoccupation also meant that there was little debate over Peel's abolition of the old, inefficient parish watchmen in London, and their replacement by the new Metropolitan Police. This was delicate ground for Wellington's government, which critics often accused of being a military dictatorship, but Peel had carefully prepared the way with a parliamentary committee in 1828, and there was no opposition in Parliament, with Lords Holland and Durham and the radical Joseph Hume all giving the scheme their support. Most of the press took a similar line, with the *Morning Chronicle, The Times* and even the *Examiner* giving it their blessing, while the caricaturists concentrated on the demise of the much-ridiculed watchmen, and their prints were either purely comic or approving. In fact the only significant opposition came from the High Tories, with Sir Richard Vyvyan citing it as evidence of Wellington's 'unmeasured ambition' and his desire 'to make all Europe a military camp & to govern upon arbitrary principles'.[1] High Tory papers like the *Standard* did not scruple to link the establishment of the Metropolitan Police to Catholic Emancipation, and suggest that it was part of a wider plot to undermine the liberties of freeborn Protestant Englishmen by introducing a political gendarmerie such as that employed in Catholic France and Austria. These arguments gained some support from ordinary Londoners, and the new police force was very unpopular at first, especially with the small shopkeepers and other rate-payers who had to pay for it. Throughout 1830 parishes across London met and angrily petitioned against the police force, condemning it as an encroachment on popular rights, unresponsive to householders and an intolerable financial burden. It was a grievance which both contributed to the revival of popular radicalism which suddenly emerged in 1830, and benefitted from it; and the government's failure to respond, by covering part of the cost of the police from the Treasury or in any other way, added considerably to its unpopularity. Nonetheless, in any but a narrowly political sense, the Metropolitan Police was a great success. It is striking proof of Peel's energy and administrative mastery that it took less than six months from the introduction of the legislation into the Commons to the launch of the police on 29 September 1829. He was delighted with the result, telling his wife 'the men look very smart, and a strong contrast to the old watchmen', and Wellington agreed, writing to Peel on 3 November: 'I congratulate you upon the entire success of the Police in London. It is impossible to see anything more respectable than they are.'[2]

The opposition of the ultras to the police was just one symptom of their vehement hostility to the government. Although never a particularly large group (most estimates suggest that they had around thirty MPs in the Commons), nor containing anyone of recognised ability (except for the aged Lord Eldon), they had disproportionate significance because of Cumberland's influence on the King. They had no agreed programme but many, including Vyvyan, objected to the government's policies on the Corn Laws, free trade, the currency, and even its foreign policy, as well as Catholic Emancipation. Not all despaired of Wellington although few could bring themselves to forgive Peel, whose one great merit in their eyes had been his support for the Protestant constitution. Others, like the Duke of Newcastle, were intensely hostile to Wellington, but felt that active opposition was futile – the battle for the constitution had been lost – and that whatever he hinted, the King would never dare to move against Wellington.[3]

A much larger number of Tories were unhappy with the government, disillusioned with Wellington and Peel, but not ready to oppose the ministry when they could see no better alternative. Many of these drifted back towards their natural place supporting the government as the months passed, but their support was much less enthusiastic and reliable than in the past; they might not vote against the ministers, but they could not be relied upon to vote with them on unpopular measures, or to attend regularly when the routine business of government was before the House. They were also far more likely to be swayed by criticism of the government coming from the ultra Tories, with whom they had much common ground, than by liberal or radical arguments; and it was this which made the ultra-Tory opposition such a worry for the ministers.

The Duke of Cumberland did everything in his power to inflame and perpetuate the divisions and discontent among the Tories, and to encourage the belief that the King was hostile to the government. At dinner one night in June

1829 he was reported to have told Sir Henry Cooke that 'the D. of Wellington had succeeded for the present but that he wd. never forgive him, that he wd. watch him narrowly, that the King hates him as he hates poison for that he coerces the King & is his master, which no King can bear, that he shd *catch him tripping* some day soon & he might depend upon it he wd take advantage of it and have him turned out'.[4] This was typical, and Wellington was well aware of the damage such talk did to the government: 'The King's Minister proposes a thing, & the King's favourite brother, fresh from the King's ear, advises that the proposal shd be rejected. This cannot go on. Nobody will support the Govt. in the House of Commons because they think the King is opposed to them.' Wellington tried to remonstrate with the King, asking him at least to avoid appearing to support Cumberland, and received ample assurances, but these soon proved worthless.[5]

Throughout the autumn Sir Richard Vyvyan was busy seeking allies in the Commons so that Cumberland could present the King with a plausible alternative ministry. Early in October he approached Palmerston suggesting that he might like to lead the Commons in such an administration, in which Lord Mansfield might be prime minister and Brougham Lord Chancellor. (It is an interesting reflection on the confused state of the parties, the dearth of talent amongst the High Tories, and the reputation that Brougham had, possibly unfairly, acquired for being unprincipled and self-serving, that this unlikely combination seemed even half-plausible.) Palmerston rejected the overture, which he regarded as both hopeless and unappealing; he believed that the government was gaining strength and that 'the Duke has a great hold upon public feelings; *no* other individual perhaps now living has as great a one'. It was a striking acknowledgement from a politician who had no fondness for Wellington. Despite this setback Vyvyan remained confident, and urged Cumberland to persuade the King to dismiss the government before Parliament met.[6] But Cumberland's influence had never extended that far, and while the King enjoyed complaining about Wellington, and may have deliberately encouraged the High Tories in order to lessen the Prime Minister's dominance, he had no intention of replacing a stable and effective government with the forlorn hope of the ultras.

Cumberland also encouraged and supported the leading ultra newspapers, the *Standard* and the *Morning Journal*, in their virulent attacks on the government. Accusations ranged from the highly specific claim that the Solicitor-General, Edward Sugden, had been appointed by the Lord Chancellor in exchange for a loan of £30,000, to more general slurs: 'As for our revered Sovereign . . . we pity him. He is the worst-used man in his extensive dominions, and in his ripe old age is openly defied, derided, held in chains.' Wellington was personally attacked in an open letter which, it emerged, was written by

Cumberland's private chaplain: 'The Most Noble Arthur D. of Wellington is proud, overbearing, grasping, dishonest & unprincipled, & capable of a design to overturn the Crown and prostrate the laws & liberties of the Country.' He was also accused of 'despicable cant', gross treachery, affected moderation, or 'treachery, cowardice and artifice united'. The government responded by prosecuting the *Morning Journal* and secured a conviction, but this did more harm than good, alienating all the liberal press while adding to the disaffection of the ultras.[7]

Wellington's concern with the attacks on him and the government in the High Tory press was heightened by the ministry's lack of a reliable voice of its own. The *Courier,* which for years had been heavily influenced by the Treasury and frequently used by ministers to refute accusations and contradict false stories, had been losing prestige for some time, and had become a laughing stock after it executed a series of somersaults in order to back whoever was in power at the moment during the upheavals of 1827–28. The government still employed it, but its support was virtually worthless. Far more important was the ministry's subterranean link to *The Times*. Great care was taken on both sides to keep this secret, for the growing reputation of *The Times* depended on the idea of its independence. Digby Wrangham, Aberdeen's private secretary at the Foreign Office, was employed as the conduit by which information and hints for stories were conveyed to the editor, the famous Thomas Barnes. *The Times* gave no pledge of loyalty in return, and could still be savagely critical of the government on particular issues (as it was over the prosecution of the *Morning Journal*), but it remained broadly supportive of the government until its final defeat.[8] That was helpful as far as it went, but ministers naturally wanted a paper that they could rely on to put their case even when it was unpopular. This led to the idea that they buy a struggling newspaper and revitalise it, but this foundered when the ministers were unable to find anyone of sufficient standing and ability willing to act as editor. Wellington had already admitted to Croker: 'I hate meddling with the Press. . . . But I am afraid that we do meddle, that is to say, the Secretary of the Treasury [Joseph Planta] does; but he does not attend to it; nor does he meddle with that degree of intelligence which might be expected from him.' The government's handling of the press did not improve and it continued to be caught between the virulence of the High Tory papers and the growing liberalism of the rest of the press.[9]

Politics in the second half of 1829 were in a curious state: the only determined opposition came from the ultras; the Whigs and liberals were fragmented, leaderless, and not ill disposed towards the government. One group of Whigs, clustered around Lord Althorp, expressed friendly neutrality and hinted broadly at a desire to join the government in return for places including a seat or two in Cabinet. Lord Lansdowne had been discredited by his coalition with Canning in 1827, but was widely assumed to be open to offers. Lord Grey remained an enigmatic, aloof figure, bitter towards those whom he blamed for the break-up of the Whig party and expressing an inclination to give the ministers credit for Catholic Emancipation, but with the potential to unite the Opposition and mount a serious challenge to the government. Huskisson, Palmerston and the other Canningites were neither trusted nor liked by any branch of the Whigs, who assumed that they were unreliable allies who would leap at any chance to return to office. Brougham aroused even more distrust, but as Peel's only serious rival in the Commons he could not be ignored; it was generally suspected that he was tired of his years in the wilderness and was more than ready to listen to any overture, even if it meant joining a Conservative government. Not even the ultras were completely irreconcilable; Cumberland may have dreamt of driving Wellington from office in ignominy and disgrace, but in cooler moments he knew that his best chance was to force Wellington to reconstruct his government and gain the support of the High Tories in exchange for seats in Cabinet and assurances on future policy.[10]

But if the Opposition was fragmented and irresolute, the government's strength had been undermined by the split in the Tory Party, the disaffection of many traditional supporters, and the poor performance of the front bench, except Peel, in the Commons. The obvious solution appeared to be a junction with one of the other groups, but Wellington demurred, saying 'he knew from experience what it was to make a junction & have a faction in the Cabinet & he wd sooner go out than do it again'.[11] Moreover, the advantages of the idea tended to evaporate on closer scrutiny. There was too much ill feeling between Wellington and Cumberland for a coalition with the ultras to be easy, while it would inevitably make the government appear reactionary, and so encourage all the other groups to unite against it. A reunion with the Canningites would be seen as rather too expedient, while their poor performance in 1828 suggested that they would do little to strengthen the government in the Commons and would be a source of discord in the Cabinet. The King was implacably hostile to Lord Grey and proposing a junction with him would inevitably mean more furious arguments and recriminations, and might possibly drive the infuriated monarch into the arms of the High Tories. In any case Wellington did not want Grey in his Cabinet; they had sat together on the coal committee and the Prime Minister had concluded that Grey 'is a very violent, arrogant & a very obstinate man ... he wd be a very disagreeable person to do public business with'.[12] Althorp's Whigs presented fewer obvious objections, but it was not clear that they had much to offer the government in either talent or numbers, while their inclusion would certainly alienate many wavering Tories and inflame the ultras. This was true of any coalition; it would gain the support of one group, but at the cost of disappointing all the others and encouraging them off the fence and into open opposition.

Wellington preferred not to seek a coalition, but to offer places to individuals from every faction as vacancies occurred. This had the advantage of showing that no one need despair of office, while the appearance of magnanimity and seeking out the best man for the job, regardless of party, might appeal to moderates of all colours. The first evidence of this policy came at the beginning of June 1829 when Wellington offered Grey's friend Lord Rosslyn the vacant Privy Seal. Rosslyn, who had declined office in 1828, now accepted and joined the Cabinet with Grey's half-hearted approval. At the same time Sir James Scarlett, a talented Whig lawyer who had held office under Canning, became Attorney General. Favouring two Whigs risked offending the Tories, but they were consoled by the appointment of Lord Edward Somerset and Colonel Trench to junior places at the Ordnance. A month later the young Lord Castlereagh was made a junior Lord of the Admiralty, at least in part in an effort to placate his father, Lord Londonderry, who had been loudly expressing his discontent with the government and in particular its failure to offer him an appointment commensurate with his vanity.[13] Further approaches were made during the autumn and winter including to Sir Edward Knatchbull and Lord Chandos the heir to the Duke of Buckingham, two leading ultras. These both declined, but two moderate Whigs and a young Canningite took office.[14]

None of these appointments did much to strengthen the government in the Commons, either by improving its performance in debate or by bringing even small blocks of votes. Indeed they probably did more to unsettle and disturb Tory waverers than they achieved in conciliating moderate Whigs and liberals. Mrs Arbuthnot had a heated argument with Wellington on the subject in late January 1830:

> The Duke considers that . . . in filling offices he ought to consider only who will best do the King's business. This *sounds* like a very grand sentiment; but the truth is, anybody can do the business of a Lord of the Treasury, & the *King's business* is, in fact, for his Minister to provide him with a *strong Govt.*
>
> . . . The Duke was furious because I told him he ought to consider his friends, tho' he agreed that I was right when I said that he never wd have a strong Govt. till there was a strong, decided Opposition. He never can have a *thick & thin* support while he goes about coquetting with all parties; he don't gain his enemies & he offends those who are well disposed to him. His theory might do very well if we were a nation of angels, but in this country we like party spirit & party violence & people will not support a Minister, however excellent, if they are to gain nothing by it. I hope, however, this session will give us the decided Opposition I wish so much for.[15]

It is unlikely that Wellington shared this hope, for it is evident that having concluded that it was impossible to construct a strong, harmonious government by coalescing with any one of the other parties and factions, he looked to keep them divided and to prevent them from combining in outright opposition to the government.

Wellington was determined to maintain the government on its chosen ground of moderate conservatism – not as liberal as the Canningites or Whigs, and not as conservative as Cumberland and the ultras. It was an uncomfortably narrow portion of the political spectrum on which to make a stand, but given the state of parties and opinion in 1829–30 it was almost certainly impossible to reconstruct the broad Tory Party which Liverpool had led. As a consequence the government was vulnerable in the Commons, having lost its liberal Canningite wing in 1828 and the High Tories in 1829. It relied heavily, much too heavily, on Peel to present its case and answer its critics. Peel was a great orator and by far the best debater in the Commons, invariably well prepared with ample information and equally capable both of rising to grand occasions and cooling the overheated atmosphere with calm good sense. When he was away attending his dying father in May 1830 Croker commented that he was 'leaving us not only without a general to lead us, but even without one fighting man; for he is himself *our host*'.[16] Far too often the rest of the government's front bench sat mute and relied entirely on Peel to carry the debate for them. Peel naturally complained of the burden and pressed Wellington to give office to ministers who would take a more active part, but Wellington suspected that much of the blame rested on Peel's leadership in the Commons. Peel did not confide in his colleagues or inform them of his intentions, and if, in their ignorance, they mistook the line he intended to pursue he abandoned them to the mercy of the Opposition. As a result they were naturally reluctant to speak, and lost confidence. Nor did Peel do much to warm the hearts of his supporters. Even his good friend Vesey Fitzgerald complained of his 'coldness and bad management', while Mrs Arbuthnot noted that he 'asks immense parties of the H. of Commons to dinner every week & treats them so *de haut en bas* & is so haughty & silent that they come away swearing they will never go to his house again, so that his civilities do him harm rather than good'.[17]

But if there was little point in recruiting talented speakers in the Commons only for them to fall mute under Peel's leadership, there were other changes which could have been made to strengthen the ministry. Sir George Murray had proved a great disappointment, not just in the Commons where he spoke little, but also at the Colonial Office, where he appeared inattentive to his duties and failed to control his officials, notably James Stephens, who was intent on pursuing a policy, especially on the slave question, quite independent of the views of the Cabinet.[18] If Murray was a failure, Vesey Fitzgerald was a cross to be borne. Wellington told Mrs Arbuthnot that he was 'an ill tempered ill conditioned blackguard with whom it is quite disagreeable . . . to be in society'; while according to the Whig Lord Althorp, although Fitzgerald was 'sharp and clever' he 'offended everybody by his ill-temper, his violence & vulgarity'.[19] It was therefore no great loss to the government when illness forced him to resign as president of the Board of Trade at the beginning of 1830, but rather than use the opportunity to make an extensive reshuffle, or at least gain a significant new recruit, Wellington simply shifted Herries to fill the vacancy. This reassured Conservatives, for whom Herries represented an alternative to the free trade policies championed by Huskisson and supported by Peel, but it did nothing to strengthen the government, and when put to the test in debate Herries failed miserably.[20]

The weakness of some ministers and the inexperience of others encouraged Wellington to take a close interest in the detail of their departments. Few of his colleagues objected to this interference, while some actively welcomed it. Lord Dudley, Wellington's first foreign secretary, told a friend that the Prime Minister:

is really a most extraordinary man. His share of trouble and of glory in this life had already been pretty large, but he goes to work just as if he had his fortune and his reputation still to make, just as if there had been no India, no Spain, no Waterloo. His industry is incessant, his attention never slumbers. If you send him a long paper, he returns it the next day with detailed observations, numbered and with proper observations, indicative in every line of the most careful examination of the whole subject. He has nobody to help him. It is all in his own hand, and it is impossible to mistake the peculiarities of his style.[21]

Lyndhurst, the Lord Chancellor, described Wellington as 'a good man to do business with, quick and intelligent', while in February 1829 the rather unsympathetic Greville discussed the Prime Minister with Vesey Fitzgerald, who 'went off in a panegyric on the Duke, and said that seeing him as he did for several hours every day, he had opportunities of finding out what an extraordinary man he was, and that it was remarkable what complete ascendency he had acquired over all who were about him'.[22]

The disadvantage of this attention to detail was that it imposed an enormous workload on Wellington. In September 1829 he complained to Mrs Arbuthnot that he 'shd be killed by it, for he was obliged to think of everything, that the persons in office had no experience &, if he did not attend in this manner, he found they got into difficulties which it was afterwards still more difficult to get them out of'. Later that month Mrs Arbuthnot worried whether the pressure of public business was affecting his temper, 'for he certainly is sometimes *very cross*'. He had just sharply snubbed her for criticising his policy towards Russia and Turkey, and while years of close friendship and a thick skin enabled her to shrug it off with a grimace, she worried that such outbursts would 'prevent people in general from speaking the truth to him'.[23] A few months later they had another altercation when Wellington was furious with Aberdeen's handling of the negotiations over Greece and Mrs Arbuthnot responded: 'Right or wrong, Lord Aberdeen was the Secy. of State & had a right to have his own opinion; he was not a clerk to do the Duke's bidding . . . He was in a great fury and I was sorry, because he is not naturally violent in matters of business &, talking in that manner of Ld Aberdeen, was shewing the dictatorial & arbitrary spirit that his enemies accuse him of having. He had been at the Coal Committee all the morning &, I suppose, he was fretted & worn with business'.[24] It is significant that Mrs Arbuthnot, who had seen so much of Wellington over the previous decade, was surprised and shocked at his irritability. He may have been harsh to his staff in the Peninsula at times, but from then until the late 1820s he seems to have been much more mellow. Presumably it was a combination of the strain of office and the tensions created by the break with the High Tories and the alienation of the King which led to the deterioration of his temper.

He was also becoming increasingly disillusioned and tired of office. As early as June 1829 he told Mrs Arbuthnot that 'he shd quite rejoice in a fit of illness that enabled him to resign honourably'. In November, after a 'very distressing' scene with the King, he complained to Knighton that 'if I had known in January 1828 one tithe of what I do now, and of what I discovered in one month after I was in office, I should never have been the King's minister, and should have avoided loads of misery!'[25] While in mid-December Mrs Arbuthnot noted: 'The object first in his view is always resigning his office, & he has certainly had great provocation. He works like a dray horse, he cannot gain by it for he is as great as he can ever be, he has no comfort in life & he says the consequence of his being Minister is that everybody quarrels with him.' She was not entirely sympathetic:

> . . . in point of fact the Duke gets everything his own way at last, but it is in a disagreeable way for he has to fight the King upon every point & is treated in a scurvy sort of way by him, and the Duke is a sort of spoiled child. He wishes to be liked by everybody; he is by nine-tenths, but the opposition of the *one* tenth irritates him.[26]

It was not that Wellington objected to criticism – he was remarkably magnanimous in his personal relations with the Opposition – but he was hurt when it came from his own side of the political fence, especially attacks from the King, the royal family and the great landowners, whose interests he believed he was protecting.

The government's political difficulties were greatly compounded by a sharp and unforeseen economic depression which began in the summer of 1829. By the end of the year most manufacturing industries were beginning to recover, although unemployment lingered and the winter brought real hardship to many. Agriculture had been in a bad way for longer, and while the picture was inevitably patchy, it would continue to be depressed throughout 1830, with another poor harvest adding to the misery. These conditions contributed significantly to the sudden revival of radicalism in 1830, and to the Captain Swing riots which expressed agrarian discontent across southern England from the middle of the year. Throughout the autumn and winter of 1829–30 there was much gloomy talk, especially among farmers and landowners, who were suffering from falling rents, and a vocal campaign was launched in the *British Farmer's Magazine* and elsewhere against the 1828 Corn Law and calling for the re-introduction of £1 notes in order to inflate the economy. Although scorned by liberal opinion, such as that expressed in *The Times*, these arguments carried considerable weight with many Tory country gentlemen, and were taken up with alacrity by the ultras.[27]

When Parliament met in February 1830 the King's Speech included the accurate statement that there was distress 'in some parts of the United Kingdom'. Lord Stanhope moved an amendment to the address in the Lords criticising the liberal economic policies pursued by successive governments ever since 1819, hinting at the need for diluting the currency and so increasing prices, and declaring that 'there was unusual distress, universal in its extent, unprecedented in its degree, intolerable in its pressure'. He was supported by Lord Carnarvon, who argued that the government had made a mistake in adopting the gold standard when silver was so much more abundant. Wellington poured cold water on such eccentricity in an excellent speech and carried the address 71 to 9.[28] Even on an issue such as this, where some trouble might have been expected in the Lords, the government's position was quite secure. Wellington's performance in the chamber helped maintain this ascendancy. The Duke of Rutland declared that the Prime Minister 'has become a capital orator. He is now one of the very best debaters in the House of Lords.' And Greville, who was inclined to deride Wellington and disliked many of his policies, nonetheless admitted: 'I like his speaking – it is so much to the point, no nonsense or verbiage about it, and he says strongly and simply what he has to say.' This was his great strength; he might not, as Greville elsewhere complained, always rise to a great parliamentary occasion, but he took immense pains to be well prepared and well informed on the subject under discussion; and it helped that the style of debate was shifting, becoming more factual and less rhetorically ornate, with more statistics and fewer quotations from the Latin and Greek classics.[29]

The government had more difficulty in the Commons, where Sir Edward Knatchbull led a concerted attack on the basis that economic distress was general, not partial. Peel's speech was not up to his usual standard, and the amendment gathered support from across the political spectrum, so that the government only secured a majority of fifty (158 to 105) because two dozen Whigs voted for the Address. It was a disconcerting start to the session and pointed to troubles ahead. Wellington wrote to the King to complain that a member of the Royal Household had voted against the Address while others had been absent, and His Majesty, whose ill humour was finally fading away, gave orders that in future all the Household were to give their support to the government. This, and other measures to tighten discipline, led to an improvement, but the government's majority never seemed entirely secure, and this impression of weakness did much to embolden the different Opposition groups.[30]

There were many subsequent debates on the economy and it proved fertile ground for the press and the cartoonists to explore while attacking the government. Curiously distress had scarcely appeared as a subject in the cartoons of 1829 when the economy actually was in recession, but became their main preoccupation in 1830 when it was recovering. Many prints depicted the ministers and Wellington in particular as heartless and blind to the sufferings of ordinary people, while the phrase 'partial distress' became a derisive catchcry. In one print Wellington is depicted as playing blind man's bluff with the poor, literally refusing to see their misery; while in another Peel drives a heavily laden waggon pulled not by horses but by men, ragged and barefoot, while Wellington rides beside them flourishing a whip and shouting: 'Go it ye *Mongrels!!!* ye can't call this anything but *Partial* while I keep a *Bit* in your Mouths.'[31]

In fact there was a good deal of discussion within the government how best to respond to the economic troubles. Peel, Goulburn and Charles Arbuthnot all favoured the reimposition of a modified Property Tax in return for the abolition of a number of indirect taxes which, they argued, pressed upon industry and the labouring poor. Wellington resolutely and in the end successfully opposed this idea, arguing that past experience, especially over tea, suggested that retailers would not pass on the full saving from any reduction in tax. He also saw the political danger in any attempt to re-establish the Property Tax, for while some liberals might approve it in theory, it would provide the perfect platform for all the different Opposition groups to combine against the government at a time when any tax would be deeply unpopular. And, most significantly, he felt that the burden of the tax would be borne principally by landowners who were already suffering severely from the parlous state of agriculture. The country gentlemen were already sufficiently disgruntled with the government; reimposing the hated Property Tax on them, even at a reduced rate and in exchange for the abolition of other taxes, would simply drive them into the arms of the ultras.[32]

Rather than introduce new taxes, the government used the savings it had already made in expenditure, and a financial sleight of hand, to fund the abolition of existing taxes on beer, cider and leather, costing the revenue a total of some £3.4 million in a full year. Parliament was assured that these taxes had been chosen on the principle of affording the greatest relief to the most distressed classes, but it was no coincidence that they would all benefit agriculture. The duty on spirits was increased, and ministers painted a bucolic picture of patriotic Britons quaffing their traditional, wholesome ale rather than being corrupted by spirits into miserable poverty and depravity. In order to ensure that the full reduction was passed on to consumers the government also lifted regulations on houses selling beer, while retaining them on those selling spirits. Like many government attempts to guide the habits of the drinking classes, this well-meant legislation produced many unintended and undesirable consequences. Beer certainly became cheaper, with a proliferation of cheap, disreputable public houses, but the effect was far less wholesome than ministers had hoped. A year later Wellington admitted that the policy had been a mistake and that the legislation had 'produced very great evils. It has occasioned and encouraged extraordinary drunkenness. It has broken up the domestic habits of the people. It has brought many families upon the poor-rates. It has tended to promote disturbances.' He proposed to give magistrates more power over public houses, but by then he was in Opposition, and this was not done for another generation.[33]

Wellington's relations with the King improved in early 1830, helped by a decline in the influence of the Duke of Cumberland. The King was ill early in the year and although he recovered, his health had become more fragile. In the middle of April his condition worsened, but the symptoms were inconsistent and the doctors puzzled. He did not appear very ill and on 10 April Wellington reported with some astonishment on the strength of his appetite:

What do you think of His breakfast yesterday morning for an Invalid? A Pidgeon and Beef Steak Pye of which he eat two Pigeons and three Beefsteaks, Three parts of a bottle of Mozelle, a Glass of Dry Champagne, two Glasses of Port [&] a Glass of Brandy! He had taken Laudanum the night before, again before his breakfast, again last night and again this Morning![34]

Nonetheless the King insisted that the 'Drawing Room' be postponed so that he did not have to come to London, and it was soon evident that he was not shamming and that his condition was worsening. He suffered attacks of severe shortness of breath when his pulse altered and he grew black in the face, leading the doctors to conclude that there was something wrong with his heart. Wellington now made frequent visits to Windsor, and the King was pleased with the attention, although he greatly disliked the necessity for the doctors to issue public bulletins describing his health.[35]

The public was not particularly concerned by news of the King's illness; indeed Mrs Arbuthnot felt that they did not really care if he lived or died. 'They are very *curious* about his state, but they feel that William the 4th will do just as well for us as George the 4th.'[36] But the King's illness had considerable political implications. If he died an election would have to be held, and the prospect of facing the electors made MPs less tractable, especially on questions of public spending. Peel told Fitzgerald on 9 May: 'The state of the King's health has still more shattered the House of Commons, already sufficiently distracted and dislocated. Everybody is looking out for the vote or question on which he can stand a chance of recommending himself to his constituents.'[37] There was also the question of the new King's attitude to his brother's ministers. The story of Clarence's dismissal from his post as Lord High Admiral less than two years before was well known, and the newspapers and caricaturists chose to assume that his views were generally liberal – probably because he had clashed with Cumberland over Catholic Emancipation, and was known to be a bluff, hearty sailor little inclined to stand on his dignity. The Opposition appeared buoyant, and there was talk that they looked to form a government including Palmerston and Grant but not Huskisson; while Cumberland and Eldon sat next to Grey and Lansdowne in the Lords, with Marquess Wellesley beside them. Yet for months Clarence had been telling anyone who would listen that he had no intention of changing the government – even though he then scrambled the message by adding that he would be delighted if Lord Grey joined the ministers in office. This was probably no more than an inept attempt to assure the world that he did not share his brother's antipathy to Grey, but it kept tongues wagging. Wellington held himself strictly aloof from such talk, going so far as to offend Clarence by ignoring compliments which clearly implied a determination to retain him in office. He told the Duke of Northumberland: 'I have communicated with nobody; nor shall I communicate with anybody upon any arrangement whatever, as long as the breath remains in the body of the King my master, without having first received his commands to do so.'[38]

The prospect of a new reign brought to the surface Wellington's desire to give up the leadership of the government. He believed that the King's death would help to unite all the Opposition groups by removing the bar to Grey taking office and by completing the destruction of Cumberland's influence. He was not willing to give Grey a Cabinet office or offer him the Lord Lieutenancy of Ireland, the only places he was likely to accept, and this meant that Grey was likely to lead the Opposition. Wellington believed that the government could hold its ground in the Lords, but he had more doubts about its success in the Commons. The best way of dealing with this might be to enhance Peel's standing by making him prime minister, and this would also open the door to the return of the Canningites, which Wellington did not think he could bring himself to swallow if he remained prime minister. He would, however, take whatever office suited Peel and give him his full support. (These views were set out in a letter which Wellington drafted but did not send to Peel, probably in early May.)[39] The cool political calculations in the draft were not the whole story, however; Wellington was tired, out of spirits and felt that his colleagues had no respect or deference for him, giving an instance when the Cabinet first decided a minor question against his wishes, and then reversed its stand when Peel changed his mind. 'He spoke of this with great bitterness, [and] said if his opinion [had] no weight he had better go.'[40] Mrs Arbuthnot was horrified when she heard this strange outburst of self-pity and over the next week had several long conversations with the Duke, endeavouring to change his mind and persuade him to stay. On 16 May they took advantage of the fine weather and walked around Buckingham House gardens, and sat on the grass, and talked for an hour and a half, at the end of which Wellington made no promises, but indicated that he would do nothing immediately.[41]

Only a small handful of confidants knew that Wellington seriously contemplated resignation in May 1830, and most politicians assumed, like Palmerston, that 'he is resolved to be minister as long as his health allows'. Hardinge, and possibly some other ministers in the Commons, were coming to the view that Peel should take the lead, and it is possible that Wellington had learnt of this and that it helped make him consider the idea. On the other hand, Lyndhurst did not believe that the ministry could stand an hour without him. A government led by Peel would certainly have been more liberal in tone than Wellington's, but it seems most unlikely that it could have survived the storms that broke in the second half of the year, while it would have widened the rift with the High Tories even further.[42]

The moment passed and Wellington dropped the idea of retiring when the King died. It was an odd, uncharacteristic incident. Clearly it arose from the weariness and disillusionment with politics which Wellington had been feeling ever since the passage of Catholic Emancipation, but why had he been so affected? Part of the explanation may be the cumulative effect of ten years in high office, with only a brief, tumultuous break in 1827. Part may have been a sense of getting old; Wellington turned sixty-one in May, no great age, but Liverpool, Canning, Castlereagh, Pitt and Wellington's own father had all died before they reached it, while the dying King, whose decline Wellington was witnessing at close quarters, was only sixty-seven. And part may have been a sense of frustration because he could not personally confront the government's opponents in the Commons, but had to rely upon proxies. But this is speculation and it is impossible to be sure just what prompted Wellington to think about kicking over the traces, and what made him settle back into harness and trot forward with his accustomed energy and self-confidence.

The King's condition gradually deteriorated during May and the first part of June, with some symptoms akin to dropsy. Several painful operations to release fluid which had accumulated in his legs brought only temporary relief, and at three fifteen in the morning on 26 June he died. He was little mourned. Mrs Arbuthnot said that 'people are sorry for the poor King but not *very*'. Wellington, as was fitting, paid the most extravagant tribute to the King in the House of Lords ('. . . one of the most remarkable Sovereigns of our time . . . no man ever approached His Majesty who did not feel instructed by his learning, and gratified by his condescension, affability, and kindness of disposition . . .'); while *The Times* veered to the other extreme, abusing him in terms hardly decent: 'There never was an individual less regretted by his fellow creatures than this deceased King . . . If George IV ever had a friend – a devoted friend – in any rank of life, we protest that the name of him or her has not yet reached us. An inveterate voluptuary . . . of all known beings, the most selfish.'[43]

On the morning George IV died Wellington went to Bushey House and was extremely well received by King William, who told him that he had full confidence in him as minister, and did not wish any changes to be made in the government. In reply Wellington assured the King that he would serve him with the same 'zeal, fidelity & honor' with which he had served his brother, and that with the King's support the government would be strong.[44] The Privy Council was summoned for noon to sign the proclamation of the new King, witness his declaration, and be sworn into office afresh. The King met the ministers and assured them that they would receive his '*entire, cordial and determined support*'. Ellenborough noted that 'there was no grief in the room', while other sources make it clear that William was delighted to have come to the throne and was in fine spirits. Croker, who was present, records: 'His voice faltered amiably at the mention of his brother, but he soon recovered that, and startled those of his Council who did not know him by exclaiming in a familiar tone against the *badness of the pen* with which he was signing the oath administered to him by the Lord President.'[45]

Over the next few weeks the King's informality and lack of pomp caused some surprise and concern. He showed himself very freely to the public in and around London, making little or no attempt to preserve the royal dignity, walking up St James's Street alone, except for the crowd of followers he soon attracted, including a prostitute who embraced and kissed him. At his brother's funeral, so far from appearing absorbed in grief, he shook one friend gleefully by the hand, nodded and grinned at others, and spent most of the service chatting to his nephew, Prince George of Cumberland. Stories of his latest eccentricity or naïve remark became the currency of the day, and while his 'affability' made him popular for the moment, it was obvious that such behaviour could soon reduce him to being a figure of fun.[46]

William IV had ten illegitimate children with Mrs Jordan – the Fitzclarences – but no legitimate offspring with Queen Adelaide. This left as his heir-presumptive his eleven-year-old niece, Princess Victoria, daughter of his late brother Edward, Duke of Kent. And this in turn raised the delicate question of whether the government should propose a Regency Bill to provide for the King's death or incapacity. It was not obvious who the regent should be. The possibilities included Queen Adelaide (at least for a year), in case she happened to be pregnant when the King died or was incapacitated; Victoria's mother, the Duchess of Kent; and, most unpalatably, the next adult male in the line of succession: the Duke of Cumberland. Peel and some other ministers afflicted with tidy minds were eager to have this uncertainty settled and a bill introduced as soon as possible; but Wellington preferred delay. He foresaw that any discussion might become heated, with different parties supporting different solutions (even within Cabinet opinion was divided), and preferred to leave it at least until after the election. He had his way, but Peel was annoyed at being over-ruled and disappointed at having nothing to say to Opposition queries on the subject.[47]

Parliament was not formally prorogued until 23 July, although most of its business had been concluded a fortnight earlier. The Opposition had been quite vociferous, with both Grey and Brougham making violent attacks on the ministry in early July, suggesting disappointment at not having received an offer from Wellington. This was, as Mrs Arbuthnot pointed out, sheer folly; Wellington could hardly have approached them before George IV's funeral (15 July), and attacking the government only created fresh obstacles to an alliance.[48] Not that Wellington had any intention of making offers to anyone, let alone Brougham or Grey. He had a furious argument with the Arbuthnots when they joined Peel in pressing him to find reinforcements in the Commons, and had rather the better of it, for when challenged they could not name anyone who would actually strengthen the front bench.[49] And despite the perennial problem of over-dependence on Peel in the Commons, the government's position in July 1830 was not bad. The King, for all his waywardness, had proved remarkably co-operative, placing the great offices of his household at the disposal of his ministers (something George IV had never done), and being quick to drop his own notions when told that they were impractical. No trace of the pigheaded Lord High Admiral appeared in these first weeks on the throne; William's new confidence in his position actually made him humbler, more ready to listen to his advisors and learn the ways of official business. As for the Commons, it was always restless before an election, and ready to work with the King's ministers afterwards. Elections almost always strengthened the hand of the executive. The Duke of Newcastle reported that some calculations suggested that the government might gain 100 seats at the poll; that seemed unlikely even to him, but half that number would be more than enough to ease the pressure on Peel in the Commons and enable the government to advance into the new reign with confidence.[50] In many ways the government's prospects seemed brighter than they had been for twelve months or more, and there appeared a good chance that Wellington might remain King William's trusted minister for many years.

CHAPTER TWENTY-ONE

THE FALL OF WELLINGTON'S GOVERNMENT
(July–November 1830)

O N 26 JULY 1830 Charles X's government dissolved the French Parliament before it could meet, imposed tight censorship on the press, and effectively suspended the constitution. This led to riots in Paris that quickly turned into an uprising which the government and army were unable to suppress despite heavy fighting. Hundreds of civilians and soldiers were killed and thousands wounded, and the streets of Paris were blocked by barricades before the exhausted and demoralised troops withdrew in disorder. Just after midday on 29 July Talleyrand declared that 'the elder branch of the House of Bourbon has ceased to reign'.[1] The situation was still extremely confused, for the uprising had been spontaneous and even the leading *libérale* politicians were unsure what to do next. Possibilities included a republic (favoured by the radicals) or Napoleon II, the nineteen-year-old son of the Emperor who was living in Austria. But neither of these suggested stability at home or peace abroad and the *libérales* looked instead to the Duc d'Orléans as a moderate compromise, and promoted him to the public as a patriotic Frenchman who had fought under the tricolour at Jemappes and Valmy in the early days of the Revolution, and who would respect their rights and liberties. In fact Orleans was reluctant to enter the fray, but once he took the plunge he proved an astute and highly successful politician. On 31 July he agreed to act as 'Lieutenant-General' of France and a week later accepted the crown as the gift of the people, reigning as King Louis Philippe, although it took months for the new regime to gain strength and stability.[2]

The British government had received no warning of Charles X's actions and it, along with all shades of British opinion, strongly disapproved. Peel condemned the ordinances as 'acts of extravagant folly' which put Polignac and the King 'completely in the wrong', while when the news first arrived Mrs Arbuthnot felt 'certain Chas the 10th cannot last a month'. British Whigs and radicals naturally welcomed the news, the former seeing in it a French version of the Glorious Revolution of 1688 just as Fox and his friends had done in 1789. Even the ultra

Tories rejoiced, for they were deeply hostile to the Catholicism of Charles X's government, and strongly committed to their own view of liberty.[3]

Wellington was clear that Britain should accept the revolution as a *fait accompli* and hope that Louis Philippe and his supporters would succeed in containing it. On 12 August he told Aberdeen:

> There are some bitter pills to swallow; the cockade, the apparently verbal, but in fact real and essential, alterations of the Charter; the act of placing it under the *sauvegarde* of the National Guard; the tone assumed by La Fayette. However, the best chance of peace is to swallow them all. If we don't quarrel with them they must set these matters to rights, or quarrel among themselves, or quarrel with us. Any one of these would be better for us, and for the world, than that we should at this moment quarrel with them.[4]

He did not greatly regret the fall of Charles X, regarding his government as inept at home and dangerous aboard, with no more morality in its foreign policy than Napoleon had shown.[5] However, the government permitted the deposed King and his family to come to Britain, affording them refuge first at Lulworth Castle in Dorset and then at Holyrood, provided that they did not intrigue against the new regime in France. Wellington studied the treaties Britain had signed in 1815 and 1818 and concluded that when Charles X violated the French constitution he voided any obligation on Britain to consult her allies before recognising the new government, and that this would take too long at a time when early recognition might help Louis Philippe consolidate his power. The allied ambassadors in London understood this very well, and Wellington believed that their governments would not mind if Britain acted unilaterally. Indeed the continental powers looked to Britain to take the lead on the question and were happy to take their cue from her.[6]

This does not mean that Wellington viewed the events in France with complacency. He was seriously alarmed and believed that there was a very considerable danger that the revolution might become more radical and follow the path of its predecessor forty years before, and that this would again plunge Europe into a long and bloody war. Louis Philippe offered the best hope of peace, but it is clear that Wellington thought that the odds were against him. And even if France was stabilised there was the obvious danger of the revolution spreading to its neighbours or further afield. An attempt to stage an uprising in Spain had been thwarted even before the revolution in Paris, when a ship laden with arms and a number of Spanish *liberales* had been detained in the Thames, while over the next few weeks and months there were revolutions in several small German states, trouble in Switzerland and Italy, growing tension in Spain, and in November a full-scale uprising against Russian rule in Poland.[7]

But the most serious trouble from a British perspective came in Brussels before the end of August. It began with a small disturbance on 25 August, but rapidly grew in scope and significance as minor local grievances led to a movement against the union with the Netherlands. The response of the authorities was initially feeble; the few troops immediately available were quickly overwhelmed and the revolt was able to consolidate its hold on the city. Indecisive attempts at conciliation then conveyed an impression of weakness, while the Prince of Orange was so indiscreet as to lead to reports that he wanted to become king of an independent Belgium, even if this meant renouncing his claim to his father's crown. Finally the authorities failed in an attempt to take Brussels by force. Wellington was privately critical of the way the Dutch government handled the crisis, and quickly recognised that any outside intervention in its favour would provoke France into supporting the Belgians and probably bring down Louis Philippe. As it was, the events in Paris had clearly provided the inspiration for the uprising and there was strong pressure, both in France and Belgium, for Belgium to again be incorporated into France (as it had been from 1794 to 1814). The risk could best be handled by including France in the consultations among the Great Powers and recognising her interests in Belgium, while expecting her in return to accept that the rest of Europe would not consent to her annexation of Belgium or her supporting liberal movements, which subverted the established government of other countries.[8]

Fortunately this accorded neatly with Louis Philippe's own views, and genuine commitment to peace and to co-operation with Britain in particular. He signalled his intentions, and offended the French radicals, by the appointment of Count Molé as foreign minister and Talleyrand as ambassador to London. King William and Aberdeen were both disconcerted by Talleyrand's appointment, but Wellington welcomed it, and the old intriguer did much to ease tension and suspicion in the relations between London and Paris in the difficult first months of the July Monarchy, as well as adding considerably to the urbanity, wit and variety of British high society.[9] An international conference to settle the problem of Belgium, essentially by determining the basis of her independence, was agreed and met in London at the end of the year after Wellington's government left office. Difficult negotiations lay ahead and in late 1832 a French army entered Belgium, besieged and captured Antwerp on behalf of the new state, and promptly left again, all with prior British consent. But it was Wellington's government which coolly handled the crisis caused by the overthrow of Charles X and the initial, and most dangerous, phase of the Belgian question, and ensured that both problems were handled by the powers through co-operation not confrontation, and so minimised the risk of them leading to a general European war.[10]

News of the Revolution in Paris reached Britain in the midst of the general election, and created a ferment of excitement which grew with the events in Brussels. The press uniformly supported the uprising and the caricaturists briefly renounced cynicism and produced prints celebrating heroic incidents of the popular struggle under titles such as *Patriots who for Sacred Freedom stood*. The *Standard* and other ultra-Tory papers linked Wellington to Polignac and accused him of supporting, even advising, the suspension of the French constitution. The liberal press generally disdained to take up this particular canard, but it gained wider currency through caricatures and the unstamped cheap papers which suddenly began to appear, and which greatly heightened the feeling of the moment. In London a revival of radicalism was encouraged by success in a series of campaigns to open parish vestries (an important form of local government), and by the rapid increase of coffee houses at which artisans could read newspapers and join in weekly political debates, where Wellington's indifference to the sufferings of the poor was as much part of the common currency as his support for reaction in France. On 5 August Joseph Hume, standing unopposed as one of the two members for Middlesex, told an election crowd that if they needed an example a glorious one might be found in a neighbouring state, although he did not believe that they would ever need to take such measures to assert their rights.[11] In October the radicals of Leeds held a public dinner to celebrate the triumph of the people in France, at which the editor of the *Leeds Patriot* declared that 'from the noble efforts made in Paris and in Belgium, from "the feast of reason" which is now spreading, the game is at last at the feet of the operative classes'. The Duke of Rutland told Mrs Arbuthnot in some alarm: 'A meeting took place last week at Leicester to congratulate the French on their revolution, & in speeches the orators promised that in a short time "there should not be a vestige of nobility in England unless the aristocracy mended their manners & sentiments", and the whole meeting responded, "the sooner it is done away with the better".'[12] While Peel noted in October:

> The success of the Mobs and either the unwillingness or inability of the soldiers to cope with them in Paris and Brussels, is producing its natural effect in the Manufacturing districts here, calling into action the almost forgotten Radicals of 1817 and 1819, and provoking a discussion upon the probable results of insurrectionary movements in this country.[13]

John Gale Jones, a 'forgotten' radical whose career went back to the 1790s and the London Corresponding Society, declared that France was 'at once our example and our reproach . . . France had done what Englishmen only talked about'. Cobbett gave a series of eleven lectures linking the French and Belgian

Revolutions to the need for parliamentary reform in Britain, at the Rotunda in Blackfriars Road between 9 September and 7 October, donating the profits to the families of Parisians killed in the fighting, and sending his son and John Bowring as 'Ambassadors of the Reformers of England' to present an address to Lafayette. And an open-air meeting at Kennington Common attracted a crowd of 10,000 people who saw Henry Hunt arrive on a van decorated with tricolours and red bonnets.[14]

Ministers felt the need to take precautions against something more dangerous than peaceful meetings after an incident at Carlisle which was believed to be an attempt to steal arms, if not seize the castle. Wellington gave orders to secure all arms depots, and bring garrisons and their supplies up to strength. Industrial disputes in Manchester also gave grounds for concern, and Peel advised the employers to grant concessions rather than risk a confrontation which might lead to collisions in other places. There were few regular troops available to deal with any trouble, and Wellington prepared a memorandum urging caution if they had to be employed so as not to run any risk of their being defeated, as the first clash would make a decisive impression on the confidence of any troublemakers.[15]

It was not only in London and the manufacturing districts that there was popular agitation in the autumn of 1830; indeed the most serious disturbances were in the rural south-east, where there was a great wave of incendiarism and machine-breaking known as the 'Swing Riots', after the many threatening letters signed 'Captain Swing' that were a feature of the unrest. The riots began in Kent in late August, although there had been some trouble going back to at least 1827. Poor harvests produced discontent directed largely at the Corn Laws (for not giving farmers sufficient protection), which was heightened by the appearance of Irish labourers and new threshing machines which threatened to reduce much-needed winter work. Over one thousand incidents occurred in less than six months, mostly in southern and eastern England, causing alarm and anxiety as well as wild rumours of conspiracies, mysterious networks of plotters and the like. The government was hampered in its response by lack of resources; few regular troops were available, while the yeomanry who were ideally suited to deal with this sort of disturbance had been largely disbanded in these counties a few years before as an economy measure. Local magistrates were often intimidated or sympathetic to the individuals facing them, so that there was at first little deterrent to the disturbances spreading. In time farmers and local gentlemen took more effective action and the riots died away during the winter. They had achieved some success, for the hated threshing machines largely disappeared for a generation, and some tithes were lowered. Special Commissions tried very large numbers of prisoners – 339 in Wiltshire, 342 in Hampshire – and appear to have been conscientious, for between one-third and one-half of the accused were either acquitted or simply bound over to keep the peace. Many others were transported to Australia or imprisoned, and while numerous rioters were condemned to death, the overwhelming majority of such sentences were commuted. It is unlikely that the news from France played any part in prompting the riots, although the member for Dover (Charles Poulett Thomson) said that the people of Kent were excited by it to 'a very great degree', and the rioters included many craftsmen as well as farm labourers.[16]

The news from France had only a limited effect on the results of the general election, while the great surge in popular radicalism and agitation mostly came after the polls had closed, although the heightened atmosphere had an important effect on the way newly elected members viewed the government. The results of the election were obscure and confused; many candidates had no strong party affiliation, and made ambiguous statements to their electors. It was common for politicians of any party to proclaim their independence and to promise to support the government so long as its measures were beneficial, but not to hesitate to oppose when it made mistakes. The confused politics of the previous four years made it particularly difficult to decide the loyalty and view of many MPs, while 141 new members included many whose allegiances could only be guessed at.

There were contests in only one-third of constituencies (128 of 380), although in many others potential candidates had tested the water and withdrawn when finding that they had little chance of success. The single most prominent issue on the hustings seems to have been a call for economy and retrenchment leading to lower taxation; this was the perennial cry of nineteenth-century Whigs and radicals, and it was undiminished, even strengthened, by the cuts introduced by Wellington's government, for it rested on assumptions about waste and extravagance that were more a matter of faith than of reason. The campaign against slavery was stirring strongly in some parts of the country, especially those with a powerful Dissenting community. It was important in the nomination of Brougham for Yorkshire, which led to the most prominent and colourful contest of a generally lacklustre election. Recriminations over Catholic Emancipation also featured largely, especially where there were High Tory candidates to give voice to the widespread sentiments of ordinary, conservative, Anglican voters. The Sale of Beer Act and the creation of the Metropolitan Police were both also much abused in places, and cost the government votes. In Ireland the dangerous issues of tithes and the union with Britain were both agitated; while the prospective renewal of the East India Company's monopoly on trade with China was discussed in some mercantile centres. And parliamentary reform, both giving representation to great new manufacturing cities such as Manchester, Birmingham and Leeds, and hostility to pocket or nomination boroughs, was widely discussed and promoted, especially in the wake of the news from Paris. Many MPs who were generally inclined to support the government pledged themselves to some measure of reform under pressure from their electors.[17]

The government does not seem to have been well prepared for the election; it did not manage to find candidates for some seats it probably should have contested, and its efforts to unseat the Canningites proved ineffective. Years later Brougham claimed that Wellington failed to use the traditional influence of the Crown; however, this is certainly untrue in many instances and probably has little foundation. On the other hand it is clear that the Crown had far less influence than it had in the past, partly because of the small reforms which had accumulated over the previous fifty years, and partly because the growing wealth of the country made men more independent, while the government had much less to offer in the way of places or rewards because of the economies and reductions which had been made ever since 1815. On 3 August, when many polls had yet to be held, Ellenborough noted: 'We have been beaten at Canterbury, and what is worse at Norwich, where a brother of Peel's has been driven out by Robert Grant, the most decided enemy of the Government. No one declares himself the opponent of Government, and as such asks support; but our candidates do not succeed at popular elections.'[18] This was not entirely true; government candidates won at Southwark, Reading and a number of other relatively open seats despite not having the advantage of incumbency, but in general the government did poorly in high-profile contests and those for prestigious county seats.[19]

There was no clear-cut result of the election, and both the government and the different Opposition groups quickly put forward confident interpretations of the composition of the new House in the hope that they would become self-fulfilling prophecies. Lord Durham claimed that the government had lost fifty seats; the *Spectator* forty or fifty; and the more cautious Duncannon still estimated it as nearly thirty. Brougham published a pamphlet, *The Result of the General Election; or, What has the Duke of Wellington gained by the Dissolution?*, in which he argued that the government had lost between twenty and twenty-six seats.[20] All this was hotly contested by the government, with an anonymous counter-pamphlet disputing many of Brougham's assumptions. Even in private the ministers were confident. Hardinge was unusually pessimistic in supposing the loss of two or three seats overall, while Billy Homes, the Whip, was reported to have put the gain at twenty-one, and Joseph Planta, the Treasury Secretary, made it a gain of twenty-two, but arithmetic was not his strong point.[21] No one would know the true result until Parliament met in November and the government's majority was tested on the floor of the Commons. Even then this would be influenced as much by subsequent events and the mood of the moment as by the election, for in the old corrupt unreformed House of Commons members were able to exercise their intelligence and vote in accordance with their perceptions of the needs of the country rather than the colour of their lapel pin.

In the middle of September, soon after the elections were concluded, the Duke went on a tour of the midlands and north of England. Grand preparations were made for his reception with lavish civic dinners, parades, and visits to factories and the Liverpool docks – commonplace events in the life of a politician later in the century, but still unusual in 1830. The enthusiastic reception he received almost everywhere, despite the disturbed state of the country, reflects both his personal popularity outside radical circles, and the novelty of the occasion. The centerpiece of the tour was the opening of the Liverpool–Manchester railway, and on the morning of 15 September Wellington and a party of twelve including Mr and Mrs Arbuthnot arrived at the station at Liverpool, 'where a magnificent car of carved & gilt wood with scarlet cloth awning, capable of holding about 40 people, was waiting to receive us'. Thousands of spectators and numerous other dignitaries were present including William Huskisson, who was one of the members for Liverpool. The train started almost immediately, and Mrs Arbuthnot wrote that: 'I don't think I ever saw a more beautiful sight than at the moment when the car attached to the engine *shot off* on its journey, that part of the railway being cut deep thro' the rock & the sides, far above our heads, being covered with people waving their hats & handkerchiefs.' They went sixteen miles in about forty minutes, at times reaching a speed of thirty miles an hour, and at other times slowing down so that other engines carrying the rest of the party (for some eight hundred people were included in the occasion) could pass on the parallel track and then be overtaken by the Duke's train in turn so that he could see the engines working. Ellenborough recorded Wellington's account of the experience:

> The rapidity of the motion is so great in the steam carriages that even the Duke with his quick eyes could not see the figures in the posts which mark the distance at every quarter of a mile, and when the two steam carriages crossed no face could be seen. It was like the whizzing of a cannon ball. The cold is great, and they must have some defence against the wind, through which they pass so rapidly.[22]

But then the delight and excitement of the carnival day turned suddenly to horror. The engine carrying Wellington's party stopped to take on water at Parkside and many of the gentlemen got out to walk around, although the company directors asked that they remain in their carriages. One of these men was Huskisson, who shook Wellington's hand and was chatting to him and Mrs Arbuthnot when there was a warning shout that another engine was approaching on the other track. There was a scramble to get back into the carriages and Huskisson panicked, got tangled in the door, and was knocked down by the engine, which passed over his leg and thigh, inflicting horrible injuries. Lord Wilton, who had studied surgery and anatomy, applied a tourniquet, but it was obvious to everyone that the injuries would be fatal. Mrs Huskisson witnessed the accident and collapsed in hysteria, but Lord Burghersh carried her to Huskisson so that he might see her before he died. The unfortunate man was lifted on a door onto the carriage and sent at utmost speed towards Manchester and then carried to the house of Mr Blackburne, a clergyman, where he died at nine o'clock that evening.[23]

Wellington and the other guests wished to cancel the rest of the festivities, but the magistrates of Manchester who were with them insisted that they proceed lest the crowds riot on being denied their treat. No one in the party had the heart to appreciate the enthusiastic welcome they received in Manchester and as soon as the engines were ready they returned to Liverpool, Wellington quitting the train a few miles from the city as a mark of respect. The remaining public events were cancelled.

By the time of his death Huskisson had become a highly divisive figure, loathed by many Tories and distrusted by many Whigs, but greatly admired by liberals, Canningites and many journalists. A reconciliation with Wellington at anything more than the most superficial level was never likely, and his inclusion in the Cabinet would have been counter-productive, bringing few votes while alienating many wavering Tories and intensifying the hostility of the ultras.

An analysis of the election results by Joseph Planta, the government Whip, was encouraging. Planta listed 311 of the 658 members of the Commons as either members or friends of the government, compared to only 188 Whigs. Other groups included Doubtful favourable (37); Moderate Ultras (37); Violent Ultras (25); Very doubtful (24); Doubtful unfavourable (23) and the Huskisson Party (11).[24] While not an outright majority, this was more than enough for practical purposes if government supporters could be persuaded to attend regularly and vote loyally. Nonetheless Wellington was again placed under great pressure, from the Arbuthnots, from Peel, and from some other ministers, to seek recruits to strengthen the government, especially its front bench in the Commons. He remained reluctant, believing that a coalition would simply introduce an element of dissension into the Cabinet, while driving all the factions who were not included into outright opposition. But staying with Peel on his journey back to London from Manchester, he gave way and agreed to an overture to Palmerston. When the offer was made, Palmerston responded by demanding the inclusion of some of his friends, specifically Lord Melbourne

(William Lamb) and Charles Grant. Wellington consulted Peel about sacrificing Herries to make room for at least one of these, but Peel thought Herries too useful at the Board of Trade to part with him. Both Wellington and Palmerston seem to have been relieved when the talks thus foundered, but while Palmerston went off to Paris to study the glorious experiment of a liberal regime at first hand, Wellington was badgered by the Arbuthnots and others with schemes to make space for the three leading liberal Tories. This resulted in a further overture when Palmerston returned to London towards the end of October. The two men had a brief interview at Apsley House (Palmerston said it lasted six minutes), which was good-humoured but decisive. The Duke offered three positions, to which Palmerston replied that the government was so weak that it needed to be entirely reconstructed, with a large infusion of Whigs as well as Canningites. Wellington was left with the impression that it would be lucky if places remained for himself, Peel and perhaps the Chancellor – in other words that nothing short of complete surrender would satisfy Palmerston. Mrs Arbuthnot consoled herself with the hope that 'the not making this junction, & the hostility that will necessarily ensure, will bring back our Tory party. If it has that effect, I for one shall be quite satisfied.'[25] However it seems much more likely that these repeated overtures, which of course soon became the talk of the town, emboldened the Opposition and created a perception that the government was weak and vulnerable.

The Whigs drew together during the autumn of 1830, and as the session approached became increasingly united and purposeful. No longer apathetic and disengaged, Grey came to London early, before the end of October, and made it clear that he would not shirk the burdens of leadership. Old resentments, particularly at Lansdowne's junction with Canning, were glossed over if not forgotten. Brougham remained a difficulty as well as an asset; he was universally distrusted and there was a fear that his election for Yorkshire might encourage his pretensions and perhaps lead him to challenge Althorp's leadership in the Commons, but there was equal recognition of his power as a speaker both in the Commons and on the hustings. Grey also made an overture to Melbourne and Palmerston through Lord Holland before the end of September, which disclosed that the Canningites were unlikely to join Wellington, and saw no obstacle of principle or personal feeling to their serving under Grey in a broadly based government. No promises were made on either side but Grey was content, for while few in number the Canningites had a wealth of ministerial experience which the Whigs sadly lacked, and which they would need if they were to offer a plausible alternative administration.[26]

Parliament assembled on 26 October for the preliminary business of swearing in new members and electing a Speaker. Ministers felt that the tide of public opinion was running against them. On 30 October Ellenborough complained that 'there is an infamous article in *The Times* today, against the conduct of the farmers and country gentlemen, and there are worse in the *Morning Chronicle*'. And the following day, at Cabinet: 'There was much conversation about the state of the Press, and a resolution taken to prosecute, notwithstanding the unwillingness of the law officers.' Confirmation of the sour mood came when Wellington was 'hissed, hooted & pelted', when riding from the House of Lords to Downing Street.[27]

The first session of the new Parliament began with much pomp and ceremony on Tuesday 2 November 1830. Debate on the King's Speech initially concentrated on a reference to events in Belgium, with the Opposition claiming that the government was considering armed intervention in conjunction with the continental powers to suppress the revolt, but Wellington and Peel both gave such clear and unequivocal assurances on this point that this line of criticism quickly fizzled out. The Whigs then turned to Wellington's elaboration of a passage in the Speech praising the system of government, in which he firmly rejected any proposal for parliamentary reform and declared that the existing system of representation was so excellent that it could not be improved.[28] This was not an unexpected shift of policy: Tory governments had always opposed parliamentary reform; Wellington had been equally decided in July; and less than four years before Canning had been even more emphatic. In the interim the movement for reform had gained considerable momentum and there had been speculation that the government might introduce a modest measure, transferring a few seats from corrupt boroughs to unrepresented towns. But Wellington and the Cabinet were determined not to give ground, fearing that any concession would excite demands for more, and effectively accept the principle that the Commons should be a popular, democratic assembly. According to Mrs Arbuthnot Wellington honestly and conscientiously believed that 'strengthening the democratic part of the H. of Commons at the expense of the aristocratic is most pernicious & dangerous', while he told Maurice Fitzgerald that if parliamentary reform 'should be carried it must occasion a total change in the whole system of that society called the British Empire; and I don't see how I could be a party to such changes, entertaining the opinions that I do'.[29] But although the stand was one of principle, it was not without potential political advantages. The passage of the Test and Corporation Acts, followed by Catholic Emancipation, had left many Tories, not just the ultras, unclear what the government stood for, or why they should support it. If the ministers had introduced a parliamentary reform measure of their own they would have appeared unprincipled, opportunistic and determined to keep their places at any price. By rejecting the measure so firmly Wellington was endeavouring to give his supporters a rallying point, and to appeal to other MPs who were alarmed by the democratic tone of the press and public opinion. However, this came at the cost of clarifying divisions between the government and Opposition, and inviting a test of strength which earlier in the year, before the election, the government had taken care to avoid.

The significance of Wellington's statement was not immediately apparent. Newcastle thought the debate 'dull', while Ellenborough wrote that 'the tone of the debate was very good, and will *do good*'. The story that, on sitting down, Wellington turned to Aberdeen, who predicted the fall of the government, while often repeated, seems to be a third-hand anecdote of Gladstone's, first recorded many years later, and almost certainly the product of hindsight. On the morning after the speech *The Times* commented that Wellington's declaration 'will not escape notice', but placed equal weight on Althorp's promise of support for some government measures, and concluded that the government's position was reasonably secure.[30] However, the statement was not well received by the public and it led to a reaction against the ministers. On 4 November Mrs Arbuthnot noted that 'the Liberals pretend we have lost immensely by the Duke's anti-reform declaration, while the Tories are delighted by it'. And a few days later Ellenborough was told by a junior colleague in the Commons that it jeopardised the government because it would prevent them gaining recruits and it was doubtful that they would have a majority on the question. Another source said the declaration had greatly injured Wellington in the City, while Hardinge told the Duke that if he was defeated on it in the Commons, or had only a small majority, he should resign. Ellenborough himself admitted that the statement had made Wellington very obnoxious and that it had been much misquoted. Meanwhile, the benefit of the stand was undermined when Sir George Murray said that he was not necessarily opposed to parliamentary reform. This was probably no more than a slip, but it made the government appear divided and uncertain, at a time when it was coming under increasing pressure.[31]

The Swing Riots were now at their height and receiving extensive coverage in the press. After one Cabinet meeting Ellenborough noted: 'The country round Battle and Hawkhurst almost in insurrection. Troops sent there.' The atmosphere in London was equally tense. According to Newcastle: 'The D. of Wellington can Scarcely move without being mobbed – on returning from the H. of Lords yesterday . . . the mob followed him to Downing Street calling him all Sorts of names & expressing their disapprobation of him; many of them Shook their fists at him close to his carriage windows – It is very Evident that we shall shortly see something very insurrectionary in London & the neighbourhood.'[32] As this suggests, there was much hostility towards the ministers, and support for reform, but opposition to the police was also an important ingredient in the trouble. Printed handbills circulated through London denouncing 'Peel's blood-thirsty gang' and warning that from 'them we can expect no mercy, for their nature, like that of their founder, is base, bloody-seeking, and villainous . . . Remember what the French and the Belgians have done! . . . One hour of true liberty is worth ages of slavery! . . . *You are not Englishmen* if you suffer your heads to be wantonly broken by that BLOODY GANG.'[33] And this was backed up by days of running street fights and riots in which the police were the prime target for attack.

On 9 November the King and his ministers were due to visit the City to attend the Guildhall Dinner for the inauguration of the new Lord Mayor, John Key. There was a general expectation of trouble, anonymous threatening letters were sent to Wellington, Peel and other officials, and rumours abounded. On 5 November the Recorder of London 'gave but a bad account of the disposition of the City'. Lyndhurst and Peel, the relevant ministers, were alarmed; Ellenborough suspected a conspiracy; and Aberdeen worried about a connection with France. Wellington's brother William was sufficiently concerned to ask Hardinge if adequate precautions had been taken to protect the Duke; and it emerged that both Hardinge and the Duke intended to carry pistols and travel in the same carriage, which had bolts on the inside of the doors. The King was said to be 'very much frightened', while Queen Adelaide 'cries half the day with fright at the idea of going'. Hardinge feared not only an attempted assassination, but also an effort 'to make London a scene of barricades like Paris and Brussels'. To prevent this 'troops will be disposed at intervals in bodies of half battalions, with provisions, and there will be 1,000 cavalry. Two guns will be ready with the marines at the obelisk, and two in the park'. Newcastle worried about the need to guard the new gasometers, 'for if the Mob got possession of them it might plunge the Town in darkness & create the most dreadful confusion'.[34]

On Sunday 7 November Wellington and Peel met at the Home Office and went through all the reports they had received warning of plans for violent disturbances in the city, including a letter from the new Lord Mayor advising that there was not sufficient force available to prevent tumult and confusion. They worried that if all the police and troops were employed keeping the route to and from the Guildhall secure, there would be none left to protect the rest of London, and they feared that fires might be lit to spread terror and create a diversion. They concluded that the risk of serious violence was too great and decided to cancel the King's visit. Cabinet met soon afterwards and Wellington explained that in his view 'we should not be justified in giving an occasion for the shedding of blood, by means of a crowd *of our own making*. The consequences of the collision would be incalculable, and might affect all parts of England.' Wellington and Peel were well aware of the implications of the decision: 'the effect it would produce on the Funds, and on public confidence – all that would be said against the Government a weighing down the King by its unpopularity'. Some of the ministers went further, Lyndhurst predicting that 'it would be said that we did it for our sakes only', and sacrificed the King; while Bathurst thought that it would put an end to the government and open the door to reform. But this reflected disquiet and the uncomfortable choice between evils rather than dissent, and when Wellington and Peel returned from the King with the news that he was pleased and relieved by their decision, the troubled ministers were satisfied.[35] The public heard the news with aston-ishment which soon turned to derision. Newcastle, who on 7 November was fearfully anticipating anarchy and rapine under cover of darkness, the next day condemned the decision as 'ill advised & injudicious' because it might make the King unpopular. *The Times* made much of the disappointment of the good citizens of London, who had for weeks been devoting themselves to prepara-tions for receiving their beloved King with all honour and reverence, and cited the radical Alderman Waithman's statement that there had been no solid ground for any alarm. More than thirty caricatures appeared, of which *The Great General frightened by Don-Key* is typical: Wellington in civil clothes runs away from a donkey dressed in the Mayor's robes and chain, the donkey brays 'Fee-fa-fum' and Wellington cries 'Oh save me, save me, Bob, run, tell the King!' The Opposition insinuated that the King was being made to suffer because of Wellington's personal cowardice, while Newcastle learnt 'from undoubted authority' that the whole thing was a stock exchange fraud perpetrated by some of Key's relations who 'imposed upon his credulity'.[36]

While much of this reaction was absurd, it fatally undermined the govern-ment's standing. Two junior ministers, Hardinge and Wortley, told Ellenborough that they considered it as dooming the government, and there was a wide-spread assumption that the decision was unnecessary and a loss of nerve.[37] That cannot be proven one way or the other, and it is worth pausing to consider the reaction if the visit to the City had gone ahead and had resulted in serious rioting and a number of civilian deaths. Would not Wellington then have been condemned for short-sighted inflexibility, indifference to human suffering, and besmirching the popular King with the blood of his subjects? All the old taunts about a military dictator ruling at the point of a bayonet would have been dusted off for another airing, and he would have been represented as being out of touch with popular sentiment. And this is on the assumption that nothing worse than rioting happened – that no one was assassinated, and that London did not follow the example of Paris and Brussels. That was unlikely, but it was not unreasonable for Wellington and Peel to be cautious, for even with hindsight we cannot be sure what would have happened if the visit had gone ahead.

Even without the King's visit there was considerable rioting in London on 9–10 November, although it was contained by the police, who for the first time employed the tactics of the baton charge as a non-lethal way of dispersing a crowd. This proved so effective that there was no need to call upon the troops who were in readiness. Wellington expected an attack on Apsley House and issued meticulous instructions for its defence, which fortunately were not put to the test.[38] The success of the police and two days of heavy rain had their effect. The riots subsided after 10 November and the Funds rose sharply, more than making up their loss on the news of the cancellation of the King's visit. Wortley, who thought the government doomed on 8 November, was much more cheerful on 11 November, while Ellenborough heard that opinion in the City was that the government would survive.[39]

Attention now concentrated on Brougham's motion for parliamentary reform which would be debated on 16 November, and which was generally expected to decide the fate of the government. Ministers were unsure whether or not they had the numbers, but were well aware that their hold on power was uncertain. Nonetheless they believed that they would have a better chance of success if they put on a bold face rather than yielding minor points, which would just emphasise their weakness. On this ground Peel refused to accept an Opposition motion for a committee to enquire into the civil list. This led to a vote on the evening of 15 November in which all the Opposition groups, including the ultras, combined to defeat the government by 204 to 233. It was the first significant test of strength in the new Parliament, and the government had lost. John Cam Hobhouse then asked Peel if the ministers intended to resign; and on not receiving an answer, he prepared to move a motion of no confidence, but was restrained by Brougham who said that the ministers should have time to consider their position.[40]

Peel, Goulburn and Arbuthnot went straight to Apsley House, where Wellington was at dinner with a large party including the Prince of Orange. Rather than bursting in with the news they sent a note upstairs to the Duke, who whispered an explanation to Mrs Arbuthnot, then went downstairs leaving his other guests none the wiser. There was no absolute need for the government to resign; the question was not very significant and many ministries, including Liverpool's, had carried on in the face of much more serious defeats. However, it was clear that even if the House had been full the government would not have had the numbers, and that this lack of support was not confined to the particular question of the civil list. This does not mean that it would necessarily have been defeated on the issue of reform; most of the High Tories voted against the government on the civil list, and while some would favour reform others would have opposed it – and the same would have been true of a number of other MPs. But victory on one great question with a small majority was not enough; ministers needed the confidence of members to carry the ordinary business of government through the Commons, and the vote on the civil list convinced them that they did not have it. And there was something else: they were ready, even eager, to resign. Earlier that day Mrs Arbuthnot had written in her journal that 'Peel is completely broken down by the fatigue & wear of mind consequent upon having no help'. That evening, when she went downstairs and joined the ministers after the other guests had gone, 'I never saw a man so delighted as Peel. He said, when Opposition cheered at the division that he did not join in it but that it was with difficulty he refrained, he was so delighted to have so good an opportunity for resigning'. Peel's reaction was extreme but a few days later Mrs Arbuthnot wrote that 'almost without exception the members of the Govt. were delighted, feeling that their situation had been irksome beyond endurance and, when such a feeling does exist, a govt. *cannot* go on'.[41]

On the following morning Wellington saw the King and told him that it would be better for the ministry to resign at once. The King was very agitated and distressed, in tears, and asked if it was really inevitable, whether some junction could not be formed or some compromise found. Wellington demurred and advised the King to send for Lord Grey, while assuring His Majesty of his unbounded gratitude for the King's kindness and support. The thanks were deserved, for the King had proved a far better friend to the government than anyone could have anticipated on his accession, but his support had not been enough and any attempt to carry on would have ended in humiliation and failure.[42]

Wellington's government fell because it lost the confidence of the House of Commons. The rioting in London, the growth of popular radicalism and the Swing Riots had all created an air of crisis, which called for a strong government. But the over-reliance on Peel in the Commons, the vain search for reinforcements, and above all the cancellation of the King's visit to the City, looked like weakness and undermined the natural assumption that Wellington was the ideal man to handle the situation. Events in France in July suggested that uncompromising opposition to the rising tide of liberalism might prove more dangerous than timely concession, while Wellington's veto on any measure of reform, and his personal unpopularity with the mob, made him appear an obstacle to the restoration of tranquillity.

In the longer term the government lost support because Wellington and Peel were unable to mount a persuasive case for the preservation of the status quo. Faith in the constitutional settlement of 1688 had been undermined by the concession of Catholic Emancipation, and this had led to calls for parliamentary reform not just from Whigs and liberals, but also from some ultra Tories who felt that Parliament no longer fairly represented the nation as a whole and the landed interest in particular. In the face of this criticism the government's arguments appeared tired and uncompelling. Warning of the dangers of undermining the constitution appeared hypocritical coming from the mouths of ministers who had themselves forced such fundamental changes in it. The almost uniform support for reform in the press was also very important, and helped ensure that the intellectual case in favour of the existing system was not properly expounded. The government badly needed a reputable newspaper to put forward the case for moderate conservatism and to counter the liberal assumptions which were rapidly coming to be taken for granted even by many conservatives. It is true that *The Times* continued to give the ministers broad support right up to the end of the ministry, but it always did so from a liberal perspective; at one level this made its endorsement more valuable, but at another it meant that the terms of the debate were set out in ways that were ultimately damaging to the government.

Another long-term trend which contributed significantly to the fall of the government was the decline in patronage and influence resulting from fifteen years of reductions in government spending and at least two generations of piecemeal reform. Together these sharply curtailed the ability of the King's ministers to 'make' a majority in the Commons. The government gained no strength at the election – indeed, based on the way MPs voted on the civil list in November it actually lost fifteen seats[43] – and this was, in part, because it had much less to offer doubtful members in order to secure their support. At the same time the growing prosperity of the country, the spread of education, and the press encouraged a spirit of independence which was evident during the poll in the agitation over pocket boroughs, and perhaps also in the behaviour of MPs themselves. Finally, a new generation was coming to the fore, full of self-confidence and intellectual complacency, convinced that the future would be better than the past; that new ways were better than old ways; and the power of reason superior to the product of experience. For such men Wellington's government was a relic, and they were impatient to see it swept aside.

And yet in less than three years in office Wellington's government had introduced a series of 'progressive' 'reforms' and 'improvements' of which any later liberal administration would have been proud, and which few could match: the repeal of the Test and Corporations Acts; Catholic Emancipation; Peel's overhaul of the criminal law; the creation of the Metropolitan Police; and a significant reduction in taxation, paid for by strict attention to economy. At the time and since Wellington has received little credit for these measures because it was felt that they were introduced despite, not because of him, and if anything ran contrary to his real wishes. To some extent this is fair; he was not a liberal, or even a reforming Tory like Peel. But nor was he a rigid conservative. His work at the Ordnance showed his commitment to administrative reform in pursuit of efficiency and economy. His support for the creation of the police was sincere, and he had come to see the necessity for Catholic Emancipation long before he became prime minister, even though he was rightly sceptical of the claims made by its proponents. He also failed to receive the credit to which he was entitled for his conduct of foreign affairs, especially his cool handling of the Eastern Question and the revolutions in France and Belgium.[44] Here he succeeded in his objective of returning Britain to the heart of Europe and restoring good relations with the Eastern Powers. The co-operative climate he fostered helped ensure their relatively calm reaction to the overthrow of the Bourbons in Paris, and this in turn paved the way for a negotiated solution to the problems caused by the Belgium revolt.

Wellington was not a great prime minister. He did not, as prime minister, preserve the nation in the hour of danger or lead her to victory against all odds. He did not dominate politics for a generation or transform the nature of the British state. And he did not strike a particular bond with the populace so that he came to represent and articulate their hopes and desires. But his reputation, like Lord Liverpool's, has suffered from the sharp shift in political outlook and attitudes which affected the British press and part of the public in the 1820s and 1830s, and which led them to dismiss almost with contempt those who did not share their new-found certainties. Wellington may not have been a great prime minister, but he was one of the leading politicians of his generation – shrewd, confident and determined, but also flexible and realistic in both his goals and methods, and entirely comparable with Canning, Castlereagh and Perceval or Grey, Melbourne and Peel.

PART IV

OUT OF OFFICE (1830–41)

CHAPTER TWENTY-TWO

OPPOSING THE REFORM BILL
(November 1830–June 1832)

WELLINGTON AND HIS colleagues formally resigned the seals of office on 22 November 1830 when Grey's new government had been formed and was ready to take their place. Except for a few months in 1814 and 1827 this was the first time Wellington had been freed from the duties and cares of a responsible position in well over twenty years. His friends worried how he would adjust to private life, with Mrs Arbuthnot protesting a little too vehemently that 'he will never be bored, for he reads a great deal, is never tired of it, has bought hunters, occupies himself setting his county to rights & Time does not hang the least upon his hands'. A few months later he assured her: 'You are quite right. I don't care about being alone. I walk, play at tennis and ride and read and write all day, so that the Hours do not at all hang heavy.'[1] Nevertheless it is clear that he did not find the adjustment easy; in October 1831 he admitted that he had lost his habitual good spirits, 'which had never before abandoned me'. He was troubled by the worsening of his deafness, which made him feel unfit for society; his temper did not improve; the behaviour of his eldest son, Lord Douro, exasperated and worried him; and he was concerned about his finances, his health and the state of the country.[2] But while he endured spells of gloom and depression, they did not settle or become pervasive, and most of the time he engaged with the world with scarcely any diminution of his keen interest and accustomed energy. There was nothing wan or forlorn about Wellington in the 1830s; he remained a powerful figure at the forefront of public life throughout the decade.

Wellington was not entirely without official duties in these years, for he retained a number of offices that were independent of the vagaries of politics. He was still Lord Warden of the Cinque Ports, Lord Lieutenant of Hampshire, Constable of the Tower of London, and colonel of the Grenadier Guards among other positions. There was some speculation in late 1830 that the new government might ask him to return to the Horse Guards as Commander-in-Chief of the army, but it does not appear that any offer was made, which spared him a difficult choice. As soon as he resigned as prime minister, Wellington went down to Hampshire to supervise operations against the Swing Rioters; however, most of the disturbances had already been brought under control, and his role in their suppression has been considerably exaggerated. He only stayed in Hampshire for a few days (23–27 November), although he returned to Winchester in December for the opening of the special commission to try the rioters.[3]

Fortunately national and international affairs soon provided a more engaging subject of interest than the riotous farm labourers of Hampshire. The new government lost no time in disappointing the hopes of its friends and vindicating the doubts of its opponents by a combination of poor judgement, over-confidence and self-indulgence. Lord Grey had spent forty years in the political wilderness, and having finally gained the promised land he fell upon the spoils of office with the same enthusiasm and lack of scruple with which his father had plundered the West Indies in the 1790s. Mrs Arbuthnot noted with gleeful disapproval: 'Ld Grey had given *good* places to his son, his three sons-in-law, three brothers-in-law, besides nephews; has made two merchants, one Sec[retar]y of the Treasury & the other Vice-President of the Board of Trade, and the same Gazette, which announced their appointments, notified the dissolution of their partnerships with houses in the City. This is all *quite new*. No merchants were ever before put into financial situations, & certainly the Duke of Wellington did not crowd the offices with his sons & nephews.' These appointments were much criticised by the liberal as well as the Tory papers and by the caricaturists, while it was later calculated that Grey's extended family received appointments, sinecures and pensions totalling £202,892 6s 2d during his ministry. To make matters worse Grey's extraordinarily wealthy son-in-law, Lord Durham, who sat in Cabinet as Lord Privy Seal and who was the darling of the radicals, was said to have benefitted by some £36,000 a year by the government's alteration of the coal duties.[4]

Radicals and liberals were further disillusioned by the government's inability to make any great savings in the King's civil list, and by its treatment of the press, which led Cobbett to complain that there had been more prosecutions of the editors and printers in the first seven months of the Whig government than in the previous seven years of Tory rule.[5] Wellington and other Tories were much more concerned by the new ministry's handling of foreign affairs, where Palmerston's mismanagement of France and the Belgian question appeared to sacrifice traditional British interests in the Low Countries. Before the end of 1830 there was real concern that this might lead to war (Wellington advised the Horse Guards 'to look to the defences of the islands of the Channel and all our sea-ports'), and although this faded over the course of the winter, there was a general sense that the government's weakness and incompetence in its first months in office had cost Britain influence on the Continent and diminished her standing.[6]

The government's budget, introduced on 11 February 1831, has been described by a sympathetic historian as a 'fiasco'. For years Whigs and liberals had accused the Tories of prodigious waste and extravagance, but now that the responsibility fell on them they proved unable to make any significant reductions in expenditure. Althorp's competence as Chancellor was cast into doubt by a succession of changes in policy on the floor of the House, in response to pressure from one industry after another. Ministers, aware that their standing was in sharp decline, carefully avoided testing the mood of the House, but when they were finally forced to a division over changes to timber duties that disadvantaged Canadian timber, they were defeated by 236 to 190. Even before this, on 26 February, *The Times* called for the reconstruction of the ministry.[7]

The Tories enjoyed the ministers' discomfiture, but were in no position to take advantage of it. Wellington was still sore over the defeat of his government and was inclined to blame the ultras for their betrayal and Peel for losing control of the Commons and giving up too easily. (This was unfair, but it is not surprising that the recollection of Peel's delight at leaving office should rankle.)[8] For his part Peel studiously distanced himself not just from the ultras but from Wellington and the main body of the Tory party, and there was a good deal of speculation that he envisaged a return to office at the head of a moderate, centrist government as soon as the Whigs had passed a modest measure of parliamentary reform. The suspicion of these plans naturally did not endear him to his former colleagues. Wellington was quite happy to accept Peel as prime minister; the defeat of his government had demonstrated the importance of the Commons, especially for a Tory administration, and Peel's dominance of the House had been increased by the elevation of Brougham, his only real rival, to the Lords. But the Duke resented Peel's lack of communication and party spirit. On 26 December he wrote to Mrs Arbuthnot: 'What is the use of talking of my making Bargains or arrangements? Can I execute them? Will Peel consent to anything? Can I do anything without Peel?' And in mid-January: 'The Theme of my letters to you is that I can do nothing; that Peel is the Person to be applied to, and according to whose Notions everything must be regulated at present; and that I only take gratuitous Trouble & expose myself to Mortification by forming and giving an opinion upon any subject.'[9]

The Tories recognised that their stand against parliamentary reform had made them, and Wellington in particular, very unpopular in the country, although even before the end of 1830 they began to see – or imagine – signs of a reaction in their favour.[10] Wellington deprecated any active opposition to the new government at first. As late as 26 January he told the Duke of Buckingham that if they were offered power they could not accept it, and that they therefore should not attempt to bring down the ministry; but equally he would not give Grey *carte blanche*: 'I certainly will not consent to any compromise of principle. I will oppose every measure which I think revolutionary. But I cannot think that it would be right to commence a regular factious opposition at the present moment.'[11] These scruples did not prove very durable and during the course of the year Wellington proved a far more energetic, effective and committed party leader than Peel. He recognised the party's weakness in the press, and encouraged the activities of Holmes and Croker, who endeavoured to provide an alternative to the liberal-radical perspective which dominated both metropolitan and provincial newspapers. They had limited success, but the reconciliation with the ultras, when it came in the spring, brought the *Standard* back into the regular Tory fold.[12] Later in the year Wellington was keen to use the network of Pitt Clubs and their annual dinners as 'a rallying point for the Conservative party', and opened the traditional Fish Dinner at Greenwich 'to all good Tories who chose to attend'. By contrast Peel would not attend the Pitt Dinner, discouraged a party gathering on the eve of the session designed to unite different strands of Tories, and refused to lend his name to party circulars.[13]

On 1 March 1831 Lord John Russell rose in the Commons to introduce the government's Reform Bill. As he spoke the House was first surprised and then shocked by the extent of the proposed changes, which were far more radical than anyone expected. No fewer than 150 seats, almost one-quarter of the House, would be stripped from their old boroughs and transferred to populous towns or, in some cases, to the counties. Existing boroughs with fewer than 2,000 inhabitants would lose both their MPs, while those with between 2,000 and 4,000 would lose one. Initially the ministers intended to create a uniform franchise giving the vote to all male householders resident in a borough whose property was rated as having a rental value of £20 per annum. However, investigation showed that this would mean that half the boroughs on Schedule B (those with populations between 2,000 and 4,000 and retaining one member) would have thirty or fewer voters, while eight boroughs would have only ten voters. Faced with the absurdity of creating a large number of new pocket boroughs in the name of reform, the Cabinet agreed to lower the property qualification to £10 per annum. This was not far short of household suffrage in London, but still not low enough to provide electorates of reasonable size in many more remote and less affluent parts of the country. A solution, of sorts, was found by extending the boundary of each borough until it included a minimum of 300 voters whose property qualified them for the franchise. Some boroughs became semi-rural in nature, which showed the absurdity of allocating seats according to one criteria (total population), but the vote according to another (value of property). The government's plans were also damaged by the extreme speed and carelessness with which they had been prepared, and the decision to base them on the 1821 census, which was not only now out of date, but which had not been designed with this purpose and which proved seriously misleading. Many boroughs were placed on the wrong schedule or not placed on a schedule at all, and although the mistakes were probably genuine, it was naturally those which favoured the ministers which made the most impression.[14]

The underlying purpose of the bill was plain, if not avowed: to create a substantial radical bloc in Parliament which, while never strong enough to hope to form a government in its own right, would support the Whigs and keep them in office whatever the wishes of the King. None of Grey's ministers, not even Durham, believed in democracy; they were, overwhelmingly, Whig aristocrats, and as the heirs of Charles James Fox their interest lay in subordinating the king to the aristocracy and in particular to a circle of great Whig families. Fox had tried to achieve this with the India Bill of 1783 but had been thwarted by George III's determination not to yield and the precocious confidence of Pitt the Younger. Now Grey, who had been excluded from power almost all his life by the hostility of George III and George IV, used his opportunity ruthlessly in an endeavour to recast the constitution in such a way that no king could afford to do without the Whigs as his rightful ministers.

The Reform Bill has often been presented, both at the time and subsequently, as the culmination of a long campaign stretching back to the 1780s and even before. While not entirely untrue, this is deeply misleading. Parliamentary reform was a minor fringe issue which at most times keenly appealed to a few devotees and was regarded by the great majority with a mixture of scepticism and boredom, rather like bimetallism later in the nineteenth century, or proportional representation in the twentieth century. On a few celebrated occasions interest in it flared among Whigs and radicals, who generally used it as a proxy for other more immediate social grievances. It had been dormant throughout the 1820s and was only revived in 1830 when the Whigs needed a cause to unite the party after Wellington had deprived them of their old totem of Catholic Emancipation. Its unexpected popularity owed something to the economic distress of 1829 and the examples of the French and Belgian revolutions of 1830, and rather more to the cumulative effect of many years of radical propagandising which spread the idea that all the ills of the country could be blamed on a wasteful and extravagant government kept in place by a corrupt House of Commons.[15] Whig ministers deliberately encouraged this discontent using their close ties with *The Times*, the *Morning Chronicle* and other liberal papers to fan the flames, and assiduously courting the radicals both in London and the country. In return even extreme radicals supported the bill, confident that far from closing the door on further reform, the bill would create a House of Commons that would be unwilling to defy the clamour of the populace and could be bullied into granting their subsequent demands.[16] This does not mean that Grey's talk, and that of the other Reformers, of the need to bring the middling classes within the fold of the constitution, weaning them with kindness away from the radicals, was either hypocritical or entirely baseless. The country had become much more prosperous during the long years of Tory rule and this wealth had spread across the land leaving the majority still very poor, but a much larger minority with more elevated tastes and pretensions than those of their grandparents. Their exclusion from power on the national stage was seldom a matter of great concern, but the domination of local politics by enclosed corporations and entrenched oligarchies was a running sore, which often had a sectarian bent – the old corporations being Anglican, while many of those who were excluded were Dissenters. And there was the resentment felt by some in the newer manufacturing towns towards a political system which, they felt, was unfairly weighted in favour of the landed interest – a resentment which frequently focussed on the Corn Laws, ignoring the extent to which agriculture had suffered and manufacturing benefitted from the economic and financial policies pursued by the government since 1815. Finally, there was an edge of moral disapproval in the way many in the provinces regarded the behaviour of the ruling class in the metropolis, which must have been strengthened by the well-publicised scandals attached to the personal lives of Cumberland, Ellenborough and many other prominent politicians, Whig as well as Tory. Whether such grievances really amounted to a serious threat to the constitution, or whether the Reform Bill was an appropriate way to address them, may be doubted, but they provided the backdrop and justification for the Whig proposals, just as the real troubles of Ireland had been used to support the claims for Catholic Emancipation.

Tories were almost equally astonished by the scope of the bill and the irresponsibility of the ministers' tactics in exciting popular agitation in its favour. They opposed Reform on many grounds, arguing that Britain's existing system of government had proved extraordinarily effective, making her the envy of the world for her prosperity, her stability and the liberty enjoyed by her people. This was all to be cast aside 'in order to imitate France, which is convulsed from one end to the other, and America, where corruption and bribery is ten times more notorious than it is here'.[17] The bill was a direct attack on private property, for those who had interests in the boroughs that would be disenfranchised would receive no compensation for their loss. Wellington complained on 14 March that:

to disenfranchise Old Sarum and Gatton, in order to make room for representatives from Birmingham and Manchester, is equally inconsistent with the principle on which every charter, every property in the kingdom, is held. I consider that if Lord John's bill or any other bill passes by which a borough will be deprived of its charter without proved delinquency, or an overpowering necessity, a shake will be given to the property of every individual in the country.[18]

The door once opened could not easily be closed and, as Mrs Arbuthnot pointed out, 'the moment the *principle* is admitted that you have *a right* to take the franchise from one town which has committed no offence & transfer it to another, I cannot see upon what *principle* you can ever stop while there is a town unrepresented with 100 inhabitants more than one with representatives'.[19] Nor would the damage stop there, as Wellington told Melville at the end of May:

> I don't in general take a gloomy view of things; but I confess that, knowing all that I do, I cannot see what is to save Church, or property, or colonies, or union with Ireland, or eventually monarchy, if the Reform Bill passes. It will be what Mr Hume calls 'a bloodless revolution'. There will be, there can be, no resistance. But we shall be destroyed one after the other, very much in the order I have mentioned, by due course of law . . .[20]

'And for what is all this risk to be run?' Mrs Arbuthnot asked, and answered her own question: 'To keep an incapable Ministry in their place, many of whom are frightened at their own bugbear. Brougham's account of his colleagues is that Ld Grey is in his dotage led by Ld Durham, that Lord Althorpe is a blockhead, Sir James Graham a puppy, and as to the Duke of Richmond, he has not brains enough to fill the smallest thimble [that] ever fitted the smallest lady's finger.' Brougham himself had so little confidence in the future of the ministry that he had made overtures to Wellington enquiring if he might retain his position as Lord Chancellor in the event of a change of government – advances which Wellington quietly ignored.[21]

There was some disagreement among the Tories how best to oppose the bill. Some, such as Lord Wharncliffe, advocated allowing it to pass its Second Reading unopposed, but then to emasculate it in committee. But Peel and Wellington both thought that this would only cause divisions in the party, while sacrificing all their strongest arguments which were based on principles that would be conceded if the Second Reading passed. This led to a dramatic debate in the Commons on the nights of 21 and 22 March, culminating in a vote at three in the morning on 23 March in which the House divided 302 to 301 in favour of the bill. Although liberal MPs rejoiced and the newspapers claimed victory, this was far too small a majority for the bill to proceed with any hope of passing the Commons, let alone the Lords. The only responsible course for the government would have been to withdraw it and prepare a more moderate scheme which could win the broad support that such a fundamental measure needed. A parliamentary committee including all shades of opinion might have been established, which could have drawn on the 1831 census and produced a bill in time for the 1832 session. Wellington and many other Tories would still have opposed it, but there were a great many MPs, and members of the Lords, who favoured some reform, but who had serious misgivings about the government's bill. However, the government refused to follow this well-established course, because this would have alienated its most zealous supporters in the press and among the radicals on whom it felt dependent. Certainly the press was in no mood for compromise, stridently attacking the opponents of reform and demanding 'the bill, the whole bill and nothing but the bill' – a slogan coined by R.S. Rintoul, the radical editor of the *Spectator*, and which was widely adopted.[22]

Parliament adjourned for the Easter recess on 30 March and returned on 12 April. Ministers used the interval to clarify and refine their proposals without offering any substantial concessions to the Opposition. Most of these changes concerned which towns and counties would receive the members taken from those that had been disenfranchised. Boroughs were required to have a minimum population of 10,000 inhabitants to receive a new member, but ministers chose which towns above this level benefitted, justifying their selection on the basis that those thus enfranchised were 'centres of manufacturing capital and skill'. Tories noted that a list which included Halifax, Oldham, the Potteries, Rochdale, Salford, and Wakefield was likely to favour liberal and radical candidates. Similarly counties with a population exceeding 150,000 were to be given two additional members (making a total of four) and to be divided into two electorates, while those with populations between 100,000 and 50,000 were to remain a single electorate but to be given a third member. The original proposal to reduce the total number of members of the Commons from 658 to 596 was modified, the new total being 627, and if this aroused too much opposition no reduction was to be made at all. This appeared to answer Opposition criticism, but the way the decision was implemented was highly partisan; Whig interests were protected, Tory interests undermined or destroyed.[23]

None of these changes had much appeal for moderate Tories or independents, with the result that the government was defeated in the early hours of 20 April when an Opposition amendment was carried in Committee by 299 votes to 291. The Cabinet responded by asking the King to dissolve Parliament and call an immediate election, with the implicit threat that if the King refused, the ministers would resign, leaving the King to find a new government where he could. William slept on the decision and then reluctantly gave way, unwilling to precipitate a political crisis and uncertain whether the Tories could provide him with a plausible alternative administration. The Tories then blundered by attempting to find a parliamentary mechanism for delaying the dissolution, which allowed the Cabinet to persuade the King that his prerogative was under attack. Amid scenes of high drama he came in person and at short notice to dissolve the Parliament, which was presented by the press as further evidence of his commitment to reform.[24]

Wellington was dismayed by the King's decision, telling Buckingham that 'I don't believe that the King of England has taken a step so fatal to his monarchy since the day that Charles I passed the Act to deprive himself of the power of proroguing or dissolving the Long Parliament'. Months later he blamed all the subsequent troubles on the King for not accepting Grey's resignation and asking the Tories to form a government. However, it seems doubtful that a Tory government could have succeeded in April 1831. There was strong popular feeling in favour of reform, the press was virulent, and Wellington was person-ally unpopular. A new government would have to bring forward some measure of reform but this would alienate many Tories and it is most unlikely that Peel would have agreed to lead or even to serve in such a ministry. These problems were to persist throughout the struggle against the Reform Bill, and effectively crippled the Tory opposition to it. On the other hand Wellington was right, for the dissolution was bound to create even greater difficulties for the Tories; their chance of success in April 1831 was not great, but it was the best they would have.[25]

The election was held over five weeks from the end of April to the begin-ning of June in an unusually partisan atmosphere. The press was unrestrained in its attacks, with *The Times* at the forefront: 'Once and again we warn [Tory boroughmongers] to desist, – not if they value the lives and happiness of others, for they are too selfish to be moved by such considerations, but if they value their own.'[26] And even more explicitly:

> Any high-born and high-bred young Tory, sent from some Club-house in St James's Street . . . with the wages of corruption in his pocket, and travelling luxuriously to some comfortable corporation constituency, consisting of some 13 or 16 persons . . . will become acquainted with every village pump; the clear river and the muddy pond will alike receive them; they will carry away undesired samples of the soil from each county, and will consider them-selves fortunate if contumely and contusions will be all they meet with.[27]

These were not entirely idle threats; at Wigan the son of one of the borough's patrons was killed by a pro-Reform mob and the Tory candidate was beaten and stripped of his clothes, while at Edinburgh the Lord Provost narrowly escaped being hurled from the North Bridge. Newark, Newcastle-under-Lyme, Stamford, Warwick and Bridgewater saw serious violence, while the election in Carmarthen was aborted due to destructive rioting. Among other, lesser, incidents a mob attacked Apsley House when Wellington was at Stratfield Saye, but were driven off when the Duke's servant John fired two blunderbusses into the air from the top of the house.[28] Overall the level of violence was not much greater than the normal turbulence of the polls, but the disturbances in 1831 had a strong party hue which was most unusual, and led many Tories to fear that this was a foretaste of elections in a post-Reform world. It was widely believed in Tory circles that some ministers actively stirred up the populace, and that the government as a whole was slow to restore order in case it discouraged their supporters. In this atmosphere of intimidation many Tory candidates refused to stand or withdrew from contests, arguing that it made sense to ride out the storm and stand again in the subsequent election. Nonetheless the government strained every muscle of political influence in favour of its supporters reportedly informing all holders of government offices, however humble, that they would be dismissed if they did not vote for pro-Reform candidates.[29]

The election resulted in very large gains for the government, especially in county seats and boroughs with relatively open electorates, giving it a majority of about 130 or 140 in the Commons. Although some of this was due to intimidation and the use of government influence, there is no doubt that the country as a whole strongly supported Reform, and greatly preferred the radical bill proposed by the ministers to more moderate schemes put forward by Tory candidates. Even Mrs Arbuthnot admitted that 'England is gone perfectly mad, and, in their desire to have this nonsensical Bill (whose authors don't pretend it will in reality do anything for the People) the people overlook every other object'.[30]

Wellington was near despair. Mrs Arbuthnot noted on 16 May:

The Duke has lost heart entirely. He thinks the revolution is begun and that nothing can save us . . . The King & his Govt are, he says, leagued with the mob to overturn the existing institutions; that, in truth, the Govt are now in the hands of the mob, for, he says, they will not be able to manage their new Parliament or direct the storm which they have raised, and he foresees nothing but civil war & convulsions.[31]

And he wrote to her:

Matters appear to be going on as badly as possible. It may be relied upon that we shall have a Revolution. I have never doubted the Inclination and disposition of the lower Orders of the People. I told you years ago that the people are rotten to the Core. You'll find that it is true. They are not blood-thirsty, but they are desirous of Plunder. They will plunder, destroy and annihi-late all Property in the Country. The Majority of them will then starve; and we shall witness Scenes such as have never yet occurred in any part of the World.

It is quite impossible that this Country can maintain half its people upon any system whatever excepting that on which we are going on at present.

I told you likewise that the Upper Orders and the Gentry were not prepared or in a State to resist the attack upon Property which would be made. They are demoralized equally with the lower orders, but in a contrary Sense. The lower orders are audacious and excited by a thirst for Plunder; the Upper Orders Timid, and excited alone by a thirst for Popularity.[32]

This was Wellington at his most gloomy and misanthropic; it was not just produced by the circumstances of the election, for there had always been an element of it in his thinking, but equally it was only one strand and not normally the dominant one. Less than a year before, when the troubles were just begin-ning, he had assured Lady Salisbury that 'this country has nothing to fear while the troops are officered by gentlemen', and that 'the spirit of the people is aris-tocratic'. He did not remain despairing for long, and was soon actively discussing the best tactics the Tories could adopt to continue to oppose the bill, while scanning the horizon for a reaction among the respectable and reason-able classes to the violence and disorder of the election.[33]

It was not only Tories like Wellington who were alarmed by the passions unleashed by the Reform campaign. The King urged his ministers to bring forward a compromise, arguing that the election had put them in a position of strength from which they could afford to be magnanimous. Palmerston agreed. He had been shaken by the hostility to the bill he had encountered, even among staunch Whigs and old reformers, at Cambridge where he had lost his seat, and he warned Grey not to be misled by the effervescent enthusiasm of the public excited by the press when more serious opinion was shifting against the bill. *The Times* aroused his particular anger, and he asked Grey: 'Is it not possible either to keep this foul mouthed paper in some control, or else to disavow it?' Cabinet considered the King's suggestion in two meetings on 29 May and 8 June, but Grey refused to countenance any retreat and Lansdowne failed to support Palmerston in the face of the Prime Minister's decided line. The King had no alternative but to accept the advice of his ministers, but his alarm at the state of the country must have been confirmed by the news that twenty-five protesters had been killed in a riot at Merthyr Tydfil on 3 June. Mrs Arbuthnot tartly noted that this attracted little interest and none of the outrage in the press at the 'Peterloo Massacre', although the number of dead was higher.[34]

The new Parliament was opened on 21 June and three days later Russell re-introduced the bill which had been modified to remove some anomalies, but with no concessions likely to conciliate doubters. The Opposition were divided over their tactics. They had no hope of defeating the bill in the newly elected Commons, and Peel was inclined to limit his resistance to a few great set-piece debates, but the bulk of the party insisted on tooth-and-nail resistance, fighting the bill clause by clause through Committee, forcing government members to accept responsibility for each individual disqualification, and making the ministers squirm as the many remaining inconsistencies and acts of partisan injustice were held up to ridicule. Croker excelled at this work and scored many hits, but they led to no victories of importance, and the result, as Mrs Arbuthnot acknowledged, was that 'every body in the House dislikes him'.[35] Peel by contrast made a fine speech on 6 July in the Second Reading debate, but scarcely concealed his distaste for the gruelling and fruitless committee work, while his coldness to his fellow Tories left them sore and alienated. But he was irreplaceable, far superior to any other talent on either side of the Commons, as Wellington told Lady Salisbury with much frustration a few months later:

> There's that fellow in the House of Commons, one can't go on without him; but he is so vacillating and crotchety that there's no getting on with him. I did pretty well with him when we were in office, but I can't manage him now at all. He is a wonderful fellow – has a most correct judgment – talents almost equal to those of Pitt, but he spoils all by his timidity and indecision.[36]

Tory obstructionism gained three months; the bill passed its Third Reading on 22 September by 345 votes to 236. The country as a whole quietened in this interlude, but the radicals became better organised and were furious with the delay. Nor was there any evidence of a wider change in public opinion; the press remained vehemently in favour of Reform, and there was no sign of the public abandoning its support for the bill, or looking to the Tories to provide a government.

Having passed the Commons, the Reform Bill was sent to the Lords where the ministers certainly did not have a majority, despite elevating five reformers in June and pressing precedent to the limit to gain a further fifteen votes through the coronation honours in September. There had already been a good deal of discussion both in private and public that the ministers might demand further creations so as to swamp the Lords with their supporters, but many Whigs intensely disliked the idea of thus subverting the independence of the Upper House. The only precedent that could be found dated from the party warfare of Queen Anne's reign, and that had involved the creation of only twelve peers. Grey himself described a mass creation as 'a measure of extreme violence . . . It is a certain evil, dangerous in itself as a precedent', and denied that Queen Anne's peers were at all comparable.[37] It was obvious that such a demand would sorely test the King's support for the government. There was, or appeared to be, a significant chance that a sufficient number of moderate Tories would decide not to oppose the Second Reading of the Bill for it to pass, even if it was then roughly handled in committee. If the ministers had been more conciliatory and made some concessions this might have been what happened, for a number of Tory peers, led by Harrowby and Wharncliffe, hesitated and made clear their hope that an open conflict between the two Houses could be avoided. But with no concessions to console them, these waverers stuck to the party line, although Wharncliffe made clear that he favoured a more moderate bill. The Second Reading debate in the Lords began on 3 October and concluded in the small hours of 8 October, and was marked by the high quality of the speeches on both sides. The bill was rejected by 199 votes to 158, a majority of 41 which was widely felt to be far too many for the ministers to counter by a creation, raising hopes that they would negotiate a compromise which could win broad support.[38]

London was quiet during the Lords debate with no crowds outside waiting for news of the vote or any immediate popular reaction, even though, as Greville remarked, 'the press strain every nerve to produce excitement'.[39] On the following day Joseph Hume and Frederick Maberley addressed a small crowd (two or three thousand people) in Regent's Park and managed to arouse some interest, but the spontaneous response of the people took four days to excite. On 12 October a crowd estimated to number 70,000 marched through the West End to present the King with an Address in favour of the Ministry and the bill. Inevitably this led to trouble and a detachment of the crowd surrounded Apsley House where, as the Duke told a friend: '[They] commenced an attack with Stones which lasted 50 minutes in broad daylight before any assistance came. They broke all the Windows on the lower floor looking towards Rotten Row, a great Number in my Room in which I was sitting, some in the Secretary's Room, and some in the Drawing Room above Stairs. All the blank windows fronting towards the Park & Piccadilly are likewise broken. They did not attempt to break into the Garden. We had Men with fire Arms ready to receive them.'[40] According to Mrs Arbuthnot one stone narrowly missed the Duke, and the outside shutters he had recently installed protected his gallery windows, 'or all his fine pictures wd have been spoiled'. At the same time Lord Londonderry was assaulted on his way to the House, although the disturbances then quickly died down. Much of the country remained perfectly quiet and Aberdeen reported that travelling from London to his estates in Scotland 'I neither saw nor heard anything of Reform'.[41]

Liberals and radicals responded to the defeat in the Lords by intensifying their campaign and increasing their demands. *The Times* launched a furious attack on the bench of bishops who had contributed significantly to the Tory majority, and hinted that they should be expelled from the House. It was also said that Grey had asked the King to dismiss Lord Hill as Commander-in-Chief for not supporting the bill, but that the King had refused, having given Hill leave beforehand to vote as he saw fit.[42] The political unions which had spread across the country over the course of the year with the tacit support and encouragement of the government launched a campaign of meetings and petitions in favour of the bill, which made it difficult for the government to offer any concessions to the Tories. Indeed there were signs that popular radicalism was increasing not diminishing, and that far from being the final answer to demands for reform the bill simply ensured that the radicals shifted their demands further to the left, with claims for household suffrage and the secret ballot now gaining plausibility which in turn forced the extremists to extend their claims to universal manhood suffrage to retain their distinctive appeal.[43] At the same time the political unions, especially the Birmingham Political Union, the largest and most prominent of them all, began to talk publicly about organising on military lines; while the press, including *The Times*, began to campaign for the creation of a National Guard purportedly to maintain order and protect the King and his government. Then, on the last three days of October, Bristol was consumed by devastating riots with many public buildings burnt, and at least twelve deaths and perhaps 300 other casualties. The riots had a strong political edge, while the local authorities were reluctant to take firm immediate action because they sympathised with the rioters. The immediate reaction of the press, other than blaming the Opposition rather than the government for this outbreak of disorder, was to redouble its calls for a National Guard, effectively urging that control of Britain's major cities be handed over to the political unions in arms.[44]

On 5 November Wellington wrote to the King enclosing a memorandum in which he pointed to the obvious dangers of permitting highly partisan political organisations to take up arms. If the political unions formed a National Guard, their opponents would also arm themselves, and the country would be on the brink of civil war, which would inevitably extend to Ireland where it would be fought on sectarian lines. It was a fundamental principle of the constitution that armed forces were the prerogative of the Crown, not Parliament, nor the people. The resources available to the Crown were perfectly sufficient for the occasion; if there was any shortage of regular troops to support the civil power, which Wellington doubted, the King had the power to call out the regular militia and to form volunteer and yeoman corps to any extent. 'If we intend then to pass our lives in a state of freedom and peace under the government and protection of a monarch, we must cling to the well-known principles of our laws and Constitution.[45]

It is clear that Wellington was genuinely alarmed by the passivity of the government in the face of the growing militancy of the political unions; but it is equally clear that he saw the occasion as an opportunity for the King to dismiss his ministers, and ask the Tories to form an administration which might hope to rally the country against the threat of revolution. A few weeks later he told the Duke of Buckingham:

> When I wrote to the King in November on the armament of the political associations, I had in hand a case in which I was certain that nineteen-twentieths of the whole country would concur with me. I did it likewise at a period of the year at which I knew that, if the King wished to get rid of the bonds in which he is held, I could assist him in doing so. There was time to call a new Parliament, and the sense of the country would have been taken on a question on which there could be no doubt.[46]

It is unlikely that Wellington would have found the country as amenable as he presents it here, or that an election could have been fought in the autumn of 1831 without serious disturbances in many parts of the country. Whether or not the political unions and the radicals really spoke for the mass of the population, they were well organised, full of confidence, and had the strong support of the press. Many Tories and independents may have flinched rather than support Wellington in a confrontation, however clear the King's support.

In fact the King either did not see or chose to ignore the implicit invitation to dismiss the government, and passed Wellington's letter on to the ministers, who composed a suitably bland response.[47] This did however prompt the government to quash the idea of a National Guard, issuing a Royal Proclamation and privately warning the leaders of the political unions and their favourite newspapers that this was going too far. Wellington was briefly delighted with the Proclamation, hoping that it would precipitate a decisive break between the government and the radicals, but was soon disillusioned by evidence that close ties remained intact.[48]

The growing tension increased the desire of moderate Tories, the King and some ministers, notably Palmerston, to find a compromise, and this led to some tentative exchanges between Wharncliffe and Harrowby and the government. However, Grey and the majority of the Cabinet proved unwilling to offer any significant concessions – having roused the radical tiger they realised that they had no hope of pacifying it with anything less than 'the whole bill' – and the talks therefore collapsed before they really got started. Neither Wellington nor Peel were surprised; they had both regarded the overture as ill advised, and feared that it would simply make the government more intransigent by revealing divisions in Tory ranks. By contrast, Cabinet solidarity held firm; neither Palmerston nor any other minister would break ranks and offer the King an alternative Whig and moderate Tory administration committed to a less extreme measure of reform.

Parliament met again on 6 December and a new Reform Bill was introduced into the Commons six days later, passing its Second Reading in the early hours of 18 December by a majority of 324 votes to 162 (exactly two to one). It went into committee on 20 January where it remained until 10 March, while the Third Reading was passed on 22 March 1832 by 355 to 239 (more MPs were always likely to attend Parliament in the spring than before Christmas). Wellington was confined to Apsley House by illness for much of December. He caught a bad cold at the beginning of the month which he endeavoured to bully, but which bullied him. On 12 December Mrs Arbuthnot described him as 'very ill . . . [and] in very low spirits'. He slept badly and was irritable with his doctors, but was soon well enough to leave his room and receive visitors; indeed the doctors thought that he saw too many people and talked too much and that this delayed his recovery. Still, he was ready to go out by 7 January and would have done so if the weather had been better, while a month later he was able to tell Aberdeen: 'I have had capital sport hunting, and bear the fatigue as well as ever. What is more, I bore six hours of rain yesterday without injury or inconvenience. So that I hope I am again fit for service, and that I can resume my old habits.'[49]

Even while the Reform Bill was slowly working its way through the Commons committee, the ministers pressed the King to pledge himself to create enough peers to ensure its passage through the Lords. The King baulked at this demand, but eventually gave some ground although the limitations he placed on his promise would still have left the government short of a majority.[50] Wellington was alarmed, telling Lord Strangford on 12 January that it did not much matter whether the government made some concessions in order to get the bill through the Lords or destroyed its independence by the creation of peers, for both were 'easy and straight roads for the destruction of the British monarchy'. And yet he did not entirely despair, going on to write:

> The King knows all this as well as you or I do. *He* alone can save himself and the country from the difficulties in which it is placed, and from the still greater difficulties for his Majesty and his people in which he will soon find himself.
>
>   Nothing is requisite but *resolution* and persevering firmness, and his Majesty will have degenerated in a rare manner from the distinguishing qualities of his family, if he should not possess these.[51]

He accepted that some measure of reform had to be passed eventually, if only because the King had pledged himself to it, but he believed that 'the passion for reform, and particularly for *the bill*, no longer rages, whatever may have passed at meetings in the autumn: the fashion is gone by; and I firmly believe that when this bill passes, if it ever should pass, it will be forced upon the country'. As for the threat of popular disturbances if the bill was not passed, he dismissed them as 'worse than ridiculous; they are contemptible'.[52]

The bill was sent to the Lords on 26 March and the Tory waverers declared that they would vote in favour of the Second Reading in order to avoid giving the government an excuse to create peers, but then attempt to amend the bill in committee. Grey made a few minor concessions and promised a degree of flexibility in committee, but there remained a large and unexplored gap between the changes the government felt were tolerable and those the waverers felt were the minimum they could accept. The bill passed its Second Reading in the Lords at six thirty in the morning on 14 April 1832 after four nights' debate, by 184 to 175 votes including proxies. Grey had gambled by not insisting on a mass creation of peers and it looked as though the gamble had paid off, giving him in many ways the best of both worlds. Yet the King, who should have been especially relieved at this outcome, was alienated and restive. He greatly resented the way that the ministers had treated him, the peremptory tone of their language, and their inability to anticipate the mood of Parliament. He was also highly critical of the government's foreign policy, especially in Belgium, where he felt that the desire to conciliate France was leading to the sacrifice of British interests.[53]

Wellington was curiously invigorated by the success of the Second Reading of the bill. The Lords had approved the principle of the bill; what remained was a fight over its detail in which the Opposition was likely to have the numbers. He told Bathurst on 27 April: 'I am very averse to the whole measure. I don't see how it is possible to govern the country under such a system, amend it as we may. But as the proposition of anything else would certainly fail, the next best thing is to endeavour to form, out of this bill, something as nearly similar as possible to what we have.' In practice this meant ensuring that freeholders in towns returning members should lose their vote for the county members, so as to 'render the counties secure to the landed interest, and free from the influence of the dissenters established in towns'. He also wanted to block the proposal to divide large counties in half, and retain as many small old boroughs as possible, in the belief that this would 'open some seats to the colonial and commercial interests of the country'. With these and other changes 'we might thus hope to confine Radicalism to the forty-four new seats created by the first bill'.[54]

The Tories discussed their tactics when the bill went to the Lords' committee, and after a little hesitation decided to use their numbers to postpone the clauses disenfranchising seats until after other provisions had been discussed. Their aim was to delay the most controversial and least palatable part of the bill in the hope that this would put pressure on the ministers to grant concessions on other clauses, but this was to overplay their hand. Grey had already told Wharncliffe that the ministers would not accept such a change, and it is clear that they felt under great pressure from their supporters in the press and the political unions not to give ground. On 7 May the Lords voted 151 votes to 116 to postpone discussion of the disenfranchisement clauses, while making it clear that following the Second Reading vote they accepted the need for a reform bill which would include the abolition of many rotten boroughs. Cabinet met and asked the King to create fifty or sixty new peers at once in order to make the Tories in the Lords irrelevant. The King considered this demand overnight and on 9 May rejected it and accepted the government's resignation. He pressed Brougham and Richmond to remain in office but both declined, and he therefore sent for Lyndhurst, not to form a government, but to advise him who might be capable and willing to do so.[55]

Many Tories welcomed the government's resignation. Charles Arbuthnot told his son: 'The great joy is that they *are out*.' And Wellington himself told Lyndhurst: 'I shall be very much concerned indeed if we cannot at least make an effort to enable the King to shake off the trammels of his tyrannical Minister. I am perfectly ready to do whatever his Majesty may command me. I am as much averse to the Reform as ever I was. No embarrassment of that kind, no private consideration, shall prevent me from making every effort to serve the King.'[56] But many other Tories proved unwilling to renounce their previous opposition to reform in order to support the King's right to choose his ministers and to obtain a less objectionable bill. Peel was crucial here. He had long made it clear that while he regarded some parliamentary reform as inevitable he would not take responsibility for it by taking office; and he reiterated this decision to Lyndhurst on 9 May when he refused either to lead or to serve in a new government. Unfortunately Peel's example influenced many other Tories in the Commons, including Goulburn, Croker and Herries, while many High Tories were also too averse to the bill to be willing to take office. This left the prospective government far too weak in the Commons; Hardinge and Murray both agreed to serve, but neither had the weight to play more than a supporting role – indeed Hardinge's standing had declined in Opposition due to the vehemence of some of his attacks on the government. Wellington and Lyndhurst concluded that their only hope of putting together a credible front bench in the Commons was to persuade the Speaker, Charles Manners Sutton, to resign his post and lead the government, and to gain the support of the respected independent Alexander Baring. But neither man proved willing, and closer acquaintance made it clear that even if they had been, they lacked the mettle to defy a hostile Commons. And the Commons *was* hostile, as heated debates on 10 and 14 May proved. In the first, a motion deploring the resignation of the ministers was passed by 288 votes to 208, and the debate was even more decided than the numbers suggest. And the second made it clear that despite the private wishes of some of their leaders, the mass of the Whigs in the Commons would not quietly let the Tories pass the bill before throwing them out of office. It was, after all, a House elected barely a year before in the midst of the Reform fever, and the members could still hear 'the bill, the whole bill and nothing but the bill' ringing in their ears. They also knew that there would be another election soon after the Reform Bill was passed and that they would have to explain their vote to their constituents; while it was possible that if a Tory government was formed it would be forced to hold an immediate election in the hope of gaining a majority in the Commons, so that they might have the joy and expense of the hustings not once but twice more before the end of the year. This was plainly not what the country needed; however imperfect the bill, however outrageous Grey's conduct, it was time the question was settled, and that could most easily be achieved by the Lords giving way and the ministers returning to office.[57]

The debate on 14 May proved decisive; up until then it had seemed possible (though never likely) that a weak Tory government might be formed which would succeed in passing the bill and which might then gain strength both at the polls and by recruiting Peel and his friends. The hostility of the House made it clear that this would not work, and leading Tories went to see Wellington that night to warn him that he had no chance of forming an administration that would have the confidence of the Commons. The Duke accepted defeat and on the following morning advised the King to send for Grey, promising to abstain from further opposition to the bill in the Lords, as a way of inducing Grey to return to office without the King being forced into the humiliation of creating peers. Grey and his colleagues made some difficulties, demanding a public guarantee from Wellington that the bill would pass without alteration, which he very properly refused, but not even the Whigs managed to convert their triumph into disaster, and as they had never actually surrendered the seals of office they simply retained their places.[58]

The resignation of Grey's government and the idea that the Reform Bill would be entrusted to the Tories produced a wave of outrage and excitement in the press, and sections of the public, particularly the political unions and other radicals. Thunderous editorials appeared, meetings were held and resolutions passed with talk of organising a general refusal to pay taxes or a run on the banks in order to make the country ungovernable. The political crisis was resolved at Westminster before such talk could turn into effective action, and it is hard to judge just how seriously to take it. Many radicals like Francis Place looked back on these 'May Days' as the high point of a life of activism that had otherwise been full of failures, and naturally exaggerated their role in determining the outcome. They liked to believe that Britain was on the brink of revolution and that only their skill and cool heads ensured both that the hated Tories were defeated, and that the bill was passed without serious violence. Yet it does not seem that any of the leading politicians were much alarmed by this threat: it was not why Wellington gave up the attempt to form a government, nor why Peel refused office; talk of trouble on the streets may have had some influence on members in the Commons, but it is hardly necessary to explain their behaviour; while Grey and his colleagues would surely not have resigned if they had believed that by doing so they ran the risk of provoking a revolution. There was strong popular support for reform in Britain in 1832, and it seems likely that if the Tories had formed a government in May there would have been considerable agitation even if the new administration promptly passed a reform bill; but the extent and implications of that agitation must remain an open question.[59]

Most of the Tory peers followed Wellington's lead and withdrew from the House, allowing the bill to complete the Committee stage in ten days. On 4 June the Third Reading passed by 106 votes to 22; and received Royal Assent by commission (the King refused to give it in person) on 7 June 1832. A Scottish Reform Bill, which blatantly favoured Whig interests, followed hard on the heels of the English bill, receiving Assent on 17 July; while a much less partisan act covering Ireland became law on 7 August. Tory hopes of forcing significant amendments to the bill had amounted to nothing. The government might have swallowed some smaller changes, although it had never shown much willingness to compromise, but this would probably have required more negotiating skill and activity on the part of the leaders of the waverers, Harrowby and Wharncliffe, and more solidarity on the part of their followers, than was ever likely. In the end some sort of confrontation was always probable; the bill was simply too unpopular in the Lords for it to be massaged through, and it was a confrontation that the Tory Lords were destined to lose. The King had left his break with the Whigs too late to have much chance of success; giving the Whigs an election in the spring of 1831 created an unassailable majority for the bill in the Commons and so greatly reduced the chance of a compromise, while Wellington had a far better chance of forming a Tory government in November 1831 than in May 1832.

The struggle over the Reform Bill and in particular the May crisis made Wellington intensely unpopular for a time. He was the subject of much obloquy in the popular press, and the caricaturists treated him roughly. In *John Bull's Picture Gallery* he was depicted as the real Captain Swing who sat on a swing made from the joined tails of two demons perched upon a gibbet. *Old England's Protector* shows him as a military despot, eager to rule by brute force; through one window the soldiery fire upon demonstrators, a guillotine can be seen through another, he holds a naked sword in his hand, the throne upon which he sits rests upon two cannon, the smoke of discord emerging from a burning torch obscures the crown, bags of treasure accumulate at his feet, his booted heels rest upon the rights of man, and the winged cap of victory is in fact a fool's cap complete with bells. In *Desperate Condition of the Tory Gang* he is the leader of a band of robbers who consult under a gallows. The accompanying text describes him as 'the mighty obstinate presumptive [*sic*] W___n: he who hath usurped the laurels of others . . . who sealed the doom of Powers, who boasted he could quiet England in three days!'[60] Wellington was burnt in effigy, and it was commonplace for radical speakers to denounce him as a military despot. 'What was to be expected', one speaker at a Coventry meeting asked, 'from a minister who had declared all public meetings to be farces, and whose first act was to send back an address from the Birmingham Political Union, saying His Majesty acknowledged no such body?'[61]

This ill feeling culminated on the morning of 18 June, the seventeenth anniversary of Waterloo, when Wellington was abused by a crowd as he rode home from the Mint, where he had sat to Pistrucci, the sculptor. His arrival had been noticed and a crowd gathered outside the Mint, which assailed him with jeers and cries of 'Buonaparte for ever!' as he left, and which followed him as he rode through the City. The mob and noise increased and became more threatening, but two Chelsea Pensioners offered their assistance, and the Duke asked them to walk close to the sides of his horse to guard against any attempt to unseat him. A policeman saw the trouble and hurried off for reinforcements, while ladies waved handkerchiefs from windows and citizens invited Wellington to take refuge in their shops and houses, but he preferred to press on to Lincoln's Inn. A young man in a buggy was very helpful keeping just behind or beside the Duke as the need arose. At Lincoln's Inn Wellington was joined by a strong detachment of Chancery lawyers and a stout body of police from Bow Street, who escorted him to Stable Yard and thence into the safety of Green Park. Yet even then the mob persisted and milled round the gates of Apsley House, yelling and hooting. Little or no actual violence was done, though the air was thick with menace and abuse, and Wellington later confessed that he was fortunate that the streets were dry with no loose stones about, and that the sight of a waggon filled with lumps of coal had given him some anxiety.[62]

News of the incident led to a reaction in the Duke's favour. On the following day *The Times*, that passionate advocate of reform, published a long editorial in which it declared its 'firm conviction' that the victory of Waterloo was the salvation of England, France and Europe, and that success was due, in large part, to an 'extraordinary combination of skill, decision, and immoveable fortitude, put forth on that day by the British General'. Having made this discovery, the paper went on to condemn the mob which had been 'so void of all generous and manly feeling, of all moral taste, and decency of nature, as to celebrate the feast of Waterloo, by base and brutal outrages upon the person of its hero! Is there on human record a fact more disgraceful than this? Would the most stupid savage have overlooked the reverence due to the actor of so mighty an achievement?'[63] The public as a whole was not quite so adept at changing direction as *The Times*, and Wellington certainly remained unpopular in many quarters, but the feeling lost some of its edge, and other voices began to make themselves heard. When Wellington attended a review of the Kentish Yeomanry later in the month he was greeted with enthusiasm, while even when changing horses at Bromley he 'was greatly cheered, without one dissentient voice'. However, as Charles Arbuthnot went on to report, Wellington was 'so disgusted with the fickleness of the People that he treats both hooting & cheering with contempt'.[64]

At first glance it appears that the long struggle of Wellington and the Tories against the Reform Bill ended in unmitigated defeat; 'the bill, the whole bill, and nothing but the bill' was passed in the teeth of their opposition, while Wellington's attempt to form a government to pass a more moderate measure ended in humiliation. This is true as far as it goes, but it is not the whole picture. It is most unlikely that the political unions and other radicals would have been satisfied with the bill if it had passed easily in the spring or autumn of 1831.[65] They would have demanded further concessions, and the ministers showed little fortitude in resisting their demands. In this light the Tory resistance can be seen as a protracted and relatively successful rearguard action, which ensured that the reform impulse was absorbed by the battle over the bill, and was largely though not completely exhausted by the time the bill was passed.

This is the most positive interpretation of events from a Tory perspective, but even if it is accepted without reservations, there remained a great deal for Tories to lament. The bill and the events leading up to its passage did great violence to the constitution, destroying the delicate balance between the King, the Lords and the Commons. The King's traditional right to choose his ministers had been cast aside; it had never been an absolute right – George III had been forced to accept the Talents in 1806, and had to part with Addington in 1804 – but the fall of Wellington's ministry in 1830, and his inability to form a Tory administration in May 1832, despite having the unequivocal support of the King in both cases, dealt the royal prerogative a blow from which it has never recovered.[66] Significantly the radicals propounded an alternative doctrine, that legitimacy was conferred exclusively by the support of the people (by which, in effect, they meant the political unions and the press, as much as the electorate or the House of Commons). Although this argument gained only limited acceptance in 1832 it helped to undermine belief in the King's authority, and in future most governments would be made and would fall as a result of general elections.

The House of Lords was also damaged by the crisis. It had never had quite the importance of the Commons, but its long-established habit of providing broad support for the government of the day had meant that direct conflicts between the two Houses had largely been confined to issues on which the government was itself divided, such as Catholic Emancipation, or which were of relatively minor importance. In these cases the Lords had generally prevailed, at least in exercising a veto if not in imposing positive action. That power was diminished by the open discussion of the possibility of creating more peers, and very large numbers of peers at that, to overturn a majority in the Lords. Henceforth if the Lords blocked any major piece of legislation it knew that it did so on sufferance, for the prime minister could demand that peerages be created and back the demand with this precedent. However, this threat could only be made by a strong prime minister with a secure majority in the Commons, willing to face the electorate; and this, together with discretion in choosing which battles to fight, ensured that the Lords remained a significant force in politics for the rest of Wellington's life and beyond.[67]

A disempowered King and a diminished Lords should have seen the Commons reign supreme. Indeed Wellington feared that the Reform Bill would make effective government impossible by simultaneously reducing the influence both of the Lords and the executive over members of the Commons, and increasing the influence of their electors and the press. Governments would be unable to secure a majority for any unpopular measures, and would have difficulty retaining a majority at all for very long unless they constantly played to the gallery. This is very much what happened in the short term as successive governments struggled with the Commons over the next few years, but in the long run the Reform Bill had the paradoxical effect of reducing the power of the Commons just as much as the Lords and the King. An enlarged electorate led, not to more individual accountability of MPs, but their subsumption under a party label, and with it the loss of their independence. This was enforced by a gradual extension of the number of questions which were defined as votes of confidence – and while in the abstract this meant that the government was submitting itself to judgement by the House, in practice it meant that few if any supporters of the government would dare break the party line and so risk forcing an election.

If the King, the Lords and the Commons all lost power, who gained it? Ideally the answer should be 'the people', specifically the half a million new voters enfranchised by the bill, but also the mass of the population as politicians took greater interest in their needs and desires. There may be some truth to this, although the provision of social welfare by governments in the later nineteenth and twentieth centuries was more a product of the economic growth that made it possible, and the inherent tendency of all organisations, particularly bureaucracies, to enlarge their scope, than it was of the need for politicians to find new things to promise voters. But the principal beneficiary of the constitutional changes of 1831–32 in the long term was the executive, and specifically the prime minister. Once a prime minister had a secure majority in the Commons, and in time that usually came to be a matter of course, there were few limits on his powers. There was still a network of informal restraints – the growing power of the press and public opinion, the fading influence of the Lords and the Crown – but these hardly compared to the Commons which forced Liverpool to abandon the Property Tax in 1816, the Lords which blocked Catholic Emancipation for a generation, or the King who kept the Whigs out of office for almost half a century. While the Reform Bill of 1832 distributed some power, in the form of votes, to a broader section of the nation, it also concentrated a great deal more power in the hands of the prime minister, and made him much less accountable. If Wellington had really aspired to despotism, he ought to have given it his warm support.

CHAPTER TWENTY-THREE

THE LIMITS OF OPPOSITION
(1832–35)

T HE LONG STRUGGLE over the Reform Bill dominated public affairs in Britain throughout 1831–32 leaving little room for other topics, but Wellington, other leading members of the Opposition, and the King, were all alarmed by the government's foreign policy. The good understanding with the Eastern Powers – Russia, Prussia and Austria – which Wellington had carefully nurtured, was discarded with distaste, for the Whig and Canningite ministers had little interest in co-operation with governments which did not share their ideological outlook. The France of the July Monarchy was a much more suitable ally, despite its instability and the residual hankering of many Frenchmen for foreign adventures and the pursuit of glory; although Palmerston never felt the same enthusiasm of some of his Whig colleagues for an exclusive alliance with France, despite the French government's excellent liberal credentials.[1]

The reversal of policy was even more marked towards Portugal. When Wellington and Aberdeen left office in 1830 they had been on the point of recognising Miguel as King of Portugal, implicitly conceding that he had as good a claim to the throne of Portugal as William III had to that of England in 1690. But Grey, his colleagues, and the liberal press, denounced Miguel as a cruel tyrant, the agent of the Holy Alliance, and made little secret of their sympathy for the defeated Constitutionalist party which supported the claim to the throne of Miguel's niece Maria. Officially the new British government proclaimed a policy of non-intervention in the Portuguese civil war – a statement which was far less even-handed than it sounded, for Miguel was in undisputed possession of the whole country, and the Constitutionalists were confined to Terceira in the Azores. Unofficially it went further, giving indirect support for a loan to the Terceira Regency, and doing nothing when a French naval squadron seized the Portuguese fleet in Lisbon harbour and distributed liberal propaganda in an unsuccessful attempt to overthrow Miguel. In April 1831 Dom Pedro was forced to abdicate as emperor of Brazil, and when he arrived in Europe that summer he was greeted as a hero and champion by liberals who knew that he had imposed constitutions on Portugal and Brazil, and who did not care to enquire why the Brazilians were so ungrateful as to depose him. Under his leadership the Constitutionalists found it easy to raise money in Paris and London, and with the money they recruited soldiers and bought arms. Palmerston proposed that Miguel should simply surrender his position and go into exile with a pension, and blamed the influence of the Eastern Powers when this 'compromise' was rejected. And he sought to gain domestic political advantage by associating Wellington and the Tories with the tyrant Miguel and the Holy Alliance in a series of articles in the *Globe* newspaper.[2]

Britain and France gave important covert support to Pedro, while insisting that Spain, which favoured Miguel, remain strictly neutral and inactive. In July 1832 Pedro landed just north of Oporto with some 7,500 men and soon captured the city, but even in this traditional liberal stronghold his arrival produced little enthusiasm, while the country as a whole viewed him with a mixture of indifference and hostility. As Miguel slowly collected forces to oppose the invasion the Constitutionalists found themselves confined to the vicinity of Oporto, and the liberal celebrations which had rung out in London, Paris and elsewhere on the first news began to appear premature if not wholly misguided.[3]

Wellington condemned the policy of the British government as both immoral and dangerous – deliberately plunging an old and faithful ally into the miseries of a civil war, which in turn risked provoking Spanish intervention, possibly leading to civil war in Spain. The abandonment of the long-standing principle of non-intervention was compounded by hypocrisy and deceit. Nor could the end result possibly be worth it, for it was obvious that the great bulk of the population favoured Miguel, and that even if the Constitutionalists triumphed in the field, their success would simply lead to more instability. In August 1832, as Parliament was about to rise, Wellington made a forthright attack on the government's Portuguese policy which angered Grey but which, Wellington believed, persuaded the government to remove a paragraph from the King's Speech at the close of the session which would have recognised Maria's right to the throne and prepared the way for open British intervention in her favour.[4]

Wellington's criticism did not echo with the public – even conservative newspapers depicted Miguel as a tyrant – but there was more disquiet over the alliance with France, especially when it involved using the navy to put pressure on Holland to acknowledge Belgium's independence and give way on points still in dispute. Wellington was strongly in favour of maintaining good relations with France, but not at the expense of ties with the other great powers, and he felt that the Whig alliance furthered French but not British interests, and that it increased, not diminished, the risk of war and revolution in Europe.[5] Recognition of Belgium's independence under Leopold of Saxe-Coburg was inevitable, but Wellington was concerned at the level of French influence in the new country, which was symbolised by Leopold's marriage to Louis Philippe's daughter in 1832. Keeping the French out of the Low Countries had been a fundamental tenet of British foreign policy for more than two hundred years, and it shocked many that less than twenty years after the defeat of Napoleon, the British government would actively encourage a French army to march through Belgium to besiege and capture Antwerp in December 1832. Like many Tories, Wellington also condemned the bad faith and hostility which surrounded Palmerston's treatment of the Dutch, and was concerned that the war might spread. Fortunately the Dutch confined themselves to a determined if futile defence of the citadel of Antwerp, while the Eastern Powers did not go beyond diplomatic pressure to ensure that the French army withdrew as soon as it fell. By the end of 1832 Wellington felt that the crisis was passed: 'The government will soon settle the Dutch affair now that the French desire of a *bully* has been gratified by the capitulation of the Citadel of Antwerp. We shall in all probability have peace abroad immediately.'[6] The French did indeed withdraw promptly, but a final settlement between Holland and Belgium was not reached for some years.

The siege of Antwerp coincided with the first general election after the passage of the Reform Act (December 1832 to January 1833). Wellington was unconvinced by the surprisingly optimistic forecasts of some leading Tories, including their election managers, but the final result was even worse than he expected. The Conservatives were reduced to only about 150 seats in the Commons compared to around 320 supporters of the government, almost 150 radicals, and 42 Irish members who followed O'Connell, although party loyalty was still very fluid and it was impossible to draw clear lines, especially between the Whigs and the radicals. The new Commons contained only eight members who were not at least nominal members of the Church of England; however, the influence of the Dissenters contributed powerfully to the success of the government on the hustings. Wellington reacted with characteristic exaggeration in March 1833: 'The revolution is made: that is to say that power is transferred from one class of society, the gentlemen of England, professing the faith of the Church of England, to another class of society, the shopkeepers being dissenters from the Church, many of them Socinians, others Atheists.' Given the resentment many Dissenters felt at the privileged position of the Church of England and its Church in Ireland, it is unsurprising that this became one of the leading issues in British politics for the next two years.[7]

The weakness of the Conservatives in the Commons and their evident lack of broad support in the country affected their tactics in Parliament. Neither Peel nor Wellington saw much point in launching a full-scale assault on the government when they could not hope to provide an alternative ministry. Wellington told Aberdeen: 'I have never relished as you know the seeking opportunities to carp at and oppose the measures of the Government. The whole course of my life has been different.' And,

> If we look at our position in the House of Lords we shall be found with a very large majority against or rather not connected with Lord Grey's Government. We cannot avoid however to consider Lord Grey's Government as the last prop of the monarchy, however bad it is and however unworthy of confidence . . . It will not be wise for us to endeavour to break down Lord Grey without knowing what is to follow him . . .[8]

Parliament opened on 29 January 1833 and the new balance of power in the Commons was shown immediately when an Amendment to the Address was moved, not by the Conservative Opposition, but by O'Connell with some support from the radicals. Peel intervened in the debate on the third night with a powerful and effective speech defending the government and in particular Edward Stanley, the Irish Secretary, who was the particular object of O'Connell's hostility.[9] This set the pattern for much of the session, with the government under constant attack from the left and never confident how many liberals and radicals would support rather than oppose them on any particular issue. Peel gave the government support wherever he could, helping the moderate ministers who were more likely to attract fire from the radicals. He constantly reiterated his support for reasonable, well-conceived reform, gradually softening the image of the party, but dismaying many Tories who hated the government and despised the weakness implicit in so many concessions.

Wellington was under great pressure from Tory peers to lead a vigorous opposition to the government in the Lords, but he firmly resisted and kept out of London a good deal in the early part of the session when there was little legislation for the Upper House to discuss. He told Rosslyn that he wished to keep the ministers in power, although 'I detest their principles and policy and object to their course of action'.[10] This uncomfortable position did not make him good company, as Charles Arbuthnot observed:

> It is quite terrible how all our friends croak. It is very disagreeable also, & makes London quite odious. Between ourselves, no one is worse than the Duke. To hear him, there is not a hope of our being saved from revolution. I

trust he is wrong: but wrong or right, the hearing from morn till night that we are going fast the way the French went 40 yrs ago is very painful . . .[11]

Although Wellington and Peel agreed that they should attempt to moderate the government rather than oppose it, relations between them had not recovered from Peel's refusal to serve the King in May 1832. There was no open quarrel between the two men, but equally there was very little communication and no warmth or trust. Their personalities were very different and rather incompatible: Peel very proud and reserved except within his own family; Wellington much more sociable, gregarious and unguarded in his conversation. Peel scarcely bothered to conceal his disapproval of Mrs Arbuthnot, whom he carelessly assumed was, or had been, Wellington's mistress; and this naturally did not predispose her in his favour, so that she tended to influence Wellington against him. Conversely Wellington believed that Peel disliked clever women, or at least that he had consciously chosen to marry one who was not clever. Given how much Wellington appreciated and enjoyed the society of intelligent, confident women, and how much he had suffered from the folly of his own misguided marriage, his comment revealed a consciousness of their differences. Even two years later, when relations between the two men were much better, Wellington told Lady Salisbury: 'There is something unconciliating about him. He has no devoted friends, for he has no confidence in anybody; he never does what I am now doing with you, for example – thinking aloud. Nothing would induce him.'[12]

Despite the lack of Tory opposition the government staggered from crisis to crisis through the session, appearing faction-ridden, incompetent and unable to command a stable majority in the Commons. Major legislation was passed, but only with Peel's help or when the ministers had accepted significant amendments from the radicals. The most important measure was probably the abolition of slavery in the British Empire, which received Royal Assent in August. The ministers were generally tepid in their enthusiasm for the idea, but it had figured prominently on the hustings, and was propelled by a broadly based and well-organised campaign that cut across the usual barriers of sect and class. The government's proposals, which included £20 million in compensation for the owners of the 800,000 slaves, were disliked by the radicals and only narrowly scraped through the Commons with Tory support. In the Lords Wellington expressed many misgivings about the details of the plan, especially those surrounding the seven-year 'apprenticeship' freed slaves were bound to serve, but did not oppose the scheme as a whole. In private he was more critical, linking the plan to other attacks on property, worrying that colonial legislatures might resist coercion from London, and fearing the financial consequences if the whole Caribbean sugar island economy collapsed. Given Wellington's important role in the negotiations for the abolition of the international slave trade in 1814–15 his coolness in 1833 is disappointing, yet many of his doubts were shared even by such progressive liberals as Lord Holland and Lord John Russell.[13]

The weakness of the Opposition's position was demonstrated clearly on the one occasion when Wellington permitted himself to make a direct attack upon the government in the Lords in 1833. On 3 June Wellington criticised the blatant activities of the Portuguese liberals in raising money and military forces in Britain, with barely concealed official assistance, in violation of the government's stated commitment to non-intervention. The ministers responded feebly and Wellington pressed his advantage to a division, the motion being carried 79 to 69.[14] But this soon proved a pyrrhic victory as the liberal press launched a torrent of abuse attacking Wellington and the House of Lords. The *Morning Chronicle* declared that 'a House of Peers without rotten boroughs to fall back upon is impotent when opposed to the nation'; while *The Times* declared that the government had lost popularity because it was not radical enough, and that the only alternative to the existing ministry was a revolution. The Commons passed a motion approving the government's policy on Portugal by 361 votes to 98 with liberals and radicals showing that a Conservative attack was the one thing that could revive their flagging enthusiasm for the ministry. On the following day the *Morning Chronicle* crowed with more delight than dignity, 'the eighty spiritual and temporal peers have received an answer from His Majesty which, in plain English, means: your opinion is not worth a straw'.[15]

The Portuguese debate was a painful demonstration of the weakness of the peers in 1833, and of the danger that a more assertive opposition would provoke a direct attack upon the House of Lords. Even before the debate some liberals had been demanding the removal of bishops from Parliament, and there were still rumours that the ministers might press the King for a mass creation of peers if the Lords proved recalcitrant. It was a lesson which influenced Wellington's handling of the most contentious issue of the session, the government's bill to 'reform' the Church of Ireland by abolishing and amalgamating many dioceses, replacing the church rates with taxes, reorganising its finances, and applying the 'surplus' funds to non-denominational charitable purposes. Wellington and many other Tories saw this as a direct attack on the position of the Church of Ireland and through it on the Protestant Establishment and the union with Britain – against which O'Connell was strongly agitating. Peel was more ready to compromise – his passion for administrative reform was excited by any ancient institution – and he extracted some important concessions, including dropping the appropriation clause; although he still voted against the Third Reading of the bill.[16]

When the amended bill came up to the Lords Wellington was under great pressure from his supporters, especially the ultra Tories, to resist it at all costs. On the other hand the Primate of the Irish Church argued that bad as it was, the bill had to be allowed to pass as the income of the clergy had already been disrupted, and that further delay would be even more damaging. Peel supported this appeal, and added that the Commons would not pass the remaining Estimates until the bill had cleared the Lords. A political crisis over the Irish Church would ensure that the Dissenters and other radicals would rally to support the government, and could hardly end other than in a serious defeat for the Lords.[17] Wellington was well aware of this, but he also knew that 'the majority in the House of Lords . . . are decidedly against the bill. It is very difficult to restrain them; and they are very much displeased.' And he went on to tell Peel:

I quite concur in your opinion of the state of the House of Commons, of the consequences of breaking down the Government by a vote of the House of Lords, and of the prospects from a new election. But it is not so easy to make men feel that they are of no consequence in the country who have heretofore had so much weight and still preserve their properties and their stations in society and their seats in the House of Lords. The true sense of their position will be imposed at last; when they will become more manageable.[18]

Rather than precipitate a crisis that could not end well, Wellington abstained from the Second Reading vote, ensuring that the bill passed with a comfortable majority.[19] His decision precipitated a revolt by the ultra peers, who, after many angry scenes, broke away from his leadership. He responded with a degree of impatience, telling Mrs Arbuthnot: 'The Question is how to attain objects practically . . . . You can settle matters very easily in your Garden. They are not so easily settled between Ultra Tory Peers on the one side, and the House of Commons and Sir Robert Peel and the Real Interests of the Country on the other.'[20]

As the long parliamentary session of 1833 finally drew towards its close Wellington remained pessimistic about the future of the country. Lady Salisbury recorded that the Duke and Lord Rosslyn agreed that 'there will be no blow-up, no bloodshed', but that 'all our ancient institutions will be destroyed by due course of law', and 'that the property of the rich will be attacked in various ways'. 'At the same time the Duke thinks there is nothing to be done – that long experience only can disgust the nation and change its feeling, and that till that is the case *we* cannot move.'[21] There were already a few small signs of a shift in public opinion in 1833. The government had steadily lost popularity, in large part because of its palpable inefficiency, and the Tories had regained some seats in by-elections. But the most that could fairly be said was that they were less unpopular than before, and in particular that the intense hostility towards Wellington that had been intermittently evident in 1831–32 had faded away. In January 1834 Wellington visited Grantham, which was then a stronghold of popular radicalism, and was well received, although more in a spirit of curiosity than acclaim, '"Let's see old Wellington", and much applause' was the general reaction.[22]

At the beginning of 1834 Wellington viewed the coming session of Parliament with little hope or enthusiasm. The quarrel with the ultras had been patched over but he was bored and exasperated with the role of party leader in opposition. He resented being lectured by Cumberland on the need to consult broadly with the Conservative peers, and resented even more the 'uncivil answers and few acceptances' he received when he invited them to a party dinner on the eve of the opening of Parliament.[23] A few months later he complained: 'To talk of my being leader of a party or anything but the slave of a party, or in other words the person whom any other may *bore* with his letters or his visits upon publick subjects when he pleases is just what I call *stuff.*'[24] But this grumbling should not conceal the fact that Wellington was an assiduous, hard-working and successful party leader, whose personal exertions did much to keep the Tory Lords together and to persuade them to restrain their opposition to the government. In this respect at least the Duke was far better at politics than Peel, with his notorious propensity to irritate friends and alienate allies.

Wellington continued to believe that the Conservatives had nothing to gain by forcing a confrontation with the government, and that vehement opposition would simply risk precipitating an attack on the Lords. This view was strengthened by a debate on 13 March 1834 when a radical motion to exclude bishops from the Lords received substantial support in the Commons and the press, despite being opposed by the ministers. Although the motion was defeated (58 to 125), the Lords remained vulnerable, and Wellington did his best to keep them out of the public eye, discouraging rhetorical attacks on the ministry. In the Commons Peel continued to support many government measures and reinforced his reputation as the friend of moderate and sensible reform. Probably the most significant piece of legislation introduced in the session was the new Poor Law, which later generations would revile as heartless and productive of endless misery. At the time, however, it was widely approved by leading radicals, although it drew vigorous opposition from *The Times* and was never popular among those likely to feel its effects directly. Both Peel and Wellington gave it their broad support without taking a prominent part in the discussion; it was very much the ministers' bill and was entirely in keeping with the intellectual spirit of their other liberal reforms.[25]

21 The portrait of Wellington painted by Lawrence for the Arbuthnots, and greatly admired by them and Wellington himself. Mrs Arbuthnot wrote that 'It is more like him than any picture I ever saw … & quite different. All other pictures of him depict him as a hero; this has all the softness and sweetness of countenance which characterizes him when he is in the private society of his friends.'

22 Princess Lieven was the wife of the Russian ambassador to London, an important figure in British society, and, until she transferred her allegiance to Canning in 1826, a close friend of Wellington. She was vivacious and entertaining as well as intensely interested in politics, and relished both gossip and intrigue.

23 Although Wellington worked hard to overcome the King's opposition to Canning's appointment as Foreign Secretary in 1822, he soon came to distrust Canning and oppose his policies. Wellington believed in close co-operation with the continental powers to preserve the peace, while Canning was more eager to appeal to public opinion and pursue a narrower vision of British interests.

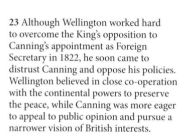

24 *Achilles in the Sulks after his Retreat; or, The Great Captain on the Stool of Repentance!!,* a satire on Wellington's resignation as Commander-in-Chief in May 1827. The Achilles statue in Hyde Park, erected in honour of Wellington's victories, can be seen through the open window.

25 *A Wellington Boot or the Head of the Army* by 'Paul Pry' (William Heath), 1827.

26 *Going to Downing Street – a sketch* by 'Paul Pry' (William Heath), 1827–29. Without obvious political point or allusion, this shows Wellington as a familiar figure on the streets of London when he was Prime Minister.

27 *Burking poor Old Mrs Constitution Aged 141* by 'Paul Pry' (William Heath), April 1829. An allusion to the recent Burke and Hare murders, showing Wellington and Peel smothering the constitution and opening the door to a return to Catholicism.

28 *Leaving the House of Lords through the Assembled Commons* by 'Paul Pry' (William Heath), March 1829. A no-popery crowd yell abuse at Wellington as he leaves Parliament in the midst of the debates over Catholic Emancipation.

29 *Partial Distress or the old Cabinet-Maker and his Man Bob Out of Employment* by John Phillips, 20 November 1830. A satire linking the fall of Wellington's government to the country's economic troubles and the statement in the King's Speech that the distress was only 'partial'.

30 A lithograph of Wellington and Mrs Arbuthnot in the park by an unknown artist, published on 27 July 1834 just a few days before Harriet's death.

31 Lady Salisbury, from a pastel portrait by C. Bartonford in the collection at Hatfield House. Following Mrs Arbuthnot's death in 1834, Lady Salisbury became Wellington's closest female confidant, and her diary gives a vivid picture of the Duke in the mid-1830s.

32 The magnificent Waterloo Gallery, which formed part of Benjamin Dean Wyatt's extension of Apsley House. To Mrs Arbuthnot's distress, Wellington insisted on covering the walls with yellow damask; it was changed to red by the second Duke.

33 *The Waterloo Banquet* by John William Salter, 1840. Wellington celebrated the anniversary of Waterloo each year with a banquet for surviving officers, which became an increasingly notable event on the London social calendar. After the Waterloo Gallery at Apsley House was completed there was room for eighty-five guests, with the table adorned by the silver gilt centre-piece given to Wellington by the Portuguese government, and which can still be seen at Apsley House today.

34 Wellington enjoyed decorating rooms at Stratfield Saye with some of his large collection of prints.

35 Wellington and Peel by Franz Xaver Winterhalter, 1844, painted for the Queen. Wellington and Peel were political allies although never close friends. Their outlook and temperaments were very different, but they had great respect for each other, and their co-operation was essential to the successful rebuilding of the Conservative Party in the mid- and late 1830s.

36 *A Cabinet Council* by 'H.B.' (John Doyle), 28 November 1834. A satire on Wellington's decision to hold almost all the chief offices of state until Peel could return from Italy and form a government.

37 *Symptoms of Insubordination* by 'H.B.' (John Doyle), 1 August 1839. Wellington as nurse or governess reproves a naughty boy (Lord Melbourne) who attempts defiance, while Peel as a second nurse comforts Lord John Russell (a toddler), and two older rough boys (Brougham and Lyndhurst) jeer at the spoiled brats. It satirises the protection given to Melbourne's government by Wellington and Peel, and the irritation this caused to both the radicals and the ultra-Tories.

38 Wellington and Colonel Gurwood by Andrew Morton, painted around 1840. Gurwood, a Peninsular veteran, edited Wellington's *Dispatches* for publication in the 1830s. Wellington was delighted to be reminded of his early letters, declaring 'I could not write them better now. I see that I had at that time all the care and foresight and attention to every detail that could forward the business which I had in charge, which is the only means of ensuring success.'

39 Bronze statue of Wellington by Carlo Marochetti unveiled in Glasgow in 1844. The popular tradition of adding a traffic cone to Wellington's head rather obscures the grandeur of the piece.

40 A daguerreotype of Wellington taken on his seventy-fifth birthday, 1 May 1844, by Antoine Claudet.

41 *Wellington and His Grandchildren* by Robert Thorburn, 1852. 'I cannot tell you how much I enjoy and prize the affection which children have for me. When they become familiar with me I believe they consider me one of themselves, and make of me a sort of plaything! They climb upon me and make toys of my Hair and my fingers! They grow up into friends.' Throughout his life Wellington enjoyed the company of children, although his attitude was far more robust and playful than the sentimentality of this picture, painted in the last year of his life.

42 The *Illustrated London News*' depiction of Wellington's funeral procession, showing the Duke's riderless horse being led, and giving a good impression of the size of the crowds.

43 The Duke of Wellington by C.R. Leslie, *c.* 1848.

The new Poor Law was introduced in the context of widespread industrial action and unrest, including the prosecution of six agricultural labourers in Dorset ('the Tolpuddle Martyrs') in March. A mass demonstration in favour of the prisoners was staged in London in late April, attracting some 25,000 protesters. This proved the last burst of the wave of popular radicalism that had gripped Britain since the summer of 1830 and which now faded away for a time, before reviving in the new form of Chartism a few years later. It also marked the final disillusionment of many radicals with the reform government; but the trend of public opinion was now running against the radicals and the Whigs alike.

The spring of 1834 also saw the Cabinet splinter, culminating in the resignation of Stanley and three other relatively conservative ministers (Graham, Richmond and Goderich, now Earl of Ripon) at the end of May. This should have left the Cabinet more united, but the fractures within it were too deep to be healed, while almost all the ministers were suffering from the strain of office and were consumed by mutual suspicions and resentments which were often played out in the press. Stanley's loss was a blow to the performance of the government front bench in the Commons, for while his vicious tongue made more enemies than friends, he was the only minister who could hope to compete with Peel, whose mastery of the chamber was now complete. Wellington was inclined to dismiss the significance of the resignations, writing a few days later: 'I believe that the Ministry has been botched up; and I confess I see no reason why it should not go on as well without as it did with the aid of the talents of Mr Stanley and Sir James Graham. In these times it is not talents that enable men to carry on the public business, much less character, but insolence, blustering and above all humbug.'[26]

Nonetheless the prospect of Stanley's resignation, which had been much discussed for weeks before it took place, encouraged leading Conservatives to put their house in order in case the government fell and the King turned to them. The lack of communication and residual ill feeling between Wellington and Peel was the central problem, and both Charles Arbuthnot and Lord Aberdeen endeavoured to organise a reconciliation, with some limited success. On 25 April Peel went out of his way in a debate on Ireland to pay warm tribute to Wellington's role as the saviour of the country in the war with Napoleon, and on 12 May Arbuthnot wrote to him outlining the Duke's views on how they should respond to a summons from the King. Crucially Wellington said that he would advise the King that the prime minister should be in the House of Commons and that he would be willing to serve under Peel in any role, although he inclined to the Horse Guards and the command of the army.[27] It is possible that by nominating the Horse Guards Wellington was indicating a desire to withdraw from the front line of politics, and that he looked to an office that he might continue to hold if a Conservative government proved short-lived; but it is equally likely that he was showing that he would not even claim a Cabinet office in the event of this proving an obstacle to Peel forming a coalition with moderate Whigs such as Stanley. Whatever the underlying meaning, the renunciation of his claim to the leadership at least removed a dangerous source of uncertainty and distrust between the two men, but it did not lead to any immediate improvement in their personal relations. As Lady Salisbury noted with some exasperation: 'Hardinge has begged of us to ask Peel and the Duke to meet each other; but one is so accustomed to be courted, and the other has so much sensitiveness and plebian pride that they are easily led to take mutual offence.'[28]

Peel's attitude to Wellington was soured at this time by the nomination of the Duke to succeed Lord Grenville as Chancellor of Oxford. Of all public honours this was probably the one Peel most coveted; his ties to the university ran deep and receiving it would have expunged the pain and humiliation he had suffered when he lost the seat in 1829. Wellington, by contrast, had never attended the university; he was no scholar and, after a quarrel, he had withdrawn his sons from Christ Church and sent them to Cambridge instead. When first approached by representatives of St John's College in November 1833 he had strongly demurred, telling them that 'I knew no more of Greek or Latin than an Eton boy in the remove; that these facts were perfectly well known, and that I must be considered incapable and unfit'.[29] He asked if it was really necessary that the Chancellor should be a peer, intending to recommend Peel, but was assured that it was, and one who attended Parliament constantly, for they already had two members for the university in the Commons. (The most obvious precedents for a commoner as Chancellor were Oliver Cromwell and his son Richard, which were hardly auspicious.) Faced with this determination Wellington suggested a number of other Tory peers, including Bathurst, Sidmouth and Talbot, but none produced any enthusiasm. In the end Wellington made no promise but agreed to consult his friends.[30] When Lord Talbot appeared willing to stand Wellington attempted to withdraw, but was warned by Bathurst that if Talbot was the Conservative candidate, the Whig Lord Carlisle 'will carry it in a hand canter'.[31] And when Grenville finally died in January, Wellington again urged the delegates 'to elect Sir Robert Peel; and pointed out to them the advantage of putting him forward as it were officially in the affairs of the Church'. However, they 'declared positively that it was impossible to carry the election either for him or for Lord Talbot'.[32] At this, Wellington finally capitulated and agreed to let his name go forward, although he remained acutely aware of his deficiencies for the position. (Indeed he probably exaggerated them, for while Grenville was a serious classicist, the

Chancellor of Cambridge was the Duke of Gloucester, the King's cousin, who even by the standards of the royal family was not renowned for sense or learning.) By any reasonable standard Wellington had been scrupulously fair to Peel, and the latter made no complaint, but nonetheless felt aggrieved, and this resentment added to the coldness with which he treated the Duke.[33]

Wellington's installation as Chancellor of the University on 10 June 1834 proved the social and political event of the season, with related ceremonies spread over several days. When Lady Salisbury arrived at the theatre quite early she found that all the seats reserved for peeresses had already been taken, although one of the proctors found seats for her party; but Princess Lieven, who arrived a little later, was forced to stand for some time until a seat in the second row could be found, and 'did not look pleased'. The undergraduates who crowded the gallery amused themselves and the rest of the audience by calling out the names of public men, which would then be greeted with suitable hissing or applause. 'The cry was always unanimous, and the feeling of the most decided Tory kind (even *I* [Lady Salisbury wrote] feel almost too liberal for the air of this place); nothing but Ultra Toryism and Ultra Protestantism will go down.' Wellington's name produced the loudest cheering, and when he entered 'the very building shook with applause' which continued for many minutes.[34]

The scene was repeated on the following day and after more degrees had been conferred the Newdigate Prize poem was recited by its author, Joseph Arnould. This included an allusion to the Duke,

And the dark soul a world could scarce subdue,
    Bent to *thy* genius, Chief of Waterloo

which, Lady Salisbury noted,

called forth such a burst of enthusiasm as I never witnessed in my life, and even the Duke told me afterwards he had never seen anything like it. The whole theatre seemed one living mass that rose in concert: the Peers, the Bishops, every creature joined to do homage to the Deliverer of Europe: the noise was positively astounding and continued fully quarter of an hour. As to the undergraduates and occupants of the arena, they scarcely knew how to give vent to their feelings; they roared, they screamed, they waved hats and handkerchiefs, they actually jumped and danced with delight. It was quite overcoming; such a moment, the witnessing such homage to the greatest man existing, was worth any trouble or any sacrifice![35]

This acclaim clearly vindicated the choice of Wellington rather than Peel or anyone else. No one cared that the Duke had mispronounced some Latin words, but they remembered that twenty years before he had been made an honorary Doctor of the University and been greeted with similar enthusiasm when he returned to England from the Peninsula, and that since then he had been one of the leading figures in the Tory Party and had championed the cause of the Anglican establishment. Seldom if ever in those twenty years had Wellington been received with such warmth, and it made up for some of the hooting and abuse he had received at times from the London mob. He told Lady Salisbury, 'if I could be spoilt by this sort of thing, they would spoil me here', and she added 'I think he feels it deeply'.[36] However, Wellington's reception at Oxford was not just a personal triumph; it was also a celebration of the High Tory principles which gave the party a renewed sense of confidence and purpose. For the past six years, ever since the Repeal of the Test and Corporation Acts, Oxford and everything it stood for had been under siege. That siege had still not been lifted, but there was a sense that the tide of battle might have turned and the garrison looked ahead with fresh hope.

Wellington and the Tories in the House of Lords were much more assertive in the last few weeks of the session of 1834. Rather against Peel's wishes they rejected the Irish Tithe Bill, which Wellington privately described as 'abominable' and containing 'not one principle ... to which we ought not to have objected'.[37] The government's attempt to force the universities to admit Dissenters was thrown out by a majority of 102, 'greater than any division of the Opposition in this century' according to Lady Salisbury, who went on to comment that 'this, I trust, will put swamping the House of Peers out of question'. Wellington was in high spirits, telling Aberdeen with satisfaction: 'I consider the destruction of the House of Lords to be now out of the question; and that we have only now to follow a plain course with moderation and dignity in order to attain very great, if not a preponderating influence over the affairs of the country'.[38]

   This new confidence reflected the weakness and gradual disintegration of the government, and a recognition that the popular tide had turned against the radicals as well as the ministers. On 7 July there was an unseemly row in the Commons between Littleton, the Chief Secretary for Ireland, and O'Connell, which involved the disclosure of secret talks and broken promises. That evening Althorp, finally driven beyond endurance, sent Grey his resignation. Grey countered with his own, and was understandably surprised and aggrieved when his colleagues and the King accepted it with equanimity, while making great and successful efforts to persuade Althorp to return to his place in Commons. Melbourne became prime minister, but before confirming him in office the King instructed him to explore the possibility of a broad coalition including Wellington, Peel and Stanley. Melbourne declined, explaining that the differences of principle between the parties were too great for such an administration to be plausible. The King then insisted that this reply be shown to Wellington and Peel and required them to respond to it. Somewhat puzzled by the oddity of the process the two Conservative leaders met at Apsley House on 11 July and discussed their answer, although they sent individual letters. Essentially they agreed with Melbourne that such a mixture of incompatible elements could not be the basis of a stable government – and Wellington could not resist the temptation of pointing to the performance of Grey's ministry in the last three months as evidence of the damage done by internal dissensions. The King expressed disappointment at the failure of the scheme, to which he 'attached great importance', but accepted the advice. Probably the King intended to send a warning to Melbourne and to encourage the Tories, but Charles Arbuthnot felt that he 'has treated us most infamously'.[39]

Melbourne's government stumbled through the rest of the session but without gaining any authority or prestige. Widely despised, the Whigs now held office only because of the lack of an obvious alternative capable of commanding a majority in the Commons. Neither Wellington nor Peel were eager to hazard the attempt to form a Conservative administration. In May Peel had told Aberdeen that 'he preferred his present situation, occupying an elevated position and enjoying great influence in the House of Commons independent of any party, to any that he could possess as part of a ministry, and that his own personal inclination was to remain there'.[40] And Wellington told Lady Salisbury in July, soon after the King's overture, 'that he thought it better the Conservatives should not take the Govt. at present', both because he 'doubted the possibility at any time of procuring a Conservative House of Commons under the Reform Bill', and because he feared that Cumberland and 'a flying squadron' of twelve or fifteen ultra Tory peers would 'thwart us whenever we came in, by a secret cabal, exactly as he used to do in George IV's time'.[41] At the end of the session Peel invited Wellington to Drayton to shoot partridges, and the visit proved a great success, easing the tension between the two men. In the middle of October Peel set off with his wife and eldest daughter for an extended tour of France and Italy, not intending to return until after the resumption of Parliament in the New Year. Obviously he had no thought of an imminent return to power.

On 10 November 1834 Lord Spencer died, meaning that his eldest son, Viscount Althorp, inherited his title and was elevated to the House of Lords. Melbourne told the King that he intended to appoint Lord John Russell to Althorp's position as leader of the government in the Commons. However, Russell was a divisive figure and his appointment would indicate that the government was shifting closer to the radicals. The King's patience with his ministers had already worn thin and on 14 November, for the last time in British history, the King exercised his prerogative and dismissed his government. Melbourne returned to London carrying a sealed package which, he realised with sardonic amusement, contained a summons to Wellington.

The Duke was not in London but at Stratfield Saye, and he received the King's message on the following day just as he was mounting his horse for the first hunt of the season.[42] He reached Brighton about five o'clock that afternoon and was invited by the King to form a government. Wellington replied that a new ministry should be led by Peel from the Commons, and the King at once agreed, indicating that he had only sent for Wellington because Peel was abroad. The Duke then said that 'nothing could be more unfair than to call upon [Peel] to put [himself] at the head of a Government which another individual should have formed'. As a solution to this difficulty Wellington suggested that he fill the most important offices in the government on a temporary basis himself until Peel got home. It might be necessary for Lyndhurst to replace Brougham as Lord Chancellor, and to appoint a few junior officials (he was thinking of the Secretaries to the Treasury, who would need as much time as possible to prepare for the election Peel would surely call), but essentially Peel would have a free hand to choose the ministry he wanted. The King agreed, even though this would create an extraordinary if temporary concentration of offices and power in the hands of a single individual, unprecedented since at least the Glorious Revolution.[43]

That evening Wellington wrote to Peel, detailing his interview with the King and adding 'I can only request you to come home as soon as you can'. In an accompanying private note he admitted that they would be unable to claim on the King's behalf that the ministers had deserted him, and implied that the King had sacrificed this tactical advantage by seizing upon the first difficulty raised by Spencer's death to dismiss them, rather than waiting for the government to fall apart of its own accord. However, he justified the King's precipitation by the strategic advantage of the rupture occurring when Parliament was not sitting, so that the new ministers would have time to consolidate their position with an election before having to face the Commons.[44] Nonetheless it is likely that both Wellington and Peel privately thought that the King had acted prematurely, before the country was entirely sickened by the incapacity of the Whigs and ready to welcome the return of the Tories to office, but that was now irrelevant; the cards had been dealt, and they must play them as best they could.

Wellington professed to believe that the outgoing ministers, and particularly Lord Melbourne, were delighted to be relieved from their difficulties, and in a sense this may have been true for the King's action gave Whigs, liberals and radicals of all shades something to unite against. Melbourne may have taken his *congé* very coolly, not even bothering to inform some of his Cabinet colleagues before they read it in the newspapers, but this did not mean that he was ready to accept the loss of power without a struggle. The news took the public completely by surprise and the liberal press expressed predictable outrage, with the *Examiner* heading its account 'The Forlorn Hope of the Oligarchy', and expressing great confidence that the attempt to form a Conservative government must fail. The *Morning Chronicle* concentrated its attacks on Wellington personally, labelling him 'The Great Dictator' in article after article, which were widely circulated by being reprinted in numerous provincial papers. A single extract gives a sense of their tone:

> How long this ambitious Chief is to enjoy his delusion, or how far he is to be permitted to insult the country, we know not. Neither can we know what means he will employ to retain his power; but this we know, that the people of England will not consent to be cheated out of the advantage of the great measure of Reform, either by the deceit and cajolery of his emissaries, or by the menacing attitudes of 'his Highness' himself. The flame of resistance is lighting up.[45]

And it was not only the partisan press that was troubled by Wellington's one-man interim administration. Creevey was both an old admirer of the Duke and greatly jaundiced with the outgoing ministers, but he was still highly critical:

> This vesting, or rather assuming, of all the power by one man, and him a soldier and with such known opinions, for a whole fortnight or perhaps three weeks, is giving opportunities for every species of criticism upon such conduct. The Whigs might have died a natural death, as they shortly would, had they been let alone; but is quite another thing to have them kick'd out of the world by this soldier, and to see him stand single-handed on their grave, claiming the whole power of the nation as his own.[46]

Nonetheless there was nothing resembling the fevered atmosphere of May 1832, and radical attempts to mobilise mass protests, either in the form of street demonstrations, or even petitions, fell flat despite every effort of the *Morning Chronicle* and other papers. A week after taking the helm Wellington wrote to Peel with evident satisfaction: 'Attempts have been made to create excitement in London and in different parts of the country. But they have failed entirely. The country was never more tranquil. The funds are rising gradually; and everything appears to go on as usual.'[47] Addresses congratulating the King were coming in from all parts of the country and Conservatives were gaining confidence. Significantly *The Times*, which had quarrelled with the Whig ministers a few months before, gave the change of government cautious support; while the cartoonists were much gentler and more equivocal than they would have been even a few years before. A print by 'H.B.' (John Doyle, the father of Dickie Doyle) depicted *A Cabinet Council* consisting of Wellington sitting at the head of the Cabinet table musing 'How is the King's Government to be carried on? – that is the question!' All the other seats at the table are empty. Lady Salisbury noted that Wellington was 'particularly diverted' by another of Doyle's prints, *Trois Dogs*, in which dogs with the faces of Durham and Brougham fight over a bone labelled 'Power' while a third dog with Wellington's face quietly carries it away.[48]

Wellington flourished in his position at the centre of events. Lady Salisbury noted that he 'looks perfectly well and as composed and cool and *"l'esprit aussi libre"* as if he had nothing on earth to do, instead of the affairs of these king-doms on his hands'. A few days later he grumbled contently to a friend that he was 'worked as no post horse at Hounslow ever was' but added with some complacency, 'I have settled every depending question, and have set right some which my predecessors had left wrong'.[49] He sent out a confidential circular to Tory peers explaining the circumstances which had led to his appointment and received a very positive response, although a number of the Lords regretted that the crisis had not come a little later.[50] For Wellington, the central issue was 'the constitutional prerogative of the King to choose his own ministers'. And, as the Duke told the Archbishop of Armagh: 'If we can secure to him the free exercise of that prerogative by the support of Parliament I may venture to say that nothing else will be in danger. If we cannot no institution will be safe.'[51]

Peel and his family landed at Dover on the evening of 8 December. The King's messenger had found them in Rome on 25 November and Sir Robert had not hesitated in returning home as quickly as possible, realising that he had no choice but to answer the King's appeal, and that the only hope of success lay in an election before he faced Parliament. It was equally obvious that his first move should be to approach Stanley and Graham, in the hope of including them in the ministry and so signalling to the country that his government would not seek to undo the Reform Bill, and would favour further moderate reform, while protecting the special place of the Anglican Church both in England and Ireland. The approach was made but failed. Stanley and his friends had already decided to decline any offer, and in reply Stanley hinted that the new ministry had been fatally tainted by Wellington's prominent role in its inception; the country would not be convinced that it would be anything more than a return of the old Tories. Given Stanley's well-known dislike tinged with jealousy of Wellington this was not implausible, but it was not the main reason for the refusal. Stanley's ambition and conceit would not be satisfied with the role of Peel's lieutenant and he calculated, quite unrealistically, that if both Peel and Melbourne failed in their attempts to form a government, he might emerge as leader of a centrist ministry drawing recruits from both sides.[52]

Stanley's refusal left Peel with little choice but to fall back on veterans of Wellington's 1828–30 ministry to fill his Cabinet. The Duke, who had offered to serve wherever he could be of most use, went to the Foreign Office. His prominence over the previous few weeks made any thought of his retiring from the forefront of politics to the Horse Guards seem unlikely and even faintly absurd. Peel himself was both First Lord of the Treasury and Chancellor of the Exchequer, while Goulburn took the Home Office and Aberdeen the Colonial Office. Fitzgerald, Melville and Croker all declined office. The only new blood of any significance came from the appointment of Earl de Grey as First Lord of the Admiralty, Alexander Baring as president of the Board of Trade, and Wharncliffe as Lord Privy Seal. None of these carried any great political weight; De Grey was Goderich's elder brother, but had not previously held political office, and was chiefly prominent in public life as president of the (later Royal) Society of Architects. Neither Baring, whose health broke down under the strain of office, nor Wharncliffe was as important in 1834–35 as circumstance had made them briefly in 1831–32. Peel did, however, include some impressive young men of talent in the junior ranks of the ministry, including W.M. Praed (a rising orator and poet who died in 1839), W.E. Gladstone, Sidney Herbert, Lord Lincoln and Lord Mahon, who served under Wellington at the Foreign Office. Mahon had attracted Wellington's notice by a speech on the Reform Bill in 1831 and the friendship had flourished, with Wellington encouraging the young man (Mahon turned thirty in 1835), who responded with admiration which extended to secretly making notes of the Duke's conversation.[53]

Peel and his colleagues were well aware that they had to do something to counter the liberal argument that they were wedded to the past and had not come to terms with the new order created by the Reform Bill. Various possibilities were considered before Peel chose the simplest: an address purportedly to the electors of his seat of Tamworth in which he outlined his political creed. This document, which has become known as the Tamworth Manifesto, was read to the new Cabinet on 17 December and approved by it before being circulated to sympathetic newspapers; it appeared in *The Times*, the *Morning Herald* and the *Morning Post* on the following day. Although the Manifesto has gained an important symbolic position in the history of the modern British Conservative Party, its actual content is closely tied to the circumstances in which it was written. Peel pointed to his record as home secretary (particularly his legal reforms) as proof that he was no 'defender of abuse', and was not possessed by any 'superstitious reverence for ancient usages'. He repeated his explicit declaration in the Commons that he regarded the Reform Bill as 'a final and irrevocable settlement of a great constitution[al] question', which he would not seek to alter or disturb. While opposed to the 'perpetual vortex of agitation', he was in favour of 'a careful review of institutions, civil and ecclesiastical, undertaken in a friendly temper combining, with a firm maintenance of established rights, the correction of proved abuses and the redress of real grievances'. He then moved on to the specific issues of the day, promising an enquiry into Municipal Corporations and outlining a number of concessions to Dissenters, although he would not force the ancient universities to admit them. He was well disposed to reform of the Church of England but not to any expropriation of its property, and he pledged himself to a peaceful foreign policy and strict economy together with 'the just and impartial consideration of what is due to all interests – agricultural, manufacturing and commercial'.[54] Essentially Peel was promising stability, good government and as many concessions to the Dissenters as he could afford without risking alienating his Tory, Anglican supporters.

On 30 December Parliament was dissolved and the election which had been universally anticipated ever since Melbourne was dismissed, was called. Despite Peel's efforts the election had a strongly sectarian hue. The United Committee of Dissenters had already deplored the change of government and called for 'decided and uncompromising' opposition to Tory candidates, and Dissenting periodicals, of which there were many, took a vigorous part in the campaign. On the other hand many conservative Whigs had begun to drift away from their traditional allegiance, disgusted by the instability of the previous five years and alarmed that each concession to the radicals had simply produced greater demands for change. The King supported his new ministers with more enthusiasm than discretion, and took a close interest in individual seats as well as in the contest as a whole.[55] Both sides had been preparing for an election since November, and while the Tories gained some advantage from incumbency, there was no time to attend to the registry of voters in Ireland and Scotland, which had been heavily stacked against them. Nonetheless Wellington was optimistic, telling Peel at the end of November: 'The reports of the committee on elections are favourable ... I reckon that we must carry two hundred elections at least that were carried in the last Parliament by Radicals and Whigs'.[56] If this was achieved the Conservatives would gain an absolute majority in the Commons – a remarkable turnaround after their disastrous showing two years before; however, as in 1832–33 these early calculations soon proved overly optimistic.[57]

The final result showed great gains for the Conservatives, but not enough to give them a secure majority in the new Commons. As usual it was impossible to be sure how all the new members (184 of them[58]) would vote, but Tory whips estimated that they had about 290 members. A generation earlier this would have been more than enough for a competent ministry backed by the King to proceed with confidence, but the influence of the Crown and the number of independent members had declined sharply, and in the polarised atmosphere of the 1830s there were relatively few uncommitted members who might be open to persuasion. So while the whips gave the government 290 supporters, they calculated on 218 Whigs (including Stanley and his small coterie) and 150 radicals and Irish. It was still possible that Peel might keep the Whigs and radicals from coalescing and gain the support of sufficient moderate Whigs to survive, but it would be a very weak government, more intent on conciliating its enemies than pleasing its friends. Still, the precedent of Pitt fifty years before gave some grounds for hope, and the Tory ministers were resolved not to abandon the King without a struggle.

Domestic issues, especially reform and the place of the Church of England, dominated the election campaign and subsequent events, but as Foreign Secretary Wellington's focus was largely on Britain's relations with the wider world. In December he told Sir Herbert Taylor, the King's private secretary, that he was hard at work mastering the details of Britain's foreign policy, 'which is certainly strangely altered in four years'. Wellington's principal aim as Foreign Secretary was to restore reasonable relations with the Eastern Powers whose governments had been so offended by Palmerston's posturing that they had withdrawn their ambassadors from London. To a considerable extent this was achieved simply by his arrival at the Foreign Office; the change was welcomed with relief in Vienna, Berlin and St Petersburg, and the ambassadors of Austria, Prussia and Russia returned to London early in the New Year. Louis Philippe and Talleyrand were also pleased, for while Palmerston had been well disposed towards France, the liberalism of the British government had strengthened the hand of the French radicals, and its fall helped the moderates reassert themselves. The Dutch government had better reason than any to welcome Palmerston's departure, but Wellington firmly quashed its hopes that he would re-open the whole Belgian question, let alone tolerate a resort to war.[59]

Otherwise Wellington felt that the position of the new government was too fragile to embark on any dramatic shift in foreign policy; he was determined to fulfil existing obligations in full and only gradually shift its emphasis. Spain had been engulfed in civil war since the death of Ferdinand VII in 1833 with the liberals supporting a regency under his infant daughter, while the conservatives supported the claim of his brother, Don Carlos, to the throne. Palmerston had actively intervened on the side of the liberals, signing the Quadruple Alliance with Spain, Portugal and France in April 1834, although the Cabinet rejected his argument for the use of British troops. Wellington strongly opposed this policy, but in office he abided by the treaty and subsequent promises, for example honouring Palmerston's promise to provide arms to the Spanish liberals. He also firmly warned Metternich against recognising Don Carlos or sending him assistance: Britain was pledged to support the Spanish Regency, and 'I could not act a double part in any transaction; and that having found His Majesty bound by treaties, I could not depart from them and must act according to their letter and spirit'. The one new initiative he took was carefully bipartisan: sending a diplomatic mission to endeavour to persuade both sides to moderate the savagery of the war, by promising not to execute prisoners or political opponents. The Eliot Convention which was the result of this mission brought some benefits – it has been estimated that the agreement saved some 5,000 lives – and it was applauded by both sides of British politics, but the war dragged on for several more years, and even when the Carlists were defeated the liberal experiment in Spain was far from successful. However well meaning, British and French intervention in both Spain and Portugal had established regimes that lacked a sufficiently broad base of support to provide an effective and tolerant government.[60]

On 16 October 1834 the Palace of Westminster was extensively damaged by fire. Temporary repairs were made over the autumn and winter, so that both Lords and Commons could continue to use the site, albeit less conveniently than before. The necessary rebuilding of the palace did not commence until 1840 and took a generation to complete. The newly elected Parliament met in these temporary quarters on 19 February 1835 to swear in members and elect a Speaker. Charles Manners Sutton had held the post for eighteen often turbulent years under governments of many shades, and was widely admired for his tact and impartiality. Two years before, after the 1833 election, Grey's government retained him in office despite his Tory background and potential role as Conservative leader in May 1832. Now, however, the Whigs and radicals decided to oppose him, encouraged by a campaign in the liberal press alleging, quite untruly, that he had encouraged the King to dismiss Melbourne. This set the scene for an immediate test of strength between the parties, and on ground which favoured the Conservatives. Stanley voted for Manners Sutton, but nonetheless the Whigs carried their man, Abercromby, by 316 votes to 306 in a very full House. While not in itself fatal, it was an ominous sign that the Whigs, radicals and Irish had overcome their differences and united to oust Peel's government before it could consolidate its position.[61]

Parliament was ceremonially opened by the King on 24 February and the Opposition moved an amendment to the address regretting the dissolution of Parliament. This was a straightforward contest and Russell and the Whigs were confident that they would have the numbers. Stanley again supported the ministers, arguing that they should be given time, while expressing disappointment with their initial proposals, and causing much offence to the Tories, especially to Wellington's friends, by personal jibes at the Duke. After three nights of debate the Opposition amendment was carried by a majority of only seven (309 votes to 302). Peel had already announced that he would endeavour to carry on even if defeated, and there remained a slight possibility that he might yet win over the handful of voters he needed to transform a minority into a majority.[62]

The following weeks were not without moments of hope for the Conservatives. On 4 March Wellington was reported to be confident that the government would stand, while Charles Arbuthnot relished signs that the unity of the Opposition was crumbling. Russell and the Whigs had to be careful not to over-reach themselves, and talk of a motion censuring Wellington for his conduct in November-December came to nothing. Nonetheless he was the subject of many of their attacks on the government, and they drew blood when they forced Londonderry to resign his appointment as ambassador to Russia. The burden of the battle fell squarely on Peel's shoulders. Lady Salisbury noted on 21 March that 'Peel rises in reputation every day; he is so immensely superior to all his opponents that they shrink into nothing before him'. He was stalwart in his defence of Wellington, assuring the Duke in February that 'he would stand or fall with him', and telling Hardinge two months later that while he would welcome an alliance with Stanley and Graham it could not be at the expense of the Duke, for 'he would never join any Administration of which the greatest man of the age, he to whom the Conservative Party owed most, was not a component part – the Duke of Wellington'.[63]

The constant struggle in Parliament wore Peel down, and by late March it had become obvious that no permanent gains were being made and that defeat was inevitable. Wellington urged him in the strongest terms to carry on to the bitter end so that when he finally resigned 'your party and your country may be satisfied it is *impossible* for you to do otherwise'.[64] The Duke's vehemence helped prolong the struggle for another week or two, although Peel was equally aware of the need to find an issue of sufficient political significance on which a defeat could justify the resignation of the government. Russell's motion for a committee to consider how to dispose of the surplus wealth of the Irish Church provided a climax of sorts – it was approved against the wishes of the ministers by 322 votes to 289 – although even then it took several days and other defeats before the Cabinet agreed to resign. The ministers informed the King and Parliament on 8 April, exactly four months since Peel's return from Italy, although they did not actually surrender the seals of office until 18 April when Melbourne's new government had been formed.[65]

Peel's biographers and historians of the Conservative Party have found much to celebrate in the events of 1834–35; Peel's reputation as a national leader was recognised beyond question and the Conservatives had re-established themselves as the obvious and legitimate alternative to the Whig-liberal-radical government. The party had shown that with the right leadership and the right spirit it could appeal to the new, broader electorate created by the Reform Act, and it had come within a whisker of gaining a majority in its own right less than three years after the humiliation of May 1832 and the election of 1833. Looking ahead it is easy to see that these months laid the foundations for the success of the Conservative Party in the years ahead.[66] But this positive interpretation obscures the implications of the defeat of 1835, for defeat it was, and arguably an avoidable one. It is quite possible that if the King had not been so hasty to dismiss Melbourne, the Whig government would have continued to unravel and public opinion would have embraced the Tories as the only competent alternative. A general election fought in the summer or autumn of 1835 might have resulted in a substantial Conservative victory. This would not in itself have reversed the effects of the Reform Bill – for the public, through elections, would remain the final arbiter – but, for better or worse, it would have salvaged a part of the King's prerogative; the precedent would have established his right to dismiss a ministry if he was confident that his decision would be endorsed by the public. That chance was lost in 1835 and the royal prerogative went the way of the royal veto, becoming a nominal or reserve power which would not be used in any normal circumstance.

Nonetheless, by the spring of 1835 the Conservative Party had recovered a great deal of lost ground and stood in a much better position than two or three years before. In part this was simply because the tide of radicalism which had begun to flow in 1829–30 had finally become exhausted, and even many liberals were disillusioned by the performance of the Reform government; but a good deal of credit also belongs to Peel and to Wellington, for the pragmatism and restraint with which they adjusted to the new order, the care with which they avoided conflicts that they were doomed to lose and that would strengthen their opponents, while not becoming irrelevant or completely alienating their most enthusiastic supporters. Wellington continued to worry about the future of the country and the risk of revolution, but the skills he was displaying in opposition had already done a great deal to lessen the danger, and the immediate future was more promising than it had been at any time since the autumn of 1830.

CHAPTER TWENTY-FOUR

PRIVATE LIFE
(1828–35)

WELLINGTON WAS FIFTY-EIGHT when he became prime minister in 1828, and sixty-five when he resigned the seals of the Foreign Office in 1835. These seven years were among the busiest, the most stressful and demanding of his life. Even the interludes of leisure which came with being out of office proved more of a challenge than a relaxation as he struggled to find a sense of purpose away from the press of public affairs. As prime minister, then the leading figure in the struggle against the Reform Bill, and Peel's coadjutor in 1834–35, he worked extremely hard. Fortunately his health in these years was generally good – better than it had been in the middle of the 1820s. He suffered bad colds in the winter of 1827 after the Duke of York's funeral, and in the spring of 1829, while in the winter of 1831–32 a cold probably turned into pneumonia, although speculation in the press that his life was in danger appears to have been exaggerated. But in general he coped well with the intense demands made upon him, and when they proved too exhausting a short interlude at Walmer or Cheltenham revived him. His deafness was increasing and was beginning to affect his pleasure in large social gatherings, and meant that it took more effort for him to follow the debates in the Lords. In 1831–32 it contributed to his poor spirits, but it diminished as a problem when his spirits revived, and he remained a fit, active man, younger in mind and body than his years would suggest.[1]

In April 1829 *The Times* published a story outlining Wellington's daily routine when in London. He rose early and walked in the park about seven o'clock or even earlier, when it was scarcely light in winter. He returned home and breakfasted, and then attended to official business, seeing Cabinet ministers, Treasury officials and foreign ambassadors. When he went to Windsor to see the King he rode the first part of the journey on horseback to get some exercise, then completed it in his carriage – the same *calèche* he had taken with him to Russia. He seldom had more than a pair of horses or a single servant accompanying him. In the evening he might attend several parties; for example 'he lately presided at the City of London Orphan Establishment, thence to the French play at the Opera-house, and from that entertainment he went to the party given by the lady of the Dutch Ambassador in Bryanston-square'.[2]

The pace did not slacken much in the country. In January 1834, on a visit to Stratfield Saye, Lady Salisbury noted: 'The Duke was up and out this morning at 7: breakfasted at 9, went out with the hounds and had nothing to eat till he returned to dinner at half past 7. He did not appear the least fatigued or sleepy in the evening, played at whist, and I left him in the drawing-room when I went to bed at 12 o'clock, talking with great animation.' At the end of that year she told him that he should rest a little more. 'I am perfectly well,' he said, 'and whether a man has a little more sleep or a little less, what does it signify?' Asked whether he never lay awake with anxiety, he replied magnificently: 'No, I don't like lying awake – it does no good. I make it a point never to lie awake . . .' However, not even his will was quite this powerful, and we know that he had endured a number of periods of poor sleep that had their inescapable effect on his health and spirits in the years after he returned from the Continent, although they may have been worse in 1819 and 1823–24 than later.[3]

The volume of Wellington's correspondence was remarkable. Between 1819 and 1832 he received some 20,000 letters, and it is clear from the draft replies that he read almost all of them, replied to most, and frequently explained his policies in detail even to complete strangers who had no influence on the national political stage. This conscientiousness has often been depicted as nothing more than a personal idiosyncrasy, but the extent of his correspondence, especially the many unsolicited letters from obscure members of the public, gave him an insight into the mood and conditions in the country outside Westminster. At the same time it is clear that it imposed a burden upon him, especially when he was prime minister, that could be exhausting and at times almost overwhelming.[4]

Wellington ate sparingly and was not much interested in food, although he employed a fine French cook who had previously worked for Napoleon, and who knew how to produce an excellent dinner for grand occasions. The Duke's breakfast was generally nothing more than a slice of dry toast and a cup of coffee and one of tea. In 1846 he vehemently complained about the new habit of taking a large luncheon in the middle of the day: 'I declare that the little Grand Duchess of Weimar ate as much at luncheon on Friday and her *Dame d'Honneur* more, than I could eat at breakfast and dinner in a week!' He was very fond of rice, eating it with most dinners at a time when this was not common in England, and attributing much of his good health in India to the large part it played in his diet. One of his friends thought that a casual observer would have considered him 'a very indiscriminate feeder; in the flow of conversation at dinner he often, without thinking or caring about it, accepted everything that was carried round, and I have seen his plate filled with the most incongruous articles, which, however, he scarcely tasted, but sent away almost untouched'. The same friend also noted that the Duke 'scarcely knew one wine from another', while the Rev. George Gleig, who was both an acquaintance and an early biographer, informs us that Wellington did not keep a large cellar but bought wine as he needed it, paying high prices for mature wines of a good vintage.[5]

He disliked smoking and refused to follow the growing fashion and establish a smoking room at Stratfield Saye. In 1845, when Commander-in-Chief of the army, he issued a General Order urging colonels to discourage the use of pipes, cigars and cheroots among their officers. He declared that smoking was 'not only in itself a species of intoxication occasioned by the fumes of tobacco, but undoubtedly occasions drinking and tippling by those who acquire the habit'. However, the warning came too late, for smoking was becoming more common and acceptable in the upper reaches of society in the last decades of the Duke's life, encouraged in part by Peninsular veterans who had acquired the habit during their service in Spain.[6]

Wellington's attire was always scrupulously neat and he dressed either in plain, well-cut civilian clothes, or the uniform appropriate to the occasion. He hated assistance and could border on rudeness in his impatient refusal of offers to hold his overcoat or button his cloak. He was quick to adopt any invention against the cold or the wet, including 'boas, capes [and] overalls of strange construction and material'. His young friend Francis Leveson Gower (later Earl of Ellesmere) noted: 'He was an early purchaser of a patent razor for safe shaving, and when he paid for the purchase with a cheque in his own hand, the inventor, instead of cashing it, framed and glazed it.' Not surprisingly he was extremely punctual and commissioned Mr Dent, the leading London watchmaker, to make him a watch with the hands so arranged that he could feel them in the dark and thus tell the time if he was awake during the night. He used to call regularly into Dent's shop in Charing Cross to correct the watch if it was not precisely accurate.[7]

He kept a close eye on the household accounts, having been defrauded by a house steward who used the money to finance his unsuccessful speculations so that Wellington was mortified to receive bills that had been left unpaid for months. He was not above making small economies and, before the penny post was introduced, sent parcels with all his London letters up to Apsley House from Stratfield Saye to take advantage of the flat tuppence charge for letters sent within the metropolis. A caricature published when he was prime minister contrasted his careful economy in using the last drop of candlewax with the lavish expenditure on building works at Apsley House and Windsor Castle; but at a time when financial retrenchment was widely regarded as the route to economic salvation, it was no political disadvantage to have a reputation for being careful with small expenses, especially when his government matched this with much larger reductions in expenditure.[8]

In 1831–32, when Wellington was depressed and full of forebodings about the state of the country, he also became anxious about the state of his finances. The rates payable on Apsley House were tripled to £1,800 per annum, leading him to comment: 'I think that the Matter will end in my shutting up the House and living in a lodging.' And a few months later he was even more emphatic: 'I have been most infamously cheated. The worst of my Position in the World is that everybody thinks that I am made of Gold, and that it is only necessary to touch me to fill their pockets. Consequently I am plundered in every direction.' The problem proved transitory and was probably as much a reflection as a cause of his poor spirits, although it is clear that he was genuinely distressed and even felt humiliated by suffering any financial difficulties.[9]

Wellington always contributed generously both to organised charities and to individuals in need. According to one account he donated over £4,000 in one year to various charitable causes; and while he took some care to ensure that this money was well spent, mistakes did occur, as he himself admitted. For years, as he told the story, 'he had helped an imaginary officer's daughter, paid for music lessons for her, given her a piano, paid for her wedding trousseau, for her child's funeral, etc etc. At last it came out that *one man* was the author of these impostures, "and then", the Duke said, "an Officer from the Mendicity Society called on me and gave me such a scolding as I never had before in my life!" '[10]

Wellington did not make a parade of his charity or of his religious feelings, but it is clear that he had a considerable private sense of religion and also accepted that, at least in Hampshire and at Walmer, he should set an example of attending church on Sunday. When he first returned from the Continent he attended early service at St James's in London, but discontinued for some years after the illness associated with the operation on his ear in 1822, fearing that the cold would deprive him of his hearing altogether. As it was, he told the Bishop of Exeter in 1831: 'I never hear more than what I know by heart of the Church service, and never one word of the sermon.' Francis Leveson Gower declared that in the course of a long friendship he never heard the Duke discuss religion, but Wellington's correspondence with both Lady Wilton and Angela Burdett-Coutts shows that he read a number of works on religion, which was a subject much in the air in the 1840s, and that while a convinced Anglican, he was by no means narrow-minded, warmly recommending lectures on Science and Revealed Religion by the Catholic Dr Wiseman.[11]

His other reading, particularly in the 1820s and the first half of the 1830s, was restricted by the demands of his work and social life. Official documents, a very extensive private correspondence and the newspapers undoubtedly formed the overwhelming bulk of what he read. However, there are occasional references to reading for pleasure which show that his taste was more for history, letters and travel than fiction or poetry. In 1819 he warmly recommended Miss Berry's life of Lady Russell to Mrs Arbuthnot, and a few weeks later declared that Lord John Russell's biography of William, Lord Russell was worth reading, although inferior to Miss Berry's work which '[is] one of the best things of the kind I have met with for some time'.[12] Years later, in 1847, he showed a surprising sensitivity in his reaction to Larmartine's *Histoire des Girondins*:

> I cannot express what an effect the reading of this work has had upon me. It has at times made me quite miserable. It has all the Effect upon the Mind of the deepest and most affecting Novel. I was perfectly aware of the Horrors of the French Revolution, and was well acquainted with its circumstances. But I did not know of the Details, particularly so minute as they are in this Work, and apparently so well authenticated. They are really Horrible! and one cannot shake off the feeling of disgust with such Horrors, and shame that Human Nature should be so bad.[13]

On a lighter note, he greatly enjoyed *Pickwick* when it appeared, and Smollet's *Peregrine Pickle* was an old favourite; he even asked Kitty to send him a copy in the Peninsula.[14]

Wellington respected Sir Walter Scott as a gentleman, but had no time for 'your professional poets . . . there never existed a more worthless set than Byron and his friends for example. Poets praise fine sentiments and never practice them, their praise of virtue and fine feeling is entirely from the imagination.' This hostility is easily accounted for by political differences and by reports of Shelley's, if not Byron's, flaunting his irreligion. However, Wellington's old sympathy for Lady Caroline Lamb, and the ruining of her life which her affair with Byron precipitated, also surely contributed to his distaste.[15]

Despite his deafness he retained an active interest in music, although by the 1830s his taste was regarded as old-fashioned, for he much preferred the work of Mozart, Handel and even Corelli to modern composers such as Beethoven. He regularly attended the opera, especially when Jenny Lind was the *prima donna*, and enjoyed private musical evenings. He was one of the patrons of the Concerts of Ancient Music, and when he had a say in the choice of works to be performed in 1847 and 1848, showed an unexpected predilection for old love songs such as *Where E'er you Walk* and *Dr Arne's Air*.[16]

When Wellington returned to England in 1818 he already possessed a magnificent collection of paintings and other works of art. The core of this collection were the 165 paintings captured from Joseph Bonaparte at Vitoria, and formally given to Wellington by King Ferdinand in 1816, including four by Velázquez and a Correggio that the President of the Royal Academy said was so fine that it deserved to be framed in diamonds.[17] In addition there were the remarkable gifts to Wellington from different emperors, kings and princes. In 1818 Louis XVIII presented the Duke with the 'Egyptian Service' of sixty-six plates and other pieces of the finest porcelain from the Sèvres factory, while the Kings of Prussia and Saxony and the Emperor of Austria followed suit with services of their own decorated with scenes from Wellington's life. The Portuguese government expressed its gratitude with an astonishing silver and silver gilt service, including an enormous and highly ornate centrepiece and more than one thousand other pieces, which was used by the Duke for the Waterloo Banquets and other grand occasions. The Merchants and Bankers of London presented Wellington with a highly decorated silver gilt shield, and two large candelabra with supporting figures representing English, Scottish and Irish soldiers, while the Prince Regent gave Wellington Canova's massive statue of a nude Napoleon as Mars the Peacemaker. Wellington added to this collection, purchasing many pictures which related to the events of his life, such as Sir William Allan's 1843 painting of the battle of Waterloo, portraits of Napoleon and his family, and scenes such as John Burnet's *Greenwich Pensioners Commemorating Trafalgar*, which was painted as a speculative companion piece to Wilkie's *Chelsea Pensioners*. The Duke commissioned many portraits of friends and contemporaries, and sat innumerable times for his own portrait, grumbling at the time it consumed, but seldom refusing. He also commissioned works unrelated to his life – such as copies of four of Raphael's finest works by Féréol Bonnemaison – and bought works including a Velásquez and many Dutch genre pieces such as Jan Steen's *Wedding Party* and *Physician's Visit*. There is no reason to believe that his own taste was particularly individual or sophisticated, and he was much influenced by his niece Lady Burghersh (herself a capable artist) and by William Seguier, who also supervised the framing and cleaning of the pictures. While not a connoisseur Wellington was an active and generous patron of the arts, who frequently lent pictures from his collection to exhibitions across the country.[18]

When Wellington acquired Apsley House from Lord Wellesley in 1817 it was a substantial town house for a member of the British aristocracy, but nothing more, although its location on Hyde Park Corner, at the very entrance to Mayfair, was unequalled – 'No 1 London', as it came to be known. In 1819–20 Wellington extended the house to the east, adding a new state dining room where the early Waterloo Banquets were held, and additional bedrooms and dressing rooms. Mrs Arbuthnot dined there for the first time on 23 April 1820 and declared that 'it is a magnificent room & the greatest improvement to the house'.[19] This extension did not affect the overall character of the house, which retained the neo-Greek style of Robert Adam, who had designed it forty years before. But in 1828 when Wellington became prime minister he decided on a further, much larger, extension which ultimately involved an extensive remod-elling of the house. The main element of the new extension was the creation of the princely Waterloo Gallery on the western side of the house, more than ninety feet long and two storeys high, which provided an appropriate setting for many of Wellington's pictures and for the Waterloo Banquet, and which could now be extended to eighty-five diners. At the same time the outside of the house was encased in Bath stone and the solid wall in front of the house was replaced by high wrought-iron railings. The interior was redecorated in the lavish, French revival style that Benjamin Dean Wyatt and his brother had made popular in the 1820s. Many other alterations were made to the rest of the house, and inevitably the original structure was found to be quite dilapidated and in need of extensive repairs.

Wellington was too busy to pay close attention to the progress of the work and allowed Mrs Arbuthnot to deputise for him in discussing details with Wyatt. She took 'infinite trouble' over the designs of the windows and the gilded overdoor decorations and was mortified when Wellington announced that he was 'going to hang it with *yellow* damask, which is just the very worst colour he can have for pictures & will kill the effect of the gilding. However, he *will* have it.'[20] The cost of the building caused even greater heartache. 'The Duke came here last night,' Mrs Arbuthnot recorded in her journal:

> [and] annoyed me dreadfully by telling me that he had received the bills of his house & that Mr Wyatt had just exceeded his estimate *three times over* & had made the sum so enormous that he did not know how to pay it & had seri-ously been thinking of selling the house. I never saw him so vexed or so annoyed. He said the shame and ridicule of being so cheated & imposed upon, & the having been lead on to an expenditure which must ruin his family, made him quite miserable, that he cd not bear the sight of the house & really did not know what to do.[21]

Mrs Arbuthnot comforted him, saying that although it was 'certainly most provoking, still the house is beautiful &, as it will hold his pictures & all his fine things, he must consider it as his Waterloo House & use part of that money'. She also suggested employing an independent agent to measure the work and pay the tradesmen's bills rather than pay everything through Wyatt, and this may be why the final cost fell from £66,000 to a still eye-watering £43,657 – as much as the whole house had been worth in 1817.[22]

The cost of the alterations to Apsley House may have been the final straw in deciding Wellington not to build a palace at Stratfield Saye, as intended by

Parliament when it made its grants in 1814 and 1815. Benjamin Dean Wyatt had drawn up detailed plans for a house that would rival or outdo Blenheim, and as late as 1825 Wellington was discussing the best location for it with his friends, although it was significant that a decade after the battle no decision had been made. In the end the decision not to build was undoubtedly wise, saving Wellington vast expense and endless trouble, and ensuring that he did not leave his heirs a house far larger than they could use or afford to maintain.[23]

Even before abandoning plans for the palace Wellington made some alterations to the existing house to make it more attractive and convenient. In 1832 Kitty enthused that 'our library is now complete . . . the room is a handsome one, the Duke has done everything to it he could to make it beautiful and comfortable'. In 1833 he enthusiastically pasted a multitude of prints onto the walls of a number of the bedrooms, telling Mrs Arbuthnot: 'I am proceeding with sticking up my Prints and Drawings. Your Room will be beautiful. The Room under it will be all Russian; others all Portuguese and Military. You can have no Idea of the Number of Prints that I have got. I shall have every bed Room in the House full of them.' In later years he added a conservatory and two outer wings to the house, as well as better heating and plumbing. He also bought a great deal more land in the vicinity, notably Sir Peter Pole's Wolverton estate in 1829 (for a figure rumoured to be in the region of £250,000), and Silchester from Lord Longford (his brother-in-law) and Lord De Vesci. By 1872 the family owned 15,847 acres in Hampshire, almost three times the size of the original Stratfield Saye estate.[24]

Wellington was a considerate and careful landlord, reinvesting heavily in agricultural improvements and assisting his tenants to do so, remitting rents in times of hardship, and personally supervising the installation of patent heating stoves in the labourers' cottages at Stratfield Saye. He preserved game to provide ample shooting for his guests until an affray between poachers and gamekeepers in which one man was killed, which led him to relax the controls, remarking that 'I would rather be without a pheasant on my lands than that such scenes should occur again'. He hunted frequently with two local packs of foxhounds, and contributed generously to their upkeep, but did not otherwise mix much in local county society.[25]

Wellington was appointed Lord Lieutenant of Hampshire on 13 December 1820 following the death of Lord Malmesbury, and retained the post for the rest of his life. Originally established to command the country's militia, the position had now become largely social and ceremonial, although the Lord Lieutenant played an important role in the appointment of magistrates. Wellington was not a very active Lord Lieutenant – he was preoccupied by national and international affairs, and his lack of close connections with the Hampshire gentry meant that he was not their natural leader. However, he did not treat the office with indifference as some Lords Lieutenant did, and he insisted that the magistrates he recommended be appointed should be willing to take the oaths of office and perform its duties, rather than regard it as a mere honour. Wherever possible he avoided appointing clergymen as magistrates, knowing that this dual role often caused great resentment, and as soon as non-conformists and Catholics became eligible to sit on the bench he recommended them. He believed that his office should be detached from party politics and went to some pains to appear neutral, for example refusing to attend a Conservative dinner in the county in 1837 or to sign any Hampshire petition that related to party politics. However, his recommendations as magistrates showed a clear bias in favour of Tories rather than Whigs, which arose because, lacking personal knowledge of many candidates, he turned for advice to John Fleming, one of the MPs for Hampshire, and Fleming disregarded the Duke's repeated injunctions to set aside political differences when considering potential magistrates.[26]

Wellington was most commonly at Stratfield Saye between early November and January, although he would also visit many other country houses in these months. He would live mostly in London between January and late July or August when Parliament was sitting, and then would go to Walmer for some weeks in September and October. He advised a prospective guest in 1833 that they could catch the steamer from London to Margate at nine, reach Margate at three and arrive at Walmer, fifteen miles away, by five o'clock.[27] In general he preferred to travel by carriage, and in 1848 expressed his dislike of travelling by rail with typical restraint:

> Certainly in my opinion people never acted so foolishly as we did in allowing of the Destruction of our excellent and commodious [post-roads] in order to expend Millions Sterling on these Rail Roads! It appears to me to be the Vulgarest, most indelicate, most inconvenient, most injurious to Health of any mode of conveyance that I have seen in any part of the World![28]

According to George Gleig, 'the Duke was never more agreeable than when you found yourself alone with him at Walmer Castle'. Gleig had served in the closing campaigns in the Peninsula as a young officer and then gone into the Church, and his parish was a few miles from Walmer. He had achieved some fame with a memoir of his service, *The Subaltern*, published in 1825, and had also written on literary and theological subjects. He approached Wellington in 1826 hoping for permission to undertake an authorised biography and, when this was declined, turned his attention to Sir Thomas Munro, who died in 1827 after a distinguished career in India. Among the mass of Munro's papers given to Gleig were a number of letters from Wellington written when he was serving in India, and Gleig approached the Duke asking for permission to print them. Wellington invited him to dine and stay at Walmer but Gleig, who was unused to mixing in such society, felt overawed at 'the prospect of becoming the guest of so great a man', and preferred driving eight miles home after dinner to staying the night. However, the Duke soon put his nervous guest at his ease: 'I had not been ten minutes in his presence before all fear of approaching him disappeared.' Wellington gave permission for the letters to be printed with the exception of a few passages 'which it might be as well to suppress, because a man in my situation is a mark for all manner of calumnies, and my meaning would be sure to be misrepresented'.[29]

Gleig stayed a number of times at Walmer and even Stratfield Saye, espe-cially during the next few years, for he took an active part in the campaign against the Reform Bill, writing in both the national and county press. In his *Reminiscences* he describes 'a clear bracing day in November', when he was the only guest and the Duke took him for a drive to Ramsgate, nine miles away, in a two-horse phaeton, or light open carriage. The Duke took his seat on the left, so as to have his better ear on the side of his guest, and drove rapidly and not very carefully, while the conversation never slackened – on this occasion being largely devoted to political economy and the measures his government had taken to reduce expenditure and encourage trade. They returned home before dark, spent an hour or so in their own rooms, then had dinner at seven. 'It [was] a very simple meal, consisting of soup, fresh herrings, an *entremet*, a small leg of Welsh mutton, a roast pheasant, and a pudding.' After coffee they went to the drawing-room and settled in two armchairs in front of the fire and read their book or paper, with the occasional outbreak of conversation until about eleven, when the Duke and his guest went to bed.[30]

It was unusual for Wellington to be that quiet and domestic even at Walmer – there were generally a number of guests – and the afternoon drive was not always a success, as a story told to Creevey by Lady Worcester makes clear. The party set off in two carriages to visit a castle ten or twelve miles away but found the road very difficult, so that eventually they all had 'to turn out and walk up to their knees in mud a mile or two to a neighbouring town, Sandwich, when the Beau's delight was to buy the ladies shoes and stockings of a tolerably homely salesman as you may suppose, and in which they came home, but his great[est] delight of all was to see my Lord Chancellor attempting to help my Lord Privy Seal (Roslyn [*sic*]) in this dirty lane, and by "*backing*" or clumsiness of some kind, knocking him over, and tumbling upon him'.[31]

Mrs Arbuthnot describes a more fortunate visit in October 1832: 'The weather is charming, and I enjoy the sea air beyond measure. I bathe every day and am out almost all day long.' On that occasion the small castle was full with the Burghershes and two boys, Lady Wilton's little girl, Lord Rosslyn and Billy

Holmes, the Tory Whip, and this seems to have been a typical party. Wellington frequently entertained his nieces, their husbands (Fitzroy Somerset and Lord Burghersh) and children at Walmer. Rose Fane, the youngest of the Burghershes, remembered Wellington as 'extraordinarily kind and indulgent, always ready to play with them, and who gave her delicious thrills by carrying her shoulder-high so that she could look down on the lighted lamps'. Lady De Ros, one of the daughters of the Duke of Richmond, recalled that when Wellington 'invited his friends to visit him, their children were always included' and that 'when we assembled for dinner, we usually found the Duke, who had dressed early, engaged in a regular game of romps with the children, who came down on purpose for what they called the Battle of Waterloo, which commenced by one of them throwing a cushion at the newspaper the Duke was reading'. There was a pleasant continuity in this, for a few weeks before Waterloo the Richmond's tutor recorded: 'In the drawing room before dinner he was playing with the children, who seemed to look up to him as to one on whom they might depend for amusement & when dinner was announced they quitted him with great regret saying, "Be sure you remember to send for us the moment dinner is over", which he promised he wd do, and was as good as his word.'[32]

The Duke continued to grumble about the demands of society upon him, especially when he was hosting a party. Staying at Stratfield Saye in January 1834, Lady Salisbury wrote in her diary: 'They were able to get out after luncheon to shoot, otherwise I think the Duke would have died of it. His royal guest [the Duke of Gloucester] is exceedingly tiresome on a wet day and pesters everyone with questions. He is perpetually calling the Duke his brother chancellor, and observed upon the curious coincidence of two Field Marshals being Chancellors of the two Universities – evidently putting their military as well as their literary talents in the same level.' Two days later she added: 'I never saw a man so relieved by the absence of the Duke of Gloucester. He declares he shall never come into his house again. But this I think is the resolution of the moment while the recollection of the bore is fresh upon him.'[33]

Nonetheless Wellington's social life continued to give him great pleasure. His most intimate friends remained the Arbuthnots, while other friendships waxed and waned. He was also close to the Salisburys; this was an old family friendship going back to Lady Mornington and her cousin the 1st Marchioness of Salisbury, and Wellington's brother Henry had tightened the connection when he married Lady Georgiana Cecil in 1816. Wellington had often hunted at Hatfield, and in 1821 he gave away Fanny Gascoyne when she married Lord Cranbourne (the eldest son of the 1st Marquess of Salisbury), Gerald Wellesley being the officiating clergyman. We know most about his friendship with Fanny in the 1830s when she began a regular diary, although it is probable that the Salisburys were a constant and pleasant ingredient in Wellington's social round throughout the 1820s. In April 1829 he was certainly present at some successful amateur theatricals at Hatfield and was much pleased at a song in his honour, and declared the whole performance great fun.[34]

Wellington was also always close to the Westmorlands, often staying at Apethorpe in the winter. Lord Westmorland, who had been Lord Lieutenant when Wellington was a twenty-year-old ADC at Dublin Castle, had sat in Cabinet with the Duke from 1818 to 1827. His son Lord Burghersh had served on Wellington's staff in the Peninsula, and had married Priscilla, his favourite niece. Mrs Arbuthnot was a cousin of the family and Lord Westmorland's eldest daughter, Lady Jersey, was a prominent figure in society, who blatantly courted Wellington to his considerable amusement.[35]

Charles Arbuthnot once told his son, 'I never see the Duke in roaring spirits but when his old military associates are around him'; however, little evidence of such occasions survives. Wellington's social life is recorded very largely by women, and in his correspondence with women, and we seldom catch more than a glimpse of his conversation when the ladies had withdrawn after dinner. Yet so far as we can tell Wellington was not especially eager to spend his evenings carousing with old comrades; his guests were mainly the leading figures of politics and society, not old soldiers, although as George Gleig found he was always happy to mix the two together. He did not spurn old friends, but he was busy living his life and he did not generally seek them out, although he welcomed them when their paths crossed.[36]

Wellington's old friend from his days in India, John Malcolm, died in 1833 – one of a series of deaths that affected Wellington in these years, severing links to the past and in some cases affecting his future happiness. Lady Mornington, Wellington's mother, died on 10 September 1831 at the age of eighty-nine – a full half-century after her husband. She had not been close to any of her children and we know little of how she spent her life, except that for years she lived in apartments at Hampton Court, but that when she died she was living in Henrietta Street, Cavendish Square. In the last year of her life her name had been included in attacks by radicals and the press on pensions (she had been granted a pension of £600 in 1813; Wellington's sister Anne receiving a similar pension from 1812), with one critic writing: 'The Duke of Wellington, when so magnificently rewarded by his country, might . . . at least, have charged himself with his mother; and the sister . . . might have been relieved by a general subscription among the brothers, since their great elevation, rather than have [been] left a Noble pauper upon the "people's industry".' These attacks, no less than the death of Lady Mornington herself, signalled the closing of an age and the breaking of the last ties to the settled world of the mid-eighteenth century. It is unlikely that Wellington felt any great grief at the death of his mother, but equally implausible that he was completely unaffected.[37]

Kitty's health gradually deteriorated in the late 1820s and by the winter of 1829–30 she was an invalid, living at Stratfield Saye, often without the company of either her husband or her sons. Yet she had welcomed his appointment as prime minister with delight, and continued to rhapsodise about his achievements with unrestrained pride. On 7 April 1829 she praised Catholic Emancipation to a friend:

> The agony of anxiety which I have felt on this most awful subject, has been unmixed with fear of the success of a measure brought forward by *Him*! And such a measure! I know what his opinion *was* upon this subject; he has explained what it *now is*, and the grounds on which his present opinion is formed. The firmest of them would not have adopted the present mode of acting had he not known it was necessary so to act! The most upright of them would not have proposed the measure had he not felt that it was *right in the sight* of his *God*![38]

Kitty travelled to London in the spring of 1830, but that summer complained that she could not go up or downstairs without pain in every muscle. Nonetheless she was a cheerful, positive and brave invalid, writing amusingly of the difficulty of accepting rather than giving assistance, and protesting that she was well on the road to recovery. She enjoyed a visit from King William and Queen Adelaide who breakfasted at Apsley House, and was delighted when the King recognised immediately a portrait of her father. She warmly approved the Duke's decision to cancel the visit to the City in November for the Lord Mayor's dinner: 'In my heart I think that in the Duke's Warlike life, he never did any thing so valiant . . . London might have been flowing with blood that night, and all England drowned in tears now!' And she even managed to rejoice at his resignation, attributing it to 'the direct Hand of that God who has ever protected him . . . Every body saw that the Duke's health was altering, that his countenance was acquiring a drawn and fallen look . . . Thank God he has resigned in time.'[39]

In January 1831 Maria Edgeworth described a visit to her old friend: 'There was no going upstairs at Apsley House for the Duke has had apartments on the ground floor appropriated – a whole suite to the Duchess's use that now she is ill she may not have the difficulty of going up and down.' She found Kitty 'on a narrow, high mattrassed sofa' looking 'paler than marble – more delicate than life'. 'Always little and delicate looking she now looked a miniature figure of herself in waxwork.' But Kitty's voice was still sweet and its tone cheerful, she still had something of the smile of former times 'and spoke with more and more animation' of past times and Maria's father. Opposite her couch was a glass case containing many of Wellington's trophies: the gold shield presented by the City of London, the Portuguese silver gilt service, and fine porcelain

plates and dishes from the King of Prussia and Emperor of Austria. 'While I
looked at these the Duchess raising herself quite up exclaimed with weak
voiced strong souled enthusiasm "All tributes to merit – there is the value! and
pure! pure! – no corruption ever *suspected* even. Even of the Duke of
Marlborough that could not be said so truly." '[40]

Wellington was both attentive and kind to Kitty in her illness, sitting with
her and talking quietly, while she was composed and quite at ease with him.
Perhaps for the first time since their youthful romance they now brought the
best rather than the worst out in each other. On 9 April he told Mrs Arbuthnot
'she is still very unwell; and I shall not go out of town again', and two days later
he admitted 'it is impossible to calculate upon the duration of her life'. The end,
when it came, was unexpectedly quick. Kitty died about half past ten on the
morning of 24 April 1831, with Wellington holding her hand and Douro beside
her. While she had never ceased to love him, his love for her had withered and
died many years before – perhaps even before they married – although it had
then left an outer shell which had deceived him as much as anyone. But if the
old romantic passion was long gone there was still the strong sentimental tie to
the days of his youth, and surely also a sense of regret at all that had happened
between them since – the things that he had not done that he should have
done, and all the ways in which he had behaved badly towards her. Wellington
was a proud man, but there was little in his behaviour to his wife of which he
could be proud, save his kindness to her at the end.[41]

Kitty's illness and death did not bring Wellington and his sons closer
together. In the following year Edward Littleton, who had married Lord
Wellesley's daughter Hyacinthe, and so was a member of the extended family,
commented: 'The duke is fond of his sons, but I never saw them riding or
walking together in my life and I believe they seldom converse. He seems to
like that he and his sons should live independently of each other. But he allows
them [to] treat Apsley House as a barrack and to use his table whenever he
dines there.'[42] And in 1834, when his sons were in their mid-twenties,
Wellington complained to Mrs Arbuthnot:

My Determination is to have no quarrel with either of my Sons. But I am
convinced that if ever I am employed again, in the Command of an Army for
Instance, I shall be under the necessity of disgracing them both. What I mean
is that they are both so inefficient and foolish that I can employ neither.

Charles is a very good Humoured, well meaning fellow. But his whole
Mind and time are employed running after Ponies and Puppy Dogs and Mrs
Browne. What I cannot bear is their grovelling partiality to low Company.

I wanted Charles to go to Oatlands with me if I had gone. No! he would
not. But he would go into any Cottage in the County in which Candles are

lighted. It quite breaks one's Heart . . . they go about like two Scamps, and in their appearance are scarcely clean; and one cannot get them to take their place among the Young Men of their own Rank and Position in life.[43]

Both young men were officers in the army. Douro became a major in 1830 at the age of twenty-three – the same age that Wellington had been when he became a major in the 33rd in 1793 – but while Wellington's career benefitted from the long war with France, neither of his sons had the opportunity to see active service in the peaceful years between Waterloo and the Crimea. Douro was offered a seat in Parliament as soon as he came of age in 1828, but Wellington declined on his behalf before accepting Aldeburgh from Lord Hertford in February 1829. The young men were on the Continent at the time, engaged in a grand tour, and did not hurry home. Douro was observed in Genoa that March, looking thin but healthy because 'some foreign princess has drawn him fine'. He took his seat in Parliament on 3 February 1830 and was re-elected for Aldeburgh in the election following the death of George IV. Naturally he supported his father's ministry, although he was absent from the vote on the civil list on 15 November which led to the government's resignation. According to William Napier, who travelled with him to Stratfield Saye, soon after: 'His politics are decidedly adverse to his father's and he is for a thorough reform. He dislikes London society for its heartlessness, and as good as told me Sir John Moore was as great a man as his father.' Nonetheless he voted with the Tories against the Reform Bill in the sessions of 1831–32. He was reluctant to stand again in 1832 but was persuaded to contest Hampshire North, where he was defeated.[44]

Mrs Arbuthnot was always generous in her assessment of Wellington's sons, praising Douro in July 1829, when he had just returned from the Continent, as 'much improved' and with 'more sense than the generality of young men of his age'. And, a few months later: 'They are both charming, tho' very different. Chas has very high spirits, great energy & great desire to learn his profession & get on in the world. Douro is more quiet, more like his father & has not such mad spirits, but I think he is very sensible, [and] had more character than any young [man] of his age that I know.' But when Wellington was ill in the winter of 1831–32 she commented to Lady Shelley, 'he has so few comforts. I don't think his sons are any use to him', and added, 'he has no daughter (which I always think so unlucky)'. It is an interesting observation, and Wellington's excellent relations with his nieces, his women friends, and, later, with his daughters-in-law, suggest that he might well have been happier, and a better parent, if he had had at least one daughter rather than just two sons.[45]

On one occasion, in February 1831, Mrs Arbuthnot's defence of Lord Douro provoked Wellington into a rage and he 'abused his son . . . & then fell to abusing me, who, he said, always took part against him & never did him justice,

& used him shamefully. I was so astounded I said nothing. I believe my silence made him more angry, & he snatched up his hat & was going out of the room. I caught hold of him by his coat, and he turned around. I said, "How can you say such things, you must know I don't care the value of my pocket hankerchief about yr son except for yr sake". I held it up as I spoke, he snatched it out of my hand, threw it upon the floor, swore a great oath, and rushed out of the room! I assure you he was like a madman, & if he had knocked me down I shd. not have been surprised. I was silly enough to sit down and *cry*.'[46] Mrs Arbuthnot was no sycophant any more than Wellington was the impassive, reserved aristocrat of legend. But the sequel helps explain the strength and resilience of the friendship, for within a couple of hours Mrs Arbuthnot received 'the kindest possible note saying he was mad & begging me to pardon'. While not unscathed, Mrs Arbuthnot could stand the storm without being cowed, knowing that such outbursts were rare, and being moved by the apology, so that she immediately replied that 'we shall be as good friends as ever again, & I hope he will not think any more about it'. No wonder that Lady Shelley, who knew them both so well, thought that Mrs Arbuthnot was particularly suited to be Wellington's 'fireside friend', because she was not shy of the Duke and was 'quite without nerves'.[47]

Wellington's confidence in Mrs Arbuthnot was absolute and he revealed more of himself to her than to anyone else. In October 1831, in the midst of the struggle against the Reform Bill, when he was depressed and out of sorts, he wrote thanking her for remaining at Stratfield Saye: 'I am very much obliged to you for staying so long with me, as I am become but a sorry Companion. I have lost my good spirits . . . One cause is that I am Deaf and feel unfit for Society. Another Cause is that I despair of Public Affairs. The last and principal one is that I am obliged to attend to my own pecuniary Affairs, which are becoming decayed.' For her part Mrs Arbuthnot admitted to Lady Shelley: 'I can't bear his being out of spirits; I think him so good and so great that I feel as if he ought not to have the ordinary ills of life.' And Lady Shelley noted that Mrs Arbuthnot 'gave him her clear and honest opinion on matters of which others were afraid to speak', and added that she (Mrs Arbuthnot) 'used to laugh at my reverence for, and my shyness with the Duke: she had no such feeling'.[48]

After the fall of Wellington's government Mrs Arbuthnot's enthusiasm for politics diminished, and she became less assiduous in keeping her journal, finally abandoning it mid-sentence early in 1832. Both she and her husband suffered great anxiety from the attacks on pensions – they were named in Parliament and feared that they would be deprived of their principal source of income – while Wellington's 'croaking' about the state of the country and the probability of revolutionary upheaval was anything but comforting. Nonetheless the friendship continued to play a central part in all their lives, and in 1833 and 1834 their spirits gradually revived, culminating in Wellington's installation as

Chancellor of the University of Oxford. Seven weeks later, while staying at her home at Woodford, Mrs Arbuthnot fell ill with cholera and died on 2 August 1834. Wellington was staying with the Salisburys at the time, and had been cheered by a report that she was recovering when the news of her death arrived. 'He threw himself in the greatest agitation on the sofa . . . and then rose and walked for a few minutes almost sobbing about the room, after which he retired.' Early the next morning he left for Woodford to comfort his surviving friend and fellow sufferer. Wellington and Charles Arbuthnot remained close for the rest of their lives; Arbuthnot lived part of the year with the Duke at Apsley House and also stayed with him at Stratfield Saye and at Walmer, but neither man ever fully recovered from the death of the woman who they had, in different ways, loved dearly. Lady Salisbury observed at the time:

> It is a dreadful loss to him – for whether there is any foundation or not for the stories usually believed about the early part of their *liaison*, she was certainly *now* become to him no more than a tried and valued friend to whom he was sincerely attached – her house was his home, and with all his glory and great-ness, he *never had a home*! His nature is domestic and as he advances in years, some female society and some fireside to which he can always resort become necessary to him. On his account I grieve most deeply for her death. I cannot bear to think what a loss it is to *him*. As I knew her more, latterly, my regard for her personally also increased: she was, I really believe sincerely attached to him – a woman of strong understanding, considerable information and perfect discretion, the quality of all others which had most attraction for the Duke. She was particularly strong and never ailed anything, so that her death has something peculiarly awful in it . . .[49]

In the space of less than four years Wellington had lost his wife, his mother, his best friend from India, and Mrs Arbuthnot, and these blows fell amid the demands and disappointments of the struggle against the Reform Bill, and Wellington's greatest unpopularity since the outcry over the Convention of Cintra. The loss of Mrs Arbuthnot was irreparable, and it required all Wellington's fortitude and strength of character to carry on, acknowledging his grief only to his closest friends, and, as always, finding solace in public affairs. Three months after Mrs Arbuthnot's death the King dismissed Melbourne's government and Wellington was plunged into six months of intense political activity; yet even politics had lost something of its savour without her to discuss it with, and in November 1835 Wellington wrote to Lady Shelley: 'Alas! our poor friend! I miss her more and more every day.'[50]

CHAPTER TWENTY-FIVE

THE MANY FACES OF FAME

WELLINGTON WAS A celebrity, the King's most famous and decorated subject. By the mid-1830s he had played a prominent part in public life for a generation, and been a familiar figure to Londoners for almost twenty years. He was often controversial, the subject of intense political debate, but his fame extended beyond politics into many other aspects of life; and his name and image appear, sometimes incongruously, in various ways in the commerce and culture of the time. All these interpretations of Wellington – the exaggerated praise and blame of political controversy, and the less obviously biased uses to which his fame was put by others – contributed to his reputation, and this in turn affected the way he was viewed by contemporaries and later generations. And while Wellington's reputation constantly evolved throughout his life, the middle and late 1830s mark an important moment of transition which makes this a good point to pause and look back over some of the ways the public had come to know him over the previous quarter of a century.

Wellington burst into the public's consciousness in 1808 with the excited reaction to his victories at Roliça and Vimeiro, and then the outrage and dismay that greeted the Convention of Cintra. He remained a highly controversial figure throughout the first half of the Peninsular War, until his continuing success eventually silenced his critics. The public learnt of his campaigns largely through press reports which mostly consisted of reprinting his official despatches in full, detailed reports of parliamentary debates about the campaigns, and large amounts of ill-informed speculation often based on inaccurate information. There were no war correspondents with the army or even based in Lisbon – professional journalism was still in its infancy – although papers would often print letters written by officers in the army to their family and friends at home. Victories were announced by the firing of the guns at the Tower and in the Park, and the grand houses in the West End of London would be brightly illuminated with a mass of candles in the windows, and often painted 'transparencies' with either mottos or scenes of a conquering Wellington displayed. Crowds of people, including many young apprentices, would turn out to see the sights, cheer loudly for the hero of the hour, and even throw stones at any houses that were not illuminated. Celebrations were quieter in the provinces, but church bells might be rung, bonfires lit, and sermons preached, and for that day at least Wellington's name would be on everyone's lips.

Numerous songs were composed to celebrate the successive triumphs of British arms and Astley's Royal Amphitheatre in London (which was more a circus than a conventional theatre) put on a succession of performances to mark the progress of his campaigns, beginning with *Lisbon or Rose de Guerre on the Banks of the Tagus* in January 1811. Henry Aston Barker displayed a panorama of the siege of Badajoz at Leicester Square in May 1813, and a number of stylised explanatory prints by George Thompson depicting Wellington's victories were published within months of the events they described. There was even elaborate stationery with a series of military vignettes forming a thick border and the centre of the sheet left blank for the purchaser to fill with a favourite patriotic poem or passage of prose copied out in their best calligraphy.[1]

Serious poets also sang Wellington's praises. In 1809 J.W. Croker published a book-length poem, *The Battle of Talavera*, which was so successful that it had run through eight editions by the end of 1810 and was reprinted again in 1812 and 1816. Similarly a poem on Salamanca, probably by J. Hamilton Roche, 'dedicated to Wellington and the brave officers and troops under his command', was into its tenth edition by 1816. By 1812 Wellington was a national hero and George Canning, in a move pregnant with irony, sought advantage from his reflected glory in his election campaign in Liverpool, where he introduced himself to the voters as 'the enlightened coadjutor of Pitt and Nelson ... [and] the illustrious friend of the immortal Wellington'. And when the Thames froze solid at the end of January 1814 and an impromptu fair was held on the ice, one stall carried the banner 'Wellington for ever – good ale'. The welcome he received on his return to England in the summer of 1814 leaves no doubt that his popularity was genuine, widespread, and cut across normal party allegiances.[2]

The first biography of Wellington was published in 1810–11 in a series of articles in a newly established periodical, the *Royal Military Chronicle*. It is likely that the author of this piece received some assistance from Wellington's brothers or their friends, but it nonetheless contained errors which the family hastened to correct. Even so the work was full of praise, which was the more welcome as it appeared at a time when Wellington's reputation still hung in the balance. The first book-length biography was written by Francis L. Clarke and was published in twenty parts from October 1812 (six pence each part or 10s 6d in boards when completed), and advertised heavily in both the London and provincial press. An updated edition appeared in 1814, while an American version appeared with the narrative from the attack on Burgos written by William Dunlap; this stopped abruptly just short of Toulouse. Clarke's work was embarrassingly laudatory, even when discussing Wellington's role in the Portland government: 'When we contemplate the records of parliament in the years 1806, 7, and 8, it is impossible not to admire that manly comprehensiveness of mind, and liberality of sentiment, which fitted him for every discussion, and carried him through many warm debates without ever creating him a single enemy.'[3]

Such eulogies were unlikely to convince the unconverted and may well have disgusted even some readers who were warmly predisposed in Wellington's favour, but Clarke's book at least made readily available the outline of his career. A second biography by George Elliott appeared in 1815, and in a new edition in 1816 which incorporated two chapters covering Waterloo. Significantly this work was dedicated to Marquess Wellesley and in the lengthy dedication the author writes: 'The following pages record the watchful solicitude with which you sought to lead the infant fortunes of him, whose transcendent exploits have nobly redeemed your fraternal love.' Canning was not the only one eager to bask in Wellington's reflected glory. As for Elliott's considered opinion of Wellington, the concluding sentence to the preface of the second edition should be sufficient: 'Justly proud as we are when we call ourselves Britons, who does not feel proud when he adds, Wellington is my countryman.'[4]

Waterloo elevated Wellington's fame and reputation to a new and unprecedented level; it is hard to think of any previous Briton who had gained such international standing. The drama of Napoleon's sudden return from Elba, his almost miraculous march on Paris, the short intense campaign, and the final dreadful climactic victory captured the public imagination. There was intense relief that the renewed war was over so quickly and great pride that British soldiers and a British general had played the decisive part in the triumph. Waterloo was much closer to London than the battlefields of Spain, Portugal and southern France, and within weeks of the fighting British tourists were visiting it, and often publishing accounts of their travels. In London Barker's panorama of the battle drew huge crowds and is reported to have made a profit of £10,000 within a few months, while Astley's spectacular show based on the battle ran for 144 performances and was frequently revived.[5] Dozens of accounts of the campaign, the battle and its aftermath ranging from letters in newspapers to instant histories appeared in the months following the news of the triumph. Public and private celebrations were held, oxen roasted, speeches made and toasts drunk. Within days of the battle the audience at Saddler's Wells was hearing Mr Sloman perform *Waterloo, or Wellington Forever*, while huge crowds attended an exhibition of artifacts associated with the battle, including Napoleon's coach and coachman, put on by the entrepreneurial William Bullock in the Egyptian Hall in Piccadilly.[6]

Sir Walter Scott, who with Byron was the greatest literary celebrity of the day, not only wrote a poem, *The Field of Waterloo* (not generally regarded as his best), but also visited the battlefield and went on to Paris where he mixed with Wellington and other leading soldiers, statesmen and even kings and emperors. He published an account of these experiences as *Paul's Letters to his Kinsfolk* – an entertaining and widely read travel book that gives a highly favourable impression of the Duke. Scott praised Wellington's personal bravery and the way he inspired his troops, constantly exposing himself to enemy fire and visiting almost every square in the front line, 'encouraging the men by his presence, and the officers by his directions'. He went on to humanise Wellington and entertain his readers by quoting some of the Duke's pithy remarks which, he says, were repeated by the soldiers 'as if they were possessed of talismanic effect'. When under heavy fire Wellington coolly commented: 'That's good practice ... I think they fire better than in Spain.' He told the 95th Rifles, who were facing a formidable body of French cavalry: 'Stand fast, 95th – we must not be beat – what will they say in England?' And again: 'Hard pounding this, gentlemen, let's see who will pound the longest.' Whether authentic or improved in the telling, such remarks were vivid and memorable and made Wellington a character in the reader's mind, not merely commander of the army. Scott praised his 'quick and decisive intellect', his 'undaunted composure', and his stern resolution, for example when he responded to a request that a much-battered brigade be withdrawn for a time to regain its composure: '"Tell him," said the Duke, "what he proposes is impossible. He, and I, and every Englishman in the field, must die on the spot which we now occupy".' But this was balanced by the much-quoted remark 'that nothing, excepting a battle lost, can be half so melancholy as a battle won'. The reader was left in no doubt that Wellington was not just a great general, but a great man, enlightened and humane.[7]

Scott was not the only writer to popularise remarks attributed to Wellington or to praise his character in the light of Waterloo. 'Would to God that night or Blücher would come', and 'Up Guards and at them' both entered popular consciousness, while within a year the word Waterloo had itself entered the lexicon, although initially meaning a bold and successful move rather than a final decisive defeat ('He met his Waterloo'). More significantly for Wellington's fame, his letters to Lord Aberdeen and the Duke of Beaufort announcing the death of the former's brother (Alexander Gordon) and the severe injury of the latter's brother (Fitzroy Somerset) were published, giving an unexpected glimpse of the emotional toll of the victory and so helping to further soften Wellington's image.[8]

The years after Waterloo saw the intense radical campaign criticising Wellington and portraying the army as a threat to the constitution, but at the same time there continued to be a steady stream of books, prints, songs and exhibitions celebrating Wellington's life and triumphs. In October 1817 on Blackdown Hills in Somerset, overlooking the town of Wellington, Lord Somerville, accompanied by a large party of gentlemen, laid the foundation stone for a pillar, 103 feet high, commemorating the Duke's achievements with an inscription at the base expressing 'Gratitude and Admiration' for victories whose benefits were summarised as 'India protected!', 'Spain and Portugal rescued!', 'Republican tyranny subdued', 'The Netherlands saved, and Europe delivered'.[9] Another monument was commenced in Dublin in the same year that when completed was over 200 feet tall, so that it is still the largest obelisk of its kind in Europe. The inscription, in Latin and English, is appropriately unequivocal:

> Asia and Europe, sav'd by thee, proclaim
> Invincible in war thy deathless name,
> Now round thy brow the civic oak we twine,
> That every earthly glory may be thine.

This inscription was composed by Marquess Wellesley, who added that they were written by:

> An Irishman for an Irishman,
> A brother for a brother.[10]

And certainly the Dublin testimonial was part of an attempt to emphasise Wellington's Irish connections and claim him as an Irishman. However, it is unlikely that he would have been comfortable with this designation, for he never showed much enthusiasm or nostalgia for the country of his birth. It is true that he spent roughly one-third of his first fifty years (to 1819) in Ireland, compared to only ten years in England, but he never returned after 1809, while he spent the last thirty-four years of his life entirely in England and on trips to the Continent. By birth he may have been Irish, but when he had the power to choose, he chose to be English, although this was a less self-conscious and exclusive term than it has subsequently become. But whatever Wellington's own opinion, friends and enemies alike, at the time and since, have made considerable play with his 'Irishness' so that it has contributed to his image if not to his character.[11]

Many commercial enterprises also sought to appropriate Wellington's name and fame for their own apolitical purposes. As early as June 1812 the proprietors of Bryant's Camp and Trunk factory in Ludgatehill advertised in *The Times* 'Wellington Bedsteads for the Army – Patent Improved Wellington Bedsteads, with Bedding (particularly adapted for Officers on foreign service) in a small portmanteau, very portable, and much lighter and cheaper than any offered to the Army'. Six months later William Caslon advertised his 'Patent Wellington Sanspareil Type', while by the end of the war Wellington's name had been used to promote snuff boxes, fans, bells, brooches, razors, barometers, coaches, door-stops and toys.[12] There was no obvious diminution in this exploitation of the name in the post-war years, and new products from poplins (fabrics) to ships were called Wellington, for no particular reason other than that this might attract custom or that it expressed a genuine enthusiasm by the manufacturer. On 10 August 1815 R. Willis of Fish Hill Street and Fleet Street included in his advertisement a reference to the Wellington Boots he had for sale. The context suggests that the style was already well known – tight-fitting leather boots designed to be worn while on foot or horseback, and to fit under trousers. There is no reason to doubt the traditional story that Wellington requested his bootmaker, Hoby of St James's, to make him a pair according to his specification, and that officers in the army and then civilian gentlemen took up the design and made it fashionable, although it is likely that the original commission occurred during or even before the Peninsular War, for it would have taken several years for the term 'Wellington boot' to become commonly understood.[13]

These post-war years also saw many property developments incorporate the names of the Duke and his last and greatest victory, including Waterlooville north of Portsmouth and Waterloo Place in London. Jane Austen satirises the trend in her unfinished novel *Sanditon*, written in the first months of 1817, when she has Mr Parker describe his new coastal resort to a visitor: 'You will not think I have made a bad exchange, when we reach Trafalgar House – which by the bye, I almost wish I had not named Trafalgar – for Waterloo is more the thing now. However Waterloo is in reserve – if we have encouragement enough this year for a little Crescent to be ventured on – (as I trust we shall) then, we shall be able to call it Waterloo Crescent'. By 1834 the Post Office Directory listed no fewer than eight Waterloos and twenty-six Wellingtons in London alone.[14]

As the radical tide faded in the 1820s there was a vogue for military memoirs and novels based on Wellington's campaigns, sparked by the success of Moyle Sherer's *Recollections of the War in the Peninsula*, and George Gleig's *The Subaltern*. Crowds flocked to the Royal Academy to see Wilkie's *Chelsea Pensioners*, and in 1825 the Dutch artist Jan Willem Pieneman exhibited his massive painting of Waterloo (27 feet by 11 feet, with the victorious Wellington calmly dominating the centre of the scene) in Hyde Park, charging a shilling admission and another shilling for a printed guide to the work. By then Waterloo Day had become established as part of the annual cycle of holidays and events in many parishes across the country, although the *Morning Post* in 1826 complained at the lack of any official commemorations of the occasion.[15]

In the years after 1818 Wellington became a familiar figure in the streets of London and the parts of the country that he visited frequently. He was a celebrity, immediately recognisable to many, a figure to be pointed out to visitors, and on occasion cheered or heckled, although the most common reaction was probably a curious stare or a respectful salute. Many images of Wellington were published in these years and the most popular at the time were not Lawrence's fine portraits, but engravings of the now less familiar portraits by Beechey and Isabey. A less flattering depiction of Wellington gained wide circulation with the publication of Harriette Wilson's *Memoirs* in 1825, which entertained and amused sophisticated audiences, but which genuinely shocked and disappointed some of Wellington's conservative admirers, while it confirmed the hostile prejudices of some radical Dissenters. The Duke's affairs – or alleged affairs – had already been the subject of much gossip and speculation in the newspapers, and one of the Cato Street conspirators is even said to have alluded to the Duke's behaviour to his wife as a justification for the attempt to kill him, but Wilson's book brought Wellington to life far more vividly and permanently than ephemeral stories in the press. She depicted Wellington not simply as immoral but, far more cuttingly, as a figure of fun, over-dressed, a bit of a bore, and left knocking on the door while she entertained a more attractive young nobleman inside.[16]

Wellington's reputation suffered greatly in the political turmoil of 1828–32 when many Tories felt betrayed by Catholic Emancipation, and the economic slump of 1829–30 led to a revival of popular radicalism. As in the years after Waterloo he was again depicted as a potential dictator, and as a wealthy aristocrat who was indifferent to popular suffering. In the popular ballads of the day Wellington was called 'Nosey' or 'Old Nosey', and Peel was 'Bob', 'Orange Peel' or 'the Ratcatcher'. Dibdin's patriotic ballad 'The Tight Little Island', composed at the height of the invasion scare during the war, was given new words to condemn Wellington's blindness to poverty; while in other songs Wellington was linked to Billy Barlow, a comic ne'er-do-well who fancied himself a great man. The fall of the Tory government in 1830 was celebrated:

What do you think of old Arthur and Bob?
Why I think they are a mess, for they can't get a job,
May Bobby sell his trap and old Nosey to the sod,
Oh how I should laugh if they both went to quod.[17]

Other songs included lines such as 'Nosey the King of Waterloo and his row dow dow iddy iddy pipe clay nose', and 'Poor old King Nosey is getting old' – this last being a theme which was deployed increasingly in the 1830s where Wellington (who turned sixty in 1829) is represented as antiquated and out-of-touch, a figure from a bygone era even though he was five years younger than Lord Grey.[18]

This was the context in which the first reference to Wellington as 'the Iron Duke' appeared in *Freeman's Journal*, the leading liberal, pro-Catholic Emancipation, newspaper in Dublin, on 14 June 1830. There had been occasional references to Wellington's 'iron manner' and 'iron hands' going back to at least 1828, even on one occasion by Wellington himself, but they never gained any great resonance and did not endure. The first use in *Freeman's Journal* was in an article encouraging opposition to the government's measure to increase some Irish taxes: 'There is no part of Ireland that would suffer more by the proposed alteration in the relative duties on rum and home-made spirits than the counties that seem to be least alive to its effects . . . Even at the eleventh hour they may display a spirit that will convince their Representatives that temporizing and half measures will not be sufficient to insure their future favour. If the Irish Question be lost, Ireland has her Representatives to accuse for it still more than the iron Duke and his worthy Chancellor.' The casual use of the phrase suggests that it may already have been current, at least in Dublin, for some time. It appears again in *Freeman's Journal* on 16 and 28 June, 26 July, 30 October and 5 November 1830 and on 4 January, 18 and 21 May and 15 June 1832, on each occasion as part of criticism of Wellington from a liberal perspective. On 15 June 1832 the paper also mentions the iron shutters Wellington had installed to protect the windows of Apsley House from stones thrown by the mob, but it does not connect this to the phrase and the link between the two appears to be a red herring.[19]

With one isolated exception the phrase does not appear in the English press until 2 December 1834, when it appeared in the *Morning Chronicle* in the report of a speech by Daniel O'Connell to the Irish Anti-Tory Association in Dublin on 28 November. This produced a riposte in the *Morning Post* which was reprinted in the *Standard* on 12 December 1834, which again used the phrase. It was picked up and used and modified by a number of papers during the political crisis of 1834–35. All these uses of the term were plainly hostile, building on the idea that Wellington was a hard, unyielding, unsympathetic figure, rigidly opposed to reform and the spirit of improvement.[20]

Significantly the term disappears for a few years after the political crisis of 1835, reappearing where it began, in *Freeman's Journal* in June 1838, and subsequently becoming a stock phrase most commonly used in reports of speeches on both sides of the Irish Sea. By this stage it had lost some of its partisan edge, although it was still more likely to be used by critics than admirers of the Duke. However, in the spring of 1840 the power of a pun overwhelmed the pejorative resonance when the proud owners of a new iron ship, the first to be built on the Clyde, named her the *Iron Duke*, complete with a full-length figurehead of Wellington in the uniform of a field marshal giving orders at the battle of Waterloo. A few months later a poem, 'They'll never Resign', which was highly critical of Melbourne's tottering government, used the phrase in a wholly sympathetic manner for the first time in a political context. Subsequently, in 1844, it appeared in both *Hansard* and *Punch* not as a newly minted term, either of affection or abuse, but as a well-established, even clichéd, sobriquet, whose origins had already been lost to sight.[21]

Wellington's popularity reached its nadir in 1832 but then recovered rapidly, with only a temporary and not very serious relapse in 1834–35. In part this was because the reformers had carried the day and Wellington and Peel conceded defeat, making it clear that no future Conservative government would seek to undo the Reform Bill. This exploded the old radical bogey of Wellington as a potential dictator, ready to use the army to overturn the constitution and oppress the people. And it coincided with a growing public interest in Wellington's military career, and in particular in the Peninsular War, which had been obscured by the political dramas of 1828–32.

For all his professed indifference to popular opinion Wellington cared about his reputation, especially as a soldier, and resented criticism when it came to his attention. However, he not only refused to write his memoirs, he consistently discouraged others from producing accounts even when he could be sure that they would be sympathetic. When John Wilson Croker wanted to write a history of Waterloo soon after the battle, Wellington told him that it would be impossible to establish the exact sequence, and hence significance, of events; and that too rigorous an enquiry would needlessly damage the reputation of many officers whose conduct on the day was less than heroic. Similarly, in 1826, he declined an offer from George Gleig to write his biography, even though this would have given Wellington the opportunity to set on record his side of the contentious episodes in his career. The reasons for his reluctance are not entirely clear, but Wellington seems to have feared that he would be held responsible for the resulting work and dragged into the controversies that it might provoke.[22]

He did not give any countenance to the early histories of the Peninsular War, and refused to give Robert Southey access to his papers. At first glance this was surprising, for Southey was well established as a Tory writer and had consider-able first-hand knowledge of Spain and Portugal. However, Wellington had a poor opinion of professional poets and may have been annoyed by an article Southey wrote on the Waterloo Campaign in which he claimed that Wellington had been surprised at the outset and that much of the credit for the victory belonged to the Prussians – both points which, while to a greater or lesser extent true, Wellington always strongly resisted. In 1820 Wellington knew that

Southey was working on a history of the war and told friends that 'he was a miserable author and could know nothing about military affairs'. And a few years later he told Samuel Rogers that he did not think much of Southey's work, although it is not clear how much of it he had read.[23]

Southey's *History* did not make a great impression on the public; its political bias was obvious and it covered the early months of the Peninsular War in immense detail, dwelling on Napoleon's crimes and Spanish bravery, while reducing the British role to that of auxiliaries and displaying a marked lack of sympathy, bordering on hostility, towards Sir John Moore. Southey's partisanship, and particularly his hostility to Moore, provoked William Napier into undertaking his own history. Napier was a complete contrast to Southey: a decade younger (he turned thirty-seven in 1822), he had served with distinction in the Light Division throughout the war, being wounded three times, one of which left a bullet lodged in his spine which caused him great pain intermittently throughout the rest of his life.[24] He was also a radical, an ardent admirer of Napoleon and fierce critic of the Tory governments that conducted the war. Wellington knew Napier and his brothers George and Charles in the Peninsula, praising their courage in the field and attention to all aspects of service, and writing personal notes to their mother (a family connection of the Duke of Richmond) whenever one or other was wounded.[25] He had far more respect for Napier than for Southey, and gave him considerable assistance, showing him some but not all his papers, answering questions, and inviting him to stay at Stratfield Saye for several months. Nonetheless their political differences ensured that their relations were never entirely comfortable or confidential. Wellington made a point of not reading the *History* as it appeared, and no one who read it could make the mistake of believing that it represented his view of the subject. He also refused to become embroiled in the disputes provoked by Napier's vehement judgements, even when these involved senior officers who had worked closely with him during the war such as Beresford and George Murray. His private opinion was that 'Napier has great materials, and means well; but he is too much influenced by anything that makes for him, even by an assertion in a newspaper'.[26]

Napier's *History* enabled Whigs and radicals, as well as those not much engaged with contemporary politics, to reconsider their attitude to the Peninsular War. Rather than telling a story of Napoleon's iniquity, the triumph of the Tory government and the misguided feebleness of the Whig Opposition, as Southey had done, Napier presented a liberal romantic view of Napoleon as the enemy of oligarchy, the British government as half-hearted and incompetent in the prosecution of the war, and the Whigs – on the rare occasions they were mentioned – as sincerely devoted to peace. And beyond this he celebrated the glorious heroism of British arms, while praising the French as worthy and honourable opponents, deriding the Spaniards and patronising the Portuguese. All this was presented in highly coloured prose, with a strong narrative drive and enough documentary and statistical support to lend it great authority. And while the hero of the first volume was unquestionably Sir John Moore, Wellington was at the centre of the remaining five, and the work as a whole was dedicated to him 'because I have served long enough under your command to know, why the Soldiers of the Tenth Legion were attached to Caesar'.[27]

Napier had completely recast the way in which the Peninsular War might be viewed, and it took some time before the mental contortions needed to adopt his perspective felt comfortable or natural to the public. The first volume of his *History* was published in 1828 and was not an immediate success, but as successive volumes appeared during the 1830s (the sixth and last was published in 1840) they became cumulatively more persuasive, despite the grumbling of many Tories who felt, with good reason, that they had been robbed of their greatest triumph by the power of purple prose and impudent legerdemain. The effect on Wellington's reputation was immense, at once helping to raise him to be a national hero whose military career stood clear of politics, and by doing so sharply distorting his career by downplaying the political components that had been integral to it ever since he first entered public life in 1790 as a member of the Irish Parliament and ADC to the Lord Lieutenant of Ireland.[28]

The publication of Wellington's *Dispatches*, in thirteen volumes between 1834 and 1839, took advantage of the interest aroused by Napier's *History* and contributed powerfully to the reassessment of Wellington's reputation in these years. Yet even here, Wellington did not take the initiative and had to be persuaded to consent to the project. As early as 1819 he had told Lady Shelley that the original letters included in Coxe's recently published *Life of Marlborough* would 'raise Marlborough very much in public esteem'. But when Colonel John Gurwood, another distinguished veteran of the Light Division, approached him in early 1832 it was with a much more modest proposal: the publication in a consolidated edition of the General Orders Wellington had issued to the army. As these General Orders were public documents, widely distributed to the army, instructing it on the routine details of service such as the posting of picquets and the distribution of rations, Wellington had no hesitation in approving their re-publication. His involvement in Gurwood's editorial work was minimal – the struggle against the Reform Bill was at its height – and he was surprised and pleased with the result. He was staying with the Arbuthnots at Woodford at the time and Charles Arbuthnot told Gurwood that the Duke 'was so delighted with reading his old orders that he did nothing else all yesterday but read them aloud'. It was a welcome fillip for his morale after the defeat over the Reform Bill, and the first edition of one thousand copies soon sold out and a second edition was published with some corrections and extending the material to include General Orders issued to the Army of Occupation of France.[29]

Gurwood was emboldened by the success of the General Orders to propose a larger scheme to Wellington: the publication of his *Dispatches*. This was initially conceived to include only formal letters, such as those to the Secretary of State, which were often published in the London *Gazette*. Wellington made no objection to this, but as Gurwood collected the official despatches together he soon realised that they gave a thin and partial account of Wellington's operations, and of the huge range of subjects – financial, logistical and diplomatic as well as military – that Wellington had dealt with throughout his career. To correct this he began to include a large amount of other official and semi-official correspondence in the drafts which he was preparing for the Duke to consider. As this suggests, Wellington was closely involved in the editorial process surrounding the publication of the *Dispatches*. Gurwood sorted the original letters, taking most from Wellington's own copies, but as time went on looking further and further afield to fill in gaps. He also at first provided a linking text, but as the number of letters to be printed increased this was abandoned. The letters were then set in type and proofs printed and sent to Wellington, who suggested cuts ranging from the suppression of a name to dropping an entire letter. He was clear that nothing written at the time should be altered, nor would he add any later explanation or justification, but some passages written in the midst of action thirty years before might read uncomfortably in a study or drawing room in 1835. So he removed a reference to twelve or fifteen men having been hanged on one occasion in India, partly because he did not believe that it was factually accurate, but also because 'in these times of impunity for thieves and vagabonds many people will be shocked by . . . [the] statement'. But he let stand the fact that *some* men had been hanged for ill-treating an officer; if this was whitewash it was very thinly applied. By far the most common cuts made by Wellington were the names of officers whose conduct or performance was being criticised. Many of these men were still alive, sometimes holding high rank in the army, while even those who were dead had left families who cherished their military reputation. It is not difficult to see why Wellington preferred not to reopen a thousand old hurts by printing these names. Politically sensitive letters received rather unexpected treatment; Wellington's occasional outbursts complaining at the criticism of his operations by the Opposition were either suppressed or softened by the removal of names, but his much more frequent letters grumbling at the government's failure to supply him with more men and limitless money were generally allowed to stand. In effect he protected the reputation of his political opponents, while exposing that of his friends and allies. This was partly due to circumstances; Castlereagh, Liverpool, Perceval and Canning were all dead, while Grey, Holland and Brougham were not only still alive but politically active. Wellington would not risk any suggestion that he was using his despatches to further current political purposes and his restraint was certainly wise, ensuring that the work was received with curiosity rather than hostility by those who differed strongly with him on the issues of the day.[30]

Working on the *Dispatches* occupied much of Wellington's time between 1833 and 1839, and he found it immensely satisfying. In January 1834 he told Lady Salisbury that he had been surprised by how well the early letters from his years in India were written: 'Tho' I was very young then, I could not write them better now. I see that I had at that time all the care and foresight and attention to every detail that could forward the business which I had in charge, which is the only means of ensuring success.' A few months later he told Francis Egerton: 'I don't know when I have been more entertained than by the perusal of my own letters. There is a freshness, activity and energy about them which is quite amusing.' And in 1836 in a conversation with George Chad he commented that 'it recalled all the feelings of youth – especially the Indian Dispatches. I felt young again – all the enterprize & excitement of that time.' Furthermore: 'They are valuable as a professional book, more so than Caesar's Commentaries because Caesar wrote afterwards for effect . . . I won't alter a word – as they were written, so let them be printed – except some proper names which must be suppressed. Nobody can tell the difficulties I had to encounter in Spain – every one was raw – I had to teach them all their business, down to the most trifling details, & they sent me out such People sometimes.' Working on the *Dispatches* helped fill the void created in Wellington's life by being out of high office in these years, and bolstered his always quite robust opinion of himself after the battering it had sustained in the political whirlwinds of 1828–35.[31]

According to Francis Egerton, the publication of the *Dispatches* had a dramatic effect on Wellington's reputation: 'Till the *Despatches* were published I do not think that either they [the Canningites] or the Whigs conceded to him any civil talent, and many Whigs are known to have believed that even his military successes had been due to such subordinates as Picton. Brougham was one of the first to do him justice, and Lord Grey, in private, did so very handsomely when the Despatches appeared.' This slightly simplifies the picture by ignoring the influence of Napier's work and the cooling of the political atmosphere after 1835, but does not appear much exaggerated. Lord Morpeth, a member of Melbourne's Cabinet, wrote that the *Dispatches* 'give the picture of the consummate man, in whom the signal aptitude for detail does not detract from, but adds largely to the impression of his even capacious greatness'. Greville records Brougham as remarking that the *Dispatches* 'will be remembered when I and others (mentioning some of the most eminent men) will be forgotten'. And Thomas Arnold of Rugby, who had supported the Reform Bill and engaged in heated controversies with Tory writers, told a friend that the Duke's correspondence 'gives one a favourable impression of him morally, I think, as well as intellectually: there is a frankness and kindliness about his letters generally which is very attractive, and one admires the activity and comprehensiveness of view which could take in so much and so execute it'.[32]

The *Dispatches* were also surprisingly successful commercially. A second edition, revised to include much new material, began to appear before the first edition was completed, and the two editions were merged from the publication of volume ten. A single-volume selection appeared in 1841 – still a weighty volume, but much more affordable and less intimidating for general readers than the full set of thirteen volumes. Nonetheless there was sufficient demand for a 'new and enlarged' edition of the whole work to be published between 1844 and 1847. This was in eight hefty volumes with smaller type and less generous spacing, which allowed the set to be sold for only six guineas or slightly less than half the price of the first edition. Gurwood received all the royalties from these various editions, amounting to over £5,700 even before the publication of the 1844 edition. In 1838 Wellington, fearing that the number of complimentary copies that had to be sent to everyone who had supplied letters or in other ways assisted the project might hurt Gurwood financially, sent him a draft for £500 and a handsome letter of thanks. Gurwood declined the money; he knew that future proceeds would make him and his family comfortable, and that the project had raised him from obscurity and given him a unique position in society, as well as proving immensely interesting if also extremely laborious. Wellington further showed his appreciation by appointing him Deputy Lieutenant of the Tower of London (worth £700 per annum) and securing him a civil list pension of £200 p.a.[33]

The success of the *Dispatches* and Napier's *History* both assisted and benefitted from the revival of Wellington's popularity that began almost as soon as the political crisis of 1832 was resolved, and waxed more strongly as the 1830s went on. In July 1835 Lady Wharncliffe was pleased to see the Duke 'cheer'd as warmly & generally as in the days of his greatest favour. It was quite a triumph to his own gates, & he was obliged continually to touch his cap in acknowledgement.' And when, in the spring of 1839, a member of the crowd hooted Wellington as he left the House of Lords, a coal-heaver grabbed the offender, 'shook him almost to death, and hurled him to the ground amid the cheers of the spectators who surrounded the Duke and followed him all the way to Apsley House'.[34]

Wellington turned seventy in 1839, and later that year he was seriously ill and widely expected to die; he recovered, but the incident and subsequent attacks prompted a surge of interest in his life and a realisation that tributes not paid promptly might have to be paid posthumously. Already, in May 1837, the

Common Council of the City of London, which had been such a vehement critic in the early years of the Peninsular War, commissioned Sir Francis Chantrey to make a mounted statue of the Duke. Chantrey died before the work was completed, but it was finished by his assistant Henry Weekes and unveiled outside the Royal Exchange on Waterloo Day 1844.[35] In December 1839 a meeting of 'noblemen and gentlemen' in Edinburgh decided to call for subscriptions for a Scottish national testimonial to Wellington. However, the proud burghers of Glasgow refused to be thus subsumed into the general mass, and instituted their own project. Possibly spurred on by this rivalry both projects went ahead, each committee raising approximately £10,000 by public subscription. Glasgow's statue, by the experienced French sculptor Carlo Marochetti, proceeded smoothly and was completed in 1844. In recent times a demotic tradition of placing a brightly coloured plastic traffic cone on Wellington's head has given the statue renewed popularity, and an official proposal to raise the height of the plinth to make this more difficult aroused strong and successful opposition. The Edinburgh statue, by John Steele, was not unveiled until Waterloo Day, 1852. Both these schemes were undertaken by Scottish Conservatives with the lukewarm participation of some Whigs, and the outright opposition of a few radicals, but they mark a further step in Wellington's gradual transition from a highly partisan figure to an apolitical national hero.[36]

A second statue of Wellington in London by Matthew Cotes Wyatt was the subject of intense controversy, but this focussed almost entirely on its artistic merits, its gigantic size (it was explicitly intended to be the largest bronze statue in the world, with the girth of Wellington's horse being more than twenty-two feet), and its placement on top of Decimus Burton's arch (which it rather overwhelmed) at Hyde Park Corner opposite Apsley House. The statue was lifted into position with great fanfare on 29 September 1846 in front of a large crowd of onlookers including Queen Adelaide, but the sceptics were not silenced. The Duke tried to avoid any involvement in the controversy, but when it appeared that the statue would be removed, he plainly indicated that he would regard this as a personal slight, and his prestige was now so great that this was immediately decisive and the statue remained in place until 1883.[37]

No fewer than seven new biographies of Wellington appeared between 1839 and 1842, although only two of these, by W.H. Maxwell and Andrew Bonar, were sufficiently successful to be reprinted. All of these biographies concentrated heavily on Wellington's military career, while Maxwell's, which was the dominant biography for the rest of the century (although it never rivalled the popularity of Napier's history) stopped abruptly after Waterloo, with an unfulfilled promise of a forthcoming memoir of Wellington's life as a statesman. The biographies present a highly favourable view of the Duke, glorying in his victories and warmly praising his character. George Soane makes explicit a common assumption: 'The life of Wellington, as displayed in his actions and letters, affords a moral lesson of deep import, from the perusal of which no one ought to rise without becoming a better and a wiser man.' And it 'shows by a multitude of examples, far beyond any precept, how indispensable patience and perseverance are even to the highest genius; it points out the real paths of success in every mode of life, for the same ways that led the soldier and the politician to his object are strictly applicable to the purposes of the humblest individual'.[38]

Numerous virtues were attributed to Wellington with varying plausibility, ranging from frankness and simplicity, dignity and grace, to patience and forebearance. He was held to represent particularly well the peculiar attributes of an English gentleman: perfect manners, restraint, self-discipline, patriotism and strong common sense. Hidden in the depths of the second volume of the first edition of the *Dispatches* Gurwood had included a story told by an unnamed friend of Wellington's who asked him after his return to England in 1805 how he could be content to command a mere brigade when he had led armies of 40,000 men in India. Wellington is supposed to have replied:

For this plain reason, I am *nimmukwallah*, as we say in the East; that is, I have eat[en] the King's salt, and therefore, I conceive it to be my duty to serve with unhesitating zeal and cheerfulness, when and wherever the King or his government may think proper to employ me.[39]

Although it was obvious from even a casual examination of Wellington's career that there were a number of occasions on which he failed to live up to this ideal, the quotation was widely seized upon as revealing the key to his life and character. It was quoted in reviews of the *Dispatches* in the *Quarterly,* in *Blackwood's,* in the *British and Foreign Review or European Quarterly,* and in the *Eclectic Review,* not to mention the *Army and Navy Chronicle* and the *London Quarterly Review.* At least four of the biographers (Soane, Alexander, Bonar and Wright) gave it prominence, as did Sir Archibald Alison in his very successful *History of Europe.* This ensured that it reached a far wider audience than those who read the *Dispatches* or even looked at any of the biographies.[40]

Liberal and radical writers ensured that such panegyrics did not have the field to themselves, and that the image of Wellington as the cold-hearted aristocrat who contemptuously described his men as 'the scum of the earth' was not forgotten, but the enthusiasm for controversies over Wellington's character and career was fading. Gradually a new consensus was emerging, which was expressed at the Coronation Banquet at Edinburgh in 1838 when the Duke was toasted as 'belonging not to any party, but as belonging to the country (cheers) – as the man who had led British armies on the field of battle'.[41] As the years passed Wellington's popularity and prestige increased, especially as he gradually withdrew from the forefront of political conflict. Yet he was still an active and important politician lending lustre to the Conservative Party and, after 1841, weight to Peel's Cabinet. At times it seemed that the living Wellington was overshadowed by his past glories, but the respect with which he was now treated, even by opponents, strengthened his influence, especially on questions where he was seen to have particular expertise: the army, most obviously, but also colonial questions with a military dimension. Even more significantly, it increased his standing in the House of Lords, especially among the Tory peers. This was important, for the Tory majority in the Lords was a double-edged sword which needed careful handling if it was not to undermine the revival of the party, and Wellington played a crucial role in its management.

CHAPTER TWENTY-SIX

LEADING THE LORDS
(1835–41)

THE CONSERVATIVE PARTY was in opposition for six years after Peel's resignation in May 1835 – the longest period of Wellington's life in which he was not in high executive office since his arrival in India almost forty years before. But he was still an immensely important figure in the political landscape – the leader of the Opposition in the House of Lords, with a powerful voice in shaping the policy adopted by the Conservative Party, while also working with the ministers on a number of questions. However, the Lords generally sat for only a few days a week, between February and August, and seldom had much legislation to discuss until after Easter, so that while important, Wellington's role was much less time-consuming and demanding than the Foreign Office or even the Ordnance. He also continued to hold numerous distinguished offices such as Lord Warden of the Cinque Ports, but while each of these offices generated a certain amount of business, they did not satisfy his appetite for work. In addition, Wellington devoted many hours to his immense private correspondence, writing long, frequent, amusing letters to friends and colleagues, and brisk notes to an innumerable army of strangers who wrote to him on a vast array of subjects. None of this was new; he had combined all these things with the demands of being prime minister, or leading the fight against the Reform Bill, or serving as Peel's Foreign Secretary. The reduction in the demands on Wellington following the fall of the Conservative government in 1835 proved timely, for in these years he began to show some signs of age (he turned sixty-six in 1835 and seventy-two in 1841), while in the later part of the period he suffered a succession of strokes which took a toll, even though he made a good recovery. Nonetheless he remained a formidable and highly respected figure in 1841.

In 1830 the loss of office had plunged Wellington into gloom, but in May 1835 his mood was buoyant, almost carefree. On 18 May Lady Salisbury encountered him riding in Hyde Park; he dismounted and strolled with her and her companion, saying 'that he was now the idlest man about town', and she noted that he was 'in great spirits'. On the following day a party including Lady Salisbury, her ten-year-old daughter Blanche, Wellington and Lord Ellenborough visited the Royal Academy exhibition, even though the Duke had already attended a private viewing. 'I walked with the Duke,' Lady Salisbury wrote in her journal, 'and looked out the numbers in the catalogue for him. He took my little Blanche in the other hand and went with great interest over the whole.' The exhibition included no fewer than three new portraits of Wellington, although none pleased Lady Salisbury. Wilkie's portrait 'is a decided failure in likeness. He [Wellington] thought so himself, and that it was too large about the body.' The portrait by Pickersgill 'is like a drunken undertaker, and that by Morton made of wood'. The good humour and gaiety of the day shines through Lady Salisbury's description, and she adds that after the Academy they went on to see a collection of Rubens' drawings that had belonged to Sir Thomas Lawrence, and then struck a lighter note with 'a panorama of the burning of the House of Lord[s] and Commons, and the learned fleas. The last is excessively laughable and really astonishing'.[1]

Ten days later another party including the Duke, Lady Salisbury and Lady G. Fane visited the Surrey Zoological Gardens. 'The Duke was in high spirits and took much interest in the animals. We saw the wild beasts fed, and among other things a young orang-outang [*sic*], just arrived, wrapped up in flannel.' The head of the zoo asked Wellington many questions about the animals he had seen in India, which the Duke enjoyed answering, while Lady Salisbury noted that he was particularly amused 'by the entertainment afforded by the animals to two little boys of Lord Burghersh's who were with us, and who ran after the different creatures, mounted on the elephants' backs etc'. The visit was so successful that the Duke went to the Zoological Gardens in Regent's Park a few weeks later, and the following year accompanied Lady Salisbury and her children 'to see the Giraffes, beautiful creatures, particularly *gentlemanlike* looking, and their shape by no means such a caricature on a quadruped as their prints had led me to believe'. Wellington had always had the capacity to enjoy himself thoroughly in moments of leisure, and these outings suggest that the slackening of the pace of business that resulted from his loss of office was not without its consolations.[2]

Wellington's good humour was encouraged by the changing mood of the country, the gains made by the Conservative Party in the 1835 election, and the revival of his own popularity. At the Royal Academy exhibition, 'the people all recognized him immediately and made way for him in the most respectful manner'. At the zoo in Regent's Park, 'our progress was rather impeded by the number of people who came round to see the Duke (the gardens were very crowded), the people hustling, running and whispering to each other, that nobody might lose the sight; children especially dragged along by their parents

and hoisted upon the most elevated places, that they might be able to say hereafter "that they had seen *him*". And on Waterloo Day 1836: 'Nothing could be
more gratifying than the reception of the Duke. The crowd followed him home,
cheering enthusiastically. Mrs Drummond and I [Lady Salisbury] with the
children endeavoured to follow but we were almost squeezed to death by the
crowd.'[3]

Conservative confidence was increased by a succession of embarrassing
defeats suffered by ministers in by-elections in the summer of 1835, the most
famous being that of Lord John Russell in Devonshire. The ministers themselves appeared to lack any great sense of common purpose or direction.
Melbourne had exerted his authority to exclude Brougham and Durham from
office, but otherwise saw no alternative but to give each minister his head in his
own department and act as mediator between them when their interests
clashed. He felt obliged to complete the unfinished business projected by Grey's
government, but had little inclination to undertake anything beyond that, for
he believed that after the upheavals of the last seven years the country needed
a period of relative tranquillity to digest all the changes that had been made. He
was also acutely aware of the weakness of his government, which was dependent
for its modest majority in Parliament on the support of the radicals, O'Connell's
Irish members, and old-fashioned Whigs whose appetite for further reform
had been exhausted. The King's hostility was palpable and, if not directly
dangerous (for the experiment of 1834 could not be repeated), it certainly
added to the strains of office. Melbourne's task as prime minister in these years
was neither easy nor obviously rewarding.[4]

The Conservative peers in the House of Lords were emboldened by the
change in popular opinion and by the government's weakness, rather than
intimidated by the failure of Peel's ministry, and did not hesitate to exert themselves in the remainder of the prolonged parliamentary session of 1835. On
14 July the Lords defeated a bill that would have opened the universities of
Oxford and Cambridge to non-Anglicans, and on 24 August they rejected the
Appropriation clauses of the Irish Tithe Bill, whose passage by the Commons
had led to the fall of Peel's government a few months before. Both measures
had also been opposed by Peel and the Conservatives in the Commons, and the
government accepted defeat on both issues, although it would re-introduce the
Irish Tithe Bill in the following year and again after that.[5]

But the most serious struggle in Parliament in 1835 after the change of
government – and indeed the most hard-fought issue of the whole six years of
Melbourne's second administration – was over the Municipal Corporations
Bill. At one level the bill simply completed the work begun with the repeal of
the Test and Corporation Acts in 1828 and the Reform Bill in 1832, by creating
an open, relatively democratic system of local government in Britain (the Act

did not extend to Ireland). But at another level it was an attack on one of the most important remaining bulwarks of Tory power in the country, and some of its provisions were blatantly partisan. Nonetheless Peel decided not to oppose the bill outright but to attempt to improve it in committee. Cases of abuse and corruption in the old corporations were too common and too notorious for reform to be rejected out of hand and, as always, Peel was acutely aware of the need to preserve his reputation as the champion of practical moderate reform if the Conservatives were to sustain their revival in the new post-1832 political system. Not surprisingly, the government used its majority in the Commons to reject Peel's amendments and sent the bill to the Lords largely unaltered.

Wellington disliked the bill even more than Peel. He had been reading Clarendon's history of the English Civil War and commented: 'The worst of this Corporation Bill is that it will form a little Republic in every town, possessing the power of raising money. In case of anything like a civil war, these would be very formidable instruments in the hands of the democratic party. Charles I was ruined by the money levied by the City of London.'[6] And he knew that most of his Conservative peers shared his attitude, and moreover were itching for another fight with the government. Nonetheless he persuaded a meeting of the Conservative Lords at Apsley House to follow Peel's lead, and let the bill pass its Second Reading and then amend it in committee. The more extreme or ultra peers were unhappy with this decision, but were consoled by an agreement to hear counsel for the Corporations at the bar of the House, and to let them call evidence. The government agreed to this most reluctantly, but was outnumbered two to one in the Lords and had little choice but to submit or withdraw the bill altogether. The evidence called by the Corporations' counsel was inflammatory and the Tory Lords became even more agitated by the issue, and appear to have slipped for the moment beyond Wellington's control, with Lyndhurst leading the attack on the details of the bill with a ruthless forensic examination.

Peel was dismayed and angry at the proceedings in the Lords. He had expected – or at least wished – the Conservative peers to follow the line he had carefully chalked out in the Commons, but he had failed to explain this clearly to Wellington, let alone attempt to persuade his noble brethren why they should accept his judgement of the issues at stake. Rather than be associated with the attack on the bill in the Lords he withdrew to his home in Staffordshire in ominous silence. Meanwhile the Lords made amendment after amendment to the bill in committee, significantly changing its character, although it was not clear whether these changes went so far that the government would abandon the bill rather than accept them.

By the end of August the amended bill was back in the Commons and Peel had returned to London. He proceeded to disown the Lords – or as some saw

it, to betray them – by repudiating many of their most controversial amendments. Wellington tried to calm feelings at a heated meeting at Apsley House,
but 'rather let out that he would surrender no principle', a stand that was warmly
cheered.[7] For a moment it looked as if the breach between the Conservative
Party in the Lords and Commons might widen and become a fissure that would
swallow all the achievement of rebuilding the party. However, at a second
meeting at Apsley House two days later Wellington, with the crucial support of
Lyndhurst, argued forcefully that they must compromise. The government
proved willing to meet them halfway, and the final bill was much less damaging
to Conservative interests than the original proposal.

Viewed with cool detachment, the result was broadly beneficial to the
Conservative Party; Peel had preserved, even strengthened, his reforming
credentials, and his willingness to throw over the aristocratic wing of his own
party rather than tamely follow their lead did him no harm among the party's
new supporters. Wellington had maintained the unity of the Conservatives in
the Lords, and had induced them to follow his lead against their inclination;
and if he had been forced to give way, they shared his pain and it strengthened
the bond between them. And the government had been deprived of a potentially popular issue, while the final bill contained many of the safeguards the
Conservatives most valued. But these advantages need to be set against the
damage done to the relations between Peel and his own party, especially (but
not only) in the Lords. It would be neither the first nor the last time that the
bonds of party loyalty were tested almost to breaking point, and some of the
wounds left lasting scars.[8]

The personal relationship between Wellington and Peel was never entirely
comfortable, even though both men recognised that it was crucial to the unity
and hopes of the party. Neither was blameless; Peel was prickly, over-sensitive
and uncommunicative, with an underlying resentment of Wellington's fame and
unique eminence. For his part Wellington found Peel clumsy and awkward, and
disliked his constant emphasis on the importance of the Commons and popular
opinion, while Peel sometimes seemed to go out of his way to slight the Lords
and the landed interest. Wellington was also accustomed to flattery and charm,
and while he had no doubt that it was right that Peel should take over the leadership of the party, he was not a man to relish taking a step back to second place.
In June 1835, Lady Salisbury told Wellington: 'Those are Peel's odd ways,
acquired from not having been used to good society from his birth. But he is a
thoroughly honest man and devoted to you.' Wellington ignored the snobbery
and replied: '"In the first position you are quite right. He *is* thoroughly honest.
I never saw a man who adhered more invariably to the truth on all occasions"
(a very rare praise for the Duke to give). "As to the second, I have my doubts
about that."' Four years later, Wellington told Mahon 'that of all the men he

had ever known, the one with the best memory was Peel, and that it was impossible for any man to be more distinguished for scrupulous veracity'. But he also declared his 'entire unbelief' in Aberdeen's statement of Peel's 'reverence and regard for the Duke'. And this was reasonable enough; each man respected, esteemed and – up to a point – admired the other, but there was no great warmth or mutual liking between them, and they remained colleagues rather than friends.[9]

Nonetheless both Peel and Wellington learnt from the rift over the Municipal Corporations Bill and in the following years took more care to co-ordinate their positions, and showed a greater willingness to compromise in order to accommodate the other. This bore fruit in the sessions of 1836 and 1837 as the renewed government attempt to appropriate the (probably non-existent) surplus revenue of the Church of Ireland was again blocked, as was an Irish Corporations Bill which would have applied much the same model of 'reformed' local government to Ireland as to England, despite their very different circumstances. The government tamely accepted these defeats, and an attempt by O'Connell and the radicals to whip up a popular cry against the House of Lords in the autumn and winter of 1835–36 spluttered and smouldered for a few months before dying out due to lack of interest. The government's standing in the country had fallen, and it was deeply unpopular in areas where the effects of its new Poor Law were being felt; while on the role of the House of Lords and on many other issues the Prime Minister felt much more in tune with his Conservative opponents than his Irish and radical supporters. Rather than resent the fact that the government could only get its measures through Parliament with the support of the Conservatives, Melbourne may have been secretly grateful for an excuse not to undertake more extensive and radical measures.[10]

In the early hours of the morning of Tuesday 20 June 1837, King William IV died at Windsor. His last wish had been to survive long enough so that his death did not force the cancellation of the Waterloo Banquet held on the previous evening (for while it was not unchristian to fight the battle and kill and wound tens of thousands of men and horses on a Sunday, it would have offended the Almighty to have celebrated the anniversary with a dinner on the Sabbath). Wellington paid tribute to the late King in Parliament, declaring that he had always found 'a firmness, a discretion, a candour, a justice, a spirit of conciliation towards others, and a respect for all' in the King's conduct. Privately, he was ruthlessly frank and clear-eyed in his assessment:

His reign was certainly a most unfortunate one for Himself, His Country and the Family. He was the most ignorant Man ever placed in a great situation. He had an unfortunate facility or rather weakness of Character; which enabled every *Charlatan* to prey upon Him. This Country will long suffer from the Measures of His Reign. His last Ministry were forced upon Him, greatly against His Inclination. He was ashamed of His Position in relation to them. He detested them; and did not treat them well. This feeling and the Conduct which it occasioned gave him a kind of Strength, which he used at times with success for the Publick Interests. At others he was obliged to give way to His own mortification and degradation. One benefit however resulted from this state of things even to the Ministers themselves. It enabled them to keep their Adherents in order. They could say the King will not consent and will go to the Tories![11]

But if there was little to lament about the late sovereign, there was good cause to be apprehensive about his successor. What could be expected of a young woman, barely turned eighteen, who had never mixed in society and who inevitably had little experience of the world? Wellington said that 'supposing her to be an angel from Heaven, she cannot have the knowledge to enable her to oppose the mischief proposed to her'. Nor was it encouraging that Melbourne had filled the Court posts with Whigs – both gentlemen and ladies, including a remarkable number of close relatives of Cabinet ministers. Far from resenting this, the Queen soon showed herself to be a warm champion of the government, and in particular a devoted friend of the prime minister.[12]

The accession of Queen Victoria had one consequence which made Wellington's life considerably easier: the dynastic union with Hanover was severed, and the Duke of Cumberland left England for his new dominion where, against Wellington's and other advice, he promptly abolished the constitution and quarrelled with the professors at the University of Gottingen. His conduct was an embarrassment for the Conservative Party in Britain, especially as he remained heir-presumptive to the British throne until the young Queen married and produced an heir. The thought of a repetition of Princess Charlotte's death in childbirth twenty years before, followed by the accession of King Ernest, was as alarming to Wellington and Peel as it was, in a rather different way, to Whigs and radicals.[13]

An election followed the King's death. Unlike in 1835, the Whigs had the advantage of incumbency and of the unconcealed support of the Queen, which they exploited to the full on the hustings. Nonetheless they lost seats as the country continued to swing back to the Conservatives, and the government's majority was halved to around twenty seats. At the same time a number of leading radicals, including Joseph Hume, lost their seats, while Lord Douro, standing as a Conservative, was elected for Norwich. Although certainly not a Conservative triumph, the election confirmed the revival of the Conservative Party and greatly encouraged its supporters. The fundamental beliefs of the

Conservative Party had evolved considerably over the previous decades as the legacy of Pitt, and even Liverpool, had receded. The power of the king to select a minister who would then find sufficient support in the Commons to carry on his government had been broken, and any lingering Tory regret at its loss was mitigated by the new Queen's extraordinary preference for the Whigs, her natural enemies. The institution of the monarchy remained important to Conservatives, but the party's main focus had shifted to a defence of the existing social order, and in particular its twin bulwarks of the Church of England and the landed interest. To this Peel added a commitment to administrative efficiency and moderate, safe reform that appealed to liberal Tories, as well as to disillusioned Whigs who were alarmed that radical demands for change had not been satisfied by all the concessions granted in 1828–32, and to the new class of sometimes self-made industrialists and merchants who did not see themselves as natural allies of Tory squires and hunting dukes.

Like most Conservatives Wellington's spirits had lifted with the revival in the party's fortunes and the waning of the radical tide. His language was still highly coloured: 'We are governed by a corrupt and ignorant faction, not supported by a corrupt court, but forced upon the court by the democracy. God help us!' But he had always expressed himself vividly and without restraint when writing to close friends, and as early as 1810 had told his brother, 'I think that Govt & Country are going to the Devil as fast as possible.'[14] Throughout the early 1830s it was common for Conservatives of all shades to talk of the risk of revolution and even civil war, but by 1835 this sense of danger was receding. That autumn Wellington told Croker:

> I am not surprised that Sir Robert Peel should be alarmed. All that I hope for is, that the change in the position of the country may be gradual, that it may be effected without civil war, and may occasion as little sudden destruction of individual interests and property as possible. We may all by degrees take our respective stations on the new order of things, and go on till future changes take place *ad infinitum*.[15]

A few months later, in January 1836, the Duke was even more positive. Lady Burghersh reported that 'his general impressions about the state of things . . . are certainly *now* not *desponding*'. And 'he feels confident the game is in our hands, and that all he wishes is to keep people *patient* and not spoil things by being in a hurry. Indeed, his very words were, "We only want time and then we shall do very well. We are *in* a revolution, but now I see the end of it".'[16]

After the election Melbourne, faced with the prospect of governing with only a small majority and relying on the radicals and Irish members, approached Wellington indirectly to see if the Conservatives might consider a coalition or, more plausibly, an informal understanding based on consultation and co-operation. Wellington was well aware that the Conservative Party, in the Commons, the Lords and the country, was too excited by its new popularity to contemplate such an arrangement, but while he rejected the overture he was impressed by it, and was perfectly sincere when he assured Melbourne that if the ministers pursued moderate policies, the Conservatives would not engage in factious opposition. Wellington and Peel both recognised that until they had a reasonable hope of forming a strong Conservative government they had nothing to gain by driving Melbourne from office, for they could keep his weak administration from doing much harm. 'The danger is,' Croker wrote at this time, 'that the Government will become so despised as to be incapable of maintaining itself, before we are strong enough to make any permanent arrangement.'[17]

The opening of Parliament in November 1837 showed that Melbourne had taken Wellington's advice to heart. The Queen's speech was so moderate that the only hostility it provoked was from the radicals, and their amendment was crushed when the Conservatives joined the ministers in voting against it. Lord John Russell underlined the point when he declared, rather more emphatically than he intended or was wise, that the government would not bring forward any further measures of parliamentary reform, and stating his opposition to the secret ballot, the next item on the radicals' wish-list. And so, at the outset, the pattern was established where the government survived only on Conservative sufferance, while the disillusioned radicals alternated between bitter attacks and grudging support.[18]

At the end of 1837 news arrived of a rebellion in Quebec, led by French Canadians, which was soon followed by a smaller rising in predominantly English Upper Canada. Although the revolts were quickly suppressed they caused alarm in England, and prompted comparisons with the beginnings of the American Revolution. The British radicals strongly criticised the government's refusal to give way to local demands sooner, and Lord Melbourne, who had little interest in colonial affairs, endeavoured to quieten them by appointing Lord Durham as Governor-General with sweeping powers to impose a settlement. Wellington and Peel believed that they should support the government so long as it took action to deal with the revolt. Wellington was particularly concerned that the trouble might attract unemployed soldiers and liberal adventurers from across Europe and the New World, including many who had already taken part in the wars of independence in Latin America, the Greek revolt, and the civil wars in Spain and Portugal. The open frontier with the United States would make it difficult to keep such men out, while if the trouble persisted it might revive American dreams of annexing the British colonies. He prepared a detailed memorandum for Lord Hill (the Commander-in-Chief) based on his study of the defence of Canada in the 1820s, and his cheerful remark – 'Why it looks as if we were at our old trade again' – rather obscures the seriousness with which he regarded the problem.[19]

When Parliament met again in the middle of January many Conservative MPs and peers anticipated a full-scale assault on the ministry for its handling of Canadian affairs. But when Brougham stood up and launched a scathing attack on the government, Wellington immediately came to its defence and acquitted it of all blame on the most vulnerable ground: of ignoring signs of trouble and not reinforcing the garrison in Canada before the rebellion occurred. This speech destroyed the chances of any attack on the government, at least for the moment, and provoked great anger and excitement inside the Conservative Party. Lord Wharncliffe, a moderate, told his wife that it had produced 'the worst effects' not only among members of Parliament, but in the country, with Conservatives in the City saying 'they will not spend money in support of a Party who throw themselves over in such a way'. And Benjamin Disraeli, who was still only a minor figure on the fringes of the party, wrote: 'Our peers mustered thick . . . but the Duke of W[ellingto]n rose and spoilt all, with his damned generosity and all that. Great disgust in Tory ranks, even among the highest; Duke supposed to be passeé [*sic*] and to like being buttered with Whig laudation.'[20]

Conversely, Lord Holland praised Wellington's 'spontaneous, noble and candid testimony', and the speech, together with the advice the Duke had privately been providing, contributed to his growing reputation as 'a man who so entirely sank all party considerations in national objects'. Only a few weeks before Brougham, of all people, had said: 'That man's first object is to serve his Country with his sword if necessary, or with a pick-axe.'[21] However it seems likely that both the praise and the blame were somewhat misplaced, and that rather than being politically ingenuous the speech was quite deliberate, even if Wellington may have gone a little further than he intended. He knew that the government would be in peril that night, and that if the ministers were beaten they would resign, and that if they resigned Peel would have to attempt to form a government without having a majority in the Commons and without any great likelihood that an election would produce one. This would be bad enough at any time but even worse if the Whigs lost office over Canada, an issue where once free of office, they could quickly coalesce with the radicals in support of granting sweeping powers to the colonial legislatures. The result would be a disaster for both the country and the party.[22]

The government had weathered the first storm but it remained weak and vulnerable, and there was strong pressure from within the party for Peel to support a radical motion censuring the government. Peel wavered, torn between the dangers of forcing the ministers from office prematurely and losing control of his followers in the Commons. Wellington was emphatic in opposing any temporary alliance with the radicals, and his influence may have been decisive. The Conservatives in the Commons moved their own censure motion, carefully framed so that the radicals could not support it. The motion was defeated, the government survived, and discontented Tories began to call Wellington the 'Lord Protector of the Government'.[23]

The value of Melbourne's weak government as a bulwark against radical pressure for further reform was demonstrated in the middle of February when a radical motion calling for the secret ballot was defeated by 198 to 315 votes. Russell and other senior ministers in the Commons voted against the proposal, but most of their followers either supported it or did not vote, and the majority was made up overwhelmingly of Conservatives. With memories of 1835 still fresh it was not hard to imagine that if the Whigs were driven from office they would soon abandon their scruples and embrace the ballot and many other radical causes.[24] But retaining Melbourne in office did not only bring negative advantages. The government finally settled the Irish Church question by abandoning the appropriation clauses that had caused so much dissension, and accepted further extensive Conservative amendments as the bill made its way through Parliament. An Irish Poor Law had already been passed and a compromise over the Irish Corporations only just fell short of being accepted by both sides. It was a vindication of the tactics employed by both Peel and Wellington and a demonstration of the continuing power of the Lords when the government's majority in the Commons was relatively slight and its popularity in decline in the country at large. Wellington was only slightly exaggerating when he told Arbuthnot: 'We have now in our Hands the Exclusive Power of Legislation. Peel has only to exercise it as he may think proper.'[25]Despite the latent humiliation of his position Melbourne was grateful for the support of his opponents and told the Queen, 'with tears in his eyes,' that 'the Duke of Wellington and Sir Robert Peel have behaved very well; they have helped us a good deal'. But the Queen was unconvinced, emotionally identifying with the Whigs and hating their opponents with youthful naïvety.[26]

The Queen's coronation was on 28 June 1838. She arrived at the abbey about noon, looking well and 'perfectly composed, her manner graceful, with as much dignity as her want of height allowed her to display'. Her arrival was marked by loud, but to Lady Salisbury's ears, not particularly enthusiastic cheering. 'When the crown was put upon her head, she seemed to suffer under its weight, but went very well through the homage and the remainder of the ceremony.' According to Lord Aberdeen a 'spontaneous and universal burst of applause' greeted Wellington's act of homage, which contrasted sharply with a feeble attempt to applaud Melbourne. O'Connell was hissed.[27]

The French representative at the coronation was Marshal Soult, and Wellington went out of his way to avoid embarrassing his old opponent, delaying the publication of the latest volume of the *Dispatches* (which covered his defeat of Soult at Toulouse), and removing any trophies specifically associated with victories over Soult from sight when the foreign ministers dined at Apsley House. Wellington also endeavoured, although unsuccessfully, to dissuade Croker from publishing an article on Toulouse in the *Quarterly Review*, telling him 'that this was a gentlemanlike country, and the Tories were the gentlemanlike party' and that this was not the time 'to publish such an article'. When his intervention failed Wellington commented ruefully: 'I am a very clever man, a very clever man indeed, except when any gentleman happens to differ in opinion with me on any point – and then I am not a clever man at all.' The dinner for the foreign ministers was more successful, but Soult left early and the two old soldiers did not strike up any great rapport.[28]

When Parliament resumed in February 1839 there was palpable frustration on the Tory benches in both Houses at their leaders' reluctance to take office. Wellington remained convinced that the party was pursuing the right policy, but even Peel was growing weary of forbearance and self-denial, however well it had worked. Nonetheless both leaders continued to manoeuvre through a number of heated debates in their Houses, ensuring that Conservative views were expressed and incorporated into legislation, but that the government was not defeated on anything that would bring it down. Gradually the government lost the will to live and when a number of radicals unexpectedly joined with the Conservatives in an attack on its handling of the colonial legislature in Jamaica, the ministers took the opportunity to resign even though they retained a majority of five on the question. Melbourne had been preparing the Queen for the possibility for some time, but when the news reached Windsor Victoria wrote that it 'struck to my heart and I felt dreadfully anxious'; she was in tears, and too miserable to appear at dinner that night. Nonetheless, she followed Melbourne's advice and summoned Wellington on the next day, 8 May, and he advised her to send for Peel, 'who was a gentleman and a man of honour and integrity'.[29]

When Peel arrived the Queen told him that she had parted from her government with reluctance, and in asking him to form an administration she indicated that she did not want him to dissolve Parliament and call an election; she hoped that he would include Wellington in his Cabinet; and that she did not intend to give up her personal friendship with Melbourne. Office on these terms was a poisoned chalice. The Conservatives did not have a majority in Parliament and the experience of 1835 showed that holding office would not, in itself, give them one; and that however complaisant Melbourne appeared at the moment, the Whigs and radicals could quickly sink their differences in order to tear the new government to pieces. Nonetheless, Peel was not daunted by the coolness of the Queen's welcome. He knew the strength of her attachment to Melbourne and hoped that her attitude to the Conservatives would soften with experience. He took the precaution of ensuring that her objections to granting a dissolution were not insurmountable, and set about forming his government. As the Queen's support for the Whigs had been so pronounced he required a clear gesture of her acceptance of the change, namely the removal of some of the Whig Ladies who held court posts near to the Queen, and who would counteract any thaw in her attitude to him. But when he returned for a second interview on 9 May the Queen cut short any discussion of changes to the Ladies with a blanket refusal even to hear what he proposed. This went far beyond any trouble Peel had anticipated, and did not bode very well for the future of his government. Peel withdrew, saying that he would consult his colleagues, and asked Wellington to endeavour to persuade her to change her mind. The Duke tried, but without success, and on 10 May Peel resigned his commission in a long, careful letter that made clear that he had only wanted to make limited changes to the Royal Household.[30]

Lady Holland expressed the Whig view of these events in a letter to her son: 'Had the D[uke] of W[ellington] conducted the negotiation it would probably have gone well; but Peel's vulgarity, stiffness and grasping, wounded the feelings of the high spirited Princess.' This was satisfying, but also quite untrue. The 'Bedchamber Crisis', as it came to be known, was neither a misunderstanding nor a result of clashing personalities. Rather it was a case of the Queen using her now limited power to achieve the result she wanted: the retention of Melbourne's government. Her methods were not subtle, and the opportunity only existed because the Conservatives did not have a majority in the Commons. She had no guarantee that Peel would not give way over the Ladies and take office anyway, but this would still have given her a significant triumph at the outset of their relationship. As it was she got her way and within a week of the vote on the Jamaica question Melbourne was re-established as prime minister, and dining and riding with the Queen as usual.[31]

The Queen paid a high price for her victory. The Conservative Party, which had always viewed her with suspicion, now became openly hostile. Peel kept his feelings to himself, but he was not a man readily to overlook the fact that he had been placed in an impossible position, nor did the Queen's continuing affection for Melbourne give him any reason to trust her in future. Comments such as Lady Holland's mortified him and added a personal element to his soreness. Even Wellington, who had no reason to regret the final outcome, was dismayed at the means by which it had been achieved, and was more inclined to be critical of the Queen than before the crisis. The public also reacted badly: ministers were hissed by the crowd when they attended a Council Meeting at Buckingham Palace; the government lost a by-election in a safe seat and came close to losing another; while at the Guildhall Dinner Melbourne received such a hostile reception that it was five minutes before he could make himself heard above the jeers. But however unpopular and enfeebled, the government had no choice but to struggle on, serving the Queen.[32]

In the autumn of 1839 Wellington lost one of his closest friends when Lady Salisbury died at the age of only thirty-seven. She had been ill for a year and was probably suffering from diabetes. To some extent she had taken the place of Mrs Arbuthnot as Wellington's confidant and the object of his affections, and her loss was all the harder to bear because it, like Mrs Arbuthnot's death, was so premature and unreasonable.

Wellington was not left without friends. He remained very close to Charles Arbuthnot, who lived at Apsley House when in London, and often stayed with the Duke at Walmer and Stratfield Saye. Business brought him into frequent contact with Fitzroy Somerset, and this would increase in the 1840s when Wellington returned to the Horse Guards. He also enjoyed, as he always had, the company of younger men and women. His niece Priscilla, Lady Burghersh, was living in England between 1831 and 1841, and her presence and that of her husband and their children brought great pleasure. Yet even this connection was touched by grief, for Lady Burghersh's daughter Louisa died in March 1837 at the age of fifteen.[33]

Other friends who became more prominent in these years included Lord Francis Leveson Gower (who had changed his name to Lord Francis Egerton in 1833 and would be made Earl of Ellesmere in 1846), and Lord Mahon (who in 1855 succeeded his father as 5th Earl Stanhope). In 1838 Wellington began writing regularly to Lady Wilton, sending her almost six hundred letters over less than ten years, in which he discussed politics and public affairs as well as social and family gossip. He also conducted a more protracted but much slighter and more intermittent correspondence with Miss Anna Maria Jenkins, an attractive young religious enthusiast whom he had first met in 1834 and who was intent on saving his soul.[34]

These years also saw greater contact between Wellington and his brothers. Henry was back in England after his years as ambassador in Vienna (senior diplomatic posts were still political appointments which changed with government; Henry was replaced in Vienna by Frederick Lamb, Melbourne's brother). William was a frequent guest at Walmer until 1838 when Wellington, as Lord Warden of the Cinque Ports, appointed him Captain of Deal Castle just a few miles along the coast, and with an attractive residence of its own. And Wellington and Lord Wellesley were finally reconciled. The Marquess had been mortified when Melbourne refused to send him back to Ireland in 1835, but had come to accept that his political career was over. He turned to literary pursuits and imitated Wellington by publishing his Indian despatches in five weighty volumes. This led to some belated recognition for his achievements, which did much to sweeten his last years, and even produced a substantial grant from the East India Company that relieved him from the worst of his financial problems. Marianne carefully orchestrated the first meeting between the two brothers, so that each felt that they were being magnanimous to the other, and once the ice was broken they derived a good deal of pleasure in discussing their early successes. Wellington congratulated Lord Wellesley on the anniversary of the fall of Seringapatam each year, and the favour was reciprocated a few weeks later on the anniversary of Waterloo. Lord Wellesley even gave the Duke his proxy for the House of Lords, implying a political as well as personal reconciliation, and the final step in turning the circle that had begun with Arthur's first election as MP for Trim, representing his brother's interest, half a century before.[35]

Unfortunately there was no comparable improvement in Wellington's relations with his sons. Lady Salisbury noted on a visit to Stratfield Saye in April 1838: 'Douro and Charles were also in the house. It is grievous to see their neglect and inattention towards the Duke, or rather their repugnance to speak to him or approach him. During the whole time I was in the house on this visit, I never heard either of them *lui addresser la parole* [speak to him]'. However, the Duke was delighted by Douro's marriage to Lady Elizabeth Hay in April 1839, and got along very well with his daughter-in-law, to whom he was both considerate and affectionate. Lady Douro was rather stiff – she had the reputation for being a glacial beauty – but she was warmed by Wellington's genuine concern for her welfare and happiness, and their shared regret at her lack of children seems to have brought them closer together.[36]

Wellington's health began to deteriorate in these years, especially from 1839 onwards. In 1835 Lady Salisbury noted that he still rode very hard when hunting, 'like a young man, and does not appear in the least tired or sleepy in the evening'. In the following summer he was knocked off his horse in a collision with a watercart and confined to his house for a few days, but he was not badly hurt and that autumn Charles Arbuthnot declared that he 'looks younger & healthier than I have seen him for a long time'.[37] He also suffered a good deal from rheumatism in his neck, 'which makes him look bent and worse than he really is'.[38]

In February 1839, while at Stratfield Saye, he suffered an 'attack' – probably a relatively mild stroke, although we know few details. This affected his voice in early March so that speaking in the Lords he was reported to be 'loud at some intervals but very low and indistinct at others, and the loudness or emphasis not according to the points he wished to urge'. But by 9 March he was reported to look 'very well' and be in high spirits, while that night he dined at the French ambassador's, went to the Opera, slipped away to put in an appearance at the Speaker's levee, returned to the Opera, and then went on to a party at Cambridge House – a sequence that was only unusual in that it was noted by one of his party.[39]

He suffered a second, much better documented, attack at Walmer on 18 November 1839. It was a very cold day with showers, and when he went riding with Lord Mahon he wore a fur collar, protected himself with an umbrella, and kept his horse to a gentle trot. He had eaten almost nothing on the preceding day or two, for when he did not have company he now ate very sparingly, and 'had left off wine almost altogether'. That afternoon he wrote a few short notes and read the paper, but finding it difficult to hold, he sent for the doctor. Soon after he rang his bell again, but he was unable to speak clearly and fell to the floor unconscious. When Doctor MacArthur arrived he feared that Wellington had suffered a stroke and might lose the use of his left side, but as the Duke gradually recovered his speech and memory it appeared that his side was unaffected, and 'that his mind displayed all its usual clearness, and that beyond all doubt the attack was not in any degree of a paralytic or apoplectic kind'. Having no other explanation, the doctors blamed it on cold and lack of food, and sensibly refrained from drawing blood and concentrated instead on simple nursing. Under this benign regime the Duke's recovery was rapid; on 20 November he was able to get up, dress, read his letters and answer a few, and on the following day he wrote many letters and attended to business, and paid bills. Mahon noted: 'He looked better than I expected – not so well as I wished – very thin and worn in the face, and his eyes not as usual. But he seemed in very good spirits, and spoke of his health with much cheerfulness and confidence ... His step was firm and steady – decidedly more so than before his attack.'[40]

The Duke suffered another similar but perhaps more severe attack three months later in London, on 13 February 1840. Although Croker had little doubt that 'the Duke's public life is over', he again recovered quickly, taking leave of his doctors on 22 February and soon resuming his normal busy life. A fourth attack came in the middle of July and a fifth in the House of Lords in February 1841 and then, as mysteriously as they had begun, they ceased.[41] The cumulative effect of these attacks was to age Wellington considerably, so that at times he appeared older than his real age (he turned seventy-one in 1840). Descriptions of him at the time vary widely, suggesting that he was much better on some days than on others. For example, on 10 April 1840 Lord Hatherton was 'painfully affected by observing the extreme feebleness of his voice and of his body', but a month later found the Duke 'as bold, clear and vigorous as if he had been twenty-five only'. Lord Mahon found him 'alas! grown very old ... On sitting down, even in the forenoon, he is apt to fall asleep for a few minutes – a very new habit with him'. But at the same time Mahon noted that 'he walks firmly and well – often four or five miles a day at once', and the Duke stoutly defended his intention to continue hunting when Lady Wilton expressed her concern. He also claimed, defiantly if implausibly, that 'I certainly am now as well as I ever was. It is astonishing what a quantity of Business I can do. I am fully equal to be dictator as I was seven Years ago; Or to take the field.' This was patently untrue, but Mahon's more judicious assessment is more convincing: 'His great mind is certainly as great as ever – not the slightest trace of decay in its powers, or obscuration in its clearness – equal, I am quite sure, in all respects to itself – but it is grown somewhat slower, both in conception and expression of ideas. He seizes upon facts less rapidly, and conveys his thoughts with longer pauses.'[42] Certainly the Duke's activity over the next few years does not suggest any impairment of his ability or serious reduction of his energy, although he made less effort to restrain his lifelong inclination to exaggeration when framing an argument, which could make him sound extreme and even almost querulous.

Five days after Wellington's attack in November 1839 he attended a meeting of the Privy Council in London, at which the Queen announced her betrothal to her cousin Prince Albert of Saxe-Coburg-Gotha. The papers had published alarming accounts of the Duke's illness and his arrival was cheered by the crowd at the Palace gates, while the Queen 'appeared to look out for me when she came into the Council Chamber'. The Queen's choice of husband was not universally popular even among the Whigs, while Conservatives were alarmed by reports that the young man (he was even younger than the Queen) had liberal if not radical views, and close ties to his uncle Leopold, King of Belgium. The Queen's declaration was closely modelled on the precedent provided by George III, except that, at Lord John Russell's suggestion, the word 'Protestant' was omitted from the description of the Prince. This appeared to be not only a slap at the establishment of the Church of England but at the Act of Succession itself, and Wellington insisted that it be restored, privately describing the government's behaviour as 'childish and foolish'.[43]

There was a further row over the Prince's allowance, which Melbourne, the Queen's minister, proposed should be £50,000 a year. This was not an unreasonable figure and was in line with precedents, but they dated to before the era of reform and economy, and Conservatives, still smarting from the Bedchamber Crisis, took great delight in reducing this to a mere £20,000, while 150 of the government's supporters in the Commons absented themselves from the vote. Even more petty was the question of whether Albert should be granted precedence over the Queen's uncles. Melbourne, who cared little for such formalities, blithely promised the Queen that this would be achieved without difficulty when consoling her for his refusal to give Albert a British peerage. But Wellington pointed out that royal precedence was established by an Act of Parliament, and that if her uncles, the Dukes of Cambridge and Sussex, did not choose to waive their rights it would be unjust to force them. The Queen was furious: 'Poor, dear Albert,' she wrote in her journal, 'how cruelly they are ill-using that dearest angel! Monsters! you Tories shall be punished. Revenge, revenge!' Wellington told Lady Wilton 'the Queen is very angry with me; but that I don't mind', and 'I am in favour with *myself*! I think I have kept the House of Lords in the Right. That is what I ought to do.'[44] The Queen was so cross that she declared that she would not invite Wellington to the royal wedding, but Melbourne insisted, reportedly telling her 'that there were some things the people of England would bear, and some that they would not – and that if she did not invite the Duke, she might depend upon it, some disagreeable consequences would follow'.[45] It was remarkable testimony to how far Wellington's popularity had revived since the Reform Crisis eight years before.

Both the Conservative Party and the country were fortunate that Albert took these insults in his stride, and far from joining in the Queen's resentment worked hard to persuade her to take a more detached view of politics. It took several years for him to acquire much influence – the Queen was most reluctant even to let him read State Papers at first – but gradually his position became stronger, and the eventual departure of Melbourne and then Baroness Lehzen marked his gradual ascent. Another man might have turned to a life of scandal and pleasure, but the very earnestness and priggishness that were Albert's least endearing qualities stood him in good stead and he reaped ample rewards in the years to come.[46]

Meanwhile Melbourne's thoroughly discredited government limped on through the parliamentary session of 1840. Against Wellington's advice but to the delight of his backbench, Peel opened the session with a direct assault on the ministry, but the radicals were not yet ready to abandon ship, and the motion was defeated by 308 votes to 287 – an unexpectedly large majority. A compromise Irish Corporations Bill was finally passed, as were the government's proposals for the future of Canada. This required a significant sacrifice of his own opinion by Wellington, which he only achieved after a struggle. He was convinced that the union of Upper and Lower Canada was a mistake and that it would lead rapidly to demands for independence. (He was not alone in this view: a confidential Colonial Office memorandum in 1835 had described the idea as 'too much of an invitation to independence'.) But to block the measure in the Lords would create a rift with Peel and give the ministers a pretext to resign, and Wellington still preferred to keep them in office.[47] He therefore contented himself with a powerful speech and entering a protest in the journals of the House, while persuading his fellow Tory peers to let the measure pass. Lord Aberdeen was filled with admiration at the way he handled the critical meeting at Apsley House:

> Of all the admirable statements I have heard him make at these meetings, I was never so much struck as on this occasion. The effect of his address was like magick; and although we had many present who were obstinate, violent, and wrong-headed, not a syllable was said in opposition to the Duke's suggestion. He treated the whole subject with the utmost dexterity and skill; and when he spoke of his own position, it was beautifully done, and the effect irresistible ... I have never known such an instance of his power and influence.[48]

That autumn Wellington was alarmed when Palmerston's bellicose diplomacy created a serious risk of war with France. The bone of contention lay far away in the eastern Mediterranean where Russia had gained great influence over the Sultan at Constantinople and France had built up considerable, though not as great, influence over Mehemet Ali the ruler of Egypt. This was bad enough, but Mehemet Ali's success in conquering Syria and threatening to advance on Constantinople made the situation far more dangerous, opening the alarming prospect of direct Russian intervention to prop up the Sultan's regime – which would transform their influence over the Porte into virtual control. Palmerston attempted to organise joint intervention by all the Great Powers to force Mehemet Ali to yield to their mediation – a result that would weaken both French and Russian influence with their protégés. But when this failed he sided with Russia and threatened Mehemet Ali with war if he did not withdraw from Syria and submit to the Sultan, in return for being permitted to keep Egypt. This would have been hard enough for the French to swallow under any circumstances, but Palmerston made it much harder by his bullying language and by his constant writing in the press, which he encouraged to be extremely chauvinistic and threatening. The French public responded with fury, which their own politicians, especially Thiers, further excited for domestic purposes. King Louis Philippe, sensing the strength of popular feeling, had little choice but to ride the wave rather than seek to curb it at least for the moment.[49]

Palmerston's policy provoked great disquiet inside the government. Melbourne supported him with many misgivings, and then only because Palmerston threatened to resign and bring down the government if he was not given a free hand. Lord Holland and most of the rest of the Cabinet disliked the Foreign Secretary's appetite for confrontation and desire to humiliate France, and both sides played out their disagreements in the press as well as the Cabinet room, Holland even going so far as to pass Cabinet secrets on to the French ambassador.[50] Wellington had no quarrel with the aim of forcing Mehemet Ali to withdraw entirely from Syria and reducing French influence in Egypt, but he was appalled that this was done in such a heavy-handed way as to drive the French into talk of war. Britain had nothing to gain by undermining Louis Philippe's regime in France, let alone by reviving the smouldering fires of Anglo-French hostility. Ministers including Lord John Russell and Melbourne consulted him on the strength of British forces in the Mediterranean and the steps that needed to be taken to prepare both for action against Mehemet Ali and the possibility of war with France. He warned them that Britain was wholly unprepared for war – years of economising had left both army and navy seriously understrength – and that she faced serious commitments in Canada and China, as well as the ever-present danger of trouble in Ireland. Louis Napoleon (the Emperor's nephew, the future Napoleon III) had recently landed near Boulogne with a handful of followers in the hope of raising a Bonapartist revolt. His attempt had been a miserable failure but it raised the possibility of French retaliation: private ventures using steam vessels raiding British coastal towns with plunder the primary motive, but also designed to provoke full-scale hostilities. Reports from France suggested that war fervour was especially strong in the maritime towns in the Channel and on the Atlantic coasts, and Wellington urged the government to take the danger seriously and take precautions.[51]

In the event, war was avoided. As soon as the excitement began to subside in Paris Louis Philippe replaced Thiers, his bellicose prime minister, with Guizot and a rapprochement was soon achieved. But while Mehemet Ali was forced to withdraw to Egypt and French influence in the Near East was curtailed, Russia's position at Constantinople was strengthened, and she emerged from the crisis with everything she wanted and with the added pleasure of seeing the two Western powers at each other's throats. If this was a diplomatic triumph for Britain, one must wonder what would constitute a diplomatic defeat.[52]

Palmerston's handling of the Eastern Crisis undermined Wellington's support for Melbourne's government; a Conservative foreign secretary (whether the Duke himself or Lord Aberdeen) would not have been so reckless and irresponsible. At the same time the mood of the country continued to favour the Conservatives, and party officials were increasingly confident that a general election would return them to power with a comfortable majority.[53] Wellington was more cautious, even gloomy, telling Charles Arbuthnot in November:

Publick affairs are in a very critical state. I don't see how the Govt. can extricate themselves from their difficulties, nor do I think that we could improve the matter much if these Ministers were beat and run, and leave the

Administration in our hands. The truth is we require to be governed. We want an Administration which will not seek popularity excepting in the strict performance of its whole duty as Government. But that is what the country will not have and will not support. We must do the best we can, therefore, and prevent as much mischief as possible, whether by the existing Ministry or our own adherents or the Radicals, and at all events delay it.[54]

When Parliament met in January 1841 the government appeared even more inert and harmless than in previous sessions, but at the end of April a series of statements connected to the budget showed that the ministers were willing to make a final bid to revive their popularity even if it offended many of their moderate supporters. Lord John Russell indicated that the Cabinet was contemplating changes to the Corn Laws, while the budget proposed significant steps towards free trade with a reduction in duties on the import of foreign sugar and timber and an increase in the duty on colonial timber. However, these moves came far too late to win over the anti-Corn Law campaigners, while the vested interests they damaged naturally mounted strong opposition. A great debate running from 7 to 18 May, with over eighty speakers, saw the government decisively defeated by 317 to 281 votes on the sugar duties. Melbourne was strongly inclined to resign but the Cabinet insisted on calling an election, not with any real hope of victory, but in order to use the advantages of incumbency to minimise their losses. The country therefore went to the polls in late June and early July, and the Conservatives gained a majority of between seventy and eighty seats. A vote in Parliament confirmed the result, and the Queen sent for Peel and asked him to form a government. The difficulty of the Queen's Ladies had already been solved quietly in private negotiations through George Anson, with Peel gaining the issues of substance, but carefully not making the concession too painful for the Queen.[55]

Between 1835 and 1841 Wellington had led the Tory Opposition in the Lords with great skill and considerable subtlety. He had to balance the strong views of his supporters, who had little or no instinctive feeling for party discipline, with Peel's preoccupations and sensitivities. He had no wish to drive the government from office but could not admit this without disgusting the party. At times, such as over the Municipal Corporations Bill and the final settlement of Canada, he sacrificed his own views to preserve party unity and keep the government captive. Naturally, being Wellington, he grumbled all through these years, complaining of his workload; of the difficulties of dealing with Peel, and Cumberland, and the Queen, and the Lords; of the state of the country; and of the difficulties facing any government after the Reform Bill. But he was remarkably stoical about his health and the death of Lady Salisbury; he kept working, and was delighted at any time to immerse himself in the constitutional status of Lower Canada, or the strength of the fleet in the Mediterranean, or Britain's relations with China and Afghanistan, whether to advise the ministers or to form his own opinions. At times, particularly between 1839 and 1841 when his health was poor, his spirits wilted and he had moments of despair, but then his immense underlying vitality revived and he plunged back into business and society with renewed vigour.

CHAPTER TWENTY-SEVEN

WELLINGTON AND THE ARMY
(1819–41)

WELLINGTON WAS BRITAIN'S most famous soldier, and his reputation was inextricably bound up with attitudes to the army. Both were subjected to fierce attacks by Whigs and radicals in the years after Waterloo, and these coloured later views on both sides. Pressure from the Opposition and its own supporters in Parliament forced Liverpool's government to reduce the army from its wartime peak of more than 250,000 men to fewer than 100,000, and even this was not enough to satisfy its critics. The scale of these reductions forced a great many officers, mostly young subalterns and captains, onto 'half-pay', a retainer that was barely sufficient to support a single man with any pretensions to respectability; while even those who remained in active service found promotion agonisingly slow, and opportunities to distinguish themselves few and far between.

Wellington had little influence over the internal affairs of the army between the end of 1818, when the troops occupying France were brought home and he relinquished his last active command, and the beginning of 1827. The Duke of York and his staff reigned supreme at the Horse Guards in these years and they had their own way of doing things, and saw no need to consult the victor of Waterloo over questions of tactics, uniforms, discipline or equipment. In 1826 Wellington told a friend with understandable bitterness:

I dare say you will be surprised to hear that in all the changes made since the war in the regulations of the army, I have never been in the most trifling or distant degree consulted on any point. As to the dress, I say nothing; though that is a matter on which one who had dressed so large an army for so long might have some experience, and an opinion as to what would wear best, and be most convenient and healthy. But upon any change in the arms and accoutring, on the establishing of cuirassiers or lancers and on things of this sort, you would have thought that I had had a good deal of practical knowledge, having had, as you know, something to do with lancers in Spain and cuirassiers at Waterloo. Well, I never knew that the Blues or any other regiment were to have cuirasses till they were actually in them. Then there was published a new book of manoeuvres and movements; as it had been my luck to move and manoeuvre a greater portion of the British army than any officer in the service, and in the field too, you would hardly credit, what I nevertheless assure you is the fact, that I never heard any more about it than you did.[1]

There is no doubt that the Duke of York was jealous of Wellington's fame and endeavoured to keep him at a distance, but he was prepared to seek his help when it came to dealing with the government. By 1823 it was obvious that the reductions in the army had been carried too far and that pressing problems first at home (in 1819–20), then in Ireland, and then in the West Indies, could only be met by temporary expedients that were expensive, inefficient and disruptive to the whole army. Towards the end of 1823 the Duke of York pressed Lord Bathurst, the Secretary of State for War and the Colonies, to approve a permanent increase in the army of nine battalions or some five thousand men. Before putting the proposal to the government, he discussed it with Wellington and adopted some of his suggestions, and Wellington supported him with a strongly worded letter to Liverpool, and a detailed memorandum which he sent to Bathurst but which was probably intended for the whole Cabinet. Even so the government agreed to raise only six new regiments (less than four thousand men), the ministers evidently fearing that any increase beyond what was absolutely necessary for immediate needs would revive the campaign against the army in Parliament.[2]

A year later the two dukes tried again, spurred by pressure to find at least five thousand men for India, where the war in Burma was proving unexpectedly costly and difficult. This time the Duke of York put forward a more ambitious and comprehensive scheme which was cleverly designed to increase the total number of rank and file by more than fourteen thousand men, but with no new field officers and only half the usual number of captains and subalterns, which made it much less expensive. Each regiment of infantry would be increased from eight to ten companies, but only six of these would serve abroad, creating something akin to a two-battalion regiment. The four 'depot' companies would be a useful unit for home defence, and would raise and train recruits and send them out to keep the field companies up to strength. The plan had disadvantages – the depot companies were often inefficient and frequently their officers were men who had little taste for active service in unhealthy climates, leading to resentment and ill feeling between the two halves of the regiment – but it was an effective expedient at the time, making the best possible use of very limited resources. Wellington explained the plan to Bathurst and strongly endorsed it, and this appears to have persuaded the Cabinet, so that the total establishment of the army was increased to just over 112,000 men. A significant portion of the cost was borne by the East India Company, and the Treasury increased its spending on the army to just under £6.5 million from just over £6 million. The army still lacked a strategic reserve and would have been severely embarrassed by a major war anywhere except India, but it had been placed on a reasonably sustainable basis for its everyday tasks of providing scattered garrisons across the empire and a modest force at home.[3]

Wellington also played the traditional role of Master-General of the Ordnance in giving strategic advice to the government on questions ranging from the wars in India and Burma to the expedition sent to Lisbon at the end of 1826. And, perhaps more significantly, he provided advice on military appointments. For example, in December 1824, with the prospect of renewed war over Bhurtpore in India, he asked Beresford if he was still interested in the command as it would soon be vacant and, although he had not yet spoken to anyone, he could probably ensure that Beresford received it.[4] Evidently Beresford declined, for when the Directors of the East India Company consulted Wellington in January 1825 over a successor to Sir Edward Paget for the post of Commander-in-Chief in India, he told them:

'You can't do better than have Lord Combermere [Stapleton Cotton]. He's the man to take Bhurtpore;' or words to that effect.

'But,' urged the deputation, 'we don't think very highly of Lord Combermere. In fact we do not consider him a man of any great genius.'

'I don't care a d__n about his genius, I tell you he's the man to take Bhurtpore,' exclaimed the Duke.[5]

Combermere was duly appointed and in April Wellington sent Charles Wynn, the president of the Board of Control, a list of generals 'fit to be employed in command in India' to serve under him.[6]

Wellington himself was appointed Commander-in-Chief following the Duke of York's death in January 1827, only to resign the appointment after his quarrel with Canning. He resumed the position in August following Canning's death, only to resign for a second time when his Cabinet colleagues ruled that he could not be both Commander-in-Chief and prime minister at the same time. Throughout the nine months that he held the office in 1827–28 he was preoccupied by the unfolding political events of the year, and he had little opportunity to make significant changes in the army, although he argued the army's case forcefully and with success when Goderich and Palmerston proposed large reductions, and he vigorously upheld the rights of the Commander-in-Chief in discussions relating to senior appointments in Ireland

and India.[7] Of greater long-term significance was Wellington's appointment of Fitzroy Somerset to the influential position of military secretary at the Horse Guards where he remained until 1852, dealing with delicate questions of officers' claims to promotions and appointment with his habitual courtesy, tact and humanity.

Wellington was succeeded as Commander-in-Chief by Lord Hill who, as Sir Rowland Hill, had been one of Wellington's most capable and reliable subordinates in the Peninsula, known for the care he took of his men, who referred to him fondly as 'Daddy Hill'. Since the end of his service with the Army of Occupation, Hill had lived the life of a country gentleman in Shropshire, seldom visiting London or attending the House of Lords. He had declined several previous offers of senior positions, but could not resist Wellington's warm solicitation to accept the command of the army in 1828. Conscientious, careful and conservative, Hill had the misfortune that for most of his fourteen years at the Horse Guards he was compelled to work with a hostile Whig government that was intent on economising and reducing the powers and independence of the Commander-in-Chief.[8]

When Wellington became prime minister at the beginning of 1828 he was attacked as a 'military dictator', and the presence of several other soldiers in the government was widely criticised. In this context it would have been politically impossible to increase the size of the army or its budget even if Wellington had wished to do so. Instead he favoured a series of modest administrative reforms which together resulted in significant savings to the public, while improving the efficiency of the army. The appointment of Henry Hardinge as Secretary-at-War was a great success. Hardinge managed the difficult feat of making savings, initiating reforms and maintaining excellent relations with the Commander-in-Chief. But his finest achievement at the War Office was a complete overhaul of the system of pensions for soldiers who had been discharged from the army. He replaced the existing patchwork of many overlapping and much-amended schemes with a much simpler and fairer system where an infantryman might be discharged after 21 years' service with a pension of one shilling a day, rising to 1s 2d if he had served for 25 years (three years longer in the cavalry). Additional sums were granted for wounds and injuries that permanently affected a soldier's ability to serve or earn an income in other ways, although soldiers whose incapacity proved to be temporary no longer received a permanent pension. Hardinge also rewarded good conduct by granting a sum of money and a medal to the soldier with the best record to be discharged each year from each regiment. Although this scheme was by no means extraordinarily generous it was as much as the country was willing to afford, and three years later the Whig government cut these pensions by more than half, so that a soldier discharged after 25 years of service would receive a pittance of 6*d* a day rather than the still meagre 1*s* 2*d* under Hardinge's scheme. Intense pressure from Hardinge, Wellington and the Horse Guards eventually persuaded the government to apply this scheme only to new recruits, but the fact that it was passed at all makes Whig claims of concern for the welfare of ordinary soldiers sound hollow.[9]

Later writers sometimes accuse Wellington of neglecting the interest of the veterans of his army and treating old soldiers who had served under him with disdain.[10] However, the contemporary evidence contradicts this; we know that Wellington was personally generous to innumerable veterans, whether it was his habit of slipping a sovereign to an old soldier met in the street, or in response to the hundreds of letters which he received asking for charity. He made a point of employing veterans on his estate at Stratfield Saye, and found places for others through offices he held, for example at Walmer Castle and the Tower of London. When he was appointed Commander-in-Chief in 1827 the *United Service Journal* commented that he had already shown himself eager 'to procure the reward and advancement of the general and field officers who served under him, by obtaining for them regiments, governments and commands as they became vacant'. It hoped that with the greater scope of the whole patronage of the Horse Guards at his disposal he would be able to do more for 'the juniors in rank [for whom] his wishes to be useful are equally strong'. At the same time the *Naval and Military Magazine* remarked on the trouble the Duke had taken to get the commissioners of Chelsea Hospital to reconsider the case of John Lowe, formerly a sergeant in the 95th Rifles who had been granted only a partial pension. But inevitably there were far more worthy cases than pensions or positions, and in April 1830 Wellington returned some papers to Beresford with the comment: 'It is heartbreaking to receive such appeals as the enclosed; and to have no means whatever of satisfying those who make them.'[11]

The arrival of the Whig ministry in late 1830 triggered a sharp deterioration in relations between the Horse Guards and the government. For years the Whigs and their radical allies had been attacking the army, especially, but not only, on the grounds of its expense, and these attacks did not cease when they came to power. For example, in July 1832 Colonel De Lacy Evans, a radical, called for the abolition of two army hospitals, two military elementary schools for orphaned children of soldiers the Royal Waggon Train, the remainder of the militia, the yeomanry, the depot companies of regiments serving abroad, district recruiting stations and royal arms factories, as well as a reduction in the number of officers in each regiment. Such talk was common and naturally caused alarm even though the government restricted itself to a few largely symbolic cuts to military spending. Clashes over patronage further embittered relations, with Grey's voracious appetite for the fruits of office bringing him into sharp conflict with the Commander-in-Chief. Equally, Hill's resolute refusal to vote in favour of the Reform Bill or several other pieces of controversial government legislation, alongside his evident lack of sympathy for the government, provoked outrage among the Whigs, and led to frequent rumours that he was about to be forced out of office and the Horse Guards made a political appointment like any other. But when Wellington resigned as prime minister the King had assured Hill that he should remain; it was the King's army, not Parliament's, and his support remained unshaken. Neither Grey nor Melbourne was willing to force the issue, conscious that removing Hill would come at a high political price, which would be much increased by the fact that they had no plausible alternative to offer in his place.[12]

Wellington was largely a spectator to these disputes, but he was nonetheless a powerful influence on them. His close ties to Hill and to Fitzroy Somerset heightened Whig suspicions of the Horse Guards, especially during the crisis over the Reform Bill; but at the same time his political weight and authority made an outright attack on the Horse Guards and the army more dangerous. Throughout the decade of Whig rule ministers continued to seek his advice on questions of strategy and senior appointments; with such consultation becoming more common as the political tensions aroused by the Reform Crisis slowly subsided. Fitzroy Somerset also kept him informed, and asked for his advice on issues ranging from the aftermath of the Bristol Riots, to the composition of an expeditionary force to Belgium that Palmerston had casually mentioned might be needed in May 1831. Wellington was careful not to abuse this influence, either with requests for patronage or unsought advice that would undermine Hill's authority, but equally Hill, and particularly Somerset, both knew him so well that they could generally anticipate his wishes unasked, and were frequently influenced by them.[13]

The army was the subject of much public discussion in the 1830s as the government and its supporters, including the radicals and the press, attempted to impose their ideas on questions ranging from recruitment and discipline to the organisation of military departments in Whitehall. Wellington played a prominent role in these controversies and they had an important effect on his reputation, suggesting that he was adamantly opposed to any reform, especially any liberal humane reform of the army, and that he was a rigid defender of social privilege and entrenched hierarchies. This was a caricature, of course, but it was very useful for his opponents, especially in the press, and as it has continued to influence his reputation, it is worth examining the issues in some detail, particularly as these debates led him to give an unusually full explanation of his views on a wide range of military and political questions.

Wellington had no illusions about the place of the army in British society: 'It is an exotic in England, unknown to the old constitution of the country; required or supposed to be required, only for the defence of its foreign possessions; disliked by the inhabitants, particularly by the higher orders, some of whom never allow one of their family to serve in it.' This view contributed to his opinion that the army was best kept out of sight. 'It is a necessary evil,' he is reported to have said to a friend, 'and we should be mad were we to make a pet of it, thus promoting one or other of two ends. For either the country will take it into its head that it is a fine thing to have an enormous armed force, in which case taxation will be largely increased and property crippled, or else an outcry will be raised, and some fine morning we may find ourselves without an army at all.'[14]

Unlike the armies of the continental powers, the British army could not be raised by conscription. Seafaring men might be impressed into the navy, and everyone held liable for service in the militia or local militia, for their purpose was the defence of the country; but the regular army might be sent to any part of the world 'not for the defence of the land of England, but of a colony or settlement – or for the conquest of a colony or settlement, or for the defence or for the conquest of any foreign territory . . . Men cannot with justice be taken from their families and from their ordinary occupations and pursuits for such objects.'[15]

The French or Prussian army was drawn from all ranks of society. There was no great gap between the social background of officers and rank and file; the army was esteemed by society, it served almost entirely at home, and misconduct would reflect badly on a soldier's family and affect his reputation in later life. The British army by contrast was much more detached from society, and most of its men at any time were serving in distant parts of the world, often in unhealthy tropical climates. Service in the army was unpopular: 'Even the common people will make an exertion to find means to purchase the discharge of a relation who may have enlisted, notwithstanding the advantages of pay, etc, which a soldier enjoys, compared with the common labourer.' This unpopularity was not primarily due to the fear of corporal punishment, which most soldiers avoided by relatively good conduct, but the harshness and dangers of the service. The only incentive to enlist was a bounty, which was largely illusory, and the opportunity to escape from difficulties at home. Consequently 'the man who enlists into the British army is, in general, the most drunken and probably the worst man of the trade or profession to which he belongs, or of the village or town in which he lives'. And 'in 99 instances out of 100, some idle or irregular, or even vicious motive is the cause of the enlistment of the volunteer'. Such men could only be turned into good soldiers by rigorous training. The recruit's 'inclinations are all to be thwarted and his habits altered, not by precept and example only, but by constant attention, observation, and exertion; and the severity, if necessary, of those placed over him, to remove those irregular or vicious habits or propensities, the hope of the indulgence of which induced the recruit to volunteer his services. Unless this is done effectually, it may be relied upon that no soldier can be formed.'[16]

Discipline needed to be strictly enforced, not just to help ensure success in battle and on campaign, but also to prevent the army becoming a danger to society. 'We forget what the army is, and what it may become, if not kept in order; and how ready the people of the country are to cry out if, by accident, they should suffer by any act of its indiscipline; or if, for want of discipline, the army should fail in obtaining success, as it certainly will fail, as it always has failed, if not in a state of discipline and good order.' The army was scattered across the world in small detachments, and the troops might spend months at a time in the narrow confines of a troopship, where loose discipline could soon lead to serious misconduct and even to mutiny. At home soldiers might be called out to support the civil power, in which case they were required to remain impassive in the face of insults, missiles and other provocations, and to act strictly as directed. The people of Britain, far more than those of the Continent, 'will not bear to be oppressed by the irregularities of an armed body, or even by individuals belonging to it'.[17]

For more than twenty years liberal reformers and radicals had argued against the use of flogging in the army, and their campaign had gained strength and support in Parliament in the 1820s, despite concessions limiting the number of lashes that might be awarded by a court martial and the crimes which might be punished in this way. Although some members of the government, including J.C. Hobhouse and Edward Ellice, successive Secretaries-at-War from 1832 to 1834, were eager to pursue the question, more senior ministers such as Grey and Melbourne had significant reservations. Nonetheless, public pressure and the strident advocacy of *The Times* meant that it could not be ignored, and Wellington himself favoured the establishment of a commission to examine the issue in 1833.[18]

The Commission into Military Punishments was promised by the Whigs, but actually established by Peel's short-lived government in March 1835, with Lord Wharncliffe in the chair, and a membership which was far from hostile to the army. It incorporated in evidence the results of a survey of senior officers established by the Adjutant-General in 1834, and oral testimony from some seventy witnesses ranging from two new recruits, six privates and a dozen non-commissioned officers (all of whom had their exact identity concealed behind initials), a number of French officers, a surgeon, and a clergyman, to Joseph Hume the radical MP, and a wide range of regimental and senior officers. Hill and Wellington both gave evidence at the very end of the enquiry, in February 1836, to avoid any risk that other witnesses should feel obliged to take the same line.

Wellington argued both in his evidence to the commission and elsewhere that flogging and the threat of flogging were essential to the discipline of the army, in part because the sentence was carried out in front of the whole regiment so that it had a powerful deterrent effect upon even the most unimaginative soldier. 'There is no punishment which makes an impression upon anybody except corporal punishment.' Soldiers would only accept lesser punishments and all the other restraints discipline imposed upon them because disobedience would be punished by flogging. 'I must say, that in hundreds of instances, the very threat of the lash had prevented very serious crimes.' He contrasted the marauding and poor behaviour of the Prussian army in the advance on Paris in 1815 with the good conduct of the British troops, pointing out (with some exaggeration in the figures) that the Prussian strength was greatly reduced by straggling, and that its plundering not only inflicted great misery on the French population, but also risked provoking reprisals, just as French misbehaviour had done in Spain. In the Peninsula constant attention to the problem had led to a great reduction in crime by the closing years of the war, and consequently in punishments. And he denied that flogging degraded a soldier in the eyes of the world or his comrades, citing instances where soldiers who had been flogged had gone on to be NCOs, including several that he had promoted himself. There was even the example of a sergeant stripped of his rank and sentenced to be flogged for stealing from the funds of his company and deserting. Wellington had intervened to spare him the flogging, as his previous record had been very good, and he had regained his sergeant's stripes, and Wellington had subsequently recommended him for a commission, which he received.[19]

Wellington also argued that none of the proposed alternatives to corporal punishment worked. Solitary confinement, the alternative most commonly put forward by reformers, was indeed a dreadful punishment if rigorously enforced, but there were no facilities for properly enforcing it even in Britain, while it was completely unsuitable for troops on board ship, in small detachments in the colonies, or on active service. It had little deterrent value, and no one who knew British soldiers would believe for a minute that those guarding a prisoner in a cell would refrain from talking to him. A soldier could not be fined, for his pay was only just sufficient to cover his needs, and debt would usually lead to further offences. Extra duties stigmatised a soldier's daily occupation, and besides, were clearly not appropriate for anything except minor offences. A soldier could hardly be sent to a civilian prison or transported to the colonies for such serious but common military offences as being drunk on duty, striking a non-commissioned officer or insubordination; but these crimes had to be punished, and be seen to be punished, swiftly and forcefully, or the discipline of even the best regiment would soon be undermined.[20]

Almost all the evidence taken by the Commission supported Wellington's arguments, with senior officers almost invariably declaring that flogging was undesirable but absolutely necessary. A rare exception was the radical soldier and MP Colonel George De Lacy Evans, who favoured its complete abolition. Significantly, Evans was a staff officer who had never commanded a regiment. Soon after giving his evidence he went to Spain to command an all-volunteer British Legion fighting for the *liberales* in the Carlist Wars. He won great applause at home from fellow radicals for his declaration that there would be no flogging under his command, but within a year the realities of active service and the lack of any practical alternative had forced him to recant and resort to the lash. Equally compelling were official figures produced by the Horse Guards which showed that while, in response to public opinion and official encouragement, the number of floggings had been reduced by more than half between 1826 and 1834, the amount of crime and consequently the number of courts martial had almost doubled. As Wellington had noted in 1832, the reluctance to resort to corporal punishment had led to a serious increase in 'the crimes of abusing, striking and even shooting non-commissioned officers and officers. Both are necessarily obliged to put themselves forward personally more frequently than formerly, in cases of violence and outrage; and it is obvious that there exists less respect for their authority and persons.'[21]

Faced with such evidence, it is hardly surprising that the Commission recommended that flogging remained essential, although it favoured a further reduction in the number of lashes different levels of courts martial could impose. The mood in the country, and increasingly the army itself, favoured the use of an alternative, if an effective substitute could be found. As early as 1834 Hill suggested the creation of a number of military prisons, but the government was deterred by the cost and it was not until 1839 that the army estimates included even a small sum for this purpose. It was left to Peel's government in the 1840s to take up the proposal seriously, and even its funding was far from generous. Nonetheless these prisons proved relatively successful with a regime of harsh conditions and quite short sentences. This in turn enabled a further reduction in the reliance on the lash during Wellington's tenure as Commander-in-Chief.[22]

But punishment alone was not enough, and Wellington and Hill were no less concerned to reduce military crimes than the most ardent of liberal reformers. Everyone agreed that drunkenness was the most common military offence, and the cause of many others. Hill described it as 'the prevailing sin of the British soldier', and Wellington said that 'if drunkenness prevails in a regiment, nothing whatever, either relating to conduct, discipline, or efficiency, can be relied upon'. Neither Wellington nor Hill were willing to encourage temperance societies in regiments, fearing that they might be used as cover for other less desirable types of meetings, but Wellington believed that 'a most desirable result would be produced if we could introduce temperance into the army . . . not only to the publick interests and to the character of the army but the individual soldiers themselves'. The problem was exacerbated by privately run regimental canteens that encouraged the sale of spirits because it was more profitable than beer and other products. Lord Howick, the strong-willed Secretary-at-War from 1835 to 1839, favoured banning the sale of spirits in the canteens, as did many commanding officers, but the licences for the canteens were issued by the Board of Ordnance not the War Office, and the Board (under pressure from the Treasury) invariably sold the licence to the highest bidder. Howick's attempts to pressure the Ordnance were fruitless, and it was not until 1848, following a campaign by George Gleig, by then Chaplain General, that a ban was imposed.[23]

In the 1830s many regiments introduced an evening meal for their men to reduce the problem of excessive drinking, but here too the Whig government's commitment to economy overrode its interest in the welfare of the soldiers, and the Treasury vetoed an allowance to cover the additional cost incurred in stations, such as North America and Gibraltar, where provisions were particularly expensive. Similarly, nothing was done to alleviate the poor quality and overcrowding in the barracks until Peel's government embarked on a building programme which slowly improved the living conditions for soldiers both at home and abroad. Howick and the reforming medical officers who advised him to do it, however, deserve credit for improving the soldiers' diet, and especially reducing the reliance on salt meat in many colonial stations.[24]

The Commission into Military Punishments also recommended that games and other recreations be encouraged to give soldiers an alternative to drinking. Wellington warmly supported the idea, saying in his evidence that 'in the East Indies we do all we can to amuse and employ [the soldiers], and to occupy their time'. Hill pressed the Secretary-at-War to support the scheme, and by 1841 numerous cricket pitches had been established; but of the 146 fives courts proposed by the Ordnance, the Treasury would only agree to pay for 29.[25]

There was general support for the introduction of badges and increased pay and pensions for soldiers who had established their good conduct over a number of years. Many regiments already had schemes along these lines, with some of them dating back to the Peninsular War, and Wellington told the commission: 'I am sure that the soldier is as sensible of such a reward, and of his merits being considered, as any other individual is.' He even approved of a proposed 'order of merit' which would recognise acts of gallantry in the field, and general good conduct, irrespective of rank. Nothing came of this at the time, but it was adopted, in more limited form, as the Victoria Cross in the Crimea nearly twenty years later. Howick was equally enthusiastic, and in this instance was able to secure the funds needed to give an additional penny-a-day pay to soldiers who had served for at least seven years and had not appeared in the defaulter's book in the previous two years. Further increments followed at seven-yearly intervals and were also reflected in the soldier's pension, while soldiers soon came to appreciate that their good conduct badges could greatly improve their prospect of finding good work after leaving the army.[26] The 1830s thus saw a modest improvement in the lives of the rank and file of the British army, and a great deal more might have been done if more funding had been available.

Wellington's views on British officers, like his views of the rank and file, are easily caricatured, but prove much more complex and interesting on closer examination. He argued that one reason why the British army required such strict discipline was the wide gulf that separated officers and men. In the Prussian army, for example, a junior officer might devote himself to studying the 'name, the character, the conduct, the family and relations, the fortune, the situation, [and] the mental acquirements of each of the men of his company', and might live with them 'as a companion, friend, and advisor'. Although something approaching this intimacy had been embraced by some British officers on active service, notably in the Light Division in the Peninsula, it was neither possible nor desirable in the British army in peacetime. 'Our officer is a gentleman. We require that he should be one, and above all that he should conduct himself as such; and most particularly in reference to the soldier, and to his intercourse with the non-commissioned officers and soldiers.' Wellington was well aware that this distance, or aloofness, had significant disadvantages:

> We carry this principle of the gentleman, and the absence of intercourse with those under his command, so far as that, in my opinion, the duty of a subaltern officer, as done in a foreign army, is not done at all in the cavalry, or the British infantry of the line. It is done in the Guards by the sergeants. Then our gentleman officer, however admirable his conduct on a field of battle, however honourable to himself, however glorious and advantageous to his country, is but a poor creature in disciplining his company in camp, quarters, or cantonments.[27]

This was the Wellington who had issued countless general orders in the Peninsula instructing the regimental officers under his command to pay close attention to their men, to prevent straggling, plunder and other misconduct, and who almost invariably blamed the crimes committed by the men on the inattention of their officers.

Nonetheless Wellington defended the existing system. In 1850 he told William Maynard Gomm: 'The British army is what it is, because it is officered by gentlemen; men who would scorn to do a dishonourable thing and who have something more at stake before the world than a reputation for military smartness.' At first sight this looks like nothing more than empty snobbery, but then we pause and recollect some of the 'dishonourable things' done by French officers in Portugal and Spain: how they set their men the example of plundering and oppressing the inhabitants, so that there was a bitter saying in the French army that the war in Spain meant death for a private, ruin for an officer and a fortune for a general. Some British officers also behaved badly, both on the field of battle and in other ways, but notorious cases attracted opprobrium which affected the officer's reputation not just in the army but in society at home, and this ensured (together with Wellington's example and strong injunctions) that such misbehaviour was rare and covert, not openly accepted as a matter of course.[28]

There was another, more fundamental advantage of officers being gentlemen and to their gaining their commissions by purchase, as Wellington explained in the early 1830s:

It is the promotion by purchase which brings into the service men of fortune and education – men who have some connexion with the interests and fortunes of the country, besides the commission which they hold from His Majesty. It is this circumstance which exempts the British army from the character of being a 'mercenary army', and has rendered its employment, for nearly a century and a half, not only not inconsistent with the constitutional privileges of the country, but safe and beneficial.[29]

The officers of the army needed to come from and identify with the landed gentry and other groups that favoured stability and the existing constitutional settlement if the army was not to be a danger to society. British suspicion of standing armies had its origins in the rule of Cromwell and the Major-Generals, but for Wellington at least these doubts had been heightened by the overthrow of civilian government in France by Napoleon at Brumaire, and the many subsequent attempts to imitate him by cliques of generally 'liberal' officers stretching from the Decemberists in St Petersburg to Riego and his comrades at Cadiz. This was why Wellington disliked having too many officers who had nothing to live upon except their pay: 'having no connexion with the property and rank of the country, they are more easily disposed to destroy its institutions, of which the primary object is to maintain the rights and protect the property of the whole community.'[30]

In any case an officer without at least some private means would find it virtually impossible to live upon his pay, which was grossly inadequate and had not been increased in decades, and would be unable to purchase promotion, so that he would stagnate as a subaltern or at best a captain. If such men were ambitious they might become disaffected; while even if they were not, they would probably become sour, lazy or inefficient as they grew old in the service, denied opportunities, recognition or rewards. There were many such officers in the British army in the 1820s or 1830s, men who had joined in 1810 or 1812 when the war seemed perpetual and opportunities boundless. Even if not reduced to that pittance inaccurately known as 'half-pay' they found peacetime soldiering slow and dispiriting, and naturally resented the wealthy and privileged young men who served the minimum period in each rank before purchasing their next step of promotion, overtaking in the process the veteran of a dozen battles (or at least a dozen years of dull garrison duty in the further reaches of empire) who lacked the means to gain their next step.[31]

Wellington acknowledged the problem, admitting that the system of purchase 'falls severely upon individuals', but nonetheless thought that it was 'highly beneficial to the service'. Purchase enabled some younger officers to rise through the ranks relatively rapidly, and this prevented the officer corps from stagnating completely in the years after Waterloo. Not that the army was then, or ever, dominated by the aristocracy. The great majority of officers were the sons of officers or clergymen, minor gentry, wealthy farmers, shopkeepers and merchants – families, in Wellington's terms, with a stake in the country, but not by and large a seat at the top table. Such men might have a small private income; £50 or £100 a year could make all the difference, especially if their family could fund their successive promotions as well. These men would give long and conscientious service for many years in a humdrum regiment of the line that never attracted public notice because it spent sixteen out of twenty years in Jamaica, Canada and the Ionian Islands (or India, the Cape or New South Wales, or a dozen other colonies), and four years at 'home' in Ireland. They were the backbone of the officer corps, not the tiny minority of gilded youths who spent a few years in the Guards or a fashionable Hussar regiment, and who caught the resentful eye of radical MPs and journalists as they lounged around the clubs of St James's.[32]

There were two other objections to the abolition of the purchase. The first was simple and decisive: it was far too expensive for any government to contemplate, for all those officers who had purchased their commissions, and who looked forward to selling them again to fund their retirement, would need to be compensated, and estimates put the bill at approximately £4 million.[33] The second was the lack of a better alternative. The artillery and engineers were promoted by strict seniority, but the result was a much greater logjam of middle-aged junior officers than in the regular army. When Wellington chaired a Commission inquiring into the system of military promotion in 1840, he found that every one of the eighty captains in the Royal Artillery was over the age of forty-eight, and that even second captains had served on average for almost twenty years. (By comparison fewer than one-third of the captains in the regular army were over the age of forty, which was still too many.) If seniority and purchase were both ruled out, there remained only selection, which both conservatives and reformers were quick to reject, believing that it would inevitably open the door to nepotism, factionalism and even corruption. The 1840 Commission recommended the retention of purchase and easing the backlog by allowing a certain number of officers of each rank to retire annually on full pay. This helped to ease the problem, as had similar measures introduced previously, but there was no complete solution and the generation of young men who joined the army as subalterns in the later years of the war against Napoleon were doomed by the post-war reductions and the long peace to many years of frustration, unless they were exceptionally lucky or left the army and found some other career.[34]

As Wellington is sometimes accused of failing to recognise the efforts of his subordinates, it is worth quoting the warm tribute he paid to ordinary regimental officers at this time. The British officer, the Duke wrote, was expected 'to serve in all climates, in all seasons, in all situations, and under every possible difficulty and disadvantage':

> He must be in turns gaoler, police officer, magistrate, judge and jury. Whether in peace or in war, in the transport in charge of convicts, or acting as a magistrate, or sitting in judgement, or as a jury man, or engaged in the more immediate and more active duties of his profession in the field, either against the internal rebel or the foreign enemy, he must never make a mistake, he must never cease to be the officer and the gentleman; cheerful, obedient, subordinate to his superiors, yet maintaining discipline, and securing the affection and attachment of his inferiors, and of soldiers placed under his command.[35]

Wellington and the Whig government worked together on the problem of ageing junior officers in the army, and were not all that far apart on the more contentious issue of military punishments. The government's constant quest to save money caused more tension, but the greatest disagreement was over the push by three successive Secretaries-at-War, J.C. Hobhouse, Edward Ellice and Lord Howick, to expand their power and authority and to make the Commander-in-Chief and the Horse Guards answerable to them, rather than directly to the King. A number of motives were at play in this dispute, although personal egotism and bureaucratic expansionism were certainly not the least significant. It was not an entirely new argument; early in his long tenure as Secretary-at-War Palmerston had provoked a similar clash with Sir David Dundas. This had left a legacy of bitterness between the War Office and the Horse Guards which played a significant part in their mutual irritation in the 1830s. Whig hostility towards Hill was also a factor, as was the desire to gain control of the patronage of the army and use it to consolidate their grip on power, just as Fox had attempted to gain control of the patronage of the East India Company fifty years before. And, as the reduction of royal power and the subordination of the King to his ministers was a central tenet of Whig policy, wresting direct control of the army from the Crown was both philosophically desirable and politically tempting.

Wellington was implacably opposed to these plans. As a Pittite and a Tory he defended the power and independence of the Crown, and he strongly believed that the efficiency of the army depended on it being insulated from direct political interference. The Duke of York had been scrupulous in giving promotion and rewards to officers according to their professional merit regardless of their politics, and Wellington, in his brief tenure at the Horse Guards, had followed his example even when it meant irritating the King at a particularly delicate moment.[36]

The different schemes advanced by Hobhouse and Howick included the transfer of part or all of the Ordnance and commissariat departments to the War Office, which would then be headed either by a new Secretary of State or a Board. These departments were notoriously inefficient; the Ordnance had declined from the high state in which Wellington left it, and the commissariat had been neglected by the Treasury for decades and was now little more than a department of accountants with no capacity to resume its wartime functions. But the War Office was just as cumbersome in its own methods, and there is no reason to believe that if the 'reforms' proposed by the Whigs in the 1830s had been put into place, the civil machinery would have worked any more smoothly when the army was sent to the Crimea nearly twenty years later. Administrative restructuring conceals more problems than it solves, and it would have been much better if Hobhouse, Howick and the other Whig Secretaries-at-War had imitated Wellington at the Ordnance, and made the old machine run efficiently, rather than waste their energies on grandiose schemes of expansion. As even a sympathetic observer commented in frustration, in the end Howick simply wanted to 'raise the Office to the Man & not humble the Man to the Office'.[37] The argument continued as long as the Whig government remained in power, causing a great deal of irritation to all involved, but neither Grey nor Melbourne was willing to stake the future of the government on this issue, and nothing less could overcome the opposition of Wellington, the Horse Guards and, while he was alive, William IV.

These disputes did not impede Wellington's co-operation with the ministers when the national interest was at stake. Indeed, for all their differences Melbourne found the Duke much easier and more pleasant to work with than Howick, who was remarkably arrogant and quarrelsome for a relatively junior Cabinet minister. Wellington threw himself with enthusiasm into giving the ministers detailed advice on how to respond to the rebellion in Canada in 1838,

the wars in China and Afghanistan two years later, and the almost simultaneous threat of war with France. The conjunction of these crises showed that
the army was stretched too thinly to cover all its responsibilities. As early as
1839 Hardinge attacked the army estimates in the Commons, urging that the
size of the army be increased. The ministers responded in 1840 by raising the
nominal strength of each battalion of infantry from 740 to 800 rank and file.
This was no more than a helpful first step for in 1840, when Palmerston was
pushing France to the brink of war, there were only 24 of the 103 battalions of
the army at home, and most of these were either under-strength regiments just
returned from long years in the colonies, or full of new recruits still finding
their feet in the army. In 1841 the situation was even more alarming, with only
eleven of the nineteen battalions at home being regarded as fit for service. A
further increase in the army was clearly necessary, and by the late 1830s the
mood of the country had changed and there was much greater support for
increased spending on national defence. However, this would be left to Peel's
new government, which would also soon have to find a successor for the ailing
Hill at the Horse Guards.[38]

PART V

BACK IN HARNESS (1841–52)

CHAPTER TWENTY-EIGHT

PEEL'S LIEUTENANT
(1841–46)

W HEN PEEL FORMED his government in August 1841 Wellington joined as Leader of the Lords, but without departmental office. This was not primarily a result of age and illness; as early as the beginning of 1838 he had told Lady Salisbury that he had no wish to take office, and that 'he should be very reluctant to be Secretary for Foreign Affairs'. In the following year, at the time of the Bedchamber Crisis, he had given way to Peel's wishes and agreed to return to the Foreign Office, but made it clear that in his opinion 'it might have been better to keep the Foreign Office for some other person, and to have left him leader of the House of Lords, in the Cabinet, and without any office'. In 1841 he was happy to leave the Foreign Office open for Aberdeen, as this would leave him free to deal with any other crisis that arose. 'We have just avoided a general war in Europe. If it had occurred . . . I should now be the Commander-in-Chief of the Allied Armies in Germany, of each of which I am the Field Marshal. God send that such an event may never occur! But considering the state of France, there can be no certainty.' It was equally possible that he might need to go to Ireland to 'settle the affair' if O'Connell caused 'trouble'; or to North America if tensions with the United States led to war. No doubt there was some bravado in these statements, but Wellington's self-confidence remained unshaken and his refusal of the Foreign Office did not reflect doubts about his capacity to combine the departmental work with his leadership of the Lords.[1]

Wellington had also taken the initiative in outlining his views on the priorities for a new Conservative government as early as December 1839. Writing before the crisis over the Eastern Question and the war with France had been completely resolved, he argued for 'an increase in the naval and military establishments of the country, so as to render these more adequate to perform the services which may be required'. He also urged the importance of 'the settlement of the Canadian question, including that of the frontier of the Province of

Maine', so that Britain would not risk facing two enemies at once; even without any actual conflict he knew that trouble in North America emboldened the French, just as poor relations with France (or trouble in Ireland) encouraged disaffected French Canadians and the opponents of conciliation in the United States. Finally, he acknowledged that new measures must be put in place to deal with the substantial budget deficit created by the Whigs, so that money would be available to fund the increase he sought in the army and navy.[2]

By the time the Conservatives took office in 1841 relations with France had improved a little, reducing the immediate danger of war, although the ill feeling and rivalry created in 1839 remained a potent force on both sides of the Channel. However, Britain's Indian Empire was committed to two significant wars, each conducted far from its natural base of operations. The Opium War with China was at least well on the way to being settled satisfactorily; but the attempt to install a sympathetic ruler in Afghanistan was going badly and would soon become very much worse. Canada remained a potential source of instability, and relations with the United States were poor, kept bad by local provocations on each side of the disputed frontier. On the other hand, Ireland was unusually quiet and confounded the doomsayers by reacting with equanimity to the change of government. Unlike Wellington, Peel's chief interest was in the domestic problems facing the government, and in particular the economy, which was entering possibly the worst trade depression of the nineteenth century. The budget deficit had deteriorated since 1839, and while this may actually have had a mildly stimulating effect on the economy, it had a much greater negative effect by shaking confidence in an era when sound finance was equated with balanced budgets or modest surpluses. These economic troubles would be exploited both by working-class Chartists, who called for radical political reform, and by the Anti-Corn Law League, which, with the support of many manufacturers, campaigned to abolish the Corn Laws so as to lower the price of food and so open the way for a reduction in wages. Although many of the supporters of the Anti-Corn Law League were respectable and often wealthy businessmen, its language was often violent and extreme in its attacks on the landed interest: and it deliberately inflamed political feelings in a manner that impeded its own cause.[3]

Peel addressed the economic and financial problems facing the government with his momentous budget of 1842. This included a significant restructuring of the Corn Law, reducing the rate of protection and correcting problems in the way the Law was enforced. While far from enough to satisfy the Anti-Corn Law League, it was a conciliatory gesture and was generally accepted by Peel's own supporters as a necessary step to place agricultural protection on ground that could be defended for many years to come. At the same time Peel introduced sweeping reductions in other tariffs, concentrating in particular on the raw materials used by industry, but including a number of farm products. In private he showed little sympathy for the farmers, even though they – and the wealthy landowners from whom they leased their farms – were the backbone of the Conservative Party. For example, in April 1842, he responded to concerns over the reduction in duty on the import of live cattle by telling Arbuthnot: 'If 10,000 head of cattle should cross the sea from foreign parts, I shall be very much surprised, but I must fairly say I hope they may. I think the price of meat unduly high.'[4]

The reduction of tariffs helped struggling manufacturers and the economy in general, but it only made the budget deficit worse, at least in the short term. Peel filled this gap by introducing a tax on all incomes over £150 p.a. at a rate of seven pence in the pound (just below 3 per cent), which, with a few other measures, was calculated to raise £4 million a year. The tax, which was a less onerous form of the old Property Tax, was introduced for a trial period of three years. Although the Whigs naturally opposed it, the general reaction was much less hostile than might have been expected, while the reduction in tariffs was widely welcomed and Peel's authority was enormously enhanced.[5] Wellington, who had been convinced since at least the previous summer that the government's financial problems could only be solved by bold measures, was warm in his praise for the Budget, telling Lady Wilton: 'I think I may venture to congratulate you upon our having laid the foundation for getting the country again upon its Legs. This is what I have been looking to for Years.' All these measures passed the House of Lords with ease.[6]

Whether Wellington also approved of the reduction in spending on the army and navy imposed by Peel may be doubted, and there is some evidence that he was not particularly happy with his position at this time. Peel – who was not the most sensitive of men – noticed that 'the contrast between [the Duke's] present position and the prominent part which, when in office he has been used to take, is occasionally painful to him'. Although he had no attacks after the strokes in February 1841, he had yet to recover fully from their effects, and his speeches in the House of Lords were sometimes delivered slowly and painfully, although they were coherent and read well. His deafness troubled him, and he found Cabinet meetings particularly hard to follow, although some ministers made a point of sitting on his good side and addressing their remarks directly to him when they had something they particularly wished him to hear. Others, including Peel, would often approach the Duke through Charles Arbuthnot, and send him papers to read so that he could master a subject before giving his opinion.[7]

Nonetheless there were undercurrents of discontent flowing in both directions, especially in the first eighteen months of the government. Wellington privately complained that Peel fussed over trifles and did not delegate enough;

this was a complaint made of many prime ministers, including Wellington, but which appears particularly well founded in Peel's case. He also grumbled more than usual about the demands made upon him, the innumerable letters and applications for patronage he received, and the burdens of society. At other times these grumbles had quite a cheerful subtext, reflecting an underlying pleasure at being at the centre of events and in great demand; but in 1841–42 they seem a little more sincere, as if Wellington was actually struggling to do everything he felt was necessary. This may also explain the worsening of his temper at this time, which is mentioned in a number of sources.[8]

None of these characteristics made him an easy colleague, and in December 1841 Fitzgerald told Greville that it would have been better if Wellington had retired and kept aloof from the government, and that he would be very glad to be without him. This was an extreme view, not widely held, and Peel in particular was well aware of Wellington's real value to the ministry, and was determined to keep him both in Cabinet and leading the Lords. The next few years were to show that Peel was right and that those who thought that the Duke was a spent force, entering his dotage and likely to prove an embarrassment, were badly mistaken.[9]

Despite these tensions Wellington was widely consulted by his colleagues and had considerable influence over the government's policies in the areas that had always interested him: defence, foreign policy, the colonies, threats of disorder at home and in Ireland, and on appointments that affected him as leader of the government in the Lords. For example, when Stanley, the colonial secretary, suggested the appointment of Lord Clare as governor of Jamaica at the end of 1841, Peel urged him to consult Wellington, adding: 'Whenever I have thought of a peer for any office, I have communicated privately with the Duke, on account of his position in the House of Lords.' Peel consulted Wellington over the appointment of a new Governor-General of India in October 1841, and they agreed on the selection of their Cabinet colleague Lord Ellenborough, despite Peel's worry at his 'tendency to precipitation and over-activity'. Wellington gave Ellenborough copious advice on the military position in India, and continued to correspond with him after he sailed, to the considerable annoyance of Fitzgerald, the responsible minister. However, such interference from a senior colleague was not unusual, especially as Ellenborough was faced first with a military disaster in Afghanistan, and then a difficult and bloody war in the Scinde, problems which Wellington was far better equipped to understand than Fitzgerald.[10]

In August 1842, a year after Peel's government took office, Lord Hill retired from the Horse Guards. His health had been in decline for some time, with the Prime Minister describing him as 'very infirm' some months before. Peel had no doubt that Wellington should succeed Hill, telling Arbuthnot:

The Duke of Wellington is perfectly well. He has recently written a letter to Ellenborough, about the general defence of the Indian Empire, which for comprehensiveness of views, simplicity and clearness of expression, and profound sagacity, is equal to any production of the meridian of his glorious career. I could not help taking it to the Queen, and asking her to read it, that she might see what a resource she had in any difficulty.[11]

This was unusually fulsome, coming from a statesman not much given to flattery, and Wellington accepted the offer with delight; he honestly believed that 'no other person is fit for that important situation', and had feared that the Queen might urge that Prince Albert be appointed. Remembering the events and arguments of 1828, the Duke expressed the view that he should pre-empt criticism by resigning from Cabinet, or at the very least give up the leadership of the government in the Lords. He did not regard this as a great sacrifice, telling Peel that because of his deafness his attendance at Cabinet meetings was 'frequently only the loss of so much time', while Arbuthnot added that the Duke often observed that 'as he had no one to answer questions for the several departments, the business [of the Lords] wore him to death'. But Peel refused to accept the proffered resignation, telling Wellington 'I could not contemplate it without the utmost pain,' and that it would destroy his satisfaction in seeing Wellington at the Horse Guards. Wellington naturally gave way: 'I have always professed to be and I am ready to take any course that may be thought desirable for her Majesty's service, and, having stated clearly my own opinion and wishes, I declare myself willing to take any course which her Majesty may command.'[12]

Wellington's appointment aroused little comment or controversy, although the *Morning Chronicle* could not resist the idea that it was the harbinger of a military government that would repress any dissent – an argument which provoked a withering response from *The Times* on the following day. But that was all; there were no accusations of politicising the Horse Guards and the army, no calls for Wellington to withdraw from politics, and the liberal constitutional arguments, which had been advanced with such passion and confidence in 1827–28, were quietly shelved. Wellington's reputation had risen to the point where he was regarded as an exception to normal rules, while he was so obviously the most suitable soldier to command the army that objections seemed carping and even slightly absurd.[13]

This does not mean that Wellington was exempt from other political criticism at this time. In the autumn of 1841 he was subjected to a barrage of abuse for the fairly banal remark: 'I have passed [a] great part of my life in foreign countries and in different parts of the world, and this is the only country I have ever known in which a poor man, if he have only industry and honesty, can acquire independence and competence.' In the hands of the press this was transformed into a suggestion that all the suffering of the working classes in the trade depression was due to their lack of industry and sobriety; with a speaker at a public meeting at Leeds citing it as proof that 'the aristocracy, as a class, are the enemies of the industrious class'. A few weeks later the attack was renewed when Wellington refused to see a delegation from Paisley – a town particularly hard hit by the depression – on the grounds that he had no departmental responsibilities relevant to their case, and that they had better direct themselves to those ministers who might actually be able to help them. This brutal disregard and callous indifference to human suffering gave the press something to write about for a few days, and led Greville to reflect sagely upon the Duke's decline from his former greatness, and the damage he risked doing to the government. But the affair was soon forgotten, and as the other ministers in the government became better known the press turned its attention to them, at least on economic and social questions.[14]

The depression of 1841–42 was extremely severe and caused real suffering, especially in the manufacturing areas of England and Scotland. Unemployment and bankruptcies multiplied, having a cascading effect as the failure of one enterprise triggered that of another. Tens of thousands of people were thrown out of work and forced to rely on local charities, which were stretched beyond their capacity, and there were innumerable cases of privation, and some even of starvation. Desperate or greedy employers tried to lower wages, leading to widespread strikes and other industrial action, including sabotage, and bands of striking workers forcing other enterprises to close down. Chartism flourished, along with other radical movements, and the experience of these years shaped the ideas of Karl Marx on the class struggle and the nature of capitalism. The ministers in London were concerned, but largely powerless to improve the state of the economy, although Peel's budget and obvious financial competence helped allay panic. Peel organised both official and private donations to attempt to relieve the worst of the suffering, and became acutely aware of the need to lessen class tensions and address popular grievances, including the perception that the Corn Laws taxed the people's bread for the benefit of wealthy aristocrats.[15]

During the summer of 1842, as the distress and the disturbances both worsened, the government was beset by calls to deploy troops to protect property and maintain order. Ministers had little sympathy for employers who were seeking to lower wages and Graham, the Home Secretary, told the commanding officer in the northern and midland district that he should encourage employers to make concessions to reasonable demands and not use his troops to break up peaceful strikes.[16] Wellington was closely involved with the precautions against disorder, even before he returned to the Horse Guards in August. The principle he had laid down in 1819 that troops not be dispersed in small parties was now widely accepted, and substantial numbers of men were quickly concentrated in the affected areas, thanks to the use of railways, and by drawing on the garrison of Ireland, which remained quiet. The combination of regular troops, the yeomanry (which generally performed well), and the use of organised bodies of army pensioners, ensured that the disturbances were generally contained, and the troubles diminished relatively quickly in the autumn as the harvest came in and the economy slowly began to improve. Nonetheless Wellington and at least some of his colleagues noted that their resources had been stretched thin, even though there was little trouble in London or Ireland. The government strengthened its hand by a modest increase in the yeomanry in 1843, and by the Enrolled Pensioners Act, which created a properly organised force of retired soldiers that could be drawn upon in an emergency. While both these steps were useful, Wellington argued that the size of the regular army needed to be substantially increased. However, Peel and Stanley (the Secretary for War as well as the Colonies) remained unconvinced.[17]

By early 1843 Wellington was clearly recovering from the lingering effect of his strokes. In January Greville noted that he was 'looking remarkably well, strong, hearty, and of a good colour . . . in very good spirits and humour'; while at the opening of Parliament in February he 'spoke with extraordinary vigour, and surprised everybody. He is certainly a much better man in all respects this year than he was two years ago, mind and body more firm.' The recovery was sustained and in March Greville thought that 'his speeches this Session have been as good, if not better than any he ever made'. However, Wellington's temper remained uncertain and may even have grown worse in 1844, with his private secretary reportedly alarmed by the asperity of some of his letters to his colleagues, although this does not seem to have affected his management of the House of Lords or his private correspondence with friends such as Lady Wilton.[18]

Ireland was the main problem facing the government in 1843, where O'Connell's campaign to repeal the Union suddenly caught fire with a series of enormous outdoor meetings in the summer and autumn, attracting crowds in the hundreds of thousands. As early as the beginning of May Lord Roden warned Wellington of 'the fearful advance which has taken place throughout this country on the subject of the repeal of the Union', and complained of 'the apparent apathy' of the Irish government. By late August Wellington agreed, telling the Home Secretary that 'those who are the leaders of these Repeal combinations in Ireland . . . [must be made to] feel the power and authority of the government and of the law, which should be brought to their very doors'.[19] When Graham responded by sending the Duke a despatch from the Lord Lieutenant asserting that everything was under control, Wellington responded furiously that the information he received was far less reassuring:

I heard of murder unnoticed; of illegal combinations excited by priests and demagogues, to refuse to work for individual landlords and farmers. I knew that large assemblies of mobs had been collected consisting of bodies marched in regular array under the head of priests, with bands and banners. That these mobs and bodies . . . defied the law and the government, terrified the whole country, threatened social order, which in Ireland is nearly annihilated.[20]

This led Graham to believe that Wellington was eager to go to Ireland and take charge of the situation himself, and he commented sarcastically to Peel that the Duke 'believes that the winds and the waves will obey him, and that in his presence there will be a great calm. I entertain an opposite opinion. If there were a rebellion, his iron hand would crush it. I doubt very much whether his preventative measures would be of a soothing character.' Peel replied that the only circumstances in which he thought that the Duke's presence in Ireland would help would be if a rebellion had actually broken out, or if there was reason to doubt the loyalty of the troops. This was not unreasonable; Wellington's appointment as Lord Lieutenant would have been seen, in Ireland and across Europe, as indicating an imminent crisis, whatever the policies he actually pursued. Whether Wellington was really eager to go to Ireland in 1843 may be doubted, although he may have feared that the weakness and lethargy of the Irish government were allowing a crisis to develop which could only be solved with his intervention.[21]

At the beginning of October Peel and Graham finally accepted that they could not let the Repeal movement continue unchecked any longer and, following the same route Wellington had suggested in August, gave orders that O'Connell and some of his leading associates should be arrested. With this, the unstoppable tide of the Repeal campaign simply collapsed, and its menaces were shown to be hollow. O'Connell's trial in the following year was mismanaged from start to finish, and led to a conviction which was overturned on appeal to the House of Lords. It was in the course of this trial that O'Connell said of Wellington: 'To be sure he was born in Ireland, but to be born in a stable does not make a man a horse.' The remark was widely circulated and then attributed to Wellington, and this in turn was used to criticise him for his lack of Irish patriotism![22]

Wellington was closely engaged with a range of subjects in these years. Much of his time was devoted to the internal administration of the army and to managing the government's business in the House of Lords when it was sitting. For some months in 1842 he was concerned by the threat of disorder in the industrial areas of England, Scotland and Wales; and in 1843 by the Repeal campaign in Ireland. He took a close interest in the unfolding events in India:

the conclusion of the Afghan War and the outbreak of the war with the Sikhs. He was perturbed by the poor state of relations with the United States when the government took office, and pleased when a diplomatic mission led by Lord Ashburton managed to resolve the line of the frontier of Maine and almost all the other issues of contention. And he continued to be anxious about the state of Canada – which remained restless – and was furious when Sir Charles Bagot, the Governor-General, admitted a number of former rebels into his council.[23]

But it was the state of Britain's relations with France that gave Wellington most concern throughout these years, and that coloured his approach to almost every other question. The war scare of 1839 had left a bitter and lasting legacy, inflaming public opinion on both sides of the Channel, and sparking a rivalry that fed off historical grievances and resentments, which even at the best of times had lurked close beneath the surface. The fall of the Whigs, and particularly Palmerston's removal from the Foreign Office, opened the door to a superficial rapprochement, and Aberdeen worked tirelessly to improve relations, and cultivated a personal understanding with Guizot, the French minister. The Queen and Prince Albert paid a private, but highly symbolic, visit to Louis Philippe at his country residence, the Château d'Eu, in the late summer of 1843, which went extremely well, and which led to the overly optimistic characterisation of relations between the two countries as an *'entente cordiale'*.

In fact the *entente* was never more than a chimera. The British government had already reacted strongly to a proposed customs union between France and Belgium, seeing it as the first step to an even closer union; and was unhappy at French moves to gain influence in Spain and Greece, the hostility of the French press, and strong popular support in Paris for increased naval spending. Wellington had not forgotten his 1839 fears of a steam-powered French invasion or coastal raids, and was not satisfied that enough had been done to make Britain more secure. And he was convinced, with good reason, that whatever the views of Guizot and the King, France as a whole was decidedly hostile. In March 1842 he told Lady Wilton: 'It is impossible to describe the Degree of detestation and abuse of us at Paris. . . . there is scarcely a House or Private Society into which an Englishman can gain admittance!' A year later Greville noted that Wellington had warned Ellenborough that 'the French Government were now busily employed in attacking our influence and undermining our interests in every quarter of the globe where they could find the means of doing so; that they despatched agents for this purpose (of various descriptions) in every direction, and he had no doubt that Ellenborough would before long hear of some French Agent in the regions about the Indus, and probably of attempts to establish some relations with the Sikh Government'. Given Wellington's strong support for close relations with France ever since the First Restoration of 1814, this level of suspicion and hostility was striking, but it is

clear that he felt that French actions belied all the fair words of Guizot and
Louis Philippe, and that Britain needed to take precautions, for any appearance
of vulnerability would risk exciting aggression.[24]

In 1845 Wellington explained his attitude to France more fully, telling Peel:

> There is no individual connected with your Government more sensible than
> I am of the absolute importance of connecting France with the councils of
> Europe, and above all of a good understanding between this country and
> France . . . Every day's experience proves that nothing can be settled in Europe
> or the Levant without war, unless by good understanding with France; nor
> can any question be settled in other parts of the world, excepting by the good
> understanding between France and this country . . .
>
> I believe the King and his Minister are wise men, and sincerely desire – the
> former for the sake of his dynasty, and both for the sake of France – to main-
> tain peace with this country. But look at the state of naval preparation in
> France. Look at the proportion of expenditure in that department, compared
> with that in all others. For what is that preparation made? . . . It is with a view
> to carry on against England offensive maritime warfare, and to make the
> British Empire the seat of the war.
>
> Who has made these preparations? Louis Philippe and in the latter years at
> least Guizot. As Frenchmen, at the head of the new Government, they are
> right. But don't let us deceive ourselves. These preparations are not symptoms
> of friendliness, or cordial understanding with, or even of a desire of peace
> with England. They are symptoms of deadly hostility.[25]

The Duke's view of French rivalry and underlying hostility was powerfully
reinforced by the events of 1844, when a series of incidents had led to serious
talk of war in both countries. None of these incidents involved any serious clash
of real interests, and if relations had been on a more secure foundation they
could all have been resolved amicably without fuss, but the public on both sides
of the Channel was primed and ready to take offence, and the press inflamed the
trouble and wildly misled its readers; Guizot's political position was too weak for
him to make concessions, while there was a dangerous divergence between his
public and private statements which left the British ministers exasperated and
distrustful. The greatest controversy was over the French annexation of Tahiti
and the supposed mistreatment of the British consul, a missionary named
George Pritchard. The affair was seized upon by British Dissenters, who championed Pritchard and abhorred the French behaviour as much on religious as
political grounds. Peel told Aberdeen: 'M. Guizot has been himself alone to
blame for what has occurred. If he chooses to send out expeditions to occupy
every place where they can find the pretence of occupation, and if the

commanders of these expeditions occupy other places not contemplated by their Government, and if M. Guizot has not the power or courage to disavow them, *he* is responsible for whatever may occur in consequence of such proceedings.' In the midst of the Tahiti affair one of Louis Philippe's sons, the Prince de Joinville, a naval officer, published a pamphlet, *Notes sur l'état des forces navales de la France*, in which he was widely, if not entirely accurately, understood to argue that steam-powered ships would give France great advantages in a naval war with Britain and even open the way to an invasion of England. Naturally this provoked a storm in Britain, where it was commonly supposed that Joinville spoke for the French government, and was either attempting to gain concessions by menaces, or had inadvertently revealed the real thinking in Paris behind the façade of the *entente*. As if this was not provocation enough, the French government now mounted a naval expedition against Morocco and gave the command to Joinville! The possibility that Morocco would follow Algiers and become a French colony was unacceptable to the British government, which saw it as a serious strategic threat, and led to unambiguous pressure which ensured that the expedition's mission never crept beyond its ostensible function of bullying the Moroccan government into granting limited French demands relating to co-operation in dealing with resistance to French rule in Algeria.[26]

The war scare of 1844 convinced Peel and the rest of the Cabinet, with the exception of Aberdeen, that Wellington was right, and that Britain must increase defence spending in order to deter France. As Peel told the Duke, 'we must not allow Louis Philippe to establish a character at our expense. The only way to prevent this is to convince him that we are in earnest and that we are prepared for a Naval War.' Aberdeen strongly disagreed, arguing that there was no real danger, and that they were being pushed by 'mere panic' into an arms race that would destroy all the trust and good understanding that he had built up with Guizot over the previous four years. But Wellington welcomed the change of policy, telling Peel that they could not ignore the fact that 'our defenceless state is at this moment as well known in France as it is in this country, if not better, and that we shall do no good by shutting our eyes to the danger'. And, in response to Aberdeen's protest: 'It may be a very foolish opinion, but I think it better to rely upon our own means for our defence than upon the good faith and forbearance of France.'[27]

But although Wellington and Peel now agreed on the need to increase defence spending, they differed over their priorities. In 1845 Peel concentrated on improving the navy, and in particular the number of steam-powered and screw-propeller-driven warships, and on fortifying ports and naval bases. But these programmes would take years to come to fruition and even then were not infallible, and Wellington was anxious that the regular army was so overstretched that it could do almost nothing if the French succeeded in landing even a comparatively small force on the south coast of England. Ideally he would have liked to have 100,000 regular soldiers ready to defend Britain, Ireland and the Channel Islands at all times. 'These, with the advantages of the use of your railroads, would enable you to defend all points and to be in security.' But that would cost £4 million a year, which the Duke knew was unrealistic. Instead he advocated a much more modest scheme to raise the strength of the regimental depots to six hundred men each, making them into a second battalion, which would increase the size of the army by 10,000 men and would only cost £200,000 a year, while the Enrolled Pensioners would provide another 10,000 and cost the same. Beyond this, Wellington looked to revive the militia, telling Peel: 'Organise the English, Scotch, and Irish Militia, which the Parliament has placed at the disposition of the Sovereign. Don't make yourself responsible for the want of preparation of that force.'[28]

Questions in Parliament from Palmerston about the capacity of the country to resist invasion added to pressure on Peel; and Wellington was so furious at the bland assurances with which the Prime Minister sought to reassure the House that he sent Peel a formal memorandum recapitulating his arguments and divesting himself of the responsibility that would otherwise attach 'to my character for leaving the country in a defenceless state'. Peel responded to this attack quite sharply, but also moved to meet Wellington's concerns. The strength of the army was increased in 1846 by some 8,000 men, while detailed plans were drawn up to call out the militia in the spring of 1846, so that Wellington seemed about to get most of what he wanted; but then these plans, like much else, got overtaken by the news of the potato blight in Ireland and the renewed discussion of the Corn Laws.[29]

The boldness and success of the 1842 Budget and Peel's dominance of the Commons had established the government on such solid foundations that Greville believed that it would remain in place as long as Peel had the health and vigour to lead it. Yet by the end of the session of 1843 its standing had fallen greatly, with its policy in Ireland subjected to vehement attacks from both flanks, and a series of 'articles of extraordinary violence' in *The Times*, leading to 'an universal opinion (just as strong among the friends as among the enemies of the Government) that Peel has fallen immensely in public opinion, and has ... shown himself unequal to a great emergency'. The arrest of O'Connell and the collapse of the Repeal movement might have repaired some of this damage, but this was soon overshadowed by the war scare with France, which was a heavy blow to the government's reputation, because it was closely associated with the, now evidently failed, policy of conciliation and the *entente cordiale*. As the general reputation of the ministry fell there was increasing discontent among its supporters on the backbench. They were less convinced than Peel that the 1842 Corn Law was working well when the price for corn remained between 50 and 52 shillings a quarter, lower than it had been for forty-three of the previous fifty years. Unlike the Prime Minister they did not rejoice when it fell as low as 47s 7d in September 1844 and remained below 50s until Christmas. They were tired of hearing Peel and some of his colleagues extolling the virtues of free trade in general, while paying only the most perfunctory and careless tribute to the importance of the landed interest which was the backbone of the Conservative Party.[30]

This simmering discontent contributed to two serious incidents in the Commons in 1844 when a number of Conservative backbenchers crossed the floor and defeated the government over factory hours (voting to reduce the working day from twelve to ten hours, contrary to Peel's wishes), and changes to the duties on imported sugar. In both cases Peel forced the Commons to reverse its vote and submit to his will by threatening to resign, but not without straining the bonds of party loyalty. Members of Parliament remembered that Lord Liverpool had calmly accepted even the loss of the Property Tax, and resented Peel's demand for complete subservience over far less significant questions. But the Reform Bill had shifted the source of the government's authority from the King to the Commons, and so any defeat in the Commons was a serious blow to the standing of the ministry of the day. But if Peel was right in maintaining that greater party discipline was essential under the new regime, he missed the corollary that ministers needed to take much greater account of the opinion inside the party in shaping policy. Loyalty needed to flow both ways if it was to continue to flow at all.[31]

Wellington was highly critical, in private, of Peel's handling of these incidents, and especially deplored the threat to resign. He told Lady Wilton:

I seldom read the Reports of these Discussions in the Newspapers; and till I received your Letter this morning I was not aware that the Intention to lay down our Arms and run away had been announced in Parliament! I have invariably done everything in my Power to prevent so disgraceful a Catastrophe. I first recommended that we should gain Time: that we should explain clearly to our friends our Intentions respecting the factory Question; our Reasons; and the Consequences which must follow our being defeated . . .[32]

Wellington's own management of the Lords was much more conciliatory and successful than Peel's handling of the Commons. There was no reason for the Tory peers to relish the government's policies any more than their fellows in the Commons, but the Duke's careful handling, and the personal respect he commanded, ensured that their grumbling remained relatively harmless. Peel himself acknowledged this in July 1844: 'It is your just influence and authority in the Lords, founded not merely on your position and high character, but on the weight which is attached to whatever falls from you in debate, that has smoothed our difficulties in the Lords, and kept that Assembly in harmony with the House of Commons.' This contemporary verdict has been confirmed by the historian Richard Davis, whose detailed study of the House of Lords in these years reveals the care and patience with which the Duke disarmed critics and ensured that differences of opinion did not grow into settled hostility.[33]

At the beginning of the Session of 1845 Wellington received a welcome reinforcement when Lord Stanley was elevated to the Lords. Stanley had been frustrated by the limited role he was playing in the Commons, where colonial affairs were attracting little attention, and thought that as he was destined to go to the Lords when his father died, he might as well make the move at once. Wellington was delighted to have his assistance, for the other ministers in the Upper House seldom played much of a part unless the debate related to their own department, and the government had been forced to rely on Brougham's help more than was desirable. Stanley made it plain that he had no thought of displacing Wellington in the leadership of the House, but looked to succeed him whenever the Duke (who was his senior by thirty years) died or retired. The arrangement worked remarkably well; Stanley softened his slashing, sarcastic style of speaking to suit the more dignified and collegial atmosphere of the Lords, and established a good relationship with Wellington after years of mutual reserve and – in earlier days – antipathy. Nonetheless, in time the move was to prove a disastrous mistake both for Stanley and for the Conservative Party that he would come to lead, which sorely missed his guidance and restraint in the Commons.[34]

The tension between the government and its supporters in both Houses, but especially the Commons, increased in 1845 with a proposal to increase funding to the Roman Catholic seminary at Maynooth. This had always been a sore point for many staunch defenders of the Church of England, and Peel was well aware that by broaching the subject he would further antagonise his already angry supporters. Nonetheless there was a strong case for increasing the grant: the college was dilapidated, its staff underpaid and not of high quality, and its graduates left with a well-established sense of grievance and resentment. Wellington expressed the view of the majority of ministers when he said that since it was impossible to withdraw the grant they might as well make it efficient; while he told the Lords that as Ireland's priests were going to be educated at Maynooth, he hoped that the increased funds might go some way towards 'making gentlemen of them'. The bill passed the Lords with a comfortable majority thanks to Whig support and despite the opposition of many Conservatives and most of the bishops. The inevitable Conservative revolt in the Commons was, if anything, rather smaller than might have been expected, but the measure aroused a sense of betrayal even among some of those who did not cross the floor. Peel had finally exhausted the great fund of goodwill, admiration and loyalty he had possessed when he became prime minister in 1841. He knew it, but was so drained by the demands of office that he scarcely cared. As Graham remarked in March: 'The country gentlemen cannot be more ready to give us the death-blow than we are to receive it.'[35]

The summer of 1845 was cold and cheerless, and by July ministers were concerned that rain might damage the harvest. In August a new problem emerged with the first reports of a blight affecting the potato crop in parts of England. This was a previously unknown fungal disease which arrived from central and eastern Europe; its effects were devastating, affecting the crop even after it was harvested, while no effective treatment was known. Potatoes played a useful, but secondary, role in the British diet; the loss of part or all the crop would cause hardship to many, but it would not be a disaster. This was not the case in Ireland, where potatoes were the mainstay of the majority of the population, and where their loss would create a risk of widespread famine. Peel and Graham understood this very well and waited anxiously for reports from Ireland. Their fears were soon realised: first reports of the disease appearing in Ireland reached London in the middle of September; by early October it was clear that Ireland was badly affected, and on 13 October Peel concluded that there was a potential catastrophe, although existing food stocks meant that it would be the New Year before it became acute.

Peel summoned a Cabinet meeting at the end of October at which he outlined an extensive programme of assistance in the form of public works to provide employment, loans and, where necessary, direct assistance. Enquiries were set on foot to purchase large quantities of grain of different sorts in the Baltic, the Mediterranean and the Black Sea, while the banking house of Barings was commissioned to spend £100,000 on the purchase of maize and meal in the United States – enough, it was calculated, to feed a million people for forty days. All this was highly commendable, but Peel looked beyond such immediate measures and asked his colleagues:

> Can we vote public money for the sustenance of any considerable portion of the people on account of the actual or apprehended scarcity, and maintain in full operation the existing restrictions on the free import of grain? I am bound to say my impression is that we cannot.[36]

Essentially Peel argued, with Graham's strong support, that they should suspend the Corn Laws at once in order to encourage the importation of as much food as possible, and that once the Laws were suspended, it would be politically impossible to reimpose them. And it was obvious that this was not a decision that Peel came to with great reluctance after seriously searching for any alternative; rather he embraced it with alacrity, having already lost faith in the principle of protection for agriculture.

However, very few of the other ministers agreed with Peel. They applauded his practical actions to avert famine in Ireland, but did not believe that this necessitated abandoning the Corn Laws – a step which they thought would fatally damage the government. At a subsequent Cabinet meeting on 6 November only Graham, Aberdeen and Sidney Herbert supported Peel, who then agreed to postpone a decision. Meanwhile public opinion was being mobilised on both sides of the question. The Anti-Corn Law League and the liberal press denounced the Laws with redoubled vigour, while the many protectionist societies which had sprung up in the counties in reaction to the activity of the League, sought pledges of faith from their local Conservative MPs. There was much speculation about the repeated Cabinet meetings, and wildly inaccurate stories were published by those who claimed to be in on the secret. It was commonly but mistakenly supposed that Wellington was the chief obstacle to repeal, with *Punch* declaring that 'the old Duke should no longer block up the great thoroughfare of Civilization, that he should be quietly and respectfully eliminated'. At the same time Lord John Russell added to the pressure on the government by publicly committing the Whigs to the immediate abolition of the Laws.[37]

Further Cabinet meetings in late November and early December produced no agreement. Peel was now arguing that the identification of the aristocracy with the Corn Laws heightened class tensions and did far more real damage to its interests than the tariff on imported corn was worth. 'I am afraid,' he told the Queen and Prince Albert, 'of other interests getting damaged in this struggle about the Corn Laws; already the system of promotion in the Army, the Game Laws, [and] the Church, are getting attacked with the aid of the League.' Against this Henry Goulburn, one of Peel's closest friends in Cabinet, argued that repealing the Corn Laws would break up the Conservative Party and open the door to democracy. It would not relieve the situation in Ireland or bring any grain into the country which could not come in under the existing law. Domestic prices of wheat were not rising as fast as in previous times of shortage. And Wellington pointed out that the Irish peasants barely engaged with the market economy, receiving their land, not money, in exchange for their labour, and that the structure of Irish society was much more of a problem than the tariff. Nonetheless, if Peel was absolutely determined on abolishing the Corn Laws Wellington would recommend that the Cabinet support him: 'A good government for the country is more important than the Corn Laws or any other consideration; and as long as Sir Robert Peel possesses the confidence of the Queen and of the public, and he has the strength to perform the duties, his administration of the Government must be supported.'[38]

Most of the Cabinet reluctantly accepted Wellington's argument, but Stanley and the Duke of Buccleuch felt that they were too strongly committed to the defence of the Corn Laws to abandon their position. Peel did not believe that he could carry the measure through the Commons without the support of the whole Cabinet, and so, on 6 December, he resigned. As neither Stanley nor any of the other ministers believed that they could form a protectionist government, Peel advised the Queen to send for Russell. But Russell was in a weak position, without a majority in the Commons or the Lords, and with a party which was itself far from united in support for repeal. In the end a quarrel over Cabinet places (the insufferable Howick, now Lord Grey, refused to serve if Palmerston returned to the Foreign Office) resulted in a humiliating failure, and Russell was forced to resign his commission on 20 December. Peel returned to office with renewed enthusiasm, and all his old ministers except Stanley agreed to take office, believing, with Wellington, that the Queen and the country must not be left without a government.

Wellington was delighted that Russell's attempt to form a government had failed, but he recognised that Peel's resuscitated ministry would have a difficult struggle to get repeal through both Houses of Parliament, and that even if this was achieved its subsequent prospects were not good. He at once set to work writing to leading Conservative peers outlining the arguments in favour of repeal and begging them at least to remain open-minded, and not to commit themselves to opposing the government on the question. It was uphill work, for Peel's abandonment of the Corn Laws – which had assumed talismanic significance for many Conservatives – released all the pent-up frustration and bitterness that had accumulated not just since 1841, but as far back as Catholic Emancipation and his refusal to support Wellington in forming a government in May 1832. Wellington hoped that while repealing the Corn Laws Peel would introduce other measures to assist farmers and landowners, and remove some of the taxes that fell particularly heavily upon them. On 26 December 1845 he told Croker: 'The truth is, that if the Government does not make an arrangement of the Corn Laws satisfactory to the landed interest, it cannot hope for its support; and it cannot carry on the Queen's business.' And early in the New Year he admitted to Lady Wilton: 'We are not in a satisfactory state. We shall, I fear, lose the support of a great proportion of our friends. I don't see daylight through our Difficulties, notwithstanding that I am taking such pains to keep, or rather to set matters right.' And: 'I don't yet know what Sir Robert Peel will propose; Still less what I shall be able to bring the great Landed Proprietors to consent to. But I am endeavouring to keep things together.'[39]

Parliament opened on 22 January and Peel chose to bury the repeal of the Corn Laws in a wider package of tariff reductions. His language was uncompromising and unconciliatory, while the compensation he offered was so paltry as to be almost insulting. There was nothing in his approach to soften the inevitable rupture with his supporters, or to entice waverers to support him, or even to remain aloof until the issue was settled. And his truculence was met with an extraordinary wave of abuse and hostility in which Lord George Bentinck and Benjamin Disraeli distinguished themselves for the violence of their sarcasm and the personal hostility that they directed at the Prime Minister. As in a particularly bitter and squalid divorce, the Opposition Whigs and liberals looked on with embarrassed astonishment as Conservative after Conservative outdid each other in venom and animus. Any hope of reconciliation or rebuilding the party, with Peel or without him, was soon gone as two-thirds of Conservative members opposed repeal and one-third followed Peel. After weeks of debates and delays the bill was finally passed by a majority of nearly one hundred, thanks to the support of the Opposition, and it went up to the House of Lords.[40]

Wellington's tactics in the Lords were very different from Peel's in the Commons. His task was easier, for he was regarded with great respect by both his old opponents and by Conservative peers committed to the defence of the Corn Laws. It was known, and helpful, that he had no great liking for the measure, but believed that it should be passed in the national interest. But even so success was not assured, for the Lords was the established bastion of the landed interest, and its members were more naturally independent, less susceptible than those of the Commons to the notions of party discipline, and relatively immune to the pressure of public opinion.

Despite his resignation from the Cabinet Stanley had hoped to be able to support Peel's proposals from the backbench, but his dismay at the lack of any significant concession to agriculture drove him slowly and reluctantly into open opposition and leadership of the protectionists. Wellington discussed the position with him with remarkable frankness, urging him to look beyond the immediate crisis to its inevitable aftermath. The Duke conceded that Peel had irretrievably lost the confidence of the Conservative Party, and that it would fall to Stanley, as the leading protectionist, to rebuild the party. Moderation and restraint in the debate would make the task much easier, by not creating barriers and bitterness between men who would otherwise be inclined to work together. This was statesmanlike advice which, if it had been heeded by the protectionists in the Commons, might have greatly improved their own political prospects. It is clear that Wellington was entirely sincere, and that he was 'most anxious' for Stanley's success as leader of the Conservatives once the immediate crisis was resolved; but he also knew that a restrained, moderate debate would facilitate the passage of the bill through the Lords. There were many peers, both ministerial and Whig or liberal, who were intending to vote for repeal, but with great reluctance or many misgivings. Their heart might fail them if they were forced to choose between a nebulous sense of duty and the passionate appeal of their friends, and all the passion, all the feeling, in the Lords at least, lay with the protectionists.[41]

Wellington's appeal was successful. Stanley opposed the bill with skill and eloquence, but without rancour and showing great personal respect for Wellington, and the bill proceeded through the Lords with little of the fury and venom of the Commons' debates. When Wellington spoke on the last night of the Second Reading debate, 28 May 1846, he pointedly avoided any discussion of the merits of the Corn Laws, and instead rested his argument solely on the dangers for the Lords if it opposed the will of the Commons, supported by public opinion, on such an important question. 'Now that, my Lords, is a situation in which I beg to remind your Lordships, I have frequently stated you ought not to stand; it is a position in which you cannot stand, because you are entirely powerless; without the Commons and the Crown, the House of Lords can do nothing.' If the Lords could not block the Reform Bill under the old constitution in 1831–32, it certainly could not block the repeal of the Corn Laws in 1846. The peers recognised their weakness, and the bill was passed by 210 to 163 votes on the evening of 25 June. Later that night, in a carefully timed move, Russell and the Opposition combined with the protectionist Conservatives to defeat the government in the Commons.[42]

On 29 June Peel made a resignation speech in the Commons that was notable for its egotism, its self-satisfaction and its delight in offending as many Conservatives – including those who had remained loyal to him – as possible. The speech culminated in an extraordinary tribute to Richard Cobden, one of the founders of the Anti-Corn Law League, and a man who for years had been exacerbating class tensions with unrestrained and often crude attacks on the aristocracy and the landed interest. It is hard to avoid the conclusion that this was a deliberate act of sabotage, a final burning of bridges between the two wings of the Conservative Party, and was Peel's revenge for the scurrilous abuse he had suffered at the hands of Disraeli and Bentinck. Both Peel and Disraeli have claims to be regarded as among the founders of the modern Conservative Party; but the arrogant selfishness of one and the immature malice of the other, as displayed in the crisis of 1845–46, helped ensure that the party remained weak and largely out of office for a generation.[43]

Wellington greatly lamented the damage done to what he still described, in February 1846, as 'the great and at this moment powerful Conservative party'. He had done everything he could to minimise the harm, with some success in the Lords, although his influence did not extend to the Commons. For five years in office, and more before that in opposition, he had acted as Peel's loyal lieutenant, deftly steering the government's legislation through the Lords, avoiding a confrontation between the two Houses, and on a number of occasions sacrificing strongly held opinions of his own for the sake of party unity, and it is a testament to his skill and influence that it was the Tories in the Commons, not the Lords, who finally revolted against Peel.[44]

After the resignation Wellington was understandably bitter at the way his loyalty, and that of the other ministers, many of them young men at the outset of their careers, had been repaid. In August Croker reported: 'He [Wellington] is very much shocked, and indeed indignant, at the apathy with which the cause of the mischief looks at the ruin, not only of the party, but of his own *followers and friends.*' Surprisingly Wellington had proved a much abler and more dedicated party politician than Peel, without ever sacrificing the overriding priority he gave to national interests. With the fall of Peel's government he largely withdrew from party politics, although not the national stage, but as he left he paused to urge forgiveness, 'Christian charity', and a willingness to forget past differences – difficult political virtues at the best of times, but ones which would be essential if the Conservative Party was to hope to regain the ground that it had lost. They were virtues that he had always practised as well as preached, in a long career that had attracted more than a common amount of abuse, but in which he had made few if any irreconcilable enemies.[45]

CHAPTER TWENTY-NINE

COMMANDER-IN-CHIEF
(1842–52)

WELLINGTON WAS COMMANDER-IN-CHIEF for the last decade of his life, and after the resignation of Peel's government in 1846 it became his principal official role, and one which kept him in frequent communication with the Cabinet on a broad range of affairs. When Peel's government first resigned in December 1845 the Queen expressed her '*strong* desire' that the Duke remain at the Horse Guards, and Wellington happily consented, once he had established that Russell had no objection. In July 1846, when Russell finally became prime minister, he called on Wellington, who assured him that while he would not actively support the new government, he would 'have no political concert with any party opposed to the Government so long as I held the office of Commander-in-Chief'. Russell was happy with this arrangement, while Peel spoke for many when he told the Queen 'that it would be monstrous to see the British army commanded by any other man than the Duke of Wellington'.[1]

Sir George Brown, one of the senior staff officers at the Horse Guards, told George Gleig that:

> Speaking from the experience which I had of him, I should say that the Duke was a remarkably agreeable man to do business with, because of his clear and ready decision. However much I may have seen him irritated and excited with the subjects which I have repeatedly had to bring under his notice, I have no recollection of his ever having made use of a harsh or discourteous expression to me, or of his having dismissed me without a distinct and explicit answer or decision in the case under consideration. Like all good men of business, who consider well before coming to a decision, his grace was accustomed to adhere strictly to precedent; to the decisions he may have previously come to on similar cases. This practice greatly facilitated the task of those who had to transact business with him, seeing that all we had to do in concluding our statement of any particular case, was to refer to his decision on some similar one.

Other sources lay rather more emphasis on Wellington's irascibility, but Brown is clear that when the Duke made a mistake, for example overlooking a change in the regulations that invalidated his decision, he 'would listen with the greatest patience to such explanations, and never made the slightest difficulty in modifying his memoranda so as to meet them'.[2]

These years saw a number of 'reforms' of the army. Some of these changes, such as the further reduction of flogging and the introduction of academic exams for junior officers, were concessions reluctantly made by Wellington. He saw much more real advantage in others, such as the construction of new barracks, which did more than anything else to improve soldiers' lives. He also oversaw the replacement of the old 'Brown Bess' musket, first with a percussion musket, and then with the Minié rifle. Wellington's main concerns in a new infantry weapon were that it should not be too complicated to load (it was critical that men did not become flurried in action), that it be robust enough to endure the hard usage of active service, and that it could use the old ammunition at a pinch, for the transition from one weapon to the next would take some years to implement throughout the army. The design, testing and supply of the weapons was the responsibility of the Ordnance not the Horse Guards, and proved fraught with difficulties, many arising from the fact that this was a decade of great innovation, so that a promising weapon would be overtaken by some fresh development before it could be approved for use by the army. These problems were compounded by the inability of the private small arms manufacturers to combine mass production with high standards, which led to constant delays. If the British army had been forced to fight against one of the great European powers in the 1840s, whether at home or abroad, it would have been seriously disadvantaged by a shortage of modern weapons, and this only increased Wellington's concern over the state of the country's defences.[3]

Despite these and many other changes, Wellington was often criticised in the military press of the day as an obstacle to progress. Papers such as the *Naval and Military Gazette* and the *United Service Gazette* strongly advocated a range of 'reforms', including the abolition of purchase for officers, short service enlistment for the rank and file, the abolition of flogging, and the expansion of the scope of the War Office to include the Ordnance and other military departments. In 1846 the *United Service Gazette* described the Duke as 'the greatest enemy, perhaps, to innovation', while in 1850 it launched a wholesale and vehement attack accusing him of giving way to the government too readily, possessing 'infirm' judgement, and not granting enough interviews to officers and consequently being out of touch with military opinion. 'It is contrary to the laws and dictates of Nature that a man, however superlatively gifted, shall reach fourscore years of age without becoming obstinate, querulous, partially incapable of active duties, given to procrastination, and prone to seek excuses for altogether putting aside matters which levy a contribution upon the thinking faculty.' Wellington should be made to resign, and the army given the benefit of 'the ingenuity of philanthropic and zealous Soldiers . . . Verily the hour is come for the intervention of the Army Reformers.'[4]

It is difficult to be know what impression remarks such as these made on their readers, who were, overwhelmingly, serving or retired officers. The circulation of these papers was not large: between one and two thousand copies per week, although some would have had more than one reader. However, the fact that both papers adopted a similar editorial line, and that the more conservative *British Army Despatch* proved short-lived, suggests that there was an appetite for such criticism, and that it struck a chord with many officers, and that Wellington was probably less generally popular and respected in the army in the 1840s than in society in general.

Much of the discontent in the army arose from years of slow promotion and under-funding which Wellington could do nothing to cure, but his refusal to urge the Queen to grant a medal to Peninsular veterans caused much unnecessary heartburn and resentment. The problem had arisen when the Waterloo Medal was issued to all soldiers of any rank who had taken part in the campaign of 1815, which left the veterans of the long and arduous campaigns in the Peninsula feeling that their service had been forgotten. The decision of the Indian government to grant medals to all ranks who had taken part in the Afghan campaign, and then the Opium War, triggered a wave of furious agitation from the Peninsular veterans, including articles in the press and petitions in Parliament. Wellington turned a deaf ear, arguing that soliciting rewards deprived them of their value, and that it was not for him to ask the Queen or her ministers for further favours. While this was consistent with his own approach to honours, it was also remarkably ungenerous to the officers and men who had served under him, and who had never received any significant reward for their service, and it is not easy to understand or sympathise with his motives on this occasion, although he may have felt that he was being bullied. Fortunately at the end of 1846 Lord John Russell intervened, suggesting to the Queen that she take the initiative. At this Wellington's objections evaporated, and in 1847 the General Service Medal was awarded to surviving veterans, not just of the Peninsula, but of many other campaigns in the long war with France. Wellington's part in the victory was recognised on the reverse of the medal where he was depicted as kneeling before the Queen, who placed a laurel wreath on his head.[5]

Waterloo produced its own retrospective controversy, with the model of the battle and subsequent history of the campaign by Captain William Siborne attracting intermittent publicity throughout the 1830s and 1840s. Siborne had not been at the battle – indeed he had never been in action at all – and he rejected advice from many of those who had, that it would be impossible to determine the precise location and strength of units once the fighting began. His attempt to portray the action at the moment of the 'crisis' of the battle, the repulse of the French Imperial Guard late in the day, sparked many claims and counter-claims from the officers of different regiments over which units deserved to be placed in the most prominent position. It also led him to depict both the French and Wellington's army as quite weak (much depleted by the day's fighting) while the Prussians appeared in great force, for he accepted at face value the very helpful information sent to him by the military authorities at Berlin. Wellington had very little to do with Siborne's work; in 1836 he answered some queries in a memorandum, but in general referred Siborne, and anyone else, to the despatch he had written immediately after the battle. In 1840 he told Lady Wilton that he had never seen the model, although 'I understand that it is beautiful; and the Shape of the Ground is accurately delineated'; but he believed that the troop locations were inaccurate and that 'the Critical Viewer of the Model must believe that the whole of each Army, without Reserve of any Kind, was engaged at the Moment supposed to be represented'. He had therefore not visited it, knowing that his visit would be represented as an endorsement of its accuracy. All this was entirely in keeping with his general attitude to historians of his campaigns, and his sensible desire to keep aloof from the disputes which their works inevitably provoked. Siborne himself later concluded that he had represented the Prussians as occupying 'too forward a position' at the moment of victory, although this did nothing to interest Wellington in a work which he regarded as fundamentally flawed in both conception and methodology. Siborne's *History* is far more useful than this suggests, although no one who has read even part of it can be surprised that it was not a commercial success.[6]

As Commander-in-Chief and Britain's pre-eminent soldier, Wellington played an active role in advising the Cabinet on questions of national defence. Russell's government was very weak, without a secure majority in either House of Parliament, and subjected to fierce if unco-ordinated attacks from both the radicals and the protectionists. It was only kept in office by the unenthusiastic support of Peel and the free-trade Conservatives who continued to follow him out of office. While much less numerous than the protectionists, Peel's faction included most of the men of recognised ability, leaving the protectionists woefully short of front-bench talent. If the two wings of the Conservative Party had been able to re-unite they would have been able to form a government, but Peel had set his face against any reconciliation, and devoted himself to keeping the protectionists out of office. His reputation in the country had never stood higher and there was a general expectation that somehow or other he would again become prime minister. He repeatedly, and apparently sincerely, denied any desire to hold office again, but by remaining active and in the Commons he was, implicitly at least, a contender and prevented his followers from gradually coalescing with either the Whigs or the protectionists. An election in 1847 did little to strengthen the government, and showed that the country was predominantly Conservative, but also, on balance, in favour of free trade.[7]

Wellington had little contact with Peel in these years and was privately critical of him for mishandling the repeal of the Corn Laws and so breaking up the Conservative Party. He had more sympathy for Stanley, and gave him some quiet, behind-the-scenes support in rallying the Conservative peers. But he recognised that the protectionists were in no position to form a government, and that there was no realistic alternative to Russell's administration. This led him to support the ministers when he believed that they were right, and to stay silent when he believed they were wrong – behaviour which Stanley understood, but nonetheless found distinctly unhelpful. Wellington worked well with Lord John Russell personally; the Prime Minister was reported to be 'very civil and deferential' to the Duke, and listened carefully and with an open mind to his advice. The appointment of Lord Howick who, having succeeded his father in 1845, was now 3rd Earl Grey, as Secretary of State for War and the Colonies was unfortunate, for Grey was convinced that he knew more of military matters than any soldier, including the Duke, and did not trouble to conceal the fact. Wellington's attitude to Palmerston, who had returned to the Foreign Office, was more ambivalent; they had never worked well together and the Duke disliked Palmerston's blustering foreign policy and constant playing to the press, but he welcomed his support for increased defence spending. However, Palmerston took advice on military matters largely from Anglesey (the Master-General of the Ordnance) and Sir John Burgoyne (the Inspector-General of Fortifications), and he and Wellington were never close allies even when they agreed.[8]

Within months of taking office Russell's government was planning to introduce a major 'reform' of the army: the introduction of 'short' service, meaning that soldiers would enlist for ten, not twenty-one, years. The experiment had been tried before, by Windham in 1806, and had not been a success, but Grey was confident that it would greatly improve the standard of recruits and lead to the creation of an effective reserve force, for the men who had served for ten years would then be enrolled as pensioners. However the ministers foolishly failed to consult Wellington in drawing up their plans, and attempted to present him with a *fait accompli*, which would not only apply to future recruits, but to all soldiers already in the army. Although Wellington was deeply sceptical of the whole idea of short service, he was willing to make the experiment with new recruits; but he was horrified that all the longest-serving soldiers in the army should at the stroke of a pen be eligible for their discharge, and feared that this would undermine the morale of the whole army. He wrote to Russell refusing to 'destroy the efficiency of the small Army which Her Majesty's Govt has at its disposition', and threatening to resign. The ministers backed down, agreeing that the bill would apply only to new recruits, and in return Wellington refused to endorse the protectionists' attack on it in Parliament. There is some evidence that Wellington's concern with the effects of the plan were exaggerated – many long-serving soldiers were already eligible for an early discharge but few took advantage of it – but his scepticism as to its benefits was fully vindicated by experience. The new scheme did not produce a different class of recruit and most men continued to volunteer for long rather than short service, or re-enlisted when their ten years was up, so that it did not produce an effective reserve. Long service was re-introduced as part of a fresh wave of 'reforms' in the 1860s, followed by another attempt at short service in the 1870s.[9]

The Whigs also made a fresh attempt to expand the powers of the War Office along the lines advocated in the 1830s. However Russell's government was no stronger, politically, than Melbourne's, and Fox Maule, the Secretary-at-War, conceded defeat when his plan encountered strong opposition from both Wellington and Anglesey, admitting that 'the House of Commons would not press changes likely to denude either especially the Duke of any . . . dignity'. And although the Ordnance was often described as notoriously inefficient, an exhaustive, two-year inquiry by the Commons Finance Committee proved unable to uncover any extravagance or recommend significant reductions.[10]

Wellington's main priority remained the threat from France. Within weeks of his taking office a fresh crisis had blown up over the role of the French government in orchestrating the simultaneous marriage of the Queen of Spain and her sister, and heir-presumptive, the former to a Spanish nobleman, the latter to the younger son of King Louis Philippe of France. Although the marriages did little or nothing to increase French influence in Spain, Palmerston reacted with great fury and bluster and encouraged the British press to whip public opinion into a frenzy. For the third time in eight years war seemed an imminent possibility, and even when the immediate fever subsided, relations remained very bad, with a clear danger that some small incident or miscalculation might lead them to spiral out of control.

Wellington was deeply concerned that the country remained vulnerable to attack from France. As soon as Parliament rose after the tumultuous session of 1846, he urged Russell to implement the plans drawn up under the previous government to revive the militia, and followed this up with a formidable memorandum dated 8 February 1847 in which he warned that there would be no time to train men once war broke out. He calculated that it would require 65,000 men just to garrison the dockyards and arsenals on which the navy depended, and that this would leave almost no disposable force with which to defend London, or any other centre threatened by a French landing. His plan was for a part-time militia, raised by conscription if necessary, whose members would receive a few weeks' training each year for several years. Such soldiers could not oppose regulars in the open field with much hope of success, but with a little additional training they could form part of the dockyard and other garrisons, releasing regulars to form a field army. A militia would be both cheap and constitutional, and after a few years it might give the country a reserve force of 150,000 men. Together with a modest increase in the regular army it would not cost more than £400,000 a year. Wellington admitted privately that he would much rather have a larger increase in the regulars, 'but I *know* I shall not have these. I may have the others.' The coasts were open to landings almost anywhere, and steam power rendered the traditional British strategy of naval blockade almost hopeless. An invasion could be launched from a dozen French ports with very little warning, and once ashore 'I know of no mode of resistance, much less of protection, from this danger, excepting by an army in the field capable of meeting and contending with its formidable enemy'. While not ideal, the measures he proposed would 'put the country on its legs in respect to personal force, and I would engage for its defence, old as I am'. But without them, if the navy was not completely successful when put to the test, 'we are not safe for a week after the declaration of war'.[11]

Wellington's assessment of the threat was fully supported by Anglesey and Burgoyne, and made a deep impression on the Prime Minister and some of his colleagues. Lord John Russell feared that the French could put 40,000 men on British soil within a week of the outbreak of war, while Palmerston declared that 20 or 30,000 Frenchmen might be landed under the cover of darkness in a single night. When another member of the Cabinet, J.C. Hobhouse, asked Palmerston privately if he really thought the French regarded Britain as this vulnerable, the Foreign Secretary replied that he had no doubt of it, and that 'Louis Philippe himself told Lord John Russell at Windsor that, had a war broken out on the Tahiti affair, he might have been compelled to take measures which he, having so strong a feeling of gratitude and affection for England, would deeply deplore'.[12]

However other ministers, including Lord Grey and the Chancellor of the Exchequer, Sir Charles Wood, were not persuaded. They felt that the government's finances were already over-stretched by the aid being given to Ireland, which was being ravaged by famine, and were unwilling to commit to an expensive programme of defence spending before the election which was due in the middle of 1847, knowing that this would give fertile ground for radical attacks on the government. It is also possible that they, and Palmerston's other opponents in the Cabinet, hoped that his awareness of the country's weakness would force him to adopt a more conciliatory policy towards France. A succession of Cabinet meetings failed to produce agreement, and Russell did not force the issue, so that little was done in 1847 to meet Wellington's concerns, although work continued on the extensive, and expensive, programme of fortifications begun under Peel.[13]

On 4 January 1848 the *Morning Chronicle* published a long letter written almost a year before by Wellington to Sir John Burgoyne, expressing his fears over the state of the country's defences, and his frustration that successive governments had not done more to strengthen the army. Wellington was furious at the publication of the letter, knowing that ministers and other observers would assume that he had deliberately leaked it in order to put pressure on the Cabinet. In fact copies of the letter had been made by Burgoyne's daughter, and one of these given to Lady Shelley who lent it to a long list of friends and influential connections, including Lord Stanley and other prominent protectionists. Lord Ellesmere wrote an article in *The Times* on the subject which was attacked in the *Examiner*, and this prompted the *Morning Chronicle* to publish the letter in full. Cobden launched a vehement attack on Wellington for war-mongering, and pretty plainly implied that he was in his dotage, 'tottering on the verge of the grave'.[14]

This controversy did not deter the government from going ahead with its plans. The ministers had finally agreed on a significant increase in defence spending including the establishment of a new militia, although they had not decided exactly what form this would take. They proposed to increase spending on the army, navy and Ordnance by a total of £358,000 and an additional £150,000 to lay the 'foundation of a militia force'. Unfortunately the sudden end of the railway boom in 1847 and a sharp trade slump had badly affected the government's revenue, and in order not to fall into deficit the ministers agreed to increase taxes. The income tax would not only need to be retained, but to rise from Peel's seven pence in the pound to twelve pence (one shilling, or a punishing rate of 5 per cent). The Prime Minister announced this proposal to the Commons on 18 February 1848 and received a cold reception. As one historian remarks, to members in the House the 'chances of invasion seemed preferable to the certain addition of fivepence to the income tax'. The mood was so hostile that within three days the government agreed to refer the proposed increase to a secret select committee, while on 29 February the Chancellor of the Exchequer announced that the planned increase in taxes and in defence spending was being dropped. Dramatic news from Paris made the immediate threat of war seem much less likely.[15]

On 24 February 1848 Louis Philippe was forced to abdicate and flee France, and the Second Republic was established. The revolution was completely unexpected and might well have been avoided with more skilful and determined handling of the protests. The news astonished the world and helped precipitate a wave of liberal risings in Italy, Germany, Prussia, Denmark, Hungary and Poland, most of which were eventually suppressed, but which left an important ideological legacy, including the cultivation of strident nationalism and greater popular participation in politics. Metternich was soon forced to join Louis Philippe and Guizot in exile in England, and stayed with Wellington at Stratfield Saye for five days in December, when the Duke treated him with great kindness and consideration.[16]

Despite the precedent of the 1790s and the spreading instability across Europe, Russell's government seized on the news to abandon its commitment to increased defence spending, and seek to recover the ground it had lost in the Commons and with public opinion. When preparing the 1849 Budget towards the end of 1848 the Cabinet demanded large reductions in spending on both the army and the navy, reversing the increases granted by Peel in 1845–46. Wellington protested, but Russell insisted that the reductions go ahead, arguing: 'A gradual and prudent course of Retrenchment will satisfy the public mind, and enable us to preserve our present safe and enviable position.'[17]

These economic troubles and the news from the Continent led to a revival of Chartism in England. Meetings were held across the country and a huge petition prepared with, it was claimed, six million signatures demanding further sweeping parliamentary reform. The Chartist leaders emphasised peaceful protests and the moral force of huge, orderly crowds; but the ministers were well aware how quickly a mass protest could change its character, and were determined to learn the lesson of the events in Paris and take ample precautions. The Chartists announced a mass meeting at Kennington Common on 10 April 1848, which would then turn into a march on Parliament to present the petition. They intended to intimidate the government by the numbers and discipline of the protesters – not by violence, but by the implicit threat of violence, and by the evident support of the population. However the government beat them at their own game, concentrating not just 4,000 police and 8,000 troops to nip any disorder in the bud, but also mobilising 85,000 special constables who provided an extraordinary demonstration of the strength of 'respectable' opinion in opposition to the Chartists' aims and methods.[18]

Wellington was closely involved in the government's response, and Hobhouse recorded in his diary the Duke's presence at the Cabinet meeting on 8 April when the ministers met to review the plan prepared by Colonel Rowan, Commissioner of the Metropolitan Police:

[The Duke] did not say much, but what he did say was decisive. He would have plenty of room for the Chartists to run away. He would not show the troops until they were to be used. He would not allow the police to be overcome at first. He thought the bridges the best place at which to stop the procession, and, if the Chartists assembled on the other side of the river, they might be stopped at the end of any street as easily as at a bridge. The great thing, he said, was to keep the parks and public offices clear. Most of this had been said by Rowan, but the authority of 'the great man,' as Hardinge called him at his dinner, gave weight to it, and we all listened and looked on respectfully.[19]

Lord Campbell, the Chancellor of the Duchy of Lancaster, also attended the Cabinet meeting on 8 April and was just as impressed as Hobhouse by Wellington, telling Sir George Campbell: 'The quickness, intelligence, and decision which the Duke displayed were very striking, and he inspired us all with perfect confidence . . . It was not I alone who was struck with the consultation of yesterday. Macaulay said to me that he considered it the most interesting spectacle he had ever witnessed, and that he should remember it to his dying day.'[20]

In the event the meeting proved an anti-climax, with the Chartists accepting the government's prohibition of a march on Parliament and peacefully dispersing, while the petition was delivered in a convoy of hackney cabs. This was not quite the end of the Chartist movement; it staged numerous further demonstrations into the summer, testing the patience of the public, the authorities and the soldiers. Nonetheless serious violence was avoided and a sense of futility, combined with the improving economy, led to the rapid decline of the movement in the second half of the year.

Russell's government struggled on through 1849 and 1850, despite its weakness in Parliament and lack of unity in Cabinet. Palmerston's high-handed foreign policy and refusal to consult his colleagues caused constant tension, but his support for the liberal revolutions of 1848–49, and his bullying of foreign governments, proved popular in the press and with the public. Disraeli became the effective leader of the protectionists in the Commons following Bentinck's sudden death in September 1848, although many of his nominal supporters viewed him with at least as much distaste and suspicion as they had ever viewed Peel. Wellington remained immensely influential within the government on military and colonial questions. On one occasion even Lord Grey commented on one of his letters on Indian affairs: 'How great he is on military matters, how clear, how comprehensive!' And the Duke continued to support the government in the Lords, because he saw no practical alternative.[21]

On 2 July 1850 the political world was shaken by the death of Sir Robert Peel after being thrown from his horse on Constitution Hill. Now in his eighties, Wellington was reconciled to the loss of his contemporaries, but Peel was still at the height of his powers and his death was the more shocking for being so sudden and unexpected. Speaking with evident emotion in the Lords, the Duke paid tribute: 'In all the course of my acquaintance with Sir Robert Peel, I never knew a man in whose truth and justice I had a more lively confidence, or in whom I saw a more invariable desire to promote the public service. In the whole course of my communication with him I never knew an instance in which he did not show the strongest attachment to truth; and I never saw in the whole course of my life the smallest reason for suspecting that he stated anything which he did not firmly believe to be a fact.' It was Wellington's answer to the furious attacks which Disraeli and the other protectionists, including many Tory peers whom Wellington regarded as friends, had made on Peel's personal reputation ever since the repeal of the Corn Laws had first been suggested.[22]

In February 1851 Russell's government resigned, having been defeated, almost by accident, on a motion calling for further parliamentary reform. Stanley made an attempt to form a government, but could not persuade either Aberdeen or Gladstone to join him, while the Peelites also refused a junction with Russell to form a stronger Whig-Liberal government. Wellington was furious at the protectionists for allowing the government to be defeated on a question of parliamentary reform, and told Prince Albert that although he 'had no feeling for Lord John Russell's Cabinet, measures, or principles . . . he felt that the Crown and the country were only safe in these days by having the Liberals in office, else they would be driven to join the Radical agitation against the institutions of the country'. This was the same line that he and Peel had pursued with Melbourne's government in the 1830s, while they waited for the underlying Conservative strength in the country to assert itself. In the meantime the crisis dragged on, with every possible combination of parties attempted and failing to produce a credible ministry. Finally, after nearly a week of inconclusive negotiations, the Queen and Prince Albert appealed to Wellington and Lansdowne, as elder statesmen half removed from the fray, for independent advice. This appeal was widely welcomed, with *The Times* describing them as 'the two Englishmen first in position, in experience and in personal character, to counsel the Crown on the course now to be pursued', while *Punch* depicted Wellington as the trusted old family doctor who was always turned to in an emergency. Fortunately the two sages, acting independently, produced the same advice: the Queen should ask Russell and his colleagues to return to office without any change to the government. This was done, and it was a matter of debate for observers whether the affair had gained or cost the ministry authority, and whether Stanley had really desired to form a ministry or whether he was privately relieved at the outcome.[23]

The proven lack of any alternative helped Russell's government survive the remainder of the session, and robbed party politics of some of its interest. At the same time, fears of war with France were reviving. In April 1849 the French had mounted an amphibious expedition of over 7,000 men, at very short notice, to restore the Pope to his temporal power in Rome, and, as one modern historian remarks, the 'implications for a Channel crossing really did not need emphasising'. But this had to be balanced against opinion in Parliament where the Peelites and radicals continued to press for further reductions in spending on the army and navy. In May 1850 Russell wrote: 'I am for remaining quiet and running a risk. But at the same time let every calculation be made as to what we could do in an emergency. I believe the French majority wish to divert attention by foreign quarrels, but we shall not give them any fair pretext.' But in September an impressive French naval review at Cherbourg sounded the alarm bells in England, and Palmerston told Russell: 'This Cherbourg review and the sight which it has afforded into the means which France has of attacking us ought I think to impress upon you the urgency of not delaying those further measures which are necessary to secure our dockyards from destruction by surprise.' The Cabinet agreed that there should be no further reduction in the army, and that work on the fortifications at Portsmouth, Plymouth and Pembroke should be completed, while in January 1851 it approved further works at Portsmouth and Plymouth.[24]

But fortifications alone were not enough: as Anglesey had warned Palmerston, '*there are no men to place behind these fine works*'. This concern led the ministers to turn their attention back to the question of reviving the militia, with the Cabinet splitting between those, like Russell and Palmerston, who wanted a large, relatively well-trained force committed to serving anywhere in Britain, and their opponents including Grey and Wood, who disliked the cost and the disruption to industry and who were reluctant to consider anything more than a modest local defence force embodied only in time of war. Before the arguments were settled and a policy agreed, Louis Napoleon had consolidated his power in a *coup d'état*. Palmerston immediately recognised the new regime, without even consulting his colleagues; but this proved the final straw for Russell's long-suffering patience, and he promptly forced the Foreign Secretary to resign. The press and public opinion were outraged by the *coup* so that Palmerston lacked popular support on the question, while fears of war were greatly heightened in its wake. On 16 February 1852 Russell introduced the government's militia bill into the Commons. It gave Wellington most of what he had long wanted: a force of 150,000 men who would each receive 28 days training in their first year, and then a fortnight in each of the next four years; and it would be raised by ballot. However, Palmerston attacked the plan in Parliament, calling for a smaller, more professional force. With the aid of the protectionists and some of the Peelites, the government was defeated and resigned on 23 February.[25]

This time Stanley (now Lord Derby) was better prepared for the consequences of success, and managed to form a minority government, even though he could not persuade Palmerston or any of the Peelites to join him. The resulting ministry lacked experience and obvious talent, and it subsequently came to be known as the 'Who? Who? government', supposedly after Wellington's repeated query on being read a list of the new ministers. The story is almost certainly too good to be true; neither it, nor the nickname, seem to have been current until the late 1870s when a popular Liberal historian gave it wide currency. Derby's government introduced its own militia bill before the end of March, proposing a force of 80,000 volunteers, who would be trained for between 21 and 56 days each year. This proved surprisingly successful; 66,280 men had joined the militia by January 1854, while a large number of separate, mostly middle-class, volunteer corps, generally weekend riflemen with smart and expensive uniforms, also sprang up during the course of 1852, as the country showed an unexpected enthusiasm for part-time military service.[26]

Wellington, speaking in the Lords' debate on the twenty-seventh anniversary of Quatre Bras, welcomed the creation of the militia as a step in the right direction. But at the same time he bluntly told the Lords: 'We have never, up to this moment, maintained a proper peace establishment – that's the real truth; and we are now in that position in which we find ourselves forced to form a peace establishment, such as this country requires, upon a militia. As to the regular army, my Lords, I will tell you that, for the last ten years, you have never had in your army more men than enough to relieve the sentries on duty at your stations in the different parts of the world.' It was almost the last time he spoke in Parliament, but after a decade of pressing successive governments, he had at last seen the foundations laid for a force that would make Britain considerably less vulnerable to a sudden attack from France.[27]

Wellington's decade as Commander-in-Chief gave him a great deal of satisfaction. He enjoyed the renewed connection with the army, and it kept him close to the centre of power when Peel's government resigned, and gave him an official platform from which to address the Prime Minister, the Cabinet and Parliament, on the questions of national defence that mattered most to him. On the other hand, his advocacy was only partially successful. He was able to persuade successive prime ministers that the country's defences were lamentably weak and needed to be strengthened, and they managed to secure some increase in spending on the navy, and on fortifications to naval dockyards and arsenals. But he was not able to gain a sustained increase in the size of the regular army; while the creation of the militia in 1852 was a very belated success, so that Britain remained vulnerable to invasion throughout his whole tenure as Commander-in-Chief. In both 1846 and 1848 he came close to success, and it is not hard to see why, faced with the crisis in Ireland and the overthrow of the Orleans Monarchy in France, Peel and Russell backed away at the last minute, making a reasonable calculation that, in Russell's words, they should run the risk of inadequate defences. Events justified their decision, but Wellington had ensured that the case for increased spending had been made with clarity and force, and if war had come, the weakness of the army would not have been his fault.

Wellington's concern with national defence did not help his reputation in the years after his death. The context soon faded from view and many writers, including some otherwise well-informed biographers, assumed that talk of a French invasion was completely spurious, if not an old man's folly. The Crimean War led to a widespread popular belief that the British army had been frozen in the decades since Waterloo, and much of the blame for this was placed on Wellington and his reluctance to embrace 'reform'. In fact the criticism was misguided on many levels; the army itself performed quite well in the Crimea, and the greatest failings were in the support services which were the responsibility, not of the Horse Guards, but of civilian departments (the Treasury in the case of the commissariat). But more fundamentally, the British army in the decades since 1815 had been given certain clearly understood roles: it was to defend British colonies in a constant succession of colonial wars, some of them quite large and demanding; it was to assist the civil power in maintaining order at home and in Ireland; and, although it was not given sufficient resources to do so, it was to defend the country against invasion. There was never any suggestion that it might be required to mount a substantial expedition to the Continent at short notice, let alone to the most remote corner of Europe. If Wellington had proposed that the army be given the resources to be able to mount such an expedition, he would not have gained the support even of his closest colleagues, let alone Parliament and the press, and he would surely have been accused of preparing to re-fight the last war. Throughout his long life Wellington regarded war as a serious business which needed proper preparation and a mastery of detail; and he knew that short cuts and impulsive decisions usually lead to long delays and heavy casualties. We must wonder whether, if he had lived a little longer, the authority of his immense experience might not have dissuaded the government from embarking on the strategic absurdity of sending the army to the Black Sea and ultimately the Crimea.

CHAPTER THIRTY

IN THE MIDST OF LIFE
(1842–52)

WELLINGTON WAS IMMENSELY popular throughout the last decade of his life and, despite being at the centre of several intense controversies (notably over the repeal of the Corn Laws in 1846 and spending on national defence in 1847–48), was generally regarded with respect bordering on veneration as the embodiment of a glorious age that was rapidly receding over the horizon. As early as 1841 Greville wrote that the Waterloo Banquet had become 'a sort of national commemoration'; and in the following year noted that when Wellington arrived at a concert at Exeter Hall the 'singing stopt at once; the whole audience rose, and a burst of acclamation and waving of handkerchiefs saluted the great old man, who is now the Idol of the people'. Another friend described walking with Wellington through the streets of London: 'Recognition and reverence of all as usual. Hats were taken off; passers made excuse for stopping to gaze. Young surgeons on the steps of St George's Hospital forgot their lecture and their patients, and even the butcher's boy pulled up his cart as he stopped at the gate of Apsley House.'[1]

He remained very close to the centre of affairs and grumbled happily about the amount of work he was expected to do: 'Rest! Every other animal – even a donkey – a costermonger's donkey – is allowed some rest, but the Duke of Wellington never! There is no help for it. As long as I am able to go on, they will put a saddle upon my back and make me go.' That was in 1839 and more than a decade later, in October 1850, he continued to compare his lot unfavourably with that of the itinerant greengrocer's beast of burden: 'They treat me worse than the Costermonger's donkey.' Grumbling had always been one of his great pleasures and, like many men, he indulged in it more freely as he grew older. He did not really regard himself as superannuated, nor did he wish that the world would remember that he was eighty years old. There was more real feeling in his frequent complaint that deafness meant that he got little pleasure from society: 'The truth [is] that I am too deaf to render society with more than one Person otherwise than irksome to me, unless there should be such a Crowd as nearly to amount to a mob! – and when there is one of these small societies, I can neither read nor write nor follow any of my usual occupations.' This led him to give up most of the country house visits that had previously filled the autumn and early winter, although he continued to entertain guests at Walmer and sometimes had large parties at Stratfield Saye. But he remained extremely active in London, often attending a succession of different social events in the one evening.[2]

His health throughout his final decade was remarkably good; there was no repetition of the strokes of 1839–41, and his chief complaints were rheumatism, deafness and a propensity to catch cold through his ears at night. He did not consult doctors: 'If I did I must do as they order me – take their medicines which would do me no good, and leave me at last to my own resources! In truth there is but little the matter with me, and I prefer to go on as I am.'[3] His regime included moderation in what he ate and drank, exercise, and rubbing himself vigorously with diluted vinegar several times a day. Less than a month before he died, he boasted to a friend:

I certainly am a good Doctor, at least for myself. I never have any other! But I am a most severe one! My only remedy is temperance, and keeping the skin in order by ablution and friction. I eat very little, and never eat or drink anything that can disagree with my Stomach in the State in which I think it is! In this I am most severe towards myself. The consequence is that I am always well! never fatigued, and I can do anything! I have none of the infirmities of old age! excepting *Vanity* perhaps! . . . My deafness is accidental! If I was not deaf, I really believe that there is not a youth in London who could enjoy the world more than myself or could bear fatigue better! but being deaf, the spirit, not the body, tires! One gets bored, in boring others, and one becomes too happy to get home.[4]

These years saw the death of many of Wellington's remaining contemporaries, including all his siblings. Lord Wellesley, as was only fitting, was the first to go, in the autumn of 1842; Anne followed in 1844; William in 1845; Henry in 1847; Gerald in 1848; and William's widow, Lady Mornington, in 1851. An even greater blow was the death of Charles Arbuthnot on 18 August 1850. Arbuthnot had been Wellington's closest friend and companion for many years, and acted as a link, not just to their shared past, but also to current events, for ministers, even prime ministers, would often choose to approach the Duke through him in the first instance if they had a delicate or difficult issue to discuss. He brought life into Apsley House for he had many friends and acquaintances who would casually call in to see him, and who might also see

Wellington, but who would not dream of calling on the Duke unless they had some particular business to transact.[5]

Fortunately Wellington proved adept at making new friends right up to the end of his life, and this did much to lighten his last years. The most important of these friends was Angela Burdett-Coutts, and in this case friendship blossomed into a late and unexpected romance. She was born in 1814, the younger daughter of Sir Francis Burdett, the radical politician, and granddaughter of Thomas Coutts the banker, from whom (via his second wife) she inherited a vast fortune. She was sickened by the false suitors who attempted to woo her, but was close to Dickens and took his advice on good causes to support. She was religious, eager to do good, and, after the death of her parents in 1844 and marriage of her companion, rather lonely. She lived not far from Apsley House in Mayfair and had known Wellington slightly for years. In the summer of 1846 their friendship developed when she asked for his advice over a dispute with the directors of the bank, who were resisting her wish to raise the salaries of the clerks. Notes and visits were exchanged and when Wellington went to Walmer in September, Miss Burdett-Coutts stayed at Ramsgate and dined and spent the night with the other guests at the castle on several occasions. Constant correspondence and many small gifts followed; he sent her flowers and gloves and fussed over her health, sending her a pair of galoshes and urging her to wear them. He reassured her that there was no reason why she should not take up skating if she wished ('I have seen Ladies skait beautifully . . . as well at least as most Men'), and advised her about her charitable schemes ('You as well as I like and endeavour to do good effectually'). By the end of the year he was warmly attached to her, and she had fallen in love with him.[6]

When he called on her in London on 7 February 1847 she quietly proposed marriage. She was thirty-three and he was seventy-eight, but her grandfather Thomas Coutts had married, very happily, when he was eighty, a woman half his age; and after his death, his widow Harriot had married the Duke of St Albans when she was twice his age, so a great disparity of ages did not seem such an insuperable barrier to her. Wellington wrote to her the next morning, declining the proposal but writing with such tenderness and affection that the friendship survived:

My Dearest Angela,

I have passed every moment of the Evening and Night since I quitted you in reflecting upon our Conversation of yesterday, Every Word of which I have considered repeatedly. My first Duty towards you is that of Friend, Guardian, Protector. You are Young, My Dearest! You have before you the prospect of at least twenty years of enjoyment of Happiness of Life. I entreat you again in this way, not to throw yourself away upon a Man old enough to be your

Grandfather, who, however strong, Hearty and Healthy at present, must and will certainly in time feel the consequences and Infirmities of Age. You cannot know, but I do, the dismal consequences to you of this certainty. Hopeless for years! during which you will still be in the prime of your Life!

I cannot too often and too urgently entreat you to consider this well. I urge it as your friend, Guardian, Protector. But I must add, as I have frequently, that my own happiness depends upon it. My last days would be embittered by the reflection that your Life was uncomfortable and hopeless.

God Bless you My Dearest! Believe me Ever Yours

Wn.[7]

She visited him at Stratfield Saye and throughout 1847 he escorted her to balls and assemblies and paid her great attention. Naturally this provoked gossip; Greville oddly regarded it as proof of the 'decay in his vigorous mind', and rumours abounded of an impending marriage. In October she spent two months in France. He wrote constantly, telling her that he was 'enjoying the fine weather . . . reflecting upon your enjoyment of it in the walks of Paris! . . . I am delighted that you are amused because it is good for you! but don't imagine I doubt for a moment where your Mind, your Heart and Soul are during all these amusements. As mine are from morning till night and during the whole night.' Even more revealingly, he longed for the return of his 'companion . . . whom I look at and caress, who is happy and delighted and smiles on me in return!'[8]

Such fervour was too intense to last and by Christmas she was pointing out that his letters were 'not as they had been before'. He responded with warmth and gentle reassurance, but over the course of 1848 the romance faded and many of his letters came to be filled with excuses, that he was too old, too deaf, or too busy with official duties to accompany her to the next event on the social calendar. Even so her trust and kindness 'were the delight of his life', while she had 'released that spring of tenderness that, even in old age, kept his heart green'. During the course of the year she became more immersed in her charities, and he was preoccupied with public affairs, but they continued to meet and exchange letters frequently. In January 1851 he told her: 'I am very happy to learn that you are satisfied with the tickets for the House of Lords. To be sure! It does amuse me mightily at times to find a veteran of eighty-two years old, deaf with all! turned into a lover.' It seems unlikely that they were ever lovers in the most obvious sense – her strong moral principles made an affair most implausible, and while there were rumours of a secret marriage, this seems fanciful – but they were very close, and Wellington displayed a tender, loving and kind side of his character that is seldom even glimpsed in his earlier affairs. However, it is not clear whether old age had softened him, or whether he had previously shown similar affection and intimacy to others, both in person and in letters which have not survived. But it is not surprising that a man who could write such letters and woo with such sensitivity should have been on excellent terms with many women over a long life.[9]

Two other women shared Wellington's attentions in the last three years (1850–52) of his life, although the available evidence does not suggest that he was ever as attached to either of them as he was to Angela Burdett-Coutts. In 1847 Wellington's friend Lord Salisbury married the twenty-two-year-old Lady Mary Sackville-West. She was intelligent and charming but not beautiful, dressed with an eccentric plainness, and took a keen interest in politics and public affairs. Her father knew Wellington well, and she had been accustomed to seeing him when she was a child; at the age of ten she had ridden with him in his carriage amidst cheering crowds when he visited Cambridge. In London after her marriage she would walk with the Duke along the north side of Green Park almost every day, taking their 'quarter-deck' exercise, with a footman following twenty paces behind. Later she recalled: 'It is to *the* Duke that I owe the best of all the good that I have learnt, and in especial the forgiveness of injuries.' He was godfather to each of her children and took a close interest in their health, sharing her anxiety whenever they were ill. He wrote to her almost every day and once told her: 'I laugh while writing them, thinking of the amusement they will afford you.'[10]

Wellington's relations with Mrs Jones of Pantglas appear closer to a flirtation than a romance or a friendship. She was the young wife of a Welsh banker with political ambitions, and they mixed in the same political and social circles as the Duke. She asked him to sit for a portrait in August 1851, and they had daily rides together in the autumn when he was at Walmer and she was staying nearby. She left her children behind with their governess when she accompanied her husband on a round of country house visits, and Wellington would often look in on them when he was in Dover, reporting on their health, and ensuring that they were well looked after when they fell ill with measles. Effie Ruskin, writing soon after Wellington's death, was censorious:

As far as he is concerned it is much better that he is dead for this love affair he had with Mrs Jones during this last Season was very unbecoming. He always was in love with someone but had never made himself ridiculous till this one which was a source of grief to his family and made him laughed at by every empty-headed fool in London. They say he never passed a day without seeing her and every where she went she took him with her and sometimes took him to very queer places. At every party Mrs Jones and the 'Dook' were ushered in together as she has never been known to blush since she came to town. I daresay she will feel no remorse at all for making the last years of so great a Hero contemptible, when perhaps she might have done him some lasting service.[11]

However, it seems likely that this reflected Mrs Ruskin's own frustrations rather than anything inherently ridiculous in a relationship that gave obvious pleasure to both parties.[12]

Nonetheless there were risks in such flirtations, as Wellington discovered when Lady Georgiana Fane threatened to sue him for breach of promise over indiscreet letters he had written her many years before. According to Greville: 'All she wants is that He should behave *kindly* to her, which is just what he will not do.' He refused to see her, so she attempted to ambush him as he came out of church, and wrote him what he described as 'daily vituperative letters'. Driven to desperation in the autumn of 1851, he wrote to her mother asking her to intercede and restrain her daughter. It is not clear if this appeal was successful, but an open scandal was avoided.[13]

Closer to home, Wellington's niece Priscilla, Lady Westmorland remained a favourite; indeed according to a friend of the Duke, she was, of all his relatives, 'certainly the one most devoted to him, and most in his confidence'. A painter herself, she acted as an intermediary with artists and, at times, with politicians; and she did something to fill the irreparable gap left by the death of Charles Arbuthnot. Wellington did not confide much in his sons, but the conflicts and disappointment of earlier years had passed and their relations had settled into an undemanding if not especially rewarding pattern. He was particularly fond of his daughter-in-law Lady Douro, shared her disappointment that she did not have children, and was concerned for her health. Lord Charles Wellesley, the Duke's younger son, was a popular member of the Queen's household from 1841 to 1846, and an unobtrusive member of the Commons from 1842 to 1855, following Peel in office and out. In 1844 Lord Charles married Sophia Pierrepont, niece of Lord Manvers, and they had six children, three boys and three girls. The eldest son Arthur died in July 1846 aged only fourteen months and Wellington felt the loss acutely, Lady Westmorland writing that 'I found the Duke yesterday very low and I think more grieved for the poor child's death than the day before'.[14]

Wellington delighted in his grandchildren, in his great-nieces and -nephews, and in the children of friends, playing with them without the slightest concern for his ducal dignity. In 1839 the artist Benjamin Robert Haydon was visiting Walmer to paint Wellington's portrait and was enjoying a hearty breakfast when:

six dear, healthy, noisy children were brought to the windows. 'Let them in,' said the Duke, and in they came, and rushed over to him saying: 'How d'ye do,

Duke, how d'ye do, Duke?' One boy, young Gray, roared: 'I want some tea, Duke.' 'You shall have it, if you promise not to slop it over me, as you did yesterday.' Toast and tea were then in demand. Three got on one side and three on the other, and he hugged 'em all. Tea was poured out, and I saw little Gray try to slop it over the Duke's frock coat . . . They all then rushed out on the leads, by the cannon, and after breakfast I saw the Duke romping with the whole of them, and one of them gave his Grace a devil of a thump . . . [The Duke] put his head out at the door . . . and said: 'I'll catch ye! – ha, ha, I've got ye!' at which they all ran away. He looked at them and laughed and went in.[15]

More than ten years later, when he was eighty-two, he told Mrs Jones: 'I cannot tell you how much I enjoy and prize the affection which children have for me. When they become familiar with me I believe that they consider me one of themselves, and make me a sort of plaything! They climb upon me and make toys of my Hair and my fingers! They grow up into friends. I have known most of the fine ladies about London as children.' Rose Fane, the youngest of Lady Westmorland's children, recalled: 'The idea of being afraid of him never entered the children's minds, and if some proposed escapade did not meet with the approval of their elders or some of the old retainers, a satisfactory solution was always felt to be assured when some one suggested, "Let's ask the Duke if we may."' And her mother commented on 'the delight he took in their prattle and remarks, and his dislike to any severity being used tow[ar]ds them. He liked to praise them, and always said the best way to make a child good was to show him that he was considered a good child.'[16]

Wellington sat to many artists besides Haydon in the last years of his life, grumbling incessantly at the time it took, but seldom, if ever, actually refusing. None of these late portraits match the brilliance of Lawrence's work, but a few are worth noting. There is the daguerreotype taken by Antoine Claudet, in May 1844, showing an impeccably dressed, white-haired old gentleman staring contemplatively, or even sadly, to one side of the viewer. Wintherhalter's twin portrait of Wellington and Peel dates from the same year; Peel is taller and twenty years younger, but Wellington's erect carriage gives him an air of greater confidence. The *Daily News* commented: 'No picture ever before gave so completely the character of both, with the additional interest accruing from the proximity of two men so long connected in life.' One of the last portraits of Wellington painted from life was an unusually large miniature on ivory of the Duke and his grandchildren by Robert Thorburn, commissioned by Angela Burdett-Coutts. Unfortunately the artist made little or no effort to avoid the risks of sentimentality implicit in the choice of subject, and the work gives a fair indication of the effect of a generation of progress on British taste.[17]

Progress and prosperity were famously celebrated at the Great Exhibition at the Crystal Palace in Hyde Park, which opened on 1 May 1851, the day Wellington celebrated his eighty-second birthday. The idea of a display of arts, products and machinery from all round the world deliberately attracting vast crowds including many foreigners was a novelty, and there were concerns, which Wellington and the Cabinet shared, of possible disorders created by local radicals or foreign revolutionaries. Wellington was officially involved both as Commander-in-Chief and as chief ranger of Hyde Park, a position to which he was appointed in August 1850. He prepared detailed plans to deal with trouble if it arose, and firmly rejected Russell's suggestion that they consult the French police for advice on how to deal with riotous crowds.[18]

In the months and weeks before the opening of the Exhibition the press was full of stories of the disasters and dangers that might occur. On 19 April the *Hampshire Advertiser and Salisbury Guardian* published a column which almost by accident launched one of the most famous and durable of Wellington anecdotes. According to this well-written *jeu d'esprit* myriad sparrows had taken up residence in the Crystal Palace and the organising committee was at a loss how to remove them. The Queen, anxious that Albert's event be a success, sent for Lord John Russell, but none of his suggestions (shooting, netting and fumigating) were of the least use. The Bishop of London was next consulted, but proved equally unhelpful. Finally the Queen appealed to Wellington. His initial response was to draft a reply in the third-person style for which he was famous: 'Field Marshal the Duke of Wellington is Commander-in-Chief of her Majesty's land forces, and as such, thinks the service upon which he is summoned out of his province. . . . Field Marshal the Duke of Wellington has had considerable experience capturing French eagles, but none in taking English sparrows.' But he repented and tore up the note as soon as it was written, and rode to Buckingham Palace where he solved the problem with the simple solution: 'A Sparrow Hawk.' Meanwhile the sparrows had kept a close eye on what was passing at Buckingham Palace. When their spies reported Lord John Russell's suggestions they were unconcerned and concluded that the Prime Minister had seen better days, while the appeal to the Bishop was met with mirthful twitterings. But the news that the Duke was sent for was met with trepidation, and as soon as they heard the word 'sparrowhawk' they decided to decamp, their leader declaring: 'That horrid old Duke, I was afraid he would hit upon an expedient.' The story became popular and was retold with many variants, with Palmerston frequently being substituted for the Bishop of London, and the punchline expanded to: 'Try sparrowhawks, Ma'am.' In time its origins were forgotten and it was treated seriously as proof of the Duke's robust common sense, although a moment's reflection should have shown that the whole tale was inherently absurd. Stories such as this simultaneously celebrated and trivialised Wellington's life and character; they began as the icing on the cake, but they were so palatable that they were remembered, while the cake – the real achievements of Wellington's life – was half forgotten; but icing without cake is sickly and unsatisfying.[19]

Wellington was intrigued by the Exhibition, visiting it almost every day and seeking out the most interesting displays to recommend to his friends. He was disappointed not to be able to purchase any of the Irish cambric on display for Lady Salisbury (the sale of exhibits was forbidden), but obtained some swatches for her to choose from, and noted the continuing progress in the French displays, which had not been completed at the time of his first visit.[20]

There were few signs of a slackening of the pace in the last year of Wellington's life. In the autumn of 1851 he was writing constantly to Angela Burdett-Coutts, Lady Salisbury and Mrs Jones, as well as all his official and miscellaneous correspondence. He took a keen and somewhat apprehensive interest in the news of Louis Napoleon's coup in Paris and, in common with the rest of the world, speculated on the implications of Palmerston's sudden dismissal from the Foreign Office. At the end of the year he was engaged in a sharp test of wills with Lord Grey over the recall of Sir Harry Smith from South Africa, while February brought the fall of Russell's government amidst discussions and debates over rival plans for the militia. In June he celebrated the thirty-seventh anniversary of Waterloo with a banquet for eighty guests including Prince Albert. After the food had been eaten and fourteen toasts had been drunk, the Prince and other guests departed and the eighty-three-year-old Duke, accompanied by Fitzroy Somerset, sallied forth to put in an appearance at the Duchess of Beaufort's reception. On 1 July he carried the Sword of State at the ceremonial closing of Parliament; according to the report in *The Times* he was in uniform under his peer's robes and looked remarkably well, but found the task of holding the massive sword upright throughout the Queen's lengthy address a considerable effort. Nonetheless on the following day he finished writing a long paper on the war in South Africa, and poured cold water on a scheme for a military *corps de reserve* for young gentlemen; then he attended a concert at the Duke of Beaufort's (where the rooms were too hot) and had a dinner for the Archbishop of Armagh and a party of Irish friends.[21]

At the end of the season Wellington left London and went to Walmer as usual, and on 25 August he wrote to Lady Salisbury of an old acquaintance he had seen: 'I never saw such a wreck! He has had the gout, and I do not think that in ten years I shall be as bad as he is now!' Grand Duchess Catherine of Russia and her husband Prince George of Mecklenburg-Strelitz stayed for a night, and although Wellington grumbled a great deal beforehand about the inconvenience, it is clear that he was charmed by the Grand Duchess and thoroughly enjoyed the visit. On 2 September he took the train from Dover to

Folkestone to visit Croker, only to find, after a long walk from the station, that Croker had gone to visit him! He repeated the journey with more success two days later and the old friends spent three hours together 'chatting in the most agreeable manner on all manner of subjects, with a vivacity and memory worth noting in a man in his 84th year. We were both deaf [Croker noted in an account of the meeting written at the time]. I worse than usual today, and he, though he walks very well in fact, seems to totter: but this he has done for some years. Both our minds, however, seem as clear as ever.'[22]

On 13 September Wellington was in good spirits welcoming Charles, Sophia and their children, writing letters, enjoying the sheltered garden, and eating a substantial dinner before retiring to bed. He looked forward to the arrival of Lady Westmorland on the following day for a brief visit on her way to the Continent, and Lady Salisbury the day after. The next morning, 14 September 1852, he felt unwell and asked Kendall, his valet, to send for the local doctor. Dr Hulke arrived and found his pulse irregular but no alarming symptoms. When he had gone, Kendall asked if the Duke would like some tea. '*Yes if you please.*' They were his last words, and were followed by a succession of seizures (possibly epileptic fits, possibly strokes) which the doctor was powerless to stop. About two in the afternoon, at Kendall's suggestion, the Duke was lifted into his favourite chair, and there, at a quarter past three, with his family, servants and doctors around him, he died.[23]

Lady Westmorland arrived at the castle barely an hour later. Lord Clanwilliam had met her in Dover and warned her that the Duke had been taken gravely ill, and she went straight upstairs and saw him 'lying on his bed in the room where I have spent so many hours with him, looking just as if he was asleep, calm and placid, and I kissed his dear face which was still warm'. And she went on to tell her husband: 'I am deeply affected, and yet I feel it is not an event which we *ought* to mourn – for it has been a happy death to him without pain or suffering and in the *full* possession of all his faculties up to the last. But what a Loss! to the Country – to the Government – to *us* – and indeed to the world!'[24]

Lady Westmorland's views were echoed in many of the reactions to the Duke's death. Queen Victoria, who heard the news when on an excursion into a wild part of the Highlands from Balmoral, wrote:

For *him* it is a blessing that he should have been taken away in the possession of his great and powerful mind and without a lingering illness. But for this country, and for us, his loss – though it could not have been long delayed – is irreparable! He was the pride and the *bon génie*, as it were, of this country! He was the GREATEST man this country ever produced, and the most *devoted* and *loyal* subject, and the staunchest supporter the Crown ever had. He was to us a true, kind friend and most valuable adviser.[25]

Brougham wrote that 'I feel as if the world were no longer the same as it has been', and Lady Georgiana Bathurst agreed: 'How it takes one by surprise . . . it seems as if it would quite alter one's existence. The world without that great name . . .' At the other end of the social and political spectrum, Thomas Cooper, a former Chartist, reflected that Wellington 'was an institution in himself. We all felt as if we lived, now he was dead, in a different England . . . I seemed myself to belong now to another generation of men; for my very childhood was passed amid the noise of Wellington's battles, and his name and existence seemed stamped on every year of our time.'[26]

The Queen and the Prime Minister agreed that the Duke should be given a state funeral, even though this would necessitate a delay of two months for Parliament to meet and grant its approval. Prince Albert was keen that the whole funeral, and in particular the design of the funeral car, 'should do justice to the immense services of the illustrious individual and at the same time do credit to the taste of the artists of England'; while the Queen expressed her desire that 'the greatest possible number of her subjects should have an opportunity of joining in it', and that it should have 'a thoroughly national character'. She also hoped that the funeral would have a wider political purpose, acting as a useful reminder to France of the allied victories of 1814 and 1815 at a time when Louis Napoleon was moving towards the proclamation of the Second Empire. *Punch* agreed that 'it was well and judicious to advertise . . . [to] the world with what enthusiasm we yet honour military heroism: that if we have abjured the love of strife, we have not renounced the spirit of valour'.[27]

The Duke's body was placed inside a simple deal shell made by the carpenter at Walmer, and this in turn was placed inside three coffins made of lead, oak and mahogany, covered in red velvet and decorated with the Garter star, the Duke's arms, and abundant gilt nails, handles and corner pieces. It lay in the little room in which the Duke died, now covered in black cloth and with a guard of honour from the Rifle Brigade, until the evening of 10 November, and on the last two days some nine or ten thousand local people were permitted to come and pay their final respects. It was transported from Walmer to Deal railway station in a torchlight procession with the family and mourners following in three coaches. In London it was met by the Lord Chamberlain and his staff who escorted it, accompanied by one hundred men of the Grenadier Guards, to Chelsea Hospital where it lay in state for a week. The hall was draped in black, the cloth trellised with silver cord. Pairs of soldiers stood like statues in niches around the walls, their heads bowed and their arms reversed. The room was illuminated by eighty-three enormous candles and the coffin sat on a dais forty-five feet wide by thirty-five feet deep, covered in cloth of gold, while on the table at the foot of the coffin lay all the Duke's medals and decorations.[28]

Although the family disliked the grandeur, the lying-in-state proved enormously popular. On the first two days admission was reserved for those granted a ticket. The Queen and Prince Albert attended on 11 November with their children, and on the next day a line of carriages two miles long blocked the entrance, and many of those with tickets had to be turned away. The weather was dreadful, but this only added to the mood of the occasion. The police completely misjudged the size of the crowd that would seek admission on the remaining days, and at least two people were killed in the crush, and there were reports of many injuries and of other deaths. The second Duke was disgusted by the mismanagement and at least half regretted agreeing to the public funeral; but the popular response was extraordinary, with more than 260,000 people attending the lying-in-state, and despite the throng outside most reports suggest that their behaviour was quiet and respectful as they filed through the hall.[29]

The shops in London were full of mourning clothes, while armlets and hatbands inscribed with 'Wellington died Sept. 14 1852' encircled with cypress and laurel were widely advertised. Opticians promoted special glasses that would enable spectators to see the details of the funeral procession from a distance, and the promotion of Wellington Funeral Cake and Wellington Funeral Wine suggests that the spirit of enterprise was flourishing. Commemorative plates and plaques, miniature and life-size busts, equestrian statuettes, prints of portraits and scenes of Waterloo and other victories, reprints of biographies and numerous catchpenny publications which purported to collect the authentic anecdotes and sayings of the great man, without any great concern for accuracy, all found a ready market.[30]

But the greatest demand was for seats with a good view of the route of the funeral procession. The coffin was moved from Chelsea to the Horse Guards on the night of 17 November, but the route from the Horse Guards to St Paul's was deliberately circuitous so that it would run past Buckingham Palace, up Constitution Hill, past Apsley House, along Piccadilly and St James's Street to Pall Mall, then Charing Cross, the Strand and Fleet Street to the cathedral. Advertisements for good seats, some with a bed for the previous night, began to appear in October. Churches along the route were assiduous in exploiting the commercial potential of their location, erecting stands in their grounds and selling seats at high prices (a guinea or more), with the proceeds going to parochial charities. A good first-floor room in Piccadilly might be let for the day for £60; while some, with a bay window, were reported to have fetched up to one hundred guineas. Near Somerset House, in the less fashionable part of town, a room that could accommodate twenty persons might be had for £25 with a cold collation included in the price; while for those with a head for heights a roof seat on the Strand cost a mere 4 shillings 6 pence.[31]

Thomas Cook organised special trains to London, both for the lying-in-state and the funeral itself, with one beginning as far north as Aberdeen and taking several days to complete the journey. For those who could not afford to go to London, church services were held in cities and towns across Britain, often preceded by civic processions, and shops and businesses were widely closed for half or the whole day. In Bristol the cathedral was packed for a memorial service, while in Exeter the large congregation 'fervently and earnestly [took] part in the solemn devotions'. At Portsmouth, flags flew at half-mast both on shore and on the ships in the harbour, minute guns were fired, muffled bells pealed, and mourning was widely worn. In Leeds, the 'silence and decorum of a Sabbath day was strictly observed in all the principal thoroughfares' and 'the feelings of sorrow on the mournful occasion of the sorrow were unanimous'. Further afield, Lord Dalhousie reported that 'the highest honours have been paid to the memory of the Duke of Wellington', not just in British India, but in Nepal, while in Mysore the Raja ordered that the festival of *dussehra* be suspended in the city as a mark of his grief. Public interest in the event was also indicated by the unprecedented sales of the *Illustrated London News*, amounting to nearly two million copies for the two issues following the funeral. In many ways the Duke's funeral marked an important point in the transition from an aristocratic world of heraldic display (which was prominent in the funeral procession but already felt by many to be archaic), to the more modern world of mass participation and media coverage.[32]

The morning of 18 November dawned dark, windy and wet after a night of heavy rain; the clouds cleared during the morning, although a bitingly cold west wind remained. At eight o'clock the first minute gun fired and the procession commenced its slow march from the Horse Guards. It was led by the second battalion of the Rifle Brigade – the old 95th from the Peninsula and Waterloo – with its band at its head playing sombre music and with muffled drums beating, and the soldiers carrying their arms reversed, marching at a slow pace. Five more battalions of infantry, seventeen guns and eight regiments of cavalry followed, together with a composite unit consisting of one man from every regiment in the British army. Eighty-three Chelsea Pensioners joined the procession at Charing Cross, while a long line of carriages contained representatives of institutions associated with Wellington and senior members of the government and judiciary, culminating in Prince Albert. The cumbrous funeral car, drawn by twelve black horses, carried the coffin on which rested Wellington's hat and sword. Wellington's sons and other male relatives followed in several mourning coaches, while the most poignant sight was generally felt to be the Duke's riderless horse, led by a groom and with his empty boots, reversed, in the stirrups. Moving slowly, the procession took nearly two hours to pass any point. The Queen, who was forbidden by protocol from attending the funeral of any subject, however distinguished, watched the procession first from Buckingham Palace (where the funeral car paused for some time), and then again from St James's Palace. She was much moved, for it was 'the first funeral of anyone I had known and who was dear to me that I had ever seen'.[33]

An immense crowd watched the procession. *The Times* estimated it at one and a half million, but it seems likely that this was no more than a guess and may well have been greatly inflated. All accounts suggest that the spectators behaved extremely well, heads were bared and the mood solemn and respectful. Just before noon the funeral car reached St Paul's, but the ingenious mechanism for lowering the body failed to work, and a delay of nearly an hour followed during which the old soldiers and eminent clerics gathered near the doorway felt the full effects of the westerly wind. The cathedral itself was densely crowded, mostly with men but with a significant section set aside for peeresses, their friends and other ladies. The service lasted some two hours and included Psalms 39 and 90 set to music composed by the Duke's father, and the *Nunc dimittis* accompanied by music adapted from Beethoven's seventh symphony. A dirge with words from the Second Book of Samuel followed: 'And the King said to all the people that were with him, "Rend your clothes and gird you with sackcloth and mourn." And the King himself followed the bier. And they buried him. And the King lifted up his voice and wept at the grave, and all the people wept. And the King said unto his servants, "Know ye not that there is a Prince and a great man fallen this day in Israel?" ' Then the coffin was slowly lowered into the crypt to the sound of Handel's 'Dead March' from *Saul*, and the Garter King of Arms read all the Duke's titles and honours. 'And thus,' as *The Times* concluded its account of the service, 'was buried, with all state and honour, the great Duke of Wellington.'[34]

The Tower Guns boomed forth, the trumpets at the western end of the cathedral played, and all across the land church bells tolled. Already the crowds in the streets were dispersing. It had been a long day and a remarkable occasion, giving rise to feelings of pride and satisfaction, but also reflections on fame and mortality. It was something to remember, something to tell the grandchildren, the day they buried the Duke of Wellington; but now it was over, and it was time to go home.

Conclusion

Few men, at least in Britain, have ever been buried with greater honours or more praise than the Duke of Wellington. The eulogies were unrestrained, describing him not just as the greatest Englishman of his age, but the greatest man of the time of any nationality, and the greatest Englishman of any age. He was the saviour of his country and of the world, the conqueror of Napoleon and, in the words of the Queen, 'Britain's pride, her glory, her hero'.[1] But while Wellington's military triumphs were described in great detail, and his private character was extolled, his political career was deliberately downplayed, old controversies were passed over, and he was presented as an essentially non-partisan national hero. However, this is at best a partial view of Wellington's career which seriously distorted the story of his life. It is easy to understand that one motive for this approach was the desire to avoid reviving past quarrels and to remember the great man – and in 1852 there was an almost universal consensus that he was a great man – in ways that old opponents, as well as allies, could embrace. But there was also a sense, which only grew stronger in the years that followed, that Wellington's career in politics in the years after 1818 was, on the whole, a mistake; and that he had failed to support the cause of progress and enlightenment. This in turn led to the depiction of Wellington as a straightforward, simple soldier, impelled by his sense of duty into the murky and distasteful world of politics where he was quite out of his depth. And, because studies of British politics up until the 1980s were almost all written from a liberal or radical perspective, it is an image that proved remarkably enduring.

Nonetheless, any examination of Wellington's life shows that his political and military careers were closely intertwined and that one cannot be properly understood without the other. As a young man he was not just a junior officer in the army but an ADC to the Lord Lieutenant of Ireland, and, thanks to his brother, had better connections in the higher reaches of government than in the army. He became an MP in the Irish Parliament before he saw a shot fired in action, and after his first experience of war he attempted to quit the army and obtain a civil office. On his return to England from India he entered Parliament to defend his brother's reputation, and was soon well known to many leading ministers and some important members of the Opposition. He held an important and difficult office in the Portland government, only one step below Cabinet rank, and was responsible both for defending the government's Irish policies in the Commons and for maintaining its influence with Irish MPs.

His early campaigns in the Peninsula provoked intense political controversy which was heightened by his political prominence. But equally it was his personal contact with ministers that convinced them of his ability and gave them the confidence to send him back to Portugal in 1809, and to support his subsequent campaigns. The return of Napoleon in 1815 brought fresh controversy with Whitbread's attack on his role in framing the declaration of the allied powers, while many Whigs and liberals opposed the renewal of the war. And in the years after Waterloo Wellington's reputation and the place of the army in British society were at the forefront of radical criticism of the government. He was depicted as a potential dictator, eager to rule through force alone and a danger to the constitution. This was another reason why the obituaries minimised the role of politics in Wellington's career: it was embarrassing to be reminded that the forces of progress and enlightenment could have been so mistaken.

When Wellington came home from France at the end of 1818 he joined the Cabinet as Master-General of the Ordnance – an office with one foot in the military and the other in the political world. In 1827 he accepted the position of Commander-in-Chief, and his subsequent resignation, re-appointment and second resignation demonstrate how closely his military and political careers interacted. In the 1830s he took a leading part in defending the army in political controversies ranging from the use of flogging to the expansion of the power of the War Office at the expense of the Horse Guards; while from 1842 to 1846 he was simultaneously a member of Peel's Cabinet, leader of the government in the Lords, and Commander-in-Chief. Even after he ostensibly withdrew from active politics in 1846 he retained great political influence and used it to strengthen his hand in his negotiations with the ministers over their plans for the army.

Wellington's whole career was made up of military and political strands woven together, each strengthening the other, although criticism of him could also spill from one field to the other. His youthful experience of Irish politics broadened his perspective and gave him confidence in dealing with the most senior figures in British India when he arrived as a twenty-seven-year-old lieutenant-colonel in 1797. In the Peninsula he was painfully aware of the vehemence of the criticism of his campaigns by the Whigs and radicals, and of the weakness and doubtful prospects of the British ministries he served, but unlike Marlborough and many other generals before and since, he firmly resisted the temptation to intervene in domestic politics. He made no attempt to build up an independent interest with George III or the Prince Regent, to cultivate the press, or seek to come to an arrangement with the Opposition. He even distanced himself from Castlereagh and Lord Wellesley when they were out of office, and gave the ministers of the day his loyal service, while making it clear that he would be willing to serve any government that wished to employ him.

From the time of his first arrival in India Wellington's correspondence shows remarkable confidence and breadth of vision, while his connection with Lord Wellesley encouraged him to consider the largest issues of war and peace, alliances and pre-emptive action. Preparing for the advance on Seringapatam brought home the crucial significance of logistics (although his experiences in the Low Countries had probably already made this plain); and he also soon displayed his lifelong concern to protect the civilian population as far as possible from the ravages of war. After defeating the Marathas in 1803 he argued for a policy of moderation and looked to establish stability and a durable settlement rather than the acquisition of as much territory and plunder as possible.

In all his campaigns, in India, the Peninsula and Belgium, he spent a great deal of time and energy in diplomacy, negotiating with allied governments and arranging the details of co-operation with their forces, whether as contingents under his command or as independent armies. He bullied and badgered the British government remorselessly for more men, equipment and above all money, and – less creditably – never gave the ministers the recognition they deserved for supporting and sustaining his campaigns. He dealt with an enormous range of miscellaneous subjects, ranging from a conspiracy in the French army against Napoleon, to the health of the bullocks that carried his supplies in India. He kept a close eye on the fluctuations in the price of specie (gold and silver coin) at Lisbon, Cadiz and throughout the Mediterranean, and was alert to the significance for the supply of grain to his army in Portugal of war in the Baltic or with the United States. The balance of forces in the Peninsula was often shaped by events in central and eastern Europe, while the possibility of the allies making peace with Napoleon influenced Wellington's strategy in 1813 and 1814. And he trod a careful line with the exiled Bourbons in both 1814 and 1815, not committing the British government to their restoration, but not discouraging risings in their favour.

Wellington was central to the British commitment to the Peninsula from 1809 to the end of the war. He grasped the underlying dynamics of the war at the very beginning, even before he landed at Mondego Bay in 1808, and saw how a British army, working with the Portuguese, could lend vital support to the Spaniards, while they in turn prevented the French from concentrating all their forces against the Anglo-Portuguese army. He recognised that French occupation would not quench Spanish resistance so long as the war continued elsewhere in the country, and that the more the French dispersed their armies to occupy territory, the fewer troops they would have available to mount fresh offensives. He anticipated the French invasion of Portugal in 1810, and prepared an extraordinarily comprehensive and thorough plan to defeat it, that converted natural weaknesses into strengths and took full advantage of the popular hatred aroused by the experience of the previous French occupations of parts of the country. Through months of long waiting he held his nerve when those around him saw no grounds for confidence, and bore the full burden of responsibility for success or failure on his shoulders, not without a good deal of grumbling, but without buckling under the strain.

Wellington always had a very clear understanding of the capabilities of his army and worked incessantly to improve it. His constant insistence that regimental officers attend to their men, and his refusal to turn a blind eye to plundering, did not make him popular, but it infused a spirit of professionalism and discipline into the army that bore an increasing harvest as the war progressed. Equally his unremitting attention to logistics underlay the improvement in the army and its growing mobility. Like most successful generals Wellington was not a great innovator; he took the tools at hand and honed them to new sharpness, and then combined them into a much more effective whole. Nonetheless his army was not, as has sometimes been suggested, an eighteenth-century army: it was much looser and more flexible than that, both on and off the battlefield, while his tactics and strategy were both thoroughly modern, building on, not ignoring, the lessons Napoleon had taught the military world. No British commander in living memory had commanded such a large army in the field in extended operations, and Wellington developed the bare idea of divisions into cohesive units that could manoeuvre and fight independently. Equally he recognised the potential of the elite light infantry created by others and employed it as his spearhead, and made good use of the rich sources of intelligence at his disposal.

In India and in his early campaigns (1808–1809) in the Peninsula, Wellington displayed ruthless aggression, seizing the initiative and taking the war to the enemy. Unlike most generals of his time he was not in the least intimidated in facing the French, and he almost never lost his nerve (the most obvious exception being a little before the outbreak of the Maratha war when the army's baggage cattle were being decimated by disease and privation). His attack at Oporto was extraordinarily bold, while the advance to Talavera was a well-calculated gamble that only failed because the French had, quite coincidentally, evacuated Galicia. Faced with the massive influx of French forces into the Peninsula in late 1809 and 1810 Wellington became much more cautious and defensive, and it is from this era that his reputation as a Fabian general is derived. Yet by the middle of 1811 he had recovered the strategic initiative, and 1812 saw a succession of triumphs including the capture of the two great border fortresses, the destruction of Marmont's army at Salamanca, the entry into Madrid, and the French evacuation of Andalusia. By abandoning so much territory the French were able to concentrate an overwhelming force against Wellington and force him to retreat back from Burgos to the Portuguese frontier, but the credibility of the Bonaparte Kingdom of Spain and the confidence of the French troops had both been dealt an irreparable blow. The advance to Vitoria in 1813 was a strategic master-stroke which prevented the French from concentrating their still superior forces against him, and which led to the rout of their demoralised army and their withdrawal to the Pyrenees. Wellington paused and consolidated his position on the French frontier for the rest of the year, waiting to see if Napoleon would accept a negotiated peace and how the allies would fare in their campaign in Germany. When the allies began their invasion of France he resumed his advance, pressing forward through Gascony and capturing Bordeaux and Toulouse before Napoleon finally abdicated. In 1815 Wellington stood on the defensive both tactically and strategically, waiting for the other powers to bring their armies into position before beginning the campaign, while his heterogeneous army was far better suited to the passive endurance required in defending a position than moving to the attack.

All generals make mistakes, and Wellington was no exception. The strangest and most unaccountable was his conduct of the Burgos campaign, and in particular his failure to bring up a siege train. But the strategic problem he was facing was probably insoluble and, even if Burgos had fallen rapidly and with little cost, it is unlikely that the allies could have maintained their advanced positions over the winter, although that does not excuse the errors committed in the operation. Other mistakes were retrieved without much harm being done; he occupied too extensive a position at Fuentes d'Oñoro, and was caught off guard at El Bodon, but in neither case were the French able to exploit their advantage. And he was clearly slow to react at the outset of the Waterloo campaign, especially as he and Blücher had decided to try to hold a very advanced line. Wellington's sieges were less successful than his battles, and although the circumstances in each case were rather different, some responsibility rests with Wellington, although much credit needs also to be given to the quality, determination and ingenuity of the French defence.

But these were small blemishes on a remarkable record of success. Wellington was victorious in every significant battle he fought – more than a dozen in the Peninsula and almost twenty in all. These ranged from meticulously planned and brilliantly executed operations against a strongly posted enemy (the passage of the Bidassoa, and Nivelle), to dour battles of attrition and endurance (Waterloo); from battles where he had to scramble to recover a misstep (Roliça, Fuentes de Oñoro), to battles where he seized an opportunity and launched his army into a sudden, unplanned attack (Assaye, Oporto, Salamanca). Some of his battles were easily won (Argaum, Busaco, the passage of the Bidassoa), and some were extremely hard-fought (Talavera, Waterloo); but his tactical ability, boldness and leadership were central to all of them. There was no single secret to his success, not 'column and line', or the use of terrain, or the handling of reserves; the tactics and methods employed varied according to circumstances, and this flexibility helps explain his success. Wellington raised the British army to an unprecedented level of efficiency and confidence until it was unmatched by any force of its size in the world. He triumphed despite the doubts of the officers of his own army and of many leading politicians at home. He made effective use in all his campaigns of allies of doubtful ability or loyalty, and took great care to gain the support of the local population even when operating in the enemy's home country. No other British general, and few generals of any nationality, have such an impressive record.

After Waterloo, Wellington told Lady Shelley: 'I hope to God that I have fought my last battle. It is a bad thing to be always fighting. While in the thick of it I am too much occupied to feel anything; but it is wretched just after. It is quite impossible to think of glory. Both mind and feelings are exhausted. I am wretched even at the moment of victory, and I always say that, next to a battle lost, the greatest misery is a battle gained.'[2] Wellington was a superb soldier, who found immense satisfaction in exercising his talents, but unlike many of his contemporaries he did not romanticise war or regard it as anything but an inescapable evil. At the Congress of Vienna, and again at Paris after Waterloo, he worked hard to smooth differences between the continental powers, and threw all his influence behind Castlereagh's efforts to moderate the terms imposed on France, so that her resentment would not breed fresh conflicts. In the years that followed he constantly endeavoured to keep Britain on good terms with all the continental powers, and to seek peaceful solutions to conflicts when they arose. He supported the restoration of 'legitimate' governments, believing that they offered the best hope of stability at home and peace abroad, but he also warned against the excesses of absolutist regimes, urging Ferdinand VII to moderate his repression of the Spanish *liberales*, being dismayed by the policies and especially the language adopted by the Eastern Powers at Troppau, and disowning the attempt by Polignac and Charles X to repress the *liberales* and retain power in France through the ordinances of

1830. His advice was frequently rejected, while liberal opinion in Britain condemned him by association. His inability, and that of Castlereagh, to persuade the public to accept their view of British foreign policy, left the way open for Canning and Palmerston to win support for their more belligerent policies.

Despite his experience of the Commons, his years as a minister and excellent political connections, Wellington was ambivalent about politics and was slow to embrace his new position when he entered Cabinet at the end of 1818. In the Peninsula he had told a friend, 'I always detested home politics', and he wrote contemptuously to his brother William of 'the Wise Gentlemen in the Debating Society'.[3] In his first years in Cabinet he concentrated his attention on the tasks of executive government: reforming the Ordnance, supporting Castlereagh's foreign policy, and advising his colleagues on the military measures needed to deal with the radical agitation of 1819–1821. He adapted to a relatively subordinate position in the government with surprising ease, especially given his difficulties with military superiors earlier in his career, while at times playing a useful role as mediator between the King and the Prime Minister. In 1822 he declined to put himself forward as the obvious successor as foreign secretary following Castlereagh's suicide; it was probably the greatest mistake of his political career, and reflects the fact that he had yet to accept fully his position as a leading politician. The long struggle with Canning over the direction of British foreign policy caused Wellington great frustration, but it also sharpened his political appetite and improved his skills. He was never a great orator, but his years as prime minister forced him to become a ready and confident speaker who excelled in laying out a straightforward argument with compelling clarity and logic. His prestige and personal experience gave his views considerable additional weight, while from the 1830s if not earlier he was assiduous in his attention to the mundane details of managing the Lords, such as arranging proxies, while taking great pains to meet with and encourage his supporters.[4] As the years passed he showed surprising tact and skill in managing men, including many for whom he felt little respect or liking, and was actually better at conciliating and consulting his followers than either Peel or Pitt. The idea that he was a stiff, upright soldier, too honourable and inflexible to flourish among the shifting sands of politics, was always a misleading caricature, even if it was one that he rather enjoyed, and occasionally exploited.

The House of Lords suited Wellington; his lack of oratory would have been more damaging in the Commons, while the effect of his personal attention would have been diluted in the larger House. But it also removed him from the critical point and left him dependent on others – notably Peel – who had their own view of events. He was not indifferent to public opinion or ignorant of the changes in society, and as prime minister he paid far more attention to managing the press than he liked to admit. He made a number of successful personal tours to northern England, visiting mines and factories and being greeted with enthusiasm. Nonetheless he never found an effective way of communicating his views to the public, either through widely reported speeches (such as those of Canning and Peel) or direct addresses (such as the Tamworth Manifesto). It was the same failing that had affected him as commander of the army: he despised the carefully contrived romantic gesture and flamboyant language that would arouse popular enthusiasm, and so excited cool admiration, not whole-hearted devotion.

Both as a soldier and as a politician he was probably a little too cynical, underestimating the strength of popular patriotism and exaggerating the appetite for plunder and disorder among the lower ranks, whether of the army or of society, although experiences from Gawilghur and Badajoz to the Cato Street conspiracy and the repeated stoning of Apsley House provided more than a little justification for his views. He also suffered, particularly as prime minister, from not having enough positive proposals of his own; he believed in providing efficient and economical administration at home and a peaceful and conciliatory foreign policy, but this provided little to excite or entertain the press or the political world. Even the creation of the Metropolitan Police, the most obvious example of his government taking the initiative, was primarily Peel's responsibility. More seriously, Wellington's largely justified criticism of the plans of the reformers was not matched by any alternative plan of his own to broaden the political nation to accommodate the newly wealthy and confident professional and manufacturing classes, who included many Dissenters and Catholics. Similarly he recognised that Catholic Emancipation would not solve the problems of Ireland, but did not bring forward more relevant measures of his own, for example to facilitate the sale of indebted estates and compel landowners to pay their labourers in cash as well as with the rent of a small parcel of land.

Wellington was, above all, a pragmatic politician. With his reputation already made and his fame secured, he could afford to be more flexible and less wedded to particular principles than other politicians. His overriding concern was always that the King or Queen's government be carried on in the most effective manner, and on a number of occasions this led him to abandon an untenable position rather than resist to the end. This underlay his change of heart on Catholic Emancipation and the Corn Laws, and even his willingness, in May 1832, to introduce a reform bill of his own in the belief that in office he could minimise the damage done. Any other politician pursuing this line would have been accused of opportunism and lack of principle, and even Wellington was not completely immune to these charges, although Peel's reputation suffered much greater damage from the events of 1829. For his part

Wellington seems to have underestimated the lack of pragmatism and sheer obstinacy of others, especially the ultra-Tories, who felt betrayed in 1829 and again in 1846. Rather than making the best of things as he did, they not only stuck to their principles but had their revenge, even though this resulted in the fall of a relatively sympathetic government and its replacement by one that was much more hostile to their interests.

In the second half of his political career, from 1835 onwards, Wellington came to be praised for his willingness to sacrifice party interests to the national good, supporting the government against the wishes of his followers, especially on questions relating to foreign policy, defence and the colonies. Indeed his example sowed the seed of the idea that such questions should, wherever possible (and especially where active military operations are involved), be dealt with in a bipartisan manner. Yet in many cases Wellington's position was underpinned by shrewd political calculation, and the long-term objective of keeping Melbourne's weak Whig administration in office until the country was ready to give the Conservatives a sufficient majority to form a strong government. This was not his only motive, and there were many other cases when he sacrificed his own strongly held views for the good of the party and the country, while he was always ready to give any government the benefit of his military and diplomatic experience without any thought of political advantage.

Still, the old view of Wellington as the 'least political' of politicians is untenable. In the 1820s he led the opposition to Canning in Cabinet and was well aware of the significance of his connections to the King. He steered a difficult course with great dexterity in the troubled waters of 1827, and emerged as prime minister in 1828 with his integrity intact and his reputation enhanced. Criticism of his political judgement in breaking with Huskisson and the Canningites in 1828, and failing to broaden the basis of his government in 1829 or 1830, dissolves on closer scrutiny. He played a vital part in rebuilding the morale and sense of purpose of the Conservative Party in the 1830s, bringing the ultras back into the fold and employing the party's majority in the Lords with great skill and discretion.[5] If Peel had been as clear in his objectives and as shrewd in his tactics, the Conservatives might well have become the natural party of government throughout the middle decades of Victoria's reign, and Wellington's role in politics would have been regarded much more highly.

As it was, by the time Wellington died in 1852, his political views appeared discredited and outmoded. Throughout his political career he had opposed the rising tide of liberal opinion. He was conservative and cynical – highly sceptical of talk of the 'march of the intellect', and of schemes of political and social reform. As the obituary in an American paper said with evident disapproval: 'He had no great faith in the progress of humanity, no lively feeling in the strength and majesty of moral powers.'[6] Looking back in 1852, in the early days of mid-Victorian complacency, it was easy to believe that all the most important legislative measures of Wellington's time – the repeal of the Test and Corporation Acts, Catholic Emancipation, the Reform Bill, and the reduction of tariffs in general and on corn in particular – were carried either against his wishes or with his grudging and reluctant consent. And this in turn led to the conclusion that Wellington was not an effective politician, and had little influence on events.

This interpretation of Wellington's political career was unchallenged in the decades that followed his death. In 1889 a great admirer of the Duke expressed the common view when he wrote: 'That he [Wellington] did his best [in the years after Waterloo] no one can doubt: that his best was a failure few will hesitate to say.' No political party had much interest in contesting this judgement. Peel had been largely, if unreasonably, claimed for the Liberals by Gladstone, while the new Conservative Party that emerged under the tutelage of Disraeli and Derby viewed its ancestry with deep suspicion, unwilling to pay homage to the achievements of men who, in 1846, had chosen another path. In the first three-quarters of the twentieth century professional historians working on the period had other interests and sympathies, recovering the story of the making of the English working class and generally contesting the liberal consensus from the left. Those few historians who looked at the Conservative side of politics between Pitt and Disraeli concentrated their attention on figures such as Canning and Peel who could be presented as liberal and progressive despite being Tories. The arrival of Wellington's papers at the University of Southampton in the early 1980s, and a changing mood among historians more generally, began a reassessment of the Duke's later life. Neville Thompson, Peter Jupp, Richard Gaunt and above all Richard Davis led the way, although many other scholars made important contributions. They showed that the Duke had been a far more active and engaged politician than had been supposed, and that the image of him as the retained servant of the crown, standing largely apart from the party fray, was misleading, representing only one of the many roles he played.[7]

Looking afresh at Wellington's political career casts some doubt over the whole liberal interpretation of British politics between Waterloo and the Great Exhibition. We can see that from Wellington's perspective the foreign policy pursued by Canning and Palmerston was mischievous and damaging, both for Britain and for Europe as a whole. It increased international tensions, it made co-operation between the great powers more difficult, and it prolonged brutal civil wars in Portugal, Spain and Greece, while making governments elsewhere more repressive. Where liberal regimes were established they generally rested on a very narrow social and political base and were corrupt, unstable and exploitative. We can also see that from Wellington's perspective the radical agitation of the post-war years in Britain, culminating in the disturbances of 1819 and the Queen's Affair of 1820–1821, could not be lightly dismissed, and that the government's response was overall both measured and effective, notwithstanding the mismanagement by the local authorities of the meeting at St Peter's Field in Manchester in 1819. We can see that Wellington, Peel and many other Tories opposed Catholic Emancipation because they understood that it was completely irrelevant to the real problems of Irish society, and that it would simply alienate the greatest supporters of British rule in Ireland, without conciliating its opponents or doing anything to pacify the country. Nonetheless Wellington came to accept that Emancipation was inevitable as early as 1825, and believed that it should be undertaken by a government sympathetic to Protestant interests in Ireland rather than one that was hostile to them. This was just one of many instances when the press and the public assumed that his views were considerably more conservative than was actually the case. Wellington opposed the Reform Bill because he saw it as a shameless grab for power by the Whigs that would overthrow a system of government that, for all its incongruities, had proved extremely successful in combining stable and strong administration with a responsiveness to public opinion, expressed through a Parliament whose members were influenced but not controlled by the executive. He also believed, unlike many of the proponents of the bill but quite correctly, that far from settling the question it would strengthen the hand of the radicals and create greater demand for further concessions. Equally, Wellington opposed the repeal of the Corn Laws without substantial and effective compensation, because he believed that it would undermine the economic base of the landed interest who were the mainstay of the country's political class (both Conservative and Whig), and encourage pressure for more political power from the manufacturing and commercial interests represented by the Anti-Corn Law League, while doing nothing to improve the economic interests of the urban poor, and worsening the plight of the rural population, including agricultural labourers, who were one of the poorest groups in society as a whole. It would also distract from, rather than assist, the government in taking effective action to deal with the threat of famine in Ireland.

The point is not that Wellington, and the many other Conservatives who shared his views, were necessarily right on all these questions, but that they had far more reasonable arguments to support their case than has generally been acknowledged. After more than one hundred and fifty years of hearing just one side of the argument it is time to look again at the other side, and to question whether things were really as simple and clear-cut as they seemed to the rising generation in 1852.

Nonetheless it is clear that Wellington's greatest achievements were not as a politician but as a soldier and statesman whose part in the defeat of Napoleon and in the post-war settlement had a profound effect on the history of Britain, Europe and indeed the world. If Pitt and Nelson played the leading roles in ensuring that Britain survived the time of greatest peril in the long war with France, it was Wellington who ensured that Britain played a prominent part in the ultimate victory, and that she emerged from the war with unprecedented prestige. Throughout the nineteenth century and well into the twentieth, Assaye and Talavera, Badajoz and Salamanca were familiar names to successive generations in Britain and beyond, while Waterloo played a large part in defining Britain's unique and pre-eminent place among the Great Powers. Britain had not just endured the storm and emerged intact, she had turned the tables on her enemy and beaten the French at their own game; it was Wellington's triumph that led, immediately and decisively, to Napoleon's final overthrow and exile to St Helena. Victory in the war, and especially the triumph at Waterloo, was the bedrock of Victorian self-confidence, pride and patriotism; underpinning a belief that if necessary Britain could defy all the rest of Europe united against her. This confidence was dimmed by the carnage of the First World War, but played an important part in underpinning morale in the Second, and while much eroded by the threat of nuclear weapons and the loss of Empire in the Cold War, some lingers even today.

Wellington's prominence undercut much radical criticism of the aristocracy, both in his lifetime and for several generations afterwards; given his role as a soldier and a statesman, and as a champion of aristocratic values, it was difficult to argue that the nobility as a class were all idle and ineffective. But his position as a soldier in politics had a more paradoxical effect, and probably encouraged the growing separation of the two professions in the course of the nineteenth century. Britain's tradition of anti-militarism predated Wellington's birth by more than a century, but the perceived failure of his political career may have discouraged other soldiers from looking to high civil office. British political culture is quite unusual in this respect; in the United States, France and many other liberal democracies the boundary between military and political office has always been much more porous.

Wellington's character was almost as celebrated as his achievements. Greville praised its 'perfect simplicity', while in 1899 the original *Dictionary of National Biography* declared that it was marked chiefly by 'manliness and public spirit'.[8] Even in his own lifetime he had been held up as a model whom young men in whatever station of life could emulate, and for several generations his selfless devotion to public duty, unswerving commitment to the truth, absolute integrity, courage, coolness and self-reliance were a common theme for improving writers, school teachers and clergymen. This praise reflected the public reputation which had been built up in Wellington's own lifetime far more closely than the actual man, but even if it was a partial, lopsided caricature, it had great influence, helping to define the ideals of masculine behaviour well into the twentieth century.

The real Wellington was never particularly cold, reserved or inscrutable; his moods, both good and bad, were palpable; he had a hot temper and a propensity to wounding sarcasm and exaggerated grumbling, while he showed little stoicism in the face of disappointment. But he could also be very considerate, was quick to apologise – at least to trusted friends – and was unexpectedly kind and tolerant, as well as playful with children. He loved the company of bright, intelligent women, and while he thoroughly enjoyed their admiration, he also listened to what they had to say and took their opinions seriously. He was frequently asked to settle family disputes, acting as peacemaker in many delicate private matters where his discretion and generosity both proved thoroughly reliable. While his relations with his own sons were never close, he was an excellent and attentive uncle, and resisted the rising tide of Victorian prudery. Until deafness ruined his pleasure he thoroughly enjoyed society, relishing its characters and absurdities, and delighting in hunting, shooting, tennis, and the horseplay and frolics at Mont St Martin. For all his determination to act as became the Duke of Wellington, and his old-fashioned formal manner of writing letters in the third person, fame and success never made him pompous or affected.

Throughout his life the greater part of Wellington's energy, passion and attention were always devoted to his official work, whether as a soldier, diplomat or politician. His appetite for business was remarkable and he had an immense capacity for sustained work. He was always eager to be employed, even in tasks that required a good deal of drudgery or that he found otherwise rather distasteful. He had been fortunate to discover a vocation early in life that suited his talents, and even more that the war gave him the opportunity to exercise them until he obtained unequalled pre-eminence. He then became the only British general since Cromwell to become head of the government; and the only prime minister to have achieved such fame in another field. He succeeded because he had a highly developed sense of what was practical, and a mastery of detail; because he examined complicated problems with great coolness, and was ingenious in finding solutions; because he had great confidence in his own judgement, and great courage in taking necessary risks, and never shirked responsibility; because he did not allow his wishes to distort his perceptions; because he had a well-deserved reputation for integrity and magnanimity which led even his opponents to respect and admire him; and because he was highly intelligent, articulate and full of immense energy. The military hero so wonderfully caught by Lawrence in his 1817 portrait was only ever part of the story.

WELLINGTON'S OFFICES, HONOURS
AND TITLES, 1814–52

(compiled with the assistance of Ron McGuigan)

When Wellington was appointed ambassador to France in 1814 his formal instructions listed his titles thus:

> Instructions for our Right Trusty and Right entirely beloved Cousin and Councillor Arthur, Duke, Marquess, and Earl of Wellington, Marquess Douro, Viscount Wellington of Talavera and of Wellington, and Baron Douro of Wellesley; a Peer of the Parliament of the United Kingdom, one of His Majesty's Most Honourable Privy Council, Field Marshal of His Majesty's Forces, Colonel of the Royal Regiment of Horse Guards, Knight of the Most Noble Order of the Garter, Duke of Ciudad Rodrigo, and a Grandee of Spain of the First Class, Duke of Vitoria, Marquess of Torres Vedras, and Conde de Vimeiro in Portugal, Knight of the Most Illustrious Order of the Golden Fleece, of the Spanish Military Order of St. Ferdinand, Knight Grand Cross of the Imperial Military Order of Maria Theresa, Knight Grand Cross of the Imperial Russian Order of St. George, Knight Grand Cross of the Royal Portuguese Military Order of the Tower and Sword, and Knight Grand Cross of the Royal Swedish Military Order of the Sword, whom we have appointed His Majesty's Ambassador Extraordinary and Plenipotentiary to our good Brother and Cousin the Most Christian King.

Subsequent honours and appointments included:

Colonel, Royal Regiment of Horse Guards, 1 January 1813–22 January 1827
Ambassador Extraordinary and Plenipotentiary to France, credentials dated 8 August 1814
GCB (Knight Grand Cross of the Order of the Bath), 2 January 1815
First Plenipotentiary to the Congress of Vienna, powers dated 18 January 1815
Commander of the Allied Army in Flanders and France, 11 April–30 November 1815
Field Marshal of the Army of the Netherlands, 23 May 1815
Plenipotentiary to the Second Conference of Paris, 1815, powers dated 30 June 1815
Commander-in-Chief of the Allied Army of Occupation in France, November 1818
Commander of the British Contingent of the Army of Occupation in France, November 1818
GCH (Knight Grand Cross of the Royal Guelphic Order), 22 March 1816
Plenipotentiary to the Conference at Aix-la-Chapelle, 1818, joint powers with Castlereagh dated 18 August 1818
Field Marshal of the Hanoverian Army, backdated to 21 June 1813–*d*
Field Marshal of the Austrian Army, 1818–*d*
Field Marshal of the Prussian Army, 1818–*d*
Field Marshal of the Russian Army, 1818–*d*

Master-General of the Ordnance, 26 December 1818–11 April 1827
Governor of Plymouth, 9 December 1819–29 December 1826
Colonel-in-Chief of the Rifle Brigade, 19 February 1820–*d*
Lord Lieutenant of Hampshire, 13 September 1820–*d*
Lord High Constable of England for the Coronations of George IV, William IV and Victoria, 1821, 1831 and 1838
Plenipotentiary on an Extraordinary Mission (to Congress of Verona), 1822, credentials dated 14 September 1822
Trustee of the Deccan Prize Fund, 1823–*d*
Commissioner for the Improvement of Windsor Castle, 1824–*d*
Special mission of condolence and congratulation on the accession of the Emperor Nicholas I of Russia, 1826, credentials dated 6 February 1826
Constable of the Tower (of London) and Lord Lieutenant of Tower Hamlets, 29 December 1826–*d*
Commander-in-Chief, 22 January–5 May 1827 (resignation submitted on 12 April), 22 August 1827–25 January 1828, 15 August 1842–*d*
Colonel, Grenadier Guards, 22 January 1827–*d*
First Lord of the Treasury (Prime Minister), 9 January 1828–22 November 1830; 9 May 1832 accepts commission to form a government (in which he might not have been prime minister); resigns commission when unable to do so; 15 November–8 December 1834 acts as interim prime minister and holds many other senior offices while awaiting Peel's return from Italy
Governor of Charterhouse, 1828–*d*
Lord Warden of the Cinque Ports, 20 January 1829–*d*
Elder Brother (Master from 1837) of Trinity House, 9 May 1829–*d*
Chancellor of University of Oxford, 10 June 1834–*d*
Foreign Secretary, 17 November 1834–18 April 1835
Cabinet minister without office and Leader of the Lords, August 1841–June 1846
Chief Ranger and Keeper of Hyde Park and St James's Park, 31 August 1850–*d*

In addition to these official positions, Wellington was president or patron of many private charities and societies including:

The Society for Foreigners in Distress
The Benevolent Society of St Patrick
The Royal Westminster Hospital for Diseases of the Eye
The Royal Western Hospital
The Middlesex Hospital
The London Hospital
The Society in Scotland for Propagating Christian Knowledge in the Highlands and Islands
The Highland Society of London
The Medico-Botanical Society

Honours in 1852 (as read out by the Garter King at Arms at his funeral and reported in the *Annual Register*):

Arthur, Duke and Marquess of Wellington
Marquess Douro, Earl of Wellington
Viscount Wellington and Baron Douro
Knight of the Most Noble Order of the Garter
Knight Grand Cross of the Most Honourable Order of the Bath
One of Her Majesty's Most Honourable Privy Council
Field-Marshal and Commander-in-Chief of Her Majesty's Forces
Field-Marshal of the Austrian Army
Field-Marshal of the Hanoverian Army
Field-Marshal of the Army of the Netherlands
Marshal-General of the Portuguese Army
Field-Marshal of the Prussian Army
Field Marshal of the Russian Army
Captain-General of the Spanish Army

Prince of Waterloo, of the Kingdom of the Netherlands
Duke of Ciudad Rodrigo and Grandee of Spain of the First Class
Duke of Vittoria, Marquess of Torres Vedras, and Count of Vimiera, in Portugal
Knight of the Most Illustrious Order of the Golden Fleece, and of the Military Orders of
St Ferdinand and of St Hermenigilde of Spain
Knight Grand Cross of the Orders of the Black Eagle and of the Red Eagle of Prussia
Knight Grand Cross of the Imperial Military Order of Maria Teresa of Austria
Knight of the Imperial Orders of St Andrew, St Alexander Newski, and St George of Russia
Knight Grand Cross of the Royal Portuguese Order of the Tower and Sword
Knight Grand Cross of the Royal and Military Order of the Sword of Sweden
Knight of the Order of St Esprit of France
Knight of the Order of the Elephant of Denmark
Knight Grand Cross of the Royal Hanoverian Guelphic Order
Knight of the Order of St Januarius and of the Military Order of St Ferdinand and of Merit of
the Two Sicilies
Knight Grand Cross of the Supreme Order of the Annunciation of Sardinia
Knight Grand Cross of the Royal Military Order of Maximilian Joseph of Bavaria
Knight of the Royal Order of the Rue Crown of Saxony
Knight Grand Cross of the Order of Military Merit of Wurtemberg
Knight Grand Cross of the Military Order of William of the Netherlands
Knight of the Order of the Golden Lion of Hesse Cassel
Knight Grand Cross of the Orders of Fidelity and of the Lion of Baden

The Times, on 19 November, prints a similar list of foreign titles and honours, but includes some inaccuracies. However, it also lists some of the offices Wellington held in Britain at the time of his death:

Lord High Constable of England
Constable of the Tower
Constable of Dover Castle
Warden of the Cinque Ports
Chancellor of the Cinque Ports
Admiral of the Cinque Ports
Lord-Lieutenant of Hampshire
Lord-Lieutenant of the Tower Hamlets
Ranger of St James's Park
Ranger of Hyde Park
Chancellor of the University of Oxford
Commissioner of the Royal Military College
Vice-President of the Scottish Naval and Military Academy
Master of Trinity House
Governor of King's College
Doctor of Laws
&c.

To these may be added:

Colonel-in-Chief of the Rifle Brigade
Colonel of the Grenadier Guards

WHO'S WHO IN WELLINGTON'S WORLD

Aberdeen, George Hamilton-Gordon, 4th Earl of Aberdeen (1784–1860): Pittite and Conservative politician, Foreign Secretary in Wellington's and Peel's governments (1828–30, 1841–46).

Alava, General Miguel Richardo de Álava y Esquivel (1770–1843): Spanish soldier who had served on Wellington's staff in the Peninsula as a liaison officer and was present at both Trafalgar and Waterloo. Exiled after the war due to his liberal views, he was protected and supported by Wellington. Became a familiar figure in London society.

Albert, Prince Albert of Saxe-Coburg and Gotha (1819–61): Prince Consort and husband (from 10 February 1840) of Queen Victoria. Albert softened Victoria's commitment to the Whigs and ensured that the court established good relations with both parties.

Alexander I, Emperor of Russia (1777–1825): In the years after 1814 Alexander became increasingly conservative and religious, forsaking his previous support for some liberal causes in western Europe.

Anglesey, Henry William Paget, 2nd Earl of Uxbridge from 1812–15, 1st Marquess of Anglesey from July 1815 (1768–1854): Lord Paget had a high reputation as a cavalry commander, and was Wellington's second-in-command in 1815. In 1809 he eloped with Henry Wellesley's wife Charlotte whom he married in November 1810. He served as Master-General of the Ordnance under Canning, Goderich and Russell (May 1827–January 1828, July 1846–February 1852), and as Lord Lieutenant of Ireland under Wellington and Grey (February 1828–March 1829, December 1830–September 1833).

Arbuthnot, Charles (1767–1850): Pittite and Conservative politician, well liked and well informed, and one of Wellington's closest friends from about 1819 to his death.

Arbuthnot, Harriet (1793–1834): Second wife of Charles Arbuthnot, keenly interested in politics, a great admirer of Castlereagh and probably Wellington's closest friend from about 1819 to her death. Wrote a detailed journal that was first published in 1950.

Bagot, Sir Charles (1781–1843): Canningite diplomat and husband of Mary (née Wellesley-Pole), Wellington's niece.

Bathurst, Henry, 3rd Earl (1762–1834): Pittite and Conservative politician, Secretary of State for War and the Colonies (1812–27), Lord President of the Council (1828–30). Bathurst was an important member of Cabinet under both Liverpool and Wellington, and was probably the senior minister whose views most closely coincided with Wellington's: more conservative than Peel or Liverpool, less so than Sidmouth or Eldon.

Beresford, William Carr, Viscount (1768–1854): Led the Portuguese army from 1809 until 1820 and remained deeply engaged in Portuguese affairs during the 1820s. Master-General of the Ordnance in Wellington's government (1828–30) but not a member of the Cabinet.

Bessborough, Henrietta [Harriet] Frances, Countess of (1761–1821): Sister of Georgiana, Duchess of Devonshire, mother of Colonel Frederick Ponsonby and Lady Caroline Lamb, and aunt of Lady Harriet Granville, she occupied a place at the pinnacle of Whig society, although her long affair with Lord Granville Leveson Gower brought her into contact with Canning's circle, and she liked and admired Wellington. Her letters, especially those to Granville Leveson Gower, are wonderfully evocative and spontaneous.

Bexley, Nicholas Vansittart, Baron (1766–1851): Chancellor of the Exchequer (1812–23), Chancellor of the Duchy of Lancaster (1823–28), and a Conservative politician allied with Lord Sidmouth.

Blücher, Gebhard Leberecht, Prince von (1742–1819): Prussian field marshal and Wellington's ally in the Waterloo campaign.

Brougham, Henry, Baron (1778–1868): Whig politician, who campaigned against the Orders-in-Council and championed Queen Caroline, and who became Lord Chancellor in Grey's government (1830–34). A man of great ability who eventually aroused the distrust of his political allies and who formed a superficial friendship with Wellington in later life.

Buckingham, Richard Temple-Nugent-Brydges-Chandos, 1st Duke of (1776–1839): Knew Wellington from youth when his father was Lord Lieutenant. He was the head of a powerful but declining political faction that joined Liverpool's government in 1821. Neither his character nor his ability were highly regarded by contemporaries.

Burdett-Coutts, Angela, *suo jure* Baroness Burdett-Coutts (1814–1906): Daughter of the radical (later Conservative) politician Sir Francis Burdett and granddaughter and heiress of Thomas Coutts the banker, she never married but gained fame as a philanthropist. Became a close friend of Wellington in 1846.

Burghersh, Priscilla Anne Fane, Lady (Countess of Westmorland from 1841) (1793–1879): Wellington's favourite niece (one of his brother William's three daughters), her husband had served on Wellington's staff at the beginning of the Peninsular War, and later had a diplomatic career that often kept them out of England.

Canning, George (1770–1827): Pittite and Liberal Tory politician, Foreign Secretary (1807–09 and 1822–27) and Prime Minister (1827). An able and engaging man who won devotion from many but aroused the distrust of more, including Wellington, who strongly disapproved of his populist style and confrontational foreign policy.

Caroline, Queen (1768–1821): Estranged wife of George IV whose return to England in 1820 precipitated a prolonged political crisis when her cause was taken up by the Whigs and radicals.

Castlereagh, Robert Stewart, Viscount (and from 1821 2nd Marquess of Londonderry – an Irish peerage which did not prevent him continuing to sit in the Commons) (1769–1822): Foreign Secretary (1812–22) and leader of the government in the Commons (1812–22). He worked closely with the allied powers in the final stages of the war against Napoleon and, with Wellington's assistance, worked for a moderate and sustainable peace in both 1814 and 1815, and subsequently to maintain friendly relations between all the powers in Europe and beyond.

Clarence, Duke of: see William IV.

Cobbett, William (1762–1835): Radical politician and journalist.

Conyngham, Elizabeth, Marchioness (1769–1861): Mistress of George IV from 1820 to his death in 1830 and a figure of considerable political influence who acquired a reputation for avarice and for pressing the material interests of her family, although she declined a substantial legacy left to her by the King.

Creevey, Thomas (1768–1838): Whig and radical politician and observer whose letters (mostly to his stepdaughter Miss Ord) are an important and amusing source for the politics and gossip of the period.

Croker, John Wilson (1780–1857): Conservative politician and writer whose letters and journals include accounts of many conversations with Wellington.

Cruikshank, George (1792–1878): Caricaturist whose works included many brilliant and savage attacks on Wellington. Mellowed in later life and became famous as an illustrator of Dickens's novels.

Cumberland, Ernest Augustus, Duke of (1771–1851): Fifth son of George III and ultra-Tory politician, his vehemence caused Wellington many problems between 1828 and 1838. On the death of William IV he inherited the crown of Hanover and soon withdrew from British politics, but remained heir presumptive until the birth of Queen Victoria's eldest son in 1841.

Disraeli, Benjamin, later Earl of Beaconsfield (1804–81): Novelist and Conservative politician who went on to twice serve as prime minister. A disaffected and ambitious Tory backbencher, Disraeli made his name through his scathing attacks on Peel in the debates over the Corn Laws in 1846 and became one of the leaders of the Protectionists.

Douro, Arthur Richard Wellesley, Marquess (1807–84): Wellington's eldest son, a soldier and a Member of Parliament (1829–32, 1837–52). He married Lady Elizabeth Hay in 1839 but the marriage proved childless. Although his relations with his father were never close he edited two series of Wellington's correspondence.

Egerton: see Leveson Gower

Eldon, John Scott, Earl of (1751–1838): Pittite and ultra-Tory politician, Lord Chancellor (1801–06, 1807–27), and the ablest of the ultra-Tories.

Ellenborough, Edward Law, Earl of (1790–1871): Conservative politician, President of the Board of Control in Wellington's government (1828–30) and Governor-General of India appointed by Peel (1841–44). His Cabinet diary during Wellington's premiership is a valuable, if sometimes prejudiced, source.

Ellesmere: see Leveson Gower

Ferdinand VII, King of Spain (1784–1833): His repression of the Spanish *liberales* following his return from imprisonment in France in 1814 made him bitterly unpopular in liberal circles in England, but modern scholarship is much less critical of his reign.

Fitzgerald, William Vesey (?1782–1843): Conservative politician and close friend of Peel.

Fouché, Joseph (1759–1820): French politician. A Jacobin responsible for atrocities during the French Revolution, he served as Napoleon's Minister of Police, and was one of the leading French liberals in 1815 playing an important part in the Second Restoration.

George IV, King (1762–1830): Prince Regent from 1811 until his accession in 1820, he was the estranged husband of Queen Caroline.

Goderich, Frederick John Robinson, Viscount (1782–1859): Created Earl of Ripon in 1833. He was a Conservative and Canningite politician popular as Chancellor of the Exchequer under Liverpool, but he proved unsuccessful as prime minister in succession to Canning and his ministry resigned after five months without ever facing Parliament.

Graham, Sir James (1792–1861): Whig, then Conservative, politician, who served under Grey and then as Home Secretary in Peel's government (1841–46). A close ally of Stanley and then of Peel.

Grant, Charles (1778–1866): Canningite and Whig politician, created Baron Glenelg in 1835. President of the Board of Trade in the early months of Wellington's government.

Granville, Harriet Leveson Gower, Countess (1785–1862): Daughter of the Duchess of Devonshire, niece of Lady Bessborough. A society figure with close connections to both Whigs and Canningites, but also a close friend of Princess Lieven and Wellington and author of entertaining letters, mostly to her sister.

Greville, Charles (1794–1865): Diarist. Greville was well informed about politics although his view of Wellington, especially in the early years, was often jaundiced.

Greville, Lady Charlotte (1775–1862): Society figure, friend and probably mistress of Wellington. Mother of Charles (the diarist) and Algernon (Wellington's private secretary).

Grey, Charles, 2nd Earl (1764–1845): Whig politician, leader of the Whigs after Fox's death in 1806, and Prime Minister (1830–34).

Grey, Henry: see Howick.

Gurwood, Colonel John (1790–1845): A Peninsular veteran who had distinguished himself at the storming of Ciudad Rodrigo and who later edited Wellington's *Dispatches* and *General Orders.*

Hardinge, Sir Henry, created Viscount Hardinge of Lahore in 1846 (1785–1856): Soldier and Conservative politician. He was Wellington's liaison officer at the Prussian headquarters in 1815, and was wounded at Ligny, losing a hand. Secretary-at-War in Wellington's government, and Governor-General of India (1844–47).

Hill, Rowland, Viscount (1772–1842): One of Wellington's ablest subordinates in the Peninsula, he served as Commander-in-Chief (1828–42), clashing frequently with the Whig government.

Hobhouse, Henry (1776–1854): Under-Secretary at the Home Office (1817–27), whose diary for 1820–27, though brief, is useful.

Hobhouse, John Cam, created Lord Broughton in 1851 (1786–1869): Friend of Byron, radical then Whig politician, Secretary-at-War (1832–33), and President of the Board of Control (1835–41, 1846–52).

Holland, Elizabeth Vassall Fox, Lady (1770–1845): Political hostess and patroness of liberal causes and writers.

Holland, Henry Richard Vassall Fox, 3rd Baron (1773–1840): Whig politician, nephew of Charles James Fox and champion of liberal causes and refugees from Europe. Cabinet minister under Grey and Melbourne.

Hone, William (1780–1842): Radical author, pamphleteer and publisher.

Howick, Henry, Lord (1802–94): Succeeded his father as 3rd Earl Grey in 1845. Whig politician, Secretary-at-War (1835–39), Secretary for War and the Colonies (1846–52). Repeatedly clashed with Wellington and the Horse Guards over proposed changes to the army.

Hunt, Henry 'Orator' (1773–1835): Radical politician famous for his speeches to mass protest meetings.

Huskisson, William (1770–1830): Canningite politician. A financial expert relied upon by Liverpool, and the *de facto* leader of the Canningites after Canning's death.

Jersey, Sarah Villiers, Countess of (1785–1867): Eldest daughter of Lord Westmorland and a society figure with an active interest in politics and close ties to the Whigs, although she later supported the Conservatives. A voluble and enthusiastic friend of Wellington. (Her mother-in-law, the previous Lady Jersey, had been the mistress of the Prince of Wales.)

João VI, King of Portugal (1767–1826): Regent for his mother Maria I from 1799 to her death in 1816, then King. Fled with the court to Brazil in 1807 and returned in 1821.

Jones, Mrs Margaret Charlotte (née Campbell; later Lady Levinge) (c. 1825–71): Society figure and politician's wife who became a friend of Wellington's in the last two years of his life.

Knighton, Sir William (1776–1836): Doctor and courtier, confidante of George IV.

Lamb, Lady Caroline (1785–1828): Society figure. The daughter of Lady Bessborough, and wife of William Lamb (the future Lord Melbourne), who had a disastrous affair with Byron.

Lawrence, Sir Thomas (1769–1830): Artist who painted the finest portraits of Wellington and many of his contemporaries.

Leveson Gower, Lord Francis (1800–57): In 1833 took the name of Egerton, and in 1846 was created Earl of Ellesmere. Conservative politician who held minor offices in Wellington's government and was his Under-Secretary at the Foreign Office (1834–35). Wrote some valuable but overused *Reminiscences* of Wellington.

Lieven, Princess Dorothea (1785–1857): Wife of the Russian ambassador to Britain from 1812 to 1834 and a influential political and society figure who had close friendships with Metternich, Wellington, Canning, Grey, Aberdeen, Palmerston and, later, Guizot.

Liverpool, Robert Banks Jenkinson, 2nd Earl of (1770–1828): Pittite politician, and Prime Minister (1812–27). The most underrated British politician of the nineteenth century.

Londonderry, Charles William Vane (formerly Stewart), 3rd Marquess of (1778–1854): Castlereagh's younger half-brother who, as Sir Charles Stewart, had served under Wellington in the Peninsula and then as a diplomat. A bitter enemy of Canning and close to the ultra-Tories although committed to Catholic Emancipation.

Louis XVIII, King of France (1755–1824): Younger brother of Louis XVI, who came to the throne with the First Restoration in 1814. He lived in exile in England from 1807 to 1814.

Louis Philippe I, King of France (1773–1850): As Duc d'Orléans he had been associated with liberal causes. Came to power with the revolution of July 1830 and established a relatively stable bourgeois monarchy which lasted until it was unexpectedly overthrown in 1848.

Lyndhurst, John Singleton Copley, Baron (1772–1863): Conservative politician and Lord Chancellor (1827–30, 1834–35, 1841–46), he was a powerful speaker in the House of Lords.

Malcolm, Sir John (1769–1833): Wellington's closest friend from his early days in India.

Melbourne, William Lamb, 2nd Viscount (1779–1848): Canningite and Whig politician. Home Secretary (1830–34), Prime Minister (1834, 1835–41), and confidante of Queen Victoria (1837–41).

Melville, Robert Saunders Dundas, 2nd Viscount (1771–1851): Pittite and Conservative politician, First Lord of the Admiralty (1812–27, 1828–30). He supported Catholic Emancipation, but resigned rather than serve under Canning in 1827. Son and heir of Henry Dundas, Pitt's right-hand man and manager of Scotland.

Metternich, Clement Wenceslas Lothar von, Prince (1773–1859): Austrian statesman and close ally of Castlereagh in the settlement of Europe after the defeat of Napoleon.

Miguel I, King of Portugal (1802–66): Highly conservative younger son of King João, he seized the throne in 1828 but was forced into exile after a prolonged civil war in 1834.

Murray, Sir George (1772–1846): Soldier and Conservative politician. Murray proved his ability as Wellington's Quartermaster-General in the Peninsula, and he went on to serve as Secretary for War and the Colonies in Wellington's government (1828–30), and Master-General of the Ordnance under Peel (1834–35, 1841–46).

Napier, Sir William Francis Patrick (1785–1860): Soldier and historian. A Peninsular veteran who wrote an immensely influential history of the war that was popular with Whigs and radicals as well as Tories.

Napoleon I, Emperor of the French (1769–1821): Returned from exile on Elba and regained power in France but was defeated at Waterloo and, following a second abdication, was exiled to St Helena.

Neumann, Philipp von (1781–1851): Austrian diplomat in London, His diary contains glimpses of Wellington and much useful information.

Nicholas I, Emperor of Russia (1796–1855): Younger brother of Alexander I; reigned 1825–55.

O'Connell, Daniel (1775–1847): Irish Catholic politician and nationalist. Led the campaign for Catholic Emancipation and the repeal of the Act of Union.

Palmerston, Henry John Temple, 3rd Viscount (1784–1865): Pittite, Canningite and Whig politician. He was Secretary-at-War (1809–28), Foreign Secretary (1830–34, 1835–41) and Prime Minister (1855–58, 1859–65).

Patterson, Marianne (née Caton), Marchioness Wellesley from 1825 (1788–1853): American-born society figure, friend and probably lover of Wellington who married Lord Wellesley in 1825.

Peel, Sir Robert (1788–1850): Pittite and Conservative politician. Chief Secretary for Ireland (1812–18), Home Secretary (1822–27, 1828–30) and Prime Minister (1834–35, 1841–46). Leader of the Commons in Wellington's government (1828–30).

Robinson: see Goderich.

Russell, Lord John (1792–1878): Whig politician. One of the architects and champions of the Great Reform Bill, Home Secretary (1835–39), Secretary for War and the Colonies (1839–41), Prime Minister (1846–52).

Salisbury, Frances Gascoyne-Cecil, Marchioness of (1802–39): First wife of the 2nd Marquess of Salisbury, friend and confidante of Wellington (especially following the death of Mrs Arbuthot in 1834), and author of a vivid and entertaining journal.

Salisbury, Mary Catherine Gascoyne-Cecil, Marchioness of (1824–1900): Second wife of the 2nd Marquess of Salisbury (married 1847), and later (1870) wife of the 15th Earl of Derby. Friend and correspondent of Wellington, especially 1850–52.

Scott, Sir Walter (1771–1832): Poet, novelist and historian who visited the Waterloo battlefield and Paris in 1815.

Shelley, Frances, Lady (1787–1873): Friend and admirer of Wellington, whose diary includes valuable material on his life especially between 1814 and the early 1820s.

Sidmouth, Henry Addington, Viscount (1757–1844): Conservative politician. Prime Minister (1801–04), Home Secretary (1812–22) and Minister without Portfolio (1822–24).

Somerset, Lord Fitzroy, created Baron Raglan 1852 (1788–1855): Wellington's ADC and military secretary in the Peninsula and at Waterloo where he lost an arm; Secretary to the Paris embassy (1814–15) and the Ordnance (1819–27); Military Secretary at the Horse Guards (1827–52). He commanded the British army in the Crimea (1854–55) and married Wellington's niece Emily (née Wellesley–Pole) in 1814.

Stanley, Edward George Smith Stanley, Lord (14th Earl of Derby from 1851) (1799–1869): Whig, Conservative and Protectionist politician. Chief Secretary for Ireland in Grey's ministry (1830–33), he resigned with three colleagues in 1834, refused to support Peel's ministry (1834–35) but subsequently joined him in opposition. Secretary for War and the Colonies (1841–45), he resigned over the repeal of the Corn Laws and became leader of the Protectionists. Prime Minister from February–December 1852, 1858–59 and 1866–68.

Talleyrand, Charles-Maurice de Talleyrand-Périgord, Prince (1754–1838): French foreign minister under the Directory, Napoleon and Louis XVIII, and ambassador to London under Louis Philippe.

Victoria, Queen, and later Empress of India (1819–1901): Succeeded William IV in 1837 five weeks after her eighteenth birthday. Formed a close bond with Lord Melbourne, her first prime minister, which weakened after her marriage to Albert in 1840.

Ward, John William, from 1823 Viscount, and from 1827 Earl of Dudley (1781–1833): Canningite politician, Foreign Secretary (1827–28).

Ward, Robert (changed name to Plumer Ward in 1828) (1765–1846): Conservative politician and novelist. Clerk of the Ordnance (1811–23). His journals (including descriptions of working with Wellington at the Ordnance) are quoted extensively in the memoir of him by Phipps.

Wellesley, Lord Charles (1808–58): Wellington's younger son; a soldier and Member of Parliament whose later life was marred by glaucoma leading to near blindness.

Wellesley, Rev. Gerald (1770–1848): Rector of St Luke's Chelsea (1805–32), Rector of Bishop Wearmouth, Co. Durham and Canon of Durham (1827–48). Wellington repeatedly but unsuccessfully pressed Lord Liverpool to make Gerald (his younger brother) a bishop.

Wellesley, Henry, created Baron Cowley in 1828 (1773–1847): Diplomat and Wellington's youngest brother. British envoy and ambassador to Spain (1811–22), ambassador to Austria (1823–31), ambassador to France (1835, 1841–46).

Wellesley, Richard Colley, Marquess (1760–1842): Wellington's eldest brother and Lord Lieutenant of Ireland (1821–28, 1833–34).

Wellesley-Pole, William, created Baron Maryborough in 1821 (1763–1845): Pittite politician and Wellington's elder brother. Served in Liverpool's Cabinet as Master of the Mint (1814–23), then held the position of Master of the Buckhounds at court (1823–30).

Wellington, Catherine (Kitty), Duchess of (1772–1831): Wellington's wife.

Whitbread, Samuel (1764–1815): Radical and Whig politician. Brother-in-law of Lord Grey. He committed suicide in 1815.

William IV, King (1765–1837): As Duke of Clarence he had served as Lord High Admiral (1827–28) until forced to resign by Wellington as prime minister. Nonetheless he supported Wellington's government when he came to the throne in 1830.

Wilton, Mary Egerton, Countess of (1801–58): Society figure, friend and correspondent of Wellington particularly between 1838 and 1848.

Winchilsea, George William Finch-Hatton, 10th Earl of (1791–1858): Ultra-Tory politician with whom Wellington fought a duel on 21 March 1829. In 1837 he married the daughter of Wellington's niece Mary Bagot.

Wyatt, Benjamin Dean (1775–1855): Architect. Wyatt worked on Marquess Wellesley's staff in India, and was Wellington's private secretary in Ireland (1807–09). He acted as Wellington's agent in looking for an estate in England after 1814 and designed the (never built) Waterloo Palace as well as conducting extensive alterations to Apsley House.

York, Frederick, Duke of (1763–1827): Second son of George III and heir presumptive of George IV. Commander-in-Chief of the Army (1795–1809, 1811–27). A conservative opponent of Catholic Emancipation.

CHRONOLOGY

31 March 1814	Allies enter Paris
6 April 1814	Napoleon abdicates
10 April 1814	Battle of Toulouse
4 May 1814	Wellington arrives in Paris
11 May 1814	Created a Duke (gazetted 3 May 1814)
13 May 1814	Returns to Toulouse
24 May 1814	Arrives in Madrid
10–15 June 1814	At Bordeaux
13 June 1814	Resigns command of the Spanish army
14 June 1814	Farewells his British army
23 June 1814	Lands at Dover
23 June–8 August 1814	In England
28 June 1814	Takes his seat in the House of Lords
1 July 1814	Thanks the Commons
7 July 1814	National Service of Thanksgiving at St Paul's
21 July 1814	Prince Regent's fete in Wellington's honour
8 August 1814	Sails for Bergen-op-Zoom
11–18 August 1814	At Brussels
22 August 1814	Arrives in Paris
24 December 1814	Treaty of Ghent ends war between Britain and the United States
28 March 1815	Wellington appointed to command of British forces on the Continent
24 January 1815	Leaves Paris
2 or 3 February 1815	Arrives in Vienna
1 March 1815	Napoleon lands in France
13 March 1815	Allied declaration against Napoleon
20 March 1815	Napoleon enters Paris
29 March 1815	Wellington leaves Vienna
4 April 1815	Arrives in Brussels
23 May 1815	Made a Field Marshal in the Army of the Netherlands
15 June 1815	Duchess of Richmond's Ball
16 June 1815	Battle of Quatre Bras
18 June 1815	Battle of Waterloo
22 June 1815	Napoleon's second abdication
3 July 1815	Convention of Paris
6 July 1815	Wellington enters Paris
16 July 1815	Napoleon surrenders to Captain Maitland of *HMS Bellerophon*
20 November 1815	Second Peace of Paris
November 1815– November 1818	Wellington commands allied Army of Occupation of France

7 December 1815	Execution of Marshal Ney
11 February 1818	Attempted assassination of Wellington
25 September–24 November 1818	Congress of Aix-la-Chapelle
November 1818	End of the Army of Occupation
21 December 1818	Wellington arrives in London
26 December 1818	Takes office as Master-General of the Ordnance
16 August 1819	'Peterloo Massacre'
1 January 1820	Army revolt in Spain demands return to Constitution of 1812
29 January 1820	Accession of George IV
23 February 1820	Cato Street Conspiracy
2 July 1820	Army revolt in Naples forces the King to accept a constitution
17 August–10 November 1820	'Trial' of Queen Caroline
27 October–17 December 1820	Congress of Troppau
13 December 1820	Wellington appointed Lord Lieutenant of Hampshire
5 May 1821	Death of Napoleon
19 July 1821	Coronation of George IV
7 August 1821	Death of Queen Caroline
12 August 1822	Castlereagh's suicide
September 1822	Wellington's illness following ear operation
16 September 1822	Canning appointed Foreign Secretary
20 September 1822	Wellington arrives in Paris
29 September 1822	Arrives in Vienna
15 October–30 November 1822	Attends Congress of Verona
9 December 1822	Arrives back in Paris
22 December 1822	Lands at Dover
April 1823	French army occupies Spain meeting little resistance
August 1823	Wellington's proposal to send troops to Portugal rejected
16 September 1824	Death of Louis XVIII, accession of Charles X
February–May 1825	Wellington puts forward plan for Catholic Emancipation
1824–1825	Speculative boom
29 October 1825	Lord Wellesley marries Marianne Patterson
1 December 1825	Death of Emperor Alexander of Russia
December 1825	Financial crash in England
8 February 1826	Wellington leaves London on Mission to St Petersburg
17 February 1826	Reaches Berlin
2 March 1826	Arrives in St Petersburg
10 March 1826	Death of King João of Portugal
6 April 1826	Wellington leaves St Petersburg
27 April 1826	Arrives back in London
December 1826–April 1828	British expedition to Portugal
5 January 1827	Death of the Duke of York
22 January 1827	Wellington appointed Commander-in-Chief
17 February 1827	Liverpool incapacitated by a stroke
10 April 1827	Canning appointed Prime Minister
11 April 1827	Wellington resigns from Cabinet
12 April 1827	Resigns as Commander-in-Chief (gazetted 5 May)
6 July 1827	Treaty of London
8 August 1827	Death of Canning, succeeded as Prime Minister by Goderich
22 August 1827	Wellington re-appointed Commander-in-Chief
September–October 1827	Tours northern England
20 October 1827	Battle of Navarino
8 January 1828	Goderich resigns
9 January 1828	Wellington appointed Prime Minister
25 January 1828	Resigns as Commander-in-Chief

April 1828	British expedition to Portugal withdrawn
26 April 1828	Russia declares war on Ottoman Empire
9 May 1828	Repeal of the Test and Corporation Acts
18 May 1828	Liberal revolt in Portugal
20 May 1828	Resignation of Huskisson followed by other Canningites
30 June 1828	Miguel claims the Portuguese crown
5 July 1828	O'Connell elected for County Clare
1828–1840	Publication of Napier's *History of the War in the Peninsula*
24 September 1828	Queen Maria of Portugal lands in England
4 December 1828	Death of Lord Liverpool
20 January 1829	Wellington appointed Lord Warden of the Cinque Ports
21 March 1829	Duel with Lord Winchilsea
13 April 1829	Catholic Emancipation receives Royal Assent
14 September 1829	Treaty of Adrianople
29 September 1829	Metropolitan Police instituted in London
1829–1830	Economic depression
May 1830	Wellington considers resignation
14 June 1830	French landings near Algiers
26 June 1830	Death of George IV, accession of William IV
5 July 1830	Algiers captured by the French
29 July 1830	Charles X of France overthrown
July–August 1830	British general election
25 August 1830	Uprising in Brussels leads to independence of Belgium
August–December 1830	Swing Riots in southern England
September 1830	Wellington tours Midlands and northern England
15 September 1830	Huskisson killed at opening of Liverpool–Manchester railway
9 November 1830	King's intended visit to the City
15 November 1830	Wellington's government defeated in vote on the Civil List
16 November 1830	Submits his resignation as Prime Minister
22 November 1830	Resignation takes effect
March 1831–May 1832	Struggle over the Reform Bill
24 April 1831	Death of the Duchess of Wellington
April–June 1831	General election gives Grey's government large majority
10 September 1831	Death of Lady Mornington, Wellington's mother
9 May 1832	William IV accepts Grey's resignation
9–15 May 1832	Wellington unsuccessfully attempts to form a government
7 June 1832	The Reform Bill receives Royal Assent
18 June 1832	Wellington harassed on his ride home from the Mint
September 1832	Publication of a selection of General Orders
28 August 1833	Slavery Abolition Act in the British Empire
1834–1839	Publication of Wellington's *Dispatches*
May 1834	Resignation of Stanley and three other ministers
10 June 1834	Wellington installed as Chancellor of the University of Oxford
7/8 July 1834	Grey resigns, Melbourne becomes Prime Minister
2 August 1834	Death of Mrs Arbuthnot
14 August 1834	New Poor Law receives Royal Assent
16 October 1834	Houses of Parliament badly damaged by fire
14 November 1834	William IV dismisses Melbourne
15 November 1834	Wellington advises the King to ask Peel to form a ministry and holds most senior offices of state until Peel returns from Italy
17 November 1834–18 April 1835	Foreign Secretary
8 December 1834	Peel lands at Dover
18 December 1834	Tamworth Manifesto published
30 December 1834	Parliament dissolved and an election called
8 April 1835	Peel's government resigns
20 June 1837	Death of King William IV and accession of Queen Victoria
November 1837	Outbreak of revolt in Canada

28 June 1838	Queen Victoria's coronation
22 February 1839	Wellington ill, possibly a stroke, at Stratfield Saye
7 May 1839	Melbourne resigns, precipitating the 'Bedchamber Crisis'
10 May 1839	Peel resigns his commission, Melbourne returns to office
15 October 1839	Death of Lady Salisbury
18 November 1839	Wellington very ill, probably a stroke, at Walmer
10 February 1840	Marriage of Queen Victoria and Prince Albert
13 February 1840	Wellington suffers another attack
15 July 1840	Suffers a further attack
August–December 1840	War scare with France
5 February 1841	Wellington suffers his fifth and final attack
June–July 1841	General election
28 August 1841	Melbourne resigns
30 August 1841	Peel appointed Prime Minister
August 1841–June 1846	Peel's government
11 March 1842	Peel's first budget and the re-introduction of Income Tax
15 August 1842	Wellington becomes Commander-in-Chief
1844	Further war scare with France
September 1845	First reports of potato blight threatening famine in Ireland
6 December 1845	Peel resigns over the Corn Laws
20 December 1845	Peel resumes office after Russell's failure to form a ministry
January–June 1846	Repeal of the Corn Laws
29 June 1846	Peel's resignation speech
1846–50	Irish famine
4 January 1848	Publication of Wellington's letter on national defence
24 February 1848	Abdication of King Louis Philippe
1848	Succession of revolutions across Europe
10 April 1848	Chartist mass demonstration at Kennington Common
2 July 1850	Death of Robert Peel
18 August 1850	Death of Charles Arbuthnot
February 1851	Russell's government resigns but returns to office when no other party can form a government
1 May 1851	Opening of the Great Exhibition
23 February 1852	Russell resigns as Prime Minister, Derby forms Protectionist government
14 September 1852	Wellington's death
18 November 1852	Wellington's funeral

ENDNOTES

Abbreviations

Castlereagh Correspondence:	Lord Castlereagh, *Correspondence, Despatches, and other Papers of Viscount Castlereagh, Second Marquess of Londonderry*, ed. Charles William Vane, Marquess of Londonderry, 12 vols. (London, William Shoberl, 1848–53)
CCA:	Charles Arbuthnot, *The Correspondence of Charles Arbuthnot*, ed. A. Aspinall (London, Royal Historical Society, 1941; Camden, 3rd series, vol. 65)
Greville, *Memoirs*:	Charles C.F. Greville, *The Greville Memoirs 1814–1860*, ed. Lytton Strachey and Roger Fulford, 8 vols. (London, Macmillan, 1938) [All citations, unless otherwise specified are to this edition]
HMC Bathurst:	*Historical Manuscripts Commission Report on the Manuscripts of Earl Bathurst preserved at Cirencester Park* (London, HMSO, 1923)
HMC Wellington:	*Wellington. Political Correspondence 1833–1835*, ed. John Brooke, Julia Gandy, R.J. Olney and Julia Melvin for the Royal Commission on Historical Manuscripts, 2 vols. (London, HMSO, 1975–86)
JMrsA:	Harriet Arbuthnot, *The Journal of Mrs Arbuthnot 1820–1832*, ed. Francis Bamford and the Duke of Wellington, 2 vols. (London, Macmillan, 1950)
JSAHR:	*Journal of the Society for Army Historical Research*
'Letters to Pole':	Wellington, 'Some Letters of the Duke of Wellington to his brother William Wellesley-Pole', ed. Professor Sir Charles Webster, *Camden Miscellany* (London, Royal Historical Society, 1948; Camden, 3rd series, vol. 79)
ODNB:	*The Oxford Dictionary of National Biography*, ed. H.C.G. Matthew and Brian Harrison (Oxford University Press, online edition, 2004–present)
W&HF:	Wellington, *Wellington and His Friends. Letters of the First Duke of Wellington to the Rt. Hon. Charles and Mrs Arbuthnot, the Earl and Countess of Wilton, Princess Lieven and Miss Burdett-Coutts*, sel. and ed. 7th Duke of Wellington (London, Macmillan, 1965)
WD:	*The Dispatches of Field Marshal the Duke of Wellington*, ed. [John] Gurwood, 8 vols. (London, Parker, Furnivall and Parker, 1844)

WND: Wellington, *Despatches, Correspondence, and Memoranda of*
                                  Field Marshal Arthur Duke of Wellington, K.G. ed. his son, the
                                  Duke of Wellington, 'in continuation of the former series', 8
                                  vols. (London, John Murray, 1857–80) [Known as *Wellington*
                                  New Despatches, these volumes cover the years 1819–32]
W P: Wellington Papers in the Special Collections of the Hartley
                                  Library, University of Southampton
WSD: Wellington, *Supplementary Despatches, Correspondence and*
                                  Memoranda of Field Marshal Arthur, Duke of Wellington, K.G.,
                                  ed. his son, the Duke of Wellington, 15 vols. (London, John
                                  Murray, 1858–72)

Preface

1 Philip Guedalla, *The Duke* (1931), p. ix.
2 Wellington to Croker, 3 June 1834, John Wilson Croker, *The Croker Papers* (1884), vol. 2,
   p. 224.

Prologue

1. Joseph Farington, *The Diary of Joseph Farington*, ed. Kenneth Garlick (1978–85) vol. 13,
   2 and 6 July 1814, pp. 4545, 4548. Farington says that this portrait was for the Prince Regent
   but Wellington's plain costume seems to show that it was for that originally commissioned by,
   and ultimately ending up with, Lord Stewart. The Service of Thanksgiving at St Paul's was
   held on the following day.
2. This portrait was commissioned in 1817 by Wellington as a present for Marianne Patterson:
   Jehanne Wake, *Sisters of Fortune. America's Caton Sisters at Home and Abroad* (2010),
   pp. 140–1 and below, p. 101. Michael Levey, *Sir Thomas Lawrence* (2005), pp. 26–7 has an
   interesting comment about it.
3. M. Dorothy George and Frederick J. Stephens, *Catalogue of Political and Personal Satires*
   Preserved in the Department of Prints and Drawings in the British Museum (1978), no. 12620,
   vol. 9, pp. 592–3.
4. Ibid., no. 12797, vol. 9, pp. 692–4; M. Dorothy George, *English Political Caricature. A Study of*
   Opinion and Propaganda (1959), vol. 2, pp. 173–4; John Wardroper, *The Caricatures of George*
   Cruikshank (1977), p. 61.

1 Celebrations and Diplomacy

1. Castlereagh to Wellington, 13 April 1814, *Castlereagh Correspondence*, vol. 9, p. 461.
2. Wellington to Castlereagh, 21 April and to Henry Wellesley, 30 April 1814, *WD*, vol. 7,
   pp. 461 and 473–4.
3. Castlereagh to Liverpool, 5 May 1814, *WSD*, vol. 9, pp. 64–5; Lord Broughton, *Recollections*
   of a Long Life, ed. Lady Dorchester (1910–11), vol. 1, p. 112; Countess Brownlow, *The Eve of*
   Victorianism. Reminiscences of the Years 1802–1834 (1940), p. 45.
4. Metternich to Laure Metternich, 26 May 1814, in Dorothy Gies McGuigan, *Metternich and*
   the Duchess (1975), p. 274.
5. Wellington to Liverpool, 9 May 1814, *WD*, vol. 7, pp. 477–8; Wellington to Henry Wellesley,
   22 May 1814, *WSD*, vol. 9, p. 100.
6. Raymond Carr, *Spain, 1808–1939* (1966), p. 118
7. Wellington to Liverpool, 9 May 1814, *WD*, vol. 7, pp. 477–8.
8. Wellington to San Carlos, 21 May 1814 (two letters); Wellington to Sir Charles Stuart, 25 May
   1814, *WD*, vol. 7, pp. 491–5 (in the version printed in Mrs Edward Stuart Wortley, *Highcliffe*
   and the Stuarts (1927), p. 204, the phrase 'great act of vigor' reads 'great act of tyranny').
9. Memorandum for Ferdinand VII, nd, *WD*, vol. 7, pp. 504–7.
10. Wellington to Castlereagh, 11 June 1814, WP 1/420, printed in *WD*, vol. 7, pp. 511–12 with
    names suppressed.
11. Wellington to Henry Wellesley, 29 July 1814, *WSD*, vol. 9, pp. 165–7; there is an incomplete
    and wrongly dated version of this letter in *WD*, vol. 7, pp. 534–5, cf WP 1/423.

12. Wellington to the Minister of War, Madrid, 29 May 1814, *WD*, vol. 7, pp. 489–99; Charles J. Esdaile, *Wellington and the Command of the Spanish Armies 1812–1814* (1990), p. 180.

13. *The Times*, 30 November 1814; Wellington to B. Sydenham, 11 June 1814, WP 1/420, printed in *WD*, vol. 7, p. 511 with names deleted; Wellington to William Wellesley-Pole, 8 December 1814, partly printed in *WSD*, vol. 9, pp. 466–7, with a further passage quoted in John Severn, *Architects of Empire. The Duke of Wellington and His Brothers* (2007), p. 377 citing Raglan Papers. Curiously there is a manuscript copy of Wellington to Pole, 8 December 1814, in WP 1/438 which does not include the paragraph. There is little doubt that Wellington's suspicions were well founded. Among other grievances Lord Wellesley deeply resented his brother's appointment to the Paris embassy, desiring the position for himself: see Political Notebook of Richard Wellesley II, undated entry, Carver Mss 54.

14. Frances, Lady Shelley, *The Diary of Frances Lady Shelley*, ed. Richard Edgcumbe (1913), vol. 1, p. 66; *The Times*, 24 June 1814, says he went to visit Lord Wellesley in Apsley House. Both, of course, may be true.

15. *The Times*, 27 June 1814.

16. *Parliamentary Debates*, vol. 28, cols. 357–9. There is a slightly different version of Wellington's speech in Wellington, *The Speeches of the Duke of Wellington in Parliament collected and arranged by Col. [John] Gurwood* (1854), vol. 1, pp. 91–4.

17. *Parliamentary Debates*, vol. 27, cols. 825–32.

18. Broughton, *Recollections of a Long Life*, vol. 1, pp. 156–7; Leslie Marchand, *Byron. A Biography* (1957), vol. 1, p. 459.

19. Details of the procession from *Annual Register for 1814*, Chronicle, pp. 57–9; Charles Abbot, Lord Colchester, *The Diary and Correspondence of Charles Abbot, Lord Colchester*, ed. his son, Charles, Lord Colchester (1861), vol. 2, p. 509; Farington, *Diary*, vol. 13, pp. 4548–9. The hissing at the Prince Regent is reported by Mrs Calvert, *An Irish Beauty under the Regency compiled from 'Mes Souvenirs' - the Unpublished Journals of the Hon. Mrs Calvert, 1789–1822*, ed. Mrs Warenne Blake (1911), p. 232.

20. Farington, *Diary*, vol. 13, p. 4549.

21. *Annual Register 1814*, Chronicle, p. 60; Abbot, *Diary and Correspondence*, vol. 2, p. 509; Captain Robert W. Eastwick, *A Master Mariner. Being the Life and Adventures of Captain Robert W. Eastwick*, ed. Herbert Compton (1891), p. 125.

22. Michael Edwardes, *Warren Hastings. King of the Nabobs* (1976), p. 190; Journal of C.W. Pasley, BL Add Ms 41,977 f 40; Sir John Kaye, *The Life and Correspondence of Major-General Sir John Malcolm* ... (1856), vol. 2, p. 92. Both these references are courtesy of the modern John Malcolm.

23. Calvert, *Irish Beauty*, p. 233.

24. Shelley, *Diary of Lady Shelley*, vol. 1, pp. 70–1.

25. R.G Thorne, The *History of Parliament. The House of Commons, 1790–1820* (1986), vol. 5, pp. 139–40.

26. Jane Wellesley, *Wellington. A Journey Through My Family* (2008), pp. 176–97 gives a useful account of Kitty's life during the Peninsular War which provides a valuable supplement to Joan A. Wilson's *A Soldier's Wife. Wellington's Marriage* (1987). See p. 179 for the suggestion that Kitty was battling depression, which seems plausible but unprovable.

27. Quoted in Wilson, *A Soldier's Wife*, p. 154.

28. Ibid., pp. 154–6.

29. Ibid., p. 158; Elizabeth Longford, *Wellington. The Years of the Sword* (1969), p. 362.

30. Memorandum on the defence of the frontier of the Netherlands, 22 September 1814, *WD*, vol. 7, pp. 564–7; also Wellington to Castlereagh, 27 September 1814, *WSD*, vol. 9, p. 289 for Mons and Namur. Wellington carelessly refers to the western or Scheldt end of the line as 'the left' - which is true as you look at a map, or if you are a French invader, but not if you are defending the country and facing south.

31. Wellington to Bathurst, 20 August 1814, *WSD*, vol. 9, pp. 187–8.

32. Castlereagh to Wellington, 6 August 1814; Prince Regent to the King of France, 9 August 1814, *WSD*, vol. 9, pp. 174–6, 176–7.

33. Wellington to Villiers, 31 August 1814; Wellington to Macaulay, 12 September 1814; Wellington to Liverpool, 12 September 1814; Wellington to Wilberforce, 15 September and 4 November 1814, *WD*, vol. 7, pp. 543–4, 553, 553–4, 557–9, 594; Liverpool to Wellington, 7 September 1814; Clarkson to the Duke of Gloucester, 27 August 1814, *WSD*, vol. 19,

pp. 225–7, 228–30 (there are many other letters on the subject in both volumes). See also Martha Putney, 'The Slave Trade in French Diplomacy from 1814 to 1815' (1975), pp. 411–27, and Robin Furneaux, *William Wilberforce* (1974), pp. 338–9.

34. Police report quoted in Philip Mansel, *Paris Between Empires. Monarchy and Revolution, 1814–1852* (2003), p. 58 – see also p. 54 for the King's favouritism. Lord Hardwicke to Charles Abbot, 16 October 1814, Abbot, *Diary and Correspondence*, vol. 2, pp. 520–2.

35. Mansel, *Paris Between Empires*, p. 59; Broughton, *Recollections of a Long Life*, vol. 1, p. 189.

36. Lady Dalrymple Hamilton quoted in Mansel, *Paris Between Empires*, p. 53; Lady Bessborough to Granville Leveson Gower, 8 November and 21 December 1814, Lord Granville Leveson Gower, *Lord Granville Leveson Gower (First Earl Granville). Private Correspondence 1781 to 1821*, ed. Castalia Countess Granville (1916), vol. 2, pp. 504, 515–17; Elizabeth Yorke to Mrs Yorke, 28 October 1814 in Augustus Hare, *The Story of Two Noble Lives. Being Memorials of Charlotte, Countess Canning and Louisa, Marchioness of Waterford* (1893), vol. 1, pp. 28–9. Madame de Staël's letters in *The Unpublished Correspondence of Madame de Staël and the Duke of Wellington*, ed. Victor de Pange (1965), p. 5; his impression is from Harriet Arbuthnot, *The Journal of Mrs Arbuthnot 1820–1832*, ed. Francis Bamford and the Duke of Wellington (1950; henceforth cited as *JMrsA*), 5 January 1832, vol. 1, p. 135.

37. Lady Elizabeth Yorke to Mrs Yorke, 28 October 1814; Hare, *Story of Two Noble Lives*, vol. 1, pp. 28–9; the Duchess of Wellington to Caroline Hamilton, 27 October 1814, quoted in Eliza Pakenham, *Soldier Sailor. An Intimate Portrait of an Irish Family* (2007), p. 140.

38. Lady Bessborough to Granville Leveson Gower, 13 November 1814, Leveson Gower, *Private Correspondence*, vol. 2, pp. 506–7.

39. Beckles Wilson, *The Paris Embassy 1814–1920* (1927), pp. 39–40. Some secondary accounts suggest that Wellington also had an affair with the actress Mlle Georges at this time; however there appears to be little or no evidence to support this story, which appears first in Longford and has then been copied from one biography to another.

40. See Castlereagh to Wellington, 21 November 1814, *WSD*, vol. 9, pp. 446–7 for a warm tribute to the importance of the role Wellington played in facilitating the Anglo-French alliance.

41. C.K Webster, *The Foreign Policy of Castlereagh 1812–1814* (1931), pp. 397–405, esp. 398 and 401; Wellington to Castlereagh, 26 December 1814, *WSD*, vol. 9, pp. 511–2; see also Wellington to Liverpool, 25 December 1814 and 23 January 1815, *WSD*, vol. 9, pp. 503–4, 543.

42. Liverpool to Wellington, 4, 13 and 18 November, and replies, 7, 16 and 21 November 1814, *WSD*, vol. 9, pp. 405–7, 430–1, 434–7 and 449.

43. Quoted in Enno E. Kraehe, *Metternich's German Policy*, vol. 2, p. 308.

44. Talleyrand to Louis XVIII, 8 February 1815, Prince Talleyrand, quoted in M.G Pallain, ed., *Correspondence of Talleyrand and Louis XVIII during the Congress of Vienna* (1881), pp. 303–4.

45. Wellington to Castlereagh, 18, 21 and 25 February, 4 March 1815, *WSD*, vol. 9, pp. 569–72, 574, 578–80, 584–7; Kraehe, *Metternich's German Policy*, vol. 2, *The Congress of Vienna 1814–1815* (1983), pp. 308–17.

46. Wellington to Castlereagh, 18 February and 4 March 1815, *WSD*, vol. 9, pp. 569–72, 584–7; see also T.I. Leiren, 'Norwegian Independence and British Opinion: January to August 1814' (1975), pp. 364–82.

47. Wellington to Castlereagh, 4 March 1815, *WSD*, vol. 9, p. 584. This considerably over-simplifies a complex story – see Webster, *Foreign Policy of Castlereagh*, pp. 397–408 for a more detailed account.

48. Wellington to Castlereagh, 4 March 1815, and Castlereagh to Wellington, 28 February 1815, *WSD*, vol. 9, pp. 584, 583.

49. Wellington to Castlereagh, 12 March 1815, *WSD*, vol. 9, pp. 588–90.

2 The Return of Napoleon

1. Kraehe, *Metternich's German Policy*, vol. 2, p. 327; Wellington to Castlereagh, 12 March 1815, *WSD*, vol. 9, pp. 588–90.

2. Declarations of the Allied Powers, 13 March 1815, *Annual Register 1815*, pp. 366–7; the original French text is in *WD*, vol. 8, p. 378; Kraehe, *Metternich's German Policy*, vol. 2, p. 330; Hilde Spiel, ed., *The Congress of Vienna. An Eyewitness Account* (1968), p. 49 quoting Humboldt.

3. Wellington to Castlereagh, Private, 12 March 1815, WP 1/453, passage deleted from version printed in *WD*, vol. 8, pp. 2–3; see also Kraehe, *Metternich's German Policy*, vol. 2, pp. 329–30.
4. Wellington to Castlereagh, 12 March, *WD*, vol. 8, pp. 2–3, 1–2 (two letters).
5. Quoted in Philip Mansel, *Louis XVIII* (1981), p. 227.
6. Queen Charlotte to the Prince Regent, Windsor, 23 March 1815, in George IV, *The Letters of King George IV 1812–1830*, ed. A. Aspinall (1938), vol. 2, pp. 46–7.
7. Samuel Romilly, *Memoirs of the Life of Sir Samuel Romilly*, ed. his sons (1840), vol. 3, pp. 159–60, diary for 22 March 1815.
8. J.W. Ward, *Letters to 'Ivy' from the first Earl of Dudley* (1905), 24 March, pp. 278–83.
9. R.I. and S. Wilberforce, *The Life of William Wilberforce by his Sons* (1838), vol. 4, diary for 27 April and 10 May, vol. 4, pp. 258, 259; Grey to Lord Wellesley, 2 and 6 April 1815, BL Add Ms 37,297, ff 236–7, 238–9; also *Parliamentary Debates*, vol. 30, cols. 344–6 and 369–72.
10. *Parliamentary Debates*, vol. 30, cols. 444–5 – the sequence of the quoted passages has been changed to clarify the argument but this does not affect their meaning.
11. Castlereagh to Wellington, 8 April 1815, *WSD*, vol. 10, pp. 44–5.
12. Wellington to William Wellesley-Pole, 5 May 1815, WP 1/464, printed in *WD*, vol. 8, pp. 61–2 with Whitbread's name deleted.
13. Memorandum by the Marquess Wellesley, nd, *WSD*, vol. 9, pp. 636–8. Lord Wellesley's views as publicly expressed in Parliament on 7 and 12 April 1815 (*Parliamentary Debates*, vol. 30, cols. 366–9, 545–57) were less negative and more conventional, although he clearly sided with the Opposition. Severn, *Architects of Empire*, pp. 378–9.
14. Wellington to Clancarty, 10 April 1815, WO 1/205, pp. 45–56 – printed with minor variations in *WD*, vol. 8, pp. 21–3. On the wider question, Castlereagh to Wellington, 'Secret and Private', 16 April 1815, *WSD*, vol. 10, pp. 80–1; Clancarty to Castlereagh, 'Private and Secret', 15 April 1815, C.K Webster, ed., *British Diplomacy 1813–1815. Select Documents* (1921), pp. 325–30; and Rory Muir, *Britain and the Defeat of Napoleon, 1807–1815* (1996), pp. 348–50.
15. Wellington to Castlereagh, 'Private and Confidential', 11 April 1815, *WSD*, vol. 10, pp. 60–2.
16. Münster to the Prince Regent, 25 March 1815, in George Herbert, Count Münster, *Political Sketches of the State of Europe from 1814–1867* (1868), pp. 230–4; Cathcart to Wellington and Cathcart to Castlereagh, 1 April 1815, *WSD*, vol. 10, pp. 11–13; Clancarty to Wellington, 1 April 1815, *WSD*, vol. 10, pp. 13–14; Wellington to Clancarty, 9 April 1815, WP 1/457 (printed, with deletions in *WSD*, vol. 10, p. 48: 'As for the contingents of the North of Germany, it appears that Metternich has as usual left us on the lurch'). Enno E. Kraehe, *Metternich's German Policy*, vol. 1, *The Contest with Napoleon, 1799–1814* (1963), pp. 332–6; Kraehe, 'Wellington and the Reconstruction of the Allied Armies during the Hundred Days' (1989), pp. 84–97, see esp. 87–93. For the mutinies of Saxon troops see Roger Parkinson, *The Hussar General* (1975), p. 210 and Peter Hofschröer, *1815, The Waterloo Campaign*, vol. 1, *Wellington, His German Allies and the Battles of Ligny and Quatre Bras* (1998), pp. 48–55.
17. Kraehe, 'Wellington and the Reconstruction of the Allied Armies', p. 94.
18. Wellington to Castlereagh, 26 March 1815, WP 1/453, printed with a silent deletion re the Austrian troops in *WD*, vol. 8, pp. 11–12; Bathurst to Wellington, 7 April 1815, *WSD*, vol. 10, pp. 27–8. Bathurst made it clear that he regarded the delay, not the cost, as the more serious problem. Wellington to the Prince Regent of Portugal, Brussels, 16 April 1815, *WD*, vol. 8, pp. 33–4; Malyn Newitt, 'Lord Beresford and the Governadores of Portugal' in Malyn Newitt and Martin Robson, *Lord Beresford and British Intervention in Portugal 1807–1820* (2004), pp. 91–3.
19. Wellington to Bathurst, 'Private', 28 April 1815, *WSD*, vol. 10, pp. 167–8 (difficulties with the King); Colborne to Bunbury, 'Private', 21 March 1815, BL Add Ms 37,052, f 77–80; see also Stuart to Castlereagh, no. 59, 31 March 1815, FO 37/78, unfoliated; Bathurst to Wellington, 2 May 1815, *WSD*, vol. 10, pp. 215–16 (two letters).
20. For Wellington's views see Harrowby to Castlereagh, 7 April 1815, *WSD*, vol. 10, pp. 31–5 (reporting Wellington's views); Wellington to Clancarty, 10 and 13 April 1815, *WD*, vol. 8, pp. 21–3, 27–9, cf Memorandum, 12 April 1815, *WD*, vol. 8, pp. 26–7, and Wellington to Sir Henry Wellesley, 2 June 1815, *WD*, vol. 8, p. 118. For Castlereagh's views see Castlereagh to Wellington, 26 March 1815, Webster, *British Diplomacy*, pp. 317–18, and Castlereagh to Clancarty, 3 April 1815, *WSD*, vol. 10, pp. 697–8.
21. Wellington to Bathurst, 'Private', 6 April 1815, WP 1/457, printed in *WD*, vol. 8, pp. 17–18, with names deleted; Memorandum by Torrens, 8 April 1815, *WSD*, vol. 10, pp. 49–51, cf Scott Bowden, *Armies at Waterloo* (1983), pp. 272, 318.

22. Duke of Cambridge to Wellington, 7 April, *WSD*, vol. 10, pp. 26–7, but cf Torrens to Bathurst, 8 April, *WSD*, vol. 10, pp. 41–3.
23. Colborne to Bunbury, 'Private', 21 March 1815, BL Add Ms 37,052, f 77–80; see also Kleist to the King of Prussia, 19 March 1815, quoted in Hofschröer, *1815*, vol. 1, p. 85; and Hon. J.W. Fortescue, *A History of the British Army* (1899–1930), vol. 10, p. 244.
24. Wellington to Stewart, 8 May 1815, *WD*, vol. 8, p. 66. See also J.C. Ropes, *The Campaign of Waterloo. A Military History* (1893), p. 43 quoting Ellesmere's essays.
25. Wellington to Bathurst, 4 May 1815, WP 1/464, printed in *WSD*, vol. 10, pp. 218–19 with a significant deletion. See also Wellington to Torrens, Brussels, 21 April 1815, *WD*, vol. 8, pp. 36–7 and reply: Torrens to Wellington, 'Private', 25 April 1815, WO 3/609, pp. 145–51.
26. Charles Dalton, *The Waterloo Roll Call* (1978), pp. 9–11, 33–9; Fortescue, *History of the British Army*, vol. 10, pp. 241–2; Sir J.E. Edmonds, 'Wellington's Staff at Waterloo' (1933), p. 240, which states that thirty-one of thirty-three officers holding senior positions on Wellington's staff at Waterloo had seen considerable service in the Peninsula.
27. Torrens to Wellington, 1 April 1815, *WSD*, vol. 10, pp. 10–11; Marquess of Anglesey, *One Leg. The Life and Letters of Henry William Paget, First Marquess of Anglesey 1768–1854* (1963), pp. 119–21; Torrens to Uxbridge, 'Private', 13 April 1815; Torrens to Combermere, 'Private and Confidential', 13 April, and 'Private', 18 April 1815, WO 3/609, pp. 114–16, 116–18, 134–7.
28. Michael Glover, *Wellington as Military Commander* (1968), p. 235; Wellington to Bathurst, 25 June 1815, WP 1/471, printed with this passage and some others deleted in *WD*, vol. 8, pp. 168–9.
29. Figures based on Bowden, *Armies at Waterloo*, pp. 272, 318. Their apparent precision is, of course, misleading and they should be taken only as a broad indication. Still, they are given to convey a sense of the overall forces at Wellington's disposal in June 1815: too many accounts concentrate exclusively on those present at Waterloo on 18 June.
30. Blücher quoted in Parkinson, *Hussar General*, p. 208; Wellington to Castlereagh, 9 April 1815, WP 1/457; see also Hofschröer, *1815*, vol. 1, pp. 104–5.
31. J.H. Rose, ed., 'Sir Hudson Lowe and the Beginnings of the Campaign of 1815' (1910), pp. 517–27, esp. Lowe to Müffling, 28 March 1815, pp. 521–2; Hofschröer, *1815*, vol. 1, pp. 90–8, and Wellington to Clancarty, 6 April 1815, *WD*, vol. 8, p. 17.
32. Gneisenau to Sir Hudson Lowe, 7 April 1815, in Rose, ed., 'Sir Hudson Lowe', p. 525. As the editor J.H. Rose points out, this letter and others printed in this article cast considerable doubt on Müffling's story that Gneisenau expressed great distrust of Wellington before the campaign began. See also Hofschröer, *1815*, vol. 1, p. 113 for more evidence of Gneisenau's commitment to co-operation.
33. Wellington to Clancarty, 3 May 1815, WP 1/464, printed with some deletions in *WD*, vol. 8, p. 57; Hofschröer, *1815*, vol. 1, pp. 116–17, 122–3; Michael V. Leggiere, *Blücher. Scourge of Napoleon* (2014), pp. 381, 385.
34. Wellington to Stewart, 8 May 1815, *WD*, vol. 8, pp. 66–9; Hardinge to Fitzroy Somerset, 2 June 1815, *WSD*, vol. 10, p. 413; see also Hofschröer, *1815*, vol. 1, pp. 122–3, but cf p. 108: the final decision was not up to either Wellington or Blücher.
35. Fanny Burney, *Diary and Letters of Madame D'Arblay (1778–1840)* (1905), vol. 6, p. 207; Spencer Madan, *Spencer and Waterloo. The Letters of Spencer Madan, 1814–1816*, ed. Beatrice Madan (1970), pp. 95–6.
36. Creevey's journal, 22 April 1815, Thomas Creevey, *The Creevey Papers. A Selection from the Correspondence and Diaries of the late Thomas Creevey, MP*, ed. Sir Herbert Maxwell (1923), p. 215; Lady Capel to her mother, *c.* 2 and *c.* 13 June 1815, Lady Caroline Capel et al, *The Capel Letters. Being the Correspondence of Lady Caroline Capel and her Daughters with the Dowager Countess of Uxbridge from Brussels and Switzerland, 1814–1817*, ed. the Marquess of Anglesey (1955), pp. 100–2, 107. For Wellington's flirtation with Lady Frances Webster at this time see below, p. 91.

3 Quatre Bras

1. Even the Bourbons had looked to war with Murat in part as a way of lessening discontent in the army. Wellington to Castlereagh, 26 December 1814, and to Liverpool, 23 January 1815, *WSD*, vol. 9, pp. 511–12, 543.
2. Henry Houssaye, *1815, Waterloo* (1990), pp. 40–8.

3. Hofschröer, *1815*, vol. 1, pp. 220–2.

4. See Hofschröer, *1815*, vol. 1, pp. 136–59, 192–3, and John Hussey, 'At What Time on 15 June Did Wellington Learn of Napoleon's Attack on the Prussians?' (1999), pp. 90–3, 99–100; Parkinson, *Hussar General*, p. 215; Wellington to Lynedoch, 13 June 1815, *WD*, vol. 8, p. 135.

5. Hofschröer, *1815*, vol. 1, pp. 187–8, and Hussey, 'At What Time', pp. 92–3, agree on this.

6. For the most recent controversy on the subject of Zieten's message and related issues see Hofschröer, *1815*, vol. 1, pp. 192–200, 331–5; Peter Hofschröer, 'Did the Duke of Wellington Deceive his Prussian Allies in the Campaign of 1815?' *War in History* (1998), pp. 176–203; Hussey, 'At What Time', and Hofschröer's reply, loc. cit., pp. 468–78; Hussey, 'Towards a Better Chronology of the Waterloo Campaign' (2000), pp. 463–80; Gregory Pedlow, 'Back to the Sources: General Zieten's Message to the Duke of Wellington on 15 June 1815' (2005), pp. 30–5; John Hussey, 'Müffling, Gleig, Ziethen, and the "Missing" Wellington Records: The "Compromising" Documents Traced' (1999), pp. 250–68; Peter Hofschröer, 'Yet Another Reply to John Hussey: What *Really* are my Charges Against the Duke of Wellington?' (2000), pp. 221–5 and 305. There is no space to discuss the details of the question here, but see the online commentary at www.lifeofwellington.com.

7. The orders are printed in *WD*, vol. 8, p. 142 and discussed in W.H. James, *The Campaign of 1815, Chiefly in Flanders* (1908), pp. 96–7&n.

8. Erwin Muilwijk, 'Waterloo Campaign 1815: The Contribution of the Netherlands Mobile Army' (online, accessed late 2007), cf Muilwijk, *1815*, vol. 1, *From Mobilisation to War* (2012), pp. 231–44, and Muilwijk, *1815*, vol. 2, *Quatre Bras, Perponcher's Gamble* (2013), p. 17.

9. Printed in *WD*, vol. 8, p. 152 and discussed in James, *Campaign of 1815*, p. 98.

10. William Verner, *Reminiscences of William Verner (1782–1871), 7th Hussars* (1965), p. 40; the Hon. Katharine Arden to her aunt, Miss Bootle Wilbraham, 9 July 1815; 'Waterloo. A Contemporary Letter' (1898) (3rd series, vol. 4), pp. 72–3.

11. Muilwijk, 'Waterloo', cf Muilwijk, *1815*, vol. 1, pp. 231–2, 239–41; Hofschröer, *1815*, vol. 1, pp. 215–17.

12. George Bowles in James Harris, 1st Earl Malmesbury, ed., *A Series of Letters of the first Earl of Malmesbury, His Family and Friends* (1870), vol. 2, pp. 445–6.

13. Prince Bernhard of Saxe-Weimar to General Perponcher, 9am, 15 June 1815, in R. Starklof, *The Life of Duke Bernhard of Saxe-Weimar-Eisenach* (1996), p. 135; see also Muilwijk, 'Waterloo', cf Muilwijk, *1815*, vol. 1, pp. 211–18 for the context.

14. Muilwijk, 'Waterloo', cf Muilwijk, *1815*, vol. 2, p. 31 based on the Prince's letter to Wellington of 7am, 16 June 1815.

15. Muilwijk, 'Waterloo', cf Muilwijk, *1815*, vol. 2, pp. 41–2.

16. Wellington's letter is printed, in English translation, in Ropes, *Campaign of Waterloo*, p. 106. It has been the subject of much controversy and discussion – see Hofschröer, 'Did the Duke of Wellington Deceive his Prussian Allies', *passim*; Hofschröer, *1815*, vol. 1, pp. 336–41, 346–7; Maj.-Gen. C.W. Robinson, 'Waterloo and the De Lancey Memorandum' (1910), pp. 582–97. For a similar Prussian letter see Gneisenau to Müffling, noon, 15 June 1815 in Hofschröer, *1815*, vol. 1, p. 198. For Wellington's letter to be significant it must be argued that Blücher would have reversed his decision to fight at Ligny on 16 June if he had received an accurate statement of the location of Wellington's troops late on the morning of 16 June. This is most implausible; it was probably too late to withdraw safely, and Blücher's eagerness to fight was proverbial.

17. For the orders to the Reserve, see [Robert Torrens], 'A Waterloo Letter' (1914), p. 840.

18. Philip Henry Stanhope, 5th Earl, *Notes of Conversations with the Duke of Wellington* (1888), p. 109; Hofschröer, *1815*, vol. 1, pp. 239–42.

19. Soult to Ney, 2pm, 16 June 1815, quoted in Capt. A.F. Becke, *Napoleon and Waterloo* (1914), vol. 2, p. 286.

20. Quoted in ibid., vol. 2, p. 284.

21. Fortescue, *History of the British Army*, vol. 10, p. 318. Mike Robinson, in his hugely detailed account of the battle, agrees: 'Les Quatre Bras was a confusing battle . . . Little is known of the sequence of events; [and] long periods of time and large areas of the fighting remain shrouded in mystery': Mike Robinson, *The Battle of Quatre Bras, 1815* (2009), p. 8.

22. N. Ludlow Beamish, *History of the King's German Legion* (1832–37), vol. 2, p. 337.

23. Ibid., vol. 2, pp. 327–8.
24. Muilwijk, 'Waterloo', cf Muilwijk, *1815*, vol. 2, pp. 110–16; private information from Erwin Muilwijk in an e-mail of 31 October 2007; Somerset in Edward Owen, ed., *The Waterloo Papers. 1815 and Beyond* (1997), p. 9.
25. Maj. George Simmons, *A British Rifleman. The Journals and Correspondence of Major George Simmons . . .*, ed. Lt.-Col. Willoughby Verner (1899), p. 366.
26. Extract from a letter from an unnamed officer of the 32nd, dated Antwerp, 25 June 1815, printed in Col. G.C. Swiney, *Historical Records of the 32nd (Cornwall) Light Infantry . . .* (1893), p. 116.
27. Beamish, *History of the King's German Legion*, vol. 2, p. 330, says it lost more than half its men but Hanoverian casualties show that the whole brigade lost only 225 casualties and that it had 70 men taken prisoner.
28. Letter from Major Robert Winchester in Maj.-Gen. H.T. Siborne, *Waterloo Letters. A Selection from Original and Hitherto Unpublished Letters* (1891), p. 386.
29. Ibid., pp. 386–7.
30. Quoted in Becke, *Napoleon and Waterloo*, vol. 1, pp. 286–7.
31. Houssaye, *1815, Waterloo*, pp. 118–20.
32. Siborne, *Waterloo Letters*, pp. 322–3.
33. 'Near Observer', *The Battle of Waterloo . . . with Circumstantial Details . . . by a Near Observer* (2nd edn, 1815; 8th edn, 1816; 11th edition, 1852), p. xlvii, quoting a letter from an officer of the Guards.
34. Sir Augustus Simon Frazer, *The Letters of Colonel Augustus Simon Frazer, K.C.B, commanding the Royal Horse Artillery in the Army under the Duke of Wellington*, ed. Edward Sabine (2001; first pub. 1859), pp. 539–40 (letter of 7.30am, 17 June 1815); Wellington to Lady Frances Webster, 3am, 18 June 1815, *WSD*, vol. 10, p. 501.
35. W. Siborne, *The Waterloo Campaign* (1900), p. 186, gives Ney's force late in the day as 16,189 infantry, 4,974 cavalry and 50 guns. This included the whole of the Twelfth Cavalry Division whereas it appears that only Guiton's brigade was present, reducing the total to barely 20,000 infantry and cavalry; however, these totals seem to be for rank and file only – adding officers, sergeants and so on, plus the gunners, would bring the total to close to 25,000 men. Siborne's figures for Wellington's army are: 24,669 infantry, 2,004 cavalry and 70 guns – this includes the Guards but not the British cavalry. Again this is apparently rank and file; but all these figures are more than usually hard to determine, and consequently no more than approximate.
36. Ney quoted in Becke, *Napoleon and Waterloo*, vol. 2, p. 287; Siborne, *Waterloo Campaign*, p. 193, 'about 4,000'; Fortescue, *History of the British Army*, vol. 10, p. 322, 4,100 or 4,200; Ropes, *Campaign of Waterloo*, p. 184, 'over 4,000'; Becke, *Napoleon and Waterloo*, vol. 1, p. 210, 'about 4,000'; James, *Campaign of 1815*, p. 146, 4,500; Houssaye, *1815, Waterloo*, p. 123, 4,300 French.
37. Peter Hofschröer, *1815, The Waterloo Campaign*, vol. 2, *The German Victory* (1999), p. 19; Fortescue, *History of the British Army*, vol. 10, p. 327; Antony Brett-James, *The Hundred Days* (1964), pp. 79–80, prints the account of one such message.
38. Felton Hervey to Mr Carroll, 3 July 1815, Sir Felton Hervey, 'A Contemporary Letter on the Battle of Waterloo' (1893), p. 432; Hofschröer, *1815*, vol. 2, p. 22.
39. Hofschröer, *1815*, vol. 2, p. 35. This is the most plausible statement of Prussian losses at Ligny; however, estimates vary widely.
40. Ibid., vol. 2, p. 24; confirmed by Frazer, *Letters*, p. 542 (letter of 9.30am, 17 June 1815).
41. Instructions to Major Gen. Colville, 17 June 1815, *WD*, vol. 8, p. 144.
42. For more on this see below, p. 56.
43. Frederick Ponsonby in Earl of Bessborough and A. Aspinall, eds., *Lady Bessborough and her Family Circle* (1941), p. 241; Siborne, *Waterloo Letters*, p. 154.
44. Bowden, *Armies at Waterloo*, p. 308.
45. cf Fortescue, *History of the British Army*, vol. 10, pp. 334–7, who is critical of Uxbridge, while Houssaye, *1815, Waterloo*, p. 149 describes him as acting like a cornet, which is certainly unfair. Casualties from W. Siborne, *History of the War in France and Belgium in 1815* (1848), p. 558 include those incurred in skirmishing before the retreat began.
46. Fortescue, *History of the British Army*, vol. 10, p. 338; Houssaye, *1815, Waterloo*, p. 151.

4 Waterloo

1. Wellington to the Duc de Berri, the governor of Antwerp and Sir Charles Stuart, all dated Waterloo, 3am, 18 June 1815, *WD*, vol. 8, pp. 145–6; Wellington to Lady Frances Webster, three o'clock, 18 June 1815, *WSD*, vol. 10, p. 501.

2. Quoted in Fortescue, *History of the British Army*, vol. 10, p. 347, cf James Stanhope, *Eyewitness to the Peninsular War and the Battle of Waterloo. The Letters and Journals of Lieutenant Colonel the Honourable James Stanhope, 1803 to 1825*, ed. Gareth Glover (2010), p. 180.

3. David Chandler, *The Campaigns of Napoleon* (1974), pp. 181–91, explains the concept and practice with characteristic elegance and clarity.

4. Hofschröer, *1815*, vol. 2, pp. 30–1.

5. Houssaye, *1815, Waterloo*, p. 176; Fortescue, *History of the British Army*, vol. 10, p. 352; it is not clear how Fortescue calculates this figure: it may simply be an attempt to count only the rank and file; Bowden, *Armies at Waterloo*, pp. 227, 271.

6. Houssaye, *1815, Waterloo*, p. 185; Bowden, *Armies at Waterloo*, pp. 131–4; Fortescue, *History of the British Army*, vol. 10, p. 354, gives 70,000 again without explaining the reduction.

7. Allied artillery: Fortescue, *History of the British Army*, vol. 10, p. 352 says 156 guns; Bowden, *Armies at Waterloo*, p. 271, says 157; Houssaye, *1815, Waterloo*, says 184. French artillery: Bowden, *Armies at Waterloo*, pp. 131–2, says 254; Houssaye, *1815, Waterloo*, p. 185, says 246.

8. Malcolm's journal, 24 July 1815, in Kaye, *Life of Malcolm*, vol. 2, p. 102.

9. Captain Oldfield's account quoted in Andrew Uffindell, *The National Army Museum Book of Wellington's Armies* (2003), pp. 292–3; T.W.J. Connolly, *History of the Royal Sappers and Miners* (1857), pp. 232–5, is unconvincing in his attempt to defend the conduct of officers and men on this occasion. See also [John Sperling], *Letters of an Officer of the Corps of Royal Engineers* (1872), pp. 131–2.

10. Oldfield in Uffindell, *National Army Museum Book of Wellington's Armies*, p. 294.

11. Beamish, *History of the King's German Legion*, vol. 2, p. 453.

12. See a very interesting letter from Sir Hew Ross to Siborne in 1835 explaining his doubts as to the accuracy of his recollections: H.D. Ross, *Memoir of Field Marshal Sir Hew Dalrymple Ross R.H.A.* (1871), p. 67.

13. Wellington to Bathurst, 19 June 1815, *WD*, vol. 8, pp. 148–9.

14. Wellington to Croker, 8 August, WP 1/478/54, *WD*, vol. 8, pp. 231–2, with Croker's name suppressed.

15. Sir James Shaw Kennedy, *Notes on the Battle of Waterloo* (2003; first pub. 1865), p. 98; Houssaye, *1815, Waterloo*, p. 203.

16. Alten to Wellington, 19 June 1815, *WSD*, vol. 10, pp. 534–5; see also Kennedy, *Notes on the Battle of Waterloo*, pp. 98–102.

17. Siborne, *Waterloo Letters*, pp. 35, 383; Rev. William Leeke, *The History of Lord Seaton's Regiment (the 52nd Light Infantry) at the Battle of Waterloo* (1866), vol. 1, pp. 73–5 and many other sources refer to being in four-deep line but few discuss it. See unpublished essay by Howie Muir.

18. Fitzroy Somerset in Owen, ed., *Waterloo Papers*, pp. 11–12; for Captain Taylor see P. Carew, 'A Hussar of the Hundred Days' (1945), pp. 302–3; and Frazer, *Letters*, pp. 553–4; for ammunition see Frazer, *Letters*, p. 545; for rations Lt.-Col. Neil Bannatyne, *History of the Thirtieth Regiment* (1923), p. 329.

19. Edmund Wheatley, *The Wheatley Diary. A Journal and Sketchbook kept during the Peninsular War and the Waterloo Campaign*, ed. Christopher Hibbert (1964), pp. 63–4.

20. All three quotes in Houssaye, *1815, Waterloo*, pp. 177–8. It is possible that Reille's remarks represent what in hindsight he wished he had said, rather than something he actually said, but even so they are interesting.

21. Houssaye argues in favour of this line of attack: *1815, Waterloo*, p. 186.

22. Ibid., pp. 185, 408.

23. Ibid., pp. 180, 190–2.

24. Ten o'clock: Wellington in his official despatch although in August he told Croker eleven o'clock; twelve noon: Wellington to Bathurst, 19 June, and to Croker, 17 August 1815, *WD*, vol. 8, pp. 146–51, 244–5; Horace Churchill to his father, 24 June 1815, in H.A. Bruce, *Life of General Sir William Napier* (1864), vol. 1, p. 176; Ney in Frederick Llewellyn, ed., *Waterloo Recollections. Rare First Hand Accounts, Letters, Reports and Retellings from the Campaign of*

1815 (2007), pp. 65–6; Rowland Hill in Edwin Sidney, *The Life of Lord Hill* (1845), p. 310 and Wheatley, *Wheatley Diary*, p. 64.

25. Malcolm's journal in Kaye, *Life of Malcolm*, vol. 2, p. 102 (for Pozzo di Borgo); Frazer, letter of 9am, 20 June 1815; Frazer, *Letters*, p. 556.

26. Rory Muir, *Tactics and the Experience of Battle in the Age of Napoleon* (1998), p. 148, quoting Jackdaw, *Battle of Waterloo*, where both notes are reproduced and transcribed.

27. Wellington to Bathurst, 19 June 1815, *WD*, vol. 8, pp. 146–51.

28. Dyneley, letter of 25 August, T. Dyneley, *Letters written by Lieut.-General Thomas Dyneley C.B., R.A., while on Active Service between the years 1806 and 1815*, ed. Col. F.A. Whinyates (1984; first pub. 1896), p. 65; Ross, *Memoir*, pp. 60–1 (diary from 18 June); and letter of Sir John May, 23 June 1815, listed for sale with transcription by Berryhill & Sturgeon in 2007 at www.berryhillsturgeon.com.

29. William Tomkinson, *The Diary of a Cavalry Officer in the Peninsular War and Waterloo Campaign*, ed. James Tomkinson (1895), pp. 288–9.

30. Sgt. William Lawrence, *The Autobiography of Sergeant William Lawrence, a Hero of the Peninsular and Waterloo Campaigns*, ed. George Nugent Bankes (1886), pp. 206–7.

31. Ibid., pp. 221–4.

32. For a more extended discussion of the subject see Muir, *Tactics and the Experience of Battle*, pp. 47–50, 193–216.

33. Houssaye, *1815, Waterloo*, p. 193.

34. 'A French Infantry Officer's Account of Waterloo' (1878), p. 460. The officer's name appears to have been Captain Duthilt.

35. W.M. Gomm, *Letters and Journals of Field Marshal Sir William Maynard Gomm . . . 1799 to 1815*, ed. Francis Culling Carr-Gomm (1881), p. 358.

36. Houssaye, *1815, Waterloo*, pp. 185–6; Erwin Muilwijk, *Standing Firm at Waterloo, 17 and 18 June 1815* (2014), pp. 135–6; Siborne, *Waterloo Letters*, p. 383.

37. A.E. Clark-Kennedy, *Attack the Colour! The Royal Dragoons in the Peninsula and at Waterloo* (1975), pp. 116–24, for the controversy in the regiment whether Captain Clark or Corporal Styles deserved the credit.

38. 'A French Infantry Officer's Account of Waterloo', p. 461.

39. Casualty figures from return printed in Siborne, *History of the War in France and Belgium* (3rd edn, 1848), p. 564; for the depletion of the brigades during the course of the day see Siborne, *Waterloo Letters*, pp. 68 and 74.

40. Fortescue, *History of the British Army*, vol. 10, p. 367 is particularly severe on Uxbridge, drawing in part on Uxbridge's own comments (printed in Siborne, *Waterloo Letters*, pp. 9–10). See also Anglesey, *One Leg*, pp. 140–2.

41. Houssaye, *1815, Waterloo*, pp. 208–11, is much fairer to the Prussians than W.H. James or Fortescue, both of whose work is marked by a strong anti-German bias, no doubt caused by the tense state of Anglo-German relations at the time (before and during the First World War respectively), exacerbated by the acrimonious controversy over the German role in the victory.

42. Ibid., p. 202.

43. Ibid., p. 203.

44. Quoted in Uffindell, *National Army Museum Book of Wellington's Armies*, pp. 298–9.

45. Ibid., p. 299.

46. Houssaye, *1815, Waterloo*, pp. 207–8.

47. Dr Haddy James, *Surgeon James's Journal, 1815*, ed. Jane Vansittart (1964), p. 47.

48. Wheatley, *Diary*, p. 66.

49. Siborne, *Waterloo Letters*, pp. 18–19. The commanding officer of the regiment was court martialled and cashiered, while the regiment was broken up and distributed through the army to perform menial duties (Gen. Cavalie Mercer, *Journal of the Waterloo Campaign* (1969), pp. 234–5). According to the figures given in Bowden, *Armies at Waterloo*, p. 265, the Cumberland Hussars lost 61 casualties including 18 killed from 516 officers and men present.

50. Quoted in Mark Urban, *Rifles* (2003), p. 272. It is not clear exactly when this panic occurred: Urban puts it at the time of D'Erlon's attack, but it may have been rather later.

51. Ibid., p. 272.

52. Clark to William Vallance, 18 July 1815, in Clark-Kennedy, *Attack the Colour!*, p. 119; see also Thomas Morris, *The Napoleonic Wars*, ed. John Selby (1967), p. 81 where the sergeant major

of the 73rd, who had been in the 43rd in the Peninsula, said: 'We had nothing like this in Spain, Sir.' Ney to Fouché, 26 June 1815, in Llewellyn, *Waterloo Recollections*, p. 66.

53. Wellington to Mulgrave, 21 December 1815, *WSD*, vol. 14, pp. 618–20.

54. Nick Lipscombe, *Wellington's Guns* (2013), pp. 379, 393–7 is far more balanced and convincing than Capt. Francis Duncan, *History of the Royal Regiment of Artillery* (1872), vol. 2, pp. 444–64, and Lt.-Col. H.W.L. Hime, *History of the Royal Regiment of Artillery 1815–1853* (1908), pp. 125–40. See also Gareth Glover, *Waterloo. Myth and Reality* (2014), p. 150, which names seven allied batteries (five of them British) that retired, but no source is cited.

55. Sidney, *Life of Hill*, p. 311.

56. Wellington to the Duke of York, 12 September 1815, *WD*, vol. 8, p. 259 (Portarlington's name supplied in an e-mail from Chris Woolgar, 14 February 2008, having consulted the original letter in the Wellington Papers). See Dalton, *Waterloo Roll Call*, p. 94 for Portarlington's implausible excuses. See also Wellington to Lt.-Gen. Sir G. Nugent, 14 November 1815, *WD*, vol. 8, p. 300: 'In general I am very averse to bringing forward instances of misconduct, after such a battle as that of Waterloo. Many a brave man, and I believe even some very great men, have been found a little terrified by such a battle as that, and have behaved afterwards remarkably well.' See Torrens to Wellington, 29 February 1816, *WSD*, vol. 11, pp. 310–11 for an instance of an officer (Maj. Clayton, Royal Horse Guards) being allowed to sell out rather than be subjected to an inquiry into his conduct.

57. Clark-Kennedy, *Attack the Colour!*, pp. 120–1; Uffindell, *National Army Museum Book of Wellington's Armies*, pp. 308–10.

58. General Order, 20 June 1815, *WD*, vol. 8, p. 156n. For the rear of the army see Tupper Carey, 'Waterloo: Reminiscences of a Commissariat Officer' (1899), p. 730; Sir Richard D. Henegan, *Seven Years Campaigning in the Peninsula and the Netherlands 1808–1815* (2005), vol. 2, pp. 175–7; Verner, *Reminiscences*, p. 47; J. von Pflugk-Harttung, 'Front and Rear of the Battle-Line of Waterloo' (1917), pp. 19–26.

59. Houssaye, *1815, Waterloo*, p. 215; Hamilton in Uffindell, *National Army Museum Book of Wellington's Armies*, p. 300. Official figures show that the 2nd King's German Legion Line Battalion had 437 officers and men on the morning of 18 June and suffered 1 officer and 18 men killed, 2 officers and 79 men wounded and 7 men missing – a total of 107 casualties; Siborne, *History of the War in France and Belgium*, pp. 532, 565 (where the total casualties are erroneously given as 97). Hamilton's figures may not be exact but they are a salutary warning that deducting the number of casualties from the initial strength of a unit is not a reliable guide to its strength at the end of the day, especially for a battle like Waterloo. See also Tomkinson, *Diary of a Cavalry Officer*, p. 289, where he prides himself on the fact that at the end of the day he had 'less than one man away assisting each wounded'.

60. Most secondary accounts put this as late as 6pm or 6.30pm. Such times are always open to debate, but Kempt's report, written on the following day, suggests that it was considerably earlier, while the cavalry charges were at their height. Kempt's report is printed in *WSD*, vol. 10, pp. 535–7.

61. Kempt's report, 19 June 1815, *WSD*, vol. 10, pp. 535–7.

62. Strength of the 1/27th from morning state in *WD*, vol. 8, pp. 392–3; casualties from Siborne, *History of the War in France and Belgium*, p. 564. Letter from an unnamed officer of the 32nd in Swiney, *Historical Records of the 32nd*, pp. 126–7. Bowden, *Armies at Waterloo*, p. 252 says Fifth Division had 6,745 officers and men at Waterloo, despite Quatre Bras casualties. The question is complicated by the issue of which Hanoverian brigade is included, Best's or Vincke's, but the figure of 6,000 is not implausible. Capt. Sir John Kincaid, *Adventures in the Rifle Brigade and Random Shots from a Rifleman* (1981), p. 170 ('Our division. . .'). See also Thomas Morris of the 2/73rd, who wrote that his battalion was reduced to 2 officers and 70 men, having begun the day with 481 all ranks: Morris, *The Napoleonic Wars*, p. 80.

63. John Fremantle to his uncle W.H. Fremantle, 19 June 1815, Lt.-Col. John Fremantle, *Wellington's Voice. The Candid Letters of Lieutenant-Colonel John Fremantle, Coldstream Guards, 1808–1821*, ed. Gareth Glover (2012), p. 211; Apsley to his father, 19 June 1815, Earl Bathurst, *Historical Manuscripts Commission. Report on the Manuscripts of Earl Bathurst preserved at Cirencester Park* (1923) (henceforth cited as *HMC Bathurst*), p. 357; Wildman in Michael Birks, *The Young Hussar* (2007), pp. 185; Frazer, *Letters*, p. 560; Alexander Gordon, *At Wellington's Right Hand. The Letters of Lieutenant-Colonel Sir Alexander Gordon, 1808–1815*, ed. Rory Muir (2003), pp. 403 and 407.

64. Wellington to Beresford, 2 July 1815, *WD*, vol. 8, pp. 185-7.
65. Houssaye, *1815, Waterloo*, pp. 209-11, 218-19.
66. Kennedy, *Notes on the Battle of Waterloo*, pp. 127-30; Houssaye, *1815, Waterloo*, pp. 218, 426.
67. The controversial works include a series of articles and counter-articles and letters in the *United Service Journal* for 1833, begun in the July issue by 'The Crisis and Close of the Action at Waterloo by an eye-witness' (George Gawler, a nineteen-year-old lieutenant in the 52nd at Waterloo), and revived by the publication in 1866 of the Rev. William Leeke's *The History of Lord Seaton's Regiment (the 52nd Light Infantry) at the Battle of Waterloo* in two volumes, which included a good deal of previously published controversial material. Leeke had been a very junior ensign (his commission was dated 4 May 1815) in the regiment at Waterloo. It is worth comparing the boldness and clarity of the claims made in these publications with a letter written on 20 June 1815 by another ensign in the 52nd, John Hart: 'A [*sic*] Ensign's Dispatch from Waterloo written and illustrated by Guy Priest' (1950), p. 1812. (The 1815 Army List shows John Hart as a lieutenant, not an ensign.) See also the scepticism expressed by many correspondents in Siborne, *Waterloo Letters*, e.g. pp. 325, 341.
68. G.C. Moore Smith, *The Life of John Colborne Field-Marshal Lord Seaton* (1903), pp. 234-7.
69. Harry Smith, *The Autobiography of Sir Harry Smith*, ed. G.C. Moore Smith (1910), p. 271; Capt. George Wood, *The Subaltern. A Narrative* (1986), pp. 210-13.
70. Vivian took part in the controversy provoked by Gawler's article (see above). See also Siborne, *Waterloo Letters*, pp. 157-60 (for Vivian) and 320-1, 329-32 (for Halkett's brigade). Vivian's claims receive some support from two letters from officers in his brigade written on 19 and 20 June: Carew, 'A Hussar of the Hundred Days', p. 304 and Capt. T.C. Fenton, 'The Peninsular and Waterloo Letters of Captain Thomas Charles Fenton' (1975), p. 225 (letter of George Luard). Houssaye, *1815, Waterloo*, pp. 220-27, 429n22; see also General Petit's *Account of the Waterloo Campaign* ed. by G.C. Moore Smith (1903), pp. 321-6.
71. Frazer, *Letters*, p. 547; Owen, ed., *Waterloo Papers*, p. 13; letter from Captain Robert Batty, dated 22 June 1815, published in 'Near Observer', *The Battle of Waterloo* (8th edn, 1816), p. lvii.
72. Wellington denied that the meeting with Blücher was at La Belle Alliance and claimed that it was at Genappe (which seems unlikely): Wellington to W. Mudford, 8 June 1816, *WD*, vol. 8, p. 332. Other witnesses affirm it, although looking at the map one would have expected the meeting to have been rather further south.
73. Wellington to Bathurst, 19 June 1815, *WD*, vol. 8, pp. 146-51.
74. Wellington to William Wellesley-Pole, 19 June 1815, 'Letters to Pole', p. 35.
75. Frazer, *Letters*, pp. 549-50 (20 June 1815); letter of Sir John May, 23 June 1815, listed for sale with transcription by Berryhill & Sturgeon in 2007 at www.berryhillsturgeon.com; Horace Churchill's letter of 25 June 1815 printed in Bruce, *Life of Napier*, vol. 1, p. 179; Wildman to his mother, 19 June 1815, in Birks, *The Young Hussar*, p. 180; Uxbridge quoted in Spencer Madan to Dr Madan (14 July 1815), Madan, *Spencer and Waterloo*, pp. 114-15; Lord Apsley to Lord Bathurst, Brussels, 19 June 1815, *HMC Bathurst*, p. 357.
76. Sir Charles Oman, 'French Losses in the Waterloo Campaign' (1904), pp. 681-93, and (1906), pp. 132-5. Bowden, *Armies at Waterloo*, p. 323, gives a figure of 43,656 for French casualties suffered at Waterloo and in the retreat. See also Houssaye, *1815, Waterloo*, pp. 443-4.
77. Allied losses from the table in Siborne's text (*Waterloo Campaign*, p. 587) and appendices (*History of the War in France and Belgium*, pp. 564-77) with some adjustment to allow for Hanoverian and Dutch-Belgian casualties suffered on 16 and 17 June (the tables give only aggregates for these contingents). Unfortunately there is a discrepancy between the figure in the text and the tables in the appendices, hence the range in the totals given. Bowden, *Armies at Waterloo*, p. 325, gives quite different figures, totalling 17,145 for total allied losses, but it is not clear what this figure is based upon.
78. Return printed in *WSD*, vol. 14, p. 633. It is possible that the return is a little distorted - it may exclude those who died during and immediately after surgery - but even so it must represent a high proportion of British casualties suffered during the campaign, and so give a fairly accurate picture of the likely fate of the wounded.
79. Fortescue, *History of the British Army*, vol. 10, p. 395. De Lancey was the acting Quartermaster-General although his formal position was Deputy Quartermaster-General.
80. [Lord William Pitt-Lennox], *Three Years with the Duke, or Wellington in Private Life* (1853), pp. 217-18.

81. Wellington to the Duke of Beaufort, 19 June 1815; Wellington to the Earl of Aberdeen, 19 June 1815, *WD*, vol. 8, pp. 153–4, 154–5.

5 Peacemaking in Paris

1. Journal of Maj. J.H. Slessor, 35th Foot, in Alethea Hayter, *The Backbone. Diaries of a Military Family in the Napoleonic Wars* (1983), p. 302.
2. John Colville, *The Portrait of a General* (1980), pp. 204–5.
3. GOs, 20 and 21 June 1815, *WD*, vol. 8, pp. 156, 159; Tomkinson, *Diary of a Cavalry Officer*, pp. 320–1; James, *Surgeon James's Journal*, p. 47.
4. Wellington to Bathurst, 23 and 25 June 1815, *WD*, vol. 8, p. 163 and WP 1/371 printed with some deletions and alterations in *WD*, vol. 8, pp. 168–9. See also Apsley to Bathurst, 25 June 1815, BL Loan Mss 57, vol. 9, no. 1007.
5. Guillaume de Bertier de Sauvigny, *The Bourbon Restoration* (1966), pp. 104–5; Mansel, *Paris Between Empires*, p. 81; Webster, *Foreign Policy of Castlereagh*, pp. 440–4; Wellington to Talleyrand, 24 June 1815, *WD*, vol. 8, pp. 163–4.
6. Wellington to Bathurst, 25 June 1815, *WD*, vol. 8, pp. 167–8.
7. Wellington to Sir Charles Stuart, 28 June 1815, WP 1/471, printed with some deletions in *WD*, vol. 8, pp. 175–6. See also Leggiere, *Blücher*, pp. 422–3, which shows that the Prussians were indeed talking of executing Napoleon.
8. Shelley, *Diary of Lady Shelley*, vol. 1, p. 105 for mention of Fort St George; Liverpool to Castlereagh, 21 July 1815, *WSD*, vol. 11, p. 47 for the grounds for selecting St Helena and Barrow's role.
9. John G. Gallaher, *The Iron Marshal* (1978), pp. 319–25.
10. Wellington to Bathurst, 2 July 1815, *WD*, vol. 8, pp. 188–93; see also Sauvigny, *Bourbon Restoration*, pp. 106–8.
11. Wellington to Bathurst, 2 July 1815, *WD*, vol. 8, pp. 188–93.
12. The text of the Convention is printed in *WD*, vol. 8, pp. 193–5, and, in English, in Siborne, *Waterloo Campaign*, pp. 754–6. Sauvigny, *Bourbon Restoration*, pp. 106–10; Bathurst to Wellington, and reply, 7 and 13 July 1815, *WD*, vol. 8, p. 206&n. See also *JMrsA*, vol. 1, pp. 340–1.
13. Wellington to Castlereagh, 23 September 1815, *WD*, vol. 8, pp. 267–70. For Wellington's bitterness at the attempt to shift all the blame onto him see Lady Bessborough to Granville Leveson Gower, 11 October 1815, Leveson Gower, *Private Correspondence*, vol. 2, p. 539; and Abbot, *Diary and Correspondence*, 1 October 1815, vol. 2, p. 554.
14. Malcolm's journal, 24 July 1815, in Kaye, *Life of Malcolm*, vol. 2, p. 108; Webster, *Foreign Policy of Castlereagh*, pp. 448–9; Stuart Wortley, *Highcliffe and the Stuarts*, p. 241; Abbot, *Diary and Correspondence*, 1 October 1815, vol. 2, p. 554.
15. Mansel, *Paris Between the Empires*, p. 86.
16. Stuart Wortley, *Highcliffe and the Stuarts*, p. 240; Captain Bowles to Lord Fitzharris, 9 August 1815, Malmesbury, *Series of Letters*, vol. 2, p. 456.
17. J.H. Slessor, 11 July and 1 August 1815, in Hayter, *The Backbone*, pp. 307, 308; Walter Scott to Joanna Baillie, Paris, 10 August–6 September 1815, Sir Walter Scott, *The Letters of Sir Walter Scott, 1787–1832*, ed. H.J.C. Grierson (1932–37), vol. 4, pp. 93–4.
18. Malcolm's journal, 24 July 1815, in Kaye, *Life of Malcolm*, vol. 2, p. 100; Scott to his wife, nd [c. 28 August 1815], *Letters of Sir Walter Scott*, vol. 12, p. 143; Journal of Frances, Lady Cole, 22 August 1815, in G.L. Cole, *Memoirs of Sir Lowry Cole*, ed. Maud Lowry Cole and Stephen Gwynn (1934), p. 173.
19. Details of honours in the *Complete Peerage*.
20. Phrase from Walter Scott to James Ballantyne, 30 August 1815, *Letters of Sir Walter Scott*, vol. 4, p. 88.
21. Shelley, *Diary of Lady Shelley*, 2 August 1815, vol. 1, p. 125.
22. Ibid., vol. 1, pp. 100–1.
23. Ibid., vol. 1, pp. 146–7, 153; Harriet Lady Granville to Lady G. Morpeth, 31 July and 1 August, Granville, Harriet, *Letters of Harriet, Countess Granville, 1810–1845*, ed. F. Leveson Gower, vol. 1, pp. 62 and 67–8, see also p. 72.
24. Shelley, *Diary of Lady Shelley*, vol. 1, p. 150, see also p. 135 and Elizabeth Longford, *Wellington. Pillar of State* (1972), pp. 19–23.

25. *JMrsA*, 4 December 1824, vol. 1, p. 362; Charles Percy to R. Sneyd, 29 September 1815, quoted in Wake, *Sisters of Fortune*, p. 125. Age may partly explain Percy's bile: he was barely twenty-one; Lady Charlotte was forty and had a son his age. John Fremantle to his uncle William, 21 July 1818, Fremantle, *Wellington's Voice*, pp. 293–4; Princess Lieven to Metternich, 1 April 1820, Princess Dorothea Lieven, *Private Letters of Princess Lieven to Prince Metternich, 1820–1826* (1938), p. 26. Longford, *Wellington. Pillar of State*, pp. 86–7 discusses the evidence that Wellington and Charlotte Greville had an affair, including two fragmentary letters, one from her husband and one from her to her son, which had not previously been published. Unfortunately these letters are useless for determining when the affair happened, and are not quite conclusive in establishing that there was an affair, although the other evidence makes it much more likely than not.

26. The portrait is reproduced in Richard Walker, *Regency Portraits* (1985), plate 1325. See Lady Shelley's comments, *Diary of Lady Shelley*, vol. 1, p. 117.

27. Castlereagh to Liverpool, 'Private and Confidential', 17 August 1815, Webster, ed., *British Diplomacy*, pp. 362–7; Webster, *Foreign Policy of Castlereagh*, pp. 470–1.

28. Gneisenau to Müffling, 29 June 1815, in Baron von Müffling, *Memoirs of Baron von Müffling* (1997), p. 275.

29. Wellington to Malcolm, 15 October 1815, BL Add Ms 38,522, f 92.

30. Castlereagh to Liverpool, 24 August 1815 (Precis), in Webster, ed., *British Diplomacy*, pp. 370–1.

31. Liverpool to Castlereagh, 10 and 15 July 1815, *WSD*, vol. 11, pp. 24–5, 32–3.

32. Wellington to Castlereagh, 11 August 1815, WP 1/478 printed in *WD*, vol. 8, pp. 235–8 with some deletions.

33. Wellington to Beresford, 7 August 1815, *WD*, vol. 8, p. 231.

34. The Emperor Alexander was so convinced that the plan could only work if Wellington commanded the army that he was inclined to make it a condition of his support. Castlereagh to Liverpool (Precis), 12 August 1815, *WSD*, vol. 11, pp. 125–6.

35. Webster, *Foreign Policy of Castlereagh*, p. 475.

36. Liverpool to Canning, 4 August 1815, *WSD*, vol. 11, pp. 94–6; see also Memorandum for Castlereagh by Liverpool, 30 June 1815, *WSD*, vol. 10, pp. 630–1: the belief that some examples were necessary pre-dates the Convention of Paris.

37. Michael Glover, *A Very Slippery Fellow. The Life of Sir Robert Wilson, 1777–1848* (1978), pp. 151–60.

38. Lady Malmesbury in Cole, *Memoirs of Sir Lowry Cole*, p. 179; Castlereagh to Liverpool, 24 July 1815, *WSD*, vol. 11, pp. 54–5; Brownlow, *Eve of Victorianism*, pp. 87–9; Lt.-Col. F.S. Garwood, 'The Royal Staff Corps, 1800–1837' (1943), p. 82; Müffling, *Memoirs*, pp. 262–3. Philip Mansel points out that much looted art remained in provincial and private collections. Of 506 pictures taken from Italy after 1796 more than half remained in France: Mansel, *Paris Between the Empires*, p. 96.

39. Malcolm's journal, 1 September 1815, in Kaye, *Life of Malcolm*, vol. 2, p. 135.

6 The Occupation of France

1. Liverpool to Castlereagh, 15 July 1815, *WSD*, vol. 11, pp. 32–3; Wellington to Castlereagh, 11 August 1815, WP 1/478, printed with some deletions in *WD*, vol. 8, pp. 235–8; Memorandum by Castlereagh, 12 August 1815, printed in part in Webster, ed., *British Diplomacy*, pp. 361–2 and in full in *WSD*, vol. 11, pp. 147–50, where it is dated 31 August 1815; Memorandum on the temporary occupation of part of France (by Wellington), 31 August 1815, *WD*, vol. 8, pp. 353–5.

2. Memorandum on the temporary occupation of part of France, 31 August 1815, *WD*, vol. 8, pp. 253–5; Thomas Dwight Veve, *The Duke of Wellington and the British Army of Occupation in France* (1992), pp. 11–24. The formal convention is in *WSD*, vol. 11, pp. 192–5; see also ibid. pp. 195–8, 208–9, 240–2.

3. Wellington to Bathurst, 1 and 22 January 1816, *WSD*, vol. 11, pp. 265, 285–6 and Wellington to William Wellesley-Pole, 20 February 1816, 'Letters to Pole', p. 37.

4. Wellington to Malcolm, June 1816, Malcolm Papers, University of Southampton, Ms 308/133; Liverpool to Bathurst, 23 December 1815, and Wellington to Arbuthnot, 7 August 1816, *HMC Bathurst*, pp. 408, 422.

5. Stuart Wortley, *Highcliffe and the Stuarts*, p. 252. See also Shelley, *Diary of Lady Shelley*, vol. 1, pp. 201–3, which gives the date and many other interesting details. This also shows that he left Paris a few days after the incident, not the next morning.
6. Duchess of Wellington to Lady Eleanor Butler and Miss Ponsonby, Cheltenham, 18 July [1816], quoted in Philip Guedalla, *The Duke* (1931), p. 299.
7. Wellington to Lady Shelley, 10 July 1816, *Diary of Lady Shelley*, vol. 1, pp. 229–31; Anne Romilly to Maria Edgeworth, 26 August [1816], S.H. Romilly, *Romilly-Edgeworth Letters, 1813–1818* (1936), p. 153.
8. Wake, *Sisters of Fortune*, pp. 101–62 (quote about Marianne's eyes from Charles Percy on p. 140; letters from Wellington to Marianne on, p. 156).
9. Guedalla, *The Duke*, p. 301; *ODNB* entry on Wilkie; Brian Winkenweder, 'The Newspaper as Nationalist Icon, or How to Paint "Imagined Communities"' (2008), pp. 85–96. Allan Cunningham, *The Life of Sir David Wilkie* (1843), vol. 2, pp. 68–78; David H, Solkin, *Painting out of the Ordinary* (2008), pp. 198–204; see also Linda Colley, *Britons. Forging the Nation, 1707–1837* (1992), pp. 364–7 for interesting interpretations of the patriotic themes inherent in the composition of the picture.
10. Sylvester Douglas, Lord Glenbervie, *The Diaries of Sylvester Douglas (Lord Glenbervie)*, ed. Francis Bickley (1992), vol. 2, p. 226, 9 May 1817; she survived until 1831.
11. Severn, *Architects of Empire*, p. 395; Iris Butler, *The Eldest Brother. The Marquess Wellesley* (1973), pp. 492–3. In fact Lord Wellesley soon bought a house on Richmond Hill: ibid., p. 496.
12. The date of Gerald's separation from his wife is unclear: Severn, *Architects of Empire*, p. 391 implies that was before Wellington's attempt to get him a bishopric, i.e. in 1815; while Robert Pearman, *The Cadogans at War, 1783–1864. The Third Earl Cadogan and His Family* (1990), p. 150 states that it was in 1818. Whichever is correct, Liverpool had previously (1813 or 1814) rejected requests for his promotion and would do so again in the 1820s. For Henry Wellesley see Severn, *Architects of Empire*, p. 399.
13. Wyatt quoted in Longford, *Wellington. Pillar of State*, pp. 44–5.
14. See H.C. Litchfield to Wellington, 22 March 1819, WP 1/621/4.
15. Longford, *Wellington. Pillar of State*, p. 45; Wellington to Priscilla Burghersh, 28 October 1817, Lady Burghersh, *Correspondence of Lady Burghersh with the Duke of Wellington*, ed. her daughter Lady Rose Weigall (1903), p. 21.
16. General Distribution of the Army, 10 April 1816, *WSD*, vol. 11, pp. 355–61; Veve, *Wellington and the Occupation of France*, pp. 33–5; John Douglas, *Douglas's Tale of the Peninsula and Waterloo*, ed. Stanley Monick (1997), pp. 103–4; Rev. Francis Kilvert, *Kilvert's Diary. Selections from the Diary of the Rev, Francis Kilvert*, ed. William Plomer (1960), vol. 1, pp. 212–13, 15 August 1870 (for John Morgan); see also Smith, *Autobiography*, pp. 312–14.
17. For example GO, 28 June 1815, *WD*, vol. 8, pp. 322–3; GO, 14 August 1817, *WSD*, vol. 12, p. 31.
18. Wellington to Lynedoch, 25 July 1817, and to Maj.-Gen. W. Cameron, 9 April 1818, *WSD*, vol. 12, pp. 16–17, 458.
19. Captain Bowles to Lord Fitzharris, 8 June 1816, Malmesbury, *A Series of Letters*, vol. 2, p. 469.
20. Georgiana, Lady De Ros, 'Personal Recollections of the Great Duke of Wellington' (1889), pp. 47–8 (also J.R. Swinton, *A Sketch of the Life of Georgiana, Lady de Ros* ... (1893), pp. 145–6). 'Lord C___' is identified as Lord Coynyngham in Wake, *Sisters of Fortune*, p. 130.
21. Quoted in Colville, *Portrait of a General*, pp. 220–1.
22. John Fremantle to W.H. Fremantle, 6 and 25 December 1815, and 20 May and 5 November 1817, Fremantle, *Wellington's Voice*, pp. 261, 275 and Wake, *Sisters of Fortune*, p. 161.
23. Creevey, *Creevey Papers*, pp. 276–8; see also Wellington to Priscilla Burghersh, 6 March 1817, Burghersh, *Correspondence*, p. 17; Mrs Calvert's journal, Calvert, *Irish Beauty*, pp. 279–80; Wellington to Hill, and reply 20 and 24 February 1816, *WSD*, vol. 11, pp. 305–6, 306–7; Sidney, *Life of Hill*, p. 321.
24. Pack to Wellington, 29 October 1818, *WSD*, vol. 12, p. 786.
25. Wellington to J.C. Villiers, 11 January 1818, *WSD*, vol. 12, pp. 212–14.
26. Mansel, *Louis XVIII*, pp. 340–3, 350–1.
27. Veve, *Wellington and the Occupation of France*, p. 84; Wellington to Bathurst, 25 February 1816, *WSD*, vol. 11, p. 308.
28. Wellington to Castlereagh, 29 January 1816, Wellington to Bathurst, 13 and 25 February 1816, *WSD*, vol. 11, pp. 295–6, 301–2, 308; Bathurst to Wellington, 9 March 1816, ibid.,

pp. 355–6 (re Stuart's views); Harriet, Countess Granville to her sister Lady G. Morpeth, June 1817, Granville, *Letters of Countess Granville*, vol. 1, pp. 104–5, and Shelley, *Diary of Lady Shelley*, vol. 1, p. 206 (re his jealousy); Webster, *Foreign Policy of Castlereagh*, p. 75.

29. This whole paragraph is based on Mansel, *Louis XVIII*, p. 307; see also ibid., p. 289, and Wellington to Bathurst, 'Private & Confidential', 4 December 1815, *HMC Bathurst*, pp. 403–4 for the Grosbois estate.

30. Wellington to Louis XVIII, 29 February 1816, *WSD*, vol. 11, pp. 309–10; Webster, *Foreign Policy of Castlereagh*, pp. 79–80. See Sauvigny, *Bourbon Restoration*, pp. 135–40, and Mansel, *Louis XVIII*, pp. 339–43 for two contrasting, sophisticated views.

31. Mansel, *Louis XVIII*, pp. 346–8, 353; Eugene N. White, 'Making the French Pay: The Costs and Consequences of the Napoleonic Reparations' (2001), p. 357

32. C. Nelson, 'The Duke of Wellington and the Barrier Fortresses after Waterloo' (1964), pp. 36–43; Memorandum on the Fortresses in the Low Countries, 22 July 1816; Wellington to Castlereagh, 22 December 1816, 14 July 1817 and 7 August 1817, *WSD*, vol. 11, pp. 447–9, 583, 735, vol. 12, pp. 22–3.

33. Wellington to the Prince of Orange, 18 April 1818, *WSD*, vol. 12, pp. 480–1; see also the Prince of Orange to Wellington, 3 April 1816, and reply, 5 May 1816, *WSD*, vol. 11, pp. 351–2, 390–2, and Creevey's journal, nd [*c*. September 1818], *Creevey Papers*, p. 285.

34. Webster, *Foreign Policy of Castlereagh*, pp. 70–3, but cf pp. 110–12.

35. There is voluminous correspondence on this question in *WSD*, vols. 11 and 12: see especially Memorandum to Ministers on the Libels published in the Low Countries, 29 August 1816; Wellington to Clancarty, 24 February 1817; Wellington to Castlereagh, 5 June 1817; Clancarty to Wellington, 14 July 1817; Wellington to Clancarty, 15 and 16 July 1817; Clancarty to Wellington, 8 September 1817; Wellington to Clancarty, 3 December 1817, *WSD*, vol. 11, pp. 464–9, 634–6, 694–6, 738–9, 746–7, 748–9; *WSD*, vol. 12, pp. 155–6.

36. Wellington to Bathurst, 12 February 1818, *WSD*, vol. 12, pp. 271–3.

37. Wellington to Clancarty, 17 July 1818, *WSD*, vol. 12, pp. 601–2; *Edinburgh Annual Register for 1819*, pt 2, pp. 306–13 has a very full and useful account of the whole affair based on the prosecution's case. Napoleon, *Napoleon's Last Will and Testament*, ed. J.P. Babeloa and Suzanne D'Huart (1977), p. 78. The printed text here reads 100,000 francs but the facsimile of the manuscript on the facing page clearly shows it to be 10,000 – the figure used in all other accounts.

38. Bathurst to Wellington, 20 and 21 (two letters) February and 3 March 1818, and Wellington to Bathurst, 25 February 1818, *WSD*, vol. 12, pp. 324–6, 333–5, 363.

39. Wellington to Beresford, 15 July 1817, to Bathurst, 12 February 1818, and to Baron Nagell, 12 November 1818, *WSD*, vol. 11, pp. 745–6, vol. 12, pp. 271–3, 829–30.

40. Wellington to Bathurst, 8 March 1818, *WSD*, vol. 12, pp. 380–1.

41. Bathurst to Wellington, 1 December 1817, 3 March 1818, *WSD*, vol. 12, pp. 151–2, 363. See also Castlereagh to Cathcart, 27 March 1818, *WSD*, vol. 12, pp. 445–9.

42. Liverpool to Castlereagh, 17 October 1815, *WSD*, vol. 11, pp. 202–3, cf Liverpool to Wellington, 3 March 1818, *WSD*, vol. 12, pp. 364–5.

43. Wellington to Bathurst, 8 March 1818; Bathurst to Wellington, 1 December 1817, *WSD*, vol. 12, pp. 380–82, 151–2.

44. Wellington to Liverpool, 4 February 1818, Liverpool to Wellington, 6 March 1818, and Baring to Wellington, 31 December 1818, *WSD*, vol. 12, pp. 247–9, 375–6, 883–4; Philip Ziegler, *The Sixth Great Power. Barings 1762–1929* (1988), p. 80; and White, 'Making the French Pay', esp. pp. 340–7, which gives a detailed and careful account of these negotiations.

45. Wellington to Castlereagh, 1 January, and to Liverpool, 26 February 1818, *WSD*, vol. 12, pp. 201–2, 343–4; Baring to Wellington, 27 and 31 May 1818; Wellington to Baring, 29 May, and to Liverpool, 30 May 1818; Liverpool to Wellington, 9 June 1818, *WSD*, vol. 12, pp. 526–40.

46. Wellington to Castlereagh, 25 July 1817, Castlereagh to Wellington, 8 August 1817, *WSD*, vol. 12, pp. 13–16, 23–4. See Muriel Wellesley, *The Man Wellington* (1937), pp. 402–5, for more on this.

47. Wellington to Castlereagh, 15 February 1818, *WSD*, vol. 12, pp. 289–90. The figure is based on the Memorandum enclosed in Wellington's letter to Castlereagh of 19 April 1818 (*WSD*, vol. 12, pp. 484–6) and is accepted by Webster, *Foreign Policy of Castlereagh*, pp. 84–5. However White, 'Making the French Pay', pp. 340–1, gives a total of 320 million francs and also refers to 180 million francs of 'additional reparations' without fully explaining what these

were. It seems likely that Wellington's memorandum is not comprehensive (it does not include British claims) and that the final total may have been higher, possibly either 320 or 500 million, which was still only a fraction of the gross.
48. Wellington to Castlereagh, 23 April 1818, *WSD*, vol. 12, pp. 491–2; White, 'Making the French Pay', p. 341.
49. Castlereagh to Bathurst, 19 November 1818, *WSD*, vol. 12, pp. 844–5; see also Webster, *Foreign Policy of Castlereagh*, pp. 119–72, esp. 145–54.
50. GO, 10 November 1818, *WSD*, vol. 12, p. 826.

7 Politics and the Duke

1. Ward to Mulgrave, 26 November 1818, Edmund Phipps, *Memoir of the Political and Literary Life of Robert Plumer Ward* (1850), vol. 2, pp. 13–14.
2. Wellington to Liverpool, 1 November 1818, *WSD*, vol. 12, pp. 812–13.
3. Liverpool to Wellington, 9 November 1818, *WSD*, vol. 12, p. 822; on Pittite distrust of the 'party' see A.D Harvey, *Britain in the Early Nineteenth Century* (1978), pp. 15–17.
4. Wellington to Liverpool, 1 March 1810, *WD*, vol. 3, pp. 759–62.
5. Sir Lewis Namier and John Brooke, *The History of Parliament. The House of Commons, 1760–90* (1964), vol. 2, p. 368.
6. J.E. Cookson, *Lord Liverpool's Administration. The Crucial Years 1815–1822* (1975), p. 53.
7. On Curwen's Act, see Denis Gray, *Spencer Perceval. The Evangelical Prime Minister* (1963), pp. 209–12.
8. Wellington to Castlereagh, 6 April, *WSD*, vol. 11, pp. 664–6.
9. Wellington to Villiers, 5 June 1810, *WD*, vol. 4, pp. 103–4; Rory Muir, *Wellington. The Path to Victory, 1796–1814* (2013), pp. 178–9.
10. Quoted in Peter Jupp, *British Politics on the Eve of Reform. The Duke of Wellington's Administration, 1828–1830* (1998), p. 52, from speech of 10 June 1828 as reported in the *Mirror of Parliament*. The version of the speech in *Parliamentary Debates* and in Wellington, *Speeches*, does not use this precise formula; however it is used in Wellington's Memorandum upon Mr Huskisson's Retirement from Office, 20 May 1828, *WND*, vol. 4, pp. 451–3.
11. See Muir, *Wellington. The Path to Victory*, pp. 306–7. Antony Brett-James, *Life in Wellington's Army* (1972), pp. 238–49 collects much other material on the subject and points to the Spanish and Portuguese refusal to permit Protestant soldiers to be buried in consecrated ground as an abiding grievance.
12. Gray, *Spencer Perceval*, pp. 100–6.
13. Wellington, *Speeches*, vol. 1, p. 178.
14. See Muir, *Wellington. The Path to Victory*, pp. 198–9.
15. Wellington, *Speeches*, vol. 1, p. 178.
16. Wellington to Lord Wellesley, 22 September 1809, *WD*, vol. 3, pp. 514–15.
17. Wellington to Sir Henry Wellesley, 4 November 1810, *WD*, vol. 4, pp. 394–5.
18. Wellington to Lord William Bentinck, 24 December 1811, *WD*, vol. 5, pp. 424–5.
19. Wellington to Charles Stuart, 13 May 1810, *WD*, vol. 4, p. 65.
20. *The Times*, 8 January 1846, p. 7.
21. Wellington to Torrens, 3 December 1816, *WSD*, vol. 11, p. 561.
22. See above, pp. 19–20, and below, p. 174. Canning had joined the Cabinet as president of the Board of Control in 1816, and was one of the government's leading spokesmen in the House of Commons; however, his influence in Cabinet appears to have been relatively slight compared to the role he played after Castlereagh's death.
23. Wellington to Lord William Bentinck, 24 December 1811, *WD*, vol. 5, pp. 424–5.
24. Stanhope, *Notes of Conversations*, 2 November 1831, p. 9; Croker's notes of conversations with Wellington at Sudborne in 1826 in John Wilson Croker, *The Croker Papers. The Correspondence and Diaries of the Late Right Honourable John Wilson Croker*, ed. Louis J. Jennings (1884), vol. 1, p. 340.
25. Memorandum on the War in Russia in 1812 by Wellington, *WND*, vol. 3, pp. 1–53, quote re French soldiers on p. 10; Wellington to Croker, 29 December 1835, *Croker Papers*, vol. 2, pp. 287–8 (quote re 'Buonaparte's whole life'); Francis, 1st Earl of Ellesmere, *Personal Reminiscences of the Duke of Wellington* (1904), pp. 98–100; Charles C.F. Greville, *The Greville Memoirs. A Journal of the Reigns of King George IV, King William IV and Queen Victoria*, ed.

Henry Reeve (1888), 2 January 1838, vol. 4, p. 5; Andrew Roberts, *Napoleon and Wellington* (2001), pp. 244–66, has an excellent account collecting all the scattered evidence of Wellington's opinion of Napoleon. See also Muir, *Wellington. The Path to Victory*, p. 431.

26. Recollections written on 28 July 1822 by Creevey, *Creevey Papers*, p. 226.

27. Creevey's journal, Saturday [12 September 1818], ibid., pp. 286–7.

28. On Russell see: Russell, *Early Correspondence of Lord John Russell, 1805–1840*, ed. his son Rollo Russell (1913), vol. 1, p. 21; Thorne, *History of Parliament*, vol. 5, pp. 63–4; *ODNB*. Although always known as Lord William Russell, he was actually Lord George William Russell, and is listed as such in these reference books. For an extended discussion of this whole question see Rory Muir, 'Politics and the Peninsular Army' (2008), pp. 72–93.

29. Wellington to Lord William Bentinck, 24 December 1811, *WD*, vol. 5, pp. 424–5.

30. *Parliamentary Debates*, vol. 30, cols. 444–5; and see above, p. 26.

31. *Parliamentary Debates*, vol. 31, cols. 976–7, 986.

32. *Parliamentary Debates*, vol. 31, cols. 987–8 (Burdett), 991 (Whitbread), 992 (W. Smith) and 1054 (Wilberforce). This and subsequent paragraphs closely follow Rory Muir, 'A Hero's Welcome: Attitudes to Wellington and the Army, 1814–1823' (2013), pp. 210–23.

33. Paul W. Schroeder, *The Transformation of European Politics, 1763–1848* (1994), argues cogently that this purpose, which was shared by Castlereagh, Metternich, Alexander and most of the other statesmen of these years, was genuine and largely successful. Relations among the Great Powers were not marked by a return to the intense competition and rivalry of the eighteenth century, let alone Napoleon's 'winner takes all' attitude.

34. J.E. Cookson, *The British Armed Nation, 1793–1815* (1997), p. 244.

35. George, *BM Catalogue of Satires*, nos. 12614, 12620 and 12797, vol. 9, pp. 585–7, 592–3, 692–4; George, *English Political Caricature*, vol. 2, pp. 167–8, 173–4; Wardroper, *Caricatures of George Cruikshank*, p. 61. (For Cruikshank's prints celebrating Wellington as the hero of Vitoria see George, *BM Catalogue of Satires*, nos. 12068 and 12071, vol. 9, pp. 258, 260.)

36. Holland to Kinnaird, 5 December 1816, Henry, Lord Holland, *Further Memoirs of the Whig Party, 1807–1821* (1905), pp. 224–8; Wellington to Cooke, 17 December 1815, *WD*, vol. 8, pp. 319–20.

37. Grey to Holland, 6 October 1816, quoted in E.A. Smith, *Lord Grey, 1764–1845* (1990), p. 209.

38. James J. Sack, *The Grenvillites, 1801–1829. Party Politics and Factionalism in the Age of Pitt and Liverpool* (1979), p. 162; *Parliamentary Debates*, vol. 32, col. 845.

39. *Parliamentary Debates*, vol. 33, cols. 243, 319 and 956 (13 and 15 March and 5 April 1816).

40. Liverpool to Huskisson, 25 November 1815, in Alex M. Delavoye, *Life of Thomas Graham, Lord Lynedoch* (1880), pp. 750–1; see also Maj.-Gen. Louis C. Jackson, *History of the United Service Club* (1937), pp. 1–6; *Parliamentary Debates*, vol. 32, cols. 1068–78.

41. William Wellesley-Pole to Charles Bagot, 5 July 1816, in Capt. Josceline Bagot, *George Canning and His Friends* (1909), vol. 2, pp. 29–31; petition quoted in Cookson, *Lord Liverpool's Administration*, pp. 47–8.

42. *Black Dwarf*, 18 June 1817, col. 330. See also Richard Hendrix, 'Political Humours and "The Black Dwarf"' (1976), pp. 108–28; *Examiner*, 22 February 1818; William Cobbett, *Selections from Cobbett's Political Works*, ed. John M. Cobbett and James P. Cobbett (1835), vol. 5, p. 446.

43. *Examiner*, 13 December 1818; *Black Dwarf*, 9 December 1818, p. 701.

44. Lord Byron, *Don Juan* (1958; first pub. 1819–24), canto 1.

45. For an example of this feeling see Sir Frederick Flood quoted in Austen Mitchell, *The Whigs in Opposition, 1815–1830* (1967), p. 77.

8 The Radical Challenge

1. *The Times*, 22, 23, 31 December 1818; Farington, *Diary*, 22–25 December 1818, vol. 15, p. 5304; Glenbervie, *Diaries*, 28 December 1818, vol. 2, p. 333.

2. Wellington, *Speeches*, vol. 1, pp. 103–4, which varies slightly from version in *Parliamentary Debates*, vol. 41, cols. 446–8 (mostly by introducing the first-person pronoun); see also Abbot, *Diary and Correspondence*, vol. 3, p. 76 (20 May 1819); see also Greville, *Memoirs*, 14 June 1819, vol. 1, p. 80.

3. Draft of Wellington to Mr Stockdale, nd February 1821, *WND*, vol. 1, pp. 155–6; the letter was not sent.

4. *The Times*, 29 May 1819; Abbot, *Diary and Correspondence*, 3 June 1819, vol. 3, p. 79; James J. Sack, 'The Memory of Burke and the Memory of Pitt: English Conservatism Confronts its Past, 1806–1829' (1987), esp. pp. 635–7.

5. Fitzgerald quoted in Nigel Cross, *The Common Writer. Life in Nineteenth-Century Grub Street* (1985), pp. 24–5. Wellington's correspondence includes numerous invitations, including from several hospitals, the Society for Propagating Christian Knowledge in the Highlands and Islands of Scotland, and a pressing invitation from Wilberforce to attend the meeting of the British and Foreign Bible Society whose work overseas would benefit greatly from his patronage: WP 1/624/5. For other invitations see WP 1/621/10, WP 1/621/19, WP 1/623/16, WP 1/624/17.

6. Shelley, *Diary of Lady Shelley*, 12 and 17 March 1819, vol. 2, pp. 32–4.

7. Maria Edgeworth, *Maria Edgeworth. Letters from England, 1813–1844*, ed. Christina Colvin (1971), 2 April 1819, p. 191.

8. Wellington to Mrs Arbuthnot, 8 August 1819, *W&HF*, pp. 4–5.

9. Stanley H. Palmer, *Police and Protest in England and Ireland 1780–1850* (1988), pp. 164–70.

10. Wellington to William Wellesley-Pole, 9 May 1810, 'Letters to Pole', pp. 33–4. See also K.O. Fox, *Making Life Possible. A Study of Military Aid to the Civil Power in Regency England* (1982), *passim.*

11. Horace Twiss, *The Public and Private Life of Lord Chancellor Eldon* (1846), vol. 2, pp. 260–4, based on Eldon's own account; on Castlereagh's close encounter see Abbot, *Diary and Correspondence*, vol. 2, p. 547.

12. Thorne, *History of Parliament*, vol. 2, pp. 267, 280–1; Shelley, *Diary of Lady Shelley*, vol. 2, pp. 28–30.

13. This whole paragraph is based closely on John Stevenson, *Popular Disturbances in England 1700–1870* (1979), p. 212; but see also Fox, *Making Life Possible*, pp. 154–6. The detail of the Waterloo veteran at Blackburn is from R.E. Foster, *Wellington and Waterloo. The Duke, the Battle and Posterity, 1815–2015* (2014), p. 105.

14. Donald Read, *Peterloo. The 'Massacre' and its Background* (1958) remains the standard account. See also Stevenson, *Popular Disturbances in England*, pp. 213–14; Ian F.W. Beckett, *The Amateur Military Tradition, 1558–1945* (1991), pp. 135–7 and Fox, *Making Life Possible*, pp. 158–69. Fox points out that all our sources are highly partisan, and that in the confusion probably no one knew exactly what was happening. While some of the doubts he raises over the accepted version of events smack of special pleading, in general his discussion is both salutary and level-headed.

15. George Pellew, *Life and Correspondence of the Rt. Hon. Henry Addington, first Viscount Sidmouth* (1847), vol. 3, p. 262; Cookson, *Lord Liverpool's Administration*, pp. 178n and 186; Shelley, *Diary of Lady Shelley*, vol. 2, p. 68. For examples of private criticism of the magistrates, see Eldon to Sir William Scott, nd, Twiss, *Life of Eldon*, vol. 2, p. 338; Canning quoted in Philip Ziegler, *Addington* (1965), p. 375; Shelley, *Diary of Lady Shelley*, vol. 2, p. 68; Liverpool to Canning, 23 September 1819, Charles D. Yonge, *The Life and Administration of Robert Banks, Second Earl of Liverpool* (1868), vol. 2, pp. 407–11.

16. Robert Walmsley, *Peterloo. The Case Reopened* (1969), p. 251, for date and paper; William Belsham, *Chronology of the Reigns of George III and George IV* (1829), unpaginated but arranged by date.

17. Quoted in George, *English Political Caricature*, vol. 2, p. 183; other details from ibid.; William Belsham, *Chronology Annual Register*, 1819 (General History), pp. 110–11; and Phipps, *Memoir of Plumer Ward*, vol. 2, pp. 36–7.

18. Palmer, *Police and Protest*, p. 279. See also Fox, *Making Life Possible*, pp. 149–50.

19. Byng to Wellington, 19 and 27 September, 28 October, 3 November 1817, WP 1/631/22 and 28; 1/633/17; 1/634/3. See also Iorwerth Prothero, *Artisans and Politics in Early Nineteenth-Century London. John Gast and his Times* (1979), pp. 124–5.

20. Wellington to Byng, 21 October 1819, WP 1/629/20 printed in *WND*, vol. 1, pp. 80–2.

21. Wellington to Byng, 21 October 1819, WP 1/629/20 printed in *WND*, vol. 1, pp. 80–2. See also Pellew, *Life of Sidmouth*, vol. 3, pp. 292–3, and Fox, *Making Life Possible*, p. 145.

22. Phipps, *Memoir of Plumer Ward*, vol. 2, pp. 21–2, 42–3.

23. Mitchell, *Whigs in Opposition*, pp. 125–9; Henry Brougham, *The Life and Times of Henry, Lord Brougham, written by himself* (1872), vol. 2, pp. 342–3, 346–7. Cookson, *Lord Liverpool's*

Administration, pp. 191-5, gives a useful account of the Acts, which are more often invoked than discussed.

24. Cookson, *Lord Liverpool's Administration*, pp. 181 and 189; see also Liverpool to Grenville, 14 November, and reply, in Yonge, *Life of Liverpool*, vol. 2, pp. 430-7; Brougham to Grey, 24 October 1819, Brougham, *Life and Times*, vol. 2, p. 348; George, *English Political Caricature*, vol. 2, p. 183.

25. Wellington, *Speeches*, vol. 1, pp. 105-6; Phipps, *Memoir of Plumer Ward*, vol. 2, p. 35, 36, 39.

26. Shelley, *Diary of Lady Shelley*, vol. 2, p. 90.

27. *The Political House that Jack Built* is reprinted in full with many other pamphlets of the period in *Radical Squibs and Loyal Ripostes*, ed. Edgell Rickword (1971); for discussion of the illustrations see George, *BM Catalogue of Satires*, vol. 9, pp. 945-8.

28. *Black Dwarf*, 24 February 1819, p. 125.

29. *Black Dwarf*, 30 June 1819, p. 430.

30. *Poor Bull & His Burden–or the Political Murraion–!!!* by G. Cruikshank, 15 December 1819; *Blockheads* by G. and I.R. Cruikshank, nd; *The Broken Crown, or, the Disasters of a Greenbag Chief!!!* [by I.R. Cruikshank], nd: George, *BM Catalogue of Satires*, nos. 13288, 13346, 14006, vol. 9, pp. 942-3, 956-7; vol. 10, pp. 140-1.

31. Rickword, ed., *Radical Squibs*, p. 94.

32. See Cruikshank's *The Belle-Alliance, of the Female Reformers of Blackburn!!!*, George, *BM Catalogue of Satires*, no. 13257, vol. 9, pp. 916-17.

33. George, *English Political Caricature*, vol. 2, pp. 182-3.

34. Reprinted in Rickword, ed., *Radical Squibs*, pp. 59-82.

35. T. Duckett to Wellington, 8 and 11 January 1819, WP 1/613/13 and 22; Kenneth Bourne, *Palmerston. The Early Years, 1784-1841* (1982), pp. 157-8; Palmerston's £10 contribution was listed as from 'P.V.' See Cruikshank's caricature of the 'Bridge Street Gang' in Wardroper, *Caricatures of George Cruikshank*, p. 99: Wellington plays a prominent part; see also A. Aspinall, *Politics and the Press, c. 1750-1850* (1949), pp. 64-5.

36. George, *BM Catalogue of Satires*, no. 13385, vol. 9, p. 970; see also no. 13407, pp. 980-1.

37. *The Times*, 1, 2 and 6 October 1819.

38. Plumer Ward's diary, 28 January 1820, quoted in Phipps, *Memoir of Plumer Ward*, vol. 2, p. 50.

9 The Queen's Affair

1. Chester New, *The Life of Henry Brougham to 1830* (1961), pp. 229-30.

2. Croker, *Croker Papers*, vol. 1, p. 160; Cookson, *Lord Liverpool's Administration*, pp. 207-8.

3. Croker, *Croker Papers*, vol. 1, pp. 160-1; Henry Hobhouse, *The Diary of Henry Hobhouse (1820-1827)*, ed. Arthur Aspinall (1947), pp. 9-10; *JMrsA*, vol. 1, pp. 1-3; Viscount Palmerston, *The Letters of the third Viscount Palmerston to Laurence and Elizabeth Sulivan, 1804-1863*, ed. Kenneth Bourne (1979), pp. 148-9, and Mitchell, *Whigs in Opposition*, pp. 138-9.

4. Mansel, *Louis XVIII*, p. 371. Berri was mortally wounded on the night of 13 February and died around 6am on 14 February. The assassin, Etienne Louvel, was an ardent Bonapartist and his motives were purely political. Wellington to Alava, 21 February 1820, WP 1/640/21, printed in *WND*, vol. 1, pp. 98-101; see also *JMrsA*, 16 February 1820, vol. 1, p. 5.

5. Prothero, *Artisans and Politics*, p. 130 (pp. 124-5 for Bentham); David Johnson, *Regency Revolution. The Case of Arthur Thistlewood* (1974), pp. 69-89; Stevenson, *Popular Disturbances*, pp. 197-8.

6. Hobhouse, *Diary*, pp. 13-14; Croker, *Croker Papers*, vol. 1, p. 163; Wellington to Mary Anne (Marianne) Patterson, 27 February 1820, Wellington, *A Selection from the Private Correspondence of the First Duke of Wellington*, ed. the Duke of Wellington (1952), pp. 185-8.

7. Mitchell, *Whigs in Opposition*, p. 143; George, *English Political Caricature*, vol. 2, p. 190; Stevenson, *Popular Disturbances*, pp. 198, 344n31. Even some modern accounts treat Edwards as the villain, for example Johnson, *Regency Revolution*, pp. 122-3.

8. Wellington to Decazes, 11 February 1820, WP 1/640/10; Wellington to Beresford, 12 February 1820, WP 1/640/13.

9. Wellington to Decazes, 11 February 1820; Wellington to Richelieu, 13 March 1820, WP 1/640/10, WP 1/642/4; Memorandum on Spain [by Wellington], 16 April 1820, *WND*, vol. 1, pp. 116-21.

10. Webster, *Foreign Policy of Castlereagh*, pp. 236–42, 245–6; John Bew, *Castlereagh. Enlightenment, War and Tyranny* (2011), pp. 478–84; the full text is printed in Sir A.W. Ward and G.P. Gooch, eds., *Cambridge History of British Foreign Policy* (1922–23), vol. 2, pp. 622–33.

11. *Parliamentary Debates*, ns, vol. 1, col. 967; Hobhouse, *Diary*, 19 June 1820, pp. 26–7.

12. Hobhouse, *Diary*, 19 June 1820, pp. 25–6; Pellew, *Life of Sidmouth*, vol. 3, p. 331; Croker to Melville, 16 June 1820, *Croker Papers*, vol. 1, pp. 175–6.

13. Croker to Melville, 16 June 1820, *Croker Papers*, vol. 1, pp. 175–6; Hobhouse, *Diary*, 19 June 1820, pp. 25–6; *JMrsA*, 17 June 1820, vol. 1, p. 24.

14. Memorandum to the Earl of Liverpool Respecting the State of the Guards, June 1820, *WND*, vol. 1, pp. 127–9; Liverpool to Wellington, 31 July 1820, *WND*, vol. 1, p. 141.

15. Liverpool to Wellington, 28 June 1820, WP 1/647/15; Fremantle to Buckingham, 19 July 1820, Duke of Buckingham and Chandos, *Memoirs of the Court of George IV 1820–1830* (1859), vol. 1, pp. 50–2; Hobhouse, *Diary*, 21 August 1820, pp. 33–4.

16. Details of this incident are obscure – it is not even mentioned in Delavoye's history of the regiment (Alex M. Delavoye, *Records of the 90th Regiment (Perthshire Light Infantry)* (1880)). The account given here is based on Sir Herbert Taylor to Wellington, 26 September 1820, *WND*, vol. 1, pp. 146–9.

17. Tom Grenville to Buckingham, 22 July 1820, Buckingham, *Memoirs of the Court of George IV*, vol. 1, pp. 52–3, cf William Wellesley-Pole to Charles Bagot, 21 July 1820, Bagot, *George Canning and His Friends*, vol. 2, pp. 96–8; John Stevenson, 'The Queen Caroline Affair', in Stevenson, ed., *London in the Age of Reform* (1977), p. 127 (for Benbow).

18. Wellington to Liverpool, 30 July 1820, BL Add Ms 38,196, f 93–4; Wellington to Mrs Arbuthnot, 6 August 1820, *W&HF*, pp. 6–7.

19. Wellington to Mrs Arbuthnot, 14 September 1820, *W&HF*, p. 9.

20. Cookson, *Lord Liverpool's Administration*, pp. 245–51.

21. There is a good account of Cobbett's role in George Spater, *William Cobbett. The Poor Man's Friend* (1922), vol. 2, pp. 398–408. One of Benbow's handbills, headed 'Proposal to Murder the Queen!', is reproduced in Lieven, *Private Letters*, pp. 82–3. Creevey to Miss Ord, 17 August 1820, *Creevey Papers*, pp. 306–7, but cf Wellington to Mrs Arbuthnot, 17 August 1820, *W&HF*, pp. 7–9. See also Prothero, *Artisans and Politics*, pp. 136–8; Stevenson, 'Queen Caroline Affair', pp. 122–5.

22. Pellew, *Life of Sidmouth*, vol. 3, pp. 327–8n; Croker, *Croker Papers*, 7 June 1820, vol. 1, p. 174; Katherine Wellesley-Pole to Charles Bagot, 24 August 1820, Bagot, *George Canning and His Friends*, vol. 2, pp. 101–2; Lady Granville to Lady G. Morpeth, 29 August 1820, Granville, *Letters of Countess Granville*, vol. 1, pp. 168–9; Creevey to Miss Ord, 7 November 1820, *Creevey Papers*, p. 337; see also Princess Lieven to Metternich, 29 August 1820, Lieven, *Private Letters*, p. 69.

23. Wellington to Lady Shelley, 4 October 1820, Shelley, *Diary of Lady Shelley*, vol. 2, pp. 103–4; *JMrsA*, 8 September 1820, vol. 1, p. 36.

24. Plumer Ward's diary for 10 November 1820 in Phipps, *Memoir of Plumer Ward*, vol. 2, pp. 87–8; Sara Hutchinson to Mrs Swaine and Mrs Wordsworth, 19 September [1820], Sara Hutchinson, *The Letters of Sara Hutchinson from 1800 to 1835*, ed. Kathleen Coburn (1954), p. 208; Benjamin Robert Haydon, *The Diary of Benjamin Robert Haydon*, ed. Willard Bissell Pope (1960-63), 19 August 1820, vol. 2, p. 279; Anglesey, *One Leg*, pp. 163–4, 366–7.

25. Lady Granville to Lady G. Morpeth, 22 August 1820, Granville, *Letters of Countess Granville*, vol. 1, pp. 160–1.

26. Hobhouse, *Diary*, 6 November 1820, p. 36; Mitchell, *Whigs in Opposition*, pp. 145–7; New, *Brougham*, pp. 250–1; George, *English Political Caricature*, vol. 1, p. 196.

27. *JMrsA*, 8 and 10 October 1820, vol. 1, pp. 41–3.

28. Plumer Ward's diary, 16, 18 and 23 October 1820, in Phipps, *Memoir of Plumer Ward*, vol. 2, pp. 59, 62, 66; Charles Arbuthnot to his wife [4 November 1820], *CCA*, pp. 19–20.

29. Plumer Ward's diary, 19 October 1820, in Phipps, *Memoir of Plumer Ward*, vol. 2, pp. 63–4.

30. *JMrsA*, 20 October 1820, vol. 1, pp. 45–6.

31. Norman Gash, *Lord Liverpool* (1984), pp. 165, 176, 205–6 and 192–5, for an excellent discussion of Liverpool's character; Liverpool to Canning, 12 September 1820, Yonge, *Life of Liverpool*, vol. 3, pp. 106–8; *JMrsA*, 10 November 1820, vol. 1, pp. 51–2, quotes a letter from her husband; Hobhouse, *Diary*, 10 November 1820, pp. 39–40.

32. Charles Arbuthnot to his wife [4 November 1820], *CCA*, pp. 19–20; Greville, *Memoirs*, 15 October 1820, vol. 1, p. 108; Burton to Colchester, 15 November 1820, Abbot, *Diary and Correspondence*, vol. 3, pp. 180–1.

33. *Parliamentary Debates*, ns, vol. 3, cols. 295–6, 5 October 1820.

34. Plumer Ward's diary, 19 October 1820, Phipps, *Memoir of Plumer Ward*, vol. 2, p. 65.

35. Plumer Ward's diary, 10 November 1820, in ibid., vol. 2, pp. 93–5; Anne Cobbett (William's daughter) quoted in Stevenson, *Popular Disturbances*, pp. 200–1; Prothero, *Artisans and Politics*, p. 140.

36. The King to Liverpool, [16 November 1820], George IV, *Letters*, vol. 2, p. 380; see ibid., pp. 386–93; Mitchell, *Whigs in Opposition*, p. 148.

37. Wellington's Memorandum is printed in *WND*, vol. 1, pp. 150–3 where it is wrongly dated 'December 1820' even though it refers to the fact that Parliament will assemble on 'the 23rd instant', which means that it must have been written before 23 November when Parliament met. The undated draft is in WP 1/656/6. The Memorandum and the King's reaction to it are discussed in *JMrsA*, 18 November 1820, vol. 1, pp. 53–4. Aspinall in George IV, *Letters*, vol. 2, p. 380, dates the letter (possibly from the original in the Royal Archives) to 16 November.

38. George IV, *Letters*, vol. 2, pp. 386–93 prints an extraordinary sequence of notes and memoranda from the King in which he weighs up the advantages and risks of dismissing the government, giving a remarkable, and far from flattering, insight into his motives and thinking.

39. Liverpool to Arbuthnot, 13 November 1820, *CCA*, p. 21; the words in the second quote are not Liverpool's but Mrs Arbuthnot's précis of what he told her husband, and as she had no love for Canning she may have coloured them a little, but the context makes clear that she was recording Liverpool's views. Her own appear in the next paragraph and are even more critical. *JMrsA*, 30 November 1820, vol. 1, p. 55.

40. Arbuthnot to Bathurst, 'Private', 29 November [1820], *HMC Bathurst*, pp. 489–90; Liverpool to Wellington, 'Private', 7 December 1820, *CCA*, p. 21; W.H. Fremantle to Buckingham, 29 December 1820, Buckingham, *Memoirs of the Court of George IV*, vol. 1, pp. 97–8; *JMrsA*, 22 December 1820, vol. 1, pp. 59–60.

41. Quoted in Francis Burton to Lord Colchester, 15 November 1820, Abbot, *Diary and Correspondence*, vol. 3, p. 181.

42. *JMrsA*, 31 August 1820, vol. 1, p. 35; Jonathan Fulcher, 'The Loyalist Response to the Queen Caroline Agitation' (1995), p. 487n, quoting from Carlile, *Republican*, 10 May 1822, p. 589.

43. George, *English Political Caricature*, vol. 2. pp. 197–201; Fulcher, 'Loyalist Response', p. 496 says that the *Courier* claimed in January 1821 that loyalist addresses outnumbered those in favour of the Queen by four to one, but it was far from an impartial source.

44. William H. Wickwar, *The Struggle for Freedom of the Press 1819–1832* (1929), pp. 168–71; Fulcher, 'Loyalist Response', pp. 493–4; Theodore Hook to Sir William Knighton, 15 February 1824, George IV, *Letters*, vol. 3, pp. 64–6; Croker diary, 11 January 1822, *Croker Papers*, vol. 1, p. 246; Lady Granville to Lady G. Morpeth, 22 December 1820, Granville, *Letters of Countess Granville*, vol. 1, p. 201; Princess Lieven to Metternich, 7 January 1821, Lieven, *Private Letters*, pp. 102–3, but cf Emily Palmerston, *The Letters of Lady Palmerston*, ed. Tresham Lever (1957), p. 68.

45. Lady Granville to Lady G. Morpeth, 11 February 1820, and to Lady Harrowby, 26 February 1831, Granville, *Letters of Countess Granville*, vol. 1, pp. 207, 209–10; Mitchell, *Whigs in Opposition*, pp. 156–7.

46. Fulcher, 'Loyalist Response', p. 501, and Stevenson, 'Queen Caroline Affair', p. 135.

10 The King and his Ministers

1. Leslie Mitchell, *Holland House* (1980), pp. 237–8; Prothero, *Artisans and Politics*, p. 146: the words are Prothero's, not Gast's; see also Bew, *Castlereagh*, pp. 479–81, 484–6; Greville, *Memoirs*, 13 August 1822, vol. 1, pp. 126–8; and Philipp von Neumann, *The Diary of Philipp von Neumann, 1819–1850*, ed. E. Beresford Chancellor (1928), 21 February 1821, vol. 1, p. 52.

2. Neumann, *Diary*, vol. 1, p. 30, 25 July 1820; Lieven, *Private Letters*, 6 January 1821, p. 102.

3. *JMrsA*, 2 January 1821, vol. 1, pp. 62–3; Webster, *Foreign Policy of Castlereagh*, pp. 298–305, 320–5.

4. Neumann, *Diary*, 23 January 1821, vol. 1, p. 49; *Parliamentary Debates*, ns, vol. 4, col. 779, 19 February 1821; Creevey, *Creevey Papers*, 24 February 1821, p. 357; *The Times*, 24 February 1821; see also Mitchell, *Holland House*, pp. 206–7.

5. Muir, *Britain and the Defeat of Napoleon*, pp. 318–19, 337–8, 370; Gash, *Liverpool*, pp. 197–8; Webster, *Foreign Policy of Castlereagh*, p. 335n; Harold Temperley, *The Foreign Policy of Canning 1822–1827* (1925), pp. 46–7.

6. Wellington to Prince Esterházy, 28 February 1821, *WND*, vol. 1, pp. 160–2: Esterházy's two memoranda are in WP 1/661/16. Webster's comments are sharp but warranted: Webster, *Foreign Policy of Castlereagh*, p. 326.

7. The *Examiner* quoted in George, *BM Catalogue of Satires*, vol. 10, p. 201; Wilson in Webster, *Foreign Policy of Castlereagh*, p. 336.

8. Wilbraham to Colchester, 26 January 1821, Abbot, *Diary and Correspondence*, vol. 3, p. 201; Fremantle to Buckingham, 24 January 1821, Buckingham, *Memoirs of the Court of George IV*, vol. 1, pp. 111–13.

9. Cookson, *Lord Liverpool's Administration*, pp. 300–1, 304–7.

10. *Parliamentary Debates*, ns, vol. 4, cols. 108–11; Creevey, *Creevey Papers*, 26 January 1821, p. 348; George, *BM Catalogue of Satires*, no. 14,051, vol. 10, p. 160 (for once Dorothy George, the immensely erudite compiler of the *Catalogue*, does not recognise the allusion); Lady Granville to Lady G. Morpeth, nd February 1821, Granville, *Letters of Countess Granville*, vol. 1, p. 204; R.E Foster, 'The Duke of Wellington in Hampshire' (2010), p. 13. A second caricature on the subject, *The Hampshire Hog*, is reproduced on the back cover of Foster's study.

11. *JMrsA*, 28 February, 2 and 11 March 1821, vol. 1, pp. 77–81; Wellington to Princess Lieven, 1 July 1821, *W&HF*, pp. 296–8; Hobhouse, *Diary*, 16 April 1821, pp. 52–3; Lieven, *Private Letters*, 9 February 1821, pp. 113–14; see also Buckingham to Wellington, 24 July 1821, WP 1/672/18, printed in *WND*, vol. 1, pp. 179–80.

12. Wellington to Mrs Arbuthnot, 29 May 1822, *W&HF*, p. 22; *JMrsA*, 30 May and 27 July 1821, vol. 1, pp. 97–9, 111–12.

13. *JMrsA*, 28 and 24 February 1821, vol. 1, pp. 77–9, 75–6; Lieven, *Private Letters*, 2 June 1822, pp. 173–5.

14. *JMrsA*, 30 May 1821, vol. 1, p. 99.

15. *JMrsA*, 10 September 1821, vol. 1, pp. 116–17; Croker, *Croker Papers*, 30 July and 16 September 1821, vol. 1, pp. 198–9, 212.

16. *JMrsA*, 24 February 1821, vol. 1, p. 76.

17. Hobhouse, *Diary*, 28 April 1821 and 8 January 1823, pp. 57, 99–101 (reporting earlier events when Bragge Bathurst did finally retire).

18. *JMrsA*, 30 May 1821, vol. 1, p. 99.

19. Memorandum by Charles Arbuthnot, nd [June 1821], *CCA*, p. 24n.

20. For Wellington's interview with the King see *JMrsA*, 27 June and 10 July 1821, vol. 1, p. 103, 105.

21. *JMrsA*, 4 July 1821, vol. 1, p. 105. For comments on the indifference with which the news was greeted see ibid., p. 104; Calvert, *Irish Beauty*, p. 356; Neumann, *Diary*, 3 July 1821, vol. 1, p. 64, and Bagot, *George Canning and His Friends*, vol. 2, pp. 115–16. For Lady Holland and the radicals see Mitchell, *Holland House*, pp. 259–63; Stuart Semmel, *Napoleon and the British* (2004), pp. 218–20; *Parliamentary Debates*, ns, vol. 4, col. 1495, 21 March 1821.

22. Wellington to Princess Lieven, 29 July 1821, *W&HF*, p. 298; Farington, *Diary*, 20 July 1821, vol. 16, p. 5703.

23. Wellington to Princess Lieven, 10 June 1821, *W&HF*, pp. 295–6. Princess Lieven commented on this indiscretion herself in passing on some of the news to Metternich: Lieven, *Private Letters*, 25 [June? or July] 1821, p. 138.

24. Wellington to Princess Lieven, 1 July 1821, *W&HF*, pp. 296–8; *JMrsA*, 1 August 1821, vol. 1, p. 113. Lady Jersey's mother-in-law had been the Prince's mistress some years before.

25. Wellington to Mrs Arbuthnot, 27 and 28 September 1821, *W&HF*, pp. 15–16; *JMrsA*, 14 October 1821, vol. 1, p. 122; A. Brialmont and G.R. Gleig, *History of the Life of Arthur Duke of Wellington* (1858), vol. 3, p. 114.

26. Quoted in Webster, *Foreign Policy of Castlereagh*, p. 362.

27. Ibid., pp. 349–81.

28. Esterházy to Metternich, 3 January 1822, quoted in ibid., p. 371; see also Lieven, *Private Letters*, 7 January 1823, pp. 218–19. For the meetings between the King and Metternich see

Hobhouse, *Diary*, 13 November 1822, pp. 76–8; Webster, *Foreign Policy of Castlereagh* pp. 369–71, and Paul. W Schroeder, *Metternich's Diplomacy at its Zenith, 1820–1823* (1977), pp. 176–7.

29. Wellington to Charles Arbuthnot, 17 November 1821, *W&HF*, pp. 16–18; *JMrsA*, 15 November 1821, vol. 1, p. 126; Londonderry to Stewart, 21 and 24 November 1821, quoted in George IV, *Letters*, vol. 2, pp. 471–2.

30. Hobhouse, *Diary*, 28 November 1821, p. 80; Harrowby to Bathurst, 24 November 1821, *HMC Bathurst*, p. 522.

31. Wellington to Mrs Arbuthnot, 10 March 1822, *W&HF*, pp. 20–1; see also Londonderry to Arbuthnot [*c.* 10 March 1822], *CCA*, pp. 29–30; *JMrsA*, 11 March and 13 April 1822, pp. 150, 155–6.

32. Lieven, *Private Letters*, 16 May 1822, p. 171.

33. Ibid., 23 March 1822, p. 165; George, *BM Catalogue of Satires*, vol. 10, nos. 14376, 14379, 14380, 14383; Alison Yarrington, 'His Achilles Heel? Wellington and Public Art' (1998), pp. 12–13.

34. On *Chelsea Pensioners* see above, p. 102, and R.E. Foster, 'Wellington and Wilkie: Money Well Spent' (2013), pp. 12–16; for the changing reception of military memoirs, and in particular the significance of Moyle Sherer's *Recollections of the Peninsula* (published in 1823) and George Gleig's *The Subaltern* (1825) see Neil Ramsey, *The Military Memoir and Romantic Literary Culture, 1780–1835* (2011), chs. 1 and 2.

35. Wellington to Bathurst, 17 June 1822, *HMC Bathurst*, p. 530; *The Times*, 19 June 1822; R.E. Foster, 'Food for Thought: The Waterloo Banquet' (2013), p. 13 suggests that there was a commemorative dinner in 1821, but that those invited mainly came from the Royal Horse Guards, the regiment of which Wellington was the colonel; so that 1822 is best regarded as the first Waterloo banquet in the form which then became established.

36. Irby C. Nicols, *The European Pentarchy and the Congress of Verona, 1822* (1971), pp. 3–5; Webster, *Foreign Policy of Castlereagh*, pp. 469–78.

37. Lieven, *Private Letters*, 2, nd and 10 June, and 1 August 1822, pp. 173, 178, 187; Hobhouse, *Diary*, 20 August 1822, p. 92 (for 15 June).

38. Wellington to Charles Arbuthnot, 9 August 1822, *W&HF*, pp. 23–5; Wellington to Mr Bankhead and reply, both 9 August 1822, *WND*, vol. 1, pp. 258 and 251.

39. Wellington to Mrs Arbuthnot, 10 August 1822, *W&HF*, p. 25.

40. See, for example, Lieven, *Private Letters*, 21 August 1822, pp. 199–200.

41. *JMrsA*, 17 March 1821, vol. 1, p. 83; see also Liverpool to Melville, 25 August 1822, in Yonge, *Life of Liverpool*, vol. 3, pp. 197–8.

42. Lieven, *Private Letters*, 21 August 1822, pp. 198–9; see also Charles Arbuthnot to his wife [2 September 1822], *CCA*, p. 31, which provides independent confirmation of Wellington's attitude.

43. It is worth comparing this argument with his position in June 1821 that the Whigs would ruin the country, and especially its foreign interests, and so must be kept out of office; see above, p. 178.

44. Wellington, Memorandum shown to Lady Londonderry, 7 September 1822, *WND*, vol. 1, pp. 277–8; see also Lieven, *Private Letters*, 10 and 14 September 1822, pp. 206–7.

45. Liverpool to Arbuthnot, 'Private & Confidential', 29 December 1822, *CCA*, p. 36; see also Gash, *Liverpool*, pp. 197–8.

46. *JMrsA*, 10 September 1822, vol. 1, p. 186; Liverpool to Charles Arbuthnot, 'Private', 7 September 1822, *CCA*, p. 32; Lieven, *Private Letters*, nd [6] September 1822, p. 203; Wellington to Mrs Arbuthnot, 6 September 1822, *W&HF*, pp. 29–30. See also Neumann, *Diary*, vol. 1, pp. 102–3.

47. Liverpool to Charles Arbuthnot, 'Most Private', 1 November 1822, *CCA*, p. 35.

48. Wellington to the King, 7 September 1822, *WND*, vol. 1, pp. 274–6.

49. This, at least, is how Princess Lieven reported it to Metternich on 8 September: the phrase 'I forgive' does not appear in Wellington's letter to the King, but it is not a bad summary of his argument. Lieven, *Private Letters*, p. 205.

50. The King to Liverpool, 8 September 1822, in Yonge, *Life of Liverpool*, vol. 3, pp. 199–200; Lieven, *Private Letters*, 13 September 1822, pp. 206–7; cf Palmerston, *Letters of Lady Palmerston*, p. 109, for a slightly different version of Canning's remark; see also A. Aspinall, 'Canning's Return to Office in September 1822' (1963), pp. 540–1.

11 Verona and Spain

1. Lieven, *Private Letters*, pp. 195–6, shows that Wellington's appointment had been decided by 17 August.
2. Charles J. Esdaile, *Spain in the Liberal Age. From Constitution to Civil War, 1808–1839* (1990), pp. 50–60; Raymond Carr, *Spain 1808–1939* (1966), pp. 129–38.
3. Webster, *Foreign Policy of Castlereagh*, pp. 470–5.
4. Wellington to Canning, 21 September 1822, *WND*, vol. 1, pp. 288–94; see also Sir C. Stuart to [the 3rd] Lord Londonderry, 30 September 1822, ibid., pp. 333–4.
5. Wellington to Canning, 21 September 1822, *WND*, vol. 1, pp. 288–94.
6. *JMrsA*, vol. 1, p. 195 citing letter of 30 September 1823 from Wellington at Vienna. The letter is partially printed in Wellington, *Wellington and His Friends. Letters of the First Duke of Wellington to the Rt. Hon. Charles and Mrs Arbuthnot, the Earl and Countess of Wilton, Princess Lieven and Miss Burdett-Coutts*, sel. and ed. 7th Duke of Wellington (1965), p. 31 but without the relevant paragraph.
7. Wellington to Mrs Arbuthnot, 30 September 1822; Wellington to Charles Arbuthnot, 2 October 1822, *Wellington and His Friends*, pp. 21, 32–3; see also Alan Heesom, 'Wellington's Friend? Lord Londonderry and the Duke of Wellington' (1999), pp. 1–34.
8. Wellington to Canning, 4 October 1822, *WND*, vol. 1, pp. 343–8.
9. Wellington to Canning, 5 November 1822, *WND*, vol. 1, pp. 491–2. This is not as unlikely as it sounds; events in Spain *did* help to inspire the 'Decemberist' conspirators: Carr, *Spain*, p. 139n; Hugh Seton-Watson, *The Russian Empire, 1801–1917* (1967), p. 185. See also Temperley, *Foreign Policy of Canning*, p. 192 on the role of Spanish diplomats in Portuguese revolution; and Neumann, *Diary*, 4 February 1823, vol. 1, p. 115, for the role of the Spanish ambassador in openly fomenting the revolution in Naples.
10. Wellington to Canning, 4 October 1822, *WND*, vol. 1, pp. 343–8.
11. Nichols, *European Pentarchy*, pp. 68–9.
12. Ibid., pp. 72–4, 84–8; Wellington to Canning, 22 October 1822, *WND*, vol. 1, pp. 408–10.
13. Wellington to Canning, 29 October 1822, *WND*, vol. 1, pp. 457–60.
14. Lord Grey quoted by Princess Lieven to Metternich, 1 February 1823, Lieven, *Private Letters*, p. 234; Creevey to Miss Ord, 15 April 1823, Thomas Creevey, *Creevey's Life and Times. A Further Selection from the Correspondence of Thomas Creevey*, ed. John Gore (1934), pp. 176–7; Canning to Wellington, 27 September 1822, *WND*, vol. 1, pp. 301–5.
15. Wellington to Canning, 29 October and 5 November 1822, Memorandum from Lord Londonderry, 8 November 1822, *WND*, vol. 1, pp. 457–60, 492–6, 510–11.
16. Nichols, *European Pentarchy*, pp. 113–19, 123–5.
17. Wellington to Canning, Verona, 29 October 1822, *WND*, vol. 1, pp. 457–60; Princess Lieven to her brother, 23 October 1822, Princess Dorothea Lieven, *Letters of Dorothea, Princess Lieven, during her Residence in London, 1812–1834*, ed. Lionel G. Robinson (1902), pp. 57–9; Londonderry to Bagot, 15 November 1827, Bagot, *George Canning and His Friends*, vol. 2, p. 139.
18. *JMrsA*, 16 November 1822, vol. 1, p. 197, refers to a letter from Somerset at Verona with Wellington; John Sweetman, *Raglan. From the Peninsula to the Crimea* (1993), p. 77 confirms his presence but adds no details; Burghesh, *Correspondence*, pp. 28–9.
19. Lieven, *Private Letters*, 26 and 25 December 1822, pp. 213–14.
20. Maria Copley to Creevey, 12 January 1823, *Creevey Papers*, p. 402; Canning to Bagot, 20 February 1823, Bagot, *George Canning and His Friends*, vol. 2, pp. 155–6.
21. *JMrsA*, 29 and 30 January 1823, vol. 1, p. 209; Creevey to Miss Ord, 11 March 1823, *Creevey Papers*, p. 409; see also Lieven, *Private Letters*, 21 March 1823, p. 244.
22. Wellington to Canning, 20 March 1823, *WND*, vol. 2, pp. 71–2; Wellington to Mrs Arbuthnot, 30 March 1823, Wellington, *Wellington and His Friends*, pp. 36–7; *JMrsA*, 17 April 1823, vol. 1, p. 227.
23. Wellington to Mrs Arbuthnot, 6 April 1823, *W&HF*, pp. 37–8.
24. *JMrsA*, 12 January and 7 February 1825, vol. 1, pp. 202–3, 213; Lieven, *Private Letters*, 28 January 1823, pp. 227–8.
25. Wellington to Fitzroy Somerset, Memorandum on Spain, January 1823, *WND*, vol. 2, pp. 1–3; Carr, *Spain*, pp. 139–40.
26. The last part of the quote from the translation in Nichols, *European Pentarchy*, p. 312; the rest from Sauvigny, *Bourbon Restoration*, p. 190, where it refers to Ferdinand VII as the 'grandson' of Henri IV, whereas he was a sixth-generation descendant.

27. Temperley, *Foreign Policy of Canning*, pp. 78–80; Nichols, *European Pentarchy*, pp. 312–13.
28. Both Alexander and Chateaubriand quoted in Nichols, *The European Pentarchy* p. 313; Alexander's letter of 15 March came after Chateaubriand's of 3 March, but it only confirmed and strengthened assurances of Russian support already given by Pozzo di Borgo in Paris.
29. Memorandum no. 2 to Mr Canning – Considerations of the Consequences of Going to War, and the Mode of Conducting that War, 10 February 1823, *WND*, vol. 2, pp. 31–3; see also *JMrsA*, 7 February 1823, vol. 1, p. 212.
30. Memorandum no. 1 to Mr Canning on the necessity of his pursuing in the House of Commons the Line chalked out in the King's Speech, 10 February 1823, *WND*, vol. 2, pp. 29–31.
31. Canning to Bagot, 'Private', 5 November 1822, Bagot, *George Canning and His Times*, vol. 2, pp. 137–8; see also ibid., p. 151, 153.
32. Sauvigny, *Bourbon Restoration*, pp. 190–1.
33. Prints that express Bonapartist sympathies: George, *BM Catalogue of Satires*, vol. 10, nos. 14501, 14511, 14521; prints with anti-Catholic themes include 14498 and 14503.
34. Ibid., vol. 10, lists 18 prints about Spain of the 32 plates on political subjects produced in 1823. Cruikshank's four are nos. 14502, 14503, 14504 and 14506. See also 14520 by his brother Robert, which depicts an impoverished John Bull so enchained by debt that he is unable to respond to an appeal for assistance from a heroic Spaniard.
35. *Parliamentary Debates*, ns, vol. 8, cols. 1301–1548; *JMrsA*, 1 May 1823, vol. 1, pp. 230–1. According to the *Annual Register* the minority of twenty included some government supporters who were unable to squeeze into the lobby: *Annual Register for 1823*, p. 46.
36. On Lord Acton's criticism see Nichols, *European Pentarchy*, pp. 277–85. It is significant that even Temperley, whose admiration for Canning is sometimes embarrassingly extravagant, rejected the charge: Temperley, *Foreign Policy of Canning*, pp. 484–6; Capt J.E.S. Green, 'Wellington, Boislecompte, and the Congress of Verona, 1822' (1918), pp. 59–76; Capt. J.E.S. Green, 'Wellington and the Congress of Verona, 1822' (1920), pp. 200–11; H.M. Lackland, 'Wellington at Verona' (1920), pp. 574–80. In fairness to Acton it should be noted that his original accusation, while intemperately worded, appears to have been nothing more than a throwaway remark in a book review.
37. Sauvigny, *Bourbon Restoration*, pp. 191–3; Carr, *Spain*, pp. 146–7; Esdaile, *Spain in the Liberal Age*, pp. 63–5.
38. Temperley, *Foreign Policy of Canning*, pp. 83–4; Neumann, *Diary*, vol. 1, pp. 118–20.
39. Quoted in Raymond Postgate and Aylmer Vallance, *Those Foreigners* (1937), p. 18.
40. Canning to Bagot, 'Private', 14 July 1823, Bagot, *George Canning and His Friends*, vol. 2, p. 183. It is interesting that Canning's description of Portuguese liberals as 'the scum of the earth' has aroused none of the criticism that has been directed at Wellington for thus describing the rank and file of his army who misbehaved after Vitoria.
41. Wellington to Canning, 31 July 1823, *WND*, vol. 2, pp. 110–12.
42. Wellington to Canning, 3 August 1823, *WND*, vol. 2, pp. 113–15.
43. *JMrsA*, 8 August 1823, vol. 2, pp. 250–1.
44. Liverpool to Canning, 1 August 1823, *WND*, vol. 2, pp. 112–13.
45. For example Hobhouse, *Diary*, 19 July 1823, pp. 102–3.
46. *JMrsA*, 26 September 1823, vol. 1, pp. 258–9. There are many earlier if rather less explicit complaints to a similar effect, e.g. 16 March, p. 223; 30 May, p. 238; 1 August, p. 248. See also Princess Lieven to Metternich, 20 April, 3 June 1823, 4 October 1823, Lieven, *Private Letters*, pp. 256–7, 268–9, 291–2.
47. Princess Lieven to Metternich, 18 July 1823, Lieven, *Private Letters*, pp. 274–5; Arbuthnot to Bathurst, 'Private and Confidential', 29 August 1823, *HMC Bathurst*, pp. 542–3.
48. For Bathurst see *JMrsA*, 3 February 1822, vol. 1, p. 211; and see also pp. 219, 220; for Peel, Arbuthnot to Bathurst, 'Private and Confidential', 29 August 1823, *HMC Bathurst*, pp. 542–3.
49. Quoted in A. Aspinall, 'The Cabinet Council 1783–1835', (1952) p. 210.
50. Gash, *Liverpool*, pp. 195–6; Liverpool to Bathurst, 4 May 1825, *HMC Bathurst*, pp. 580–1; see also Boyd Hilton, 'The Political Arts of Lord Liverpool' (1988) pp. 155–9, although even Hilton refers to Liverpool exercising a degree of 'policy co-ordination' – a phrase which still underestimates Liverpool's real power.
51. Princess Lieven to Metternich, 7 January 1823, Lieven, *Private Letters*, pp. 218–19.

52. For example Princess Lieven to Metternich, 5 March and 28 March 1823, Lieven, *Private Letters*, pp. 241–2, 245–8.

12 Latin America and the Catholic Question

1. Princess Lieven to Metternich, 2 August 1824, Lieven, *Private Letters*, pp. 323–5; Wellington to Mrs Arbuthnot, 10 August 1824, *W&HF*, p. 45; see also *JMrsA*, 21 January 1824, vol. 1, p. 282.
2. *JMrsA*, 24 September 1824, vol. 1, p. 339.
3. Wellington to Mrs Arbuthnot, 13 April 1825, *W&HF*, p. 53.
4. Wellington to Canning, 19 January 1824, enclosed Memorandum, and reply from Canning, 22 January 1824, *WND*, vol. 2, pp. 189–92.
5. *JMrsA*, 3 February 1824, vol. 1, p. 284.
6. Ibid., p. 285.
7. Charles Arbuthnot to Bathurst, 'Private and most confidential', 24 March 1824, *HMC Bathurst*, p. 565.
8. *JMrsA*, 21 and 24 March and 11 April 1824, vol. 1, p. 293, 294–5, 300; Charles Arbuthnot to Bathurst, 'Private and most confidential', 24 March 1824, *HMC Bathurst*, p. 565.
9. *JMrsA*, 10 June 1824, vol. 1, p. 321; see also ibid., 31 March, 7 and 11 April, and 24 May 1824, pp. 297, 299–300, 314–15; Gash, *Liverpool*, pp. 226–7; Abbot, *Diary and Correspondence*, vol. 3, p. 330.
10. On Liverpool's talk of retirement see *JMrsA*, 11 April 1824, vol. 1, p. 300; on the King's enthusiasm for Wellington see George IV to Wellington, 23 July 1824, WP 1/796/15; on the Lord Mayor's dinner affair see *JMrsA*, 29 April 1824, vol. 1, pp. 305–6, *WND*, vol. 1, pp. 250–1, 262–3; on Wellington's rebuff to the Duke of York see Princess Lieven to Metternich, 17 June 1824, Lieven, *Private Letters*, p. 318.
11. *JMrsA*, 10 June 1824, vol. 1, p. 322.
12. Princess Lieven to Metternich, 17 June 1824, Lieven, *Private Letters*, pp. 318–19.
13. Princess Lieven to Metternich, 17 June 1824, ibid., pp. 317–18; for other speculation about a possible coalition see Croker to Bloomfield, 10 May 1824, *Croker Papers*, vol. 1, pp. 265–7 and *JMrsA*, 6 June 1824, vol. 1, p. 320.
14. Princess Lieven to Metternich, 2 September 1824, Lieven, *Private Letters*, pp. 328–9.
15. Fremantle to Buckingham, 23 December 1823, Buckingham, *Memoirs of the Court of George IV*, vol. 2, p. 21; *JMrsA*, 15 January 1824, vol. 1, p. 280; see also ibid., 13 and 28 December 1823, vol. 1, pp. 276, 277.
16. Fremantle to Buckingham, 22 May 1824, Buckingham, *Memoirs of the Court of George IV*, vol. 2, p. 79; Croker to Bloomfield, 10 May 1824, *Croker Papers*, vol. 1, pp. 265–7; *JMrsA*, 12 February, 22 April, 21 May 1824, vol. 1, pp. 286, 301–2, 311–12.
17. *JMrsA*, 24 September and 21 October 1824, vol. 1, pp. 337, 353.
18. *JMrsA*, 15 January 1824, vol. 1, p. 280; Princess Lieven to Metternich, 30 August 1824, Lieven, *Private Letters*, p. 328. Canning was ill again in February–March 1825: see *WND*, vol. 2, pp. 421, 427–8.
19. *JMrsA*, 20 February 1824, vol. 1, p. 289.
20. Wellington to Princess Lieven, 23 March 1824, *W&HF*, pp. 303–4.
21. *JMrsA*, 14 and 18 November 1823, vol. 1, pp. 273–6.
22. Temperley, *Foreign Policy of Canning*, p. 199; see also two long letters from Beresford to Wellington describing events as they unfolded dated 5, 12 and 14 May 1824, WP 1/792/4 and 14.
23. Princess Lieven to Metternich, 4 July 1824, Lieven, *Private Letters*, pp. 320–1.
24. Princess Lieven quoting Wellington's conversation in her letter to Metternich of 22 July 1824, ibid., p. 322; see also *JMrsA*, 16 July 1824, vol. 1, pp. 327–8.
25. For example Temperley, *Foreign Policy of Canning*, pp. 202–3.
26. Ibid., pp. 205–7.
27. *JMrsA*, 16 July 1824, vol. 1, p. 328.
28. Canning to Wellington [private], 8 November 1822, *WND*, vol. 1, pp. 511–12.
29. Wellington to Canning, 18 October and 10 November 1822, *WND*, vol. 1, pp. 385, 516–17.
30. *JMrsA*, 18 December 1824, vol. 1, p. 367; Wellington to Canning, 18 October 1822, *WND*, vol. 1, pp. 384–5, cf Canning to Wellington, 29 October 1822, ibid., pp. 463–6, which points out that such products were already permitted entry to Britain for re-export.

31. The declared value of British exports to Central and South America rose from £2.5m in 1815 to almost £4m in 1818; fell sharply due to the depression of 1819; was around £3m p.a. in 1820–22; £4.2m in 1823; £5.6m in 1824; £6.4m in 1825; then fell back to only £3m in 1826 and £4m in 1827. (By comparison in 1823 exports to southern Europe were £6.8m, to the USA £5.4m, and to Asia £3.9m.) B.R. Mitchell and Phyllis Deane, *Abstract of British Histories Statistics* (1962), p. 313. Economic cycles and peace or war in the principal markets affected trade far more than the establishment of diplomatic relations, which in 1824–25 simply applied an unhelpful stimulus to an already overheated economy.

32. *JMrsA*, 19 July 1824, vol. 1, p. 329.

33. Plumer Ward to Buckingham, 31 July 1824, Buckingham, *Memoirs of the Court of George IV*, vol. 2, p. 109; *JMrsA*, 19 July 1824, vol. 1, pp. 328–9; Cabinet Memorandum, 23 July 1824, in Augustus Granville Stapleton, *George Canning and His Times* (1859), pp. 327–400; Aspinall, 'Cabinet Council', pp. 217–18.

34. Wellington to Liverpool, and reply, 7 and 8 December 1824, *WND*, vol. 2, pp. 364–6.

35. *JMrsA*, 10, 16 and 18 December 1824, vol. 1, pp. 364–8; Princess Lieven to Metternich, 4 December 1824, Lieven, *Private Letters*, pp. 338–9.

36. *JMrsA*, 18 December 1824, vol. 1, pp. 366–7.

37. *JMrsA*, 18 December 1824, vol. 1, p. 368. See also Liverpool to Wellington, 16 December 1824, *WND*, vol. 2, p. 368, and Aspinall, 'Cabinet Council', pp. 220–1.

38. The King to Liverpool, 17 December 1824, *WND*, vol. 2, p. 368. See also the King to the Cabinet, nd, George IV, *Letters*, vol. 3, p. 97.

39. Canning to Granville, 'Most private', 17 December 1824, Stapleton, *George Canning and His Times*, pp. 411–13.

40. *JMrsA*, 7 April 1825, vol. 1, p. 387.

41. O'Connell quoted in Abbot, *Diary and Correspondence*, 20 December 1824, vol. 3, p. 354; Wellington to Peel, 2 January 1825, *WND*, vol. 2, pp. 394–5.

42. *JMrsA*, 19 February 1825, vol. 1, pp. 376–7.

43. *JMrsA*, 31 May 1824, vol. 1, pp. 317–18; see also Wellington to Clancarty, 6 June 1822, *WND*, vol. 1, pp. 240–1, which shows his thinking moving in this direction.

44. Richard W. Davis, 'Wellington and the "Open Question": The Issue of Catholic Emancipation, 1821–1829' (1997), p. 44; G.I.T. Machin, *The Catholic Question in English Politics 1820 to 1830* (1964), pp. 51–2; see Muir, *Wellington. The Path to Victory*, pp. 24–5.

45. *JMrsA*, 19 February 1825, vol. 1, pp. 376–8.

46. Memorandum on the case of the Roman Catholics in Ireland (by Wellington), [May] 1825, *WND*, vol. 2, pp. 592–607, esp. 592–5.

47. Ibid., pp. 592–607, esp. 595–6.

48. Ibid., pp. 592–607, esp. 596–9, 601–2.

49. Ibid., pp. 592–607, esp. 602–7; see also *JMrsA*, 5 and 25 March 1825, vol. 1, pp. 379–81, 385–6.

50. *JMrsA*, 12 May 1825, vol. 1, pp. 396–7.

51. *JMrsA*, 25 May 1825, vol. 1, p. 401.

52. *JMrsA*, 23 April and 6 May 1825, vol. 1, pp. 389, 392–3; see also Abbot, *Diary and Correspondence*, 25 April 1825, vol. 3, pp. 379–80.

53. *JMrsA*, 28 April 1825, vol. 1, p. 390; *Parliamentary Debates*, ns, vol. 13, cols. 138–42; Abbot, *Diary and Correspondence*, 10, 12 and 17 May 1825, vol. 3, pp. 372–4, 383.

54. Gash, *Liverpool*, p. 234 ('most vehement'); *JMrsA*, 18 May 1825, vol. 1, p. 397; Abbot, *Diary and Correspondence*, 16 May 1825, vol. 3, pp. 385–6; Liverpool to the King, 18 May 1825, *WND*, vol. 2, p. 451.

55. *JMrsA*, 20–27 May 1825, vol. 1, pp. 398–401; Gash, *Liverpool*, pp. 234–5.

56. Wellington to Liverpool, and reply, 22 and 23 June 1825, *WND*, vol. 2, pp. 463–5; Croker to Lord Hertford, 22 September 1825, *Croker Papers*, vol. 1, pp. 281–2; *JMrsA*, 21 September 1825, vol. 1, p. 414; Davis, 'Wellington and the "Open Question"', p. 46; Machin, *Catholic Question*, pp. 65–7.

13 The Last Year of Liverpool's Government

1. Princess Lieven to Metternich, 27 January 1825, Lieven, *Private Letters*, p. 343; see also *JMrsA*, 16 March 1825, vol. 1, pp. 381–2. Figures from Frank Griffith Dawson, *The First Latin American Debt Crisis. The City of London and the 1822–25 Loan Bubble* (1990), pp. 139–40.

2. Liverpool quoted in George, *English Political Caricature*, vol. 2, p. 210, possibly from a newspaper report, cf *Parliamentary Debates*, vol. 12, cols. 1194–5, where similar sentiments are expressed in slightly different words. Huskisson quoted in Boyd Hilton, *Corn, Cash, Commerce. The Economic Policies of the Tory Governments 1815–1830* (1977), p. 205; David Williams and John Armstrong, 'Promotion, Speculation and their Outcome: The "Steamship Mania" of 1824–1825' (2008), p. 645.

3. *JMrsA*, 16 March 1825, vol. 1, p. 382.

4. *The Times*, 8 August 1825, lists the directors; Maurice Fitzgerald, hereditary Knight of Kerry, to Wellington, 19 July 1824, WP 1/796/12; Wellington to Huskisson, 14 September 1824, WP 1/801/15, and reply 19 November 1824, WP 1/805/6; Wellington to Fitzgerald, 13 December 1824, WP 1/808/7.

5. *JMrsA*, 17 December 1825, vol. 1, p. 428.

6. *JMrsA*, 20 December 1825, vol. 1, pp. 428–9; Niall Ferguson, *The House of Rothschild*, vol. 1, *Money's Prophets 1798–1848* (1999), pp. 135–7; Hilton, *Corn, Cash and Commerce*, pp. 215–20.

7. *JMrsA*, 10 February 1826, vol. 2, pp. 10–11; Hilton, *Corn, Cash and Commerce*, p. 224; Dawson, *First Latin American Debt Crisis*, pp. 214–15, gives examples of consequences for individuals.

8. Williams and Armstrong, 'Promotion, Speculation and their Outcome', pp. 654–5, quotes from *The Times*.

9. Details of defaults from Dawson, *First Latin American Debt Crisis*, p. 173; Wellington's prediction, Princess Lieven to Metternich, 4 February 1825, Lieven, *Private Letters*, p. 343.

10. *JMrsA*, 15 January and 21 February 1826, vol. 2, pp. 4–5, 13; see also C.W. Crawley, *The Question of Greek Independence. A Study of British Policy in the Near East 1821–1833* (1930), p. 52.

11. 'Extract from the Memorandum of a Conference between Mr Canning and Count Lieven', 25 October 1825; Stratford Canning to Canning, 16 December 1825, *WND*, vol. 2, p. 547, 580–5; Canning to Wellington, 19 February 1826, *WND*, vol. 3, pp. 85–93; see also Wellington to Canning, 22 November 1825, *WND*, vol. 2, pp. 569–71.

12. Schroeder, *Transformation of European Politics*, p. 640. See also Loyal Cowles, 'The Failure to Restrain Russia: Canning, Nesselrode and the Greek Question 1825–1827' (1990), pp. 688–720 *passim*, esp. pp. 693–4; and A.B. Cunningham, 'The Philhellenes, Canning and Greek Independence' (1978), pp. 168–76. All three works are highly critical of Canning's policy, disputing his commitment to the Greek cause, and his control over events. Temperley's *Foreign Policy of Canning* now appears seriously outdated and its conclusions in need of revision.

13. Wellington to Canning, 10 November 1824, and 22 November 1825; Wellington to Bathurst, 17 February 1826, *WND*, vol. 2, pp. 338–9, 569–71, vol. 3, pp. 113–16.

14. Wellington to Canning, 22 November 1825, *WND*, vol. 2, pp. 569–71; Bathurst to Wellington, 2 March 1826, *WND*, p. 142; Cowles, 'The Failure to Restrain Russia', pp. 699–704; Steven Schwartzberg, 'The Lion and the Phoenix – [pt] 1 British Policy toward the "Greek Question" 1831 [*sic* 1821]–1832' (1988), pp. 157–60.

15. *JMrsA*, 27 January 1826, vol. 2, pp. 6–7; the King to Wellington, 27 December 1825, *WND*, vol. 3, pp. 53–4.

16. Wellington to Bathurst, 17 February 1826, *WND*, vol. 3, pp. 113–16.

17. Wellington to Mrs Arbuthnot, 2 and 5 March 1826, *W&HF*, pp. 56–8; Shelley, *Diary of Lady Shelley*, 16 August 1826, vol. 2, pp. 142–3 (the camp bed).

18. Wellington to Canning, 5 March 1826, *WND*, vol. 3, pp. 148–50; Wellington to Mrs Arbuthnot, 28 March and 4 April 1826, *W&HF*, pp. 62–4.

19. *JMrsA*, 29 April 1826, vol. 2, p. 23.

20. Wellington to Granville, 27 March 1826, *WND*, vol. 3, pp. 220–1; Wellington to Bathurst, 7 March 1826, ibid., pp. 159–60, and Wellington to Canning, 4 April 1826, ibid., pp. 224–31; W. Bruce Lincoln, *Nicholas I. Emperor and Autocrat of all the Russias* (1978), p. 115.

21. Bathurst to the Lords Commissioners of the Admiralty, 8 February 1826, *WND*, vol. 3, pp. 82–3.

22. Quoted in Schwartzberg, 'Lion and Phoenix', pp. 167–8.

23. Cowles, 'Failure to Restrain Russia', pp. 709–10ff; Schroeder, *Transformation of European Politics*, pp. 646–7, cf Schwartzberg's intriguing alternative interpretation, in 'Lion and Phoenix', pp. 167–9.

24. Mrs Arbuthnot to Lady Shelley, 1 May 1826, Shelley, *Diary of Lady Shelley*, vol. 2, p. 137; see also Palmerston, *Letters of Lady Palmerston*, pp. 148–9.

25. *JMrsA*, 29 April 1826, vol. 2, p. 23; Canning to Wellington, 28 April 1826, *WND*, vol. 3, p. 310; Greville, *Memoirs*, 12 February 1826, vol. 1, p. 155; see also *The Times*, 11 February 1826, and compare the *Examiner* of 26 March with that of 16 April 1826.

26. *JMrsA*, 23 April 1826, vol. 2, pp. 20–2; Princess Lieven to Metternich, 14 May 1826, Lieven, *Private Letters*, p. 367. See also Mitchell, *Whigs in Opposition*, pp. 192–3, and Aspinall, 'Canning's Return to Office', pp. 544–5n.

27. Princess Lieven to Metternich, 28 December 1822 and 6 January 1823, Lieven, *Private Letters*, pp. 214, 216.

28. *JMrsA*, 6 May, 31 July 1825, vol. 1, pp. 392–3, 410, and 26 April 1826, vol. 2, p. 24; Bagot, *George Canning and His Friends*, vol. 2, p. 305.

29. Princess Lieven to Metternich, 20 and 28 March, 16 April and 4 June 1826, Lieven, *Private Letters*, pp. 362–70; *JMrsA*, 22 June and 17 July 1826, vol. 2, pp. 31, 37–8; Wellington to Mrs Arbuthnot, 3 and 4 September 1826, *W&HF*, pp. 68–9.

30. Hobhouse, *Diary*, 25 July 1826, p. 121; *JMrsA*, 1 July 1826, vol. 2, p. 34.

31. Abbot, *Diary and Correspondence*, 14 December 1826, vol. 3, p. 452, mentions Wellington's statement; see also Hobhouse, *Diary*, 25 July 1826, p. 121, and Mitchell, *Whigs in Opposition*, p. 185.

32. *JMrsA*, 14 May and 1 September 1826, vol. 2, pp. 26 and 45. See Mitchell, *Whigs in Opposition*, pp. 186–9, for another view of this.

33. Wellesley to Wellington, 15 August 1826, and reply 20 August 1826, WP 1/860/14 and 1/861/16; Yonge, *Life of Liverpool*, vol. 3, pp. 383–95; Bathurst to Arbuthnot, 13 September 1826, *CCA*, p. 83; Arbuthnot to Bathurst, 1 September 1826, *HMC Bathurst*, pp. 614–15; *JMrsA*, 1 September 1826, p. 45.

34. *JMrsA*, 16 February 1827, vol. 2, pp. 80–1; *The Times*, 24 October 1848.

35. Beresford to Wellington, 8 November 1826, *WND*, vol. 3, pp. 446–9.

36. Beresford to Wellington, 30 November and 1 December 1826, *WND*, vol. 3, pp. 470–3.

37. Canning to Liverpool, 3 December 1826, *WND*, vol. 3, pp. 473–4; *JMrsA*, 5 and 9 December 1826, vol. 2, pp. 61–2; Wellington to Beresford, 5 December 1826, *WND*, vol. 3, pp. 476–7.

38. Clinton's Instructions, dated 17 December 1826, are based on a Memorandum prepared by Wellington dated 10 December 1826: *WND*, vol. 3, pp. 489–90, 480–2. Details of the force are given in Sir Herbert Taylor to Wellington, 9 December 1826, *WND*, vol. 3, p. 480; see also *JMrsA*, 12 December 1826, vol. 2, p. 63.

39. Canning to Wellington, 11 December 1826, *WND*, vol. 3, p. 484; *Parliamentary Debates*, ns, vol. 16, cols. 347–8; Wellington, *Speeches*, vol. 1, pp. 120–1; *JMrsA*, 15 December 1826, vol. 1, pp. 63–4.

40. *Parliamentary Debates*, ns, vol. 16, col. 369.

41. Palmerston to his brother quoted in Bourne, *Palmerston*, p. 249.

42. Greville, *Memoirs*, 14 December 1826, vol. 1, pp. 161–2.

43. *JMrsA*, 15 December 1826, vol. 2, pp. 63–4.

44. Beresford to Wellington, Lisbon 30 December 1826, *WND*, vol. 3, pp. 507–8.

45. Princess Lieven to Metternich, 30 June 1826, Lieven, *Private Letters*, p. 372.

46. *JMrsA*, 22 January and 4 February 1827, vol. 2, pp. 73–4, 75; see also Charles Arbuthnot to Bathurst, 30 January 1827, *HMC Bathurst*, pp. 628–9, and Greville, *Memoirs*, 12 February 1827, vol. 1, pp. 167–8; Norman Gash, *Mr Secretary Peel. The Life of Sir Robert Peel to 1830* (1961), p. 425.

47. *JMrsA*, 7 September 1826, vol. 2, p. 49.

48. Wellington to Bathurst, 9 January 1827, *WND*, vol. 3, p. 537 where the last two sentences are suppressed but printed in *HMC Bathurst*, p. 622; Arbuthnot to Bathurst, 'Confidential', 14 January 1827, ibid., pp. 625–6; Liverpool to Peel, 6 January 1827, Charles Stuart Parker, *Sir Robert Peel . . . from his Private Papers* (1891–99), vol. 1, pp. 435–6; Peel to Wellington, 6 January 1827, *WND*, vol. 3, p. 531; Liverpool to Bathurst, 'Private & Confidential', 8 January 1827, *HMC Bathurst*, p. 622; *JMrsA*, 28 January 1827, vol. 2, pp. 74–5.

49. *JMrsA*, 22 January and 6 February 1827, vol. 2, pp. 74–7; see also Arbuthnot to Bathurst, 14 and 22 January 1827, *HMC Bathurst*, pp. 625–7; and Aspinall, 'Cabinet Council', p. 159. Wellington himself later stressed the importance of keeping the Commander-in-Chief detached from politics: Memoranda of 25 March 1837 and 4 January 1838 printed in Charles M. Clode, *The Military Forces of the Crown. Their Administration and Government* (1869),

vol. 2, pp. 759–63. Grey to Princess Lieven, 27 January 1827, Princess Dorothea Lieven and Charles, 2nd Earl Grey, *Correspondence of Princess Lieven and Earl Grey*, ed. Guy Le Strange (1890), vol. 1, p. 35.

50. Abbot, *Diary and Correspondence*, 16 February 1827, vol. 3, pp. 462–3; *JMrsA*, 15 February 1827, vol. 2, p. 79.

14 Master-General of the Ordnance

1. *Parliamentary Papers: Second Report of the Select Committee on Public Income and Expenditure* in House of Commons, *Reports from Committees* (1828; henceforth cited as the *Finance Committee Report*), pp. 9–12; 'Papers related to the reduction of the Ordnance Establishment', *c.* 4 June 1821, WP 1/695/3.

2. Torrens to Wellington, 19 August 1813, *WSD*, vol. 8, pp. 198–9.

3. Wellington to Lady Charlotte Greville, 25 December 1818, Ellesmere, *Personal Reminiscences*, pp. 114–15.

4. Wellington to Liverpool, 21 December 1809, *WD*, vol. 3, pp. 659–660; Thorne, *History of Parliament*, vol. 5, pp. 186–7; Charles Ross, *Correspondence of Charles, First Marquis Cornwallis* (1859) vol. 1, p. 10n; Wellington to Mulgrave, nd February 1819, *WND*, vol. 1, pp. 20–1.

5. Hime, *History of the Royal Regiment of Artillery*, p. 59, quoting Dickson's unpublished journal. For a useful if eulogistic account of Macleod's life see the obituary in *United Service Journal*, July 1834, pp. 380–5; other evidence of his conflicts with Wellington in Hime, op. cit., pp. 61 and 68. For Mann see *ODNB* and George Raudzens, 'The British Ordnance Department 1815–1855' (1979), pp. 95–6.

6. Phipps, *Memoir of Plumer Ward*, vol. 2, p. 15.

7. Ward's diary, 16 and 25 November 1819 (in the midst of the debates in Parliament over the Peterloo Massacre), and 8 January 1820, ibid., vol. 2, pp. 23, 35, 45–6.

8. Charles, Viscount Hardinge, *Viscount Hardinge by his Son* (1981), pp. 10–30; *ODNB*; Canning to Wellington, 27 February 1824, WP 1/785/16; *Finance Committee Report*, p. 11; *JMrsA*, vol. 1, 29 August 1824, p. 333. It is remarkable that there has not been a full biography of Hardinge.

9. Wellington to Dickson, 27 February 1821, WP 1/662/25; and to Sir Herbert Taylor, 31 March 1825, WP 1/815/22.

10. 'Papers relating to Proposals for the Reduction of the Ordnance Establishment', *c.* 4 June 1821, WP 1/695/3; *Finance Committee Report*, pp. 8 and 17.

11. 'Papers relating to Proposals for the Reduction of the Ordnance Establishment', *c.* 4 June 1821, WP 1/695/3.

12. *Finance Committee Report*, pp. 9.

13. 'Report of the Commissioners appointed to Inquire into and state the mode of Keeping the Official Accounts in the Principal Departments connected with the Receipts and Expenditure for the Public Service', 9 February 1829, pp. 76–7.

14. *Finance Committee Report*, pp. 4, 9.

15. *Parliamentary Debates*, ns, vol. 8, 14 March 1823, cols. 597–9.

16. Wellington to Hopetoun, 11 September, and to Hill (including the quote), 5 October 1822, *WND*, vol. 1, p. 281 and 355; Wellington to Beresford, 11 November 1822, and 9 December 1822, WP 1/738/14, WP 1/746/8; Knighton to Wellington, 17 January 1823, WP 1/754/28; *Parliamentary Debates*, ns, vol. 8, 19 February 1823, cols. 140–72. See also Phipps, *Memoir of Plumer Ward*, vol. 2, pp. 104–5, and *JMrsA*, 21 February 1823, vol. 1, p. 216 for accounts of this debate.

17. Hime, *History of the Royal Artillery*, pp. 9, 17–19. The artillery suffered proportionally more because almost all the drivers were discharged, and perhaps also because it was less immediately useful for the principal tasks of the post-war army: colonial garrisons and preserving order at home. The *Finance Committee Report*, pp. 20–1, gives somewhat different but broadly consistent totals.

18. Hime, *History of the Royal Artillery*, pp. 19–23.

19. Wellington to the Duke of York, 9 January 1819, Wellington to Sir Herbert Taylor, 11 April 1821, *WND*, vol. 1, pp. 1–2, 167–8.

20. Wellington to Sir Herbert Taylor, 11 April 1821, *WND*, vol. 1, pp. 167–8.

21. Wellington to Melville, 2 March 1821, *WND*, vol. 1, p. 163.

22. Wellington to Malcolm, 21 September 1825, *WND*, vol. 2, p. 501 – see also p. 484 for his previous letter to Malcolm on the subject.

23. Ross to Somerset, and reply 24 and 28 June 1824, Ross, *Memoir*, pp. 70–1. For the significance of the position – one of the choicest pieces of patronage at Wellington's disposal – see Wellington to Malcolm, 7 September 1825, *WND*, vol. 2, p. 484.

24. For example Wellington to Lady Shelley, 20 March 1826, *Diary of Lady Shelley*, vol. 2, p. 135, promising to ensure that a protégé of Sir John's would be made a clerk as soon as he was old enough; and Wellington to Henry Goulburn, 17 September 1823, *WND*, vol. 2, pp. 120–1, regarding the appointment of two barrack-masters.

25. Wellington to Melville, and reply, 31 August and 3 September 1825, WP 1/826/12, WP 1/827/2.

26. Wellington to Sir William Congreve, 22 August 1824, *WND*, vol. 2, p. 302.

27. On Perkins and his steam gun see S.G. Goodrich, *Recollections of a Lifetime, or Men and Things I Have Seen...* (1857), vol. 2, pp. 226–7; George, *BM Catalogue of Satires*, vol. 10, p. 491. Wellington attended the public exhibition of the steam gun in London but was rightly sceptical of its practical utility; see Wellington to Beresford, 12 December 1829, *WND*, vol. 6, pp. 321–2. For the claimed improvements in Congreve's Rockets see Sir William Congreve to Wellington, 9 August 1822, *WND*, vol. 1, p. 252.

28. Wellington to Melville, 9 December 1820, WP 1/658/2.

29. Entry on Thomas Frederick Colby in *ODNB*; *Finance Committee Report*, p. 23; Lord Wellesley to Wellington, and reply, 17 and 23 February 1824, *WND*, vol. 1, pp. 218–19, 220–1.

30. Memorandum on the Defence of Canada [for] Lord Bathurst, 1 March 1819, *WND*, vol. 1, pp. 36–44. See Kenneth Bourne, *Britain and the Balance of Power in North America 1815–1908* (1967), chs. 1 and 2 for the context and previous plans as well as a good discussion of Wellington's ideas.

31. Ibid., pp. 16 and 23 (for it being an encumbrance); pp. 10 and 37 (for possibility that the Americans might turn their gaze to the Caribbean).

32. Wellington to Huskisson, 20 July 1826, *WND*, vol. 3, pp. 350–1; on wider suspicion of US in British government see Bourne, *Balance of Power in North America*, pp. 6–10, 28–9.

33. Wellington to Sir Herbert Taylor, 27 December 1824, *WND*, vol. 2, pp. 381–3.

34. On such disputes see Bathurst to Wellington, 16 August 1819, WP 1/623/13; Wellington to Bathurst, 6 August 1820, WP 1/652/3; Wellington to Bathurst, 20 March and 6 May 1824, *WND*, vol. 2, pp. 238–9, 263; Neville Thompson, *Earl Bathurst and the British Empire* (1999), pp. 156, 168–9 and 141, 144–5 (on Wilmot).

35. Peter Burroughs, 'The Ordnance Department and Colonial Defence, 1821–1855' (1982), p. 127, quoting a minute by Wellington dated 23 March 1823.

36. On the Duke of York see Wellington to Mrs Arbuthnot, 4 March 1822, *W&HF*, pp. 19–20; Mann to Crew, 8 April 1822, WO 44/265, f 328–30.

37. Wellington to Goulburn, 17 September 1823, *WND*, vol. 2, pp. 130–1; see also R.B. McDowell, *The Irish Administration, 1801–1914* (1964), p. 16 which provides additional evidence of the abuses.

38. Wellington to Mr Griffin, 23 September 1823, WP 1/772/17.

39. Burgoyne to Burgh, 3 April 1823, in George Wrottesley, *Life and Correspondence of Field Marshall Sir John of Burgoyne* (1873), vol. 1, pp. 343–4; Wellington to Crew, 8 July 1823, WP 1/768/1.

40. Wellington to General Mann, 14–21 May 1823, *WND*, vol. 2, pp. 94–6.

41. Order dated 21 May 1823 included in Wellington to General Mann, 14–21 May 1823, *WND*, vol. 2, pp. 94–6.

42. Wellington to General Mann, 14–21 May 1823, *WND*, vol. 2, pp. 94–6: Wellington's letter was written in response to objections from Mann and the proposed Order also included provisions for records to be kept in the Engineer's office of the performance of individual officers on their projects.

43. Burroughs, 'Ordnance Department and Colonial Defence', pp. 125–6.

44. Hime, *History of the Royal Artillery*, pp. 29–36, 65–6, quotes a story in the *Morning Herald* of 6 June 1827 purporting to be from an artillery officer in Lisbon, although this was officially denied and the timing of its publication, immediately before an important parliamentary debate on Portugal, casts further doubt on its credibility. Ross, *Memoir*, pp. 75–7 prints several interesting letters from artillery officers at home giving details of the composition of the force and reaction to Webber Smith's recall.

15 Family and Friends

1. Marchioness of Douro, 'Housing a Great Duke' (1999), p. 7; see also Longford, *Wellington. Pillar of State*, p. 45 and Edna Healey, *Lady Unknown. The Life of Angela Burdett-Coutts* (1978), p. 91.
2. Edgeworth, *Letters from England*, 19 September 1818, p. 103; Wellington's letter quoted in Longford, *Wellington. Pillar of State*, pp. 74–5.
3. Wellington to Duchess of Wellington, 5 and 11 May, and reply 10 May 1821, quoted in ibid., pp. 75–6.
4. Duchess of Wellington to Wellington, 9 July 1821, quoted in ibid., pp. 76–7.
5. *JMrsA*, 27 October 1825, vol. 1, pp. 422–3.
6. *JMrsA*, 26 January 1826, vol. 2, pp. 5–6.
7. Shelley, *Diary of Lady Shelley*, vol. 2, pp. 311–13; Duchess of Wellington quoted in Muriel Wellesley, *Wellington in Civil Life* (nd [1939]), p. 56. For Kitty's relations with her children, and the remarkable way in which she let them write to her, see Longford, *Wellington. Pillar of State*, pp. 82–3.
8. Duchess of Wellington to Lady Eleanor Butler and Miss Caroline Ponsonby, 18 July [1816], quoted in Guedalla, *The Duke*, p. 299: see above, p. 101.
9. Duchess of Wellington to Lady Shelley, 11 January 1821, and Wellington to Lady Shelley, 22 and 18 March 1820, Shelley, *Diary of Lady Shelley*, vol. 2, pp. 109 and 101–3. The Duke's sons were accompanied to Eton by their private tutor, Mr Wagner: *Wellington Private Correspondence*, p. 19.
10. Sir A. Wellesley to the Duke of Richmond, 2 April 1809, *WSD*, vol. 5, pp. 633–5.
11. Wellington to Maj.-Gen. Sir J.W. Gordon, 28 May 1817, *WSD*, vol. 11, pp. 687–8; Wellington to Lord Charles Wellesley quoted in Longford, *Wellington: Pillar of State*, p. 84.
12. Wellington, *Private Correspondence*, pp. 26–55 contains a variety of correspondence and memoranda on which this paragraph is based.
13. Lady Granville to Lady G. Morpeth, Paris, 21 July 1825, Granville, *Letters of Countess Granville*, vol. 1, pp. 352–3; William Napier [to his wife], February 1824, Bruce, *Life of Napier*, vol. 1, p. 249; *JMrsA*, 27 October 1825, vol. 1, p. 422.
14. *JMrsA*, 27 October 1825, vol. 1, pp. 421–2.
15. Wellington to Mrs Arbuthnot, 28 July 1826, *W&HF*, pp. 65–6.
16. *JMrsA*, 16 July 1826, vol. 2, pp. 35–6.
17. Ibid.
18. A selection of Wellington's letters to the Arbuthnots are printed in *W&HF*, pp. 3–112; details of their opening and closing from ibid., p. 3. For the relationship in general see E.A. Smith, *Wellington and the Arbuthnots* (1994), pp. 57–67, and also the introduction to her published *Journal*.
19. *JMrsA*, 26 September 1823 and 7 September 1826, vol. 1, pp. 256–60, vol. 2, p. 47; for examples of Mrs Arbuthnot acting as Wellington's copyist see ibid., 14 and 25 October 1825 and 15 September 1829, vol. 2, pp. 213, 216, 305.
20. *JMrsA*, 16 November 1828, vol. 2, p. 220.
21. *JMrsA*, 23 November 1830, vol. 2, p. 404; Smith, *Wellington and the Arbuthnots*, p. 59; Rev. G.R. Gleig, *Personal Reminiscences of the First Duke of Wellington* (1904), pp. 200–1.
22. Henry Greville quoted in Smith, *Wellington and the Arbuthnots*, pp. 64–5; Henry was the younger brother of Charles, the diarist, and Algernon, Wellington's private secretary.
23. *JMrsA*, 20 October 1825, vol. 1, pp. 420–1; Wake, *Sisters of Fortune*, pp. 183–95.
24. Quoted in Wake, *Sisters of Fortune*, p. 196.
25. Ibid., pp. 194–9, 206–12, 219–26.
26. Greg Roberts, 'The Forgotten Brother [William Wellesley-Pole] (nd)', pp. 63–5; Abbot, *Diary and Correspondence*, vol. 3, p. 294; see also Hobhouse, *Diary*, 17 September 1823, pp. 105–6; Bagot to Binning, 23 September 1823, Bagot, *George Canning and His Friends*, vol. 2, p. 194; see also Peel to Bathurst, 26 August 1823, *HMC Bathurst*, p. 542.
27. The Wellington Papers at Southampton contain about a dozen letters from Wellington to Henry between 1819 and 1832 and the same number from Henry to Wellington, although other letters are mentioned. More private letters, and Wellington's correspondence with Gerald, may be preserved at Stratfield Saye.

28. *JMrsA*, 11 and 23 May 1821, vol. 1, pp. 93–6; Greville, *Memoirs*, 12 May 1821, p. 119; see also Lieven, *Private Letters*, pp. 114–15. Some of Wellington's letters to his niece Mary are printed in Bagot, *George Canning and His Friends*, and his letters to Priscilla are printed in Burghersh, *Correspondence*.
29. William L. Wellesley, *Two Letters to the Right Hon. Earl Eldon, Lord Chancellor* (1827); Longford, *Wellington. Pillar of State*, pp. 250–7; D.R. Fisher, ed., *The History of Parliament. The House of Commons, 1820–32* (2009), vol. 6, p. 816.
30. Denys Forrest, *The Oriental. Life Story of a West End Club* (1968), pp. 25, 29.
31. Shelley, *Diary of Lady Shelley*, 16 August 1826, vol. 2, pp. 145–6.
32. Wellington to [Col. Frederick Ponsonby], 21 March 1822, *WND*, vol. 1, pp. 220–1; Bessborough and Aspinall, eds., *Lady Bessborough and Her Family Circle*, p. 279n.
33. Frederick Ponsonby to Wellington [*c.* 22 July 1822], ibid., p. 279; Fisher, *History of Parliament, 1820–32*, vol. 6, pp. 829–32. Ponsonby was an MP and, of course, a loyal member of the Whig Opposition, but Wellington never let political differences stand in the way of his private friendships.
34. Shelley, *Diary of Lady Shelley*, vol. 2, p. 310.
35. Lady Burghersh, 'On the Duke of Wellington, 1852', Burghesh, *Correspondence*, p. 212; Wellington to Hyacinthe Littleton quoted in Severn, *Architects of Empire*, p. 390; Lawrence Stone, *Broken Lives. Separation and Divorce in England, 1660–1857* (1993), pp. 284–346 for a detailed account of the Westmeath affair, esp. pp. 308–11 for Wellington's mediation; Lieven, *Private Letters*, pp. 195–203; Greville, *Memoirs*, 15 June and 15 August 1839, vol. 4, pp. 179, 198–9.
36. *JMrsA*, 23 June 1823, vol. 1, p. 324.
37. *JMrsA*, 5 Aug 1822, and 14 July 1825, vol. 1, pp. 175–6, 408.
38. Wellington to Mrs Arbuthnot, 9 September 1822, *W&HF*, pp. 30–1; *JMrsA*, 10 September 1822, vol. 1, p. 185.
39. *JMrsA*, 5 January 1822, vol. 1, p. 136; ibid., p. 279 shows that Wellington was also at Apethorpe on 1 January 1824, and *WND*, vol. 3, p. 56 shows that he was there on 1 January 1825.
40. Shelley, *Diary of Lady Shelley*, vol. 2, pp. 73–4.
41. Wellington to Lady Shelley, 31 October 1819, and 14 January 1820, *Diary of Lady Shelley*, vol. 2, pp. 82 and 94.
42. Wellington to Mrs Arbuthnot, 6 January 1822, *W&HF*, pp. 18–19.
43. Quoted in Brialmont and Gleig, *Life of Wellington*, vol. 4, pp. 168–9.
44. Lady Granville to Lady G. Morpeth, January 1821, January 1820 and January 1822 and to Lady Harrowby, 18 January 1822, Granville, *Letters*, vol. 1, pp. 203, 149, 220–1; a note by Samuel Rogers written in April and June 1821 after staying with Wellington at Woburn Abbey and dining with him at Apsley House, Samuel Rogers, *Reminiscences and Table-talk of Samuel Rogers*, ed. G.H Powell (1903), p. 250.
45. Wellington to Mary Bagot, 14 December 1817, Bagot, *George Canning and His Friends*, vol. 2, p. 63.
46. Neumann, *Diary*, vol. 1, p. 13; Sir Robert Peel, *The Private Letters of Sir Robert Peel*, ed. George Peel (1920), pp. 87 and 88.
47. Shelley, *Diary of Lady Shelley*, vol. 2, pp. 312–13: a passage of recollections written in 1852 on the day of the Duke's funeral.
48. Wellington to Mrs Arbuthnot, 7 September 1824, *W&HF*, pp. 49–50.
49. It will be seen from this that I disagree with Longford's contention that Wellington was best suited to the life of an army mess and a family of ADCs: Longford, *Wellington. Pillar of State*, p. 81.

16 The Ins and Outs of 1827

1. Peel to Wellington, 17 and 18 February 1827, *WND*, vol. 3, p. 596; *JMrsA*, 20 February 1827, vol. 2, pp. 81–2.
2. *The Times*, 20 and 22 February 1827; New, *Life of Brougham*, p. 308; Aspinall, *Politics and the Press*, pp. 100–1, 221, 326–7; Arbuthnot to Huskisson, 'Private', 19 April 1827, A. Aspinall, *The Formation of Canning's Ministry, February to August 1827* (1937), pp. 125–6.
3. Peel made it clear from the outset that he would not serve under Canning because of his support for Catholic Emancipation: Peel to Eldon, 9 April 1827, and Peel to Canning, 17 April, Parker, *Sir Robert Peel*, vol. 1, pp. 460–2, 466–8.

4. *JMrsA*, 10 March 1827, vol. 2, pp. 87–9.
5. A. Aspinall, 'The Coalition Ministries of 1827', pt. 1, 'Canning's Ministry' (1927), p. 214n; Londonderry to Wellington, 12 April 1827, WP 1/887/14. Canning's family background was somewhat less respectable but no humbler than that of Eldon or Sidmouth; while Grey's family were hardly the ancient aristocracy, his father only being ennobled in 1801. The first Lord Grey was a fine soldier but had a reputation with regard to plunder and prize money that would have abashed the most avaricious courtesan, let alone Canning's poor (in every sense) mother.
6. *JMrsA*, 20 February 1827, vol. 2, pp. 82–3.
7. *JMrsA*, 22 June 1826, 10 March 1827, vol. 2, p. 33, 87–8; Rutland to Lady Shelley, 23 April 1827, *Diary of Lady Shelley*, vol. 2, pp. 153–5; Buckingham to Wellington, 21 February 1827, WP 1/883/12.
8. *JMrsA*, 23 March 1827, vol. 2, p. 94.
9. *JMrsA*, 10 March, 22 March and 22 February 1827, vol. 2, pp. 87–8, 92 and 83–4.
10. *JMrsA*, 3 April 1827, vol. 2, pp. 100–1; see also a Memorandum dated 14 April 1827 enclosed in Canning to Wellesley, 24 May 1827, Richard, Marquess Wellesley, *The Wellesley Papers* 'by the editor of "The Windham Papers" ' (1914), vol. 2, p. 165. This supports the argument but its value is uncertain as it is not clear who wrote it.
11. Wellington to the King, 20 February 1827; Sir William Knighton to Wellington, 23 February 1827, *WND*, vol. 3, pp. 597–600; see also *JMrsA*, 22 February 1827, vol. 2, p. 84; and Muir, 'Politics and the Peninsular Army', pp. 72–93 *passim*.
12. *The Times*, 8 and 15 March 1827; *Morning Chronicle*, 17 March 1827; Wellington to Messrs Farrers & Co, 16 and 19 March 1827, with answers written on the same letter, WP 1/886/8 & 9.
13. *JMrsA*, 22 and 25 March 1827, vol. 2, pp. 92–3, 95; Wellington to Buckingham, 21 March 1827, *WND*, vol. 3, p. 611; Richard A. Gaunt, 'The Fourth Duke of Newcastle, the Ultra-Tories and the Opposition to Canning's Administration' (2003), pp. 574–6; Wellington to Londonderry, 20 April 1827, *WND*, vol. 3, pp. 654–5; the charges are repeated in Temperley, *Foreign Policy of Canning*, p. 523, and rebutted by Aspinall, *Formation of Canning's Ministry*, p. xxxix.
14. *JMrsA*, 22 February 1827, vol. 2, p. 85; Abbot, *Diary and Correspondence*, 15 May 1827, vol. 3, p. 501; Wellington to Mrs Arbuthnot, 28 March 1827, *W&HF*, p. 72; Aspinall, intro. to *Formation of Canning's Ministry*, pp. xxxiv–v.
15. *The Times*, 24 March 1827; Princess Dorothea Lieven, *The Unpublished Diary and Political Sketches of Princess Lieven*, ed. Harold Temperley (1925), p. 117; Stapleton, *George Canning and His Times*, pp. 585–6 quoting the account Canning dictated to Stapleton, his secretary; Wellington's Memorandum on Quitting the Cabinet, 13 April 1827, *WND*, vol. 3, pp. 636–42 (esp. p. 640); Wellington's speech in Lords on 2 May 1827, *WND*, vol. 4, pp. 1–14 (esp. p. 11): Canning to Wellington, 5 May 1827, *WND*, vol. 4, pp. 16–20 (esp. p. 19).
16. Canning to Wellington, 6pm, 10 April 1827, *WND*, vol. 3, p. 628; compare Canning to Bexley, 10 April 1827, Aspinall, *Formation of Canning's Ministry*, p. 58; Wellington to Canning, 10 April 1827, *WND*, vol. 3, p. 628.
17. Canning to Wellington, 11 April 1827, *WND*, vol. 3, pp. 628–9; Bathurst to Wellington, 15 April 1827, WP 1/887/22, has some interesting comments on Canning's letter and the significance of the King's approval; Wellington to Canning, 11 April 1827, Wellington to the King, 12 April 1827, *WND*, vol. 3, pp. 629, 630–1.
18. Wellington's speech of 2 May 1827, *WND*, vol. 4, p. 10.
19. Wellington was aware of this: Abbot, *Diary and Correspondence*, 15 May 1827, vol. 3, p. 502.
20. For some details of discussions about how to replace Wellington see Memorandum by Sir Herbert Taylor, 29 January 1828, *WND*, vol. 4, pp. 222–4. Anglesey, *One Leg*, pp. 169–72: for evidence of his presumption see ibid., pp. 166–7 and 177; and also *JMrsA*, 11 February 1827, vol. 2, pp. 78–9.
21. For example, Henry Hobhouse: see letters to Sidmouth of 23 and 27 April and 3 May 1827, printed in his *Diary*, pp. 144–5.
22. *JMrsA*, 7 September 1827, vol. 2, p. 142.
23. Croker to Blomfield, 21 March 1823, *Croker Papers*, vol. 1, pp. 264–5.
24. Mitchell, *Whigs in Opposition*, pp. 184–201; Aspinall, 'The Coalition Ministries of 1827, pt. 1, 'Canning's Ministry', pp. 201–11. For a nice example of the tensions created by the junction within the Whig Party see the exchange between Sefton and Creevey in *Creevey Papers*, pp. 459–61.

25. *Examiner*, 15 April 1827; *Morning Chronicle*, 16 April 1827; *The Times*, 16 April 1827.
26. George, *BM Catalogue of Satires*, no. 15386, pp. 668–9, reproduced in Edward Du Cann, *The Duke of Wellington and his Political Career after Waterloo - The Caricaturists' View* (2000), p. 39; see also nos. 15377, 15385 and 15399, vol. 10, pp. 663, 668 and 679.
27. Peel to Wellington, and reply, both 22 April 1827, in Parker, *Sir Robert Peel*, vol. 1, pp. 483–4, which may have been prompted by letters from Mr and Mrs Arbuthnot of 17 and 19 April, ibid., pp. 482–3; see also Wellington to Bathurst, 15 April 1827, *WND*, vol. 3, pp. 642–3.
28. Wellington to Mrs Arbuthnot, 20 April 1827, *W&HF*, p. 74.
29. *Parliamentary Debates*, ns, vol. xvii, cols. 392–3; *JMrsA*, 2 May 1827, vol. 2, pp. 113–14.
30. *Parliamentary Debates*, ns, vol. 17, 1 May 1827, col. 411.
31. Rutland to Lady Shelley, 9 May 1827, *Diary of Lady Shelley*, vol. 2, p. 156.
32. Abbot, *Diary and Correspondence*, 2 May 1827, vol. 3, pp. 492–3; *JMrsA*, 5 May 1827, vol. 2, pp. 114–15; Newcastle's diary, 2 May 1827, Fourth Duke of Newcastle, *Unrepentant Tory. Political Selections from the Diaries of the Fourth Duke of Newcastle-under-Lyne, 1827–1838*, ed. Richard A. Gaunt (2006), pp. 24–5; for Newcastle's previous dislike of Wellington see ibid., pp. 3, 13 January 1827 and Gaunt, 'Newcastle, the Ultra-Tories and the Opposition', p. 579.
33. Wellington's speech, 2 May 1827, in *WND*, vol. 4, pp. 1–14 (quotation on pp. 7–8), also printed in Wellington, *Speeches*, vol. 1, pp. 121–33, and *Parliamentary Debates*, ns, vol. 17, cols. 454–67.
34. Hilton, *Corn, Cash, Commerce*, pp. 282–6; Wellington to Bathurst, 1 June 1827, *HMC Bathurst*, p. 633; Huskisson to Wellington, 24 May, 2 June (2 letters) and 5 June 1827, WP 1/889/23, WP 1/891/1, 2 & 5; Goderich to Wellington, 6 June 1827, WP 1/891/7; Wellington to Huskisson, 2 & 4 June 1827, WP 1/892/1 and 2. *Parliamentary Debates*, ns, vol. 17, cols. 1097–8, 1238–41; Wellington, *Speeches*, vol. 1, pp. 136–45.
35. *Morning Chronicle*, 19 and 20 June 1827; George, *BM Catalogue of Satires*, vol. 10, nos. 15414 and 15415, the third print *Les Roses de Guerre* is no. 15409.
36. *JMrsA*, 17 June 1827, vol. 2, pp. 126–7; Charles Arbuthnot reporting Peel's views to Bathurst, 'Private and Confidential', 15 July 1827, *HMC Bathurst*, pp. 637–41.
37. A. Aspinall, 'The Coalition Ministries of 1827', pt. 2, 'The Goderich Ministry' (1927), gives a detailed and sympathetic account of all these negotiations.
38. The King to Wellington, and reply, 21 and 22 May 1827, *WND*, vol. 4, p. 35, 36–7; *JMrsA*, 23 and 24 May, vol. 2, pp. 121, 122; Charles Arbuthnot to Bathurst, 15 July 1827, *HMC Bathurst*, pp. 639–41: Abbot, *Diary and Correspondence*, 15 May 1827, vol. 3, p. 502.
39. Wellington to Westmorland, 17 August 1827, *WND*, vol. 4, pp. 97–8; Peel to Wellington, 19 August 1827, *WND*, vol. 4, p. 102; Peel to Arbuthnot, 17 September 1827, *CCA*, pp. 94–5; Bathurst to Wellington, 12 and 22 August 1827, *WND*, vol. 4, pp. 81–2, 104–5; Melville to Arbuthnot, 21 August 1827, *CCA*, pp. 92–3; Hardinge to Wellington, 11 August 1827, *WND*, vol. 4, pp. 77–9; Londonderry to Wellington, 12 August 1827, *WND*, vol. 4, pp. 83–6; Rutland to Lady Shelley, 12 August 1827, *Diary of Lady Shelley*, vol. 2, pp. 162–4; Cumberland to Countess Bathurst, 11 July 1827, *HMC Bathurst*, pp. 633–6.
40. *JMrsA*, 21 August 1827, vol. 2, pp. 137–8. See also Charles Arbuthnot to Peel, 12 August 1827, Parker, *Peel*, vol. 2, pp. 4–5.
41. *JMrsA*, 21 August and 7 September 1827, vol. 2, pp. 137–8, 140; Wellington to Charles Arbuthnot, 21 August 1827, *W&HF*, pp. 76–7.
42. *The Times*, 17 August 1827; George, *BM Catalogue of Satires*, vol. 10, nos. 15429, 15430, pp. 699–700.
43. Wellington to Eldon, 1 September 1827, *WND*, vol. 4, pp 121–2; *JMrsA*, 7 September 1827, vol. 2, p. 141; Londonderry to Wellington, nd [early Sept 1827], WP 1/897/1; Huskisson to Granville, 8 January 1828, quoted in Aspinall, 'The Coalition Ministries of 1827', pt. 2, 'The Goderich Ministry', p. 555.
44. Wellington to Mrs Arbuthnot, 8 October 1827, *W&HF*, p. 78; earlier letters in the same source hint at some impatience. There is an excellent account of the visit in Alan Heesom, 'The Duke of Wellington's Visit to the North East of England, September–October 1827' (1999), pp. 3–35, which is the source of the bulk of this paragraph.
45. Wellington to Canning, 20 March 1827, *WND*, vol. 3, p. 610; see also same to same, 26 March, ibid., p. 612; Bathurst to Charles Arbuthnot, 4 July 1827, *CCA*, pp. 87–8.
46. This account is largely based on the entry for Codrington in the *ODNB* which, surprisingly, is more objective than that in Douglas Dakin's *The Greek Struggle for Independence,*

1821–1833 (1973), pp. 226–8. See also Crawley, *Question of Greek Independence*, pp. 83–92. Casualty figures for the Turkish Egyptian fleet are very uncertain.

47. Wellington to the King, 13 November 1827, *WND*, vol. 4, p. 158; Wellington to Bathurst, 13 November 1827, *HMC Bathurst*, p. 648; Philip Ziegler, *King William IV* (1971), p. 137.

48. Wellington to Bathurst, 13 November 1827, *HMC Bathurst*, p. 648; Dakin, *Greek Struggle for Independence*, pp. 228–9, confirms the point about Captain Hamilton.

49. Creevey to Miss Ord, 14 November 1827, *Creevey Papers*, p. 476; Bathurst to Wellington, 15 November 1827, *WND*, vol. 4, pp. 158–9.

50. *JMrsA*, 2 and 14 December 1827, vol. 2, pp. 147–52.

17 Cabinet-Making

1. Wellington to Peel, 9 January 1828, *WND*, vol. 4, pp. 183–4.

2. Wellington to Mrs Arbuthnot, 9 January 1828, *W&HF*, pp. 80–1; Wellington to Peel, 9 January 1828, *WND*, vol. 4, pp. 183–4.

3. Peel to Julia Peel, 9 January 1828, Peel, *Private Letters*, pp. 103–4; Peel to the Bishop of Oxford, 15 January 1828, Parker, *Sir Robert Peel*, vol. 2, pp. 30–1.

4. A. Aspinall, 'Last of the Canningites' (1935), p. 640, quoting Lyndhurst to Knighton, 11 January 1828; Ward, *Letters to 'Ivy'*, p. 331.

5. Wellington to the King, 14 October 1828, *WND*, vol. 5, pp. 133–6; Creevey to Miss Ord, 8 February 1828, *Creevey Papers*, p. 494; Hardinge to Arbuthnot, 14 August [1827], *CCA*, pp. 89–90.

6. Huskisson to Granville, 18 January 1828, quoted in Aspinall, 'Last of the Canningites', p. 642; Wellington to the King, 12 January 1828, *WND*, vol. 4, pp. 186–8; Wellington to Westmorland, 18 to 21 January 1828, *WND*, vol. 4, pp. 201–2, 209–10; Wellington to Bexley, and reply, 18 January 1828, ibid., pp. 202–3; Wellington to Peel, 13 January 1828, Parker, *Sir Robert Peel*, vol. 2, pp. 29–30, on the King's emotion at losing Bexley.

7. *ODNB*, see also entry for his wife under her maiden name.

8. *Complete Peerage* and *ODNB* – although both incorrectly state that Rosslyn was the Tory Whip in the House of Lords. As a soldier he is probably better known as St Clair Erskine. Wellington to Rosslyn, 15 January 1828, and Wellington to the King, 24 January 1828, *WND*, vol. 4, pp. 193–4, 214. For Rosslyn's Whig credentials see Mitchell, *Whigs in Opposition*, pp. 54, 88, 165, 207–9.

9. Wellington to Mrs Arbuthnot, 23 January 1828, and to Charles Arbuthnot, 26 January 1828, *W&HF*, pp. 82–3.

10. Peel to the Bishop of Oxford, 15 January 1828, Parker, *Sir Robert Peel*, vol. 2, pp. 30–1; Wellington to the King, 14 January 1828, *WND*, vol. 4, pp. 190–1; Huskisson to Wellington, 17 January 1828, and 'Proposed Questions to be put to the Duke of Wellington', William Huskisson, *The Huskisson Papers*, ed. Lewis Melville (1931), pp. 282–4; Charles Arbuthnot to Huskisson, 'Confidential', 19 January 1828, *CCA*, pp. 99–100.

11. Wellington to Mrs Arbuthnot, 13 January 1828, *W&HF*, pp. 81–2.

12. Hardinge to Mrs Arbuthnot, 15 and 26 January 1826, *CCA*, pp. 98 and 101–2.

13. George, *BM Catalogue of Satires*, vol. 11, nos. 15500, 15509, 15510, pp. 2–3, 8–9; Edward Law, Lord Ellenborough, *A Political Diary, 1828–1830* (1881), 24 and 25 January 1828, vol. 1, pp. 6–8.

14. Newcastle, *Unrepentant Tory*, 15 February 1828, p. 46; George, *BM Catalogue of Satires*, vol. 11, nos. 15515 and 15518, pp. 11–12, 14–15, cf Gordon L. Teffeteller, *The Surpriser. The Life of Rowland, Lord Hill* (1983), pp. 194, 198–201.

15. Wellington's speech of 2 May 1827, in *WND*, vol. 4, pp. 1–14 (quote on p. 8); Grey to Creevey, 25 January 1828, *Creevey Papers*, pp. 486–7 alludes to it, as does a famous caricature, *The Prime-Ear of Great Britain*, depicting Wellington with the body and ears of an ass: George, *BM Catalogue of Satires*, vol. 11, p. 2, no. 15499; *Morning Chronicle*, 22 January 1828, thought that as a soldier he could not possess the knowledge which it felt was indispensable in a minister, let alone a prime minister. Ashley to Mrs Arbuthnot, [1 Feb 1828], *CCA*, pp. 103–4.

16. Hardinge to Mrs Arbuthnot, 12 January 1828, *CCA*, p. 98.

17. Creevey to Miss Ord, 28 February 1828, Creevey, *Life and Times*, p. 259.

18. Wellington to the Prince of Orange, London, 5 April 1828, *WND*, vol. 4, pp. 335–6.

19. Ellenborough, *Political Diary*, 22 and 24 January 1828, vol. 1, pp. 1–7 (quote on p. 7).
20. Ibid., 25, 26, and 28 January 1828, pp. 7–11; for the text of the King's Speech see *Parliamentary Debates*, 1828, ns, vol. 18, cols. 1–4.
21. *Parliamentary Debates*, ns, vol. 18, cols. 25–7; Ellenborough, *Political Diary*, 29 January 1828, vol. 1, pp. 13–14.
22. Creevey to Miss Ord, 21 February 1828, *Creevey Papers*, p. 495; the *Annual Register* confirms that the Rev. R. Ponsonby was made Bishop of Killaloe in February 1828 (Appendix to the Chronicle, p. 206).
23. *JMrsA*, vol. 2, 22 March, 27 and 29 June, 19 July 1828, p. 174; Palmerston to William Temple, 25 April 1828, Evelyn Ashley, *The Life and Correspondence of Henry John Temple, Viscount Palmerston* (1879), vol. 1, p. 140, comments on the role of the Finance Committee in general. See Mitchell, *Whigs in Opposition*, p. 209, on divisions among the Whigs.
24. *JMrsA*, vol. 2, 29 February and 17 March 1828, pp. 166–7, 171–2.
25. *JMrsA*, 17 March 1828, vol. 2, pp. 171–2; Littleton to Anglesey, 16 May 1828, quoted in Jupp, *British Politics on the Eve of Reform*, p. 59; Creevey to Miss Ord, 12 February and 20 March 1828, *Creevey Papers*, pp. 494, 498, cf Edward Littleton Hatherton, *The Hatherton Diaries. Extracts from the Personal Diary Between the Years 1817–1862 of Edward Walhouse Littleton afterwards the First Lord Hatherton, 1791–1863* (nd [*c.* 2003]), 22 July 1828, where he was less impressed by Wellington's reception of a delegation.
26. G.I.T. Machin, 'Resistance to the Repeal of the Test and Corporation Acts, 1828' (1979), p. 124n, lists 20 MPs who voted against repeal in 1828 despite supporting Emancipation and 37 who supported repeal of the Test and Corporation Acts, but who opposed Catholic Emancipation.
27. Ellenborough, *Political Diary*, 20, 25 and 26 February 1828, vol. 1, pp. 35–6, 40, 42.
28. *Parliamentary Debates*, ns, vol. 18, cols. 676–784: col. 781 for numbers and cheering; Ellenborough, *Political Diary*, 23 February and 3 March 1828, vol. 1, pp. 38–9, 46–7; see also Richard A. Gaunt, 'Peel's Other Repeal: The Test and Corporation Acts, 1828' (2014), pp. 243–62, for Peel's role in negotiating with the Anglican bishops the safeguards to be added to the bill.
29. *John Bull*, 10 and 24 March, *Standard*, 4 March, quoted in Machin, 'Resistance to Repeal', pp. 127–8.
30. Machin, 'Resistance to Repeal', pp. 135–7.
31. Newcastle, *Unrepentant Tory*, 27 February 1828, p. 47; see also *JMrsA*, 29 February 1828, vol. 2, pp. 166–7.
32. *JMrsA*, 17 March 1828, vol. 2, pp. 171–2.
33. For Huskisson see: *JMrsA*, 15 February 1828, vol. 2, p. 162; Ellenborough, *Political Diary*, 7 February 1828, vol. 1, pp. 20–1, and Greville, *Memoirs, 25 February 1828, vol. 1, pp. 204–6; for Palmerston: *Parliamentary Debates*, ns, vol. 19, col. 722, 14 May 1828; *JMrsA*, 29 January 1828, and 20 May 1828, vol. 2, p. 159, 187; Ellenborough, *Political Diary*, 17 and 19 May 1828, vol. 1, pp. 106–7, 109; Palmerston to William Temple, 18 January 1828, Ashley, *Life of Palmerston*, vol. 1, pp. 123–4; Palmerston to Laurence Sulivan, 21 August 1827, Palmerston, *Letters to the Sulivans*, p. 196.
34. Dudley to Ivy, nd [March 1828], Ward, *Letters to 'Ivy'*, pp. 333–4.
35. For examples of Dudley supporting the other Canningites when he thought they were wrong see *JMrsA*, 24 March 1828, vol. 2, p. 175. Ellenborough, *Political Diary*, 11 May 1828, vol. 1, pp. 103–4 – which was based on a conversation with Charles Arbuthnot, not Wellington. See also ibid., 2 May 1828, p. 98; *JMrsA*, 29 March 1828, vol. 2, p. 179.
36. Palmerston's journal, 2 April 1828, and letter to William Temple, 8 May 1828, Ashley, *Life of Palmerston*, vol. 1, pp. 136–7, 142–3.
37. Palmerston to William Temple, 25 April 1828, ibid., vol. 1, pp. 139–42; Ellenborough, *Political Diary*, 18 March 1828, vol. 1, p. 62, indicates that Huskisson did make an attempt to keep the troops there but was defeated.
38. *JMrsA*, 29 March 1828, vol. 2, p. 179; Ellenborough, *Political Diary*, vol. 1, pp. 51–74 (quote on p. 72); Palmerston's journal, 28 March 1828, in Ashley, *Life of Palmerston*, vol. 1, pp. 133–6.
39. *JMrsA*, 29 March 1828, vol. 2, pp. 179–80; Ellenborough, *Political Diary*, 28 March 1828, vol. 1, p. 72 and, for Peel, ibid., 19 March, p. 64.
40. Newcastle, *Unrepentant Tory*, 31 March 1828, p. 49. Newcastle went on to express some disappointment with the details of the bill.

41. Palmerston to William Temple, 25 April 1828, in Ashley, *Life of Palmerston*, vol. 1, pp. 140–1.
42. *JMrsA*, 21 March 1828, vol. 2, p. 173.
43. Ellenborough, *Political Diary*, 19 March 1828, vol. 1, pp. 63–4; see also Palmerston's journal, 12 March 1828, in Ashley, *Life of Palmerston*, vol. 1, p. 129.
44. Ellenborough, *Political Diary*, 23 May 1828, vol. 2, p. 114; Huskisson to Wellington, 2am, 20 May 1828, *WND*, vol. 4, p. 449.
45. Wellington to Huskisson, 20 May 1828, *WND*, vol. 4, p. 449; see also Wellington's Memorandum upon Mr Huskisson's Retirement from Office, 20 May 1828, and Memorandum upon Lord Palmerston's Retirement, 20 May 1828, *WND*, vol. 4, pp. 451–3, 453–5 and Ellenborough, *Political Diary*, 23 May 1828, vol. 1, pp. 113–20.
46. Ibid., vol. 1, p. 115.
47. Ward, *Letters to 'Ivy'*, 29 May [1828], pp. 338–9.
48. George, *BM Catalogue of Satires*, vol. 11, pp. 24–5, nos. 15531, 15532 (the latter reproduced in Du Cann, *Wellington. The Caricaturists' View*, p. 49): these are the only two prints on the resignation in the *BM Catalogue*.
49. Ellenborough, *Political Diary*, 21 and 24 May 1828, vol. 1, pp. 112 and 120–1; Creevey to Miss Ord, 4 June 1828, *Creevey Papers*, p. 501.
50. Ellenborough, *Political Diary*, 26 May 1828, vol. 1, p. 122; *JMrsA*, 29 May 1828, vol. 2, p. 189.
51. Newcastle, *Unrepentant Tory*, 27 May 1828, p. 54 – see also preceding and following entries.
52. Ellenborough, *Political Diary*, 28 May 1828, vol. 1, pp. 125–8; see also A. Aspinall, *Three Early Nineteenth-Century Diaries* (1952), p. xiii, paraphrasing an unpublished memorandum by Ellenborough.
53. *JMrsA*, 4 June 1828, vol. 2, p. 191; Charles Arbuthnot to his wife, 13 July 1828, *CCA*, p. 105.

18 Catholic Emancipation

1. On Philpotts see *ODNB* and G.C.B. Davies, *Henry Phillpotts Bishop of Exeter, 1778–1869* (1954).
2. Sir Robert Peel, *Memoirs by the Right Honourable Sir Robert Peel*, ed. Lord Mahon and Edward Cardwell (1858), vol. 1, pp. 127–8.
3. Oliver Macdonagh, *The Hereditary Bondsman Daniel O'Connell* (1988), pp. 251 and 249–55 *passim*.
4. Peel to Sir Walter Scott, 3 April 1829, Parker, *Sir Robert Peel*, vol. 2, pp. 99–100; see also Wellington's Memorandum of 1 August 1828, *WND*, vol. 4, pp. 565–70. Anglesey's ADC Baron Tuyll, who was on the spot, gives a first-hand account which largely supports these descriptions – see Anglesey, *One Leg*, p. 199.
5. Memorandum by Wellington, 1 August 1828, *WND*, vol. 4, pp. 565–70, quote on p. 570.
6. Wellington to the King, 1 August, and reply, 3 August 1828, *WND*, vol. 4, pp. 564–5, 573.
7. Richard W. Davis, 'The Tories, the Whigs and Catholic Emancipation, 1827–29' (1982), p. 98. This was an early piece in a series of erudite articles by Professor Davis, frequently exchanging views with Professor Machin, which concentrated on Wellington's pledge to the King when taking office that the issue of Catholic Emancipation would not be discussed in Cabinet without the King's prior permission; the constitutional significance of this pledge; the attitude of previous governments to the point; and the effect the pledge had on the unfolding of events in 1828–29. There is no space to discuss properly the intricacies of the debate here, but in summary although I think Professor Davis has fully made his case that the pledge given by Wellington was unusual, I am less convinced by his argument as to its significance or consequences. I do not believe that Wellington ever contemplated recalling Parliament in the autumn of 1828 to pass Emancipation, nor do I think that he would have been wise to do so – in my view the urgency bordering on panic implied in such a measure would have heightened, not calmed, the atmosphere of crisis, and this would not have lessened opposition either in Ireland or Britain. Given this, I do not think that Wellington was concerned that he could not discuss the question in Cabinet until early 1829, especially as he placed such a high premium on secrecy. It is true that in January 1829 Wellington told Francis Leveson Gower that 'during the whole summer I have been employed in endeavouring to prevail upon the King to allow his servants to take into consideration the whole case of Ireland' (Wellington to Lord Francis Leveson Gower, 19 January 1829, *WND*, vol. 5, pp. 456–7); but examining

Wellington's correspondence for the second half of 1828 does not support the idea of Wellington banging his head futilely against a brick wall of royal opposition, but rather of him edging a half-stuck door open while being cautious not to make the hinges squeak too loudly. It is worth noting that the Whigs preserved similar secrecy over the details of the Reform Bill, as did Peel over the terms of the repeal of the Corn Laws; while other examples could be given from this period of governments keeping secret the details of particularly important and controversial legislation until the last moment. Nonetheless it must be acknowledged that the interpretation of Wellington's tactics is largely conjectural, as there is very little evidence explaining why he acted as he did. Other articles by Davis and Machin on the subject include Richard W. Davis, 'Wellington, the Constitution and Catholic Emancipation' (1996), pp. 20–14; Davis, 'Wellington and the "Open Question"', pp. 39–55; Davis, 'A Last Blast?' (2001), pp. 359–62, and 'A Last Blast (Again)' (2002), p. 246. G.I.T. Machin, 'The Catholic Question and the Monarchy, 1827–1829' (1997), pp. 213–20; Machin, 'Canning, Wellington, and the Catholic Question, 1827–1829' (1984), pp. 94–100.

8. Charles Arbuthnot to Bathurst, 17 August 1828, *HMC Bathurst*, pp. 655–6.

9. Memorandum by Wellington, 7 August 1828, *WND*, vol. 5, pp. 254–68, quote on pp. 256–7; *JMrsA*, 29 July 1828, vol. 2, pp. 197–200.

10. Ibid.; Bathurst to Wellington, 3 August 1828, *WND*, vol. 4, p. 574. For Lyndhurst: Wellington to Mrs Arbuthnot, 10 August 1828, *W&HF*, pp. 83–4; Wellington to Peel, 9 August 1828, *WND*, vol. 4, pp. 582–3, summarises Lyndhurst's ideas; Dennis Lee, *Lord Lyndhurst. The Flexible Tory* (1994), pp. 73–4.

11. Peel to Wellington, 11 August 1828, Peel, *Memoirs*, vol. 1, pp. 181–7, quote on p. 185, and the accompanying Memorandum, pp. 189–200.

12. The controversy can be traced from Wellington's perspective in dozens of letters in *WND*, vol. 4 and a few in vol. 5. See also Bathurst to Charles Arbuthnot, 19 August 1828, *CCA*, p. 106; *JMrsA*, 17 and 28 August 1828, vol. 2, pp. 202–5; and Wellington to Peel, 26 August 1828, *WND*, vol. 4, pp. 665–6. There is a good account of the affair by Roger Morriss, 'Military Men Fall Out: Wellington, Cockburn and the Last Lord High Admiral, 1827–8' (1998), pp. 117–35, and see also Andrew Lambert, 'Politics, Administration and Decision-making: Wellington and the Navy 1828–30' (2008), pp. 199–215.

13. Quoted in MacDonagh, *Hereditary Bondsman*, p. 258; see also p. 255.

14. Anglesey to Wellington, 24 September 1828, and Peel to Lord Hill, 23 September 1828, both *WND*, vol. 5, pp. 81–2.

15. Fitzroy Somerset to Wellington, 24 September 1828, *WND*, vol. 5, p. 80; Wellington to Anglesey, 28 September 1828, ibid., pp. 92–3; Peel to Anglesey, 14 August 1828; Peel, *Memoirs*, vol. 1, pp. 203–4; Francis Leveson Gower to Wellington, 29 December 1828, *WND*, vol. 5, pp. 376–7.

16. Machin, *Catholic Question*, pp. 131–45, gives a good overview.

17. Wellington to Westmorland, 16 October 1828, *WND*, vol. 5, p. 142.

18. Wellington to the King, 14 October 1828, *WND*, vol. 5, pp. 133–6.

19. Wellington to the King, 16 November, enclosing memorandum of 7 August, and reply 17 November 1828, *WND*, vol. 5, pp. 252–4, 254–68, 268.

20. Wellington to Mrs Arbuthnot, 18 November 1828, *W&HF*, pp. 84–5.

21. Memorandum on the Catholic Question by Charles Sumner, Bishop of Winchester, nd December 1828, and the Bishop of Chester to Wellington, 22 December 1828, *WND*, vol. 5, pp. 324–5, 350–1; *JMrsA*, 9 December 1828, vol. 2, pp. 224–6, for Lloyd.

22. Ellenborough, *Political Diary*, 17 January 1829, vol. 2, p. 298; Wellington to Mrs Arbuthnot, 27 December 1828, *W&HF*, pp. 85–6.

23. Curtis to Wellington, 4 December 1828, and reply, 11 December 1828 (the letter that was published); Curtis to Wellington, 22 and 29 December 1828; Wellington to Peel and to Curtis, both 26 December 1828, *WND*, vol. 5, pp. 308–9, 352–3, 375–6, 357, 358; Machin, *Catholic Question*, pp. 128–30; Anglesey, *One Leg*, pp. 213–16; for other reactions to the publication of the letter see Newcastle, *Unrepentant Tory*, 29 December 1828, p. 67.

24. Wellington to Anglesey, 11 and 19 November 1828, and replies 14 and 23 November 1828; Wellington to the King, 26 December 1828, *WND*, vol. 5, pp. 240–1, 270–4, 244–8, 278–80, 356. Memorandum by Croker, 9 January 1829, *Croker Papers*, vol. 2, pp. 2–5, and Anglesey, *One Leg*, pp. 213–16.

25. Wellington to Mrs Arbuthnot, 27 December 1828, *W&HF*, pp. 85–6.

26. Wellington to the King, 4 December 1828, George IV, *Letters*, vol. 3, p. 448; the King's reply does not appear to survive but see Charles Arbuthnot to Bathurst, 16 December 1828, *HMC Bathurst*, pp. 657–8.

27. Wellington to Francis Leveson Gower, 19 January 1829, *WND*, vol. 5, pp. 456–7, on the importance of secrecy; Rutland to Charles Arbuthnot, 8 February 1829, *CCA*, p. 114; Wellington to Camden, 6 February 1829, *WND*, vol. 5, pp. 487–8.

28. Peel to Wellington, 12 January 1829, *WND*, vol. 5, pp. 435–6; Peel, *Memoirs*, vol. 1, pp. 276–81; Gash, *Mr Secretary Peel*, pp. 546–7; for a report of the criticisms of Peel see Croker to Lord Hertford, 2 February 1829, *Croker Papers*, vol. 2, p. 12.

29. Memorandum by Peel, nd January 1829, *WND*, vol. 5, pp. 436–40.

30. Note by Peel on his Memorandum of 12 January, Peel, *Memoirs*, vol. 1, pp. 297–8 (also in Parker, *Sir Robert Peel*, vol. 2, p. 82); Peel to Francis Leveson Gower, 'most Private', 17 January 1829, in Parker, *Sir Robert Peel*, vol. 2, pp. 82–4; Ellenborough, *Political Diary*, 15 January 1829, vol. 1, p. 295. A formal minute expressing this qualified consent, oddly dated 26 January, is in *WND*, vol. 5, p. 470. Aspinall, *Cabinet Council*, p. 220n, notes that this must have been one of the last instances of such consultation with ministers individually.

31. Ellenborough, *Political Diary*, 23 January 1829, vol. 1, p. 317.

32. Ibid., 2 February 1829, vol. 1, pp. 331–2.

33. *JMrsA*, 2 and 4 February 1829, vol. 2, pp. 234–7.

34. *JMrsA*, 14 January 1829, vol. 2, pp. 231–2, cf Francis Leveson Gower to Charles Arbuthnot, 3 January 1829, *CCA*, p. 133; Ellenborough, *Political Diary*, 21 January 1829, vol. 1, p. 310, and Palmerston, *Letters to the Sulivans*, p. 227&n; Wellington to Northumberland, and reply, 11 and 18 January 1829, *WND*, vol. 5, pp. 428–9, 453–4.

35. Wellington to Beaufort, and reply, 30 and 31 January 1829; Wellington to the King, 1 and 3 February 1829; Westmorland to the King, 3 February 1829, *WND*, vol. 5, pp. 478–9, 483–4. See also *JMrsA*, 2 and 4 February 1829, vol. 2, pp. 234–7.

36. Newcastle's diary, 4 and 7 February 1829, *Unrepentant Tory*, pp. 68–9.

37. Lady Holland to her son, 6 February 1829, Lady Elizabeth Holland, *Elizabeeth Lady Holland to Her Son, 1821–1845*, ed. the Earl of Ilchester (1946), pp. 94–6.

38. Creevey to Miss Ord, 6 March 1829, *Creevey Papers*, p. 540.

39. Croker, *Croker Papers*, 10 February 1829, vol. 2, p. 10; see also Ellenborough, *Political Diary*, 6 February 1829, vol. 1, p. 339.

40. Wellington to Rutland and Lonsdale, 7 February 1829, *WND*, vol. 5, pp. 489–92; see also *JMrsA*, 8 February 1829, vol. 2, pp. 237–9.

41. It is only quite recently that the Ultras have begun to receive the scholarly attention they deserve, with important articles by Richard Gaunt, Douglas Simes, B.T. Bradfield and Edwin Jaggard, among others, together with Gaunt's edition of Newcastle's diary.

42. Machin, *Catholic Question*, pp. 163–9.

43. *JMrsA*, 15 February 1829, vol. 2, p. 241; see also Croker's diary, 16 February 1829, *Croker Papers*, vol. 2, p. 11; Wellington to the King, 16 February 1829, *WND*, vol. 5, pp. 504–5.

44. *Parliamentary Debates*, ns, vol. 20, col. 378; Newcastle, *Unrepentant Tory*, 20 February 1829, p. 73; *JMrsA*, 26 February 1829, vol. 2, pp. 242–4.

45. Ellenborough, *Political Diary*, 26 February 1829, vol. 1, pp. 361–3; *JMrsA*, 26 February 1829, vol. 2, pp. 243–4; see also Greville, *Memoirs*, 2 March 1829, vol. 1, pp. 260–2.

46. Newcastle, *Unrepentant Tory*, 24 and 28 February, 1 and 2 March 1829, pp. 74–6.

47. *JMrsA*, 28 February 1829, vol. 2, pp. 244–6; see also Ellenborough, *Political Diary*, 28 February 1829, vol. 1, pp. 366–9.

48. Ellenborough, *Political Diary*, 2 March 1829, vol. 1, p. 372.

49. *JMrsA*, 4 March 1829, vol. 2, pp. 246–8; see also Ellenborough, *Political Diary*, 4 March 1829, vol. 2, pp. 376–8.

50. The King to Wellington, 8pm, 4 March and 5 March, and Wellington's reply, 4 March 1829, *WND*, vol. 5, p. 518; see also Ellenborough, *Political Diary*, 4 and 9 March 1829, vol. 1, pp. 376–8, 384, and *JMrsA*, 4 March 1829, vol. 2, pp. 246–9. According to Ellenborough the letter, although dated 8pm, was actually written at 9.30pm and this seems confirmed by it not reaching Wellington until after he returned home, having seen the Cabinet and called on the Arbuthnots. Peel, *Memoirs*, vol. 1, pp. 349–50; *Parliamentary Debates*, ns, vol. 20, cols. 727–80.

51. *JMrsA*, 28 February 1829, and 4 March 1829, vol. 2, pp. 246, 248.
52. Ellenborough, *Political Diary*, 4 March 1829, vol. 1, p. 377.
53. Ibid., 2 and 9 March 1829, vol. 1, p. 373 and 385; *JMrsA*, 8 and 10 March 1829, vol. 2, pp. 250–1; Wellington to Marquess of Salisbury, 7 March 1829, *WND*, vol. 5, p. 520.
54. *Parliamentary Debates*, ns, vol. 20, col. 780; see also Gash, *Mr Secretary Peel*, p. 576.
55. This summary of the Tory press is based closely on James J. Sack, 'Wellington and Tory Press, 1828–30', in *Wellington. Studies in the Military and Political Career*, ed. Norman Gash (1990), pp. 163–6.
56. Ibid., pp. 160–3; George, *English Political Caricature*, vol. 2, pp. 222–3, on the overall balance.
57. George, *BM Catalogue of Satires*, vol. 11, nos. 15707, 15660 and 15719, reproduced in Du Cann, *Wellington. The Caricaturists' View*, pp. 79, 77 and 73.
58. *JMrsA*, 16 and 20 March 1829, vol. 2, pp. 254, 256; Newcastle, *Unrepentant Tory*, 6, 9 and 10 March 1829, pp. 77–9; Machin, *Catholic Question*, pp. 145–8, 155–6, 175.
59. *JMrsA*, 12 March 1829, vol. 2, pp. 252–3.
60. *Parliamentary Debates*, ns, vol. 20, cols. 930–5, cf *JMrsA*, 12 March 1829, vol. 2, p. 252.
61. Lord Winchilsea to Henry Nelson Coleridge, Secretary to the Committee for Establishing King's College London, 14 March 1829, published in the *Standard*, 16 March 1829, *WND*, vol. 5, pp. 526–7.
62. Wellington to Winchilsea, 19 March 1829, *WND*, vol. 5, pp. 533–4.
63. Winchilsea to Falmouth, at night, 20 March 1829, *WND*, vol. 5, p. 539n.
64. Dr Hume's account, 21 March 1829, *WND*, vol. 5, pp. 539–45; Ellenborough, *Political Diary*, 21 March 1829, vol. 1, p. 403 says that Falmouth suggested eighteen paces, but that Hardinge insisted on the much more usual twelve.
65. The text of the apology with Hume's addition is printed in *WND*, vol. 5, pp. 538–9.
66. Dr Hume's account, 21 March 1829, *WND*, vol. 5, pp. 539–45.
67. Winchilsea to Falmouth, Friday night, 20 March 1829, *WND*, vol. 5, p. 539.
68. Ellenborough, *Political Diary*, 21 March 1829, vol. 1, p. 403.
69. Quoted in Wellesley, *Wellington in Civil Life*, p. 132.
70. Greville, *Memoirs*, 26 March 1829, vol. 1, pp. 279–80; Mrs Arbuthnot to Lady Shelley, 21 March 1829, *Diary of Lady Shelley*, vol. 2, pp. 188–9.
71. Greville, *Memoirs*, 21 and 26 March 1829, vol. 1, p. 277, 279; *JMrsA*, 22 March 1829, vol. 2, pp. 257–8.
72. *The Times*, 23 March 1829; George, *BM Catalogue of Satires*, vol. 11, nos. 15696 and 15697 (the latter reproduced in Du Cann, *Wellington. The Caricaturists' View*, p. 74).
73. Newcastle, *Unrepentant Tory*, 26 March 1829, p. 83: see also entry for 22 March; Ellenborough, *Political Diary*, 21 March 1829, vol. 1, p. 403.
74. Broughton's diary, 2 April 1829, in his *Recollections of a Long Life*, vol. 3, pp. 315–16.
75. Newcastle, *Unrepentant Tory*, 4 April 1829, p. 85; *JMrsA*, 6 April 1829, vol. 2, p. 264.
76. *JMrsA*, 7 April 1829, vol. 2, pp. 264–5; the King to the Lord Chancellor, 13 April 1829, *WND*, vol. 5, p. 580.

19 The Foreign Policy of Wellington's Government

1. The only exception is Churchill in 1951, but he was then seventy-seven and there was a sense that his time had passed. Wellington was fifty-eight when he became prime minister in 1828.
2. Palmerston's account of Cabinet meetings over Greece in 1828 makes this clear: Ashley, *Life of Palmerston*, vol. 1, pp. 136–9, 142–6. See also Peter Jupp, 'The Foreign Policy of Wellington's Government' (1999), pp. 163, 166, 178–9.
3. Neumann, *Diary*, vol. 1, p. 181, 30 December 1827, and subsequent entries pp. 181–2; Dudley to Wellington, 14 January 1828; Herries to Wellington, 15 January 1828, *WND*, vol. 4, pp. 192, 195–6; D.C.H. Smith, 'Wellington, Aberdeen and the Miguelist Crisis in Portugal' (1973), pp. 130–2; Ferguson, *House of Rothschild*, vol. 1, *Money's Prophets*, p. 152.
4. Frederick Lamb to Wellington, 28 January 1828, *WND*, vol. 4, pp. 218–19.
5. Frederick Lamb to Wellington, 15 March 1828, *WND*, vol. 4, p. 309.
6. Wellington to Frederick Lamb, 24 March 1828, *WND*, vol. 4, pp. 321–3.
7. Wellington to Frederick Lamb, 7 and 11 May 1828, *WND*, vol. 4, pp. 427–30.
8. See above, p. 314.

9. Smith, 'Wellington, Aberdeen and the Miguelist Crisis in Portugal', pp. 155–8, 13–16; Frederick Lamb to Wellington, 28 May 1828, *WND*, vol. 4, p. 479.

10. *The Times*, 14 and 15 July 1828; *Morning Chronicle*, 4 June 1828.

11. Letter dated Lisbon, 30 August, in *The Times*, 13 September 1828; editorial of the same date; letter from 'An English Officer' in *The Times*, 14 May 1828.

12. Ellenborough, *Political Diary*, 2 October 1828, vol. 1, p. 234; Croker to Wellington, and reply, 13 and 14 September 1828, *WND*, vol. 5, pp. 53, 54–5.

13. 'Observations on a Despatch upon the Affairs of Portugal' [by Wellington, July 1828], *WND*, vol. 4, pp. 545–8; see also Ellenborough, *Political Diary*, 4 August 1828, vol. 1, pp. 188–9.

14. Smith, 'Wellington, Aberdeen and the Miguelist Crisis in Portugal', pp. 226–35, 253–60, 269–81; Wellington to Aberdeen, 10 September 1828, *WND*, vol. 5, pp. 37–8; Ellenborough, *Political Diary*, 4 August 1829, vol. 1, pp. 188–9.

15. Wellington, Memorandum on a despatch from Sir Frederick Lamb, 9 May 1828, *WND*, vol. 4, pp. 433–4.

16. Wellington to Peel, 29 October 1828, *WND*, vol. 5, p. 183.

17. Wellington to Aberdeen, 30 October 1828, *WND*, vol. 5, pp. 186–8.

18. Memorandum for the Earl of Aberdeen [by Wellington], 19 September 1828, *WND*, vol. 5, p. 63.

19. Wellington to Aberdeen, 23 September 1828, *WND*, vol. 5, pp. 73–5; Lady Holland to her son, 5 January 1829, *Lady Holland to Her Son*, p. 93; *The Mirror of Literature, Amusement and Instruction*, vol. 13, no. 370, p. 321, Saturday 16 May 1829.

20. Quoted in Crawley, *Question of Greek Independence*, pp. 100–1.

21. Lincoln, *Nicholas I*, pp. 122–4, makes this suggestion, and the readiness with which the Turks had given way in 1826 makes it seem plausible.

22. Wellington to the Comte de la Ferronays, 26 February 1828, *WND*, vol. 4, pp. 274–8.

23. Wellington to Aberdeen, 1 and 3 January 1829, *WND*, vol. 5, pp. 408–9, 417.

24. *JMrsA*, 30 August 1828, vol. 2, pp. 205–6; Duke of Rutland to Lady Shelley, 25 September 1828, *Diary of Lady Shelley*, vol. 2, pp. 182–4; George, *BM Catalogue of Satires*, vol. 11, nos. 15507, 15533, 15534, 15552 *The Nest in Danger*, 15553 *The Turkey at Bay*, 15554, 15555, 15566 *A Ruse*; Mitchell, *Holland House*, pp. 212–14.

25. Wellington to Aberdeen, 29 July 1829, *WND*, vol. 6, pp. 56–8.

26. Wellington to Heytesbury, 8 September 1829, *WND*, vol. 6, pp. 145–6.

27. Ellenborough, *Political Diary*, 4 and 16 August 1828, vol. 1, pp. 190, 198, cf entry for 17 July 1828, p. 165 which gives a more rounded account of the official purpose of the expedition.

28. Ellenborough, *Political Diary*, 1 November 1828, vol. 1, p. 250.

29. In his defence it seems that he had been misled by unguarded remarks in Aberdeen's private letters which differed from his official instructions: *ODNB* entry on Stratford Canning by Muriel E. Chamberlain, see also Muriel Chamberlain, *Lord Aberdeen. A Political Biography* (1983), pp. 213–15.

30. Memorandum upon the Affairs of the Turks and Greeks etc [by Wellington], 10 November 1828, *WND*, vol. 5, pp. 231–9; see also Wellington to Aberdeen, 2 November 1828, Memorandum on Turkey and Greece, 16 November 1828, and Memorandum on Mr Stratford Canning's despatches, 14 December 1828, ibid., pp. 198–9, 249–52, 331–4.

31. Wellington to Aberdeen, 18 and 31 December 1828, *WND*, vol. 5, pp. 340–2, 382–3.

32. M.S. Anderson, *The Eastern Question, 1774–1923* (1966), pp. 70–1; Lincoln, *Nicholas I*, pp. 128–9; Kulcheva is sometimes dated to 30 May, the equivalent of 11 June in the Julian calendar used in Russia.

33. Wellington to Aberdeen, 21 August 1829, *WND*, vol. 6, pp. 98–9.

34. Aberdeen to Wellington, 24 August 1829, *WND*, vol. 6, pp. 104–5; Wellington to Aberdeen, 11 September 1829, ibid., pp. 151–3, but cf same to same, 4 October 1829, ibid., p. 192 when he despaired of building a substitute for Turkish power from Greece.

35. This summary from Anderson, *Eastern Question*, pp. 72–3.

36. Observations on the Treaty of Adrianople [by Wellington], 10 October 1829, *WND*, vol. 6, pp. 212–9, esp. 218; see also Memorandum upon the Seventh Article of the Treaty of Adrianople, 29 October 1829, and another memorandum with the same title, 4 November 1829, ibid., pp. 268–71; 286; Anderson, *Eastern Question*, p. 73 for Metternich.

37. Even Mrs Arbuthnot was highly critical in the wake of the Russian victory: see *JMrsA*, 15 October 1829, vol. 2, pp. 309–10.

38. Palmerston to Sulivan, 7 October 1829, Palmerston, *Letters to the Sulivans*, p. 232; Ellenborough, *Political Diary*, 13 August 1829, vol. 2, p. 86.
39. Schroeder, *Transformation of European Politics*, pp. 663–4.
40. Chamberlain, *Aberdeen*, pp. 245–6; Jupp, 'Foreign Policy of Wellington's Government', p. 156.
41. Wellington to Aberdeen, 31 July, and Aberdeen to Wellington, 30 July 1829, *WND*, vol. 6, pp. 66–7, 63–4; Chamberlain, *Aberdeen*, pp. 245–6.
42. Wellington to Charles Grant, 8 April 1828, *WND*, vol. 4, pp. 349–51; Bourne, *Balance of Power in North America*, p. 37; Jupp, 'Foreign Policy of Wellington's Government', pp. 156–8.
43. Wellington to Aberdeen, 22 September 1828, *WND*, vol. 5, pp. 69–70; Palmerston to Laurence Sulivan, 19 January 1829, Palmerston, *Letters to the Sulivans*, pp. 225–6.
44. Wellington to Aberdeen, 21 August 1829, *WND*, vol. 6, pp. 98–9; Wellington to the King, 26 August 1829, ibid., pp. 109–10; *JMrsA*, 12, 24 and 28 July 1829, vol. 2, pp. 296, 299, 300.
45. Palmerston to Sulivan, 11 Dec 1829, *Letters to the Sulivans*, pp. 237–8; Pamela Pilbeam, 'The Growth of Liberalism and the Crisis of the Bourbon Restoration 1827–30' (1982), pp. 363–4.
46. Sauvigny, *Bourbon Restoration*, pp. 456–9.
47. Wellington to Aberdeen, 18 April 1830, *WND*, vol. 6, p. 576; [Wellington], Memorandum of a Conversation with the French Ambassador, 24 January 1830, ibid., pp. 437–9; G.W. Chad, *The Conversations of the Duke of Wellington with George William Chad*, ed. 7th Duke of Wellington (1956), pp. 21–2.
48. Chamberlain, *Aberdeen*, p. 245.

20 Domestic Difficulties

1. Palmerston to Sulivan (paraphrasing Vyvyan), 7 October 1829, Palmerston, *Letters to the Sulivans*, p. 233; *Parliamentary Debates*, ns, vol. 21, cols. 867–84, 1487–8, 1750–3; *Morning Chronicle*, 24 September 1829; *The Times*, 25 September 1829; *Examiner*, 19 April 1829 (where it quotes criticism in the *Standard* in order to ridicule it). George, *English Political Caricature*, vol. 2, p. 227; Palmer, *Police and Protest*, pp. 286–308, esp. 293.
2. Peel to Mrs Peel, 10 October 1829, Peel, *Private Letters*, p. 117; Wellington to Peel, 3 November 1829, *WND*, vol. 6, pp. 282–3; Palmer, *Police and Protest*, pp. 286–308, esp. pp. 303–5 on the popular reaction against the police in London. The Whig government in 1833 undertook to provide one-quarter of the cost of the Metropolitan Police from the Treasury: Palmer, *Police and Protest*, p. 308.
3. B.T. Bradfield, 'Sir Richard Vyvyan and the Fall of Wellington's Government' (1968), pp. 143–8; Newcastle, *Unrepentant Tory*, 23, 24 and 30 June 1829, pp. 92–4.
4. *JMrsA*, 5 June 1829, vol. 2, pp. 280–1.
5. *JMrsA*, 25 and 26 May 1829, vol. 2, pp. 276–7.
6. Palmerston to Sulivan, 7 October 1829, Palmerston, *Letters to the Sulivans*, pp. 235–6; Bradfield, 'Sir Richard Vyvyan and the Fall of Wellington's Government', p. 148.
7. Passages quoted in Newcastle, *Unrepentant Tory*, 12 September 1829, p. 95, and Wickwar, *Struggle for Freedom of the Press*, pp. 285–7; see also Aspinall, *Politics and the Press*, pp. 342–4.
8. Ibid., pp. 222–32, on the *Courier*; *The Times, The History of the Times*, vol. 1, The '*Thunderer*' in the Making 1785–1841 (1935), pp. 258–70, esp. 261–2. Wrangham's position is identified in J.M. Collinge, *Office Holders in Modern Britain*, vol. 8, *Foreign Office Officials* (1979), p. 82.
9. Wellington to Croker, 14 September 1828, *WND*, vol. 5, pp. 54–5.
10. Wellington to the Duke of Northumberland, 16 March 1830, *WND*, vol. 6, pp. 532–3; *JMrsA*, 21 and 25 May, 16 June 1829, vol. 2, pp. 273–5, 285–8; Hardinge to Mrs Arbuthnot, [19 June 1829], *CCA*, pp. 116–17; Charles Arbuthnot to Wellington, 5 October 1829, *WND*, vol. 6, pp. 198–201.
11. *JMrsA*, 25 May 1829, vol. 2, p. 275.
12. *JMrsA*, 26 June 1829, vol. 2, p. 291.
13. Mitchell, *Whigs in Opposition*, pp. 217–18; *JMrsA*, 28 May, 1 and 10 June 1829, vol. 2, pp. 277–80, 282–3.
14. James Abercromby, a Lansdowne Whig, became Chief Baron of the Exchequer in Scotland; Maurice Fitzgerald, the Knight of Kerry, another Lansdowne Whig, became Vice Treasurer of Ireland; and the young John Stuart Wortley, a Canningite and son-in-law of Lord Harrowby, was made Secretary to the Board of Control: Fisher, *History of Parliament*, vol. 4, p. 14, vol. 5, pp. 133–4, and vol. 7, pp. 336–7.

15. *JMrsA*, 31 January 1830, vol. 2, p. 329.
16. Croker to Vesey Fitzgerald, 3 May 1830, *Croker Papers*, vol. 2, pp. 57-9.
17. *JMrsA*, 15 March 1830, vol. 2, pp. 344-5; ibid., 24 October 1829, pp. 311-12 (Vesey Fitzgerald), 5 February 1830, p. 331 (Wellington), and 16 July 1830, p. 373.
18. Wellington to Murray, 27 January and 17 June 1830, Murray Papers, National Library of Scotland, Adv 46.8.10 f 15, 132-4; D.M Young, *The Colonial Office in the Early Nineteenth Century* (1961), pp. 110-12; *JMrsA*, 5 January 1829, vol. 2, pp. 229-30; Greville, *Memoirs*, 21 December 1828 and 24 July 1830, vol. 1, p. 227; vol. 2, p. 11.
19. *JMrsA*, 5 January and 16 June 1829, vol. 2, pp. 229-30, 285-6.
20. *JMrsA*, 31 January and 18 March 1830, vol. 2, pp. 327-9, 345-6 (welcoming the appointment of Herries then deploring his failure); Bathurst to Wellington, 10 January 1830, *WND*, vol. 6, p. 401 (urging his appointment).
21. Ward, *Letters to 'Ivy'*, nd [March? 1828], pp. 332-3.
22. Greville, *Memoirs*, vol. 1, 29 June 1828, and 22 February 1829, pp. 213-14, 256-8.
23. *JMrsA*, 15 and 24 September 1829, vol. 2, pp. 305, 307.
24. *JMrsA*, 22 February 1830, vol. 2, p. 339.
25. *JMrsA*, 26 June 1829, vol. 2, pp. 289-90; Wellington to Knighton, 10 November 1829, *WND*, vol. 6, pp. 293-4.
26. *JMrsA*, 16 December 1829, vol. 2, pp. 320-1.
27. William Smart, *Economic Annals of the Nineteenth Century* (1910-17), vol. 2, pp. 466-74 (esp. 467, 474), 510-15; Charles Arbuthnot to Wellington, 28 October 1829, *WND*, vol. 6, pp. 265-7. For more on the Swing Riots see below, pp. 387-8.
28. *Parliamentary Debates*, ns, vol. 22, cols. 1-4 (the Lords Commissioners' speech); cols. 4-56 (Lords' debate): Stanhope's speech, cols. 10-18, quote in col. 10; Wellington's speech, cols. 34-41. The debate is summarised in Smart, *Economic Annals*, vol. 2, pp. 518-22.
29. Rutland to Lady Shelley, 24 February 1830, *Diary of Lady Shelley*, vol. 2, pp. 199-200; Greville, *Memoirs*, 19 and 26 February 1830, vol. 1, pp. 374, 376; *JMrsA*, 19 February 1830, vol. 2, p. 337 comments on Wellington's preparations for a debate.
30. Lt.-Gen. Sir J.W. Gordon to Sir H. Taylor, 6 February 1830, Sir Herbert Taylor, *The Taylor Papers*, ed. Ernest Taylor (1913), pp. 313-15; Mitchell, *Whigs in Opposition*, pp. 222 and 226; Gash, *Mr Secretary Peel*, pp. 608-9; Wellington to the King, 7 and 8 February 1830, *WND*, vol. 6, pp. 470, 471-2.
31. George, *BM Catalogue of Satires*, nos. 16032 and 16039, *There is None So Blind as Him Who Will Not See* by William Heath, 12 February 1829 [*sic* 1830], and *Partial Distress by Sharpshooter*, 16 February 1830, reproduced in Du Cann, *Wellington. The Caricaturists' View*, pp. 65 and 62. George, *English Political Caricature*, vol. 2, pp. 229-31 gives the wider context.
32. Wellington to Charles Arbuthnot, 14 October 1829, *WND*, vol. 6, pp. 222-5; Charles Arbuthnot to Peel, 'Private', 16 February 1830, Peel Papers, BL Add Ms 40,340, f 218-19; reply, 16 February 1830, *CCA*, p. 124; *JMrsA*, 16 February, 12 and 15 March 1830, vol. 2, pp. 335, 343, 345.
33. Memorandum upon the Beer Bill [by Wellington], 18 August 1831, *WND*, vol. 7, pp. 499-500; Smart, *Economic Annals*, vol. 2, pp. 538-9; Neville Thompson, *Wellington After Waterloo* (1986), p. 100; Norman Gash, *Robert Surtees and Early Victorian Society* (1993), p. 230.
34. Wellington to Mrs Arbuthnot, 10 April 1830, *W&HF*, p. 90.
35. *JMrsA*, 22 April 1830, vol. 2, pp. 351-2; Wellington to Peel, 19 April 1830, *WND*, vol. 6, pp. 581-2.
36. *JMrsA*, 23 April 1830, vol. 2, p. 352.
37. Quoted in Gash, *Mr Secretary Peel*, p. 631.
38. Wellington to Northumberland, 23 May 1830, *WND*, vol. 7, pp. 58-9; Clarence to Wellington and reply, 29 April and 1 May 1830, ibid., pp. 8-10; Stanhope, *Notes of Conversations*, 30 November 1840, p. 258; *JMrsA*, 17 and 27 May 1830, vol. 2, pp. 357-8, 360. On Clarence's behaviour see Croker to Vesey Fitzgerald, 3, 11, 14 May 1830, *Croker Papers*, vol. 2, pp. 57-61; *JMrsA*, 3 May 1830, vol. 2, p. 354; Palmerston to Sulivan, 22 April 1830, Palmerston, *Letters to the Sulivans*, p. 239.
39. Memorandum of a letter from the Duke of Wellington to Sir Robert Peel, nd 1830, *WND*, vol. 7, pp. 106-8; see also Gash, *Mr Secretary Peel*, pp. 634-5.
40. *JMrsA*, 10 May 1830, vol. 2, p. 355.

41. *JMrsA*, 10, 12, 17 May 1830, vol. 2, pp. 355–8.
42. Palmerston to Sulivan, 22 April 1830, Palmerston, *Letters to the Sulivans*, p. 239; Ellenborough, *Political Diary*, 29 June and 2 July 1830, vol. 2, pp. 289–90, 297–8; *JMrsA*, 12 May 1830, vol. 2, pp. 356–7.
43. *JMrsA*, 29 June 1830, vol. 2, p. 365; *Parliamentary Debates*, ns, vol. 25, cols. 707–10; *The Times*, 28 June and 16 July 1830; E.A. Smith, *George IV* (1999), pp. 272–3; for one version of Wellington's real opinion of George IV see Gleig, *Personal Reminiscences*, p. 107.
44. *JMrsA*, 29 June 1830, vol. 2, pp. 364–5.
45. Croker to Vesey Fitzgerald, 27 June 1830, *Croker Papers*, vol. 2, pp. 65–7; Ellenborough, *Political Diary*, 26 June 1830, vol. 2, pp. 276–80; Greville, *Memoirs*, 18 July 1830, vol. 2, pp. 2–4.
46. Greville, *Memoirs*, 18 and 20 July 1830, vol. 2, pp. 2–4, 7–9; *JMrsA*, 16 July 1830, vol. 2, pp. 370–1.
47. Ellenborough, *Political Diary*, 26, 27, 28 June 1830, vol. 2, pp. 280–4, 288; *JMrsA*, 8 July 1830, vol. 2, pp. 364–5; Cecil Woodham-Smith, *Queen Victoria from her birth to the Death of the Prince Consort* (1973), pp. 79–81. When Parliament met again in November the government introduced legislation naming the Duchess of Kent as regent if anything incapacitated King Willliam before Victoria came of age at eighteen. The possibility of Queen Adelaide being pregnant was left unresolved; ibid., p. 81.
48. *JMrsA*, 3 July 1830, vol. 2, pp. 366–8.
49. *JMrsA*, 16 July 1830, vol. 2, p. 373. Mrs Arbuthnot was ambivalent – agreeing that the government needed strengthening and that Herries and Murray should be moved, but seeing the logic of Wellington's argument that no recruits on offer would do much, if anything, to strengthen the government.
50. Newcastle, *Unrepentant Tory*, 10 July 1830, p. 120.

21 The Fall of Wellington's Government

1. Talleyrand quoted in H.A.C. Collingham, *The July Monarchy. A Political History of France 1830–1848* (1988), p. 11. According to Mansel, *Paris Between Empires*, p. 250, the 'glorious' three days saw about 150 troops and 600 civilians die and 600 troops and 2,000 civilians be wounded. Munro Price, *The Perilous Crown. France Between Revolutions, 1814–1848* (2007), p. 161, cites official records for figures of 496 civilians killed and 849 wounded, and approximately 150 soldiers killed and 580 wounded with a further 137 missing.
2. Collingham, *July Monarchy*, pp. 6–21; Mansel, *Paris Between Empires*, pp. 257–65.
3. Peel to Wellington, 1 August 1830, *WND*, vol. 7, pp. 142–3; *JMrsA*, 28 July 1830, vol. 2, p. 375; Newcastle's diary, 1 and 13 August 1830, *Unrepentant Tory*, p. 124; Norman Gash, 'English Reform and the French Revolution in the General Election of 1830', in *Essays Presented to Sir Lewis Namier*, ed. Richard Pares and A.J.P. Taylor (1956), pp. 266–7.
4. Wellington to Aberdeen, 12 August 1830, *WND*, vol. 7, pp. 156–8. Wellington told Ellenborough as early as 31 July that he considered Charles X dethroned and that they would soon need to consider recognising the new government. Ellenborough, *Political Diary*, 31 July 1830, vol. 2, pp. 327–30.
5. Ellenborough, *Political Diary*, 31 July 1830, vol. 2, pp. 327–30, cf Schroeder, *Transformation of European Politics*, p. 668 which goes a long way towards agreeing with this assessment.
6. Memorandum, 14 August 1830, *WND*, vol. 7, pp. 162–9; Ellenborough, *Political Diary*, 23 August and 5 September 1830, vol. 2, pp. 340, 351–5; Aberdeen to Peel, 20 August 1830, Parker, *Sir Robert Peel*, vol. 2, pp. 158–9.
7. Memorandum, 14 August 1830, *WND*, vol. 7, pp. 162–9; for the ship with Spanish *liberales* see Ellenborough, *Political Diary*, 28 July 1830, vol. 2, pp. 325–7 and Memorandum from Wellington to Aberdeen, 27 July 1830, *WND*, vol. 7, p. 133.
8. Wellington to Aberdeen, 3 and 10 September, 8 and 19 October 1830, *WND*, vol. 7, pp. 235–6, 253–4, 293, 309–11; Memorandum by Wellington, 3 September and 1 October, nd, ibid., pp. 237–8, 281–3, 330–4; Greville, *Memoirs*, 31 August 1830, vol. 2, pp. 39–40.
9. Aberdeen to Wellington, and reply, 13 and 16 September 1830, *WND*, vol. 7, pp. 259–60, 267, Collingham, *July Monarchy*, p. 188, *JMrsA*, 25 October 1830, vol. 2, pp. 393–4, Philip Ziegler, *The Duchess of Dino* (1986), pp. 190–6.
10. A.C.F. Beales, 'Wellington and Louis-Philippe, 1830' (1933–34), pp. 352–6.

11. George, *English Political Caricature*, vol. 2, pp. 235–6; Prothero, *Artisans and Politics*, pp. 272–5; Roland Quinault, 'The French Revolution of 1830 and Parliamentary Reform' (1994), p. 386; Hume paraphrased in Gash, 'English Reform and the French Revolution', pp. 263–4.

12. *Leeds Patriot* quoted in Gash, 'English Reform and the French Revolution', p. 265; Rutland to Mrs Arbuthnot, 21 September 1830, *CCA*, pp. 130–1.

13. Quoted in Gash, 'English Reform and the French Revolution', pp. 265–6.

14. Quinault, 'The French Revolution of 1830 and Parliamentary Reform', p. 385; Gash, 'English Reform and the French Revolution', p. 264.

15. Memorandum, 26 October 1830, *WND*, vol. 7, pp. 321–2; Memorandum for Fitzroy Somerset, 12 October 1830, ibid., pp. 300–1; Ellenborough, *Political Diary*, 11 and 25 October 1830, vol. 2, pp. 389–402; Gash, *Mr Secretary Peel*, pp. 618–20.

16. On the Swing Riots see Ruth Newman, 'The "Swing" Riots: Agricultural Revolt in 1830' (1985), pp. 436–47; Pamela Horn, 'Some Hampshire Ladies and the 1830 "Swing" Riots' (1987), pp. 187–93; Shirley Burgoyne Black, 'Swing: The Years 1827–30 as Reflected in a West Kent Newspaper' (1989), pp. 89–106. E.J. Hobsbawm and George Rudé's *Captain Swing* (1969) remains the most detailed and authoritative source. For the yeomanry see Beckett, *Amateur Military Tradition*, pp. 132–3. For Poulett-Thomson see Fisher, *History of Parliament*, vol. 1, p. 230.

17. Fisher, *History of Parliament*, vol. 1, pp. 228–9.

18. Ellenborough, *Political Diary*, 3 August 1830, vol. 2, pp. 332–3; see also Fisher, *History of Parliament*, vol. 1, pp. 229–30.

19. Mitchell, *Whigs in Opposition*, p. 233; Gash, 'English Reform and the French Revolution', pp. 274–9 (on Southwark and Reading).

20. Fisher, *History of Parliament*, vol. 1, p. 231. In private Brougham was even more confident, claiming that the government lost 34 and the Whigs gained 25: Mitchell, *Whigs in Opposition*, p. 232n.

21. Mitchell, *Whigs in Opposition*, p. 233; Fisher, *History of Parliament*, vol. 1, p. 231.

22. Ellenborough, *Political Diary*, 28 September 1830, vol. 2, p. 370; *JMrsA*, 26 September 1830, vol. 2, pp. 385–6.

23. *JMrsA*, 26 September 1830, vol. 2, pp. 385–8.

24. Aspinall's introduction to *Three Early Nineteenth-Century Diaries*, pp. xxii–xxiii, cf Ellenborough, *Political Diary*, 7 October 1830, vol. 2, p. 380 gives slightly different figures e.g. Huskisson 13.

25. *JMrsA*, 30 October 1830, vol. 2, pp. 395–6; see also ibid., 10 and 23 October, pp. 390, 392; Ashley, *Life of Palmerston*, vol. 1, pp. 211–12; Wellington to Lord Clive, 30 September 1830, *WND*, vol. 7, p. 281; extract of a letter from Lord Palmerston, nd, *WND*, vol. 7, p. 328; Bourne, *Palmerston*, pp. 316–23 gives a very detailed account of these negotiations.

26. Mitchell, *Whigs in Opposition*, pp. 236–40; Bourne, *Palmerston*, pp. 317–19.

27. Ellenborough, *Political Diary*, 30 and 31 October 1830, vol. 2, pp. 407–9; George, *BM Catalogue of Satires*, nos. 16,287–98, vol. 11, pp. 351–4; Newcastle's diary, 30 October 1830, *Unrepentant Tory*, p. 128.

28. *Parliamentary Debates*, 3rd series, vol. 1, cols. 44–53; Wellington, *Speeches*, vol. 1, pp. 379–88.

29. *JMrsA*, 4 November 1830, vol. 2, pp. 397–8; Wellington to Maurice Fitzgerald, 6 November 1830, *WND*, vol. 7, pp. 352–3. Canning's declaration against reform is in *Parliamentary Debates*, ns, 3 May 1827, vol. 17, col. 541; in 1826 William Lamb, who would serve as home secretary in Grey's Cabinet, had also spoken strongly against reform: Fisher, *History of Parliament*, vol. 6, p. 18.

30. Newcastle's diary, 2 November 1830, *Unrepentant Tory*, pp. 129–30; Ellenborough, *Political Diary*, 2 November 1830, vol. 2, pp. 411–12; *The Times*, 3 November 1830.

31. *JMrsA*, 4 November 1830, vol. 2, p. 397; Ellenborough, *Political Diary*, 6 November 1830, vol. 2, pp. 416–17; Arbuthnot to Peel, 5 November 1830, Parker, *Sir Robert Peel*, vol. 2, p. 167.

32. Ellenborough, *Political Diary*, 11 November 1830, vol. 2, p. 429; Newcastle's diary, 3 November 1830, *Unrepentant Tory*, p. 130.

33. Quoted in Palmer, *Protest and Police*, p. 310.

34. Ellenborough, *Political Diary*, 5 and 6 November 1830, vol. 2, pp. 415–18; *JMrsA*, 7 November 1830, vol. 2, pp. 398–9 (on the King and Queen); Newcastle's diary, 7 November 1830, *Unrepentant Tory*, p. 130.

35. Ellenborough, *Political Diary*, 7 November 1830, vol. 2, pp. 418–22; cf Prothero, *Artisans and Politics*, pp. 278–9, which gives some details of the radical agitation from the perspective of the radicals.

36. Newcastle's diary, 8 and 11 November 1830, *Unrepentant Tory*, pp. 130–2; *The Times*, 9 November 1830; George, *English Political Caricature*, vol. 2, p. 239; George, *BM Catalogue of Satires*, vol. 11, no. 16,305, p. 35; caricature reproduced in Du Cann, *Wellington. The Caricaturists' View*, p. 99; Broughton, *Recollections of a Long Life*, vol. 4, p. 63.

37. Ellenborough, *Political Diary*, 8 November 1830, vol. 2, p. 423.

38. Palmer, *Police and Protest*, p. 310; Memorandum – Precautions to be taken to defend Apsley House in case of Attack [by Wellington], 9 November 1830, *WND*, vol. 7, pp. 354–5.

39. Prothero, *Artisans and Politics*, p. 279; Ellenborough, *Political Diary*, 10–12 November 1830, vol. 2, pp. 427–31.

40. *Parliamentary Debates*, 3rd series, vol. 1, col. 548–9; Ellenborough, *Political Diary*, 13–16 November 1830, vol. 2, pp. 431–7.

41. *JMrsA*, 20 November 1830, vol. 2, pp. 401–3; Ellenborough, 19 [*sic* 17] November 1830, vol. 2, pp. 437–41. Ellenborough himself was not sorry to leave office: ibid., 10 and 16 November 1830, vol. 2, pp. 429, 435.

42. *JMrsA*, 20 November 1830, vol. 2, pp. 401–2; Ellenborough, *Political Diary*, 19 [*sic* 17] November 1830, vol. 2, pp. 437–41.

43. Fisher, *History of Parliament*, vol. 1, p. 232.

44. For example Greville, *Memoirs*, 31 August 1830, vol. 2, pp. 40–1.

22 Opposing the Reform Bill

1. *JMrsA*, 22 December 1830, vol. 2, pp. 406–9; Wellington to Mrs Arbuthnot, 5 May 1831, *W&HF*, p. 96.

2. Wellington to Mrs Arbuthnot, 22 October 1831, and 15 August 1832, *W&HF*, p. 100, 102–3; Mrs Arbuthnot to her husband, [17] and [18] February 1831, *CCA*, pp. 138–9, 139–40. See below, pp. 461–2, for more on Douro.

3. Hardinge to Mrs Arbuthnot [16 Nov 1830], *CCA*, p. 132; R.E. Foster, *The Politics of County Power. Wellington and the Hampshire Gentlemen, 1820–1852* (1990), pp. 78–9; Greville, *Memoirs*, 23 and 28 November 1830, vol. 2, pp. 69 and 72.

4. *JMrsA*, 29 November 1830, vol. 2, p. 405; Smith, *Lord Grey*, p. 261; Michael Brock, *The Great Reform Act* (1973), p. 134; George, *English Political Caricature*, vol. 2, pp. 242, 244.

5. Brock, *Great Reform Act*, p. 134.

6. Wellington to Fitzroy Somerset, and reply, 19 and 20 December 1830, *WND*, vol. 7, pp. 374–5; Wellington to Maurice Fitzgerald, 26 December 1830, *WND*, vol. 7, pp. 382–5; Aberdeen to Wellington, 21 January 1831, *WND*, vol. 7, pp. 394–5; Wellington to Aberdeen, 5 February 1831, *WND*, vol. 7, pp. 404–5; *JMrsA*, 11 February 1831, vol. 2, pp. 412–14; Bourne, *Palmerston*, pp. 336–7, confirms that the talk of war was not limited to the Tory Opposition.

7. Brock, *Great Reform Act*, pp. 135–6, 173–4; *JMrsA*, 21 March 1831, vol. 2, p. 414; *The Times*, 26 February 1831.

8. Wellington to Mrs Arbuthnot, 26 and 28 December 1830, *W&HF*, pp. 91–2.

9. Wellington to Mrs Arbuthnot, 26 December 1830, and 12 January 1831, *W&HF*, pp. 91–2, 93; Brock, *Great Reform Act*, pp. 135–6; Norman Gash, *Sir Robert Peel. The Life of Sir Robert Peel After 1830* (1972), pp. 7–9; *JMrsA*, 16 January 1831, vol. 2, pp. 410–12 (Wellington's recognition that Peel not himself should be prime minister).

10. Hardinge to Mrs Arbuthnot, 31 December 1830; Charles Arbuthnot to his wife, 13 February 1831, *CCA*, pp. 133–5, 135–6.

11. Wellington to Buckingham, 26 January 1831, *WND*, vol. 7, pp. 399–400.

12. Wellington to Mrs Arbuthnot, 28 December 1830, *W&HF*, p. 92; Aspinall, *Politics and the Press*, pp. 329–41, esp. 333–4; Croker to Mrs Arbuthnot, 4 April 1831, *CCA*, p. 140.

13. Wellington to Aberdeen, 23 May 1831, *WND*, vol. 7, pp. 442–3; William Holmes to Mrs Arbuthnot, 24 August 1831, *CCA*, pp. 142–3; Gash, *Sir Robert Peel*, pp. 18–19; Wellington did not go to the Pitt dinner either, but he was in mourning for the Duchess who died on 24 April: see below, pp. 461–2.

14. Brock, *Great Reform Act*, pp. 161–2, 136–44, 147.

15. George, *English Political Caricature*, vol. 2, pp. 242–4.

16. Brock, *Great Reform Act*, pp. 164–5.

17. *JMrsA*, 22 December 1830, vol. 2, p. 407. There was no secret ballot in America until the 1880s, or in Britain until 1872.

18. Wellington to Buckingham, 14 March 1831, *WND*, vol. 7, pp. 409–10.

19. *JMrsA*, 29 March 1831, vol. 2, p. 415.

20. Wellington to Melville, 30 May 1831, *WND*, vol. 7, pp. 450–1; see also *JMrsA*, 29 March 1831, vol. 2, pp. 414–18.

21. *JMrsA*, 29 March 1831, vol. 2, p. 417.

22. Brock, *Great Reform Act*, pp. 165, 176–9.

23. Ibid., pp. 183–5.

24. Ibid., pp. 152–4, 171, 174–5, 188–92; George, *English Political Caricature*, vol. 2, p. 245.

25. Wellington to the Duke of Buckingham, 21 May and 28 July 1831, *WND*, vol. 7, pp. 440, 478–9.

26. Quoted in *The Times, History of the Times*, vol. 1, p. 274.

27. Ibid.

28. Brock, *Great Reform Act*, p. 198; Fisher, *History of Parliament*, vol. 1, p. 237; Wellington to Mrs Arbuthnot, 28 and 29 April 1831, *W&HF*, pp. 94–5.

29. *JMrsA*, 16 May 1831, vol. 2, pp. 418–20; Brock, *Great Reform Act*, pp. 198–9.

30. *JMrsA*, 8 June 1831, vol. 2, p. 421; Brock, *Great Reform Act*, pp. 195–6; Fisher, *History of Parliament*, vol. 1, pp. 233–4.

31. *JMrsA*, 16 May 1831, vol. 2, p. 420.

32. Wellington to Mrs Arbuthnot, 1 May 1831, *W&HF*, pp. 95–6.

33. Brock, *Great Reform Act*, p. 133, citing Lady Salisbury's notes, 18 September 1830; Wellington to Maurice Fitzgerald, 21 May, *WND*, vol. 7, pp. 439–40.

34. Bourne, *Palmerston*, pp. 508–9, including quote; Brock, *Great Reform Act*, pp. 202–3, 211; *JMrsA*, 8 June 1831, vol. 2, p. 424.

35. *JMrsA*, 23 October 1831, vol. 2, p. 430; Brock, *Great Reform Act*, pp. 211, 215–16.

36. Quoted in Sir Herbert Maxwell, *The Life of Wellington and the Restoration of the Martial Power of Great Britain* (1900), vol. 2, p. 257; see also Brock, *Great Reform Act*, p. 217 and Gash, *Sir Robert Peel*, pp. 19–21.

37. Richard W. Davis, *A Political History of the House of Lords, 1811–1846* (2008), pp. 169, 163.

38. Brock, *Great Reform Act*, pp. 231–44.

39. Greville, *Memoirs*, 14 October 1831, vol. 2, pp. 208–9.

40. Wellington to Mrs Arbuthnot, 12 October 1831, *W&HF*, p. 99; see also Wellington to Maurice Fitzgerald, 13 October 1831, *WND*, vol. 7, pp. 561–2.

41. *JMrsA*, 23 October 1831, vol. 2, pp. 431–2; Aberdeen to Wellington, 5 November 1832, *WND*, vol. 8, pp. 36–7; Brock, *Great Reform Act*, pp. 247–8.

42. Charles Arbuthnot to his son Charles, 31 October 1831, Arbuthnot Papers, 3029/1/2/35; *JMrsA*, 23 October 1831, vol. 2, pp. 428–31.

43. See Prothero, *Artisans and Politics*, pp. 282–93, esp. 287; Brock, *Great Reform Act*, pp. 156–7, 165–7.

44. Lord Granville Somerset to Wellington, 3 November 1831, *WND*, vol. 8, pp. 26–8; Palmer, *Police and Protest*, p. 389; Brock, *Great Reform Act*, pp. 248–55. Brock says that there were probably more than 400 casualties, Palmer 12 dead and 94 wounded, but Brock's account is more detailed.

45. Memorandum on the Constitutional Forces of the Country, and upon the Forming and Arming of Political Unions [by Wellington], 5 November 1831, enclosed in Wellington to the King, 5 November 1831, *WND*, vol. 8, pp. 30–4.

46. Wellington to Buckingham, 2 January 1832, *WND*, vol. 8, pp. 143–5.

47. The King to Wellington, 9 November 1831, *WND*, vol. 8, pp. 43–4.

48. Wellington to Wharncliffe, 23 November 1831, *WND*, vol. 8, pp. 79–80; Charles Arbuthnot to his son Charles, 28 November 1831, *CCA*, p. 149; Wellington to Scarlett, 27 November 1831, *WND*, vol. 8, pp. 85–6. Brock, *Great Reform Act*, p. 259, confirms Wellington's suspicion that Attwood received prior warning of the Proclamation.

49. Wellington to Aberdeen, 7 February 1832, *WND*, vol. 8, pp. 212–13; Wellington to the Bishop of Exeter and to Lord Bute, 6 and 7 January 1832, *WND*, vol. 8, pp. 147–9, 149; Charles Arbuthnot to his wife, 15, 21 and 22 December 1831, Arbuthnot Papers, 3029/1/1/10–12.

50. Brock, *Great Reform Act*, pp. 268–70.
51. Wellington to Strangford, 12 January 1832, *WND*, vol. 8, pp. 155–8.
52. Wellington to Wharncliffe, 3 February 1832, *WND*, vol. 8, pp. 205–9.
53. Brock, *Great Reform Act*, pp. 279–82.
54. Wellington to Bathurst, 27 April 1831, *WND*, vol. 8, pp. 285–8, cf Wellington to Cumberland, 27 April 1832, ibid., pp. 283–5.
55. Brock, *Great Reform Act*, pp. 284–92.
56. Charles Arbuthnot to his son Charles, 9 May 1932, Arbuthnot Papers, 3029/1/2/55; Wellington to Lyndhurst, 10pm, 10 May 1832, *WND*, vol. 8, p. 304.
57. Brock, *Great Reform Act*, pp. 292–5, 299–302; John Cannon, *Parliamentary Reform, 1640–1832* (1980), pp. 233–6.
58. Brock, *Great Reform Act*, pp. 301–4.
59. Cannon, *Parliamentary Reform*, pp. 236–40.
60. Quoted in George, *English Political Caricature*, vol. 2, p. 254, which also discusses the other prints described here. *The Real Swing* is reproduced in ibid., plate 95; *Old England's Protector* in Du Cann, *Wellington. The Caricaturists' View*, p. 113.
61. Quoted in N. LoPatin, 'Wellington and Political Unions: Rumours, Misinformation and the Great Reform Act of 1832' (1999), p. 197.
62. Rogers, *Reminiscences and Table-talk*, pp. 256–8, recording Wellington's own account a few days later; J.R. Swinton, *Sketch of the Life of Lady de Ros . . .* (1893), pp. 166–8, Wellington's account in conversation, 15 September 1842; *The Times*, 19 June 1832, prints a number of accounts which vary in their details, e.g. some have Wellington alone, others with just a groom, one suggests that an attempt was actually made to unseat him, and another says that he *was* pelted with 'every description of missile'.
63. *The Times*, 19 June 1832.
64. Charles Arbuthnot to his son Charles, 30 June 1832, Arbuthnot Papers, 3029/1/2/70.
65. Brock, *Great Reform Act*, pp. 156–7.
66. As the fall of Wellington's government in 1830 shows, the reduction in the power of the Crown was the result of a long process of 'reform' which the Bill of 1832 extended and consolidated. Nonetheless before 1832 the King had a very significant influence over who became prime minister; while after 1832, except in very rare and unusual circumstances, the monarch's influence was negligible.
67. For a fascinating argument that the Lords did not lose as much power as previously thought in 1832 see Davis, *Political History of the House of Lords*, pp. 178–80.

23 The Limits of Opposition

1. The best modern accounts of Palmerston's foreign policy are in Bourne, *Palmerston*, pp. 332–407 and David Brown, *Palmerston. A Biography* (2010), pp. 143–88. For this paragraph see in particular Bourne, pp. 342–3, 349–52 and Brown, pp. 144, 151–3.
2. Roger Bullen, 'Party Politics and Foreign Policy: Whigs, Tories and Iberian Affairs, 1830–36' (1978), p. 40.
3. Ibid., pp. 38–40; Smith, 'Wellington, Aberdeen and the Miguelist Crisis in Portugal', pp. 299–303.
4. Memorandum on Portugal and Dom Miguel [by Wellington], July 1832; Wellington to Aberdeen, 11 and 18 August 1832, and reply, 22 August 1832, *WND*, vol. 8, pp. 375–8, 381–2, 388–9, 390–1; Wellington, *Speeches*, vol. 1, pp. 569–80.
5. Wellington to Sir Henry Cooke, 14 November 1832, *WND*, vol. 8, p. 445.
6. Wellington to Melville, 26 December 1832, *WND*, vol. 8, pp. 502–3; see also Wellington to Rosslyn, 31 October 1832, and Wellington to Lord Francis Leveson Gower, 15 December 1832, *WND*, vol. 8, pp. 431–2, 482–6.
7. Hardinge to Wellington, 15 November 1832, *WND*, vol. 8, pp. 449–50; Charles Arbuthnot to his son Charles, 20 November and 9 December 1832, *CCA*, p. 164; Gash, *Sir Robert Peel*, pp. 40–1; Ian Newbould, *Whiggery and Reform 1830–1841* (1990), pp. 82–3; S.F. Woolley, 'The Personnel of the Parliament of 1833' (1938), p. 242; Wellington to Croker, 6 March 1833, *HMC Wellington*, vol. 1, pp. 106–7.
8. Wellington to Aberdeen, 18 January 1833, *HMC Wellington*, vol. 1, pp. 32–3; see also Wellington to Roden, 13 March 1833, ibid., vol. 1, pp. 120–1.

9. Gash, *Sir Robert Peel*, pp. 43–6.

10. Wellington to Rosslyn, 13 March 1833, *HMC Wellington*, vol. 2, pp. 119–20.

11. Charles Arbuthnot to his son Charles, 15 March 1833, *CCA*, pp. 167–8. Four months later Arbuthnot described Wellington as Job's comforter whose talk 'depressed & oppressed me', Charles Arbuthnot to Mrs Arbuthnot, 9 July 1833, ibid., p. 171.

12. Lady Salisbury's diary, 1 April 1835 (Wellington on Peel's choice of a wife), and 13 May 1835 (the quote), Carola Oman, *The Gascoyne Heiress. The Life and Diaries of Frances Mary Gascoyne-Cecil, 1802–1839* (1968), pp. 163, 164–5; on Mrs Arbuthnot's influence, ibid., 11 May 1834, pp. 114–15, and Mrs Arbuthnot to Lady Shelley, 23 August 1833, *Diary of Lady Shelley*, vol. 2, pp. 245–7; Gash, *Mr Secretary Peel*, p. 659; Gash, *Sir Robert Peel*, p. 61.

13. Newbould, *Whiggery and Reform*, pp. 83, 113–19; Davis, *Political History of the House of Lords*, pp. 189–90; Wellington to Alexander Finlay, 2 April 1833, Wellington to the Duke of Buckingham, 13 June 1833, Wellington to Lord Harewood, 16 July 1833, *HMC Wellington*, vol. 1, pp. 154–5, 230, 262.

14. Bullen, 'Party Politics and Foreign Policy', pp. 42–3; the full text of Wellington's speech is in Wellington, *Speeches*, vol. 1, pp. 611–20; see also Smith, 'Wellington, Aberdeen and the Miguelist Crisis in Portugal', p. 305.

15. *The Times*, 5 June 1833; *Morning Chronicle* quoted in Bullen, 'Party Politics and Foreign Policy', pp. 43–4.

16. Gash, *Sir Robert Peel*, pp. 48–51; Davis, *Political History of the House of Lords*, p. 182, argued that the government's withdrawal of the appropriation clause was a direct result of the Opposition's show of force in the debate over Portugal.

17. Peel to Wellington, 'Private', 20 July 1833, *HMC Wellington*, vol. 1, pp. 263–5; Lady Salisbury's diary, 10 July 1833, ibid., p. 248.

18. Wellington to Peel, 23 July 1833, *HMC Wellington*, vol. 1, p. 265.

19. Davis, *Political History of the House of Lords*, p. 184, gives a circumstantial account, cf Gash, *Sir Robert Peel*, p. 52, who says Wellington voted with the ministers in favour of the bill.

20. Wellington to Mrs Arbuthnot, 22 July 1833, *W&HF*, pp. 106–7.

21. Lady Salisbury's diary, 21 August 1833, *HMC Wellington*, vol. 1, p. 283; the same passage is also in Oman, *Gascoyne Heiress*, p. 85 with trifling differences of punctuation.

22. Lady Salisbury's diary, 9 January 1834, Oman, *Gascoyne Heiress*, p. 107; see also 22 December 1833, ibid., pp. 100; Lord Strangford to Wellington, 26 October 1833, *HMC Wellington*, vol. 1, p. 347, and Edward Sugden to Hardinge, enclosed in Hardinge to Wellington [11 November 1833], *CCA*, pp. 175–6.

23. Wellington to Cumberland, 1 January 1834; Wellington to Roden, 17 January 1834, *HMC Wellington*, vol. 1, pp. 406–8, 422–3.

24. Wellington to Londonderry, 19 June 1834, *HMC Wellington*, vol. 1, p. 569.

25. Newbould, *Whiggery and Reform*, pp. 128–30; *The Times, History of the Times*, pp. 295–7; Gash, *Sir Robert Peel*, pp. 65–7, 75; Wellington to Londonderry, 17 June 1834, *HMC Wellington*, vol. 1, pp. 561–2. In fact Wellington unsuccessfully moved an amendment to soften the harsh provisions of the law in relation to the financial responsibility for bastard children, see Davis, *Political History of the House of Lords*, pp. 190–4; Wellington, *Speeches*, vol. 1, pp. 749–52.

26. Wellington to Roden, 3 June 1834, *HMC Wellington*, vol. 1, p. 552.

27. Arbuthnot to Peel, 'Private and Confidential', 12 May 1834, Parker, *Sir Robert Peel*, vol. 2, pp. 240–2; Gash, *Sir Robert Peel*, p. 67.

28. Lady Salisbury's diary, 11 May 1834, *HMC Wellington*, vol. 1, pp. 528–9, also in Oman, *Gascoyne Heiress*, pp. 114–15. See also Wellington to Aberdeen, 23 May 1834, *HMC Wellington*, vol. 1, pp. 541–2.

29. Wellington to Bathurst, 28 November 1833, *HMC Wellington*, vol. 1, pp. 361–3.

30. Wellington to Hardinge, 28 November 1833, and Wellington to Bathurst, 28 November 1833, *HMC Wellington*, vol. 1, p. 363.

31. Wellington to the Rev T. Wintle, 30 November 1833; Bathurst to Wellington, 5 December 1833, *HMC Wellington*, vol. 1, pp. 367, 376.

32. Wellington to Hardinge, 17 January 1834, *HMC Wellington*, vol. 1, pp. 420–1.

33. Gash, *Sir Robert Peel*, pp. 61–3, admits that 'Peel was less than just' towards Wellington, but it is not hard to sympathise with his feeling even though he had no fair ground for complaint.

34. Lady Salisbury's diary, 10 June 1834, Oman, *Gascoyne Heiress*, pp. 116–17.

35. Lady Salisbury's diary, 11 June 1834, ibid., pp. 118–20.
36. Lady Salisbury's diary, 13 June 1834, ibid., pp. 121–2.
37. Wellington to Aberdeen, 4 September 1834, *HMC Wellington*, vol. 1, pp. 663–5; Lady Salisbury's diary, 11 September 1834, Oman, *Gascoyne Heiress*, pp. 136–7.
38. Lady Salisbury's diary, 2 August 1834, ibid., p. 132; Wellington to Aberdeen, 23 August 1834, *HMC Wellington*, vol. 1, pp. 639–41.
39. Charles Arbuthnot to his son Charles, 15 July 1834, *CCA*, pp. 186–7; Wellington to the King, and reply, 12 and 14 July 1834, *HMC Wellington*, vol. 1, pp. 602–4, 607; Gash, *Sir Robert Peel*, pp. 70–2.
40. Lady Salisbury's diary, 11 May 1834, *HMC Wellington*, vol. 1, pp. 528–9. This is hearsay but it is confirmed by other sources: see Gash, *Sir Robert Peel*, pp. 75–6.
41. Lady Salisbury's diary, 22 July 1834, Oman, *Gascoyne Heiress*, p. 132.
42. Wellington to Lord Wilton, 25 November 1834, *HMC Wellington*, vol. 2, pp. 88–9 for this detail; Gash, *Sir Robert Peel*, pp. 78–90, provides a convenient summary of the circumstances surrounding Melbourne's dismissal.
43. Wellington to Peel, 15 November 1834, *HMC Wellington*, vol. 2, pp. 19–20.
44. Wellington to Peel, 15 November 1834 (2 letters), *HMC Wellington*, pp. 18–21.
45. *Examiner*, 23 November 1834; *Morning Chronicle*, 19 November 1834.
46. Creevey to Miss Ord, 22 November 1834, *Creevey Papers*, pp. 640–1.
47. Wellington to Peel, 22 November 1834, *HMC Wellington*, vol. 2, p. 55; see also Greville, *Memoirs* (the 1888 edition), 26 November 1834, vol. 3, p. 164.
48. *The Times, History of the Times*, vol. 1, pp. 290–1, 300, 333–40; *Trois Dogs* by H.B., BM online catalogue, *Doyle Political Sketches*, no. 349; Lady Salisbury's diary, 26 November 1834, Oman, *Gascoyne Heiress*, p. 146 where it is strangely attributed by the editor to the caricaturist Henry Bunbury, who died in 1811.
49. Lady Salisbury's diary, 20 November 1834, Oman, *Gascoyne Heiress*, pp. 143–5; Wellington to Lord Francis Egerton, 29 November 1834, *HMC Wellington*, vol. 2, pp. 108–9.
50. Wellington's circular to Conservative Peers, marked 'Private & Confidential', 21 November 1834, is printed in *HMC Wellington*, vol. 2, pp. 49–51, as are many of the responses e.g. from Rutland (pp. 66–7), Londonderry (pp. 68–9), Harrowby (p. 69) and Lonsdale. Wellington explained his reasons for not publishing the circular to Lord Harewood on 28 November 1834, ibid., p. 96.
51. Wellington to the Archbishop of Armagh, 4 December 1834, *HMC Wellington*, vol. 2, p. 155.
52. Angus Hawkins, *The Forgotten Prime Minister. The 14th Earl of Derby*, vol. 1, *Ascent, 1799–1851* (2007), pp. 153–4; Gash, *Sir Robert Peel*, pp. 85–7.
53. Gash, *Sir Robert Peel*, pp. 87–93; Stanhope, *Notes of Conversations*, preface, pp. v–vi.
54. The Tamworth Manifesto is printed in Peel, *Memoirs*, vol. 2, pp. 58–67, and is also available in full at Wikisource.
55. For example see the King to Wellington, 29 November 1834, *HMC Wellington*, vol. 2, p. 122.
56. Wellington to Peel, 30 November 1834, *HMC Wellington*, vol. 2, pp. 130–1; Gash, *Sir Robert Peel*, pp. 99–100.
57. Wellington to Rutland, 10 January 1835; Lord Francis Egerton, 23 January 1835, *HMC Wellington*, vol. 2, pp. 318, 384; *Morning Post*, 15 September 1830, mentions the visit to both works.
58. Figure from Woolley, 'Personnel of the Parliament of 1833', p. 242.
59. Wellington to Sir Herbert Taylor, 27 December 1834, *HMC Wellington*, vol. 2, pp. 249–50; Memorandum by Wellington of a Conversation with Baron Zuylen van Nyevelt, 11 January 1835, ibid., vol. 2, pp. 331–2; see also Wellington to Sir Robert Adair, 30 December 1834, ibid., vol. 2, p. 253.
60. Wellington to Karl von Hummelauer, 23 January 1835, *HMC Wellington*, vol. 2, pp. 376–7; Alava to Wellington, 24 November 1834, ibid., p. 74; Bullen, 'Party Politics and Foreign Policy', pp. 49–55; F. Darrell Munsell, 'Wellington's Iberian Policy, 1834–1835' (1989), pp. 555–6.
61. Gash, *Sir Robert Peel*, pp. 106–7; Charles Arbuthnot to his son Charles, 20 February 1835, *CCA*, p. 189.
62. Gash, *Sir Robert Peel*, pp. 107–10; Hawkins, *Forgotten Prime Minister*, vol. 1, pp. 169–71.

63. Lady Salisbury's diary, 21 March, 26 February and 26 April 1835, Oman, *Gascoyne Heiress*, pp. 158, 154, 164.
64. Lady Salisbury's diary, 29 March 1835, *Gascoyne Heiress*, pp. 159–61.
65. Gash, *Sir Robert Peel*, pp. 110–21.
66. For example ibid., pp. 122–5.

24 Private Life

1. On Wellington's health, see *JMrsA*, 22 and 28 January 1828, 8 and 10 March 1829, 12 December 1831, 17 January 1832, vol. 2, pp. 74, 250, 251, 437, 439; Wellington to the Bishop of Exeter, 6 January 1832, *WND*, vol. 8, p. 147; Longford, *Wellington. Pillar of State*, p. 299; on his deafness, Wellington to Mrs Arbuthnot, 22 October 1831, *W&HF*, p. 100.
2. *The Times*, 2 April 1829, p. 4.
3. Lady Salisbury's diary, 24 January, 26 November 1834 and 1 April 1835, Oman, *Gascoyne Heiress*, pp. 110, 146, 163–4. For Wellington's previous poor sleep see above, pp. 141 and 213 and *JMrsA*, 15 January 1824, vol. 1, p. 280.
4. Shaun Robert Durham, 'The Duke of Wellington and the People, 1819–1832' (1999), p. 5; see above, pp. 373–4.
5. Wellington's breakfast: James Hall's account of his visit to Walmer in 1836 in W.M. Parker, 'A Visit to the Duke of Wellington' (1944), p. 79; Wellington to Miss Burdett-Coutts, 4 July 1847, *W&HF*, pp. 244–5; Ellesmere, *Personal Reminiscences*, p. 94; Gleig, *Personal Reminiscences*, p. 141.
6. Wellesley, *Wellington. A Journey Through My Family*, p. 70; Gash, *Robert Surtees and Early Victorian Society*, p. 314. Wellington's dislike of the habit was neither new nor limited to smoking: in 1810 he made William Warre promise to give up taking snuff: William Warre, *Letters from the Peninsula, 1808–1812* (1999), 15 May 1810, p. 79.
7. Ellesmere, *Personal Reminiscences*, pp. 77–8; Gleig, *Personal Reminiscences*, p. 336; Rev. G.R. Gleig, *The Life of Arthur, Duke of Wellington* (1909 'Everyman' edn), p. 342 for the watch.
8. Management of household finances: Gleig, *Personal Reminiscences*, pp. 141–2; Ward, *Letters to 'Ivy'*, pp. 333–4; re postage: Gash, *Robert Surtees and Early Victorian Society*, p. 367, and Stanhope, *Notes of Conversations*, 29 October to 4 November 1839, p. 193; *The Saveall or – economy*, a print by William Heath, nd, George, *BM Catalogue of Satires*, no. 15,563, reproduced in Du Cann, *Wellington. The Caricaturists' View*, p. 56.
9. Wellington to Mrs Arbuthnot, 15 August and 12 December 1832, *W&HF*, pp. 102–4; see also same to same, 22 October 1831, ibid., p. 100, and Ellesmere, *Personal Reminiscences*, pp. 136–7.
10. Swinton, *Sketch of Lady De Ros*, pp. 147–8; Brialmont and Gleig, *Life of Wellington*, vol. 1, p. 10, for the figure of £4,000.
11. Wellington to the Bishop of Exeter, 6 January 1832, *WND*, vol. 8, pp. 147–9; Ellesmere, *Personal Reminiscences*, p. 78; Wellington to Lady Wilton, 20 December 1840, *W&HF*, pp. 153–4; Wellington to Angela Burdett-Coutts, 29 August 1847, ibid., pp. 249–50 (recommending Wiseman's book).
12. Wellington to Mrs Arbuthnot, 8 and 27 August 1819, *W&HF*, pp. 4–6.
13. Wellington to Angela Burdett-Coutts, 29 August 1847, *W&HF*, p. 249.
14. Swinton, *Sketch of Lady De Ros*, p. 147; Elizabeth Longford, 'The Duke of Wellington's Books' (1967), p. 26.
15. Lady Salisbury's diary, 26 October 1833 and 8 June 1837, in Oman, *Gascoyne Heiress*, pp. 91 and 240; Wellington to Lady Shelley, 12 November 1824, *Diary of Lady Shelley*, vol. 2, p. 121.
16. Gleig, *Personal Reminiscences*, p. 283; Ellesmere, *Personal Reminiscences*, pp. 79–80; Healey, *Lady Unknown*, pp. 101–2.
17. C.M. Kaufmann, *Catalogue of the Paintings in the Wellington Museum* (1982), p. 47.
18. Julius Bryant, *Apsley House. The Wellington Collection* (2011), *passim*; Kaufmann, *Catalogue of the Paintings in the Wellington Museum*, esp. pp. 5–13, 18, 46–8, 144–5; Jonathan Voak, 'The Wellington Collection at Apsley House' (1996), *passim*; Ellesmere, *Personal Reminiscences*, pp. 88–9.
19. *JMrsA*, 24 April 1820, vol. 1, p. 14.
20. *JMrsA*, 11 February 1830, vol. 2, p. 333; see also 16 November 1828, p. 219.
21. *JMrsA*, 16 February 1830, vol. 2, pp. 335–6.
22. *JMrsA*, 16 February 1830, vol. 2, pp. 335–6; Longford, *Wellington. Pillar of State*, p. 262; J.M. Robinson, *The Wyatts. An Architectural Dynasty* (1979), pp. 105–6.

23. Ibid., p. 105; *JMrsA*, 20 October 1825, vol. 1, pp. 420–1.
24. Duchess of Wellington to Sir Thomas Lawrence, 9 October 1822, quoted in Pakenham, *Soldier, Sailor*, p. 179; Wellington to Mrs Arbuthnot, 7 April 1833, *W&HF*, p. 106; Foster, *Politics of County Power*, p. 9; Pakenham, *Soldier, Sailor*, p. 174.
25. Gleig, *Personal Reminiscences*, pp. 320–1, 332–3 (the quote), Ellesmere, *Personal Reminiscences*, p. 77 (also on game); pp. 61, 76 (on hunting); Longford, *Wellington. Pillar of State*, p. 206 (remitting rents); Foster, *Politics of County Power*, p. 14 (patent stoves).
26. Foster, *Politics of County Power*, *passim*, esp. pp. 23–33; Stanhope, *Notes of Conversations*, 2 November 1840, p. 243.
27. Wellington to Strangford, 14 September 1833, *HMC Wellington*, vol. 1, pp. 296–7.
28. Wellington to Angela Burdett-Coutts, 20 September 1848, *W&HF*, pp. 266–7: see also ibid., pp. 118 and 244. There seems no reason to believe that this dislike of rail travel arose from the circumstances of Huskisson's death despite Gleig's suggestion to this effect: Gleig, *Personal Reminiscences*, p. 41.
29. Ibid., pp. 25–30, 285.
30. Ibid., pp. 285–8.
31. Creevey, *Life and Times*, October 1829, pp. 309–10.
32. Mrs Arbuthnot to Lady Shelley, 2 October 1832, *Diary of Lady Shelley*, vol. 2, p. 219; Rachel Weigall, *Lady Rose Weigall. A Memoir based on her Correspondence and Recollections of her Friends* (1923), pp. 4–5; Swinton, *Sketch of Lady de Ros*, pp. 152–3; Madan, *Spencer and Waterloo*, p. 96.
33. Lady Salisbury's diary, 22 and 24 January 1834, Oman, *Gascoyne Heiress*, pp. 109, 111; see also Wellington to Mrs Arbuthnot, 14 December 1833, *W&HF*, pp. 109–11.
34. Oman, *Gascoyne Heiress*, pp. 52–3; Emily Eden, *Miss Eden's Letters*, ed. Violet Dickinson (1919), pp. 176–7; cf *JMrsA*, 10 June 1829, vol. 2, p. 281, where some further theatricals later in the year are warmly praised.
35. See above, Ch. 10.
36. Charles Arbuthnot to his son Charles, 22 July 1833, *CCA*, pp. 171–2.
37. *Morning Post*, 19 September 1831; *Morning Chronicle*, 8 February 1831; *Sheffield Independent*, 1 January 1831; *JMrsA*, 23 October 1831, vol. 2, p. 428; Wellesley, *Wellington. A Journey Through My Family*, pp. 251–2.
38. Quoted in Pakenham, *Soldier, Sailor*, p. 194.
39. Ibid., pp. 199–200.
40. Maria Edgeworth to Mrs Edgeworth, 22 January 1831, *Letters from England*, pp. 474–7.
41. Longford, *Wellington. Pillar of State*, pp. 266–7; Wellington to Mrs Arbuthnot, 24 April 1831, *W&HF*, p. 94; Pakenham, *Soldier, Sailor*, pp. 202–3 (quoting Mrs Arbuthnot's account).
42. Quoted in Fisher, *History of Parliament*, vol. 7, pp. 682–3.
43. Wellington to Mrs Arbuthnot, 21 February 1834, *W&HF*, pp. 111–12.
44. William Napier to his wife, nd December 1830, Bruce, *Life of Napier*, vol. 1, p. 333; Fisher, *History of Parliament*, vol. 7, pp. 682–3.
45. *JMrsA*, 29 July and 14 November 1829, vol. 2, pp. 297, 316; Mrs Arbuthnot to Lady Shelley, nd, *Diary of Lady Shelley*, vol. 2, pp. 178–9: references to Wellington's illness and depression make it probable that this letter was written in December 1831 or January 1832: see *JMrsA*, vol. 2, pp. 436–9 for evidence that supports this supposition.
46. Mrs Arbuthnot to Charles Arbuthnot [17 February 1831], *CCA*, pp. 138–9.
47. Mrs Arbuthnot to Charles Arbuthnot [18 February 1831], *CCA*, p. 139; Shelley, *Diary of Lady Shelley*, vol. 2, p. 311.
48. Wellington to Mrs Arbuthnot, 22 October 1831, *W&HF*, p. 100; Mrs Arbuthnot to Lady Shelley, nd [late 1831 or early 1832], and diary, 14 September 1852, *Diary of Lady Shelley*, vol. 2, pp. 178–9, 310–11.
49. Lady Salisbury's diary, 2 August 1834, Oman, *Gascoyne Heiress*, pp. 132–3.
50. Wellington to Lady Shelley, 16 November 1835, *Diary of Lady Shelley*, vol. 2, p. 257.

25 The Many Faces of Fame

1. *The Times*, 11 January 1811 and 10 May 1813. George Thompson's prints and other popular images celebrating Wellington's victories, including the decorated stationery, are not included in George, *BM Catalogue of Satires*, as they are not satirical and have been little studied;

however, they are reproduced and discussed in Conrad Kent, *Estampas de la Guerra de la Independencia en la Provincia de Salamanca* (2010), pp. 47–71 and Professor Kent has very kindly elaborated on this material in private correspondence with me.

2. Myron F. Brightfield, *John Wilson Croker* (1940), pp. 267–70; election material quoted in Stephen M. Lee, *George Canning and Liberal Toryism* (2008), p. 69.

3. *Royal Military Chronicle*, vol. 1, no. 2 (December 1810), p. 99; Francis L. Clarke and William Dunlap, *The Life of the Most Noble Arthur, Marquis and Earl of Wellington* (1814), p. 112. See advertisement in the *Ipswich Journal*, 3 October 1812, and many other newspapers of around the same date. This form of publication explains why the first edition of Clarke's work is extremely rare.

4. George Elliott, *The Life of the Most Noble Arthur Duke of Wellington . . .* (1816), pp. iv and xii.

5. Peter Hofschröer, *Wellington's Smallest Victory. The Duke, the Model Maker and the Secret of Waterloo* (2004), pp. 19–20, 24–5.

6. Foster, *Wellington and Waterloo*, pp. 82–3; Hofschröer, *Wellington's Smallest Victory*, pp. 19–20, 24–5, 29.

7. Sir Walter Scott, *Paul's Letters to His Kinsfolk* (1834), pp. 124–8.

8. Foster, *Wellington and Waterloo*, pp. 79–82.

9. *Morning Post*, 31 October 1817.

10. P.E. Garnett, 'The Wellington Testimonial' (1952), pp. 48–61, inscription quoted on p. 58.

11. As recently as October 2013 an academic conference at Kells, Co. Meath, was held under the heading 'The Irishness of the Hon. Arthur Wesley, First Duke of Wellington'. See also Peter W. Sinnema, *The Wake of Wellington. Englishness in 1852* (2006), pp. 94–111 for a sophisticated discussion of the debates over Wellington's Irishness at the time of his death.

12. *The Times*, 29 June and 23 December 1812 (this was not the original, most famous, William Caslon who died in 1766); Foster, *Wellington and Waterloo*, p. 42.

13. See Longford, *Wellington. The Years of the Sword*, p. 409; *The Times*, 10 August 1815; and also 'The Hunter Wellington Boots Story', www.wellie-boots.com/wellington-boots-hunter-story (accessed 2014) and Adam Edwards, *A Short History of the Wellington Boot* (2006), *passim*.

14. Jane Austen, *Sanditon* (1925), ch. 4, pp. 44–5; Foster, *Wellington and Waterloo*, p. 98; *The Small Edition of the Post Office London Directory* (1843), p. 1047.

15. Ramsey, *Military Memoir and Romantic Literary Culture*, pp. 137, 162–3; *The Times*, 23 June 1825; Foster, *Wellington and Waterloo*, pp. 111–13.

16. Harriette Wilson, *The Memoirs of Harriette Wilson Written by Herself* (1909), vol. 1, pp. 55–65, 81–4, 163, 203–5, 253 (hammering on the door, pp. 203–5). For the mention of Wellington's private conduct by the Cato Street conspirators see Longford, *Wellington. Pillar of State*, p. 74.

17. Durham, 'Wellington and the People', p. 206; Karen Robson, 'The Depiction of the Duke of Wellington in the Broadside Ballad' (2013), pp. 194–9. 'The Tight Little Island' is also known as 'The Snug little Island'. 'The Odds and Ends of the Year 1830', printed in *Keystone Folklore Quarterly* (1964), p. 53.

18. Robson, 'Depiction of Wellington in the Broadside Ballad', pp. 194–7.

19. *Freeman's Journal* for these dates accessed through the online Nineteenth-Century British Newspapers database, searches of which, and other tools, do not reveal any earlier use of the phrase. For Wellington's 'iron manner' see Broughton's diary, 2 April 1829, in his *Recollections of a Long Life*, vol. 3, pp. 315–16; for his 'iron hands' see Newcastle's diary, 11 March 1829, *Unrepentant Tory*, p. 81; for Wellington's reference to his 'iron hand' see Neumann, *Diary*, 16 October 1828, vol. 1, pp. 192–3.

20. Newspapers as mentioned accessed through the online Nineteenth-Century British Newspapers database. See also the *Morning Chronicle*, 31 January and 6 February 1835 for references to the 'iron Duke'.

21. *Freeman's Journal*, 20 June 1838, 20 September 1838, and 6 April 1839. The *Leicester Chronicle*, 11 May 1839. For the ship, see *Morning Chronicle*, 12 May 1840; and for the poem, *Morning Post*, 5 October 1840; *Parliamentary Debates*, 4th series, vol. 73, col. 788. For *Punch's* use of the sobriquet see R.E. Foster, 'Mr Punch and the Iron Duke' (1984), pp. 36–42.

22. Wellington to Croker, 8 August 1815, WP 1/478 (printed with Croker's name suppressed in *WD*, vol. 8, pp. 231–2); Gleig to Wellington, 10 and 15 November 1826, WP 1/865/11 and 1/865/17; Gleig's preface to Brialmont and Gleig's *Life of Wellington*, vol. 1, p. xv. See also Wellington to Gleig, 4 November 1829, WP 1/1059/8.

23. Wellington's opinion of Southey: Edward Littleton Hatherton, 'Extracts from Lord Hatherton's Diary', ed. A. Aspinall (1964), 19 May 1820, p. 19; Rogers, *Reminiscences and Table-talk*, p. 239; see also Lady Salisbury's diary, 8 September 1836, Oman, *Gascoyne Heiress*, p. 211. See commentary for discussion of Southey's article on Waterloo and Wellington's purported role in its editing.

24. Bruce, *Life of Napier*, vol. 1, p. 114.

25. Wellington to Lady Sarah Napier, 30 September 1810, *WD*, vol. 8, pp. 303–4; 16 March 1811, *WD*, vol. 4, pp. 674–5; 20 January 1812, *WD*, vol. 5, p. 478; internal evidence makes it clear that these were not the only such letters Wellington wrote to Lady Sarah.

26. Rogers, *Reminiscences and Table-talk*, p. 239; see also Wellington to Lord Francis Egerton, 14 May 1834, Ellesmere, *Personal Reminiscences*, p. 140, and *JMrsA*, 24 November 1829, vol. 2, p. 319.

27. Maj.-Gen. Sir W.F.P. Napier, *History of the War in the Peninsula and the South of France, from the Year 1807 to the Year 1814* (1853), vol. 1, p. xiii.

28. The impact of Napier's work on British culture more generally is examined in Eleanor N. Morecroft, '"For the British Soldier is Keenly Sensitive to Honour": Military Heroism and British Identities in the Works of William Napier' (2011).

29. Shelley, *Diary of Lady Shelley*, March 1819, vol. 2, p. 34; Arbuthnot quoted in Chris Woolgar, 'Wellington's *Dispatches* and their Editor, Colonel Gurwood' (1996), p. 192.

30. This whole paragraph is based on Woolgar's excellent article 'Wellington's *Dispatches* and their Editor', pp. 193–200 (quote re time of impunity on p. 195). See also C.H. Dudley Ward, *A Romance of the Nineteenth Century* (1923), for Gurwood's life and letters shedding light both on his character and his work editing the *Dispatches*.

31. Lady Salisbury's diary, 22 January 1834, Oman, *Gascoyne Heiress*, p. 109; Ellesmere, *Personal Reminiscences*, 16 May 1834, p. 140; Chad, *Conversations of the Duke of Wellington*, 3 July 1836, p. 19; see also Greville, *Memoirs*, 2 January 1838, vol. 4, p. 3.

32. Ellesmere, *Personal Reminiscences*, p. 86; Morpeth's diary for 4 December 1844 quoted in the UK Reading Experience Database Record Number 28519, www.open.ac.uk/Arts/reading/UK/record_details.php?id=28519 (accessed January 2014); Greville, *Memoirs*, 4 January 1838, vol. 4, p. 10; Thomas Arnold to Sir Thomas Pasley, Rugby, 21 April 1837, in A.P. Stanley, *The Life and Correspondence of Thomas Arnold D.D.* (1868), vol. 2, pp. 83–4.

33. Woolgar, 'Wellington's *Dispatches* and their Editor', pp. 202–4.

34. Lady Wharncliffe to Lady Erne, 11 July 1835, Lady Wharncliffe, *The First Lady Wharncliffe and Her Family, 1779–1856* (1927), vol. 2, pp. 261–2; newspaper report quoted in Foster, *Wellington and Waterloo*, p. 133.

35. John Physick, *The Wellington Monument* (1970), pp. 1–2; Yarrington, 'His Achilles Heel?', pp. 31–2.

36. J.E. Cookson, 'The Edinburgh and Glasgow Duke of Wellington Statues: Early Nineteenth-Century Unionist Nationalism as a Tory Project' (2004), pp. 23–40.

37. Physick, *Wellington Monument*, pp. 2–17; Wellington to Croker, 14 June 1847, *Croker Papers*, vol. 3, p. 128.

38. George Soane, *Life of the Duke of Wellington compiled from His Grace's Despatches* (1839–40), vol. 1, p. viii. The other six biographies are those by Sir James Alexander; Andrew R. Bonar; Basil Jackson and C. Rochfort Scott; W.H. Maxwell; Rev. G.N. Wright; and the anonymous *Life and Exploits of . . . the Duke of Wellington including a complete History of the Peninsular War* published by Berger. Full details in the bibliography.

39. Wellington, *The Dispatches of Field Marshal the Duke of Wellington during his various campaigns in India, Denmark, Portugal, Spain, the Low Countries and France from 1799 to 1818*, ed. Lt-Col. [John] Gurwood (1834–39), vol. 2, p. 616 of this first edition; it was made much more prominent in the new and enlarged edition of 1844–47 appearing on the first page of the introduction to volume three (*WD*, vol. 3, p. vii), but as is shown in the text it had already aroused much notice by then. See Muir, *Wellington. The Path to Victory*, pp. 184–5 for further discussion of the quote.

40. *Quarterly Review*, vol. 58 (September–December 1836), p. 106; *Blackwood's Edinburgh Magazine*, vol. 41 (May 1837), p. 714; *The British and Foreign Review or European Quarterly*, vol. 10 (1840), p. 158; *Eclectic Review*, vol. 15 (3rd series, 1836), p. 307; *Army and Navy Chronicle or Scientific Repository*, vol. 11 (1840), p. 164; *London Quarterly Review*, vol. 69 (February 1837), p. 58; Soane, *Life of the Duke of Wellington*, vol. 1, p. 74; Sir James Alexander, *Life of Field Marshal, His Grace the Duke of Wellington* (1839–40), vol. 1, pp. 163–4; Andrew R. Bonar, *Life of Field Marshal His Grace the Duke of Wellington* (1842), p. 87; Rev.

George N. Wright, *Life and Campaigns of Arthur, Duke of Wellington* (1841), vol. 1, p. 97; Archibald Alison, *History of Europe from the Commencement of the French Revolution in 1789 to the Restoration of the Bourbons in 1815* (1833–42), vol. 6, p. 748. It also appeared in the *Morning Post*, 6 March 1835, and other publications could readily be added to this list.

41. Newspaper account quoted in Cookson, 'The Edinburgh and Glasgow Duke of Wellington Statues', p. 28.

26 Leading the Lords

1. Lady Salisbury's diary, 18 and 19 May 1835, Oman, *Gascoyne Heiress*, pp. 165–6.
2. Lady Salisbury's diary, 30 May and 28 June 1835, and 31 May 1836, ibid., pp. 166, 170, 203.
3. Lady Salisbury's diary, 19 May and 28 June 1835, and 18 June 1836, ibid., pp. 165–6, 170, 204.
4. Leslie Mitchell, *Lord Melbourne, 1779–1848* (1997), pp. 142–208 gives a fascinating but by no means flattering portrait of the Prime Minister: see esp. pp. 164, 182 and 188 for Melbourne's lack of interest in launching a fresh wave of reform.
5. Davis, *Political History of the House of Lords*, pp. 200, 215; Gash, *Sir Robert Peel*, pp. 136–7.
6. Lady Salisbury's diary, 8 September 1835, Oman, *Gascoyne Heiress*, p. 177.
7. Fitzgerald to Peel, nd, quoted in Davis, *Political History of the House of Lords*, pp. 211–12.
8. Gash, *Sir Robert Peel*, pp. 131–40, and Davis, *Political History of the House of Lords*, pp. 201–14, give complementary accounts while differing widely in their interpretation especially of Peel's behaviour. The Duke of Newcastle's diaries give an important first-hand account of the first half of proceedings from the perspective of an ultra-Tory who would have voted against the Second Reading and endeavoured to prevent the bill going into Committee (Newcastle, *Unrepentant Tory*, pp. 277–85). For Peel's point of view see Peel to Croker, 26 August 1835, *Croker Papers*, vol. 2, pp. 282–4; and for Wellington's see Wellington to Peel, 25 April 1835, WP 2/33/23.
9. Lady Salisbury's diary, 10 June 1835, and 26 January 1838, Oman, *Gascoyne Heiress*, pp. 167–8, 270–1; Stanhope, *Notes of Conversations*, 14 October 1839, p. 185.
10. Gash, *Sir Robert Peel*, pp. 142–62; Davis, *Political History of the House of Lords*, pp. 219–27; Mitchell, *Lord Melbourne*, pp. 180–5.
11. Wellington to an unknown correspondent, 26 July 1837, Wellington, *Private Correspondence*, pp. 203–5; Wellington's tribute in Parliament quoted in Thompson, *Wellington After Waterloo*, p. 167. But see also Wellington's more generous comments to Lord Mahon in 1840: Stanhope, *Notes of Conversations*, 30 November 1840, p. 258.
12. Wellington to Lady Burghersh, 23 June 1837, Burghersh, *Correspondence,* pp. 98–9.
13. For the annoyance Cumberland caused Wellington in 1836 see Wellington to Peel, 11 February 1836, Parker, *Sir Robert Peel*, vol. 2, pp. 323–4; Greville, *Memoirs*, 4 January 1838, vol. 4, pp. 6–7; and Wellington to Lord Egerton, 7 December 1837, Ellesmere, *Personal Reminiscences*, pp. 163–4.
14. Wellington to Lady Burghersh, 23 June 1837, Burghersh, *Correspondence,* pp. 98–9; Wellington to William Wellesley-Pole, 9 May 1810, 'Some Letters of the Duke of Wellington', p. 34.
15. Wellington to Croker, 26 October 1835, *Croker Papers*, vol. 2, p. 286. For Peel's alarm see Croker to Lord Hertford, 30 September 1835, ibid., p. 284.
16. Lady Burghersh to Lord Burghersh, 20 January 1836, Burghersh, *Correspondence,* pp. 64–6.
17. Thompson, *Wellington After Waterloo*, p. 169, for Melbourne's overtures which are not fully documented elsewhere; Gash, *Sir Robert Peel*, pp. 202–3; Wellington to Arbuthnot, 15 February 1838, WP 2/49/91–3; and Croker to Peel, 15 August 1837, *Croker Papers*, vol. 2, pp. 319–21.
18. Philip Ziegler, *Melbourne* (1976), pp. 275–9; Gash, *Sir Robert Peel*, pp. 197–8.
19. Peel to Wellington, 7 January 1838, Parker, *Sir Robert Peel*, vol. 2, pp. 355–7; Wellington to Hill, 23 December 1837, and memorandum for Hill of same date, WP 2/48/123–4; Greville, *Memoirs*, 2 and 5 January 1838, vol. 4, pp. 2, 6 and 10.
20. Lord Wharncliffe to Lady Wharncliffe, nd 'Monday', *First Lady Wharncliffe and Her Family*, vol. 2, pp. 288–9; Benjamin to Sarah Disraeli, 20 January 1838, Benjamin Disraeli, *Benjamin Disraeli Letters*, ed. J.A.W. Gunn (1982–2004), vol. 3, no. 709, pp. 9–10; Davis, *Political History of the House of Lords*, pp. 231–2.
21. Lord Holland quoted in ibid., pp. 231–2; Greville, *Memoirs*, 5 January 1838, vol. 4, p. 10.

22. There is no direct evidence for this interpretation but see Wellington to Arbuthnot, 15 and 19 February 1838, WP 2/49/91–3, and 2/49/102–3, and Charles Arbuthnot to his son Charles, 13 February 1838, *CCA*, pp. 196–7.

23. Stanhope, *Notes of Conversations*, 6 July 1839, pp. 146–7; Lady Salisbury's diary, 3, 17 and 19 February 1838, Oman, *Gascoyne Heiress*, pp. 272–4.

24. Gash, *Sir Robert Peel*, pp. 202–3.

25. Wellington to Arbuthnot, 19 February 1838, WP 2/49/102–3, cf Lady Salisbury's diary, 19 February 1838, Oman, *Gascoyne Heiress*, pp. 273–4, where he said something very similar.

26. Queen Victoria's journal quoted in Mitchell, *Lord Melbourne*, pp. 186–7, and Ziegler, *Melbourne*, p. 261.

27. Lady Salisbury's diary, 28 June 1838, Oman, *Gascoyne Heiress*, pp. 286–7; Aberdeen quoted in Ziegler, *Melbourne*, pp. 268–9.

28. Lady Salisbury's diary, 22 and 28 June and 28 July 1838, Oman, *Gascoyne Heiress*, pp. 285, 288, 293.

29. Ziegler, *Melbourne*, pp. 290–2; Lady Cowper's diary, 8 May 1838, Mabel, Countess of Airlie, *Lady Palmerston and Her Times* (1922), vol. 2, p. 12; Queen Victoria's journal quoted in Stanley Weintraub, *Victoria. An Intimate Biography* (1987), p. 122.

30. Gash, *Sir Robert Peel*, pp. 220–4; Memorandum by Peel in Parker, *Sir Robert Peel*, vol. 2, pp. 390–2.

31. Lady Holland to her son, nd, *Lady Holland to Her Son*, p. 177; Ziegler, *Melbourne*, pp. 292–8 gives a fascinating account of the crisis from the Whig point of view including the reaction of different ministers, some of whom greatly surpassed Melbourne in their determination to support the Queen.

32. Gash, *Sir Robert Peel*, pp. 224–7; Ziegler, *Melbourne*, pp. 299, 304.

33. Burghersh, *Correspondence*, pp. 52, 55, 91–2; Lady Salisbury's diary, 28 March 1837, Oman, *Gascoyne Heiress*, pp. 237–8; Stanhope, *Notes of Conversations*, 4 May 1841, p. 264.

34. Ellesmere, *Personal Reminiscences*; Stanhope, *Notes of Conversations*; extracts of Wellington's letters to Lady Wilton are published in *W&HF* (see esp. pp. 115–16 and 201), Wellington, *The Letters of the Duke of Wellington to Miss J., 1834–1851*, ed. Christine Herrick (1880); see Longford, *Wellington. Pillar of State*, pp. 300–1n for her full name.

35. Severn, *Architects of Empire*, pp. 499–517, esp. 505–7; Lady Salisbury's diary, 16 May 1838, Oman, *Gascoyne Heiress*, p. 283.

36. Lady Salisbury's diary, 12 April 1838, Oman, *Gascoyne Heiress*, p. 279; Wellesley, *Wellington. A Journey Through My Family*, p. 173; Longford, *Wellington. Pillar of State*, p. 387; Charles Arbuthnot to his son Charles, 15 February 1840, Arbuthnot Papers, 3029/1/2/223.

37. Lady Salisbury's diary, 9 December 1835, and 1 July 1836, Oman, *Gascoyne Heiress*, pp. 188 and 205; Charles Arbuthnot to his son Charles, 21 July and 1 November 1836, Arbuthnot Papers, 3029/1/2/171, and *CCA*, pp. 194–5.

38. Lady Salisbury's diary, 16 May 1838, Oman, *Gascoyne Heiress*, p. 283; see also Croker to the King of Hanover [22 Nov 1838 ?], and Wellington to Croker, 15 December 1838, *Croker Papers*, vol. 2, pp. 324–5, 332–3.

39. Stanhope, *Notes of Conversations*, nd February, 4 and 9 March, and 23 November 1839, pp. 135–6 and 04; Croker to the King of Hanover, 21 November 1839, *Croker Papers*, vol. 2, pp. 357–8.

40. Stanhope, *Notes of Conversations*, 23 November 1839, pp. 197–212, gives a very detailed account of the attack and Wellington's recovery (quotes from pp. 199 (wine), 202 (nature of the attack), 210–11 (his appearance)).

41. Charles Arbuthnot to his son Charles, 15 and 22 February, 19 July and 6 August 1839, and 7 February 1841, Arbuthnot Papers, 3029/1/2/233, 228, 246, 249 and 293; Croker to the King of Hanover, 17 February 1840, *Croker Papers*, vol. 2, pp. 360–2; Stanhope, *Notes of Conversations*, 18 March, and nd [July?] 1840, and 5 February 1841, pp. 217, 241–2, 262–3.

42. Hatherton quoted in Davis, *Political History of the House of Lords*, p. 253; Stanhope, *Notes of Conversations*, 27 April 1840, pp. 236–7; Wellington to Lady Wilton, 18 October 1840, *W&HF*, p. 148.

43. Croker to Lady Hardwicke, 24 November 1839, *Croker Papers*, vol. 2, pp. 358–9; Wellington to Lady Wilton, 25 and 27 November 1839, *W&HF*, pp. 125–6; Ziegler, *Melbourne*, pp. 311–12.

44. Ziegler, *Melbourne*, pp. 311–13 (Albert's allowance and the quote from the Queen's private journal); Wellington to Lady Wilton, 3 and 5 February 1840, *W&HF*, pp. 128–30.

45. Lord Cowley to Charles Arbuthnot, 11 February 1840, *CCA*, p. 217.
46. Daphne Bennett, *King Without a Crown. Albert, Prince Consort of England, 1819–1861* (1977), pp. 37–84.
47. Gash, *Sir Robert Peel*, pp. 241–5; Davis, *Political History of the House of Lords*, pp. 254–8; Colonial Office Memorandum quoted in Chamberlain, *Lord Aberdeen*, p. 279; Wellington's desire to keep Melbourne in office: Wellington to Croker, 12 November 1839, *Croker Papers*, vol. 2, p. 357; Wellington to Peel, 18 December 1839, Parker, *Sir Robert Peel*, vol. 2, pp. 416–20. See also Stanhope, *Notes of Conversations*, 8 November 1840, p. 252.
48. Aberdeen to Arbuthnot, 14 July 1840, *CCA*, pp. 220–1.
49. This account of the 'Eastern Question' largely follows the revisionist interpretation advanced in Schroeder, *Transformation of European Politics*, pp. 736–56, esp. 739–42. Brown's account in his *Palmerston. A Biography*, pp. 223–37 is naturally more sympathetic to Palmerston and critical of the French, but nothing in it undermines Schroeder's central arguments.
50. Ziegler, *Melbourne*, pp. 318–29; Brown, *Palmerston. A Biography*, pp. 323–4.
51. For Wellington's views on the Eastern Question see his letters to Lady Wilton between 3 August and 20 November 1840, in *W&HF*, pp. 135–51, esp. 6 August (Lord John Russell consulting him), pp. 135–6, 19 August (talks with Lord Melbourne), p. 140.
52. Schroeder, *Transformation of European Politics*, pp. 749–56.
53. Gash, *Sir Robert Peel*, pp. 248–9.
54. Wellington to Charles Arbuthnot, 16 November 1840, *CCA*, pp. 223–4.
55. Gash, *Sir Robert Peel*, pp. 249–70.

27 Wellington and the Army

1. Croker's 'Notes on Conversations with Wellington', September 1826, *Croker Papers*, vol. 1, pp. 342–3.
2. Duke of York to Wellington, 7 November 1823; Memorandum by the Duke of York, 6 November 1823; Liverpool to Wellington, 11 November 1823; Wellington to Liverpool, 12 November 1823; Wellington to Bathurst, 12 November 1823; Memorandum by Wellington, 'Insufficiency of our Military Establishments, and means of arguing them', 12 November 1823; Bathurst to Wellington, 14 November 1823, *WND*, vol. 2, pp. 168–77, 180; Fortescue, *History of the British Army*, vol. 11, p. 86, cf *WND*, vol. 2, p. 379, for strength of this augmentation.
3. Duke of York to Wellington, 3 and 24 December 1824, WP 1/807/1 and WP 1/807/23; Wellington to Bathurst, 26 December 1824, *WND*, vol. 2, pp. 378–80; Fortescue, *History of the British Army*, vol. 11, pp. 87–9; Gleig, *Personal Reminiscences*, p. 305.
4. Wellington to Beresford, 18 December 1824, *WND*, vol. 2, p. 374.
5. Lord Combermere, *Memoirs and Correspondence of Field Marshal Viscount Combermere . . .* by Mary, Viscountess Combermere and Capt. W.W. Knollys (1866), vol. 2, pp. 29–30.
6. Wellington to Charles Wynn, 7 March 1825, *WND*, vol. 2, p. 425.
7. Palmerston to Wellington, 1 August 1827; Wellington to Goderich, 25 August, enclosing a copy of Wellington to Palmerston, 4 August 1827, *WND*, vol. 4, pp. 104, 106–18; Huskisson, *Huskisson Papers*, pp. 247–53; Taylor to Wellington, 12 and 19 August 1827, *WND*, vol. 2, pp. 82–3, 100–1; *JMrsA*, 24 October 1827, vol. 2, p. 146.
8. Wellington to Hill, 1 February 1828, *WND*, vol. 4, pp. 252–3; Hill to Wellington, 2 February 1828, in Sidney, *Life of Hill*, pp. 336–7, and more generally, pp. 331–7; Teffeteller, *The Surpriser*, pp. 195, 198–9.
9. Philip D. Jones, 'The British Army in the Age of Reform, 1830–1854' (1968), pp. 27–31, 59–62; Hew Strachan, *Wellington's Legacy. The Reform of the British Army, 1830–54* (1984), p. 69.
10. For example Fortescue, *History of the British Army*, vol. 10, p. 224 and Sir Charles Oman, *Wellington's Army, 1809–1814* (1913), p. 49.
11. See the contemporary evidence quoted in Wellesley, *Wellington in Civil Life*, pp. 7–9; *United Service Journal*, June 1827, p. 539; *Naval Military Gazette*, quoted in Neil Ramsey, 'The Military Author and Romantic War: British Military Memoirs and the Emergence of the Soldier Hero, 1809–1835' (2008), ch. 2, p. 35; Wellington to Beresford, 21 April 1830, *WND*, vol. 7, p. 1.

12. Jones, 'British Army in the Age of Reform', pp. 38 (Evans), 35–6 (only symbolic savings); Teffeteller, *The Surpriser*, pp. 205–6 (clashes over patronage); Sidney, *Life of Hill*, pp. 352–3 (Hill's refusal to support the Reform Bill, and the King's statement that it was not a political office); Jones, op. cit., pp. 39, 104, 111–13, and Strachan, *Wellington's Legacy*, pp. 6–7, on Whig hostility to Hill and calls for his resignation.

13. Fitzroy Somerset to Wellington, 18 May 1831, *WND*, vol. 7, pp. 436–7; Sweetman, *Raglan*, pp. 99–100; *JMrsA*, 12 March 1829, vol. 2, p. 253; Jones, 'British Army in the Age of Reform', pp. 41–2.

14. Wellington, Memorandum on the Proposed Plan for altering the Discipline of the Army, 22 April 1829, *WND*, vol. 5, pp. 592–7; Gleig, *Personal Reminiscences*, p. 307.

15. Wellington, Memorandum on Corporal Punishment, 4 March 1832, *WND*, vol. 8, pp. 233–9, quote on p. 234.

16. Wellington, Memorandum on the Proposed Plan for altering the Discipline of the Army, 22 April 1829, *WND*, vol. 5, pp. 592–7; Wellington, Memorandum on Corporal Punishment, 4 March 1832, *WND*, vol. 8, pp. 233–9, quotes on p. 235.

17. Wellington, Memorandum on the Proposed Plan for altering the Discipline of the Army, 22 April 1829, *WND*, vol. 5, pp. 592–7; Wellington, Memorandum on Corporal Punishment, 4 March 1832, *WND*, vol. 8, pp. 233–9 (quote on p. 236).

18. Wellington to Sir John Macdonald, 9 April 1833, *HMC Wellington*, vol. 1, pp. 192–3; Jones, 'British Army in the Age of Reform', pp. 69–71; Strachan, *Wellington's Legacy*, pp. 80–2; see also J.R. Dinwiddy, 'The Early Nineteenth-Century Campaign against Flogging in the Army', in his *Radicalism and Reform in Britain 1780–1850* (1992), pp. 125–48.

19. Wellington's evidence in the 'Report of the Commission on Military Punishments', *Parliamentary Papers*, 1836, vol. 22, pp. 322–32, esp. p. 327. See also Wellington's Memorandum on Corporal Punishment, 4 March 1832, *WND*, vol. 8, pp. 233–9.

20. Wellington's evidence in the 'Report of the Commission on Military Punishments', *Parliamentary Papers*, 1836, vol. 22, pp. 322–32, esp. pp. 327–8; Wellington, Memorandum on Corporal Punishment, 4 March 1832, *WND*, vol. 8, pp. 233–9, esp. pp. 236–8.

21. Wellington Memorandum on Corporal Punishment, 4 March 1832, *WND*, vol. 8, pp. 233–9, esp. p. 238; Strachan, *Wellington's Legacy*, pp. 80–2.

22. Strachan, *Wellington's Legacy*, pp. 81–2.

23. Hill quoted in Teffeteller, *The Surpriser*, p. 201; Wellington, Memorandum upon Sir Herbert Taylor's Proposed Circular to Commanding Officers of Regiments Regarding the Mode of Punishing Soldiers etc., 22 December 1829, *WND*, vol. 6, pp. 343–5; Wellington to Lt.-Col. Woodford, 21 December 1833, *HMC Wellington*, vol. 1, pp. 392–4; Strachan, *Wellington's Legacy*, pp. 66–7.

24. Strachan, *Wellington's Legacy*, pp. 58–62; Jones, 'British Army in the Age of Reform', pp. 147–50.

25. Wellington's evidence in the 'Report of the Commission on Military Punishments', p. 330; Strachan, *Wellington's Legacy*, p. 85.

26. Wellington's evidence in the 'Report of the Commission on Military Punishments', p. 330; Strachan, *Wellington's Legacy*, pp. 99–101; Jones, 'British Army in the Age of Reform', pp. 137–8.

27. Wellington, Memorandum on the proposed plan for Altering the Discipline of the Army, 22 April 1829, *WND*, vol. 5, pp. 592–7 (quote on p. 596). The previous quotations in this paragraph also come from this memorandum.

28. Gomm, *Letters and Journals*, p. 373.

29. Wellington to Lord Hill, 7 March 1833, printed in *WD*, vol. 8, pp. 366–74 (quote on p. 369), and also in the *United Service Journal* (1833), part 3, pp. 277–82 (quote on p. 278).

30. Wellington to Sir Herbert Taylor, 11 April 1821, *WND*, vol. 1, pp. 167–9.

31. For an eloquent if possibly a little overstated example of the problem see 'Grievances of a Veteran', a letter from an anonymous officer to the editor of the *United Service Journal* (1833), pp. 536–8.

32. Wellington, Memorandum for Hill, 7 March 1833, *WD*, vol. 8, pp. 366–74; Strachan, *Wellington's Legacy*, pp. 109–11, 139–40.

33. Ibid., p. 117.

34. There is an excellent account of the 1840 Commission in Jones, 'British Army in the Age of Reform', pp. 171–7 which includes the figures on the age of captains in the artillery and the rest of the army. See also Strachan, *Wellington's Legacy*, p. 115, for the reason why the Commission's recommendations did not have a greater effect.

35. Wellington, Memorandum for Hill, 7 March 1833, *WD*, vol. 8, pp. 366–74 (quote on p. 373).
36. See above, p. 282; and Fortescue, *History of the British Army*, vol. 11, p. 92 for the Duke of York, and Lady Salisbury's diary, 15 April 1838, Oman, *Gascoyne Heiress*, p. 280 for Wellington.
37. Lord Vivian quoted in Strachan, *Wellington's Legacy*, p. 252; see ibid., pp. 246–54 and Jones, 'British Army in the Age of Reform', pp. 101–19. See also two important memoranda by Wellington (to Fitzroy Somerset, 25 March 1837, and to Lord Melbourne, 4 January 1838) printed in Clode, *Military Forces of the Crown*, vol. 2, pp. 759–63.
38. Jones, 'British Army in the Age of Reform', pp. 178–9; Strachan, *Wellington's Legacy*, pp. 181–3.

28 Peel's Lieutenant

1. Lady Salisbury's diary, 26 January 1838, Oman, *Gascoyne Heiress*, pp. 270–1; Arbuthnot to Peel, 8 May 1839 and 12 May 1841, Parker, *Sir Robert Peel*, vol. 2, pp. 391, 460–1; Wellington to Peel, 17 May 1841, ibid., vol. 2, pp. 461–2; Greville, *Memoirs*, 1 September 1841, vol. 4, p. 405 confirms that there had been an overture from Prussia for Wellington to take command of the allied armies in Germany in the event of war.
2. Wellington to Peel, 18 December 1839, Parker, *Sir Robert Peel*, vol. 2, pp. 416–21.
3. Gash, *Sir Robert Peel*, pp. 295, 340.
4. Peel to Arbuthnot, 5 April 1842, Parker, *Sir Robert Peel*, vol. 2, p. 527.
5. Gash, *Sir Robert Peel*, pp. 303, 319–22.
6. Wellington to Lady Wilton, 14 March 1842, *W&HF*, pp. 181–2.
7. Peel to Stanley, 29 December 1841, Parker, *Sir Robert Peel*, vol. 2, p. 512; Davis, *Political History of the House of Lords*, p. 271; Greville, *Memoirs*, 9 February 1844 and 26 April 1846, vol. 5, pp. 177 and 316; Peel to Arbuthnot, nd, 4 August and 29 September 1841, *CCA*, pp. 230–3; Peel to Arbuthnot, 21 October 1842, and Peel to Wellington, 24 October 1842, Parker, *Sir Robert Peel*, vol. 3, pp. 384–5.
8. Wellington to Lady Wilton, 7 and 15 September and 29 October 1841, *W&HF*, pp. 169–73; Gash, *Sir Robert Peel*, pp. 526–30 (Peel overworked and unable to delegate); Thompson, *Wellington After Waterloo*, p. 202; Greville, *Memoirs*, 7 September and 24 November 1841, vol. 4, pp. 413 and 427.
9. Greville, *Memoirs*, 3 December 1841, pp. 430–1; Davis, *Political History of the House of Lords*, p. 271.
10. Peel to Stanley, 29 December 1841, Parker, *Sir Robert Peel*, vol. 2, p. 512; Peel to Wellington, and reply, 6 and 7 October 1841, ibid., vol. 2, pp. 575–7; Wellington to Lady Wilton, 1 April 1812, *W&HF*, p. 182; Fitzgerald to Peel [8 September] and 11 October 1842, Parker, *Sir Robert Peel*, vol. 2, pp. 590, 593–4.
11. Peel to Arbuthnot, 5 April 1842, ibid., vol. 2, p. 535, which also includes the remark about Hill's infirmity.
12. Arbuthnot to Peel, 9 April and 29 July 1842; Peel to Wellington, 10 August 1842; Wellington to Peel, 10 August 1842, 'at night', Parker, *Sir Robert Peel*, vol. 2, pp. 535–7; Peel to the Queen, 10 August 1842, Queen Victoria, *The Letters of Queen Victoria*, ed. A.C. Benson and Viscount Esher (1908), vol. 1, pp. 420–1.
13. *Morning Chronicle*, 18 August 1842; *The Times*, 19 August 1842.
14. Wellington, *Speeches*, 24 August 1841, vol. 2, p. 477; *Spectator*, 2 October 1841, pp. 944–5; *Punch*, vol. 1, 1841, p. 102; Greville, *Memoirs*, 30 November 1841, vol. 4, pp. 429–30; Foster, 'Mr Punch and the Iron Duke', p. 38.
15. Gash, *Sir Robert Peel*, pp. 339–40, 358, 360.
16. Ibid., p. 350; F.C. Mather, *Public Order in the Age of the Chartists* (1959), p. 158.
17. Gash, *Sir Robert Peel*, pp. 342–3, 358–9; Mather, *Public Order in the Age of the Chartists*, pp. 149–51, 156, 161–4, 174–5; Greville, *Memoirs*, 1 September 1842, vol. 5, pp. 29–30; Peel to Graham, 15 October 1843; Stanley to Peel, 16 and 23 December 1843; Peel to Stanley, 19 December 1843, Parker, *Sir Robert Peel*, vol. 2, pp. 572–3.
18. Greville, *Memoirs*, 19 January, 7 February, 19 March 1843, and 9 February 1844, vol. 5, pp. 70, 77, 83, and 157. Extracts from his letters to Lady Wilton in 1843–44 are printed in *W&HF*, pp. 186–98; see also Burghersh, *Correspondence*, pp. 144–60.
19. Davis, *Political History of the House of Lords*, pp. 282 (Roden) and 289 (Wellington).
20. Wellington to Graham, 3 September 1843, quoted in ibid., p. 290.

21. Graham to Peel, 6 September 1843, and Peel to Graham, 18 September 1843, Parker, *Sir Robert Peel*, vol. 3, pp. 63–4.

22. Gash, *Sir Robert Peel*, pp. 402–11; John Flanedy, *A Special Report of the Proceedings in the Case of the Queen against Daniel O'Connell, Esq. M.P.* (1844), pp. 161, 179.

23. Correspondence between Arbuthnot, Peel, Stanley and Wellington between 18 and 25 October 1842 in Parker, *Sir Robert Peel*, vol. 3, pp. 382–6.

24. Wellington to Lady Wilton, 21 March 1842, *W&HF*, p. 182; Greville, *Memoirs*, 9 February 1843, vol. 5, p. 80, see also p. 188; Wellington to Peel, 22 September 1845, Parker, *Sir Robert Peel*, vol. 3, pp. 404–7; C. I. Hamilton, *Anglo-French Naval Rivalry, 1840–1870* (1993), pp. 9–13; Chamberlain, *Aberdeen*, pp. 343–56.

25. Wellington to Peel, 22 September 1845, Parker, *Sir Robert Peel*, vol. 3, pp. 404–7.

26. Peel to Aberdeen, 12 August 1844, ibid., vol. 3, pp. 394–5; C. J. Bartlett, *Great Britain and Sea Power, 1815–1853* (1963), pp. 155–64; Chamberlain, *Aberdeen*, pp. 359–67; Gash, *Sir Robert Peel*, pp. 507–12.

27. Peel quoted in ibid., pp. 510–11; Aberdeen to Peel, 31 December 1844, Wellington to Peel, 27 December 1844, and 7 January 1845, in Parker, *Sir Robert Peel*, vol. 3, pp. 396, 198–200 and 397.

28. Bartlett, *Great Britain and Sea Power*, pp. 155–74; Hamilton, *Anglo-French Naval Rivalry*, p. 26; Michael S. Partridge, *Military Planning for the Defense of the United Kingdom, 1814–1870* (1989), p. 127; Wellington to Peel, 7 August 1845, Parker, *Sir Robert Peel*, vol. 3, pp. 202–6.

29. Wellington to Peel, 7 August, and reply, 9 August 1845; Peel to Graham, 13 August 1845, Parker, *Sir Robert Peel*, vol. 3, pp. 202–6, 207–16, 217–18.

30. Greville, *Memoirs*, 13 March 1842 and 1 August 1843, vol. 5, pp. 16, 121–2; Gash, *Sir Robert Peel*, pp. 386, 429, 453, 455 and 467.

31. Ibid., pp. 438–53, esp. 452–3.

32. Wellington to Lady Wilton, 29 March 1844, *W&HF*, pp. 195–6.

33. Peel to Wellington, 29 July 1844, Parker, *Sir Robert Peel*, vol. 3, p. 157; Davis, *Political History of the House of Lords*, pp. 291, 314. See also Richard W. Davis, 'Leaders in the Lords: Introduction' and 'Wellington' in *Parliamentary History*, vol. 22 (2003), pp. 1–12, 43–55, esp. 10–11, 44, 53–5.

34. Stanley to Peel, 27 July 1844; Wellington to Peel, 28 July 1844; Peel to Wellington, 29 July 1844; Peel to Stanley, 30 July 1844, Parker, *Sir Robert Peel*, vol. 3, pp. 154–9; Hawkins, *Forgotten Prime Minister*, vol. 1, pp. 287–91; Gash, *Sir Robert Peel*, pp. 453–4; Greville, *Memoirs*, 14 September 1844, vol. 5, p. 190.

35. Gash, *Sir Robert Peel*, pp. 414–17, 472–8; Davis, *Political History of the House of Lords*, pp. 315–20; Graham to Croker, 22 March 1845, Parker, *Sir Robert Peel*, vol. 3, p. 172. (Wellington's support for making the college efficient: Gash, *Sir Robert Peel*, p. 417; his remark about making them gentlemen: Davis, *Political History of the House of Lords*, p. 317.)

36. Quoted in Gash, *Sir Robert Peel*, p. 539; see pp. 531–44 for the blight and the government's response.

37. Ibid., pp. 538–45; Robert Stewart, *The Foundation of the Conservative Party, 1830–1867* (1978), pp. 206–12; *Punch* quoted in Foster, 'Mr Punch and the Iron Duke', pp. 38–9.

38. Gash, *Sir Robert Peel*, pp. 538–56, esp. 556 (quote from Peel), 547–8 (Goulburn's argument) and 547 (Wellington quote). See also Wellington to Peel, 17 October 1845, Parker, *Sir Robert Peel*, vol. 3, p. 225, and Wellington to Croker, 11 December 1845, *Croker Papers*, vol. 3, pp. 39–40. I. McLean, 'Wellington and the Corn Laws', 1845–6: A Study in Heresthetic' (1999), pp. 243–4, points out that Wellington's diagnosis of the problem was correct: there was no absolute shortage of food in Ireland, which continued to export grain throughout the famine; rather the problem was ensuring that the Irish poor had access to it. This was also the thinking behind Peel's schemes for public works and other attempts to create employment in the first instance, with direct aid used only when the problem had become acute.

39. Wellington to Croker, 26 December 1845, *Croker Papers*, vol. 3, pp. 43–4; Wellington to Lady Wilton, 7 January 1846, *W&HF*, pp. 201–3; Greville, *Memoirs*, 13 January 1846, vol. 5, pp. 282–3; Davis, *Political History of the House of Lords*, pp. 328–30.

40. Gash, *Sir Robert Peel*, pp. 567–91.

41. Wellington, Memorandum on the Conservative Leadership in the House of Commons, nd [7 July 1846], in Maxwell, *Life of Wellington*, vol. 2, pp. 355–6; McLean, 'Wellington and the Corn Laws', pp. 250–1, 255–6; Davis, *Political History of the House of Lords*, pp. 331–4; Hawkins, *Forgotten Prime Minister*, vol. 1, pp. 305–7.

42. Davis, *Political History of the House of Lords*, pp. 334–6.
43. Gash, *Sir Robert Peel*, pp. 603–7; Richard A. Gaunt, *Sir Robert Peel. The Life and Legacy* (2010), pp. 105–7 and 81–2; Robert Blake, *Disraeli* (1966), p. 243.
44. Davis, *Political History of the House of Lords*, p. 332 ('great and . . .').
45. Croker to Lockhart reporting a conversation with Wellington, 19 August 1846, *Croker Papers*, vol. 3, p. 76; see also Lady Westmorland to Lord Westmorland, 13 July 1846, Lady Westmorland, *The Correspondence of Priscilla, Countess of Westmorland*, ed. her daughter Lady Rose Weigall (1909) p. 85.

29 Commander-in-Chief

1. Queen Victoria to Wellington, 12 December 1845, *Letters of Queen Victoria*, vol. 2, pp. 55–7; Wellington to Peel, 2 July 1846 (describing his interview with Russell), and Peel to Arbuthnot, 4 July 1846 (recounting what he told the Queen), in Parker, *Sir Robert Peel*, vol. 3, pp. 454–7; Greville, *Memoirs*, 3 July 1846, vol. 5, p. 330.
2. Sir George Brown (Deputy Adjutant-General at the Horse Guards, 1828–50; Adjutant-General, 1850–53) quoted in Gleig, *Life of Wellington* (Everyman edn), pp. 337–8, 346–7.
3. On barracks Strachan, *Wellington's Legacy*, pp. 60–2; on new weapons Hew Strachan, *From Waterloo to Balaclava. Tactics, Technology, and the British Army, 1815–1854* (1985), pp. 31–42; Gleig, *Life of Wellington* (Everyman edn), pp. 339–40; Peel to Graham, 13 August 1845, Parker, *Sir Robert Peel*, vol. 3, pp. 217–18.
4. This whole paragraph closely based on Strachan, *Wellington's Legacy*, pp. 19–24.
5. Charles D. Yonge, *The Life of Field Marshal Arthur, Duke of Wellington* (1860) vol. 2, pp. 554–8; Queen Victoria to Wellington, 25 November and 1 December 1846; Wellington to the Queen, 27 November and 2 December 1846; the Queen to Lord John Russell, 14 December 1846, *Letters of Queen Victoria*, vol. 2, pp. 109–13; Greville, *Memoirs*, 12 December 1846, vol. 5, pp. 364–5.
6. Wellington to Lady Wilton [23 April 1840], *W&HF*, pp. 133–4; Hofschröer, *Wellington's Smallest Victory*, *passim* (pp. 193–4 for Siborne's conclusion that he had placed the Prussians too far forward); Foster, *Wellington and Waterloo*, pp. 141–7.
7. Greville, *Memoirs*, 13 July 1847, and 7 March 1848, vol. 5, p. 460, vol. 6, p. 34; Arbuthnot to his son Charles, 7 September 1846, *CCA*, p. 241.
8. Croker to Lockhart, 19 August 1846, *Croker Papers*, vol. 3, p. 76 (Wellington critical of Peel); Wellington to Stanley, 27 October 1847, quoted in Thompson, *Wellington After Waterloo*, pp. 231–2 (Wellington sympathetic); Stanley to Arbuthnot, 7 October 1847, *CCA*, pp. 244–6 (Stanley understands but still irritated by Wellington's support for government); Greville, *Memoirs*, 16 September 1846, pp. 347–8 (Russell's tact with Wellington); Robert Morton, 'A Melancholy Sight: Wellington and the Protectionists' (2013), pp. 291–4 (Wellington does not support the protectionists in Parliament); Strachan, *Wellington's Legacy*, p. 17 (Grey's arrogance); Wellington, *A Great Man's Friendship. Letters of the Duke of Wellington to Mary, Marchioness of Salisbury, 1850–52*, ed. Lady Burghclere (1927), p. 241 (Wellington's dislike of Palmerston's foreign policy); Partridge, *Military Planning*, p. 12 (Palmerston's connection with Anglesey and Burgoyne).
9. Strachan, *Wellington's Legacy*, pp. 70–4 (including the quote from Wellington); Wellington's Memoranda of 15 December 1846 and 22 January 1847, WP 2/190/49–52, 64–9; Jones, 'British Army in the Age of Reform', pp. 256–62; Partridge, *Military Planning*, pp. 74–6. Curiously both Strachan and Jones acknowledge the failure of short service but nonetheless criticise Wellington for opposing it.
10. Jones, 'British Army in the Age of Reform', pp. 277–80.
11. Memorandum by Wellington of 8 February 1847 quoted in Thompson, *Wellington After Waterloo*, p. 233; earlier correspondence summarised in Spencer Walpole, The Life of Lord John Russell (1891), vol. 2, pp. 14–16; Wellington to Burgoyne, 9 January 1847, in Wrottesley, *Life of Burgoyne*, vol. 1, pp. 444–51; an incomplete but still extensive version of this letter is also printed in Shelley, *Diary of Lady Shelley*, vol. 2, pp. 272–8.
12. Hobhouse's diary, 24 April and 19 October 1847, in Broughton, *Recollections of a Long Life*, vol. 6, pp. 189, 199–200; Wrottesley, *Life of Burgoyne*, vol. 1, pp. 433–4, Anglesey, *One Leg*, pp. 322–3, and Partridge, *Military Planning*, pp. 9–11.

13. Walpole, *Life of Lord John Russell*, vol. 2, pp. 16–17; Roger Bullen, *Palmerston, Guizot and the Collapse of the Entente Cordiale* (1974), pp. 201–2 and 202n.
14. *Morning Chronicle*, 4 January 1848; Wrottesley, *Life of Burgoyne*, vol. 1, pp. 444–51 and 469–81, and Shelley, *Diary of Lady Shelley*, vol. 2, pp. 272–89, print Wellington's letter and extensive correspondence and recriminations about how it came to be published. Wellington to Lord John Russell, 7 January 1848, in Walpole, *Life of Lord John Russell*, vol. 2, pp. 19–20. *The Times*, 25 December 1847; *Examiner*, 1 January 1848. For Cobden's speech see Wrottesley, *Life of Burgoyne*, vol. 1, pp. 476–7, and also Greville, *Memoirs*, 8 February 1848, vol. 6, p. 12.
15. Walpole, *Life of Lord John Russell*, vol. 2, pp. 25–6.
16. Stanhope, *Notes of Conversations*, pp. 325–9; Alan Palmer, *Metternich* (1972), pp. 315, 320, 322, 323.
17. Russell quoted in Michael S. Partridge, 'The Russell Cabinet and National Defence' (1987), p. 245; see also Greville, *Memoirs*, 19 January 1849, vol. 6, pp. 147–8, for the pressure the government was under from Cobden's call for drastic cuts in expenditure.
18. Palmer, *Police and Protest*, pp. 484–9.
19. Hobhouse's diary, 8 April 1848, Broughton, *Recollections of a Long Life*, vol. 6, p. 214.
20. Lord Campbell to Sir G. Campbell, 9 April 1848, quoted in Maxwell, *Life of Wellington*, vol. 2, pp. 368–9.
21. Grey quoted in Hobhouse's diary, 26 January 1849, Broughton, *Recollections of a Long Life*, vol. 6, pp. 231–2. For Wellington's political position and the difficulties it created for Stanley see Morton, 'A Melancholy Sight', pp. 292–4.
22. Wellington's speech in Parliament, 4 July 1850, Wellington, *Speeches*, vol. 2, pp. 720–1; for evidence of the effect of Wellington's tribute, see Greville, *Memoirs*, 6 July 1850, vol. 6, pp. 234–5; see also Hobhouse's diary, 3 July 1850, Broughton, *Recollections of a Long Life*, vol. 6, pp. 259–60.
23. Memorandum by Prince Albert, 23 February 1851, *Letters of Queen Victoria*, vol. 2, pp. 293–6; Naotaka Kimizuka, 'Elder Statesmen and British Party Politics: Wellington, Lansdowne and the Ministerial Crises of the 1850s' (1998), pp. 359–63 (including quotes from *The Times* and *Punch*); Greville, *Memoirs*, 25 February to 4 March 1851, vol. 6, pp. 273–9; Hawkins, *Forgotten Prime Minister*, vol. 1, pp. 400–6; Thompson, *Wellington After Waterloo*, pp. 255–6.
24. The modern historian quoted is Hamilton, *Anglo-French Naval Rivalry*, p. 53; Russell quoted in Bartlett, *Great Britain and Sea Power*, p. 272; Palmerston quoted in Partridge, 'The Russell Cabinet and National Defence', pp. 246–7.
25. Partridge, *Military Planning*, pp. 132–4; Strachan, *Wellington's Legacy*, pp. 205–7.
26. Details of Derby's militia bill from Partridge, *Military Planning*, pp. 133–4, and Strachan, *Wellington's Legacy*, pp. 209–10 (figures for its success). The first reference in print to the 'Who? Who? government' appears to be in Justin McCarthy's immensely popular but by no means impartial or reliable *History of Our Own Times* which was first published 1879: passage in vol. 2, p. 122, of the 1897 Boston edition.
27. Wellington, *Speeches*, 15 June 1852, vol. 2, pp. 733–6.

30 In the Midst of Life

1. Greville, *Memoirs*, 23 June 1841 and 5 June 1842, vol. 4, p. 387 and vol. 5, p. 25; Ellesmere, *Personal Reminiscences*, 11 June 1844, p. 177.
2. Stanhope, *Notes of Conversations*, 29 October–4 November 1839, p. 194; Wellington to Lady Salisbury, 18 October 1850, Wellington, *Great Man's Friendship*, p. 137; Wellington to Angela Burdett-Coutts, 2 October 1847, *W&HF*, p. 251.
3. Wellington to Lady Salisbury, 10 January 1851, Wellington, *Great Man's Friendship*, p. 173; see also pp. 162, 167 and 168.
4. Wellington to Lady Salisbury, 29 August 1852, ibid., pp. 314–15.
5. Greville, *Memoirs*, 25 August 1850, vol. 6, pp. 254–5; Ellesmere, *Personal Reminiscences*, p. 91; Wellesley, *Wellington in Civil Life*, pp. 355–7.
6. Healey, *Lady Unknown*, pp. 83–8; extracts from some of the 842 letters Wellington wrote to Angela Burdett-Coutts are printed in *W&HF*, pp. 235–90 (quotes from those of 1 and 5 January 1847, pp. 238–40), and also (though less accurately transcribed) in Clara Burdett

Patterson, *Angela Burdett-Coutts and the Victorians* (1953), pp. 65–127; but the full warmth of the relationship only emerges from Healey's biography.

7. Wellington to Angela Burdett-Coutts, 8 February 1847, *W&HF*, pp. 242–3.

8. Greville, *Memoirs*, 13 July 1847, vol. 5, pp. 460–1; Wellington quoted in Healey, *Lady Unknown*, pp. 95–6.

9. Healey, *Lady Unknown*, quotes on pp. 97, 101 and 109, and discussion of the nature of the relationship on pp. 109–10.

10. Wellington, *A Great Man's Friendship, passim*, quotes pp. 4 and 129–30.

11. Effie Ruskin to her mother quoted in Euphemia Ruskin, *Effie in Venice. Unpublished Letters of Mrs John Ruskin written from Venice between 1849–1852*, ed. Mary Lutyens (1965), p. 164n, also pp. 169–75 for her social life in London.

12. Wellington's letters to Mrs Jones were first published as 'Selections from Wellington's Letters' by her daughter Mary Davies-Evans in *The Century Magazine*, vol. 30, no. 2 (December 1889), pp. 163–83 and reprinted as *My Dear Mrs Jones* in a slim volume by the Rodale Press in 1954.

13. Greville, *Memoirs*, 25 July 1851, vol. 6, pp. 297–8; Wellington to the Countess Dowager of Westmorland, 22 October 1851, described and quoted in Sotheby's catalogue of the Contents of Fulbeck Hall, Lincolnshire, auctioned on 8 October 2002, p. 187.

14. Ellesmere, *Personal Reminiscences*, pp. 56–7; *The Times*, 11 October 1858; Wellesley, *Wellington, A Journey Through My Family*, pp. xii–xiii; Lady Westmorland to Lord Westmorland, 9 July 1846, Burghersh, *Correspondence*, pp. 175–6.

15. Benjamin Robert Haydon, *The Autobiography and Journals of Benjamin Robert Haydon*, ed. Malcolm Elwin (1950), p. 569; the same passage is in Haydon, *Diary*, vol. 4, p. 587.

16. Wellington to Mrs Jones, 6 October 1851, Weillington, 'Selections from Wellington's Letters', p. 172, *My Dear Mrs Jones*, pp. 8–9; Weigall, *Lady Rose Weigall*, pp. 4–5; Memorandum on the Duke of Wellington by Lady Westmorland, Burghersh, *Correspondence*, p. 211.

17. See Richard A. Gaunt, 'Wellington, Peel and the Conservative Party' (2013), pp. 266–8, for a perceptive and interesting discussion of Winterhalter's painting, including the quote from the *Daily News*.

18. Thompson, *Wellington After Waterloo*, p. 252.

19. *Hampshire Advertiser and Salisbury Guardian*, 19 April 1852; a number of other newspapers of around the same date published the column, and it is not clear in which it first appeared although several papers credit it to the *Bristol Times*, a paper which is not included in the Nineteenth-Century British Newspapers database; Wemyss Reid, *Memoirs and Correspondence of Lyon Playfair* (1900), pp. 119–20.

20. Wellington to Lady Salisbury, 15 May 1851, Wellington, *Great Man's Friendship*, p. 187, also p. 190 where he refers to his 'daily visit to the Glass Palace', and many other references in his letters in these months.

21. Wellington to Lady Salisbury, 20, 22 and 26 December 1851; 9, 10 and 14 January 1852; 1–6 July 1852, Wellington, *Great Man's Friendship*, pp. 233–6, 243–8, 274–8; Wellington to Angela Burdett-Coutts, 30 December 1851, 7 January 1852, *W&HF*, pp. 286–7; Sweetman, *Raglan*, p. 150 (Waterloo banquet); *The Times*, 2 July 1852.

22. Wellington's letters to Lady Salisbury, 25 and 28 August 1852, Wellington, *A Great Man's Friendship*, pp. 310–13; Croker's memorandum, 4 September 1852, *Croker Papers*, vol. 3, pp. 272–80.

23. Kendall to Georgiana, Lady de Ros, 14 September 1852, Swinton, *Sketch of the Life of Lady de Ros*, p. 47; Longford, *Wellington. Pillar of State*, pp. 398–400. Different sources, all written at the time, differ over small details, for example the time the Duke went to bed the previous night. Nor does any source appear to give an authoritative statement as to the cause of death, although the words most commonly used to describe the fatal attacks were 'fits' or 'seizures'.

24. Lady Westmorland to Lord Westmorland, [14 September 1852], Burghersh, *Correspondence*, pp. 202–4.

25. Queen Victoria to the King of the Belgians, 17 September 1852, *Letters of Queen Victoria*, vol. 2, pp. 394–5.

26. Brougham to Lady Westmorland, 15 September 1852, Burghersh, *Correspondence*, p. 209; Lady Georgiana Bathurst to Lady de Ros, 15 September 1852, in Swinton, *Sketch of Lady de Ros*, p. 48; Thomas Cooper quoted in Foster, *Wellington and Waterloo*, p. 165.

27. Prince Albert and *Punch* quoted in Michael Greenhalgh, 'The Funeral of the Duke of Wellington' (1973), pp. 220 and 225; Queen Victoria quoted in Foster, *Wellington and Waterloo*, p. 165; John Wolffe, *Great Deaths, Grieving, Religion and Nationhood in Victorian and Edwardian Britain* (2000), pp. 38–9; see also R.E. Foster, 'Bury the Great Duke: Thoughts on Wellington's Passing' (2013), pp. 307–8.

28. Gerald, 7th Duke of Wellington, 'The Great Duke's Funeral' (1952), p. 778; *The Times*, 11 November 1852; *Annual Register 1852*, Chronicle, pp. 188–90; Foster, 'Bury the Great Duke', pp. 308–9.

29. Foster, 'Bury the Great Duke', pp. 308–9; John Morley, *Death, Heaven and the Victorians* (1971), pp. 81–3; 2nd Duke of Wellington to Angela Burdett-Coutts, 13 and 15 November 1852, quoted in Wellington, 'The Great Duke's Funeral', p. 784.

30. Morley, *Death, Heaven and the Victorians*, pp. 87–8.

31. Ibid., p. 85.

32. Wolffe, *Great Deaths*, pp. 45–6; *The Times*, 19 November 1852; *Leicester Chronicle*, 30 October 1852 (details of the train from Aberdeen); Lord Dalhousie to Queen Victoria, 23 November 1852, *Letters of Queen Victoria*, vol. 2, pp. 400–1.

33. *The Times*, 19 November 1852; *The Order of Proceeding of the Public Funeral of . . . Wellington*, *passim*; Foster, 'Bury the Great Duke', p. 311 (quoting Queen Victoria).

34. *The Times*, 19 November 1852; *Annual Register 1852*, Chronicle, pp. 192–4, 494–6; Morley, *Death, Heaven and the Victorians*, p. 87; Foster, 'Bury the Great Duke', pp. 311–12.

Conclusion

1. Queen Victoria, quoted in Neville Thompson, 'Immortal Wellington: Literary Tributes to the Hero' (1999), p. 258.

2. Shelley, *Diary of Lady Shelley*, vol. 1, p. 102.

3. Wellington to Lt.-Gen. A. Campbell, 18 June 1812, *WD*, vol. 5, p. 712; Wellington to William Wellesley-Pole, Wellington, 'Some Letters of the Duke of Wellington to his brother William Wellesley-Pole', ed. Professor Sir Charles Webster (1948), p. 29.

4. Davis, *Political History of the House of Lords*, pp. 10–11.

5. Richard Gaunt, 'Wellington, Peel and the Conservative Party', p. 278, quotes Norman Gash's judgement that Wellington was the 'least political' of party leaders in order to dispute it and argue that he was rather 'one of the most political'.

6. Quoted in Foster, 'Bury the Great Duke', p. 305.

7. Sir William Fraser, *Words on Wellington, The Duke – Waterloo – the Ball* (1889), p. 94; Gaunt, *Sir Robert Peel*, pp. 154–5; Gaunt, 'Wellington, Peel and the Conservative Party', pp. 278–81.

8. Greville, *Memoirs*, 18 September 1852, vol. 6, p. 360; *Dictionary of National Biography*, 1922 edition, vol. 20, p. 1114.

BIBLIOGRAPHY

The essential source for Wellington's later life remains his correspondence and papers. For the period up to the end of the occupation of France in 1818 this continues to be covered by the published *Dispatches* (*WD*) and *Supplementary Despatches* (*WSD*) as well as the original manuscripts at the University of Southampton. From the beginning of 1819 to the end of 1832 the published series continues with eight volumes edited by the second Duke in a format very similar to the *Supplementary Despatches*, which have long been informally known as *Wellington New Despatches* (*WND*). The weighting of these volumes is to the later part of the period, so that the first two volumes cover seven years (1819–25 inclusive), the same period covered by the last six. These years are also exceptionally well covered by the extremely detailed, searchable calendar of the correspondence at the University of Southampton, which provides a comprehensive description of every letter, and frequently includes a full transcription of its contents. The years between the beginning of 1833 and the end of April 1835 (the fall of Peel's short-lived first administration) are covered by two volumes of Wellington's political correspondence prepared and published by the Historical Manuscripts Commission (*HMC Wellington*). But from 1835 until Wellington's death in 1852 there is no series of his published correspondence to assist the biographer, who must rely on the manuscripts in Southampton, and letters published in other collections and biographies such as Parker's three-volume biography of Sir Robert Peel. The unpublished material for these years is very extensive, and fortunately there is a preliminary listing of individual letters (not, alas, as yet available online), which saves a great deal of time in identifying letters of particular interest. Wellington's speeches (collected in two volumes by Gurwood) can be useful, although his correspondence is both much more extensive and, generally, much more revealing.

Far less of Wellington's private correspondence has been published, but the selection of letters produced by the seventh Duke, *Wellington and His Friends* (*W&HF*), is immensely useful for both his private life and his views on politics, from 1819 onwards. Less generally useful, but with some fascinating letters, is the *Selection from the Private Correspondence* published by the Roxburghe Club in 1952. These can be supplemented by Wellington's correspondence with his niece Lady Burghersh, and by a number of letters appearing in Lady Shelley's diary, the correspondence of Charles Arbuthnot, the *Croker Papers*, and the biographies of Angela Burdett-Coutts by Patterson and Healey. Wellington's letters to the second Lady Salisbury (*A Great Man's Friendship*) are disappointing and lack much political content; while his letters to 'Miss J.' (Anna Maria Jenkins) do not deserve the attention they have received, being largely inconsequential. A very slim volume of letters to Mrs Jones of Pantglas, written in the last year of his life, adds a little to the record of his social life, but is most interesting for what is left unsaid.

The best insight into Wellington's character and opinions in the 1820s and early 1830s comes from the *Journal of Mrs Arbuthnot* (*JMrsA*). Mrs Arbuthnot was a close friend and confidante whom Wellington thoroughly trusted, but she was also a highly intelligent woman and skilled observer who was by no means uncritical in her devotion to Wellington, and the picture she paints of him is the more interesting and attractive for its honesty and occasional sharpness. She had her own biases, and was as full of admiration for Castlereagh as she was critical of Canning, and while her attitude to Peel is more complex, she was seldom able to do him justice. The picture presented in the *Journal* is supplemented and confirmed by the extracts from Wellington's letters to her published in *Wellington and His Friends*, while there is also much good material in the *Correspondence of Charles Arbuthnot* and in the unpublished Arbuthnot papers at the University of Aberdeen. E.A. Smith's study *Wellington and the Arbuthnots* fills in the background, and his considered comments on the nature of the relationship between both the Arbuthnots and Wellington are particularly valuable.

Many of Wellington's other female friends left rewarding accounts of him in these post-war years. The *Diary of Frances, Lady Shelley* is particularly good for the early years from 1814 to the early 1820s, while Jehanne Wake's excellent group biography of the Caton sisters sheds a great deal of light on Wellington's relationship with Marianne Patterson. Princess Lieven's private letters to Metternich are a very rich source for the period between 1820 and 1826, full of politics and foreign policy, but also showing Wellington relishing the absurdities of the court and society. For a few years in the mid-1830s (largely 1834–38) the diary of the first Lady Salisbury (strictly the first wife of the 2nd Marquess and 22nd Earl of Salisbury) goes some way to filling the gap left by Mrs Arbuthnot's death. Edited by Carola Oman and published as *The Gascoyne Heiress*, this is an extremely useful source for both Wellington's public and private life during this period. After Lady Salisbury's death Wellington wrote frequently to Lady Wilton and, later, to Angela Burdett-Coutts, mixing politics with other news, although neither woman was as engaged with the political world as his earlier confidantes. A selection of these letters is published in *Wellington and His Friends*. There are also good glimpses of Wellington in the letters of Harriet, Countess Granville, her aunt Lady Bessborough, and Lady Palmerston, and in the *Sketch of the Life of Georgiana, Lady de Ros* by her daughter, Mrs J.R. Swinton.

The *Creevey Papers* contains a great deal of vivid and entertaining material that sheds light on the politics of the period from the perspective of a radical Whig who nonetheless was strongly disposed to like and admire Wellington. And there is even more useful material, although it is generally less entertaining, in the *Croker Papers*. The *Diary of Philipp von Neumann* adds a foreign point of view (he was an Austrian diplomat who mixed in London society); while Wellington makes occasional, revealing appearances in the journals of the artist Benjamin Robert Haydon and Thomas Raikes. However, the most important source of this kind is the diary kept by Charles Greville, which becomes particularly useful in the 1830s and 1840s. Greville's attitude to Wellington was complicated, and he needs to be treated quite warily when writing directly about the Duke. He was never an intimate friend or close associate and he appears to have resented the fact that his mother had probably been Wellington's mistress in the years after Waterloo. Nonetheless he was fascinated with politics and extremely well connected with both Whigs and conservatives, and his journal adds flesh, colour and detail to the records of these years. The best edition is that revised and edited from the manuscripts by Lytton Strachey and Roger Fulford, published in a limited edition in eight volumes in 1938 as *The Greville Memoirs*, as this includes a number of passages previously suppressed.

Stanhope's *Notes of Conversations with the Duke of Wellington* and Ellesmere's *Personal Reminiscences of the Duke of Wellington* have been heavily used by biographers since their first appearance (in 1888 and 1903 respectively). They are most useful on particular points (for example Stanhope on Wellington's illness in 1839) but as a record of Wellington's opinions, let alone as a source for his actions in the past, they need to be treated with considerable care. Gleig's *Personal Reminiscences* is a late work with some very strange quirks, and needs to be approached with caution. The *Table-talk of Samuel Rogers* is another tempting but unreliable source; as gossip recorded at the time it has some value, but no one is on oath when the company is relaxed and the wine is flowing freely.

Mention should be made here of Sir William Fraser's *Words on Wellington* (1889) and G.W.E. Russell's *Collections and Recollections* (1898). Both these works, as sources for information about Wellington (as opposed to later attitudes to him), are utterly unreliable and have had a pernicious influence in spreading inaccurate or unconfirmed anecdotes about him and remarks attributed to him. As the old quip goes, they contain material both original and accurate, but what is original is not accurate, and what is accurate is not original! If a story or saying cannot be traced back further than either of these books it should be discarded as a red herring, and any historian who cites them for a matter of fact loses credibility in the process. Yet so significant has been their influence that there are numerous details and stories about Wellington's life which have been repeated from one biography to another, and which continue to be widely accepted, that have their origin in these books, and I cannot be sure that I have identified and excluded all these base coins even from my own account.

There have been many biographies of Wellington, and some of the earliest are discussed in Chapter 25 above. From the point of view of a modern biographer the most useful and significant include Brialmont and Gleig's four volumes and Gleig's one-volume abridged edition which contains some original material not found anywhere else: for example a fascinating first-hand account by Sir George Brown of Wellington's working methods at the Horse Guards in the 1840s. Sir Herbert Maxwell's biography includes some otherwise unpublished material from the Salisbury papers, while the lives by Philip Guedalla, Muriel Wellesley (for some good material from family papers), Christopher Hibbert and Jane Wellesley (also for good family material including on the later generations) all have value for Wellington's life after Waterloo, as does Eliza Pakenham's account of Kitty's family. John Severn's *Architects of Empire* is excellent for Wellington's relations with his brothers, particularly Lord Wellesley, while Andrew Roberts' study of Wellington and Napoleon is particularly useful for Wellington's attitude to the French Emperor. Elizabeth Longford's two-volume biography remains significant and has often proved useful for Wellington's private life or for tracking down an elusive quotation or anecdote. Sitting next to these works Neville Thompson's *Wellington After Waterloo* appears to be placed on the wrong shelf, for it seriously engages with Wellington's political career, and was one of the first works in the 1980s to begin the revival of interest in his place in the politics of the age of reform. While I frequently disagree with Thompson's interpretation of events, I have found his work immensely stimulating and helpful, and I would have found it much harder to come to my own view of Wellington's later life if I had not been able to use his book as a foundation. Norman Gash's entry on Wellington in the *Oxford Dictionary of National Biography* also deserves mention for its coverage of Wellington's political career.

Looking through the second half of Wellington's life chronologically, it is remarkable that there is no modern, scholarly, balanced account of the Hundred Days of 1815. By default the best secondary source is probably still Henry Houssaye's *1815, Waterloo*, published over a hundred years ago. This can be supplemented by W.H. James's *Campaign of 1815* and the relevant chapters of volume ten of Fortescue's *History of the British Army*, although both these accounts (written just before and during the First World War) show a marked bias against the Prussians which needs to be taken into account. Scott Bowden's *Armies at Waterloo* provides a very thorough listing of the forces engaged and contributes to the discussion of their strength, while Oman's article on 'French Losses in the Waterloo Campaign' remains relevant. Mike Robinson's *The Battle of Quatre Bras* gives a highly detailed picture of events from a wide range of allied sources, with very little in the way of analysis and no attempt to cover the French perspective; while Erwin Muilwijk's three volumes on the contribution of the Dutch-Belgian army to the campaign contain fascinating and very useful material that helps to correct the bias in most British sources. Yet for many details of the campaign and the battle of Waterloo itself we must still go back to Siborne's massive, unwieldy and often flawed history, first published less than thirty years after the battle.

The campaign of 1815 has always been controversial, with competing attempts to explain the French defeat and apportion blame to Napoleon, Grouchy or Ney; give credit to Wellington, the British troops and the other allied troops in his army; and assess the weight of the Prussian contribution to the victory. This last controversy was revived in the 1990s by two substantial books and numerous articles by Peter Hofschröer, whose work was highly critical of Wellington and who argued that the Prussians had never received the recognition they deserved. Unfortunately the debate this triggered soon became heated and in the process the real contribution made both by Hofschröer and his critics (notably John Hussey, but including many others) tended to be obscured. Now that the dust appears to have settled (although this may be tempting fate), it can be seen that many of Hofschröer's specific allegations have failed to win general acceptance, but that some of his criticisms of Wellington are, at least partly, justified, and that there is, or should be, a better general recognition of the Prussian contribution to the allied victory. A good summary of some of the controversial points is given in Greg Pedlow's article 'Wellington versus Clausewitz'.

Many new accounts of the Waterloo campaign will certainly be published as we approach the bicentenary. Writing this in October 2014 I have seen only Gareth Glover's *Waterloo. Myth and Reality*, a fairly conventional study which includes some interesting discussion of controversial points (not just those related to the Prussians), but which is marred by its lack of scholarly apparatus. Glover's most useful work has been in the publication of a large number of hitherto forgotten or unpublished accounts of the battle including a series of volumes entitled *The Waterloo*

Archive. However, these voices mostly come from Wellington's army, and we badly need more French and Prussian accounts to balance the very heavy preponderance of British and allied sources.

Wellington's role in command of the allied Army of Occupation of France is discussed in Veve's monograph, although this needs to be supplemented with broader accounts of French and British domestic politics and the international relations of these years. Philip Mansel's stylish biography of Louis XVIII and study of Paris between Empires are very helpful here, in addition to Sauvigny's *Bourbon Restoration*.

Sir Charles Webster's study of Castlereagh's foreign policy has aged well and remains the essential secondary source for the negotiations around the Second Peace of Paris, and for Britain's part in the diplomacy of the next seven years. The best and most recent of the biographies of Castlereagh is by John Bew, which adds many points of interest, although our interpretations of Castlereagh's policy in the final years of his life differ considerably. Harold Temperley's *Foreign Policy of Canning* is much too substantial a work to be ignored, but it is deeply flawed, partisan in its arguments and untrustworthy in its use of evidence. More recent secondary accounts clearly establish the need for a radical revision of Temperley's conclusions; see especially articles by Cowles, Cunningham and Schwartzberg, and D.C.H. Smith's thesis on Portugal. Chamberlain's biography of Aberdeen is also a useful corrective, although its main value is for British foreign policy in Wellington's government and later. Paul Schroeder's magisterial overview *The Transformation of European Politics* is a work of great learning and sophistication, which puts British policy into a broader perspective and which is thought-provoking and challenging as well as, largely, convincing. A glaring gap in the literature is any detailed study of the interaction between foreign affairs and British public opinion in the years between 1814 and 1830. A hint of how fruitful this approach might be can be gained from a couple of chapters of L.G. Mitchell's *Holland House*, and an excellent article by Roger Bullen, but they only whet the appetite.

John Cookson's study of Lord Liverpool's government between 1815 and 1822 probably came out a decade too soon to receive the recognition that it deserved, but it is thorough, perceptive and immensely useful. Norman Gash's biography of Liverpool is naturally much less detailed, but provides an excellent and much-needed overview of the most neglected politician of the nineteenth century. Boyd Hilton's article on Liverpool's 'Political Arts' contests some of Gash's interpretation and enriches the picture. Hilton's monograph *Corn, Cash, Commerce* details the economic policies of Liverpool's government – a subject which did not greatly interest Wellington, or most of his Cabinet colleagues, at least until the financial crash of 1826. Aspinall's articles on Canning and his followers are full of wonderful material; while the attractive, beguiling side of Canning's character emerges clearly from Wendy Hinde's enjoyable biography. Aspinall also edited the slim but useful diary of Henry Hobhouse, the Under-Secretary at the Home Office, which sheds much light on Cabinet politics between 1820 and 1827 (especially the first half of the period). The Opposition's role in politics between Waterloo and the fall of Wellington's government is admirably detailed in Austin Mitchell's informative monograph; which can usefully be supplemented by Chester New's biography of Brougham to 1830, and William Hay's work on the revival of the Whigs. The repeal of the Test and Corporation Acts is discussed in excellent articles by G.I.T. Machin and Richard Gaunt; while Machin and Richard Davis have covered many aspects of Catholic Emancipation in numerous articles and Machin's monograph, and Wellington's evolving attitude to the question is charted in Karen Piggott's thesis.

The nature, workings and activities of government in this period are explored in two original and important books by Peter Jupp, one concentrating on Wellington's government (although I do not find Jupp's interpretation of Wellington's role and personality particularly convincing). Other sources of particular relevance to the three years when Wellington was prime minister include Ellenborough's Cabinet diary, and, for the early months, the letters of Palmerston and J.W. Ward. Norman Gash's wonderful biography of Peel now comes into its own, as one of the most relevant and important secondary studies for Wellington's political career, and remains so for the rest of Peel's life. Relations between Wellington and Peel were never entirely comfortable, and their approach and perspectives differed greatly, while their personalities were not particularly compatible. Nonetheless Gash is far too good a historian simply to use Wellington as Peel's foil, and provides the most detailed and useful account of Conservative politics from the early 1820s to the mid-1840s. His biography is also a pleasure to read. Richard Gaunt's study of Peel's life and legacy is an intelligent and stimulating discussion of Peel's career and reputation that has influenced my thinking in many ways, both direct and indirect; while Douglas Hurd has contributed a popular modern biography which does not aspire to replace Gash's work.

Boyd Hilton's *A Mad, Bad and Dangerous People?* is the best and most detailed general history of Britain in the period; while Frank O'Gorman's *Emergence of the British Two-Party System* and Michael Bentley's *Politics without Democracy* give lively overviews of politics over a longer perspective. J.C.D. Clark's *English Society, 1688–1832* sparked a debate which still resonates and which has had the beneficial effect of forcing subsequent historians to consider assumptions that had previously been taken much too easily for granted.

The successive waves of popular radicalism that played such an important part in British politics from the Convention of Cintra to the early 1830s have received a good deal of scholarly attention. Their origins are investigated in Peter Spence's intriguing study; while John Stevenson gives a most useful overview. Donald Read's account of Peterloo is probably still the best account of that notorious incident; while David Johnson gives a popular account of the Cato Street Conspiracy. George Spater's biography of Cobbett is invaluable, while Iorwerth Prothero's life of John Gast proved unexpectedly useful and interesting. Stanley Palmer's study of the reaction of the authorities to political protests is hugely impressive, while K.O. Fox's monograph adds some interesting perspectives and F.C. Mather's study of *Public Order in the Age of the Chartists* is helpful for the later period. Edgell Rickword's reprint of Hone's *Political House that Jack Built* and other pamphlets of the day is both convenient and illuminating; while Jonathan Fulcher gives a fascinating account of loyalist responses to the ideological attack mounted by the radicals. The caricatures which give us such a colourful, full-blooded and irreverent view of the politics of the period are meticulously catalogued by Dorothy George in the *British Museum Catalogue of Personal and Political Satires* (volumes 9–11 cover the period from 1811 to 1832), while her *English Political Caricature* provides an excellent overview. The *Catalogue* in particular contains an enormous amount of detailed information about day-to-day politics of these years, illuminating many issues that would otherwise remain obscure, and George writes with immense learning and understanding of the period. Edward Du Cann's handsome volume reproduces many of these prints in colour, while most can also be found on the British Museum's website along with some further acquisitions.

The ultra-Tories who caused so many problems for Wellington, in government and in opposition, have attracted a good deal of study in the last twenty years or so, having previously been dismissed with scorn (except for the articles by B.T. Bradfield, published in the 1960s). Richard Gaunt's meticulous edition of the Duke of Newcastle's diary, *Unrepentant Tory*, reveals just how impractical and eccentric were some of the ultra Tories. There is also a good deal of primary material in the diary of Charles Abbot, Lord Colchester. Articles by Richard Davis, Richard Gaunt, Alan Heesom, Edwin Jaggard and Douglas Simes, and entries in the *History of Parliament, 1820–32* (edited by D.R. Fisher) help to fill out the picture. (While the *History of Parliament* is a wonderful resource, its use to Wellington's biographer will be enormously enhanced when its coverage is extended to include the House of Lords, and perhaps even the Crown; for at least until the twentieth century there has always been much more to Parliament than the Commons.)

Wellington's years as Master-General of the Ordnance have never received much attention. The most useful secondary source is the article by George Raudzens, which can be supplemented by an article by Peter Burroughs and Hime's *History of the Royal Regiment of Artillery 1815–53*. But the real meat lies in the primary sources: Wellington's correspondence (the Southampton calendar is particularly useful here), the memoir of Robert Plumer Ward by Phipps (which prints long extracts of Ward's diary), Clode's *Military Forces of the Crown*, the *Parliamentary Debates*, and the report of the Finance Committee.

Michael Brock's *The Great Reform Act* gives an excellent account of the politics of Wellington's first years in opposition, which can be supplemented by John Cannon's *Parliamentary Reform*. Ian Newbould's *Whiggery and Reform* is a most useful study of the Whig government, while the biographies of Grey by E.A. Smith and Melbourne by both Ziegler and Leslie Mitchell are revealing. The diaries of Ellenborough, Littleton and Le Marchant for the period of Lord Grey's government, edited by Aspinall and published as *Three Early Nineteenth Century Diaries* is a useful addition to other primary sources already discussed above. Our understanding of the conservative perspective and of the vital role of the House of Lords in these years has been transformed by the work of Richard Davis, in both his articles and his *Political History of the House of Lords*, which should bury forever the idea of Wellington as a simple soldier out of his depth in politics. Richard Gaunt's article on 'Wellington, Peel and the Conservative Party' adds to this picture; while the wider context continues to be provided by Gash's life of Peel and by studies such as Robert Stewart's *Foundation of the Conservative Party*.

The history of the British army between Waterloo and the Crimea has not attracted a great deal of scholarly attention. Fortescue's work remains essential for the colonial campaigns of the period; but is less reliable for the political battles over the army that played an important part in Wellington's life in the 1830s and 1840s. Two modern studies cover these in some detail: Philip Jones's unpublished thesis, and Hew Strachan's *Wellington's Legacy*. Unfortunately both works are beguiled by the idea of 'reform' and tend to assume that any change advanced by 'reformers' must have been beneficial, even when they present ample reason to doubt this assumption. Strangely, Strachan appears unaware of Jones's thesis (submitted sixteen years earlier), or even of his article in *Albion* published twelve years before his own book; while he is overly influenced by the hostile depiction of Wellington in the military press in the 1840s. Nonetheless there is much good material in both works. The emotive subject of flogging in the army, and the radical campaign against it, is admirably covered by an article by J.R. Dinwiddy; while Wellington's own views on the army are best taken from his considered evidence to official enquiries and the memoranda he drew up, rather than casual remarks over dinner recorded by Stanhope and other gossips.

The excellent modern biographies of Palmerston by Kenneth Bourne and David Brown explain the context of Wellington's growing alarm over the foreign policy pursued by Melbourne's government between 1839 and 1841, and the consequent risk of war with France. Aberdeen worked hard to repair the damage (see Chamberlain's biography), but Wellington was unconvinced of the depth of the rapprochement and his fears of war and invasion were far from being an old man's folly. Michael Partridge's monograph on military planning, and the accounts of naval policy by Bartlett and Hamilton, add greatly to the evidence in political biographies such as Gash's life of Peel. Wellington's role in the politics of Peel's government continues to be discussed in works mentioned above ranging from Neville Thompson's *Wellington After Waterloo* to Davis's *Political History of the House of Lords*. The fine scholarly biography of Stanley by Angus Hawkins is most relevant to Wellington in the 1840s, in its discussion of Peel's government and the crisis over the Corn Laws. Dorothy George's account of the caricatures stops at 1832, but Richard Gaunt has provided an admirable supplement with his selection of John Doyle's works relating to Peel, in which Wellington also figures prominently. A few of these images are famous, but many more had been largely forgotten and it is a pleasure to be able to see them, handsomely reproduced and with a reliable and informative text.

There is abundant evidence for the way Wellington's reputation changed over the years, but the only work which has seriously examined this directly is Russ Foster's admirable study *Wellington and Waterloo: the Duke, the Battle and Posterity*. Christopher Woolgar has explained the story behind the publication of Wellington's *Dispatches* and Wellington's relations with their editor, Colonel Gurwood; and Peter Jupp's article on 'Pictorial Images of the Duke of Wellington' opened several new lines of enquiry and remains full of interest. The old *Wellington Iconography* has now been superseded by *Wellington Portrayed* – a marvellous collection of portraits and statues of Wellington, beautifully reproduced, which shows the many forms of the public face that he presented to the world. The story behind the Edinburgh and Glasgow statues of Wellington is described in an excellent article by John Cookson which shows the political overtones to any celebration of Wellington's reputation even in the last decade of his life.

Wellington's funeral has been described and discussed from a range of perspectives in a number of complementary articles and books, notably those by Foster, Wolffe, Morley, Wellington, Thompson and Greenhalgh; while Peter Sinnema's discussion of Wellington's reputation at the time of his death contains interesting information struggling to emerge from a surfeit of academic jargon.

Despite his pungent turn of phrase and many quotable remarks, Wellington was no great stylist; his letters are read for the interest of their content rather than for simple pleasure. But much that has been written about him is immensely enjoyable to read, including many of the primary sources. The journals of Mrs Arbuthnot, Lady Salisbury and Charles Greville; the letters of Lady Bessborough and Princess Lieven; and the accounts of soldiers such as Francis Larpent, George Bell and Sergeant William Lawrence, are as vivid and entertaining as any novel; and like a nineteenth-century novel they broaden our understanding and sympathy of people belonging to a different time and place, with different outlooks and values. And that, surely, is the best of all the reasons why we study the past.

MANUSCRIPTS

University of Southampton

Ms 61 Wellington Papers: WP 1/408–1244 Wellington's correspondence, April 1814–December 1832; WP 2 Wellington's correspondence, 1833–52
A detailed calendar of Wellington's correspondence from 1819–32 (including a partial or complete transcription of most letters) is freely available through the University of Southampton website
Ms 63 Carver Papers: Papers of Marquess Wellesley and his son Richard Wellesley II
Ms 69 Collins Papers: Papers of Wellington's servant Christopher Collins
Ms 272 Minor collections including a small group of letters from Wellington to William Holmes, 1832–38
Ms 308 Malcolm Papers: Correspondence between Sir John Malcolm and Wellington, including some after Wellington left India

British Library

Bathurst Papers: Loan Ms 57 vol. 9
Broughton Papers (Supplementary): Add Ms 56,552
Bunbury Papers: Add Ms 37,052 (including letters from Colborne to Bunbury, 1815)
Gurwood Papers: Add Ms 38,522
Liverpool Papers: Add Ms 38,196
Pasley Papers: Add Ms 41,977
Peel Papers: Add Ms 40,340 Correspondence with Charles Arbuthnot, 1822–34
Wellesley Papers: Add Ms 37,297

The National Archives (formerly The Public Record Office), Kew

Foreign Office Papers: FO27/113 France 1815, Fitzroy Somerset; FO 37/76–78 Holland, Charles Stuart and Lord Clancarty, 1815; FO 92/13 To Wellington, 1815; FO 92/14 From Wellington, Feb–May 1815
War Office Papers: WO 1/205 In Letters, Belgium, January–June 1815; WO 3/609 Torrens Correspondence, 1815; WO 6/16 Out Letters: Holland, Flanders, France, 1813–18; WO 17/1760 General Returns, France, 1815; WO 37 Scovell Papers incl. printed Memorandum of Service at Waterloo by Scovell, in 37/12; WO 44/265 Ordnance Papers; WO 80/2 Murray Papers (post-war correspondence with Wellington)

Special Libraries and Archives, University of Aberdeen

Arbuthnot Papers: Ms 3029/1/1 Letters of Charles Arbuthnot to his wife Harriet; Ms 3029/1/2 Letters of Charles Arbuthnot to his son Charles G.J. Arbuthnot; Ms 3029/2/1 Letters of Harriet Arbuthnot to her husband Charles; Ms 3029/3 Letters from Charles G.J. Arbuthnot to his father, Charles Arbuthnot

National Library of Scotland, Edinburgh

Murray Papers: Adv Ms 46.8.7 Letterbook, 1828; Adv Ms 46.8.8 Letterbook, 1829; Adv Ms 46.8.10 Letterbook, 1830; Adv Ms 46.8.16 Correspondence, 1831–34

Centre for Buckinghamshire Studies, Aylesbury

D/FR46/11/46–50 Five letters from the Marquess of Buckingham to W.H. Fremantle, 14–26 March 1821

DIGITAL RESOURCES

Calendar of the Wellington Papers, 1819–32, University of Southampton
The Times Digital Archive
Nineteenth-Century Newspapers database, British Library

Illustrated London News Historical Archive
Oxford Dictionary of National Biography online
National Portrait Gallery online catalogue
British Museum online catalogue
National Army Museum online catalogue
Hansard, 1803–2005
The Napoleon Series (www.napoleon-series.org)
UK Reading Experience Database Record (www.open.ac.uk/Arts/reading/UK/)
Broadside Ballads Online, Bodleian Library (http://ballads.bodleian.ox.ac.uk)

BOOKS AND ARTICLES

Abbot, Charles, Lord Colchester, *The Diary and Correspondence of Charles Abbot, Lord Colchester*, ed. his son, Charles, Lord Colchester, 3 vols. (London, John Murray, 1861)
Airlie, Mabel Countess of, *In Whig Society* (London, Hodder & Stoughton, 1921)
——, *Lady Palmerston and Her Times* (London, Hodder & Stoughton, 1922)
Aldington, Richard, *Wellington* (London, Heinemann, 1946)
Alexander, Sir James, *Life of Field Marshal, His Grace the Duke of Wellington*, 2 vols. (London, Colburn, 1839–40)
Alison, Archibald, *History of Europe from the Commencement of the French Revolution in 1789 to the Restoration of the Bourbons in 1815*, 10 vols. (Edinburgh, Blackwood, 1833–42)
——, *Lives of Lord Castlereagh and Sir Charles Stewart . . .*, 3 vols. (Edinburgh, Blackwood, 1861)
Ambrose, Tom, *The King and the Vice Queen* (Stroud, Sutton, 2005)
Anderson, M.S., *The Eastern Question, 1774–1923* (London, Macmillan, 1966)
Anglesey, Marquess of, *One Leg. The Life and Letters of Henry William Paget, First Marquess of Anglesey (1768–1854)* (London, Jonathan Cape, 1963)
Annual Biography and Obituary, vols. 1–13 (London, Longman, Hurst, Rees, Orme & Brown, 1817–29)
Annual Register, or A View of the History, Politics, and Literature for the Year . . . (published annually)
Anton, James, *Retrospect of a Military Life* (Cambridge, Trotman, 1991; first published 1841)
Arbuthnot, Charles, *The Correspondence of Charles Arbuthnot*, ed. A. Aspinall (London, Royal Historical Society, 1941: Camden, 3rd series, vol. 65)
Arbuthnot, Harriet, *The Journal of Mrs Arbuthnot 1820–1832*, ed. Francis Bamford and the Duke of Wellington, 2 vols. (London, Macmillan, 1950)
Arden, the Hon. Katharine, Letter to her aunt, Miss Bootle Wilbraham, Brussels, 9 July 1815, 'Waterloo. A Contemporary Letter', *Cornhill Magazine*, vol. 77 (3rd series, vol. 4) (January 1898) pp. 72–3
Ashley, Evelyn, *The Life and Correspondence of Henry John Temple, Viscount Palmerston*, 2 vols. (London, Richard Bentley, 1879)
Aspinall, A., 'The Cabinet Council, 1783–1835', *Proceedings of the British Academy*, vol. 38 (1952)
——, 'Canning's Return to Office in September 1822', *English Historical Review*, vol. 78 (1963), pp. 531–45
——, 'The Canningite Party', *Transactions of the Royal Historical Society*, 4th series (1934), vol. 17, pp. 177–226
——, 'The Coalition Ministries of 1827', pt. 1 'Canning's Ministry', pt. 2 'The Goderich Ministry', *English Historical Review*, vol. 42 (April and October 1927), pp. 201–26, 533–59
——, 'English Party Organization in the Early Nineteenth Century', *English Historical Review*, vol. 41 (1926) pp. 389–411
——, *The Formation of Canning's Ministry February to August 1827* (London, Royal Historical Society, 1937; Camden, 3rd series, vol. 59)
——, 'George IV and Sir William Knighton', *English Historical Review*, vol. 55 (1940), pp. 57–82
——, 'The Irish "Proclamation" Fund, 1800–1846', *English Historical Review*, vol. 56 (1941), pp. 265–80
——, 'Last of the Canningites', *English Historical Review*, vol. 50, no. 200 (October 1935), pp. 639–69
——, 'The Old House of Commons and its Members (*c.* 1783–1832)', *Parliamentary Affairs*, vols. 14–15 (1960–62); vol. 14, pp. 13–25, 162–77, 291–311, 435–50; vol. 15, pp. 15–38, 171–7, 284–93, 424–49

——, *Politics and the Press c.1780–1850* (London, Home & Van Thal, 1949)

——, ed., *Three Early Nineteenth-Century Diaries* (London, Williams & Norgate, 1952) [Diaries of Denis Le Marchant, Lord Ellenborough and Edward Littleton, 1830–34]

Aspinall, A. and E. Anthony Smith, *English Historical Documents*, vol. XI, *1783–1832* (London, Eyre & Spottiswoode, 1969)

Aspinall-Oglander, Cecil, *Freshly Remembered. The Story of Sir Thomas Graham, Lord Lynedoch* (London, Hogarth Press, 1956)

Austen, Jane, *Sanditon* (Oxford University Press, 1925)

Bagot, Capt. Josceline, *George Canning and his Friends*, 2 vols. (London, John Murray, 1909)

Balfour, Lady Frances, *The Life of George, Fourth Earl of Aberdeen*, 2 vols. (London, Hodder and Stoughton, nd [1922])

Ballard, Joseph, *England in 1815. A Critical Edition of the Journal of Joseph Ballard*, ed. Alan Rauch (New York, Palgrave Macmillan, 2009)

Bannatyne, Lt.-Col. Neil, *History of the Thirtieth Regiment* . . . (Liverpool, Littlebury, 1923)

Barczewski, Stephanie L., *Myth and Identity in Nineteenth-Century Britain. The Legends of King Arthur and Robin Hood* (Oxford University Press, 2000)

[Barnes, Thomas], *Parliamentary Portraits; or Sketches of the Public Character of some of the Most Distinguished Speakers of the House of Commons* (London, Baldwin, Cradock and Joy, 1815)

Bartlett, C.J., *Great Britain and Sea Power, 1815–1853* (Oxford, Clarendon Press, 1963)

Bartlett, Thomas, *The Fall and Rise of the Irish Nation. The Catholic Question, 1690–1830* (Dublin, Gill and Macmillan, 1992)

Bathurst, Earl, *Historical Manuscripts Commission Report on the Manuscripts of Earl Bathurst preserved at Cirencester Park* (London, HMSO, 1923) [cited as *HMC Bathurst*]

Batty, Capt. Robert, *An Historical Sketch of the Campaign of 1815* . . . (London, Rodwell and Martin, 1820)

Beales, A.C.F., 'Wellington and Louis-Philippe, 1830', *History*, vol. 18 (1933–34), pp. 352–6

Beales, Derek, 'Parliamentary Parties and the "Independent" Member, 1810–1860', *Ideas and Institutions of Victorian Britain*, ed. Robert Robson (London, G. Bells & Sons, 1967)

Beamish, N. Ludlow, *History of the King's German Legion*, 2 vols. (London, Boone, 1832–37)

Becke, Capt. A.F., *Napoleon and Waterloo*, 2 vols. (London, Kegan Paul, Trench, Trübner, 1914)

Beckett, Ian F.W., *The Amateur Military Tradition, 1558–1945* (Manchester University Press, 1991)

Beckett, J.C., *The Making of Modern Ireland, 1603–1923* (London, Faber & Faber, 1967)

Beckett, John, *The Rise and Fall of the Grenvilles Dukes of Buckingham and Chandos, 1710–1921* (Manchester University Press, 1994)

Belsham, William, *Chronology of the Reigns of George III and George IV* (London, John Cumberland, 1829)

Bennett, Daphne, *King Without a Crown. Albert, Prince Consort of England, 1819–1861* (Philadelphia and New York, J.B. Lippincourt, 1977)

Bentley, Michael, *Politics without Democracy. Great Britain, 1815–1914* (Oxford, Blackwell, 1985)

Beresford, Kathryn, 'The Duke as Hero and Villain during the Emancipation Crisis and After', *Wellington Studies IV* (2008), pp. 274–98

Berry, Mary, *Extracts from the Journals and Correspondence of Miss Berry from the Year 1783 to 1852*, ed. Lady Theresa Lewis, 3 vols. (London, Longmans, 1866)

Bessborough, Earl of, and A. Aspinall, eds., *Lady Bessborough and her Family Circle* (London, John Murray, 1941)

Bessborough, Lady: see also Leveson Gower, Granville

Best, G.F.A., 'The Constitutional Revolution, 1828–1832 and Its Consequences for the Established Church', *Theology*, vol. 62 (1959), pp. 226–34

——, 'The Protestant Constitution and its Supporters, 1800–1829', *Transactions of the Royal Historical Society*, 5th series, vol. 8 (1958), pp. 105–27

Bew, John, *Castlereagh. Enlightenment, War and Tyranny* (London, Quercus, 2011)

Bindoff, S.T., E.F. Malcolm Smith and C.K. Webster, *British Diplomatic Representatives, 1789–1852* (London, Royal Historical Society, 1934; Camden, 3rd series, vol. 50)

Birks, Michael, *The Young Hussar* (Brighton, Book Guild, 2007)

Black, Shirley Burgoyne, 'Swing: The Years 1827–30 as Reflected in a West Kent Newspaper', *Archaeologia Cantiana*, vol. 107 (1989), pp. 89–106

Blake, Robert, *Disraeli* (London, Eyre & Spottiswoode, 1966)

Blakiston, Georgiana, *Lord William Russell and his Wife, 1815–1846* (London, John Murray, 1972)

Blanco, Richard L., 'Reform and Wellington's Post Waterloo Army, 1815–1854', *Military Affairs*, vol. 29 (1965), pp. 123–32

Bonar, Andrew R., *Life of Field Marshal His Grace the Duke of Wellington* (Halifax, William Milner, 1842)

Bourne, Kenneth, *Britain and the Balance of Power in North America 1815–1908* (London, Longmans, 1967)

——, *The Foreign Policy of Victorian England, 1830–1902* (Oxford, Clarendon Press, 1970)

——, *Palmerston. The Early Years, 1784–1841* (London, Allen Lane, 1982)

Bowden, Scott, *Armies at Waterloo* (Arlington, Empire Games Press, 1983)

Bradfield, B.T., 'Sir Richard Vyvyan and the Country Gentlemen, 1830–34', *English Historical Review*, vol. 83 (1968), pp. 729–43

——, 'Sir Richard Vyvyan and the Fall of Wellington's Government', *University of Birmingham Historical Journal*, vol. 11 (1968), pp. 141–56

Brereton, J.M. and A.C. Savory, *The History of the Duke of Wellington's Regiment (West Riding) 1702–1992* (Halifax, Duke of Wellington's Regiment, 1993)

Brett-James, Antony, *General Graham, Lord Lynedoch* (New York, St Martin's Press, 1959)

——, *The Hundred Days* (London, Macmillan, 1964)

——, *Life in Wellington's Army* (London, George Allen & Unwin, 1972)

Brialmont, A. and G.R. Gleig, *History of the Life of Arthur Duke of Wellington*, 4 vols. (London, Longman, Brown, Green, Longmans & Roberts, 1858)

Brightfield, Myron F., *John Wilson Croker* (London, George Allen and Unwin, 1940)

British Museum, *Catalogue of Political and Personal Satires*: see George

Brock, Michael, *The Great Reform Act* (London, Hutchinson, University Library, 1973)

Brock, W.R., *Lord Liverpool and Liberal Toryism 1820–1827* (Hamden, Archon Books, 1967; first published 1941)

Brougham, Henry, *The Life and Times of Henry, Lord Brougham, written by himself*, 3 vols. (New York, Harper & Brothers, 1872)

Broughton, Lord (John Cam Hobhouse), *Recollections of a Long Life*, ed. Lady Dorchester, 6 vols. (London, John Murray, 1910–11)

Brown, David, *Palmerston. A Biography* (New Haven and London, Yale University Press, 2010)

——, *Palmerston and the Politics of Foreign Policy, 1846–55* (Manchester University Press, 2002)

Browne, T.H., *The Napoleonic War Journal of Captain Thomas Henry Browne, 1807–1816*, ed. Roger Norman Buckley (London, Bodley Head for the Army Records Society, vol. 3, 1987)

Brownlow, Emma Sophia, Countess, *The Eve of Victorianism. Reminiscences of the Years 1802 to 1834* (London, John Murray, 1940)

Bruce, H.A., *Life of General Sir William Napier*, 2 vols. (London, John Murray, 1864)

Bryant, Julius, *Apsley House. The Wellington Collection* (London, English Heritage, 2011)

Brynn, Edward, *Crown and Castle. British Rule in Ireland, 1800–1830* (Toronto, Macmillan of Canada, 1978)

Buckingham and Chandos, Duke of, *Memoirs of the Courts and Cabinets of William IV and Victoria*, 2 vols. (London, Hurst and Blackett, 1861)

——, *Memoirs of the Court of George IV 1820–1830*, 2 vols. (London, Hurst and Blackett, 1859)

——, *Memoirs of the Court of England during the Regency, 1811–1820*, 2 vols. (London, Hurst and Blackett, 1856)

Bullen, Roger, *Palmerston, Guizot and the Collapse of the Entente Cordiale* (London, The Athlone Press, 1974)

——, 'Party Politics and Foreign Policy: Whigs, Tories and Iberian Affairs, 1830–36', *Bulletin of the Institute of Historical Affairs*, vol. 51 (1978), pp. 37–59.

Burghersh, Lady (Priscilla Fane, née Wellesley-Pole), *Correspondence of Lady Burghersh with the Duke of Wellington*, ed. her daughter Lady Rose Weigall (London, John Murray, 1903)

Burghersh, Lord, *Correspondence of Lord Burghersh, afterwards eleventh Earl of Westmorland, 1808–1840*, ed. his granddaughter Rachel Weigall (London, John Murray, 1912)

Burnham, Robert and Ron McGuigan, *The British Army against Napoleon. Facts, Lists, and Trivia 1805–1815* (Barnsley, Frontline, 2010)

Burney, Fanny, *Diary and Letters of Madame D'Arblay (1778–1840)*, ed. her niece Charlotte Barrett, 6 vols. (London, Macmillan, 1905)

Burrell, J.R., ed., *Official Bulletins of the Battle of Waterloo* . . . (London, Parker, Furnivall and Parker, 1849)

Burroughs, Peter, 'The Ordnance Department and Colonial Defence, 1821–1855', *Journal of Imperial and Commonwealth History*, vol. 10, no. 2 (January 1982), pp. 125–49

Butler, Iris, *The Eldest Brother. The Marquess Wellesley* (London, Hodder and Stoughton, 1973)

Butler, Marilyn, *Maria Edgeworth. A Literary Biography* (Oxford, Clarendon Press, 1972)

Byron, Lord, *Don Juan* (Boston, Houghton Mifflin, 1958, first published 1819–24)

Cahill, G.A., 'The Popular Movement for Parliamentary Reform, 1829–32', *Historian*, vol. 37 (May 1975), pp. 436–52

Calvert, the Hon. [Frances] Mrs, *An Irish Beauty under the Regency compiled from 'Mes Souvenirs' – the Unpublished Journals of the Hon. Mrs Calvert, 1789–1822*, ed. Mrs Warrenne Blake (London, John Lane The Bodley Head, 1911)

Canning, George, *Some Official Correspondence of George Canning*, ed. E.J. Stapleton, 2 vols. (London, Longmans, Green, 1887)

Cannon, John, *Parliamentary Reform, 1640–1832* (Cambridge University Press, 1980)

Cannon, Richard, *Historical Record of the Fourth, or the King's Own, Regiment of Foot* (London, Longman, Orme & Co, 1839)

Cantlie, Sir Neil, *A History of the Army Medical Department*, 2 vols. (Edinburgh and London, Churchill Livingstone, 1974)

Capel, Lady Caroline et al, *The Capel Letters. Being the Correspondence of Lady Caroline Capel and her Daughters with the Dowager Countess of Uxbridge from Brussels and Switzerland, 1814–1817*, ed. the Marquess of Anglesey (London, Cape, 1955)

Caquet, P.E., 'The Napoleonic Legend and the War Scare of 1840', *International History Review*, vol. 35, no. 4 (2013), pp. 702–22

Carew, P., 'A Hussar of the Hundred Days', *Blackwood's Magazine*, vol. 258 (November 1945), pp. 299–305

Carey, Tupper, 'Waterloo: Reminiscences of a Commissariat Officer', *Cornhill Magazine*, vol. 79 (June 1899), pp. 724–38

Carr, Raymond, *Spain 1808–1939* (Oxford, Clarendon Press, 1966)

Castlereagh, Lord, *Correspondence, Despatches, and other Papers of Viscount Castlereagh, Second Marquess of Londonderry*, ed. his brother Charles William Vane, Marquess of Londonderry, 12 vols. (London, William Shoberl, 1848–53)

Chad, G.W., *The Conversations of the Duke of Wellington with George William Chad*, ed. the Seventh Duke of Wellington (Cambridge, St Nicolas Press, 1956)

Chamberlain, Muriel, *Lord Aberdeen. A Political Biography* (Harlow, Longman, 1983)

——, 'The Soldier and the Classicist: Wellington, Aberdeen and the Eastern Question, 1828–30', *Wellington Studies III* (1999), pp. 136–51

Chambonas, Comte, *Anecdotal Recollections of the Congress of Vienna* . . . (London, Chapman & Hall, 1902)

Chandler, David, *The Campaigns of Napoleon* (New York, Macmillan, 1974)

Clark, J.C.D., *English Society 1688–1832* (Cambridge University Press, 1985)

Clarke, Francis L. and William Dunlap, *The Life of the Most Noble Arthur, Marquis and Earl of Wellington* . . . (New York, Van Winkle and Wiley, 1814)

Clark-Kennedy, A.E., *Attack the Colour! The Royal Dragoons in the Peninsula and at Waterloo* (London, Research Publishing, 1975)

Clausewitz, Carl von, *On Waterloo. Clausewitz, Wellington and the Campaign of 1815* trans. and ed. Christopher Bassford, Daniel Moran and Gregory Pedlow (Createspace.com, 2010)

——, *On Wellington. A Critique of Waterloo* trans. and ed. Peter Hofschröer (Norman, University of Oklahoma Press, 2010)

Clode, Charles M., *The Military Forces of the Crown. Their Administration and Government*, 2 vols. (London, John Murray, 1869)

Cobbett, William, *Selections from Cobbett's Political Works*, ed. John M. Cobbett and James P. Cobbett, 6 vols. (London, Anne Cobbett, nd [1835])

Cole, G.L., *Memoirs of Sir Lowry Cole*, ed. Maud Lowry Cole and Stephen Gwynn (London, Macmillan, 1934)

Colebrooke, Sir T.E., *Life of the Honourable Mountstuart Elphinstone*, 2 vols. (London, John Murray, 1884)

Colley, Linda, 'The Apotheosis of George III: Loyalty, Royalty and the British Nation 1760–1820', *Past and Present*, vol. 102 (1984), pp. 94–129

——, *Britons. Forging the Nation, 1707–1837* (New Haven and London, Yale University Press, 1992)

Collinge, J.M., *Office Holders in Modern Britain*, vol. 8, *Foreign Office Officials 1782–1870* (University of London, Institute of Historical Research, 1979)

Collingham, H.A.C., *The July Monarchy. A Political History of France 1830–1848* (London and New York, Longman, 1988)

Collins, Bruce, 'The Limits of British Power: Intervention in Portugal, 1820–30', *International History Review*, vol. 35 (2013), pp. 744–65

——, *War and Empire. The Expansion of Britain, 1790–1830* (Harlow, Longman, 2010)

Colville, John, *The Portrait of a General* (Salisbury, Michael Russell, 1980)

Combermere, [Stapleton Cotton], Lord, *Memoirs and Correspondence of Field Marshal Viscount Combermere . . .* by Mary, Viscountess Combermere and Capt. W. Knollys, 2 vols. (London, Hurst & Blackett, 1866)

The Complete Peerage by G.E.C[ockayne], 2nd edn, 12 vols. (1910–59; printed in microprint edition in 8 vols., Sutton Publishing, 2000)

Connolly, T.W.J., *History of the Royal Sappers and Miners*, 2 vols. (London, Longmans, 1857, first published in 1855 with slightly different title)

Cookson, J.E., *The British Armed Nation, 1793–1815* (Oxford, Clarendon Press, 1997)

——, 'The Edinburgh and Glasgow Duke of Wellington Statues: Early Nineteenth-Century Union Nationalism as a Tory Project', *Scottish Historical Review*, vol. 83 (April 2004), pp. 23–40

——, *Lord Liverpool's Administration. The Crucial Years, 1815–1822* (Edinburgh and London, Scottish Academic Press, 1975)

Corrigan, Gordon, *Wellington. A Military Life* (London and New York, Hambledon and London, 2001)

Coss, Edward J., *All for the King's Shilling. The British Soldier under Wellington, 1808–1814* (Norman, University of Oklahoma Press, 2010)

Costello, Edward, *The Peninsular and Waterloo Campaigns*, ed. Antony Brett-James (London, Longmans, Green, 1967)

Cowles, Loyal, 'The Failure to Restrain Russia: Canning, Nesselrode and the Greek Question 1825–1827', *International History Review*, vol. 12 (November 1990), pp. 688–720

Cox, Montagu H. and Philip Norman, eds., *Survey of London*, vol. 14, *The Parish of St Margaret, Westminster* (London, Batsford for the London County Council, 1931)

Crawley, C.W., 'Anglo–Russian Relations, 1815–1840', *Cambridge Historical Review*, vol. 3 (1929), pp. 47–73

——, *The Question of Greek Independence. A Study of British Policy in the Near East, 1821–1833* (Cambridge University Press, 1930)

Creevey, Thomas, *Creevey's Life and Times. A Further Selection from the Correspondence of Thomas Creevey*, ed. John Gore (London, John Murray, 1934)

——, *The Creevey Papers. A Selection from the Correspondence and Diaries of the late Thomas Creevey, MP*, ed. Sir Herbert Maxwell (London, John Murray, 1923)

Croker, John Wilson, *The Croker Papers: The Correspondence and Diaries of the Late Right Honourable John Wilson Croker*, ed. Louis J. Jennings, 3 vols. (London, John Murray, 1884)

Cross, Nigel, *The Common Writer. Life in Nineteenth-Century Grub Street* (Cambridge University Press, 1985)

Cunningham, A.B., 'The Philhellenes, Canning and Greek Independence', *Middle Eastern Studies*, vol. 14 (1978), pp. 151–81

Cunningham, Allan, *The Life of Sir David Wilkie*, 3 vols. (London, John Murray, 1843)

Dakin, Douglas, *The Greek Struggle for Independence, 1821–1833* (London, Batsford, 1973)

Dalton, Charles, *The Waterloo Roll Call* (London, Arms & Armour, 1978)

Daunton, Martin, *Trusting Leviathan. The Politics of Taxation in Britain, 1799–1814* (Cambridge University Press, 2001)

Davies, G.C.B., *Henry Phillpotts Bishop of Exeter, 1778–1869* (London, S.P.C.K., 1954)

Davies, Godfrey, *Wellington and His Army* (Oxford, Blackwell, 1954)

——, 'Wellington, the Man', *JSAHR*, vol. 30 (1952), pp. 96–112

Davies, Huw J., *Wellington's Wars. The Making of a Military Genius* (New Haven and London, Yale University Press, 2012)

Davis, Richard W., 'Deference and Aristocracy in the Time of the Great Reform Act', *American Historical Review*, vol. 81 (June 1976), pp. 532–9.

——, *Dissent in Politics, 1780–1830. The Political Life of William Smith, MP* (London, Epworth Press, 1971)

——, 'The Duke of Wellington and the Ultra Peers', *Wellington Studies III* (1999), pp. 35–55

——, *The English Rothschilds* (London, Collins, 1983)

——, 'The House of Lords, the Whigs and Catholic Emancipation 1806–1829', *Parliamentary History*, vol. 18 (1999), pp. 23–44

——, 'A Last Blast?' and 'A Last Blast (Again)', *Parliamentary History*, vol. 20 (2001), pp. 359–62, vol. 21 (2002), p. 246

——, 'Leaders in the Lords: Introduction' and 'Wellington' in *Parliamentary History*, vol. 22 (2003), pp. 1–12, 43–55

——, ed., *Lords of Parliament. Studies, 1714–1914* (Stanford University Press, 1995)

——, *A Political History of the House of Lords, 1811–1846* (Stanford University Press, 2008)

——, 'The Strategy of "Dissent" in the Repeal Campaign, 1820–1828', *Journal of Modern History*, vol. 38 (1966), pp. 374–93

——, 'The Tories, the Whigs and Catholic Emancipation, 1827–29', *English Historical Review*, vol. 97 (1982), pp. 89–98.

——, 'Toryism to Tamworth: The Triumph of Reform, 1827–1835', *Albion*, vol. 12 (1980), pp. 132–46.

——, 'Wellington, the Constitution and Catholic Emancipation', *Parliamentary History*, vol. 15 (1996), pp. 209–14

——, 'Wellington and the "Open Question": The Issue of Catholic Emancipation, 1821–1829', *Albion*, vol. 29 (Spring 1997), pp. 39–55

——, 'Wellington, Peel and the House of Lords in the 1840s', *Partisan Politics, Principle and Reform in Parliament and the Constituencies, 1689–1880. Essays in Memory of John A. Phillips*, ed. Clyve Jones, Philip Salmon and Richard W. Davis (Edinburgh University Press for the History of Parliament Trust, 2005) pp. 164–82

Dawson, Frank Griffith, *The First Latin American Debt Crisis. The City of London and the 1822–25 Loan Bubble* (New Haven and London, Yale University Press, 1990)

Delaforce, Patrick, *Wellington the Beau* (Moreton-in-Marsh, Windrush, 1990)

Delavoye, Alex. M., *Life of Thomas Graham, Lord Lynedoch* (London, Richardson and Marchant Singer, 1880)

——, *Records of the 90th Regiment (Perthshire Light Infantry)* (London, Richardson and Marchant Singer, 1880)

Denmark and the Dancing Congress of Vienna, exhibition catalogue, Christiansborg Palace (Copenhagen, 2002)

De Ros, Georgiana, Lady, 'Personal Recollections of the Great Duke of Wellington', *Murray's Magazine* (January and February 1889), pp. 37–53, 193–201

Dinwiddy, J.R., 'The Early Nineteenth Century Campaign against Flogging in the Army', *Radicalism and Reform in Britain, 1780–1850* (London, Hambledon, 1992)

——, 'The "Influence of the Crown" in the Early Nineteenth Century: A Note on the Opposition Case', *Parliamentary History*, vol. 4 (1985), pp. 189–200

Disraeli, Benjamin, *Benjamin Disraeli Letters*, ed. J.A.W. Gunn, 9 vols. (Buffalo, University of Toronto Press, 1982–2004)

——, *Disraeli's Reminiscences*, ed. Helen M. Schwartz and Marvin Schwartz (London, Hamish Hamilton, 1975)

Douglas, John, *Douglas's Tale of the Peninsula and Waterloo*, ed. Stanley Monick (London, Leo Cooper, 1997)

Douglass, Paul, *Lady Caroline Lamb* (Palgrave Macmillan 2004)

Douro, Marchioness of, 'Housing a Great Duke' (11th Wellington Lecture, University of Southampton, 1999)

Dropmore: Historical Manuscripts Commission Report on the Manuscripts of J.B. Fortescue preserved at Dropmore, 10 vols. (London, HMSO, 1892–1927)

Du Cann, Edward, *The Duke of Wellington and his Political Career after Waterloo – The Caricaturists' View* (Woodbridge, Antique Collector's Club, 2000)

Duncan, Capt. Francis, *History of the Royal Regiment of Artillery*, 2 vols. (London, John Murray, 1872)

Durham, Shaun Robert, 'The Duke of Wellington and the People, 1819–1832' (PhD, University of Southampton, 1999)

Durham, Shaun, 'The Uses of Celebrity: The Attempted Exploitation of the Duke of Wellington, 1819–32', *Wellington Studies III* (1999), pp. 88–116

Dyneley, T., *Letters written by Lieut.-General Thomas Dyneley C.B., R.A., while on Active Service between the years 1806 and 1815*, ed. Col. F.A. Whinyates (London, Ken Trotman, 1984, first published 1896)

Eastwick, Captain Robert W., *A Master Mariner. Being the Life and Adventures of Captain Robert W. Eastwick*, ed. Herbert Compton (London, T. Fisher Unwin, 1891)

Eden, Emily, *Miss Eden's Letters*, ed. Violet Dickinson (London, Macmillan, 1919)

Edgeworth, Maria, *The Life and Letters of Maria Edgeworth*, ed. Augustus Hare, 2 vols. (London, Edward Arnold, 1894)

——, *Maria Edgeworth. Letters from England, 1813–1844*, ed. Christina Colvin (Oxford, Clarendon Press, 1971)

Edghill, Keith, 'Dangerous Doctrines! The Battle for Anglican Supremacy in the British Army, 1810–65', *JSAHR*, vol. 80 (Spring 2002), pp. 36–57

The Edinburgh Annual Register for 1819, vol. 12 (Edinburgh, Constable, 1823)

Edmonds, Sir J.E., 'Wellington's Staff at Waterloo', *JSAHR*, vol. 12 (1933), pp. 239–47

Edwardes, Michael, *Warren Hastings. King of the Nabobs* (London, Hart Davis, 1976)

Edwards, Adam, *A Short History of the Wellington Boot* (London, Hodder & Stoughton, 2006)

Ellenborough, Edward Law, Lord, *A Political Diary, 1828–1830*, 2 vols. (London, Richard Bentley, 1881)

Ellesmere, Francis, 1st Earl, *Personal Reminiscences of the Duke of Wellington* (London, John Murray, 1904)

Elliott, George, *The Life of the Most Noble Arthur, Duke of Wellington . . .* (2nd edn, London, Sherwood, Neely and Jones, 1816)

Esdaile, Charles J., *The Duke of Wellington and the Command of the Spanish Armies, 1812–1814* (Basingstoke, Macmillan, 1990)

——, *Spain in the Liberal Age. From Constitution to Civil War, 1808–1939* (Oxford, Blackwell, 2000)

Farington, Joseph, *The Diary of Joseph Farington*, ed. Kenneth Garlick et al, 16 vols. (new edn, Yale University Press, 1978–85)

Farmer, Hugh, *A Regency Elopement* (London, Michael Joseph, 1969)

Fenton, Capt T.C., 'The Peninsular and Waterloo Letters of Captain Thomas Charles Fenton', *JSAHR*, vol. 53 (Winter 1975), pp. 210–31

Ferguson, Niall, *The House of Rothschild*, vol. 1, *Money's Prophets, 1798–1848* (New York, Penguin, 1999)

Fisher, D.R., ed., *The History of Parliament. The House of Commons, 1820–1832*, 7 vols. (Cambridge University Press for the History of Parliament Trust, 2009)

Flanedy, John, ed., *A Special Report of the Proceedings in the Case of the Queen against Daniel O'Connell, Esq. M.P.* (Dublin, James Duffy, 1844)

Flick, Carlos, 'The Fall of Wellington's Government', *Journal of Modern History*, vol. 37 (1965), pp. 62–71

Foord, A.S., 'The Waning of "The Influence of the Crown"', *English Historical Review*, vol. 62 (1947), pp. 484–507.

Forrest, Denys, *The Oriental. Life Story of a West End Club* (London, Batsford, 1968)

Fortescue, Hon. J.W., *A History of the British Army*, 13 vols. in 20 (London, Macmillan, 1899–1930)

——, *Wellington* (London, Ernest Benn, 1960; first published 1925)

Foster, R.E., ' "Bury the Great Duke": Thoughts on Wellington's Passing', *Wellington Studies V* (2013), pp. 299–328

——, 'The Duke of Wellington in Hampshire, 1817–1852', *Hampshire Papers*, no. 30 (July 2010)

——, 'Food for Thought: the Waterloo Banquet', *The Waterloo Journal*, vol. 35, no. 2 (Summer 2013), pp. 13–17

——, 'Mr Punch and the Iron Duke', *History Today*, vol. 34 (May 1984), pp. 36–42

——, *The Politics of County Power. Wellington and the Hampshire Gentlemen, 1820–1852* (New York, Harvester Wheatsheaf, 1990)

——, 'Waterloo Bridge: National Memorial or National Disgrace?', *The Waterloo Journal*, vol. 35, no. 3 (Winter 2013), pp. 8–12

——, *Wellington and Waterloo. The Duke, the Battle and Posterity, 1815–2015* (Stroud, Spellmount, 2014)

——, 'Wellington and Wilkie: Money Well Spent', *The Waterloo Journal*, vol. 35, no. 1 (Spring 2013), pp. 12–16

Fox, K.O., *Making Life Possible. A Study of Military Aid to the Civil Power in Regency England* (privately published, 1982)

Franklin, Robert, *Lord Stuart de Rothesay. The Life and Times of Lord Stuart de Rothesay of Highcliffe Castle, 1779–1845* (Upton-upon-Severn, Images, 1993)

Fraser, P., 'Party Voting in the House of Commons, 1812–1827', *English Historical Review*, vol. 98 (October 1983), pp. 763–84

Fraser, Sir William, *Words on Wellington. The Duke – Waterloo – the Ball* (London, John C. Nimmo, 1889)

Frazer, Sir Augustus Simon, *The Letters of Colonel Sir Augustus Simon Frazer, K.C.B. commanding the Royal Horse Artillery in the Army under the Duke of Wellington*, ed. Edward Sabine (Uckfield, Naval & Military Press, 2001, first published 1859)

Fremantle, Lt.-Col. John, *Wellington's Voice. The Candid Letters of Lieutenant-Colonel John Fremantle, Coldstream Guards, 1808–1821*, ed. Gareth Glover (Frontline Books, 2012)

'A French Infantry Officer's Account of Waterloo', *United Service Magazine* (December 1878, and January 1879), pp. 453–62, 66–76 [The author appears to have been a Captain Duthilt]

Fry, Michael, *The Dundas Despotism* (Edinburgh, John Donald, 2004)

Fulcher, Jonathan, 'The Loyalist Response to the Queen Caroline Agitation', *Journal of British Studies*, vol. 34, no. 4 (October 1995), pp. 481–502

Furneaux, Robin, *William Wilberforce* (London, Hamish Hamilton, 1974)

Gallaher, John G., *The Iron Marshal* (Carbondale, Southern Illinois University Press, 1978)

Garlick, Kenneth, *Sir Thomas Lawrence. A Complete Catalogue of the Oil Paintings* (Oxford, Phaidon, 1989)

Garnett, P.F., 'The Wellington Testimonial [Dublin]', *Dublin Historical Record*, vol. 13 (June–August 1952), pp. 48–61

Garston, J., 'Armies of Occupation I: The British in France, 1815–1818', *History Today*, vol. 11 (June 1961), pp. 396–404

Garwood, Lt.-Col. F.S., 'The Royal Staff Corps, 1800–1837', *Royal Engineers Journal*, vol. 57 (1943), pp. 81–96, 247–60

Gash, Norman, 'After Waterloo: British Society and the Legacy of the Napoleonic Wars', *Transactions of the Royal Historical Society*, 5th series, vol. 28 (1978), pp. 145–57

——, 'English Reform and the French Revolution in the General Election of 1830', *Essays Presented to Sir Lewis Namier*, ed. Richard Pares and A.J.P. Taylor (London, Macmillan, 1956)

——, entry on Wellington in the *Oxford Dictionary of National Biography*

——, *Lord Liverpool* (London, Weidenfeld and Nicolson, 1984)

——, *Mr Secretary Peel. The Life of Sir Robert Peel to 1830* (London, Longmans, 1961)

——, *Robert Surtees and Early Victorian Society* (Oxford, Clarendon Press, 1993)

——, *Sir Robert Peel. The Life of Sir Robert Peel After 1830* (London, Longman, 1972)

——, ed., *Wellington. Studies in the Military and Political Career of the First Duke of Wellington* (Manchester University Press, 1990)

——, 'Wellington and Waterloo', *Wellington Studies II* (1998), pp. 215–38

Gaunt, Richard A, 'The Fourth Duke of Newcastle, the Ultra-Tories and the Opposition to Canning's Administration', *History*, vol. 88 (October 2003), pp. 568–86.

——, ed., *Peel in Caricature. The 'Political Sketches' of John Doyle ('H.B.')* (The Peel Society, 2014)

——, 'Peel's Other Repeal: The Test and Corporation Acts, 1828', *Parliamentary History*, vol. 33 (2014), pp. 243–62

——, *Sir Robert Peel. The Life and Legacy* (London, Tauris, 2010)

——, 'Wellington in Petticoats: The Duke as Caricature', *Wellington Studies IV* (2008), pp. 140–72

——, 'Wellington, Peel and the Conservative Party', *Wellington Studies V* (2013), pp. 262–85

[Gawler, George], 'The Crisis and Close of the Action at Waterloo by an Eye-witness', *United Service Journal* (July 1833), pp. 299–310, with further correspondence in ibid., Pt. 3, pp. 1–16 (1835), Pt. 1, pp. 303–4, and (1836), Pt. 2 pp. 357–8.

George III, *The Later Correspondence of George III*, ed. A. Aspinall, 5 vols. (Cambridge University Press, 1962–70)

George IV, *The Letters of King George IV 1812–1830*, 3 vols., ed. A. Aspinall (Cambridge University Press, 1938)

George, M. Dorothy, *English Political Caricature. A Study of Opinion and Propaganda*, 2 vols. (Oxford, Clarendon Press, 1959)

George, M. Dorothy and Frederick G. Stephens, *Catalogue of Political and Personal Satires Preserved in the Department of Prints and Drawings in the British Museum*, 11 vols. (London, British Museum Publications, 1978; first published 1870–1954) (cited as George, *BM Catalogue of Satires*)

Geraghty, Anthony, 'Pared and Starved for the Lord', *Times Literary Supplement* (12 January 2007), p. 18

Gibson, William T., 'Wellington, the Whigs and the Exeter Vacancy of 1830', *Report on the Transactions of the Devonshire Association for the Advancement of Science, Literature and Art*, vol. 122 (1990), pp. 41–6

Gleig, Rev. G.R., *The Life of Arthur, Duke of Wellington* (London, J.M. Dent, 1909, the Everyman edn)

——, *The Light Dragoon* (London, Routledge, 1850)

——, *Personal Reminiscences of the First Duke of Wellington* (Edinburgh, Blackwood, 1904)

——, *The Subaltern. A Chronicle of the Peninsular War*, ed. Ian C. Robertson (Barnsley, Leo Cooper, 2001; first published 1825)

Glenbervie, Sylvester Douglas, Lord, *The Diaries of Sylvester Douglas (Lord Glenbervie)*, ed. Francis Bickley, 2 vols. (London, Constable, 1928)

Glover, Gareth, *From Corunna to Waterloo. The Letters and Journals of Two Napoleonic Hussars, 1801–1816* (London, Greenhill, 2007)

——, *Letters from the Battle of Waterloo. The Unpublished Correspondence by Allied Officers from the Siborne Papers* (London, Greenhill, 2004)

——, ed., *The Waterloo Archive*, vols. 1–4 (Barnsley, Frontline, 2010–12)

——, *Waterloo. Myth and Reality* (Barnsley, Pen & Sword, 2014)

——, ed., *Wellington's Lieutenant, Napoleon's Gaoler. The Peninsula and St Helena Diaries and Letters of Sir George Ridout Bingham 1809–1821* (Barnsley, Pen & Sword, 2004)

Glover, Michael, *A Very Slippery Fellow. The Life of Sir Robert Wilson, 1777–1849* (Oxford University Press, 1978)

——, ' "An Excellent Young Man": The Rev. Samuel Briscall, 1788–1848', *History Today*, vol. 18, no. 8 (1968), pp. 578–84

——, 'Purchase, Patronage and Promotion in the Army at the time of the Peninsular War', *Army Quarterly*, vol. 103 (1972–73), pp. 211–15, 355–62

——, *Wellington as Military Commander* (London, Batsford, 1968)

Glover, Richard, *Peninsular Preparation. The Reform of the British Army, 1795–1809* (Cambridge University Press, 1963)

Gomm, W.M., *Letters and Journals of Field Marshal Sir William Maynard Gomm . . . 1799 to 1815*, ed. Francis Culling Carr-Gomm (London, John Murray, 1881)

Goodrich, S.G., *Recollections of a Lifetime, or Men and Things I Have Seen . . .*, 2 vols. (New York, Auburn, Miller, Orton & Mulligan, 1857)

Gordon, Alexander, *At Wellington's Right Hand. The Letters of Lieutenant-Colonel Sir Alexander Gordon, 1808–1815*, ed. Rory Muir (Thrupp, Sutton Publishing for the Army Records Society, 2003)

Granville, Harriet, Countess, *Letters of Harriet, Countess of Granville, 1810–1845*, ed. F. Leveson Gower, 2 vols. (London, Longmans, Green, 1894)

Grattan, William, *Adventures with the Connaught Rangers, 1809–1814* (London, Greenhill, 2003)

Gray, Denis, *Spencer Perceval. The Evangelical Prime Minister* (Manchester University Press, 1963)

Green, Capt. J.E.S., 'Wellington, Boislecompte, and the Congress of Verona, 1822', *Transactions of the Royal Historical Society*, 4th series, vol. 1 (1918), pp. 59–76

——, 'Wellington and the Congress of Verona, 1822', *English Historical Review*, vol. 35 (April 1920), pp. 200–11

Greenhalgh, Michael, 'The Funeral of the Duke of Wellington', *Apollo*, vol. 98 (1973), pp. 220–6

Greville, Charles C.F., *The Greville Memoirs. A Journal of the Reigns of King George IV, King William IV and Queen Victoria*, ed. Henry Reeve, 8 vols. (London, Longmans, Green, and Co., 1888)

——, *The Greville Memoirs 1814–1860*, ed. Lytton Strachey and Roger Fulford, 8 vols. (London, Macmillan, 1938) [All citations, unless otherwise specified, are to this edition]

'Grievances of a Veteran', *United Service Journal* (December 1833), pp. 536–8

Griffith, Paddy, ed., *Wellington Commander. The Iron Duke's Generalship* (Chichester, Antony Bird, nd [1985])

Griffiths, Dennis, *Plant Here the Standard* (Basingstoke, Macmillan 1996)

Gronow, Capt. R.H., *The Reminiscences and Recollections of Captain Gronow . . .* (Nunnery, Surtees Society, 1984)

Guedalla, Philip, *The Duke* (London, Hodder and Stoughton, 1931)

Gunn, J.A.W., 'Influence, Parties and the Constitution: Changing Attitudes, 1783–1832', *Historical Journal*, vol. 17 (1974), pp. 301–28

Guy, Alan, ed., *The Road to Waterloo* (London, National Army Museum, 1990)

Hamilton, Albert J., ' "Une position nouvelle en Europe": The Duke of Wellington in France, 1815–1818', *Duquesne Review*, vol. 16 (1971), pp. 91–100

Hamilton, C.I., *Anglo-French Naval Rivalry, 1840–1870* (Oxford, Clarendon Press, 1993)

——, 'John Wilson Croker: Patronage and Clientage at the Admiralty, 1809–1857', *Historical Journal*, vol. 43 (2000), pp. 49–77

Hamilton, Lt.-Gen. Sir F.W., *The Origin and History of the First or Grenadier Guards*, 3 vols. (London, John Murray, 1874)

Hannay, Prudence, 'The Duke of Wellington and Lady Shelley', *History Today*, vol. 25, no. 2 (February 1975), pp. 98–109

Hansard's Parliamentary Debates Third Series commencing with the Accession of William IV, vol. 1 (London, T.C. Hansard, 1831–27)

Hardinge, Charles, Viscount, *Viscount Hardinge by his Son* (Oxford, Clarendon Press, 1981)

Hardy, John, 'The Building and Decoration of Apsley House', *Apollo*, vol. 98, no. 139 (September 1973), pp. 170–9

Hare, Augustus, *The Story of Two Noble Lives. Being Memorials of Charlotte, Countess Canning and Louisa, Marchioness of Waterford* (London, G. Allen, 1893)

Harrington, Peter, *British Artists and War. The Face of Battle in Paintings and Prints, 1700–1914* (London, Greenhill, 1993)

Harris, [Benjamin], *Recollections of Rifleman Harris as told to Henry Curling*, ed. Christopher Hibbert (Hampden, Archon Books, 1970) [Hibbert says 'John' but research by Eileen Hathaway has established that the author's name was Benjamin: see her edition entitled *A Dorset Rifleman*]

Hart: see Priest

Harvey, A.D., *Britain in the Early Nineteenth Century* (London, Batsford, 1978)

Hatherton, Edward Littleton, Lord, 'Extracts from Lord Hatherton's Diary', ed. A. Aspinall, *Parliamentary Affairs*, vol. 17 (1964), pp. 15–22, 134–41, 254–68, 373–88

——, *The Hatherton Diaries. Extracts from the Personal Diary between the Years 1817–1862 of Edward Walhouse Littleton afterwards the First Lord Hatherton, 1791–1863* (Trowbridge, Cromwell Press, nd [c. 2003])

Havard, Robert, *Wellington's Welsh General. A Life of Sir Thomas Picton* (London, Aurum, 1996)

Hawkins, Angus, *The Forgotten Prime Minister. The 14th Earl of Derby*, vol. 1, *Ascent, 1799–1851* (Oxford University Press, 2007)

Hay, William Anthony, *The Whig Revival, 1808–1830* (Basingstoke, Palgrave Macmillan, 2005)

Haydon, Benjamin Robert, *The Autobiography and Journals of Benjamin Robert Haydon*, ed. Malcolm Elwin (London, Macdonald, 1950)

——, *The Diary of Benjamin Robert Haydon*, ed. Willard Bissell Pope, 5 vols. (Harvard University Press, 1960–63)

Hayter, Alethea, *The Backbone. Diaries of a Military Family in the Napoleonic Wars* (Edinburgh, Pentland Press, 1983)

Haythornthwaite, Philip J., *The Armies of Wellington* (London, Arms & Armour, 1994)

Healey, Edna, *Coutts & Co 1692–1992. The Portrait of a Private Bank* (London, Hodder & Stoughton, 1992)

——, *Lady Unknown. The Life of Angela Burdett-Coutts* (New York, Coward, McCann & Geoghegan, 1978)

Heathcote, Ralph, *Ralph Heathcote. Letters of a Young Diplomatist and Soldier during the time of Napoleon*, ed. Countess Gröben (London, John Lane, 1907)

Heesom, Alan, 'The Duke of Wellington's Visit to the North East of England, September–October 1827', *Durham County Local History Society Bulletin*, no. 60 (November 1999), pp. 3–35

——, 'Wellington's Friend? Lord Londonderry and the Duke of Wellington', *Wellington Studies III* (1999), pp. 1–34

Hemingway, Private George, 'A New Account of Waterloo: A Letter Home from Private George Hemingway of the Thirty-Third Regiment of Foot', ed. Daniel Waley, *British Library Journal*, vol. 6 (1980), pp. 61–4

Hendrix, Richard, 'Political Humours and "The Black Dwarf"', *Journal of British Studies*, vol. 16, no. 1 (1976), pp. 108–28

Henegan, Sir Richard D., *Seven Years Campaigning in the Peninsula and the Netherlands 1808–1815*, 2 vols. (Stroud, Nonsuch, 2005 – first published 1846)

Herries, Edward, *Memoir of the Public Life of the Right Hon. John Charles Herries*, 2 vols. (London, John Murray, 1880)

Hervey, Sir Felton, 'A Contemporary Letter on the Battle of Waterloo', *Nineteenth Century*, vol. 33 (March 1893), pp. 430–5.

Hibbert, Christopher, *Wellington. A Personal History* (London, HarperCollins, 1997)

Hicks, Geoffrey, ed., *Conservatism and British Foreign Policy, 1820–1920. The Derbys and their World* (Farnham, Ashgate, 2011)

——, *Peace, War and Party Politics. The Conservatives and Europe, 1846–1859* (Manchester University Press, 2007)

Hilton, Boyd, *Corn, Cash, Commerce. The Economic Policies of the Tory Governments 1815–1830* (Oxford University Press, 1977)

——, *A Mad, Bad, Dangerous People? England 1783–1846* (Oxford, Clarendon Press, 2006)

——, 'The Political Arts of Lord Liverpool', *Transactions of the Royal Historical Society*, 5th series, vol. 38 (1988), pp. 147–70

Hime, Lt.-Col. H.W.L., *History of the Royal Regiment of Artillery, 1815–1853* (London, Longmans, Green & Co., 1908)

Hinde, Wendy, *Castlereagh* (London, Collins, 1981)

——, *George Canning* (London, Collins, 1973)

Hobhouse, Henry, *The Diary of Henry Hobhouse (1820–1827)*, ed. Arthur Aspinall (London, Home & Van Thal, 1947)

Hobhouse, J.C., see Broughton

Hobsbawm, E.J. and George Rudé, *Captain Swing* (London 1969)

Hofschröer, Peter, *1815, The Waterloo Campaign*, vol. 1, *Wellington, His German Allies and the Battles of Ligny and Quatre Bras* (London, Greenhill, 1998), vol. 2, *The German Victory* (London, Greenhill, 1999)

——, 'Death of Colonel John Gurwood', *JSAHR*, vol. 81 (2003), pp. 379–81

——, 'De Lacy Evans – What was his Role in the Waterloo Campaign?', *JSAHR*, vol. 80 (2002), pp. 163–6

——, 'Did the Duke of Wellington Deceive his Prussian Allies in the Campaign of 1815?', *War in History*, vol. 5, no. 2 (1998), pp. 176–203

——, 'The Model of the Battle and the Battle of the Model: Wellington, Siborne and the Waterloo Model', *JSAHR*, vol. 79 (2001), pp. 269–77

——, *Wellington's Smallest Victory. The Duke, the Model Maker and the Secret of Waterloo* (London, Faber and Faber, 2004)

——, 'Yet Another Reply to John Hussey: What *Really* are my Charges Against the Duke of Wellington?', *JSAHR*, vol. 78 (2000), pp. 221–5 and p. 305

——, 'Zieten's Message to Wellington', *JSAHR*, vol. 81 (2003), pp. 286–8

Holland, Elizabeth Lady, *Elizabeth Lady Holland to Her Son, 1821–1845*, ed. the Earl of Ilchester (London, John Murray, 1946)

Holland, Henry Lord, *Further Memoirs of the Whig Party, 1807–1821* (London, John Murray, 1905)

Holmes, Richard, *Wellington. The Iron Duke* (London, HarperCollins, 2002)

Holroyd, Richard, 'The Bourbon Army, 1815–1830', *Historical Journal*, vol. 14 (September 1971), pp. 529–52

Holyoake, Gregory, *Wellington at Walmer* (Dover, Buckland, 1996)

[Hone, William], *The Political House that Jack Built* is reprinted in full with many other pamphlets of the period in *Radical Squibs and Loyal Ripostes*, ed. Edgell Rickword (Bath, Adams & Dart, 1971)

Hope, Lt. James, *The Iberian and Waterloo Campaigns. The Letters of Lt. James Hope*, ed. S. Monick (Heathfield, Naval and Military Press, 2000)

Horn, Pamela, 'Some Hampshire Ladies and the 1830 "Swing" Riots', *Hatcher Review*, no. 24 (1987), pp. 187–93

Horsburgh, E.L.S., *Waterloo. A Narrative and a Criticism* (London, Methuen, 1900)

Houssaye, Henry, *1815, Waterloo* (London, A&C Black, 1900)

Howard, Michael, ed., *Wellingtonian Studies* (Aldershot, privately printed, 1959)

Howarth, David, *Waterloo Day of Battle* (New York, Galahad, 1968)

Hunt, Giles, *The Duel. Castlereagh, Canning and Deadly Cabinet Rivalry* (London, Tauris, 2008)

'The Hunter Wellington Boots Story', www.wellie-boots.com/wellington-boots-hunter-story

Hurd, Douglas, *Robert Peel. A Biography* (London, Weidenfeld and Nicolson, 2007)

Huskisson, William, *The Huskisson Papers*, ed. Lewis Melville (London, Constable, 1931)

Hussey, John, 'At What Time on 15 June Did Wellington Learn of Napoleon's Attack on the Prussians?', *War in History*, vol. 6, no. 1 (1999), pp. 88–116, and Hofschröer's reply, *loc. cit.*, vol. 6, no. 4 (1999), pp. 468–78

——, ' "Evening" and the Waterloo Despatch', *JSAHR*, vol. 79 (2001), pp. 336–8 and subsequent correspondence in vol. 80 (2002), p. 260, and vol. 81, pp. 62–3

——, ' "Let No Man Lay to Wellington's Charge the Suicides of these two Men": The Problems of Reminiscence and the Failings of Old Age', *JSAHR*, vol. 80 (2002), pp. 98–109

——, 'Müffling, Gleig, Ziethen, and the "Missing" Wellington Records: The "Compromising" Documents Traced', *JSAHR*, vol. 77 (1999), pp. 250–68

——, 'Towards a Better Chronology of the Waterloo Campaign', *War in History*, vol. 7, no. 3 (2000), pp. 463–80

——, ed., 'Two Letters from the Prince of Orange to Wellington, June 1815', *JSAHR*, vol. 77, no. 311 (Autumn 1999), pp. 225–6

Hutchinson, Sara, *The Letters of Sara Hutchinson from 1800 to 1835*, ed. Kathleen Coburn (London, Routledge and Kegan Paul, 1954)

Hyde, H. Montgomery, *The Strange Death of Lord Castlereagh* (London, Heinemann, 1959)

Ingilby, Lt. W.B., 'Diary of Lieutenant Ingilby, R.A. in the Peninsular War and during the Waterloo Campaign', ed. Major E.A. Lambert, *Minutes of the Proceedings of the Royal Artillery Institution*, vol. 20 (1893), pp. 241–62, 315–23

Ingram, Edward, 'The Role of the Duke of Wellington in the Great Game in Asia, 1826–1842', *Indica*, vol. 25 (1988), pp. 131–42

Jackson, Basil and C. Rochfort Scott, *The Military Life of Field Marshal the Duke of Wellington*, 2 vols. (London, Longman, Orme, Brown, Green and Longmans, 1840)

Jackson, Basil, *Notes and Reminiscences of a Staff Officer* (London, John Murray, 1903)

Jackson, George, *The Bath Archives. A Further Selection from the Diaries and Letters of Sir George Jackson, K.C.H. from 1809 to 1816*, ed. Lady Jackson, 2 vols. (London, Richard Bentley, 1873)

Jackson, Maj.-Gen. Louis C., *History of the United Service Club* (London, United Service Club, 1937)

Jaggard, Edwin, 'Cornwall Politics 1826–1832: Another Face of Reform?', *Journal of British Studies*, vol. 22 (1983), pp. 80–97

——, 'Lord Falmouth and the Parallel Political Worlds of Ultra-Toryism, 1826–32', *Parliamentary History*, vol. 33, pt. 2 (2014), pp. 300–20

James, Dr Haddy, *Surgeon James's Journal, 1815*, ed. Jane Vansittart (London, Cassell, 1964)

James, Lawrence, *The Iron Duke. A Military Biography of Wellington* (London, Weidenfeld and Nicolson, 1992)

James, W.H., *The Campaign of 1815, Chiefly in Flanders* (Edinburgh, Blackwood, 1908)

Jarrett, Mark, 'Castlereagh, Ireland and the French Restorations of 1814–1815', (PhD thesis, Stanford University, 2006)

Jenkins, Brian, *Era of Emancipation. British Government of Ireland, 1812–1830* (Kingston and Montreal, McGill-Queen's University Press, 1988)

——, *Henry Goulburn 1784–1856. A Political Biography* (Montreal and Kingston, McGill-Queen's University Press, 1996)

Jenkins, Susan, 'Sir Thomas Lawrence and the Duke of Wellington: A Portraitist and his Sitter', *Wellington Studies IV* (2008), pp. 126–39

——, 'The "Spanish Gift" at Apsley House', *English Heritage Historical Review*, vol. 2 (2007), pp. 112–27

Jennings, Lawrence C., *French Anti-Slavery. The Movement for the Abolition of Slavery in France, 1802–1848* (Cambridge University Press, 2000)

Johnson, David, *Regency Revolution. The Case of Arthur Thistlewood* (Salisbury, Compton Russell, 1974)

Johnson, Edgar, 'Sceptred Kings and Laureled Conquerors: Scott in London and Paris, 1815', *Nineteenth Century Fiction*, vol. 17 (March 1963), pp. 299–319

——, *Sir Walter Scott. The Great Unknown*, 2 vols. (London, Hamish Hamilton, 1970)

Jones, Philip D., 'The British Army in the Age of Reform, 1830–1854', (PhD thesis, Duke University, 1968)

——, 'British Military Reform during the Administration of Lord Grey, 1830–34', *Albion*, vol. 4 (1972), pp. 82–93

Jones, W.D., *Prosperity Robinson. The Life of Viscount Goderich, 1782–1859* (London, Macmillan, 1967)

Jupp, Peter, *British Politics on the Eve of Reform. The Duke of Wellington's Administration, 1828–1830* (Basingstoke, Macmillan, 1998)

——, 'Continuity and Change: British Government and Politics, 1770–1850', *Wellington Studies IV* (2008), pp. 1–21

——, 'The First Duke of Wellington in an Irish Context' (9th Wellington Lecture, University of Southampton, 1997)

——, 'The Foreign Policy of Wellington's Government', *Wellington Studies III* (1999), pp. 152–83

——, *The Governing of Britain, 1688–1848. The Executive, Parliament and the People* (Abingdon, Routledge, 2006)

——, 'Irish Parliamentary Elections and the Influence of the Catholic Vote, 1801–1820', *Historical Journal*, vol. 10 (1967), pp. 183–96

——, 'The Landed Elite and Political Authority in Britain, ca1760–1850', *Journal of British Studies*, vol. 29 (January 1990), pp. 53–79

——, *Lord Grenville 1759–1834* (Oxford, Clarendon Press, 1985)

——, 'Pictorial Images of the First Duke of Wellington', *Avenues to the Past. Essays presented to Sir Charles Brett on his 75th Year*, ed. Terence Reeves-Smyth and Richard Oram (Ulster Architectural Heritage Society, 2003) pp. 105–34

Kanter, 'Robert Peel and the Waning of the "Influence of the Crown" in Ireland 1812–1813', *New Hibernian Review*, vol. 5 (2001), pp. 54–71

Kaplan, Herbert H., *Nathan Meyer Rothschild and the Creation of a Dynasty. The Critical Years 1806–1816* (Stanford University Press, 2006)

Kaufmann, C.M., *Catalogue of Paintings in the Wellington Museum* (London, HMSO, 1982)

Kaye, Sir John, *The Life and Correspondence of Major-General Sir John Malcolm . . .* 2 vols. (London, Smith Elder, 1856)

Keegan, John, *The Face of Battle* (New York, Viking, 1976)

——, *The Mask of Command* (London, Cape, 1987)

Kennedy, Sir James Shaw, *Notes on the Battle of Waterloo* (Staplehurst, Spellmount, 2003, first published 1865)

Kent, Conrad, *Estampas de la Guerra de la Independencia en la Provincia de Salamanca* (Salamanca, Instituto de las Indentidades, Diputación de Salamanca, 2010)

Kilvert, Rev. Francis, *Kilvert's Diary. Selections from the Diary of the Rev. Francis Kilvert*, ed. William Plomer, 3 vols. (London, Cape, 1960)

Kimizuka, Naotaka, 'Elder Statesmen and British Party Politics: Wellington, Lansdowne and the Ministerial Crises of the 1850s', *Parliamentary History*, vol. 17, pt. 3 (1998), pp. 355–72

Kincaid, Capt. Sir John, *Adventures in the Rifle Brigade and Random Shots from a Rifleman* (Glasgow, Richard Drew, 1981)

Knight, Roger, *Britain against Napoleon. The Organization of Victory, 1793–1815* (London, Allen Lane, 2013)

Kraehe, Enno E., *Metternich's German Policy*, vol. 1, *The Contest with Napoleon, 1799–1814* (Princeton University Press, 1963), vol. 2, *The Congress of Vienna, 1814–1815* (Princeton University Press, 1983)

——, 'Wellington and the Reconstruction of the Allied Armies during the Hundred Days', *International History Review*, vol. XI (1989), pp. 84–97

Kurtz, Harold, *The Trial of Marshal Ney* (London, Hamish Hamilton, 1957)

Lackland, H.M., 'Wellington at Verona', *English Historical Review*, vol. 35 (October 1920), pp. 574–80.

Lambert, Andrew D., 'Politics, Administration and Decision-making: Wellington and the Navy 1828–30', *Wellington Studies IV* (2008), pp. 199–215

——, 'Preparing for the Long Peace: The Reconstruction of the Royal Navy, 1815–1830', *Mariner's Mirror*, vol. 82, no. 1 (February 1996), pp. 41–54

Large, D., 'The Decline of "the Party of the Crown" and the Rise of the Parties in the House of Lords, 1783–1837', *English Historical Review*, vol. 78 (1963), pp. 669–95

Laqueur, Thomas, 'The Queen Caroline Affair: Politics as Art in the Reign of George IV', *Journal of Modern History*, vol. 54, no. 3 (September 1982), pp. 417–60

Las Cases, Count, *Memorial de Sainte Hélène. Journal of the Private Life and Conversations of the Emperor Napoleon*, vol. 3 (London, Colburn, 1823)

Lawrence, Sgt. William, *The Autobiography of Sergeant William Lawrence, a Hero of the Peninsular and Waterloo Campaigns*, ed. George Nugent Bankes (London, Sampson Low, Marston, Searle & Rivington, 1886)

Leach, Lt.-Col J., *Rough Sketches of the Life of an Old Soldier* (Cambridge, Ken Trotman, 1986; reprint of 1831 edn)

Lee, Dennis, *Lord Lyndhurst. The Flexible Tory* (Niwot, University Press of Colorado, 1994)

Lee, Stephen M., *George Canning and Liberal Toryism* (Woodbridge, Boydell & Brewer for the Royal Historical Society, 2008)

Leggiere, Michael V., *Blücher. Scourge of Napoleon* (Norman, University of Oklahoma Press, 2014)

Leeke, Rev. William, *The History of Lord Seaton's Regiment (the 52nd Light Infantry) at the Battle of Waterloo*, 2 vols. (London, Hatchard, 1866)

Leiren, T.I., 'Norwegian Independence and British Opinion: January to August 1814', *Scandinavian Studies*, vol. 47 (1975), pp. 364–82

Leveson Gower, Granville, *Lord Granville Leveson Gower (First Earl Granville) Private Correspondence 1781 to 1821*, ed. Castalia, Countess Granville, 2 vols. (London, John Murray, 1916)

Levey, Michael, *Sir Thomas Lawrence* (New Haven and London, Yale University Press, 2005)

Lieven, Princess Dorothea, *Letters of Dorothea, Princess Lieven, during her Residence in London, 1812–1834*, ed. Lionel G. Robinson (London, Longmans, 1902)

——, *Private Letters of Princess Lieven to Prince Metternich, 1820–1826* (New York, Dutton, 1938)

——, *The Unpublished Diary and Political Sketches of Princess Lieven*, ed. Harold Temperley (London, Cape, 1925)

Lieven, Princess Dorothea, and Charles, 2nd Earl Grey, *Correspondence of Princess Lieven and Earl Grey*, ed. Guy Le Strange, 3 vols. (London, Bentley, 1890)

Linch, Kevin, *Britain and Wellington's Army. Recruitment, Society and Tradition, 1807–1815* (Basingstoke, Palgrave Macmillan, 2011)

Lincoln, W. Bruce, *Nicholas I. Emperor and Autocrat of all the Russias* (London, Allen Lane, 1978)

Lipscombe, Nick, *Wellington's Guns* (Botley, Osprey, 2013)

Littleton, see Hatherton

Livermore, H.E., *A New History of Portugal* (Cambridge University Press, 1966)

Llewellyn, Frederick, ed., *Waterloo Recollections. Rare First Hand Accounts, Letters, Reports and Retellings from the Campaign of 1815* (no place, Leonaur, 2007)

London County Council, *Survey of London*, vol. 23, *South Bank and Vauxhall*, Pt. 1, ed. Sir Howard Roberts and Walter H. Godfrey (London, London County Council, 1951)

Longford, Elizabeth, 'The Duke of Wellington's Books', *History Today*, vol. 17 (January 1967), pp. 22–8

——, *Wellington. Pillar of State* (London, Weidenfeld and Nicolson, 1972)

——, *Wellington. The Years of the Sword* (London, Weidenfeld and Nicolson, 1969)

LoPatin, N., 'Wellington and Political Unions: Rumours, Misinformation and the Great Reform Act of 1832', *Wellington Studies III* (1999), pp. 184–202

Low, E.B., *With Napoleon at Waterloo and Other Unpublished Documents*, ed. Mackenzie MacBride (Philadelphia, Lippincott, 1911)

Macaulay, Neill, *Dom Pedro. The Struggle for Liberty in Brazil and Portugal, 1798–1834* (Durham, NC, Duke University Press, 1986)

Macaulay, Rose, *They Went to Portugal* (London, Cape, 1946)

MacCahill, M.W., 'Peerage Creations and the changing Character of the British Nobility, 1750–1830', *English Historical Review*, vol. 96 (1981), pp. 259–84

McCarthy, Justin, *History of our Own Times*, 4 vols. (Boston, Estes and Lauriat, 1897)

MacDonagh, Oliver, *The Hereditary Bondsman Daniel O'Connell* (London, Weidenfeld and Nicolson, 1988)

McDowell, R.B., *The Irish Administration, 1801–1914* (London, Routledge & Kegan Paul, 1964)

McGuigan, Dorothy Gies, *Metternich and the Duchess* (New York, Doubleday, 1975)

Machin, G.I.T., 'Canning, Wellington, and the Catholic Question, 1827–1829', *English Historical Review* (1984), pp. 94–100

——, 'The Catholic Question and the Monarchy, 1827–1829', *Parliamentary History*, vol. 16 (1997), pp. 213–20

——, *The Catholic Question in English Politics 1820 to 1830* (Oxford, Clarendon Press, 1964)

——, 'The Duke of Wellington and Catholic Emancipation', *Journal of Ecclesiastical History*, vol. 14 (1963), pp. 190–208

——, 'The No-Popery Movement in Britain, 1828–29', *Historical Journal*, vol. 6 (1963), pp. 193–211

——, 'Resistance to the Repeal of the Test and Corporation Acts, 1828', *Historical Journal*, vol. 22, no. 1 (March 1979), pp. 115–39

McLean, I., 'Wellington and the Corn Laws, 1845–6: A Study in Heresthetic', *Wellington Studies III* (1999), pp. 227–56

Macleod, Lieutenant-General John, obituary in *United Service Journal* (July 1834), pp. 380–5

Mackenzie, Capt. T.A. et al, *Historical Records of the 79th Queen's Own Cameron Highlanders* (London, Hamilton Adams; Devonport, A.H. Swiss, 1887)

Madan, Spencer, *Spencer and Waterloo. The Letters of Spencer Madan, 1814–1816*, ed. Beatrice Madan (London, Literary Services, 1970)

Malcolm, John, *Malcolm. Soldier, Diplomat, Ideologue of British India* (Edinburgh, John Donald, 2014)

Malmesbury, ed., *A Series of Letters of the first Earl of Malmesbury, His Family and Friends*, 2 vols. (London, Richard Bentley, 1870)

Mansel, Philip, *Louis XVIII* (London, Blond and Briggs, 1981)

——, *Paris Between Empires. Monarchy and Revolution, 1814–1852* (New York, St Martin's Press, 2003)

——, 'Wellington and the French Restoration', *International History Review*, vol. 11 (1989), pp. 76–83

Marchand, Leslie, *Byron. A Biography*, 3 vols. (London, John Murray, 1957)

Martin, Theodore, *The Life of His Royal Highness the Prince Consort*, 5 vols. (New York, Appleton, 1880)

Martinien, A., *Tableaux par corps et par batailles des Officiers Tués et Blessés pendant les Guerres de l'Empire (1805–1815)* (Paris, Éditions Militaires Européennes, nd)

Mather, F.C., *Public Order in the Age of the Chartists* (Manchester University Press, 1959)

Mathews, Shirley, 'The Wellington Pamphlets, Catholic Emancipation and National Identity', *Wellington Studies IV* (2008), pp. 244–73

Maurice Maj.-Gen. Sir F., *The History of the Scots Guards*, 2 vols. (London, Chatto & Windus, 1934)

Maurice, J.F., 'Assye [*sic*] and Wellington', *Cornhill Magazine*, 3rd series, vol. 73 (September 1896), pp. 291–304

Maxwell, Sir Herbert, *The Life of Wellington and the Restoration of the Martial Power of Great Britain*, 2 vols. (4th edn, London, Sampson Low, Marston and Co., 1900)

Maxwell, W.H., *Life of Field Marshal His Grace the Duke of Wellington*, 3 vols. (London, A.H. Baily, 1839–41)

May, Sir John, letter of 23 June 1815 listed for sale with transcription by Berryhill & Sturgeon in 2007 at www.berryhillsturgeon.com

Mercer, Gen. Cavalié, *Journal of the Waterloo Campaign* (London, Peter Davies, 1969)

Middleton, Charles R., *The Administration of British Foreign Policy, 1782–1846* (Durham, Duke University Press, 1977)

——, 'The Formation of Canning's Ministry and the Evolution of the British Cabinet, February to August 1827', *Canadian Journal of History*, vol. 10 (April 1975), pp. 17–34

——, 'The Irish Representative Peerage Elections and the Conservative Party, 1832–1841', *Proceedings of the American Philosophical Society*, vol. 129 (1985), pp. 90–111

Milkes, Elisa R., 'A Battle's Legacy: Waterloo in Nineteenth-Century Britain' (PhD thesis, Yale University, 2002)

Mill, Major James, 'Service in Ireland, the Peninsula, New Orleans and at Waterloo', *United Services Magazine* (April–September 1870), pp. 493–503, 43–51, 210–20, 390–9, 550–9 and 70–80

Miller, David, *The Duchess of Richmond's Ball, 15 June 1815* (Staplehurst, Spellmount, 2005)

Milne, Maurice, 'Archibald Alison: Conservative Controversialist', *Albion*, vol. 27 (1995), pp. 419–45

Milton-Smith, J., 'Early Grey's Cabinet and the Objects of Parliamentary Reform', *Historical Journal*, vol. 15 (1972), pp. 55–74

Mitchell, Austin, *The Whigs in Opposition, 1815–1830* (Oxford, Clarendon Press, 1967)

Mitchell, B.R. and Phyllis Deane, *Abstract of British Historical Statistics* (Cambridge University Press, 1962)

Mitchell, Leslie, *Holland House* (London, Duckworth, 1980)

——, *Lord Melbourne, 1779–1848* (Oxford University Press, 1997)

Molé, Count, *The Life and Memoirs of Count Molé (1781–1855)*, ed. the Marquis de Noailles, 2 vols. (London, Hutchinson, 1923)

Moody, T.W., F.X. Martin and F.J. Byrne, eds., *A New History of Ireland*, 9 vols. (Oxford, Clarendon Press, 1976–2005)

Moore Smith, G.C., *The Life of John Colborne, Field-Marshal Lord Seaton* (New York, Dutton, 1903)

Moorsom, W.S., *Historical Record of the Fifty-Second Regiment . . .* (London, Bentley, 1860)

Morecroft, Eleanor N., ' "For the British Soldier is Keenly Sensitive to Honour": Military Heroism and British Identities in the Works of William Napier' (PhD thesis, University of Queensland, 2011)

Morley, John, *Death, Heaven and the Victorians* (London, Studio Vista, 1971)

Morris, Thomas, *The Napoleonic Wars*, ed. John Selby (London, Longman, 1967) [Memoir of a ranker in the 73rd]

Morriss, Roger, 'Military Men Fall Out: Wellington, Cockburn and the Last Lord High Admiral, 1827–8', *Wellington Studies III* (1999), pp. 117–35

Morton, Robert, 'Greatest Living Englishman? The Standing of the Duke of Wellington as Seen at Queen Victoria's Coronation', *Wellington Studies IV* (2008), pp. 323–37

——, 'A Melancholy Sight: Wellington and the Protectionists', *Wellington Studies V* (2013), pp. 286–98

Müffling, Baron von, *History of the Campaign of the British, Dutch, Hanoverian and Brunswick Armies under the Command of the Duke of Wellington, and of the Prussians . . . in the Year 1815* (London, Egerton, 1816)

——, *Memoirs of Baron von Müffling* (London, Greenhill, 1997) [Other editions of this work appear with title *Passages from My Life and Writings* with the same pagination]

Muilwijk, Erwin, *1815*. vol. 1, *From Mobilisation to War* (Bleiswijk, Sovereign House Books, 2012)

——, *1815*. vol. 2, *Quatre Bras, Perponcher's Gamble* (Bleiswijk, Sovereign House Books, 2013)

——, *Standing Firm at Waterloo, 17 and 18 June 1815* (Bleiswijk, Sovereign House Books, 2014)

——, 'Waterloo Campaign 1815: The Contribution of the Netherlands Mobile Army', http://home.tiscali.nl/erwinmuilwijk (accessed late 2007) [This work has now been published in a series of books, as listed]

Münster, George Herbert, Count, *Political Sketches of the State of Europe from 1814–1867* (Edinburgh, Edmonston & Douglas, 1868)

Muir, Howie, unpublished essay on the use of four-deep line in the allied army at the battle of Waterloo

Muir, Rory, *Britain and the Defeat of Napoleon, 1807–1815* (New Haven and London, Yale University Press, 1996)

——, 'A Hero's Welcome: Attitudes to Wellington and the Army, 1814–1823', *Wellington Studies V* (2013), pp. 210–23

——, 'Politics and the Peninsular Army', *Wellington Studies IV* (2008), pp. 72–93

——, *Salamanca 1812* (New Haven and London, Yale University Press, 2001)

——, *Tactics and the Experience of Battle in the Age of Napoleon* (New Haven and London, Yale University Press, 1998)

——, *Wellington. The Path to Victory, 1769–1814* (New Haven and London, Yale University Press, 2013)

Muir, Rory, Robert Burnham, Howie Muir and Ron McGuigan, *Inside Wellington's Peninsular Army* (Barnsley, Pen & Sword, 2006)

Munsell, F. Darrell, 'Wellington's Iberian Policy, 1834–35', *Consortium on Revolutionary Europe*, vol. 19 (1989), pp. 548–57

Murphy, Paula, *Nineteenth-Century Irish Sculpture. Native Genius Reaffirmed* (New Haven and London, Yale University Press, 2010)

Namier, Sir Lewis and John Brooke, *The History of Parliament. The House of Commons, 1760–1790*, 3 vols. (HMSO for the History of Parliament Trust, 1964)

Napier, Maj.-Gen. Sir W.F.P., *History of the War in the Peninsula and the South of France, from the Year 1807 to the Year 1814*, 6 vols. (London, Thomas and William Boone, 1853)

——, 'Letters from Colonel William Napier to Sir John Colborne', ed. Prof. Moore Smith, *English Historical Review*, vol. 18 (1903), pp. 725–53

Napoleon, *Napoleon's Last Will and Testament*, ed. J.P. Babeloa and Suzanne D'Huart (New York, Paddington Press 1977)

'Near Observer', *The Battle of Waterloo . . . with Circumstantial Details . . . by a Near Observer* (London, Booth, 2nd edn, 1815; 8th edn, 1816; 11th edn, 1852)

Nelson, C., 'The Duke of Wellington and the Barrier Fortresses after Waterloo', *JSAHR*, vol. 42, no. 169 (March 1964), pp. 36–43

Neumann, Philipp von, *The Diary of Philipp von Neumann, 1819–1850*, ed. E. Beresford Chancellor, 2 vols. (London, Philip Allan, 1928)

New, Chester, *The Life of Henry Brougham to 1830* (Oxford, Clarendon Press, 1961)

Newbould, Ian, *Whiggery and Reform 1830–1841* (Stanford University Press, 1990)

Newcastle, Fourth Duke of, *Unrepentant Tory. Political Selections from the Diaries of the Fourth Duke of Newcastle-under-Lyne, 1827–1838*, ed. Richard A. Gaunt (Woodbridge, Boydell Press for the Parliamentary History Yearbook Trust, 2006)

Newitt, Malyn and Martin Robson, *Lord Beresford and British Intervention in Portugal 1807–1820* (Lisbon, Imprensa de Ciências Sociais, 2004)

Newman, Ruth, 'The "Swing" Riots: Agricultural Revolt in 1830', *Hatcher Review*, vol. 2 (1985), pp. 436–47

Nicols, Irby C., *The European Pentarchy and the Congress of Verona, 1822* (The Hague, Nijhoff, 1971)

Nicholson, Harold, *The Congress of Vienna. A Study of Allied Unity, 1812–1822* (London, Constable, 1946)

Noyce, Karen A., 'The Duke of Wellington and the Catholic Question', in Norman Gash, ed., *Wellington. Studies in the Military and Political Career of the First Duke of Wellington*

O'Brien, P.K., 'The Security of the Realm and the Growth of the Economy, 1688–1916' in Peter Clarke and Clive Trebilock, eds., *Understanding Decline. Perceptions and Realities of British Economic Performance* (Cambridge University Press, 1997)

'The Odds and Ends of the Year 1830', *Keystone Folklore Quarterly*, vol. 9 (Summer 1964), p. 53

O'Gorman, Frank, *The Emergence of the British Two-Party System, 1760–1832* (London, Edward Arnold, 1982)

——, 'Party Politics in the Early Nineteenth Century', *English Historical Review*, vol. 102 (January 1987), pp. 63–88

Olphin, H.K., *George Tierney* (London, George Allen & Unwin, 1934)

Oman, Carola, *The Gascoyne Heiress. The Life and Diaries of Frances Mary Gascoyne-Cecil, 1802–1839* (London, Hodder and Stoughton, 1968)

Oman, Sir Charles, 'French Losses in the Waterloo Campaign', *English Historical Review*, vol. 19 (October 1904), pp. 681–93, and vol. 21 (January 1906), pp. 132–5

——, *A History of the Peninsular War*, 7 vols. (Oxford, Clarendon Press, 1902–30)

——, *Wellington's Army, 1809–1814* (London, Edward Arnold, 1913)

Owen, Edward, *The Waterloo Papers. 1815 and Beyond* (Tavistock, AQ & DJ Publications, 1997)

Pakenham, Eliza, *Soldier, Sailor. An Intimate Portrait of an Irish Family* (London, Weidenfeld & Nicolson, 2007)

Palmer, Alan, *Metternich* (London, Weidenfeld and Nicolson, 1972)

Palmer, Stanley H., *Police and Protest in England and Ireland 1780–1850* (Cambridge University Press, 1988)

Palmerston, Emily, *The Letters of Lady Palmerston*, ed. Tresham Lever (London, John Murray, 1957)

Palmerston, Viscount, *The Letters of the third Viscount Palmerston to Laurence and Elizabeth Sulivan, 1804–1863*, ed. Kenneth Bourne (London, Royal Historical Society, 1979; Camden, 4th series, vol. 23)

——, *Selections from Private Journals of Tours in France in 1815 and 1818* (London, Bentley, 1871)

Parker, Charles Stuart, *The Life and Letters of Sir James Graham . . .*, 2 vols. (London, John Murray, 1907)

——, *Sir Robert Peel . . . from his Private Papers*, 3 vols. (London, John Murray, 1891–99)

Parker, W.M., 'A Visit to the Duke of Wellington', *Blackwood's Magazine*, vol. 256 (August 1944), pp. 77–82

Parkinson, Roger, *The Hussar General* (London, Peter Davies, 1975)

The Parliamentary Debates from the Year 1803 to the Present Time, published under the superintendence of T.C. Hansard (1814–20)

The Parliamentary Debates . . . new series, 'published under the superintendence of T.C. Hansard (1820–30)

Parliamentary Papers: Report of Commissioners for Inquiring into Naval and Military Promotion and Retirement (London, Clowes, 1840)

Parliamentary Papers: Report of the Commissioners Appointed to Inquire into and State the Mode of Keeping the Official Accounts in the Principal Departments Connected with the Receipts and Expenditure for the Public Service (9 February 1829)

Parliamentary Papers: Report from His Majesty's Commissioners for Inquiring into the System of Military Punishments in the Army (London, Clowes, 1836)

Parliamentary Papers: Second Report of the Select Committee on Public Income and Expenditure [the Finance Committee], 1828, in House of Commons, *Reports from Committees*, vol. 5 (1828)

Partridge, Michael S., *The Duke of Wellington, 1769–1852. A Bibliography* (Westport, Meckler, 1990)

——, *Military Planning for the Defense of the United Kingdom, 1814–1870* (New York, Greenwood Press, 1989)

——, 'The Russell Cabinet and National Defence, 1846–1852', *History*, vol. 72 (June 1987), pp. 231–50

Patterson, Clara Burdett, *Angela Burdett-Coutts and the Victorians* (London, John Murray, 1953)

Pattison, Frederick, *Personal Recollections of the Waterloo Campaign by Lieutenant Frederick Hope Pattison*, ed. Bob Elmer (Association of Friends of Waterloo Committee, 1997 – first published Glasgow, for private circulation, 1870)

Pearman, Robert, *The Cadogans at War, 1783–1864. The Third Earl Cadogan and His Family* (London, Haggerston Press, 1990)

Pears, Iain, 'The Gentleman and the Hero: Wellington and Napoleon in the Nineteenth Century', *Myths of the English*, ed. Roy Porter (Cambridge, Polity, 1993)

Pedlow, Gregory W., 'Back to the Sources: General Zieten's Message to the Duke of Wellington on 15 June 1815', *First Empire*, no. 82 (2005), pp. 30–5

——, 'Wellington versus Clausewitz', *On Waterloo. Clausewitz, Wellington and the Campaign of 1815* by Carl von Clausewitz, trans. and ed. Christopher Bassford, Daniel Moran and Gregory W. Pedlow (Createspace.com, 2010)

Peel, Lady Georgiana, *Recollections of Lady Georgiana Peel* (London, John Lane, 1920)

Peel, Sir Robert, *Memoirs by the Right Honourable Sir Robert Peel . . .*, ed. Lord Mahon and Edward Cardwell, 2 vols. (London, John Murray, 1858)

——, *The Private Letters of Sir Robert Peel*, ed. George Peel (London, John Murray, 1920)

Peers, Douglas, 'The Duke of Wellington and British India during the Liverpool Administration, 1819–1827', *Journal of Imperial and Commonwealth History*, vol. 17 (October 1988), pp. 5–25

Pellew, George, *Life and Correspondence of the Rt. Hon. Henry Addington, first Viscount Sidmouth*, 3 vols. (London, John Murray, 1847)

Percival, Victor, *The Duke of Wellington. A Pictorial Survey of his Life (1769–1852)* (London, HMSO, 1969)

——, 'Mementoes of the Iron Duke', *Apollo*, vol. 98, no. 139 (September 1973), pp. 216–19

Petit, Gen., *General Petit's Account of the Waterloo Campaign*, ed. G.C. Moore Smith, *English Historical Review*, vol. 18 (April 1903), pp. 321–6

Pflugk-Harttung, J. von, 'Front and Rear of the Battle-Line of Waterloo', *Military Historian* (January 1917), pp. 19–26

Philips, W. Alison, *The War of Greek Independence, 1821–1833* (New York, Scribner's, 1897)

Phipps, Edmund, *Memoir of the Political and Literary Life of Robert Plumer Ward*, 2 vols. (London, John Murray, 1850)

Physick, John, *The Duke of Wellington in Caricature* (London, HMSO, 1965)

——, *The Wellington Monument* (London, HMSO, 1970)

Piggott, Karen, 'Wellington, Ireland and the Catholic Question, 1807–1827' (PhD thesis, University of Southampton, 1990)

Pilbeam, Pamela, 'The Growth of Liberalism and the Crisis of the Bourbon Restoration 1827–30', *Historical Journal*, vol. 25 (1982), pp. 351–66.

Pimlott, J.L., 'The Administration of the British Army 1783–1793' (PhD thesis, Leicester University, 1975)

[Pitt-Lennox, Lord William], *Three Years with the Duke, or Wellington in Private Life* (London, Saunders & Otley, 1853)

Plumer Ward, Robert: see Phipps

Pole Tylney Long Wellesley, William: see Wellesley, William L.

Porter, Whitworth, *History of the Corps of Royal Engineers*, 2 vols. (London, Longmans, Green, 1889)

Postgate, Raymond and Aylmer Vallance, *Those Foreigners* (London, Harrap, 1937)

Prest, John, *Lord John Russell* (London, Macmillan, 1972)

Price, Munro, *The Perilous Crown. France Between Revolutions, 1814–1848* (London, Macmillan, 2007)

Priest, Guy, 'A [*sic*] Ensign's Dispatch from Waterloo Written and Illustrated by Guy Priest', *Country Life* (16 June 1950), p. 1812

Prothero, Iorwerth, *Artisans and Politics in Early Nineteenth Century London, John Gast and his Times* (Folkestone, Dawson, 1979)

Putney, Martha, 'The Slave Trade in French Diplomacy from 1814 to 1815', *Journal of Negro History*, vol. 60 (July 1975), pp. 411–27

Quinault, Roland, 'The French Revolution of 1830 and Parliamentary Reform', *History*, vol. 97 (October 1994), pp. 377–93

Raikes, Thomas, *A Portion of the Journal of Thomas Raikes*, 4 vols. (London, Longman, Brown, Green, and Longmans, 1856)

Ramsey, Neil, 'The Military Author and Romantic War: British Military Memoirs and the Emergence of the Soldier Hero, 1809–1835' (PhD thesis, Australian National University, 2008)

——, *The Military Memoir and Romantic Literary Culture, 1780–1835* (Farnham, Ashgate, 2011)

Raudzens, George, 'The British Ordnance Department 1815–1855', *JSAHR*, vol. 57, no. 230 (Summer 1979), pp. 88–107

Read, Donald, *Peterloo. The 'Massacre' and its Background* (Manchester University Press, 1958)

Reid, Wemyss, *Memoirs and Correspondence of Lyon Playfair* (London, Cassell, 1900, the 'popular edition')

Rhinelander, Anthony L.H., *Prince Michael Voronstov* (Montreal and Kingston, McGill-Queen's University Press, 1990)

Rickword, Edgell, ed., *Radical Squibs and Loyal Ripostes* (Bath, Adams & Dart, 1971)

Roberts, Andrew, *Napoleon and Wellington* (London, Weidenfeld & Nicolson, 2001)

Roberts, Frederick, Lord, *The Rise of Wellington* (London, Sampson Low, Marston, 1902)

Roberts, Greg, 'The Forgotten Brother [William Wellesley-Pole]' (MA thesis, Queen Mary University, London, nd)

Robinson, Maj.-Gen. C.W., 'Waterloo and the De Lancey Memorandum', *Journal of the Royal United Services Institution*, vol. 54 (1910), pp. 582–97

Robinson, J.M., *The Wyatts. An Architectural Dynasty* (Oxford University Press, 1979)

Robinson, Mike, *The Battle of Quatre Bras, 1815* (Stroud, The History Press, 2009)

Robson, Karen, 'The Depiction of the Duke of Wellington in the Broadside Ballad', *Wellington Studies V* (2013), pp. 180–209

——, 'What Every "Official" Man Seeks – Patronage and the Management of Parliament: The Experience of Two Chief Secretaries for Ireland, 1802–09', *Wellington Studies II* (1999), pp. 87–103

Rodger, N.A.M., *The Command of the Ocean. A Naval History of Britain, 1649–1815* (London, Allen Lane, 2004)

Rogers, Samuel, *Reminiscences and Table-talk of Samuel Rogers*, ed. G.H. Powell (London, Brinley Johnson, 1903)

Romilly, Samuel, *Memoirs of the Life of Sir Samuel Romilly*, ed. his sons, 3 vols. (London, John Murray, 1840)

Romilly, S.H., *Romilly–Edgeworth Letters, 1813–1818* (London, John Murray, 1936)

Ropes, J.C., *The Campaign of Waterloo. A Military History* (London, G.P. Putnam's Sons, 1893)

Ros, Georgiana, Lady de, 'Personal Recollections of the Great Duke of Wellington', *Murray's Magazine* (January and February 1889), pp. 37–53, 193–201 [See also Swinton]

Rose, J.H., ed., 'Sir Hudson Lowe and the Beginnings of the Campaign of 1815', *English Historical Review* (July 1910), pp. 517–27

——, 'The Unstamped Press, 1815–1836', *English Historical Review*, vol. 12 (1897), pp. 711–26

Ross, Charles, *Correspondence of Charles, First Marquis Cornwallis*, 3 vols. (London, John Murray, 1859)

Ross, H.D., *Memoir of Field Marshal Sir Hew Dalrymple Ross R.H.A.* (Woolwich, Royal Artillery Institution, 1871)

Ross-Lewin, Harry, *With 'The Thirty-Second' in the Peninsular and other Campaigns*, ed. John Wardell (Dublin, Hodges, Figgis & Co, 1904, reprinted Trotman, 2000)

Ross-of-Bladenburg, Lt.-Col., *History of the Coldstream Guards from 1815 to 1895* (London, Innex, 1896)

Royal Military Calendar, 5 vols. (3rd edn, London, Egerton, 1820)

Royal Military Chronicle, 7 vols. (London, Davis, 1811–14)

Ruskin, Euphemia, *Effie in Venice. Unpublished Letters of Mrs John Ruskin written from Venice between 1849–1852*, ed. Mary Lutyens (London, John Murray, 1965)

Russell, George W.E., *Collections and Recollections*, 2 vols. (London, Nelson, nd [*c.* 1903])

Russell, *Early Correspondence of Lord John Russell, 1805–1840*, ed. his son Rollo Russell, 2 vols. (London, T. Fisher Unwin, 1913)

Rutz, Michael A., 'The Politicizing of Evangelical Dissent, 1811–1813', *Parliamentary History*, vol. 20 (2001), pp. 187–207

Sack, James J., *From Jacobite to Conservative. Reaction and Orthodoxy in Britain, c.1760–1832* (Cambridge University Press, 1993)

——, *The Grenvillites, 1801–1829. Party Politics and Factionalism in the Age of Pitt and Liverpool* (Urbana, University of Illinois Press, 1979)

——, 'The House of Lords and Parliamentary Patronage in Great Britain, 1802–1832', *Historical Journal*, vol. 23 (1980), pp. 913–37

——, 'The Memory of Burke and the Memory of Pitt: English Conservatism Confronts its Past, 1806–1829', *Historical Journal*, vol. 30, no. 3 (1987), pp. 623–40

——, 'Wellington and Tory Press, 1828–30', in *Wellington. Studies in the Military and Political Career*, ed. Norman Gash

Sainty, J.C., 'The Evolution of the Parliamentary and Financial Secretary of the Treasury', *English Historical Review*, vol. 91 (1976), pp. 566–85

Sauvigny, Guillaume de Bertier de, *The Bourbon Restoration* (Philadelphia, University of Pennsylvania Press, 1966)

Scherer, Paul, *Lord John Russell. A Biography* (Selinsgrove, Susquehanna University Press, 1999)

Schroeder, Paul W., *Metternich's Diplomacy at its Zenith, 1820–1823* (Austin and London, University of Texas Press, 1977)

——, special issue of *International History Review*, vol. 16, no. 4 (November 1994), discussing Schroeder's account of the International System and the Concert of Europe

——, *The Transformation of European Politics, 1763–1848* (Oxford, Clarendon Press, 1994)

Schumpeter, 'English Prices and Public Finance 1660–1822', *Review of Economic Statistics*, vol. 20 (1938)

Schwartzberg, Steven, 'The Lion and the Phoenix – [pt] 1 British Policy Toward the "Greek Question" 1831 [*sic* 1821]–1832', *Middle Eastern Studies*, vol. 24 (1988), pp. 139–77, 287–311

Scott, I., 'Counter-Revolutionary Diplomacy and the Demise of Anglo-Austrian Co-operation, 1820–23', *Historian*, vol. 34 (1972), pp. 465–84

Scott, Sir Walter, *The Letters of Sir Walter Scott, 1787–1832*, ed. H.J.C. Grierson, 12 vols. (London, Constable, 1932–37)

——, *Paul's Letters to His Kinsfolk* (Edinburgh, Cadell, 1834)

Seaforth, Anonymous, 'Seaforth Papers: Letters from 1796–1843', published in [Littell's] *The Living Age* (12 December 1863), p. 493, where it was reprinted from *The North British Review* [Includes a number of letters from the Duchess of Wellington to Lady Hood]

Semmel, Stuart, *Napoleon and the British* (New Haven and London, Yale University Press, 2004)

Senior, H., *Orangeism in Ireland and Britain, 1795–1836* (London, Routledge & Kegan Paul, 1966)

Seton-Watson, Hugh, *The Russian Empire, 1801–1917* (Oxford, Clarendon Press, 1967)

Severn, John, *Architects of Empire. The Duke of Wellington and His Brothers* (Norman, University of Oklahoma Press, 2007)

Shattock, Joanne, *Politics and Reviewers* (Leicester University Press, 1989)

Shaw, Philip, *Waterloo and the Romantic Imagination* (Basingstoke, Palgrave Macmillan, 2002)

Shelley, Frances, Lady, *The Diary of Frances Lady Shelley*, ed. Richard Edgcumbe, 2 vols. (New York, Scribners, 1913)

Sherer, Moyle, *Recollections of the Peninsula* (Staplehurst, Spellmount, 1996; first published 1824)

Sherwig, John M., *Guineas and Gunpowder. British Foreign Aid in the Wars with France, 1793–1815* (Cambridge, Mass., Harvard University Press, 1969)

Siborne, Maj.-Gen. H.T., *Waterloo Letters. A Selection from Original and Hitherto Unpublished Letters* (London, Cassell, 1891)

Siborne, W., *History of the War in France and Belgium in 1815* (3rd edn, London, Boone, 1848)

——, *The Waterloo Campaign* (5th edn, Westminster, Constable, 1900)

Sidney, Edwin, *The Life of Lord Hill* (London, John Murray, 1845)

Simes, Douglas, ' "The Champions of the Protestant Cause Will Not Lightly Abandon It": The Ultra Tory Press and the Wellington Adminstration', *Wellington Studies IV* (2008), pp. 299–322

——, 'Fearing "The Bold Unflinching McBeath": Ultra Tory Concerns About the Duke of Wellington and his Administration in the Aftermath of Catholic Relief', *Wellington Studies V* (2013), pp. 224–61

——, 'A Long and Difficult Association: The Ultra Tories and "the Great Apostate" ', *Wellington Studies III* (1999), pp. 56–87

Simmons, Maj. George, *A British Rifleman. The Journals and Correspondence of Major George Simmons . . .* ed. Lt.-Col. Willoughby Verner (London, A&C Black, 1899)

Simpson, James, *Paris After Waterloo* (Edinburgh, Blackwood, 1853)

Sinnema, Peter W., *The Wake of Wellington. Englishness in 1852* (Athens, Ohio University Press, 2006)

Sked, Alan, ed., *Europe's Balance of Power, 1815–1848* (London, Macmillan, 1979)

Smart, William, *Economic Annals of the Nineteenth Century*, 2 vols. (London, Macmillan, 1910–17)

Smith, D.C.H., 'Wellington, Aberdeen and the Miguelist Crisis in Portugal, 1826–1831' (MA thesis, University of Kent, 1973)

Smith, E.A., *George IV* (New Haven and London, Yale University Press, 1999)

——, *Lord Grey 1764–1845* (Oxford, Clarendon Press, 1990)

——, *The Queen on Trial. The Affair of Queen Caroline* (Stroud, Alan Sutton, 1993)

——, *Wellington and the Arbuthnots* (Stroud, Alan Sutton, 1994)

Smith, Harry, *The Autobiography of Sir Harry Smith* ed. G.C. Moore Smith (London, John Murray, 1910)

Snow, Peter, *To War with Wellington. From the Peninsula to Waterloo* (London, John Murray, 2010)

Soane, George, *Life of the Duke of Wellington compiled from His Grace's Despatches*, 2 vols. (London, E. Churton, 1839–40)

A Soldier of the 71st. The Journal of a Soldier in the Highland Light Infantry, 1806–1815, ed. Christopher Hibbert (London, Leo Cooper, 1975)

Solkin, David H., *Painting out of the Ordinary* (New Haven and London, Yale University Press for the Paul Mellon Centre for Studies of British Art, 2008)

Sotheby's catalogue of the Contents of Fulbeck Hall, Lincolnshire, auctioned on 8 October 2002

Southey, Robert, *History of the Peninsular War*, 6 vols. (new edn, London, John Murray, 1837)

——, *New Letters of Robert Southey*, ed. Kenneth Curry, 2 vols. (New York and London, Colombia University Press, 1965)

Spater, George, *William Cobbett, The Poor Man's Friend*, 2 vols. (Cambridge University Press, 1982)

Speck, W.A., *Robert Southey. Entire Man of Letters* (New Haven and London, Yale University Press, 2006)

Spence, Peter, *The Birth of Romantic Radicalism. War, Popular Politics and English Radical Reformism, 1800–1815* (Aldershot, Scolar Press, 1996)

Spencer-Stanhope, Lady Elizabeth, *Letter Bag of Lady Elizabeth Spencer-Stanhope*, ed. A.M.W. Stirling, 2 vols. (London, John Lane, 1913)

[Sperling, John], *Letters of an Officer of the Corps of Royal Engineers* (London, Nisbet, 1872)

Spiel, Hilde, ed., *The Congress of Vienna. An Eyewitness Account* (Philadelphia, Chilton, 1968)

Staël, Madame de, *The Unpublished Correspondence of Madame de Staël and the Duke of Wellington*, ed. Victor de Pange (London, Cassell, 1965)

Stanhope, James, *Eyewitness to the Peninsular War and the Battle of Waterloo. The Letters and Journals of Lieutenant Colonel the Honourable James Stanhope, 1803 to 1825*, ed. Gareth Glover (Barnsley, Pen & Sword, 2010)

Stanhope, Philip Henry, 5th Earl, *Notes of Conversations with the Duke of Wellington* (2nd edn, London, John Murray, 1888)

Stanley, A.P., *The Life and Correspondence of Thomas Arnold D.D.*, 2 vols (Boston, Ticknor and Fields, 1868)

Stanley, Lady, 'Letters from Maria Josepha, Lady Stanley to her father, Lord Sheffield', ed. Lord Stanley of Alderley, *History Today*, vol. 4 (1954), pp. 628–37

Stapleton, Augustus Granville, *George Canning and His Times* (London, Parker, 1859)

Starklof, R., *The Life of Duke Bernhard of Saxe-Weimar-Eisenach* (University Press of America, 1996)

Stedman, Heather, 'Monuments to the Duke of the Wellington in Nineteenth-Century Ireland: Forging British and Imperial Identities', *Irish Geography*, vol. 46 (2014), pp. 129–59

Stevenson, John, *Popular Disturbances in England 1700–1870* (London, Longman, 1979)

——, 'The Queen Caroline Affair', *London in the Age of Reform*, ed. John Stevenson (Oxford, Basil Blackwell, 1977)

Stewart, Robert, *The Foundation of the Conservative Party, 1830–1867* (London and New York, Longman, 1978)

Stites, Richard, *The Four Horsemen. Riding to Liberty in Post-Napoleonic Europe* (Oxford University Press, 2014)

Stocqueler, J.H., *The Life of Field Marshal the Duke of Wellington*, 2 vols. (London, Ingram, Cooke & Co, 1852)

Stone, Lawrence, *Broken Lives. Separation and Divorce in England, 1660–1857* (Oxford University Press, 1993)

Strachan, Hew, 'The Early Victorian Army and the Nineteenth-Century Revolution in Government', *English Historical Review*, vol. 95 (October 1980), pp. 782–809

——, *From Waterloo to Balaclava. Tactics, Technology, and the British Army, 1815–1854* (Cambridge University Press, 1985)

——, *Wellington's Legacy. The Reform of the British Army, 1830–54* (Manchester University Press, 1984)

Strauchen, Elizabeth Bradley, 'Giovanni Puzzi, His Life and Work: A View of Horn Playing and Musical Life in England from 1817 into the Victorian Era (c. 1855)' (D. Phil thesis, Somerville College, University of Oxford, 2000)

Stuart Wortley, Mrs Edward, *Highcliffe and the Stuarts* (London, John Murray, 1927)

Sutton, Denys, 'The Great Duke and the Arts', *Apollo*, vol. 98, no. 139 (September 1973), pp. 161–9

Sweetman, John, *Raglan. From the Peninsula to the Crimea* (London, Arms & Armour, 1993)

Swiney, Col. G.C., *Historical Records of the 32nd (Cornwall) Light Infantry . . .* (London, Simpkin, Marshall, Hamilton, Kent & Co., 1893)

Swinton, J.R., *A Sketch of the Life of Georgiana, Lady de Ros . . .* (London, John Murray, 1893)

Talleyrand, Prince, *The Correspondence of Prince Talleyrand and King Louis XVIII during the Congress of Vienna*, ed. M.G. Pallain (New York, Scribner's, 1881)

Taylor, Sir Herbert, *The Taylor Papers*, ed. Ernest Taylor (London, Longmans, Green and Co., 1913)

Teffeteller, Gordon L., *The Surpriser. The Life of Rowland, Lord Hill* (Newark, University of Delaware Press, 1983)

Teignmouth, Lord, *Reminiscences of Many Years*, 2 vols. (Edinburgh, David Douglas, 1878)

Temperley, Harold, 'Canning, Wellington and George IV', *English Historical Review*, vol. 38 (April 1923), pp. 206–25

——, *The Foreign Policy of Canning 1822-1827* (London, G. Bell & Sons, 1925)

Thackeray, W.M., *The Letters and Private Papers of William Makepeace Thackeray*, collected and ed. Gordon N. Ray, 4 vols. (London, Oxford University Press, 1945)

Thompson, F.M.L., *English Landed Society in the Nineteenth Century* (London, Routledge, 1963)

Thompson, Neville, *Earl Bathurst and the British Empire* (Barnsley, Leo Cooper, 1999)

——, 'Immortal Wellington: Literary Tributes to the Hero', *Wellington Studies III* (1999), pp. 257–80

——, *Wellington After Waterloo* (London, Routledge & Kegan Paul, 1986)

Thorne, R.G., *The History of Parliament. The House of Commons, 1790-1820*, 5 vols. (Secker & Warburg for the History of Parliament Trust, 1986)

Tilney, Chrystal, '"A Compleat Trial of Principle": Southey, Wellington and the *Quarterly Review*', *Cylchgraw Llyfrgell Genedlaethol Cymru/The National Library of Wales Journal*, vol. 20 (1977–78), pp. 377–86

The Times, *The History of the Times*, vol. 1, *The 'Thunderer' in the Making 1785-1841* (London, The Times, 1935)

Tomkinson, William, *The Diary of a Cavalry Officer in the Peninsular War and Waterloo Campaign*, ed. James Tomkinson (London, Swan Sonnenschein, 1895)

[Torrens, Robert], 'A Waterloo Letter', *National Review*, vol. 63 (1914), pp. 834–49

Towle, Philip, *Enforced Disarmament from the Napoleonic Campaigns to the Gulf War* (Oxford, Clarendon Press, 1997)

Trevelyan, G.M., *The Seven Years of William IV. A Reign Cartooned by John Doyle* (London, Avalon Press and William Heinemann, 1952)

Tristram, Henry, 'The Repeal of the Corporation and Test Acts, 1828', *Dublin Review*, vol. 183 (1928), pp. 105–15, 201–7

Twiss, Horace, *The Public and Private Life of Lord Chancellor Eldon . . .*, 2 vols. (London, John Murray, 1846)

Tylden, G., ed., 'The Union Brigade at Waterloo' (letter or diary of Lt. Archibald James Hamilton), *JSAHR*, vol. 24 (Spring 1946), pp. 46–7

Tylden, Major G., 'The First Duke of Wellington as a Horseman', *JSAHR*, vol. 43, no. 174 (June 1965), pp. 67–72

Uffindell, Andrew, *The Eagle's Last Triumph* (London, Greenhill, 1994)

——, *The National Army Museum Book of Wellington's Armies* (London, Sidgwick & Jackson, 2003)

Urban, Mark, *The Man Who Broke Napoleon's Codes. The Story of George Scovell* (London, Faber and Faber, 2001)

——, *Rifles* (London, Faber and Faber, 2003)

Vaughan W.E., ed., *A New History of Ireland*, vol. 5, *Ireland Under the Union, I. 1801-1870* (Oxford, Clarendon Press, 1989)

Verner, William, *Reminiscences of William Verner (1782-1871), 7th Hussars* (Society for Army Historical Research, Special Publication no. 8, 1965)

Veve, Thomas Dwight, *The Duke of Wellington and the British Army of Occupation in France, 1815-1818* (Westport CT, Greenwood, 1992)

Victoria, Queen, *The Letters of Queen Victoria*, ed. A.C. Benson and Viscount Esher, 3 vols. (London, John Murray, 1908)

Vivian, Claud, *Richard Hussey Vivian, First Baron Vivian. A Memoir* (London, Ibister, 1897)

Voak, Jonathan, 'The Wellington Collection at Apsley House' (8th Wellington Lecture, University of Southampton, 1996)

Wade, John, *The Extraordinary Black Book. An Exposition of Abuses in Church and State . . .* (New York, Kelley, 1970; first published 1819)

Wake, Jehanne, *Sisters of Fortune. America's Caton Sisters at Home and Abroad* (New York, Simon and Schuster, 2010)

Walker, Richard, *Regency Portraits*, 2 vols. (London, National Portrait Gallery, 1985)

Walmsley, Robert, *Peterloo. The Case Reopened* (Manchester University Press, 1969)

Walpole, Spencer, *The Life of Lord John Russell*, 2 vols. (London, Longmans, Green, 1891)

Ward, Sir A.W. and G.P. Gooch, *Cambridge History of British Foreign Policy*, 3 vols. (Cambridge University Press, 1922–23)

Ward, C.H. Dudley, *A Romance of the Nineteenth Century* (London, John Murray, 1923)

Ward, J.W., *Letters from the Earl of Dudley to the Bishop of Llandaff* (London, John Murray, 1840)

——, *Letters to 'Ivy' from the first Earl of Dudley*, ed. S.H. Romilly (London, Longmans, Green and Co., 1905)

Ward, Robert Plumer, see Phipps

Ward, S.G.P., 'General Sir George Murray', *JSAHR*, vol. 58, no. 236 (Winter 1980), pp. 191–208

——, 'General Sir Willoughby Gordon', *JSAHR*, vol. 31, no. 126 (Summer 1953), pp. 58–63

——, *Wellington* (London, B.T. Batsford, 1963)

Wardroper, John, *The Caricatures of George Cruikshank* (London, Gordon Fraser, 1977)

Warre, William, *Letters from the Peninsula, 1808–1812* (Staplehurst, Spellmount, 1999)

Wasson, Elias A., 'The Coalitions of 1827 and the Crisis of Whig Leadership', *Historical Journal*, vol. 20 (1977), pp. 587–606

——, 'The Whigs and the Press, 1800–1850', *Parliamentary History*, vol. 25 (February 2006), pp. 68–87

Webster, C.K., ed., *British Diplomacy 1813–1815. Select Documents* (London, G. Bell & Sons, 1921)

——, *The Congress of Vienna* (London, Thames and Hudson, 1965)

——, *The Foreign Policy of Castlereagh, 1812–1814* (London, G. Bell and Sons, 1931)

——, *The Foreign Policy of Castlereagh 1815–1822* (London, G. Bell and Sons, 1958)

Weigall, Rachel, *Lady Rose Weigall. A Memoir based on her Correspondence and Recollections of her Friends* (London, John Murray, 1923)

Weintraub, Stanley, *Victoria. An Intimate Biography* (New York, Truman Talley/E.P. Dutton, 1987)

Wellesley, Charles, Marquess of Douro, *Wellington Portrayed* (London, Unicorn Press, 2014)

Wellesley, Lord Gerald and John Steegmann, *The Iconography of the First Duke of Wellington* (London, J.M. Dent & Sons, 1935)

Wellesley, Henry, *The Diary and Correspondence of Henry Wellesley, First Lord Cowley, 1790–1846*, ed. the Hon. F.A. Wellesley (London, Hutchinson & Co., [1930])

Wellesley, Jane, *Wellington. A Journey Through My Family* (London, Weidenfeld and Nicolson, 2008)

Wellesley, Muriel, *The Man Wellington* (London, Constable, 1937)

——, *Wellington in Civil Life* (London, Constable, nd [1939])

Wellesley, Richard, Marquess, *The Wellesley Papers* 'by the editor of "The Windham Papers"', 2 vols. (London, Herbert Jenkins, 1914)

Wellesley, William L., ('Wicked William' or William Pole Tylney Long Wellesley), *Two Letters to the Right Hon. Earl Eldon, Lord Chancellor* (London, John Miller, 1827) [William's name is given on the title page of the pamphlet as 'the Hon. W.L. Wellesley']

Wellington, Arthur Wellesley, 1st Duke of, *Despatches, Correspondence, and Memoranda of Field Marshal Arthur Duke of Wellington, K.G.*, ed. his son, the Duke of Wellington 'in continuation of the former series', 8 vols. (London, John Murray, 1857–80 [Known as *Wellington New Despatches* or *WND*, these volumes cover 1819–32]

——, *The Dispatches of Field Marshal the Duke of Wellington*, ed. Col. [John] Gurwood, 8 vols. (London, Parker, Furnivall and Parker, 1844) [This enlarged and revised edition is generally the best and is used here, cited as *WD*]

——, *The Dispatches of Field Marshal the Duke of Wellington during his various campaigns in India, Denmark, Portugal, Spain, the Low Countries and France from 1799 to 1818*, ed. Lt.-Col. [John] Gurwood, 13 vols. (London, John Murray, 1834–39) [This is the first edition, which lacks significant material included in the 'enlarged' edition of 1844]

——, *A Great Man's Friendship. Letters of the Duke of Wellington to Mary, Marchioness of Salisbury, 1850–1852*, ed. Lady Burghclere (London, John Murray, 1927)

——, 'Letter of the Duke of Wellington (May 22, 1815) on the Battle of New Orleans', *The Louisiana Historical Quarterly*, vol. 9 (January 1926), pp. 5–10

——, *The Letters of the Duke of Wellington to Miss J., 1834–1851*, ed. Christine Herrick (New York, Dodd, Mead, 1889)

——, *The Life and Exploits of . . . the Duke of Wellington including a Complete History of the Peninsular War . . . with Sixty Engravings* (London, Berger, 1840)

——, *Military Dispatches*, ed. and intro. Charles Esdaile (London, Penguin, 2014)

——, *A Selection from the Private Correspondence of the First Duke of Wellington*, ed. the Duke of Wellington (printed by the Dropmore Press for the Roxburghe Club, 1952)

——, 'Selections from Wellington's Letters [to Mrs Jones of Pantglas]' by her daughter Mary Davies-Evans in *The Century Magazine*, vol. 30, no. 2 (December 1889), pp. 163–83, and reprinted as *My Dear Mrs Jones* in a slim volume by the Rodale Press in 1954

——, 'Some Letters of the Duke of Wellington to his brother William Wellesley-Pole', ed. Professor Sir Charles Webster (London, Royal Historical Society, 1948; Camden, 3rd series, vol. 79)

——, *The Speeches of the Duke of Wellington in Parliament* collected and arranged by Col. [John] Gurwood, 2 vols. (London, John Murray, 1854)

——, *Supplementary Despatches, Correspondence and Memoranda of Field Marshal Arthur, Duke of Wellington, K.G.*, ed. his son, the Duke of Wellington, 15 vols. (London, John Murray, 1858–72)

——, *Wellington. Political Correspondence 1833–1835*, ed. John Brooke, Julia Gandy, R.J. Olney and Julia Melvin for the Royal Commission on Historical Manuscripts, 2 vols. (London, HMSO, 1975–86) [Known as *HMC Wellington*]

——, *Wellington and His Friends. Letters of the First Duke of Wellington to the Rt. Hon. Charles and Mrs Arbuthnot, the Earl and Countess of Wilton, Princess Lieven and Miss Burdett-Coutts* selected and ed. the Seventh Duke of Wellington (London, Macmillan, 1965)

——, *Wellington at War, 1794–1815. A Selection of his Wartime Letters*, ed. Antony Brett-James (London, Macmillan, 1961)

Wellington, Catherine (Kitty), Duchess of, 'Seaforth Papers: Letters from 1796–1843' [letters to Lady Hood], published in Littell's *The Living Age* (12 December 1863), p. 493, reprinted from *The North British Review*

Wellington, Gerald, Seventh Duke, 'The Great Duke's Funeral', *History Today*, vol. 2 (1952), pp. 778–84

Westmorland, Lady, *The Correspondence of Priscilla, Countess of Westmorland*, ed. her daughter Lady Rose Weigall (New York, E.P. Dutton, 1909)

Wharncliffe, Lady, *The First Lady Wharncliffe and Her Family, 1779–1856*, 2 vols. (London, Heinemann, 1927)

Wheatley, Edmund, *The Wheatley Diary. A Journal and Sketchbook kept during the Peninsular War and the Waterloo Campaign*, ed. Christopher Hibbert (London, Longmans, 1964)

Wheeler, Private William, *Letters of Private Wheeler*, ed. B.H. Liddell Hart (London, Michael Joseph, 1951)

White, Eugene N., 'Making the French Pay: The Costs and Consequences of the Napoleonic Reparations', *European Review of Economic History*, vol. 5 (2001), pp. 337–65

Whitehorne, Major A.C., *The History of the Welch Regiment*, vol. 1 (Cardiff, *Western Mail and Echo*, 1932)

Wilberforce, R.I. and S., *The Life of William Wilberforce by his Sons*, 5 vols. (London, John Murray, 1838)

Wickwar, William H., *The Struggle for Freedom of the Press 1819–1832* (London, George Allen & Unwin, 1929)

Williams, David and John Armstrong, 'Promotion, Speculation and their Outcome: The "Steamship Mania" of 1824–1825', *Aslib Proceedings*, vol. 60 (2008), pp. 642–60

Willis, Clive, 'Wellington and the Clinton Expedition to Portugal 1826–1828', *Wellington Studies IV* (2008), pp. 173–84

Wilson, Beckles, *The Paris Embassy, 1814–1920* (London, Fisher Unwin, 1927)

Wilson, Frances, *The Courtesan's Revenge. Harriette Wilson, the Woman who Blackmailed the King* (London, Faber and Faber, 2003)

Wilson, Harriette, *The Memoirs of Harriette Wilson Written by Herself*, 2 vols. (London, Eveleigh Nash, 1909 – first published 1825)

Wilson, Joan, *A Soldier's Wife. Wellington's Marriage* (London, Weidenfeld and Nicolson, 1987)

Winkenweder, Brian, 'The Newspaper as Nationalist Icon, or How to Paint "Imagined Communities"', *Limina*, vol. 14 (2008), pp. 85–96

Wolfe, John, *Great Deaths. Grieving, Religion, and Nationhood in Victorian and Edwardian Britain* (Oxford University Press for the British Academy, 2000)

Wood, Capt. George, *The Subaltern. A Narrative* (Cambridge, Ken Trotman, 1986)

Woodham-Smith, Cecil, *Queen Victoria from her Birth to the Death of the Prince Consort* (New York, Knopf, 1973)

Woolgar, C.M., 'Conversations with the Duke of Wellington', *Wellington Studies IV* (2008), pp. 338–58

——, 'Wellington, His Papers and the Nineteenth-Century Revolution in Communication' (Inaugural Lecture, University of Southampton, 2009)

——, 'Wellington's *Dispatches* and their Editor, Colonel Gurwood', *Wellington Studies I* (1996), pp. 189–210

——, 'Writing the Despatch: Wellington and Official Communication', *Wellington Studies II* (1999), pp. 1–25

Woolley, S.F., 'The Personnel of the Parliament of 1833', *English Historical Review*, vol. 53, no. 210 (April 1938), pp. 240–62

Wright, Rev. George N., *Life and Campaigns of Arthur, Duke of Wellington*, 4 vols. (London, Peter Jackson, 1841)

Wrottesley, George, *Life and Correspondence of Field Marshal Sir John Burgoyne*, 2 vols. (London, Bentley, 1873)

Wu, Duncan, *William Hazlitt. The First Modern Man* (Oxford University Press, 2008)

Yarrington, Alison, *The Commemoration of the Hero, 1800–1864* (New York, Garland, 1988)

——, 'His Achilles Heel? Wellington and Public Art' (10th Wellington Lecture, University of Southampton, 1998

Yonge, Charles D., *The Life and Administration of Robert Banks, Second Earl of Liverpool*, 3 vols. (London, Macmillan, 1868)

——, *The Life of Field Marshal Arthur, Duke of Wellington*, 2 vols. (London, Chapman and Hall, 1860)

Young, D.M., *The Colonial Office in the Early Nineteenth Century* (London, Longmans, 1961)

Ziegler, Philip, *Addington* (London, Collins, 1965)

——, *The Duchess of Dino* (London, Collins, 1986)

——, *King William IV* (London, Collins 1971)

——, *Melbourne* (London, Collins, 1976)

——, *The Sixth Great Power. Barings 1762–1929* (London, Collins, 1988)

INDEX